THE OXFORD ENCYCLOPEDIA OF

ECONOMIC HISTORY

THE OXFORD ENCYCLOPEDIA

OF

ECONOMIC

HISTORY

Joel Mokyr

Editor in Chief

VOLUME 4

Monte di Pietà

—

Spain

OXFORD

UNIVERSITY PRESS

2003

OXFORD

UNIVERSITY PRESS

Oxford New York

Auckland   Bangkok   Buenos Aires   Cape Town   Chennai
Dar es Salaam   Delhi   Hong Kong   Istanbul   Karachi   Kolkata
Kuala Lumpur   Madrid   Melbourne   Mexico City   Mumbai   Nairobi
São Paulo   Shanghai   Taipei   Tokyo   Toronto

Published by Oxford University Press, Inc.
198 Madison Avenue, New York, New York 10016
www. oup.com

Library of Congress Cataloging-in-Publication Data

The Oxford encyclopedia of economic history / Joel Mokyr, editor in chief.
p. cm.
Includes bibliographical references and index.
ISBN 0-19-510507-9 (set)
ISBN 0-19-517090-3 (v. 1: alk. paper)
ISBN 0-19-517091-1 (v. 2: alk. paper)
ISBN 0-19-517092-X (v. 3: alk. paper)
ISBN 0-19-517093-8 (v. 4: alk. paper)
ISBN 0-19-517094-6 (v. 5: alk. paper)
1. Economic history–Encyclopedias. I. Title: Encyclopedia of
economic history. II. Mokyr, Joel. III. Oxford University Press.
HC15 .O94 2003
330'.03–dc21

2003008992

1 3 5 7 9 8 6 4 2
Printed in the United States of America
on acid-free paper

Common Abbreviations Used in This Work

AD	*anno Domini*, in the year of the Lord
ASEAN	Association of Southeast Asian Nations
b.	born
BCE	before the common era (= BC)
c.	*circa*, about, approximately
CE	common era (= AD)
CEO	chief executive officer
cf.	*confer*, compare
d.	died; penny (pl., pence)
diss.	dissertation
EC	European Community
ed.	editor (pl., eds), edition
EEC	European Economic Community
EU	European Union
f.	and following (pl., ff.)
FAO	Food and Agriculture Organization
FDI	foreign direct investment
fl.	*floruit*, flourished
FTA	free trade area
GATT	General Agreement on Tariffs and Trade
GDP	gross domestic product
GNP	gross national product
G-10	Group of Ten industrialized countries
IMF	International Monetary Fund
ISI	import-substitution industrialization
l.	line (pl., ll.)
LDC	less developed country (pl., LDCs)
MDC	more developed country (pl., MDCs)
MFN	most-favored nation
MITI	Ministry of International Trade and Industry (Japan)
MNC	multinational company (pl., MNCs)
n.	note
NAFTA	North American Free Trade Association
NBER	National Bureau of Economic Research
n.d.	no date
NGO	nongovernmental organization
no.	number
n.p.	no place
n.s.	new series
OECD	Organization for Economic Cooperation and Development
OEEC	Organization for European Economic Cooperation
OPEC	Organization of Petroleum Exporting Countries
p.	page (pl., pp.)
pt.	part
r.	reigned
R&D	research and development
rev.	revised
s.	shilling
SEC	Securities and Exchange Commission (United States)
ser.	series
supp.	supplement
UNESCO	United Nations Educational, Scientific, and Cultural Organization
UNRRA	United Nations Relief and Rehabilitation Administration
USD	U.S. dollar(s)
USSR	Union of Soviet Socialist Republics
vol.	volume (pl., vols.)
WHO	World Health Organization
WIPO	World Intellectual Property Organization

M

(CONTINUED)

MONTE DI PIETÀ. The purpose of the *monte di pietà* (literally, "mountain of compassion"), or pawnshop was to provide small amounts of credit to anyone, even if poor, who was in a position to provide collateral with a value at least a third more than what was received. During the late Middle Ages, this institution moved into the credit the credit arena, which Christians and above all Jewish lenders previously dominated, by acquiring agreements, called *condotte*, from various cities to provide credit at stipulated conditions.

The Observant Friars Minor, a branch of the Franciscan order, assumed the task of promoting the first pawnshops, persuading the richest inhabitants and the civic authorities to offer the capital necessary for its operation. A series of theoretical passages, from Pietro di Giovanni Olivi (1248–1298), a Franciscan philosopher and thelogian, to Bernardino da Siena (1380–1444) one of the most famous Franciscan preachers of the late Middle Ages, had led Observant Franciscans to experiment with the pawnshop as a concrete economic action that encouraged social harmony. After attempts made in Ancona in 1454 and in Ascol: Piceno in 1458, the first pawnshop was founded in Perugia in 1462. Often the commune granted the office and some funds.

The clients of the pawnshop were the less poor of the poor, defined as the *pauperes pinguiores* ("fat paupers"), that is, those who needed financial support but not charity. Many statutes demanded that the client swear to use the borrowed money for an authentic need and not to use it to gamble or to undertake commercial activity. The statutes show that the average time given to make restitution for the security was one year, after which an unredeemed security was put up for auction.

Many pawnshops required a reimbursement of expenses when the loan was made, about 5 percent. The question of interest divided the members of the Franciscan order and above all divided the Franciscans from the Dominicans and the Augustinians. With few exceptions, the members of the two last orders opposed the reimbursement of expenses, which they judged to be a dangerous weakening of the strictures against usury. Many treatises were written on this theme in the second half of the fifteenth century, and a wide debate developed. The discussion abated in 1515, when the Fifth Lateran Council established the lawfulness of the application of moderate interest, although the council held it better to operate without requiring it. Not requiring it, however, would have meant compromising the capital of the pawnshop and quickly condemning it to extinction.

From the very beginning the *monti* accepted deposits of money, and although in itself the practice of deposits was crucial because it gave the pawnshop economic resources, the remuneration of depositors also increased the availability of funds. Thus the pawnshops were also able to serve classes of the population different from the clients of the first period. Soon the prohibition against using the money of the pawnshop for commercial purposes was dropped, and the institution could support artisans in temporary crises and in general when they found themselves short of money for any number of reasons. From 1462 to 1562 over two hundred pawnshops were founded in Italy, twenty-one in Umbria alone.

For a long time historians maintained that a direct relationship existed between Jewish bankers and the pawnshops and that the latter were fated to compete with the former on their own terrain. Today the frequent coexistence of the Jewish banks and the pawnshops is proven. The two institutions handled different credit needs and were therefore compatible, at least from the point of view of the signori and of the clientele. However, the Franciscans, who intended to cleanse Christian society of any usurious comportment and of the Jewish presence in the credit sector, did not recognize a compatibility.

From central and Northern Italy the pawnshop spread to southern Italy (1520 in Lecce, 1539 in Rome and Naples, 1578 in Barletta) but had little or no success outside of Italy. The exceptions were Belgium and the Low Countries, where it assumed from the beginning a banking character.

As an instrument of economic politics and public assistance at the disposal of city governments, the pawnshop constituted a place of power that local nobility often occupied. In the space of a few decades, the activities and functions of pawnshops expanded until they assumed the appearance of a bank, but in the last years of the eighteenth century, during the Napoleonic era, they suffered spoliations and modifications that limited their sphere of action, and they once again became institutions of charity. But in the late nineteenth century, the institution openly resumed its banking functions while retaining the provisions of traditional loans on suitable collateral.

[*See also* Banking, *subentry* on Middle Ages and Early Modern Period.]

BIBLIOGRAPHY

Banchi pubblici, banchi privati e Monti di pietà nell' Europa preindustriale, Atti del Convegno, Genova 1–6 ottobre, 1990. Genoa, Italy, 1991.

Garrani, Giuseppe. *Il carattere bancario e l' evoluzione strutturale dei primigeni Monti di pietà.* Milan, Italy, 1957.

Langholm, Odd. *Economics in Medieval Schools: Wealth, Exchange, Value according to the Paris Theological Tradition.* Leiden, 1992.

Meneghin, Vittorino. *I Monti di pietà in Italia dal 1462 al 1562.* Vicenza, Italy, 1986.

Menning, Carol Bresnahan. *The Monte di Pietà of Florence: Charity and State in Late Renaissance Italy.* Ithaca, N.Y., and London, 1993.

Muzzarelli, Maria Giuseppina. *Il denaro e la salvezza: L' invenzione del Monte di pietà.* Bologna, 2001.

Noonan, John T. *The Scholastic Analysis of Usury.* Cambridge, 1957.

Pullan, Brian. *Rich and Poor in Renaissance Venice: The Social Institution of a Catholic State, to 1620.* Oxford, 1971.

Soetaert, P. *Le livre de règlements des monts-de-piété aux Pays-Bas Méridionaux* (1618). Brussels, 1976.

Todeschini, Giacomo. *Il prezzo della salvezza: Lessici medievali del pensiero economico.* Rome, 1994.

MARIA GIUSEPPINA MUZZARELLI
Translated from Italian by Sylvia J. Cannizzaro

MONTREAL, city in French Canada, on the Saint Lawrence River, settled in 1642 by Roman Catholic missionaries. While its roots were religious, Montreal's location ensured its commercial importance; it is located on an island at the confluence of the Ottawa and Richelieu Rivers with the Saint Lawrence. Quebec City to the northeast of Montreal was the region's transatlantic port, but Montreal was the gateway to the interior of northern North America. Boats seeking goods that were harvested or collected from the western hinterland stopped there because of the series of impassable rapids immediately to the west of the city. Beyond the rapids, the Ottawa and Saint Lawrence rivers offered western access to the Great Lakes; to the south, through the Richelieu and Lake Champlain, travelers might reach Albany, on the Hudson River, and even Manhattan Island (the Dutch port of New Amsterdam that became the British port of New York). Fur was the colony's most important export commodity until overtaken by timber in the early nineteenth century, and Montreal was the center of the fur trade. In the early 1600s, native people trapped and transported the furs (primarily beaver pelts) to Montreal. Later in the seventeenth century, the trade expanded west, more fur trading posts were built in the interior, and *voyageurs* (primarily French traders) transported furs to Montreal for export.

In 1763, after years of warfare, Montreal and the rest of New France were ceded to Britain. The British conquest did not appreciably alter Montreal's economy, although it led to a change in the city's ethnic composition. Some of the elite export–import merchants returned to France and were replaced by English-speaking merchants who, with superior ties to Britain, came to dominate these trades. Yet the French maintained their dominance in artisan trades. By 1844, however, Montreal's dominant ethnic group was English, although later that century the French regained the majority.

Throughout the seventeenth and eighteenth centuries, Quebec City was the largest city in the colony. By the 1820s, however, Montreal came to the fore. During the next few decades, the gap between the two cities widened, as Montreal became the leading city within both the province of Quebec and Canada. Given its proximity to Upper Canada (Ontario) and natural waterways that offered inexpensive transportation routes and, later, an important source of hydroelectric power, Montreal became the transshipment port for goods flowing into and out of the west, especially as Upper Canada attracted settlers and grew in importance during the nineteenth century. Shipping routes and transport routes by road and by railway were improved, and financial services were expanded in the early nineteenth century. More important to its growth, though, was the range of goods flowing through its port (potash and wheat, for example); Montreal became the country's leading manufacturing center. Important industries included railroad and railcar manufacturing, marine engineering, flour milling, brewing, and sugar refining. In 1967, the city hosted a world's fair, EXPO '67, and added a baseball team (the National League's Montreal Expos), both of which helped boost the modern tourism industry of Canada's key industrial, commercial, and financial center. Not long afterward, however, Toronto replaced Montreal as Canada's largest city and financial epicenter.

BIBLIOGRAPHY

Dechêne, Louise. *Habitants and Merchants in Seventeenth Century Montreal.* Translated into English by Liana Vardi. Montreal, 1992. An indispensable study that draws on a wide variety of archival sources; it covers the native populations and the fur trade, offers demographic and social profiles of the French population, and describes in some detail settlement and farming.

Dickinson, John, and Brian Young. *A Short History of Quebec.* 2d ed. Toronto, 1993. Up-to-date overview, with annotated bibliographies for each chapter.

Tulchinsky, Gerald. *The River Barons: Montreal Businessmen and the Growth of Industry and Transportation, 1837–53.* Toronto, 1977. Offers a detailed historical examination of Montreal's shipping and rail development, as well as discussion of the rise of Montreal as a manufacturing center.

GILLIAN HAMILTON

MORGAN, J. P. (1837–1913), American banker.
John Pierpont Morgan, in the last twenty years of his life, was the most powerful banker in U.S. history, ar-

guably the most powerful private banker who ever lived. His firm, J. P. Morgan and Company, dominated the New York financial market and had a powerful presence in both London and Paris, making it the premier international bank of its day.

It is not the least of history's ironies that Morgan's life began the year after Andrew Jackson had destroyed the nation's central bank, the Second Bank of the United States, and ended a few months before the creation of the present central bank, the Federal Reserve. In the interim, the United States was the only major nation to lack such an institution. As a result, J. P. Morgan and Company twice effectively functioned as the de facto central bank of the United States. It was Morgan's remarkable, commanding personality as much as his great bank and his international connections that made this possible. Edward Steichen, who took the most famous photographic portrait of Morgan, said that meeting his gaze was like confronting the headlights of an express train.

Unlike many of the major economic figures of the late nineteenth century, Morgan was born to wealth. His paternal grandfather moved in 1817 to Hartford, Connecticut, where Morgan was born. There he invested in steamboat lines, railroads, and real estate and later was a founder of the Aetna Insurance Company. Morgan's father, Junius Spencer Morgan, in 1854 was invited to join the major London banking house of the American expatriate George Peabody. After Peabody's retirement in the early 1860s, Junius Morgan took over the firm, renaming it J. S. Morgan and Company.

Thus J. P. Morgan was exposed from his earliest days to international banking at its highest level and absorbed from his father the idea that personal integrity was indispensable to such an enterprise. Asked at the end of his life if money and property were the basis of credit, Morgan replied, "No, sir, the first thing is character. . . . Money cannot buy it. . . . Because a man I do not trust could not get money from me on all the bonds in Christendom."

Educated both in the United States and Europe, he studied at the University of Göttingen in Germany and was fluent in both French and German. In 1857 Morgan went to work for the New York firm of Duncan and Sherman as a junior accountant. He soon acquired a reputation for spotting opportunities and making quick decisions on business matters.

Morgan always had a romantic and impulsive side to his nature. In 1861 he married Amelia Sturges, of a distinguished New York family, although she had contracted tuberculosis that year and her health was deteriorating rapidly. She died only four months later, leaving Morgan a widower at the age of 24. He married again in 1865, to Frances Tracy, daughter of a prominent New York lawyer.

J. P. MORGAN. Aboard the yacht *Corsair*, watching the Yale-Harvard race in New London, Connecticut, June 1910. (Pierpont Morgan Library, New York/Art Resource, NY)

They had three daughters, Anne, Juliet, and Louisa, and a son, J. P. Morgan, Jr., who would head the House of Morgan for thirty years after his father's death.

In the great Wall Street boom of the Civil War, Morgan soon opened his own firm and quickly prospered. In 1864 he took on a senior partner, Charles H. Dabney, and the firm was renamed Dabney, Morgan and Company. Morgan mastered the art of banking in this era, one of great prosperity, lawless markets, and deep corruption in both business and government. Like others who came of age at this time, such as John D. Rockefeller and Andrew Carnegie, Morgan always looked upon government not as a means to regulate the markets, but as part of the problem. To Morgan, it was up to businessmen such as himself, men of personal integrity, to police the market.

In 1872, on Dabney's retirement, Morgan joined with John Drexel of Philadelphia to form Drexel, Morgan and Company. The firm flourished and Morgan's share of the profits averaged half a million dollars a year, even in the depressed mid-1870s. In this period and the following decade, Morgan was principally engaged in reorganizing railroads, the number and size of which grew enormously in the post–Civil War era. But they were sometimes badly managed, with complicated securities structures. In the frequent economic downturns of the late nineteenth century, they often defaulted and had to be reorganized. The deep depression that began in 1893 gave Morgan many new opportunities in these reorganizations, improving the capital structures with new, lower interest bonds while making handsome profits for the bank. He often put a partner on the board of these reorganized railroads to see that they were well managed, but did not seek to control them directly.

On the death of his father in 1890, Morgan reorganized Drexel, Morgan and Company in New York and J. S. Morgan in London as J. P. Morgan and Company. Its headquarters, at the corner of Wall and Broad Streets, quickly became known, simply, as The Corner, the very symbol of Wall Street power and money.

In that decade Morgan began participating in the formation and consolidation of industrial concerns as well as railroads, including General Electric, AT&T, International Harvester, and United States Steel, the world's first billion-dollar corporation, formed in 1901. In 1895 the depression nearly forced the United States government off the gold standard when Congress refused to authorize a bond issue to fund the depleted U.S. Treasury gold reserve. Morgan, working with the Rothschild Bank in Europe, devised a means to legally supply the government with gold.

Again, in 1907, when panic swept Wall Street, Morgan took charge of the situation, summoning the other New York bankers to work out a plan to provide the stock market and the banks with sufficient liquidity to abort the panic. The need to turn to a private banker in times of financial crisis, because the government had been powerless to help, finally convinced the country that the United States could no longer do without a central bank.

After his father's death, Morgan began collecting art, including paintings and rare manuscripts and books, on a massive, almost unprecedented scale. After his death, the books and manuscripts were donated to the Pierpont Morgan Library in New York and most of the paintings were given to the Metropolitan Museum of Art in New York and the Wadsworth Atheneum in Hartford, Connecticut.

BIBLIOGRAPHY
Carosso, Vincent. *Investment Banking in America.* Cambridge, Mass., 1970.

Carosso, Vincent. *The Morgans: Private International Bankers, 1854–1913.* Cambridge, Mass., 1987.

Chernow, Ron. *The House of Morgan: An American Banking Dynasty and the Rise of Modern Finance.* New York, 1990.

Cooper, John Milton, Jr., *Pivotal Decades: The United States, 1900–1920.* New York, 1990.

Kirkland, Edward C. *Industry Comes of Age: Business, Labor, and Public Policy, 1860–1897.* New York, 1961.

Satterlee, Herbert L. *J. Pierpont Morgan: An Intimate Portrait.* New York, 1939.

Strouse, Jean. *Morgan: American Financier.* New York, 1999.

Taylor, Francis Henry. *Pierpont Morgan as Collector and Patron.* New York, 1970.

JOHN STEELE GORDON

MORRIS, WILLIAM (LORD NUFFIELD) (1877–1963), English manufacturer and philanthropist.

William Richard Morris's forebears came from Oxfordshire, and he attended the Church School at Cowley, leaving it at fifteen to become apprenticed to a bicycle repairer. Morris was very good with his hands, a natural mechanic; but he was said never to have learned to read a blueprint, and so was not a designer. After nine months, he left his employer to branch out on his own with a capital of four pounds, to make bicycle repairs, and later he began making his own bicycles in a shed behind his father's home in James Street, Cowley Saint John, Oxford. Further small premises were acquired for cycle storage and repairs, and he obtained a contract for the repair of the cycles used by the Oxford Post Office telegraph boys. Hard work and tremendous energy characterized Morris all his life.

Before the end of the century, Morris took up cycle racing with great success, becoming champion of Oxfordshire, Buckinghamshire, and Berkshire. On 9 April 1904, at age twenty-six, Morris married Elizabeth Anstey, a former schoolteacher. By 1905, Morris had begun hiring out cars and drivers, and driving instruction was also given. Morris became an agent for motorcycles, six British and one American (Hupmobile). The notice "Motor Repairs a Speciality" was prominently displayed in an area of his shop that was Morris's favorite department. By 1912, Morris had developed a four-cylinder car, the Morris Cowley two-seater, a composite vehicle. "To use the assembly method," Morris wrote later, "involves a detailed knowledge of scores of trades." He had that knowledge, acquired over the years in the Birmingham and Coventry areas.

Always looking to the future, in early 1914 Morris made two trips to the United States to study American production methods, the second with a young Norwegian, Hans Landstad, White & Poppe's chief draftsman, who became Morris's chief designer. A bigger Morris car was required, and in place of the T-head 1,018-cubic-centimeter engine of the White & Poppe came the L-head 1,548-cubic-centimeter American Continental engine, considered too small for the American market. So greatly did Morris improve manufacturing methods for munitions that he was awarded the Order of the British Empire (OBE) after World War I. In 1921, Morris countered a serious slump in the motor trade by reducing the prices of his cars; but, always competitive, he doubled their production each year. His 1925 output of fifty-three thousand cars was a European record. In the years leading up to World War II, Morris bought firms that had been his rivals, such as Wolseley and Riley. During the war, he built Tiger Moth training air-craft, tanks, and so forth. Morris was equally known as a philanthropist, in particular for the foundation of Nuffield College (1937) and the Nuffield Foundation (1943), a charitable trust endowed with stock in Morris Motors Ltd., and valued at £10 million. Morris received a peerage in 1934 and became Viscount Nuffield in 1938.

BIBLIOGRAPHY

Andrews, P. W. S., and Elizabeth Brunner. *The Life of Lord Nuffield*. Oxford, 1955.

Jackson, Robert. *The Nuffield Story*. London, 1964.

Jarman, L. P., and R. I. Barraclough. *The Bullnose and Flatnose Morris*. London, 1976.

PETER HULL

MORTALITY. One of the most fundamental dimensions of the human condition is mortality. Among the most outstanding achievements of the modern era have been the reduction of death rates, the prolongation of human life, and the control and even virtual elimination of many infectious and parasitic diseases. This article aims at a brief discussion of mortality measurement and estimation, data sources, and techniques of analysis followed by a discussion of the history of human mortality.

Measurement, Data, and Analysis. The standard way to measure and summarize mortality is the calculation of death rates by combining statistical counts of deaths with base populations at risk, usually obtained from census data. The simplest measure is the crude death rate, usually given as deaths per one thousand midperiod population for a year or group of years. The midperiod population is a common means to approximate person years at risk.

One of the main shortcomings of the crude death rate is that individuals do not die with equal probability at all ages. Risk is relatively high at birth and then declines rapidly with age until it reaches its nadir between the ages of five and twenty. Risk of dying then increases with age, gradually at first and then much more rapidly after about age forty or fifty. In addition, risk of dying differs significantly by sex. Females usually have lower mortality rates at all ages than males, though there are both historical and present-day examples of "crossover," in which females experience higher mortality. Consequently, it is preferable to have mortality rates calculated separately by sex and age, either by single years of age or in standard five-year age groups (for example, five to nine, ten to fourteen). It is preferable also to have single years in the first five years of life (ages zero to four) because of the rapid decline in mortality in that period.

The resulting age-specific death rates produce an abundance of data. To summarize these rates, two techniques are frequently employed. The first is adjusted or standardized death rates. The preferred method is direct standardization, in which a set of age-specific death rates for the population of interest (for example, urban, black females in the United States, 1939–1941) is weighted by a common "standard" population age distribution. This facilitates comparisons across groups and over time if the same standard is used. A less-satisfactory procedure, indirect standardization, is used when age-specific death rates of the population of interest cannot be calculated. It consists of weighting a standard set of known age-specific death rates by the age distribution of the population of interest.

A more sophisticated way to summarize age-specific death information is with the life table, developed in the late seventeenth century by Sir Edmund Halley but put into its modern form by Joshua Milne in the early nineteenth century. It has been used extensively for determining premiums for life insurance and annuities as well as for demographic research. The procedure creates probabilities of dying between any two "exact" ages (for example, ages ten and fifteen) from age-specific death rates. This is the $q(x)$ function from which the rest of the life table is derived. The life table may be calculated from period data, that is, a cross section of death rates in a brief period of time, or with data from actual birth cohorts, that is, the actual death rates of an age group as it moves through time. For period life tables, there is a "synthetic cohort" of individuals at increasing ages from the cross section. Expectations of life at various exact ages are calculated. The most commonly reported is the expectation of life at birth, $e(0)$, which may be interpreted for a period life table as the average number of years an infant would live from birth if he or she experienced the same death rates over life as prevailed in the cross section. For a cohort life table, $e(0)$ would be the actual average number of years lived by an infant in that region and group born in some specified time period. The data requirements are, however, greater and require, for a complete life table, that the cohort has no more living members. The cohort analysis of mortality is more realistic in that it deals with the actual experiences of groups over time, but it is much less common in practice because of the data requirements. Consequently, appeal is often made to the "synthetic cohort" based on the cross section in a period life table. Life tables may be constructed for single years of age or may only cover grouped ages. The latter is known as an "abridged" life table and is the most common type encountered, again because the basic underlying data often come from grouped ages.

For many societies historically or even present-day developing countries with missing or defective data, it may be necessary to use life tables for such purposes as population projections or estimating fertility, and no reliable life tables exist. In such instances, systems of model life tables have been created that can be fitted to the limited actual data of such societies and time periods. The most well known of these are by Coale and Demeny (1983) and by the United Nations (1973, 1982, 1983). Model life tables are also useful when actual life tables are of suspect quality.

A mortality measure of particular interest is the infant mortality rate (IMR). This is calculated as the number of deaths of infants (persons aged zero, that is, not having reached the first birthday) per one thousand live births. Stillbirths are excluded by convention. Mortality is relatively high in the first year of life. Historically, the IMR has often exceeded 250 or even 300 infant deaths per 1,000 live births. That is, 25 percent to 30 percent of all infants died before reaching their first birthday. Infant mortality is divided into subperiods: perinatal mortality (mortality in the first week), late neonatal mortality (mortality at 7–28 days), and post neonatal mortality (mortality at 29–365 days). Neonatal mortality (perinatal and late neonatal mortality) is more affected by congenital conditions at birth. Post neonatal mortality is heavily influenced by environmental circumstances, infectious diseases, and infant feeding practices. Thus historically the decline of the IMR occurred disproportionately in the post neonatal period with the increasing effectiveness of public health measures, medical interventions, health education, more sanitary infant feeding, and the reduction of the incidence of infectious and parasitic diseases.

Another measurement issue involves the cause of death. In 1900, the International Statistical Institute (founded in 1853) held a conference that approved the first standard international list of causes of death (ICD-1). The list has been revised a number of times since then, now under the direction of the World Health Organization. Currently the ninth revision (ICD-9) is used. There has been a shift from symptomatic diagnosis of cause of death to etiological, organic, and epidemiological cause attributions as a consequence of improved medical and scientific knowledge.

Cause of death data furnish a further complication to mortality analysis by introducing another large dimension (to age, sex, race, nativity, residence, regions, marital status, occupation, time period, and so forth). In addition to the primary cause of death, there are also secondary and tertiary causes. For example, diabetes is a major contributing cause to death from cardiovascular disease. A solution to this complication has been the multiple decrement life table with an abbreviated list of causes. The idea is that the "synthetic" population in the life table is reduced not just by age but also by specific primary causes of death. One common abbreviated grouping comprises respiratory tuberculosis; other infectious and parasitic diseases; neoplasms (cancers); cardiovascular disease; influenza, pneumonia, bronchitis; diarrheal disease; certain degenerative diseases; maternal mortality; certain diseases of infancy; motor vehicle accidents; other accidents and violence; and other and unknown. Particular problems for historical research are misdiagnoses of cause of death and large numbers of cases in the category "unknown."

When basic census data or vital statistics are lacking, resort is often made to survey data (such as the recent Maternal and Child Health Surveys or the World Fertility Surveys) and to indirect methods of estimation. For historical research, survey data are usually not present, but indirect estimation methods may still be usable. For example, infant and childhood mortality may be estimated from data in a census or survey on children ever born (parity) and children surviving, cross classified by age or marriage duration of mother. This is possible with samples of the 1900 and 1910 U.S. censuses, the 1896 census of Argentina, and with published and manuscript data from the 1911 census of England and Wales. Adult mortality may be estimated from data on the ages of individuals and whether one or both parents were alive; the same is possible for information on marriage duration and whether the spouse was alive. The distribution of deaths by age (for a stable population) can be used to determine age-specific death rates. Finally, for closed populations (that is, those not subject to significant in and out migration), survivorship from one census to the next for specific age-sex groups can provide estimates of adult mortality.

A particular problem historically is the lack of proper data for many places extending even into the recent past. The periodic taking of censuses with significant demographic detail has been the product of modern data collection systems. Although ancient China had a series of enumerations of "doors" (households) and "mouths" (individuals) and while other premodern societies collected censuslike data, the modern demographic data regimes had their origins in the Scandinavian countries (Sweden, Denmark, Norway, Iceland, and at times Finland) in the seventeenth and eighteenth centuries.

Later in the eighteenth century, some European nations, including Spain (1768–1769, 1787, 1797) and Portugal (1768), took irregular and often rather incomplete censuses. Regular enumerations truly began with the United States, whose federal Constitution (1788) mandated a decennial census for apportionment of the House of Representatives. The first census was taken in 1790, and since then twenty-two national censuses have been taken. A much more general trend to regular national-level enumerations began in the early to mid-nineteenth century, both for governmental and general scientific purposes. This required the improvement of the bureaucratic mechanisms for collecting, tabulating, and publishing the results. There were also increases in the types and details of the types of information collected. Most important for the study of mortality is detail by age and sex. Sometimes questions were asked about deaths in the household in the year prior to the census (for example, in the U.S. censuses of 1850 to 1900), although there are serious issues of understatement of deaths. Questions on children ever born and children surviving began to be asked in the late nineteenth century, and they permit the estimation of childhood mortality.

The collection of data on vital events was instituted in many countries in the course of the nineteenth century, but much earlier the Christian churches established the practice of recording the religious events of baptism, marriage, and burial. The new Church of England parish registers began in 1538. France began the parish register system gradually, but registers were of usable quality only by about 1670. In 1563, the Council of Trent decreed that all Catholic countries should keep parish registers. This system was extended to colonial areas in Latin America and New France (Quebec). Baptisms and burials are not precisely the same as births and deaths, of course, but parish records have yielded important insights into demographic patterns. Elsewhere, ancient China created the institution of family registers that was made official in 1721 and was adopted in Japan. Japan compiled national totals every six years up to 1852. Korea also took up the system and made compilations from 1395. But, as mentioned, the modern system began in Scandinavia in the seventeenth century.

The life table in single or multiple decrement format (or even increment-decrement form) has been a mainstay of mortality analysis, as has straightforward tabular presentation of various mortality measures. In recent years, however, the use of multivariate statistical modeling has popularized some newer methods, such as limited value dependent variable multiple regression, proportional hazards and other Cox models, and Poisson regression. Proportional hazards and related models are similar to multiple regression but consider the dependent variable as waiting time until some vital event, in this case death, as a function of a number of independent variables, such as age, sex, race, residence, and socioeconomic status. It is appropriate for individual-level data. Poisson regression is suited to analysis of aggregated data in the form of rates (for groups, regions, years, and so forth).

Mortality History. There have been significant improvements in human survival over the past several centuries. Much of this has been from reduced mortality from infectious and parasitic diseases and especially diminished mortality peaks (that is, years of severe excess mortality). Before the eighteenth century, epidemics and plagues were major killers in the Western world. Since then the incidence and importance of mortality peaks has sharply diminished, and in addition many other infectious and parasitic diseases have diminished greatly. Now most people die of chronic and degenerative diseases, such as cancer, cardiovascular diseases, and diabetes.

These developments are related to the modern agricultural revolution (beginning in the seventeenth century in Europe), the Industrial Revolution (dating from the late eighteenth century), and modern advances in public health and medicine since the late nineteenth century. Unlike most other species, human beings have suffered disproportionately from infectious and parasitic diseases. This is likely the consequence of living in close proximity with domesticated animals, who also suffer from a similar cause of death structure. For example, tuberculosis, measles, and smallpox likely came from cattle (and some other animals), while influenza and whooping cough probably came from pigs. This was exacerbated by the Neolithic revolution (from about 8000 BCE), which induced humans to shift to sedentary agriculture and nucleated settlements. The increase in population growth from the Neolithic revolution more likely arose from higher birthrates than lower death rates, since settled agriculture and the proximity of livestock were more hazardous to life and health.

History abounds with references to catastrophic epidemics and plagues: the destructive plague in 430 BCE in Athens during the Peloponnesian War, possibly smallpox or typhus; the repeated epidemics in the Roman Empire during the reign of Marcus Aurelius (c. 165–180 CE), likely measles and smallpox; the great plague of Justinian (542–565 CE) and the Black Death of medieval Europe (1346–1349 and subsequent waves), identified with bubonic plague but possibly a viral hemorrhagic fever; numerous references to periodic human mortality peaks in China; and the tremendous decline in the indigenous population of the New World after contact with Old World inhabitants after 1492 from a variety of diseases but particularly smallpox, influenza, and measles.

Human viability is a balance with the environment that includes availability of food, adequate clothing, shelter, and the ecology of the parasitic microorganisms. The Neolithic revolution increased food supplies but at the same time brought people together in situations favoring greater microparasitism and death through infectious disease. Changes in human mobility, densities, locations, and activities have often disturbed that balance and resulted in serious increases in infectious disease and mortality and population stagnation or decline. The appearance of serious epidemics (probably measles and smallpox) from Mesopotamia in the Roman Empire in the second century CE resulted in the longer-term decline of the demographic and economic basis of urban, commercial Roman civilization. It remained for these two highly contagious viral diseases to establish themselves as chronic endemic childhood diseases rather than periodic epidemic adult diseases to restore demographic balance. The effect of exposure to these infections on the indigenous populations of the New

World after 1492 and of the populations of Oceania in the nineteenth century is better documented than earlier serious disturbances to the human-microparasite balance.

The "epidemiological transition" to a low mortality regime is accompanied by a dramatic shift in the cause of death structure. In a simulation exercise, the United Nations constructed four hypothetical populations with accompanying causes of death. In the high fertility, high mortality population (with an $e(0)$ of fifty years and a young age structure from the high fertility), infectious and parasitic diseases accounted for 34 percent of all mortality, while degenerative diseases (cancer and cardiovascular disease) caused 25 percent of deaths. In the low fertility, low mortality population (with an $e(0)$ of seventy years and an older age structure caused by low fertility), infectious disease was responsible for only 6.5 percent of deaths, and degenerative diseases caused 63 percent of mortality.

Many of history's great killers came in epidemic forms: bubonic plague, smallpox, measles, typhus, scarlet fever, influenza. These diseases remained after the eighteenth century, but the mortality peaks began to subside. Plague disappeared from most of Europe in the early eighteenth century. But many diseases (for example, smallpox, measles) were more commonly endemic. The generic forms of gastrointestinal disease (diarrhea, gastritis, enteritis) and of respiratory disease (bronchitis, pneumonia) were important killers of both children and adults. Periodic large-scale epidemics recurred even in the nineteenth century in Europe and other areas, notably when cholera moved from South Asia in the 1820s and created worldwide epidemics in the 1830s, late 1840s, 1860s, and early 1890s. By the nineteenth century, many endemic infectious diseases also began to diminish.

Unfortunately the historical record lacks much standard demographic data, particularly on causes of death, until the eighteenth and nineteenth centuries. Even when they are available, the data are of suspect quality, and the category "other and unknown" is often quite large. England and Wales have the longest time series of consistent data on deaths by age and cause (from 1850 onward) and have been widely studied for the origins of the historical mortality decline. They clearly experienced a sustained decline in the respiratory tuberculosis death rate from at least 1861, well before any specific medical interventions, although some reclassification of deaths from tuberculosis to other respiratory infections contributed to this. The tuberculosis bacillus was not identified by Robert Koch until 1882, and specific chemotherapy and vaccination (BCG) were not available until the 1940s and 1950s respectively. About 18 percent of the mortality decline from all causes during the period from 1848 to 1971 was owed to respiratory tuberculosis. For the period from 1851 to 1860 and from 1891 to 1900, the portion of the mortality decline in England and Wales owed to respiratory tuberculosis was even larger (44 percent), and the share of the decline over the same period attributable to infectious disease was 92 percent.

This English case is likely atypical. For instance, the average share of the decline in age and sex standardized death rates from respiratory tuberculosis was only 11 to 12 percent in the comparable stage of the mortality transition. The cool climate, urban crowding, and polluted air probably all contributed to the high incidence of tuberculosis. For Italy, the share of the early mortality decline (1881–1910) was only about 8 to 10 percent for respiratory tuberculosis, but it was 58 to 60 percent for all infectious diseases. Tuberculosis also may not have always been the major killer among infectious diseases. In Sweden and Finland, respiratory tuberculosis death rates increased in the eighteenth century and into the nineteenth century as the effects of increased population density, crowding, urbanization, and (later) some industrialization took hold. In Italy, with its drier and warmer climate, gastrointestinal infections were of relatively more importance than respiratory infections as a cause of death.

The control of infectious diseases proceeded unevenly. For smallpox, inoculation existed in Europe from the early eighteenth century (and earlier in the Middle East) and vaccination from the 1790s. Inoculation actually gave the patient a case of smallpox under controlled conditions. Vaccination infected the patient with a case of the related cowpox, a much milder and less-dangerous infection in humans. Both conferred partial or total immunity. These measures, gradually adopted over the eighteenth and nineteenth centuries, brought this highly contagious killer under control. For England and Wales, for example, smallpox was responsible for only 1.2 percent of all deaths and 3.6 percent of deaths from airborne infections between 1848 and 1854. It had become negligible as a cause of death by 1901. Much of the reduction in both epidemic and endemic incidence of smallpox had taken place before the mid-nineteenth century. Today, because of assiduous public health measures, smallpox is extinct or close to extinct as a human disease.

Plague, as already mentioned, basically disappeared from Europe in the eighteenth century and only intermittently occurred in the rest of the world (usually Asia). This may have been due to ecological and biological changes in the transmission process, but government quarantines likely played some role. Scarlet fever and diphtheria (responsible for 4.6 percent of deaths in England and Wales in 1848–1854) experienced significant declines in the late nineteenth century. Diphtheria was finally treatable with antitoxin (developed by Emil Behring in 1890 and first produced commercially in 1894), but scarlet fever appeared to diminish in virulence. Measles is a highly contagious viral infection whose effects are similar to smallpox: epidemic course with a high adult incidence and a high case fatality rate in populations without immunity acquired in childhood (for example, the indigenous population of the New World in the sixteenth and seventeenth centuries, Pacific Island populations in the nineteenth century). Both measles and smallpox became largely endemic diseases of childhood with fewer catastrophic demographic consequences as populations became sufficiently dense.

Progress in the control of infectious diseases may have been uneven, but much of the advance has been made since the second half of the nineteenth century. So, for example, the decline in infectious diseases in Italy (from 1881) was more rapid than in England and Wales and was concentrated in gastrointestinal diseases (as opposed to respiratory infections). In England and Wales, the course (and hence control) of these infections was uneven until after about 1890. New Zealand demonstrated a slow decline from much lower levels. Japan exhibited inconsistent progress until after World War II, whereas the United States had a steady and relatively rapid decline in infectious diseases after 1900.

The causes of the decline are varied and may be grouped into four basic categories: improvements in the standard of living (including better nutrition, housing, and clothing), direct medical intervention, public health (including quarantine, improved water supplies and sewage disposal, hygienic milk supplies, compulsory immunizations, and health and hygiene education programs), and ecobiological factors (that is, changes in the basic biological disease environment, organisms, method of disease transmission). A leading hypothesis on the origins of the modern mortality decline is that of Thomas McKeown. He argues that, prior to the twentieth century, specific medical intervention was usually ineffective or nonexistent and that ecobiological changes were rare (affecting possibly plague, scarlet fever, and diphtheria). Thus he placed most of the credit with rising standards of living, particularly better nutrition, although his later work accords a greater role to public health measures. In contrast, Samuel Preston (1976) attributes less than half of the mortality decline in the twentieth century to increases in income per capita, the remainder owing to medical, public health, and ecobiolgical factors.

The answers to the questions on the origins of the modern mortality transitions are not simple, however. As examples, public health measures succeeded in controlling cholera in a number of places before the microorganism was identified. Better water and sewage disposal already had significant effects on urban mortality before the widespread acceptance of the germ theory of disease. It is clear that medical science had contributed to and had an impact on public health in the nineteenth century. Improved standards of living were generated by the economic development process, which also created greater urbanization and, sometimes with a lag, industrialization. Cities had much higher mortality than rural areas, and the positive effects of rising incomes generated by the higher productivity of cities was often more than offset by the negative health externalities of the urban environment. Urban crowding, housing problems, and poor sanitation created increased mortality risks that were only controlled from the late nineteenth century, onward with increased public health programs, administration, and expenditures. These measures were increasingly effective, and several decades into the twentieth century, cities were healthier places than the countryside because of better public health, including water supplies and sewage disposal, more available medical care, and higher incomes. The industrialization process itself also produced new health and mortality risks.

Apportioning the contributions of modern economic growth versus the technology of medical science and public health has been controversial. Current thinking suggests that the extent and timing of the "mortality revolution" was largely dependent on the accidents of technological change, especially the impact of the germ theory of disease (pioneered by Louis Pasteur and Robert Koch, among others) and, in the twentieth century, the "therapeutic revolution" of effective chemotherapies, better diagnostic technology, and modern surgical techniques. Thus the modern mortality revolution, dating from about 1870, is seen as largely independent of the Industrial Revolution and agricultural revolution and as impeded by the rapid urbanization that accompanied the early stages of modern economic growth.

BIBLIOGRAPHY

Cipolla, Carlo M. *The Economic History of World Population*. 3d ed. Baltimore, 1965.

Coale, Ansley J., and Paul Demeny with Barbara Vaughn. *Regional Model Life Tables and Stable Populations*. 2d ed. Princeton, 1983.

Easterlin, Richard A. "The Nature and Causes of the Mortality Revolution." In *Growth Triumphant: The Twenty-first Century in Historical Perspective*, pp. 69–82. Ann Arbor, 1996.

Haines, Michael R., and Richard H. Steckel, eds. *A Population History of North America*. New York, 2000.

Kiple, Kenneth F., ed. *The Cambridge World History of Human Disease*. New York, 1993.

Lancaster, H. O. *Expectations of Life: A Study in the Demography, Statistics, and History of World Mortality*. New York, 1990.

Lee, James Z., and Wang Feng. *One Quarter of Humanity: Malthusian Mythology and Chinese Realities*. Cambridge, Mass., 1999.

Livi-Bacci, Massimo. *A Concise History of World Population*. 2d ed. Malden, Mass., 1997.

McKeown, Thomas. *The Modern Rise of Population*. New York, 1976.

McNeil, William H. *Plagues and Peoples*. Garden City, N.Y., 1976.

Mokyr, Joel. "Technological Progress and the Decline of European Mortality." *American Economic Review* 83.2 (1990), 324–330.

Preston, Samuel H. *Mortality Patterns in National Populations with Special Reference to Recorded Causes of Death*. New York, 1976.

Preston, Samuel H., Nathan Keyfitz, and Robert Schoen. *Causes of Death: Life Tables for National Populations*. New York, 1972.

Shryock, Henry S., Jacob S. Siegel, and Associates. *The Methods and Materials of Demography*. U.S. Bureau of the Census. Washington, D.C., 1971.

Trussell, James, and Timothy Guinnane. "Techniques of Event-History Analysis." In *Old and New Methods in Historical Demography*, edited by David S. Reher and Roger Schofield, pp. 181–205. Oxford, 1993.

United Nations. *The Determinants and Consequences of Population Trends: New Summary of Findings on Interaction of Demographic, Economic, and Social Factors*. New York, 1973.

United Nations. *Model Life Tables for Developing Countries*. New York, 1982.

United Nations. *Indirect Techniques for Demographic Estimation*. Manual X. New York, 1983.

Wrigley, E. A., and R. S. Schofield. *The Population History of England, 1541–1871*. Cambridge, Mass., 1981.

MICHAEL R. HAINES

MORTGAGE BANKS. Already in ancient Greece, real estate (usually land) served as a guarantee to secure the repayment of loans. In contrast to commercial credit, it took a very long time before the provision of mortgages became institutionalized. Until deep into the nineteenth century, notaries (continental Europe) and scriveners (Great Britain) dominated the mortgage market, acting as intermediaries between private creditors and borrowers. This age-old system met increasing criticism by Physiocrats and other observers in the course of the eighteenth century because it led to an inefficient fragmentation of the mortgage market. In areas remote from cities, mismatches between the supply and demand of credit resulted in "unreasonably" high mortgage rates or in some instances even in an absolute lack of capital. Nevertheless, the argument should not be stretched too far. In the eighteenth century, England's traditional mortgage market grew rapidly, so that for landowners, indebtedness became a normal condition of real estate management. Mortgages arranged by scriveners played an important role in financing industry and enclosures in addition to construction of residences.

The institutionalization of mortgage credit started with the creation of the Schlesische Landschaft in 1771. This public land company, organized as a cooperative of Junker landowners, financed its credit operations by issuing mortgage bonds. It was an initiative of the Prussian government to provide the landed aristocracy of Silesia with the necessary funds to restore their estates after the extensive devastation of the Seven Years' War (1756–1763). In the next decades, other Prussian regions and neighboring states, including Bavaria and France, would establish similar mortgage institutions. In the first half of the nineteenth century, despite international diffusion, the land companies failed to gain a substantial share of the agricultural mortgage market. A major reason was that the landed aristocracy often opposed the extension of the system to ordinary farmers. Large landowners preferred to provide mortgage credit themselves as part of a strategy to maintain their grip on the local rural communities. A possible exception to this general picture of relative failure was the Kantonalbanken in Switzerland, which played an important role in improving the infrastructure of the region.

The establishment of Crédit Foncier de France in 1852 gave the institutionalization of mortgage credit a new boost. In contrast to the public Landschaften, France's Crédit Foncier was one of the first private mortgage banks in Europe. As a private institution, it broke with the tradition of class-based provision of mortgage credit (a policy orientation that was maintained when Crédit Foncier later became a semipublic corporation). Moreover, being organized as a joint stock bank, it could rely on a much larger capital basis. Consequently, mortgage bonds could be issued on an unseen scale, so that the number of mortgages granted soared rapidly. Although originally intended to support the development of French agriculture, most credit soon flowed to the promising construction sector, especially in Paris, where Baron Haussmann had just launched his ambitious projects of urban renewal.

In the 1860s, the success of Crédit Foncier and favorable general economic conditions inspired entrepreneurs in many continental European countries to create similar private mortgage banks (e.g., in Germany, the Frankfurter Hypothekenbank). During that period, the rapid development of western Europe's industrial cities attracted thousands of migrants from the countryside, thereby creating a huge demand for new housing. In these circumstances, the notaries were swamped by an overwhelming demand for new mortgages. The general and long economic crisis after the spectacular boom of the early 1870s did not harm the newly created mortgage banks. To the contrary, in this uncertain climate, bonds issued by mortgage banks were considered as secure investments compared with shares.

Great Britain followed a different path toward the institutionalization of mortgage credit. In the first half of the nineteenth century, building societies were established as self-help and self-build organizations. Typically, a group of people agreed to contribute regularly in order to finance the purchase of land and the construction of dwellings. When all members were housed and all debts settled, the society was disbanded. From the mid-nineteenth century, this system of terminating building societies gradually gave way to permanent ones. During the process most building societies grew in size and obtained interests over large districts. At the same time, the emphasis shifted from direct sponsorship of specific building projects to providing mortgage loans to entrepreneurs. These entrepreneurs usually built several properties, which they made available on the rented market.

A somewhat similar system developed in the United States. In the first half of the nineteenth century, savings and loan associations emerged as specialized savings and home financing institutions. They were not banks, as their savings and investment accounts cannot be considered as deposits. Most associations were organized on a mutual basis, with the owners of accounts as shareholders and part owners. Until the early 1930s, savings and loan associations operated solely under state laws, which gave rise to a considerable diversity in the scope of their operations. Most states' laws, however, limited the activity of an association to a certain geographical area.

An important result of the more rational organization of the mortgage market on both sides of the Atlantic was that the balance between demand and supply was more easily achieved. This indirectly brought about a downward pressure on the interest rate. The institutionalization of the mortgage system also paved the way for a considerable extension of the average term of a mortgage. Given the same interest rate, a longer term meant an alleviation of the annual repayment burden. In that way, home ownership became a realistic financial possibility for a somewhat wider public.

Despite these favorable developments, politicians in Europe gradually realized by the late nineteenth century that low-income housing remained a relative unattractive market for private investors. Therefore, the government somehow had to intervene, also in the provision of mortgage credit. In 1889, Belgium authorized the Caisse Générale d'Épargne et de Retraite/Algemene Spaar en Lijfrentekas, a semipublic savings bank, to invest part of its funds in the construction or purchase of working-class housing at a reduced interest rate. In the following decades, the initiative inspired similar cheap credit arrangements in other countries (e.g., France, Germany, and Portugal).

Around the turn of the twentieth century, several private mortgage banks had to change their funding strategy. From the mid-1890s, the traditional method of issuing bonds came under pressure as the revival of the stock market lured many investors. In their search for new financial resources, mortgage banks in some countries started developing networks of agents. In this way it became possible to collect ordinary savings on a large scale and to reinvest them in mortgages. By doing so, the traditional divide between savings banks and mortgage institutions gradually diminished.

Apart from Scandinavia, most mortgage banks, including the British building societies, were not very active in the field of agricultural credit. By the late nineteenth century, cooperative savings banks inspired by the ideas of Raiffeisen had filled up the gap in countries such as Germany and Belgium. Great Britain, however, had to wait until the late 1920s before a specialized agricultural mortgage institution was established.

Despite the turbulent macroeconomic environment, the 1920s proved a relatively prosperous decade for most mortgage banks. The postwar reconstruction period and later the strong drive among the middle classes and better-off workers toward home ownership resulted in a strong demand for mortgage credit. Nevertheless, in their search for deposits, many mortgage institutions felt increasing competition from deposit banks (e.g., in England and France) and universal banks (e.g., in Germany, Belgium). In the early 1920s, merger waves among deposit or universal banks had created powerful financial conglomerates. To broaden their funding base, they rapidly established large numbers of branches in provincial cities.

In the 1930s, these big banks lost market share again. In the early years of the Great Depression, they showed greater vulnerability to bank runs than mortgage institutions. This was certainly not the only reason for the relative success of mortgage institutions, however. The public considered loans guaranteed by mortgages on real estate as more secure investments compared with the risky financing of industrial activities by big banks. Moreover, mortgage institutions benefited from the housing boom that occurred in many European countries during the first half of the 1930s, driven by low (nominal) interest rates, falling building prices, and increasing real incomes for those at work.

Another effect of the severe banking crises in the early 1930s was that government control on banking activities increased substantially. The main concerns of the authorities were the financial sector's stability and the protection of depositors. Therefore, they usually encouraged the avoidance of price competition and, to this aim, froze the banking sector in a specialized and oligopolistic structure. In this framework, the deposit banks were often restricted in their possibilities to offer mortgage loans.

In Britain, the building societies took advantage from the tight control on deposit banks, which gave them a virtual monopoly on the mortgage market. They expanded vigorously, benefiting from the very rapid increase in owner occupation during the second half of the twentieth century. Their total number of offices grew spectacularly, and by 1980, their liabilities to the public in sterling were 20 percent larger compared with those of the deposit banks. At the same time a merger wave took place that created some very big building societies. In 1986, the building societies were allowed to offer a broad range of financial and nonfinancial products. Some big building societies took the opportunity to become full-fledged commercial banks.

In some continental European countries (e.g., France and Belgium), the gradual deregulation process from the late 1960s produced a somewhat different result. The deposit banks aggressively entered the market of real estate finance and pushed the mortgage and savings banks clearly into the defensive. In Germany, the universal banks developed a similar strategy, albeit less successfully. The German mortgage banks responded to the threat with a merger wave and by producing tailor-made solutions for individual customers. The Mediterranean world provided again a different picture as the deregulation process proceeded there very slowly.

[*See also* Banking, *subentry on* Modern Period; Housing, Investment in; *and* Pawnbroking and Personal Loan Markets.]

BIBLIOGRAPHY

Buyst, Erik. *An Economic History of Residential Building in Belgium between 1890 and 1961.* Brussels, 1992.

Cassis, Youssef, Gerald D. Feldman, and Ulf Olsson, eds. *The Evolution of Financial Institutions and Markets in Twentieth-Century Europe.* London, 1995.

Krooss, Herman E., ed. *Documentary History of Banking and Currency in the U.S.* London, 1982.

Pohl, Hans, ed. *Europäische Bankengeschichte.* Frankfurt a.M., 1993.

Pooley, Colin G., ed. *Housing Strategies in Europe 1880–1930.* Leicester, 1992.

ERIK BUYST

MOZAMBIQUE. *See* Southern Africa.

MULK LANDS. *Mulk* land is land held in complete ownership by an individual or group and is recognized as the private property of its cultivators or occupiers. *Mulk* land is also called *mamluk* or *milk* land in Egypt and Iran (formerly Persia). According to conventional adoption of land law in the former Ottoman Empire, the Middle East, and other Muslim areas, *mulk* land represents an unrestricted mode of land ownership in which individuals exercise full rights to dispose of in any way. Such right is considered perpetual. Ownership of *mulk* land is associated with *manfa'a* (usufruct), which, according to Muslim jurist al-Suyuti, is governed by legal recognition, "giving its beneficiary the right to profit from it or receive compensation for it according to the attribution which he possesses." *Mulk* or milk right on property extends to slaves, landed estates, and houses based on the conservative definition of the *raqbe* overlordship (complete ownership right of an estate by an individual) vested in the owner.

The origin of *mulk* land is linked to the transformation of land ownership and administration during the early period of Islam, through the classical period of Ummayad and Abbasid dynasties up to the Ottoman Empire. Land was originally apportioned to individuals in the form of *ushr* (tithe) or *kharaj* (tax paying) and was regarded as the private property of the owner. Because of complications associated with the separation of the two categories of land, owners of *kharaj* land were said to be forbidden from exercising absolute ownership and inheritance of the land. New terminologies were then introduced to distinguish the two forms of land. *Ushr* land was called *mulk* or *milk* land, while *kharaj* land was named *khalisah*, which is further transformed as *miri* or *emiri* land designated as pure crown or state property. *Mulk* land is held in perpetual ownership.

An owner of *mulk* land exercises the most complete legal form of ownership of land under the Ottoman Land Code of 1858. Article 2 of this code divides *mulk* land into four categories:

1. site (for houses) within towns or villages
2. land separated from state land and made *mulk* in a valid way according to the dictates of the Islamic sacred law
3. tithe-paying land that was distributed at the time of conquest among the victors and given to them in full ownership
4. tribute-paying land, which was left and confirmed in the possession of the non-Muslim inhabitants

Mulk land ownership is also associated with the exercise of the absolute right, *dominium*, the real right that incorporates the use, exploitation, and disposal. *Mulk* land ownership is however limited under three conditions:

1. It does not infringe upon other persons' rights.
2. The state protects the public interests against private interests.
3. The rights shall not be abused.

An *emiri* land can be incorporated into a *mamluk* land owing to growing demand for land in such areas as Egypt, where one-third of the land was said to have been turned into *mulk* in the nineteenth century. The difference between mulk and emiri land is, therefore, narrow in historical and political perspectives because *emiri* land can now be inherited while *mulk* land is being governed by the principles of personal property law defined by the *Shari'a* law.

[*See also* Emiri Lands *and* Waqf.]

BIBLIOGRAPHY

Anderson, J. N. D. *Islamic Law in the Modern World.* New York, 1959.

Fisher, Sir Stanley, ed. *Ottoman Land Laws Containing the Ottoman Land Code and Later Legislation Affecting Land with Notes and an Appendix of Cyprus Laws and Rules Relating to Land.* London, 1919.

Gibb, Hamilton Alexander Rosskeen, ed. *The Encyclopaedia of Islam.* New ed. Leiden, 1960.

Liebesny, Hebert J., and Majid Khadduri. *Law in the Middle East,* vol. 1, *Origin and Development of Islamic Law.* Washington, D.C., 1955.

Liebesny, Herbert J. *The Law of the Near and Middle East: Readings, Cases, and Materials.* Albany, N.Y., 1975.

Ongley, F., and Horace Edward Miller. *The Ottoman Land Code.* London, 1892.

IBRAHIM HAMZA

MULTINATIONAL CORPORATIONS.

The phrase *multinational corporation* is used to designate a business that extends across political boundaries. The word *corporation* is frequently used interchangeably with the terms *firm, enterprise, business,* and *company;* in short, the noun indicates that the subject studied is a producer of goods and/or services. So, too, in the literature (and in this essay) the term *multinational* is used interchangeably with the terms *international, transnational, global,* and, most recently, *metanational.* The adjective tells us that the entity does not merely operate "domestically" but under more than a single political sovereignty (it extends as a firm over political boundaries).

Early Multinational Enterprise. Aspects of multinational enterprise were present in ancient times. Sumerian merchants as far back as 2500 BCE realized that in pursuing foreign trade they should have representatives located abroad to handle, warehouse, and distribute goods. Centuries before the birth of Christ, Phoenicians engaged in long-distance commerce (to Africa, Europe, and Asia), and the traders placed men in far-off locales to receive, store, and sell their wares. This type of extension of the trading firm was replicated to some extent in Greek and Roman commerce. After the fall of the Roman Empire, it seems probable that in the first millennium CE, Arab traders' business organizations bore a shadow of resemblance to the networks of prior (and more modern) times.

By the twelfth and thirteenth centuries, Italian and German bankers had offices in a number of European cities. Moving forward, we know little about the institutional structures linked with the global trade in silver of the sixteenth, seventeenth, and eighteenth centuries. Yet, clearly, in the sixteenth and seventeenth centuries, the giant trading companies, for example, the Muscovy Company, Dutch East India Company, and the British East India Company, with their extensive intracompany transactions, arc amenable to study and, indeed, have been studied as multinational enterprises. In short, before the Industrial Revolution, associated with trade and to a lesser extent banking, there had emerged businesses that crossed over political boundaries.

These were the precursors of modern multinational enterprise, which dates from the mid- to late nineteenth century. Before the age of steam across the Atlantic and railroads that connected the interiors of countries, coordination and control within a business organization was impeded by the absence of speed. Letters took months, as did travelers. Yet, managerial structures evolved, based on trust, customs, and established norms. And, indeed, with modern multinational enterprises, corporate cultures have often superceded hierarchical structures in the administration of the firm.

Free-Standing Companies and Classic Multinational Enterprises. Modern multinational enterprise, beginning in the mid- to late nineteenth century, disseminated capital, technology, and ways of doing business on a global scale. Capital did not move simply through markets; it was transferred by companies in connection with the products and processes of modern times. In the late nineteenth century, two types of multinational corporations came of age. The first was what Mira Wilkins called the "free-standing company," a company formed in a locale where capital was abundant, with an eye to doing business abroad. The United Kingdom was by far the most significant nation for the headquarters of free-standing companies, albeit many were based in other capital-rich countries. Investors did not want to send their moneys to unknown ventures abroad; they wanted to know how their moneys were being used. They wanted inside information on the business activities in which they were investing. The free-standing company was used to mobilize capital. It attracted a cluster of related businesses—for example, promoters, accountants, engineers, trading companies, specialists in the region or the industry—and it channeled modern practices to countries around the world. There were literally thousands of free-standing companies in banking, in breweries, in plantations, in mining, in oil concessions, and in public utilities. All the British overseas banks started as free-standing companies (that is, they were not outgrowths of existing British commercial banks). Large capital investments in breweries in the United States and South Africa, for instance, by Britishers were free-standing companies (they did not have breweries as parent firms, but rather were developed to match British resources with opportunities overseas). From India to the Congo, free-standing companies set up plantations. Rio Tinto in Spain began as a free-standing company, as did the predecessors of British Petroleum in Iran. Many of the earliest power and light facilities around the world were initially established as free-standing companies.

At the same time, in other industries, those that required the management of manufacturing *and* distribution, those that involved new products, process technologies, and brand names, the more familiar, so-called "classic" multinational enterprises emerged. Whether it was Singer sewing machines, or Lever soap, or Siemens electrical equipment, there came into existence in the late nineteenth century national and then international business. It was not only manufacturing companies that expanded their business on a broad scale through direct investments abroad. Insurance companies, for example, became multinational enterprises, starting first at home and then spreading more broadly on a global basis. By the early twentieth century such modern multinational enterprises were proliferating. The leading German chemical companies were all multinational, with extensive direct investments abroad. The French Pathé film developed a global business. Ford Motor Company, founded in 1903, had a plant in Canada in its second year and was soon establishing itself as an international enterprise. A 1907 letter from a vice president of Western Electric (the U.S. manufacturer of telephones and telephone equipment) to an agent in Bangkok, Thailand, reveals the breadth of one multinational corporation's operations:

> You speak of an anti-American attitude on the part of the [Government] Commission. We have offices and factories making our standard apparatus in Great Britain, Belgium, Germany, France, Russia, Austria, Italy, and Japan so that so far as this matter goes we are international rather than American. If there were time we could arrange to have the order go to any one of those countries that might be preferred (Wilkins, 1970, p. 200).

World War I disrupted the global economy. German multinational enterprises were sequestered by Allied governments. There were sharp curtailments in their business abroad, with a revival, however, in the late 1920s. There had been extensive multinational enterprise involvements in Russia, which ended with the Russian Revolution (1917). In the 1920s, however, U.S. multinationals expanded in a formidable manner. On a global scale, free-standing companies were still present in this decade, but were of relatively less importance. The most successful of these had internalized the skills and abilities that at origins had been borrowed from the clusters of outsiders, and they came to resemble the "classic" multinational enterprises, containing within the business the "core competencies." Everywhere during the 1920s, after the early postwar crises, there was an expansion of international business operations, particularly those of Americans. The multinational enterprise extended its managerial expertise across borders, operating under the rules of sovereign states.

After the Crash of 1929 and in the 1930s, as the world economy fragmented, multinational enterprises faced political and economic adversity. Most of the leading multinational enterprises persisted, but, with some major exceptions, curtailed their activities. The decade saw rising governmental intervention that sharply affected the behavior of multinational corporations. New barriers to trade meant that if a multinational industrial enterprise was to reach a particular market, it had to manufacture within that market. Companies vaulted over the tariff walls. Foreign exchange restrictions, including blocked currencies, made the life of the manager of a multinational enterprise ever more difficult. When revenues were in local currencies that depreciated, profits were squeezed. The problems of the multinational corporations mirrored those within the world economy.

World War II created new circumstances for multinational enterprises. Assets of "revived" German multinational corporations were once more (as in World War I) taken over by Allied governments. American businesses in Germany and Japan lost their ability to influence, much less control, their foreign affiliates. Because multinational enterprises had operations on both sides of the war, they became suspect. Both enemy and allied governments tried to use these enterprises and their affiliates abroad for national purposes. The tissue of intracompany transactions within the multinational enterprises was torn asunder; control and potential for control by the parent of its affiliates became nonexistent.

Postwar Years. When World War II ended, businesses everywhere turned to domestic concerns. Political and economic risks abroad were formidable. Some companies (General Electric is a splendid example) sharply reduced their international businesses. Initially, only the international oil companies (because oil was so critical to recovery) made large new foreign investments. Gradually, however, the renewal of multinational enterprise occurred. By the 1960s, such books as the one by Jean Jacques Servan-Schreiber were talking about the "American Challenge" in Europe, a challenge of U.S. technology and management, carried across the Atlantic by multinational corporations. Such a refrain echoed views that had been expressed at the start of the century, when American business had presented a range of new products through direct investments in Europe; it echoed similar views of the 1920s on U.S. business abroad. In the 1960s, IBM was introducing the entire world to the beginning of the age of computers. Coca-Cola was the global symbol of America. Such books as Richard Barnet and Ronald Muller's *Global Reach* (New York, 1974) reflected the vast international expansion of American business.

European multinational enterprises were, overall, slower to resume their spread around the world, but by the late 1960s, when the first stage of the "miracle of European unification" had come to pass, European businesses were prepared to extend themselves not only over borders within Europe but farther afield. Japanese multinational enterprises had a long history, yet their historical experience had been modest compared with that of multinational enterprises headquartered in Europe and the United States. Moreover, the Japanese multinationals before World War II had been mainly in trade and banking. Now Japanese multinational enterprises emerged in manufacturing, slowly at first and then by the 1970s quite dramatically. Japanese production methods in automobiles and electronics, demonstrated globally by multinational enterprises, suddenly became the new challenge. By the 1980s, U.S., European, and Japanese multinational enterprises were ubiquitous in the world economy. A sizable portion of world trade was done within companies. Much of the world's technologies were transmitted between parents

MULTINATIONAL REACH. Women shopping for imported merchandise at a store in Saudi Arabia, 1999. (© Katz/Tin Stoddart/Woodfin Camp and Associates, New York)

and affiliates. To the surprise of many (but not to the historians of multinational enterprises), multinational corporations were making their largest investments in developed rather than less-developed nations. Smaller markets and unstable political conditions meant less-developed countries were not particularly attractive to multinational enterprise. In the post–World War II years, many third world countries had expropriated or nationalized properties of multinational enterprises. Developed nations, where property rights were respected and consumers had the ability to buy goods and services, were the most appealing to global corporations. It was in developed countries that the ideas and knowledge could be incorporated and disseminated. The United States was the largest host as well as home to multinational enterprise.

Students of multinational enterprise talked increasingly of the Triad: the United States, Europe, and Japan, and of the bypassing of less-developed countries, whereas in the 1970s, less-developed countries were denouncing transnational corporations and complaining about exploitation. By the 1980s and 1990s, many such nations, while remaining wary of multinational enterprises, eagerly were seeking to attract the latter, perceiving them as "engines of growth."

When the cold war came to an end, and when privatization and deregulation became the global norm, multinational enterprises adapted. Alliances and networks were not new, but as international businesses expanded, these interrelationships took on complex and novel dimensions.

As in times past, so in the 1990s multinational enterprises pioneered in spreading new technologies and new marketing practices, new knowledge, along with corporate cultures. Whether it was cell phones, McDonald's, or Gap, multinational enterprise contributed to the smaller world economy. Industries had become totally internationalized. This was true from the newer biotechnology to the older automobile industries. Banks became multinational. Industries became ill-defined, with single multinational enterprises involved in a number of different overlapping sectors. Internet and e-commerce became incorporated in multinational enterprises' behavior.

Multinational enterprises had often been the results of mergers, of restructuring, and of reorganizations through time. Multinationals would grow to be giants and then would cut back. General Motors in 1990 had 767,200 employees, of which 251,130 were outside the United States (*World Investment Report 1993*, p. 26). In 1999, GM had 398,000 employees, of which 162,300 were outside the United States (*World Investment Report 2001*, p. 90). There was, in short, not a constant linear expansion in size; companies learned of the limits of organization. Companies exited from particular markets and product lines as well as entered into new businesses. The story of multinational enterprises was the story of the jagged growth of firms.

Ebbs and flows in corporate expansion notwithstanding, there is no question but that throughout the entire twentieth century and at the dawn of the twenty-first century, multinational enterprises were in the vanguard of economic innovation, contributing to economic growth, economic change, and the transformations of the world economy. This was true in all sectors. By the start of the twenty-first century, multinational corporations were leading actors in the world economy. They did not transcend sovereign states; they operated under the laws of a multiplicity of nations worldwide; they had a wide variety of relationships with governments. They led in making the world's leading industries thoroughly international.

BIBLIOGRAPHY

Carlos, Ann, and Stephen Nicholas. "Giants of an Early Capitalism: The Chartered Trading Companies as Modern Multinationals." *Business History Review* 62 (Autumn 1988), 398–419. Argues that the early trading companies shared important characteristics with modern international businesses.

Jones, Geoffrey. *The Evolution of International Business.* London, 1996. The only existing history of multinational enterprise, covering all nationalities and sectors.

Jones, Geoffrey, ed. *British Multinationals: Origins, Management, and Performance.* Aldershot, U.K. 1986. A collection of essays on the development of British business overseas.

Jones, Geoffrey, and Lina Gálvez-Muñoz, eds. *Foreign Multinationals in the United States: Management and Performance.* London, 2002. An up-to-date group of articles on foreign multinational enterprises in the United States in the post–World War II era.

Teichova, Alice, Maurice Lévy-Leboyer, and Helga Nussbaum, eds. *Multinational Enterprise in Historical Perspective.* Cambridge, 1986. A set of original papers, by leading scholars on multinational enterprise, with materials on the growth of international business and data on governments and multinationals.

Wilkins, Mira. *The Emergence of Multinational Enterprise: American Business Abroad from the Colonial Era to 1914.* Cambridge, Mass., 1970. The first history of American multinational enterprise and the standard work in the field.

Wilkins, Mira. *The Maturing of Multinational Enterprise: American Business Abroad from 1914 to 1970.* Cambridge, Mass., 1974. The second volume of Wilkins's history of American business abroad; *The Emergence* was the first. *The Maturing* was nominated for a National Book Award and like *The Emergence* has gone through a number of printings. These two volumes are considered the basic work on the history of U.S. business abroad.

Wilkins, Mira. *The History of Foreign Investment in the United States to 1914.* Cambridge, Mass., 1989. A comprehensive history of foreign investment in the United States that is heavily weighted to cover foreign multinationals in the nation that attracted the most investments by foreign multinational enterprise. Two sequels to this volume are forthcoming, one on 1914 to 1945, and the other on the years subsequent to 1945.

Wilkins, Mira. "Japanese Multinationals in the United States: Continuity and Change, 1879–1990." *Business History Review* 64 (Winter 1990), 585–629. A narrative on the rise of Japanese multinational enterprise in the United States, revealing how far back such investments existed.

Wilkins, Mira, ed. *The Growth of Multinationals.* Aldershot, U.K. 1991. An anthology of previously printed articles on the history of multinational enterprise, which charts the surveys of multinational enterprise, pioneering essays on the subject, new perspectives, case studies, and data on countries that were hosts to multinational enterprise.

Wilkins, Mira, and Harm Schröter, eds. *The Free-Standing Company in the World Economy, 1830–1996.* Oxford, 1998. A collection of original essays that discusses the role of this important, special type of multinational enterprise.

Wilkins, Mira. "The History of Multinational Enterprise." In *The Oxford Handbook of International Business*, edited by Alan M. Rugman and Thomas L. Brewer, pp. 3–35. Oxford, 2001. A survey of the subject with an extensive bibliography on the history of multinational enterprise.

MIRA WILKINS

MUMFORD, LEWIS (1895–1990), American intellectual, historian, architectural critic, and social commentator.

Mumford's most significant contribution to economic history is his series on the history of technology. The first book in this series, *Technics and Civilization* (1934–1963), was pioneering in its sweeping cultural and social interpretation of technology, even if it was not quite as precise as A. P. Usher's *History of Mechanical Inventions*, from which it borrowed. Mumford's book became a precursor of modern constructivist interpretations of the history of technology, regarding technology as fundamentally a social phenomenon. Mumford adhered to a stage theory of technological development. He regarded history as consisting of three stages—eotechnic, paleotechnic, and neotechnic—largely based on advances in energy usage, which he borrowed from the Scottish writer Patrick Geddes. The distinction most critical to his thinking was between machines and "the Machine," meaning a technological system of growing complexity, with which he became increasingly concerned.

Mumford viewed the paleotechnic age, roughly the period of the first Industrial Revolution, with disdain, referring to it at one point as a "new barbarism," a mixture of bourgeois culture and environmental degradation. Yet in his earlier work, he was persuaded that new and clean sources of energy, coupled with urban planning, could raise the curtain on a new age. Electrical power was to liberate industrial capitalism from its youthful foibles.

Mumford had little interest in the Marxist notions of class struggle, but his criticism of the early industrial age was just as trenchant, if more hopeful. As Mumford observed, Marx was concerned mostly about questions of distribution (for whom were goods produced?), whereas Mumford was concerned about the possibility of the wrong goods being produced and about scientists producing the wrong kind of knowledge, serving the industrial complex rather than the population at large. Although *Technics and Civilization* is ambiguous in its view of the historical role of technology, in its closing sentence Mumford wrote that although modern science and technics have fallen short of their inherent possibilities, the lesson from history is that "nothing is impossible."

In the aftermath of World War II, and especially in view of the use of the atomic bomb, Mumford became increasingly pessimistic and a radical skeptic of technology. This thinking culminated in *The Myth of the Machine* (1967), especially the second volume, entitled *Pentagon of Power* (1970). In that book, Mumford argued that human history was driven by "megamachines," and he was appalled rather than fascinated by the use of science in large production systems. The Machine, as he saw it, embodied the entire technological society or military-industrial complex. In some ways, Mumford's writings resemble those of antitechnological philosophers such as Jacques Ellul and Herbert Marcuse, although his despair was never quite as complete as theirs. Mumford feared the coming of a technological culture in which a small scientific elite with a monopoly of knowledge controlled every manifestation of life by reducing it to its mechanical components. His lifelong sense of social justice made it impossible for him to reconcile the technological system with basic human values, and his later writing combined a deep pessimism about the future of industrial society with a technological determinism he had been able to avoid in his earlier work.

BIBLIOGRAPHY

Hughes, Thomas P., and Agatha C. Hughes, eds. *Lewis Mumford: Public Intellectual*. New York, 1990.

Mumford, Lewis. *Technics and Civilization*. (1934) New York, 1963.

Mumford, Lewis. *The Myth of the Machine: Technics and Human Development*. 2 vols. New York, 1967.

MUSEUMS. The museum is often understood as a characteristically modern western European institution. In fact, its origins may be traced to classical Greece and the great Hellenistic Museion of Alexandria, founded by Ptolemy Sotor around 290 BCE. The emphasis here was on education and philosophical inquiry, rather than the accumulation of historical material. The temples of ancient Rome contained a greater profusion of works of art, paintings, weapons, and curiosities.

The revival of the museum idea during the Renaissance began with the formation of several important Italian collections, notably those of the Venetian republic, the Vatican, and, above all, Florence, under the influence of the Medicis. It was the building and collecting activity of the elder Cosimo de' Medici (1389–1464) that turned the new Medici palace into "the first museum of Europe," albeit a private one. The princely collections of Renaissance Italy placed a relatively low value on paintings and contained a baffling variety of objects: antique sculpture, precious stones, natural history specimens, and a variety of curiosities. The emphasis was on similitude, resemblance, and correspondences between objects. A more restricted collection of paintings and sculpture would be described as a gallery. From the late sixteenth century in England, noble and gentry houses often included a long gallery, usually occupying an entire upper floor or a wing, which could be used for exercise in wet weather, or increasingly, for display.

More common than either, from the sixteenth to the eighteenth centuries, was the gentleman's "cabinet," a single room containing decorative art and curiosities, especially natural history specimens. Several well-known examples were described and illustrated by contemporaries, such as those of the Neapolitan naturalist and chemist Ferrante Imperato (1599), Frances Calceolari in Verona (1622), and Olaf Worm in Copenhagen (1655). These *Kunstkammers* or *chambres des merveilles* attempted in some degree to create a partial world picture, a theater of the world, at a time when Europe was poised on the edge of new scientific discoveries. They attempted to "bring all of nature indoors," setting it alongside *artificialia*, or manmade objects.

The scientific revolution and the rationalism of the eighteenth-century Enlightenment provided the context for a new approach to collecting: that of comprehensiveness. Rather than representing a random assembly of exotic objects, the ideal museum collection was increasingly seen as one that contained a systematic classification of all the known materials in the universe. Diderot expressed the idea in volume 9 of his *Encyclopédie* in 1765, but the British Museum, founded in 1759, was the first institution to embody the encyclopedic ideal of universality, both in the range and classification of the collections and in terms of public access. Its precursor was the Tradescant Museum, a small natural history collection opened to the public in Lambeth in 1625, cataloged by Elias Ashmole in 1656, which later formed the core of Oxford University's Ashmolean Museum (opened in 1683).

The British Museum operated with a small annual grant from Parliament, but public entry was restricted to sixty visitors a day until 1808, when the quota was doubled. It was the egalitarianism of the French Revolution that ushered in a genuinely democratic concept of public access to museums, with the opening of the new Louvre in 1793. With Napoleon's rise to power, the idea of a democratic, national museum was overlain with the spoils of conquest to create an aggressive kind of cultural imperialism. From 1803 to 1813, the Musée Napoleon (as the Louvre was known) brought together major works of art from the conquered territories of Europe, and for the first time arranged them into a series of national schools, set out in separate rooms and galleries. After the Congress of Vienna of 1815, most items were restored to their original owners, but a new art-historical principle had been established, based on differentiated categories. The centralization of

MUSEUM. Interior of the Guggenheim Museum, New York. (Robert E. Mates/Solomon R. Guggenheim Museum, New York)

previously dispersed works was justified on the grounds of public education.

The restitution of looted works of art in 1815 was often accompanied by a reevaluation of their significance, and the creation of new national museums and galleries followed in many European countries, including Spain (the Prado, opened 1819), the Netherlands (the Rijksmuseum, 1815), and Germany (the Altesmuseum, Berlin, 1830, and the Alte Pinakothek, Munich, 1836). In many cases, the founding or refounding of national museums and galleries was the accompaniment of nationalist movements and struggles for national independence, particularly in Germany, Hungary, and Czechoslovakia. In Britain, nationalistic expression in museums remained weak, but Anglo-French industrial rivalry after 1815 and fears about the impact of mechanization produced a new determination to improve the quality of industrial design, the outcome of which was the foundation of design schools and the South Kensington Museums (1852), later renamed the Victoria and Albert Museum (1899). The 1850s also saw the establishment of a national museum in the United States, the Smithsonian, which, like the Victoria and Albert, had a well-articulated educational role.

In the core museum countries of Europe—Britain, France, Germany, and Italy—the classical tradition shaped the museum establishment and its concerns, but from the late nineteenth century, Celtic, Nordic, and Scandinavian sources gained ground. European industrial growth and the loss of vernacular buildings stimulated interest in "folk life" museums, pioneered in Sweden by Artur Hazelius at the Nordiska Museet at Stockholm (1873). A century later, deindustrialization created the opportunity and the demand for open-air industrial museums, particularly in Britain, where the Beamish and Ironbridge Gorge museums pioneered new approaches.

The late twentieth century saw a much-enhanced educational role for museums, together with substantial increases in government funding in many countries. Today, Europe has about 15,000 museums, with another 20,000 across the rest of the world, and their economic benefits in terms of urban and rural regeneration are widely recognized. The International Council of Museums (ICOM, founded 1946) is now represented in 140 countries of the world and operates as a nongovernmental professional organization representing museum interests. ICOM has advisory status to the United Nations Educational, Scientific, and Cultural Organization (UNESCO) and the United Nations Economic and Social Council, and maintains close links with the International Council on Monuments and Sites (ICOMOS), the international body dedicated to the conservation of the world's historic monuments and sites.

BIBLIOGRAPHY

Bazin, Germain. *The Museum Age*. Brussels, 1967.

Hooper-Greenhill, Eilean. *Museums and the Shaping of Knowledge*. London, 1992.

Hooper-Greenhill, Eilean. "The Museum in the Disciplinary Society." In *Museum Studies in Material Culture*, edited by S. M. Pearce, pp. 61–72. Leicester, 1989.

Impey, Oliver, and Arthur MacGregor. *The Origins of Museums: The Cabinet of Curiosities in Sixteenth- and Seventeenth-Century Europe*. London, 1985.

Lewis, Geoffrey. "Museums and Their Precursors: A Brief World Survey." In *Manual of Curatorship: A Guide to Museum Practice*, edited by J. M. A. Thompson, pp. 5–21. London, 1984.

McClellan, Andrew. *Inventing the Louvre: Art, Politics, and the Origins of the Modern Museum in Eighteenth-Century Paris*. Cambridge, 1994.

DAVID ORMROD

MUSIC INDUSTRY.

> Birds do it, whales do it,
> Folks dressed up in tails do it . . .

What they do, of course, is make music—one of the most ancient modes of social interaction. The oldest known musical instrument, a seven-hole Chinese flute, has been carbon dated to 7000 BCE. King David of Israel was famed not only for his military prowess but also for his skills in composing and playing on diverse musical instruments. The development of music in medieval Europe can be characterized by events three centuries apart in the Wartburg, a fortress towering over the town of Eisenach, Germany. From the *Codex Manesse*, dating from the early thirteenth century CE, we know that Landgraf Hermann von Thüringen staged a singing competition in the Wartburg that attracted the leading minstrels of central Europe (excluding Tannhäuser, who was placed there posthumously through the confusion of names in early legends and then by Richard Wagner). In 1521, Martin Luther (1483–1546) took refuge in the Wartburg from death warrant-bearing agents of the Holy Roman Emperor, and there composed the great Protestant anthem, "A Mighty Fortress Is Our God."

Church and Court Support. The Protestant Reformation that Luther precipitated ended the monolithic control of Rome over acceptable forms for church music. The multiplicity of approaches to religious music that followed ranged from the intricate polyphony of Giovanni Palestrina (1525–1594), to the Lutheran organ chorales of Dietrich Buxtehude (1637–1707), to the predations of Cromwellian thugs during the 1650s, who entered English churches to destroy their organs. During the quarter millennium after Luther's Worms trial in 1521 composition and performance for religious services became the vanguard for a great flowering of classical music. This, in turn, induced a demand for improved musical instruments: notably, the violins, violas, and violoncellos whose perfection, not since surpassed, was centered in the Austrian Tyrol and Cremona, Italy, culminating in the creations of Antonio Stradivarius (1644–1737). Paralleling these advances in instrument technology, but more decentralized geographically, was the perfection of organs by the great organ builders of Flanders, France, Germany, and Italy.

In the eighteenth century, a new vanguard emerged. The performance of music had long been cultivated in noble European courts. As the population of central Europe was restored following the devastations wrought by the Thirty Years' War (1618–1648), food prices and hence land rents began to recover from their post war depression, enriching feudal landlords. By a process whose exact dynamics have not been fully illuminated, a kind of cultural arms race occurred. The central European and northern Italian lands that had previously formed the core of the Holy Roman Empire were divided into hundreds of principalities and dukedoms. Many, especially in what is now Germany, were largely autonomous, free of any central control; others were subservient to the Habsburg monarchy. Enjoying enhanced land rents and the tariffs collected on internal commerce, they began competing with one another for prestige—among other things, through the ostentatious

splendor of the operas, concerts, and table music performed within their courts. See Elias (1983; 1993) and Raynor (1972). This competition among noble courts created a vibrant market for musicians and encouraged the composition of innovative works that would enhance the noble patron's prestige. With more musicians employed, there was an increased probability that a few individuals of extraordinary creative genius would emerge, gravitating to the most affluent or most progressive courts. Surveying this historical epoch, Baumol and Baumol (1994) argue that

> Obviously, economic and political conditions cannot create talent, but they certainly can either inhibit it or provide opportunities for its exercise. Our main hypothesis . . . suggests that the political division of the Holy Roman Empire and the Habsburg possessions into many petty states worked to produce the circumstances that . . . help to explain the profusion of musical productivity in the eighteenth century.

Eventually, however, the competition among noble courts for musical talent abated. There were at least four intersecting reasons. For one, the extravagant expenditures required to keep abreast brought many courts, especially those that borrowed heavily to support their conspicuous consumption, into precarious financial straits. Second, as in arms races and oligopolistic competition, when virtually all courts had orchestras, the distinction of maintaining one faded, so many mended their finances by dropping out of the race. Third, the French Revolution and the ensuing Napoleonic Wars (1789–1814) engulfed much of central Europe and forced temporary dispersions of many noble courts. And fourth, the reform or abolition of feudal master-peasant tenure relationships was accelerated by the French Revolutionary invasions and the ensuing economic distress, encouraging many landlords to become active farmers and not mere rent receivers.

Free Market–Oriented Activity. Meanwhile, new and even more powerful forces were materializing. At first gradually but then with increasing speed and geographic scope during the nineteenth century, the Industrial Revolution led to a greatly expanded and prosperous middle class. Emulating customs that were once mainly the province of the noble orders, the newly prosperous bourgeoisie began to make music an important part of their social lives. For the female children of bourgeois families, ability to perform on the cembalo, the newer pianoforte, or the flute was a symbol of social status and often enhanced a maiden's chances for an advantageous marriage. Middle-class citizens' attendance at operas and public orchestral concerts increased, and well-to-do families entertained themselves and their friends at home with chamber music salons. The demand for home performance of music created a derived demand for music lessons provided by professional musicians and for sheet music supplied by a rapidly growing publishing industry, which in turn paid honoraria and (later) royalties to composers for their creations. As public concerts began to draw growing middle-class audiences, opportunities for freelance music performers and composers expanded. With rising demand for public concerts came a demand for larger performance halls, which in turn induced technological innovations affecting musical instruments to improve their versatility (e.g., with the addition of keys and valves to wind instruments) and their carrying power, especially with continuing improvements in the strength and resonance of the pianoforte, invented by Bartolomeo Cristofori (1655–1731) in the early years of the eighteenth century and improved initially by German organ-builder Gottfried Silbermann (1683–1753). My analysis of data on U.S. piano sales during the nineteenth and twentieth centuries reveals an income elasticity of demand in the range of 3.2 to 4.3. As income per capita rose, demand for home pianos rose much more than proportionately.

The decline in noble court and church support of music and the rise of private-sector demand for freelance musicians is shown quantitatively by Figure 1, which is derived from Scherer (2001a). A broad sample of music composers born between 1650 and 1849 was drawn, using as a reference point composers whose works were available in recorded form, as compiled in the *Schwann Opus* guide to recorded classical music for fall 1996. Altogether, adequate information on 645 such composers was available, with the number of composers born in fifty-year intervals rising from 141 for the 1650 to 1699 cohort to 148 from 1700 to 1749, 168 from 1750 to 1799, and 188 from 1800 to 1849. The bar graph heights in Figure 1 show the percentage of each fifty-year cohort's members who pursued as a principal or secondary vocational activity three categories of work: employment with or direct subsidy from a noble court, employment with the church, and composing as a freelance unaffiliated music provider. Many composers were coded as having been active in two or even three of these alternatives during their careers. Johann Sebastian Bach (1685–1750), for example, was employed as church organist and music director in Arnstadt, Muehlhausen, and Leipzig; as composer in the ducal courts of Weimar and Coethen; and as director of and composer for a privately organized and financed orchestra, the Collegium Musicum, during his later years in Leipzig. Even Johannes Brahms (1833–1897), one of the most independent-minded of nineteenth-century freelance composers, spent brief intervals as an employee of the Detmold principality court. For all 645 sampled composers, the trend away from church and court support and toward market-oriented freelance activities is unmistakable, even though freelance composing activity is already evident among the 1650 to 1699 birth cohort.

Opera was one of the first organized musical activities to provide freelance composition opportunities. Although there were scattered nonpublic antecedents associated with noble courts, the first public opera house, San Cassiano, opened in Venice during 1637. It established patterns widely emulated elsewhere in Italy, England, and parts of northern Europe, such as the free Hanseatic city of Hamburg. New opera houses were brought into being by a consortium of wealthy citizens, sometimes ennobled and sometimes not, who contributed capital for the building and who usually received permanent rights to a theater box in compensation. A committee representing the founding contributors chose an impresario to manage the opera's affairs under contract. The impresario typically assumed some financial risks for a season, lurching perilously between success and ruin and sometimes fleeing town ahead of creditors when the chosen performances cost too much or attracted too few paying spectators. When deficits occurred, as they often did, the original investors were called upon to add new subventions. The impresario contracted with performers, composers, and librettists and organized the intricate series of events that had to occur before a new opera (there were typically several per season) mounted the stage.

Composers were normally paid a fixed fee, varying with their past success record, some in advance and the remainder only when the opera was staged. Would-be composers competed for contracts to compose not only for operas in the city in which they resided, but all over Italy and often in the principal cities of other European nations. Thus, even as early as the seventeenth century, opera composing was characteristically a freelance activity. It was not unusual for a composer to write several operas per year, most of which failed quickly and were withdrawn. Up to the nineteenth century, composers surrendered all rights in their compositions to the impresario in exchange for a fixed fee. The impresario in turn contracted with copyists, whose payment often consisted in part of the right to make additional copies they would sell to smaller provincial opera houses.

This was not the only organizational pattern. Especially in Austria and Germany but also in Naples, the opera was maintained as an enterprise by the ruling local sovereign, who provided a theater and subsidies, appointed an impresario to organize the activities, and often retained one or more composers as regular court employees responsible for churning out several new operas per year. Sometimes the composer was paid a bonus for each new opera he completed; sometimes not. The more able court-employed opera composers were occasionally given leave to compose operas for noncompeting geographic venues, and in this respect, they also became freelance composers.

For instrumental and orchestral music, a variety of other market-oriented organizational forms emerged. In the

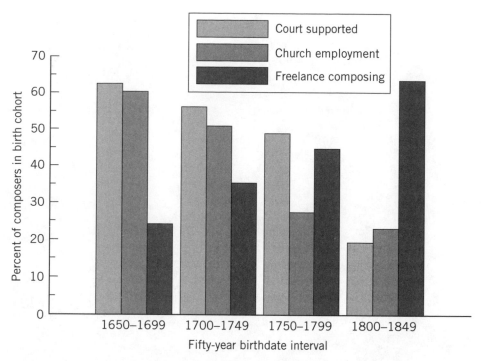

FIGURE 1. Trends in the occupational roles of classical music composers. SOURCE: Scherer, 2001a.

wealthier cities, solo and chamber music performance took place in the salons of nobles or affluent bourgeoisie. Composers would be invited to present their works, participating in and directing multiperformer pieces and hoping for an honorarium whose magnitude was not always fixed in advance, and which frequently proved disappointing. Composers and freelance performers during the eighteenth and nineteenth centuries often traveled from city to city and arranged, through the good offices of an acquaintance or a prominent citizen to whom a letter of recommendation was carried, an ad hoc performance in a local hall or theater. Risks for such performances varied widely, depending on the affluence and goodwill of the local sponsor. For out-of-the-way cities like Riga (Latvia), seldom graced by prominent talent, halls and accompanying musicians were often provided gratis.

A venue that yielded appreciable profits for Wolfgang Amadeus Mozart (1756–1791) in his early Vienna years was the subscription concert, under which a hall would be reserved for a series of concerts and subscriptions would be sold in advance. The number and quality of musicians hired to complement each performance could be adapted to the magnitude of early receipts, and if advance bookings were insufficient, as Mozart found when Austria went to war against Turkey in 1788, the series could be canceled altogether.

For many composers and performers, an important source of financial support was the benefit concert; a hall was secured and friendly musicians donated their comple-

mentary services in the expectation of later reciprocity. Substantial net receipts might then be retained by the beneficiary. Finally, beginning in the eighteenth century and expanding during the nineteenth and twentieth centuries, regular concert series were sponsored by entrepreneurs or musical organizations in the larger cities.

Composition for and performance in such series became a significant source of earnings for capable freelance composers and performers. A particularly successful example was that of Franz Joseph Haydn (1732–1809), who, after toiling for decades as a salaried music director for the Princes Esterhazy, traveled to London twice during the 1790s for concerts arranged by Johann Peter Salomon (1745–1815) and returned to Vienna with a substantial fortune.

Music Publishing and Copyright. Selling their compositions to publishers was one way freelance composers could earn the money required to keep body and soul together. Firms specializing in music publishing began to emerge in the seventeenth century, appeared in larger numbers during the eighteenth century, and proliferated during the nineteenth century. In the eighteenth century there were two main technologies for printing sheet music. The staffs, notes, and other markings could be cut or stamped onto a smooth copper or pewter plate and then printed by the method known as engraving; or individual lines, notes, notations, and text could be set in movable type following a much more complex variant of the processes believed to have been invented by Johann

MUSICAL PERFORMANCE. *A Concert,* pen and ink drawing by Giuseppe Zocchi (1711–1767). (Gabinetto dei Disegni e delle Stampe, Galleria degli Uffizi, Florence/Scala/Art Resource, NY)

Gutenberg (1397–1468). Engraved music tended to be of higher quality than typeset music, but the typesetting method was greatly improved during the 1750s by Johann G. I. Breitkopf (1719–1794) of Leipzig. In the early years of the nineteenth century a new process, stone lithography, reduced music publishing costs. Further cost reductions and quality improvements followed with the adoption of photo offset lithography beginning in the 1860s. During the eighteenth century and the early decades of the nineteenth century, music publishers faced competition from copyists, sometimes acting individually and sometimes employed by firms, who laboriously copied musical manuscripts, one sheet at a time, by hand. Because engraving, typesetting, and lithography all required substantial front-end setup costs, hand copyists had a speed advantage over the more mechanical processes. When demand was quite limited, their unit costs were also lower.

The success of hand copyists was facilitated, and the profits of mechanical music publishing were constrained, by the paucity of well-defined intellectual property rights in music compositions. At first, composers and publishers sought royal privileges to prevent others from copying their musical works. Such privileges were granted in many parts of Europe, especially in France, but required good political connections—something many composers lacked. The prototype of modern copyright laws was the so-called Statute of Anne, enacted in England in 1709. It shift-ed emphasis from protecting publishers to protecting authors (and under later interpretations, music composers), established systematic and open procedures for obtaining protection, and provided exclusive rights in new works for a period of twenty-eight years (later extended). France abandoned the privilege system and embraced a copyright approach after the Revolution of 1789. Article I, Section 8, of the U.S. Constitution expressly authorized the granting of copyrights; enabling legislation followed in 1790. Copyright laws spread to the Habsburg empire, Italian territories controlled by Austria, and various German states between 1828 and 1840.

Due to the fragmented governmental organization of central Europe until well into the nineteenth century, privileges and copyright often offered ineffective protection against copying. A composer or publisher might obtain an exclusive privilege to publish music in Berlin, but could not restrain the dissemination of pirated works from Mainz or Paris. National unification eliminated part of this problem, and reciprocity treaties among some European nations reduced cross-border copying. The principle that copyright in one national jurisdiction could restrain copying in another, reciprocating nation achieved worldwide scope beginning with the Berne Convention of 1886.

Copyright laws strengthened the bargaining position of composers vis-à-vis potential publishers, increased publishers' profits by reducing the loss of sales to pirates, and led to the development of a new approach to derivative performance rights. Following precedents originating in France, Giuseppe Verdi (1813–1901) was one of the first composers to utilize the new system of rights aggressively. Up to the establishment of copyright in northern Italy in 1840, opera impresarios pursued one of two courses. They either licensed hand copies of new opera scores to provincial theaters wishing to replicate the opera, dispatching an overseer to ensure that additional copies were not made, or they allocated the right to disseminate the scores in this way to their copyists. Once a copyright law existed, Verdi insisted on retaining the rights to his scores, which he then licensed through his agent and publisher, Giovanni Ricordi (1785–1853). At first Verdi proposed to collect a fixed honorarium for each subsequent performance of his operas, but Ricordi convinced him that this strategy would choke off performances in smaller towns or induce theaters to use pirated works adapted just enough to dodge legal restraints. As a result, Verdi and Ricordi adopted a system of performance fees graduated to what the traffic would bear. Verdi then received an agreed-upon percentage of the receipts from Ricordi, who maintained the requisite enforcement organization. Verdi could now relax the frenzied pace at which he had been composing and live a life of luxury.

Substantial transaction costs had to be incurred to manage performance rights systems like those implemented by Ricordi and Verdi. Ricordi employed a sizable team of field agents and retained attorneys in all the principal cities of Italy. Recognition of this problem led to the creation of copyright collecting societies that serve all composers, monitoring the media in which music might be performed, collecting royalties for the use of individual works, launching exemplary lawsuits to bring free riders into line, and distributing royalties to the copyright owners in proportion to measured usage rates. The pioneer in this genre, carrying forward the provincial performance rights licensing approach used by the Paris Opera, was France's Société des Auteurs et Compositeurs Dramatiques, established in 1829. In the United States, similar functions are performed by ASCAP (the American Society of Composers, Authors and Publishers, organized in 1914) and BMI (Broadcast Music Incorporated). In the United Kingdom, the parallel organization is the Performing Right Society Ltd., created in 1914.

Growing Prosperity and Technological Revolutions. As prosperity gradually increased, the demand to hear others perform music was extended into a much larger segment of the population, first into the middle class and then into the working classes. Musical institutions responded, and performance moved from being an élite to a mass culture. An early antecedent was John Gay's (1685–1732) *Beggar's Opera*, first performed in London during 1728. Featuring jaunty tunes on popular themes sung in English, it proved wildly popular, draining patronage away from traditional Italian-language operas performed at the time and tapping new, less wealthy, audiences. It set a precedent for later nineteenth-century operettas written by Jacques Offenbach (1819–1880), Johann Strauss Jr. (1825–1899), Gilbert and Sullivan, and many others. In Italy, opera houses began shifting in the 1850s from offering more or less original operas to repertory, sparing creative and set-building outlays and permitting less affluent individuals to buy tickets. Verdi became a national hero whose works were known and loved by virtually all. In Vienna, ballrooms proliferated during the 1830s until they could accommodate 50,000 participants simultaneously. "Waltz King" Johann Strauss Sr. (1804–1849) responded entrepreneurially to the new demand, increasing the size of his private orchestral forces to employ under contract 200 musicians, who were deployed in smaller contingents to numerous ballrooms scattered across the city (see Fantel, 1971). His son Johann Jr. assumed leadership of the family enterprise upon the father's death, and in 1872 he reached what was undoubtedly the pinnacle of nineteenth-century commercial music. For the unprecedented fee of $100,000 (plus traveling expenses), he joined the Boston Peace Jubilee, conducting an orchestra of 2,000 that performed Strauss waltzes before audiences (sheltered by a giant wooden shed) estimated at 100,000 persons.

The demographic changes in music appreciation and performance might have continued evolving along this trajectory but for a series of revolutionary technological innovations that began toward the end of the nineteenth century and continued throughout much of the twentieth century. Among the most important were the phonograph (or gramophone), whose facilitating inventions are attributed to Leon Scott in 1857, Thomas Edison in 1877, and Emil Berliner in 1897; the radio, over which the first music transmission was achieved by Reginald Fessenden in 1906, with public broadcasting expanding rapidly in the 1920s; the telephone, over whose wires commercial radio broadcasts were transmitted between cities; talking (and singing) motion pictures, which appeared in the late 1920s; television, whose use exploded in the years following World War II; coaxial cable, radio relay, and fiber optical cable transmission of radio and video signals over long distances; the long-playing high-fidelity record, which became popular in the 1950s; the commercial videocassette recorder, introduced during the 1970s, and the compact disc audio player, introduced in 1981.

These technological developments made performed music available at affordable prices to persons in every income stratum, at least within the economically developed nations. They gave rise to whole new industries—most notably, the music recording industry and (as part of a broader sector) the music broadcasting business. Consumer purchases of recorded music accelerated when phonographs began embodying electrical (or, in newer terminology, electronic) principles in place of mechanical acoustic methods in 1925. The sale of musical records in diverse and technologically improving formats expanded more or less steadily from that time on. In the United States, sales of one billion individual music recordings, mostly in the form of compact discs and tape cassettes, were first achieved in 1994. The growth rate of unit shipments continued at a brisk rate of 4.2 percent per year between 1982 and 1998.

Although the exact chain of causation needs more systematic exploration, the nearly simultaneous emergence of broadcast radio and electrical phonographs appears to have had a profound impact on the way musical performances were enjoyed. In the estimation of an income elasticity of demand for pianos mentioned above, additional explanatory variables included the number of phonographs and radio sets owned by U.S. households. Competition from phonographs (initially of poor sound quality) was found to have little impact on the demand for pianos, but as radio set usage increased, the sale of new pianos plummeted. No longer, it would appear, did the middle-class American family gather around the piano for an evening of homemade musical entertainment. Instead, the urge to hear music was satisfied by listening to radio broadcasts of the Hit Parade, Bing Crosby, the Metropolitan Opera (Saturday afternoons), the NBC Symphony Orchestra, and much else. Enjoying music became less active and more passive. An era approached its end.

Changes in technology also affected another phenomenon—the economics of superstardom (see Rosen, 1981). Superb talent is rare, and consumers have always been willing to pay a premium to enjoy it. Farinelli (aka Carlo Broschi) (1705–1782), by universal acclaim the greatest of all eighteenth-century castrati, earned £5,000 during the 1735–1736 opera season in London, the richest of markets, at a time when a master building craftsman employed full-time earned £30 per year. Castrati in general received much higher fees than other singers, who were in turn better paid than orchestral players. A century later, in 1831, the most brilliant violinist of all time, Nicolò Paganini (1782–1840), netted £10,200 from six concerts in London, capping a European tour that brought wealth of which few contemporary musicians could even dream. As rail transportation displaced tedious, backbreaking stage coach transit and reliable steamships entered the coastal and ocean routes, the most distinguished musicians traveled with increasing frequency to the metropolitan centers—Paris, London, Saint Petersburg, and New York—where their superstar status would yield the largest fees.

The electronic revolutions of the twentieth century allowed superstars to reach out to even larger audiences and hence to extend their financial advantage over more mundane musicians by increasing margins. The "three tenors"—Jose Carreras, Placido Domingo, and Luciano Pavarotti—reached tens of millions of listeners through their worldwide television broadcasts during the 1990s, earning performance fees and subsequent record royalties dwarfing those of the most successful nineteenth-century stars. Record sales and performance fees allow the most successful performers of popular music to become millionaires many times over. Like market-dependent indices such as the returns to technological innovation, the sales of popular records follow a skew distribution; a relatively few big hits capture a disproportionate share of sales. In 1997, for example, the best-selling musical album, by the Spice Girls, achieved sales of 5.3 million units in the United States alone; seventy albums had U.S. sales of 1 million units or more. The best-selling single record in 1997, Elton John's "Candle in the Wind" (commemorating the death of Diana, princess of Wales) sold 8.1 million units in the United States, or 6 percent of all the singles purchased that year. Warren Hamlen (1991) estimated that dollar sales in the United States between 1955 and 1987 totaled $80 million for records featuring Barbra Streisand, $68 million for Billy Joel, $63 million for the Beatles, and $18 million for the twentieth most purchased star's records. Electronic amplification also made possible huge public concerts at Woodstock (New York), Central Park, and other open venues, drawing audiences far larger than those of the 1872 Boston Peace Jubilee. The most lucrative known North American concert tour, by the Rolling Stones in 1994, had gross receipts of $121 million.

Changing Fashion. Fashion has always been an important determinant of musicians' success. Patrons' and later middle-class consumers' tastes for musical styles tended to change with each passing generation. George Frideric Handel (1685–1759) hovered on the brink of bankruptcy when the Italian operas he was offering Londoners fell out of favor, but rebounded by composing English-language oratorios. Asking to be released from his salaried job with the archbishop of Salzburg in 1781 to become a freelancer in Vienna, W. A. Mozart was warned presciently that in Vienna "a person's fame lasts only a short time; at the beginning one hears only praises and earns a great deal, that is true—but for how long? After a few months the Viennese want something new." And indeed, Mozart died in debt, in part because he lost the support of his most affluent adherents. Similar lapses from fashion befell many prominent composers during the nineteenth century. In the twentieth century, changes in musical taste occurred with even greater rapidity. But since the tastes of many consumers, once acquired in youth, often remain durable, there has also been a proliferation of musical styles, all available in recorded format. Thus, in the realm of popular music, the period following World War II saw the emergence from already existing "popular," country/western, jazz, swing, blues, and calypso forms such innovations as bebop, rock'n'roll, hard rock, soft rock, techno, and rap, among others. More variants seem certain to follow. Conventional revealed preference theory suggests that humankind has gained something from the innovations, although when preferences can be molded under the pressure of peer-group fads, theory provides less definitive guidance. The individual historian, recognizing that "de gustibus non disputandum est," is well advised to avoid personal judgment.

[*See also* Theater Arts.]

BIBLIOGRAPHY

Baumol, William J., and Hilda, Baumol. "On the Economics of Musical Composition in Mozart's Time." In *On Mozart*, edited by James H. Morris, pp. 72–101. Washington, D.C., 1994.

Elias, Norbert. *The Court Society*. Trans. by Edmund Jephcott. Oxford, 1983.

Elias, Norbert. *Mozart: Portrait of a Genius*. Trans. by Edmund Jephcott. Berkeley, 1993.

Fantel, Hans. *Johann Strauss: Father and Son, and Their Era*. Newton Abbot, U.K., 1971.

Hamlen, William A., Jr. "Superstardom in Popular Music: Empirical Evidence." *Review of Economics and Statistics* 73 (November 1991), 729–733.

Jensen, Luke. *Giuseppe Verdi and Giovanni Ricordi, with Notes on Francesco Lucca*. New York, 1989.

McFarlane, Gavin. "Copyright Collecting Societies." In *The New Grove Dictionary of Music and Musicians*, vol. 4, pp. 748–760. Macmillan, 1980.

McVeigh, Simon. *Concert Life in London from Mozart to Haydn*. Cambridge, 1993.

Moore, Julia. "Beethoven and Musical Economics." Ph.D. diss., University of Illinois, Urbana-Champaign, 1987.

Pohlmann, Hansjörg. *Frühgeschichte des musikalischen Urheberrechts*. Kassel, 1962.

Raynor, Henry. *A Social History of Music from the Middle Ages to Beethoven*. New York, 1972.

Rosen, Sherwin. "The Economics of Superstars." *American Economic Review* 71.5 (December 1981), 845–858.

Rosselli, John. *The Opera Industry in Italy from Cimarosa to Verdi: The Role of the Impresario*. Cambridge, 1984.

Rosselli, John. *The Life of Verdi*. Cambridge, 2000.

Scherer, F. M. "The Evolution of Free-Lance Music Composition, 1650–1900." *Journal of Cultural Economics* 25 (2001a), 307–319.

Scherer, F. M. "The Innovation Lottery." In *Expanding the Boundaries of Intellectual Property*, edited by Rochelle C. Dreyfuss et al., pp. 3–21. Oxford, 2001b.

Scherer, F. M. *Quarter Notes and Bank Notes: The Economics of Music Composition in the 18th and 19th Centuries*. Forthcoming.

F. M. SCHERER

MUTUAL FUNDS. Mutual funds are financial products that invest pools of monies into a variety of securities, such as stocks and bonds. Mutual funds are generally classified into two types: closed-end and open-end. Closed-end funds trade on financial markets, like common stocks, where their prices are determined by the interaction of supply and demand. The investment product often trades at a discount or premium to its underlying net asset value. Open-end mutual funds, on the other hand, buy and sell shares directly with investors at the prevailing net asset value less any redemption fee.

The origin of the modern closed-end mutual fund can be traced to investment trusts formed in Europe during the nineteenth century. King William I of the United Kingdom of the Netherlands established trusts in the 1820s that allowed investors to purchase shares in foreign government stock. London's Foreign and Colonial Government Trust, founded in 1863, invested in foreign and Commonwealth securities. The first U.S. mutual funds, the New York Stock Trust (1889) and the Boston Personal Property Trust (1893), primarily purchased shares in railroad companies.

One of the most important early mutual funds was Philadelphia's Alexander Fund, established in 1907. Twice a year the trust offered shares at a price of $100 and a 6 percent yield. The manager received a fee equal to 10 percent of income and profits. The distinguishing feature of the issue was that subscribers could redeem their shares on demand minus a 10 percent fee to the manager, foreshadowing modern-day open-end funds. Moreover, anyone dissatisfied with a stock in the portfolio could challenge the pick with the elected Board of Overseers. If the board agreed, they could force the manager to sell the contested investment (Rottersman and Zweig, 1994).

Participation in nineteenth-century and early-twentieth-century mutual funds was generally limited to wealthy individuals, however. Most Americans placed their savings in banks or purchased shares of stock in individual companies. The emergence of mutual funds in the mid-1920s forever changed the way Americans invested their savings. The number of funds increased from a handful to nearly seven hundred by the end of the 1920s. Most funds were of the closed-end variety, although open-end funds also benefited from the bull market. On the eve of the great stock market crash in October 1929, the assets of mutual funds exceeded three billion (Rottersman and Zweig, 1994).

The 1929 crash drove many mutual finds out of business, especially closed-end trusts that had purchased securities on margin (DeLong and Schliefer, 1991). The crisis and ensuing depression prompted reform of America's financial system as well as the mutual fund industry. The Securities Protection Act, passed by Congress in 1933, required companies to provide investors with a prospectus that described the composition and administration of funds. The Securities and Exchange Commission, created in 1934, placed mutual funds under the jurisdiction of the National Association of Securities Dealers, which sets advertising and distribution rules.

The most important legislation for the mutual fund industry included the Investment Company Act and Investment Advisers Act of 1940. The Investment Company Act requires funds to price their assets based on the market value, places limitations on transactions between a fund and its manager, and sets leverage limits. The law also mandates that funds redeem an investor's shares within seven days of a request. The Investment Advisers Act requires most investment advisers to register and contains some antifraud provisions (Campbell, 1994).

The mutual fund industry struggled in the years following the stock market crash and Great Depression. Mutual fund companies did not bring a single new closed-end fund to market in the 1930s. By 1951 there were slightly more than one hundred mutual funds with approximately one million shareholders. A resurgent equity market in the 1950s and 1960s renewed investor confidence in security markers, sparking renewed growth in mutual funds. The industry expanded to 269 funds with $48.3 billion in assets under management by the end of the 1960s (*Mutual Fund Fact Book*, 1970).

The 1970s were a period of innovation in the mutual fund industry. Most funds had traditionally limited their portfolios to common stocks. New financial products, such as balanced funds with both stocks and bonds, ushered in an era of diversified investment products. Money market mutual funds offered check writing privileges and higher interest rates than savings accounts. Tax-exempt municipal bond funds and Individual Retirement Accounts (IRA) were created as well. Investors now had many choices to create a diversified portfolio and to invest in tax-free and tax deferred accounts.

Some innovations were also inspired by academic research. Proponents of the efficient markets hypothesis (EMH) argued that stock prices reflected all currently available public information (Fama, 1970). One implication of the EMH is that investors cannot consistently pick stocks that will outperform the market. The Vanguard Company introduced indexed mutual funds in 1976 to track the overall performance of the stock market as measured by the Standard and Poor's Index of five hundred companies. The passive investment approach has gained increasing popularity as index funds have generally outperformed actively managed funds (Jensen, 1968; Malkiel, 1977).

The mutual fund industry expanded in the 1980s with the beginning of the greatest bull market in American history. The assets of mutual fund companies increased 939 percent during the 1980s. Mutual funds began to offer financial products ranging from real estate to closed-end emerging market country funds in addition to standard investments in U.S. securities. Mutual fund growth continued in the 1990s as the number of funds rose to over 8,000 with $6.8 trillion in assets and over 80 million investors (*Mutual Fund Fact Book*, 2000–2002).

The downturn in American equity markets at the beginning of the twenty-first century has led to some consolidation in the mutual fund industry. Although it is difficult to predict the long-term effects of the stock market drop, it is clear that mutual funds have become an important savings vehicle for the average investor.

BIBLIOGRAPHY
Campbell, William A. "The Investment Act of 1940: Reasonable and Intelligent." *Friends of Financial History* 51 (1994), 14–18.
DeLong, J. Bradford, and Andrei Schleifer. "The Stock Market Bubble of 1929: Evidence from Closed-End Mutual Funds." *Journal of Economic History* 51.3 (1991), 675–700.
Fama, Eugene F. "Efficient Capital Markets: A Review of Theoretical and Empirical Work." *Journal of Finance* 25.2 (1970), 383–417.
Jensen, Michael C. "The Performance of Mutual Funds in the Period 1945–1964." *Journal of Finance* 23.2 (1968), 389–416.
Malkiel, Burton. *A Random Walk down Wall Street*. Princeton, 1977.
Mutual Fund Fact Book. Investment Company Institute. New York, 1970.
Mutual Fund Fact Book. Investment Company Institute. New York, 2000–2002.
Rottersman, Max, and Jason Zweig. "An Early History of Mutual Funds." *Friends of Financial History* 51 (1994), 12–20.

MARC D. WEIDENMIER

MYANMAR. Formerly Burma, Myanmar is the name given to the country by the military regime that refused to accept the results of the 1990 elections. The boundaries of the state are, like those of other countries in Southeast Asia, inherited from the colonial period, when Burma was conquered by the British, based in India, in three wars: that from 1824 to 1826, when they acquired Arakan and Tenasserim; that from 1852 to 1854, when they acquired Pegu; and that of 1885, when they dislodged the monarchy in what they called Upper Burma. They went on to establish their supremacy over the chiefs in the Shan states.

The state that the British acquired bit by bit had not been integrated previously. The core of the kingdom was in the dry zone of central Burma, where Mandalay was the last of several royal capitals. Based there, the monarchs sought to bring under their control not only the Burmans but other peoples, too. Besides the Shans, those included the "hill" peoples—Kachins, Chins, and Karens—over whom they were generally content to exercise a loose suzerainty, and the Aakanese, whose kingdom was conquered between 1784 and 1785. Their main struggle was with the Mon people to the south. King Alaungpaya's suppression of their revolt in the 1750s was marked by the foundation of Rangoon (Yangon), "the end of the strife." But that city was never the focus of the Burman realm, though it became the capital of British Burma and remains the capital of the successor-state.

The Kyaukse area is one of the first in Southeast Asia for which there is documented evidence of wet-rice cultivation. The productivity of the system was the source of the kingdom's strength and aspiration. Only one of the dynasties—the first Taung-ngu—sought to base itself in the delta of the Irrawaddy rather than in the traditional dry zone, and so take a larger part in maritime commerce. For Alaungpaya, Rangoon was an end rather than a beginning. Like other traditional monarchies, moreover, Burma prohibited the export of rice.

In general the kingdom was, like most of Southeast Asia in the precolonial period, thinly populated: perhaps 4 million in 1824. The extent of the depopulation of the Mon region after its reconquest may have been exaggerated. Certainly, however, the delta of the Irrawaddy was almost empty.

The British conquest thus not only shifted the focus of the realm, it also led to an economic transformation. Burma became a major rice exporter, first to Europe, particularly after the opening of the Suez canal in 1869, and then increasingly to India and other parts of Asia. That was made possible by the settlement of the delta by cultivators from other parts of Burma. Their success was itself made possible not only by back-breaking and disease-ridden labor, but by the availability of loans from wealthier Burmans and, more controversially, from Chettiars, members of a trading and banking caste from the Madras presidency.

The British administration also made this transformation feasible by abandoning the prohibition on rice exports and by changing the traditional attitude to tenure. Traditional rulers in scantily populated Southeast Asia valued people, not land; service, not tax. Influenced by Smithian liberalism and anxious to establish a taxable base, colonial rulers took a different view. In Burma, they produced the Land and Revenue Act of 1876, which established property in land and made it possible to use it as a security, enhancing the advantage conferred by the regularity of the monsoon in Lower Burma.

The British, as elsewhere, hoped to establish a peasant proprietary. The result, however, was rural indebtedness and foreclosures. Burmese lenders were no less exacting than Chettiars, perhaps more, but increasingly it seemed that the delta was coming into the hands of non-Burmese.

The communal antagonisms stimulated by the Depression in the 1930s nevertheless focused on the urban areas. There, Burmans had been much slower to take up the opportunities that the new administration offered, while Indian migrants, often already experienced in its ways, had an advantage. Rangoon, its capital, became increasingly an Indian city. By 1901, Indians formed 51 percent of its population. The riots of 1930 occurred because Burmese labor had been driven by economic pressures to compete with Indian labor in the rice-processing industry and on the docks.

Nationalists seeking to challenge British rule saw this as part of a pattern: their country had fallen under a double imperialism, that of India as well as Britain. When the Japanese overthrew the British, indeed, the position of the Indians was destroyed as well—more than four hundred thousand joined the chaotic evacuation of 1942—and it was never restored.

Nationalists had also criticized the role of major British firms. The Irrawaddy never became a means of opening up a major trade effort with western China, but its superb accessibility made the fortunes of the Irrawaddy Flotilla Company. British firms also dominated the extraction of teak, of which Burma was the major source. Long used in shipbuilding, it was used also for railway sleepers as well as housing and furniture. Its importance led to the first attempts at a well-conceived timber policy, those initiated by Governor-General Dalhousie on the acquisition of Pegu. Mines in Karenni and the Shan states offered lead, silver, and tungsten. But, most significant in an empire deficient in the newer sources of energy, Burma was a source of oil. The Yenangyaung fields were developed by Burmah Oil, the parent of Anglo-Iranian, starting in 1886. A pipeline to Syriam was laid in 1908.

Nationalism—together with wartime destruction—made it unlikely that these firms would play a large part in the economy of Burma after it secured its independence in 1948. Attempting to respond to agrarian unrest and to preempt communist opposition, the government adopted a left-wing program. Like other Southeast Asian countries, it also associated independence with a program of import-substitution industrialization. That seemed all the more necessary because, neighbor of India, Burma was even less industrialized than other Southeast Asian countries, but it was all the more risky. Its failure—not simply due to insurgency on the part of what had become "minorities" as well as of the communists, nor to the fall in rice prices after the Korean War—helped to erode the position of the civilian elite. The military took over in 1962 and has retained power ever since.

Myanmar has rejected the paths that the other Southeast Asian countries took—encouraging foreign investment, moving from import-substitution industrialization (ISI) to export-oriented industrialization (EOI)—and no doubt avoided some of the problems that development brought. Its determination to retain power, however, gave China an opportunity: it became a source of arms and a major trading partner. Was there a risk that Myanmar was exchanging the dominance of one great neighbor for another?

BIBLIOGRAPHY

Adas, Michael. *The Burma Delta: Economic Development and Social Change on an Asian Rice Frontier, 1852–1941.* Madison, Wis., 1974.

Aung, Tun Thet. *Burmese Entrepreneurship: Creative Response in the Colonial Economy.* Stuttgart, 1989.

Cady, John F. *A History of Modern Burma.* Ithaca, N.Y., 1958.

Chakravarti, Nalini Ranjan. *The Indian Minority in Burma: The Rise and Decline of an Immigrant Community.* London, 1971.

Cheng Siok-hwa. *The Rice Industry of Burma, 1852–1946.* Kuala Lumpur, 1968.

NICHOLAS TARLING

N

NAMIBIA. *See* Southern Africa.

NAPLES. Naples traditionally has benefited from its strategic position as a gateway between an unusually fertile agricultural hinterland and the central and western Mediterranean. Founded as a "new town" serving as a feeder to the city of Cuma in the sixth century BCE, Naples became the seat of an independent duchy in the eighth century CE. Falling increasingly into the orbit of Rome, it appears to have been economically and politically less dynamic than the neighboring cities of Amalfi, Gaeta, Capua, and Salerno. The creation in the twelfth century CE of a unified Norman kingdom in southern Italy marked a turning point in Neapolitan fortunes. In 1224, Frederick II (1198–1250) founded a university there (including law and medical schools, as well as a faculty of theology, established in 1231, where Thomas Aquinas studied), in competition with the University of Bologna. By 1266, the new Angevin regime had moved the main seat of government from Palermo to Naples; when Sicily broke away from the mainland in 1282, Naples became the capital of the mainland south. Under Robert Anjou (1309–1343), Naples became the hub of Florentine merchant banking, based on an exchange of credit to the Crown for export rights to wheat.

However, Naples felt the benefits of capital status most strongly from the mid-fifteenth century on, when the pace of political centralization rose sharply. Naples rose from about 50,000 inhabitants in 1450 to 150,000 around 1500, and doubled in size again by the early 1600s. The city stagnated during the seventeenth-century depression, but growth resumed in the 1730s; by the 1790s, Naples was the third largest European city with nearly 500,000 inhabitants. The second largest southern Italian city in the same period was Lecce, which reached 30,000 inhabitants. The two phases of strongest demographic growth also marked peaks of economic and cultural achievement: first during the mid-fifteenth century when Alfonso I of Aragon (king of Naples 1442–1458) took up residence in Naples at the head of a Mediterranean empire that included Castile, Aragon, Catalonia, Sicily, Sardinia, and Naples; and then in the eighteenth century under the Bourbons, when the city became a leader of the European Enlightenment. Both phases ended with French-inspired wars: the invasion of Italy by Charles VIII (r. 1483–1498) in 1494–1495 and the short-lived anti-Bourbon revolution of 1799.

NAPLES. Panoramic view of the city and its harbor, engraving, eighteenth century. (Alinari/Art Resource, NY)

The causes of Naples's demographic dominance were twofold. First, southern Italian rulers granted Naples a vast portfolio of commercial and tax privileges—including full exemption from tariffs on grain supplies and from direct taxes—that significantly lowered the city's relative cost of living and led to the wholesale immigration of the provincial feudal elite and their retinues and hangers-on. This influx generated a huge, self-reinforcing source of concentrated demand funded by rural incomes and turned Naples into the main source of investment and commercial capital in the kingdom. Modern Italian historians—influenced by the French Physiocrats and by Naples's relative economic and cultural decline since Italian unification (1860), when it lost its traditional privileges—consequently have analyzed premodern Naples as a parasitical consumer of rural wealth and as the source of many of the lasting imbalances in southern Italy's economy and society. This view must be mitigated by the second factor at play, namely, a lack of urban competitors elsewhere in the kingdom, which was due as much to the persistence of high feudal barriers to trade and market fragmentation as to Neapolitan privilege, and which explains why centralized demand from metropolitan Naples did not have more positive consequences for market integration and growth.

BIBLIOGRAPHY

Bentley, Jerry H. *Politics and Culture in Renaissance Naples*. Princeton, 1987.

Chorley, Patrick. *Oil, Silk, and Enlightment: Economic Problems in XVIIIth Century Naples*. Naples, 1965.

Davis, John A. *Merchants, Monopolists, and Contractors: A Study of Economic Activity and Society in Bourbon Naples, 1815–1860*. New York, 1981.

Imbruglia, Girolamo, ed. *Naples in the Eighteenth Century: The Birth and Death of a Nation State*. Cambridge, 2000.

Società Editrice Storia di Napoli. *Storia di Napoli*. 15 vols. Naples, 1967–1978.

S. R. EPSTEIN

NATIONAL DEFENSE. The financing of the military and its weaponry has proved the crucial problem of governance for most cultures. Among the early civilizations, such as the river valley empires, financial administration and government were inseparable. Governments were organized on hierarchical bases, with the rulers possessing control over military decisions. Taxes in these agricultural economies were paid in kind, which made it more difficult to utilize the revenue for military campaigns over great distances. Supporting a large standing army was the most expensive item. The optimal size of an empire was determined by the efficiency of its taxation, resource extraction, and transportation systems, whereas the supply of weaponry was seldom a crucial variable. Some changes were brought on by the diffusion of cheap iron weaponry after about 1200 BCE.

Other civilizations, nonetheless, paled in comparison with the military efficiency and economy of the Roman Empire. Military spending was the largest item in the public budget throughout Roman history. During the first two centuries of the Empire, the Roman standing army consisted of about 160,000 men, with another 150,000 troops available to it. For example, in republican and imperial Rome more than half the revenue went to military pay.

In the early Middle Ages, a diverse system of European feudalism emerged in which feudal lords provided protection for a price to smaller communities. Prior to 1000 CE, the command system was still preeminent, on a contingency basis, in the mobilization of military resources. This system of patrimonialism, as Charles Tilly (*Coercion, Capital, and European States*, AD *990–1990*, Cambridge, 1990) defines it, began its slow decline with the twelfth century Crusades. The feudal kings were forced to supplement the ordinary revenues to finance their armies. Because of the political ambitions and the expansionary drives of the medieval rulers, however, they usually had to rely on short-term deficits in military financing.

Innovations in warfare and military technology, driven by the gunpowder revolution of the fifteenth century, permitted armies to attack and defend larger territories. Warfare then became commercialized in the fourteenth and fifteenth centuries as volunteer feudal armies had to give way to professional mercenary forces. Accordingly, medieval states needed still more revenue, relying increasingly on indirect taxes, to support the growing costs of warfare. The commercialization of warfare was accompanied by the rising importance of sea power as the European states began to build their overseas empires. States like Portugal, the Netherlands, and England became the "systemic leaders" due to their extensive fleets and commercial expansion.

The early winners in the fight for world leadership were usually supported by the availability of inexpensive credit. This pattern can be perceived in England. Between 1535 and 1547, the English defense share (military portion of state expenditures) averaged 29.4 percent, with large yearly fluctuations. Between 1685 and 1813 its mean defense share increased to 74.6 percent, never falling below 55 percent, and England became the most feared fiscal-military power of the period.

The newly emerging nation states began to develop more centralized and productive revenue-expenditure systems, especially in the absolutist era. The cost and scale of warfare grew: during the Thirty Years' War (1618–1648) between 100,000 and 200,000 men fought under arms on the average, whereas fifty years later, in the War of the Spanish Succession (1701–1714), some 450,000 to 500,000 men went to battle. The proportion of populations serving in the armed forces increased dramatically. For example, from about 1500 to 1700, the French armed forces share of the population increased from 0.1 to 2.1 percent, the English share increased from 1.0 to 5.4 percent; and the Swedish share during its short bid for greatness increased spectacularly to 7.1 percent. The warring participants' reliance on long-term credit was extensive. Spain's decline in the seventeenth century can be linked to the lack of long-term credit as well as poor financial management.

The new style of warfare, prominent in the revolutionary wars of the latter part of the eighteenth century, and the rapid population growth, lowering the percentage of the population in the armed forces, increased the European warring potential even further. The French army grew more than 3.5 times in size from 1789 to 1793, up to 650,000 men, the British army grew from 57,000 men in 1783 to 255,000 in 1816, and the Russian army retained a massive army of 800,000 men even after 1815. This kind of mobilization, encouraged by the introduction of conscription by the French during the revolutionary wars, became more or less permanent in the nineteenth century, requiring new sources of financing.

Reforms were introduced, such as reliance on balanced budgets, innovations in public debt management, and direct taxation. These reforms were supported by the industrial revolutions and rising productivity levels, and were accompanied by an industrialization of war and armaments production from the mid-nineteenth century on. The economic challenges posed by these changes differed. For the French, the mean defense share remained roughly the same between 1870 and 1913, about 35 percent, whereas its military burden (military expenditures share of gross domestic product) rose modestly to 4.2 percent. For Great Britain, the mean defense share from 1870 to 1913 declined slightly, to 36.7 percent, compared with the early nineteenth century. However, the strength of the British economy actually enabled its military burden, slight to begin with, to decline to 2.6 percent. Germany incurred a similar percentage in the same period.

For most countries the period leading to World War I meant comparatively higher military burdens. The United States, the new economic leader, incurred a meager 0.7 percent average military burden, similar to the interwar period. In World War I (1914–1918), this military potential was unleashed in Europe, with a war of attrition causing immense suffering and property damage amounting to some $36 billion. After the war, especially in the 1920s, public spending in most countries was plagued by budgetary immobility. However, although the defense shares of democracies dropped noticeably, their respective military burdens either stayed at similar levels as before or actually increased. The French military burden rose to a mean level of 7.2 percent. The British average military burden increased, despite efforts to cut military spending, although its mean defense share dropped to 18.0 percent.

For these countries, the mid-1930s marked the beginning of rearmament, their authoritarian challengers having begun even earlier. Hitler's Germany increased its military burden from 1.6 percent in 1933 to 18.9 percent in 1938, its rearmament program promising both "guns and butter." Mussolini's efforts in Italy were less successful, producing a military burden of only 4 to 5 percent in the 1930s. The Japanese rearmament drive was the most extensive, amassing a military burden as high as 22.7 percent in 1938.

In World War II (1939–1945), the initial phase from 1939 to early 1942 favored the Axis as far as strategic and economic potential were concerned. After that, the war of attrition, with the United States and the USSR joining the Allies, turned the tide in favor of the economically superior Allies. The economic demands of the war were unprecedented. The British maximum military burden of about 27 percent of gross domestic product (GDP) in 1918 grew to more than 50 percent and remained there throughout World War II. The United States assumed a new military-political leadership role afterward, especially within the North Atlantic Treaty Organization (NATO), founded in 1949. The USSR, rising to new prominence during and after the war, established the communist Warsaw Pact in 1955. The war also gave impetus to welfare states that brought the Organization for Economic Cooperation and Development (OECD) government expenditure average from under 30 percent of GDP in the 1950s to more than 40 percent in the 1970s.

Military burdens and military-industrial complexes grew at the same time, with military spending levels peaking during the early Cold War. The American military burden rose above 10 percent in 1952–1954, and retained a high mean value of 6.7 percent for the postwar period. Great Britain and France followed the American example, albeit more warily. The Cold War embodied a relentless armaments race between the two superpowers, with the USSR spending about 60 to 70 percent of the American equivalent in the 1950s. CIA estimates analyzed by Noel E. Firth and James H. Noren (*Soviet Defense Spending: A History of CIA Estimates, 1950–1990*, College Station, Tex., 1998) indicate that the cost of U.S. military programs in 1965–1989 continued to exceed the equivalent dollar cost of the Soviet programs until 1972. From 1972 to 1985, the USSR surged ahead. All in all, during this period American military spending amounted to a total of $6.1 trillion (in 1988 prices), whereas the USSR spent an estimated $6.3 trillion. Nevertheless, figures by the Stockholm International Peace Research Institute (*SIPRI Yearbooks of World Armaments and Disarmament*, Stockholm and Oxford, 1969/70–2000) point toward a two-to-one lead in favor of NATO over the Warsaw Pact throughout the 1970s and 1980s. Part of this armaments race was due to technological

NATIONAL DEFENSE. *The Parade of the Red Army,* painting (1923) by Konstantin Yuon (1875–1958). (Tretyakov Gallery, Moscow/Scala/Art Resource, NY)

advances that produced a mean annual increase in real costs of about 5.5 percent. Still, consumption spending on personnel and operations has remained the biggest expense.

Military spending levels began a slow decline throughout the world from the 1970s onward, with the exception of the early 1980s. The American military burden was 6.5 percent in 1986, dropping to 3.0 percent by 1999. The decline was mostly triggered by the downfall of the Soviet bloc. The USSR's challenge to American military dominance began to crumble after the mid-1980s, but the Soviet military burden remained high until 1990 (12.3 percent). In the 1990s, with a declining GDP, the Russian military burden dropped rapidly, to 3.2 percent in 1998.

Other nations also downscaled their military spending in the 1990s. For example, German military spending in 1991 was more than $52 billion in constant U.S. dollars (in 1995 prices), whereas by 1999 it had declined to less than $40 billion. The French had a more modest decline; its military burden decreased from 3.6 percent to 2.8 percent. Overall, the world spent about a third less on its military in real terms in between 1989 and 1996.

Globally, military expenditures remain highly concentrated. The fifteen big spenders accounted for 80 percent of the world total in 1999. In terms of the scale of violence,

the twentieth century seems to have been the most war-prone in human history by any indicator, yet wars involving great powers have declined in frequency, duration, and number of participants. Interdisciplinary research on conflicts, as superbly summarized by Daniel S. Geller and J. David Singer (*Nations at War: A Scientific Study of International Conflict*, Cambridge, 1998), provides insights into economic capabilities and cycles of war. At the state level, static and dynamic capability balances, measured especially by military variables, seem to suggest that approximate parity or shifts toward parity were consistently associated with conflicts in the nineteenth and twentieth centuries. Moreover, advocates of hegemonic perspective like Paul Kennedy (*The Rise and Fall of the Great Powers. Economic Change and Military Conflict from 1500 to 2000*, London, 1988) have argued that uneven economic growth "inevitably" causes the world's leading states to increase costly military spending, opening opportunities for challengers. The results of empirical research on hegemonic cycles are, however, still mixed. Research on the economic growth impact of military spending, mostly performed with post–World War II data using demand-side models, has discovered a negative growth impact based on the argument that military spending crowds out investment. In contrast, most supply-side models have pointed toward a small positive growth impact or none at all. If there is a peace dividend from cutting military spending, it is in its effect on investments; unfortunately, with a lag of five years or more.

BIBLIOGRAPHY

Bonney, Richard, ed. *The Rise of the Fiscal State in Europe, c. 1200–1815*. Oxford, 1999.

Feinstein, C. H. *National Income, Expenditure and Output of the United Kingdom, 1855–1965*. Cambridge, 1972.

Fontvieille, Louis. *Evolution et croissance de l'État français: 1815–1969*. Economies et sociétés. Institut de Sciences Mathématiques et Économiques Appliquées. Vol. 10, October 1976.

Harrison, Marke, ed. *The Economics of World War II: Six Great Powers in International Comparison*. Cambridge, 1998.

Historical Statistics of the United States, Colonial Times to 1970. U.S. Bureau of the Census. Washington, D.C., 1975.

Hobson, J. M. "The Military-Extraction Gap and the Wary Titan: The Fiscal-Sociology of British Defence Policy 1870–1913." *Journal of European Economic History* 22.3 (1993), 461–506.

Maddison, Angus. *Monitoring the World Economy, 1820–1992*. Paris, 1995.

McNeill, William H. *The Pursuit of Power: Technology, Armed Force, and Society since A.D. 1000*. Chicago, 1982.

Mintz, Alex, and Chi Huang. "Defense Expenditures, Economic Growth, and the Peace Dividend." *American Political Science Review* 84.4 (1990), 1283–1293.

Sandler, Todd, and Keith Hartley. *The Economics of Defense*. Cambridge Surveys of Economic Literature. Cambridge, 1995.

Singer, J. David, and Melvin Small. *National Material Capabilities Data, 1816–1985*. Ann Arbor, 1993.

Webber, Caroly, and Aaron Wildavsky. *A History of Taxation and Expenditure in the Western World*. New York, 1986.

JARI ELORANTA

NATIONAL INCOME ACCOUNTS *[This entry contains six subentries, a historical overview and discussions of exports and imports, public expenditures, investment and savings, wages and labor income, and rental income.]*

Historical Overview

National accounts are an important analytical tool to those practicing the macroeconomic history of nation-states. It tracks the flows of output, income, and expenditure at the aggregate level and for each of their subcategories. It also provides links to the stock of wealth of nations. National accounts series are distinguished from stand-alone series, such as series on real wages and commodity prices. National accounts represent an integrated framework that provides balances to control for the consistency of the aggregated income, output, and expenditure totals. It therefore puts the quantitative study of economies on a much stronger footing. Historical national accounts series assist economic historians in analyzing long-term economic growth, distribution, and structural change. The use of national accounts also contributes to international compar-

isons of economic performance, and it facilitates the study of topics in social and political history.

National accounts are rooted in the politically motivated interests of its pioneers around the end of the seventeenth century, including Sir William Petty, Gregory King, and Pierre Boisguillebert. These interests mainly concerned the taxable capacity of the nation-state and the redistribution issues associated with it. But over time the purposes of national accounting changed and became much broader in scope, in particular after the beginning of the twentieth century. In an overview of the policy purposes of national accounting in the United States since 1933, Mark Perlman summarizes these as: "(1) the distribution of income and of the costs of government; (2) the extent of unused capacity in various sectors of the economy; (3) the sources of economic growth; (4) pecuniary well-being; and (5) the fluctuations of the business cycle so as to design economic stabilization policies" (Perlman, 1987, p. 134). Indeed during the heydays of developmental work in national accounting during the 1940s and 1950s, the overriding aim was toward more intensive management of the macroeconomy. National accounts series have been extensively used as an input in macroeconomic modeling and forecasting. Developments in economic theory, in particular Keynesian demand theory and neoclassical growth theory, have been important driving forces for national income accounting. Finally, from a broader worldwide perspective, the rapid increase in coverage by national accounts for low-income countries indicates its usefulness to promote development.

An Integrated Measurement Framework. National accounts represent the macroeconomic bookkeeping system of an economy. It brings together a mass of primary statistics that measure the behavior of individual households, firms, and governments, which are integrated into a unique statistical framework, describing the macroeconomic performance of an economy. The national accounts system consists of three main components. Its core and most well-known component, the national income and product accounts, describes the flows of output, income, and expenditure. During the second half of the twentieth century, input-output tables that measure the transfers of such flows between industries and expenditure categories became an integral part of the income and product accounts. The second component of the national accounts tracks the financial flows, including those not directly associated with production, such as transfer payments (the capital account and flow-of-funds account). The third component of the system provides a link between the production, income, and financial flows on the one hand and the related stock of wealth on the other (national balance sheets). The latter includes the value of nonreproducible and reproducible assets as well as net claims on foreign assets. In economic history the national income and product accounts are most widely used. The other two components have been much more difficult to reconstruct for longer time periods, although major contributions to historical capital and wealth accounts were made by Raymond Goldsmith (1985).

The international comparability of national income and product accounts is based on a number of important conventions concerning concepts and definitions of the entities measured. Nowadays these are laid down in the United Nations System of National Accounts (SNA). Most important among these conventions are the definitions of the boundaries of economic activity and the precise valuation concepts of production, investment, intermediate inputs, and so forth. The main convention on boundaries is that any production, consumption, saving, or investment activity is included when it is reflected in a sale and a purchase transaction in a legalized market. A much narrower definition of production, which took into account the production and distribution of physical goods only, was applied by former socialist countries in the now-abandoned Material Product System. Over time SNA introduced various exceptions to the rule of recording market transactions only, including imputations for owner-occupied housing, unpaid services rendered by financial intermediaries, and some imputations for own consumption on, for example, farms. Still, according to the SNA, most activities outside markets—most importantly those in households—as well as illegal market activities remain largely unaccounted for. In a similar vein national balance sheets restrict themselves largely to assets that yield an annual return derived from its service flows. These definitions of the production and capital boundaries are an important limitation for historical economic research because of major shifts from nonmarket to market activities (and to a lesser extent also the other way around) over time. Critics such as Robert Eisner (1988) suggest that output and investment concepts should be extended to include, among other things, household production, investment in research and development, and the impact of depletion of natural resources on GDP and investment. Indeed the most recent versions of SNA have created substantial room for measuring economic activities beyond the core concepts of GDP and investment.

History of National Accounts Construction. The early days of national accounts construction from the late seventeenth century up to the middle of the twentieth century have been extensively documented by Paul Studenski (1958) and John Kendrick (1970). The first steps toward the construction of a national bookkeeping system were made by Sir William Petty (1623–1687), who laid out the framework of income ("Annual Value of the Labour of the People") and capital ("Annual Proceed of the Stock or Wealth of the Nation") on the one side of his account and expenditure ("Annual Expense of the People") on the other. In his estimate for England in 1688, Gregory King (1648–1712) added the excess of income over expenditure ("Yearly Increase in Wealth") to Petty's framework. According to Kendrick, this approach "was quite similar to the present-day concept of national income and product at factor cost" (Kendrick, 1970, p. 286). Other important pioneering attempts were made in France by Pierre Boisguillebert (1646–1714) and Marshal Vauban. The work by the French Physiocrats, including François Quesnay's *Tableau Économique*, foreshadowed the later work on sector accounts and input-output tables.

But a comprehensive system of national income accounts, covering output, income, and expenditure and matching those using a system of double bookkeeping, was not constructed until the twentieth century. By the late 1930s national income figures of a reasonable quality had been produced for a number of advanced countries, which are documented by Simon Kuznets (1933) and Colin Clark (1940). Apart from Clark and Kuznets, other pioneering contributors during this period include James Meade and Richard Stone (in the United Kingdom), Milton Gilbert (in the United States), Ragnar Frisch and Odd Aukrust (in Norway), and Jan Tinbergen and Johannes B. D. Derksen (in the Netherlands).

Zoltan Kenessey characterized the postwar era of national accounting by: (1) the systematic application of macroeconomic (mainly Keynesian) theory in the national accounts system; (2) the introduction of double-entry bookkeeping to enforce consistency among the production, expenditure, and income accounts; (3) increased policy orientation in the era of postwar reconstruction; (4) the portrayal of the whole economic process, including the integation of macroeconomic accounts and interindustry accounts; (5) the internationalization of methodological development through subsequent revisions of the System of National Accounts and coordination efforts at the Organization for Economic Cooperation and Development (OECD), United Nations, and Eurostat; and (6) the mathematization and computerization of the work (Kenessey, 1993, pp. 34–40). Toward the end of World War II the first attempts at international standardization of the income and product accounts were undertaken under the auspices of the League of Nations and subsequently the United Nations, under the leadership of Richard Stone (Stone, 1947). Stone's study was the predecessor of the first System of National Accounts (SNA), which was published in 1953. This was followed by a flow of books and papers on methods and procedures, of which many were published in the Income and Wealth series of the International Association for Research in Income and Wealth. The third revision of the SNA (SNA 1968) signaled a move toward integration of the income and product accounts with financial and wealth accounts. SNA 1968 was subsequently adopted by most countries in the nonsocialist world. In the former Soviet Union and its satellite states and China the national accounts were based on the Material Product System (MPS), but during the late 1980s various countries (notably China) began to switch to the SNA.

A fourth revision of the SNA (SNA 1993) was introduced during the 1990s and is presently being implemented by the vast majority of countries in the world. According to Kendrick (1996), a leading scholar in U.S. national accounts, the latest SNA has not been meant to make major conceptual changes or extensions but largely provides clarifications and refinements of concepts and definitions. For example, the production boundary with regard to household production has been somewhat expanded, yet production of household services remains excluded to the extent that these services are not marketed but currently consumed by the same household. SNA 1993 also extended the investment concept, though somewhat arbitrarily, to include intangible assets, such as mineral exploration, computer software, entertainment, literacy or artistic originals, patented entities, leases and other transferable contracts, and purchased goodwill. The new system also explicitly creates room for satellite accounts, for example, in the areas of health, environment, and tourism as well as for social accounting matrices that link the core economic accounts with structural features of an economy and with the distribution of income and expenditure among household groups.

The key measurement issues in contemporary national accounts relate to the measurement of output in the services sector and the measurement of prices in general. During the twentieth century the services sector in advanced countries has rapidly expanded its GDP share to up to 75 percent. A large share of these services are not (entirely) market-based and provided by government or private nonprofit institutions. Much of the output from these industries is still imperfectly measured using input-based measures, such as wage series. Even for market services, real output series are often difficult to obtain, as quality adjusted price indexes to deflate nominal output are not as reliable as for the goods-producing sector. As for prices, SNA 1993 advocates the use of chain-weighted price indexes that take account of annual changes in the composition of components in output, income, and expenditure. The latter creates a substantial challenge for the reconstruction of historical national accounts, as detailed weighting systems are often difficult to obtain on an annual basis.

Historical Reconstruction of National Accounts. As far as consistent series of national income accounts for the post–World War II period are concerned, one can now rely on annual series provided by each country's national statistical offices or, in some instances, their central banks. For OECD countries, internationally comparable series are provided by the OECD or (for European countries) Eurostat. The United Nations National Accounts also contains series of national accounts for lower-income countries beyond OECD. Unfortunately with the emergence of subsequent versions of the System of National Accounts and changes in classifications and measurement methods, the series often contain breaks. Some national statistical offices have themselves revised their national accounts series backward in time. For example, the U.S. National Income and Product Accounts provide a large range of series using the latest methodologies back to 1929. For other countries (in particular some of the Nordic countries) statistical offices have been directly involved in historical national accounts reconstruction. But the majority of contributions to the reconstruction of historical national accounts, in particular for the pre–World War II period, for which no commonly accepted framework such as the SNA was as yet available, are by individual academic scholars and research groups. The first attempts to reconstruct national accounts backward in time started during the 1950s, even though the first historical national income series for Sweden back to 1861 was already made in the 1930s (Lindahl, Dahlgren, and Kock, 1937). In the United States the first historical national accounts series emerged from a project by the National Bureau of Economic Research, including studies by Solomon Fabricant, Arthur F. Burns, Moses Abramovitz, and John W. Kendrick. The seminal works of Simon Kuznets (1961) and Kendrick (1961) represent the state of the art of American historical national accounts by the early 1960s. In Europe major contributions emerged during the 1960s and 1970s, including the work by Jean Marczweski (1961) for France, the series for Germany by W. G. Hoffmann (1965), and Charles Feinstein's (1972) series for the United Kingdom. Thanks to the work of Kazushi Ohkawa, a major system of historical national accounts is available for Japan in a series titled *Estimates of Long-Term Economic Statistics of Japan since 1868*, which appeared during the 1970s (Ohkawa et al., 1966–1988). Long national accounts series are also available for Australia and Canada. Even for some major countries in the developing world, such as Brazil, China, and India, important steps toward reconstruction of historical national accounts were made. Some scholars have done a great deal to put historical national accounts into an international comparative perspective, among which the seminal works of Angus Maddison (1995, 2001) feature predominantly. Although Maddison's estimates largely focus on aggregate measures of GDP, his work provides a major reference source for most historical national accounts studies in the world. Bart van Ark (1995) provides an overview of historical national accounting in European countries, showing that for several countries historical national accounts are now in their second, third, or (in particular in the Nordic countries) even fourth generations.

As in contemporary national accounts, the major problems in historical national accounting relate to the estimation of output in service industries and traditional handicraft industries and the measurement of prices using frequently changing weights. But for many countries even estimates of real output series for the goods sector can be problematic due to lack of data. Some scholars have therefore applied ingeneous methods to proxy national income indirectly. One approach, developed under the leadership of Ferenc Jánossy (1971), made use of physical indicators related to living standards, which were statistically related to per capita income estimates from the national accounts for recent periods and then backwardly extrapolated to periods for which no national income data are available. Anthropometric estimates looking at differences in height of people between regions have also sometimes been used as a proxy for differences in income levels (Steckel, 1983). Another approach, which was suggested as early as 1951 by E. M. Doblin, makes use of Irving Fisher's quantity equation ($MV = PQ$) to estimate real national income (Q) on the basis of exsisting measures of prices (P), money supply (M), and the velocity of money (V). Even though these methods are useful proxies to estimate national income series in the absence of detailed production, income, and expenditure data, they are an imperfect alternative to a consistent historical national accounts system as advanced in the studies described above.

Historical national accounts have become an important tool in studies of the determinants of long-term economic growth and living standards. For example, traditional growth accounting studies, such as those for France, Japan, the United Kingdom, and the United States, are strongly rooted in historical national accounts. Studies of structural change, as well as those focusing on the distribution of factor income, such as wages and factor shares, also heavily rely on historical national accounts. More generally a historical national accounts framework of indicators of economic growth and development provides an indispensable background for the study of issues in economic, political, and social history alike.

BIBLIOGRAPHY

Clark, Colin. *The Conditions of Economic Progress*. London, 1940.
Doblin, E. M. "The Ratio of Income to Money Supply: An International Survey." *Review of Economics and Statistics* 33 (1951), 201–213.
Eisner, Robert. "Extended Accounts for National Income and Product." *Journal of Economic Literature* 26. 4 (1988), 1611–1684.
Feinstein, Charles H. *National Income Expenditure and Output of the United Kingdom, 1855–1965*. Cambridge, 1972.
Goldsmith, Raymond W. *Comparative National Balance Sheets: A Study of Twenty Countries, 1688–1978*. Chicago, 1985.
Hoffmann, W. G. *Das Wachstum der deutschen Wirtschaft seit der Mitte der 19. Jahrhunderts*. Berlin, 1965.
Janossy, F. "Kann eine short-cut Methode mehr als ein Notbehelf sein?" *Acta Oeconomica* 7 (1971), 3–4.
Kendrick, John W. *Productivity Trends in the United States*. Princeton, 1961.
Kendrick, John W. "The Historical Development of National-Income Accounts." *History of Political Economy* 2.2 (1970), 284–315.
Kendrick, John W. "Introduction and Overview." In *The New System of National Accounts*, edited by J. W. Kendrick, pp. 1–23. Boston, Dordrecht, Netherlands, London, 1996.
Kenessey, Zoltan E. "Postwar Trends in National Accounts in the Perspective of Earlier Developments." In *The Value Added of National Accounting*, edited by W. F. M. de Vries, G. P. den Bakker, M. B. G. Gircour, S. J. Keuning, and A. Lenson, pp. 33–70. Voorburg and Heerlen, Netherlands, 1993.
Kuznets, Simon. "National Income." In *Encyclopaedia of the Social Sciences*, vol. 11. New York, 1933.
Kuznets, Simon. *Capital in the American Economy*. Princeton, 1961.
Lindahl, E., E. Dahlgren, and K. Kock. *National Income of Sweden, 1861–1930*, vol. 3. Stockholm and London, 1937.
Maddison, Angus. *Monitoring the World Economy, 1820–1992*. Paris, 1995.
Maddison, Angus. *The World Economy: A Millennial Perspective*. Paris, 2001.
Marczweski, J. "Histoire quantitative—Buts et méthodes." *Cahiers de l'ISEA*. Paris, July 1961.
Ohkawa, Kazushi, M. Shinohara, and M. Umemura, eds. *Estimates of Long-Term Economic Statistics of Japan since 1868*. 14 vols. Tokyo, 1966–1988.
Perlman, Mark. "Political Purpose and the National Accounts." In *The Politics of Numbers*, edited by W. Alonso and P. Starr, pp. 133–151. New York, 1987.
Steckel, R. "Heights and Per Capita Income." *Historical Methods* 16 (Winter 1983), 1–7.
Stone, Richard. "Definition and Measurement of the National Income and Related Totals." Appendix to *Measurement of National Income and Construction of Social Accounts*. Studies and Reports on Statistcal Methods, No. 7, United Nations. Geneva, 1947.
Studenski, Paul. *The Income of Nations: Theory, Measurement, and Analysis: Past and Present*. New York, 1958.
Van Ark, Bart. "Towards European Historical National Accounts." *Scandinavian Economic History Review* 43.1 (1995), 3–16.

BART VAN ARK

Exports and Imports

Exports are goods and services that are produced in a given region and sold outside that region. Imports are goods and services that are purchased in a given region but produced outside of that region. Exports and imports are the main element in the current account of the balance of payments.

The terms *exports* and *imports* make the most sense in the context of an international system of nation-states. Studies of production data for a particular country can determine how much of each good is sold within the nation; the portion that is not sold domestically is counted as an export. Similarly if the data show that a good is being purchased in a country but is not produced there, the good is an import.

The fact that countries have imposed tariffs and quotas on imports and exports for centuries means that such data are extremely plentiful. However, the basic theoretical concepts run aground when the way these statistics are actually collected is examined more closely.

First, there are measurement issues. Usually movements of goods and services are recorded at ports, airports, and border crossings. This leads to two ways that exports and imports are actually counted. The first is "general trade," whereby all goods that enter a country are counted as imports and all goods that leave a country are exports. Notice that this avoids many important complications. For example, goods that have been brought into a country and then sold abroad are counted as both imports and exports. Yet neither transaction had anything to do with the production and consumption decisions of the country except insofar as the business that conducted the transaction earned income for its services.

To deal with this problem, countries also measure "special trade." This consists of goods and services that are imported for internal use (that is, not reexported) and goods that are actually produced within a country and then shipped abroad. This method is what is relevant for the national income accounts, since the purpose of national income accounting is to measure flows of final goods and services, income, and production, not transfers of goods, income, or production.

Tariffs and quotas clearly affect the accuracy of these figures. National income accounts for countries with relatively high tariffs will show undervalued imports and will not report imports that were smuggled into the country. Similarly trade in illegal goods and services will not be recorded in the official accounts.

Another measurement problem concerns prices. Until the nineteenth century many countries only collected data on physical volumes of exports and imports, for example, barrels of rum, pounds of pepper. When a monetary value was calculated, it was done by counting the physical units moved and then valuing them at a fixed price rather than at the actual market transaction price. This means that one must be careful to check the price movements of individual goods before 1800. The more the fixed prices diverged from the market prices, the less accurate are the statistics on exports and imports (see Clark, 1938).

A second measurement problem concerns geographic boundaries. Exports and imports are relatively easy to measure when boundaries are stable but quickly become difficult to gauge when boundaries are disputed or change over time. For example, in computing export statistics for Germany from 1870 to 1945, one must be careful to identify what areas are included in "Germany" at any particular time since the territorial boundaries were constantly shifting.

Similarly one must look closely at statistics collected for countries with extensive colonies and other overseas territories. In some countries, such as the United Kingdom, clear records of origins and destinations exist that allow a scholar to calculate exports and imports for Great Britain separately from its colonies and possessions. In other countries this is not possible, and one must utilize these data with care.

A simple way to examine general trends in exports and imports is to compute the ratio of exports plus imports to gross domestic product; this is known as the trade-to-GDP ratio. In 1700 the world trade-to-GDP ratio ranged from 2 percent to 6 percent. By 1800 this had risen to between 3 percent and 8 percent (O'Rouke and Williamson, 2002; Maddison, 2001). By 1900 the ratio had grown to over 20 percent, but it fell dramatically between 1914 and 1950 to approximately 10 percent. The ratio has grown steadily since then, reaching over 25 percent by 2000 (Estevade-ordal, Frantz, and Taylor, 2002; Maddison, 2001).

These numbers tell a story of gradual trade expansion from 1700 to the mid-1800s. According to Kevin H. O'Rourke and Jeffrey G. Williamson (2002), this was not driven by increased integration of international commodity markets. Rather, a combination of strong European import demand and expanding export supplies outside of Europe caused an expansion of international trade.

The period from roughly 1870 to 1914 reveals a different story. Prices for a wide range of commodities in Europe and the Americas converged, allowing countries to specialize and trade at lower costs. The sources of this convergence include improved communications (especially via the telegraph), faster and more reliable transportation (especially steamships and railroads), and increased productivity in loading and unloading cargoes at ports and depots. These advancements were aided by declining tariffs through the 1870s but were slowed by rising protection after 1880 (for details see O'Rourke and Williamson, 1999; Bairoch, 1989).

The collapse of trade during the early twentieth century was driven by two world wars, retaliatory tariff policies between the wars, and the general economic collapse of the Great Depression. Starting in 1947 tariffs and quotas were gradually reduced through successive rounds of the General Agreement on Tariffs and Trade (GATT) and after 1994 through the World Trade Organization (WTO).

The composition of trade varied considerably over time. During the eighteenth century and into the early nineteenth century, trade consisted primarily of goods that a country could not produce for itself. For example, European imports consisted primarily of timber and tobacco from America, sugar products from the Caribbean, and spices, silk, and drugs from Asia. An important element of this trade also consisted of human beings: slaves transported from Africa to the Americas and the Caribbean.

Beginning in the mid-nineteenth century intra-industry trade grew in importance. For example, Europe and the Americas produced textiles, with European countries producing finer grades of cloth and American factories coarser products. Specialization remained important, however; the most important example of this is the "European grain invasion" of 1870 to 1914, whereby American and Russian grain poured into European markets. This was also the case for manufactured goods, which became increasingly important in the late nineteenth century and the early twentieth century.

Trade patterns were disrupted during the interwar period, leading many nations to doubt the benefits of trade. After World War II many countries, especially in Latin America, pursued import-substitution policies and thus reduced their participation in international markets. However, other countries, especially in East Asia, took the opposite approach and promoted exports as a way of industrializing their economies. In particular manufacturing became the focus in many of these countries, beginning with simple products and moving up the value chain to higher value-added goods.

Since 1950 intra-industry trade in manufactured goods has dominated the scene, with exports and imports of primary products continuing to be important factors in Latin America and Africa. Oil imports were especially vital for Europe, North America, and East Asia, and this brought oil-producing regions such as the Middle East into the international trading system to a greater extent than ever.

Finally, services have always been a significant part of international trade. In the eighteenth century the most important were shipping, insurance, and foreign exchange services. These continued to be crucial in the nineteenth century and were joined (and often overshadowed) by banking and other financial services, especially after 1870. Since the 1950s and especially since the 1970s, service trade has grown rapidly, with financial services and entertainment media being the most important growth areas.

BIBLIOGRAPHY

Bairoch, Paul. "European Trade Policy, 1815–1914." In *The Cambridge Economic History of Europe*, vol. 8, edited by Peter Mathias and Sidney Pollard, pp. 1–160. Cambridge, 1989. A clear and accessible overview of nineteenth-century trade policy. Despite the title, Bairoch does not restrict his attention solely to Europe.

Clark, George Norman. *Guide to English Commercial Statistics, 1696–1782*. London, 1938. Provides a detailed picture of "general" versus "special" trade and how exports and imports were valued before the nineteenth century.

Estevadeordal, Antoni, Brian Frantz, and Alan M. Taylor. "The Rise and Fall of World Trade, 1870–1939." National Bureau of Economic Research, Working Paper 9318, November 2002. Forthcoming in *Quarterly Journal of Economics*. Provides an explanation of both the expansion of trade from 1870 to 1914 and its collapse from 1919 to 1939 along with good data sources for further research.

Maddison, Angus. *The World Economy: A Millennial Perspective*. Paris, 2001. This is an excellent source of aggregate data on exports and imports from 1820 to 1998 for all regions of the world.

Mitchell, B. R. *International Historical Statistics*. 2d rev. ed. New York, 1995. This is the best source for data on individual countries before 1960.

O'Rourke, Kevin H., and Jeffrey G. Williamson. *Globalization and History: The Evolution of a Nineteenth-Century Atlantic Economy*. Cambridge, 1999.

O'Rourke, Kevin H., and Jeffrey G. Williamson. "After Columbus: Explaining the Global Trade Boom, 1500–1800." *Journal of Economic History* 62 (March 2002), 1–31. These two works by O'Rourke and Williamson provide an excellent overview of world trade patterns from 1500 to 1900. The bibliographies also contain a rich array of data sources.

UNCTAD Handbook of Statistics. New York, 2001. Available online at <www.unctad.org>. This is the best source for data on individual countries after 1960.

LOUIS D. JOHNSTON

Public Expenditures

From an accounting point of view, there are three ways to classify public expenditure. Administrative classification catalogs public expenditure according to the organization or administrative agency that manages it. Accounting registers are established by the laws of administration and accountancy in place at each historical moment. This is the oldest classification system because historically the concerns of public accounting were limited to administrative and political control of public expenditure, which became more pronounced after liberal revolutions. Since the parliament had to control the smallest details, the administrative organization of the public budget was split into many parts, thereby permitting detailed analysis of specific categories of expenditure. Generally, the large categories were grouped according to ministries (foreign affairs, interior, treasury, public works, war, education, and so on) or organizations (parliament, higher court, and so on).

After World War II, once Keynesian public finance programs were established, ministers of finance wanted not only to control administrative responsibilities but also to assess the economic effects of the state's budgetary decisions. To this end, economic classification of public expenditure was established, which implied the reorganization of public expenditure and income using economic criteria, independent of the administrative agencies that managed them. This allowed budgetary variables to be consolidated into national accounts. In general, economic classification distinguishes two kinds of accounts: current accounts and capital accounts. Current expenditure is composed of spending on goods and services, personnel, finance, social allowances, subsidies, and other current transfers; saving is the net balance of this current account. Capital expenditure includes gross fixed capital formation and land acquisition (both constitute real investments) and capital transfer.

Functional classification organizes state expenditure according to the aims it serves, independent of the administrative unit that manages funds and their economic significance. Other distinct types of functional classifications can exist, according to the aspects of state activity emphasized. The most conventional classification distinguishes the following functions: general services, including state and public administration expenditures, foreign relations, justice, and police; defense, for expenses occurred in national defense; social security, which includes the expenses of pensions, social assistance, and charity; economic services, for expenditures made in different economic sectors, such as infrastructure, research, and economic regulation; the functions of education, health, housing and community services, and social services; and a function that includes the financial expenditures of public debt.

In Europe, from the middle of the nineteenth century on, governments set up annual public budgets for approval by parliament, so that an account tribunal would audit the government's budgetary performance. An excellent summary of budgetary statistics in Europe by Flora (1983) permits an analysis of changes in governments' priorities over the long term and an evaluation of the extent to which government programs have been achieved. However, the analysis of budgetary statistics poses serious problems to the historian, as best seen in the German example. It is difficult to reconstruct consolidated budgets from all the public administrations because there is normally a lack of data from autonomous organizations, municipalities, social security, and other agencies. In some cases, there is no other solution but to concentrate on an analysis of the central government's expenditures. In dealing with a federal country, it is essential to include the member states because they deal with an important part of the administrative activity of the public sector themselves. In any case, institutional diversity makes it impossible to make exact and precise comparisons among countries because centralized countries channel most of their budgetary operations through the central government, whereas federal countries do this basically through states and municipalities. There is also the problem of multiple large transfers made among the public organizations, and calculation of total net statistics would require a complex consolidation. In addition, when the country under analysis has suffered significant institutional changes, comparisons between different periods are impossible. The constitutions of Bismarck (1871) and the Weimar Republic (1919), as well as the institutional changes that Germany underwent in 1933–1934 and from 1945 to 1951, indicate changes in the way in which fiscal responsibilities were shared between the Reich, the states, and the municipali-

ties. Thus it is very hard to establish continuity in studying German budgets.

A second problem arises because of periods lacking the historical records of the budgetary activities of central and regional governments. In some instances, documents have been lost; in other cases, the documents are not available because they were systematically destroyed by the same authorities that drew them up, as occurred in Germany between 1914 and 1918 and between 1933 and 1945. A third drawback is the difficulty of estimating the real value of income and budgetary expenditures, particularly in periods of high inflation (such as the periods after the two world wars) and deflation (for instance, the 1930s crisis). The problem is so great that some public finance scholars have excluded analysis of the periods from 1914 to 1923 and from 1935 to 1948, as indicated by Witt (1987). However, despite these serious drawbacks, it is still possible to make a comparative analysis of the historical evolution of public expenditures in Europe.

The evolution of the volume of expenditures in relation to national income during the nineteenth century varies according to the nation in question. However, a general deadlock, even a decline, can be noted from the period of the Napoleonic Wars until the end of the nineteenth century, followed by a small increase until the beginning of World War I. A decline during the nineteenth century is explained by the high initial public expenditures that occurred during the Napoleonic Wars; an increase from the end of the nineteenth century reflects budgetary trends with the emergence of social security and education and health expenditures, all antecedents of the welfare state. In the twentieth century, public expenditures increased notably. Of particular significance are the two leaps in public expenditures produced on the occasion of the two world wars, which more than doubled the resources spent by the state as a proportion of national income. In the United Kingdom, the relationship between central government expenditures and national income rose from 7.6 percent to 25.5 percent between 1910 and 1920, and from 18.6 percent to 57.8 percent between 1930 and 1940 (this increase takes into account the possible effect of the 1930s crisis). In Italy, Germany, and France, the relative increase in government expenditures due to the two world wars was of a similar magnitude. Although smaller, the increase in central government expenditures as a percentage of national income due to the 1970s economic crisis is also important. It increased from 36.4 percent to 42.5 percent in the United Kingdom between 1970 and 1975, while in Italy the budgetary volume grew from 30.6 percent to 42.5 percent of GDP in the same years. The evolution in Spain was different, as there was an increase between the middle of the nineteenth century and the 1870s; there was stagnation until the 1920s, followed by level spending until the 1970s.

To study the structure of public expenditure it is useful to return to a functional classification although there is always the problem of the fragile homogeneity of the data. It does not appear that there is a common pattern of evolution among the European countries, as the percentages of the distinct functions vary widely among countries and through time. The following statistics refer to the structure of central government expenditures for Italy, France, and Spain, whereas the statistics for general government expenditures are used for the United Kingdom and Germany. This choice, which inevitably divides the analysis, is made because the two latter countries traditionally have had more decentralized expenditures than the other three. Also the available statistics for the general government are older in these two countries. In any case, two large categories greatly influenced the composition of expenditures, because of their size and variations through time: interest of the debt and defense expenditure. Another large category of public expenditure was general services, whose percentage was relatively stable in different countries and through time. Despite national diversity, there is a tendency for resources devoted to these three categories to diminish as the size of total public expenditures increases.

These three categories have been considered by public finance scholars as impediments to the modernization of public expenditures, as they have absorbed large amounts of budgetary resources, leaving very little to be assigned to other, more modern functions. Until 1960 defense spending was significant in the main European countries; with few exceptions, by country and during phases of peace, it was over 15 percent and sometimes made up more than 40 percent of total budgetary expenditure. During the nineteenth century debt interest expenditure was around 40 percent of total expenditures in countries such as the United Kingdom, Italy, France, and Spain. This percentage diminished throughout the century, in particular in the United Kingdom, where by the end of the century only 7 percent of the budget was used for this purpose. However, Spain, France, and Italy continued to devote considerable percentages, over 30 percent, to debt interest expenditures, although the amounts did diminish until the onset of World War I. Financing this war caused an increase in the financial burden of the United Kingdom and Germany, but not that of Italy or France, and even less that of nonbelligerent countries. Given the large rise in budget totals, the increase of public debt after World War II did not mean an increase in the percentage of the financial burden (which in 1950 fell to 11.2 percent and 5.7 percent in the United Kingdom and in France and Italy, respectively). In subsequent decades, this function decreased although it increased again during the 1970s crisis.

When the expenditures for debt interest and defense were significant, the percentages of the rest of the categories were reduced. In particular, economic services, which were the second largest expenditure, accounted for over 15 percent between the middle of the nineteenth century and the middle of the twentieth century, but afterward rose to over 20 percent in the United Kingdom and Italy, and settled at around this level in France and Germany. There were also notable amounts in Italy destined for economic services from unification until 1920 (above 20 percent). Huge resources were again channeled to economic expenditures in Italy after 1950. Likewise, in France, spending for economic services was high until 1880 (14.2 percent) and again reached considerable levels after 1950. Until 1920, expenditures for economic services in the United Kingdom and Germany were greater, though not much more, than those in Spain. It was after the 1930s, and especially after World War II, that economic services grew in Europe. Between 1950 and 1975 they were around or above 20 percent; however, after 1975 economic expenditures generally declined.

Aside from these expenditures, other functions that defined the emergence of the welfare state were further developed well into the beginning of the twentieth century. Public spending for education was always important in Germany. After unification it increased, from 10.8 percent to 19.8 percent by 1910, and then it decreased; but it recovered after 1970. In other countries, education expenditures became more significant much later, owing to changing ideas about public-service policy, increased treasury receipts, and a decrease in spending on debt, general services, and defense. In the United Kingdom, public education advanced from the beginning of the twentieth century on, particularly between the 1920s and the 1960s. Meanwhile, in France, public education grew between 1880 and 1910, and then again much later, between 1950 and 1970. In Italy, public education expanded after World War II, especially from 1945 to 1970. In Spain, on the contrary, although spending on public education grew at the beginning of the twentieth century, it did not develop significantly until the 1970s. It was inferior in comparison to other Latin nations such as France and Italy, which already had improved their spending on education, particularly after World War II. Similarly, the expansion of social security spending was delayed, as it started to play a role worth mentioning in the United Kingdom, France, and Germany only after World War I (in 1930, being 21 percent, 16 percent, and 26 percent, respectively), and in Italy after World War II (13 percent in 1950). World War II and the economic crisis of the 1970s also contributed to an increase in social security spending, particularly in France and Germany (above 40 percent in 1980); in England and in Italy these expenditures were somewhat less (around 31 percent). In Spain, social security spending did not take off until the end of the 1960s, and it became more important with the democratization of the country after 1975 (accounting for only 18 percent in 1980). In 1990, social security expenditures in all these countries were greater than 30 percent, and in France and Germany it reached nearly 40 percent of all public spending.

In view of the deadlock of the nineteenth century, one of the phenomena that will attract the most attention of future economic historians studying the first eight decades of the twentieth century will be the remarkable development of the public sector in Western economies, a growth in public expenditures that was accompanied by structural transformation. In the functional classification, there was a general trend to reduce the weight of pure public goods (such as administration, defense, public security, and justice), and to increase the relative size of merit goods (education and health) and of social expenditures and income redistribution. A variety of factors may explain this increase in public spending. The previous analysis highlights the great importance that the two world wars had on the growth and the change in structure of public expenditures (above all in the application of Keynesian theory after World War II), the 1970s crisis, and the political system of each country. Political variables have been as significant as economic variables, in times of crisis as well as expansion. However, the analysis of public expenditures through time is complex because of the numerous variables involved; so an abundance of explanatory theories and multiple causal factors are offered.

At the end of the nineteenth century, Wagner's law (1897) showed that the relationship of public expenditure/gross domestic product would grow in proportion to the increase in GDP per capita of a country. The theory of the displacement effect of Peacock and Wiseman (1961) challenged this law, explaining that the increase in public expenditure was due to the existence of wars. To this, their adherents added economic crises and social uprisings. According to this theory, it was not phases of growth that made public expenditure increase, but the two world wars and the economic depressions that began in 1929 and 1973. These critical circumstances allowed governments to increase the tolerable fiscal burden on taxpayers, which remained stable in times of peace, and to maintain the new level of tax once the conflict was over. This allowed the financing of additional public expenditure that increased with the wars.

Other hypotheses also are used to explain the large increase in public expenditure during the twentieth century. From a supply point of view (i.e., the public choice school), it is held that democracies create excessively large budgets and public deficits, because voters are blinded by a fiscal illusion that leads them to underestimate the cost of financing increases in public spending. Other theories blame the increase in public expenditure on bureaucracies; public servants are motivated to increase public spending, since this in turn results in maximizing their own power, extending their administrative bodies, hiring more staff, and increasing their wages. Finally, technological models support the concept that the increase in budgetary obligations is determined essentially by technological and organizational factors. In effect, as the productivity of the public sector advances less than that of the private sector, the prices of the public sector increase more than those of private goods. Consequently, the size of public expenditure increases in proportion to national expenditure, if both are measured in current terms.

Among demand-based theories, it is worth mentioning those that point to the existence of a demonstration effect, as in demand for private consumption, that involves the relationship of public expenditure/national income in underdeveloped countries, which try to emulate countries with a larger income and do so with relatively larger amounts of public spending.

BIBLIOGRAPHY

Borcherding, Thomas E., ed. *Budgets and Bureaucrats: The Sources of Government Growth.* Durham, N.C., 1977.

Borcherding, Thomas E. "The Sources of Growth of Public Expenditure in the United States, 1902–1970." In *Budgets and Bureaucrats,* edited by T. E. Borcherding, pp. 45–70. Durham, N.C., 1977.

Comín, Francisco. *Historia de la hacienda pública en Europa.* Barcelona, 1996.

Flora, Peter. *State, Economy, and Society in Western Europe, 1815–1975: A Data Handbook,* vol. 1, *The Growth of Mass Democracies and Welfare States.* London, 1983.

Peacock, Alan T., and Jack Wiseman. *The Growth of Public Expenditure in the United Kingdom.* Princeton, 1961.

Tussing, A. Dale, and John A. Henning. "Long-Run Growth of Nondefense Government Expenditures in the United States." *Public Finance Quarterly* 2.2 (1974), 202–222.

Tussing, A. Dale, and John A. Henning. "Measuring the Effect of Structural Change on Long-Term Public Expenditure Growth: The United States, 1929 to 1981." *Public Finance Quarterly* 4 (1991), 393–411.

Wagner, Adolf. "Three Extracts on Public Finance." In *Classics in the Theory of Public Finance,* edited by R. A. Musgrave and A. L. Peacock. London, 1897.

Witt, Peter-Christian, "Tax Policies, Tax Assessment and Inflation: Towards a Sociology of Public Finances in the German Inflation, 1914–1923." In *Wealth and Taxation in Central Europe,* edited by P. C. Witt, pp. 137–160. New York, 1987.

Witt, Peter-Christian, ed. *Wealth and Taxation in Central Europe: The History and Sociology of Public Finance.* New York, 1987.

FRANCISCO COMÍN

Investment and Savings

Modern economies are large and complex, so it is difficult to isolate and explain such key processes as savings and investment. Instead, imagine the other extreme: a desert island with only one inhabitant—the proverbial shipwrecked sailor.

The Fable of the Shipwrecked Sailor. To begin, life is very hard. The only way the sailor can survive is to catch fish with his bare hands. It is a slow, difficult, process, and only by working long hours can he catch enough to stay alive. Unless he can change this pattern, he is condemned to a permanent subsistence existence at a very low level. How might his condition improve? Nature might become more bounteous: a favorable change in the temperature of the water could bring more fish swimming into his hands. Or he might learn by repeated activity to become more adept.

Imagine the latter happens, so that eventually he needs only ten hours to catch the same quantity for which he previously toiled for twelve hours. He could then spend fewer hours fishing, leaving more time for leisure. Or he could continue working exactly as before, but eat more each day. Or he could devote only ten hours to fishing and spend the remainder of his working day building a net. If he chooses to do this, when the net is ready he can catch more fish. The time he spends fishing can then be further reduced and used instead to build a small boat.

With this accomplished, his position improves dramatically. He can catch enough fish in four days to feed him comfortably for the rest of the week. The remainder of his time can be spent improving the quality of his life in other ways: building a shelter, improving his supply of fresh water, enjoying more leisure time. Every time he elects to refrain from an immediate increase in his consumption of food or leisure by allocating time and effort to the construction of physical equipment, he enhances his ability to enjoy an even higher level of consumption in the future.

The sailor's sacrifice of current consumption constitutes the essence of the macroeconomic concept of *saving*. The construction of durable capital goods that will make possible higher levels of output in future periods represents the matching concept of *investment*. In a more complex monetary economy, saving and investment are undertaken by different people at different times, and the relationship between them is obscured in many ways, but these remain their essential features.

This simple story illustrates the basic themes that are important to an understanding of the crucial role played by investment and savings in economic development. Large parts of the world are effectively locked into positions like that of the lone sailor when he first arrived. The proportion of their income that the population can save remains very low; they have very little capital equipment; and they are forced to spend all of their energies desperately struggling to maintain themselves in conditions in which there seems to be no prospect that the future will be any better than the past.

Other countries were potentially more fortunate. By some means (the possibilities include better climatic conditions, more favorable endowments of natural resources, easier access to trade routes, military conquest and plun-

der, greater receptivity to innovation) they were able to achieve an initial surplus above their minimum subsistence needs. In developed economies, this surplus was allocated primarily for productive purposes, and a cumulative process of economic growth was initiated and sustained. Construction of more capital led to higher output and better standards of living. Some of the benefits of this were then used for other growth-enhancing outlays—education and training, research and development—leading to still higher levels of output per worker and yet more physical and human capital. Unfortunately, in other cases this potential source of growth was wasted, the ruling elites preferring instead to build grand palaces and pyramids, wage futile wars, or—in recent times—to transfer it to their private banking accounts abroad.

The Evolution of Savings and Investment. For many centuries and for millions of peasant farmers, the crucial form of savings consisted of setting aside a proportion of each year's harvest as seed for the following year. Another historically important form of self-financing involved mine owners, industrialists, and merchants allowing part of their annual profit to remain in the business as the basis for future expansion. The fixed assets they used were relatively small and cheap, and their main requirement was for working capital and trade credit to bridge the interval between payments for raw materials and labor and receipts from sales of the finished product. As long as activities were conducted on a relatively small scale, it was generally possible for individuals and partnerships to obtain the necessary savings from internal "plowed-back" profits, or by limited borrowing from family members and local associates. But from the late eighteenth century, this began to change as a result of two interrelated developments. On the demand side, the scale of activity in canal building, gas lighting, and similar projects increased to the point where it was no longer possible for owner-entrepreneurs to provide all the necessary funds from their own savings. In the nineteenth century, this process was powerfully stimulated by the immense program of railway construction, and by the expansion of steel manufacture and other capital-hungry industries employing substantial fixed assets.

On the supply side, small local sources of finance gradually merged to become large national capital markets. What had begun as a market in domestic and foreign government securities—strongly boosted by need to finance large outlays during the Napoleonic wars—came to play an increasingly prominent role in the financing of industry and commerce. One major element in this development was legislation permitting joint stock companies to issue shares for which individuals could subscribe without incurring any responsibility for the management of the enterprise, and with no further liability—in the event of losses—beyond the value of their shares. The other vital development was the steady growth of banks, mutual savings institutions, life insurance companies, and other financial intermediaries. They assembled massive sums from the many small savers who wished to save but not to acquire physical assets. These funds were then channelled by means of loans and share purchases to those with schemes for the construction of assets on a scale that could not be matched by their personal savings.

Both savers and investors benefited from the development of an efficiently functioning capital market. Economies of scale reduced the costs of financial intermediation; and larger, more stable, and—as a rule—better regulated institutions diminished the degree of risk that savers faced in entrusting their funds to the care of another party. In consequence, savers were encouraged to lend more freely and borrowers could obtain finance at lower rates.

With this divorce of savings from investment, the motives for saving were also transformed. For most individuals, the dominant reason for refraining from immediate consumption was no longer to create physical assets. Instead, they wanted to leave a bequest for their widows or children, or to protect themselves against a possible loss of income caused by illness, unemployment, or retirement. Their prime concerns in relation to their savings were now the security and liquidity of their portfolio of paper assets, and the rate of return they could expect relative to the degree of risk they were willing to take.

Up to this point, we have considered only voluntary saving by persons within a single country. There are, however, three important ways in which the concept must be extended. First, much saving is not voluntary; it is enforced in various ways. One of the more obvious involves serfs, who are compelled to work without remuneration on roads and other projects. In planned economies, such as the USSR under Stalin, a smaller share of current production was allocated to consumption goods and services, and a higher share to capital goods, than the population would have selected if allowed to express their preferences. In monetary economies, more subtle forms of taxation can be used to suppress consumption and increase saving, a technique especially invoked in times of war. Yet another form of forced saving occurs when inflation erodes the real value of incomes and assets fixed in nominal terms.

Second, it is not only persons and partnerships that save. Companies do so when they distribute only part of their profits as dividends and retain the balance; governments do so when their revenue from taxes and other sources exceeds their current expenditures. Third, over time the allocation of saving has become an increasingly international process. By 1914, the United Kingdom, France, and other European nations had diverted a substantial fraction of their total savings to foreign countries.

This process continued with renewed momentum in the 1920s and again after World War II, with the United States prominently involved as both a major overseas investor and a leading borrower. Personal savers, industrial and financial institutions, governments, and international agencies are today deeply involved in an extensive network of global saving and investment.

Investment and the Stock of Capital. We turn next to the matching flows of investment. As it is used in national accounting and macroeconomics, this concept covers three separate categories: fixed capital formation, changes in inventories, and net investment abroad. It must be emphasized that this is totally different from its use as a financial term (as in, "I sold all my investments in technology companies and now hold only government securities").

Fixed capital formation (FCF) relates to reproducible tangible assets that are used repeatedly in processes of production for more than a year. Certain assets come obviously and unambiguously within this heading, for example, factory buildings and shops; such structures as highways, railroads, and distribution networks for electricity or telecommunications; and machinery, vehicles, ships, and aircraft. Other types of assets are less clear cut and their treatment is a matter of convention. To mention only a few of many examples, the standard methodology includes residential housing but not private automobiles and other consumer durables; military infrastructure but not destructive weapons; major improvements to assets but not routine repair and maintenance. The definition may be substantially widened by different decisions on these borderline cases, or by the inclusion of intangible assets (such as software programs), and additions to human capital.

The initial production or acquisition of fixed assets constitutes gross FCF. However, assets are "used up" in the course of production by wear and tear, and their contribution to income also diminishes as a result of technical obsolescence. The joint process constitutes capital consumption. This is a difficult concept, and is not directly measurable. There is scope for disagreement as to the way in which it develops through time, and the pattern is not necessarily the same for all types of assets. Nevertheless, it is clear that most assets have only a finite economic life because technological progress makes it profitable to replace them even before they are physically worn out, for example, where an innovation results in a new machine that can produce the same output with less labor. Some part of gross FCF is thus required to offset this capital consumption, and any excess over this represents net FCF.

The second type of investment is the change in inventories of materials and supplies that are to be used up in production. These inventories include raw materials, finished goods, and work in progress (for example, houses under construction at the end of the period, and crops not yet harvested). The third category, net investment abroad, represents the change in the value of overseas assets acquired by the citizens of one country, less the change in the value of domestic assets acquired by nonresidents. Here "net" refers to this balance, not to a deduction for capital consumption, and the balance may be positive (net lending) or negative (net borrowing). Unlike the two previous categories, investment abroad covers financial as well as physical assets, and also holdings of monetary gold and silver.

The three categories of investment all refer to flows during a year. However, by their nature, successive flows of investment can be cumulated to form the stock of capital. The national accounting concept of capital refers only to assets as defined above for investment and must not be confused with other uses of the term. For fixed capital there are two measures of the stock, corresponding to the gross and net flows of FCF. Either of these might be supplemented to cover stocks of inventories and overseas assets, as broader definitions might also include stocks of consumer durables, intangible assets, and human capital.

It is easiest to think of the stock of fixed capital in terms of separate groups of assets, each with their estimated economic life as defined above. For example, for assets with a life of thirty years, the end-2000 gross stock would be the sum of all gross FCF over the thirty years, from 1971 to 2000, and similarly for other life spans. Aggregation over all categories gives the stock at that date, and this can be extrapolated to subsequent years by the perpetual inventory system. Thus, the end-2001 gross stock equals the end-2000 gross stock plus gross FCF in 2001 less assets retired (sold or scrapped) in 2001. For this calculation, all items must be adjusted to the prices of the same year, so the initial perpetual inventory estimates are made at constant prices, but alternative series at current prices can be derived from this.

The deduction for retirements is based on the original FCF in those assets. In the simplest scheme, it is assumed that all thirty-year assets added to the stock in 1971 are removed in 2001, and so on. Alternative procedures recognize that this "sudden-death" convention is unrealistic and assume instead some appropriate distribution of retirements around the average life.

The fundamental characteristic of the gross stock is that assets are included in the stock at the same value up to the moment when they are retired; a ten-year machine is thus assumed to make the same contribution to income in its last year as in its first. By contrast, the alternative measure of the net stock of capital allows for a continuous decline in the value of the assets in accordance with the pattern of capital consumption.

Measurement of Savings and Investment. It is difficult to get accurate estimates of savings. They can be measured indirectly as the (small) difference between two (large) estimates of income and consumption, but this residual is inevitably subject to wide margins of error. Alternatively, direct measurement can be based on information from banks and other institutions in which the savings were deposited. This normally requires the authority of an official enquiry, and so estimates are generally only available for recent years, though Goldsmith has provided series for the United States from 1897.

In the absence of such evidence, it is necessary to rely on estimates of investment, since actual saving is by definition equal to actual investment. How then is investment estimated? Until the late eighteenth century, there is almost no statistical basis for the measurement of gross FCF. After that, the problem can be approached from four main directions. The first involves a detailed classification of censuses of production and related statistics to identify such capital goods as machinery. These must be distinguished from finished consumer goods, such as shirts, and from intermediate goods consumed in the process of production, such as cotton yarn. There is an inevitable degree of arbitrariness in any such classification, but the broad outlines of the distinction are clear enough. A corresponding classification of the foreign trade statistics is also required so that imports of capital goods can be added to the domestic supply and exports excluded.

The second approach is to work with data on the physical quantities of specific assets compiled for other purposes (number of houses built, tonnage of ships newly registered) and to value these at an appropriate cost per unit. The third possibility is to use estimates of expenditure on capital goods either given explicitly in the owners' accounts, or provided in returns to official statistical agencies. The final approach is to infer capital outlays from the change in the value of the stock of assets at successive dates—as shown, for example, in balance sheets or fire insurance valuations. If these stock estimates give net values of fixed assets, the difference will be net FCF, and capital consumption must be added back to get gross FCF; if they are at book values, the difference will be a measure of gross FCF net of retirements. In practice, no one method provides all the required information, and historical estimates—such as those used in Table 1—are based on combinations of these different procedures.

For inventories, accounts and balance sheets provide the main source of information. Annual series for net investment abroad are generally derived from estimates of the balance of payments on current account, and the cumulated flows can be checked against direct estimates of net holdings of foreign assets obtained from periodic surveys.

Investment, Savings, and Economic Growth. Savings and investment are of interest and importance for

TABLE 1. *National Savings and Investment as a Percentage of Gross National Product, Selected Countries, 1770–1969*

	(1) UNITED KINGDOM	(2) UNITED STATES	(3) FRANCE	(4) GERMANY	(5) ITALY	(6) SWEDEN	(7) DENMARK	(8) SPAIN	(9) JAPAN	(10) RUSSIA	(11) AUSTRALIA	(12) CANADA
1770–1800	4	(8)										
1800–1809	7[a]	}										
1810–1819	13[a]	}										
		}(8)										
1820–1829	13[a]	}	11									
1830–1839	8	}	11									
1840–1849	10	16[b]	13									
1850–1859	10	20[b]	16	(14)				5				
1860–1869	12		17	(18)	7[e]	9[e]		8			7[e]	
1870–1879	13	18[b]	12	(20)	8	11	10	8			11	9
1880–1889	13	18[b]	15	(18)	10	8	7	9	14[h]	(13)[h]	10	10
1890–1899	12	20	16	(22)	10	11	9	9	14	(14)	9	8
1900–1909	13	19	18	(23)	18	11	11	12	12	(15)	16	16
1910–1913	15	17	17	(24)	17	14	11	14	15	(*18*)	16	17
1920–1929	11	17	33[c]	13[d]	14	14	11[f]	19	16	25[i]	15	17
1930–1938	9	8	9	14	16	17	14	18[g]	17	26[i]	13	10
1950–1959	16	18	19	25	21	22	24	22	28	28[i]	24	23
1960–1969	18	19	25	32	24	24	20	23	37		25	23

Notes: Ratios are based on estimates at current market prices and are averages of percentages in individual years. Except for Spain, all estimates are for gross national capital formation (GNCF) as a percentage of gross national product (GNP). GNCF equals GDCF (gross domestic fixed capital formation plus the change in inventories) plus net foreign lending or less net foreign borrowing. Estimates for Spain are for GDCF and GDP.

Estimates are shown in parentheses where the original sources give national product and capital formation net of capital consumption, and a rough adjustment was made to obtain GNP and GNCF.

[a]1770 to 1830 is for Great Britain; the 1830–1839 ratio for this region would be 11 percent. Decades are 1801–1810, 1811–1820 and 1821–1830. [b]Decades are 1839–1848, 1849–1858, 1869–1878, and 1879–1988. [c]Begins 1922. [d]Begins 1925. [e]Begins 1861. [f]Begins 1921. [g]Ends 1935. [h]Begins 1885. [i]GNP is at ruble factor cost; estimates are for 1928, 1937, and 1950–1955.

SOURCES: The estimates were obtained from or based on the sources listed below. Where an estimate was available only for net domestic fixed capital formation, it was assumed that capital consumption was two-thirds of this, and a corresponding addition was made to NNP to obtain GNP. Where no estimate was available for the change in inventories, it was assumed that the change at constant prices was equal to 40 percent of the change in GNP at constant prices, and this measure was then multiplied by the GDP deflator to obtain the required estimate at current prices. Both procedures follow Simon Kuznets "Quantitative Aspects of the Economic Growth of Nations: VI. Long-Term Trends in Capital Formation Proportions." *Economic Development and Cultural Change* 9 (July 1961), part 2, and "Quantitative Aspects of the Economic Growth of Nations: VII. The Share and Structure of Consumption." *Economic Development and Cultural Change* 10 (January 1962), part 2. Estimates for 1950–1969 were generally taken from OECD, *National Accounts of OECD Countries*. Paris, 1969. **United Kingdom before 1913:** Feinstein, Charles H., and Sidney Pollar, eds. *Studies in Capital Formation in the United Kingdom, 1750–1920.* Oxford, 1988, pp. 462–463; Mitchell, Brian R. *British Historical Statistics.* Cambridge, 1988, pp. 831–832. **United Kingdom from 1920:** Feinstein, Charles H. *National Income, Expenditure, and Output of the United Kingdom, 1855–1965.* Cambridge, 1972. pp. T9, T11, and T82–3. **United States before 1859:** Gallman, Robert E. "Economic Growth and Structural Change in the Long Nineteenth Century." In *The Cambridge Economic History of the United States*, vol. II, edited by Stanley L. Engerman and Robert E. Gallman, 39–40, Cambridge, 2000. **United States from 1870:** Kendrick, John. *Productivity Trends in the United States.* Princeton, 1961, p. 296; U.S. Department of Commerce. *Historical Statistics of the United States.* Washington, D.C., 1975, pp. 224, 229, 230, and 263. **France before 1913:** Lévy-Leboyer, Maurice, and François Bourguignon. *The French Economy in the Nineteenth Century.* Cambridge, 1990, Tables A-I to A-III; Lévy-Leboyer, Maurice. "La balance des paiements et l'exportation des capitaux français" in *La position internationale de la France aux XIXe and XXe siècles.* Paris, 1977, p. 119. **France from 1920:** Carré, J.J-., P. Dubois, and E. Malinvaud. *French Economic Growth.* Stanford, Calif., 1976, pp. 24, 528, and 546–547; Sauvy, Alfred. *Histoire économique de la France entre les deux guerres.* Paris, 1965–1976, vol. I, p. 312 and vol. II, p. 460. **Germany:** Balderston, Theo. *The Origins and Causes of the German Economic Crisis, 1923–1932.* Berlin, 1993, pp. 333–334; Hoffmann, Walther G. *Das Wachstum der deutschen Wirtschaft seit der Mitte des 19 Jahrhunderts.* Berlin, 1965, pp. 825–826 and 698–699; Klein, Burton H. *Germany's Economic Preparations for War.* Cambridge, Mass., 1959, pp. 251–255. **Italy:** Fuà, Giorgio. *Notes on Italian Economic Growth 1861–1964.* Milan, 1965, pp. 60, 65, and 83. **Sweden:** Krantz, Olle, and Carl-Axel Nilsson. *Swedish National Product, 1861–1970.* Lund, 1975, pp. 150–155. **Denmark:** Bjerke, K., and N. Ussing. *Studier over Danmarks Nationalprodukt, 1870–1950.* Copenhagen, 1958, pp. 146–153. **Spain:** Carreras, Alberto. *Industrialización Española: Estudios de Historia Cuantitativa.* Madrid, 1990, pp. 185–188; Prados de la Escosura, Leandro. *Spain's Gross Domestic Product, 1850–1993, Quantitative Conjectures.* Madrid, 1995, Tables C1 and C6. **Japan:** Ohkawa, Kazushi, and Miyohei Shinohara, eds. *Patterns of Japanese Economic Development, A Quantitative Appraisal.* New Haven, Conn., 1979, pp. 251–255 and 349–363. **Russia:** Bergson, Abram. *The Real National Income of Soviet Russia since 1928.* Cambridge, Mass., 1961, pp. 245 and 282; Gregory, Paul R. *Russian National Income, 1885–1913.* Cambridge, 1982, pp. 58–59. **Australia:** Vamplew, Wray, ed. *Australian Historical Statistics.* Broadway, N.S.W., 1987, pp. 133–139, 185, 191, and 198. **Canada:** Urquhart, M. C. "New Estimates of Gross National Product, Canada, 1870–1926." In *Long-Term Factors in American Economic Growth.* edited by Stanley L. Engerman and Robert E. Gallman, Chicago, 1986, p. 33; Urquhart, M. C., and K. A. H. Buckley, eds. *Historical Statistics of Canada.* Toronto, 1965, p. 131.

economic historians because of their role in economic growth. Before looking at this relationship, one vital point must be clarified. In a Robinson Crusoe economy, the two concepts are identical: the act of saving (not consuming) is simultaneously the act of investing (building a boat). In more realistic historical settings, the two acts were separated in time, and savings typically preceded investment, as with seed corn and plowed-back profits.

But in a modern economy, no previous savings are required in order for the banking sector to be able to increase its deposits to provide finance for prospective investment. One of the great insights of the revolution in economic theory initiated by the famous British economist John Maynard Keynes (1883–1946), was to show that in these circumstances the crucial relationship is reversed: savings are determined by investment. Provided only that there are spare resources, an initial act of investment will lead to an increase in output and income (via the multiplier), and this additional income will in turn generate the required level of savings. Whatever might be the initial desires or intentions of savers, the amount they actually save will be equal to, and governed by, the amount of investment.

The measure normally used in discussions of the relationship between savings and economic growth is the ratio of savings (S) to national income (Y), known as the savings rate, S/Y. Since savings equals investment, this will also be the investment rate, I/Y. In 1954, the Nobel Laureate, W. Arthur Lewis, offered a quantitative assessment of the crucial role of S/Y in promoting economic growth:

> The central problem in the theory of economic development is to understand the process by which a community which was

previously saving and investing 4 or 5 percent of its national income or less, converts itself into an economy where voluntary saving is running at about 12 to 15 percent of national income or more.

Rough estimates of the ratio are shown for twelve developed economies in Table 1. In most cases, the available statistics begin after the process of development was already underway, but they suggest that Lewis was broadly correct in setting the preindustrial ratio at about 4 or 5 percent. As these countries developed, the proportion of income saved and invested increased. It had typically risen to about 15 to 20 percent in the years immediately before 1913, and in the long boom following World War II it climbed even higher, with ratios well above 20 percent in most of these countries.

What factors lie behind this three- or fourfold rise in the savings and investment ratios? In a short article, it is possible to outline only some of the possible answers to this large and complicated question. As a starting point, consider two schedules: one sloping upward and relating the supply of savings (S/Y) to the rate of interest, the other sloping downward and relating the demand for investment (I/Y) to the rate of interest. In both cases there may be movements along the curve as supply or demand responds to changes in the rate of interest; and the curves themselves may shift if there are changes in any of the underlying factors that are taken as given, for example, the structure of the economy or the state of technology.

At one extreme (illustrated in Figure 1a), the rise in the ratios might be the outcome of a shift to the right in the investment demand schedule as a consequence of changes in one or more of the given factors. This would lead to a higher

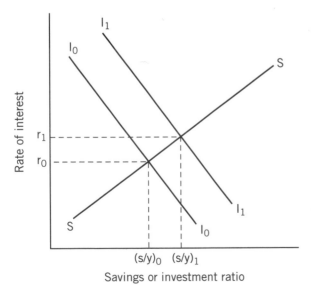

FIGURE 1a. A shift to the right in the investment demand schedule.

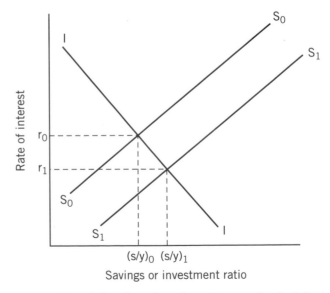

FIGURE 1b. A shift to the right in the savings supply schedule.

rate of interest and a movement along the savings supply schedule in response to this. At the other extreme (Figure 1b), the savings supply schedule could have shifted outward, leading to a lower interest rate and a movement along the investment schedule in response to this. In practice, of course, it is likely that both curves shifted over time, and the elasticity of the schedules, that is, their responsiveness to changes in the rate of interest, would also be a crucial aspect of the process.

There is a rich menu of possible changes in the underlying conditions that could explain such outward movements in the two schedules. For the savings supply schedule these include (1) the growth of financial intermediaries and their role in increasing opportunities for saving by cutting transaction costs and reducing risk; (2) structural changes in favor of groups with a higher propensity to save, for example, shifts in the income distribution to the advantage of the recipients of profits and rents, or demographic trends leading to a smaller proportion of young or old in the population; (3) changes in savings behavior within particular age or income groups because, for example, a weakening of the extended family made it more necessary for individuals to provide for their old age; and (4) changes in government policies, such as reductions in the share of income taken in tax, or specific tax inducements to save for certain purposes, notably retirement. Movements in any of these factors in the opposite direction could similarly be invoked to explain periods when the savings ratio has fallen, as it did for the United States in the twentieth century.

The main explanations for an outward shift in the investment demand schedule include (1) increases in capital intensity as a result of a bias in technological progress in favor of capital-using and labor-saving innovation; (2) structural changes in the direction of sectors (for example, transportation or housing) with higher capital requirements per unit of output; (3) a fall in the relative price of capital goods; and (4) the impact of population growth on population-sensitive investment, such as housing.

It is difficult to isolate and quantify these possible influences on the two schedules, and even harder to determine their respective elasticities, so there is rarely a consensus on the relative importance of the difference factors in any particular case.

Finally, it remains to mention briefly the relationship between investment and economic growth. Quantitative studies leave little doubt that there is a positive association, but the relationship is complex and has almost certainly changed over time. In the earlier stages of economic development, increases in the stock of physical capital accounted for a large part of the rise in output per man hour: workers were able to produce more because they had more capital to work with. More recently, however, advances in the quality of the equipment have become progressively more important, and the primary role of investment has been to act as the carrier for technological change. Scientific and technical innovations in productive processes must be embodied in physical equipment in order to be economically effective, and it is this aspect of capital formation that has contributed so powerfully to enonomic growth and made investment and saving so crucially important. These same innovations have also created the need for higher levels of skill, and so made human capital formation increasingly significant as a source of economic advance.

[*See also* Consumption.]

BIBLIOGRAPHY

Crouzet, F. *Capital Formation in the Industrial Revolution.* London, 1972. A useful collection of articles on savings and investment in Great Britain.

David, Paul A. "Invention and Accumulation in America's Economic Growth: A Nineteenth-Century Parable." *Journal of Monetary Economics* 6 Suppl. (1977), 179–228. A leading contribution to the debate about the reasons for the rise in the savings ratio in the United States in the nineteenth century.

Davis, Lance E., and Robert J. Cull. *International Capital Markets and American Economic Growth, 1820–1914.* Cambridge, 1994.

Davis, Lance E., and Robert E. Gallmann. "Savings, Investment, and Economic Growth: The United States in the Nineteenth Century." In *Capitalism in Context,* edited by John A. James and Mark Thomas, pp. 202–229. Chicago, 1994. A very clear and balanced survey of different views on this topic.

Edelstein, Michael. *Overseas Investment in the Age of High Imperialism.* New York, 1982. The major study of the determinants of British overseas investment before 1913 and its impact on investments in the main borrowing countries.

Feinstein, Charles H., and Sidney Pollard, eds. *Studies in Capital Formation in the United Kingdom 1750–1920.* Oxford, 1988.

Gallmann, Robert E. "The United States Capital Stock in the Nineteenth Century." In *Long-term Factors in American Economic Growth,* edited by S. L. Engerman and R. E. Gallman, pp. 165–213. Chicago, 1986.

Gallmann, Robert E. "Investment Flows and Capital Stocks: U.S. Experience in the Nineteenth Century." In *Quantity and Quiddity, Essays in U.S. Economic History,* edited by Peter Kilby, pp. 214–254. Middletown, Conn., 1987.

Goldsmith, Raymond W. *A Study of Saving in the United States.* 3 vols. Princeton, 1955.

Hudson, Pat. *The Genesis of Industrial Capital: A Study of the West Riding Wool Textile Industry c.1750–1850.* Cambridge, 1986. An excellent investigation of the financing of a leading British industry.

Imlah, A. H. *Economic Elements in the Pax Britannica.* Cambridge, 1958. The standard estimates of British foreign investment before 1913.

Kuznets, Simon. *Capital in the American Economy, Its Formation and Financing.* Princeton, 1961. The final volume in a series of studies covering different sectors of the U.S. economy.

Mathias, Peter, and M. M. Postan, eds. *The Cambridge Economic History of Europe,* vol. 7, parts I and II. Cambridge, 1978. Includes articles on capital formation in nineteenth-century Great Britain, the United States, France, Germany, Russia, and Japan.

Matthews, R. C. O., C. H. Feinstein, and J. C. Odling-Smee. *British Economic Growth, 1856–1973.* Oxford, 1982. Includes a systematic analysis of the trends in both investment and savings.

Ohkawa, Kazushi, and Henry Rosovsky. *Japanese Economic Growth: Trend Acceleration in the Twentieth Century.* Stanford, Calif., 1973. Includes a detailed study of the role of investment in Japanese economic growth.

CHARLES FEINSTEIN

Wages and Labor Income

Income distribution has been a main topic in economics since the days of Gregory King and William Petty. For the classical economists, as Irving B. Kravis (1962) noted, the distribution of income among the suppliers of labor, land, and capital was the most efficient indicator of the relative welfare of different social groups. Thus wages, profits and rents represented the income of workers, entrepreneurs, and proprietors, respectively. Such a direct identification of social groups with particular types of income cannot, however, be made so readily for the recent past. The remuneration of production factors is today central to the various kinds of studies. As Alan B. Krueger (1999) pointed out, factor shares can be used to (1) describe the functional distribution of income, (2) estimate the factor shares in the aggregate production function, and (3) infer the division of rents between workers and firms.

The largest share of national income is the labor's share, and within labor income the most important component is wages, although labor income includes other kinds of labor remunerations in addition to wages. In the following sections some empirical issues in the study of labor income are surveyed in the light of economic history, including the hypothesis of the stability of factor shares across time and space and the relative importance of raw labor and human capital in labor income.

The Historical Study of Labor Income. How the income of owners and the self-employed should be treated in the labor-capital dichotomy has provoked a great deal of controversy over time. Jean-Baptiste Say and Richard Cantillon held that the remuneration of owners and the self-employed was a return for the risk of their activities. However, classical economists considered that the remuneration of business people was simply a return for capital previously invested. Hence for physiocrats and classical economists the remuneration of owners should not be considered in labor's share but in capital's share. In a sharp contrast, Alfred Marshall was the first economist to point out that a part of the income earned by self-employed workers and owners is a compensation for their work, while another part represents a return on investment and risk or simply economic profit from their entrepreneurial activities. Marshall's argument is widely accepted today in the standard analysis of income shares. Its implication is that, in the functional distribution of income, labor's share should include not only the compensation of employees but also the opportunity costs of the work of proprietors, unpaid family workers, and the self-employed.

According to the United Nations publication *System of National Accounts* (1995), the compensation of workers includes wages, piece payments, salaries (cash and in-kind), tips, bonuses, fringe benefits, commissions, and employer contributions to social security programs, pension schemes, health plans, and other benefit packages. Lack of evidence often prevents historians from measuring labor income correctly, though some historical studies that succeeded in quantifying the main components of labor income can be cited. A good example is provided by Robin Matthews, Charles Feinstein, and John Odling-Smee's (1982) study of Britain, in which they estimated four main components in labor's share: wages, salaries, the part of self-employed income that rewards labor, and employers' contributions to public and private insurance and pensions. In any case, total compensation of workers should not be identified simply with wage rates as is sometimes implicitly assumed in the historical literature.

To measure labor income correctly, it is important to establish which proportion of the income of proprietors, unpaid family workers, the self-employed, and retired workers represent returns to labor. It should be noted that self-employment, rather than wage employment, dominates in developing countries, as it did in most historical cases. In particular, allocating agricultural value added to the different functional components of income in societies of the past represents a major challenge for historians. In addition the empirical analysis of the functional distribution of income and in particular of labor's share is handicapped by the fact that data has not been determined by the requirements of economic analysis but rather by the legal and institutional arrangements of the society. Thus indirect methods have to be used to quantify these shares.

Alternative methods to estimate the income of proprietors and the self-employed accruing from their work have been designed. Colin Clark (1957) and Simon Kuznets (1966) favored the approach of attributing to entrepreneurs and self-employed workers a labor income per head equal to per worker compensation of employees, and most empirical studies have accepted it. An alternative proposed by Edward F. Denison (1967) was to assume the division between labor and property (capital and land) income to be the same in incorporated and nonincorporated firms.

A more sophisticated alternative procedure has been applied by Dale W. Jorgenson (1988) and his collaborators and more recently by Alwyn Young (1995) according to the principle that the remuneration of the self-employed is equal to the opportunity cost of their work. To estimate labor income, hourly incomes of employees by industry, sex, age, and education must be constructed. Compensation data and hours of work by industry, sex, age, education, and class of worker are used to estimate the incomes of employees and the implicit labor incomes of employers, unpaid family workers, and the self-employed under the assumption that the last three earn an implicit wage equal to the hourly wage of employees with similar sex, age, educational, and industrial characteristics. However, while this approach is theoretically preferable, lack of data often impedes its historical application. However, as Kuznets argued, the underlying assumption that the labor service of the self-employed can be equal to wage employees "is far too crude to warrant the refinement in calculation" (1996, p. 178).

Recently Douglas Gollin (2001) suggested a less data-demanding approach by making adjustments to the national income on the reported operating surplus of unincorporated enterprises since most of the self-employed fall into this category. Then either all the private surplus of private unincorporated enterprises is allocated to labor income, or it is assumed to comprise the same mix of labor and capital income as the rest of the economy.

Are Factor Shares Stable over Time? The perception that income distribution between capital and labor has been relatively stable over time goes back to the 1930s. "The stability of the proportion of the national dividend accruing to labor," J. M. Keynes wrote, was "one of the most surprising, yet best established, facts in the whole range of economic statistics, both for Great Britain and for the United States" (1939, pp. 48–49).

The validity of the stability hypothesis is supported by empirical evidence for the present, provided labor income (including employee compensation and the remuneration of the self-employed) is considered. The share of labor remains quite stable across countries, ranging, according to Gollin, from two-thirds to four-fifths of national income despite the fact that its distribution between wage employ-

ment and self-employment varies considerably. Gollin has noted that large differences in national rates of the self-employed are closely associated to per capita income levels. Differences in labor's share across countries reflect more disparities in the structure and scale of firms than in sectoral composition of output. Thus in the poor countries rates of self-employment are larger than in the rich countries because the share of larger firms is smaller. Consequently today's differences in employee shares across countries are basically explained by the relative sizes of the earnings obtained by the self-employed, unpaid family workers, and business owners.

Are these generalizations confirmed by historical evidence? Data for a number of countries confirms that the share of employee compensation has shown a tendency to grow over the last one and a half centuries, in particular between the mid-nineteenth century and the mid-twentieth century (see Table 1). Kravis and Kuznets pointed to historical explanations of the growing share of wages in total income. Kravis stressed structural change as a major reason behind the increase in wage ratios to GDP. The shift of labor away from agriculture and the increase in the size of firms implied that the proportion of the self-employed and small entrepreneurs declined. Hence the operating surplus (that is, entrepreneurial income) as a share of national income decreased over time as long-term employment reallocation simultaneously increased workers' compensation. Demographic changes and urbanization, Kuznets suggested, also mattered, as the rise of the age of entry in the labor market, the rise of the average age of retiring, and the incorporation of working women into wage labor contributed to explaining the rise in the wage ratio.

Evidence assembled in Table 2 tends to reject the idea of a stable labor's share in national income. Labor income, broadly defined to include nonwage employment, increased

TABLE 1. *Wages and Salaries as a Percentage of National Income*

	UNITED KINGDOM	GERMANY	JAPAN	FRANCE	UNITED STATES	NETHERLANDS
1856	50.4			36.0	40.0	53.0
1873	47.7				41.1	52.0
1913	48.5	47.0		45.0	47.0	43.0
1924	57.9	64.0		50.0	60.8	43.1
1937	56.7		40.4		65.1	41.7
1953	61.0	60.0	53.1	59.0	67.3	
1964	62.0		52.2			
1973	60.9		47.3			
1973–1982	59.5	52.1	50.8	45.7	56.9	48.9
1992	57.4		56.4	52.5	60.4	53.3

SOURCES: Matthews, R. C. O., et al., 1982, p. 164; Kuznets, S., 1966, pp. 168–169; Ohkawa, K., and M. Shinohara, 1979, pp. 379–381; Smits, J. P., et al., 2000, pp. 173–174; Bakker, G. P. den, et al., 1990, p. 201; Maddison, A., 1987, p. 659; Gollin, D., 2001, p. 19 ("naïve" calculation); Budd, E. C., 1960, p. 373; Kravis, I. B., 1968, p. 134.

TABLE 2. *Labor Share as a Percentage of Gross National Income*

	UNITED KINGDOM	GERMANY	JAPAN	FRANCE	UNITED STATES	NETHERLANDS
1856	57.8	77.8		56.0	66.7	
1873	54.4	77.8			63.0	
1913	56.0	70.9		67.0	62.4	
1924	66.6	87.3		71.0	71.5	
1937	65.1	78.1	59.7		76.5	
1953	70.0	74.0	76.6	81.0	77.3	
1964	71.4		69.5			
1973	72.8		67.0			
1973–1982	74.5	70.0	70.8	69.5	73.3	70.4
1992	71.9		72.5	68.1	66.4	68.0

Average employee compensation used to impute compensation for entire workforce.
SOURCES: Matthews, R. C. O., et al., 1982, p. 164; Hoffmann, W. G., 1965, p. 503; Ohkawa, K., and M. Shinohara, 1979, pp. 379–381; Kuznets, S., 1966, p. 168; Maddison, A., 1987, p. 659; Gollin, D., 2001, p. 19 (Adjustment 3); Budd, E. C., 1960, p. 382; Kravis, I. B., 1968, p. 134.

its share of GDP in all cases considered, except for Germany (whose data Walther G. Hoffmann [1965] computed in a different fashion) over the period 1850–1950, to stabilize (and even decline) thereafter. Explaining why historical evidence contradicts economists' empirical regularities represents a challenge for economic historians.

Total hours worked (both by the self-employed and by wage earners) have fallen with industrialization, while there was not a declining response but an increasing one of the labor's share of income. Why? Historical evidence shows that factory supplies increased at different rates. How was income distribution affected? Two offsetting forces were at play. On the one hand the supply of capital has been growing faster than the supply of labor, but on the other the productivity of labor has risen relative to the productivity of capital. The extent to which these forces matched each other has been translated into the stability of factor shares. Kuznets's stress on the changes in the composition of the labor force, with a relative increase in skilled labor, could be suggested as an explanation. Thus increases in relative marginal productivity of labor translated into relatively higher returns to labor compared to capital, solving the paradox of an increasing labor's share in income while worked hours per capita tended to decline. Education, broadly defined to include on-the-job training, was suggested by Kuznets as the key explanatory factor, though he also pointed to gains from total factor productivity accruing to labor that could be the result from non-Hicks neutral technological advances. As Kuznets put it in 1966, "The share of labor in growing output has increased . . . because greater investment has been made in maintaining and increasing the quality of labor; also, a larger proportional share of the net gains, after the input of resources adjusted for quality has been taken into account, has gone to labor" (1966, p. 185).

Hence changes in the composition of labor income need to be explored.

What Is in Labor Income? Labor's share of national income is, broadly speaking, composed of returns to unskilled and skilled labor (human capital). Human capital compensation is the result of past investments in education (broadly defined), training, and experience. Raw labor remuneration is the zero-skilled, nonexperienced worker's compensation. Thus each worker's earnings consists of two additive components, raw labor and human capital.

In the early empirical literature on human capital, literacy and enrollment rates were employed as proxies for human capital. However, average years of schooling are not necessarily a good measure of human capital. Firstly, formal education is not the only source of human capital, since workers can acquire skills through training and experience. In historical terms this is particularly important. Formal education was not universal up to the twentieth century in many countries, and multiple forms of education and training were previously available. Secondly, its rationale is that one year of schooling delivers the same returns always and everywhere, independently from the field of study or the quality of education. Thirdly, it assumes that workers in each education category are perfect substitutes, even if they are occupied in different jobs and sectors. Fourthly, it considers that different levels of education explain all differences in productivity across workers.

There are two alternative ways to solve the problems of education-based measures of human capital and to separate raw labor from human capital. One is based on the direct estimate of labor income shares and another on regression analysis. Each has its advantages, but the former is less data demanding and has already been employed in economic history studies.

Casey B. Mulligan and Xavier Sala-i-Martín (1997) constructed a direct measure of the shares of human capital and raw labor. Starting from the intuition that a worker's quality would be related to the wage rate received in the marketplace, they defined wages as the sum of the returns on past investments in human capital and the value of raw labor. In other words, the wage of any person is equal to the sum of human capital's returns and the wage rate of the zero-skilled worker. Therefore their measure of human capital for a given economy is the weighted sum of all workers, where the weights are the ratio of their wages to the wage of the zero-skilled worker. This is equivalent to the aggregate wage bill divided by the wage of the zero-schooling worker.

This measure had a series of conceptual and practical advantages. It is consistent with variable elasticity of substitution across the different types of workers. Also it considers not only education but training and experience as measures of human capital, allowing for the existence of differences in productivity across different workers with the same education levels. Finally, it is consistent with changes in the relative productivity of workers across countries and over time. However, it has also a series of shortcomings. Particularly relevant is that it assumes that market prices reflect perfectly human capital and raw labor remuneration. In other words, this approach necessarily implies that the zero-schooling worker had always the same amount of skill and that he or she is a perfect substitute for all the others.

Jonas Ljundberg's (1998) historical study of human capital in Sweden resembles Mulligan and Sala-i-Martín's approach. Also Joan R. Rosés's (1998) study of the Catalan cotton industry uses a similar approach and provides a measure of human capital and raw labor consistent and efficient in the presence of some labor market failures, such as sex discrimination and specific-sector findings. Rosés separated human capital shares into the returns of broad education, on-the-job training, and experience returns. Then he hypothesized that the remuneration of any worker could be divided into three parts, one owed to unskilled labor (equal to the minimum wage), another owed to education (equal to the minimum wage of the skilled worker minus the unskilled work remuneration), and the rest owed to experience and on-the-job training (the remaining remuneration). This worker-level measure of human capital can be transformed easily in an aggregate measure of the returns of raw labor, education, and training. Specifically the total payments of raw labor are equal to the minimum wage of each sector multiplied by the number of days (hours) worked in that sector. Similarly the total payments to education are equal to the minimum skilled wage in each sector, commonly the initial (entry) wage of skilled workers, multiplied by the number of days (hours) worked

by skilled workers minus the remuneration of raw labor in these skilled workers. Finally, training is equal to the residual of the total labor's share. This method would be easily extended to eliminate discrimination from the calculations separating the estimation by sex, race, or any other category. It has a major shortcoming, however, since it does not allow for the fact that accumulation of experience and on-the-job training could differ between unskilled and educated workers.

An alternative approach is to estimate raw labor and human capital based on regression analysis, as proposed by Krueger. Following Finis Welch's model of linear skill, Krueger derived the wage of raw labor from the following Mincerian earnings regressions:

$$\ln W_i = b_0 + b_1 S_i + b_2 X_i + b_2 X_i^2 + e_i,$$

where $\ln W_i$ is the natural log of worker i's yearly earning, S_i equals years of schooling, X_i is potential experience (age minus education minus 6), X_i^2 is potential experience squared, and e_i is error term. In this framework the average remuneration of each worker down to raw labor is approximately the exponential of the intercept plus half of the mean square error of the regression. Thus obviously the share of wages owing to raw labor is the sum of all raw labor remuneration divided by total labor remuneration, and the residual is the human capital remuneration.

An advantage of this method is its relative simplicity, but it also suffers from several major shortcomings. Particularly any monopoly return from labor, like unionization, is reflected immediately in human capital share. Instead, minimum wage legislation tends to raise the intercept and to increase in turn raw labor share.

BIBLIOGRAPHY

Abramovitz, Moses, and Paul A. David. "Reinterpreting Economic Growth: Parables and Realities." *American Economic Review* 63.2 (1973), 428–439.

Bakker, Gert P. den, Theo A. Huitker, and Cornelius A. van Bochove. "The Dutch Economy, 1921–39: Revised Macroeconomic Data for the Interwar Period." *Review of Income and Wealth* 36.2 (1990), 187–206.

Budd, Edward C. "Factor Shares, 1850–1910." In *Trends in the American Economy in the Nineteenth Century*, edited by W. N. Parker, pp. 365–406. NBER Studies in Income and Wealth, vol. 24. Princeton, 1960.

Clark, Colin. *The Conditions of Economic Progress*. 3d ed. London, 1957.

Denison, Edward F. *Why Growth Rates Differ: Postwar Experience in Nine Western Countries*. Washington, D.C., 1967.

Gollin, Douglas. "Getting Income Shares Right." Mimeo, Williams College. Williamstown, Mass., 2001.

Hoffmann, Walther G. *Das Wachstum der deutschen Wirtschaft seit der Mitte des 19. Jahrhunderts*. Berlin, 1965.

Johnson, D. Gale. "The Functional Distribution of Income in the United States, 1850–1952." *Review of Economics and Statistics* 36 (1954), 175–182.

Jorgenson, Dale W. "Productivity and Economic Growth." In *Fifty Years of Economic Measurement*, edited by E. R. Berndt and J. E. Triplett, pp. 19–118. Chicago, 1990.

Keynes, J. M. "Relative Movements of Real Wages and Output." *Economic Journal* 49 (1939), 34–51.

Kravis, Irving B. *The Structure of Income: Some Quantitative Essays.* Philadelphia, 1962.

Krueger, Alan B. "Measuring Labor's Share." NBER Working Paper 7006. Cambridge, Mass., 1999.

Kuznets, Simon. *Modern Economic Growth: Rate, Structure, and Spread.* New Haven, 1966.

Ljundberg, Jonas. "Human Capital in Sweden." University of Lund, Mimeo. Lund, 1998.

Maddison, Angus. "Growth and Slowdown in Advanced Capitalist Economies: Techniques of Quantitative Assessment." *Journal of Economic Literature* 25.2 (1987), 649–679.

Matthews, R. C. O., C. H. Feinstein, and J. C. Odling-Smee. *British Economic Growth, 1856–1973.* Oxford, 1982.

Mulligan, Casey B., and Xavier Sala-i-Martín. "A Labor Income-Based Measure of the Value of Human Capital: An Application to the States of the United States." *Japan and the World Economy* 9.2, (1997), 159–191.

Ohkawa, Kazushi, and Miyohei Shinohara, eds. *Patterns of Japanese Economic Development: A Quantitative Appraisal.* New Haven, 1979.

Phillips, Joseph. "Labor's Share and 'Wage Parity.'" *Review of Economics and Statistics* 42.2 (1960), 164–174.

Rosés, Joan R. "Measuring the Contribution of Human Capital to the Development of the Catalan Factory System (1830–61)." *European Review of Economic History* 2.1 (1998), 25–48.

Smits, Jan Pieter, Edwin Horlings, and Jan Luiten van Zanden. *Dutch GNP and Its Components, 1800–1913.* Groningen, Netherlands, 2000.

Young, Alwyn. "The Tyranny of Numbers: Confronting the Statistical Realities of East Asian Growth Experiences." *Quarterly Journal of Economics* 110.3 (1995), 641–680.

LEANDRO PRADOS DE LA ESCOSURA AND JOAN R. ROSÉS

Rental Income

In the modern period, it is important to distinguish ground rents paid for the use of land (*rente foncière*) from fees paid for land use under the feudal or seigneurial system (*rentes féodales* or *seigneuriales*). The former are based on short-term rental contracts, whereas the latter are charges imposed in perpetuity and assessed in cash or in kind. Furthermore, from the Middle Ages to the early nineteenth century, the evolution of judicial and political systems gradually led to unqualified freehold of land that had been leased for rent payments (under the feudal system) or for fixed fees to tenant farmers, which differentiates these forms of leasing from ground rent.

In the feudal or seigneurial type of contract, the landowner gave his tenant the right to exploit his lands for a fee. This fee took various forms over the centuries. One of its primitive forms, not found everywhere, was sharecropping (*métayage*). In this case, landowners and tenants shared expenses and income in a proportion that varied over time. As for ground rents, they were first payable in kind, then partly in kind and partly in cash, before being entirely payable in currency. However, even when the principal was paid in cash, certain minor charges in kind (chickens or capons, for example) were part of the contract.

The length of leases gradually increased, with differences in timing from region to region. This was especially true from the end of the eighteenth century on, owing to investments made by farmers. From an initial three-year time period in the north of France, for example, leases increased to six, nine, or eighteen years in length and sometimes more. Nevertheless, this evolution underwent some reversals, especially during the French Revolution, when for monetary reasons landlords specified farm rents in kind even when in principle these remained payable in cash.

Ground rents applied both to large farm holdings and to small patches of land rented by farmers to increase their tillage or by day laborers who cultivated them either for their own subsistence or to supplement their income.

Karl Marx interpreted the passage from peasant proprietorship to tenant farming and then to rent in kind and in cash as embodying the development of capitalism. If, as he thought, capitalism is defined by the exploitation of labor, in which the capitalist pockets part of the proceeds, ground rents were only a further development of the form of debiting to which the tenant farmer was bound by his landlord. This evolution made it easier for the farmer to accumulate wealth, for he thus gradually gained increasing control of the commercialization of his farm's products, along with—in the final phase—the monetary payment, which for him represented control over the entire process of commercialization (part of which, in the case of ground rents paid in kind, was assured by the landowner or his representative). Whether the rent was assessed in kind or in cash, the farmer relied on salaried labor to work his farm. From this point of view, rent in kind is identical in form to rent in cash, since exploitation of the land by salaried work corresponds to both sorts of payments. Thus, I cannot accept Karl Marx's reasoning that these steps represented a development of capitalism. It must be noted that wages could also be paid in kind. The shift to monetary exchanges, even if it modified the relations among landowners, farmers, and wage earners, was thus independent of the forms taken by work during the same period.

Around 1300 in England, between 20 and 30 percent of the land that belonged to lords (the rest being worked by free peasants or villeins) was cultivated in overwhelming proportions by the owners. From this period on, two circumstances gradually gave preeminence to tenant farming in England as well as in France. The lords' estates increased considerably in size, and their owners tended more and more to lease them. However, it is possible that in certain regions ground rent arrangements were made earlier, for the Abbey of Saint-Denis began to rent or lease its lands in the twelfth century. It is unknown whether the lands were then sublet to multiple tenants or whether the taker was a true tenant farmer. This evolution partly contradicts the view of the nineteenth-century thinkers who saw a long process of expropriation of peasants unfolding from the Middle Ages to the nineteenth century. This belief was shared by Marx and a large number of twentieth-century historians, including, for example, Marc Bloch. However, this view does not take into account the fact that peasants never possessed all the land or the fact that the peasantry never constituted a homogeneous class.

Starting in the late Middle Ages, when most of the lords had shifted to tenant farming, the broad outlines of the development of the tenant farm base were apparent, thanks to the distribution of real property. In the countryside near Paris in the mid-sixteenth century, peasants no longer owned more than 30 percent of the land. By the end of the seventeenth century, their share had fallen to 10 percent. In contrast, where the population was smaller and nature less fertile, their share rose to 30 percent or even more by the end of the eighteenth century.

In England, the peasants' share of land fell away more rapidly than in France. It went from 70 to 80 percent in the Middle Ages to 20 percent in 1700, 24 to 30 percent in 1800, and 15 percent in 1900. In England, as in France, practices diverged widely. In Cumbria, for example, whereas the lands devoted to tenant farming covered only 6 percent of certain estates around 1600 and 50 percent at the end of the eighteenth century, in Nottinghamshire, 80 percent of the lands were used for tenant farming as early as the mid-sixteenth century.

From the Middle Ages to the nineteenth century in both countries, the constitution of great estates were rented as larger and larger farms. This growth in the surface area of the lands farmed shows the burgeoning wealth of the tenant farmers, for in addition to the increased capital necessary for this growth, farmers needed to provide for their children. This was true only where natural conditions, as in the north of France, made it possible to produce in large volumes. For these reasons, as Véron de Forbonnais (an eighteenth-century French political economist) hoped, one cannot forget that agriculture was practiced in spaces that were not equivalent from the agricultural viewpoint and that did not have the same natural potential.

A more precise image of the tenant farm base is discernible during the period when the system was at its apogee. In England around 1890, the statistics show roughly 440,500 farmers, of whom 12.5 percent cultivated lands they owned themselves, while a little more than 83 percent rented their lands, and 4.4 percent added leased lands to those they owned. In terms of surface area, 85.4 percent of agricultural lands were farmed by tenants, as opposed to 14.6 percent farmed by owners. Moreover, in

this period the geographical distribution seems to have been fairly homogeneous. These statistics are not exhaustive, for they do not take parcels smaller than one acre into account. If the entire surface area of all farmed land is compared with the total surface area represented by the statistics, there is a deficit of more than 5 million acres (2 million hectares). This deficit can only be attributed to the small parcels not included in the statistics. If cottagers are incorporated into these statistics, the number of farmers jumps to 700,000. Landowners who farmed their own lands then represent 66.3 percent of all farmers, but with only 15 percent in surface area, their share in land holdings remains modest. In contrast, if one considers that the deficit comes primarily from the failure to take small landowners into account, the proportion of lands farmed by their owners would be 28 percent. If this were confirmed, one could conclude that England, like France but without a French-style revolution, experienced an increase in farming by landowners during the latter part of the nineteenth century.

In France, according to the 1892 statistics, the group of farmer-owners was a little larger than in England. Indeed, of 5.6 million farmers, 74.6 percent cultivated lands they owned themselves, while 6.2 percent were sharecroppers (*métayers*) and 36.4 percent tenant farmers (*fermiers*). As for the surface area, farmer-owners accounted for 52.8 percent of the territory, as opposed to 10.8 percent for sharecropping and 36.4 percent for tenant farming. But, unlike England, France presented significant regional variations. Thus, farmer-owners accounted for only 34 percent of the lands in the Seine-et-Oise department as opposed to 68 percent in the Gers, a department in which only 5 percent of the lands were leased. Ground rents were thus a much more important factor in England than in France.

Historians have used ground rent to study the evolution of production and productivity. In the first case, ground rent, thought to indicate the evolution of production, is taken as an indicator of cereal yield. In the second case, it is used to provide an estimate of the productivity of work and capital. To do so, the use of series of data is required. These methods are not without interest, but they must be used with caution. In fact, ground rent can by no means be defined mechanically in relation to production or to the costs involved in production. As rent is also a power relation between owners and farmers, fluctuations observed in the evolution of production and productivity actually only reflect these power relations. Furthermore, the evolution of a series of leases may at any given point reflect the landowner's approach to management. In fact, one can find a series of leases in which a value that has remained stagnant suddenly rises significantly. The constitution of sufficiently large series is supposed to compensate for this disadvantage, but the results are not always convincing. Another disadvantage to be overcome is that tenant farmers quite often had to pay bribes to the landowners. This has to be taken into account in the constitution of the series, as well as the existence of agreements signed under private auspices that indicate a fee rate different from the one included in the lease signed before a notary. This relativizes the theories devoted to ground rents. These methods are only an imperfect indication of the evolution of production and productivity, but, for want of anything better, they are not to be disdained.

It is relatively easy to constitute a series of leases, but the process may take a long time. First, when the lease was the object of a contract between landlord and tenant, leases can be found in notaries' records. To locate them, it is necessary to go through whole sets of documents or to consult registers in which leases were recorded, where such registers exist. For small parcels, notaries are the principal if not the sole source of information. Leases for larger farm properties can be found in notaries' records as well, but they can also be located in rent books or account books in estate archives.

BIBLIOGRAPHY

Béaur, Gérard. "Le marché foncier éclaté: Les modes de transmission du patrimoine sous l'Ancien Régime." *Annales ESC* (January–February 1991), 189–203.

Campbell, Bruce. *English Seignorial Agriculture, 1250–1450.* Cambridge, 2000.

Chevet, Jean-Michel. *La terre et les paysans en France et en Grande-Bretagne: Du début du XVIIème siècle à la fin du XVIIIème siècle.* 2 vols. Paris, 1998–1999.

Gregson, Nicky. "Tawney Revisited: Custom and the Emergence of Capitalist Class Relations in North-East Cumbria, 1600–1830." *Economic History Review* 42 (1989), 18–42.

Hoffman, Philip T. *Growth in a Traditional Society: The French Countryside, 1450–1815.* Princeton, 1996.

Turner, Michael Edward, John V. Beckett, and Bethanie Afton. *Agricultural Rent in England, 1690–1914.* Cambridge, 1997.

JEAN-MICHEL CHEVET
Translated from French by Catherine Porter

NATIONALIZATION AND PRIVATIZATION. Both terms were largely unknown before the twentieth century. They are rooted in *property* and *ownership*, which are older concepts, but even they should not be considered here before the nineteenth-century rise of industrial capitalism. The Marxist analysis of industrial capitalism and the countervailing defence of market and laissez-faire economies set the scene for the popular concepts of nationalization and privatization as the shift of production from the private sector to the public sector. That shift has been related to products and services that carry prices, often produced by enterprises under financial constraints. Nationalization was an institutional change toward socialism in many

European countries after World War I (1914–1918), associated then with the perception that capitalism had broken down along with the collapse of the three large Eurasian empires (the Russian, Austro-Hungarian and Ottoman). After World War II (1939–1945), the wave of nationalizations was repeated in India, Malaya, Uganda, and other countries where various colonies and imperial possessions became independent but wanted a social-welfare state. Often a distrusting Western capitalism and the ongoing Cold War provided motivation for their alignment with the Soviet bloc; foreign aid and political ideals led many new third-world countries into nationalizing industries that had been set up under colonialism. Australia and Canada tried some of the European developments. The United States had a mild ripple of social concern during the Great Depression, but by the end of World War II, U.S. investments in markets and private ownership continued to be strong. By the late 1970s, U.S. influence, growing economic problems in eastern European communist regimes, and the financial and fiscal problems of the state sector in the mixed economies of western Europe and the third world, resulted in almost worldwide reversal of emphasis to private enterprise. The People's Republic of China, Cuba, North Korea, and Vietnam remained communist states after the 1991 demise of the Soviet Union.

Although these phases were unambiguously associated with questions of ownership, the actual transitions had two other features. One was a change in market structure. The railways in France were brought under full public ownership in the 1930s, as were the coal mines in the Netherlands and the electricity supply in Japan; all were national monopolies. In the United Kingdom, the privatization of water, gas, and electricity from 1985 onward brought competition for electricity generation—but a national private monopoly in gas supply and a set of franchised regional private monopolies in water supply. (The term *privatization* has also been used for contracting some services previously operated by government departments—refuse collection, hospital catering services—but such issues and the deregulation of airlines, for example, will not be covered here.) Another feature of the twentieth-century transitions was the role of government. The term *nationalization* means that physical assets owned by individuals, firms, municipalities, or subnational states were taken over by the central government: the Reichspost (postal system) on the establishment of the German empire in 1871, the railways in Italy in 1905, the Reichsbahn (roadways) during Germany's Weimar Republic in the 1920s. The few acts of denationalization in Europe in the 1950s differed significantly from the privatizations of the 1980s and 1990s; in the 1950s, the Netherlandse Soda Industrie, the U.K.'s Iron and Steel Corporation, and Volkswagenwerk in West Germany were sold to indigenous buyers. By the 1980s, the liberalization of the capital markets meant that privatization often involved sales to foreign buyers—individuals or multinational companies—a source of concern for many governments. For example, in the late 1980s, Turkey's government wanted to bring private capital and entrepreneurship into its economy but knew that important manufacturing sectors would go to foreign owners.

Public Ownership: Theory and Actuality. Karl Marx wrote economic and political philosophy in the mid-nineteenth century, and his ideas were taken seriously by the turn of the twentieth century. The classic Marxist diagnosis of capitalism distinguished two groups in society (capitalists and proletariat) according to their ownership of the "means of production"—plant, machinery, vehicles, and land. Under socialism, the means of production are owned by the proletariat who, under capitalism, depended on wage labor in the factories and on the farms of capitalists. In the early 1900s, that was translated into action in Russia, and state ownership of assets became a central feature of the Soviet Union. The influence of Marxism was, as late as 1967, reflected in the Arusha Declaration: "major means of production and exchange [in the newly independent African state of Tanzania were to be] . . . under the control of the peasants and workers." In other developing countries and in western Europe, the impact of Marxist ideas was less direct. The promotion of more equal income distributions and of lower prices for commodities for working-class families were common threads in all nationalizations. Where Marxist terminology was present, it was not always taken literally: the constitution of Britain's Labour party included, from 1918, a commitment to "the common ownership of the means of production, distribution and exchange, on the best obtainable system of popular administration and control of each industry and service." Most historians interpreted that as just a part of a political package, to unite the various party subgroups.

Few other conceptual frameworks for thinking about public ownership existed except for that of Marx. A very different diagnosis emerged in the property rights approach, first set out by Armen Alchian in 1965. Under unfettered private property rights, individuals have the unilateral ability to sell the rights they own, including shares in publicly quoted companies; this ability creates an incentive for managers to perform efficiently, since any underperformance will lead to financial losses, sales of shares, and collapse of share prices. In contrast, for public firms, ownership is invested in the state or municipality, so individuals can relinquish ownership rights only by moving to another polity or by engaging in political action. In this argument, there is less pressure on managers to perform: public enterprises will be characterized by poor economic performance and large budgets, which give prestige and big salaries to both managers and the civil servants who supervise them. This hypothesis was articulated repeatedly in the American economics literature of the 1960s and 1970s, and it provided a clear rationale for the standard critique of public enterprises, as espoused by such international bodies as the World Bank. Many of the nationalized industries in the mixed economies of the Western world had a set of public-interest objectives that were difficult to reconcile with their financial objectives. As a result, by the 1970s, state-owned sectors in many countries registered large financial losses, which provided useful ammunition for the proponents of privatization.

The political statements and ideological pronouncements accompanying nationalizations and privatizations contained two other ingredients, only tenuously related to narrow principles of ownership. First, there was the case—embedded in some of the earlier versions of neoclassical economics—for government intervention, because of market-structure problems. In the nineteenth century, municipal governments in Europe and the United States bought out the assets of water-supply companies, or they initiated municipal water-supply programs. The case rested on the public-health hazards associated with poor quality water. Then, too, there were economic gains to be had from coordinating public transport investments, timetables, and construction work. None of the policy objectives required public ownership; rather, they implied the setting of standards, with regulations and monitoring: water quality; adequate sewage systems; safety and punctuality on the rails and roads. If the private standards were not consistent with commercial viability, the neoclassical policy implication was government subsidy, not public ownership. Nonetheless, such an approach often proved inadequate and, historically, was often followed by public ownership.

Similar issues were involved in the classic market structure case for government intervention—for a "natural monopoly"—where the technology of the product or service was such that one firm could produce more cheaply than two or more firms. Here, private ownership led either to monopoly profits or to cut-throat competition, putting product-quality standards and profit rates below acceptable levels. Edwin Chadwick (1859) recognized that situation in the water supply of urban Britain in the mid-nineteenth century. In the nineteenth century, streetcar systems were sometimes described as monopolies of a public necessity and the editor of *Traction and Transmission*, an American journal, suggested that "services . . . which are in the nature of monopoly should by preference be in the hands of the Municipalities . . . private companies cannot be trusted to exercise the power of monopoly with discretion." (1901, p. 294). In neoclassical terms, the issue was not one of ownership but rather of market structure, and the policy implication was regulation of fares, tariffs, freight rates, and profit rates. Again, the experience with regulation was often perceived in the late nineteenth century and the early twentieth as unsatisfactory, so public ownership followed, suggesting that other factors were involved. Another dimension of market structure linked with the question of managerial efficiency included rivalry among producers, which could take the form either of competition in the field (when railway companies competed over a common rail track, when water-supply utilities duplicated distribution networks) or of competition for the field (as contestants for airline or television franchises). Examples of competition in the field were not restricted to private enterprise and occurred, as in electricity supply, where conditions of natural monopoly existed. The argument, then, was that such competition could improve managerial performance and offset the high costs associated with duplication of facilities in the natural monopoly setting. In some U.S. cities (about fifty in the 1960s, for example), competition existed among the electric utility companies, often between a municipal and a private utility. In some cases, customers could not switch suppliers after connection to one firm; in other cases, they could switch at any time.

Second, because public ownership, by definition, involved government, periods of nationalization and privatization were involved with the wider objectives of the government in power, whether the context was local, regional, or national. Historically, that became important where there was a high expectation for government action on economic and social issues. In some cases, the institutional changes were but part of a fundamental reorientation of the society, as in Russia (the Soviet Union) after 1917 or in the 1990s restoration of eastern Europe's private-sector economy. In other cases, the context was that of changing the balance of a mixed economy, as in the early nineteenth-century United States, where the prospect of expansion and economic growth prompted municipalities to invest in canals. In Sweden, both canals and railroads had government subsidies and investments. In the same era, the more densely populated parts of Europe had the problem of urbanization and public-health concerns and intrusive effect of canals and railways, which resulted in collective action. Although nineteenth-century governments played some part, the main agent of change was the municipality—pressed on one side by cholera epidemics and rising infant mortality rates and on the other by property owners and other taxpayers unwilling to finance civic improvements. After World War II, the liberal democracies in Europe took large sections of infrastructure and, in some cases, manufacturing into the public sector. With independence from colonial rule in Africa and Asia, from the 1960s onward some new countries instituted five-year plans for economic development and used state-owned industry as an integral element.

Nineteenth Century. In turning to specific historical phases of nationalization and privatization, the focus of the nineteenth-century venture into industrial public ownership was a concentration on infrastructure. The pace of industrialization and urbanization in northwest Europe was so rapid, and government was so weak in administrative terms that, in the beginning, the initiative was seized by private operators—with railway and telegraph companies, water companies, and textile manufacturers making their own gas supplies. By the mid-1900s in Britain, Belgium, France, and the United States, many such operators had a local monopoly and came under government scrutiny. Postal services had been a government responsibility since the 1800s, but railways, gas, water, telegraph, electricity, and streetcars (later, local buses) came to be regulated or brought into public ownership; all were network industries that had elements of natural monopoly, and some had important environmental spillovers—safety, health, the transmission of knowledge. Railroads in Prussia and several other German states, in Belgium, and in Sweden were run by central governments, while in France and the Netherlands the planning of the rail network was subject to the central government's guidance and financial support. Even Austria, as part of one of Europe's oldest empires, saw public ownership at both city and state levels—of parts of water supply, railroads, electricity, and urban transport. In the United States, in the early 1800s, competition among the East Coast cities yielded what has been called an urban-centered mercantilist era of canal construction. New York City linked its ports with the Erie Canal via the Hudson-Mohawk River traffic, to become the country's leading commercial and financial center.

Government became involved in infrastructure sectors because operators needed rights of way, and the power to grant them rested with governments. Once granted, such rights often led to local monopolies. These did not always lead to public ownership, and railway companies, for example, had only indirect regulation of fares, rates, and land grants in Britain and the United States. Strategic objectives were present in small countries like Belgium, where many forms of communication had an international significance, so were taken over by the state. In France, fear of foreign domination resulted in the involvement of municipal and central governments in the collective supply and regulation of railroads, canals, roadways, harbors, and coal. Prussia had used railroad revenues as a supplement to taxes. Such "cash cows" also existed at the municipal level in Britain, where the local governments of some industrial cities (Leeds, Manchester, Birmingham) had public-health problems and little wealth from property, so they ran the gas supply, markets, tramways, and electricity generation and distribution and milked them to stave off the complaints of local taxpayers. These municipal programs were not as closely motivated by socialist ideals as has sometimes been supposed. In Britain, the main surge of municipal involvement in gas and water was from 1850 to 1880, well before the Webbs and the Fabians tried to popularize socialism in London at the turn of the twentieth century. In Germany, municipal enterprise in gas and electricity developed from 1860 to 1900. In the Netherlands, it dated from the 1880s. Clean water supplies were a central element in public-health programs that dominated much municipal activity in nineteenth-century urban Europe and the United States.

Twentieth Century. Technology and political forces pushed twentieth-century public ownership issues away from the town and municipality and toward the central government. Nineteenth-century economies of scale had been of such a modest size, in the provision of streetcars and in the production and distribution of gas, electricity, and water, that they could be exploited by cities like Glasgow, Lyon, Barcelona, Milan, and New York. Developments in the generation and transmission of electricity were, by the early twentieth century, making regional and national operations economical—in addition, the benefits of good water supplies and sewage systems were increasingly recognized as a national responsibility. On the political front, the overthrow of the tsarist government in Russia in 1917 and the introduction of five-year plans by the Soviet Union gave public ownership an increasing appeal throughout Europe. Regional electricity grids were established with government holdings, leading in the 1930s to some national grids, as in Japan and Britain. The United States then organized the Tennessee Valley Authority as a federal dam and electricity-generating project. The unemployment in Europe of the interwar era and the Great Depression (1919–1939), together with the reconstruction and nationbuilding that came after World War II, provided the final push. Britain's airlines were nationalized in the early 1940s, followed by coal, the railways, the ports, gas, and electricity. The strong regional government traditions in Germany, with its large geographical area, yielded electricity networks of mixed private/public ownership (a nationalization law drafted in 1919 never reached the statute books). In Italy, not until 1962 was a state-owned monopoly formed for production and distribution of electric power. Public ownership had not been a major ideological issue for the fascist regimes of Germany and Italy (1920s and 1930s). As long as private companies cooperated with those states' political and rearmament programs, there was little interference. The Hermann Goring Steel Works was started by Nazi Germany in 1938 because German steel barons were unwilling to exploit the domestic supplies of iron ore in the central regions. The Volkswagenwerk automobile plant was set up as a state-owned enterprise by engineers from the Ford Motor Company of Detroit, Michigan, because other German carmakers were unwilling to manufacture the "Beetle." Italy's Institute for Industrial Reconstruction (IRI) was transformed into a permanent public agency in 1937, as much a child of Italy's late industrial development as a product of designs from the fascist era.

The effect of World War II on West Germany was that suspicion of the state justified the use of the term *privatization* to describe the disposal of major government holdings in coal and manufacturing. In postwar Japan, the government's involvement in the electric-power industry was relinquished for similar reasons. In Spain, strategic considerations following its political isolation during World War II, prompted government involvement in industry when huge new state undertakings were set up for railroads, telecommunications, electricity, oil refining, maritime transport, and parts of manufacturing; Spain's distinctive postwar autarky meant that these enterprises remained a striking feature of the economy. France's fear of foreign domination in the 1920s had prompted government involvement in the chemical industry and in oil drilling, refining, and retailing—as well as formation of the airline Air France and of the Société Nationale des Chemins de Fer for railroads in 1937. As in Britain, France's post-1945 reconstruction led to nationalization of coal, gas, and electricity supplies—but in France, the commitment to building a strong industrial base in coal, iron, and the infrastructure industries was to secure against any future German threats, which gave a more lasting dimension to economic planning.

The wave of nationalizations in the mixed economies of western Europe in the immediate post–World War II period was dwarfed by the shift to communist governments in eastern and central Europe from the Balkans through Czechoslovakia to East Germany and Poland. Their political and economic links with the Soviet Union resulted in the Eastern bloc, with regulation and monitoring of their small-scale economic activities (in retailing and agriculture) those not under the umbrella of the large-scale enterprises. In the 1960s and 1970s, some third-world countries in Africa and Asia opted for large public sectors, in part a Marxist influence, a desire to break with what was perceived as the imperialist dimension of capitalism. "African Socialism" took many forms—it was claimed as the rationale for Julius Nyerere's Tanzania of the 1960s and 1970s, as well as for Jomo Kenyatta's freewheeling Kenya, into whose tourism and manufacturing sectors the Western world continued to invest; the actual form of state enterprise often mirrored Western practices, since many of the technical advisers were Western expatriates. The "public corporation"—state owned but with a separate corporate legal identity and in principle independent of direct government administration—was the characteristic form of nationalized industry in Britain, and similar structures were adopted in, for example, East African postal systems, telecommunications, airlines, railways, and harbors. They then experienced the same problems as the Western public sector—but with the added difficulty of a raw group of politicians and civil servants burdened with the high expectations that followed independence from colonial rule.

Since the 1980s, the process of privatization was not a simple return of state assets to the private sector. Even in western Europe where the process started first, the capital markets of the 1980s were much more open internationally than in earlier decades of the twentieth century, so new owners of the former state assets were not necessarily the citizens of that state—but often foreign, multinational firms. That liberation of ownership may be difficult to reverse. After World War II, when transport and fuel companies were nationalized in several European countries, a simple exchange of paper was involved—equity-share certificates surrendered for government bonds; there were no resource effects for the nation as a whole, simply an internal transfer of ownership. When in the late 1980s and 1990s, privatization often involved sale of state assets to noncitizens, there was effectively an inflow of resources to pay for the assets. Their repurchase by any future nationalizing government might involve payment, unless uncompensated expropriation were to be used. From 1988 to 1992, nearly one third of the proceeds of privatization, worldwide, came from foreign exchange.

Most of the privatizations from the early 1980s were fairly slow moving. In Britain, which accounted for 75 percent of the value of all privatization proceeds in western Europe from the mid-1980s to the mid-1990s, the initial forays by the first Conservative government of Prime Minister Margaret Thatcher were tentative, with only takeovers of small firms. The sale of local government housing (at subsidized prices) proved popular for tenants and led the second and third, more confident, Conservative governments to sell the major public utilities. As in other parts of western Europe, privatization in Britain was followed by regulation of prices and profit rates until more competition developed. Sales of state assets in the developing countries were, by the mid-1990s, fairly modest, having only a small effect on their governments' fiscal problems. Reliance on foreign capital (especially in Africa) was politically difficult, but it often accompanied conditional loans from such bodies as the World Bank. Manufacturing and commerce was privatized in the developing world more than in Europe, where in eastern Europe and the former territories of the Soviet Union, privatization was painfully slow. Initially, the concentration was on retail trade, the service sector, and small-scale manufacturing. The shift of the Eastern-bloc economies to a private-market economy first required fundamental changes in their

laws—with respect to market entry, property rights, and sensitivity for the welfare of the workforce. Nonetheless, the commitment to privatization was clear in the developing world, in Russia, and in eastern and western Europe. A full retrospective interpretation by historians should be extremely interesting.

BIBLIOGRAPHY

Alchion, Armen. *Economic Forces at Work*. Indianapolis, 1977.

Anderson-Skog, Lena, and Ollie Krantz, eds. *Institutions in the Transport and Communications Industries: State and Private Actors in the Making of Institutional Patterns, 1830–1990*. Canton, Mass., 1999.

Chadwick, Edwin. "Results of Different Principles of Legislation and Administration in Europe: Of Competition for the Field, as Compared with Competition within the Field, or Service." *Journal of the Royal Statistical Society* 22 (September 1859).

Clarke, Thomas, and Christos Piteli, eds. *The Political Economy of Privatisation*. London, 1993.

Cook, Paul, and Colin Kirkpatrick, eds. *Privatisation Policy and Performance: International Perspectives*. Hemel Hampstead, U.K.,1995.

Dobson, Frank. *Forging Industrial Policy: The United States, Britain and France in the Railway Age*. Cambridge, 1994.

Millward, Robert, and John Singleton, eds. *The Political Economy of Nationalisation in Britain, 1920–1950*. Cambridge, 1995.

Nove, Alex. *An Economic History of Russia*. Harmondsworth, U.K., 1973.

Roll, Eric. *The Mixed Economy*. London, 1984.

Toninelli, Pier, ed. *The Rise and Fall of State-Owned Enterprise in the Western World*. Cambridge, 2000.

Yarrow, George, and Piotri Jasinski, eds. *Privatisation: Critical Perspectives on the World Economy*. 3 vols. London, 1996.

ROBERT MILLWARD

NATURAL RESOURCES *[This entry contains three subentries, a historical overview and discussions of property rights and regulation.]*

Historical Overview

Economic history provides the antidote to the assumption that there is a static and readily exhaustible resource base. Historical experience shows that recurrent, though uneven and intermittent, technological developments have continually revised our definition of the resource base. Fears that resources will run out go back a long way. They were prevalent with respect to a possible "timber famine" in seventeenth-century England and even in colonial America. In 1863 a Royal Commission into overfishing was appointed in Great Britain. In 1865 Stanley Jevons asserted in *The Coal Question* that British economic growth would soon slow down because it depended on steam coal. He thought little more could be mined and there was no substitute.

Fears of these kinds are hydra-headed and astonishingly resistant to contrary evidence. An early lesson is that resources are a function of the prevailing technology. All reasonable projections of past behavior have made and continue to make predictions of resource exhaustion implausible: technological change has economized on the materials in use or permitted a shift to more abundant—hence cheaper—substitutes. Additional sources of energy and raw materials have repeatedly been found, often because the techniques for searching have themselves been improved. Trade, too, is a substitute for resources, exposing as chimerical many fears of local or regional scarcities. Admittedly, stocks of fish, whales, and other animals are susceptible to overuse. Laws regulating the "take" or the size of individual fish that might be caught are ancient—Richard I ordered the removal of weirs and fixed nets from the Thames in 1196. Leaving aside such enactments and the modern international moratoria on catching various species, search costs in any case rise steeply when yields decline. Fishing and hunting are seldom likely to continue until a resource is completely extinguished. From the point at which they cease, commercial species have often shown an astonishing propensity to recover. The survivors, after all, have the food and breeding sites to themselves.

A Panglossian view would overstate the case, but glosses on historical experience persist in implying that resources have been and will be terminally exhausted at human hands. But economic growth has seldom been accompanied by the total depletion of any resource. Estimates of known reserves of oil and minerals, usable with current technologies, have continually been raised. Nor do prices throughout the nineteenth and twentieth centuries reveal a trend toward scarcity. Indexed against either the consumer price index or wages, the prices of coal, oil, electricity, and copper fell steadily, except during the two world wars, when trade was interrupted.

The resource base was obviously limiting for small, isolated populations that were not adept at inventing new technologies or well integrated into transportation networks. Location is a resource in itself; river or sea access was particularly important before the railway. Until then, the overland carriage of freight is said to have been typically fifteen times more expensive than waterborne transit. Commercial entrepôts like Constantinople, Venice, and Amsterdam traded on their maritime access; interior regions were much harder to develop.

Resources, then, were a function of technology for premodern as much as for later societies. Weak technologies, as well as inefficient institutions, actually constrained the use of resources more tightly than after industrialization. Some raw materials that were known to be present could not be exploited. In an oft-cited example, American Indians were aware of seepages of petroleum oil and dabbled with these for medicinal purposes. But oil was not much of a resource for them nor for any other population until the sinking of "Colonel" Drake's well in Pennsylvania in 1859.

There was no means of extracting oil until Drake adapted a technique long used in China to bore for brine salt. Even then most of the purposes for which oil has since been employed had still to be devised. The temptation is to agree with the opinion that "there are no resources, only human resourcefulness."

One powerful tool of immense antiquity is the fire stick. Many societies cleared forest by burning it, judging land for farming more valuable. Others regularly burned scrub to improve grazing and browsing for the deer, say, or kangaroos that they hunted. This aboriginal activity unintentionally reduced the costs of resource acquisition for later white colonists. The populations of settlers and aborigines were so small they ought never to have clashed, but they did, because both valued the same stretches of open land. The most elementary technology accordingly paved the way for relatively wild country to be reevaluated as an agricultural resource. Where settlement became dense, rural resources were used more and more intensively. Stealing the honey of wild bees gave way to hives from which honey could be harvested; gathering the eggs and young of colonially nesting birds led to the building of dovecotes from which eggs and "squabs" could more conveniently be taken; fishing in streams was supplemented by fishponds and carp netting. These simple technologies squeezed more product out of the same units of land.

Nevertheless, technology alone will not convert a resource-using economy—and all economies use resources—into one with sustained economic growth. Greek colonists in Sicily had produced large iron-reinforcing members by 470 BCE. Song China (eleventh to thirteenth centuries CE) had water-spinning machines for hemp and smelted as much iron per capita as Great Britain did about 1800, yet failed to maintain, let alone elaborate, these advances. There are plenty of examples of other early achievements. But regular, greater, and faster technological change awaited British and European industrialization, which undeniably brought about an enormous increase in the consumption of raw materials incorporated in the manufactures of the period. In a broad and long sense, Europe's achievement was to industrialize at the same time as it gathered in extra-European resources. There may have been, in Adam Smith's famous phrase, "no necessity" to seek the outer world, at least with respect to resource scarcities in the fifteenth century. The eventual outcome was to suck resources into a Europe that did not, however, use them to rest on its laurels but employed them to fuel demographic and economic growth.

A determined effort to relate both economic performance and structure to natural resources was "staple theory." This was the brainchild of the Canadian economic historian Harold Innis, arising from his studies of specific export industries. Others in Canada extended the theory and tried hard to justify historical research by integrating it into the development economics fashionable in the 1960s and 1970s. They applied staple theory to a longer sequence of products, and later, with rather less success, to other primary-product exporting countries like Australia.

The central notion of staple theory was that export economies were dominated in successive periods by a single staple product. Canada first exported codfish, next furs, then lumber; Australia exported wool, gold, wheat. The dominant export acted as a "leading sector" determining the pace of growth in the remainder of the economy, influencing the level of income, selecting the relevant technology, and shaping the institutions. An economy might fall into a staple trap and find it hard to shift to another export or, more harmfully, to diversify its domestic economy because of the political stranglehold that those with interests in the existing staple could exert. The economy might then decline as receipts fell, because it would be overexposed to competition from overseas producers of the same good. While approximately congruent with the early experience of countries like Canada, which had prompted the theory, the role of the staple was undoubtedly exaggerated (in Australia, relative to import substitution in the domestic sector). Dominant staples in any case faded because these economies actually did succeed in diversifying.

Almost paradoxically, it has since been shown that growth in the late-nineteenth-century United States relied more on resource-intensive exports and less than used to be thought on the superior efficiency of America's own manufacturing. Yet the point has been added that the ability of the United States to develop in this way, at a period when its economy was overtaking that of Great Britain, did not depend straightforwardly on the blessing of an excellent resource endowment. A wide range of resources, especially minerals, were incorporated in exports, not just a few where American reserves were outstanding. This suggests that the more meaningful assets of the United States were markets and institutions capable of vigorously exploiting its endowment. We go back to the point that it is less helpful to think of "natural" resources in terms of their physical existence than to see them as functions of evolving technology, and of institutions, too. The relationship between resources and economic change goes two ways. Economic growth is not guaranteed by an abundance of this or that raw commodity in nature. On the other hand, technological advance is not necessarily induced by the opposite: an increasing shortage of some particular resource.

Notwithstanding this observation, as well as the waning of interest in staple theory, resources continue to be credited with commanding effects on the pace and shape of economic growth in resource-exporting countries. They are also held responsible for the direction that change takes. Resource scarcities, or, better expressed, the relative price of resources, signals the wisdom of inventing tools and machines to economize on them. Although logically it does not matter which costs are reduced, this signaling effect is intrinsically plausible. Take the woodman's axe: nineteenth-century American axes were lighter and had handles that were easy to grasp; British axes had heavier heads, with stouter, straighter handles. The suggestion is that scarcer timber (and land?) in Great Britain put a premium on axes that could chop out tree stumps that Americans could afford to burn. Yet American labor was dearer and the price of labor, rather than the relative prices of timber, may have prompted invention down the channels it took. On the other hand, in terms of prevailing technologies, the American resource endowment was more lavish than that of, say, Russia. This contrast suggests that, despite the formative role of technology and institutions, endowments could affect the overall level of economic performance as well as the bias of development. We do not really know how far technologies and institutions were themselves artifacts of the resource base.

Many early studies of British industrialization saw the rising prices of certain materials as the key to the technological breakthroughs of the late eighteenth century. The chronology seemed to fit and, after all, adjustment to change in relative prices is a prime tool of economic thought. There was a literature on the "timber famine" that could be made to chime with the switch from charcoal to coal in the iron industry. The central breakthrough to which the necessity-is-the-mother-of-invention school referred was Abraham Darby's coke smelting of iron in 1709. But there was no definite sign of a shortage of charcoal at the time of Darby's experiments. For all the later importance of coke smelting, his discovery was more a reflection of the intellectual inquisitiveness of eighteenth-century British society than a direct reflection of resource availability. The relative ease with which technological substitutes for resources have been found in the modern world does not mean that substitutes automatically appear for every rare commodity—merely that our enormous research efforts continue to be broadly efficacious.

It is seductively easy to portray increasing resource scarcities at any given moment as stimulating resource-saving technologies, which they do—except when they don't. This paradox is called the "vasty deep" problem. The allusion is to a passage from Shakespeare which points out that anyone may call forth spirits from the vasty deep—but they may not come. If the severity of problems guaranteed their solution, the shortages that most vex us would be overcome, and overcome first. Nature has usually proved to be surprisingly forgiving, but not quite as forgiving as all that.

[*See also* Common Goods; Fossil Fuels; *and* Public Goods.]

BIBLIOGRAPHY

Blainey, Geoffrey. "A Theory of Mineral Discovery: Australia in the Nineteenth Century." *Economic History Review*, 2d ser., 23 (1970), 298–313. Shows that apparently chance finds were related to variations in search costs connected to the business cycle.

Flinn, Michael W. "Technical Change as an Escape from Resource Scarcity: England in the Seventeenth and Eighteenth Centuries." In *Natural Resources in European History*, edited by Antoni Maczak and William N. Parker, pp. 139–159. Washington, 1978. Interesting essay, one of a useful set of conference papers, giving reasons for doubting the common assumption that important industrial breakthroughs were responses to particular resource scarcities.

Grigg, David B. *The Agricultural Systems of the World*: *An Evolutionary Approach*. Cambridge, 1974. Comprehensive descriptions of the world's main agricultural resources and their historical development.

Jones, Eric L. "The Environment and the Economy." In *The New Cambridge Modern History*, vol. 13, *Companion Volume*, edited by Peter Bourke, pp. 15–42. Cambridge, 1979. Surveys resource-using aspects of long-term European economic development, notably industrialization.

Rosenberg, Nathan. *Perspectives on Technology*. Cambridge, 1976. Includes discussions of relationships between technological change and resource use by the author most responsible for bringing the issue to the notice of modern economists.

Simmons, Ian G. *Changing the Face of the Earth*: *Culture, Environment, History*. Oxford, 1989. Important volume, especially with regard to sources of energy; has a comprehensive bibliography.

Simon, Julian L., ed. *The State of Humanity*. Oxford, 1995. Major analysis by scholars, including economic historians; it contains eight chapters on natural resources.

Watkins, Mel. "A Staple Theory of Economic Growth." In *Approaches to Canadian Economic History*, edited by W. T. Easterbrook and M. H. Watkins, pp. 49–73. Toronto, 1969. Overview of the genesis of staple theory applied to the work of Canadian economic historians, who originated it.

White, Colin. M. *Russia and America*: *The Roots of Economic Divergence*. London, 1987. Valuable comparative discussion of "Risk, Resources and the Natural Environment."

Williamson, Harold F. "Prophecies of Scarcity or Exhaustion of Natural Resources in the United States." *American Economic Review* 35 (1945), 97–109. Shows that recurrent prognostications of resource scarcity are of ancient vintage and have repeatedly been overtaken by fresh discoveries.

Wright, Gavin. "The Origins of American Industrial Success, 1879–1940." *American Economic Review* 80 (1990), 651–668. Finds the origins in resource-intensive exports.

Wrigley, Edward A. "The Supply of Raw Materials in the Industrial Revolution." *Economic History Review*, 2d ser., 15.1 (1962), 1–16. Classic paper by the modern author most associated with the argument that coal was vital to Britain's industrial success.

ERIC JONES

Property Rights

Natural resources are valuable assets that are not man-made. Examples are minerals, petroleum, water, fish, wildlife, timber, pastures, and farmland. Historically, they have been critical inputs in the process of economic growth. Property rights are ownership institutions, and they too have played a vital role in economic growth. Property rights assign access to natural resources and define the array of sanctioned uses, investments, and exchanges. Ownership institutions rights also distribute the associated rewards and costs of resource use. Therefore, property rights determine who has decision-making authority, who will claim the resulting net income stream, and what their incentives and time horizons will be.

Property rights institutions seek to avoid the "tragedy of the commons," whereby too many individuals competitively exploit a scarce resource too completely and too rapidly (Hardin, 1968). With no controls on access and use, individuals rush to seize the resource, spurred by private self-interest with little concern for the full social costs of their actions. The ensuing competition results in rapid and wasteful production, little investment, and reduced trade. With ownership uncertain, individuals are forced to devote valuable labor and capital from production and exchange to defense, to counter the predatory actions of others. Common-pool outcomes have been formalized as a prisoner's dilemma, whereby the lack of cooperation among two resource users leads to the least-optimal result for both (Clark, 1976).

Historically, local customs have loosely defined and enforced some natural resource property rights. Small, cohesive communities have held group ownership rights or "common property." These local customary rights have been effective for long time periods so long as resource values have remained comparatively low and competitive entry by outsiders has been minimal (Ostrom, 1990). Other historical property rights arrangements have been much more formally defined and enforced and assigned to individuals as private property rights. Typically, private rights are assigned to the most valuable resources in market economies. Finally, some property rights to natural resources have been withheld by the state or crown with access either sharply restricted to elites, such as for royal hunting privileges in Europe, or alternatively, open for all citizens, as is the case for wildlife in the United States (Libecap, 1986, 1989).

Generally, property rights to natural resources can be grouped into two categories according to whether the resource is mobile or stationary. Stationary resources, such as agricultural land, timber stands, and mineral deposits, have had relatively clear definitions of property rights. Historically, they have been valuable and worth claiming, and the costs of defining rights have been comparatively low. Mobile resources, such as water, petroleum, fish, and wildlife, have presented greater challenges. Historically, some resources, like fish, wildlife, and water in eastern North America, were so abundant and valued so little that few efforts at assigning rights were undertaken. Even with depletion and higher values, the costs of controlling access and use have been so high that few arrangements have materialized.

Property rights are political institutions. That is, the state must recognize and support them, even if they are local, communal ownership arrangements. Distributional issues have been critical factors in determining when and how property rights to natural resources have emerged. For property rights to be effective, exclusive access is required. This condition means that some parties will be denied the ability to use and benefit from a natural resource. Other parties will be granted access; the associated allocation of ownership rights to natural resources, especially agricultural land, has been a defining factor in the observed distribution of wealth and political power in Western societies. Distributional conflicts over the allocation of ownership of valuable resources have delayed the development of property rights and have led to the persistence of the "tragedy of the commons."

Fisheries. Fisheries have been very valuable sources of food and wealth throughout economic history, especially the North Atlantic cod fisheries near Iceland, Norway, and the Georges and Grand Banks. Yet deep-sea ocean fisheries are extremely vulnerable to overharvest because there are no effective controls on the number of boats that exploit the stock. Ownership is by the rule of capture, meaning that fishers can own what they catch, but not the stock of fish in the sea. Gradually, incessant fishing pressure has driven the stock down to low levels, reducing the average catch and making the stock subject to the vagaries of shifting water temperatures and disease.

Few deep-sea fisheries have escaped the tragedy of the commons. Even in-shore fisheries like the California sardine fishery have suffered from excessive entry and catch. Although the California sardine fishery was one of the most valuable in the United States in the 1930s, for all practical purposes it was extinct by the 1950s. More stationary species, including oysters, crabs, and lobsters, occasionally have been given territorial property rights to protect the stock. Some mobile fisheries, like the Pacific salmon, appear to have had effective native property regimes along the rivers of the Pacific Northwest and Canada. But these institutions often have been displaced by political demands for greater access by sport and commercial fishers, and the stock has suffered (Higgs, 1982; Johnson and Libecap, 1982). Similar harvest pressures have developed in fisheries elsewhere, including the Mediterrian Sea and western Pacific Ocean, where local arrangements historically managed the fishery. On the supply side, new technology has increased boat size and range, allowed for the tracking of fish, and improved the effectiveness of harvest techniques. On the demand size, growing world populations have increased reliance on fishery stocks as sources of protein, raising prices. Both effects have brought unprecedented levels of fishing throughout the world, dramatically depleting most fish stocks.

Wildlife. As with fish, most wildlife are migratory and pose difficulties in the assignment of property rights. Where they can be confined with fencing or herding, as is sometimes possible with deer, moose, elk, and reindeer, restrictions on hunting can avoid the tragedy of the commons. In Europe, royal hunting preserves maintained the stocks of some species. In the United States, wildlife law has explicitly maintained access to the stock open to all and assigned ownership only to the catch or harvest under the common-law rule of capture. Certain species have suffered from intense overharvest—the passenger pigeon and western buffalo are notorious examples. In the nineteenth century, wildlife were an important part of the diet in the United States. With no effective restrictions on catch or harvest, many species were dramatically reduced. Hunting seasons and catch limits to provide some protection to the stock did not appear until the twentieth century, and those laws have had varying success (Tober, 1981).

Petroleum. As with fish and wildlife, ownership of petroleum in the United States is assigned by the rule of capture. Oil reservoirs are commonly found beneath numerous, independently owned surface tracts. Mineral rights usually are reserved to the surface landowner and are leased, not permanently transferred, to third parties. Through leasing, multiple firms gain access to the reservoir and compete for oil. Ownership is assigned only upon extraction. Oil in the reservoir is migratory and compressed under high pressure. A firm can drain neighboring leases by drilling multiple wells and extracting oil rapidly. Each well sunk creates a pocket of low pressure around the well base, which stimulates oil migration toward the well as oil rushes to the low-pressure area. Rapid drilling and extraction also allow firms to take advantage of high subsurface pressures that expel the oil to the surface at low cost. As those pressures are dissipated, extraction becomes more costly. These conditions encourage the competitive drilling and draining of the reservoir.

The classic costs of open access include rent dissipation because of high capital costs from redundant wells and extensive surface storage, a time path of production that does not reflect future returns, and reduced total oil recovery. As much as two-thirds of the oil may be left trapped in the ground from too rapid production. The problem of the common pool in oil production was recognized when oil was first discovered in the United States in 1859, but private efforts to constrain competitive extraction through unitization have been difficult. They have been blocked by distributional concerns in negotiations and by politics in state efforts to force unitization. Alternative government regulations to control production through prorationing also have had varying conservation benefits (Libecap and Wiggins, 1994). Although the state typically owns subsurface mineral deposits elsewhere in the world, mitigating competitive common-pool extraction, problems still arise where international boundaries cut through hydrocarbon deposits, such as in the North Sea, the Caucasus, the Caspain Sea, and the Middle East (especially between Kuwait and Iraq).

Water. In areas of abundant water, such as in northern Europe and the eastern United States and Canada, water ownership and use historically have not been critical issues. Fresh, clean water has not been scarce, although upstream users sometimes inflict externalities on downstream users. In the eastern United States, ownership has been granted by riparian rights, whereby the landowner has property rights to the adjacent surface water. Upstream owners have had first access, and during dry periods, downstream owners have received smaller allocations. Historically, upstream users have been known to pollute water from time to time before the water reaches downstream.

As water values rose, the government adopted regulations to address pollution problems in the nineteenth and, more especially, in the twentieth century. In drier climates, such as the Mediterranean and Middle East, fresh water has been scarcer and subject to more exact ownership arrangements. In the western United States, water ownership has been assigned by prior appropriation. That is, property rights to water have been separated from land rights and are based on the priority of the claim. This arrangement grew out of the mid-nineteenth century mining industry where mining camps required water, generally from other areas. Dams, ditches, and canals were constructed to catch and transport water from its natural location to where it was to be used. Western agriculture developed around irrigation, and prior appropriation rights allowed water to be moved from one site to farm areas.

With urban population growth in the late twentieth and early twenty-first centuries, agricultural interests have lobbied for government restrictions on the transfer of water rights from traditional farm uses to higher-valued urban consumption. Political conflict over the ownership and use of water has limited the development of water markets in many western states. With rising populations and economic development in other semiarid regions, historical water allocation, which has favored agriculture, will have to be redirected toward urban and industrial uses. This process of institutional change is unlikely to be smooth, given the politically charged nature of water ownership and use.

Minerals. Minerals, such as gold and silver, have a clearer history of property rights development for two reasons: they have been very valuable and they are stationary. In central and western Europe, the aristocracy seized ownership of mineral deposits, notably silver, early; ownership passed to the state in the nineteenth century. The process

of property rights allocation was more open in the United States and Australia because private individuals could compete for them. The discovery of valuable ore deposits in the western United States after 1848 brought dramatic increases in land values in an area where property rights were not well defined or recognized by European immigrants. Because of the high expected returns from ownership and the associated high costs of failing to agree on some property arrangement, private mineral rights were adopted quickly and without significant violence.

Secure property rights were assigned to the stock of ore in the ground, separate from the surface land (unlike oil). Mining could take place over time in a manner that maximized private returns. This ownership structure facilitated investment in aqueducts, deep tunnels, mills, and equipment necessary for capital-intensive deep-vein mining. Stock markets emerged after 1850 in San Francisco and other cities for the sale of mine equities to support development of the Comstock Lode in Nevada and other mining regions in the West. Mining often was the first major economic activity in the settlement of frontier regions (Libecap, 1978).

Agricultural Land. Throughout history all over the world, agriculture lands have always been desirable, scarce assets, subject to competitive control. Granary lands in Siciliy, the Po and Danube valleys, and other parts of Europe, Asia, South America, Australia, and Africa have attracted settlement and a corresponding need to develop ownership institutions. Most agriculture requires investment in clearing, cultivation, planting, and harvest, and without reasonably secure property rights, long-term agricultural development cannot take place. The nature of property rights to agricultural land has had an important effect on how societies have developed.

As argued by Pipes (1999), the absence of clear private property rights to land for most farmers in Russia hindered the development of a market economy. In contrast, in the United States and Canada, granting well-defined and enforced private property rights to the most valuable asset in an agricultural society, farmland, became an important precedent for creating a market economy. The practice established the legal and social underpinnings for secure property rights to other assets, such as commercial property and financial instruments. Private farmland could be held exclusively, sold or leased without restriction, passed on to heirs, modified through investment, and used as collateral for loans. The state policed against trespass and the courts arbitrated ownership disputes.

The allocation of surface land was molded by the distributional goals of federal land policy in the United States. The general aim in the North, particularly after 1862, was to promote the development of small farms of approximately 160 acres by restricting the number and size of individual claims that could be patented. In the East, this arrangement worked well to facilitate the rapid transfer of land from the federal government to private claimants. In the more arid West, where larger farms were necessary to be viable, the homestead size restriction worked less well. Marginal adjustments were made to the land laws in the early twentieth century to allow claims of 320 and 640 acres in some areas, but these allocations were still too small. Vast tracts of low-valued arid land were never claimed under the land laws, and they reverted to permanent federal government ownership with the establishment of the National Forests in 1891 and the passage of the Taylor Grazing Act of 1934.

Timberland. Property rights to timber resources have been assigned to the surface landowner in the United States, and there were no separate provisions for timber rights as existed for mineral rights. With a heavily forested continent, timber was a lower-valued resource than most minerals. Under federal land laws, property rights were assigned in small plots for agricultural use. Although some individuals assembled large timbered areas through the use of land scrip and railroad grants, including Cornell in Wisconsin and Weyerhaeuser in Washington State, there was no way for lumber companies to procure large sections of forested land from the government directly. As early as the mid-nineteenth century, logging operations were highly capital-intensive, and there were economies of scale in production. As a result, lumber companies resorted to fraud to acquire land, ostensibly for farms (Libecap and Johnson, 1979; Johnson and Libecap, 1980). Even so, much of the forested lands of the western states were never claimed privately, and were placed under the National Forests in 1891; production has occurred since through concessions from the government. In the South, timber companies could acquire private land for their timber stocks, and they could adjust production to maximize economic returns.

[*See also* Common Goods *and* Public Goods.]

BIBLIOGRAPHY

Clark, Colin W. *Mathematical Bioeconomics.* New York, 1976.

Hardin, Garrett. "The Tragedy of the Commons." *Science* 162 (1968), 1243–1248.

Higgs, Robert. "Legally Induced Technical Regress in the Washington Salmon Fishery." *Research in Economic History* 7 (1982), 55–86.

Johnson, Ronald N., and Gary D. Libecap. "Efficient Markets and Great Lakes Timber: A Conservation Issue Reexamined." *Explorations in Economic History* 17 (1980), 372–385.

Johnson, Ronald N., and Gary D. Libecap. "Contracting Problems and Regulation: The Case of the Fishery." *American Economic Review* 75.5 (1982), 1005–1022.

Libecap, Gary D. "Economic Variables and the Development of the Law: The Case of Western Mineral Rights." *Journal of Economic History* 38 (1978) 338–362.

Libecap, Gary D. "Property Rights in Economic History: Implications for Research." *Explorations in Economic History* 22 (1986), 227–252.

Libecap, Gary D. *Contracting for Property Rights.* New York, 1989.

Libecap, Gary D., and Ronald N. Johnson. "Property Rights, Nineteenth-Century Federal Timber Policy, and the Conservation Movement." *Journal of Economic History* 39 (1979), 129–142.

Libecap, Gary D., and Steven N. Wiggins. "Contractual Responses to the Common Pool: Prorationing of Crude Oil Production." *American Economic Review* 74 (1984), 87–98.

Ostrom, Elinor. *Governing the Commons: The Evolution of Institutions for Collective Action.* New York, 1990.

Pipes, Richard. *Property and Freedom.* New York, 1999.

Tober, James A. *Who Owns the Wildlife? The Political Economy of Conservation in Nineteenth Century America.* Contributions in Economics and Economic History, No. 37. Westport, Conn., 1981.

GARY D. LIBECAP

Regulation

For many natural resources in Europe, North America, and Australia, property rights were defined clearly and markets operated effectively through most of the nineteenth and twentieth centuries, with little regulation of access, exploitation, or prices, especially in North America. This situation generally still characterizes agricultural land, timber resources, hard-rock minerals such as gold and silver and other mineral deposits such as coal. However, it does not describe natural resources where common-pool or open-access problems have long existed, such as fisheries and petroleum. Because government regulation of the latter resources has involved competing political constituencies, it has been designed both to mitigate the losses of the common pool and to give an advantage to one group over another. In many cases, this second objective has defeated the conservation effort. In addition, regulation has been used to control output in order to fix prices, an objective that also has not always been consistent with conservation. Two examples from North America are surveyed here.

Petroleum Production Regulation. The production of crude oil and natural gas potentially suffers from serious common-pool losses that arise when firms compete for migratory oil and gas lodged in subsurface reservoirs. Since the first commercial production of petroleum in the United States in 1859, firms have been confronted with technical and pecuniary losses of the common pool as they have competed with each other to extract oil from common reservoirs. In 1910, estimates of oil losses from fire and evaporation due to reliance upon surface storage in California were as high as 11 percent of the state's production. In 1914, the director of the U.S. Bureau of Mines estimated that annual losses from excessive drilling were $50 million, a quarter of the value of U.S. production. The race to produce oil also resulted in huge quantities being dumped on the market, depressing prices. Following discovery of a cluster of very large oil fields in Oklahoma and Texas in the late 1920s and early 1930s, U.S. crude oil prices fell from

$2.29 per barrel in 1926 to $0.18 per barrel in 1931 and $0.10 in 1933. Three solutions to the common-pool problem were attempted: oil lease consolidation, unitization of oil production under a single firm, and prorationing of field output among oil firms. The latter two solutions involved regulation.

Prorationing, adopted in the United States in the 1930s, was the most common remedy because it did not involve agreement on the relative value of oil leases, a problem that plagued both lease consolidation and unitization. Under prorationing rules, a state regulatory agency, such as the Texas Railroad Commission or the Oklahoma Corporation Commission, established production quotas for each lease or well, depending on the regulatory rule, which were designed to limit overall extraction from reservoirs. The quota allocation rule was the source of intense political debate. Large producing firms, with extensive leases on many separate reservoirs, sought production quotas based on acreage. Small firms sought per-well quotas, which could allow them to drain a larger portion of the reservoir by drilling additional wells. Monitoring compliance also was a difficult problem, with small firms cheating more frequently because they bore fewer of the overall common-pool losses with their small holdings than did the larger firms, and because they could capture a neighbor's oil with clandestine output. In general, small oil firms were so numerous and politically influential in Texas that they achieved favorable quotas, with a production allocation rule based on 50 percent wells and 50 percent acreage. Further, very high-cost stripper wells were exempt from state prorationing rules. Minimum spacing regulations were adopted to limit the number of wells drilled, but small firms also typically received exemptions from the spacing rules. Small firms took advantage of the per-well quota rule by drilling additional wells, whereas larger firms held back. The Cole Commission of the U.S. House of Representatives estimated in the 1930s that prorationing rules in East Texas contributed to the drilling of 23,000 unnecessary wells. Moreover, cheating was so rampant that the country's largest field, East Texas, had to be placed temporarily under martial law by the governor of Texas in August 1931.

Despite these problems, state prorationing regulations controlled total field production and costs, relative to common-pool settings, and prolonged field life (Libecap and Wiggins, 1984). Prorationing controls, however, could be used not only to address the technical losses of the common pool but for price fixing. In the 1920s there was a national market for crude oil, with most producing regions connected by pipelines and railroads to domestic users. The midcontinent states of Kansas, Oklahoma, and Texas were the leading producing states, accounting for 54 percent of total U.S. crude oil production. Old fields in Kansas and Oklahoma were particularly vulnerable to the enormous quantities of new, low-cost oil being brought to market from new fields in Texas. Interstate efforts to coordinate production and maintain price levels began in 1926.

Representatives from Kansas, Oklahoma, and other high-cost producing states argued that Texas should disproportionately constrain its output, but little concrete action was taken. In 1930, following the discovery of the East Texas field and a corresponding collapse of oil prices, the governor of Oklahoma organized the Oil States Advisory Committee to set total production quotas for Kansas, New Mexico, Oklahoma, and Texas. State agencies were to allocate each state's quota across the fields, leases, and wells within its jurisdiction. The quotas were quickly violated. For example, in March 1933 East Texas production approached one million barrels per day, despite a production quota from the Texas Railroad Commission of 400,000 barrels (Libecap, 1989b). Governors of oil-producing states sought federal government enforcement of state quotas, and, as a result, interstate crude oil prorationing was placed in the NRA (National Recovery Administration) Oil Code, adopted in September 1933. A target price was selected, and interstate shipments were held to an amount commensurate with estimated demand at that price. Any shipment in excess of state quotas, "hot oil," was declared illegal. When the NRA fair practice codes were struck down by the U.S. Supreme Court in 1935, Congress passed the Connally Hot Oil Act within a month to regulate the interstate shipment of oil. The law, however, did not authorize federal government regulation of production, despite the desires of the governors of Kansas and Oklahoma. Texas remained strongly opposed to such intervention. An Interstate Oil Compact to coordinate state oil production to meet targeted prices was drafted along the lines desired by Texas in 1935. The Interstate Oil Compact set target prices and state production quotas, with Texas playing a central role through 1972, when this organization was largely displaced by the Organization of Petroleum Exporting Countries (OPEC). In addition to interstate production rules, the United States adopted import quotas in 1959 to protect domestic producers from low-cost foreign oil. The net result of these quotas was the premature depletion of U.S. oil reserves, forcing increased reliance on foreign sources of supply by the 1970s.

Solutions with more limited adoption included private agreements to reduce the losses of the common pool through lease purchase and consolidation and through production unitization. Widespread lease purchases to reduce the number of drilling firms did not occur because of disagreements over lease values. Accordingly, most U.S. fields remained covered with a crazy quilt of leases and multiple firms competing for the same oil.

Under the alternative remedy of unitization, the firms on a reservoir were to select a single producer to extract the oil, and all other firms would receive shares of the net returns, with the shares based on relative lease values; but disagreements over lease values, and thus unit shares, thwarted many unit agreements. Share negotiations often took from four to eight years, during which the losses of the common pool continued. Although unitization had been recognized as a solution to the common-pool problem early in the history of U.S. production, as late as 1975 only 38 percent of Oklahoma production and 20 percent of Texas production came from fieldwide units. State regulatory efforts to force unitization through compulsory unitization laws were met with opposition from small, independent oil firms that feared they would be made worse off by such rules. They achieved more favorable unitization rules in Oklahoma and blocked any compulsory unitization legislation in Texas (Libecap and Wiggins, 1986).

Fishery Regulation. Fisheries also are plagued by open-access losses. With few effective constraints on entry and catch and with ownership of the fish assigned under the rule of capture, fishers have little incentive to protect the stock. As fishing pressure has increased, the stock of key species has declined, sometimes dramatically. Most offshore, migratory fisheries, with rich historical roots, such as those for cod and whales, have suffered from serious overfishing. Other newer, deep-sea fisheries, such as tuna, also face intense harvest rates. Even closer inshore fisheries, such as those for shrimp, salmon, sardines, and shellfish, are under assault. Some, such as those for California sardines, have been totally depleted and are no longer commercial fisheries (Libecap, 1989a). Threats have come both from greater numbers of fishers harvesting the same stock and from new technology that allows fishers to be more productive. Rising prices, new entry, and new technology also have undermined traditional commons management regimes that have existed for some inshore fisheries.

In response to these open-access losses, governments have adopted domestic and international regulations to control harvest rates. The record of success, however, is very mixed. Two problems have thwarted effective regulation. One is that fishers cannot agree on the kinds of restrictions to be enacted. More productive fishers who have adjusted to open-access conditions fear disproportionate controls on their fishing by comprehensive regulatory schemes. Generally, a consensus among fishers and politicians can be reached only on a set of limited regulations that reduce the worst abuses of uncontrolled production, such as fishing seasons, catch limits, equipment controls (size of boat, technology used, net mesh size), and hatcheries. These regulations often are difficult to enforce, but more critically, they do not strictly limit access, nor do they provide incentives for fishers to privately limit their catch. Property-rights arrangements to the catch, such as individual transferable quotas (ITQs), have been adopted only in a few fisheries, generally after the fishery faces depletion. The resistance to ITQs comes from the allocation mechanism. If the quotas are based on historical catch to reflect the different abilities of fishers, new entrants are disadvantaged. If the quotas are assigned uniformly, better fishers are made worse off, perhaps relative to the open-access status quo (Johnson and Libecap, 1982). Moreover, once assigned, quotas can be very valuable, and there has been political opposition to granting lucrative property rights to naturally occurring resources such as fish.

These same distributional issues have confronted international fishery regulators. Countries have resisted constraints on their fishers, seeking instead to limit the harvests of others. Further, they often have objected to overall catch limits and to the quotas they have received. Ongoing conflicts over international whaling agreements, which have provided relatively successful regulations for some species, illustrate the problem.

A second problem with regulation is that it often is directed by the political process away from conservation concerns toward the access objectives of influential constituencies and the administrative agency. Higgs (1982) has examined the gradual outlawing in Washington state, since 1860, of cheaply enforceable property rights to the salmon fishery and the corresponding prohibiting of the most efficient production techniques. Salmon are anadromous and thus can be caught at low cost when they return from the ocean to spawn in freshwater streams. Early commercial fishers employed gill nets, traps, and fish wheels along rivers; and, with a limited number of sites, total fishing could be controlled. In the 1930s, however, commercial and sports fishers using ocean boats lobbied the Washington legislature to exclude their low-cost competitors from the fishery. They were successful. Traps and other fishing gear were outlawed. Fishing shifted to the ocean, the number of fishers increased, and the salmon stock gradually declined.

This is a common outcome in fishing regulation. Johnson and Libecap (1982) describe the conflicts that have taken place historically between more productive fishers and their less effective competitors, and between inshore and offshore fishers, that have blocked the adoption of comprehensive regulations in the Texas Gulf shore fishery. Finally, even where private fisher unions and trade associations have successfully limited the catch to mitigate open-access losses, politics have intervened. In the 1930s through the 1950s, fisher unions along the U.S. coasts adopted rules to limit entry by nonunion members and to restrict the catch of members. Yet, the arrangements were found in violation of the Sherman Antitrust Act after complaints were filed from excluded fishers, and the restrictions were dismantled despite their ability to reduce the losses of the common pool (*Gulf Coast Shrimpers' and Oystermen's Association v. U.S.*, 236, F. 2d, 658, 1956). Similar practices in other areas, such as Monterey Bay, also were halted, allowing entry and increased harvest.

BIBLIOGRAPHY

Higgs, Robert. "Legally Induced Technical Regress in the Washington Salmon Fishery." *Research in Economic History* 7 (1982), 55–86.

Johnson, Ronald N., and Gary D. Libecap. "Contracting Problems and Regulation: The Case of the Fishery." *American Economic Review* 72.5 (1982), 1005–1022.

Libecap, Gary D. *Contracting for Property Rights.* New York, 1989a.

Libecap, Gary D. "The Political Economy of Crude Oil Cartelization in the United States, 1933–1972." *Journal of Economic History* 49.4 (1989b), 833–855.

Libecap, Gary D., and Steven N. Wiggins. "Contractual Responses to the Common Pool: Prorationing of Crude Oil Production." *American Economic Review* 74.1 (1984), 87–98.

Libecap, Gary D., and Steven N. Wiggins. "The Influence of Private Contractual Failure on Regulation: The Case of Oil Field Unitization." *Journal of Political Economy* 93 (1986), 690–714.

GARY D. LIBECAP

NAVIGATION ACTS, the British Acts of Trade, were a series of laws promulgated by the British Parliament between 1651 and 1849 (when they were repealed) to define the mercantilist commercial relations between Britain and its colonies. The Acts were intended to protect British merchants, shippers, and manufacturers from their Dutch and French counterparts. The Acts reserved most commerce between the colonies and other countries to British citizens, which included the colonists themselves. The Acts required that the colonies' most important exports and imports be "reexported," that is, transshiped through Britain, thus incurring transaction costs and duties. The Acts also mandated certain subsidies; the most important were for ships, pitch, turpentine, and indigo. Historical interest in the Navigation Acts centers on their role in possibly provoking the American Revolution (1776–1781). The Revolution was a war against the British but also a civil war between the supporters and the opponents of independence, in which many American colonists tried to remain neutral. Support of, opposition to, and indifference to the Revolution corresponded closely with the distribution of burdens and the benefits of the Acts.

The colonists who bore the most substantial burdens included tobacco and rice growers and exporters, since reexportation meant lower prices for their crops. Also, certain provisions of the Acts virtually excluded almost all colonial merchants from the lucrative transatlantic trade in tobacco, then the colonies' most desired export. One of the greatest burdens imposed by the Acts arose from the competitive pressures they created for colonial merchants, manufacturers, artisans, and their employees, since in addition to excluding foreign merchants, the Acts defined what amounted to a common market for Britain and its colonies. The result was benefits, as well as burdens, for colonial commerce and industry. The Acts did serve to block competition from Dutch and French merchants and they penalized European manufactures, but the colonies' undercapitalized and inexperienced merchants and industrialists were forced to compete directly with the most advanced commercial and industrial country in the world. Moreover, colonial artisans and mechanics had to compete with low-wage British workers.

Colonial competition with English and Scottish merchants and the incoming flood of British manufactures was first felt in the 1750s. The Seven Years' War (French and Indian War, 1756–1763) provided a respite from these competitive pressures, but afterward the distress of colonial merchants and manufacturers multiplied—and with it their demands for an independent government that would enact tariffs to provide protection from British competition. As transatlantic freight costs steadily fell, British imports became ever cheaper, which put American manufacturing at a growing disadvantage. In the wake of Britain's fiscal crisis spawned by the Seven Years' War, the Crown attempted to generate higher revenues by enforcing the Acts in earnest; this especially hurt prominent colonial merchants who had prospered by the smuggling of goods to and from Holland and the Caribbean. When the British defeated the French in 1763 at Quebec, protection from foreign merchants that the Navigation Acts provided became irrelevant. The burdens of the Navigation Acts rose steadily, while the benefits dwindled.

The Patriot leadership and much of the rank and file were drawn from the merchants, tobacco and rice planters, manufacturers, artisans, and workers who were driven to ruin by increasingly harsh competition from the British and Scots. The first mass protests against British colonial policy were the nonimportation movements directed against British goods. The drive to restrict competition with the British continued after the American Revolution. In the 1780s, many of the states imposed duties on British goods, and the first two acts of the U.S. Congress were laws to protect shipping and manufacturing from foreign competition.

In contrast, the Navigation Acts benefited other colonists—especially producers of subsidized goods, representatives of British merchants, and others closely linked to England—and they tended to be Loyalist, as for example, the Carolina backcountry, principal beneficiary of the pitch and turpentine subsidies.

Most small farmers in the North American colonies produced no exports and so were not penalized by reexportation. They even received modest benefits from the Acts, which led to lower prices of the tobacco, rice, and imported British manufactures that they consumed. The small farmers of Virginia and Maryland especially profited by trading directly with Scottish factors, sidestepping the traditional middlemen, the tidewater tobacco planters. All of this encouraged the view that British rule was benign, thus undermining enthusiasm for independence. Since most colonists either benefited from or were unaffected by the Acts, the Patriots emphasized, in their speeches and pamphlets, liberty and democracy as concerns, rather than the burdens of British mercantilism.

Britain pursued a number of other policies that harmed important economic interests in the American colonies. Especially infuriating were new taxes on sugar and on documents, the banning of settlements beyond the Appalachian Mountains, and the prohibition of colonial currencies. British merchants and manufacturers were able to get Parliament to pass laws—often contrary to the spirit of the Navigation Acts—that prejudiced American colonial interests. For example, the East India Company obtained a monopoly from Parliament over the tea trade, and British hatters secured the prohibition of fur-hat manufacture in the colonies (hats made from North American beaver pelts were in high demand in Europe).

Many historians believe that the Navigation Acts did not lead the thirteen American colonies to revolt. Robert Thomas, in "A Quantitative Approach to the Study of the Effects of British Imperial Policy on Colonial Welfare" (*Journal of Economic History* 28 [1965], 336–355) transformed the debate over the Acts, by constructing a counterfactual that measured their quantitative effect on the colonists; it was one of the first counterfactuals to be rigorously specified and empirically estimated by economic historians. Other economists have refined Thomas's methodology and his estimates, but they agreed with his conclusion that the net burden (the sum of the costs and benefits) was no more than 3 percent of the average colonist's income. The modest size of the burden reinforced the prevailing view that the Revolution was largely about ideological issues, not narrowly economic grievances.

Thomas's analysis, by focusing on the net burden, disguises the widely varying impact of the Navigation Acts on the American colonists. Most patriots came from groups and regions that were harmed by the Navigation Acts, loyalists tended to come from groups and regions that benefited from the British presence, and those who did not take sides, at least initially, tended to be unaffected. Thomas's counterfactual completely ignores one of the most important burdens, the costs of competing with British and Scottish merchants and manufacturers; it relates only to the period from 1764 to 1776, when the burdens were rising rapidly and the benefits were falling. The Patriots had good reason to believe that the situation would only worsen. Thus, to under-

stand what drove the thirteen colonies to war, a "prospective" counterfactual— one that looks at what the burdens might have been after 1776, if they had not gained independence—is more appropriate than the conventional "retrospective" counterfactual. An analysis that focuses on the distribution of economic burdens and benefits, recognizes the competition forced on the colonies by British mercantile policy, and uses a prospective counterfactual can best illuminate the important role of the Navigation Acts in bringing about the American Revolution.

BIBLIOGRAPHY

McCusker, John J. "British Mercantilist Policies and the American Colonies." In *The Cambridge Economic History of the United States*, vol. 1, edited by Stanley L. Engerman and Robert E. Gallman, pp. 337–362. Cambridge, 1996. An overview of the Navigation Acts.

ECONOMIC SOURCES OF THE AMERICAN REVOLUTION
Breen, T. H. *Tobacco Culture: The Mentality of the Great Tidewater Planters on the Eve of the Revolution*. Princeton, 1985.
Egnal, Marc. *A Mighty Empire: The Origins of the American Revolution*. Ithaca, N.Y., 1988.
Egnal, Marc, and Joseph A. Ernst. "An Economic Interpretation of the American Revolution." *William and Mary Quarterly* 29.1 (1972), 3–32.
Greene, Jack P. *The Reinterpretation of the American Revolution, 1763–1789*. New York, 1968.
Tyler, John W. *Smugglers and Patriots: Boston Merchants and the Advent of the American Revolution*. Boston, 1986.

NON-PATRIOT COLONISTS
DePauw, L. G. "Politicizing the Politically Inert: The Problem of Leadership in the American Revolution." In *The American Revolution: Changing Perspectives*, edited by William M. Fowler, Jr. and Wallace Coyle, pp. 3–26. Boston, 1979.
Mason, Keith. "Localism, Evangelicalism, and Loyalism: The Sources of Discontent in the Revolutionary Chesapeake." *Journal of Southern History* 50.1 (1990), 25–54.

USING THE STANDARD COUNTERFACTUAL
Loschky, David J. "Studies of the Navigation Acts: New Economic Non-History?" *The Economic History Review* 26.4 (1973), 689–691.
McClelland, Peter D. "The New Economic History and the Burdens of the Navigation Acts: A Comment." *The Economic History Review* 26.4 (1973), 679–686.
Sawers, Larry. "The Navigation Acts Revisited." *The Economic History Review* 42.2 (1992), 262–284. For a critique of this approach.

LARRY SAWERS

NEPAL. The modern Kingdom of Nepal has an area of 147,181 square kilometers and in 2001 had a population of 23 million people. It was founded in 1768–1769 by Prithvi Narayan Shah, ruler of Gorkha, a small state in the hill region 144 kilometers west of Kathmandu Valley, through the conquest of the three independent states of Kathmandu, Lalitpur, and Bhaktapur. For almost a century between 1846 and 1950 the kingdom was actually ruled by the Rana family, while the Shah kings remained mere titular heads of state. The Ranas established a new political system under which only the senior-most member of the family in each generation would be designated as head of the government. The Ranas' monopoly of political power gave them a monopoly of economic power as well. All surplus revenues of the state became the personal income of the prime minister, and little was spent for the nation's development and public welfare. The Ranas also followed a policy of isolation that helped Nepal preserve its independence at a time when the whole of South Asia, including India, was under British colonial rule, but that isolation came at the cost of social and economic development. In early 1951 the Rana rule was toppled by a people's revolution. This allowed the return of the Shah family to power but bred acute political instability. The nation witnessed a series of political experiments, alternating between a royal autocracy, a nonparty system, and a multiparty parliamentary system under three different constitutions as well as five successive governments in as many years after 1990. The pattern of short-lived governments persists with three Nepali Congress prime ministers holding office during the period from mid-1998 to mid-2001.

Largely as a result of political instability, Nepal has become one of the poorest countries of the world, with a per capita income of approximately U.S. $220. Indeed the number of people living below the line of poverty increased from 4.89 million (36 percent of the population) in 1977 to 9.5 million (45 percent) in 1996. Approximately 66 percent of the population spends more than 70 percent of its expenditure on food, and 71 percent has an annual per capita income of less than U.S. $150. This shows that over half of Nepal's population is poor and that one-quarter is extremely poor. One of the lowest per capita figures in the world, it is a result of low GNP growth associated with a high population growth rate. Nepal's population increased to more than 23 million in 2001, a growth rate of 2.27 percent, and is likely to double in the next 30 years. The national growth rate, expected to rise by 4.6 percent, in 2001 actually declined by 0.63 percent.

Agriculture is the single largest source of employment and production in Nepal. Until 1951, 93.8 percent of the economically active population depended on agriculture. By 1991 the figure had declined to 81.2 percent, but three-fourths of the economically active population is still engaged in agriculture. In 1975 agriculture contributed 71.6 percent to the gross domestic product (GDP). This figure declined to 35.3 percent in 2001. The industrial sector contributed 4.2 percent of GDP in 1974 and increased to 9.9 percent in 2001, an annual rate of increase of just 0.25 percent.

The political changes of the early 1950s brought about important changes in the process of economic development. Nepal adopted development planning as an instrument of national development. The first five-year plan was started in 1956. Since then nine development plans have

been completed, but these plans have failed to live up to the expectations of the people. The emphasis over the years has shifted from urban-industrial growth to regional growth, rural development, fulfillment of basic needs, and alleviation of poverty. These changes reflect the general failure of the planning strategy. Nevertheless the ruling elites seem to be even more committed than ever to planned development because it provides both political legitimation and access to foreign assistance.

With the aim of reducing the gap between development expenditure and its own available resources, Nepal has received assistance from various nations and international organizations for the past forty-eight years totaling U.S. $5,215.7 million in grants and loans. In 2001 foreign aid totaled Nepali Rs. 31,287.0 million, of which 54 percent was in the form of loans. At the current exchange rate of Rs. 76.10 to the dollar, the total aid inflow would amount to Rs. 3,969.13 million. This is almost double the amount if computed on an annual basis at each year's exchange rate. Between 1980 and 1999, the exchange rate fell from Rs. 12 to Rs. 68.25. Debt-servicing charges increased from Rs. 2,407 million in 1991 to Rs. 10,032.8 million in 2000, an average of 32.8 percent of the regular budget expenditure.

At present foreign aid has become all-pervasive in Nepal. Consequently economic, social, and political policy making is planned and conducted with foreign aid. The general belief is that aid has not brought about the promised economic and social development. On the contrary, it is charged with having widened gaps in economic opportunities between the rich and the poor and increased the base and magnitude of corruption. Indeed it is said to have disempowered the Nepali state, its people, and its government.

Another factor that has had a negative impact on Nepal's economy is the worsening law and order situation. On 13 February 1996 the Communist Party of Nepal (Maoist) declared a "people's war" demanding the establishment of a "new democracy" as a "historical revolt against feudalism, imperialism, and so-called reformists." The main demand of the Maoists was the establishment of a republican system and elections for a constituent assembly. The attempts of the government to arrive at a negotiated settlement have proved fruitless. More than 7,000 people, including 4,050 Maoists, were said to have been killed in the course of the people's war. During the previous five years the number was only 2,700. The Maoists killed an estimated eight hundred civilians considered "enemies of the revolution"; destroyed a number of government buildings, banks, telecommunication installations, bridges, and other infrastructure; set fire to the houses of people; and kidnapped and murdered a number of people in different parts of the country. All this has had a negative impact on development efforts and the quantum of development assistance, particularly from foreign multilateral agencies and international nongovernmental organizations. Therefore joint police and army operations were launched in "search and destroy" efforts against Maoist bases in the country. Amnesty International reported that half of these killings were unlawful and accused both the security forces and the Maoists of gross abuses of human rights.

The World Bank, in a report in 2000, pointed out that the unrest was due to "widespread poverty, significant disparities in incomes, employment opportunities, and access to resources and basic social and economic services, and infrastructure between urban and rural areas and between regions, frustrated public expectations from successive governments and perceptions of increasing corruption and weak governance. Solutions cannot focus only on security measures." The report added, "At best Nepal appears to have stood still, while most of her South Asian neighbors have been taking strides in reducing poverty." Whether or not Nepal will be able to meet the challenge of maintaining law and order, increasing agricultural and industrial production, eradicating corruption and social and economic disparities, and improving the administration are questions that can be answered only in the future.

BIBLIOGRAPHY

Acharya, Keshav P. *Action Aid Nepal: A Brief Review of Foreign Aid in Nepal.* Kathmandu, Nepal, 2002.

Joshi, Bhuwan Lal, and Leo E. Rose. *Democratic Innovations in Nepal: A Case Study of Political Acculturation.* Berkeley and Los Angeles, 1966.

Nepal: A Deepening Human Rights Crisis. Amnesty International. 2002.

Regmi, Mahesh C. *Land Tenure and Taxation in Nepal.* 4 vols. Berkeley, 1963–1968.

Regmi, Mahesh C. *A Study in Nepali Economic History: 1766–1846.* New Delhi, 1971.

Regmi, Mahesh C. *Landownership in Nepal.* Berkeley, 1976.

Regmi, Mahesh C. *An Economic History of Nepal, 1846–1901.* Varanasi, 1988.

Stiller, Ludwig F. *The Rise of the House of Gorkha: A Study of the Unification of Nepal, 1768–1846.* New Delhi, 1973.

Stiller, Ludwig F. *Nepal: Growth of Nation.* Kathmandu, Nepal, 1993.

World Bank. *Nepal: 2000 Economic Update Report.* Kathmandu, Nepal, 2000.

Mahesh C. Regmi

NETHERLANDS. *See* Low Countries.

NEWCOMEN, THOMAS (1663–1729), English inventor of an early steam engine.

Although most people associate James Watt with the invention of the steam engine, the honor ought really to fall to his predecessor, Thomas Newcomen. Several "engines" had been invented and a few made to work before Newcomen, but it was Newcomen who, in a remarkably short space of years, developed the dominant design for the steam engine, with piston and rocking beam, which was to last through the heyday of the Industrial Revolution until the engine became locomotive in the nineteenth century. The engine that Newcomen developed has few rivals to its reputation as the most complex technological object of its time anywhere in the world. Newcomen solved almost all of the most pressing technical problems of the many individual components of his complex machine. It is, in fact, extremely rare for any major innovation to develop so rapidly, let alone at the beginning of the eighteenth century before industrialization took hold, and considering that it was the most complex technological achievement of its time, developed mostly through the agency of a single individual. According to Joel Mokyr, the Newcomen engine must be the clearest example ever of a "macro-innovation" (1994).

The only predecessor to Newcomen of any commercial importance was a steam pump developed by Captain Thomas Savery. Compared with the Newcomen engine, it was technically very simple. But for Newcomen, the Savery "engine" raised a serious problem of intellectual property rights, because Savery's patent was sufficiently loosely worded to potentially block Newcomen's vastly more sophisticated engine. Long negotiations were entered into, and in effect Newcomen came to take on much of the responsibility for the patent rights by buying into the Savery shares, though clearly he never made a fortune out of his remarkable contribution.

Equally remarkable was the lack of obvious technological training or background that Newcomen brought to his accomplishment. Born and brought up in Dartmouth, close to the tin and copper mines of southwest England but far from the leading industrial and coal-mining districts, he was described as a blacksmith or ironmonger, hence with skills in execution, not conception.

The economics of the Newcomen engine, which was less efficient in fuel consumption than its successor, the Watt engine, dictated that it was cost-effective primarily in regions with access to cheap coal. Engines not infrequently lasted for many years on coalfields, where they could burn otherwise unsalable "slack" coal. Here, costing very little to run, it was cheaper to purchase than the Watt engine, and after the lapsing of the Savery patent in 1733 did not involve a royalty payment on the patent. Until the Watt engine emerged, itself at first basically a Newcomen engine with the condensation of the steam carried out in a separate vessel, there was little option if a concentration of power was required at a site not served by other motive forces, such as waterwheels. The engine was soon exported, first to Belgium by 1720, then to other northwest European countries by 1730, though only later to America. In Britain, probably around 1,500 were built altogether, capable of supplying perhaps 25,000 horsepower.

The steam engine became what has recently been termed a "general purpose technology," able to be extended to new areas of application, such as manufacturing. By the early 1750s, it was being used in mills and factories, but it needed the intermediate use of a water wheel to convert its jerky up-and-down motion into the stable, rotative power required to drive machinery. Improved Watt engines were later able to drive machinery directly, though even they often needed a flywheel to regulate the transmission. Development of the machinery, however, occurred largely independently of the steam engine. The Industrial Revolution in technological terms represented the recruitment of the steam engine developed—principally by Newcomen—for mining and pumping to its own dynamic of mechanization.

BIBLIOGRAPHY
Dickinson, Henry W. *A Short History of the Steam Engine*. Cambridge, 1939.
Mokyr, Joel. "Technological Change, 1700–1830." In *The Economic History of Britain since 1700*, edited by Roderick Floud and Donald McCloskey, 2d ed., vol. 1, *1700–1860*, pp. 12–43. Cambridge, 1994.
Rolt, L. T. C., and John S. Allen. *The Steam Engine of Thomas Newcomen*. New York, 1997.
Von Tunzelmann, G. N. *Steam Power and British Industrialization to 1860*. Oxford, 1978.

NICK VON TUNZELMANN

NEW DEAL. Between 1933 and 1939, the structure of American government underwent a profound transformation. The New Deal created a stronger and larger national government, expanded the scope of social welfare services at all levels of government, established a permanent program of social insurance, and dramatically increased government regulation of the private economy. The New Deal is remarkable both for the speed with which the reforms were introduced and their permanence. With few exceptions, the major policy initiatives of the New Deal are still in place at the beginning of the twenty-first century. At the heart of the New Deal legacy are such programs as Social Security, Unemployment Insurance, the minimum wage and maximum hours regulations, the Securities and Exchange Commission, the Federal Deposit Insurance Corporation, and agricultural price supports. The New Deal was framed, however, by the Great Depression, a major shift in the balance of political power, and the normal cycles of American electoral politics.

The Great Depression and American Politics. Between 1929 and 1933, the American economy suffered its deepest depression in recorded history. By the spring of 1933, 25 percent on the nation's labor force was unemployed and the real value of output and income had fallen by 30 percent. Prices had fallen by 25 percent in four years, and gross national product (GNP) valued in nominal prices had declined by 46 percent. GNP had been $104 billion in 1929; in 1933 it was only $56 billion. The Hoover administration found itself caught between traditional economic policy that emphasized the importance of keeping government finances in order by raising taxes and cutting expenditures, both of which Hoover proposed, and the need to ameliorate the social dislocation caused by the Great Depression through more active government policies. Hoover, who came to national prominence in World War I as a humanitarian through his administration of food relief to the Belgians, failed to show comparable compassion for the suffering of unemployed Americans. The Democratic nominee for president in 1932, Franklin Roosevelt, campaigned against Hoover's budget deficits. There was nothing in Roosevelt's campaign message to suggest the New Deal that followed his election.

The election was a turning point for the Democratic Party. Between 1896 and 1930, the Democrats had elected only one president and controlled the House of Representatives for four terms and the Senate for three terms, all in the 1910s. When the Democrats came to power in 1933, they had been the minority power for forty years. It was the Great Depression that put them in office. But could Roosevelt and the Democrats form a stable coalition of interests from a party of disparate groups with little in common other than not being Republican?

Roosevelt was inaugurated on 4 March 1933, and he immediately called for a special session of Congress to meet on 9 March. The special session was called to deal with the banking crisis that had spread throughout the nation. The Emergency Banking Act was introduced to Congress at 1:00 PM on 9 March and passed at 8:36 PM. But Congress stayed in session until June, and in those "first hundred days" passed legislation creating the elements of the New Deal: banking and securities regulation, support for unemployment relief and social welfare through the Federal Emergency Relief Administration (FERA), price supports and assistance for agriculture through the Agricultural Adjustment Administration (AAA), and a measure of self-regulation for industry through the National Recovery Administration (NRA). Roosevelt, concerned about the budget, also urged economy measures. One of the first bills passed by Congress was an economy act, cutting the budgets of government agencies and the salaries of government employees by 10 percent. The large appropriations for relief of farmers and the unemployed were placed in the "emergency" budget. The first hundred days contained something for every potential major group in the Democratic Party: farmers (AAA), labor (FERA), and business (NRA).

The winter of 1933–1934 was bitter, and the economy, which had shown signs of recovery in late summer, went back into a slump in the fall. Over the winter, Roosevelt and his relief administrator, Harry Hopkins, with the

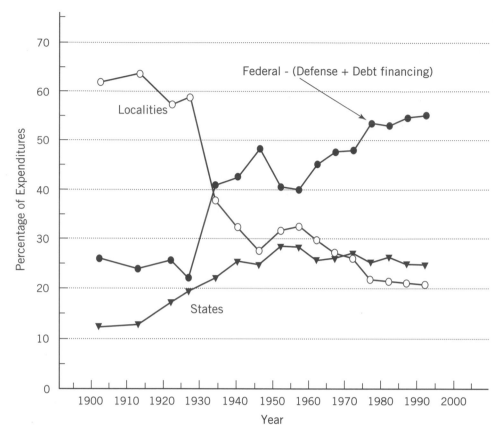

FIGURE 1. Shares of domestic expeditures: intergovernmental grants attributed to granting government, 1902–1992. Federal government expenditures are total federal expenditures minus expenditures for defense, international relations, and interest on government debt. SOURCE: 1902–1982, U.S. Census of Governments (1985); 1987 and 1992, Advisory Council on Intergovernmental Relations (1995).

support of Congress, provided work-relief jobs for 2 million individuals. Between the summer of 1933 and the summer of 1934, national, state, and local governments combined spent more than $2 billion for unemployment relief, more than 4 percent of GNP in 1933. Would voters support this level of expenditure and the New Deal in general? In the elections of 1934, the number of Democrats elected to the House and the number of Democratic Senators each rose by nine seats. The midterm elections of 1934 clearly indicated popular support for the New Deal.

Armed with this mandate, the Democrats returned to Washington, D.C., in the winter of 1935 and fashioned a more permanent New Deal. Between 1935 and 1937, Congress and Roosevelt together created a "Second New Deal." They created a permanent social welfare system through the Social (Economic) Security Act and permanent reform of the banking system and federal deposit insurance through the Federal Deposit Insurance Corporation (FDIC). Although the New Dealers allowed the NRA to slip forever into obscurity, they recognized the rights of labor to form

unions and bargain collectively through the National Labor Relations Act, which established the National Labor Relations Board (NLRB) to oversee the certification of unions and to mediate and arbitrate labor disputes. Despite a constitutional challenge to the agricultural price supports of the AAA, the New Dealers passed the Domestic Allotment and Soil Conservation Act, which reinstated the AAA and provided the framework for continuing price supports and crop limitations in agriculture. And, not least, they recognized the need to continue battling the social effects of the Depression by passing the Emergency Relief Appropriations Act of 1935, which gave Roosevelt the authority to create agencies to deal with unemployment. He created the Works Progress Administration (WPA), the National Youth Administration (NYA), and the Rural Electrification Administration (REA).

The Second New Deal was a smashing political success. In the face of growing opposition by business leaders, Roosevelt allowed the Supreme Court's challenge to the NRA to stand. The Democrats built a coalition of urban workers, northern and southern farmers, and the solidly Democratic (although conservative) South. In the elections of 1936, Roosevelt carried 61 percent of the popular vote, the number of Democrats in the House increased from 319 to 331, and in the Senate from 69 to 76 (U.S. Bureau of the Census, 1975, pp. 1077, 1083). By 1939, however, an alliance of Republicans and conservative southern Democrats had weakened the Democratic coalition. No major New Deal policies were reversed, but there were no new policy initiatives after 1938. The growing tensions in Europe began occupying more of FDR's attention.

New Deal Federalism. Not surprisingly, New Deal history is about the national government and FDR. Two important historical elements qualify the notion that the main consequence of the New Deal was the growth of big government. The first is the fact that between 1902 and 1922, total government expenditures—combined federal, state, and local expenditures—grew from 7.8 to 12.6 percent of GNP, and between 1922 and 1940 to 17.9 percent. Figure 1 shows the share of total government expenditures at each level of government from 1902 to 1982. The figure shows that expenditure shares were roughly stable before and after the 1930s, but during the decade, a reversal in the relative importance of national and local governments took place.

The figure also shows that the share of government spending at the state level did not decline during the New Deal; in fact, it increased. State government expenditures were 2.8 percent of GNP in 1932 and 5.1 percent of GNP in 1940. The reason that state expenditures grew as the federal government expanded points to a second important fact about the New Deal: it involved state and local governments. New Deal programs for public works, relief, and agricultural support relied heavily on state and local governments for their operation. The New Deal had two components: the "national" New Deal, programs involving only the national government, and the "federal" New Deal, programs involving the mutual cooperation of the national, state, or local governments.

New Deal Programs. The most important national New Deal programs had wide-ranging impact on the economy, yet they carried little weight within the federal budget. Reforms in the banking sector, beginning with the Glass-Steagall Act of 1932 and continued in a series of banking acts, reorganized the Federal Reserve System, divorced investment banking from commercial banking, took the country off the gold standard, and established deposit insurance through the FDIC. Reform and regulation of the stock market began with the Securities Act of 1933 and was made permanent with the creation of the Securities and Exchange Commission (SEC). The SEC oversaw the operation of securities markets and required publicly listed firms to make regular and accurate information available to investors.

The regulations instituted later in the New Deal were a response to larger social goals rather than an immediate reaction to the Depression. The Wagner Act of 1935, which created the National Labor Relations Board, was a major triumph for organized labor. The NLRB created a mechanism through which labor unions could gain official recognition and enter into bargaining with employers. In 1936, organizational battles in the steel and automobile industries led to a series of massive strikes. In 1938, the Fair Labor Standards Act created a national minimum wage and standards for overtime and maximum hours legislation. Labor market regulation reflected the important role that labor, organized and otherwise, had come to play in the New Deal.

The field of public works was an area of both national and federal programs, and one with a much larger impact on the budget. The Public Works Administration (PWA) set out to help the economy recover and to improve national resources through infrastructure investment. Massive projects begun under Hoover, such as the Grand Coulee Dam, Hoover Dam, and Fort Peck Dam, were completed under the PWA. The Tennessee Valley Authority and the Bonneville Power Authority brought electricity and flood control to the Tennessee and Columbia River Valleys, and a permanent federal government presence in the generation of electrical power. Billions of dollars were spent on dams, highways, bridges, water systems, and other public projects.

New Deal programs in agriculture involved relief and regulation. The Agricultural Adjustment Administration (AAA) was created in 1933 to raise farm prices and assist farmers. It did so by paying farmers to reduce the amount of crops that they planted and, through the Commodity Credit Corporation, directly purchasing farm products. The AAA was financed through taxes on food processing. When the Supreme Court declared the processing taxes unconstitutional in 1935, Congress responded by funding the program from general revenues in the Soil Conservation and Domestic Allotment Act of 1936 and a second Agricultural Adjustment Act in 1938. Crop allotments were a distinctly "federal" program. National officials set national annual crop output targets, but the negotiation of contracts for crop restriction by individual farmers was left to committees of farmers and extension agents organized at the county level. Because of its structure, relief for agriculture largely took the form of relief for large and wealthy farmers, who stood to gain the most from higher farm prices and payments for crop restrictions, rather than assistance for poor, small, marginal farmers, and regulation of crop output.

By far the largest New Deal programs were the relief programs, designed explicitly to deal with the suffering caused by the Depression. The Federal Emergency Relief Administration (FERA) was created in the first hundred days and charged with assisting state unemployment relief programs. The agency was given a budget of $500 million for two years. Because there was no national welfare system in place, FERA worked with state and local relief offices. It soon became apparent that the relief problem was far larger than Congress thought. In the winter of 1933–1934, FERA organized the Civil Works Administration, which put 2 million people to work, half from the relief roles and half from the unemployed not receiving relief. By the summer of 1935, when FERA was replaced by the WPA and the Social Security programs, it had spent more than $4 billion and provided relief to an average of 2 million families each month.

In 1935, the temporary relief administration put in place with FERA was overhauled. The new system had two parts. The permanent component was put under the Social Security Board and consisted of Old Age Insurance (Social Security—a national program), Unemployment Insurance, Aid to the Blind, Old Age Assistance, and Aid to Dependent Children—all programs administered jointly by the national, state, and local governments. The "emergency" relief programs continued in the Works Progress Administration and other agencies created under the authority of the Emergency Relief Appropriations Act of 1935, including the National Youth Administration and the Rural Electrification Administration, and continued funding for the Civilian Conservation Corp. Through the end of the decade, relief programs provided support for roughly 2 million families every year.

Accomplishments and Legacies. During a fireside chat, FDR declared the goals of the New Deal to be "relief, recovery, and reform." Whether the New Deal promoted or retarded the American economy's recovery from the Great Depression is an unanswered question. Viewed purely as an economic recovery program, the New Deal was filled with contradictions. The NRA encouraged businesses to raise prices, and the AAA encouraged farmers to raise prices, which would have reduced, not increased, consumption. It hoped that higher profits would encourage businesses to increase employment, but at the same time FERA offered relief benefits that kept some workers out of the labor market. The FDIC increased depositor confidence and all but eliminated banking panics after 1933, but uncertainty over the direction of the regulation of banking and securities markets surely reduced the amount of investment in new plants and equipment in 1934 and 1935. The New Deal probably promoted and retarded recovery simultaneously. Economic historians have also debated whether relief, recovery, and reform or political interests influenced New Deal spending (see Wallis, 1998).

On the relief front, the New Deal was an unparalleled success. The various New Deal programs provided assistance to an average of 2 million families each month. The Social Security Act established a permanent American welfare system, providing for insurance in old age and assistance for the needy of any age. Again, the system failed to cover everyone, but it was a significant accomplishment nonetheless. How much reform the New Deal accomplished often depends on the speaker. There is no doubt that the New Deal had very small effects on the distribution of income, the extent of poverty, or long-standing differences in income between regions and races. What cannot be denied is that the reforms in banking and security regulation, social welfare policy, agricultural price supports, and labor market regulation are legacies of the New Deal today.

Perhaps the greatest accomplishment of the New Deal was the ability of the American people and political system to adapt. The 1930s were a decade of worldwide depression that produced political reaction and oppression, ultimately leading to World War II. The United States was able to face the economic crisis and remake its system of government in a constitutional and orderly manner. Amid contention and debate, the American political system delivered a New Deal for the American people.

[*See also* Great Depression.]

BIBLIOGRAPHY
Bernstein, Barton." The New Deal: The Conservative Achievements of Liberal Reform." In his *Towards a New Past: Dissenting Essays in American History*, pp. 263–288. New York, 1968.
Chandler, Lester. *America's Greatest Depression*. New York, 1970.
Higgs, Robert. *Crisis and Leviathan: Critical Episodes in the Growth of American Government*. New York, 1987.
Howard, Donald S. *The WPA and Federal Relief Policy*. New York, 1973.
Kennedy, David M. *Freedom from Fear: The American People in Depression and War, 1929–1945*. New York, 1999.
Leuchtenburg, William E. *Franklin D. Roosevelt and the New Deal, 1932–1940*. New York, 1963.
Patterson, James T. *Congressional Conservatism and the New Deal*. Lexington, Ky., 1967.
Patterson, James T. *The New Deal and the States*. Princeton, 1969.
U.S. Bureau of the Census. *Historical Statistics of the United States*. Washington, D.C., 1975.
Wallis, John Joseph. "The Political Economy of New Deal Spending, Revisited, with and without Nevada." *Explorations in Economic History* 35 (1998), 140–170.
Williams, E. A. *Federal Aid for Relief*. New York, 1939.

JOHN JOSEPH WALLIS

NEWSPAPERS [*This entry contains two subentries, a historical overview and a discussion of industrial organization and regulation.*]

Historical Overview

Journalists, when recounting the history of their profession, like to push its foundations back before the use of printing in Europe—to feudal courts or even to the *Acta diurna* (Daily Events) that were written on the walls of the Forum in ancient Rome. In fact, the periodical publication of news constitutes a clearly definable industry, with a specific starting point in the early seventeenth century and, thereafter, with a continuous and connected existence.

Origins and Issues. The newspaper, as such, did not appear spontaneously in any one country but developed on an interconnected and global basis as political and economic conditions, technical possibilities, and secure lines of supply and distribution emerged. In China, during the Tang dynasty (618–906 CE) a court gazette was produced by woodcut; the Chinese invented movable type centuries before it was used by Johannes Gutenberg of Mainz in the mid-fifteenth century. The Fugger family, German bankers, issued regular newsletters in the fifteenth century and are generally recognized as the initiators of news dissemination in the West. In Japan, newssheets, pressed from ceramic tiles, circulated in the higher reaches of society in the seventeenth century.

The early centuries. The organized circulation of news is essentially a European industry, based on the Western-style printing press, the invention of which is ascribed to Johannes Gutenberg of Mainz in about 1445. At first, news appeared in nonperiodical book form (often entitled *Occurrences*). By the 1620s, the Blaeuw printing press, developed in Holland, underwent improvements that effectively doubled its capacity per unit of labor, while the transportation routes of Europe made it possible for weekly information to move across the continent. *Corantos* (from Latin, *currere*, "to run"), the weekly summaries of seventeenth-century military, political, and other information, printed with the same type font and format as brief books (usually with four pages), were then published in Holland. Some five hundred titles of those "running" publications have been identified, and many arrived weekly in London from the Low Countries; their material was then translated into English and added to more locally originated news, which then passed out of London and across the British countryside. Armies of carriers transported them along the roads out of London, with some five or six individuals responsible for a single route between the capital and a country town or group of towns. By the 1620s in London, almost 80 percent of the adult male population (some 60,000) could read; in the countryside of the British Isles, perhaps 30 percent. Organized public readings of the *corantos* were therefore established at country inns for the interested. A simultaneous industry of manuscript newsletter writing enabled the better educated to receive, by subscription, a more sophisticated account of contemporary events.

Professional editors quickly emerged, such as Thomas Gainsford in London, who collected and translated incoming *corantos*, arranged the ongoing accounts in proper sequence, and clarified conflicting accounts for the convenience of puzzled readers. London and Amsterdam thereby witnessed the foundation of the "public sphere" (as it would be called by social theorist Jürgen Habermas), for the reading community of London surely acquired a good knowledge and understanding of the political intrigues of both Europe and of the English court. The first recorded newssheet in English, dated September 1621, was entitled *Corante, or, Weekly News from Italy, Germany, Hungarie, Spaine and France*. A single *coranto* might enjoy an edition of five hundred copies or perhaps one thousand. Within a few years, the writing of news had evolved from the staccato printing of brief statements, each headed by its European dateline, into a flowing narrative discourse. As Gainsford put it: "to avoid breakings off. And fractions of matter, I will not precisely name either the Letters, or the time of their mission. Let it suffice that you know we were not eyewitnesses of the business, but we must trust other mens relaciouns, as you are curteous enough to give credit to our secondary reports." (English spelling and punctuation have changed during the ensuing four hundred years.)

Typefounding and typesetting then constituted formidably heavy work. For example, to set up a page of type for the Gutenberg Bible would take a skilled man a day, then another day to print sixteen sheets off the hand press. Enormous sums of money were thus invested in the creation of such books, and printers were eager for jobs that would create a faster cash flow. The newsbooks were only slapdash jobs, so pressmen could pull a quick 150 copies an hour. In France, printers were producing three thousand copies of a two-sheet joblot publication with two machines in one long day's work. Moreover, in France, the inward newsflow and the onward distribution were better organized than elsewhere; the *grands courriers* covered minor as well as major routes and at so great a pace that the two-day trip from Paris to Bordeaux was not bettered until the installation of the electric telegraph in the 1820s.

Birth of English journalism. The English Civil War of the mid-1600s (1644–1653) had a drastic effect on journalism (as did the *Fronde* in France, rebellions of 1648–1653, to oppose the court of Louis XIV and Cardinal Mazarin). The effective restraints on the licensing of publications through the Stationers' Company and Britain's Star Chamber were removed. England's news made gripping reading and domestic news then overtook foreign news. One of the new band of newswriters remarked: "And now by a strange alteration and vicissitude of times we talke of nothing else but what is done in England, and perhaps once in a fortnight we hearken after newes sent out of Scotland." The first great flowering of English journalism was underway. England's Civil War soon created a furious journalistic counterpart in the conflict between rival *Mercurius* writers who sometimes, like Marchamont Nedham, defected from side to side. About twenty thousand editions of such periodicals survive, some with circulations that lasted, at weekly intervals, for years.

After the removal of the monarchy in England, Oliver Cromwell (1599–1658), the Puritan general who led the forces of Parliament in victories over Charles I, advocated the king's trial and execution, then ruled the new Commonwealth and Protectorate until his death as the Lord Protector. The Cromwellian era saw the more efficient reapplication of government controls over the emerging newspaper press, and only two publications were permitted—the *London Gazette* and Nedham's *Mercurius Politicus*. The Stationers' Company, at arms' length from government, was entrusted with the task of supervision. With the death of Cromwell, General George Monck's royalist troops commenced their slow advance on London, to restore the monarchy with Charles II in 1660; a kinsman of the general, Henry Muddiman, was then appointed to oversee the press. To ensure the safety of the monarchy, the Restoration became a bleak era for the British press—secretaries of state controlled incoming flows of information and a new post, Surveyor of the Press, was granted draconian powers of search in an effort to control both the news and the public. Yet in two respects the newspaper of that era grew in quality—in the elegance and clarity of expression and in the growth of advertising, much of it generated by trade with the new British colonies (for tobacco, coffee, tea, and the sale of land in North America). Financial information also grew in importance. In London, an hourly penny post was established to serve the suburbs and city, bringing both general communications and newspapers.

During the Restoration, of major importance to the evolution of newspapers was the establishment of the coffeehouse, which became their principal means of distribution in the eighteenth century. Coffeehouses were associated with political factions, so Charles II attempted to close them; with the expiration of the Licensing Act of 1662, however, controls on the press ended. Opposition papers had, however, been imported from Holland. Elsewhere in Europe, despite the growing sophistication and diversity of newspaper production, the press remained under various systems of absolutist control, since Europe's sovereigns watched the developments in England with disdain—and scurrilous and untruthful newssheets filled London. In Paris, meanwhile, the illiterate could hear news read aloud daily for 6 *sous* in public halls. Another oral news system in France, that of the *nouvellistes*, existed simultaneously; as licensed diplomatic gossips, they shifted from spoken to written publication in later years. French streetsellers of printed news (*colporteurs*) were licensed, and they were expected to be able to read. Because of social unrest in France, the death penalty existed for illegal papers that aroused feelings against the government or religion; the news was therefore dominated by three official gazettes—one bearing the royal arms and founded by Théophraste Renaudot.

Arrival of a daily press. In London in 1702, the first daily newspaper was printed—Samuel Buckley's *Daily Courant*—which thrived on the news flowing out of France during the War of the Spanish Succession (1701–1714, in which the European powers disputed the rights to the Spanish throne). Buckley announced the intention "to give news, give it daily and impartially." This paper continued into six thousand editions; in the mid-1700s, it gave way to five London dailies, each with a circulation averaging fifteen hundred. In addition, there were six London thrice-weeklies and five weeklies. The total circulation amounted to some one hundred thousand a week, which probably meant a million readers. With average wages of 10 shillings a week, purchasing a paper was within many household budgets. The press economy also supported some 150 job printers by 1750, each with a pair of presses and several apprentices. In the eighteenth century, provincial newspapers were started in large numbers, existing mainly on the transcription of London papers, "the quintessence of every print." In the late 1700s, these gathered sufficient readers to initiate the collection and printing of local news. Only in Holland was there a press more free and profuse than that of London, where the view prevailed that published opinions, within limits, were not a threat to constitutional authority; after all, the papers that circulated such opinions might be manipulated, harassed, bribed, or taxed. In the eighteenth century, women's papers, social and political sheets, and entertainment papers proliferated: Richard Steele's *Tatler* and Joseph Addison's *Spectator* after 1709 popularized the new genre of the weekly moral essay, which brought the novelists and men of letters Henry Fielding, Daniel Defoe, and Jonathan Swift into political journalism and, thus, into a new form of political power.

The eighteenth-century English press was distributed on the streets by networks of hawkers, controlled by two major dealers, Mrs. Nutt and Mrs. Dodd. They both continued in business into their seventies and frequently spent time in jail, since they bore the first brunt of any prosecution for illegal content. The coffeehouses then organized into a loose federation, to limit the number of newspaper titles in circulation—an effort in cost control. By the 1740s, they had prevailed, and a vast array of cheap (1 farthing), untaxed, and illegal papers ceased publishing. Provincial papers were sent out of London by professional carriers and by the agents of the six government Clerks of the Road, who were given the privilege of free franking (and skimmed £4,000 a year for themselves); sometimes they published and distributed their own newspapers. Throughout England and Scotland roamed the agents of the secretaries of state, who reported on the content of the press and who organized prosecutions for profanity or seditious libel, their great weapon being the infamous general warrant.

Britain's Stamp Act of 1712 had inaugurated the tax system, designed both to curb newspapers and enrich government. At first, the publisher had to pay a penny per sheet used, plus a shilling for every advertisement. The tax was increased steadily until 1836, when it began to be reduced. There had been several methods of tax evasion, however, and the most popular turned the paper into a pamphlet, by printing it flat on one and a half folio–size printer's sheets. In that era of rapidly increasing interest in news, the higher the tax grew, the greater was the propensity of readers to rent their papers or to read them in a coffeehouse, where they were shared.

American journalism. On 25 September 1690, Benjamin Harris, a Boston bookseller who was frequently in trouble with the licensing authorities, both in London and the American colonies, issued his *Publick Occurrences, Both Foreign and Domestick*. It survived one edition of four days (since Harris had no official permission), and it was 24 April 1704 before the Boston postmaster John Campbell's News-Letter appeared and lasted until 1776. Other Colonial-era newspapers included the Boston *Gazette* (1719), Philadelphia *American Mercury* (1719), Boston's *New England Courant* (1721), New York *Gazette* (1725), Maryland *Gazette* (1727), and Philadelphia's *Pennsylvania Gazette* (1728). The North American colonies were poised for the rapid growth of a newspaper industry; the seaboard population increased from 300,000 to more than 1 million from 1700 to 1750. The internal postal routes were well developed, and the postmasters were government appointed. In 1769, Isaac Doolittle's printing press was made in the colonies, so they no longer had to import them; this was the veritable technology of independence. It ensured that press freedom was among the founding principles of the Republic (from 1776 to 1781), and the new United States of America quickly developed its own newspaper and journalistic style. As publisher of the *Pennsylvania Gazette* (1729–1766), Benjamin Franklin imported from London the weekly essay format, pioneered there by Addison's *Spectator* and Steele's *Tatler* (and further developed in Samuel Johnson's *Idler*). His brother James Franklin created a number of papers in which he appealed for contributions that were "Serious, Sarcastic, Ludicrous or otherwise Amusing." Franklin introduced the cartoon and provided much of the iconography that gave the American colonists their material of common allusion.

After the American Revolution and during George Washington's presidency, so great was the interest in news that circulations of eight thousand were achieved by the *Connecticut Journal*, which also manufactured its own paper because of the paper shortage during the British blockade. Yet dozens of papers came into being and the institution fanned out northward, across the U.S.–Canada border into Quebec and Halifax (Nova Scotia). Popular agitational journalism provided the chief stylistic developments of the late eighteenth century on both sides of the Atlantic: Thomas Paine's sixteen pamphlets, *The Crisis* (1776–1783) were read aloud to American troops before battle. Alongside the provision of news, the constant advocacy of a cause became the mainstay of newspapers, as well as the chief means by which circulations were increased and readerships defined.

Press Freedoms in Europe. The demand for a free press began to sweep across Europe. It was linked to the American and French Revolutions and the rising demand for individual liberty (which reached a climax in Europe's 1848 revolutions). Sweden in 1776 was the first country to acquire a law guaranteeing press freedom, but its king tended to ignore it. In England, the anonymous *Letters of Junius* demanded the admission of reporters to the galleries of Parliament, and they pressed for the rights of juries to decide both fact and law in cases of libel (which in New York had been highlighted since the 1720s, when a jury trying the case of John Peter Zenger had defied authority and English common law to acquit him. Yet the truth did not become an accepted defense in libel in New York State until 1804).

The social status of journalism. In Britain, journalism long remained a socially stigmatized profession, called "Grub Street"; only in the 1830s did editors begin to dine with dukes and printers stand for Parliament. In the United States, publisher-patriots like Franklin and Paine had made it respectable, as the guardian for government corruption. On both sides of the Atlantic, newspapers became quarrelsome and vituperative instruments of political factions. Then, in 1835, the founding of the New York *Herald* by James Gordon Bennett introduced a new ethic—impartiality—and, with it, a new journalism. Bennett also printed the interview form for the first time. Impartiality became an economic tool in the circulation wars of New York City after the arrival of Benjamin Day's *Sun* (1833) and Horace Greeley's *Tribune* (1841). When Joseph Pulitzer arrived in New York and bought the *World* in 1883 and William Randolph Hearst started the *Journal* in 1896, another highly competitive and populist "new journalism" arose; they used sensational news, crusades against powerful interests, political cartoons, and, later, comic strips. The new circulations were fed by the burgeoning advertising industry, so turn-of-the-century newspapers became big business. In London as in New York, the entrepreneurial role of the printers was superseded as they came to be locked into shareholding corporate structures.

New presses and the birth of **The Times.** Modern journalism began in Britain with the founding of *The Times* in London (1785) by John Walter and his descendants. So

NEWSPAPERS. At the headquarters of *La République Française,* painting by Henri Gervex (1852–1929). (Musée d'Orsay, Paris/Giraudon/Art Resource, NY)

powerful were its early editors Thomas Barnes and John Delane that it earned the soubriquet "The Thunderer." *The Times* became the authoritative ideological representative of the new Victorian Empire's middle class—William Hazlitt called it "the greatest engine of temporary opinion in the world"—unrivaled until the introduction of the *Daily Telegraph* in the mid-1800s. *The Times* helped to pioneer new, steam-driven, printing presses. The Stanhope cast-iron press had once replaced its largely wooden predecessors, while reducing the amount of human effort entailed in printing, as its metal parts moved relatively easily. In 1816, the central screw of the printing press (from William Caxton's original converted winepress) was replaced for the hand pressing of a printing plate, and steam was used to move the machinery. In the United States, George Clymer's Columbia press accommodated larger page sizes, with four or five columns to a page, and it was then that banner headlines came in: DETROIT IS TAKEN! Soon, even towns with a population of 300 often had their own press and newspaper. Sunday papers were started in the United States and the British Isles in imitation of London's *Observer* (founded 1791). So great was the competition between newspapers that fast "newsboats" were constructed to sail a hundred miles or so into the Atlantic, to intercept approaching European ships and bear away their cargoes of newspapers for rapid copying. Americans often bought and read several papers in those days (morning and evening and extra editions), some in English, some in other languages (since many were relatively recent European immigrants).

Newspapers and radicalism. The American patriot Thomas Jefferson had called the newspaper "the tocsin of nations," and throughout the nineteenth century, the medium became inseparable from the business of nation building, party construction, and class formation. In England, William Cobbett's *Weekly Register*, selling at two pence after the Napoleonic Wars (1804–1815), gathered a radicalized following of sixty thousand readers, evading Britain's Stamp Act when one copy was passed from hand to hand. As the British and French colonial empires expanded, so too did their respective newspaper formats (and even today the presses of Latin America, Africa, and India still reveal elements of their historical models). Britain developed a group of national newspapers, while the U.S. industry was based on its city-oriented papers. Electronic transmission systems of the late twentieth century facilitated nationwide U.S. publication of *The Wall Street Journal, USA Today, The Christian Science Monitor, The National Observer,* and *The New York Times.* Tabloid and specialty papers (*The National Enquirer, Baseball World,* etc.) and foreign-language papers are distributed nationally, as well, throughout the United States.

In most industrial societies, governments and their constitutions came to terms with the roles of newspapers—at varying paces and with different levels of enthusiasm. The press became accepted as a necessary part of the sociopolitical and industrial system. A great range of forms were developed: Sundays, evenings, mornings, regional and local editions, as well as financial papers and specialty papers. As millions of new consumers came into the manufacturing economy, there also arrived the electric telegraph, news agencies, syndication, and serialization. New forms of home lighting (gas light, electricity) expanded the hours of reading. New cities were established, which created additional sources of news and helped widen the readership, the public interest, and the cultural criticism.

The end of taxes on knowledge. The abolition of newspaper taxes ("the taxes on knowledge") was one of the great issues that divided British Victorian society, for to end them would place the press, it seemed to some, in the hands of the uneducated classes. The taxes were reduced during the 1830s and repealed in 1861. *London's Daily Telegraph* was the first new paper to benefit from the change and, by 1865, enjoyed a circulation larger than all its rivals combined (including *The Times* of London). It borrowed from *The New York Herald* the multilayered headline (the assassination of U.S. President Abraham Lincoln in 1865 merited no fewer than seventeen lines to *The Times* of London's three). After the U.S. Civil War (1861–1865), news collecting became ever more specialized; covering a war eventually entailed massive and ingenious handling of technical and human resources. Owner-editors were driven ever farther into management; they made deals with professional intermediaries, advertising agencies, wire services, and syndication companies. The acquiring of readerships also became a specialized business.

In the mid-1800s, sixty men were needed to print a daily paper: a dozen or so political reporters, six court reporters, correspondents in European capitals, and a squad of leader writers, provincial reporters, and dozens of "penny-a-liners" (Am., stringers). Profits were high because all the new consumer businesses depended upon the paper—Mr. Lipton could not sell his tea without it and the new department stores would not long survive.

Improved technology. By 1860, newspapers were being produced on rolls of paper instead of on single stamped sheets. From rolls 3.5 miles long, four thousand copies could be run off, cut, and folded without stopping the presses. In the 1860s, 5,429 new papers were founded in the United States. By 1880, new methods for making newsprint (paper) brought the U.S. price down to five cents per pound (in England the halfpenny paper was in sight).

In 1846, the American Richard Hoe had produced the first rotary press. A decade later, English and French papers started the use of page molds (from *papier maché*) instead of printing from the wood or metal type. Various improvements in typesetting were also made, culminating in the invention of Ottmar Mergenthaler, who had emigrated from Germany to the United States in 1872. His used molten metal (lead) to set up the lines of type and was called Linotype. In London, the powerfully organized typographers managed to delay its use for decades.

Twentieth Century. For more than a century, the newspaper has played an important role in industrialized society. It has shared political power with legislatures; it has been an economic mainstay; it has contributed to the iconography and the morale of nations. In the twentieth century, its hegemony among the information media was progressively challenged by radio (1920s), television (1950s), and the newer electronic media (1990s)—the World Wide Web and the Internet in particular. Still, in the twenty-first century it remains a profitable and ubiquitous industry, with links to its rival information technologies. The twentieth century had begun with a proliferation of new papers that practiced a new popular journalism; it ended with fears of amalgamations, takeovers, monopolies, and cross-ownerships. The competitive pursuit of truth—first guaranteed by the First Amendment, to the U.S. Constitution (1791), by the French Press Law of 1881, by the ending of Britain's Taxes on Knowledge—now seems to depend on the ease of expression that has been granted by the computer, the Internet, and the Web.

Popular journalism and the penny press. The *Daily Mail* of 1896 incorporated, for England, many of the advances in popular journalism that had been pioneered in the United States. Those new papers catered to the masses and tried to shape them around the emerging political causes. In the United States, mass dailies and the yellow press used simple but persuasive English for the undereducated and immigrants. W. T. Stead (creator of England's upscale *Pall Mall Gazette*) also prepared the way for the new mass dailies, which fought with sensational banner headlines for the attention of buyers. The politics of a paper tended to be a less important "hook" for late twentieth-century readers, who looked to newspapers for special information, entertainment, exposure of political mismanagement, scandals, cultural data, sports, business, and lifestyle news. In 1880, some 40 million U.S. dollars were spent on advertising; by 1904, that had grown to 140 million dollars. By the 1970s, that had grown to 6 billion; by 1985, to 12 billion; by 2000, 24 billion. The newspaper needs a large portion of that pot for its survival, so its contents are shaped to secure the readers that the different kinds of advertisers require.

In the United Kingdom, where a dozen or more newspapers have long competed nationally, a very firm division developed between the broadsheet "qualities" and the tabloid "populars," which have sometimes enjoyed readerships of more than 10 million per day. In the United States, with its city-based press, the division was between the "newspaper of record" and the other metropolitan and small-town papers, with fewer of their own sources of information. Gradually the U.S. newspaper became a natural, local-advertising-dependent monopoly, but sometimes with an evening and a morning paper competing in the same market. Great chains of newspapers were established under one owner, which has often aroused alarm in both the U.S. and the European industry. By 1980, two-thirds of the seventeen hundred U.S. dailies (75 percent of total sales) were in group ownership and, of these, five were predominant. Legislation was repeatedly attempted to prevent or delay this phenomenon—and also that of cross-ownership with broadcasting—with varying degrees of failure. Independence has given way to commercialism and economic survivalist strategies.

Technology transformed. Newspapers grew with the speed and size of the printing, but no change of technological principle occurred before the move from linotype to offset printing (practical for newspapers as of the 1960s) and the 1970s computerization of typesetting (from hot type to cold type).

Electricity had replaced steam in 1900, then folding and stuffing devices for supplements were used; the teletype machine replaced the dot-and-dash telegraph signal. From the 1920s, a perforated tape was used to drive the typesetting machines, saving great amounts of time and energy. U.S. newspapers grew to a hundred pages (*The New York Times* on Sundays and others of that ilk). The telephone created a new division between "leg-men" and "rewrite men."

Photography and wire transmission transformed and smartened the look of papers and generally replaced drawings (*The Wall Street Journal* is still a holdout). The photographer Frederic Ives of Cornell University perfected the half-tone system in the 1880s and enabled photography to become a new subdivision of journalism.

By the end of the twentieth century, the newspaper ceased to be a mechanical industry (no more clacking typewriters, teletypes, Telexes, or Linotypes) and became a relatively silent electronic world that employed a small fraction of its once great workforce. Only the presses still rumble a bit as they print the news, often illustrated by brilliant color photography.

[*See also* Advertising; Information and Communication Technology; *and* Magazines.]

BIBLIOGRAPHY

Breed, Warren. *The Newspaperman, News and Society*. New York, 1990.
Chalaby, Jean K. *The Invention of Journalism*. New York, 1998.
Collet, Collet D. *A History of the Taxes on Knowledge*. London, 1933.
Curran, James, and Seaton, Jean. *Power without Responsibility*. London, 1991.
Garnham, Nicholas. *Capitalism and Communication: Global Culture and the Economics of Information*. London, 1990.
Harris, Michael. *London Newspapers in the Age of Walpole*. London and Toronto, 1987.
Lee, Alan J. *The Origins of the Popular Press, 1855–1914*. London and Totowa, N.J., 1976.
Morison, Stanley. *The English Newspaper, 1621–1932*. Cambridge and New York, 1932.
Morison, Stanley. *History of the Times*. 5 vols. London, 1945–1952.
Mott, Frank L. *American Journalism: A History, 1690–1960*. New York, 1969.
Schudson, Michael. *Discovering the News*. New York, 1976.
Seymour-Ure, Colin. *The British Press and Broadcasting since 1945*. Oxford, 1996.
Smith, Anthony. *The Newspaper—An International History*. London and New York, 1979.
Smith, Anthony. *Goodbye Gutenberg—The Newspaper Revolution of the 1980s*. Oxford and New York, 1980.
Tebbel, John. *The Compact History of the American Newspaper*. New York, 1973.
Wickwar, William H. *The Struggle for Freedom of the Press, 1819–1932*. London, 1928.

ANTHONY SMITH

Industrial Organization and Regulation

Newspapers typically echo modern economic growth in that they emerge with cities and they take advantage of evolving technology. They widely influence both governments and economies. In government they form a key component of policy as they both reflect and lead public opinion. So important has been their role in history that they have been called the fourth estate, a term that has spread around the world. (Nineteenth-century English historian Thomas Macauley referred to reporters and editors as an influential body akin to the three "estates"—lords spiritual, lords temporal, and commons—of England). Today newspapers compete with television for the public's attention globally, but locally they are without peer in their influence on government policy and on regional economies. In local markets they provide a daily vehicle for businesses to advertise their wares to customers at reasonable rates. Newspapers have been valuable to customers for generations because they penetrate deeply into communities. Some weekly newspapers reach nearly 90 percent of the homes in their areas, and most of the subscribers renew as automatically as they pay their property taxes.

A common definition of a newspaper is that of a daily or a weekly publication that gathers and comments on the news. However, some periodicals barely fit that definition. They seldom cover breaking news, or they offer no informed opinion. Perhaps the only definition that fits every newspaper would be that of a publication that runs through a high-speed press on a roll of coarse paper called newsprint. Even that definition may be too narrow because some newspapers use the bright paper that is common to magazines.

The cords that bind disparate newspapers into an industry are competition, regulation, readership, and advertising. Virtually every newspaper has strengths and weaknesses within those categories. So similar are their business issues that newspaper publishers and editors tend to be active participants in trade associations. They gather constantly to swap information and to educate each other about common problems. Some newspapers may have regional rivalries so fierce that their managers are not on speaking terms, but they may speak openly with managers of similar papers only a few dozen miles away.

Newspapers have challenges common to every industry—competition, regulation, and markets; yet their birth has been unlike that of any other commercial endeavor, originating in the human desire to speak freely. On every continent, newspapers have been created not primarily because of someone's desire to make a living, but rather because an editor has wanted to give voice to viewpoints that have seemed oppressed. Once some measure of freedom of speech has been established, newspapers have the luxury of acting like an industry; and although industries such as high-rise construction and deep-sea fishing certainly are dangerous to workers, only journalism has employees who so voluntarily insert themselves into physical danger. As long as there are photographers and reporters, some of them will risk their lives to bring news to the public. When war comes, such as in Vietnam, Kosovo, and Afghanistan, they beg to accompany an attack. When violence breaks out locally, someone from a newspaper is close to it. A prime example is Colombia, where journalists were assassinated in the drug wars of the late twentieth century.

Many industries can consolidate, leaving each branch a clone of the others and allowing promotion of a single brand. Newspapers, because of their geographic character, can come under the same corporate umbrella but must remain distinct. So, as long as there are newspapers, there will be many of them. The United States has close to fifteen hundred dailies, down from a peak of above two thousand. Europe has an estimated twenty-six hundred, Asia twenty-five hundred, South American more than seven hundred, and Canada about one hundred.

History. Sheets of handwritten news, pegged up in public places, were the first newspapers. One, *Acta Diurna* (Daily Events), appeared in Rome in 59 BCE. The Chinese printed with wooden blocks during the eighth century CE, traders created newsletters in the Middle Ages, pamphlets on single events appeared in the sixteenth century, and the printing press brought newspapers to Europe as the Reformation gathered momentum during the early seventeenth century. In the early 1600s, newspapers also appeared in Japan.

By 1704 America had a newspaper, the *Boston News-Letter*, appearing regularly, and sixty years later the colonies had thirty newspapers. That number rose to a thousand early in the next century, but they cost too much for common people to buy them. Primary audiences were the wealthy, politicians, and merchants. In 1833 Benjamin Day started a "penny" newspaper called the *New York Sun*, and soon presses running at increasingly high speeds brought newspapers to the masses of America's large cities. Publishers added entertaining material to the steady diet of government news, broadening appeal as they slashed prices. Newspapers' popularity blossomed as people were migrating to cities, and as literacy grew. Newspapers became unifying and socializing factors in their cities. Immigrants used the daily product to learn their new country's language and customs; at the end of the day they also had something for wrapping the fish or starting a fire. By the mid-nineteenth century, railroads, the telegraph, and the postal service had shrunk the country, and were helping newspapers expand by bringing fresh news to people hundreds of miles away from a city where the paper was printed. James Gordon Bennett's *New York Herald* helped forge the modern newspaper, which heavily emphasizes entertainment and promotion. Papers built circulation through stunts such as sending reporter Nellie Bly around the world and dispatching Henry Morton Stanley to Africa in search of Dr. David Livingstone.

The number of U.S. papers reached 2,250 in 1914 and stabilized at roughly 1,800 after World War II. Then began a slow decline in numbers. Daily papers sank from 1,772 in 1950 to 1,480 in 2000. Yet as total daily circulation slid a little, Sunday circulation soared, and employment rose to 445,000. Evening papers vanished in favor of morning editions; but the newspaper industry itself continued to grow financially, heavily expanding its influence into weekly newspapers, special-interest papers, and the Internet.

The pattern of industry growth has been similar in each industrialized nation, with the exception of communist countries where government control has created an artificial industry. Newspaper readership is highest in Sweden, Japan, Germany, and Finland.

Regulation. Conflict over press freedom began most remarkably in England, and since then the issue worldwide has wavered between two poles: authoritarian and libertarian. Countries in Asia, Latin America, and Africa often restrict the press, which is freest in Europe, English-language nations, and Japan. The Middle East restrains its press; even Israel, which enjoys the freest press in that region, curbs military news. European papers tend to have a more political orientation than those of Canada or the United States.

English poet and political activist John Milton struck one of the great blows for press freedom in 1644 when he published *Areopagitica*. Like Oliver Cromwell, Milton was a Protestant offended by the House of Stuart. Censorship laws roused his anger, and he argued for unfettered expression: "whoever knew Truth put to the worse, in a free and open encounter?" Ironically Milton became a censor himself as a Protectorate official when he suppressed Catholic writings, an early example of how politics twists its own rhetoric when issues of press freedom surface. Countless times around the world, revolutionary governments claiming to represent "the people" have sought immediately to muzzle television stations and newspapers, and populist rebels often try to seize media outlets. A popular saying in the modern newsroom is that freedom of the press "belongs to those who own one."

Milton and others had a powerful impact, and freedom of the press grew and flourished in England and elsewhere. A 1662 law regulated printing, but seventeen years later Parliament declined to renew it, allowing twenty newspapers to start up within three years. In 1690 there began a lengthy history of skirmishes between American colonial governments and the Continent's newspapers. Benjamin Harris, a staunch advocate of free speech and a free press, established America's first newspaper, *Publick Occurrences Both Forreign and Domestick* (the spelling used most often in sources). Harris was a London publisher who had run afoul of the English courts, and in America his Boston paper was shut down after one day by order of the colonial government. Benjamin Franklin gained control of a newspaper in 1721 when his brother was jailed for contempt and was ordered to cease being a publisher. Franklin later started a paper in Philadelphia that set the stage for modern newspapering; he avoided rambling discourses in favor of short, lively articles and also took in advertising. The formula made him wealthy in his forties, like so many newspaper publishers who came after him.

The concept of freedom of the press had begun its worldwide struggle, which continues today. Sweden passed a free-press law in 1766. A year earlier in the American colonial government, the Stamp Act of 1765 imposed a tax that was about 50 percent of the cost a newspaper. Publishers fought to win repeal, and in doing so they realized how powerful they could be in the arena of public policy. The Townshend Act, also taxing paper, provided another test. The U.S. Constitution itself did not mention freedom of the press although the writings of James Madison, Thomas Jefferson, Franklin, and others certainly echoed Milton's sentiments. The First Amendment (1791) gave newspapers clear protection that no other industry had, stating that "Congress shall make no law . . . abridging the freedom . . . of the press." Jefferson wrote in 1816, "Where the press is free, and every man able to read, all is safe." Six years later, after long experience as a public official, Madison wrote that "a popular government without popular information or the means of acquiring it, is but a prologue to a farce or tragedy, or perhaps both." Winds of freedom were blowing in Europe too. In 1771, just before its own great upheaval, France got its first daily. Many more new papers followed during the French Revolution.

After America won independence, the press had leanings toward Jeffersonian or Federalist politics. Editors spent years attacking public officials and losing libel suits, beginning around 1840 to adopt a shared sense of responsibility to both the public and to their profession. In a famous case, New York publisher John Peter Zenger won a libel case on grounds that facts were the basis of the political commentary he printed.

Although in England and the United States in the late 1800s adverse publicity was considered part of the punishment for committing a crime, the next century saw tighter restrictions on court reporting in those and many other nations. Wartime brought tougher oversight of the press to many nations in the twentieth century. England passed an Official Secrets Act in 1911 that restrained the press. The year 1917 saw the Espionage Act and the Trading-with-the-Enemy Act in the United States, potentially creating censorship and punishing disloyalty; papers carrying articles critical of government could not pass through the mail. In China and the Soviet Union, communist regimes controlled and owned newspapers; freedom of speech was curtailed. Meanwhile legal cases against the Western press continued to sprout, and the courts have not yet resolved the issue of judges holding reporters in contempt of court for refusing to reveal sources of stories.

In the twentieth century, an offshoot of a libertarian view of the press became known as social responsibility. It received impetus in the 1920s with the rise of radio, which was required by law to observe responsibilities to the public. Newspapers willingly adopted codes of ethics that aimed for fair treatment of news and advertising. Then, hit by economic downturns in large cities, some American newspapers sought regulation. The Newspaper Preservation Act of 1970 allowed them to combine advertising and printing in order to reduce costs. The justification for a "joint operating agreement" was to preserve independent editorial voices in cities. Newspapers, which had fought trusts during the muckraking heyday of the late nineteenth century, now had the ironic distinction of their own form of antitrust exemption. Meanwhile, the U.S. government prevented companies from owning television stations in the same city where they owned newspapers. Advertising largely was self-regulated, but the U.S. Federal Trade Commission was on guard for illegal advertising.

Competition. Newspapers evolved through a relatively brief period of ferocious competition with one another, especially in large U.S. cities. Circulation wars around the turn of the twentieth century actually drew blood, with a few of the so-called circulation sluggers using methods that served them well in their later careers in organized crime. A

NEWSPAPERS. Telegraph department at the *New York Herald,* 1905. (George Grantham Bain/Prints and Photographs Division, Library of Congress)

large city in Europe and America then had more than a dozen papers; their numbers declined gradually through merger or collapse. Late in the nineteenth century in New York City came the most spectacular examples of head-to-head competition. Sensationalism and promotional antics combined to create journalistic excess on a grand scale. Joseph Pulitzer's *World* and William Randolph Hearst's *Journal* earned a place in history texts for helping start the Spanish-American War. That brand of sensationalism, once called yellow journalism, lives on today in supermarket newspapers and "tabloid" television news. As papers declined in number to one or two in large cities, newspapers settled into their modern period of competing essentially with other media. They depend on a few wire services—Associated Press, Dow Jones, Reuters, Agence France-Presse—for national and international news; but they have no peer in local news gathering. They remain powerful but no longer dominant in their advertising markets.

The typical newspaper derives 60 to 70 percent of its revenues from advertising. (Perhaps two-fifths of each issue is news.) The rest of the money comes from sales in stores or on the street and from home-delivery subscriptions or mail. Roughly half of the advertising dollars can come from classified ads. A newspaper is in some ways a factory, running raw material (paper) into a machine (the press), adding value (information in the form of news), and

producing a finished product that slides into a truck after automatically being coded for its destination. In the 150 years of its modern existence, the newspaper has had a nearly unrivaled record of profitability. Its margins are two or three times the profits of the average factory. It competes well against other forms of news and entertainment, suffering downturns only when the business cycle shrinks companies' advertising budgets.

As an advertising medium, the newspaper is fortunate in that it has diverse sources of income: national, local, classified, and legal advertisements. Advertisers have the options of changing their audiences or their costs by buying space in the paper next to news, buying "freestanding" inserts on slick paper, or buying "zone" ads that go to geographic slices of the readership. Today they also can buy ads in combination with a newspaper's Web sites or as partners in other media.

Few industries face the variety of competition that confronts newspapers on all fronts. A shipper, for instance, must deal with the complexity of trucks, planes, and the postal system; but each day a newspaper faces rivals from a huge array of sophisticated industries: television, radio, magazines, information databases, billboards, books, direct mail, special-event marketing, public relations, wire services, movies, video games, entertainment rentals, and now the Internet. Each delivers a message of advertising, entertainment, or information to a changeable public. Studies suggest that branches of the media do not steal customers one-for-one from each other, but rather that they fragment audiences, causing each other to evolve. For instance, children have dropped part of their television viewing in favor of the Internet. They have gone back to reading, but in a new way. Television news viewers tend to be newspaper readers. Since the 1960s, surveyed Americans have said that they get their news more from television than from newspapers, and that television has more believability.

One overpowering message of newspaper research is that newspapers' chief competitor is time itself. It takes time to read a newspaper, and subscribers are spending as little as twenty minutes with the paper today. Worldwide, other vehicles of entertainment and information increasingly vie for a consumer's attention; many people are working longer hours and holding down more jobs; commuting times are growing. Advertisers worry that readers will not spend enough time with a paper to read the ads. Newspapers respond by tailoring their coverage to audiences and by using tactics that ensure faster reading.

Another response has been to grow by acquisition, a trend that has occurred worldwide but especially in the United States. Groups of publications were amassed first by companies bearing the great newspaper names: Hearst, Scripps, Gannett, Knight, Ridder, Thomson, Chandler, McCormick. As competition accelerated in the 1960s and 1970s, the groups floated stock to the public and grew into horizontal or vertical conglomerates. The "family newspaper" became a rarity, especially if it was a large one. Roughly 80 percent of the dailies became group-owned. Less visibly, chains of newspapers also grew in other categories: suburban, ethnic, business, legal, free distribution (so-called shoppers), and alternative.

The result of group ownership and large scale can be remoteness and standardization that eventually rob a product or service of its individuality; but newspapers by nature must serve a geographic locale or an affinity of interests, and the best papers have remained intensely local. As both good business and good strategy, most publishers have adhered to the notion of a newspaper as "a community talking to itself." Larger newspaper companies also have meant increased access to capital markets. Newspapers could tap the stock markets for major investments in buildings, equipment, and acquisition. Full-color printing, long possible but long too expensive, has become the norm.

One trait that has helped newspapers to compete over the years is their avid embrace of new technology. Part of that bias must come from the nature of newspapers: their business is to find and report the new. They thus were among the first industries to put every worker on a desktop computer. Reporters took the earliest laptop computers out on assignment. Presses and mailrooms were put under computer control. Sky satellites delivered information around the globe. Photographers eliminated the darkroom as soon as they could. At the dawn of Internet use, newspapers provided some of the best Web sites. Newspapers now have tended to cross-fertilize worldwide, and not just because some large companies own papers in two or more nations. Freelance designers, for instance, have redone newspapers all over the world. Many countries have developed national newspapers, such as *USA Today*, and the World Wide Web has allowed newspapers to overcome the limits of geographic distribution to start becoming global products.

[*See also* Advertising.]

BIBLIOGRAPHY

Bogart, Leo. *Press and Public: Who Reads What, When, Where and Why in American Newspapers*. Hillsdale, N.J., 1981.

Folkerts, Jean. *Media Voices: An Historical Perspective*. New York, 1992.

Hodgson, F. W. *Modern Newspaper Practice*. London, 1986.

Newspaper Association of America. < http://www.naa.org/>.

Newsom, D. Earl. *The Newspaper: Everything You Need to Know to Make It in the Newspaper Business*. Englewood Cliffs, N.J., 1981.

Udell, Jon G. *The Economics of the American Newspaper*. New York, 1978.

Ulloth, Dana, Peter Klinge, and Sandra Eells. *Mass Media: Past, Present, Future*. Saint Paul, 1983.

GEORGE HARMON

NEW YORK. On 11 September 2001, international terrorists attacked the United States, crashing two fuel-laden planes into the twin towers of New York City's World Trade Center, which collapsed several hours later. As pretentious as the title "World Trade Center" might once have sounded, in 2001 it was an accurate description of the global reach and importance of that corner of Manhattan, and foreign nationals from more than ninety countries were among those killed. Although the city's global dominance is a relatively recent phenomenon, it has long held a position of prominence in the Atlantic economy.

The city grew around an easily defended, strategic position initially established by the Dutch West India Company at the southern tip of Manhattan, a thirteen-mile long, two-mile wide island at the mouth of the Hudson River. The main river lies on the island's west side with branches of the Hudson—the Harlem River to the north and the East River—protecting two other sides. The sea lay to the south. Despite the protection afforded by these waters, the Dutch fort at New Amsterdam fell to the British in 1664, and the community was shortly renamed for the king's brother, the Duke of York.

By 1840, New York City had become the largest city in the United States, and it has remained so. It grew rapidly

TABLE 1. *NYC Population, 1790–2000*

	POPULATION BY BOROUGH					NEW YORK CITY (CONTEMPORARY BOUNDARIES)
	MANHATTAN	BRONX	BROOKLYN	QUEENS	STATEN ISLAND	
1790	33,131	1,781	4,495	6,159	3,835	33,131
1800	60,515	1,755	5,750	6,642	4,564	60,515
1810	96,373	2,267	8,303	7,444	5,347	96,373
1820	123,706	2,782	11,187	8,246	6,135	123,706
1830	202,589	3,023	20,535	9,049	7,082	202,589
1840	312,710	5,346	47,613	14,480	10,965	312,710
1850	515,547	8,032	138,882	18,593	15,061	515,547
1860	813,669	23,593	279,122	32,903	25,492	813,669
1870	942,292	37,393	419,921	45,468	33,029	942,292
1880	1,164,673	51,980	599,495	56,559	38,991	1,216,653
1890	1,441,216	88,908	838,547	87,050	51,693	1,530,124
1900	1,850,093	200,507	1,166,582	152,999	67,021	3,437,202
1910	2,331,542	430,980	1,634,351	284,041	85,969	4,766,883
1920	2,284,103	732,016	2,018,356	469,042	116,531	5,620,048
1930	1,867,312	1,265,258	2,560,401	1,079,129	158,346	6,930,446
1940	1,889,924	1,394,711	2,698,285	1,297,634	174,441	7,454,995
1950	1,960,101	1,451,277	2,738,175	1,550,849	191,555	7,891,957
1960	1,698,281	1,424,815	2,627,319	1,809,578	221,991	7,781,984
1970	1,539,233	1,471,701	2,602,012	1,986,473	295,443	7,894,862
1980	1,428,285	1,168,972	2,230,936	1,891,325	352,121	7,071,639
1990	1,487,536	1,203,789	2,300,664	1,951,598	378,977	7,322,564
2000	1,537,195	1,332,650	2,465,326	2,229,379	443,728	8,008,278

SOURCE: U.S. Bureau of the Census, *Census of Population* (various years).

during periods of mass immigration (e.g., the late 1840s and the late 1890s), when its population increased more than 6 percent per year. Ellis Island in New York's harbor served as the port of entry for 16 million immigrants between 1892 and 1924, many of whom went no further than New York City. New York's foreign-born population peaked at almost 41 percent in 1910. It reached its nadir in 1970 at just 18.2 percent.

Until 1874, the city was coterminous with Manhattan Island (see Table 1). In that year, it expanded onto the mainland, annexing the towns of Morrisania, West Farms, and Kingsbridge in the Bronx and setting in motion a process of consolidation that led to the five boroughs—the Bronx (1874), Brooklyn (at the time, 1898, the third largest city in the nation), Manhattan, Queens (1898) and Staten Island (1898)—that comprise today's city.

Despite the expansion of its physical boundaries through annexation, the city's population density increased until 1910. Nowhere was this more true than on Manhattan. In 1790, the population of Manhattan averaged 1,466 persons per square mile; a hundred years later, density was 63,770 per square mile. The peak of 103,166 per square mile was reached in 1910. However, even before densities reached these levels, the city was planning for its growth. In lower Manhattan, where earliest settlement occurred in what be-

came the Financial District, the Lower East Side, and Greenwich Village, development had been haphazard, characterized by winding streets of varying widths, irregularly shaped building lots, and variable street frontages. In response, in 1811, the city adopted what became known as of the "Commissioner's Plan," which provided for a rectangular grid of streets and property boundaries without regard to topography for the island from Fourteenth Street northward. There were to be twelve numbered avenues running north-south connected by 155 cross-streets in the (erroneous) expectation that most commerce and travel would take place crosstown between the two rivers (Spann, 1988).

Housing New York's growing population was a major challenge to its construction industry. The influx of poor immigrants, especially to lower Manhattan, led to the conversion of many structures into low-rent, cramped, often windowless, high-density housing known as rookeries. These proved so successful in housing the masses that they quickly became the model for the construction of inexpensive, multistory, utilitarian housing until the passage of Tenement Laws. Cramped, overcrowded conditions facilitated the spread of such infectious diseases as typhoid fever and cholera, leading to various public health regulations, particularly the Tenement Laws of 1867, 1879, and 1901, which set standards regarding ventilation, daylight,

NEW YORK. View of the skyline from the Hudson River, 1997. (© Bernard Boutrit, Woodfin Camp and Associates, New York)

and access to a privy (Jackson, 1976). Fresh water and sanitation needs began to be met in 1842, when abundant fresh water began to flow to the city via the Croton Aqueduct. This system served the city's needs for the rest of the century, although continued growth forced the city to look further afield to the Catskills to meet the demand for water (Weidner, 1974).

Single-family housing, catering to middle-class residents, continued to be built "uptown" in the 1840s and 1850s. The middle class lived in the relative comfort of brownstones (named for the color of the New Jersey sandstone that faced them) and, eventually, in luxury apartments, such as the Dakota built in 1884 (Lockwood, 1972). "Filtering" occurred as buildings formerly occupied by the middle and upper classes were converted to rental housing for the working class. Manhattan's relatively small area led to high land prices that put home ownership out of reach of the vast majority of workers and, indeed, much of the middle class.

High land values encouraged high-density vertical housing; but until the perfection of the passenger elevator and new construction methods (e.g., steel framing), heights were limited. The seven and one-half-story Equitable Building, constructed between 1868 and 1870, was the first to incorporate the elevator as part of its design; by 1875, there were several ten-story buildings in the city. Strictly speaking, none of these were skyscrapers, a term that applies only to buildings with a full skeleton frame carry-

ing the walls and the floors. The first skyscraper was the Tower Building built in 1888–1889 (Jackson, 1995, 1073–1075). With the proliferation of skyscrapers, the city adopted new zoning laws in 1916 that required the upper floors on tall buildings be "stepped back" above a certain height; buildings of unlimited height were allowed on just 25 percent of the lot. It was during this regime that many of the more famous skyscrapers were built—the Chrysler Building (1930) and the Empire State Building (1931), for example (Makielski, 1966).

While tenements and skyscrapers permitted high density housing close to the central business district, transportation improvements made it increasingly economical for people to live at greater distances. Horse-drawn omnibuses provided the first mass transit, but the sad state of the city's streets meant that these were relatively inefficient people carriers. Street railroads proved more successful. The first, the New York & Harlem Railroad, opened in 1832 and others followed in the 1850s (Jackson, 1995, 1127–1128). Each, however, suffered from the same disadvantages: they competed with private carriages and pedestrians for space on the city's streets, and they created a sanitation problem as horses still drew them. One solution to the former problem was the construction of elevated track, the first opened in 1868; another was the subway, which opened in 1904.

The island of Manhattan was critically dependent upon chartered ferry companies until bridges were built to the mainland. As ferry traffic grew, the more important crossing points increasingly operated on fixed schedules. In the 1850s, for example, the Union Ferry Company made 1,250 crossings a day to Brooklyn for a standard fare of two cents. By 1860, passenger traffic across the East River averaged about one hundred thousand persons per working day. A decade later, that figure had doubled. The opening of the Brooklyn Bridge in 1883 dealt a severe blow to the commuter ferry system, and soon thereafter New York was also connected with the Bronx and Queens (Jackson, 1995, pp. 397–401).

Commerce has played a key role in New York's development from the start. The site was established as a trading port for transatlantic trade and as an entry to the American hinterland via the Hudson River. It was here that Robert Fulton ushered in the era of steam navigation in 1807. The commercial importance of New York was vastly enhanced by the opening of the Erie Canal in 1825, which brought the American Midwest into its commercial orbit. By the mid-nineteenth century, this single avenue of commerce carried more cargo than all the nation's railroads and the Mississippi and Ohio River systems.

While New York never achieved preeminence as a manufacturing center (except in the needle trades) despite its national and international trade connections and its abundant labor, it quickly achieved national, then international, prominence as a center for finance. In 1784, Alexander Hamilton penned the charter for the first bank in the city—the Bank of New York (one of the country's largest bank holding companies today). This link to the nation's founding fathers (plus New York's role as national capital between 1785 and 1790) led to the bank's successful underwriting of the first loan to the federal government in 1789. To Hamilton, this was a critical step in establishing the "full faith and credit of the United States." New York's role as a trading center for the nation and the Atlantic economy ensured that its banks had strong international ties. With the demise of the First and Second Banks of the United States, New York City's leading banks also became the nation's largest commercial banks (Klebaner, 1990).

In 1792, twenty-four brokers in the Wall Street area subscribed to an agreement establishing a formal securities market that became the New York Stock Exchange (NYSE). While this market is now the world's largest market for industrial equities, the NYSE was slow to develop. Instead, it concentrated on bonds (corporate and governmental) until the 1890s, leaving much of the equity trading that dominates today's finance to street traders and to other markets, notably the Boston Stock Exchange (Sobel, 1975). The exchange celebrated its first million-plus-share trading day in 1886. It reached the 100-million-plus level in 1982, and the billion-plus level in 1997.

New York's already dominant position in domestic banking and finance was solidified by the establishment of the Federal Reserve System (referred to as the FED) in 1913. Although nominally based in Washington, D.C., the FED's most important actions—the buying and selling of U.S. government securities to influence domestic interest rates, fund the national government, and affect the exchange rate—are conducted through the Federal Reserve Bank of New York, which, along with the NYSE, give the city global financial importance. It also serves as the repository for much of the world's gold reserves.

As America replaced Great Britain as the leading military power, center of international finance, and home of the dominant culture, so, too, New York replaced London as *the* cosmopolitan metropolis, a position it still occupies.

BIBLIOGRAPHY

Jackson, Anthony. *A Place Called Home: A History of Low-Cost Housing in Manhattan*. Cambridge, Mass., 1976.

Jackson, Kenneth T., ed. *The Encyclopedia of New York City*. New Haven, 1995. This is the single-best source and reference to most everything about New York.

Klebaner, Benjamin Joseph. *American Commercial Banking: A History*. Boston, 1990.

Lockwood, Charles. *Bricks and Brownstones: The New York Row House, 1783–1929: An Architectural and Social History*. New York, 1972.

Makielski, S. J. *The Politics of Zoning: The New York Experience*. New York, 1966.

Sobel, Robert. *N.Y.S.E.: A History of the New York Stock Exchange, 1935–1975*. New York, 1975.

Spann, Edward K. "The Greatest Grid: The New York Plan of 1811." In *Two Centuries of American Planning*, edited by D. Schaffer, pp. 11–39. Baltimore, 1988.

Weidner, Charles H. *Water for a City: A History of New York City's Problem from the Beginning to the Delaware River System*. New Brunswick, N.J., 1974.

JEREMY ATACK

NEW ZEALAND. A small group of South Pacific islands, New Zealand became integrated into the international economy in the nineteenth century. Its cultural, political, and social institutions are much indebted to its inheritance from the native Polynesian inhabitants, known as Maori. It also owes much to what was brought by the predominantly British immigrants, and much else was developed within New Zealand by local activity shaped by a continuing inflow of ideas and people from abroad. The economy, however, stems very little from the Maori heritage; rather, Maori had to adapt themselves to participate in an economy that owed the most to imported ideas and integration with economic activity abroad.

Nineteenth Century. The modern New Zealand economy was developed as local resources were contributed to a nineteenth-century economy centered on Europe and North America. Some natural resources such as whale oil and seal skins were valuable as soon as they were collected and transported internationally, others required only a little additional domestic activity, and for a while gold mining was a major component of the New Zealand economy. However, the principal resource of New Zealand was its combination of land and climate, which provided a long grass-growing season and made it possible to raise farm animals cheaply. Wool grown in New Zealand could compete successfully in the North Atlantic economy while providing incomes in New Zealand that were high in relation to those that could be earned elsewhere. By the end of the nineteenth century, wool exports were joined by refrigerated products, especially butter and cheese and frozen lamb. These exports financed a wide range of imports so that New Zealanders had access to much the same pattern of consumption as was available in the industrialized countries of Europe and North America, and in other similar economies such as Australia.

New Zealand never had a subsistence agricultural sector that was gradually transformed through the influence of a more productive industrial sector, as was the case in much of Europe. Still, it very quickly developed a complex economy. The relatively high incomes that could be earned in New Zealand attracted a continuing inflow of immigrants and induced a high rate of natural population increase. Most people did not work directly on farms but were employed in urban centers. Agriculture required many services and inputs and, especially with the development of refrigerated products, some processing before products were exported. Some imports could be transported more cheaply in bulk or as components, with the final packaging or assembly done in local industries or services. New Zealand towns, though small from an international perspective, supported their own economic activity, with both production and consumption entirely within New Zealand. "Modernization" was significantly different from the kind of "industrialization" with which it was often regarded as synonymous elsewhere.

New Zealand attracted not only migrants but also investment from abroad. The available returns gradually reached an equilibrium with international experience, and some analysts write about a "long depression" in the late nineteenth century. There were disequilibria in local labor markets and distributional issues as interest rates fell less than output prices, but deceleration of growth is a better description than depression. Refrigeration initiated a new acceleration.

Because Britain did not restrict imports and had a strong demand for the goods that New Zealanders could produce most efficiently, it was overwhelmingly important among New Zealand's export markets. Because the settlers mostly had British ancestry and because the continuing inflow of newspapers and magazines was mostly from Britain, British goods largely satisfied consumption demand in New Zealand. This trade was also convenient for firms that could organize both exporting and importing. The political relationship between Britain and New Zealand was of secondary importance as New Zealand had very early gained de facto control of its own trade relations; and although New Zealand governments provided some tariff preferences for British goods, they were not very important either.

New Zealand governments did play an important economic role in the nineteenth century. Although there was little interest anywhere in the idea of real income per capita, New Zealanders were aware that their standards of living were better than those of Britain; and the prevailing implicit economic objective was to maintain that position while building a larger population. "Development" meant extensive growth subject to the constraint that average real income should be maintained, but contemporary discussion was much more in terms of concrete examples of new railways, new industries, or newly farmed land. Whenever the government apparatus could promote development in this sense, there was little resistance to its use. So the government was directly responsible for building and operating railways, and when gaps in the institutions available were not otherwise filled, as with insurance companies and some forms of financial institutions, a government agency was created. Governments depended heavily on customs duties for their revenue and, in designing tariffs, gave preference to activities that were established in New Zealand, but, as far as possible, not at the expense of exporters.

Twentieth Century. In the 1930s, in New Zealand as elsewhere, the government's economic responsibilities increased. Unemployment increased in the 1920s, as more and more work was organized as continuous employment rather than periodic contracts; but in the 1930s, the unemployment rose to unprecedented levels. The problems were international in scope, and were transmitted to New Zealand through lower export prices. Both the New Zealand government and the private sector found it very hard to respond other than by waiting for the problems to be solved overseas although there were some determined efforts at developing local initiative. Contrary to the myth that New Zealanders came together in the face of a malevolent international economy, the experience of the 1930s was actually one of considerable social tension. Recollections of the impact of unemployment played a key role in thinking about the economy for many years thereafter. Furthermore, the traditional acceptance of a wide field for state activity was reinforced by changed international thinking, which held that governments should be responsible not only for the public sector but for ensuring that the economy as a whole was as productive as possible.

One particular event joined with this historical background to shape the economy that emerged in the years after World War II. As incomes in New Zealand recovered from Depression levels, the country's demand for imports rose; and, in December 1938, faced with a balance-of-payments crisis, the first Labour Government, which had been elected to office in reaction to the Depression, introduced import and exchange controls. Unwilling to restrain imports by deliberately cutting incomes because a recurrence of unemployment was unacceptable, the government attempted instead to protect overseas reserves by licensing commodity imports and instituting exchange controls for other items involving overseas payments.

Import and exchange controls varied in severity from time to time and gradually declined in importance before their abolition in 1984, having survived largely because of the protection they afforded particular industries. Although they were introduced mainly because of the balance-of-payments crisis, their protective implications were quickly recognized. Politicians defended them in terms of their ability to promote industrial growth, even if they knew that New Zealand's real income was reduced if local industry grew only because cheaper imports were excluded. The profits and the jobs of many firms came to depend on the shelter afforded by import controls, and fear that they might be jeopardized made it politically difficult to use controls for their original purpose, to contain foreign exchange payments within the limit of export earnings.

In retrospect, the 1938 measures can be seen as a crucial component of the post-Depression policy of "insulating" the New Zealand economy from overseas influences. The government soon would have had many more direct economic responsibilities in any case since all countries use controls in wartime. What was unusual in New Zealand is that controls were associated with deliberate government policy. They became part of the contemporaneous extension of the welfare state rather than the result of a wartime emergency.

At the end of World War II, many controls were dismantled, but not import and exchange controls. Throughout the 1950s and 1960s, the basic structure of the economy depended on them, although precisely how was far from clear at the time. Import controls worked not through limiting the total value of imports but through ensuring that imports were mostly materials and equipment used in New Zealand activity. Businesses in New Zealand knew that they would be protected from competing final goods while generally being able to acquire needed inputs. Domestic investment was thereby enhanced since entrepreneurs could be confident about their markets; and even if they had misjudged the level of demand, errors would not be greatly penalized since population and income growth would before long enable the investment to be utilized. High levels of private investment ensured that demand for labor would be high, and New Zealand maintained a remarkably low level of unemployment. High levels of employment and aggregate demand meant that there was always a tendency for the demand for imports to run ahead of what could be financed from export receipts. The economy experienced a foreign-exchange constraint.

The low level of unemployment was a major benefit of this structure. Not only was aggregate employment high, but a wide variety of jobs could be provided to suit the aptitudes and interests of individual New Zealanders. The value of this advantage was realized only when it was lost in more recent years. The cost of the structure was that resources in New Zealand were not directed toward their most valuable use, and incomes were lower on average than they could have been. In relation to other countries, New Zealand got a lower return from its high level of investment, and consumer goods available overseas were excluded from New Zealand or available only to customers who were somehow able to get themselves into a preferential position—especially in the case of motor vehicles.

The structure gave a special role to exports. However, as the New Zealand economy grew at a rate that was quite high in relation to earlier periods of history, it was soon apparent that export growth was not going to facilitate growth at a rate equal to what was being achieved by other countries. At the same time, growth of per capita real incomes was a much more prominent policy objective than it had been in earlier years. Although New Zealand's indigenous idea of "development" in terms of expansion at a constant average income did not die overnight, it gradually became less important than growth of average incomes.

The British market for New Zealand's exports did not offer the scope for such faster growth. Britain was growing less rapidly than many other countries; it was becoming concerned about its own farmers and wanted to protect their domestic market; and, from the late 1950s onward, there was the prospect that Britain would eventually join the European Economic Community and accede to its protectionist regime for agriculture. So the objective for New Zealand became diversification—diversification of markets for traditional exports and diversification of the range of goods exported. This approach enjoyed considerable success, but its limitations were exposed when, in the 1970s, Middle East oil producers succeeding in implementing and sustaining a very sharp increase in the price of oil. In effect, a significant slice of world income was redistributed away from oil importers to oil producers, and New Zealand's export markets, although markedly more various than they had once been, were overwhelmingly oil importers. Diversification proved to be no answer when all markets contracted together.

By 1984, it was clear that existing policies were leading New Zealand into increased overseas debt while not removing its disparity of incomes compared with other countries. The mechanisms that had produced full employment in the 1950s and 1960s had been lost; the fundamental problems remained.

New Zealand then embarked on a major change of direction toward an economy characterized by an international orientation. "The New Zealand experiment" attracted much international attention, both positive and critical, but it was essentially a response to local circumstances. At the time of the Closer Economic Relations Agreement with Australia in the early 1980s, the focus was turned from industry as a social instrument for employment promotion to economic growth through servicing the consumer demand that most valued New Zealand resources. That demand increasingly came from the Asia-Pacific region although Europe, into which Britain had been submerged, remained a significant market.

BIBLIOGRAPHY

Bassett, Michael. *The State in New Zealand, 1840–1984.* Auckland, 1998.

Condliffe, John B. *New Zealand in the Making.* 2d ed. London, 1959.

Condliffe, John B. *The Welfare State in New Zealand.* London, 1959.

Easton, Brian. *In Stormy Seas: The Postwar New Zealand Economy.* Dunedin, 1997.

Gould, John D. *The Muldoon Years.* Auckland, 1985.

Gould, John D. *The Rake's Progress? The New Zealand Economy since 1945.* Auckland, 1982.

Hawke, Gary R. *The Making of New Zealand. An Economic History.* Cambridge, 1985.

Lloyd Prichard, Muriel F. *An Economic History of New Zealand to 1939.* Auckland and London, 1970.

Silverstone, Brian, Alan Bollard, and Ralph Lattimore, eds. *A Study of Economic Reform: The Case of New Zealand.* Amsterdam, 1996.

Sutch, William B. *Colony or Nation?* Sydney, 1966.

GARY R. HAWKE

NICARAGUA. *See* Central American Countries.

NIGERIA. Before 1860, the states of the region, which became modern Nigeria, traded with various European powers in the south along the Atlantic coast, while states in the north were equally active in the caravan trade across the Sahara to North Africa and beyond. Precolonial industries included ironworks, leather, and cloth, which were traded within West Africa and to the north. After the transatlantic slave trade ended, agricultural products became the prime trading good with Europe.

Agricultural Economy. Since precolonial times, agriculture has been the centerpiece of the Nigerian economy. Until the early 1970s, about 70 percent of Nigeria's labor force was employed in the agricultural sector. Involvement in the agricultural sector, however, differed from place to place. In the rural communities, virtually everyone was, and still is, engaged in agriculture, while the percentage of the people involved in agriculture was low in the cities, especially in places like Lagos and Abuja, where the bulk of the population engaged in trade, manufacturing, administration, and educational activities. Nigeria is a vast territory of cultivable land spanning the forest vegetation of the south to the open savannah and semiarid region of the north, and this allowed for the cultivation of a vast array of crops for local consumption as well as for export. Several crops were also produced both for local and foreign markets, such as palm oil, peanuts, cotton, rubber, and cocoa. According to Olufemi Ekundare (1973) in 1968 the average acreage per person under cultivation was 1.02 (0.4 hectare) for eastern Nigeria, 4.28 (1.7 hectares) for northern Nigeria, 2.43 (0.97 hectare) for western Nigeria, 2.07 (0.8 hectare) for the midwest, and 2.45 (0.98 hectare) for the whole country. Each region was noted for the production of specific crops—peanuts and cotton in the north, cocoa and kola nut in the west, rubber in the midwest and palm products in the east. Since these products, especially those produced in the west, east, and mid-west, fetched more revenue than those from northern Nigeria, people in these regions largely neglected food production. Hence, people in northern Nigeria have become renowned as food producers, especially in the production of yams and grains.

Between 1860 and 1890, Nigeria's foreign trade fluctuated widely due to conflict, poorly developed transport and communication lines, the lack of a stable and unified currency, and economic problems in Europe. Although Nigerian traders were responsible for moving goods from the interior to the coast, Nigeria's foreign trade remained firmly under the control of European merchants who could obtain the necessary capital to finance imports and exports. In the latter part of the nineteenth century, the most important agricultural products exported to Europe were palm products. Palm oil was superior to other vegetable fats and became important in the European production of soap and candles and in manufacturing, while palm kernels were viewed as superior cattle feed.

In the late nineteenth century, palm products made up about 75 percent of all Nigerian exports, with Germany taking more than 70 percent of the annual exports between 1862–1899. In the same period, Great Britain was the main consumer of Nigerian palm oil. Cotton exports fluctuated and were dependent on domestic demand, and the disparity in price between cotton and other products influenced the farmer's choice in growing it. In the last few decades of the nineteenth century, exports of peanuts and rubber increased while exports of cocoa, which was not native to Nigeria but was deliberately introduced as a cash crop, also skyrocketed after 1886. Other exports included beninseed, hides, maize, and mahogany. During this time, the main imports into Nigeria were cotton goods from Great Britain, which constituted between 35–50 percent of yearly imports; luxury goods such as looking glasses, scissors, and jewelry; and substitutes for local products such as alcohol, salt, kerosene, medicine, boats, canoes, guns, and gunpowder.

Twentieth Century. The first three decades of the twentieth century saw the creation of the foundation of the colonial economic system. During this period, measures such as direct taxation and wage employment were introduced to help shift the economy that was "traditionally based" to one that better served colonial needs. It is from this period that some observers trace the roots of rural neglect. Owing to the possibility of garnering higher profits, emphasis was placed on the growth and export of cash crops and the importation of manufactured goods. According to Olasiji Oshin, rural underdevelopment was caused by the British decision to build administrative and commercial centers at strategic points along trade routes, which, according to his argument, led to urban overdevelopment and rural underdevelopment. For example, following the discovery of coal at Udi in the 1915, Port Harcourt and Enugu emerged as colonial towns, with Port Harcourt as the port through which to export the coal while Enugu developed around the colonial government station and the railway junction. Starting at the turn of the century, mining grew in importance to the Nigerian economy: tin in Bauchi, gold deposits in various parts of northern Nigeria in the 1910s and 1920s, and coal in Igboland in 1915.

One of the biggest changes in the Nigerian economy in the mid-twentieth century was the rapid increase in manufacturing. The country deliberately shifted from cash crops toward industrialization via import substitution. Hence, the manufacturing sector became dominated by multinational firms that controled more than 60 percent of the nation's industrial output. Between 1950 and 1960, the total value of manufacturing production increased by 398 percent. The three largest manufacturing areas were rubber processing, bakeries, and textiles, while oil milling, margarine, beer and soft drinks, tobacco, tanning, saw milling, and cement were also important. Owing to its heavy dependence on imported raw materials, the manufacturing sector has often been affected by the vagaries of the Nigerian international trade. For example, the economic crisis that started in the 1980s caused many companies to collapse as a result of the inability to raise enough capital to source imported materials and machineries. This resulted in industrial closures, job layoffs, underutilization of capacity, and an increased pace of divestment of foreign firms from the country. Similarly, some of the measures adopted toward addressing the crises were disastrous for the manufacturing sector. Trade liberalization opened the country's borders for imported goods, thereby encouraging smuggling, dumping, and product adulteration. This left industries unprotected from foreign competition.

From the mid-1960s to the mid-1980s, the agricultural industry declined as more emphasis was placed on the petroleum industry. Nigeria went from basic self-sufficiency in food production to being heavily dependent on food imports. This process was aided by urbanization, underinvestment in agriculture, and a growing preference on the part of the populace for imported food goods. Production of subsistence food crops and cash crops increased in the late 1980s, which was due in part to the abolishment of the federal marketing boards and the devalued naira. This in turn contributed to higher producer prices and, therefore higher output.

In the last two decades of the twentieth century, Nigeria's most important cash crop was cocoa, but its share of the international cocoa market was reduced due to aging and sick trees, low producer prices, smuggling, and labor shortages. Since 1990, Nigeria has been Africa's largest rubber producer, but production decreased in the late 1990s due to a lack of a decent rubber tree replanting program. Since the mid-1980s corporate investment in agriculture has centered on palm oil and cotton. In 1971, Nigeria was overtaken by Malaysia as the world's top exporter of palm products and began importing palm oil to meet its domestic needs. Output of palm produce had suffered because of labor shortages, inefficient harvesting methods, and a lack of investments. Production increased in the mid-1980s owing to a massive replanting effort in eastern Rivers state and a dramatic reduction of imported palm products. At the same time, trade liberalization and a change in the exchange rate policy made it more profitable to export palm products and therefore encouraged increased production. Production of raw cotton increased from 189,000 tons (170,100 metric tons) in 1989 to 276,000 tons (248,400 metric tons) in 1990, which was due in large part to government and private investment. Local production increased because of government incentives given to local companies and the imposition of higher tariffs on imported cotton. Further, the government was willing, as shown by its buying of 400,000 bales of excess cotton in 1990, to help cotton farmers.

In the last couple of decades of the twentieth century, other cash crops included peanuts, soybeans, wheat, sugar cane, cashew nuts, karate nuts, carrots, ginger, tobacco leaves, green coffee, beef, veal, goat meat, fish, and timber. Subsistence crops that are largely traded outside of the cash economy include sorghum, maize, yams, cassava, rice, and millet.

The discovery of oil in the Niger River Delta region had a huge impact on the Nigerian economy. Nigeria began exporting oil in 1958, and by the 1970s, petroleum

NIGERIA. Agricultural land, 1971. (Eliot Elisofon/Eliot Elisofon Photographic Archives/National Museum of African Art, Smithsonian Institution, Washington, D.C.)

production had replaced agriculture as the dominant sector of the economy. In 1986, the petroleum industry's share of the gross domestic product (GDP) was 18 percent and made up 97 percent of all exports and 70 percent of government revenues. Nigeria uses petroleum sales to meet its debt payments and to pay for imports. Oil is such an important resource that the ambition to control oil resources has been mentioned as one of the underlying reasons for the Biafra secessionist bid of the late 1960s. Indeed, since the 1970s, oil has become central to the country. Nigeria is a leading member of the Organization of Petroleum Exporting Countries (OPEC) and Africa's largest petroleum-producing state. The United States buys, on average, approximately half of Nigeria's yearly petroleum exports. Spain, Germany, France, Portugal, and Great Britain are also major importers of Nigerian petroleum. In 1970, Nigeria produced 54.2 million metric tons (59.6 million tons) of oil, but this increased to 104.4 million metric tons (114.8 million short tons) in 1980 and to 915.8 million metric tons (1 billion short tons) in 1992. Earnings from the sale of oil rose from $8.5 billion to $10.6 billion in 1989 and 1990. This figure, however, constantly fluctuates, depending on OPEC decisions and the political situation in the Middle East. For example, oil exports fell to 74.1 million metric tons (81.5 million short tons) in 1985, while earnings also dropped to about $9.7 million in 1996. Nevertheless, income from oil enabled the government to embark on expanded public expenditures in industrialization, transport, social welfare, and other forms of infrastructural development.

The pattern of Nigerian economic changes has influenced several sectors of the society, such as the family, the legal system, and government. For instance, polygamous marriages are prevalent in areas where agriculture was or is the most important economic system. One main explanation for this is that marriage to several women leads to the production of multiple children who provide "free" agricultural labor. In the nonagricultural sectors, monogamy is the order of the day. With the depressed economy, especially with the developments arising out of the Structural Adjustment Program, the family system has gone through some modifications. For example, unlike in previous eras, Nigerians, especially young males, now delay marriage by two to three years. Thus, since 1986, there has been a pool of eligible bachelors and single women who could not marry because of the high cost of marriage and the higher cost of maintaining a home. Similarly, family planning measures have gained more popularity as families adjust to harsher economic circumstances.

Role of Government. Until 1980, the economic boom enabled the government to dabble into commercial investments; economic decline, on the other hand, has meant a regime of divestment. Thus, the government has set up several bodies and parastatals to address the privatization of many investments. In 1972, the government, through the Nigerianization/Indigenization plan, embarked on a policy that would reduce the role of expatriate firms in the economy. Thus, expatriate holdings in industries such as breweries, textiles, hotels, rubber, and plastic were reduced to between 40 and 60 percent. The remaining percentages were sold to Nigerians, and if Nigerians lacked the resources, the government stepped in as primary investor.

Government's involvement in the economy has a dual implication in the system of governance. While it quickened the pace of economic development and thereby created jobs for thousands of people, it also became an avenue for corruption in public places. One of the popular slogans is "Government Job Is Nobody's Job." Hence, officials appointed to oversee public enterprises see this as an avenue to quick wealth. Since independence, cases of corruption and looting of the treasuries of public enterprises are frequently reported. Indeed, since the 1980s accounting offices of some parastatals have been set ablaze to cover up frauds. Even with privatization, government officials have colluded with entrepreneurs to undervalue certain establishments after having received payments from the latter. On the other hand, some of the entrepreneurs were actually fronts for public officers. Thus, with the avenue to enrich themselves, many people have taken to politics as it guaranteed their access to strategic positions in the commanding sectors of the economy.

Nigeria's economy has affected the city-countryside structure. Since better economic activities revolve around the cities, Nigerians have often drifted to them. Some of these cities, such as Sokoto, Kano, Zaria, and Benin, have played important roles in commerce and industries like textiles, dairy, leatherwork, and bronze casting. In western Nigeria, virtually all the modern cities were creations of the slavery, agricultural, and colonial economies of the past two centuries. For example, Ibadan, Ogbomoso, Abeokuta, and Lagos received a substantial number of slaves for distribution to other communities and to the Atlantic trade. The importance of Lagos as a slaving port in the nineteenth century attracted European traders, missionaries, and others settlers, and by 1861 it had emerged as Nigeria's most important port town. This continued with the immigration of others from the Americas, Europe, and the Nigerian interior as traders and workers. To boost this position, Lagos was provided with a seaport, airport, and railway facilities, and it also became the meeting point of many roads radiating from other Nigerian towns. In eastern Nigeria, major cities include Enugu, Aba, Onitsha, and Port Harcourt.

Because of inadequate records, it is relatively difficult to assess the pattern of demographic changes. Hence, international organizations have resorted to projections, which are used here. Nigerian censuses in 1963 and 1991 put the population at 55.5 million and 88.5 million, respectively.

The latter figure was far short of the UN projections, which had put the population 99 million in 1991. Another major difference was that the UN estimated Nigeria to have more women than men, but the 1991 census put the gender component at 44.5 million males and 43.9 million females. An increasing part of this population has moved into the cities in search of employment, education, and other services. Hence, the percentage of urban population has increased from 30.26 million in 1984 to 38.44 million in 1994. Urban migration has led to rapid annual population growth of around 5.7 percent from 1970 through 2000. These figures contrast with the national population growth of between 2–3 percent and rural growth of around 1.8 percent during the same period.

BIBLIOGRAPHY

Africa South of the Sahara, 1990–2000. London, n.d.

Aigbokhan, Ben E. *Poverty, Growth, and Inequality in Nigeria: A Case Study.* Nairobi, Kenya, 2000.

Anunobi, Fredoline O. *The Implications of Conditionality: The International Monetary Fund and Africa.* Lanham, Md., 1992.

Ekundare, Olufemi R. *Economic History of Nigeria, 1860–1960.* London, 1973.

Falola, Toyin. *The History of Nigeria.* Westport, Conn., 1999.

Falola, Toyin, and Paul E. Lovejoy, eds. *Pawnship in Africa: Debt Bondage in Historical Perspective.* Boulder, 1994.

Kayode, M. O., and Ibi Ajayi, eds. *Nigerian Economy under the Military: Proceedings of the 1980 Annual Conference of the Nigerian Economic Society.* Kano, Nigeria, 1980.

Kayode, M. O., and Y. Bala Usman, eds. *Proceedings of the National Conference on Nigeria since Independence: The Economic and Social Development of Nigeria.* Zaria, Ethiopia, 1983.

Lovejoy, Paul E. *Transformations in Slavery: A History of Slavery in Africa.* Cambridge, 2000.

Olukoshi, Adebayo. *Economic Crisis, Structural Adjustment, and the Coping Strategies of Manufacturers in Kano, Nigeria.* Geneva, 1996.

Teriba, O., and M. O. Kayode. *Industrial Development in Nigeria: Patterns, Problems, and Prospects.* Ibadan, Nigeria, 1977.

United Nations African Statistical Yearbook, 1990–1996.

Uwadibie, Nwafejoku O. *Decentralization and Economic Development Nigeria: Agricultural Policies and Implementation.* Lanham, 2000.

OLATUNJI OJO AND JENNIFER LOFKRANTZ

NILE. The watershed of the river Nile defines a very ancient zone of economic interaction in the northeastern quarter of the continent of Africa. One branch of the great river, the White Nile, has its origins in the highlands of the lake country of East Africa; a second, the Blue Nile, arises on the Ethiopian plateau. From the confluence of the Blue and White Niles the river flows northward toward the Mediterranean through increasingly harsh desert conditions, and about a hundred miles from the sea branches into a broad delta.

In early times the White Nile contributed a steady flow and the Blue a seasonal spate that annually overflowed the adjacent riparian flood plains below the confluence. This inundation facilitated the early flowering of an ancient agriculture-based high civilization along the banks of the Egyptian Nile. The introduction of the animal-driven waterwheel during the last half of the first millennium before the common era stimulated the elaboration of more substantial cultures south of Egypt in the northern Sudan, where the kingdoms of Meroë and Nubia flourished through late antiquity and the Middle Ages. The numerous cultures that existed above the confluence, and along the lesser eastern and western tributaries of the Nile, also availed themselves of the resources provided by the great river; in no case, however, was their dependence upon the Nile as great as that of the Egyptians and the northern Sudanese.

Over the course of five millennia the Egyptians have steadily refined technologies through which the resources of the Nile may be exploited and made more reliable. This process accelerated greatly during the nineteenth and twentieth centuries with the rapid modernization of Egypt, including both the introduction of more effective techniques of water management and vastly increased demand with the industrialization of agriculture and population growth. Egypt's strategic vision has perforce risen to embrace all the lands of the vast Nile basin. For the first half of the twentieth century not only Egypt but also much of the rest of the Nile watershed answered to British colonial conceptions of correct Nile waters allocation. During the second half of the century, however, the independent African heirs to erstwhile European empires did not find it easy to reach an understanding concerning the sharing of a precious and limited resource. The construction of the Aswan high dam (1960–1970) assured a more reliable supply of water to Egypt, free of yearly natural fluctuations, while the development of large irrigated agricultural schemes in the central Sudan foreclosed on additional potential resources.

Perhaps the last major untapped supply of Nile water is the quantity lost to evaporation in the vast southern Sudanese swamps of the *sadd*. Attempts to make this water available to users downstream by channeling the course of the White Nile around the swamps through a proposed Jonglei Canal thus far have failed because of the opposition of southern Sudanese communities. Other upstream lands, notably Ethiopia and Uganda, also are reluctant to mortgage their future development to the immediate needs of the northern Sudan and Egypt.

BIBLIOGRAPHY

Adams, William Y. *Nubia: Corridor to Africa*. Princeton, 1977.

Collins, Robert O. *The Waters of the Nile*. Oxford, 1990.

Collins, Robert O. *The Nile*. New Haven, 2000.

Egyptian Ministry of Public Works. *Water Master Plan*. Cairo, 1981.

Trigger, B. G., B. J. Kemp, D. O'Connor, and A. B. Lloyd. *Ancient Egypt: A Social History*. New York, 1983.

JAY SPAULDING

NOBEL, ALFRED (1833–1896), Swedish inventor, donor of the Nobel Prizes.

Since the Middle Ages, black powder had been the only explosive available, for either military or civilian purposes, until, in the early 1860s, Alfred Nobel found a way to use nitroglycerine as a blasting agent. He invented a detonator cap for initiating a controlled explosion of nitroglycerine, which made it possible to market that very powerful explosive. This invention has been called the greatest discovery ever made in both the principle and practice of explosives, on which the entire modern practice of blasting has been built (Miles, 1955). Nobel's second important invention, dynamite, patented in many countries in 1867, facilitated the transport and handling of nitroglycerine. An entirely new industry grew up, based on Nobel's patents and with Nobel as initiator. Within ten years, sixteen explosives manufacturing factories had been founded in fourteen countries with Nobel as co-owner. During the following hundred years, dynamite was the dominant blasting agent throughout the world: in the construction of railroads, tunnels, canals, and harbors and in mining.

Nobel was born in Stockholm. After spending his poverty-stricken early years there, he lived in Saint Petersburg, Russia, from 1842 to 1863. He obtained an excellent private education in Russia and later began working in his father's engineering firm. He also wrote poems, drama, and two novels.

When Nobel started experimenting with nitroglycerine, he moved back to Sweden. In 1864, he obtained patents in several countries on his process for industrial manufacturing of blasting oil (nitroglycerine) and on his cap. The first four explosives companies—in Sweden (1864), Norway and Germany (1865), and the United States (1866)—produced blasting oil. Several accidental explosions occurred; Nobel's youngest brother was killed in one such explosion, and Nobel—who, in 1865, had moved to Germany—continued his experiments, hoping to make the new explosive safer. Thus he invented dynamite.

Fully aware of the great potential of his new invention, Nobel packed a suitcase with dynamite and went on a demonstration tour to France and Britain. In France, he soon found a partner, Paul Barbe, who arranged the financing of dynamite companies in France, Switzerland, Italy, and Spain, Nobel receiving half of their shares for his patents. In 1871, after years of negotiation, the British Dynamite Company was founded by Nobel and some Scottish financiers. Nobel received three-eighths of the company's shares for his patents and bought another eighth. Demand for dynamite soared. The German firm built four new factories, two of them in Austria-Hungary. After just five years, the British Dynamite Company increased its share capital tenfold and changed its name to Nobel's Explosives, a sign of Nobel's prominence.

In 1873, Nobel moved to Paris, where he built a laboratory and, for the first time, employed a research assistant. Nobel's strenuous research resulted in a new explosive, blasting gelatin. Stronger and more versatile than dynamite, it could be used underwater. The patents he obtained in between 1875 and 1876 were transferred to his dynamite companies against royalties on sales.

Nobel was the largest shareholder in all the dynamite companies. He acted as their product developer and traveled incessantly to all the factories to introduce new processes and oversee security, but he seldom took part in their commercial decisions. The Nobel companies were separate entities, and keen competition arose among them, especially between the British and German companies regarding exports to the large markets in Australia and South Africa. In the mid-1880s, Nobel took the initiative in negotiating a merger of the companies. Two holding companies—supposedly the first of their kind in the world—were founded, Nobel-Dynamite Trust Company in 1886 by the British and German explosives manufacturers and La Société Centrale de Dynamite in 1887 by the French, Italian, Swiss, and Spanish Nobel companies. Their head offices, in London and Paris, respectively, coordinated production, sales, investments, and purchases of raw material. A market-sharing and price-fixing agreement was signed between the two trusts, soon joined by the DuPont and other dynamite companies in the United States, whereby the world market for civilian explosives was divided among the three parties. Ten years later, this agreement was extended to include military propellants.

Nobel's later research included work on a military propellant based on nitroglycerine. In 1887, he obtained patents on ballistite, a smokeless powder, an invention as revolutionary for the production of military propellants as Nobel's dynamite had been for the production of civilian explosives. Nobel withdrew from business to continue his research and was granted patents on, for example, artificial silk, artificial leather, and celluloid. In all, he held 355 patents.

In 1896, Nobel died in San Remo, Italy, his home since 1891. He had never married. According to his will, his property was to constitute a fund whose yearly proceeds would be awarded in five prizes: the world-renowned Nobel Prizes in physics, chemistry, physiology or medicine, literature, and the promotion of international peace.

BIBLIOGRAPHY

Lundström, Ragnhild. *Alfred Nobel som internationell företagare* (Alfred Nobel as an International Entrepreneur). Uppsala, 1974. Based on material (correspondence, accounts, etc.) in the archives of the original Nobel companies in the various countries, deals with Nobel's business enterprises. Summary is given in English.

Reader, W. J. *Imperial Chemical Industries: A History*, vol. 1, *The Forerunners, 1870–1926*. London, New York, Toronto, 1970. Discusses the development of Nobel's Explosives and the Nobel-Dynamite Trust. As regards negotiations about formation of the Nobel-Dynamite Trust, it differs somewhat from Lundström. It gives a well-informed account of the agreements with the American explosives manufacturers, among them foremost DuPont, which are not found elsewhere.

Schück, Henrik, and Ragnar Sohlman. *The Life of Alfred Nobel.* 1929. Translation of *Alfred Nobel och hans släkt*. Stockholm, 1926. Still the best biography of Nobel. Sohlman was Nobel's research assistant from 1893 on. In his will, Nobel entrusted Sohlman, then only twenty-six years old, with being executor of the will.

RAGNHILD LUNDSTRÖM

NORDIC COUNTRIES *[This entry contains five subentries, an overview and discussions of the economic history of Denmark, Finland, Norway, and Sweden in modern times.]*

General Overview

In several aspects, the Nordic countries, Denmark, Norway, Sweden, Finland, and Iceland, have a common history and, except the Finns, languages with close similarities. Yet from the early modern period, the countries developed in different directions.

Iceland was colonized by Norwegians in the ninth and tenth centuries and later was under the Danish crown until 1944. Finland was acquired by Swedish kings in the early and high Middle Ages and became a part of the kingdom of Sweden, with representatives in the Diet (Estates), until captured by tsarist Russia in 1809. Within the Russian Empire, Finland was an autonomous grand duchy until it gained its independence in 1917. In 1397, Denmark, Norway, and Sweden with Finland had entered the Kalmar Union, a type of federation under the Danish crown. While Sweden-Finland finally fought its way out of the union in 1523, Norway stayed under the Danish crown until the end of the Napoleonic wars, when the country was surrendered to Sweden. In the union with Sweden, Norway had its own Diet and government until it won independence in 1905.

Important territorial changes occurred during the modern period. Sweden originally had no coast to the sea in the west or in the south. In 1645–1658, those provinces as well as inland counties in the north were captured from Denmark-Norway. Sweden was at war for two-thirds of the period 1560–1720, and through expansionist policies the Baltic countries as well as Polish and German provinces became ruled and taxed from Stockholm. But at the end of the period, this "Greatness of Power" broke down. Through centuries, Schleswig and Holstein, situated around the root of the Jutland peninsula and with mixed Danish- and German-speaking populations, had been annexed to the kingdom of Denmark. In 1864, these provinces, and thereby a third of the population, was relinquished to Germany.

Demography. In 1720, about 0.6 million people lived in Denmark, not including close to 0.3 million in Schleswig-Holstein. Norway comprised between 0.5 and 0.6 million people, Sweden slightly less than 1.5 million, Finland close to 0.3 million, and Iceland 50,000. Population figures for 1800 are more accurate (figures for 1900 are in parentheses): Denmark inhabited 926,000 (2.4 million); Norway, 883,000 (2.2 million); Sweden, 2.3 million (5.1 million); Finland, 833,000 (2.6 million); and Iceland, 47,000 (78,000).

In all countries, population growth attained a higher level in the nineteenth century, yet in Norway the growth rate had already approached a higher level by the eighteenth century. Outstanding with an early start, however, was Finland, growing 1.37 percent annually from 1750 to 1850 and increasing its population almost fourfold in one hundred years, even faster than England. The crude fertility ratio was stable, slightly above 0.3 percent until the late nineteenth century, again with Finland as an exception. Finland in the mid-eighteenth century had a crude fertility ratio well above 0.4, though due to later marriages it fell off but stayed at a higher level than the other countries. Iceland also was an outlier with violent fluctuations in both mortality and fertility almost until 1900.

The primary cause of the rapid population growth in the mainland Nordic countries was the decrease in mortality. Traditionally, the decrease has been explained by the diffusion of the potato (where more people could be fed from the same piece of land), vaccination against smallpox, better hygiene, and so forth. However, it has been pointed out that all these factors came too late to explain the simultaneous reduction of child mortality from the 1780s onward in Denmark, Norway, and Sweden. An alternative explanation is that the virulence of smallpox microbes had become weaker. Later in the nineteenth century, better living standards reduced mortality rates, especially among adults.

At that time, emigration, foremost to North America, emerged as a break on population growth. Based on the size of the population, Norway came second after Ireland as to the number of emigrants. In the period from 1850 to 1914, about 0.7 million Norwegians, 1.2 million Swedes, and 0.3 million each of Danes and Finns traveled over the Atlantic, and only about one-fifth came back. The Norwegian mass emigration started first and the Finnish was last. The biggest wave of Nordic emigrants came in the 1880s.

The Economy of the Modern Period. The diverging Danish and Swedish paths of development had an origin in the early sixteenth century. In the struggle for independence, the Swedish higher nobility was severely tolled. Power became concentrated in the king, who leaned upon the Diet, which was composed of four estates, including the peasantry. The Danish king, on the contrary, was dethroned, and the new one had to share power with the higher nobility. Although the Danish nobility was ousted

from state power with the introduction of absolutism in 1660, landlords did not lose economic power. Whereas the Swedish peasantry retained its freedom, the Danish tenants sank halfway to feudal serfdom, although they typically had access to large farms of 10 to 20 hectares. Even if independent, Swedish peasants were sitting on small farms of 3 to 8 hectares. Half the agricultural land belonged to the peasantry, who paid tax to the state. In Denmark, peasants held one-tenth of the land. The nobility possessed about one-fifth of Sweden and one-third of Denmark. Before the Reformation, similar shares accrued to the church, while the crown (state) held the rest. In 1527, the Swedish crown and, in 1536, the Danish crown, though less radical, confiscated clerical land. In Finland, the nobility at this time owned less than one-tenth of the land. Norway had old property rights, and with the land register of 1661, the distribution of land can be discerned. The nobility was feeble, according to one hypothesis, since the once imposing Norwegian nobility was almost extirpated in the Black Death and in 1661 held less than one-tenth of the land. Despite Reformation, the Norwegian church, although formally subordinated to the state, had retained one-fifth, while the (Danish) crown held one-third. One-fifth was owned by rich townsmen and the last fifth by peasants. In the following centuries, considerable changes occurred in the distribution of land, in particular in Sweden and Finland. As payment for military services, the nobility war rewarded with homesteads, manors, and noble lands, totalling more than two-thirds of the country's area. In the 1680s, the king recaptured the gifts. In the eighteenth and nineteenth centuries, considerable crown lands were acquired by tenants, thereby increasing the economic and political power of the free peasantry.

In the later Middle Ages, foreign trade of the Nordic countries was largely controlled by the German Hanseatic towns. A major import was salt, and a major export was fish. In the sixteenth century, the Dutch opposed the Hanseatic hegemony in the Baltic trade. The Nordic countries thereupon managed their foreign trade themselves, even if immigrated Dutch merchants were influential. In the seventeenth and eighteenth centuries, the Danes in particular organized overseas trade in the East Asia and western India through monopolistic joint-stock companies. The Icelandic trade also was monopolized by the Danes, from 1602 to 1787, in the form of regulated companies. A large share of the merchant companies' loot was re-exported from Copenhagen.

When monopolizing the Icelandic trade, other foreign merchants were expelled from Iceland. On the other hand, Danish merchants were not even allowed to settle in Iceland or engage in local production. In that way, Iceland maintained an archaic way of life, based on pasture farming and fishing. Land ownership was concentrated but divided into independent farms, almost all managed by tenants. A large share of the population could not acquire a farm and therefore were not able to establish a household. Thus, according to the census in 1703, about one-third of all adults lived as unmarried servants in a household. When the trade monopoly was canceled in 1787, a new brake on modernization had just been instituted (1783). Free labor was prohibited until 1863, thereby posing a serious constraint on capitalist development. The barter economy highlights an old-fashioned society, and until 1776 the units of value were: 1 cow = 6 ewes = 120 ells of cloth = 240 dried fishes.

The so-called inflationary period of the European economy, about 1520–1620, in particular saw a change in relative prices. For example, grain and beef prices increased more than most other commodities, and this fundamentally influenced even remote parts of the Nordic countries. In Denmark, where one can reach a port to the sea from virtually anywhere, grain was shipped to the Netherlands. However, compared to the Baltic grain trade passing the sound, Danish grain exports can be estimated to barely one-tenth. More important was the Danish export of oxen, which from 1601 to 1620 was valued to half the value of the Baltic grain trade. About 40,000 to 50,000 stall-fed oxen were tended southward across the border in these years, three times the number of the smaller grazed cattle a century before. Commercialization permeated Danish society, and in the seventeenth century, a network of towns flourished, turning Copenhagen into a metropolis.

In northern Norway and in Finland, the changing relative prices meant harder times. Fishermen from the north sailed to Bergen, Norway, where one kilogram of dried fish could buy more than six kilograms of rye meal in the late sixteenth century, while a hundred years later the price relations were one to one. People retreated from specialized fishery to more self-sufficient agriculture, and those left behind intensified their production of dried fish. The Finns sailed to Stockholm or other towns at the Gulf of Bothnia and exchanged fish, butter, and diverse handicrafts for salt and cereals. Facing disadvantageous prices, they first withdrew from the market and then took up tar production, which for centuries became an important export trade of Sweden-Finland.

The main Swedish export commodity from the sixteenth to the eighteenth century was iron, first a sort of pig iron but increasingly a more processed iron, bar iron. Actually, later mercantilistic legislation prohibited export of pig iron to 1855. Initially, Hanseatic merchants had been involved with the peasant-ironmasters (*bergsmän*) in small-scale production. In the seventeenth century, however, manorlike works (*bruk*) emerged, and they relied on merchant houses in Stockholm, Gävle, and Göteburg for financial resources and marketing. Heckscher estimated that Sweden furnished around 35 percent of world (European) iron production around 1720. The forests, providing charcoal for the smelting, were the basis of Swedish iron making, besides the iron ore. Before the breakthrough of puddling in the British iron industry, Sweden was the main supplier of the west European market during the eighteenth century, in competition with Russia.

Although conducted by private enterprises, iron exports were important in the financing of the Swedish military state. Mainly situated in the Bergslagen region, stretching across the country west and northwest of Stockholm, these exports promoted interregional trade of oxen, grain, and handicrafts. A more direct financial support for the expansionist policy, however, was copper production. It had been monopolized by the state and, in the seventeenth century, was totally dominating in Europe. In the Swedish exports of that century, iron constituted roughly 50 percent and copper 30 percent. However, iron displayed a sustained growth, while copper declined after 1650.

Another major Nordic export was sawn wood from southern Norway. Peasants erected water sawmills in the sixteenth century, and exports attained a peak in 1620, not regained until 1800 when its value was more than twice the income of the likewise significant merchant marine. Together with the preceding examples, this may illustrate that although dominated by agriculture, the rural populations of Norway, Sweden, and Finland were engaged intensely in complementary trades, such as fishery, metallurgy, tar boiling, handicrafts, and sawing. Denmark, on the other hand, was dominated by agriculture and foreign trade. Despite these indications of a growing economy, the literature points to an old controversy about a European crisis during the seventeenth century. The records of Nordic countries support the view that the crisis had its epicenter in state absolutism.

Preindustrial Change. After a depression in the second quarter of the eighteenth century and a cattle plague that severely reduced the Danish stock, economic growth diffused through agriculture and foreign trade. Population growth added to demand for grain, and despite higher Norwegian self-sufficiency, the total volume of Danish grained shipped to Norway increased. It is estimated that the Danish merchant tonnage in 1786 was the fourth highest in Europe, after Great Britain, France, and the Netherlands, and ranked first when tonnage is counted per capita. Nevertheless, in the two following decades, Denmark's total was overtaken by the Norwegian flag. While the Danish and Norwegian economies increased their foreign trade, in Sweden the old established export trade in iron stagnated because of increased competition from Great Britain's domestic production and growing Russian exports.

Everywhere, however, dynamic change pervaded agriculture, and rural handicrafts also expanded. This development is mirrored in the composition of the agricultural population and in land ownership. In 1750, there were five peasants for every landless male adult in Sweden. In 1870, the relation was one to one, and the proletarianization had accelerated after 1820. Basically, the process was similar in the other Nordic countries, yet more extreme in Finland and more moderate in Norway. In Denmark, it began earlier and was drawn out over centuries.

More land was put under the plow, and peasants also bought land from the crown and from the nobility. In Sweden (1700–1870), peasant land expanded from one-third to two-thirds. In Norway, peasants' share of the land increased from one-fifth in 1661 to four-fifths in 1855. Most remarkable, however, was the change in Denmark, where landlords in 1780 still held 80 percent of the land. In three decades, half this share was sold out, and the class of peasant-proprietors emerged from insignificance to a major economic and political force.

Also of fundamental importance was the change from the open field system to consolidated holdings. Different from Great Britain, where enclosures promoted large-scale capitalist agriculture, enclosures in the Nordic countries primarily promoted the propertied peasant class. In Denmark, the bulk of enclosures took place from 1760 to 1800, in Sweden from 1820 to 1860, and in Norway from the 1850s, whereas in Finland consolidation was still incomplete in 1900. The received view is that the agricultural reforms were implemented from above, by the king (Denmark) or by landlords (Sweden). An alternative perspective, however, is that market-oriented peasants were major actors in a movement that further enhanced commercialization.

Industrialization. In some regions of Europe, proto-industry was a precursor of modern factory industry. In the Nordic countries, household industries grew from the eighteenth and into the nineteenth century, but only in few instances can a continuity to modern industries be traced. It also seems as if the putting-out system, with a merchant capitalist in a network of homeworkers, was sparsely represented, for example in the Jutland knitting industry and in the Swedish textile industries. Even if producing for distant markets, the household industries resembled a rural handicraft more than the typical proto-industry.

The timing of industrialization is still a debated question. As in other countries, a gradual perspective has gained assent, even if a decisive breakthrough may be assigned to the 1890s in Denmark and Sweden and a decade later in Norway. The traditional view is that the British introduction of free trade around 1850 sparked off a handful of export industries based on primary resources. Actually, exports had exhibited decisive growth in the second half of the eighteenth century but was interrupted by protectionist measures in the wake of the Napoleonic wars. Much of

the resumed expansion took place within the primary sector—agriculture in Denmark and Sweden and forestry in Sweden and Finland. As a result, the expansion further strengthened the countryside and contributed to the delay of urbanization.

In recent decades, research has emphasized the role of the domestic markets in industrialization, drawing attention to commercialization of agriculture and the growth of rural industries before 1850. The Danish exports surged from the 1840s, first with barley, but in the last quarter of the century agriculture transformed to livestock production. In the 1880s, butter became the most important export, though it is often forgotten that butter is an industrial commodity. The raising of capital for the exploding growth of Danish dairies was possible through the cooperative organization of the firms. Other Danish industries, such as iron foundries and steam-engine makers that also expanded from the 1840s, were oriented toward the home market. In the 1890s, technological innovations constituted the basis for new developments in a couple of branches in engineering.

In Norway, the traditional export staples, fish and sawn wood, were overtaken by shipping services. Roughly speaking, while the former commodities constituted one-fifth each of the exports of goods and services, shipping accounted for two-fifths during the last third of the century. Norwegian sail shippers were successful in tramp freight markets, and they also managed, after some hesitation, to transform to steam from the 1880s. In tonnage, Norway now ranked third in the world. About the same time, ashore pulp processing grew to a significant industry. It lasted until after 1900, before technological innovations and hydroelectric energy widened the scope and increased the pace of Norwegian industrialization.

In Sweden, the old staple, iron, resumed growth and in 1850 still made up half of the exports. Yet it was soon overtaken by sawn wood and oats, the latter designed as energy for horses in British urban transports. Wood exports created a Klondike in the north, whereby foreign demand turned the vast, formerly worthless forests into highly valued capital. In 1870, wood accounted for above one-third, oats for almost one-third, and iron for one-fourth of Swedish exports. Around 1890, oats exports suddenly expired, and the growth of sawn wood stagnated. However, technological innovations in pulp and paper had already created a new growth industry. And the same applied, in particular from 1890 onward, for electrical engineering and several other branches of engineering. Moreover, the basic Bessemer steel process created a German demand for phosphoric ores, thereby opening for exploitation the fields and mines in the far north of Sweden.

In Finland, wooden shipbuilding furnished the merchant marine before iron and steam extinguished both

TABLE 1. *Sectoral Shares of GDP/Employment in Percent, and GDP Per Capita in 1990 Geary-Khamis Dollars*

	DENMARK		NORWAY		SWEDEN		FINLAND	
	1870	1900	1865	1900	1870	1900	1870	1900
Agriculture	50/52	30/41	46/60	25/41	42/72	27/55	58/75	49/70
Industry	20/26	26/30	18/14	28/26	18/15	33/26	17/16	22/19
Services	30/22	44/29	38/27	47/30	39/13	39/17	25/8	28/11
GDP per capita	1927	2902	1303	1762	1289	2178	1107	1620

SOURCE: GDP per capita from Maddison, A., *Monitoring the World Economy, 1820–1992*, p. 194 f. Swedish figures from the Lund project on Historical National Accounts. Sectoral shares for the other countries from Bjerke, J., *Trends in Norwegian Economy, 1865–1960*, p. 54 f.; Hansen, S. A., *Okonomisk vaekst i Danmark*, vol. 1, p. 142, vol. 2, pp. 202 f., 210 f.; Hjerppe, R., *The Finnish Economy, 1860–1985*, pp. 231 f., 264 f.

these trades. Modern industry already entered, however, in 1820, when a Scotchman started a cotton factory, enticed by the low tariff barrier to Russia. Despite new textile factories in the 1840s, when Britain lifted the prohibition on machinery exports, neither textiles nor the old iron industry were dynamic elements in industrialization in Finland as well as in other Nordic countries. Such a role was performed by the industries connected to forestry, sawmills and pulp and paper, despite a lagging technology. Their export volumes increased about 5 percent annually from 1870 to 1900 and made up two-thirds of total exports in 1900. However, manufacturing was still a small fraction of the economy in Finland.

Imports grew even faster than exports, and toward the end of the nineteenth century, the Nordic countries had substantial deficits in their trade balances. The difference was paid through capital imports and foreign debts accumulated until 1914. Consequently, domestic consumption and living standards rose rapidly, as did huge investments in industrialization.

Capital imports primarily financed railways. The first railway in Denmark was opened in 1847; in Norway, 1854; in Sweden, 1856; and in Finland, 1862. Railway building peaked in the 1870s and 1890s. In Sweden, the backward linkages to industry became important, and in all four countries, railways contributed to the development of the financial sector.

Table 1 highlights some characteristics of the historical national accounts, although the income levels are sensitive to future research. While it is probably true that Denmark was closer to western Europe in its economic standing, other Nordic countries appeared as the poor northern periphery of Europe. Except Norway, all the countries grew rapidly in the late nineteenth century. From the sectoral shares of GDP and employment, it can be concluded, for example, that Danish agriculture had a very high productivity—double that of the other countries. The table also shows that industry developed earlier in Denmark, although Sweden and Norway rapidly shifted employment from agriculture to industry. Near the end of century, Swedish industry appears to have had the highest productivity.

BIBLIOGRAPHY

Unfortunately, the rich literature on Nordic economic history is sparsely available in foreign languages and the titles below cover only a few areas. However, for the scholar some journals represent a mine: *Economy and History* that was edited by the Department of Economic History at Lund University, 1958–1980; *Scandinavian Journal of History*, for example with a special issue on literacy in the Nordic countries, 1550–1900 (1990, vol. 15, no. 1); and, first and foremost, *Scandinavian Economic History Review*. It is impossible to justify only a few references to the rich supply of that journal, but Hodne (1994) and Schön (1997), below, could not be omitted here since they represent the opposing views on the industrialization, the Export Model and the Domestic Market Model, respectively. Moreover, three special issues should also be mentioned: on shipping in Scandinavia (1980, vol. 28, no. 2), on proto-industrialization in Scandinavia (1982, vol. 30, no. 1), and on the standard of living in Scandinavia, 1750–1914 (1986, vol. 34, no. 2). Most useful is also the *Bibliography 1953–1989* on *Scandinavian Economic History Review* and *Economy and History* (Lund, 1990).

Ahlström, Göran. *Technological Development and Industrial Exihibitions, 1850–1914: Sweden in an International Perspective*. Lund, 1996.

Bengtsson, Tommy, Rolf Ohlsson, and Gunnar Fridlizius, eds. *Pre-Industrial Population Change*. Lund, 1984. Conference reports mirroring the controversy on mortality decline in northern Europe.

Bengtsson, Tommy. "La pays nordiques de 1720 à 1914." In *Histoire des populations de l'Europe, II: La révolution démographique 1750–1914*, edited by J-P. Bardet and J. Dupâqier, pp. 371–395. Paris, 1998.

Bruland, Kristine, ed. *Technology Transfer and Scandinavian Industrialisation*. New York, 1991.

Dybdahl, Vagn. "Dänemark, 1650–1850." In *Handbuch der europäischen Wirtschafts- und Sozialgeschichte*, edited by Wolfram Fischer, et al., pp. 281–297. Stuttgart, 1993.

Dyrvik, Ståle, ed. *The Satellite State in the Seventeenth and Eighteenth Centuries*. Bergen, Norway, 1979. Informative conference reports on Norway and Great Britain.

Fladby, Rolf. "Norwegen, 1650–1850." In *Handbuch der europäischen Wirtschafts- und Sozialgeschichte*, edited by Wolfram Fischer et al., pp. 298–310. Stuttgart, 1993.

Gunnarsson, Gisli. *Monopoly Trade and Economic Stagnation: Studies in the Foreign Trade of Iceland, 1602–1787.* Lund, 1983.

Gustafsson, Bo. "The Industrial Revolution in Sweden." In *The Industrial Revolution in National Context*, edited by Mikulas Teich and Roy Porter, pp. 201–225. Cambridge, 1996.

Hansen, Svend Aage. *Early Industrialisation in Denmark.* Copenhagen, 1970. A booklet by the author of the Danish historical national accounts.

Heckscher, Eli F. *An Economic History of Sweden.* Cambridge, Mass., 1954. A popularized version of Heckscher's four-volume work that has been the point of departure for much research in Swedish economic history.

Heikkinen, Sakari. *Labour and the Market: Workers, Wages and Living Standards in Finland, 1850–1913.* Helsinki, 1997.

Hildebrand, Karl-Gustaf. "Labour and Capital in the Scandinavian Countries in the Nineteenth and Twentieth Centuries." In *The Cambridge Economic History of Europe*, edited by Peter Mathias and Michael M. Postan, vol. 7.1, pp. 590–628. Cambridge, 1978.

Hildebrand, Karl-Gustaf. *Swedish Iron in the Seventeenth and Eighteenth Centuries: Export Industry before the Industrialization.* Södertälje, Sweden, 1992.

Hjerppe, Riitta. *The Finnish Economy, 1860–1985: Growth and Structural Change.* Helsinki, 1989. Summarizes and analyzes a large research project by many scholars on the historical national accounts.

Hodne, Fritz. "Export-Led Growth or Export Specialization?" *Scandinavian Economic History Review* 43.3 (1994), 296–310.

Hornby, Ove. "Dänemark, Norwegen und Schweden, 1850–1914." In *Handbuch der europäischen Wirtschafts- und Sozialgeschichte*, edited by Wolfram Fischer et al., pp. 209–260. Stuttgart, 1993.

Jörberg, Lennart. *A History of Prices in Sweden, 1732–1914.* 2 vols. Lund, 1972. Documents and analyzes prices and agricultural day wages in twenty-four counties.

Jörberg, Lennart. "The Industrial Revolution in the Nordic Countries." In *The Fontana Economic History of Europe*, edited by Carlo Cipolla, pt. 4:2. Glasgow, 1973.

Kaukiainen, Yrjö. "Finnland, 1860–1913." In *Handbuch der europäischen Wirtschafts- und Sozialgeschichte*, edited by Wolfram Fischer et al., pp. 261–285. Stuttgart, 1993.

Maarbjerg, John P. *Scandinavia in the European World-Economy, ca. 1570–1625: Some Local Evidence of Economic Integration.* New York, 1995.

Martinius, Sture. "Schweden und Finnland, 1650–1850." In *Handbuch der europäischen Wirtschafts- und Sozialgeschichte*, edited by Wolfram Fischer et al., pp. 235–280. Stuttgart, 1993.

Magnusson, Lars. *An Economic History of Sweden.* London, 2000.

Magnússon, Magnus S. *Iceland in Transition: Labour and Socio-Economic Change before 1940.* Lund, 1985.

Schön, Lennart. "Internal and External Factors in Swedish Industrialization." *Scandinavian Economic History Review* 45.3 (1997), 209–223.

Söderberg, Johan, Ulf Jonsson, and Christer Persson. *A Stagnating Metropolis: The Economy and Demography of Stockholm, 1750–1850.* Cambridge, 1991.

JONAS LJUNGBERG

Modern Denmark

The Danish economy in the late nineteenth century was still dominated by agriculture, and foreign trade was to a large extent that of a peripheral country exporting foodstuffs to Britain and receiving industrial goods—and coal—in return.

The 1890s, however, had seen the first indications of the modernization process that in the following century would transform the country into a rich welfare society. Agriculture had modernized its production into dairy farming, several industrial plants had been built, the infrastructure had been improved, early social reforms had been introduced, and a new phase in the demographic transition had started with simultaneous declines in the rates of fertility and mortality.

During the twentieth century the population grew from 2.4 million in 1900 to 5.3 million in 2000. This was the result of a decline in the gross mortality rate from seventeen to ten per thousand inhabitants and a decline in the fertility rate from thirty in 1900 to less than twenty in the 1930s. After a baby boom in the 1940s a new decline began, and a minimum of less than ten per thousand was reached in 1983, with a net reproduction rate of 662 followed by a modest rise in the following years. Before 1914 there was a large outmigration, especially to the United States, whereas the migration pattern in the last decades of the century was dominated by inmigration, to a large extent from southeast-European and non-European countries. A consequence of these changes was that a much higher proportion of the population around 2000 consisted of elderly citizens, whereas there were relatively few children, and the family pattern had changed to a smaller average household size. In the late 1990s half of all households had only one member, and every third Dane lived in a one-person household.

The primary sector, mostly agriculture, continued its dominance of the economy until about 1930; then the secondary sector became agriculture's equal, and in the following decades would surpass it in importance. From the 1960s on, the number of workers employed in manufacturing stagnated, and in the last decades of the twentieth century the service sector grew very rapidly, not least its public part.

Agriculture's economic problems after World War I were created first by the "back to gold" crisis of the mid-1920s and later by protectionist policies of many European countries in the 1930s. Commercial treaties with Britain secured part of the export of bacon, butter, and eggs, but under less profitable conditions than during the preceding liberalist era. During World War II food products could be sold at good prices in the domestic market and in central Europe; but after the war agriculture suffered again from difficult export conditions in the two main markets, Britain and Germany, especially after the failure of attempts to create a large European Free Trade Area in the late 1950s and with discriminatory trade barriers created by the Common Agricultural Policy of the European Common Market after 1963. Denmark's 1973 membership in the European Economic Community (EEC) (later the European Union) changed this situation, but by that time agriculture had been reduced to employing less than 10 percent of the population and had lost its importance as the main earner of foreign exchange. The number of farms declined from about 200,000 early in the twentieth century to about 50,000 in year 2000; but the larger consolidated farms were run very efficiently with large machines and were more productive than ever, although with a higher proportion of vegetable products than in the heydays of dairy farming. One effect of this development was a massive outflow of people from rural districts into the towns.

In manufacturing most of the early firms were producing exclusively for the home market, with the cement industry and shipbuilding the most noteworthy exceptions. The leading sectors were the food processing, textile, and machine industries. During the 1920s there were large fluctuations in output, and it was not until the 1930s that a new expansion started, sheltered by an import restriction scheme introduced during the international crisis to combat a deficit in the balance of payments and widespread unemployment. Most of the new firms, among them many in the textile industry, were not internationally competitive and succumbed to the liberalization taking place within the Organization for European Economic Cooperation (OEEC) in the 1950s. The real transformation of Danish society from an agrarian society to an industrial one, however, took place between 1958 and 1972, assisted by international boom years and a deliberate industrialization policy initiated to create new jobs in internationally competitive firms and to earn foreign exchange as compensation for dwindling income from agricultural exports. Many of the new industrial plants were built in rural areas, and several of the firms gained worldwide reputations, among them Lego (toys), Danfoss (thermostats), and the Lindø shipyard, which for a time had the largest capacity in Europe for building supertankers. After the first oil crisis, manufacturing continued to modernize with labor-saving investments in the food-processing industry and the machine industry as the leading sectors.

This development resulted in a gross national product (GNP) in constant prices that by the end of the twentieth century was about ten times of that one hundred years earlier. Development of a higher standard of living has been accompanied by a deliberate welfare policy, begun in the 1890s with old-age pensions and state-subsidized health insurance societies and continuing early in the twentieth century with legislation concerning unemployment benefits and disability pensions. These policies were developed gradually at first and then especially rapidly after 1958 into an all-embracing social security system, accompanied by a large public sector and one of the highest burdens of taxation in the world. Another consequence has been a very even distribution of income.

BIBLIOGRAPHY

Dansk Pengehistorie, vols. 1–5. Copenhagen, 1968–1993.
Dansk Socialhistorie, vols. 1–7. Copenhagen, 1979–1982.
Det danske Landbrugs Historie, vols. 1–4. Odense, 1988.
Hansen, Svend Aage. *Økonomisk vækst i Danmark*, vols. 1–2. Copenhagen, 1972–1974.
Johansen, Hans Christian. *Dansk historisk statistik, 1814–1980* (Danish Historical Statistics, 1814–1980). Copenhagen, 1985.
Johansen, Hans Christian. *The Danish Economy in the Twentieth Century*. London, 1987.
Johansen, Hans Christian. *Industriens vækst og vilkår, 1870–1973*. Odense, 1988.
Ølgaard, Anders. *The Danish Economy*. Brussels, 1979.

HANS CHRISTIAN JOHANSEN

Modern Finland

Finland in 2000 was a small industrialized country with a standard of living that ranked among the top twenty countries in the world. At the beginning of the twentieth century it was a poor agrarian country with a gross domestic product (GDP) per capita less than half that of the United Kingdom and the United States, world leaders at that time in this respect. Finland was part of Sweden until 1809 and a grand duchy of Russia from 1809 to 1917, with a relatively wide autonomy in internal economic affairs. It became an independent republic in 1917. Not directly involved with the fighting in World War I, Finland experienced a civil war at early independence in 1918 and fought against the Soviet Union during World War II. Finland has large forest areas of coniferous trees, and forests have been an important factor in its economic development. Other natural resources are scarce; there is no coal or oil, relatively few minerals, and little water power, despite the large number of lakes.

Economic Activities. In 1900 Finland was an agrarian country. Half of its production was in agriculture and forestry and more than half of its population worked in these primary industries. The structural change into an industrial economy took place relatively late; not until the 1950s did industry and construction outrank the former primary sector. By 2000 two-thirds of Finland's economy was in services, about one-third in manufacturing and construction, and only 4 percent in agriculture and forestry.

Finland imported a large share of its grain in 1900. A protectionist agricultural policy, starting in the 1920s, made the country more self-sufficient but led to continuous overproduction in the 1960s. The land reform of 1918 secured land to tenant farmers and that of 1944 to evacuees from eastern Finland and war veterans. These land reforms decreased the average size of farms. The last decades of the twentieth century saw the number of farms gradually decrease again and the average size of farms gradually increase to western European levels.

Before World War I the protected Russian market was important for the development of Finnish industry, because Finnish products could be sold mainly without tariffs. The paper industry grew in significance before World War I because St. Petersburg provided a large market. Textile and metal industry products were sold as well. The opening of the British market for timber in the 1980s together with the lowering of freight rates boosted sawmilling, which made sawn timber Finland's most important export from the 1860s to the 1930s.

In the interwar period Finland was among the five most important producers of sawn timber in the world, and an important producer of pulp, paper, and plywood. Forest products were Finland's most important industry, but from the 1930s on, the metal industries started to increase their share of production. They produced machinery and tools for agriculture, industry, and transport; weapons for the army; and bridges and other equipment for the infrastructure. The wartime needs of the army as well as war reparations to the Soviet Union boosted the metal industries further. Starting in the 1950s, Finnish metal industries became important suppliers of paper machinery, special ships like icebreakers and luxury cruisers, cranes, elevators, cables, and other products for both the domestic and foreign markets. The electronics industry began to be significant in the 1980s, with mobile phones and their transmission stations leading by 2000. Nokia is the big developer and producer of mobile phones.

Shipbuilding has lost in importance, as well as the textile and clothing industries, which had rather favorable conditions in the 1960s and 1970s because of large sales to the Soviet market. The paper industry is among the few largest producers of fine and printing paper in the world, with UPM-Kymmene, Stora Enso, and Metsä-Serla as the leading companies. Timber and the sawmill industry have lost their relative position in industry and exports but the production volumes have not shrunk. Sawn goods, plywood, and other wood-based construction boards are still exported all over the world.

The large share of forestry industry has caused cyclical fluctuations in the economy because of the big fluctuations in the world market prices of timber and paper products. The political events in Russia (and formerly in the Soviet Union) have caused big changes in the export conditions of Finnish products. The Eastern market was almost closed after the revolutions of 1917. The Soviets bought Finnish products on a bilateral basis between the end of World War II and 1991. The collapse of the Soviet Union stopped the trade again; it had only revived to a small extent by 2000.

Population. The population was 2.7 million in 1900 and 5.2 million in 1999. The country is among the larger ones in Europe by area, but it is sparsely populated, with 44 people per square mile. The population is very homogeneous. It has a small number of people of foreign origin, but two language groups, a Finnish-speaking majority and a Swedish-speaking minority. The number of foreigners has increased in the 1990s to only about 1–2 percent of the population. Population growth decreased from 1 percent per annum in the early 1900s to 0.3 percent in the late 1990s.

The level of education was low in the early 1900s, much behind the country's Nordic neighbors. Basic education increased in the interwar period and in the 1960s the educational system was widened to educate the majority of people either in vocational, trade, or technical schools or universities. By 2000 education was at the same level as in the most advanced European countries.

As with industrialization, urbanization was slow. In 1900 an ample tenth of the population was living in urban areas; by 1999 the figure was about two-thirds. A growing problem is the emptying of the remote rural areas and how to keep up services in sparsely populated areas. The rising standard of living, better health care, and education have raised the average life expectancy from below 50 years in 1900 to 77 in 2000. Of importance since the 1950s has been the common Nordic labor market, which has allowed many Finns to find work in Sweden, particularly in the 1960s and early 1970s.

Institutions. The public sector is large nowadays, as in the other Nordic countries, and Finland follows the so-called Nordic welfare model, although it was adopted later than in the neighboring countries. Public child health centers, cash allowances for children, and maternity leaves were established in the 1940s, and pension schemes have covered the whole population since the 1950s. Unemployment programs had their beginnings in the 1930s depression and have widened since. A public health care program has covered the whole population since the early 1970s. Economic support to the disabled is a rule. Almost all education is government run and free. Some social benefits were cut slightly during the 1990s depression, but income distribution is among the most even in the world. The Nordic democratic corporate model of three-party negotiations between employers, employees' unions, and the government for the development of working conditions has been prevalent since the 1960s, but central wage negotiations were losing some of their popularity during the 1990s.

Finland, like many other small countries, has and has had a very open economy, with high export and import shares. The most important trade partners have been the United Kingdom, Germany, Russia (including the former

Soviet Union), and Sweden. In foreign trade policy Finland has been flexible. The tariffs were relatively low and trade unrestricted before World War I. Finland enjoyed a favorable situation—the almost complete lack of tariffs in Russia. In the interwar period Finland moderately followed the rise of protectionism, and after withdrawal from the gold standard, belonged to the Sterling Bloc. In 1948 Finland became a member of the World Bank, the International Monetary Fund (IMF), and the Bretton Woods agreement. Two years later it became a member of the General Agreement on Tariffs and Trade (GATT). Finland had a bilateral trade agreement with the Soviet Union from 1947 to 1991. Finland had a special FINNEFTA agreement with the European Free Trade Association (EFTA) since 1961 and became a full member of EFTA in 1985. A free-trade agreement of industrial products with the European Economic Community (EEC) opened trade in 1974, and in 1995 Finland became a member of the European Union. In 1999 Finland became part of the Economic and Monetary Union (EMU), with a central European bank and a common European currency, the euro. The main economic connections have been with the western countries all through the twentieth and into the twenty-first century.

Foreign direct investments in Finland and by Finnish companies abroad were insignificant until the 1970s. Since the 1980s many more international trade and financial markets have opened and increased foreign ownership in companies. About 70 to 80 percent of the stocks in the Finnish stock exchange were in foreign hands by the early twenty-first century. Finnish companies increased their ownership in foreign companies even more through purchases and expansion into foreign subsidiaries. The government has been an important economic initiator, with government investments in mining, basic industries, power production and transmission, and the construction of infrastructure. However, the government's role started to decrease in the 1990s.

BIBLIOGRAPHY

Heikkinen, Sakari, and Riitta Hjerppe. "The Growth of Finnish Industry in 1860–1913; Causes and Linkages." *Journal of European Economic History* 16.2 (1987); and P. K. O. Brien, ed. *The Industrial Revolutions in Europe*, Pt. 2, *The Industrial Revolutions*, vol. 5, pp. 227–244, 1994.

Heikkinen, Sakari. *Labour and the Market: Workers, Wages and Living Standards in Finland, 1850–1913*. Commentationes Scientiarum Socialium 51. Rauma, 1997.

Hjerppe, Riitta. *The Finnish Economy, 1860–1985: Growth and Structural Change*. Helsinki, 1989.

Hjerppe, Riitta. "Finland's Foreign Trade and Trade Policy in the 20th Century." *Scandinavian Journal of History* 18 (1993), 57–76.

Kaukiainen, Yrjö. *A History of Finnish Shipping*. London, 1993.

Kaukiainen, Yrjö. "Finland, 1860–1913." In *Handbuch der europäischen Wirtshafts- und Sozialgeschichte*, vol. 5. Stuttgart, 1985.

Myllyntaus, Timo. *Electrification of Finland: The Transfer of a New Technology into a Late Industrialising Economy*. Worcester, Mass., 1991.

Peltonen, Matti. "The Peasant Economy and the World Market. Finnish Peasant Farming in the Age of Agrarian Crises, 1880's–1910's." *Review Fernand Braudel Center* 16.3 (1993), 357–381.

RIITTA HJERPPE

Modern Norway

At the close of the nineteenth century Norway was one of the poorest countries in Europe, with one of its highest emigration rates and significant social problems. Yet, according to Angus Maddison's data, between 1913 and 1950 Norway had the highest growth rate among the advanced countries. Further acceleration, beginning in the 1970s as the oil economy emerged, took Norway to third place in the world in terms of gross domestic product (GDP) per capita. The key to this turnaround lies in the exploitation of natural resources and the active diffusion of foreign technologies, accompanied by significant state ownership and intervention.

In 1900 Norway had a population of 2.2 million people. The economy was predominantly rural and dominated by fishing, shipping, and forestry—despite modernization, particularly of textiles and mechanical engineering, based on technology importation from the 1850s on and innovation and growth in paper and pulp production from the 1890s. In the early twentieth century, however, the direction of industrial development changed; large-scale industrial concerns based on electricity, chemistry, and metallurgy emerged.

A primary development was hydropower, harnessed for the production of electricity, partly by local authorities and partly by the state. Small power stations were constructed for local energy consumption, and some higher waterfalls were exploited by private investors for large-scale industrial uses (including electrochemical and electrometallurgical processes). The latter relied on foreign capital and technology, and gave rise to enclaves that were integrated into international labor markets but had few up or downstream effects within Norway itself. The fertilizer producer Norsk Hydro was an exception. Parallel to large-scale industrialization was increased investment in smaller-scale production. Through a locally funded, decentralized savings-bank system, investment flowed into small firms, farms, and fisheries. Agriculture was increasingly mechanized, and the fishing fleet changed from oars and sail to motors. Small-scale industrialization was extensive, based on broad adoption of mechanical processes.

Post–World War I development was uneven and severely affected by external shocks: the international crisis of 1920–1921, the depression of 1930–1933, and then World War II. Access to hydropower turned out to be critical to the industrial growth that followed the years of crisis during the 1920s in the electrochemical and metallurgical sectors. After foreign acquisition of several firms, production shifted toward alloys and aluminum, using electrolysis techniques. The country's longstanding marine capabilities also paid off, as shipping and whaling experienced the greatest export growth in the interwar period. This development depended on major technological changes. The diesel engine was adopted in shipping, which now turned to oil transport, and floating whale factories were introduced in whaling. Powerful groups of shipowners emerged in Oslo and Bergen. By the 1930s the Norwegian merchant fleet was the fourth largest fleet in the world.

Although rural conditions deteriorated, in many small towns small-scale industry was established, employing relatively cheap rural labor and excess electrical energy supplies. Powered by small electrical engines, the production of clothing, furniture, and metals was decentralized, located in small towns along the coast, and focused on domestic or local markets. The closing of foreign markets by World War I and subsequent protection strengthened this trend.

During the "period of long growth" (1950–1974) growth rates were historically high but low relative to other OECD (Organization for Economic Cooperation and Development) countries, despite very high investment rates. This discrepancy is explained by decreasing returns on invested capital because of slow growth in employment and by substantial investments made in infrastructure, which produced gradual growth effects.

The government took an active economic role after World War II, through regulation of credit, a corporatist industrial policy, and significant ownership stakes in industrial companies. The ownership stakes, combined with a wide range of support measures, became the vehicle for major public investment in the economy. Expansion of the merchant fleet, electricity, and large-scale industry continued, but extensive investments were made to modernize all sectors. As a consequence, rural labor was increasingly drawn to new job opportunities in the cities, and the urban share of the population increased. Small-scale industry experienced both contraction and increased productivity; faced by international competition, low-productivity firms closed down, as survivors responded with technological upgrades. By the start of the 1960s the industrial sector encompassed a set of smaller, relatively low-productivity firms producing finished goods for the domestic market (still somewhat protected from international competition) and an outward-looking and competitive set of firms producing semifinished goods (electrochemical products) or services (shipping), in areas of natural competitive advantage. This dual industrial structure was weakened during the following two decades as many of the smaller, finished-goods producers grew in size and improved their productivity and export performance.

Norway's development changed radically in the 1970s as an oil economy emerged. The OPEC price shocks of 1973 and 1979 prompted exploitation, and by the mid-1980s offshore production of oil and gas accounted for 15 percent of GDP, where it has remained. In the wake of oil developments, the traditional industries, heavy industry, and shipping all declined markedly. Loss of market share in oil transport, especially after the Middle East war in 1973, affected shipping and shipbuilding. These industries then turned toward more specialized roles largely related to North Sea oil and gas activities. Oil also impacted mechanical engineering, which became a growth sector as engineering production turned toward the North Sea. The North Sea investment followed the industrial model of the postwar period: significant state involvement via regulation and industrial support measures, research-and-development investment, and the creation of a wholly owned state oil company. As a result, Norway became a major player in offshore technologies.

Development was checked following a fall in oil prices in 1986 and the crisis of the late 1980s and early 1990s, which hit financial services severely. During the following years employment in the service sectors (both public and private) rose, and growth continued in exports of products from natural-resource-based industries. But new growth opportunities also were exploited; fish farming, for example, became an important growth sector in the 1990s. There was a resurgence in shipping (following the establishment of the Norwegian International Shipping Register in 1991).

The Norwegian model has essentially been one of significant state activism and ownership, directed toward the exploitation of natural resources. This model continues to be important: government holdings in industry remain extensive, and their value considerably exceeds the entire value of the Oslo stock exchange. By the beginning of the twenty-first century, Norway (now with a population of 4.4 million) had one of the world's highest GDP per capita ratios. However, unlike those of the rest of Scandinavia, it had not been achieved by the development of high-technology companies and sectors. Rather, the economy remained specialized in production tied to natural advantages and resources: oil and gas, fish, electrochemical/metallurgical production, and shipping.

BIBLIOGRAPHY

Basberg, Bjorn L., Jan Erik Ringstad, and Einar Wexelsen, eds. *Whaling and History: Perspectives on the Evolution of the Industry*. Sandefjord, 1993.

Bruland, Kristin. *British Technology and European Industrialization: The Norwegian Textile Industry in the Mid-Nineteenth Century*. Cambridge, 1989.

Fischer, Lewis R., and Helge W. Nordvik, eds. *Shipping and Trade, 1750–1950: Essays in International Maritime Economic History*. Ponterfract, 1990.

Hanisch, Tore Jorgen. "The Economic Crisis in Norway in the 1930s: A Tentative Analysis of Causes." Special issue. *The Scandinavian Economic History Review* 26 (1978), 145–155.

Hodne, Fritz. *An Economic History of Norway: 1815–1970.* Trondheim, 1975.

Hodne, Fritz. *The Norwegian Economy, 1920–1980.* London, 1983.

Maddison, Angus. *Phases of Capitalist Development.* Oxford, 1982.

OLAV WICKEN AND KRISTINE BRULAND

Modern Sweden

Sweden is one of the highly industrialized nations; but compared to, for example, Britain, its industrialization started late. Before the 1850s, Swedish economic growth was very slow; but then it accelerated, as industrialization commenced. Between the 1890s and the late 1940s the country's economic growth was very rapid internationally; but then it declined to the European average, and since the 1960s Swedish growth has been below this average. Agriculture's share of total production and employment has decreased, from its position of dominance until the middle of the nineteenth century to a few percentage points today. The industrial share rose until the 1960s and then decreased; whereas the share held by services grew slightly until the 1960s and then accelerated, so that today it is by far the largest of these three sectors. Thus Sweden has followed the general pattern of industrialized countries. These variations have many causes; here some of the important variables are discussed: industrial development, population, and institutions.

In the second half of the nineteenth century industrial growth was mainly concentrated in forest and iron and steel industries, which, together with agriculture, contributed to rapid growth in exports compared to the gross domestic product (GDP). In the 1890s the pattern of industrial expansion changed. Home-market industries grew in importance, causing exports to stagnate and even to go down slightly relative to GDP in the decades around the turn of the twentieth century. At the same time engineering industries started to expand. A number of firms that later became large and international rather than Swedish were established, many based on domestic inventions. Examples are: LM Ericsson, later Ericsson, which specialized in telephones and telecommunications systems; SKF, producer of ball bearings; and ASEA, today part of ABB (ASEA-BrownBoveri), a company based on generation and long-distance transmission of electricity. These firms resulted from an enduring Swedish technical tradition, fostered, for example, by the iron and steel industries. From the turn of the century other endeavors expanded as well, such as the pulp and paper industry, the chemical industry, and iron ore mining. All these were or became important export industries.

No long-term expansion of total exports compared to GDP occurred in the twentieth century until the 1970s, but fluctuations were great. In the 1920s, for instance, the export share rose when new industries reaped the fruits of the preceding period of innovation. In the 1930s Sweden followed the world trend with stagnating exports. The Swedish currency formed part of the sterling bloc, which suspended the gold standard in 1931; and in the rest of the decade the growth rate was comparatively high. Also, new areas of Swedish industry that had to do with consumer durables and automobiles stimulated economic growth.

After World War II, Swedish economic growth was triggered in a number of areas, particularly the engineering, electric, automobile, and shipbuilding industries. However, starting in the late 1960s Swedish industrial development encountered structural problems. A number of industries had become saturated or outmoded. Shipbuilding is a conspicuous example, along with the iron and steel industry and some engineering. In earlier structural crises, old parts were creatively destroyed rather swiftly, but now the government—whether liberal or social democratic—tried by financial and other support to maintain operation of the old systems, perpetuating the structural problems. However, in the long run it was impossible, for example, to "rescue" the shipyards producing very large ships, mainly tankers, and an entire industry that had led the world had to close down.

Industrial policies and the institutional composition of the government sector—the democratic corporate model—helped to make economic growth slower in Sweden than in most of the rest of the industrialized world, causing severe economic—and social—crises in the early 1990s. In the late 1980s a reorientation of economic policy had begun, and in the nineties it strengthened; but it is too early, as the twenty-first century dawns, to judge whether the problems have been overcome. Fundamental changes in the last half-century, summarized in the term economic globalization, probably have had a decisive impact, so that a thorough-going adaptation to the international economy is well under way. Furthermore, in the very recent years economic growth has accelerated, supposedly because of the so-called new economy; but it remains to be seen whether these tendencies are long- or short-term phenomena.

The population of Sweden is close to 9 million inhabitants, making it one of the small European countries. In the middle of the nineteenth century, the population was 3.5 million, but the increase was uneven. In the early twentieth century, up to the 1930s, the population growth declined because of a falling excess of births over deaths and a net emigration that represented the final stage of the great emigration movement, which peaked in the second half of the nineteenth century. In the 1930s, however, population growth again began to accelerate because of a great natural increase, especially in the 1940s, and a

MODERN SWEDEN. View of rail yard in Stockholm, 2001. (© Suzi Moore/Woodfin Camp and Associates, New York)

beginning net immigration, which soared later. The natural increase declined again in the second half of the century, but with fluctuations, and population growth would have been extremely low, had it not been for the immigration.

Sweden is one of the largest European countries and thus is sparsely populated with 20 inhabitants per square kilometer around the year 2000, when the figures for Belgium, Britain, and Germany were 335, 244, and 230, respectively. There has been a concentration of population in some areas as others have stagnated or declined in population. Large parts of the country are extremely sparse, for instance, the interior of Norrland, the northernmost part of the country. The skewed distribution of the people is due to urbanization. Around 1850, only 10 percent of the population lived in urban areas, a share that rose to 22 percent in 1990, 55 percent in 1950, and 84 percent in 1995.

The rapid expansion of Swedish industry in the first half of the twentieth century had to do with new and dynamic industries and with the fact that Sweden was nonbelligerent in the world wars. Furthermore, appropriate institutions prevailed in the form of laws and regulations, traditions, and attitudes. Early in the century there was often unrest in the labor market, but this did not impede growth possibilities. In the 1930s wage negotiations were centralized to a greater extent than previously, and other rules and regulations were introduced.

In 1932 the Social Democrats came into office, where they remained for over forty years. Their ascendancy marked the start of the welfare state, which was consented to by the liberal political parties. In fact a rivalry developed between the parties as to which was most reform-minded. Thus the Swedish welfare state was formed basically by political consensus. This was clearly seen from 1976 to 1982 and from 1991 to 1994, when there were liberal governments; they did not try to change the predominant political pattern of the country.

A policy launched in the 1930s, with its heyday in the 1950s and 1960s but with a clear imprint even on the following decades, has been called the Swedish model. It was characterized by democratic corporatism, by which is meant cooperation between employers' and employees' organizations and with government authorities. There were central negotiations on wages and working conditions, and a consensus on economic and social policy and the public sector grew. This development, however, was not special for Sweden but characteristic of a number of European countries, particularly the small ones. Thus it could instead be considered "small state model." However, there were special traits for individual countries. The Swedish characteristics were visible from the 1970s onward with a public sector growing faster than in most other countries. Furthermore, there were special "socialist" measures such as union representation on corporate boards of directors and codetermination in all questions at all places of work—although in practice, this meant obligatory information only. Another example is the provision of "wage-earner funds" aiming at changing ownership of companies, which, however, did not materialize before the funds were dissolved.

In general the Swedish governance system became rigid at the same time that internationalization and globalization expanded greatly. These rigidities seem to have hampered structural changes and adaptations, and have slowed economic growth as described above.

A characteristic of Sweden is the predominance of giant corporations. When they became increasingly internationalized in the last decades of the twentieth century, the balance between the constituent parts of the so-called Swedish model was changed. For example, central wage negotiations were given up, and there was decentralized wage formation. Furthermore, increased consensus between the labor force and management within the giant companies caused tensions within the trade unions.

It is too early to say whether the institutional rigidities have vanished, but there are signs of a greater ability to adapt. Probably Sweden's changing attitude toward the European Union is an indication of this. In order to counteract the escalating economic and social crisis, around 1990 the Social Democrats changed their attitude and started to work for a Swedish membership in the EU, which was achieved in the mid-1990s.

BIBLIOGRAPHY

Fridlizius, Gunnar. "Sweden." In *European Demography and Economic Growth*, edited by W. R. Lee. London, 1979.

Henrekson, Magnus, Lars Jonung, and Joakim Stymne. "Economic Growth and the Swedish Model." In *Economic Growth in Europe since 1945*, edited by Nicholas Crafts and Gianni Toniolo, pp. 240–289. Cambridge, 1996.

Jonung, Lars, and Rolf Ohlsson, eds. *The Economic Development of Sweden since 1870*. Cheltenham, U.K., 1997.

Jörberg, Lennart. "The Industrial Revolution in the Nordic Countries." In *The Fontana Economic History of Europe, 1700–1914*, vol. 4, edited by C. Cipolla. London, 1970.

Jörberg, Lennart, and Olle Krantz. "Scandinavia 1914–1970." In *The Fontana Economic History of Europe*, vol. 6, no. 2. London, 1976.

Jörberg, Lennart, and Olle Krantz. "Economic and Social Policy in Sweden 1850–1939." In *The Cambridge Economic History of Europe*, vol. VIII, *The Industrial Economies: The Development of Economic and Social Policies*. Cambridge, 1989.

Lindbeck, Assar. *The Swedish Experiment*. Stockholm, 1997.

OLLE KRANTZ

NORFOLK SYSTEM. *See* Crop Rotation *and* Open-Field System.

NORTH, DOUGLASS CECIL (born 1920), economic historian.

A native of Cambridge, Massachusetts, who spent most of his professional career at two institutions—first, the University of Washington in Seattle and then, from 1983 on, Washington University in Saint Louis—North was a founder of cliometrics (also known as the New Economic History), the systematic application of statistical methods and economic theory to the study of history. Later, he was a pioneering researcher and founder of the New Institutional Economics, an ambitious attempt to expand the reach of standard economics through a fusion of price theory, political analysis, transactions-cost theory, and the historical study of institutions, to gain a better understanding of why some nations are rich and some poor. In 1993, North and Robert Fogel jointly shared the Nobel Memorial Prize in Economic Sciences for their work in economic history.

Although best known for his contributions to the theory of economic history, North began his career with a series of important empirical studies in U.S. business and economic history. As a college student, North had initially intended to become a professional photographer, having won various prizes in international competition and having had the privilege of working with the eminent photographer Dorothea Lange. However, her husband, Paul Taylor, convinced North to become an economist. North eventually received his undergraduate and doctoral degrees from the University of California, Berkeley, where his Ph.D. dissertation focused on the history of the American insurance industry. He then took an appointment at the University of Washington, where he remained for over three decades, eventually serving as chairman of the department.

North's initial research centered on studies of American regional economic growth. An invitation from Solomon Fabricant to become a research associate at the National Bureau of Economic Research in 1956–1957 permitted him to work with Simon Kuznets, under whose influence he compiled the first quantitative historical series of the U.S. balance of payments. This work, in conjunction with his studies of regional development, led to his first book, on the economic growth of the United States from 1798 to 1860, which analyzed America's historical development in terms of an export-led model of growth.

Beginning in 1959–1960, North helped found the Cliometric Society; and through his writings and personal advocacy, and during his subsequent five-year tenure as coeditor of the *Journal of Economic History*, he worked to promote this new, cliometric approach to economic history. This work provoked the ire of many traditional historians, who were leery of economic theory and unfamiliar with modern statistical and mathematical techniques. Indeed, the split between cliometric and traditional economic historians has not entirely healed to this day.

At the very moment in the late 1960s when cliometrics was nearly ascendant, North began to evolve his ideas about institutional analysis, which paved the way for the bulk of his research for the next thirty years. Partly as a result of a year spent at Cambridge University, where he served as Pitt Professor and decided to switch from American to European economic history, and partly because of his work on nineteenth-century transatlantic shipping, which argued that technological developments per se had less to do with rising productivity in the industry than changes in organization and structure, North began to feel that standard neoclassical analysis was inadequate to the task of explaining the economic rise of the West. His search for a framework within which to meld institutional and neoclassical economic ideas was advanced by his adoption of the transactions-cost perspective first outlined by Ronald Coase at the beginning of the sixties.

This work led to two important collaborations, first with Lance Davis and then with Robert Paul Thomas. His book with Davis sought to outline their theoretical perspectives on institutional and transactions-cost analysis in history, whereas the book with Thomas applied these ideas to explain the rise or the fall of the various western European economies, beginning with the feudal period. North developed these ideas further in 1981 in *Structure and Change in Economic History.*

North's move to Washington University in Saint Louis in 1983 led to increased collaboration with political scientists and scholars from other noneconomic disciplines and to the creation of the Center for Political Economy. In a 1990 book, he argued for the need to include ideas about historical path dependence in analyzing political institutions. His shared receipt of the 1993 Nobel Memorial Prize in Economics attracted worldwide attention to his ideas. In 1997–1998 he served as the first president of the International Society for the New Institutional Economics, in which the ideas of North, Coase, Oliver Williamson, and Mancur Olson figured prominently. He believed that economists had lost interest in many of the big ideas characteristic of earlier economic research, and he worked ceaselessly to promote work at the boundaries of the various social sciences. Most recently, North has developed an interest in cognitive science and has been trying to use insights from experimental psychology to understand how imperfect rationality on the part of individuals is mitigated by institutions or leads to the persistence of growth-suppressing behavior. His work is widely cited not only in economics but in the related fields of political science, sociology, and the law.

BIBLIOGRAPHY

Davis, Lance, and Douglass C. North. *Institutional Change and Economic Growth.* Cambridge, 1970.

Drobak, John, and John V. C. Nye, eds. *Frontiers of the New Institutional Economics.* San Diego, Calif., 1997.

North, Douglass C. *Economic Growth of the United States, 1790 to 1860.* New York, 1961.

North, Douglass C. *Structure and Change in Economic History.* New York, 1981.

North, Douglass C. *Institutions, Institutional Change, and Economic Performance.* Cambridge, 1990.

North, Douglass C., and Robert P. Thomas. *The Rise of the Western World.* New York, 1973.

JOHN V. C. NYE

NORTH AFRICA *[This entry contains three subentries, on the economic history of North Africa during the ancient period, independent Islamic period, and colonial and modern periods.]*

Ancient Period

The North African Paleolithic era was a Stone Age hunting-and-gathering economy, with patterns of culture similar to the Eurasian cultures of that time. The later Mesolithic era was one of specialized collecting near the Nile River and Saharan oases, as the Pleistocene big game went south or were hunted to extinction. Specialized collecting resulted in the domestication of some animals and food plants in the increasingly warmer and dryer North African ecology. By 10,000 to 8,000 years ago, herding and settled farming economies typified the North African Neolithic era, one linked to parts of the Mediterranean, in its "maritime character," and associated with coastal trade. The limited cultivation of cereal grains (barley and wheat) and pulses (lentils and peas) fed both people and animals (goats and sheep). By about 2000 BCE, camels were herded and donkeys were added as beasts of burden. In much of pre-Roman north Africa, the economic base was a system of mixed dry farming in combination with livestock raising, with some seasonal transhumance (migrations). Some Saharan peoples never settled but became camel herders and long-distance traders, who linked the Mediterranean with sub-Saharan Africa.

About 630 BCE, Cyrene was founded by the Greeks as a colony of Thera; it retained its Hellenic culture and orientation throughout the various early conquests of ancient Egypt and North Africa, as well as that of the Romans of the first century BCE to the fifth century CE. Cyrene established wide territorial claims into a region known to have produced grain, olives, and wine. It was also noted for horse raising and the production of the silphium plant (*Symphytum officinale,* comfrey), a well known cure-all in antiquity. The region was incorporated into the expanding Persian Empire, then became part of Ptolemaic Egypt after conquest by Alexandar the Great, with a period of independence in between. Only then was it annexed as a Roman province in 74 BCE. The Phoenician city-state of Carthage (in present-day Tunisia) was won by Rome after the three Punic Wars (264–262 BCE; 218–202 BCE; 149–146 BCE). Carthage and its extensive territories were annexed in 146 BCE, but the recurring warfare caused the Romans to burn the city and plow it under with salt, thereby condemning the land to infertility. Surviving Carthaginians continued to live in the new Roman province of Africa. The Romans took Numidia in 46 BCE, then Mauretania in 40 CE.

At its height, Rome held six provinces, from Algeria to Cyrenaica, but political control of the region was accomplished only through the building of roads, harbors, and new cities. With 10,000 to 30,000 inhabitants, the new cities were still dwarfed by Carthage, which had some 250,000. Pre-Roman irrigation works in North Africa included the Punic and the Numidian (present-day Sudan) terraced hillsides to farm with the water runoff, some earthen dams, and the canals that routed water onto the fields. Although North Africa had supplied grain to Mediterranean markets before Roman annexation, it became the major supplier to the empire, shipping perhaps two-thirds of Rome's grain during the first century CE, when the armies also occupied Europe, Egypt, and the Near East. After Roman annexation, North Africa had much economic growth, with increased wealth for the indigenous elite. Large estates were established by citizens, but imperial estates also became important. Intensive economic growth continued for Africa Proconsularis and for Numidia during the second to the fourth centuries CE, but the densest population remained in the Punic area of Carthage and its environs.

Under Roman administration, North African agriculture and arboriculture were intensified. Roman interest in Tunisia expanded grain-producing estates. Olive oil was soon the most important cash crop; the North African province of Tripolitania produced the largest amount of olive oil in the Roman world by the third century CE. Other North African commodities included wine, fish and fish products, pottery, marble, and wood. The third century CE was a period of growth. The Vandal invasion of 429 CE did not alter the regional economy. Despite economic decline elsewhere in the Mediterranean and bitter local religious disputes in the fourth and fifth centuries CE, archaeological evidence shows that African exports until the seventh-century Islamic invasions were indicative of prosperity.

[*See also* Egypt *and* Timbuktu.]

BIBLIOGRAPHY

Camps, G. "Beginnings of Pastoralism and Cultivation in North-west Africa and the Sahara: Origins of the Berbers." In *The Cambridge History of Africa*, vol. 1, pp. 548–623. Cambridge, 1982. From the earliest times to c. 500 BCE.

Cherry, David. *Frontier and Society in Roman North Africa*. Oxford, 1998.

Clark, J. Desmond. "The Cultures of the Middle Palaeolithic/Middle Stone Age." In *The Cambridge History of Africa*, vol. 1, pp. 248–341. Cambridge, 1982.

Kehoe, Dennis P. *The Economics of Agriculture on Roman Imperial Estates in North Africa*. London, 1988. Detailed survey of the economy of large estates in the Bagradas Valley, Africa Proconsularis, during the second century CE. A useful model of the economic relationships of ancient agriculture as relating to production for Rome.

Mattingly, David J. *Tripolitania*. London, 1995. A thorough study of that Roman province.

Mattingly, David J., and R. Bruce Hitchener. "Roman Africa: An Archaeological review." *Journal of Roman Studies* 85 (1995), 165–213.

Shaw, Brent D. "Lamasba: An Ancient Irrigation Community." *Antiquités africaines* 18 (1982), 61–103.

Shaw, Brent D. *Environment and Society in Roman North Africa: Studies in History and Archaeology*. Brookfield, Vt., 1995.

J. G. MANNING

Independent Islamic Period

Arab interest in North Africa began in 642 CE with the invasion of Cyrenaica from Egypt and the capture of Tripoli the following year. The next few years saw a period of raids into the Byzantine areas of Ifriqiya (Tunisia), although these were not followed up by a permanent settlement until 670 with the founding of Kairouan in south-central Tunisia, which remained the religious and political capital of the Maghrib for two and a half centuries. A period of military setbacks slowed the Arab advance, and it was not until 698 that they captured Carthage and founded the city of Tunis. Early in the eighth century, Ifriqiya became a governorship independent of Egypt. The invading armies found converts to Islam and recruits for their armies from among the settled Berber inhabitants of North Africa, who enabled them to pacify the nomadic people away from the coast, complete their conquest of Algeria and Morocco, and successfully invade Spain in 711. Although administrative ties between Morocco and Islamic Spain were never tight, there was a great deal of labor movement between the two, with families migrating in both directions.

The Berbers were converted fairly quickly to Islam, with the only holdouts being Jews who were settled in the area. Some of the newly converted moved to the cities from the countryside to benefit from escaping from the land and head taxes and in expectation of receiving an annuity as did the Arabian Muslims. While this policy increased the speed of conversion to Islam, it drained the treasury of the caliphate in the Middle East. A later caliph was forced to reinstate land taxes on converted (non-Arab) Muslims. This unequal fiscal treatment and exclusion from public service caused much resentment and violent uprisings in later years. Women played a limited part in the economic life of North Africa, mainly as domestic servants, singers and dancers, and as helpers in their husbands' trade.

Religious fugitives and merchants from the Middle East settled among the Berbers over the centuries, strengthening Islamic and Arab influences in North Africa. There were clearly defined dispute resolution procedures and a sharing of the taxation burden among the Berber people, throughout the Islamic period in the Maghrib. Although they did not practice collective farming, families tended to farm that which they had traditionally cultivated. Agriculture was a fairly low-technology affair with only the swivel plow used until European conquest. Trade was vital between farming communities and nomads and between both and the cities, where they obtained manufactured goods. Cities were generally grouped into regions based on race and origin, with narrow streets and few public facilities beyond a mosque and communal oven, and no public squares.

The city of Fès was founded in the early ninth century by Moulay Idrīs II and flourished because of its location on a river, providing waterpower and a strategic trade location. Fès remained the industrial center of Morocco throughout the Middle Ages, with the dominance of its artisans such as jewelers, blacksmiths, and clothes makers.

Trans-Saharan trade developed soon after the Arab conquest of North Africa and was flourishing by the ninth century, with Arabs trading salt for gold and slaves from the lands south of the desert. Slaves were used as field laborers and also as recruits for the army since they had loyalties to no particular people. The Arabic traders were the primary means by which Islam spread across sub-Saharan Africa, with a journey taking three months or more in each direction. The Saharan trade slowly died off after European explorers and traders managed to navigate down the western coast of Africa. But it was the banning of the slave trade in the nineteenth century, first by the French in Algeria after the conquest in 1830 and in Tunisia a decade later, that made overland trade across the Sahara uneconomic. Morocco only banned the slave trade late in the nineteenth century.

The tenth and first half of the eleventh centuries saw a period of flourishing in the Maghrib, with an expansion of agriculture and settled towns. Food was generally plentiful, in particular cereals, olives, dates, and animal products, and there was a surplus to export. Farmers were interested in keeping and expanding their knowledge and would often carry seeds and cuttings to exchange with others on their pilgrimages to Mecca. New plants such as cotton, sugar cane, oranges, apricots, peaches, rice, sorghum, bananas, and mangoes came to North Africa from the eastern part of the Islamic world, bordering on India and Southeast Asia.

However, in the mid-eleventh century, the Egyptian caliph encouraged the nomadic Beni Hilal Arabs to migrate west from upper Egypt. The nomads headed west, destroying settlements and bringing their families with them as they turned portions of Tripolitania (Libya) and Ifriqiya into wasteland. This second Arab invasion was more important than the first in that the second wave relegated Berber culture and language from its position of prominence in the countryside in favor of Arabic, which was already dominant in the cities. Olive plantations and grain fields were abandoned and towns deserted as sections of the population were driven from the land that the Arab people used as pasture. The remaining farmers were heavily taxed and under constant threat of raiding. Kairouan was sacked between 1050 and 1052 and much reduced in population. Coastal cities fared better at maintaining their independence and local trade and agriculture

until the capture of many coastal cities by the Normans in the mid-twelfth century.

The Almoravid Berbers rose in the middle of the eleventh century to become rulers of Morocco, western Algeria, and Andalusian Spain. They were nomadic people from southern Morocco and Mauritania who relied on stock raising and the Saharan caravan traffic and later expanded their rule and Islam south to Senegal. The rule of the Almoravids saw an elimination of the various heresies that had been present in Morocco since the advent of Islam and the facilitation of greater ties with Spain, which enriched the learning and industries of the towns of Fès, Marrakech (founded by the Almoravids), and Algiers.

The next empire formed in Morocco was that of the Almohads, who came from the Atlas Mountains in southern Morocco and took over the country and parts of western Algeria, including the newly founded trading port of Bejaïa. Life in Morocco was generally good under the new reign with a period of peace and public works, particularly in and around Rabat and Marrakech. This period saw the growth of industry, such as paper manufacturing and metal smelting, and growing trade with Spain, Italy, and France. It was during this period that the city of Tlemcen in western Algeria grew rich through the Saharan trade and had a large vibrant port with trade links to Europe.

The twelfth and thirteenth centuries saw the beginnings of normal commercial relations across the Mediterranean, with European merchants allowed to settle and trade in the major ports. Islamic and Arabic influences had slowly spread up the Nile to Sudan, with the migration of Arabic people from Egypt displacing the original Christian kingdoms that were found there from 1300 onward.

Trade with Italy was important for Morocco in the thirteenth century, which imported metals, hardware, textiles, woolen clothes, spices, and wine and exported slaves, leather, hides, carpets, wool, grain, and sugar. As the *reconquista* drew to a close in Spain, the kingdoms of Spain and Portugal attempted to carry it over the sea to Morocco. From the late fifteenth century and continuing on into the sixteenth, both European countries captured coastal ports on both the Mediterranean and Atlantic coasts. The ports of Ceuta and Melilla have continued in Spanish hands through the present day. The purpose of these conquests, although motivated by religion, was economic in nature, since these were places from which Spain could purchase grain and wool for retrade with black Africa. Gradually, these ports were retaken militarily by the Moroccans, mostly owing to the absence of support from the Iberian governments.

Morocco from this point on became less attached to the eastern Maghrib and more inward and European focused. In the late sixteenth century, Morocco sent military expeditions across the Sahara, capturing Timbuktu and the lands around the Niger River, but, because of the long distances, failed to maintain effective control. Many Muslim inhabitants and Jews from Spain were expelled between 1492 and 1614 and migrated to North Africa, in particular northern Morocco and Tunisia. These newcomers were generally well educated and skilled and provided a useful new source of urban labor. The seventeenth century saw a period of political instability and economic decline, in particular the sugar mills of southern Morocco and the desert trade, which was diverted to the French base in Senegal and farther east to Algeria and Tunisia. The eighteenth century saw a tax reorganization in favor of the urban over the rural and the beginning of large-scale migrations from the Atlas Mountains down to the plains.

Piracy developed in the Mediterranean in the thirteenth century as Christian and Muslim corsairs raided the other religion's boats to capture slaves and booty. The developing commercial trade and weak governmental control (and often support) of piracy facilitated its emergence. The decline in Turkish power in the seventeenth century saw an increase in piracy within Tunisian and Algerian ports, directed against Christian shipping. It brought in great wealth and increased the population drawn to Algiers and the other pirate ports. The eighteenth century saw the decline of piracy. This decline was due to stronger European fleets and to the confiscation of booty by the Islamic governments.

Algiers was founded in the tenth century and grew in importance as a trading and pirating center, increasing in size with the arrival of Spanish Muslims after the capture of Granada in 1492. The period of Turkish rule in Algeria (1516–1830) was an attempt by the Turks to squeeze the maximum amount of surplus out of Algeria, which functioned by selling off the rights to collect taxes, often to tribal chiefs, who became de facto rulers of their part of the country. Although power was nominally in the hands of the beys appointed from Turkey, in effect the military made the major decisions. The southern and western parts of the country were primarily pastoral regions, while the more heavily populated eastern Algeria was a region of subsistence agriculture, with some grain surplus exported. Declining returns from piracy in the 1700s saw the levying of more and higher taxes without a corresponding attempt to improve the infrastructure of the country. A diplomatic incident in 1827 was the excuse the French used to invade Algeria in 1830.

Tunis was not as devoted as Algiers to piracy, as its commercial links were too important to completely sever by these illegal activities. The population of Tunisia was estimated at around 1 million in the period of Ottoman rule, with 15 percent urban, a higher percentage than the other countries of the Maghrib. The main items produced were agricultural: cereals, olive oil, and wool, which were exported under a monopoly by the state. Taxation was generally heavier on the rural population, which enabled an urban intellectual elite to develop. In Tunisia, the ruling Turks gradually became assimilated and, except for a few customs and words, had lost their separate identity by the start of the nineteenth century. During this time, Tunisia became subservient to European economic interests, allowing foreigners to buy land, borrowing heavily to finance a larger army and new palaces, and abolishing state monopolies in agriculture at the behest of European merchants. Tax rates were raised so much that they created civil unrest and discouraged agricultural production. This forced Tunisia to import wheat at times, leading to a trade deficit. The prospects of a debt default led to the imposition of an International Financial Commission, which collected taxes on behalf of foreign creditors. Eventually, in 1881 the French took advantage of a Tunisian raid into Algerian territory to invade the country and establish a protectorate.

North Africa was sparsely inhabited up until the twentieth century. Estimates have the population of the Maghrib at 3 to 4 million in 750 CE, rising to levels in 1800 of 4 million people for Morocco, 4 million for Algeria, and between 1.5 and 2 million for Tunisia.

Morocco was an insular country in the early nineteenth century. As in other North African countries, the diffusion of technology from the Industrial Revolution in Europe was almost nonexistent. Europeans were restricted to a few ports in the country. The sultan began a process of monopolizing all trade, both import and export, which was complete by midcentury. This restriction of trade caused a war with Spain in 1860, after which Spain forced the Moroccans to open up their country to foreign trade and investment. A fiscal deficit, owing to the difficulty of raising taxes, saw the sultan raise three foreign loans in 1902 and 1903, which had as surety 60 percent of the customs duties, to be collected by French officials. Lack of centralized control contributed to raids against French establishments in Morocco, giving the French the excuse to take over portions of the country beginning in 1907. This was completed with the establishment of a French protectorate in 1912.

Libya in the seventeenth and eighteenth centuries saw revenue drawn from exporting cattle, sheep, and dates—often to the British fleet based in Malta—plus some proceeds from piracy, which was curtailed under British and French pressure in 1816. The ban on the slave trade in Algeria and Tunisia triggered an increase in the trade through Libya in the mid-1800s, although this wound down toward the end of the century. This latter period under Turkish rule was one of virtual autarky, with visitors and traders strongly discouraged from visiting. The country remained backward, with little infrastructure investment well into the nineteenth century, although the Ottomans modernized the legal and education systems. Encouraged by the Ottomans, southern Tunisians moved to Libya after the French takeover. Italian companies expanded their presence in Libya in the early twentieth century, and the country was taken over militarily by Italy in 1911.

BIBLIOGRAPHY

Abun-Nasr, Jamil M. *A History of the Maghrib in the Islamic Period.* Cambridge, 1987.

Brett, Michael, ed. *Ibn Khaldun and the Medieval Maghrib.* Norfolk, U.K., 1999.

Dîrî, 'Abd al-Azīz, *The Historical Formation of the Arab Nation.* Translated by Lawrence I. Conrad. New York, 1987.

Fisher, Sydney Nettleton. *The Middle East: A History.* New York, 1959.

Hourani, Albert. *A History of the Arab Peoples.* Cambridge, Mass., 1991.

Joffé, George, ed. *North Africa: Nation, State, and Region.* London, 1993.

Julien, Charles-André. *History of North Africa.* Translated by John Petrie. London, 1970.

Kissling, H. J., et al. *The Last Great Muslim Empires: History of the Muslim World.* Princeton, 1996.

Marmon, Shaun E. *Slavery in the Islamic Middle East.* Princeton, 1999.

The Middle East and North Africa: Medieval and Modern History, vol. 2, no. 3, *Trends in History.* New York, 1982.

Morsy, Magali. *North Africa, 1800–1900.* New York, 1984.

Udovitch, A. L., ed. *The Islamic Middle East, 700–1900: Studies in Economic and Social History.* Princeton, 1981.

Valensi, Lucette. *On the Eve of Colonialism: North Africa before the French Conquest.* Translated by Kenneth J. Perkins. New York, 1977.

Welch, Galbraith. *North African Prelude: The First Seven Thousand Years.* New York, 1949.

LYNDON MOORE

Colonial and Modern Periods

The region called North Africa corresponds to what can be precisely described as Arabo-Berber Africa. North Africa is physically distinct from Africa south of the Sahara and is culturally typified by its Arabo-Berber Islamic identity, which forms the core of the region's unity. The region covers almost six million square kilometers, or one-fifth of the African continent. It extends for twenty-five hundred kilometers from north to south, between the shores of the Mediterranean and the southern Sahara, and for five thousand kilometers from west to east, between the Atlantic Ocean and the Red Sea. The countries of North Africa, which extend from 20 to 37 degrees latitude north, lie within the zone of subtropical climate. More specifically there is a Mediterranean climate in the north, contrasted by a desert climate in the south.

Although the population and geographical characteristics grant certain physical characteristics to the North African countries, the region is divided into two separate entities. The Maghrib, which means "Land of Sunset," was first adopted by the Arab conquerors to refer to the area

west of Egypt and is thereby distinguished from Arab East or the Middle East. The Maghrib is the region once referred to by Europeans as "Barbary," the Land of the Berber. As a historiogeographical term, *Maghrib* has been used collectively to refer to Northwest Africa, comprising Algeria, Morocco, Libya (except Cyrenaica, the eastern part of Libya bordering on Egypt), Tunisia, and Mauritania. All of these countries, with the exception of Libya, were during the colonial period part of the French colonial empire with a Spanish presence in parts of Morocco. Libya was first occupied by Italy and then administered by Britain and France. Besides demarcating North Africa as Maghrib, French colonialists have adopted Afrique du Nord to refer to their former possessions in this region, thus excluding Egypt, Libya, and the western Sahara. A second entity of North Africa, which is not part of Maghrib or northeastern Africa, is Egypt. Egypt was seen in terms of British spheres of influence as opposed to the French presence in Maghrib. This division still largely prevails, even though the region underwent a decisive change from the postindependence period. Following World War II the ambition for Arab union in search for unity, cooperation, and economic integration led to the creation of the North African Arab Maghrib Union (AMU) on February 1989 by Algeria, Libya, Morocco, Tunisia, and Mauritania. The union attracted Mauritania, a northwest African country usually not considered part of North Africa that borders the Atlantic Ocean, Senegal, Mali, and the Spanish Sahara. The total population of the region is more than 72 million, or about 20 percent of the total population of Africa. Moors (people of mixed Arab and Berber ancestry) make up the majority of the population. Egypt is the most heavily populated state of the region, and Mauritania in Northwest Africa is the least populated with less than three million inhabitants.

Colonial Period. The beginning of the nineteenth century marked a starting point for the rapid political and economic transformation of North Africa. The most obvious characteristic of this transformation was the gradual integration of the North African economy into European-dominated world markets triggered by the impact of the Industrial Revolution in Europe. Europe's expansion into the region by way of colonial presence and control led to an intensification of commerce and the diminishing political importance of the local rulers. Because the colonial period had a profound impact on existing patterns of economic activity in the region, North African economic history from the colonial to the modern period is closely connected to the European dominance of the world economy.

In the precolonial period North Africa's geographical location on the southern Mediterranean shores and its long-distance caravan trading networks linked the region to both the southern Mediterranean and the Islamic world. At the beginning of the nineteenth century, with the exceptions of

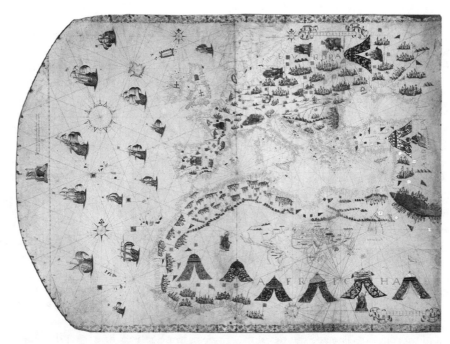

NORTH AFRICA. Map of Europe and North Africa by Jacobus de Maiolo, 1561. (Museo Navale di Pegli, Genoa, Italy/Scala/Art Resource, NY)

Mauritania and Morocco, which existed as independent states, the region was ruled by autonomous dynasties established by Ottoman military generals. Although these dynasties were vassal states of the Ottoman sultan, they nevertheless enjoyed economic independence from the Porte. Economies of the region chiefly based on the long-distance caravan trade with the western Sudan and the Levant were characterized by thriving commerce. The volume of commercial traffic between Tunisia and the Levant up until the early nineteenth century accounted for 12.3 percent of Tunisia's exports. By 1824 the total volume of exports was on the rise, reaching 5.876 million francs, of which *chéchias* (fezzes) alone accounted for 2,253,835 francs.

Corsair activities with the southern Mediterranean also favored rulers of the North African region. By 1800, for instance, maritime activities involving the control of European ships along the southern shores of the Mediterranean provided the Tunisian government's treasury with two-fifths of its central revenues. Although a shrinking source of revenue, economically privateering also significantly furnished the Algerian and Moroccan treasuries, even though income from this activity was irregular.

Access to the Mediterranean Coast also attracted European merchants, who had conducted trade and business with the Barbary Coast since the sixteenth century. Consequently when European imperial powers carved up North Africa in the early nineteenth century, they found economic structures that had been partly facilitated by early European merchants and brokers in established commercial outposts along the Barbary Coast. These precolonial European merchants were, in a sense, not part of the colonial force. However, they were vital in the process of incorporating the region into a European-dominated world economy. Beginning in the 1830s formal European colonial penetration in the region marked a *fin de siècle des temps* for the region's long-distance economy and commercial activities with European merchants. By 1816 economic activities stemming from corsairing were suppressed by the European powers. Subsequently European imperial penetration into the region over several decades marked the beginning of a pattern of economic expansion overseas for North Africa. Among the significant aspects of the colonial period were the European dominance of the North African economy, the commercialization of the rural economy, and the introduction of large-scale European exports to North Africa. Consequently North Africa underwent a fundamental transformation that ultimately brought it under Europe's financial and political control. Thus through trade expansion and disputes, Algeria fell victim to French occupation (1830–1962), and Tunisia was a protectorate (1881–1956). Egypt was occupied by the British in 1882. Libya fell to the Italians in 1911 and did not gain independence until 1951 under the mandate of the United Nations. Morocco was jointly occupied by France and Spain (1912–1956).

Once a colonial presence was established, European penetration and rule in North Africa introduced a new course for a number of institutional developments, including economic and political changes that shaped the domestic and international affairs of North Africa throughout the colonial period. However, these changes, depending on whether the colonial powers were French, English, Italian, or Spanish, were not uniform. Indeed there were wide variations, particularly in the social and economic reforms created by European-inspired legal codes, in land tenure systems, in modern technology, and in commercial development.

However, with the exceptions of Libya, Morocco, and Mauritania, a shared legacy of financial and economic insolvency was also a common pattern of the transformation of North Africa's economy under European domination. The mid-nineteenth century, which was overshadowed by two important developments, both of which resulted from colonization, best illustrates the pattern of the region's economic development under colonial rule. The first development had to do with the early European nationals, especially merchants and bondholders, and their respective consuls vis-à-vis the Mehkzan (the central government) of North African countries that favored European merchants—France being one of the largest beneficiaries—in lieu of local merchants. The second development is in fact the result of the first. The effect of European merchants' activities disturbed not only governments of the region but also the commercial activities of the local merchants and the rural economy. In the long run the rural population was drawn into the consumption of Western manufactured goods in lieu of goods produced by rural economies. One of the drastic effects of this European influence was the inability of local merchants to compete with large-scale maritime trade monopolized by European merchants, who gradually weakened and eventually superceded the traditional, long-distance caravan trade. This led to a decline of local and rural economies. The mass infiltration of European manufactured goods into North Africa also raised the value of imports above the value of exports, therefore discouraging local industry. In Tunisia, for instance, the *chéchia* makers, whose guilds produced prestigious craft products famous throughout the Ottoman Empire and the western Sudan, were undermined by unfair competition from French merchants in the form of synthetic copies of *chéchia* made in Marseille and exported to the Levant. The pattern of such economic change not only drained the financial resources of the Mehkzan, it also discouraged local industry except in Libya and Mauritania, where European merchants had little presence at the time. It is commonly believed that the introduction of a monetary system into the economy also led to an increase in indiscriminate moneylending to central governments, which in turn resulted in financial bankruptcy. Demographically, however, the change in economic patterns in North Africa resulted in the population increasing from seven million to twelve million following trade expansion.

Naturally one of the main characteristics of North African economic development was the economic insolvency arising from the drastic effects of indiscriminate borrowing from the Europeans. In 1867, for instance, the bey of Tunis was facing impending bankruptcy owing to heavy borrowing from European creditors resident in Tunis. The result was dramatic, for it brought the regency to the verge of European intervention. However, Great Britain, Tunis's friend and ally at the time, hoped to introduce reforms to the regency of Tunis and forced Ahmed Bey (1837–1855) to adopt the *el-Ahd el-Aman* (1857), which was modeled after the Ottoman Hatti Sheriff from 1839–1856. The British consul in Tunis, Richard Wood (1806–1900), who engineered the strategy, was met with opposition from European merchants and creditors as well as from the French and Italian governments. Caught in the trap of European capitalist expansion, the bey of Tunis faced bankruptcy in 1867 and ultimately brought Tunis under European control in 1869. A financial collapse of this sort was a typical pattern of nineteenth-century European imperialism, and it set the stage for European control over the North African economy.

Egypt was another case in point. Successors of Mohammad Ali hoped to advance the Westernization of Egypt by borrowing heavily from European creditors. For instance, after Ismail became khedive (1863–1879), he put the country heavily in debt. His strong desire to Westernize Egyptian society, reform Egypt's administration, and modernize its economy proved costly. His modernization project, including enlargement of the army and other heavy expenditures, increased the national debt from three million pounds sterling in 1863, when he took over, to ninety to one hundred million pounds sterling in 1876. Apart from the Suez Canal, only 10 percent of the 90 million pounds borrowed by Ismail was actually directed to modernization plans. In fact much of the money was used to reduce earlier debts, to finance war with the Sudan, and to settle indemnity payments. In a desperate effort to check the growth of the debt, the taxation of the fellahin (peasants) was increased. Yet similar to what had transpired in the regency of Tunis, Ismail's last attempt to avoid economic insolvency was in vain, and in May 1876 the European powers declared Egypt insolvent. An international *caisse de la dette publique* was established by representatives of Britain, France, Austria, and Italy with a mandate to organize the servicing of the debt. As did Tunis, Egypt gave up its economic sovereignty to the commission. Inevitably the difficult situations the governments of North African countries experienced in paying their European creditors coupled with the resulting huge tax burden on their own population soon created difficulties for the North African urban economy. In both Egypt and Tunisia, where agriculture remained one of the main sectors of the economy, taxation increases led to the discontent of the fellahin.

Settler Economy. One of the dominant traits of North African economic history during the colonial period was the exploitation of its local economies by European settlements. Former European nationals who were provided incentives to migrate from their metropolises and settle in the region formed a dominant part of the colonial force. The motives for settlements in part were to gain control over land tenure and agriculture, to create economic buffers, and to exclude other European colonizers from spheres of interest. Yet not all North African countries were affected by the settlers' colonial economy. French Algeria, where the French presence on the Algerian coast dates back to the 1830s, set a precedent for settler economies and initiated a systematic land tenure policy consistent with the doctrines of French "official colonization." In Algiers and its environs, lands were taken from indigenous people and allocated to European settlers, who were in turn provided incentives, including loans, housing, and an agricultural infrastructure, largely for grape production. In Tunisia, as soon as the French had established a protectorate over the unstable Ottoman regency in 1881, the process of dispossessing the fellahin began. The official colonization policy of the regency, "colonization by capital" (1881–1882), was to ensure the elimination of Italian imperials and Maltese implants by the British and allow large French corporations (Compagine des Batignolles, Societe Marseillaise de Credit, Societe Fonciere de Tunisie, and so forth) to gain control of nearly 430,000 hectares. The decree of 13 November 1898 required a transfer of Tunisian-owned land, that is, *habus* (pious foundations), to the French administration of at least two hundred hectares annually.

When North African countries were gaining independence, the region was experiencing mixed results from its incorporation into the European economy, largely because the rural economics of the region that existed before the colonial period were not only lucrative according to the local standards but were regular and balanced. The long-distance trade through overland and overseas trade with the Levant and the southern Mediterranean rim had previously comprised much of the region's economy, although the local agricultural and pastoral economies were superceded by a European-based economy. Therefore the opening up of the region to European commercialization in lieu of rural economies and the resulting bankruptcies of North African countries followed a pattern of European imperialism, a complex modernization of the region, that came at a massive cost.

Modern Period. During the modern period the main pattern of economic structures of North Africa was complex. On the one hand, the economies of North Africa entered into a decade of independence with imbalanced economies bearing the marks of colonial legacies. On the other hand, from the 1960s to the 1970s, with the exception of South Africa, North Africa became the most rapidly growing industrial region on the African continent. The discovery of oil and gas, which made possible the spread of processing industries on a large scale over many parts of the region, was in some sense a striking economic change from past eras. The discovery of oil in the Sahara was one of the most significant of all the economic developments of the region's economy in the modern period. Along with oil came a series of related industrial economic activities that can be seen as some of the most significant economic transformations in the region since the colonial period. The processing industry, for instance, accounted for 10 percent of the gross national product (GDP) in Algeria, 14 percent in Morocco, 17 percent in Tunisia, and 20 percent in Egypt. In 1970 Libya, Algeria, and Egypt were the continent's first, third, and fourth largest oil producers, with 160 million, 47 million, and 16 million tons respectively. Oil revenues served as the main source of finance for industrial and other development projects. Oil and gas refineries were built in most parts of North Africa. Refineries were built in the Algerian ports of Algiers, Arzew, and Skikda and were linked to the principal oil fields by pipelines. There were also gas liquefaction plants in Arzew and Skikda. In Tunisia there were gas and oil refineries in Bizerte. Libya's chief refineries included Zawia, Brega, Misurata, and Ras Lanuf. In the 1970s Morocco had two mining refineries, one at Sid Kacem and the other at Mohammedia. Tunisia, on the other hand, was a less-important producer of hydrocarbonates (four million tons in 1970).

Politically the discovery of oil in the region meant a lot to North African states. Owing to their strong economic importance in the modern period, there was a general increase in assertiveness in political activities of the region, especially vis-à-vis the former colonial powers. This assertiveness was made particularly clear during some historical changes that dominated the modern period. Some aspects of this assertiveness were results of the broader changes in world political-economic strength partly inspired by the Organization of Petroleum Exporting Countries (OPEC) in the 1970s. The political importance associated with the oil economy was particularly obvious in the aftermath of the "oil shock," when the region and its Middle East OPEC counterparts played a significant political role in the use of oil as an economic weapon to punish supporters of Israel in the Arab-Israeli conflict.

Besides oil and gas, North Africa is also rich in several other natural resources, such as phosphates, iron, zinc, and fish. For phosphate Morocco, Tunisia, and Egypt are Africa's first, second, and fourth largest producers. Morocco was the world's third largest producer and exporter (ten million tons a year) in 1970. For natural gas Algeria and Libya were the leading exporters. Natural resources were of secondary importance to the Egyptian economy.

On the other hand, Mauritania, Algeria, Morocco, and Tunisia led the region in iron, zinc, and mercury production. However, the growth of processing industries linked to these mining industries as well as oil and gas were constrained by a number of internal and external factors. Except in Libya, both private and state industries encountered shortages of skilled local labor and at the same time were unable to recruit a sufficient amount of skilled foreign labor.

Advances in industrial processing in turn stimulated the growth of traditional economic sectors. In agriculture olive oil and grapes in Tunisia and Algeria and the cotton and textile industries in Egypt were accelerated by the growing industrial processing. In Morocco the industrial sector in the early 1970s remained relatively concentrated on the Atlantic littoral, with 52 percent of modern industrial factories located in the Casablanca-Mohammedia area in 1972 and a further 7 percent in other parts of the Atlantic Coast.

In the modern period tourism has also proved one of the biggest sources of foreign revenue for Egypt, Morocco, Tunisia, and Algeria. In 1971 the tourism sector accounted for increases in their GDPs and attracted foreign investment in North Africa in general. It created over forty thousand jobs directly, and in Egypt, Morocco, and Tunisia it indirectly stimulated local crafts industries.

The Cold War context also introduced important economic developments in North Africa. Following a global Mediterranean plan, the European Economic Commission (EEC) set a policy of contributing to the economic, social, and cultural development of the North African states. By 1971 the EEC had initiated bilateral association and cooperation agreements with all the North African countries except for Libya. During this period North Africa was a politically volatile region where the USSR was trying to develop influence. To maintain political stability and strengthen its own influence, the EEC adopted the Global Mediterranean Policy in 1972. However, various economic and trade agreements were negotiated separately in an ad hoc manner. By 1995 the European Union (EU) wanted to overhaul its relationship with the Mediterranean countries, and Egypt, Tunisia, Algeria, and Morocco signed the Barcelona Declaration of November 1995 with the EU for economic and financial partnership through an industrial free trade area that has been negotiated separately with each of the North African countries. Until today these agreements, which now include Algeria, remain a major factor in economic development in the region.

BIBLIOGRAPHY

Abun Nasr, J. M. *A History of the Maghrib in the Islamic Period.* Cambridge, 1987. Reprinted 1990, 1993.

Anderson, Lisa. *The State and Social Transformation in Tunisia and Libya, 1830–1980.* Princeton, 1986.

Berque, Jacque. *French North Africa: The Maghrib between Two World Wars.* Translated by Jean Stewart. London, 1967.

Burke, Edmund, III. *Prelude to Protectorate in Morocco: Precolonial Protest and Resistance, 1860–1912.* Chicago, 1976.

Dumett, Raymond E., ed. *Gentlemanly Capitalism and British Imperialism: The New Debate on Empire.* New York, 1999.

Joffé, George, ed. *North Africa: Nation, State and Region.* London and New York, 1993.

Kanya-Forstner, A. S. *The Conquest of the Western Sudan: A Study in French Military Imperialism.* London, 1969.

Knapp, Wilfred. *North West Africa: A Political and Economic Survey.* 3d ed. Oxford, 1977.

Laroui, Abdallah. *The History of the Maghrib: An Interpretive Essay.* Translated by Ralph Manheim. Princeton, 1977.

Mahjoubi, Ali. *L'establishment du protectorat francais en Tunisie.* Tunis, Tunisia, 1977.

Morsy, Magali. *North Africa, 1800–1900: A Survey from the Nile Valley to the Atlantic.* London, 1984.

Owen, Roger. *State and Power Politics in the Making of the Modern Middle East.* New York, 1992.

Parker, B. Richard. *North Africa: Regional Tensions and Strategic Concerns.* New York, 1984.

Valensi, Lucette. *On the Eve of Colonialism: North Africa before the French Conquest.* Translated by Kenneth J. Perkins. New York and London, 1977.

ISMAEL M. MONTANA

NORWAY. *See* Nordic Countries.

NUCLEAR POWER. The nuclear power industry history is rooted in international competition to develop and deliver nuclear weapons and control their proliferation, and to dominate markets for commercial nuclear power plants (NPPs) and nuclear fuel.

Nuclear Fuel Cycle. Figure 1 shows the Nuclear Fuel Cycle. Uranium (U) is 99.3 percent U-238 and 0.7 percent U-235. With fission, U-235 releases energy and neutrons, which either are captured by U-238 to become plutonium (e.g., Pu-239), or "split" (fission) U-235 atoms, releasing more energy and neutrons in a chain reaction. Nuclear weapons require nearly pure U-235 or plutonium. To produce electricity, NPPs use natural or enriched uranium, a mix of uranium and plutonium (mixed oxide, MOX), or plutonium. In NPPs, a controlled chain reaction produces heat to generate electricity.

The "front end" of the cycle involves uranium mining and milling, conversion and enrichment, and fuel fabrication. Uranium mining for nuclear weapons started in the early 1940s. Since the commercial market emerged in the 1960s, Australia, Canada, Namibia, and South Africa have come to dominate the uranium market with nearly 60 percent of global production (NEA, 1999). To increase the percentage of U-235 (by removing U-238), uranium is converted to Uranium Hexafluoride and enriched using two (commercial) methods: diffusion and centrifuge. Enriched uranium

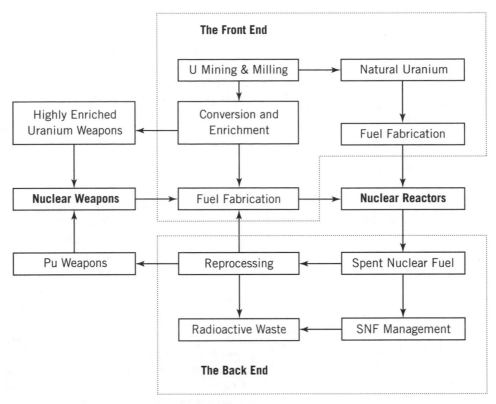

FIGURE 1. Nuclear fuel cycle.

(1 to 4 percent U-235) is then used to fabricate nuclear fuel (EIA, 1996). Environmental consequences of the "front end" include uranium mining and milling tails and depleted uranium from enrichment. Historically, most tails and depleted uranium are from nuclear weapons production.

The "back end" includes spent nuclear fuel (SNF) management, reprocessing, and high-level radioactive waste disposal. The "back end" is the most environmentally contentious aspect of commercial nuclear power. There are two types of back ends: "open" and "closed." Under the open cycle, SNF is cooled at the NPP, stored, and finally shipped to a geologic repository. The closed cycle involves reprocessing SNF to extract uranium and plutonium for fuel. Because of nuclear weapons proliferation and economics, the United States does not currently use commercial reprocessing. France and the United Kingdom dominate the reprocessing market.

Commercial Nuclear Power Reactor Technologies. Commercial NPPs can be classified as follows. First, reactors have either a "fast" or "slow" (thermal) chain reaction. With a fast chain reaction, *fast* reactors are more efficient in using plutonium as a fuel and in converting uranium to plutonium. Therefore, they are known as "fast breeder reactors," or as "liquid metal reactors" (LMRs), because liquid metals (e.g., sodium) cool the reactor.

Second, *thermal* reactors can be classified along two dimensions: the moderator (to slow neutrons) and the coolant (to remove heat). Water (light and heavy) and graphite are used as moderators. Water (light or heavy) and gas (air, carbon dioxide, or helium) are used as coolants.

Third, NPPs use either direct (boiling) or indirect (pressurized) cycles to transfer energy to the turbine generator.

Although there have been many experimental reactors combining these options, only five types of commercial NPPs have been built (IAEA, 2002):

(1) Light Water Reactors (LWRs), including (1) Pressurized light-Water-moderated and cooled Reactors and Soviet/Russian pressurized Water-moderated, Water-cooled Electricity Reactors (PWRs and WWERs) and (2) Boiling light-Water-moderated and cooled Reactors (BWRs) and Advanced BWRs (ABWRs);

(2) Heavy Water Reactors (HWRs), including Pressurized Heavy-Water-moderated and cooled Reactors (PHWRs);

(3) Gas-Cooled, graphite-moderated Reactors (GCRs), including (1) early British and French GCRs, (2) later British Advanced GCRs (AGRs), and (3) High-Temperature Gas-cooled, graphite-moderated Reactors (HTGRs);

(4) Light-Water-cooled, Graphite-moderated Reactors (LW-GRs); and

(5) Liquid Metal Reactors (LMRs).

Many national programs foresaw three stages of NPP deployment: (1) GCRs and HWRs that can use natural uranium, (2) LWRs and HTGRs that require enriched uranium or MOX, and (3) LMRs that can create more plutonium than they use. Until the 1970s, GCRs had the largest market share. In the 1970s LWRs became dominant. In 1999 these plants generated over 75 percent of the electricity in France and Lithuania, about 20 percent in the United Kingdom and the United States, and less than 5 percent in China and India. Although costs vary between technologies and across countries, approximately 60 percent of total cost is for plant construction, 20 percent for fuel, and 20 percent for operations and maintenance (see, for example, NEA, 1998).

National Programs. Each country developed nuclear power under a unique set of constraints.

United States. The world's first reactor was an air-cooled, graphite-moderated, natural-uranium "pile" built in Chicago in December 1942 (ANS, 1992). Soon after both uranium and plutonium weapons were used in Japan in August 1945, the Atomic Energy Act of 1946 restricted ownership of radioactive materials to the U.S. government, restricted foreign access to nuclear research and development (R&D), and established the Atomic Energy Commission (AEC). The AEC directed R&D from the late 1940s to the early 1970s. Under AEC R&D, the USS *Nautilus* became the first nuclear-powered submarine in 1954.

The Atomic Energy Act of 1954 allowed private ownership of nuclear reactors (but not nuclear fuel). Immediately, construction began on a 60-MW PWR prototype at Shippingport, Pennsylvania. The Shippingport PWR began operating in 1958. The U.S. built several reactor types (LWR, HWR, HTGR, and LMR) between 1956 and 1965 (see Arthur D. Little, Inc., 1968). To encourage NPP orders, turnkey contracts for LWRs were negotiated in the mid-1960s between electric utilities and four reactor manufacturers: Westinghouse, General Electric (GE), Babcock & Wilcox, and Combustion Engineering. Dozens of orders followed. More than 100 LWRs were built, but no construction started after the 1979 Three Mile Island (TMI) accident in Pennsylvania as capital costs rose to satisfy new safety requirements. While NPPs are now much safer than they were in 1979, U.S. public perception and debate is still influenced by the TMI accident.

United Kingdom and Commonwealth. Although the United Kingdom and Canada participated in the U.S. nuclear weapons program during World War II, the United States restricted them from its R&D in 1946. The United Kingdom began its nuclear program in 1945 using GCRs.

A graphite reactor started operation in 1947. By 1953, the United Kingdom developed a new fuel type for its GCR design, Magnox (metallic uranium clad in a magnesium alloy), providing efficient electricity generation, and started building eight 50-MW Magnox units to produce both plutonium and electricity. Construction started in 1960 on eighteen 220-MW Magnox units. Fourteen Advanced GCRs (AGRs) were built by 1989. The United Kingdom also built two LMRs, one HWR, and one PWR (completed in 1995). No NPPs have been built since. British Nuclear Fuels Limited (BNFL, which now owns the nuclear divisions of Westinghouse, Combustion Engineering, and others) operates the GCRs and fuel facilities. British Energy operates the AGRs and the PWR.

Four Commonwealth members have nuclear programs: Canada, India, Pakistan, and South Africa. Only Canada and India are discussed here. In 1944, Canada began research on HWRs with the United States and United Kingdom, completing the first HWR in September 1945. Atomic Energy of Canada Limited (AECL) further demonstrated HWR technology during the 1950s. This led to the CANDU (Canadian Deuterium Uranium), a PHWR using natural uranium in 1962. Since then, AECL has built twenty-three CANDUs in Canada, four in South Korea, two in India, and one each in Pakistan, Argentina, and Romania. Two units are under construction in China and another in Romania.

India imported two GE BWRs in 1964. A year later India began constructing two CANDUs, in a joint venture between AECL and the Indian Department of Atomic Energy (DAE), and a reprocessing plant. The first unit began operating in December 1973. After India's 1974 nuclear weapons test, Canada ended cooperation with India, and DAE completed the second unit in 1980. India completed ten more PHWRs between 1984 and 2000. Under construction are two 500-MW PHWRs and two Russian WWER-1000s.

France. France formed the Commissariat à l'Energie Atomique (CEA) in 1945. Although the CEA conducted early research on HWRs, by the mid-1950s it focused on GCRs to produce both plutonium and electricity. The first unit began operating in 1959 at Marcoule with a reprocessing plant on site. Between 1960 and 1966, France built five GCRs. Also, a Westinghouse PWR was built at Chooz and operated with Belgium, beginning in 1966. For various reasons, France began building PWRs in 1970 under Westinghouse licenses held by Framatome. By 2001, Framatome built fifty-eight units in France and five elsewhere. (France also built a series of LMRs; a 250-MW unit is operating at Marcoule.) Framatome is building two PWRs in China. France uses a closed fuel cycle with the world's largest commercial reprocessing plant at La Hague.

Western Europe. Nine other western European nations built NPPs. These nations were either NPP "developers"

NUCLEAR POWER PLANT. Gien, Loire Valley, France, 1992. (© Walter Mayr/Woodfin Camp and Associates, New York)

(Germany and Sweden) or "importers" (Belgium, Finland, Italy, Netherlands, Slovenia, Spain, and Switzerland), not discussed here.

West Germany imported two BWRs from GE in 1958 and 1962, built with Allgemeine Elektricitaets-Gesellschaft (AEG). AEG built three more BWRs before forming a subsidiary, Kraftwerk Union (KWU), with Siemens in 1969. KWU completed six BWRs by 1985. Siemens initially focused on HWRs but began building PWRs in 1965. It completed twelve PWRs with KWU by 1989. Only LWRs built by KWU now operate in Germany. In June 2000, Germany announced it would phase out nuclear power. By 2001, Siemens merged its nuclear power division (AEG/KWU) with Framatome.

Sweden began its nuclear program in 1957 with Asea's 10-MW PHWR. After finishing it in 1964, Asea switched to BWRs, starting its first BWR in 1966 and finishing its ninth unit in 1985. Sweden also built three Westinghouse PWRs by 1983. A 1980 referendum on nuclear power prompted the Swedish parliament to ban new NPPs and to attempt to retire all units by 2010.

Former Soviet Union, Eastern Europe, and Central Asia. The Soviet Union deployed two reactor types: a LWGR (the RBMK) and a PWR (the WWER). (A series of LMRs were built; one 600-MW unit is operating in Beloyarsky in the South Urals.) Soviet research on uranium began in the early 1940s, allowing the construction of enrichment facilities during the mid-1940s. A graphite reactor was completed in 1946. Based on it, the world's first continuously operating NPP began producing electricity (at five MW) in 1954 in Obninsk (a LWGR using enriched uranium). Construction on two LWGR prototypes began at Beloyarsky in 1958. The Soviets scaled this up to one thousand MW by 1970 and deployed it in Russia, Ukraine (at Chernobyl), and Lithuania. No RBML construction was started after the Chernobyl accident in 1986.

Like the United States, the Soviets developed PWRs to power submarines. Two WWER prototypes were built, providing experience for a standardized WWER-440 (440 MW), deployed starting in 1967 in Russia, Bulgaria, East Germany, and Armenia. A second-generation WWER with enhanced safety features was deployed starting in 1970 in Finland, Ukraine, Hungary, Russia, East Germany, and Czechoslovakia. A third-generation WWER-1000 was deployed starting in 1974 in Russia, Ukraine, and Bulgaria. While construction on several units was started in the 1980s, only one was completed. Russia is building two WWER-1000s in China, two in India, and finishing a KWU unit in Iran.

East Asia. Japan, China, Taiwan, and South Korea lead the world with NPPs under construction (on nuclear power in Asia, see Rothwell, 1998). After initial Japanese research in the 1950s, a GE BWR prototype was built between 1960 and 1965. General Electric completed two more BWRs between 1966 and 1971 and began building BWRs with Toshiba in 1969 and with Hitachi in 1970. Since then, Toshiba has built sixteen BWRs and Hitachi has built eight BWRs. In the 1990s, GE started building

ABWRs with both Toshiba and Hitachi. Two ABWRs were completed by 1997. Two ABWRs and one BWR are under construction. The first Westinghouse PWR was ordered in 1967. Westinghouse built two more PWRs and began working with Mitsubishi in 1970. Since then, Mitsubishi has built nineteen PWRs. Japan built three other reactor types, including a 250-MW LMR, but accidents at the LMR, and associated fuel facilities, have slowed Japan's nuclear program.

In the 1980s, China started constructing PWRs. The China National Nuclear Corporation (CNNC) built Qinshan 1, a 300-MW PWR similar to a unit it built in Pakistan. At Daya Bay, two Framatome 944-MW PWRs were built with French and British engineering, equipment, and financing. All three PWRs began operating in 1994. China's Ninth Five-Year Plan (1996–2000) approved construction of eight units at four sites. Four different suppliers from China, France, Canada, and Russia are each building two units. There are no plans for more NPPs in China's Tenth Five-Year Plan.

Taiwan started its nuclear program by organizing research and training in the 1960s. Taiwan started ordering Westinghouse PWRs in 1972. It completed four PWRs by 1983. In 1978, it began building two GE BWRs, completing them by 1985. Two GE ABWRs are being built.

The South Korea Electric Power Company (KEPCO) ordered six Westinghouse PWRs between 1972 and 1981, a CANDU from AECL in 1977, and two Framatome PWRs in 1983. In the 1980s, KEPCO formed the Korean Heavy Industry Company (KHI) to build four more PWRs and three more CANDUs. These units were completed in 1999. KHI is now building four PWRs.

Nuclear Power in the Twenty-First Century. The international nuclear power industry is actively building two dozen LWRs and PHWRs; most are in Asia. The industry expects new NPP designs to compete against fossil-fueled plants, particularly as nations come into compliance with the Kyoto Protocol (DOE, 2001). On the other hand, electricity market liberalization and deregulation favor less capital-intensive technologies. Future orders will depend on the development of cheaper and safer designs.

BIBLIOGRAPHY

American Nuclear Society (ANS). *Controlled Nuclear Chain Reaction: The First 50 Years*. La Grange Park, Ill., 1992.

Arthur D. Little, Inc. *Competition in the Nuclear Power Supply Industry*. Washington, D.C., 1968.

Department of Energy (DOE). *A Roadmap to Deploy New Nuclear Power Plants in the United States by 2010*. Washington, D.C., 2001.

Energy Information Administration (EIA). *Nuclear Power Generation and Fuel Cycle Report 1996*. Washington, D.C., 1996.

International Atomic Energy Agency (IAEA). *Power Reactor Information System (PRIS) Database*. Vienna, 2002.

Nuclear Energy Agency (NEA). *Projected Costs of Generating Electricity: Update 1998*. Paris, 1998.

Nuclear Energy Agency (NEA). *Uranium 1999: Resources, Production, and Demand*. Paris, 1999.

Rothwell, Geoffrey S., ed. "Special Issue on Nuclear Energy in Asia." *Pacific and Asian Journal of Energy* 8.1 (1998).

GEOFFREY ROTHWELL

O

OCEANIA. *See* Pacific Islands.

OIL CROPS. The use of certain agricultural crops for the production of oil for culinary purposes, for illumination, and as a cosmetic is as old as history. Olives have been produced in the Mediterranean basin for thousands of years; evidence suggests that olives were cultivated on Crete about 3500 BCE and in Israel/Palestine in Neolithic times. Palm oil, from the fruit of the oil palm, has been used in Africa for just as long. Oil derived from cottonseed has a lengthy history of use in China and India as does oil from the kernel of the coconut palm, in Southeast Asia and the Pacific. Such crops were collected from wild trees or plants. The oil was processed through a combination of treading or crushing with stones, boiling, and then skimming the oil after an infusion of water.

The trade in such oils has an equally long history. Olive oil has been a major trade item across the Mediterranean basin for centuries. North Africa, particularly the island of Djerba, was an important center of export in Roman times, as was Andalusia. Andalusia's olive oil output grew sharply with the development of American trade in the sixteenth century. Over time, however, olive oil proved costly in comparison with other oils, which increasingly began to replace it in the market. The key was the development brought on by the Industrial Revolution in Great Britain from the eighteenth century that sharply increased demand for oils for lubricants, for illumination by candles, and for soap.

The main competitors of vegetable oils for these purposes came from fish oils and animal fats, such as tallow. With industrialization, however, it was oil crops that expanded in output. In particular, palm oil, and later palm kernel oil, were ideally placed to meet this new demand. From the 1820s, West African exports of palm oil soared because these oils were particularly well suited for the production of soap and candles and also as a source of lubrication for railways and machinery. Merseyside was the main destination for these oils in Great Britain, as was Marseilles in France. The development of new transportation links between Europe and Africa, especially with the growth of steamshipping after the 1850s, helped meet this demand, while the spread of railways and improvements in port facilities were additional important factors.

However, the discovery of major sources of petroleum in Pennsylvania in 1859 and the development of electrical illumination had a significant impact on the demand for such oil crops. Petroleum proved far more appropriate for lubrication and helped generate a major fall in vegetable oil prices from the 1860s. However, the invention of margarine by the French chemist Hippolyte Mège-Mouriès, in 1869 opened a major new market. The growth in European population and the need for new sources of fats for foodstuffs meant that the margarine industry, based initially in Germany and the Netherlands, was able to produce a cheap commodity to replace lard in the working-class diet. Improved processing methods with the development of new mechanical techniques for crushing in Germany further increased demand for vegetable oils.

In the early twentieth century, the development of hydrogenation—the passing of hydrogen over an oil, thereby allowing the use of liquid vegetable oils in margarine manufacture—was of critical importance. One of the main crops to benefit from this new process was the oil of the groundnut (peanut) from West Africa. Groundnuts had been exported from Africa since the 1830s, but after 1900 there was a major increase in European imports, particularly from Nigeria after 1912. Groundnuts, along with olive oil, palm kernel oil, coconut oil, and soybean oil, proved particularly suitable for margarine manufacture, with the residue cake from the processing being used for animal feed. Beginning with World War I, margarine manufacture began to increase considerably in Great Britain.

The growth in demand for oil crops in this period marked the increased incorporation of agricultural producers into the world market and led to changes in both cultivation and processing methods in the twentieth century. One visible change was the increase in the size of the area used for oil crops. The acreage under olive cultivation in Spain, for example, virtually doubled between the late nineteenth century and the 1970s. Another change was in the attempt to develop plantation farming of oil crops in such places as Africa, where Lever Brothers led the way. Processing methods developed, too, with new techniques that increased the volume of oil expressed from the crop and enabled vegetable oils to be used in an extensive variety of products, such as foodstuffs, animal feeds, soaps, detergents, paints, adhesives, and cosmetics.

BIBLIOGRAPHY

Frankel, R., S. Avitsur, and E. Ayalon. *History and Technology of Olive Oil in the Holy Land*. Arlington, Va., 1994. A study of the growth and processing of olive oil in one of the crop's earliest centers of production.

Hogendorn, Jan S. *Nigerian Groundnut Exports: Origins and Early Development*. Zaria, Nigeria, 1978. A study of the reasons behind the growth of the West African (more particularly Nigerian) groundnut trade in the early twentieth century.

Lynn, Martin. *Commerce and Economic Change in West Africa: The Palm Oil Trade in the Nineteenth Century*. Cambridge, 1997. A study of the development of one oil crop from cultivation of the oil palm in West Africa to the production of soap and other commodities in Great Britain.

Stuyvenberg, Johannes Hermanus van, ed. *Margarine: An Economic, Social and Scientific History*. Liverpool, U.K., 1969. A study of the historical origins and the scientific development of margarine, published a century after its invention.

Wilson, Charles. *The History of Unilever: A Study in Economic Growth and Social Change*. 2 vols. London, 1954. A comprehensive study of the major twentieth-century firm involved in the processing of oil crops in Great Britain and the Netherlands.

MARTIN LYNN

OIL INDUSTRY *[This entry contains four subentries, a historical overview, and discussions of technological change, property rights, and industrial organization.]*

Historical Overview

The oil industry is a particularly important part of modern industrial society. Crude oil, or petroleum, and its derivatives provide energy for manufacturing, transportation, and various heat processes. Petroleum is a dark liquid with moderate to high viscosity. Chemically it is a hydrocarbon, meaning it consists of hydrogen and carbon compounds. Petroleum is also referred to as a fossil fuel as it is derived from once living organisms, particularly plankton and algae. It is refined into gasoline of various grades, kerosene, and fuel oil, and petroleum derivatives are used as lubricating fluids and in the manufacture of literally hundreds of products, including road pavement, floor coverings, waxes, roofing materials, plastics, medicines, fertilizers, insecticides, and synthetic fibers.

The United States pioneered the modern oil industry, and petroleum played an important role in the buildup of U.S. economic, political, and military power. This was especially true in the late nineteenth century and early twentieth century. After World War II, the U.S. dominance of world oil began to decline as producer nations increasingly exerted control over their own oil resources.

Most of the world's crude oil reserves are located in relatively few regions. The Middle East contains about 65 percent of the worlds' crude oil reserves. Saudi Arabia alone accounts for approximately 260 billion barrels of oil, while Iran, Iraq, Kuwait, and the United Arab Emirates each claim about 100 billion barrels. Venezuela, Mexico, and nations of the former Soviet Union have about 50 to 60 billion barrels of oil each. The United States, Libya, Nigeria, and China individually have approximately 18 to 25 billion barrels of oil.

Early Oil Utilization. It was not until the mid-nineteenth century that oil began to fuel modern industrialization. Prior to that time, and for as many as five thousand years earlier, humans collected crude oil that seeped to the earth's surface and utilized it for various heating and lighting purposes. Asphaltic bitumen, a form of petroleum, has been used for thousands of years in architecture, roadwork, medicine, and waterproofing everything from ship hulls to baskets and mats.

The first known attempts to refine crude oil occurred in about 100 CE, when Coptic alchemists in Egypt and Syria developed a method to distill it. Oil was also used for military purposes. In the Middle Ages armies used oil in grenades and other armaments to create "Greek fire" that often devastated opposing armies and their fortifications.

During the age of European transatlantic exploration, asphalt deposits became increasingly important for waterproofing ships. In the Americas, European explorers noted that Native Americans used oil for medicinal purposes. Subsequently Europeans in some cases began using oil as an ointment for a variety of ailments, including headaches, rheumatism, and toothaches.

The medicinal use of petroleum in the United States reached new heights in the mid-nineteenth century. Samuel Kier, a canal boat operator, began manufacturing and marketing "rock oil" as a cure for numerous ailments. He was not the first promoter to sell medicinal oil, but his marketing efforts were widespread. He later stated that he had sold about 240,000 half-pint bottles of medicinal oil for $1 each. He recommended that three doses per day might even cure blindness.

Kier's efforts at marketing rock oil brought increased attention to petroleum and its possible uses. Others were interested in oil for its potential curative powers as well as for more practical purposes. George H. Bissell, a young New York lawyer, suspected that Kier's rock oil might be similar in chemical composition to coal oil, derived from the distillation of bitumen, which was used during the mid-1850s as a fuel for illumination.

Believing that large underground oil supplies were located in eastern Pennsylvania, Bissell and a partner, J. G. Eveleth, found investors to help finance the purchase of oil properties in Titusville, Pennsylvania. The investors required that the partners personally visit the land and contract for a scientific report on the oil there. Benjamin

OIL INDUSTRY. First functioning oil well, Titusville, Pennsylvania, 1859. (Prints and Photographs Division, Library of Congress)

Silliman, Jr., a Yale University professor, and Luther Atwood, a chemist and pharmaceutical manufacturer, drafted the report in April 1855. It confirmed Bissell's belief that oil could be utilized as an illuminant. Satisfied, the New Haven investors stipulated that the new oil firm be incorporated in Connecticut. Bissell and Eveleth formed the Pennsylvania Rock Oil Company on 18 September 1855 and leased twelve hundred acres of land.

James M. Townsend, president of Pennsylvania Rock Oil Company, hired Edwin L. Drake to drill for oil at Titusville. A thirty-eight-year-old former dry goods salesman and express agent for the Boston & Albany Railroad, Drake was a conductor for the New York, New Haven, and Hartford Railroad; he was not an experienced oilman. Drake moved to Titusville, and Townsend sent mail addressed to "Colonel" Drake to improve Drake's standing among Titusville's residents. Drake hired W. A. "Uncle Billy" Smith, an experienced salt well operator, to do the drilling. On 28 August 1859 they struck oil at 69.5 feet.

Modern Oil Industry. The Titusville oil discovery commenced the modern oil industry. Crude oil, however, was not easily utilized. First, it had to be refined into a more usable form, such as kerosene. D. S. Stombs and Julius Brace of Virginia established in 1861 the first major U.S. refinery that produced kerosene. By the 1870s and 1880s, kerosene lamps provided much of the domestic illumination for the urban working class.

The burgeoning oil industry attracted other entrepreneurs as well. In 1863 the partnership of Maurice B. Clark, Samuel Andrews, and John D. Rockefeller formed the Excelsior Works refinery. Rockefeller bought out Clark in 1865, the same year their refinery became the largest in Cleveland, Ohio. By 1869 the Cleveland refinery complex had become the largest in the world and produced one-tenth of the nation's refined petroleum output. In 1870 a variety of related partnerships were consolidated into the Standard Oil Company (Ohio) with Rockefeller as president.

Standard soon monopolized the U.S. refining business. By 1880 Standard's control of U.S. refining capacity grew to between 90 and 95 percent of total domestic refining. As the firm increased its dominance in refining operations, it began integrating vertically into petroleum pipelines and wholesale marketing. Standard Oil's monopolistic position allowed it to gain favorable rates for railroad transportation as well.

Rockefeller's drive to create a large and efficient oil company led to management innovation. Standard used decentralized managerial structures that allowed it to adapt more readily to changing business conditions. Standard also embarked on research and development programs that produced technological advances, particularly in production and refining operations.

By the end of the nineteenth century Standard was one of the largest and most highly integrated companies in the world. In 1899 Standard Oil of New Jersey became the new holding company for all of the Standard Oil divisions. Although its market share of U.S. refining capacity dropped to 82 percent in 1899, Standard's vertically integrated structure gave it a strong competitive advantage. Standard also controlled 87 percent of domestic oil production and 85 percent of the domestic petroleum marketing business.

Standard began to lose market share in the early twentieth century for reasons beyond its control. The discovery of massive southwestern oil fields in states where Standard had little or no business presence led to the emergence of substantial competitors.

On 10 January 1901, Anthony F. Lucas, Al Hamil, and Curt Hamill discovered oil at Spindletop, a salt dome formation south of Beaumont, Texas. The Pittsburgh wildcatters John H. Galey and James M. Guffey, associated with the Mellon interests, financed Lucas's efforts. When his well hit oil at a depth of 1,139 feet, a stream of "black gold" blew more than 100 feet high. It continued to flow until capped nine days later. The Lucas gusher produced an estimated 100,000 barrels a day and marked the beginning of the Texas oil boom and the decline of Pennsylvania dominance in oil. New companies that emerged after Spindletop included the Texas Company (Texaco) and Gulf Oil (later merged with Chevron).

The demand for oil, and gasoline in particular, increased dramatically in the early twentieth century. The gasoline-powered automobile produced in large numbers on Henry Ford's assembly line and others created an ever increasing demand for gasoline as a fuel and oil as a lubricant. Relatively inexpensive cars meant that more people could afford them and the oil products necessary to fuel and maintain them. During World War I, gasoline-powered tractors, trucks, and later airplanes further increased demand.

During the 1920s a scandal involving oil and the administration of President Warren G. Harding symbolized the pervasive importance, politically and economically, of the oil industry. U.S. Secretary of the Interior Albert Fall had leased U.S. Navy oil reserves located at Teapot Dome, near Caspar, Wyoming, to Harry F. Sinclair's Mammoth Oil Company. Fall also leased the Elk Hills, California, oil reserve to Edward L. Doheny's Pan-American Petroleum and Transport Company. Fall then received gifts and "loans" amounting to about $400,000. Consequently Fall was convicted of bribery, was sentenced to one year in prison, and was fined $100,000.

Additional oil discoveries in Texas and Oklahoma rekindled the oil boom there. In October 1930 Columbus M. "Dad" Joiner discovered oil at the Daisy Bradford well near Kilgore, Texas. Joiner had discovered the East Texas field that comprised about 140,000 acres and 5.5 billion barrels of oil. At the time this was the largest oil field ever discovered. Within three years of Dad Joiner's original discovery well, about twelve thousand new wells had been drilled in the area, and East Texas oil flooded the market. The price of high-grade oil fell from $1.10 to below $.10 per barrel within a year. In addition issues related to conservation, both of oil and the underground water that forced the oil to the surface, became paramount. Competitive chaos in the oil fields led to imposition of new regulations by the Texas Railroad Commission (TRC) in Texas and the federal government.

World War II imposed new challenges on the oil industry. Oil was a vital part of the war effort, and the combatants regularly attempted to disrupt or destroy each others' fuel supplies. Soon after the Japanese bombing of Pearl Harbor, German U-boats attacked U.S. oil tankers transporting petroleum from the Gulf Coast up the Atlantic seaboard. The submarine attacks and the continuing threat of attack disrupted U.S. oil trade to northeastern refineries. This threatened not only an East Coast oil shortage but an Allied forces oil shortage as well. During 1942 oil tanker shipments from the Gulf Coast to the New York Harbor area fell from an average of 1.5 million barrels per day to approximately 75,000 per day.

Subsequently the U.S. Reconstruction Finance Corporation (RFC) agreed to finance two "war emergency pipelines" to alleviate the northeastern oil shortage and ensure oil supply for the war effort. Completed in 1943, the Big Inch (twenty-four inches in diameter) and Little Big Inch (twenty inches) delivered more than 350 million barrels of crude and refined products to the New York Harbor area during the war. In 1946 the federal government auctioned the Inch Lines as war surplus property to Texas Eastern Transmission Corporation, a newly formed natural gas firm that converted the Inch Lines for natural gas transportation.

The oil industry fueled U.S. prosperity in the 1950s and 1960s. New discoveries in offshore Gulf Coast, California, Alaska, and North Sea brought additional supply to the U.S. and world market. In the North Sea massive offshore oil platforms produced oil and gas in often extremely dangerous conditions. The 1968 Prudhoe Bay discovery in Alaska represented the largest petroleum reservoir ever discovered in the United States. It is also, however, located in an climatologically extreme environment.

Oil Crises. The increasing oil production and transportation has created more opportunities for major accidents, and the oil industry became a chief concern for the emerging environmental movement. On 29 January 1969 Union Oil Well A-21 on federal leaseholds off the Santa Barbara, California, coast blew out. The well itself was quickly capped, but a fissure on the ocean floor associated with the well released 235,000 gallons of crude oil. This

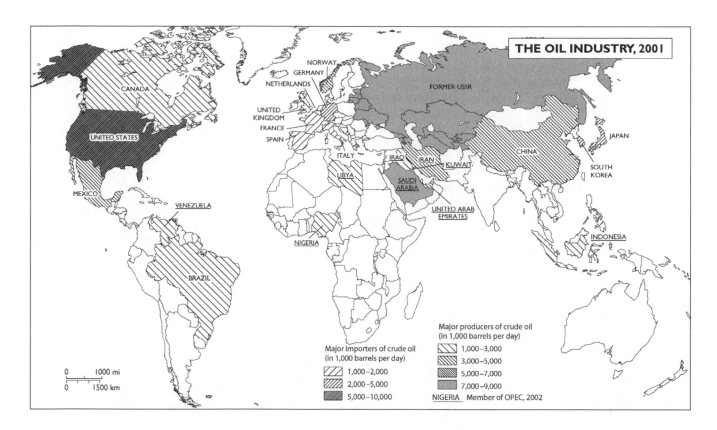

THE OIL INDUSTRY, 2001

Major importers of crude oil
(in 1,000 barrels per day)
- 1,000–2,000
- 2,000–5,000
- 5,000–10,000

Major producers of crude oil
(in 1,000 barrels per day)
- 1,000–3,000
- 3,000–5,000
- 5,000–7,000
- 7,000–9,000

NIGERIA Member of OPEC, 2002

created an oil slick that killed birds and fish, interrupted commercial fishing, and created difficulties for local tourism extending from Santa Barbara to San Diego. The Santa Barbara oil spill galvanized environmental action on the West Coast and led to a moratorium on drilling new wells on state-owned submerged lands.

An even more serious oil spill occurred in 1989 at Prince William Sound, Alaska. The *Exxon Valdez* oil tanker grounded on Bligh Reef, causing a rupture of its oil storage tanks. Eleven million gallons of oil spewed into the sound and spread across 10,000 square miles of water and 1,300 miles of shoreline. It was estimated that 300,000 to 645,000 sea birds and 4,000 to 6,000 marine mammals died as a result of this spill, the worst in U.S. history. Exxon subsequently spent $2.1 billion on the cleanup and paid a fine.

U.S. dominance in the global oil industry shifted during 1973, when Arab oil-producing nations used oil as an economic weapon against the United States and other nations that supporting Israel in the Yom Kippur War. After the United States agreed to resupply Israel during that war, the Organization of Arab Petroleum Exporting Countries (OAPEC), a subgroup of the Organization of Petroleum Exporting Countries (OPEC), agreed to either reduce or terminate oil exports to nations supporting Israel. In particular OAPEC initiated an embargo against the United States and curtailed overall production. This caused spot prices to increase six fold from pre-embargo levels. Nations that depended upon oil imports

bid for spot market oil, and prices increased dramatically from $3 per barrel to $20 per barrel during the next several months. At that time the United States imported approximately 36 percent of its oil supply.

In 1979 another oil supply crisis occurred. An Islamic revolution forced the shah of Iran to flee his country. The turmoil of the Iranian revolution thrust that nation's oil industry into disarray, and its daily oil production of 3 to 4 million barrels practically ceased. In September 1979 Iraq attacked Iran, and the Iran-Iraq War effectively removed Iraq's 3 million barrel-per-day production from the market. Once again the worldwide cost of oil increased dramatically. The price of OPEC–produced oil increased from $16 per barrel in September 1979 to more than $36 per barrel by January 1980. This price increase had enormous global economic implications. In the United States a serious economic downturn followed, and long lines of cars at gasoline stations symbolized this era.

The oil disruptions of the 1970s prompted the United States to seek energy independence. The National Energy Security Act of 1980 set in motion a new U.S. policy designed to promote energy conservation and reduce U.S. dependence upon foreign oil. This act created the Synthetic Fuels Corporation (SFC) to develop methods for extracting oil and gas from coal. Although it was originally capitalized at $88 billion, the SFC became a casualty of the Reagan administration, which disliked government involvement in energy. There was also renewed interest in developing coal, new oil sources such as those in Alaska, and nuclear power systems.

The U.S. did establish an emergency oil supply. In 1975 President Gerald Ford signed the Energy Policy and Conservation Act (EPCA). This act created the Strategic Petroleum Reserve (SPR) intended to store up to 1 billion barrels of petroleum. By policy, the SPR is the U.S. emergency supply of crude oil. Oil is stored in large underground salt caverns on the Gulf of Mexico coastline. The U.S. president has authority to allow oil withdrawal from the SPR during an emergency. The first oil deliveries to the SPR on 21 July 1977 consisted of 412,000 barrels of Saudi Arabian light crude. In the twentieth century the United States withdrew oil from the SPR only during Operation Desert Storm in 1991. As of 2002 the SPR contained approximately 561 million barrels of oil.

Despite the actions of OPEC and major oil-producing nations, the global oil market has experienced volatile price and supply swings. By the late 1990s the relative price of oil had fallen to levels approximate to those prior to the oil crises of the 1970s. Additionally the number of rotary oil rigs working in the United States has varied considerably since the 1940s and generally declined following an upswing after the 1970s oil crises. The weekly rig count reached a high of 4,530 on 28 December 1981 and hit a low of 488 on 27 April 1999 inspite of new technologies permitting enhanced oil recovery of low yield oil wells, 3-D seismic technology, and directional drilling techniques.

Oil is a limited natural resource. The United States, despite its policy to reduce dependence on foreign oil, has imported increasingly higher volumes of oil since World War II. Imports in 1950 accounted for about 13 percent of total U.S. consumption, 19 percent in 1960, 23 percent in 1970, 40 percent after the 1973 embargo, and about 50 percent or 9 million barrels per day by the mid- to late 1990s. As more easily produced oil is consumed, oil companies will spend increasing amounts of time exploring for and producing oil that is more difficult and costly to locate and produce.

Worldwide oil consumption increased at an average annual rate of 7 percent per year from 1859 through 1973. Since 1973 the annual consumption rate has declined significantly. It is estimated that between 1985 and 1995 world oil consumption increased by approximately 16 percent. However, during this ten-year period new global oil discoveries of about 9 billion barrels annually were more than offset by average consumption rates of 23 billion barrels, 45 percent of which represents gasoline consumption. Under the current world oil consumption rate of approximately 25 billion barrels per year, humans by the year 2011 will have consumed approximately one-half of the 2.4 trillion barrels of consumable oil on earth. It is therefore quite probable that in the twenty-first century an increasing demand for oil and gradually decreasing supply will result in further shortages.

BIBLIOGRAPHY

Castaneda, Christopher J., and Joseph A. Pratt. *From Texas to the East: A Strategic History of Texas Eastern Corporation.* College Station, Tex., 1993.

Hidy, Ralph W., and Muriel E. Hidy. *Pioneering in Big Business, 1882–1911.* New York, 1955.

Nevins, Allan. *John D. Rockefeller: The Heroic Age of American Enterprise.* New York, 1940.

Olien, Diana Davids, and Roger M. Olien. *Oil in Texas: The Gusher Age, 1895–1945.* Austin, 2002.

Pratt, Joseph A. *The Growth of a Refining Region.* Greenwich, Conn., 1980.

Prindle, David F. *Petroleum Politics and the Texas Railroad Commission.* Austin, 1981.

Rees, Judith, and Peter Odell. *The International Oil Industry: An Interdisciplinary Perspective.* New York, 1987.

Sampson, Anthony. *The Seven Sisters: The Great Oil Companies and the World They Shaped.* New York, 1975.

Vietor, Richard H. K. *Energy Policy in America since 1945.* Cambridge, 1984.

Williamson, Harold F., and Arnold R. Daum. *The American Petroleum Industry: The Age of Illumination, 1859–1899.* Evanston, Ill., 1959.

Williamson, Harold F., and Arnold R. Daum. *The American Petroleum Industry: The Age of Energy, 1899–1959.* Evanston, Ill., 1963.

Yergin, Daniel. *The Prize: The Epic Quest for Oil, Money, and Power.* New York, 1991.

CHRISTOPHER J. CASTANEDA

Technological Change

In its natural state crude oil, or petroleum, is a liquid hydrocarbon typically found beneath the earth's surface. Oil and other hydrocarbon fuels developed through the long-term decomposition of algae, plankton, and other ocean-based microscopic plant and animal life. The decomposition of these organisms into "fossil fuels" occurred in anaerobic environments under the pressure of top layers of sediment and rock.

Historical Development. Throughout recorded history there have been many instances of oil seeping to the earth's surface (the La Brea tar pits in Los Angeles are one well-known example). Oil tends to flow naturally toward the earth's surface, from high to low pressure, but it is usually prevented from reaching ground level by rock and other geologic structures. When a market for kerosene and oil developed in the mid-nineteenth century, oil exploration and production efforts mounted and likewise stimulated the development of oil producing and refining technology.

In the mid-nineteenth century, entrepreneurs, such as those associated with the American Medical Oil Company of Kentucky, bottled and sold oil for medicinal purposes. Strong demand for oil, however, did not occur until scientific studies revealed that refined oil could be used for lighting. Benjamin Silliman, Jr. of Harvard University published a report on petroleum (1885) confirming that refined oil, or kerosene, could be used as a fuel for illumination.

Subsequently, a group of investors hired Edwin L. Drake to search for oil in eastern Pennsylvania. Drake discovered oil at Titusville, Pennsylvania, and managed the first oil well that commercialized the petroleum industry. His well consisted of a wooden derrick about thirty feet tall. After two years of drilling, Drake's well reached a depth of only 69.5 feet. However, on 28 August 1859, W. A. "Uncle Billy" Smith, who was Drake's experienced salt mine driller, realized they had struck oil. The burgeoning supply and demand for oil resulted in new technologies to produce, store, transport, and refine crude oil.

Production. To locate possible oil reservoirs, geologists search for geological structures that might contain oil. The anticline, a domelike structure, is one of the more common geological structures that indicates trapped oil. Aerial photography and satellite images are also used to uncover geological formations possibly indicative of oil. The seismic survey is a sophisticated method of determining geological formation through measurements of sound waves directed into the earth. Seismic surveys are used both on land and at sea.

To create a pathway for oil to flow to the earth's surface, a well must be created. The earliest technology related to oil well drilling came from salt mine drillers. In West Virginia near the Kanawha River during 1806, two brothers, David Ruffner and Joseph Ruffner, experimented with drilling techniques to bring brine water to the surface. Salt extracted from brine water was essential for preserving meat, food, and hides. In one effort they used a hollow sycamore tree with a four-foot interior diameter. The tree, or "gum," was propped up over the location of the well, and a workman inside of the tree dug into the earth and deposited the dirt and rocks into a bucket that was pulled up by other men who emptied it. Innovations in drilling technology during the second decade of the nineteenth century included replacing wood tubing with tin tubing. During the 1820s drillers began using copper tubing with screw joints, and wells reached depths of one thousand feet. Later, steel drill pipe and improved bits enabled drillers to explore deeper into the earth. Modern drilling is conducted with a drilling rig. On land the rig is positioned over the desired location. Drilling commences when a drill bit is forced into the ground. The particular type of bit used depends upon the type of rock through which it will drill. The drill bit is connected to a drill collar that is in turn attached to sections of drill pipe. The rotary table on the rig rotates the downhole assembly, or "drill string," and its combined weight and rotation cause the drill bit to push through rock. Oil wells typically drill to depths of three thousand to seventeen thousand feet, but some deep wells have

reached about five miles. When the drill bit becomes dull, it must be replaced. This requires removal of the entire drill stem, which may weigh as much as one hundred tons, section by section until the bit is recovered. This process was conducted manually until the modern period, when automated drilling rigs were built to handle this dangerous job automatically.

Casing is typically installed inside the drill hole. Casing is metal tubing that decreases in diameter from the top of the drill hole to the bottom. It prevents the influx of water and other contaminants, and it also prevents cave-ins. Drilling mud, a mixture of clay, water, and chemicals, is forced down into the drill hole. The mud helps keep the drilling bit cool, and it also flushes rock cuttings back to the surface. Manipulation of the drilling mud is required to control well pressure and prevent blowouts.

In the twentieth century offshore drilling commenced. It began first on piers that extended off the southern California coast. In the 1920s at Baku on the Caspian Sea, oil operators located a rig on the end of a trestle system that extended into the offshore. Trestles were less successful off the Texas Gulf Coast due to the soft soil conditions, so drillers used other methods, including constructing drilling platforms in the ocean. A drilling platform located one mile offshore in the Gulf of Mexico began producing oil in 1938, becoming the first oil producer in open waters in the Gulf of Mexico. In 1947 the first well beyond the sight of land in 18 feet of water and 10.5 miles offshore Louisiana began producing oil. Two decades later, in the North Sea and deep Gulf of Mexico, offshore drilling continued from huge platforms that had all the services of a small city. By the end of the twentieth century approximately one-third of the world's oil production came from offshore wells.

In some instances drillers must make a drill hole that is not vertical. They employ directional or slant drilling techniques that can deviate from the vertical by as much as 90 degrees. Drilling at 90 degrees is referred to as horizontal drilling. The first known episode of slant drilling occurred in California during the 1920s. Oil well operators produced oil from state oil fields in offshore water. The drillers had discovered how to bore a slanted hole in the subsurface, so there was no indication aboveground that the well was slanted. Slant drilling occurred later in East Texas as well. Although slant drilling became illegal, it was difficult to detect.

When a well produces oil, a system of valves and pipes referred to as a Christmas tree is installed at the wellhead. This assembly controls the oil's flow, whether aided by pumps or collected through natural well pressure. The oil then flows to a gathering station for initial processing.

Storage and Transportation. Storing oil was one of the first major problems early successful oil drillers encountered. Early storage containers were typically wooden barrels or vats. Vats typically had no more than a

OIL INDUSTRY. Oil fields in Irkuk, Iraq, about one hundred and fifty miles north of Baghdad, 1958. (*New York World-Telegram* and the *Sun* Newspaper Photograph Collection/Prints and Photographs Division, Library of Congress)

one-hundred-gallon capacity, compared to a barrel's forty-two-gallon capacity. Horse-drawn carriages provided short-distance transportation, although even a few fully loaded barrels comprised an extremely heavy load. Railroads initially offered only open flatcars for transportation, and exposure to wind, rain, intense sun, and cold caused deterioration of the barrels and leakage or fire hazards.

By the early 1860s the necessity for large-scale petroleum storage and transportation facilities was evident. The New York Kerosene Company in 1860 owned one steel storage tank with a capacity of thirty thousand barrels. Railroads soon adopted tank cars, first wooden and then steel, to transport oil long distances. The wooden tank cars often suffered from leaks and proved generally unsatisfactory. In 1865 J. F. Keeler of Pittsburgh built a car twenty-five feet long and eight feet wide with a rounded bottom. The car, with iron plates, became the predecessor of modern oil tank cars. Also in the 1860s several oilmen utilized cast-iron pipe to successfully transport oil, and by the late nineteenth century oil firms commonly transported oil overland by pipeline. In 1878 Ludwig Nobel commissioned the first ocean going oil tanker, the *Zoroaster*, which operated on the Caspian Sea.

In the twentieth century gasoline-powered tank trucks transported oil by road. This allowed easy access to the numerous gas stations built to supply fuel for the rapidly increasing number of gasoline-powered automobiles. In addition, approximately 200,000 miles, of oil pipeline operated in the United States. By the end of the twentieth-century oceangoing oil tankers with capacities of 3 million barrels transported oil from the Middle East to oil-consuming nations.

Refining. Crude oil must be refined to transform it into a usable fuel. Early oil refiners used methods similar to those used for refining coal oil. These methods required heating the oil in a distillation unit. Vapors from the heated crude were allowed to condense into liquids, such as kerosene. During the early 1860s many small refiners operated nothing more than a portable, five-barrel still costing no more than $400.

Various forms of distillation have been used to refine oil. These include direct-fire distillation, steam distillation, superheated distillation, vacuum distillation; and cracking. Cracking is particularly important for increasing the yields of refined oil. Also referred to as destructive distillation, cracking involves the application of high temperatures to break larger molecules into smaller ones, thereby increasing the overall yield.

Modern refineries process crude oil through a fractionating column. The column is heated at its base, and the temperature declines toward the top of the column. As the vapors rise in the column, they condense back into liquids, from heavy to light, at special trays designed to maintain a temperature just below the liquid's boiling point. These various liquids include gasoline, lubricating oils, kerosene, waxes, asphalt, and other hydrocarbons. Modern refineries are dramatically larger in size, capacity, and technological sophistication than earlier ones, yet the basic process of distillation through heat remains the same.

BIBLIOGRAPHY

Coyne, Mark S., et al. *Natural Resources*, vol. 2. Pasadena, Calif., 1998.

Moore, Preston L. *Drilling Practices Manual*. Tulsa, Okla., 1986.

Nevins, Allan. *John D. Rockefeller: The Heroic Age of American Enterprise*. New York, 1940.

Pratt, Joseph A., Tyler Priest, and Christopher J. Castaneda. *Offshore Pioneers: Brown and Root and the History of Offshore Oil and Gas*. Houston, 1997.

Sampson, Anthony. *The Seven Sisters: The Great Oil Companies and the World They Shaped*. New York, 1975.

Shell Oil Company. *Oil*. Houston,1998.

Stobaugh, Robert, and Daniel Yergin, eds. *Energy Future: Report of the Energy Project at the Harvard Business School*. New York, 1979.

Williamson, Harold F., and Arnold R. Daum. *The American Petroleum Industry: The Age of Illumination, 1859–1899*. Evanston, Ill., 1959.

Williamson, Harold F., and Arnold R. Daum. *The American Petroleum Industry: The Age of Energy, 1899–1959*. Evanston, Ill., 1963.

Yergin, Daniel. *The Prize: The Epic Quest for Oil, Money, and Power*. New York, 1991.

CHRISTOPHER J. CASTANEDA

Property Rights

Due to the subsurface formation and reservoir environment of petroleum, legal issues related to property rights have had an enormous influence on the history of oil production. In the United States during the nineteenth century and into the 1930s, the "rule of capture" doctrine ruled the oil fields. This provision of English common law treated oil essentially the same way it treated wild game. Landowners were within their rights to capture the game as well as the oil that crossed over their land.

In the late nineteenth century some U.S. courts cited the English case *Acton* v. *Blundell* (1843) in oil property rights disputes. It was first applied to a petroleum dispute in Pennsylvania decided in 1875, in which the court affirmed the rule of capture while acknowledging the legislature's authority to establish alternative guidelines. This decision and others provided legal precedent with ramifications experienced in later oil booms.

The *Acton* v. *Blundell* case, however, involved a water well that was drained by a nearby coal pit. The owner of the water well sued on the basis that each landowner had a right to the water crossing his or her land. The coal pit owner prevailed because the water flowed underground. Therefore, the judge determined, it was impossible to know exactly where the water flowed or how much water crossed into each landowner's property. This decision distinguished between surface flows and underground flows, but it affirmed the "rule of capture."

Booms. Unlike solids, such as coal, gold, and copper, oil, like subsurface water, flows below the earth's surface; it is considered to be "fugacious." This characteristic, bolstered by the rule of capture doctrine, led property owners to produce as much oil underneath their own property as quickly as possible, before neighbors could produce and profit from the same oil reservoir.

Rampant overproduction resulted in the creation of "boomtowns," where a myriad of oil derricks crowded small areas of land or parts of developed towns. With the "boom" came the "bust" when the oil reservoirs became unproducible either because of a lack of oil or the loss of pressurization from the depletion of natural gas or water from the well. Thus it is estimated that in oil boom situations, some wells produced only 5 to 10 percent of the reservoir's capacity before the loss of the well's gas or water drive. Rapid overproduction also created storage capacity problems and tended to lower overall prices.

Such unregulated and wasteful production characterized the early Pennsylvania oil fields as well as the Texas oil industry from Spindletop (1901) to the East Texas boom of the 1930s. Similar boom and bust situations arose in many locations where large quantities of oil were first discovered, such as in Oklahoma, Venezuela, and the Middle East. Generally the large oil companies, or majors, tended to call for conservative production of new wells, while smaller firms and wildcatters preferred no regulation. Small oil producers charged that the large firms sought to exercise monopolistic control under the guise of promoting conservation.

In the United States oil-leasing agreements also encouraged rapid oil production. In 1890 leaseholders controlled about four-fifths of the approximately 1.6 million acres of oil property. Leases typically contained clauses that required the lessee to begin exploration and drilling operations within a short time period. These provisions were intended to prevent a neighboring landowner or lessee from draining the oil reservoir first.

Leases often included provisions that protected the landowner when the producer did not act quickly. These leases contained a "delay rental" provision stipulating that the lessee, or producer, pay a monthly fee during periods of postponed exploration or drilling activity. Producers had to show "due diligence" to maintain their leases and not pay delay rental fees.

In some instances oil and gas firms in the Southwest sought to gain maximum coverage through leasing arrangements, known as "checkerboarding." In this system leasing agents, often using multiple names to avoid scrutiny, arranged for as many leases as possible near and around a competitor's acreage. In this manner a new entrant had a chance to tap into an existing oil reservoir being produced by a competitor.

Regulation. New oil discoveries and increasing production levels in Oklahoma and Texas during the 1920s and 1930s prompted imposition of state regulation. After 1919 the Texas Railroad Commission (TRC) held authority to issue conservation orders, and during the 1920s the TRC issued Rule 37, which generally prohibited placement of more than one well per two acres. Wells also were to be located at least three hundred feet apart. Oil drillers, however, generally ignored these spacing rules, and the TRC did not have the means to enforce Rule 37.

Ultimately the East Texas oil boom forced the TRC to make a concerted effort to control production. Within three years of Columbus M. "Dad" Joiner's 1930 discovery of the East Texas field, which measured forty-five miles by twelve miles, twelve thousand oil wells were completed there, and lease prices had risen from $1.50 per acre in 1929 to as much as $3,000 per acre by 1932. Excessive waste and "competitive suicide" threatened to ruin the field and its producers.

Consequently the TRC attempted to control production levels through prorationing production among the wells operating in a field. In 1931 the TRC issued its first proration order, which limited production in each well in the East Texas field to about one thousand barrels per well per day. Legal challenges overturned the order, and Texas governor Ross Sterling declared martial law. He ordered troops into the oil fields to regain order. The TRC established its authority in April 1933, when it set an allowable production level of 750,000 barrels per day for the East Texas field with individual well quotas based on each well's production characteristics.

Texas continued to enforce oil well prorationing through the 1960s. Prorationing had stabilized the oil industry and promoted conservation. During the late 1950s and early 1960s the United States had a surplus oil capacity of approximately 4 million barrels per day, but this level of overproduction fell to no more than 1 million per day by 1970. Also in 1970 U.S. oil production hit its highest level of the twentieth century at 11.3 million barrels per day. With U.S. oil demand surging along with U.S. dependence on foreign oil, in March 1972 the TRC ceased prorating oil to market demand so long as the reservoir was not damaged by increased production.

Unitization is another form of oil production control mandated by some states. Under unitization, a single operator who represents all interested property owners manages the production operation. The unitization agreement determines how the production will be divided among the owners. Unitization in the United States has become more common since the 1940s with the application of enhanced oil recovery techniques on mature wells.

Oklahoma instituted compulsory unitization in 1945, but Texas has not had compulsory unitization. Typically smaller firms have opposed this practice.

Foreign Access. In the Middle East and Latin America local oil exploration and production technology was not generally available. Therefore a host nation's leaders or government officials sought to attract U.S. or European oil firms to discover and produce oil. In the Middle East oil property rights generally had to be negotiated with individual leaders or host governments, and oil firms took concessions leased through the host nation's leaders or government. A variety of partnerships and profit-sharing agreements among Western oil firms and concessions between those firms and host governments generally characterized international oil producing property rights.

The famed "Seven Sisters," consisting of Gulf, Standard of California (Socal), Texaco, and Standard Oil of New York, operated as a cartel from the late 1920s through the early 1970s. Collectively they purchased concessions in Latin America, North Africa, and the Persian Gulf. Also, in the 1920s a consortium of European and U.S. firms established the Iraq Petroleum Company (IPC). The IPC, along with British, Dutch, French, and U.S. oil firms, signed what was later known as the Red Line Agreement that prohibited signatory oil companies operating within the defined boundaries of the old Ottoman Empire (Saudi Arabia, Iraq, Syria, and Turkey) from competing with each other. If one member purchased a concession, all members participated in it.

In Saudi Arabia during 1936, Socal purchased a concession for $50,000 to develop that country's oil fields. After Socal and Texaco formed the Arabian-American Oil Company (Aramco) in 1939 and added new partners in 1946, the Red Line Agreement had effectively ended, and the Middle Eastern oil "play" opened up to new competition and new entrants.

In both the Middle East and Latin America, host nations sought increasing control over their oil-producing properties as production levels and profits increased. In 1938 the Mexican government nationalized its oil industry and subsequently consolidated it under Petroleos Mexicanos or Pemex. In Venezuela, where Shell and Exxon operated, the government in 1948 passed a law calling for a 50-50 profit-sharing agreement. Also, King Saud demanded a 50-50 profit sharing system for Saudi Arabia. Similar arrangements were made between Kuwait and the Kuwait Oil Company, Ltd., a partnership of Gulf Oil and British Petroleum (BP). In Iran nationalization of the domestic oil industry contributed to a coup that replaced the leader and restored foreign control over Iran's oil industry.

Oil property rights remain complex. They are influenced by a variety of factors, including legal precedent, politics, technology, knowledge of geology, and price swings.

BIBLIOGRAPHY

Coyne, Mark S., et al. *Natural Resources*, vol. 2. Pasadena, Calif., 1998.

Libecap, Gary D., and James L. Smith. "The Economic Evolution of Petroleum Property Rights in the United States." Unpublished paper, 2002.

Prindle, David F. *Petroleum Politics and the Texas Railroad Commission*. Austin, 1981.

Rees, Judith, and Peter Odell. *The International Oil Industry: An Interdisciplinary Perspective*. New York, 1987.

Sampson, Anthony. *The Seven Sisters: The Great Oil Companies and the World They Shaped*. New York, 1975.

Williamson, Harold F., and Arnold R. Daum. *The American Petroleum Industry: The Age of Illumination, 1859–1899*. Evanston, Ill., 1959.

Williamson, Harold F., and Arnold R. Daum. *The American Petroleum Industry: The Age of Energy, 1899–1959*. Evanston, Ill., 1963.

Yergin, Daniel. *The Prize: The Epic Quest for Oil, Money, and Power*. New York, 1991.

CHRISTOPHER J. CASTANEDA

Industrial Organization

The modern oil industry began in the mid-nineteenth century. Since that time it has been characterized by episodes of "boom" and "bust," intense competition for market share, various types of cartel-like agreements, governmental efforts to either regulate or control, the promise of great wealth, and mergers and consolidation. In the late twentieth century the oil industry confronted an environmental movement that sought to reduce fossil fuel consumption and prevent toxic wastes from polluting human and animal habitats.

The oil industry is capital intensive. Immense sums of money are spent on oil discovery, exploration, and development projects. Marketing, transportation, and distribution systems likewise require enormous amounts of financing and logistical planning. Therefore the oil industry has developed an industrial structure that emphasizes scale and scope to maximize profits.

Nineteenth Century Beginnings: Standard Oil. Standard Oil was the largest U.S. oil company in the late nineteenth century and early twentieth century, and its corporate growth provided a model for other big firms. Standard grew by first expanding horizontally into refining and then consolidating legal and administrative functions. Subsequently Standard integrated vertically into production, transportation, and marketing.

Standard Oil dominated the nineteenth-century oil industry, but Edwin Drake's oil discovery at Titusville, Pennsylvania, in 1859 started it. Four years after Drake's momentous find, John D. Rockefeller and two partners formed the Excelsior Works refinery in Cleveland, Ohio. During the next several years Rockefeller increased his control over the refinery complex, and it soon became the world's largest.

As a business organization, a partnership worked best when capital requirements were relatively low and the business had a singular function. As the need for capital increased and the business became more complex, the corporate form became appropriate. Rockefeller understood this, and in 1870 he consolidated a variety of partnerships into the Standard Oil Company (Ohio), of which he was president.

Rockefeller was a ruthless businessman who aggressively moved to buy out competitors, principally through exchange of stock. As Standard grew larger, Rockefeller's ability to pressure competitors to sell out to him increased. By 1872 Standard controlled virtually all of Cleveland's daily refining capacity of twelve thousand barrels, or one-fourth of the industry's total refining capacity. Pittsburgh and the New York–New Jersey area were also large petroleum refining centers.

Attempts to bring stability to the oil industry came in many forms. Generally the oil corporations themselves had the most influence on shaping the domestic oil market. In the nineteenth century Standard Oil was involved in numerous and ongoing attempts to bring supply and price stability to the otherwise volatile industry.

One attempt to make the industry more stable was the pooling agreement. In 1871 Thomas A. Scott of the Pennsylvania Railroad invited several petroleum refiners, including Standard Oil, to participate in an oil pool. Under the auspices of a newly formed company, the South Improvement Company (SIC), the Pennsylvania Railroad planned to coordinate the allocation of oil shipments with the selected oil refiners. Members of the SIC would receive rebates and commissions on their shipments, while nonmembers would pay the full published rates. After news of this scheme became public, angry oil producers and other refiners attempted to boycott members of the SIC. The company never transacted any oil, but this scheme and other cases of rebating and cutthroat competition stigmatized Standard Oil for years to come.

Rockefeller continued to pursue control over production and prices. A group of refiners formed the National Refiners Association in 1872 with Rockefeller as president. This organization sought to make pricing agreements with the Petroleum Producers Association. The arrangement was also short-lived, as new producers continued to bring more oil to the market, effectively nullifying any agreement.

Standard thereafter sought to control the market primarily through its own corporate power rather than through pooling or associations. It gained control over petroleum pipelines and railroad transportation routes, thereby squeezing other refiners and forcing them to merge with Standard. By 1879 Standard controlled more than 90 percent of total U.S. refining capacity.

Standard Oil pioneered the "trust" corporate form in 1882, and transferred its headquarters from Cleveland to

New York City. The trust was based on a legal agreement in which trustees managed all Standard Oil properties. Legal challenges forced Standard to dissolve the trust in 1892, although Standard's corporate organization remained effectively the same. In 1899, Standard adopted a holding company structure.

Standard had many detractors. Ida Tarbell's *The History of Standard Oil Company* (1904) publicly exposed Standard Oil's business practices and fanned anti–Standard Oil public opinion. Standard continued to lose market share in the early twentieth century. The discovery of massive southwestern oil fields, the first at Spindletop, Texas, led to the emergence of significant competitors.

The federal government was not impressed with industry-generated attempts to self-regulate. In 1906 the U.S. Justice Department filed an antitrust suit against Standard Oil. In 1909 a U.S. circuit court ruled that Standard Oil was in violation of antitrust laws, and in 1911 the U.S. Supreme Court heard Standard Oil's appeal. That Court affirmed the circuit court's ruling. Subsequently the Standard Oil corporate structure was divided into twenty-six separate firms based on geographical lines. These included Standard Oil of New Jersey (Exxon); Standard Oil of New York or Socony (Mobil); Standard Oil of California or Socal (Chevron); Standard Oil of Indiana (Amoco); Standard Oil of Ohio or Sohio (later part of British Petroleum); Continental Oil (Conoco); and Atlantic (ARCO).

Oil industry expansion had brought forth calls for more government regulation of the oil business. Continuing problems with rebates led to congressional action. The Interstate Commerce Commission (ICC) had been created in 1887 to regulate railroad transportation. Later the Elkins Act (1903) and the Hepburn Act (1906) enhanced the ICC's regulatory power to prohibit rebates and impose penalties on firms that offered them. The Hepburn Act also expanded the scope of the ICC over interstate oil pipelines.

The U.S. government became more involved in the oil industry during World War I. Recognizing the vital role of petroleum in national security and national defense, President Woodrow Wilson in 1917 created the Fuel Administration, which had among other responsibilities the authority to work with U.S. oil companies to ensure a stable petroleum supply for the Allied governments.

After the war, in 1919, the American Petroleum Institute (API) was established to develop industry standards, statistics, and research. Some independent oil firms believed that the API favored the large integrated, or major, oil firms. Consequently independents, such as Tom Slick, vocally opposed the API's attempt to set national standards. Small producers later formed the Independent Petroleum Association of America (IPAA) to represent their interests.

International Oil. Europeans also entered the oil industry in the nineteenth century. Marcus Samuel of Britain established Shell Transport and Trading. Shell began operations in the 1870s as a trade and transportation company, and it originally transported and marketed crude oil produced in Russia. Shell established a worldwide system of oil tankers and storage tanks to move Russian oil to market. In 1906 Royal Dutch merged with Shell to become Royal Dutch Shell.

The British government, having "lost" Shell to the Netherlands, decided to reenter the oil industry itself. It purchased the Anglo-Persian Oil Company and transformed it into British Petroleum (BP). BP developed substantial oil-producing properties in Persia, while Shell worked in Russia, Mexico, and the East Indies.

In Russia during the 1870s, Robert Nobel and Ludwig Nobel from Sweden entered the burgeoning oil business at Baku. Later members of the Rothschild family formed an oil company to operate in the Caspian Sea as well. Russia quickly became a leading oil-producing nation.

In the early twentieth century various intercompany agreements sought to stabilize an increasingly volatile oil market. In August 1928 Walter Teagle of Standard Oil (New Jersey), John Cadman of BP, and Henry Deterding of Shell met at Achnacarry Castle in Scotland. The three men agreed to follow a seven-point plan known as the "As Is" agreement to end the global price wars that had created corporate instability. Not long afterwards four other firms—Gulf, Standard of California (Socal), Texaco, and Standard Oil (New York)—joined the pact and together formed the famed "Seven Sisters." Despite ongoing disagreements and other problems, the Seven Sisters cartel persisted until the early 1970s.

The Seven Sisters operated as a cartel and controlled a significant portion of the world oil industry. Collectively the Seven Sisters had developed fields in Latin America, North Africa, and the Persian Gulf. By 1950 they controlled about 90 percent of world oil production, excluding the United States and Soviet Union, as well as 80 percent of refining and 70 percent of marketing operations. The Seven Sisters had a variety of relationships with the oil-producing countries, including partnerships, profit-sharing arrangements, and concession systems. The Seven Sisters retained their dominance in world oil during the two decades following World War II although their market share gradually diminished as new firms and oil-producing nations entered the industry.

In the 1920s Middle East nations attracted attention from foreign oil companies. A consortium of European and U.S. firms established the Iraq Petroleum Company (IPC) in 1928. This company consisted of four partners with equal shares of 23.5 percent, British Petroleum, Compagnie Française des Pétroles, Royal Dutch Shell, and the Near East Development Corporation (representing U.S. interests), and the entrepreneur Calouste Gulbenkian had 5 percent.

In conjunction with the IPC, the corporate participants signed an additional agreement, later known as the Red Line Agreement. This agreement essentially prohibited all the oil companies operating within the defined boundaries of the old Ottoman Empire from competing with each other. Considering the size of the signatory firms, the Red Line Agreement served as the establishment of a new Middle Eastern oil cartel.

The IPC was soon overshadowed by a new entrant. In 1936 Socal purchased for $50,000 a concession to develop oil in Saudi Arabia. Previously both Standard Oil of New Jersey and Gulf Oil had passed on the opportunity to develop the concession. Socal later formed a partnership with Texaco called Caltex. After oil production commenced in 1939, Socal and Texaco formed the Arabian-American Oil Company (Aramco). Responding to security concerns, the U.S. government at one point during World War II sought to purchase Aramco through the Reconstruction Finance Corporation, but the effort failed.

Aramco controlled a vast oil supply, but it lacked markets. King Saud pushed Aramco for additional revenue, and the company considered adding partners. In 1946 Standard Oil of New Jersey and Socony-Vacuum joined Aramco. Together these firms offered Aramco access to an international oil distribution system and capital. Essentially a partnership among major U.S. oil firms and Saudi Arabia, Aramco's operations effectively scuttled the Red Line Agreement.

Host nations increasingly sought more control over their oil. In Latin America foreign oil-producing companies confronted nationalist tendencies. U.S. and British oil firms had developed Mexican oil fields in the early twentieth century, and by the 1920s imported Mexican oil accounted for more than 20 percent of total U.S. oil consumption. The Mexican Eagle, a British company, produced about 65 percent of Mexico's oil, but Mexican popular opinion blamed the U.S. companies (including Standard) that produced most of the remaining 35 percent for manipulating the Mexican oil market. As a result the Mexican government in 1938, nationalized its oil industry and subsequently consolidated it under Petroleos Mexicanos or Pemex. In Venezuela, where Shell and Exxon operated, the government in 1948 passed a law calling for a 50-50 profit-sharing agreement. Soon thereafter King Saud began to demand a 50-50 system. An agreement was reached in 1950 that effectively lowered Aramco's U.S. tax liability while greatly increasing Saudi Arabia's oil revenue. Similar arrangements were made between Kuwait and the Kuwait Oil Company, Ltd., a partnership of Gulf Oil and BP.

The struggle for control of the oil supply occurred most dramatically in Iran. After unsuccessful negotiations to raise Iran's share of oil revenue in its partnership with BP, the Iranian government nationalized the domestic oil industry and placed its assets under the newly formed National Iranian Oil Company. Foreign oil companies then refused to purchase Iranian oil, while the Iranian communist Tudeh grew in power, creating political concerns for the U.S. government. Political turmoil in Iran forced the shah to flee the country, and Mohammed Mossadeq, the former Iranian Oil Commission chairman, assumed political power as prime minister. In 1953 a subsequent coup reportedly supported by the CIA brought the shah back to power. A new Iranian oil consortium was established that included five major U.S. oil firms (8 percent each), BP (40 percent), Shell (14 percent), and Compagnie Francaise de Petroles (6 percent).

Texas Oil and Regulation. On 10 January 1901 Anthony F. Lucas's team hit oil at Spindletop near Beaumont, Texas, on the Gulf Coast. The Lucas gusher produced an estimated 100,000 barrels a day and marked the beginning of the Texas oil boom. Many new oil companies, some of which became large oil firms, benefited from of the Spindletop discovery. These new companies included the Texas Company (later Texaco), Gulf Oil Corporation (later merged with Chevron), Sun Oil Company, Magnolia Petroleum Company, and Humble, which in 1919 merged with Standard Oil of New Jersey.

New oil discoveries in Texas solidified that state's growing reputation as the nation's most important oil-producing state. In particular Columbus M. "Dad" Joiner's 1930 discovery of the massive East Texas field, the largest oil field to that date, set in motion a new era of government regulation of the oil industry.

The proliferation of wildcat drilling and rampant production in the East Texas field had several ramifications. The unrestrained East Texas oil production flooded the market with oil. The price of high-grade oil at the time of Dad Joiner's first discovery well was $1.10 per barrel. A year later the price of East Texas crude fell below $.10 per barrel, forcing oil prices to a similar level nationwide. The price plummet caused many U.S. producers to temporarily halt oil production. In addition issues related to conservation, both of oil and the underground water that forced the oil to the surface, became paramount.

In response the Texas Railroad Commission (TRC) attempted to gain control of the East Texas situation. The TRC sought to impose a prorationing scheme on East Texas oil producers to control production in an equitable manner. Many oil producers opposed any type of production controls and ignored the TRC's prorationing policy. During August 1931 Texas governor Ross Sterling declared martial law and sent troops into the oil fields to prevent production and sale of "hot oil."

Other states followed Texas' lead. They formed the Interstate Oil Compact (IOC) in 1933 with the purpose of coordinating member states' prorationing plans. States, however, lacked adequate enforcement authority until 1935, when the U.S. Congress passed the Connally Hot Oil Act. This act prohibited the interstate movement of illegally produced oil and gave the TRC, other state commissions, and the IOC the authority they needed to regulate intrastate oil production.

World War II imposed new challenges on the oil business. As in World War I, the federal government became actively involved in the industry. The Petroleum Administration for War (PAW) lead by Harold Ickes sought to coordinate the petroleum industry during the wartime emergency. The PAW centralized U.S. petroleum policies and coordinated supply allocations. After German U-boats began sinking U.S. oil tankers transporting petroleum from the Gulf Coast up the Atlantic seaboard, the Reconstruction Finance Corporation (RFC) agreed to finance two "war emergency pipelines" to alleviate the northeastern oil shortage and ensure wartime oil supply. After the war the federal government auctioned the so-called "Inch Lines" as war surplus property to Texas Eastern Transmission Corporation, which converted the Inch Lines for natural gas transportation.

Post–World War II. A cartel of oil-producing nations, the Organization of Petroleum Exporting Countries (OPEC), was a nationalist response to foreign corporate control of the member nations' oil. Five nations—Saudi Arabia, Iran, Iraq, Kuwait, and Venezuela—formed OPEC during a meeting in Baghdad during 1960. OPEC's members were interested principally in receiving a stable income for their oil rather than a fluctuating market-based revenue.

Later other countries, including Libya, Nigeria, and Indonesia, joined OPEC. Substantial oil discoveries in Libya occurred relatively late. In 1959 Standard Oil of New Jersey struck oil at Zeltin, Libya; the oil was particularly high quality. Libya soon thereafter ranked as the sixth-largest oil exporter, accounting for 10 percent of worldwide oil exports.

Occidental Petroleum, led by Armand Hammer, participated in the Libyan oil boom. After winning concessions in 1965, Occidental struck huge oil deposits, including one at the Idris field, which became one the highest producing oil fields yet discovered. Since Libya was outside of the Middle East, its oil supply was not subject to that region's political strife or access via the Suez Canal. After Muammar al-Qaddafi's military coup of 1969, however, Hammer and other oil company representatives negotiated to remain active in Libya. The oil companies were allowed to stay after agreeing to royalty and tax payment increases. This Libyan episode restarted the earlier movement of producer nation control over its natural resources.

In 1974 the United States lost its ranking as the largest volume oil-producing nation. The Soviet Union then became the highest volume producer. However, Soviet oil production began to decline between 1988 and 1995. In 1996 Saudi Arabia, with its massive oil reserves, became the world's leading crude oil producer, followed by the Soviet Union and the United States. However, neither the Soviet Union nor the United States could claim the huge oil reserves enjoyed by Saudi Arabia.

Mergers and Consolidation. The oil industry remains one of the world's largest industries. During the 1980s and 1990s oil firms began to merge and create astoundingly large corporations, and even larger mergers took place early in the twenty-first century. Not all oil companies saw their economic prospects increase during the last two decades of the twentieth century, as international competition, conservation efforts, and environmental liability taxed some oil firms' profit lines.

A series of large oil company mergers occurred in the mid-1980s. In 1984 Standard Oil of California acquired Gulf Oil; the new company became Chevron Corporation. Three years later BP completed its acquisition of Sohio, or Standard Oil of Ohio, the original Standard Oil firm. In 1998, BP acquired another former Standard Oil company, Amoco, formerly Standard Oil of Indiana.

Even larger mergers took place during the next several years. During 1999 Exxon (formerly Standard Oil of New Jersey) and Mobil (formerly Standard Oil of New York) combined. By 2001 the new Exxon Mobil Corporation ranked number one on the Fortune 500 list of the largest U.S. corporations with total revenues of $210 billion and assets of $149 billion. Not far behind was the combined ChevronTexaco Corporation with approximately $100 billion in revenue. Early in the twenty-first century the corporate trend is clearly toward merger and consolidation in the oil industry.

BIBLIOGRAPHY

Castaneda, Christopher J., and Joseph A. Pratt. *From Texas to the East: A Strategic History of Texas Eastern Corporation.* College Station, Tex., 1993.

Coyne, Mark S., et al. *Natural Resources*, vol. 2. Pasadena, Calif., 1998.

Hidy, Ralph W., and Muriel E. Hidy. *Pioneering in Big Business, 1882–1911.* New York, 1955.

Miles, Ray. *"King of the Wildcatters": The Life and Times of Tom Slick, 1883–1930.* College Station, Tex., 1996.

Nevins, Allan. *John D. Rockefeller: The Heroic Age of American Enterprise.* New York, 1940.

Pratt, Joseph A. *The Growth of a Refining Region.* Greenwich, Conn., 1980.

Rees, Judith, and Peter Odell. *The International Oil Industry: An Interdisciplinary Perspective.* New York, 1987.

Sampson, Anthony. *The Seven Sisters: The Great Oil Companies and the World They Shaped.* New York, 1975.

Stobaugh, Robert, and Daniel Yergin, eds. *Energy Future: Report of the Energy Project at the Harvard Business School.* New York, 1979.

Vietor, Richard H. K. *Energy Policy in America since 1945.* Cambridge, 1984.

Williamson, Harold F., and Arnold R. Daum. *The American Petroleum Industry: The Age of Illumination, 1859–1899.* Evanston, Ill., 1959.

Williamson, Harold F., and Arnold R. Daum. *The American Petroleum Industry: The Age of Energy, 1899–1959.* Evanston, Ill., 1963.

Yergin, Daniel. *The Prize: The Epic Quest for Oil, Money, and Power.* New York, 1991.

CHRISTOPHER J. CASTANEDA

OPEN-FIELD SYSTEM (*Gewanndorf* in German, *champs ouverts* in French; *vangebrug* in Danish), a distinctive, highly communal agricultural system that emerged only in preindustrial Europe. From the Middle Ages onward, it dominated the plains of western Europe in northern France, the southern German lands, and eastern Denmark, including the islands, the central as well as the midland regions of England and central and eastern Sweden. (See map on page 00.) In a somewhat different form, and at a later date, it was also found in northern Russia. Despite its dominance in some regions, it did not develop throughout Europe; some regions never used the system and were characterized by less-communal and/or enclosed field systems.

The open-field system comprised an entire social world that shaped the lives of a large proportion of rural Europeans for almost a thousand years. In outward appearance, the system was characterized by big fields and a lack of fences, trees, and hedges. This gave a wide-open look to the landscape, hence "open fields." The following general description applies to the system in western Europe in the late Middle Ages—the earliest point at which there are clear records of it in most of the places mentioned above. It is a general description, as the system did vary somewhat from place to place. In terms of physical layout, there were four elements:

(1) communal arable land for growing the primary food crops and for communal grazing of herds;

(2) communal meadows for the production of hay;

(3) wasteland or commons, used by the collectivity for the gathering of firewood and grazing; and

(4) private gardens attached to houses in the village, used for growing vegetables, fruit, herbs, and so on.

The first of these elements, the communal arable village land, was typically split into many long thin strips: each was called a *lanière* in French, *Streif* in German, *teg* in Swedish. Strips could be very long, sometimes up to a kilometer in length, although quite narrow; they were divided by grassy balks (unplowed ridges), by boundary stones, and by the pattern of ridge and furrow left by the plow. Each cultivator owned a share of these strips, which were scattered throughout the village fields. Strips were grouped into blocks, called *furlongs* in English, *quartiers* in French, *Gewänne* in German; these were in turn organized into one, two, or three large fields (rarely more), depending on

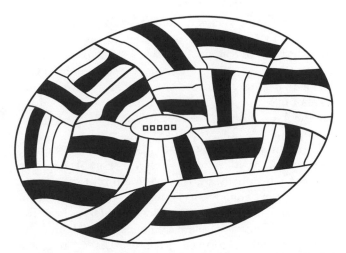

FIGURE 1. Open-field system, depicted without common. Shaded area represents one landholding.

the type of rotation system used by the village or by other conditions. The great fields of the village were referred to as *sols* in French, *Zelgen* or *Schläge* in German, *vångar* in Swedish. This layout of farms in the fields gave the landscape the checkerboard pattern, as well as the pattern of ridge and furrow that can still be seen in aerial photographs (see M. W. Beresford and J. K. St. Joseph, *Medieval England: An Aerial Survey* 1979).

Typically, the strips were organized in a regular way in the fields, often going in a clockwise direction (the sun's course in the Northern Hemisphere), in the same order as the houses along the village street. This way, every farmer's strips were adjacent to those of his neighbors in the village. In Denmark, this sun division (*solskifte*) was referred to in the saying "the toft is the mother of the acre"; that is, the position of the house garden (the "toft") gave rise to the position of the strips in the open fields. Similarly, in Sweden, the medieval Provincial Codes expressed this as "lot is acre's mother." According to the sun division, a person given land "toward the sun" had strips in the east or south of each furlong, while a person with land "toward the shade" had strips in the west or north of each furlong. In the same fashion, the glebe lands (those belonging to the church) usually occupied the same relative position in each furlong. Figure 1 shows a stylized depiction.

The size of holdings in the common arable fields differed somewhat from region to region and from country to country. The basic unit in England was the *hide*, which was more or less equivalent to the German *Hufe*, the French *manse*, and the Swedish *mantal*. Each measure of land was originally large enough to support an extended family and its dependents. Since these units tended to become fragmented with time and inheritance (until they eventually disappeared), most cultivators had some fraction of the original unit to farm. In late medieval England, a typical farm size was a yardland or virgate (quarter-*hide*, or about 30 acres). In Sweden at this same time, farms were usually some fraction of a *mantal*, perhaps about 9 or so hectares (about 22 acres). Average German farms may have been about the same size in the late Middle Ages. In France, farms ranged in size from about 5 to 30 hectares in the Middle Ages, with an average holding size of perhaps 13 hectares (about 32 acres).

Communal Rotations and Grazing. A diagnostic characteristic of the system was that strips of arable land were cropped individually, yet they were subject to communal crop rotations, communal grazing, and sometimes to communal regulation of cropping. Crop rotations ranged from relatively extensive to relatively intensive use of the land. The most extensive form of agriculture was to have no fallowing (rest) or rotation of fields, and simply to abandon land when the soil was exhausted. This was the one-field system, where all the village land was contained in one large common unit or field. One-field systems of this sort could be found in medieval Sweden (see Mats Widgren in *Medieval Farming and Technology*, edited by Grenville Astill and John Langdon, Leiden, 1997). When the abandonment of land was not feasible, a two-course rotation could be used, during which half the village land sat fallow (was rested) each year. In that case, all the village land was arranged into two great fields; one was cropped while the other lay fallow and supported communal grazing. The following year, the fallow field became the cropped field, and vice versa. This system was also common in Sweden and parts of the Rhineland, as well as in areas of Denmark, England, and France.

The most intensive form of agriculture left only a third of the land fallow each year. In that case, there were typically three great fields; two were cropped while one lay fallow to support communal grazing. The next year the fields were rotated. Generally, in a three-field system, one field would have the spring crop (planted in the spring, e.g., barley or oats), one would have the winter crop (planted in the fall, e.g., wheat or rye), while the fallow field supported the herds. By the late Middle Ages, a three-field system dominated in regions of open-field agriculture, in the midlands of England, and in eastern Denmark, northeastern France, and the southern German lands.

Collective rotations made possible a large block of fallow land for communal grazing (except in the one-field system, where there was no fallow field). Collective rotations also facilitated grazing the stubble after harvest, since it was all grouped within one compact block. Yet collective rotations and communal grazing in the open-field system meant that each farmer was required to follow the same time schedule for planting, harvesting, and fallowing his strips or the entire system would be disrupted. For this reason, there were always regulatory bodies of some sort

to ensure the rules were followed: called the *byelaw* in England, *marken* in the eastern provinces of the Netherlands, the *Dorfgenossenschaft* (or other name) in Germany, and *bystämman* in Sweden. The regulators were responsible for coordinating field rotations, cropping, harvesting, and grazing, as well as appointing the village shepherds and fence keepers. They were also responsible for sanctioning those who violated the rules. In the late Middle Ages, if admonishment by the village council was not enough, manorial law and the manor court further enforced agricultural rules.

It is important to distinguish between a three-field *system* and a three-course *rotation*: although a three-field system always followed a three-course rotation, and a two-field system always followed a two-course rotation, the reverse was not true. It was possible to have a three-course rotation and yet not have three great fields—in fact, this was typical in less-communal regions. In less-communal regions, rotations were typically based on subdivisions of fields, not on whole fields, so the number of fields and the number of rotations were not related. In such regions, the type of rotation simply reveals the proportion of land left fallow every year (a three-course rotation means that one third of the land sits fallow each year; two rotations means one half, etc.)—and does not refer to the field system *per se*.

In the open-field system, animals were grazed not only on the fallow field and the common arable fields after harvest but also on the village commons. The common land was separate from the arable fields and could include rough grazing land, marshland, woodland, and wasteland. Sometimes there was also a high-quality hay meadow, typically located by a stream. Flooding the meadow with water from the stream ensured a lush crop of grass for hay. Once the hay was cut, the meadow was made available for common grazing. All in the village had at least some rights to the commons and to products of the common land, such as wood and hay. Regulating the use of the commons and the resources of the commons were important responsibilities of the village or town council. Only private gardens or tofts surrounding the houses in the village were not regulated by the council. These were often intensively cultivated to produce vegetables, fruits, and herbs for home use and also specialty crops, such as vines, hops, hemp, and flax.

Open Fields and Local Culture. In open-field regions, communal regulation of agriculture and land use was accompanied by strong traditions of communitarianism. In these regions, the villages tended to be large and compact, and people lived in houses built side by side. The church, centrally located within the village, was often the center of community life. In many villages, the village associations and councils met in the church—since it was typically the

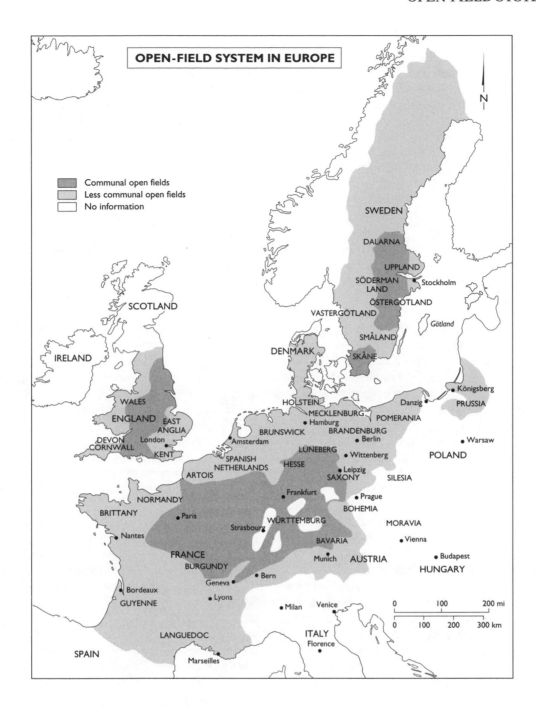

largest public building. (Other locations could be used, for example, under a linden tree in southwestern Germany). Church functions and village functions were frequently combined, and church officials were often village officials as well. These were regions where people "thought instinctively in terms of the community" (see M. Bloch, *French Rural History.* Berkeley, 1966). English open-field villagers "felt that they were bound to help their neighbors and do what they could, each man in his office, to further the common good of their village"(see *English Villagers of the Thirteenth Century.* Cambridge, 1941). Communal solidarity was further reflected in the custom—common in open-field regions—of holding all members of a village responsible for the debts of one member. Community celebrations and ceremonies that took place at various times in the agricultural year were more common in open-field regions than other regions.

Open Fields and Class Relations. In the late Middle Ages, open-field regions tended to be heavily manorialized, and the influence of the feudal lord pervaded all aspects of rural life, economic and social. Strips of land of both the lord (the demesne land) and the peasants were often intermingled in the open fields. Most peasants were "customary tenants," those who farmed the land of the manor and/or those who were bound personally to their lord in some way (e.g., as villeins). In these regions there were few freeholders who owned their lands outright and were largely free of manorial obligations. Customary tenants were responsible for the cultivation of the lord's land, as well as their own (although this was less true outside England, where the use of labor services was in decline). Customary tenants were also tied to their lords by a variety of other rules and obligations. In addition to labor services, customary tenants were held responsible for a variety of other feudal dues—in kind, in fees, and in services. These often included money rents for using the land, mandatory fees for using manorial facilities (the mill, ponds, ovens, etc.), transfer dues for land or goods sold or inherited, and a miscellany of others.

Customary tenants were subject to the authority of the manorial court—the court run by the feudal lord. In late medieval England, typically, there was only one lord per village, although on the continent several lords commonly shared jurisdiction over a village and its lands. The manor court judged any conflicts and disputes that arose in the village. The lord sometimes attended his court and served as judge, although often such duties were delegated to manorial servants, who were chosen from among the peasant community. Similarly, other duties—supervising the cultivation of the demesne, for example—were often delegated to well-off, trusted members of the village community. Village governance typically worked in conjunction with manorial officials, and vice versa. Thus, village associations depended on the manorial court for the enforcement of its rulings and the punishment for noncompliance. Some exceptions to these generalizations existed. The association of the open-field system with strong manorial control was not found everywhere. For example, in Scandinavia, open-field regions were comparatively lightly manorialized in the late Middle Ages, and there were many "free villages," where there was no manor at all.

Origins. Since the origins of the open-field system are lost in a poorly documented past, we may never know for sure how this distinctive economic system was created. Some scholars have suggested that it resulted from dealing with the functional problems created by the scattering of each farmer's strips of land throughout the village lands. This has lead to an interest in explaining the scattering. An older generation of scholars theorized scattering as a product of joint plowing (F. Seebohm, *The English Village Community*. London, 1883; 4th ed., 1905); asa means of equalizing shares of land among villagers P. Vinogradoff, *Villainage in England*. Oxford, 1892); oras a product of the piecemeal colonization of new land(T. A. M. Bishop, 1935, "Assarting and the Growth of Open Fields," *Economic

History Review* 16.2 (1935), pp. 145–147; see also Robert Dodgshon in *The Origins of Open-field Agriculture*, edited by Trevor Rowley, London, 1981). In his *French Rural History* (1966), Bloch suggested that scattering was a risk-management system; that is, scattering was implemented so that each cultivator had a share of the different kinds of land and, therefore, all cultivators shared the same risks and opportunities (see also D. McCloskey "The Open Fields of England: Rent, Risk, and the Rate of Interest, 1300–1815." In *Markets in History: Economic Studies of the Past,* edited by David W. Galenson. Cambridge, 1989). However sound these explanations of scattering may be, they cannot explain the open-field system completely. The scattering of landholdings was nearly universal in preindustrial Europe, but the open-field system was found only in some regions and not others.

Current evidence dates the formation of the open-field system to the Middle Saxon period in England, from the late ninth century to the twelfth century, where its introduction was associated with the settlement of the more fertile clay lands of the plains and the nucleation of settlement. Similarly, the development of the system has been dated to around the eleventh century in Sweden, the eleventh century to the thirteenth in Denmark, before the thirteenth century in France, and it was in evidence by the thirteenth century in the German lands (see the contributions in Astill and Langdon, eds., 1997, cited above). There is evidence that the development of the system was associated with the establishment of compact villages. The argument has been made for England and for France that in order to farm the heavier clay soils, a technological innovation was introduced, in the form of the heavy wheeled plow with moldboard (plate attached to the side of the plowshare for turning the sod). The ridge-and-furrow pattern the plow produced served to drain the soil. Since the plow was heavy and difficult to turn, fields were arranged in long strips, with each strip being the equivalent of a day's plowing. According to Bloch (1966), the resulting long, narrow, scattered strips of arable land were farmed most conveniently in a collective fashion. Therefore areas where the heavy wheeled plow was used were areas of strip fields, communal agriculture, and the open-field system (Eric Kerridge, *The Common Fields of England.* Manchester, 1992, makes a similar argument). This argument does not hold up everywhere, since in some open-field regions the use of the wheeled plow with moldboard was rare.

Others suggest population growth as the catalyst for the development of the open-field system. According to this argument, the introduction of the open-field system resulted from shortages of pasture for animals caused by population growth. The arguments of Joan Thirsk (*The Rural Economy of England.* London, 1984) have been influential;

she suggests that population growth caused a shortage of pasture land for grazing animals, while partible inheritance customs (dividing land among all the heirs) led to fragmentation of land holdings into many narrow, scattered strips. In response to the difficulties of grazing the herds on many scattered fragments of land, the village land was rearranged, so as to distribute the holdings of all farmers throughout the arable land of the village and to group those holdings into two or three large fields. This would ensure that every year there would be one large block of land (the fallow field) for the village herds to graze, although it also necessitated communal cropping and crop rotation. Communal grazing had advantages, since it saved each villager the time, effort, and cost of fencing any fallow field individually. By grouping the entire village herd into one large field, only one fence needed to be constructed to keep the herd from the growing crops. It also saved on supervision costs—only one shepherd was necessary to watch the entire village herd, rather than each villager having to watch over the family's animals. According to this argument, the need for pasture was the primary motivation behind the establishment of the open-field system. Hence, the system was never established in regions where pasture was abundant. The importance of the need for grazing land as the motivating force behind the creation of the open-field system is also stressed by H. S. A. Fox (in Rowley, ed., 1981, cited above) and Eric Kerridge (1992, above).

Bruce Campbell (in Rowley, ed., 1981, above, pp. 112–129) notes that in places such as eastern England, land was divided into smaller and smaller parcels in response to population growth, yet these small strips of land never were arranged in a regular two-field or three-field system (as Thirsk's theory would predict). Instead, a chaotic arrangement of small strips of land was the final result. Similar processes occurred in other areas of Europe, which were characterized by growing populations and less-communal field systems, for instance, in areas of southern France, northern Italy and the Low Countries. Campbell also notes logistical problems in the change to the highly organized open-field system; he suggests that it would have been easier to implement the system in a period of declining population, not rising population. He also suggests that this may have occurred in the ninth and tenth centuries, implemented by the feudal lord as a labor-control strategy, in response to labor shortages. Circumstantial evidence that supports his argument is that open-field regions tended to be regions of strong manorial control, although, as noted above, this was not universally the case. Further, there is evidence that overlords were responsible for the nucleation of settlement (as a labor-control strategy) in Russia in the seventeenth and eighteenth centuries, also in Latin America in the early nineteenth century.

Other scholars have pointed to the complete lack of correspondence between each of these factors that are hypothesized as responsible for the open-field system—scattering of land holdings, the use of the heavy wheeled plow with moldboard, a dense population, strong manorial overlordship—and the presence of the open-field system. Instead, they have noted the existence of dissimilar field systems in otherwise quite similar locales, and they have suggested that the system cannot be explained without reference to local institutional arrangements and the customs and culture of the people who lived in the different regions (e.g., see Carenza Lewis, Patrick Mitchell-Fox, and Christopher Dyer, *Village, Hamlet and Field: Changing Medieval Settlements in Central England.* Manchester, 1997; Rosemary L. Hopcroft, *Regions, Institutions and Agrarian Change in European History.* Ann Arbor, 1999).

Economic Effects. Was the open-field system an efficient economic system compared to other, less-communal field systems? Answers to this question are confounded by the lack of evidence on agricultural matters in preindustrial Europe and by the fact that the open-field system often was located on the best land of Europe—while other, less-communal systems often were found in marginal areas. As noted above, one scholarly tradition suggests that the communal open-field system was a developmental stage in the intensification of agriculture, a sensible response to problems posed by population growth and a shortage of pasture. Accordingly, it was an efficient economic system in its day because it successfully dealt with those problems. Yet there is another tradition of scholarship dating from the eighteenth century that proclaims the communal open-field system to be an inefficient system of agriculture, compared to those based on private property rights in land. For example, after his tours across Europe in the late eighteenth century, the popular writer and agronomist Arthur Young derided open fields as backward and primitive (*Travels in France during the Years 1787, 1788 and 1789.* Cambridge, [1789] 1929). The communal open-field system has also been criticized as being inflexible and a retardant on individual initiative and innovation. Scholars have noted the higher rents paid for enclosed land compared to open-field land, and some suggest the comparative inefficiency of open fields (see, for example, J. A. Yelling, *Common Field and Enclosure in England.* London, 1977); this was the rationale for the enclosure movements that swept across Europe beginning in the eighteenth century.

Much research challenges the view that the open-field system was inefficient, at least before the modern period. For example, Carl Dahlman (*The Open-field System and Beyond.* Cambridge, 1980) argues that the open-field system was an economically efficient way of dealing with problems faced by preindustrial cultivators as it facilitated large-scale grazing. Robert C. Allen (*Enclosure and the Yeoman*, Oxford, 1992) has shown how cropping was more flexible than initially thought and that the open-field system could sustain considerable agricultural advance and innovation. Gregory Clark ("Commons Sense: Common Property Rights, Efficiency and Institutional Change" *Journal of Economic History* 58.1 (1998), pp. 73–102) showed that the gains from enclosure were not as great as once thought.

This revisionist literature may not have succeeded in proving that the open-field system was as efficient as farming systems that embodied fewer communal rights. Throughout preindustrial Europe, rents typically were higher for enclosed land than for common land. Further, many of the then most productive agricultural regions, such as in the Low Countries, were not characterized by the open-field system and never had been (see Jan de Vries and Ad van der Woude, *The First Modern Economy*, Cambridge, 1997). In general, agricultural progress in western Europe from the late Middle Ages onward was more common in regions *not* characterized by the open-field system—that is, in regions where there were fewer and weaker common rights (see Hopcroft, 1999, above). Even the ecologically marginal areas (mountains, forests, and marshes) outside the open-field regions made important contributions to the economic development of Europe (see Sidney Pollard, *Marginal Europe*, Oxford, 1997). In an econometric analysis of a contemporary descendant of Europe's common fields, in the Swiss Alps, Glenn Stevenson found higher productivity (measured by milk production) on private pastures than on common grazing lands, despite the existence of careful regulation and oversight of the commons (see *Common Property Economics*, Cambridge 1991).

Not only were other agricultural systems typically more productive than the open-field system, but other systems seem to have been more successful at promoting nonagricultural production as well. There is evidence that early industries, such as the cloth-making industry, were more common outside the open-field regions. Many rural industries were characteristic of pastoral and ecologically marginal regions, which were never open-field regions. Such industries were also based in other less-communal regions of Europe; for example, the cloth industry of late medieval and early modern England was concentrated in less-communal regions, notably in the southwest, around Bristol, and in the east, in East Anglia. The Low Countries, where the classic open-field system was largely absent, was the center of cloth making on the continent as early as the Middle Ages. Home industries of various sorts were more common in the less-communal west of Sweden than in the open-field regions of the east; the west was where the Swedish furniture industry began. Similarly, the rural cloth industry in the German lands tended to be located outside the open-field regions, that is, in the east and north (e.g., in Westphalia, Saxony, and Silesia). In France also, less-communal regions in the west (e.g., in Brittany and Normandy) and the south were important textile-producing regions.

In sum, the open-field system, while it provided subsistence for peasants in Europe for perhaps a thousand years, was not a system that notably promoted economic development and change. Other systems were better at this. In the long run, the priority for development and change won. The open-field system was eventually dismantled, and, like many other past social creations, it has become a historical curiosity; it persists only as a maintained tourist attraction (e.g., in Laxton, England). Nonetheless, it has left its mark on the landscapes and villages of the plains of Europe, a legacy that can be seen to this day.

[*See also* Agricultural Revolution; Crop Rotation; Enclosures; *and* Property Rights in Land, *subentry on* Communal Control.]

BIBLIOGRAPHY

Ault, W. O. *Open-Field Farming in Medieval England*. London, 1972. Discussion of the functioning of the open-field system.

Beckett, J. V. *A History of Laxton—England's Last Open-Field Village*. Oxford, 1989. Describes the last current, functioning open-field system in England.

Darby, H. C. *A New Historical Geography of England*. Cambridge, 1973.

Dodgshon, R. A., and R. A. Butlin, eds. *An Historical Geography of England and Wales*. 2d ed. London, 1990.

Göransson, S. "Regular Open Field Pattern England and Scandinavian Solskifte." *Geografiska Annaler* 43 (1961), 80–101.

Gray, H. L. *English Field Systems*. Cambridge, Mass., 1915. An old, but largely accurate, discussion of field systems, including the open-field system.

Heckscher, Eli F. *An Economic History of Sweden*. Translated by Göran Ohlin. Cambridge, 1954. An older but sound economic history, with information on farming systems in Sweden.

Mayhew, Alan. *Rural Settlement and Farming in Germany*. London, 1973.

Mead, W. R. *An Historical Geography of Scandinavia*. New York, 1981.

Planhol, Xavier de, with Paul Claval. *An Historical Geography of France*. Translated by Janet Lloyd. Cambridge, 1994. Includes a discussion of field systems.

Pounds, N. J. G. *An Historical Geography of Europe*. Cambridge, 1990. A regional view of European history; includes a discussion of the open-field system and other farming systems.

Robisheaux Thomas. "The World of the Village." In *Handbook of European History 1400–1600*, edited by Thomas A. Brady, Jr., Heiko A. Oberman, and James D. Tracy, vol. 1, pp. 79–112. Leiden, 1994.

Rösener, Werner. *Peasants in the Middle Ages*. Translated by Alexander Stützer. Urbana, Ill., and Chicago, 1992. A focus on the German lands, with much information about the rural economy, including the open-field system.

Scribner, Bob, ed. *Germany: A New Social and Economic History*, vol. 1, *1450–1630*. New York, 1996. Essays with a variety of information about the German rural economy, including the open-field system.

Smith, C. T. *An Historical Geography of Western Europe before 1800*. New York, 1967. Includes a still useful overview of field systems in western Europe.

ROSEMARY L. HOPCROFT

OPIUM AND NARCOTICS. Opium is a narcotic drug obtained from opium poppy (Papaver somniferum). The narcotic effects are mainly attributable to morphine, which constitutes 9–12 percent of raw opium. Morphine was first isolated from opium at the beginning of the nineteenth century. At the end of the nineteenth century it was discovered that heroin could be made from morphine. Opium for many centuries was the principal painkiller, taken in the form of pills or added to beverages. Opium use increased rapidly when it was consumed through smoking to generate a state of euphoria. When it became more popular trade increased and with the increase in demand came new areas of production, although the opium poppy was native to what is now Turkey.

In the eighteenth and nineteenth centuries opium was big business in Asia. Traders brought opium from British India and the Ottoman Empire and exported it in large quantities to China. In smaller quantities opium was exported to other areas in Southeast Asia with Chinese communities. The British East India Company established a monopoly on opium cultivation in the Indian province of Bengal. Private traders sold the opium to smugglers along the Chinese coast, who in their turn spread it across large parts of China.

Efforts of the Chinese government to enforce opium restrictions resulted in a trading conflict between China and Great Britain known as the First Opium War (1839–1842). This war did not legalize the trade, but it did halt Chinese efforts to restrict it. In the Second Opium War (1856–1860) with Great Britain and France the Chinese government was forced to legalize opium trade. The British were not the only ones making money on the opium business. For financial reasons European colonial governments established opium tax farms. Auctions were held and monopoly rights were sold to the highest bidder, usually a consortium of Chinese (Rush, 1990; Trocki, 1990). Later on, governments took control over the opium business themselves. The French were the first to implement a government opium monopoly, in Indo-China in the late nineteenth century. Other countries followed. The Dutch, for example, introduced a similar system in what is now Indonesia. By the early twentieth century, opium and its derivatives had become a major global commodity.

The attitude of many governments toward opium, morphine, and heroin changed, mainly for two reasons. The first was the change in medical technology. With the introduction of new types of medicine to alleviate pain and cure other diseases, the need for a broad-spectrum medicine like opium and its derivatives vanished. The second was ethical. Under the pressure of an anti-opium movement, control treaties were established through the League of Nations in 1925. In countries in Asia opium was under government control, but in many other countries opium was banned. Criminal organizations entered the market to satisfy consumer demand.

During World War II, restrictions on shipping and strict port security made global opium trafficking very difficult, and new production areas opened. The Golden Triangle (Lao PDR, Myanmar, Thailand) became a major opium producer, and today is one of the two main opium production areas. The other is the Golden Crescent (Afghanistan, Iran, Pakistan). Because the United States and Europe are today's largest consumers there is a lot of (mainly) heroin trafficking between these regions.

The history of cocaine and cannabis (marijuana and hashish) has important similarities to that of opium. After a period of limited and traditional chewing and smoking for medical and recreational purposes, more sophisticated trade routes spread consumption worldwide. Cocaine is derived from the leaves of the coca plant (Erythroxylon coca), which originates in Latin America, still the source of most cocaine. Cannabis, derived from the hemp (Cannabis sativa) plant that is grown primarily for fiber production, originates in central Asia.

Current estimates (United Nations, 1997) indicate that there are 8 million users of heroin and other opiates. In addition, there are 13 million cocaine users and 141 million cannabis users. Because of their addictive properties heroin and cocaine are considered to be hard drugs, while cannabis is considered to be a soft drug. Originally it was thought that due to their addictive properties, demand for heroin and cocaine was fairly inelastic. Empirical estimates show that the price of drugs is influencing demand much more than had been imagined at first. In part these estimates are based on historical numbers from government monopolies on opium (Van Ours, 1995). The new theory of rational addiction supports these empirical findings (Becker and Murphy, 1998). According to this theory rational addicts take the past and future into account and thus react more strongly to changes in prices.

BIBLIOGRAPHY
Becker, G. S., and K. M. Murphy. "A Theory of Rational Addiction." *Journal of Political Economy* 96 (1998), 675–700.
Ours, J. C. van. "The Price Elasticity of Hard Drugs: The Case of Opium in the. Dutch East Indies 1923–1938." *Journal of Political Economy* 103 (1995), 261–279.
Rush, James R. *Opium to Java: Revenue Farming and Chinese Enterprise in Colonial Indonesia, 1860–1910.* Ithaca, N.Y. and London, 1990.
Trocki, Carl A. *Opium and Empire: Chinese Society in Colonial Singapore, 1800–1910.* Ithaca, N.Y. and London, 1990.
United Nations. *World Drug Report.* Oxford, 1997.

J.C. Van Ours

ORGANIZED CRIME. Even if only its contemporary manifestations are taken into account, providing a working definition of organized crime is not an easy task. Academic

ORGANIZED CRIME. Police bust an illegal vodka deal, Moscow, 1990. (© Jeremy Nicholl/Woodfin Camp and Associates, New York)

scholarship has swung back and forth between an approach that seeks to identify the characteristics of organized crime groups and another that focuses on the activities that can be classified as organized crimes. Since organized crime groups often thrive within legitimate social organizations and operate a mix of legal and illegal activities, it is necessary to draw from both approaches.

Criminal organizations have existed in diverse fashions in most human societies sufficiently organized to support them, venturing into almost every form of illegal activity. While their universe is highly diverse, a few common traits are nonetheless clearly distinguishable. First, organized crime can exist only in reference to one or more established societies and their respective form of government and legal structure; in the likeness of a disease, its ultimate goal is not to destroy its host society, but to acquire wealth and power by draining from its resources and infiltrating its control system. This characterization rules out organizations that challenge the state itself, in the fashion of terrorist organizations or revolutionary movements, which respond to political rather than economic motives. Second, organized crime groups aim to persist in time regardless of individualities; armed bands that respond to a charismatic leader and dissolve after his or her death do not fall into this category, and neither do occasional associations of criminals for the purpose of committing one or a few specific crimes. While some authors would disagree with this restriction, it serves the purpose of highlighting the institutional nature of criminal organizations. The third feature common to organized crime groups is the need to specialize in the supply of protection, and the use of corruption and violence (or effective intimidation) toward achieving that goal. By operating in markets and venues outside state protection, organized crime groups need to shield their customers and themselves from both law enforcement and rival groups. While successful criminal groups have better dealt with law enforcement through corruption and infiltration, keeping contenders at bay often requires a display of strength and the eventual use of violence.

The systematic study of organized crime is handicapped by a severe lack of reliable primary sources. Whatever information is available derives either from criminals, in the form of court supervised confessions or epic memoirs aimed at legitimizing themselves, or from law enforcement agencies, which rely on the crimes and criminals they are able to uncover (and therefore the less successful of the lot) and often pursue self-legitimization goals as well. As a result, myth and legend disguised as more or less reliable information plagues the historiography of organized crime, and the scant hard data available allows only for quite wide bounds on the object of study, a problem that becomes more acute as the focus moves further back in history.

While breaking the law in the ancient world was extremely common by rich and poor alike, with the exception of piracy there is little or no evidence pointing to widespread organized crime. Existing studies of antiquity focus on small groups or factions that resemble modern criminal organizations only in the type of crimes they carried out, such as loansharking (lending at interest rates above the legal limit and using violence to enforce payment), but that lack the continuity element or even a sufficiently organized structure. A noteworthy exception is the case of the circus factions, groups charged with organizing public sporting events in the Eastern Roman Empire, which became the route to gain both the emperor's attention and access to administrative posts in the imperial bureaucracy. In the fifth and sixth centuries, a series of riots and street battles marked the underlying struggle for power, which subsided only when the factions were given formal roles and when the hippodrome was substituted for the cathedral as the venue of public imperial appearances.

The first modern criminal enterprises were perhaps the Chinese secret societies, which originated as religious orders and participated in rebellions against colonial governments and foreign missionaries but were widely known to provide cover for gambling, opium trade, and prostitution, among other activities. The Triple Harmony Society, also known as Triad, was likely founded in the early seventeenth century; its rituals, structure, and paraphernalia persisted through the centuries and are currently used by an array of groups that operate local and international criminal networks out of Hong Kong.

The Japanese Yakuza traces its roots back to associations of peddlers and gamblers in the feudal society of the mid-seventeenth century, organized in families that were almost invariably formed through adoption and where practices were passed on through a system of mentorship known as *oyabun-kobun*, or father-child. The Yakuza (which takes its name from the worst possible hand in a game of cards) carved its position in Japanese society by running gambling dens and extracting protection money from farmers. After the 1867 imperial restoration and its accompanying widespread political reform, the Yakuza took great care in building strong links with the new political leadership, bureaucracy, and law enforcement, to the point that it enjoys an almost symbiotic relationship with those structures and that real crackdowns on its activities have been rare occurrences.

The iconic criminal organization *par excellence* has been the Sicilian Mafia, the most prominent of the southern Italian groups that filled in the power vacuum left by the Spanish departure in the 1860s and never quite filled by the Italian monarchy. Its basic unit is the Family, a hierarchical structure headed by a *capo*, or boss, and governed by strict membership rules of allegiance and secrecy. Although the Mafia has operated in a variety of illegal activities through time, its core competence remains the supply of protection in an environment where the state often fails to do it, either through absenteeism or corruption. The Mafia sells protection from counterparties in legal or illegal transactions, from rival crime groups and, most important, from itself. Virtually no economic activity can take place in eastern Sicily without the blessing of the local Mafia family, and the price for that blessing usually includes a cut for local law enforcement. Mafia families are extremely territorial, and the disputes that break out between rival organizations are often marked by a high degree of violence. While the evidence points to occasional attempts at forming regional coordinating bodies, the lack of enforcement mechanisms meant that they had no real weight on the distribution of activities.

The combination of wealth accumulated by the capitalist system and the proliferation of civic and economic liberties has made the United States of America the most fertile territory for organized crime. American cities are host to the most diverse criminal organizations: Italian-American "families," who escaped Italy after the fascist government cracked down on them in the 1920s; black and Chicano street gangs, usually serving as retail outlets for illicit goods; Asian societies, offshoots of the triads, the Yakuza, or other Southeast Asian organizations; and motorcycle gangs, which organize loud runs through public thoroughfares as displays of strength. The activities in which these groups engage are equally broad, but they have mainly concentrated on trade in illicit goods and services rather than on crimes against persons or property, using violence as an enforcement mechanism rather than as a primary source of income. Local and federal laws have provided no shortage of forbidden markets, epitomized by the 1920s prohibition of the manufacture and distribution of alcoholic beverages, which fueled their illegal trade and brought diverse fame to such characters as Lucky Luciano, Al Capone, and Eliot Ness. An all-important branch of organized crime is the introduction of the proceeds of illegal activities into the financial system, best known as money laundering, which is often achieved with the complicity of high-ranking officials in financial institutions.

Controlling organized crime poses two major problems for law enforcement. First, the secrecy of the organizations, their shielding of key figures from direct involvement in criminal operations, and their several mechanisms to prevent infiltration make it difficult to gather evidence, which in most cases is useful only against noncrucial figures. Second, the successful infiltration of law enforcement agencies and political structures by organization members usually reduces the intensity with which they are prosecuted. The evidence problem has been less severe in totalitarian regimes, where the standards of proof for prosecuting crimes tend to be lower, while modern technology has recently proven a key factor in breaking the secrecy codes of old. Infiltration is often a more severe issue, and only major confrontations between the political establishment and the underworlds, such as the assassination by the Mafia of two prominent Italian magistrates in the early 1980s, have provided motive to undertake thorough purges, and even then with mixed success.

Organized crime imposes large direct and indirect costs on the economies in which it operates. Direct costs include those faced by legitimate economic actors (through extortion and violence), and the diversion of otherwise taxable resources to illicit operations. Indirect costs include increasing law enforcement structure, negative externalities generated by illicit goods (such as increased healthcare costs for drug rehabilitation treatments), and the foregone income that would have been generated by the legitimate businesses that were deterred from entering the market by criminal organizations. Both the volume of criminal operations and the indirect costs are unobservable, making it virtually impossible to estimate the impact of organized crime, even in modern economies. Modern economic growth has provided a rapidly increasing pool of resources for criminal organizations to prey on, thereby ensuring that their absolute impact does not decrease. However, the opposing forces of stronger institutional structures (including law enforcement) and increasing legal regulations (mainly the outlawing of specific markets) make the evolution of the relative impact of organized crime very difficult to gauge.

[*See also* Gambling and Gambling Industry; Opium and Narcotics; Piracy; Prostitution; *and* Smuggling.]

BIBLIOGRAPHY

Abadinsky, Howard. *Organized Crime*. 2d ed., Chicago, 1985. One of the standard sources of organized crime in America. Its theoretical framework is echoed in many other works, and it contains detailed historical accounts on the criminal organizations of Chicago and New York.

Block, Alan A. *Space, Time, and Organized Crime*. 2d ed., New Brunswick, N.J., 1994. A survey of selected organized crime issues between the progressive era and present times. Especially noteworthy is the chapter on history and historiography, which addresses the pervasive reliance on myth and legend, often due to the lack of primary source material.

Gambetta, Diego. *The Sicilian Mafia*. Cambridge, 1993. A masterful analysis of the Mafia from the point of view of economic theory. The book provides an exhaustive description of the industry of protection in terms of its players, markets, and resources, and then applies it to the Sicilian case from the origins of the Mafia to modern days. Primary evidence from court records is complemented with personal on-site interviews to provide a vivid picture of the presence of the Mafia in Sicilian economic life.

Herbert, David, L., and Howard Tritt. *Corporations of Corruption: A Systematic Study of Organized Crime*. Springfield, Ill., 1984. Particular emphasis is placed on legal and law enforcement issues. The chapter on history is somewhat incomplete and contains some commonplace inaccuracies.

Hopwood, Keith, ed. *Organised Crime in Antiquity*. London, 1999. A collection of articles on crime in ancient Greece, Rome, the Roman provinces, the Eastern Roman Empire, and the Aztec Empire, providing little or no evidence of widespread criminal organization. Of particular interest is the article by Michael Whitby on the circus factions.

Kaplan, David E., and Alec Dubro. *Yakuza: The Explosive Account of Japan's Criminal Underworld*. Reading, Pa., 1996. A complete history of Japan's organized crime, although more elaboration on the pre-twentieth-century periods would have been desirable. No economic analysis is presented, but the historical account of modern times is rather complete, with particular emphasis on the pervasiveness of the Yakuza in Japan's political system and economic life.

Kelly, Robert J. Ko-Lin Chin, and Rufus Schatzberg, eds. *Handbook of Organized Crime in the United States*. Westport, Conn., 1994. A comprehensive collection of articles on the several groups operating in America and on law enforcement strategies. The article by Michael Maltz presents an overview of the problems arising in the search for a definition of organized crime.

Lyman, Michael D., and Gary W. Potter. *Organized Crime*. 2d ed., Upper Saddle River, N.J., 2000. A comprehensive textbook on organized crime in the United States, with a detailed chapter on its historical evolution.

McMullan, John L. *The Canting Crew: London's Criminal Underworld, 1550–1700*. New Brunswick, N.J., 1984. An attempt to reconstruct the criminal environment of sixteenth- and seventeenth-century London through the dialect used by criminals (cant), recorded in court documents, confessions, and popular plays. A clear example of the difficulties encountered when working with almost nonexistent evidence, the work is complemented with an analysis of economic conditions and labor markets in the leading up to the capitalist era and creating the conditions for the spread of organized crime.

MAURICIO DRELICHMAN

OTTO, NIKOLAUS AUGUST (1832–1891), German inventor.

Most modern automobiles are powered by "Otto cycle" engines, direct descendants of the first four-stroke compression internal combustion engine built by Nikolaus August Otto in 1876. These and earlier Otto engines were a boon to Europe's craftspeople and small businesspeople because previously only large firms could afford to buy, accommodate, and run steam engines to mechanize their operations. Otto's inventions and their influence on economic history are more impressive because his family's economic difficulties forced him to leave high school early, despite an excellent record. Born near Frankfurt, Germany, he later sold tea, coffee, and sugar to stores in small towns around Cologne, where he began his work on engines.

A long search for alternatives to steam engines accelerated in the nineteenth century, culminating in the first internal combustion engine put into production, built by Belgian Jean Lenoir in 1860. Otto experimented with the noncompression Lenoir engine initially but found success developing atmospheric and compression types of internal combustion engines.

In 1864 Otto joined forces with Eugen Langen, a successful businessman with a technical background who worked part-time with Otto and bankrolled the company.

Their patented atmospheric engine won the grand prize at the 1867 Paris Exposition based on its startling improvement in fuel efficiency. Though the engine was large, heavy, and not powerful (one to three horsepower) by today's standards, demand quickly outran production capacity. Otto and Langen found other investors. In 1872 they founded Gasmotoren-Fabrik Deutz AG, in which Gottlieb Daimler and Wilhelm Maybach, who later became auto industry pioneers, also played key roles. Deutz and its licensees in Great Britain, the United States, and continental Europe built almost five thousand atmospheric Otto engines.

In 1876 Otto completed his radically new compression-type four-stroke engine: fuel and air were drawn in, compressed, ignited and expanded, and exhausted as the piston moved out and back in twice. Dubbed the "Silent Otto" for its quieter operation, the engine was patented in major countries. Deutz, its licensees, and its patent infringers poured resources into producing these engines in quantity and made rapid, substantial improvements in them. The German patent was broken when a patent attorney discovered that the Frenchman Alphonse Beau de Rochas had received an unpublished patent in 1862 for his description of how a four-stroke engine working on Otto's principles could be built, though Beau de Rochas neither built one nor pursued the technology. Otto had not documented his earlier work well enough to defend the German patent, though the British one survived a challenge. Scholars are convinced Otto made his discoveries independently but are not sure when.

The detailed story of Otto's accomplishments was relatively neglected in the writing of economic history in English until the 1960s, though much was written in German. Otto is featured in a book by C. Lyle Cummins, Jr., *Internal Fire* (2000), first issued on the one hundredth anniversary of the 1876 invention of the "Silent Otto." His contributions have been recognized by others writing on the history of invention and patterns of technological change.

BIBLIOGRAPHY

Cummins, C. Lyle. *Internal Fire: The Internal Combustion Engine, 1673–1900.* Warrendale, Pa., 2000. In its third edition, the most comprehensive work in English on Otto's role in developing the internal combustion engine, with fine coverage of both the history and the technological details.

Hardenberg, Horst O. *The Middle Ages of the Internal-Combustion Engine, 1794–1886.* Warrendale, Pa., 1999. This excellent book, written under the auspices of the Society of Automotive Engineers Historical Committee, covers exhaustively all of the work done on internal combustion engines during the period in question. Though the historical work is excellent, the volume is intended for and would be most interesting to professional engineers.

Klemm, Friedrich, et al. *A History of Western Technology.* Ames, Iowa, 1991. A short section on Otto explains clearly why his work was expected to help small firms and curb the expanding power of firms large enough to afford steam engines.

Kranzberg, Melvin, and Carroll W. Pursell, Jr., eds. *Technology in Western Civilization*, vol. 1, *The Emergence of Modern Industrial Society.* New York, London, and Toronto, 1967. Includes an essay by Lynwood Bryant, author of two definitive articles on aspects of Otto's work, on the beginnings of the internal combustion engine and Otto's role in it.

Mokyr, Joel. *The Lever of Riches: Technological Creativity and Economic Progress.* New York and Oxford, 1992. There are only two short sections on Otto, but the descriptions of his work in the context of automobile development are informative for those interested in the complex development of technology.

BRADLEY LEWIS

OTTOMAN EMPIRE. The Ottoman Empire stood at the crossroads of intercontinental trade, stretching from the Balkans and the Black Sea region through Anatolia, Syria, Mesopotamia, and the Persian Gulf to Egypt and most of the North African coast for six centuries until World War I. For most of the seventeenth and eighteenth centuries, its population exceeded 30 million (of which the European provinces accounted for half or more, Anatolia and Istanbul for 7 to 8 million, and other Asian and North African provinces for the rest) but declined thereafter due to territorial losses. One might have expected that the economic institutions that sustained this large, multiethnic entity for so long would be of interest to economic historians.

Unfortunately, the recent studies by E. L. Jones and David Landes that provide surveys of non-European empires as well as explanations for the rise of the West, like many of their mainstream predecessors, have shown little interest in understanding the Ottoman land regime, manufacturing and state economic policies, or the daily existence of ordinary men and women. These accounts depict the empire as a centralized, monolithic entity lacking in internal dynamism and differentiation. Moreover, they rely heavily on the pamphlets of European travelers, a genre whose pitfalls have been examined extensively in recent decades. In the more recent account by Landes, the Ottoman Empire is reduced to a caricature of nomads and raiders, despotism, military conquest, looting, and corruption. "The Ottoman empire was a typical despotism, only more warlike" (Landes, 1998, p. 398). With this perspective, however, the longevity of the Ottoman Empire becomes an anomaly and even a mystery. "The empire of the Ottoman Turks proved more durable [than the Mughal dynasty of India]. That in itself is a mystery, because after some two hundred and fifty years of expansion [1300–1550], its downhill course should have brought about fragmentation and liquidation in a matter of decades" (p. 396).

Economic Institutions. Until the end of the sixteenth century, the rise of the Ottoman Empire was closely associated with military conquest. Military success, in turn, depended closely on the land-tenure regime that supported a large cavalry-based army. The Ottoman bureaucracy always took care to undertake detailed censuses of the new territories in order to assess their fiscal potential. Even after territorial expansion slowed down in the second half of the sixteenth century, agriculture continued to provide the economic livelihood for close to 90 percent of the population and key fiscal support for the Ottoman state. The durability of the empire, its achievements as well as limitations during the next three centuries, cannot be understood without studying its agrarian institutions.

The peasant family farm was the basic economic and fiscal unit in the countryside in most of Anatolia and the Balkans, the core areas of the empire where the relatively high land/labor ratios favored small holdings (İnalcık, 1994). The state established ownership over most of these lands early on and did not relinquish it until the second half of the nineteenth century. Hereditary usufruct of the land was given to peasant households, which typically cultivated with family labor and a pair of oxen. Plagues in urban areas were frequent, but large-scale famines were rare in the Ottoman Empire thanks to the favorable land/labor ratios.

The state utilized the *timar* system to tax the rural population and support a large provincial army. Under this system, *sipahis*, state employees often chosen for their wartime valor, lived in the rural areas, collected taxes from the agricultural producers, and spent the revenues locally on the training and equipment of a predetermined number of soldiers as well as their own maintenance.

The Ottoman central administration did not attempt to impose the *timar* regime in all of the conquered territories. In many of the more distant areas such as eastern Anatolia, Iraq, Egypt, Yemen, Walachia, Moldavia and the Maghrib, the Ottomans were eager to collect taxes but altered the existing land regimes either to a limited extent or none at all. The most important reason for this preference was the wish to avoid economic disruption and possible popular unrest. It was also not clear whether the central government had the fiscal, administrative, and economic resources to establish a new regime in these areas. The central government thus handled the task of establishing the land-tenure-cum-fiscal regime for the expanding empire with a large degree of pragmatism. This approach was in fact quite similar to Ottoman practices in other areas. As a result, zones with varying degrees of administrative control emerged inside the empire. At the core were areas most closely administered by the capital with institutions most closely resembling those in the Istanbul region. With increasing distance from the capital, the institutions and administrative practices reflected the power balances between the capital and the local structures and forces. For example, the land regime and the fiscal practices in Ottoman Egypt remained closely attuned to the demands of irrigated agriculture along the Nile valley.

In the urban economy, manufacturing and trade remained under the control of the guilds. The guilds sought and obtained the support of the government whenever merchants tried to organize alternative forms of production. In part because of this support, putting-out activities remained weak in Ottoman lands. The government, in turn, needed the guilds for the preservation of the traditional order. At the same time, a considerable amount of tension existed between the government and guild membership, both Muslim and non-Muslim. While the guilds tried to preserve their independence, they were viewed with suspicion for the heterodox religious beliefs of their membership (Faroqhi, 1984).

It has often been assumed that the prohibition of charging of interest in Islam prevented the development of credit or, at best, imposed rigid obstacles in its way. Similarly, the apparent absence of deposit banking and lending by banks has led many observers to conclude that financial institutions and instruments were, by and large, absent in Islamic societies. However, Islamic law had provided several means by which the antiusury prohibition could be circumvented, just as the same prohibitions were circumvented in Europe in the late medieval period. Thus, there was no insurmountable barrier against the use of interest-bearing loans for commercial credit. Nonetheless, in the medieval Islamic world this option was not exercised. Instead, numerous other commercial techniques were used, including a variety of business partnership forms such as *mudaraba* or commenda and other credit arrangements sanctioned by religious theory.

Ottoman institutions of credit and finance retained their Islamic lineage and remained mostly uninfluenced by the developments in Europe until the end of the seventeenth century (Çizakça, 1996). Dense networks of credit developed in and around Ottoman urban centers despite the Islamic prohibitions against interest. Muslims were equally active in trade and finance as the non-Muslims until the seventeenth century. Muslim entrepreneurs continued to make use of the varieties of business partnerships that flourished in most parts of the Islamic world.

State Economic Policies. Until late in the fifteenth century, tension existed in Ottoman society between the Turkish landed aristocracy of the provinces and the bureaucracy at the center made up mostly of converted slaves (*devshirme*), with the balance of power often shifting between the two. The successful centralization drive of Mehmed II in the second half of the fifteenth century moved the pendulum again, this time decisively. The landed aristocracy was defeated, state ownership was established over privately held lands, and power was concentrated in the hands of the central bureaucracy. After this shift, the economic policies of the government in Istanbul began to reflect much more strongly the priorities of this bureaucracy. The central bureaucracy tried, above all, to create and reproduce a traditional order, with the bureaucracy at the top. The state tolerated and even encouraged the activities of merchants, domestic manufacturers more or less independent of the guilds, and money changers as long as they helped reproduce that traditional order. These groups could accumulate wealth and capital, but the properties of government bureaucrats were often confiscated after their death. Despite the general trend toward decentralization of the empire during the seventeenth and eighteenth centuries, merchants and domestic producers never became powerful enough to exert sufficient pressure on the central government to change or even modify these traditional policies. Only in the provinces were locally powerful groups able to exert increasing degrees of influence over the provincial administrators.

One main Ottoman priority in economic matters was the provisioning of the urban economy, including the army, the palace, and state officials. Foreign merchants were especially welcome because they brought goods not available in Ottoman lands. To this end, beginning in the sixteenth century, the Ottomans granted European merchants various privileges and concessions. The Ottoman government did not hesitate to intervene in local and long-distance trade to regulate the markets and ensure the availability of goods. When compared with both Islamic law and the general practice in medieval Islamic states, the early Ottomans were more interventionist in their approach. However, they soon recognized that they did not have the capacity to intervene in markets in a comprehensive and effective way. The mixed success of their actions inevitably led them to move toward more selective interventionism after the sixteenth century (Pamuk, 2000a).

Promoting long-distance trade and gaining control over trade routes, both overland and maritime, was an important part of the Ottoman strategy across the eastern Mediterranean. Ottoman naval buildup in this region was thus designed to serve both military and commercial purposes. The Ottomans also supported the flourishing trade across the Black Sea and across Anatolia to and from Persia. After gaining control of Egypt early in the sixteenth century, they attempted to establish a permanent presence in the Indian Ocean. Because of their technological disadvantages against the Portuguese in ocean-going navigation and warfare, however, they were forced to retreat to the Mediterranean.

The emphasis on provisioning necessitated an important distinction between imports and exports. Imports were encouraged, as they added to the availability of goods in the urban markets. In contrast, exports were tolerated only after the requirements of the domestic economy were met. As soon as the possibility of shortages emerged, however, the government did not hesitate to prohibit the exportation of basic necessities, especially foodstuffs and raw materials.

The contrasts between these policies and the practices of mercantilism in Europe are obvious. It would be a mistake, however, to identify the concern with the provisioning of urban areas solely with Ottomans or Islamic states. Frequent occurrences of crop failures, famine, and epidemics combined with the primitive nature of available transport led most if not all medieval governments to focus on the urban food supply and more generally on provisioning as the key concerns of economic policy. These Ottoman priorities and practices had strong parallels in the policies of the governments in western and southern Europe during the late Middle Ages. The contrasts between Ottoman and European economic policies emerged later, during the era of mercantilism in Europe. The Ottomans were not unaware of mercantilist thought and practice. One important reason that mercantilist ideas never took root in Ottoman lands was that merchants and domestic producers, whose perspectives were so influential in the development of these ideas in Europe, did not play a significant role in Ottoman economic thought (Pamuk, 2000a).

Long-Term Trends. Most economic historians agree that the sixteenth century until the 1580s was a period of demographic and economic expansion, at least in the core regions of the empire. The growing population increased the pace of exchange in the urban areas and incorporated large segments of the rural population into the local markets. The Ottoman economy and state finances began to face serious difficulties, however, toward the end of the century. While population growth began to put pressure on land and the rural economy, the changing technology of warfare and the need to maintain larger permanent armies created fiscal problems for the central government. With the growing need to collect a larger part of the rural taxes at the center, the *timar* system began to be abandoned in favor of tax farming.

Another adverse development for both the economy and state finances was the impact of the discovery of a sea passage to Asia over the intercontinental trade routes that passed through the Ottoman Empire. When the ocean finally triumphed over the mainland around 1600, towns of the Levant along the caravan route, as well as the Ottoman state finances, felt the decrease in commercial activity. Moreover, with the decline of the central government's administrative and political power, urban-based provincial notables known as the *ayan* began to capture an increasing share of the tax revenues at the expense of the central government. In comparison to these developments, the earlier attempts by historians to single out the so-called "price revolution" as a key event triggering "Ottoman decline" at the end of the sixteenth century appear misplaced today.

The economic and fiscal difficulties lasted well into the seventeenth century. Demographic and economic difficulties culminated in the social and political upheavals known as the Celâli Revolts. As the peasants took flight or returned to nomadism, agriculture, especially commercial agriculture, and tax revenues were adversely affected. Population and economic activity stagnated and probably declined in many parts of the empire during the seventeenth century. In Suraiya Faroqhi's apt characterization, the seventeenth century was a period of "crisis and partial recovery" for the Ottoman economy (1984).

Until recently, Ottoman historiography had depicted an empire in decline after the sixteenth century. This paradigm is now being replaced by one that places greater emphasis on the state's and society's ability to reorganize as a way of adapting to changing circumstances. As a corollary to this shift, economic historians have questioned whether the seventeenth and eighteenth centuries were simply a period of crisis and stagnation. Recent studies have shown that Ottoman agriculture and industry did not enter a period of irreversible decline after the sixteenth century.

In fact, most of the eighteenth century was a period of relative peace, stability, and economic expansion. Available evidence on production is limited, but it does point to an increasing trend toward agriculture and artisanal activity as well as investment in manufacturing in many parts of the Balkans and Anatolia. In the Balkans, large-scale farms (*çiftlik*) began to emerge, specializing in grain production for Istanbul and other long-distance markets. Also, trade with central and western Europe expanded, which facilitated the incorporation of the Ottoman economy into the European network of multilateral payments. Until the nineteenth century, however, technological change in the Ottoman Empire in agriculture, manufacturing, mining, shipbuilding, and other areas remained limited. Despite their geographical proximity, the Ottomans did not keep up with European developments and did not adopt European innovations quickly (Issawi, 1996).

The nineteenth century was a period quite different from the earlier era. In the face of the growing European challenge and territorial losses of the empire in the Balkans and North Africa (including Egypt), the period was characterized, on the one hand, by major efforts of the central bureaucracy aimed at the elimination of the provincial *ayan*, centralization of the empire, and Western-style reform in administration, education, law, and justice as well as economic, fiscal, and monetary affairs. It was also a period of integration into world markets and rapid expansion in trade with industrial Europe, which transformed the Ottoman economy into an exporter of primary products and importer of manufactured goods. This process was facilitated by the construction of ports and railroads and the establishment of modern banking institutions, mostly with European capital. As a result, the commercialization of agriculture proceeded rapidly in Macedonia, western and central Anatolia, and along the Syrian coast. The rural population was drawn to markets not only as producers of cash crops but also as purchasers of imported goods, especially cotton textiles (Owen, 1981).

Institutional changes and integration into world markets combined to create a slow but significant trend of economic growth in the decades leading up to World War I and possibly earlier. Per capita incomes probably rose at an average of about 1 percent per annum after 1880. Export-oriented agriculture was the leading sector, and the more commercialized coastal regions along with the port cities participated to a greater extent in this process. Estimates place per capita incomes for 1913 in the range of 12 to 14 current pounds sterling, or more than $1000 in purchasing power parity adjusted in 1990 U.S. dollars. This would put average incomes in the Ottoman Empire below those of most countries in southeastern Europe but above those of Egypt and Iran.

Evidence of long-term changes in the standard of living during these centuries is beginning to emerge from the Ottoman archives. A recent study indicates real wages of construction workers in Istanbul and other cities were already below those of northwestern Europe in the sixteenth century. After declining by 30 to 40 percent during the sixteenth century, probably due to population growth, urban real wages remained roughly unchanged until late in the eighteenth century. They almost doubled from the late eighteenth century until World War I, even as the real wage gap with northwestern Europe began to widen after the Industrial Revolution. On the eve of World War I, real wages of urban construction workers in the Ottoman Empire were about 40 percent above their levels in 1500 (Pamuk, 2000b). The state research does not yet permit historians to make generalizations about the standard of living of the rural population.

Based on Central Bureaucracy. For most of its six-hundred-year existence, the Ottoman Empire is best characterized as a bureaucratic, agrarian empire. The economic institutions and policies of this entity were shaped to a large degree by the priorities and interests of a central bureaucracy. With its pragmatism, flexibility, and habit of negotiation, the bureaucracy managed to contain many challenges, both internal and external, and succeeded in maintaining a traditional order (Barkey, 1994). Even the reforms of the nineteenth century are best understood as attempts to maintain the privileged position of the center as well as the territorial integrity of the empire.

Before the Industrial Revolution and the European expansion of the nineteenth century, the central bureaucracy faced its most serious challenge from the *ayan* of the provinces. Despite a protracted struggle lasting almost two centuries, however, the *ayan* were unable to establish alternative institutions and channels of capital accumulation. Although they were interested in trade, agriculture, and manufacturing, tax farming remained the most lucrative enterprise for them. Key economic institutions of the traditional Ottoman order, such as state ownership of land, urban guilds, provisionism, and selective interventionism, remained mostly intact during this period. In the early part of the nineteenth century, the center, supported by new technologies, was able to reassert its power over the provinces. On the whole, this environment did not prove conducive to either technological change or the emergence of new forms of economic organization.

[*See also* Levant, *subentry on* Islamic Rule.]

BIBLIOGRAPHY

Barkey, Karen. *Bandits and Bureaucrats: The Ottoman Route to State Centralization.* Ithaca, N.Y., 1994.

Çizakça, Murat. *A Comparative Evolution of Business Partnerships, the Islamic World, and Europe.* Leiden, 1996.

Faroqhi, Suraiya. *Towns and Townsmen of Ottoman Anatolia: Trade, Crafts, and Food Production in an Urban Setting, 1520–1650.* Cambridge, 1984.

İnalcık, Halil, and Donald Quataert, eds. *An Economic and Social History of the Ottoman Empire, 1300–1914.* Cambridge, 1994.

Issawi, Charles. "The Economic Legacy." In *Imperial Legacy: The Ottoman Imprint on the Balkans and the Middle East,* edited by L. Carl Brown, pp. 227–245. New York, 1996.

Jones, Eric. L. *The European Miracle.* 2d ed. Cambridge, 1981.

Landes, David. *The Wealth and Poverty of Nations.* New York, 1998.

Owen, Roger. *The Middle East in the World Economy, 1820–1914.* London and New York, 1981.

Palairet, Michael. *The Balkan Economies, circa 1800–1914: Evolution without Development.* Cambridge, 1997.

Pamuk, Şevket. *A Monetary History of the Ottoman Empire.* Cambridge, 2000a.

Pamuk, Şevket. *Five Hundred Years of Prices and Wages in Istanbul and Other Cities, 1469–1998.* Ankara, Turkey, 2000b.

ŞEVKET PAMUK

OUIDAH (or Whydah) is a town in the Republic of Benin (until 1975 called Dahomey), West Africa, in the region formerly called the "Slave Coast." It originally belonged to the small coastal kingdom of Hueda (whence the name Ouidah), but in 1727 it was conquered by the hinterland kingdom of Dahomey, to which it remained subject until the French colonial occupation in 1892. Functioning as a seat of Dahomian provincial administration as well as a commercial center, it grew into a substantial town, with a population of around 15,000 by the nineteenth century.

Ouidah became a place of embarkation for the Atlantic slave trade from 1671, when the French opened a trading post (subsequently fortified) there; later, English (1682) and Portuguese (1721) forts were also established. Over the following two centuries, Ouidah probably supplied over 10 percent of all transatlantic exports, over a million slaves, making it the second most important African "port" of the slave trade (exceeded only by Luanda, Angola). It sent slaves mainly to Brazil and secondarily to the French West Indies, but relatively few to the British West Indies and North America. Ouidah remained a major supplier of slaves after the legal prohibition of the trade in the early nineteenth century, when exports continued illegally to Brazil and Cuba; the last transatlantic shipment of slaves from Ouidah was to Cuba in 1863. In this period, several Brazilian slave traders settled in the town, notably Francisco Felix de Souza (died 1849), who became commercial agent to the Dahomian king Gezo (r. 1818–1858).

Ouidah was not strictly a "port," being situated 3.5 kilometers (2.2 miles) from the coast, north of a lagoon that runs parallel to the shore. Indeed, this lagoonside situation was as critical for its commercial role as its proximity to the sea, slaves often being delivered to Ouidah by canoe along the lagoon. Slaves exported had to be taken overland and across the lagoon to the shore, rather than being embarked directly into European ships. Moreover, at the coast there is no "port," in the sense of a sheltered harbor, but only an open roadstead. Because of dangerous surf and sandbars, ships could not approach close to the shore, but had to stand some distance off and land goods and embark slaves in smaller craft, for which purpose African canoes were normally employed.

Beginning in the 1830s, exports of palm produce developed, surpassing slaves in value by the 1850s. Ouidah participated in this transition, but its commercial preeminence was eroded by the development of an alternative outlet for Dahomey's trade at Cotonou, 35 kilometers (22 miles) to the east. This diversion was initially due to Cotonou's more advantageous situation in relation to waterways connecting with the interior, which became critical with the shift in trade to palm produce, whose greater bulk placed a premium on cheap waterborne transport. The process was accelerated under French colonial rule by the construction of modern port facilities at Cotonou, beginning with a wharf in the 1890s. Ouidah had ceased to handle any export trade by the 1940s, when its customs post was closed, and remains nowadays economically marginalized.

BIBLIOGRAPHY

Agbo, Casimir. *Histoire de Ouidah du XVe au XXe siècle.* Avignon, France, 1959. History of the town, by a local amateur historian.

Berbain, Simone. *Le Comptoir français de Juda (Ouidah) au XVIIIe siècle.* Paris, 1942.

Law, Robin. *The Slave Coast of West Africa, 1550–1750: The Impact of the Atlantic Slave Trade on an African Society.* Oxford, 1991.

Law, Robin. "Ouidah, 1727–1892: A Pre-Colonial Urban Community in Coastal West Africa." In *Africa's Urban Past,* edited by David Anderson and Richard Rathbone, pp. 55–70. London, 2000.

Newbury, C. W. *The Western Slave Coast and Its Rulers: European Trade and Administration among the Yoruba and Adja-speaking Peoples of South-western Nigeria, Southern Dahomey and Togo.* Oxford, 1961.

ROBIN LAW

OWEN, ROBERT (1771–1858), British self-made cotton-spinning entrepreneur, who sought substantial improvements in the working conditions and characters of his work force at the New Lanark mills.

Founded by David Dale in 1801, Owen assumed management of the mills. During the next quarter century, the New Lanark Twist Company generated extraordinary profits, of which, after the formation of a new partnership in 1806, Owen gained about 40 percent of the profits (estimated at 12.5 percent per annum). Owen reduced the hours of labor, organized a system of infant education, and discouraged illegitimate pregnancy and excessive drinking. Attempts to persuade his fellow manufacturers to limit the hours of labor and improve factory conditions largely failed, however. In 1817, with widespread social unrest and unemployment, following the post–Napoleonic Wars demobilization and the consequent slackened demand, Owen became persuaded that the poor should be housed in communities of "co-operation," in which labor and profit would be shared in common.

By 1820, and particularly in Owen's *Report to the County of Lanark* (1821), he contrasted his own "social" system to the "individual" system of competition among and between individuals. By 1825, his own system—whose theory of justice was founded the concept of universal labor and the exchange of products on an "equitable" principle of equivalent labor-time and materials costs—was being termed *socialism*. The remainder of Owen's career was dedicated to implementing these principles, first at a ready-made community in the United States—in New Harmony, Indiana—bought from a German pietist sect; that lasted from 1825 to 1827. Then he tried various social experiments in Britain, of which the most important was the Queenwood community, begun in 1839 and lasting until 1845. Owen was involved in efforts to find the first union for all trades, the Grand National Consolidated Trades Union: he also worked on the foundation of "labor exchanges" in London and Birmingham during the early 1830s, where artisans traded their wares directly, thus eliminating middlemen.

By 1825, Owen's system had been linked to ideas of worker-ownership, called "co-operation," a term that also encompassed retail "shopkeeping" endeavors, which, by contrast with Owen's system, retained private property. Also in the 1820s, a number of key works of economic theory were published, inspired by Owen's views. These included William Thompson's *An Inquiry into the Principles of the Distribution of Wealth Most Conducive to Human Happiness* (1824) and his *Labor Rewarded* (1827), as well as John Gray's *Lecture on Human Happiness* (1825) and his *The Social System* (1831). Owen's greatest period of popular success came during the "sectarian" phase of the movement (1839–1845), when some fifty branches of the Association of All Classes of All Nations were established, chiefly in the manufacturing districts, to raise funds for a community. Among those attending lectures at the main, Manchester, branch was the young Friedrich Engels, whose early writings in economics evince a marked Owenite inspiration.

Besides the *Report to the County of Lanark*, Owen's main economic writings are *Observations on the Effect of the Manufacturing System* (1815) and *The Book of the New Moral World* (7 parts, 1836–1844). His autobiography, with various writings, was published as *The Life of Robert Owen Written by Himself* (2 vols., 1857–1858). Modern editions of his works include *A New View of Society and Other Writings*, edited by G. Claeys (Harmondsworth, Penguin Books, 1991), and *Selected Works of Robert Owen*, edited by G. Claeys (4 vols., Pickering and Chatto, 1993).

BIBLIOGRAPHY

Claeys, Gregory, ed. *Selected Works of Robert Owen.* 4 vols. London, 1993.

Harrison, J. F. C. *Robert Owen and the Owenites in Britain and America.* London, 1969.

Podmore, Frank. *Robert Owen: A Biography.* London, 1923.

GREGORY CLAEYS

P–Q

PACIFIC ISLANDS. The Pacific Islands were a final frontier of human settlement on the planet. Whereas Homo Sapiens reached New Guinea perhaps forty to fifty thousand years ago, Austronesians started to spread into Oceania only around six thousand years ago, passing beyond those areas of western Melanesia previously reached by Pleistocene hunter-gatherers. Contrary to theories of the South American origins of modern Polynesians, settlement initially moved eastward from Southeast Asia through coastal New Guinea, to New Caledonia (around four thousand years ago), to Fiji, Samoa, and Tonga (approximately three thousand to thirty-five hundred years ago), and to the Marquesas Islands (perhaps two thousand years ago). From the Marquesas Islands, settlers voyaged as far afield as Easter Island (Rapanui), Hawaii, and New Zealand.

How were Austronesians able to navigate across such vast expanses of empty ocean? New maritime technologies, including use of sail and outrigger canoes, enabled passage across previously impassable oceans. Navigation techniques, including use of horizon and zenith stars, winds, and currents, and cloud, reef, and bird flight patterns as methods of targeting landfall, made possible triple voyages (of discovery, return to point of origin, and finally deliberate settlement). Cultivation of root crops and rearing of pigs, dogs, and chickens allowed survival in otherwise inhospitable circumstances. Archaeological evidence of a distinct Lapita ceramic tradition, dated between thirty-six hundred and two thousand years ago and stretching from the Bismarck Archipelago and New Caledonia eastward to Tonga and Samoa, has been associated with the Austronesian advance.

The Neolithic material cultures of the Pacific were based on cultivation of root crops (taro, yams, and sweet potatoes), animal husbandry, and fishing. Complex trading patterns based on resource complementarity did exist (for example, between interior and coastal regions, wet and dry islands, or areas with distinct specializations), although the primary context of exchange was usually to underpin reciprocal or ceremonial bonds. On the larger continental islands of Melanesia, settlements were often concentrated on river deltas or leeward sides of islands capable of supporting rotational slash-and-burn agriculture. In highland New Guinea, extensive forest clearance some five thousand years ago paved the way for continuous cultivation, eventually of the sweet potato. Toward the east of Oceania, yam and taro provided the staple crops, although the coral atolls only a few meters above sea level found in many parts of Micronesia and Polynesia could support only limited taro, coconut, and breadfruit cultivation and were highly reliant on exploitation of reef and deep-sea areas.

On the authority of a papal bull of 1493, Spanish territorial claims extended westward from Europe through the Americas. In November 1520, Ferdinand Magellan rounded Cape Horn and led the first European voyage across the Pacific. Further Spanish transpacific navigations, the establishment of a galleon trade from Acapulco to Manila after 1565, and the foundation of a colony on Guam in 1676 strengthened the Spanish presence. But the British and French explorations of the late eighteenth century, in particular Captain James Cook's three Pacific voyages, paved the way for the incorporation of the South Pacific into the world economy.

Early Nineteenth-Century Trade Expansion. British establishment of a penal colony in New South Wales in 1788 proved the key impetus to the early nineteenth century expansion of South Pacific commerce. A provisioning trade in salt pork and live pigs grew up with Tahiti, and settlers became involved in sealing and bay whaling along the eastern Australian coast, in the Bass Strait and later around New Zealand. Conversely, the interior of the continent seemed at first inaccessible owing to the absence of navigable waterways and the obstacle posed by the Blue Mountains. As late as 1817, Governor Lachlan Macquarie noted:

> This country is not so fortunate as to furnish almost any one article of its own growth or produce worthy of export; and the consequence has been that its efforts to obtain Exports have been turned to the procuring of the Oil, Skin, Shells etc., which the surrounding seas and South Sea Islands produce. (Macquarie, 1817, p. 401)

Until the mid-1830s, whale oil, sealskins, and whalebone remained Australia's leading exports, while earnings from the repair and revictualing of foreign vessels were mainstays of the expanding ports at Sydney and Hobart Town.

Nevertheless, there were obstacles to the expansion of South Pacific trade. British restrictions limited colonial shipbuilding, and the British East India Company had a monopoly over the China trade. China was an obvious target market because British ships arriving with supplies regularly departed in ballast to pick up cargoes at Canton or Manila before returning to Europe. Like Britain, Australia also imported large quantities of tea from China and financed this primarily with specie exports. Island produce to supply the China market, such as *bêche-de-mer* (sea slugs), sandalwood, pearl, and turtle shell, could potentially diminish Australia's trade deficit with China. Early Sydney traders used elaborate measures to circumvent the company's monopoly over trade with China. Restrictions on colonial shipbuilding were abolished in 1819, and the East India Company's China monopoly was finally ended in 1834.

From the 1790s onward, British, French, and American whalers hunted their quarry in South Pacific waters. In an age before electric or gas lighting, whale oil supplied fuel for illumination of streets and houses. The sperm whale, usually found in deeper tropical waters, provided particularly fine oil, spermaceti, used both for interior lighting and as a lubricant for precision instruments. Pacific whalers required supplies of timber, water, and fresh food. Hawaiian and Maori agriculture were transformed by servicing whaling vessels, and prostitution thrived in the port towns of Hawaii, Tahiti, and Guam. Large numbers of Pacific Islanders were engaged as crew aboard whalers. New England vessels, for example, deliberately departed shorthanded, taking on their full complement only when they reached Hawaii. By the 1840s, when American vessels dominated the whaling trade, islanders comprised perhaps 20 percent of all Pacific whaling crews.

In the early phases of expansion of commerce, fishhooks, nails, and other iron goods found ready markets among Stone Age Pacific societies, as eventually did alcohol, cloth, and tobacco. By the 1830s, guns and ammunition comprised 68 percent of New South Wales's exports to the Maori of New Zealand. Firearms obtained as trade goods assisted the centralization of chiefly authority in Fiji, Tahiti, Hawaii, Samoa, and Tonga. In those countries, missionary activity largely preceded trade expansion, fostering new demands for clothing, Bibles, and other goods. In Tonga, the Wesleyan missionary Shirley Baker became prime minister in the government of King George Tupou I. He assisted the passage of reformist legislation diminishing the authority of the nobility and, through a land redistribution program, providing for individual land ownership. But the key stimulus to Tongan cash cultivation was the desire for incomes to participate in competitive church collections, also controversially organized by the Reverend Baker. Tonga was easily the largest coconut oil producer in the South Pacific in the 1870s.

Although estimates of the size of precontact indigenous populations are notoriously uncertain, high death rates followed contact with Europeans. Exposure to hitherto unknown infectious diseases against which islanders had no immunities, such as measles, smallpox, whooping cough, and influenza, decimated island populations. On Spanish Guam, a smallpox epidemic reduced the Chamorro population by 70 percent in the thirty years after 1688. A quarter of all indigenous Fijians were carried away by measles in 1875. Higher death rates may have correlated with the intensity of European visits and with the extent of settler intrusion, while larger populations with better nutrition experienced smaller declines and more rapid recoveries. Severe falls in population sizes due to contagious diseases continued into the twentieth century. An influenza epidemic, carried along shipping routes in 1918–1919, hit most of the Pacific Islands, killing around a quarter of the Samoan and Tahitian populations. Leaving aside those areas demographically overwhelmed by settlers (Australia, New Zealand, and Hawaii), indigenous populations on average more than trebled in the following half century.

The Shift to Plantation Agriculture. German firms controlled perhaps 70 percent of South Pacific commerce by the 1870s. Having initially established operations in Apia (Samoa) in 1857, the Hamburg firm J. C. Godeffroy & Sohn developed a network of agents as far westward as island New Guinea, northward into Micronesia, and eastward to the Society Islands. Small schooners serviced the smaller islands, while larger brigantines shipped produce back to Europe. Apia general manager Theodor Weber revolutionized the coconut trade by shifting to copra exports, involving export of the dried white meat of the nut for milling in vast hydraulic presses in Germany rather than crude oil processing in the Pacific. Copra became the staple of Pacific commerce despite low value per unit of weight and consequent high freight charges on shipment back to Europe. Because coconuts were important in the diets of Pacific Islanders, European traders could procure coconuts wherever a surplus was available. The coconut palm was also a land-intensive rather than labor- or capital-intensive crop and therefore was well suited to prevailing relative factor scarcities in the Pacific.

Until the 1860s, South Pacific commerce typically involved small-scale resident traders engaged in barter trade with islanders. By interrupting the supply of raw cotton from the southern United States and raising world prices, the U.S. Civil War (1861–1865) stimulated cotton cultivation in Fiji, Samoa, Tahiti, and Queensland (Australia). German plantations in Samoa, for example, were laid out in the 1860s with cotton interplanted among rows of coconut palms. Unlike coconut palms, which took around seven years to bear fruit, cotton was a labor-intensive crop that produced up to three harvests a year. Yet the cotton boom proved short-lived. The end of the U.S. Civil War permitted a resumption of U.S. cotton exports, and falling world prices left many planters bankrupt, particularly in Fiji.

In Queensland, Fiji, and Hawaii, sugar plantations close to heavily capitalized milling operations expanded rapidly in the 1870s and 1880s. All faced severe problems with labor shortages, as did cotton and copra production in Samoa and the nickel mines and colonial apparatus of French New Caledonia. In Hawaii during the 1840s and 1850s, poll taxes and statutes against "idleness" and "vagrancy" pushed over 50 percent of adult males into plantation labor. Yet even this proved insufficient. Following the 1876 Reciprocity Treaty with the United States, the volume of Hawaii's sugar exports rose tenfold between 1876 and 1890 owing to duty-free access to the American market. Hawaii became the Pacific's largest overseas labor recruiter with around a quarter of a million contract laborers arriving between 1860 and 1900, mostly from Japan and China. By contrast, the colonial government kept native Fijians in their villages under traditional chiefs, leaving plantations dependent on labor brought from other Pacific Islands and India (60,553 Indian migrants arrived between 1879 and 1916). During the last quarter of the nineteenth century, Queensland was by far the largest importer of Pacific Island indentured labor (62,000 recruits) and was in direct competition with recruiting ships from Fiji (27,000) and Samoa (12,500).

Former interpretations of the Melanesian labor trade emphasized its coercive aspects, such as the "blackbirding" (kidnapping) of islanders and the harsh conditions they faced on plantations. More recent "islander-oriented" historians, such as Deryck Scarr, Clive Moore, and Peter Corris, have highlighted considerable voluntary recruitment. Along similar lines, Ralph Schlomowitz analyzed markets for Melanesian time-expired workers (those on second or subsequent contracts) and found that they bargained successfully for higher wages and that "beach" payments to recruits' kin or communities tended to rise markedly during the 1870s and 1880s. Both trends were taken as indicative of the emergence of a flexible labor market with remuneration adjusted upward to equilibrate demand and supply of labor. Schlomowitz showed that high death rates for plantation laborers were particularly severe for first-time recruits at early stages in their contracts, implying that lack of immunity to unfamiliar infectious diseases rather than ill treatment played the major role in premature mortality.

Indenture contracts were normally for a fixed duration and with stipulated remuneration set by conditions in the country of origin rather than in the vicinity of plantations (where labor scarcity would presumably have exerted greater upward pressure on wages). Penal clauses were widely used as means of extending contracts or clawing back wages. In Fiji during the 1890s and 1900s, for example, some 85 to 90 percent of Indian laborers were prosecuted for breaches of the labor ordinances, including failure to complete specified daily "tasks." As a result, wages did not reach their contractual level of 1s. per day until 1909. Open market determinants of wages also were limited in other respects. Despite increased competition, wage differentials between Fiji and Queensland persisted during the 1880s, when first-time Melanesian recruits for Fiji were offered around £3 per annum, as compared with Queensland's £6 per annum, and when Fiji's time-expired workers secured only around half the rate of their Queensland counterparts. Recruiting ships bound for Fiji were progressively squeezed out of the New Hebrides and then the Solomon Islands as the recruiting frontier moved northeastward.

Ultimately, intensified competition in the Melanesian labor reserve was dealt with by colonial partition of labor supplies rather than by a shift toward greater flexibility in remuneration. Fiji's labor shortages were met by resorting to the import of labor from British India, while French Indo-China provided workers for the nickel and chrome mines of New Caledonia. French authorities excluded rivals from recruiting Loyalty Islanders, and Queensland's recruiters were barred from German New Guinea after 1884. Even the British Solomon and Gilbert Islands were eventually closed to overseas recruiting vessels. As local sources of cash incomes expanded, islanders in any case proved increasingly reluctant to sign contracts as overseas laborers. In the aftermath of Australian federation (1901), the new government adopted a policy of exclusion of colored labor, and the Queensland leg of the Melanesian labor trade was finally ended in 1906.

Early Twentieth Century. By 1900, the imperial partition of the South Pacific was complete. France had acquired Tahiti and surrounding archipelagos (1842 onward), New Caledonia (1853), and a stake in the joint Anglo-French Naval Commission in the New Hebrides (1887). Germany had secured control over Northern New Guinea (1884), the Marshall Islands (1885), Nauru (1888), the Caroline Islands and northern Marianas (1899), and Samoa (1900). In the aftermath of the Spanish-American War (1898), the United States took Guam from the Spanish, annexed Hawaii (in support of a coup by American settlers five years earlier), and by agreement with Germany and Britain, formalized its control over the eastern Samoan port of Pago Pago. Britain had possessions in Fiji (1874), Papua (1884), the Cook Islands (1888), the Gilbert and Ellice Islands (1892), and the Solomon Islands (1893) and a loose protectorate over Tonga (1900).

Germany's defeat in World War I brought a repartition of the Pacific. At the outset of the war, German naval forces in the Pacific attempted to reach Europe via Cape Horn.

Most were destroyed off the Falkland Islands. Japan secured Germany's former Micronesian territories north of the equator despite protests from the Americans. Subsidized Japanese concerns took over German copra and other trading operations and established a sugar industry on Saipan and elsewhere in the southern Marianas, mainly based on employment of migrant Okinawans, before the islands were heavily fortified in the run up to the Pacific war. Western Samoa and New Guinea likewise became "Class C" League of Nations mandated territories under, respectively, New Zealand and Australia. In both countries German planters were expropriated. Phosphate-rich Nauru became a British Empire mandate, in practice administered by Australia.

Commodity price deflation in the aftermath of World War I and a slowdown in the Australian and New Zealand economies depressed export earnings in many parts of the Pacific. Postwar resumption of European sugar beet production led to falling world sugar prices, reducing Fiji's export earnings. The end of Indian indentured migration (1916) also slowed cane supplies as plantations were converted to small Indian-run tenant farms. Yet Fiji's sugar industry was eventually assisted by devaluation of the Fiji pound and by Britain's shift to "imperial preference," which gave the country a protected sugar quota destined for the United Kingdom market.

The copra industry, the lynchpin of virtually all the Pacific Island economies, fared less well. Falling copra prices led to severe cuts in wages and work forces, and many plantations were abandoned. Phosphate prices also fell, although during the 1930s exports from Nauru and Ocean Island nevertheless expanded to meet the needs of Antipodean agriculture. Despite severe falls in output between 1931 and 1934, restructuring of New Caledonia's nickel industry and centralization of operations under Société le Nickel enabled the industry to survive, and rapid expansion accompanied European rearmament in the late 1930s. Rising interwar gold prices stimulated exploratory activity in the Pacific. New mines opened at Mount Kasi and Vatukoula in Fiji in the early 1930s, and there were major gold strikes at Edie Creek (1926) and elsewhere in the mountains of New Guinea's Morobe district.

The depression increased the power of larger firms, such as Burns Philp and Carpenters, at the expense of smaller concerns and white planters. Cuts in plantation work forces implied for many Pacific Islanders an involuntary return to subsistence cultivation, yet indigenous cash cultivation of copra nevertheless contributed an increasing fraction of total exports in many parts of Melanesia. Incorporation into the market economy was too well established to be reversed even by falling world market prices.

The Japanese attacked Pearl Harbor on 7 December 1941, and three days later they seized Guam from the Americans. At its height, the Pacific segment of Japan's "Great East Asia Co-Prosperity Sphere" extended south to New Guinea and eastward into the Gilbert Islands. But the reversals came swiftly. On 7 May 1942, Japanese forces heading for Port Moresby were defeated in the Battle of the Coral Sea, and a month later the Americans won a major victory in the Battle of Midway Island. Ferocious fighting on and around Guadalcanal ended in February 1943, after which the Japanese were gradually pushed back northward through Micronesia. Commerce collapsed, plantations were closed, and shipping lines discontinued operations in many of the Melanesian and Micronesian areas of conflict. Yet the Pacific war proved a significant stimulus to commercial activity in areas occupied by American forces. By 1943, there were at least 500,000 American troops dispersed among the islands. U.S. bases were established in New Caledonia, on Efate and Espiritu Santo (New Hebrides), on Bora Bora (French Polynesia), and in Nuku'alofa (Tonga), Nadi (Fiji), and Apia (Samoa). Wage rates offered by the incoming American forces tended to be far in excess of those previously paid under the prewar colonial administrations, and sales of curios, trinkets, and foodstuffs, as well as prostitution, thrived. Protest movements, such as the John Frum cult on Tanna (New Hebrides) and the Maasina Rule movement on Malaita (Solomon Islands), were strongly influenced by the wartime experience of American prosperity.

Post–World War II Era. The nature of political ties with metropolitan powers was a powerful determinant of living standards in the postwar Pacific. French Polynesia and New Caledonia, for example, sustained relatively high per capita income through a combination of French aid, nickel export earnings, and nuclear testing–related military expenditures. Similarly, Hawaii, the fiftieth American state after 1959, became the richest of the Pacific Islands, largely owing to American finance and tourism. Despite considerable mineral, forestry, and agricultural resources, most Melanesian economies, conversely, faced relatively low levels of GDP per capita. Populations remained heavily dependent on village-based subsistence production, with small formal sectors centered on copra, sugar, forestry, and fisheries exports. Only Papua New Guinea and Fiji diversified into manufacturing and longer-run sustained mineral production.

One reason for this contrast is explored in the migration, remittances, aid, and bureaucracy model (MIRAB). Geoff Bertram pointed out that from the 1960s onward many of the Polynesian and Micronesian Islands sustained high levels of import consumption despite long-run trade deficits. In Niue, Tokelau, the Cook Islands, Kiribati, and Tuvalu, government expenditure also remained considerably in excess of locally generated revenue. These countries nevertheless fully financed their current accounts through aid receipts, various service incomes, and remittance inflows from migrants working overseas. Bertram argued that such earnings "crowded out" export production. The comparative advantage of MIRAB countries was to concentrate instead on exporting factors of production (particularly labor) and sustaining aid inflows, as opposed to the preferred World Bank path of boosting exports and cutting back state expenditure.

Where populations have unlimited access to metropolitan labor markets, as for Niue and the Cook Islands (to New Zealand) and the Marshall Islands and Federated States of Micronesia (to America), relatively high overseas wage rates may have provided a floor below which export industries became unviable. Conversely, for Kiribati and Tuvalu migration possibilities have been limited to work aboard overseas merchant ships, and GDP per capita has remained significantly lower, at least following the termination of phosphate mining on Ocean Island (Banaba) in 1979. Despite facing immigration controls, Samoans and Tongans have proved adept at exploiting migration possibilities. Around half their populations today reside overseas in Australia, New Zealand, and North America. Strong kinship ties underpinned migrant remittance flows and relatively high living standards, but export earnings nevertheless continued to finance nearly half the total current account earnings.

More generally, there is no evidence of a direct correlation between export collapse and aid or remittance inflows as implied by the "crowding out" thesis. In the former American-controlled Trust Territory of Micronesia, for example, earnings from phosphate and copra and other island produce collapsed well before the commencement of large U.S. aid subventions in the 1960s. With the end of the indentured labor–dependent plantation systems, Pacific Island economies faced other difficulties in establishing viable export industries. World market prices for traditional staples, such as copra, declined. Despite rapid urbanization, village-based subsistence cultivation continued to provide an alternative to waged employment. Although research has found little correlation between small country size and low GDP per capita, Pacific microeconomies nevertheless faced serious problems with vulnerability to natural disasters, internal dispersion, and remoteness from major markets hindering participation in the postwar acceleration in economic growth witnessed in other parts of the Pacific Rim.

[*See also* Contract Labor and the Indenture System *and* New Zealand.]

BIBLIOGRAPHY

Bennett, Judith. *The Wealth of the Solomons: A History of a Pacific Archipelago, 1800–1978.* Honolulu, Hawaii, 1987.
Bertram, Geoff. "Sustainable Development in the Pacific Micro-Economies." *World Development* 14.7 (1986), 801–822.
Bertram, Geoff. "The MIRAB Model Twelve Years On." *Contemporary Pacific* 11.1 (1999), 105–138.
Corris, Peter. *Passage, Port, and Plantation: A History of Solomon Islands Labour Migration, 1870–1914.* Carlton, Australia, 1973.
Denoon, Donald, et al. *The Cambridge History of the Pacific Islanders.* Cambridge, New York, and Melbourne, 1997.
Howe, Kerry. *Where the Waves Fall: A New South Sea Islands History from First Settlement to Colonial Rule.* Sydney, 1984.
Irwin, Geoffrey. *The Pre-Historic Exploration and Colonisation of the Pacific.* Cambridge, 1992.
Knapman, Bruce. *Fiji's Economic History, 1874–1939: Studies of Capitalist Colonial Development.* Canberra, 1987.
La Croix, Sumner, and Christopher Grandy. "The Political Instability of Reciprocal Trade and the Overthrow of the Hawaii Monarchy." *Journal of Economic History* 57.1 (1997), 161–189.
Macquarie, Lachlan. "Letter to the Earl of Bathhurst, 15 May 1817." *Historical Records of Australia* 9.1 (1914–1925).
Maude, Harry. *Of Islands and Men: Studies in Pacific History.* Melbourne, 1968.
Moore, Clive. *Kanaka: A History of Melanesian Mackay.* Port Moresby, Papua New Guinea, 1985.
Munro, Doug, and Stewart Firth. "Companies Strategies and Colonial Policies." In *Labour in the South Pacific*, edited by Clive Moore, Jacqueline Leckie, and Doug Munro, pp. 3–29. Townsville, Australia, 1990.
Newbury, Colin. "The Melanesian Labour Reserve: Some Reflections on Pacific Labour Markets in the Nineteenth Century." *Pacific Studies* 4.1 (1980), 1–25.
Peattie, Mark. *Nan'yō: The Rise and Fall of the Japanese in Micronesia, 1885–1945.* Honolulu, Hawaii, 1988.
Shineberg, Dorothy. *They Came for Sandalwood: A Study of the Sandalwood Trade in the Southwest Pacific, 1830–1865.* Melbourne, 1967.
Scarr, Deryck. *Fragments of Empire: A History of the Western Pacific High Commission, 1877–1914.* Canberra and Honolulu, Hawaii, 1967.
Schlomowitz, Ralph. "Markets for Indentured and Time-Expired Melanesian Labour in Queensland, 1863–1906: An Economic Analysis." *Journal of Pacific History* 16.2 (1981), 70–91.

JON FRAENKEL

PAKISTAN. Pakistan entered the twenty-first century fearful of its future, and with good reason. The 1990s were a devastating decade. Instead of achieving consolidation and a sense of direction, it floundered. Internal dislocation, regional conflicts, and social disruption were reflected in its economic performance. During the second half of the 1990s, the average annual growth rate of per capita gross domestic product (GDP) was 1.2 percent. The output of large-scale manufacturing fell during the same period. For the first time since partition, India outperformed Pakistan, with a per capita growth rate nearly treble that of Pakistan. Foreign direct investment remained insignificant. Indeed, during the latter part of the 1990s there was a capital outflow, as private sector confidence plummeted because of policy inconsistencies and conflict-related sanctions. The export base has remained shallow.

The country is effectively bankrupt, frequently unable to meet its external debt-servicing obligations without further

PAKISTAN. Fruit stall, Peshawar, 1992. (© Geoffrey Clifford/Woodfin Camp and Associates, New York)

infusion of loans from international financial institutions. Added to this is a rapidly rising domestic debt burden. Collectively, debt-servicing obligations are equal to 65 percent of total revenue, with debt servicing having emerged, since 1995, as the largest single item of current expenditure. The second largest item is defense.

These distorted priorities have led to inadequate performance in all three aspects of human development: advancing health and education, providing equitable economic growth, and expanding civil freedoms. Pakistan has had the sharpest rate of population increase for any country of over ten million people; the literacy rate is a shocking 30 percent. The number of people below the official poverty line, defined by a basic minimum level of nutrition, has risen exponentially, increasing from 17.8 million in 1987 to 34.7 million by 1999, with the level of inequality now worse than it was in 1963. In 1999 the democracy suffered a reversal. Recent elections have led to the induction of civilians, but the political system remains fragile.

Conflict is at the core of Pakistan's unstable economic performance. Its deep embroilment in two regional conflicts, with India over Kashmir and in Afghanistan's wars, has created a conflict economy. Further, ethnic and sectarian conflicts have taken a heavy toll, not least on the principal commercial city and port, Karachi. Uncertainty due to conflict has had an adverse effect on investment and savings, thereby undermining future prospects. Foreign capital is scanty, and domestic capital has been leaving the country. A look back at the country's brief history explains its instability.

The groundwork for the unraveling of Pakistan's economy was laid in the 1980s, under the Islamic authoritarianism of the Zia era. At first glance the eighties seemed spectacular, with a growth rate of 6 percent per annum and rapid rise of remittances to a level where they became larger than aid inflows. The economy was liberalized, helping Pakistan revert to a private-sector-led development strategy. Poverty fell. However, the economy's underlying fragility was disguised by the flashes of wealth accompanying migrants' remittances, large aid inflows due to war in Afghanistan, and a few years of buoyancy in agriculture. Meanwhile, huge debt was accumulated, the fiscal deficit became unsustainable, the export base remained narrow, and—most devastating of all—domestic and regional conflicts led to a menacing proliferation of light weapons.

The 1970s had witnessed the dismemberment of Pakistan, as East Pakistan seceded to become Bangladesh in December 1971. The elected civilian government of Z. A. Bhutto subsequently tried to pick up the pieces of a truncated and internationally humiliated country. In the economic arena, there were signs of early progress, as exports responded to a sharp devaluation, and later an oil shock led to large exports of labor for a Middle Eastern construction boom. However, these encouraging developments were overshadowed by major errors in economic policy. The supposed consensus on the private sector's leading role was shaken by the widespread nationalization of industrial, financial, and agro-processing units. The result was a sharp drop in private sector confidence as investment plummeted, and the growth rate slowed. Despite the intentions of a left-leaning government, social-sector investments did not take place, partly because of a lack of revenues in a stagnating economy. Equity issues were not addressed through the land reform program, primarily because they were circumvented, and implementation was far from rigorous.

Before that, the early 1960s had seemed to promise a very different future. Pakistan was in the company of the East Asian "tigers," with high growth rates generated under a private-sector-led strategy. Industries were established from scratch. The foundations of a modern banking system were laid. In the agricultural sector, Pakistan became one of the key beneficiaries of international research. The irrigation-fertilizer-seeds package of the Green Revolution found fertile ground in Pakistan, and a boom in agricultural production fueled a sense of optimism about the country's economic future. Yet during that decade, the 1965 war became the first conflict that seriously undermined the economy. There were short-term costs of that war, associated with the freezing of aid and resultant foreign exchange constraints; but much more serious were the longer-term implications. The 1965 war marked the beginning of the end of united Pakistan. It weakened the Ayub regime, accentuated the sense of regional grievances in the unprotected eastern wing, and unleashed a dynamic that culminated in India's military intervention in 1971. In addition, social unrest was aggravated because of a development strategy that actively promoted inequality in order to increase growth.

Over half a century has passed since Pakistan's independence. The country's first decade consisted of laying its economic foundations; and Pakistan's economy did far better than most anticipated, for a country that was not expected to cope with a refugee crisis and a lack of industry and skilled manpower. There have been short bursts of exceptional performance since then. Yet over the whole period, human development progress has been sporadic and disjointed. A conflict-ridden economy inevitably generates insecurity, which undermines sustainable development. The depth of the current crisis requires a major change in direction and priorities. Past performance suggests this is unlikely, but there is enough resilience and dynamism to prove the pessimists wrong.

[*See also* Bangladesh *and* India.]

BIBLIOGRAPHY
Ahmed, R., and Ahmed, A. *The Management of Pakistan's Economy*. Karachi, 1995.
Baqai, M., and Haq, M., eds. *Employment, Distribution, and Basic Needs in Pakistan*. Lahore, 1986.
Burki, S, J., and Korson, J., eds. *Contemporary Problems of Pakistan*. Boulder, 1994.
Griffin, K., and Khan, A., eds. *Growth and Inequality in Pakistan*. London, 1972.
Husain, I. *The Economy of an Elitist State*. Karachi, 1999.
Hussain, A. *Strategic Issues in Pakistan's Economic Development*. Lahore, 1990.
Nasim, A., ed. *Financing Pakistan's Development in the 1990s*. Karachi, 1992, Press,
Noman, O. *Economic and Political History of Pakistan*. London, 1990.
Noman, O. *Why Pakistan Did Not Become a Tiger — Economic and Social Progress in Asia*. Karachi, 1998.

OMAR NOMAN

PALESTINE. *See* Levant.

PANAMA. *See* Central American Countries *and* Panama Canal.

PANAMA CANAL. A transit across the forty-seven-mile-wide Isthmus of Panama reduced the sea distance between the Atlantic and Pacific seaboards of North America by seventy-eight hundred miles. During the California gold rush of the late 1840s it consequently became a Prime focus of U.S. interest. Such was the flood of transients that in 1855 a railroad opened, connecting Colón, on the Atlantic, with Panama City, on the Pacific.

The first attempt to cut a canal through the isthmus was made in the 1880s by a French consortium, headed by Ferdinand de Lesseps, promoter of the Suez Canal. Though it ended in failure, in 1904 the project was taken up by the United States, which regarded a canal as vital for both its naval strategy and its maritime commerce. Construction began after President Theodore Roosevelt abetted Panama's secession from Colombia, and the new nation had to ratify a treaty giving total control over the Canal Zone to the United States.

The huge task of construction was completed in 1914 by the U.S. Army Corps of Engineers, which employed a segregated labor force of skilled white Americans and unskilled blacks, primarily from the British West Indies. The loss of Panamanian sovereignty over the Canal Zone, the marginal role of Panamanians in the enterprise, and the exclusion of Panama from canal revenues generated strong local resentment, which Washington occasionally appeased.

Although the U.S. Navy had seen the canal as its main life artery, the increasing size of capital ships and the rise of airpower soon reduced the canal's strategic value. In the 1930s the canal locks were seen as dangerously open to sabotage and aerial bombing. During World War II, the waterway stayed beyond enemy reach, and it operated to the immense advantage of the United States. But the advent of the atom bomb clouded its future, and the new locks project begun in 1940 was never to be restarted.

The canal was also initially a major commercial asset. Since its opening merchant ships have accounted for over 80 percent of transits. In 1914, its first year of operation, 1,108 vessels carrying 4.9 million tons of cargo passed through. By 1955 the figures reached 9,811 vessels and 41.5 million tons of cargo, and in 2000 over 13,000 ships transported 200 million tons of cargo or 4 percent of world maritime trade through the canal.

The canal's commercial value has been substantially compromised by its inability to handle the volume of traffic without long delay or to accommodate the largest vessels, since the locks limit ships to a beam of 106 feet. Supertankers began bypassing the canal in the late 1950s, and the largest container ships cannot use it. Such vessels now transship their cargoes across the isthmus.

The military vulnerability of the canal and its growing commercial obsolescence explains why the United States eventually acceded to Panamanian demands to transfer the canal to its control. A 1977 treaty abolished the Canal Zone in 1979 and transferred operation of the canal to Panama in 1999. Schemes for an alternative sea-level canal have so far remained on paper.

BIBLIOGRAPHY

Conniff, Michael. *Black Labor on a White Canal: Panama, 1904–1981.* Pittsburgh, 1985.

Du Val, Miles. *And the Mountains Will Move: The Story of the Building of the Panama Canal.* Stanford, Calif., 1947.

Major, John. *Price Possession: The United States and the Panama Canal, 1903–1979.* New York, 1993.

McCullough, David. *The Path between the Seas: The Creation of the Panama Canal, 1870–1914.* New York, 1977.

Richard, Alfred. *The Panama Canal in American National Consciousness, 1870–1990.* New York, 1990.

JOHN MAJOR

PANICS. *See* Financial Panics and Crashes.

PAPAL STATE. *See* Rome and the Papal State.

PAPERMAKING. One of the oldest branches of manufacturing, its origins lie in China, where in 105 CE, the court official Cai Lun developed a technique for making paper from the fibers of hemp, old rags, fish nets, and the bark of the mulberry tree (genus *Morus*). From there, the art gradually spread westward and, by the beginning of the second century CE, centers of papermaking could be found throughout the Near East and North Africa. European contact with the Islamic world eventually brought the technology to Spain in 1151, from where it spread to Italy by 1276, France by 1348, Germany by 1390, England by 1494, and the North American Colonies by 1690. Before that, Europeans and Near Easterners wrote and painted on the Egyptian-style papyrus or on fine-grained vellum (lambskin, kidskin, or calfskin).

Technological Development. Despite the slowness of its diffusion, the technique of papermaking that was introduced into Europe in the twelfth century was not substantially different from the process developed in China a thousand years earlier; production remained very much small-scale and manual.

Mechanization. In the second half of the eighteenth century, this stability of technique was disrupted by developments in two areas. The first of these concerned the mechanization of production. In 1798, the Frenchman Nicholas-Louis Robert invented the first machine capable of producing a continuous web of paper. This machine, which came to be known as the Fourdrinier, in honor of the two brothers Henry and Sealy Fourdrinier who had made Robert's device commercially viable, quickly became and has remained the mainstay of papermaking. The first working machine was installed at Frogmore mill in Hertfordshire, England, in 1804. In 1809, another paper machine was developed by the Hertfordshire papermaker John Dickinson; called the cylinder machine, this rival design proved less adaptable than the Fourdrinier in all branches of the trade other than boardmaking (cardboard). The advent of such machinery had a profound effect on the industry, dramatically reducing costs and raising productivity. Since these machines emerged first in Britain, the British papermakers held the paramount position in the industry until the second half of the nineteenth century, by which time Continental European and North American papermakers were beginning to reach comparable levels of mechanization.

Raw materials. The second major development of the late eighteenth century and the early nineteenth was the improvement in the range and quality of available papermaking materials. In an industry where typically more than half of the running costs are spent on raw materials, considerable attention is directed toward assuring that they are kept cheap and available. While all plant life is capable of yielding the fibers necessary for papermaking, the number of materials for which this can be done economically is limited. Traditionally, the papermaker's favored materials have been linen (flax) and cotton rags. This preference began to be problematic by the mid-nineteenth century, as the supply of rags failed to keep up with the expanding needs of the trade. There followed an intensive search for a new raw material—a search that literally spanned the world. Two materials in particular attracted the attention of papermakers: esparto and wood pulp. A process using esparto, a grass indigenous to Spain and North Africa, was developed by the Englishman Thomas

Routledge in 1856; from 1860 to 1900, it became the chief raw material of the British industry.

Elsewhere, however, attention fixed on finding a way to use wood. In 1840, the German Frederich Gottlob Keller secured a patent for a woodgrinding machine that was capable of making pulp for papermaking. In 1851, the first practical wood pulp made by chemical means (using the soda process) was invented in England by Hugh Burgess and Charles Watt. A drawback to the early mechanical process and the soda process wood pulp was the poor quality of paper both produced; the advance of wood as a viable papermaking material awaited the discovery of more effective chemical processes. Two such processes eventually emerged: the sulfite process developed by the American Benjamin C. Tilghman in 1857 and the sulfate, or kraft, process invented by the German chemist Carl F. Dahl in 1884. With these two processes, wood pulp quickly became the dominant raw material for papermaking—a development that has had important implications for the location of the industry, since it has afforded timber-rich countries like the United States, Germany, Canada, Japan, Sweden, Finland, and Norway a comparative advantage in the trade ever since the 1880s. This advantage remains to the present with more than 50 percent of current world capacity (around 218 million tons) produced, in the United States, Canada, and Japan; a further 21 percent is produced in Germany, Sweden, Finland, France, Italy, and the United Kingdom.

Apart from pulp, the other vital input for papermaking is water. So significant is this consideration that the location of the industry has for most of its history been governed by its availability, a condition that stemmed from the fact that water is not only a crucial ingredient in the production process, but before the steam engine was also the industry's only source of energy. One consequence of this heavy reliance on water has been the pollution of national waterways, an especially acute problem for the industry since the latter half of the nineteenth century, following the development of various chemical processes for extracting papermaking fibers from esparto and wood. The byproducts were often discharged into the nearby rivers. Although still a concern, this problem was steadily brought under control during the twentieth century with the development of purification technologies and the introduction of legislation, such as the Control of Pollution Act enacted in the United Kingdom in 1974, which imposes strict regulation of the amount and composition of effluents released into rivers and other waterways.

Production Process. Chemically, the basis of all paper is cellulose, a complex organic compound found in all plant tissue. When cellulose is separated into individual filaments, then matted together and dried, the sheets of cellulose it forms is, in essence, paper. There are three distinct

stages to this process that have remained fundamentally unaltered since the early days of hand production. The first involves the preparation of the raw material into a form (called "stuff") suitable for transformation into paper; this is accomplished by beating the raw material into pulp. Although the traditional method of doing this was by mortar, by 1750 the Hollander beater—a machine invented in Holland in 1680, which vigorously pounds the raw material against a set of sharpened metal bars—had largely supplanted the older technique. This beating not only separates the strands of cellulose from other unwanted substances found in plant flesh but also ensures that these strands are shortened and fibrillated into the form most suitable for matting. After the beating is completed, the pulp is mixed with water to make a paper stock, usually of a consistency of 99.5 percent water and 0.5 percent pulp.

Following the preparation of the pulp, the formation of sheets of paper begins with the so-called wet end of the process. Here, the appropriately mixed stuff is taken from the vat where it was stored and allowed to run over wire-meshed cloth (with traditional handmade paper, this was a wire mold), through which water drains by means of gravity, leaving behind a residue of intermeshed cellulose fibers. Although still wet and unfinished, this is, in structure, paper. The next and final stage of production, the dry end of the process, sees the drying, finishing, and winding onto reels of the finished product. With traditional hand production this was an exacting and time-consuming process, requiring numerous skilled craftsmen working independently of the actual formation of the paper. With the advent of the paper machine, however, the dry end of papermaking was for the first time united to the wet end as a single continuous process. It is interesting to note that, despite continuous piecemeal improvement to the Fourdrinier since its invention, the basic construction and workings of the modern machine remains true to Robert's original 1798 machine.

Industrial Organization. Since the 1850s, survival in virtually all branches of the paper trade has demanded machine production; a fact that has necessarily made the industry far more capital intensive than it had been when hand production was unopposed. In 1849, an average machine mill in the United States required a capital investment of $16,100—considerably more than the $5,000 needed to establish a comparable hand mill. By 1914, the cost of a machine mill had risen to around $745,000; by the 1930s, that figure was closer to $6 million. Capitalization on such a scale inevitably made fixed costs a prominent feature of the industry's cost structure. In turn, this importance of fixed costs and the slow rate of capital turnover provided a strong incentive for producers making standardized products to lengthen production runs. Maximizing throughput in turn, encouraged manufacturers to integrate vertically.

PAPERMAKING. In the heart of the papermill, the mold is first dipped into a large vat of pulp (figure 1) and the excess water is drained. Next, the mold is blotted between sheets of felt slightly larger than the paper (figure 2). When the blotter has accumulated 260 sheets, the felt and paper are separated and the sheets are again pressed (figure 3). Plate from Diderot and d'Alembert's *Encyclopédie*, 1762–1772.

An early example of this was the International Paper Company; incorporated in the United States in 1898, its assets in 1900 amounted to $41.6 million in mill plant and $4.2 million in woodlands and other property located in New York, Michigan, and various New England states. The growth of such large, integrated firms also intensified concentration within the industry.

Despite these trends, which *ceteris paribus* should have bestowed some degree of market power, the industry has in most places remained surprisingly competitive. The most important factor in compelling firms to operate with competitive pricing and profits has been the practice of grade shifting, which involves the rapid switching of a mill from the manufacture of relatively unprofitable kinds of paper to those that appear at the time more remunerative. The ability to do this is a distinct feature of the industry and its machinery, for with minor changes most paper machines can produce almost any grade of paper desired. Grade shifting keeps prices close to break-even levels, simply because as prices increase (or decrease) firms can easily enter (or exit) the market and stabilize them. Moreover, by injecting a significant degree of contestability into the larger paper markets, this has also often acted as a defence against the establishment of monopolies.

Consumption. One of the most important features of the industry's development, particularly since 1800, has been the vast growth in demand. Paper consumption in the United States, the biggest market, has grown from 65 pounds per capita in 1913 to 660 pounds in 1986. Newsprint, which accounts for more than 30 percent of the world's paper output, has been the most important source of demand—a consequence of the emergence of the modern daily newspaper at the end of the nineteenth century. The growth in demand, however, is due not only to the spread of literacy and cheap wood-pulp paper, which has sparked the proliferation of newspapers with ever larger circulations, but is also related to the increasing number of uses that have been found for paper. Such vast changes in consumption habits have been called a "paper revolution." From the 1850s onward, various mass-produced paper bags, boxes, containers, and other forms of packaging have become popular, as well as stationery, the postcard, wrapping paper, cheap fiction, school supplies, greeting cards, sanitary papers, and tissues. New technologies, like photography and telegraphy, required new varieties of paper; older technologies using papers developed in new directions. In the printing trade, for example, special new surfaces—like coated stock for reproducing half-tone photographic images, as well as colored stock—have been developed. As might be expected from a product considered an intermediate good, the demand for paper has been typically price inelastic; it has also been significantly income elastic, a characteristic that has ensured the progress of the industry has been closely tied to the rise and spread of prosperity worldwide.

[*See also* Printing Industry.]

BIBLIOGRAPHY

Clapperton, Robert H. *The Paper-Making Machine: Its Invention, Evolution, and Development*. London, 1967. The best technical history of the paper machine; many excellent illustrations and photographs.

Cohen, A. J. "Technological Change as Historical Process: The Case of the U.S. Paper and Pulp Industry, 1915–1940." *Journal of Economic History* 44.3 (1984), 775–799. A thoughtful analysis of the nature and process of technological change in the modern industry.

Coleman, Donald C. *The British Paper Industry, 1495–1860: A Study in Industry Growth*. Oxford, 1958. The best work on the economics and technology of papermaking prior to mechanization.

Evans, John, ed. *Trends and Developments in Papermaking*. San Francisco, 1985. A useful account of the changes that have occurred in the paper industry of the mid-twentieth century.

Guthrie, John A. *The Economics of Pulp and Paper*. Pullman, Ohio, 1950.

Hunter, Dard. *Papermaking: The History and Technique of an Ancient Craft*. 2d ed. New York, 1974. The definitive history of the art and practice of papermaking since ancient times.

Magee, Gary Bryan. *Productivity and Performance in the Paper Industry: Labour, Capital, and Technology in Britain and America, 1860–1914*. Cambridge, 1997. Provides a detailed comparative analysis of the paper industry in the second half of the nineteenth century and is particularly useful on productivity growth, technological change, and the adoption of new papermaking materials.

McGaw, Judith A. *Most Wonderful Machine: Mechanization and Social Change in Berkshire Paper Making, 1801–1885*. Princeton, 1987. A fascinating study of the introduction and social impact of the paper machine in the United States.

Munsell, Joel. *Chronology of the Origin and Progress of Paper and Paper Making*. New York, 1980.

Ohanian, Nancy K. *American Pulp and Paper Industry, 1900–1940: Mill Survival, Firm Structure, and Industry Relocation*. Westport, Conn., 1993. Particularly useful for its statistical analysis of changes in firm location, size, and organization in the twentieth century.

Spicer, Albert D. *The Paper Trade*. London, 1907. Illuminating account of the paper industry at the beginning of the twentieth century; although it chiefly focuses on the British industry, it draws many interesting international comparisons and is notable for the wealth of statistical information supplied.

GARY B. MAGEE

PARAGUAY. *See* American Indian Economies; Central South American States; *and* Spain, *subentry on* Spanish Empire.

PARIS. In the thirteenth century, Paris, already a capital, was Europe's leading city, and it remained so until the eighteenth century. It long remained a case apart, differing from known urban norms. In 1328, it had 200,000 inhabitants. Its population fluctuated with periods of prosperity and crisis, both economic and political, until 1815. At the beginning of the fifteenth century, Paris lost one-half of its population, but the city's population returned to 200,000 in 1500 and rose to 350,000 in 1550. The religious wars caused the Parisian population to fall to 250,000 or 300,000 in 1600, it rose to 500,000 in 1700 and had reached 650,000 on the eve of the French Revolution (1789). According to the first census of 1801, the Revolution reduced the population to 547,000. By 1811, Paris had regained its population level of 1789.

Growth accelerated during the nineteenth century. Paris annexed its outlying municipalities in 1860. Moreover, the nearby suburbs outside the new city limits were populated quickly, creating a conurbation. After 1860, the growth of Paris *intra muros* slowed, stagnating at 2.9 million in the 1920s, then dropping to 2.2 million in 1997. But the greater Paris area counted almost 6 million inhabitants in 1931, and 9.5 million in 1997.

Parisian growth has depended on immigration since the Middle Ages. At that time, it was not only the small and the humble, but all those who were seeking their fortune who came to the city: nobles attracted by the court, officers of the king, artisans, students, and teachers at the university. This multiform immigration, whether French or foreign, has always existed. Among many possible examples are the "Lombard" artisans and financiers of the fourteenth century, the merchants from Lucca in the fifteenth century, the Swiss bankers, the German cabinetmakers in the eighteenth century, and the Italian masons in the nineteenth century. Inside France itself, the "catchment" zone for Paris, which was at first limited to the northern section of the country, never ceased to expand. It was immigrants who populated the suburbs of Paris in the 1800s. The wave of foreign arrivals, already considerable before 1914 and during the 1920s, grew after World War II. Initially coming from nearby European countries or North Africa, they later came from all continents. By 1982, immigrants made up 12 percent of the population of the greater Paris area.

It is the diversity of the activities characterizing a capital city that has been responsible for Parisian growth. In the twelfth century, Paris became the center of the French monarchy, with the court established there permanently in the thirteenth century. This political capital attracted all ranks of the aristocracy as well as officers, lawyers, merchants, bankers, and money-changers. It was also a religious and university center of the first order, the main intellectual center of Western Christendom. The religious orders remained powerful until the Revolution. If the court left Paris for Versailles under Louis XIV, the city retained the administrative functions of government. The University of Paris is still by far the most important French university center.

The greater Paris area, or Île-de-France region, accounts today for more than half the French domestic expenditure in research and development. Paris is also an economic capital, situated in the heart of a rich region, at the center of a network of roads and waterways. The convergence on Paris of the transportation system has been continuously reinforced, first by the road-building program of the eighteenth century, then by the railway network of the 1800s, and finally by the highway system of the twentieth century.

Since the twelfth century, commercial activity has focused on supplying the capital. At that time, this trade was controlled by the *Hanse des marchands de l'eau*, which had been founded in the eleventh century and had instigated the creation of the municipal administration of Paris. Several fairs, including that of Saint-Denis, were held in the environs of Paris at that time. They began to decline in the fourteenth century. Merchants in Paris maintained privileged relations with the surrounding area and with all the regions situated north of the Loire River, but the involvement of Paris in international trade remained limited.

Commercial activity developed at the same rate as the growth of the city and its surrounding area. The areas supplying the capital were in a continuous process of expansion beyond the Île-de-France region. The big Parisian traders gradually came to exercise influence over increasingly distant areas, particularly in northern and western France.

The trade in grains and flours, controlled by merchants in ports or markets, was subject to strict controls until the nineteenth century, when the Parisian major merchants were able to obtain control of the markets for numerous products, thanks to the convergence of the national transportation network on the capital. In addition, retail trade underwent a radical transformation with the development first of department stores, then of stores with multiple branches. After World War II, the 1969 transfer of the Parisian central markets from Les Halles to Rungis, a site south of the city, was part of a vast program to restructure the capital's food supply system.

In the eighteenth and nineteenth centuries, the wealth of Paris attracted an increasing number of bankers and financiers from the provinces or from abroad, leading to the formation of the Parisian *haute banque*. On the eve of World War I, Paris was the second-largest financial market in the world. The war brought a decline in the Parisian market. After World War II, strict government control of the financial markets slowed their expansion; but since the 1970s, increased liberalization allowed Paris to acquire an

PARIS. L'Avenue de l'Opéra, before 1895. (Snark/Art Resource, NY)

honorable place. Since the construction of the new La Défense quarter, the business center of the city has been moving toward the west.

The French capital has never ceased to be a vast construction site. Whether for the monarchy or the Republic, the church or the city government itself, urban planning and architecture have always been a means to affirm power and magnificence. Networks for distribution of water and energy began to develop in the 1840s. In the twentieth century, pharaonic projects, such as the Défense business district were built in the greater Paris area, the *mégapole*.

Extremely refined social practices, which reached their apogee in the eighteenth century, were developed by Parisian high society. Paris thus became the city of fashion and taste, on international as well as national levels, giving the market for *articles de Paris* an international dimension.

The great majority of wage earners work in the service sector, and financial activity is the primary source of office jobs. But despite the increase in the importance of the service sector, Parisian industries have not disappeared. Throughout history, they have been producers either of goods for general consumption or of luxury or semiluxury goods. In 1300, Paris had more than three hundred trades.

Those related to food and clothing were always well represented. Art-related trades did more or less well depending changes in fashion. Thus, goldsmithing, which prospered in the thirteenth century, declined at the end of the Middle Ages, and cabinet-making reached its apogee in the eighteenth century. At the end of the nineteenth century, the high-fashion and new perfume industries developed.

During the nineteenth century, the intensive industrialization of Paris took place in two waves. The first, from 1830 to 1870, was dominated by the chemical, food, and mechanical-engineering industries, while the electrical, automobile, and aeronautic industries predominated during the second wave from 1880 to 1914. Some factories were built in Paris during the eighteenth century, but the vast majority of Parisian workers worked from home or in small workshops. The typical industrial establishment of the nineteenth century employed between one hundred and five hundred workers. The gigantic factories such as those—now closed down—built by the automobile industry in west Paris date from the twentieth century. But the dominant model has remained that of a medium-sized business operating a human-scale establishment in a highly skilled sector.

BIBLIOGRAPHY

Beaujeu-Garnier, Jacqueline. *Nouvelle histoire de Paris: Paris, hasard ou prédestination.* Paris, 1993.

Bergeron, Louis, ed. *Paris, genèse d'un paysage.* Paris, 1989.

Bertier de Sauvigny, Guillaume de. *Nouvelle histoire de Paris: La Restauration, 1815–1830.* Paris, 1977.

Chadych, Danielle, and Dominique Leborgne. *Atlas de Paris: Évolution d'un paysage urbain.* Paris 1999.

Evenson, Norma. *Paris: A Century of Change.* New Haven and London, 1979.

Favier, Jean. *Nouvelle histoire de Paris: Paris au XV siècle, 1380–1500.* Paris, 1974.

Jacquemet, Gérard. *Belleville au XIXe siècle.* Paris, 1984.

Kaplan, Steven L. *Provisioning Paris: Merchants and Millers in the Grain and Flour Trade during the Eighteenth Century.* Ithaca, N.Y., 1984.

Lavedan, Pierre. *Nouvelle histoire de Paris: Histoire de l'urbanisme à Paris,* Paris, 1975.

Noin, Daniel, and Paul White. *Paris.* Chichester, U.K., 1997.

FRANÇOIS CARON

PASTORALISM refers to the social organization in which livestock raising is the primary economic activity and the basis of livelihood. It is a people's mode of existence and subsistence based, directly or indirectly, on the herding of certain domesticated animals. Pastoralism has been called "a biocultural system," "an ecosocial system," and "a complex ecological system." Pastoral societies were widespread in Africa, Europe, and Asia, and varied from truly nomadic to semi-nomadic communities. Pastoralists often do not eat the animals they herd for food. However, many sedentary communities depend on pastoral animals to meet their dietary needs for animal protein—from meat and blood to milk and its by-products, such as cheese, butter, yogurt, and clarified butter fat. Many nonfood items, like wool, hides, skins, manure, and bones, used for a variety of purposes, may also be derived from pastoral activities.

According to Theodore Monod (1975, p. 106), pastoralism is a chain whose links cannot be separated arbitrarily: man depends on the animal, which itself depends on the plant, which in turn depends on water and soil. Lawrence Krader (1968, p. 455) considers this "chain" as an ecological relation of "symbiosis and parasitism." According to him, pastoralism combines the symbiotic relations of agricultural system with the parasitic relations of hunting, fishing, and gathering to produce a "man-herd symbiosis."

Herding must be differentiated from pastoralism. The key is the pasture. Herding is care of a flock of wild or tame domestic or domesticated animals, but herding can take place in environments other than the pasture. Raising pigs, chicken, horses, and asses is not usually considered a pastoral activity because it could take place in and around the village and, according to Krader, "in barns, stalls, pens, tethers, sties, or simply roaming loose." Domesticated elephants in Asia fall in this category. Increasingly, too, traditional pastoral animals—cattle, camels, sheep, goats—have been herded in contemporary times under nonpastoral conditions.

The organization of pastoralism varies widely. For the most part, pastoral communities consider the activity a way of life. Many see it as the affair of the whole village, clan, or ethnic group. Both situations hold true for pastoralism among the Fulani, Maasai, Tuaregs, and Bedouins of Africa and the Middle East.

One of the major characteristics of pastoralism is migration. Scholars have debated the causes of pastoral migrations. Many emphasize ecological factors, others the need of the animals or pastoralists. Monod argues that pasture is more important than water, since animals can survive without water, but not without pasture. P. H. Gulliver (in Monod, p. 369) contends that nomadic movement is a response not only to "physico-biotic conditions" and sociopolitical factors over which pastoralists have no control, but also to the internal context of the pastoralist's sociocultural system. Moses Awogbade (1983) proposes the "eco-social linkages" as the cause of pastoral migration. Thus, pastoral migrations can be viewed as a cultural method of adaptation to various ecological factors.

Reviewing the whole complex of variables to which the pastoralists react makes it clear that the movement of herdsmen cannot be regular from season to season. Moreover, each time the nomad decides to move, he is making a delicate choice; and he also has to decide on timing, direction, distance, and new location. In the debate on the direction of pastoral migrations, scholars have proposed cyclical and noncyclical explanations. It is important to stress empirical forces also. The pastoralist sometimes has to choose between pastures and water. In addition, he has to consider the likely movements of other herds to a potentially good area, which may quickly become overcrowded. Other factors are the general political stability in the region, friendly agricultural hosts, nearness to markets for grains and other foodstuffs consumed but not cultivated by the pastoralist, and the presence of animal diseases or epidemics such as trypanosomiasis and rinderpest.

From the foregoing, it is apparent that the pastoralist must live a highly flexible lifestyle, one that allows a high degree of freedom of movement and avoids any sentimental attachment to a particular place as home. Thus, a paradox emerges in pastoralism: movement is a necessity, but movement affords a degree of freedom of action.

Scholars divide pastoralists into three categories or groups. The categories are exceedingly overlapping, and a pastoral society may be classified as belonging in more than one category. The first are agro-pastoralists or mixed farmers. They are semi-settled pastoralists who cultivate enough crops to feed their families or engage in fishing, foraging, and beekeeping during the off-season. Agro-pastoralists often have rights to land and use labor (their family or hired hands) to cultivate the land. They tend to grow a variety of food crops for subsistence and for market or nonmarket exchange. They raise livestock for domestic and agriculturally related uses (e.g., bulls for plowing the farm and cow dung for fertilizing the land). These animals are kept for their economic values also, but agro-pastoralists' herds tend to be small because there is a progressive shift away from dependence on livestock to some level of crop cultivation. Many pastoral groups in Africa currently fall into, or seem to be progressing toward, this category.

The second are the transhumant pastoralists. Primarily livestock producers, they possess a semi-permanent place at which older members remain throughout the year, and where they practice some farming or supplement their diet and income by fishing. Herders migrate over long distances for grazing during the dry season, or during periods of prolonged drought, but return to base camp at the start of the rainy season to help with field preparation and crop cultivation. The structure and complexity of their housing are affected by the length of time they planned to spend in a place. In the past, the most common form used to be a more ecologically balanced shelter of sticks and woolen tent. Currently, the most basic form is a shelter made of a sheet of polythene as cover. This shelter tends to litter the landscape because when camp is broken, torn and discarded plastics are not absorbed in the soil. Many Fulbe clans, especially those on Jos and Mambilla plateaus, are tran-

shumant; so are the Dinka of Sudan and many Bedouin groups in Israel and Jordan today.

The third are the "exclusive pastoralists," often categorized in earlier studies as "true nomads," although the term is misleading. Pastoralists in this category often do not cultivate crops, and do not stay long enough in a place to have land rights. They tend to migrate frequently (but not aimlessly) for ecosocial and other reasons. Nomads have fascinated sedentary people, and are the subject of tales and short stories; tourist videos, photographs, and photojournalism; even cookbooks, bodybuilding and fashion articles, and herbal remedies. Two extremely successful photographic books on African nomads were produced by Carol Beckwith—*Maasai* with Tepilit Ole Saitoti (New York, 1980) and *Nomad of Niger* with Marion van Offelen (New York, 1983). A Nigerian Federal Department of Livestock's survey finds that exclusive or nomad pastoralists have set migration routes and often very long-standing arrangements with farmers to make use of crop residues. Historical examples of nomad pastoralists included the Hebrews, Bedouins, Aryans, Mongols, and Turks, and the Germanic invaders of the Roman Empire. Contemporary examples include the Fulbe, Turkana, Koyam, Shuwa, Tuareg, North Arabian Bedouins, Kurds, Basseri, Bakhtiaris, Uled Suliman, Kababish, and Maasai.

Historians view pastoralism as an offspring of the transition from the hunting/gathering of the Paleolithic Age to Neolithic agriculture. The key component of that transition was domestication. Of the pastoral animals, the sheep was the oldest, descending from the wild sheep (*ovis orientalis*) in the mountains of Turkey and Iran in about 9000 BCE. About three millennia later, the goat was domesticated in the same general region of Mesopotamia and spread faster and more widely than any of the other animals. Pigs emerged in Southeast Asia and the Middle East about 6000 BCE, cattle from Mesopotamia around 5500 BCE, and transport animals—horses from Southern Russia, asses or donkeys from Egypt, and camels from Arabia—in about 2000 BCE. The domestication of the reindeer occurred in the Tundra region of Finland, Norway, and Sweden about five centuries ago.

In general, herd size is small among pastoralists. The largest number of animals held by pastoralists (milkers, breeders, etc.) are usually not for sale but are kept as insurance against the risks of drought, disease, and epidemics. This "insurance" concept may partly explain the intense care that pastoralists bestow on their animals and the wide range of taboos and superstitions to which they subscribe. It may also help to explain the resistance against recent attempts to modernize the pastoral production process.

There are many threats to the future of pastoralism in the contemporary world. They include the modern state system with firm borders that reduce migratory drifts;

agricultural expansion and changes in land tenure systems that reduce grazing resources; bovine diseases that spread across international borders; and several environmental factors—low rainfall, inadequate pastures, and so forth. Others are commercialization of the family herd; class, gender, and social differentiation; and the adverse effects of certain government policies, such as taxation, nomadic education, reforestation, and construction of dams.

BIBLIOGRAPHY
Awogbade, Moses. *Fulani Pastoralism: Jos Case Study*. Zaria, 1983.
Beckwith, Carol, and Tepilit Ole Saitoti. *Maasai*. New York, 1980.
Beckwith, Carol, and Marion van Offelen. *Nomad of Niger*. New York, 1983.
Ekvall, Robert B. *Fields on the Hoof: Nexus of Tibetan Nomadic Pastoralism*. New York, 1968. A short account of Tibetan pastoralism. Very useful in the discussion of yak, goat, and sheep herding; care of the animals; sociocultural life of the Tibetan nomads; and relationship with farming communities.
Ephal, Israel. *The Ancient Arabs: Nomads on the Borders of the Fertile Crescent, 9th–5th Century BC*. Leiden, 1982. Originally published in Hebrew, this is the English translation of a controversial work on pre-Islamic Arabian nomadism.
Galaty, John G., and Pierre Bonte, eds. *Herders, Warriors, and Traders: Pastoralism in Africa*. Boulder, 1991. A good book on the conditions of African pastoralists in the contemporary period.
Gulliver, P. H. In *Pastoralism in Tropical Africa*, edited by Théodore Monod, p. 369. London, 1975.
Irons, William, and Neville Dyson-Hudson, eds. *Perspectives on Nomadism*. Leiden, 1972. A very useful book on theoretical approaches to understanding pastoralism, a good resource on researches already done on nomads.
Johnson, Douglas L. *The Nature of Nomadism: A Comparative Study of Pastoral Migrations in Southwestern Asia and Northern Africa*, 2d printing. Chicago, 1974. First published in 1969, the book covers exactly what the title suggests, except that "Southwestern Asia" is actually the region from Afghanistan and Iran through Turkey to Arabia.
Krader, Lawrence. "Pastoralism." In *International Encyclopedia of the Social Sciences*, vol. 11, edited by David L. Sills. New York, 1968.
Majok, Aggrey Ayuen, and Calvin W. Schwabe. *Development among Africa's Migratory Pastoralists*. Westport, Conn., 1996. Ayuen Majok was born to a Southern Sudanese pastoralist. The postcolonial history of development in the pastoral society. It emphasizes the inadequacy of the response of many NGOs after the 1970s drought. Chap. 4, "Animal Diseases and Their Social Consequences," is highly recommended.
Marx, Emanuel, and Avshalom Shmueli, eds. *The Changing Bedouin*. New Brunswick, N.J., 1984. Contributors examine the changing position of Bedouin Arabs in the borders of the state of Israel.
Monod, Theodore, ed. *Pastoralism in Tropical Africa*. London, 1975.
Paine, Robert. *Herds of the Tundra: A Portrait of Saami Reindeer Pastoralism*. Washington, D.C., 1994. A first-hand account of reindeer herding in the tundra.
Rigby, Peter. *Persistent Pastoralists: Nomadic Societies in Transition*. London, 1985. Focuses on East African pastoralists, especially the Maasai.
Salzman, Philip C., ed. *When Nomads Settle: Processes of Sedentarization as Adaptation and Response*. New York, 1980. An indispensable work on the processes of sedentarization among nomad pastoralists.
Stenning, Derrick J. *Savanna Nomads: A Study of the Wodaabe Pastoral Fulani of Western Bornu Province, Northern Region, Nigeria*. London, repr. 1994. Originally published in 1959, it traces the history of the Fulani in igeria, focusing on the Wodaabe clan in Bornu, and discussing the social and cultural context of herding, fertility of women and cattle, and transhumance and migratory drifts.

AKANMU G. ADEBAYO

PATENTS. A patent for invention gives the patentee limited exclusive rights to use an invention. The origin of patent systems reaches back more than five hundred years, and the institution has evolved along with the emergence of modern economies. Today, adoption of patent systems is nearly universal, with some country-to-country variation in the scope of patent rights, and within a broad international framework.

A patent system presents complex questions for the inventor and for society. The inventor must consider the benefit of the exclusive right obtained with a patent but bear in mind the out-of-pocket costs of patent and legal fees and implicit costs such as the loss of secrecy. Society must weigh the benefits of any added invention that may occur with a patent system against the cost of restrictions on innovation. The patent system has evolved to increase its value to inventors and, therefore, enhance inventive contribution to economic development. Society's efforts to balance the interests of society against those of inventors have also contributed to the institutional development of the patent system.

Extensive literature exists that exploits data on patent applications and/or grants to investigate the relation between invention and economic development. This literature has been controversial, in large part because some scholars view patent statistics as having serious drawbacks as measures of invention. Carefully used, however, patent data have yielded important information regarding the history of inventive activity.

Origin and History of Patents for Invention. A patent for invention is a special case of letters patent, or open letters, which are documents with which a government can grant certain special privileges (official appointments, commercial rights, pardons, and so on). Although patents are still issued for reasons other that invention, the term *patent* is generally associated with invention.

By the fifteenth century, there were a number of examples of patents granted for invention in Europe, but they were too isolated to say they were part of a broad, conscious policy to systematically promote invention. The first formal patent system that specifically aimed to encourage invention appeared in Venice during the late fifteenth century. Venetian patentees obtained exclusive use of their invention for ten years. Authorities reviewed the invention for novelty and usefulness, and if the patent was granted, the patentee was required to use the invention within a specified period of time. Novelty, usefulness, and requirements for applying the invention are characteristics of patent systems that have survived to the present day.

Many European governments granted patents before 1700, but it is in England that the most dramatic elements of patent history took place during the sixteenth and seventeenth centuries. In the reigns of Elizabeth I and James I (1558–1625), patent monopolies awarded for purposes such as rewarding favored subjects, fostering loyalty among allies, and raising revenue for the government contributed to tension between the monarchy and Parliament. This conflict was resolved in 1623 when Parliament passed the Statute of Monopolies, which proclaimed that monopolies were illegal and allowed injured persons to seek damages.

Monopoly for invention was the significant exception, defined in Section 6 as ". . . any letters patent and grants of privilege for the term of fourteen years or under, hereafter to be made of the sole working or making of any manner of new manufactures within this Realm, to the true and first inventor and inventors of such manufactures, which others at the time of making such letters patents and grants shall not use, so as also they be not contrary to the law nor mischievous to the State by raising prices of commodities at home, or hurt of trade or generally inconvenient."

It was the end of the eighteenth century before other countries established patents system in statutory law. In France, the king issued an edict in 1762 that instituted reforms regarding grants of privileges to inventors, such as limiting the exclusive right to fifteen years and requiring that the invention be applied in industry. A formal statute for patents of invention became French law in 1791. Based on authority granted to Congress in the Constitution, the United States passed a patent law in 1793. In the early nineteenth century, formal patent systems became widespread in Europe. Between the years 1810 and 1843, patent laws were adopted in Austria, Russia, Prussia, Belgium, the Netherlands, Spain, Bavaria, Sardinia, the Vatican, Sweden, Württemberg, Portugal, and Saxony. Although non-European countries would pass their own patent laws in later years, by the early nineteenth century, the practice of granting exclusive rights to inventors emerged outside of Europe.

Institutional Development. The patent institution is defined by procedures through which a patent is granted, specific rules that determine whether an invention is patentable, and limits to the scope of a patent right. These institutional details address a number of questions required for a workable system. What specific rights does the patentee receive? How will disputes be resolved? What consideration does the government receive in return for the patent grant? Should the inventor be required to disclose information about the patent and, if so, with what

detail? Who will administer the patent system? What fees should the inventor pay? Must the invention be novel and workable? If so, should there be a review process for patent applications? What resources will be available to a review process? These practical details changed over time, owing to institutional innovation at both the national and international levels.

England's early patent system served as an incubator for institutional arrangements. The Statute of Monopolies set some standards, such as the term of a patent right (a maximum of fourteen years, thought to be twice the length of an apprenticeship) and the use of common law to settle disputes over patents. Without further statutory guidance, however, the early patent system could operate within a range of discretion that is wider than we see today. For example, patents obtained to promote stock speculation were particularly rampant from 1691 to 1694 and from 1717 to 1720. In response, the law clerks who processed patent applications instituted controls to curb these abuses. These controls, such as requiring specifications of the invention and limiting to five the number of persons named on a patent, were put in place during the period from 1700 to 1720.

After 1750, institutional reform came from the courts and Parliament. Judicial decisions defined the legal meaning of invention, the function and level of detail of the specification, and the social contract implicit in a patent grant. The English Parliament passed a new patent law in 1852, which created the English Patent Office and simplified the patenting procedure. A renewal fee structure was introduced, allowing the patentee to pay a fraction of the total cost of fees upon application, with further sums paid at the end of the third and seventh years of the grant. The law also created the Commissioners of Patents, who (following the French practice) were required to publish specifications upon submission. Later reforms reduced patent fees, made licensing compulsory under certain circumstances, limited patents to a single invention, formally required a specification, established an international patent rights agreement, extended the term of the patent from fourteen to sixteen years, and broadened examination to include limited review for novelty.

Institutional arrangements of other countries' patent systems also changed over time. This change could be incremental, as in the United States, where patent applications in the late eighteenth century were at first subject to a strict review for novelty and usefulness. But early in the nineteenth century, the review was abandoned, making the system one of simple registration. Legal reform put in place in 1836 reinstituted a review process. Holland had more dramatic institutional development, adopting a patent law in 1817, repealing it in 1869, and reintroducing a patent system in 1912.

International Development. Patent law and practice among nations differed in details, and as international economic ties expanded during the nineteenth century, inventors became more concerned with these differences. Foreigners could be subject to discriminatory patent fees, as in the United States after 1836. Definition of patentable invention could differ from country to country, with restrictions most common on food and medicine. A requirement of novelty presented particular difficulties, especially if the inventor was obligated to disclose details of the invention, because disclosure could destroy the newness of the invention for patent purposes in another nation.

Efforts to find a remedy for these difficulties began in 1873, culminating in the Paris Convention of 1883, in which the signatories agreed to abide by a number of international patent protocols. First, foreigners should be treated on an equal basis as nationals. Second, the convention established a right of priority, which makes the effective filing date of a foreign patent application the same as the filing date of the original application, subject to the laws of the second country—provided an application is made within a specified period of time. Third, the patentee does not forfeit the ability to obtain a patent in a participating country if the patentee imports to that country a product manufactured using the patented invention, although the patentee is obligated to work the invention in the foreign country if required by the nation's laws.

The Paris Convention instituted a process to introduce changes to international patent practice and to allow additional nations to participate. The convention also created a bureau to carry out administrative tasks, which evolved into the World Intellectual Property Organization (WIPO). As an arm of the United Nations, WIPO administers treaties for intellectual property rights, maintains an International Patent Classification system that organizes information on inventions, and administers international patent applications under the authority of the Patent Cooperation Treaty.

There are several vehicles for international patent cooperation, among which the Patent Cooperation Treaty is particularly important. Signed in 1970, the treaty allows inventors to make a single patent application that is valid in many countries. Recent negotiations regarding international intellectual property rights have been conducted within the World Trade Organization and its predecessor, the General Agreement on Tariffs and Trade (GATT). The 1994 revision of GATT included an agreement on Trade Related Aspects of Intellectual Property Rights, which established enforceable national standards for patent protection.

The patent institution has undergone continual change at both the national and international levels. Some of these efforts aimed at rationalizing patent administration. In the background, however, was the question of balancing the interests of inventors and society. These interests revolve around the incentives to invent and innovate.

Patents and the Incentives to Invent and Innovate. Modern patent law is justified as an appropriate grant for an inventor's efforts, but the interests of society requires limitations on the property right invested in the patent. Thus, the patent has limited life and scope, and the inventor is required to disclose details of the invention. One attractive feature of this arrangement is that the government need not make any judgment as to the economic value of the invention. If it is highly valued in the marketplace, then the inventor would obtain a large reward. Moreover, if highly valued inventions are expensive to research and develop, the market may provide sufficient revenues to the inventor to cover the expense. Thus, the market will furnish a desirable incentive structure for inventions: inventive effort is directed toward inventions that are useful in proportion to the cost of their development.

This argument ignores the considerable uncertainty regarding the ultimate value of an invention. This uncertainty implies that some inventions are made that have little value, and that desirable inventions may not be developed. Nevertheless, a patent system's incentive structure does help to (imperfectly) direct scarce inventive resources toward their most useful purposes.

Productivity's advance depends upon invention, but it also depends upon innovation, the process whereby an invention is applied in production. A patent monopoly limits innovation. The patentee has an incentive to encourage innovation by licensing the patent, but because the ideas behind most inventions can be reproduced at little additional cost, the optimal social price for a license will be close to zero. Patentees typically set a high price for a license and so will limit innovative activity below what might be best for society.

A patent has a limited life to reduce, in part, the social cost of restrictions on innovation. Other policies, such as compulsory licensing and complete disclosure, may also help to limit the cost of restricted innovation. The practical effort to balance the incentive to invent and the need to innovate spurred much of the evolution of the patent institution described above. The question of this balance formed the basis for a widespread debate about the merits of the patent institution during the middle of the nineteenth century.

Economists have had varied judgments on the net economic effect of patents. Some have argued that a patent system would not raise the total volume of invention because much invention is autonomous and, therefore, independent of incentives. Others have argued that the patent system is a major causal factor behind modern economic growth. Research has shown many instances in which the social return to invention is higher than the

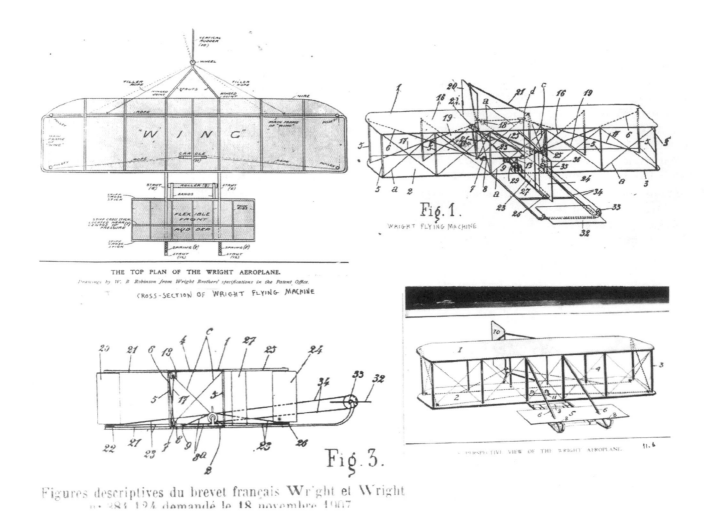

return that private firms and individuals have obtained from invention. If generally true, then the amount of resources devoted to invention may be less than optimal for society, and patenting, by raising the private rate of return to invention, will induce more resources towards inventive effort.

Little direct evidence exists of the impact of patent systems on economic development. Both the Netherlands and Switzerland did not have national patent systems in the late nineteenth century. The evidence from this natural experiment is mixed: In Switzerland, modern industrial development was possible without patents, while reintroduction of a patent system in the Netherlands led to a greater amount of invention after 1912. Other studies have looked closely at the actual working of patent systems and have also led to mixed conclusions. Because the early English patent system was on shaky legal footing, had many instances of worthless but patented invention, and had few

significant patents in innovative industries, the patent system may have done little to promote economic development in England. By the middle of the eighteenth century, many of the system's problems had been resolved. Although it remained imperfect, it became workable, and the patent system contributed significantly to the flowering of English ingenuity during the Industrial Revolution.

The impact of a patent system may extend beyond simply altering the private rate of return to invention and the overall rate of invention. During the nineteenth and twentieth centuries, the nature of production and application of technology changed from a primitive invention industry to formalized, large-scale efforts in research and development, with patented invention playing an important role throughout this transformation. An infant invention industry appeared in England during the early part of the nineteenth century. In this period, most major inventions were patented, quasi-professional inventors emerged who actively used patents to protect their inventive efforts, and trade in patented invention became vigorous. Similarly, formal institutions that facilitated trade in invention developed in the United States during the period from 1840 and 1920. The patent system may have been central to the evolution of the market for technology, which in turn stimulated inventive activity by enabling individual inventors to flourish.

Patents as Economic Indicators in Historical Research. Historians have sought to understand the determinants of invention because of inventor contribution to humanity's intellectual heritage and because of the role of invention in modern economic growth, such as the competitive advantage that inventiveness may give to regions or industries. Historians have also explored the sources of invention, such as the extent to which scientific discovery contributes to technological advance or whether market forces are important in the modern inventive process.

Progress on these questions hinges on measuring invention. Proxies are available, such as numbers of technical and scientific personnel, expenditure on research and development, total factor productivity, and the number of patent applications and grants. Patent data have a number of advantages: They have a well-defined connection to invention, are issued with objective standards, and are available across a wide expanse of time and space. This line of research, however, has been controversial because patent data have serious limitations as measures of invention. Deficiencies include whether patents are closely tied to inventive resources or productivity growth, limitations on the patentablility of invention, changes in the ratio of patents to patentable invention, and the wide range of the economic value of patented invention.

Careful use of patent data can address most of these deficiencies, and recent research that exploits patent data has yielded a number of important insights. Over the period from 1751 to 1850, English inventors became specialized in their inventive efforts and diversified their inventive "portfolio" by patenting in multiple industries. U.S. patentees of the early nineteenth century were concentrated near waterways, suggesting that growth of markets stimulated invention. Australian inventors of the late nineteenth century directed activity at areas in which their skills, knowledge, and experience were most suited and the return to invention was greatest. Relative to gross fixed capital investment, investment in patented invention (as measured by the aggregate value of patent rights) increased in Great Britain and Ireland by approximately 100 percent in the period from 1870 to 1970.

Recent advances in economic analysis have led to new methods of teasing out useful information in patent data by exploiting patent renewals or foreign patenting. The economic value of a patent right will be higher if the patent is renewed or a patent is sought in foreign countries because the expected value of the patent right must rise to justify the added expense of renewal or foreign patents. Assuming that the economic value of a patent is positively associated with the value of a patent right, renewal rates and rate of foreign patenting can provide information with which to weight patent counts to obtain more accurate measures of the economic value of patented invention. This source of information on the historical value of patent rights is particularly useful because renewal fees have been required by most countries since the mid-nineteenth century.

In summary, patents have had a prominent, if controversial, place in economic history. Patent systems are nearly universal in the world economy and became so through a long history of development. The development helped to improve the administration, legal status, and economic role of patent systems. Debate continues on the best way to balance the interests of inventors and of society, and continued research holds the promise of improving the patent system so as to provide the optimal incentives to inventors while at the same time minimize the social cost of limiting innovation.

Inventions are unique discoveries that add to economically valuable knowledge and can be best understood in a historical context. Difficulties with the use of patent statistics (such as differences in the propensity to patent between individuals and corporations, and the growth of the proportion of patents awarded to foreigners) may be less prominent before the twentieth century, which suggests that patent data may be particularly valuable for historical research. As an example, scholars have found that the average value of patented invention varied considerably in England, France, and Germany for the period from 1950 to 1976, but the average value of patented invention in Great Britain and Ireland was relatively stable over the period from 1852 to 1876. Research that carefully investigates the patent record through history can therefore contribute significantly to our understanding of invention.

[*See also* Technology.]

BIBLIOGRAPHY

Boehm, Klaus. *The British Patent System*. Cambridge, 1967.

Dutton, Harold I. *The Patent System and Inventive Activity during the Industrial Revolution, 1750–1852*. Manchester, 1984. Review of the evolution of the English patent institution and the impact of patents on inventive activity; concludes that the patent system contributed significantly to the flowering of English ingenuity during the Industrial Revolution.

Federico, Pasquale J. *Renewal Fees and Other Patent Fees in Foreign Countries*. Study no. 17, prepared for the Subcommittee on Patents, Trademarks, and Copyrights of the Senate Committee on the Judiciary, 1958.

Gomme, Arthur A. *Patents of Invention: Origin and Growth of the Patent System in Britain*. London, 1946, 1948. Details on the early history of the English patent system.

Gomme, Arthur A. "The Centenary of the Patent Office." *Transactions of the Newcomen Society* 27 (1951, 1953), 163–167.

Griliches, Zvi. "Patent Statistics as Economic Indicators: A Survey." *Journal of Economic Literature* 28.4 (December 1990), 1661–1707.

Lamoreaux, Naomi R., and Kenneth L. Sokoloff. "Inventive Activity and the Market for Technology in the United States, 1840–1920." National Bureau of Economic Research, Working Paper No. W7107, 1999. Argues that the patent system was central to the evolution of a market for technology, which in turn stimulated inventive activity by enabling individual inventors to flourish.

Lanjouw, Jean O., Ariel Pakes, and Jonathan Putnam. "How to Count Patents and Value Intellectual Property: The Uses of Patent Renewal and Application Data." *Journal of Industrial Economics* 46.4 (1998), 405–432.

Machlup, Fritz, and Edith Penrose. "The Patent Controversy in the Nineteenth Century." *Journal of Economic History* 10.1 (1950), 1–29.

MacLeod, Christine. *Inventing the Industrial Revolution*. Cambridge, 1988. Skeptical that the early patent system contributed to English economic development.

Magee, Gary Bryan. "Technological Development and Foreign Patenting: Evidence from Nineteenth-Century Australia." *Explorations in Economic History* 36.4 (October 1999), 344–359.

Mokyr, Joel. *The Lever of Riches*. Oxford, 1990. See especially pages 247–252 on the impact of patent systems on economic development.

North, Douglas. *Structure and Change in Economic History*. New York, 1981. Chapter 12 argues that the patent institution raised the private return to invention, which helped stimulate a sustained effort to improve technology.

Penrose, Edith. *The Economic of the International Patent System*. Baltimore, 1951. Also contains information on the origin of the patent system in Europe.

Plant, Arnold. "The Economic Theory Concerning Patents for Inventions." *Economica*, n.s. 1.1 (1934), 30–51.

Schankerman, Mark, and Ariel Pakes. "Estimates of the Value of Patent Rights in European Countries during the Post-1950 Period." *Economic Journal* 96 (1986), 1052–1076.

Schiff, Eric. *Industrialization without National Patents*. Princeton, 1971. Study of nineteenth-century economic development in the Netherlands and Switzerland when they did not have patent systems.

Schmookler, Jacob. *Invention and Economic Growth*. Cambridge, Mass., 1966. Uses patent data to support the hypothesis that demand for invention has been important in directing U.S. inventive activity.

Sokoloff, Kenneth L. "Inventive Activity in Early Industrial America: Evidence from Patent Records, 1790–1846." *Journal of Economic History* 48 (1988), 813–850. Patented invention was concentrated near waterways, suggesting that larger markets stimulated invention.

Sullivan, Richard. "Estimates of the Value of Patent Rights in Great Britain and Ireland, 1852–1876." *Economica* 61 (1994), 37–58. Shows that for this historical period the average value of patent rights was stable, and compares the aggregate investment in patent rights in 1870 to that in 1970.

ONLINE RESOURCES

Ladas and Parry. "A Brief History of the Patent Law of the United States." <http://www.ladas.com/Patents/USPatentHistory.html> Essay written by a partner in the Ladas and Parry law firm (specialists in intellectual property law). Includes a chronology of U.S. patent law. Web site also has information on international patent agreements.

World Intellectual Property Organization. <http://www.wipo.org> Provides basic facts and history about WIPO, and details on the development of international intellectual property law.

RICHARD J. SULLIVAN

PAWNBROKING AND PERSONAL LOAN MARKETS. Lending money or goods is ubiquitous throughout human history and in all societies. Much lending has been informal, though we see a rich variety of formal institutional arrangements for both large-scale and small-scale loans. Often loans are secured by collateral (e.g., land, animals, structures, future output, personal property, labor services) though loans are made without security, especially if the lender has reason to be confident that the borrower can and will repay. Ancient Greeks (including Demosthenes, Aristophanes, and Plato) refer to lending and borrowing. The Bible contains many references to money lending in both the Old and New Testaments. The Qu'rān details laws of commercial interchange, including rules for borrowing and lending. Both Mosaic and Roman law spelled out rules governing credit relations. Lending was well developed in Asian and African societies.

It is common to distinguish between loans for production and loans for consumption. Such a distinction has been important in moral judgments about debt where "consumptive loans" have been widely condemned as imprudent—even sinful. Borrowing to fund commerce or a productive activity is expected to generate returns that can repay the loan, and is properly thought of as investment. Borrowing to fund consumer wants is motivated by a desire to smooth consumption over time. Because the desire to consume often does not match the timing of the receipt of income, individuals regularly engage in consumption-smoothing behavior. The most commonly employed consumption-smoothing strategies are saving (consuming income from the past) and borrowing (consuming income from the future). Consumption smoothing is ordinary, everyday behavior, though emotions that lead people to borrow vary from desperation (e.g., crop failure or unemployment threatens starvation) to something far milder (a preference for having an item now rather than later).

This essay focuses on small-scale loans for consumption, though the distinction between credit for consumption and credit for production is not always clear or easily made. A few examples will illustrate the difficulty. Credit extended to farmers funds production through the purchase of land, seed, implements, and supplies, but farmers also borrow on the security of future crops in order to fund consumption. Poor farmers in many parts of the world, including the postbellum American South, have found that such borrowing can lead to a state of permanent indebtedness called debt-peonage. Merchants borrow by receiving wholesale goods for which payment will be made later and then facilitate the borrowing of their retail customers by extending book credit—allowing customers to "run a tab" and so pay for goods at a later date. Even pawnshops, which principally met the needs of those who borrowed for consumption purposes, did lend some funds to merchants and artisans who pawned inventories to increase liquidity for business purposes.

Pawnbroking. Common throughout history are loans by pawnbrokers who made loans secured by a pledge of personal property, which was surrendered and remained with the lender while the loan was outstanding. In this way, loans on pledges differ from other collateralized loans, such as mortgages, where the debtor retains use of the property and surrenders it only if the loan is not repaid.

Although lending on pledges was practiced in many ancient societies, the first clear evidence of specialized pawnbrokers comes in the fifth century CE from China, where pawnshops were run as commercial enterprises by Buddhist monasteries. Moneylenders operated in China and other societies long before the appearance of pawnshops. Some scholars have argued that Buddhist-run pawnshops may have existed in India prior to their appearance in China. Later, Buddhist monks introduced pawnshops to Japan. Temple pawnshops thrived in China for many centuries, lending the funds that temples collected from their "inexhaustible treasury" of donations. Some early temple loans to the poor may have been made without interest for charitable motives, but increasingly Buddhist-run pawnshops charged interest on all loans. Over time, lay pawnbrokers joined the business, wearing black robes in imitation of monks' garments so that by 1000 CE, China had a large number of pawnshops used by people of all economic classes. By the1200s, the government began to operate official pawnshops, with proceeds used to fund military expenditures. By the 1500s, temple pawnshops had disappeared, and the government increasingly regulated pawnshops.

In medieval Europe, pawnbroking and other forms of money lending were mostly in the hands of Jews and Italians. Christians were prohibited from charging interest by the usury laws of the church. Since Jews were not bound by this prohibition and were restricted from entering most other occupations, a specialized class of Jewish moneylenders emerged. Jews were persecuted and suffered periodic confiscation and expulsion but continued to provide much of the credit available in Europe. Christians who lent money were generally called Lombards because so many had been merchants from Lombardy in northern Italy. They entered the money-lending business through their handling of papal remittances through bills of exchange, which provided profits on exchange rates that did not contravene the usury prohibition (as long as the rates were not predetermined).

Jews and Lombards operated pawnshops throughout Europe in the thirteenth through the sixteenth centuries. The church regarded pawnshops as evil—clear violations of the prohibition of usury. Governments had a more complex evaluation, since they earned substantial revenues from fines and taxes levied on pawnshops. In 1462, Franciscan monks in Perugia devised a new plan to combat pawnshops. They engineered the establishment of the first municipally run pawnshop, the *monte di pietà*, which made loans to the poor on terms more favorable than those provided by private lenders. Soon *monti* were operating in other Italian cities. Some *monti* tried free lending on the smallest loans, but charging of interest (or fees) was usual. The *monte di pietà* in Padua charged 5 percent per annum when local moneylenders were demanding 20 percent. Because of the canon laws on usury, interest-taking on pawns by the *monti di pietà* led to controversy that was finally settled by the Pope's decision in 1517 following the fifth Council of the Lateran that the *monti di pietà* "which take small sums . . . without making a profit . . . have committed no sin and are not usurers."

Over the next few centuries, municipalities, usually with the support of the church, established charitable pawnshops on the *monte di pietà* model in most continental European countries. European imperialists brought these institutions to their colonies. For example, a large *montes pietatis* functioned in Mexico City. In most places, the *monts-de-piété* coexisted with private pawnbrokers whose operation was subject to increasingly stringent regulation, including licensing provisions and maximum interest and fees.

The most notable exception is France, in which pawnbroking was taken over by the state after 1804—Napoleonic reforms made pawnbroking a state monopoly with rules governing details of operation and interest charges. The state-run *monts-de-piété* had favorable access to the capital market, which helped keep interest charges low compared to private pawnshops. Throughout much of the nineteenth century, the *mont-de-piété de Paris* charged 9 percent per annum. Most loans were for small amounts. In 1891, 65 percent of articles pawned in Paris were for loans under ten francs, and the most commonly pawned items were clothing. Conservative lending by the *monts-de-piété*, which was allowed to lend up to two-thirds of the auction value of items but often lent less, gave rise to a secondary market of pledge brokers who lent on the security of pawn tickets.

In Great Britain, pawnbroking was a private business with state regulation and oversight. The first statutory regulation was in 1603. Major national legislation in 1800 and 1872 required licenses, set maximum interest rates, and regulated the relationship between pawnbroker and pledger. In *Making Ends Meet: Pawnbroking and Working-Class*

Credit (New York, 1983), Melanie Tebbutt describes how working-class Britons, especially women, were regular users of pawnshops and other forms of credit. Pawnshops were the "poor person's bank," but ordinary people also used other forms of credit, including store credit, loan sharks, and dolly shops (illegal pawnshops that lent on very small pawns at high interest rates).

The United States never had government-run pawnshops, but states and municipalities passed laws regulating pawnbroking and other small loan activities. These laws varied greatly in their particulars and in the degree to which they were enforced. Around the turn of the twentieth century, Progressives campaigned to pass uniform laws regulating money lending. Philanthropic reformers, inspired by the *monts-de-piété* founded private semicharitable pawnshops called "remedial loan banks."

Lending on pledges has been practiced in both urban and rural settings throughout the world, but specialized pawnbroking is a largely urban phenomenon, which expanded tremendously following the Industrial Revolution. In rural areas, most credit relationships are connected with agriculture, with land and crops serving as collateral. With the development of large urban populations engaged in manufacturing and commercial pursuits, pawnshops increasingly provided the credit that allowed urban workers to meet their consumption-smoothing needs. In 1870, 50 percent of the English population but 84 percent of pawnbrokers were located in cities and boroughs. In industrial areas, there was one pawnshop for every four thousand people. For many members of the urban working classes, a trip to the pawnbroker, euphemistically called "visiting uncle" by the British (*ma tante* by the French), was a common occurrence. Happy occasions and sad occasions were likely to send one to the pawnshop to convert clothing, bedding, jewelry, or household goods into cash to fund a celebration or a funeral, to meet a pressing bill or the quarterly rent payment, to survive a spell of slack work, or to tide one over till Saturday payday.

Pawning People. Pawnshops solved the problem of security for loans by accepting a wide variety of goods as pledges. Labor services have also been used as collateral. In African pawnship, persons served as security for loans in an indenture system. An individual could surrender himself or herself or a family member to work for the creditor until a loan was paid. While the pawnship system has ties to indigenous slavery and the taking of hostages, the Yorubá clearly differentiated pawning labor from slavery. The practice of pawning labor is not limited to Africa. In many societies, moneylenders could enslave someone who failed to honor a debt. British indenture contracts in which individuals wishing to migrate to the New World traded their future labor services for transportation is a clear case of securing a loan with labor services.

Buying on Time. Consumption smoothing is all about time. People borrow in order to consume earlier than their resources allow. Lenders must be compensated by interest payments and have reasonable security that they will be repaid. Pawning solves the security problem by having lenders hold the collateral until the loan is paid. Many other arrangements have been developed that allow buyers to consume in advance of payment. The names for such arrangements are many—we will call them "buying on time."

Throughout history, moneylenders have advanced funds in exchange for a promise of future payment with interest. What provides security for such loans? What happens if the loan is not repaid? In many societies, lenders could enslave debtors who did not repay. Property could be seized, as in the cases of foreclosed mortgages or repossessed goods. Sometimes the state punished debtors with imprisonment or in other ways (e.g., in England, transportation to the colonies). Loan sharks threaten violence if they are not repaid.

Store credit (or book credit) is a common "buying on time" arrangement where sellers allow buyers to take possession of goods in advance of payment. In Colonial New England, most buying took place "on the book" with accounts settled later by payments in goods or money. With store credit, the interest is often embedded in a two-price structure of "cash prices" and higher "credit prices" for the same good. Such pricing circumvents religious strictures against charging interest or legal rules setting maximum allowable interest.

A large number of "buying on time" arrangements have become increasingly common during the last two centuries, especially in developed countries. Credit unions, mutual savings banks, consumer finance companies, revolving credit, hire-purchase, and payday loans are among the rich variety of loan opportunities that have been added to, and in large part replaced, pawnshops and other forms of money lending that were common in the past. In Europe, pawnshops are far less common than they were in the nineteenth century, though there is evidence of a revival of these and other forms of "fringe banking" to serve the poor in the United States.

In the developing world, credit provision remains problematic at many levels. One interesting development is the spread of Grameen-type banks that provide microcredit to poor people seeking to operate small businesses.

BIBLIOGRAPHY

Calder, Lendol. *A Cultural History of American Credit.* Princeton, 1999. A survey of many types of consumer credit in the United States, with emphasis on the moral and political debates about personal debt.

Caskey, John P. *Fringe Banking: Check-Cashing Outlets, Pawnshops, and the Poor.* New York, 1994. Contains a good chapter on the history of pawnbroking in the United States in a book devoted to the recent rise of pawnbroking.

Danieri, Cheryl L. *Credit Where Credit Is Due: The Monte-de-Piété of Paris, 1777–1851*. New York and London, 1991.

Falola, Toyin, and Paul E. Lovejoy, *Pawnship in Africa: Debt Bondage in Historical Perspective*. Boulder, 1994.

Hudson, Kenneth. *Pawnbroking: An Aspect of British Social History*. London, 1982. A business history of pawnbroking in England, with emphasis on the law.

Johnson, Paul. *Saving and Spending: The Working-Class Economy in Britain, 1870–1939*. Oxford, 1985. Describes the many ways that Britons saved, borrowed, and insured.

Olney, Martha L. *Buy Now, Pay Later: Advertising, Credit, and Consumer Durables in the 1920s*. Chapel Hill, N.C., and London, 1991.

Stiansen, Endre, and Jane I. Guyer, eds. *Credit, Currencies, and Culture: African Financial Institutions in Historical Perspective*. Stockholm, 1999. Articles on credit in Islamic and non-Islamic areas of Africa before and after the slave trade.

United Nations. *The Role of Microcredit in the Fight against Poverty*. New York, 1998. Study of the operation and spread of Grameen-type banks in developing countries.

Whelan, T. S. *The Pawnshop in China*. Ann Arbor, 1979. Translation of a study of Chinese pawnbroking by Yang Chao-yü.

ELYCE J. ROTELLA

PEASANTRY.

PEASANTRY. Who is a peasant? The English word *peasant* derives from the French *paysan*, which means nothing more or less than "country dweller." But the term *peasant* and even more the collective term *peasantry* have gained currency in English by promising something more specific than this. Unfortunately, neither term possesses a stable meaning across the social sciences. For some, *peasant* is a technical term with a formal, if contested, definition; for others it has primarily a political meaning; while still others hold that it belongs to the realm of informal speech and carries an unavoidable pejorative connotation.

Anthropology. Social and cultural anthropologists have gone furthest in formalizing the concept of peasantry. A generation of anthropologists ending in the 1970s defined *peasants* as a social type, standing between the primitive tribes from which they emerged and the industrial society into which they would in time merge. On this spacious historical stage the distinctive characteristic of peasantries was that they always existed as "part societies with part cultures" (Kroeber, 1948). Peasants endured asymmetric relations with their social, political, and economic superiors. Culturally peasants cultivate the "little tradition," while their superiors uphold the "great tradition."

To anthropologists, peasants are neither autonomous (like primitive peoples) nor the citizens of an industrial society, the legal and moral equals of the economic and political elites. Instead, they stand between these benchmarks as a structurally subordinated social type; they emerge with the emergence of the state, and their culture reflects this unalterable fact. Consequently peasants seek to limit their contact with the larger society. According to Robert Redfield (1956), "the market is held at arm's length," and

their primary economic aim is to limit their exposure to the risks that could bring ruin to their families and communities. Eric Wolf (1966) summarized these characteristics by asserting that "the peasant . . . runs a household, not a business concern." Anthropologists saw peasants as exposed to a multitude of risks and uncertainties with no financial buffer to absorb the shocks. Consequently community was important to peasants, because reciprocal obligation was a form of insurance against misfortune. Community obligations and risk avoidance combined to form a culture that informed peasant decision making, and this decision making diverged substantially from that of the "rational farmer." Instead, peasants viewed their economic options from the perspective of what James Scott (1976) called the "moral economy," a social norm in which community reciprocity transcends individual profit maximization.

In this anthropological framework, peasant "backwardness" appears to be a matter of choice, based on culture rather than on economic factors. Moreover this culture bears a structural character that is quite independent of historical change. If peasants studied by the past generation of anthropologists are the remnant of a once much larger phenomenon, it is a fair question to ask how the marginal and impoverished conditions of contemporary peasantry might differ from historical peasantries.

Marxism. Peasants were a problem for Marxists, and for this reason many leading Marxian theorists devoted considerable attention to the concept of peasantry. The problem, in a nutshell, is this: in the feudal stage of production, peasants are the social class that produces the surplus necessary for the reproduction of feudal social relations. The feudal elites extract this surplus via obviously nonmarket mechanisms. Much of what the anthropologists describe as the peasant social type is compatible with Marxian thinking. But under capitalism peasant production is no longer central to the system. The proletariat is now the key social class, and their exploiters are capitalists. In this social context, the position of peasants is ambiguous. With access to land—the means of production—peasants can reproduce themselves autonomously. Via market relations, they can participate in the capitalist mode of production. On the other hand, as poor producers on the brink of ruin, they are one step away from joining the proletariat. If peasantry under feudalism could be seen (rightly or wrongly) as a unified social type, under capitalism the divisions within peasantry seemed to be their most compelling feature. According to Sidney Mintz (1974), peasant societies are "always and everywhere typified . . . by internal differentiation along many lines."

"The central debate in Marxian theoretical work on peasants," according to Frank Ellis (1993), "concerns the sustainability, or persistence, of peasant forms of production within the dominant capitalist mode of production." In 1899 V. I. Lenin concluded that social differentiation under capitalism made the persistence of a "peasant mode of production" untenable. He argued that peasants must disappear as a distinct social class, as social differentiation led them to divide into capitalist farmers and rural wage laborers. Karl Kautsky shared this view, but he went on to note that peasantry has staying power as a reserve army able to resist proletarianization. Its internal reproduction ability offers some advantages to capitalists, who therefore step back from crushing it altogether. These caveats did not impress Leon Trotsky and Rosa Luxemburg, for whom peasants could only be a counterrevolutionary force. In their view, the sooner peasants were cleared from the historical stage the better—and this view informed the collectivization of the Russian peasantry under Joseph Stalin in the 1930s.

Opposed to this position were "neopopulists," who argued that a distinctive peasant mode of production existed, was sustainable within a capitalist context, was not necessarily a threat to the construction of socialism, and could be the basis of an efficient smallholder agricultural sector. The economist A. V. Chayanov (1966) offered the most influential exposition of a distinctive "peasant economics," and this has led to a succession of "propeasant" social scientists, such as Michael Lipton (1977) and Teodor Shanin (1990), advocating land reform, "fair price" policies, and other forms of support for small cultivators that extends to the present day.

Economics. Within economics the concept of peasantry has no settled meaning. But when economists speak of peasants rather than farmers, they usually intend to refer to small cultivators (family farmers) functioning within a specific institutional context. Neoclassical economists are suspicious of the claim that peasantry, or any group, constitutes a separate category of humankind with its own economic rules. Instead, the economist's approach to peasants considers them primarily as economic agents interacting with their markets, their natural environment, and the political institutions that conditioned their activities. While this approach does not have to assume that peasants were perfectly rational and fully informed agents, it certainly attributes to them the ability and the motivation to do as well for themselves as they could.

If, then, economists speak of peasants rather than farmers, it is usually because of specific, historical conditions that constrain their behavior, and these constraints are primarily various forms of market imperfection. Chayanov's "peasant mode of production," for example, is driven almost entirely by the assumption that peasants had no access to a labor market. They could neither hire the labor of others nor sell their own. Consequently the peasant household was driven by the demographic imperatives of its own generational cycle, in which an ever-changing mix of able-bodied workers and dependents required the purchase and sale of land and in which production was focused primarily on the consumption norms of the household itself. This focus on household needs could cause households to work with great industry when necessary and to avoid drudgery when possible, all according to an economic calculus unique to the household and little influenced by external price signals.

Chayanov, basing his work on the Russian rural economy, believed peasant economies had no access to labor markets but did have access to an active land market. In many other parts of the world, it is limitations to and imperfections in the land market that are thought to constrain peasants in their economic decision making. Where land is monopolized by elites, or its sale is legally restricted, or it is simply scarce, peasant households are encouraged to expend their labor on the available land in amounts far beyond what would be justified by the prevailing wage rate. Since peasants paid family members their average product rather than their marginal product, household production decisions were characterized by self-exploitation.

Others have emphasized the absence of insurance markets, which impose efficiency-reducing farming practices on peasants in their quest to avoid risks that could bring disaster to the household. Donald McCloskey (1975) argued that the open fields of medieval and early modern Europe persisted to allow peasants to distribute their crops among multiple fields and thereby avoid failure owing to localized climatic extremes. An additional argument holds that specialized production was held back for the same reason and that crop and technical innovations are met with skepticism out of a time-tested aversion to risk.

More generally peasant economies are thought to suffer from imperfect and incomplete input and product markets. The peasant, unable to depend on markets to supply necessities or without access to transparent and competitive markets on which to sell crops, limits his or her exposure to the market—holds the market at arm's length—preferring to supply the household first, before seeking to market surpluses. Likewise, in the absence of input markets, the cultivator must produce on-site all of the inputs for the production process, such as seed, manure, fodder, and draft power. This constrains the peasant in her or his technological choices, since the highly interrelated character of agricultural production in the absence of a market for inputs and intermediate products makes it difficult to introduce changes to any single part of the production process.

The mixed farming systems of western Europe offer a good example of this condition. To produce grain, the peasant needed not only arable land but also manure to

kets for many of their inputs. Only then could they abandon "organic" farming and become highly specialized. In light of the above, the following definition, offered by Ellis (1993), fairly summarizes the economist's approach to peasants:

> Peasants are households which derive their livelihoods mainly from agriculture, utilize mainly family labour in farm production, and are characterized by partial engagement in input and output markets which are often imperfect or incomplete.

Historical Peasantry. Historians have no general definition of *peasantry*. They use the term innocently to refer to rural households with ties to the soil in some places and times (France until the 1950s, for example) but not others (the United States in any time period). Historically there were rich peasants and poor ones, even landless peasants. Typically historians follow local nomenclature, which speaks of *Hofbauer, Meier, Kötter,* and *Seldner* in parts of Germany, *fermier, laboureur,* and *manouvrier* in France, and *yeoman, husbandman,* and *cottager* in England. Historians are suspicious of essentializing generalizations and have long focused their attention not on commonalities but on the ways in which peasants differ one from another, whether for reasons of ecology, inheritance rights, technology, consumption, or configurations of power relations.

The emergence of peasant societies is not a major focus of historical research, being left usually to archaeologists and other specialists in prehistory. But historians, especially economic historians, have developed an intense and abiding interest in the long era of "classic peasantry." In Europe, according to Tom Scott (1976), "the formation of a distinctive peasantry—as a separate caste or social group—was an achievement of the High Middle Ages." Thus, while peasants had long existed, a "peasantry" as a social order crystallized in the eleventh and twelfth centuries. Only then did medieval thinkers define the social system as consisting of the three orders of the clergy, the knights, and the peasantry: those who pray, those who fight, and those who labor. In most of Europe the concept of a peasant social order maintained a certain integrity until well into the nineteenth century. Much historical writing on this long era has focused on two great themes: the character and dynamic of peasant economy and the processes by which traditional peasantry came undone and gave rise to commercial agriculture.

The first of these themes was studied and analyzed by a succession of economic and social historians, including Wilhelm Abel (1980), B. H. Slicher van Bath (1963), M. M. Postan (1975), and French historians of the Annales School, such as Marc Bloch (1966), Pierre Goubert (1960), and Emmanuel Le Roy Ladurie (1966). A common thread ran through their work: a substantially autonomous peasantry working with relatively stable technologies and

PEASANTRY. An Indian peasant plowing the fields. Illustration from *Boileau Album,* folio 19, Madras School, 1785. (Victoria and Albert Museum, London/Art Resource, NY)

fertilize the land and draft animals to pull plows and other equipment. This required access to meadows and pastures to maintain livestock. Peasants needed access to a variety of inputs, and as population growth made this access costlier, various measures were introduced to intensify the production process. Ester Boserup's (1965) influential model of long-term agrarian change emphasizes how the agronomic factors common to all agricultural production placed cultivators without access to input markets before inexorable trade-offs between land productivity and labor productivity. Mitigating the impact of these trade-offs led to more complex, interrelated forms of organizing production. They often led to cooperative action by neighbors and communities to share certain inputs or to coordinate activities. What might appear to the outsider as an ancient way of life expressing noneconomic cultural values could actually be relatively recent adaptations intended to intensify production. One might conclude that many European peasants became farmers when they gained access to mar-

imbedded in restrictive village institutions was confined in an *histoire immobile*. This "motionless society" experienced sudden shocks *(crise de subsistence)* owing to harvest failures and other misfortunes, and it experienced long, slow oscillations of population growth and contraction driven by the Malthusian forces that held it in thrall. But it was incapable of sustained economic growth. Le Roy Ladurie (1977) summarized the age of "classic peasantry": "Twelve to thirteen generations of peasants were busy reproducing themselves within limits of finite possibilities whose constraints proved inexorable."

An alternative historical approach to economic life in the age of "classic peasantry" rejected the notion of a binding demographic constraint and insisted instead on the primacy of political institutions. This Marxian historiography, developed by Dobb, Rodney Hilton (1978), and most recently by Robert Brenner (1985), emphasized nonmarket constraints exerted by the social property relations of European feudalism. With feudalism's gradual demise, European peasantries became geographically differentiated and socially differentiated into three forms of agricultural labor: landless wage laborers (in England), enserfed peasants working large estates (in East-Elbian Europe), and an independent peasantry (in much of western Europe). This last form supported the sort of economic stasis celebrated by the Annales School historians, but the others forced peasants—shorn of their autonomy—into closer market relations and hence into forms of capitalist agriculture. The comparative study of European peasantry has long attracted scholarly attention, for differences in institutions, social stratification, and agricultural technologies are profound, rarely follow political boundaries precisely, and have led to significant differences in economic performance and political structure.

A third approach to peasant agriculture, that of the past generation of economic historians, has shifted the focus from demography and political institutions toward markets. Skeptical of the conventional wisdom that markets were a threat to peasant aspirations, these scholars investigated medieval and early modern economies of several western European countries with the assumption that peasants were rational decision makers confronting historically specific institutions and technologies. For example, Jan de Vries (1974), in a study of sixteenth- and seventeenth-century Dutch agriculture, argued that under appropriate institutional settings "peasants" could become "farmers," investing and specializing to improve productivity in response to market incentives. Later Robert Allen (1992) offered evidence for a substantial long-term growth of agricultural output in England. Moreover in this classic land of the large capitalist landowner and landless laborer, Allen found the supposedly vanquished small-scale family farmer responsible for an im-

portant part of a productivity growth that averaged 0.2 to 0.3 percent per annum over the seventeenth and eighteenth centuries. Philip T. Hoffman (1996) studied French agriculture, exploiting evidence of land rents and agricultural wage rates to estimate changes in total factor productivity. He found that French peasants in proximity to the Paris market achieved sustained long-term productivity growth on the order of 0.13 percent per annum over the long period 1500 to 1789. None of the estimated rates of output growth is large by modern standards, but as averages for long time periods, they sufficed to make possible important changes in occupational structure, urbanization, and material culture. Preindustrial European peasantry was not synonymous with an unchanging traditionalism. Far from "holding the market at arms length," peasants embraced market opportunities, whether they arose in medieval Flanders, early modern Holland, or northern France.

These productivity improvements were rarely the products of truly new technologies. The technical basis for achieving the advances in productivity existed by the early fourteenth century. The agenda for the next four to five hundred years was to exploit fully this "medieval potential." George Grantham (1993) summarized these findings succinctly with the observation that "it is the history of markets rather than the history of technology which explains the growth of agricultural labour productivity" in the long era preceding the Industrial Revolution. None of this is to deny the specific character of the constraints facing peasants; what it does seek to deny is the need to deploy a distinct "theory of peasantry."

Historical peasantries in non-European societies are often still treated as "peoples without history," although the study of Ching dynasty China and Tokugawa Japan are notable exceptions. The long-regnant Malthusian approach to Chinese rural society is now vigorously challenged by Kenneth Pomeranz (2000), James Lee and Wang Feng (1999), and Philip Huang (1990), while in Japan the concept of the "industrious peasant" economy has been influential since the pioneering work of Thomas Smith (1959). In both cases peasants are viewed as rational economic actors who shape not only their physical assets but also the composition of their families to optimize production and consumption. The study of peasantry elsewhere, especially in Africa and Latin America, has been less deeply influenced by the market-focused approach of economic historians. In part because of the emphasis placed on concepts of "indigeneity" in the interpretation of rural peoples in these regions, the anthropological traditions remain influential.

Demise of Peasantry. Today the concept of peasantry is largely confined to the rural populations of the third world. They usually grow cash crops rather than subsistence crops and are highly dependent on markets—as often as not international markets. They may or may not own land and other capital, and while some employ nonhousehold labor, many others combine agriculture with industrial employments. They are highly differentiated, even though economic success is often a disqualification from being considered a peasant. If the term *peasant* remains useful today, it is not so much to define a category of economic actors as to identify a "subaltern" political stratum. This postmodern concept views peasantry primarily as a force of resistance "against history."

Historians and social scientists once saw peasant rebellion as instrumental in the achievement of some great (and irresistible) social objective. The numerous peasant rebellions of fourteenth- and fifteenth-century Europe (Flanders in 1323–1328, the French Jacquerie of 1358, and the English peasant revolt of 1381 among others) are often interpreted as integral to the late-medieval crisis of feudalism. The German Peasant's War of 1525 is in a class by itself, implicated in the Reformation as well as in the course of later German state building. The prominence of the twentieth-century peasant movements that supported the revolutions of Mexico (1911), Russia (1917), and China (1949) led social and political theorists to inquire into the purpose and potential of peasant mobilization in contemporary societies. For example, Barrington Moore, Jr. (1966) argued that the prevalence of democracy or dictatorship depended on whether or not revolutionary movements toppled the traditional elites before the onset of industrialization. If so, peasants could combine with the bourgeoisie around market economies and political democracy. If not, the old social classes could combine with the new industrialists to support authoritarian rule.

Such theorizing is no longer in fashion. Today the historian's shift of attention from politics and economics to culture leaves past and present forms of peasant rebellion stripped of grand designs. What is left is "everyday forms of resistance," devoid of emancipatory objectives. Its larger meaning can only be supplied by privileged interpreters. Most recently meaning has been infused into peasant rebellion, as into an empty vessel, by antiglobalization and proenvironmental groups. Meanwhile peasants, as always, will continue to make decisions for themselves.

BIBLIOGRAPHY

Abel, Wilhelm. *Agrarian Fluctuations in Europe from the Thirteenth to the Twentieth Centuries.* London, 1980.

Allen, Robert C. *Enclosure and the Yeoman: The Agricultural Revolution of the South Midlands, 1450–1850.* Oxford, 1992.

Bloch, Marc. *French Rural History: An Essay on Its Basic Characteristics.* Berkeley, 1966.

Boserup, Ester. *The Conditions of Agricultural Growth: The Economics of Agrarian Change under Population Pressure.* Chicago, 1965.

Brenner, Robert. "The Agrarian Roots of European Capitalism." In *The Brenner Debate: Agrarian Class Structure and Economic Development in Pre-Industrial Europe,* edited by T. H. Aston and C. H. E. Philpin, pp. 213–327. Cambridge, 1985.

Chayanov, A. V. *The Theory of Peasant Economy.* Homewood, Ill., 1966.

Ellis, Frank. *Peasant Economics: Farm Households and Agrarian Development.* 2d ed. Cambridge, 1993.

Goubert, Pierre. *Beauvais et le Beauvaisis de 1600 à 1730.* 2 vols. Paris, 1960.

Grantham, George. "Division of Labour: Agricultural Productivity and Occupational Specialisation in Pre-Industrial France." *Economic History Review* 46 (1993), 478–502.

Hilton, Rodney, ed. *The Transition from Feudalism to Capitalism.* London, 1978.

Hoffman, Philip. *Growth in a Traditional Society: The French Countryside, 1450–1815.* Princeton, 1996.

Hoppenbrouwers, Peter, and Jan Luiten van Zanden, eds. *Peasants into Farmers? The Transformation of Rural Economy and Society in the Low Countries (Middle Ages to Nineteenth Century) in Light of the Brenner Debate.* Turnhout, Belgium, 2001.

Huang, Philip. *Peasant Family and Rural Development in the Yangzi Delta.* Stanford, Calif., 1990.

Kroeber, A. L. *Anthropology.* New York, 1948.

Lee, James Z., and Wang Feng. *One Quarter of Humanity: Malthusian Mythology and Chinese Reality.* Cambridge, Mass., 1999.

Lenin, V. I. "The Development of Capitalism in Russia." In *Collected Works,* vol. 3, pp. 21–607. Moscow, Russia, 1964.

Le Roy Ladurie, Emmanuel. *The Peasants of Languedoc.* Urbana, 1966.

Le Roy Ladurie, Emmanuel. "Motionless History." *Social Science History* 1 (1977), 115–136.

Lipton, Michael. *Why Poor People Stay Poor.* London, 1977.

McCloskey, Donald. "The Persistence of English Common Fields." In *European Peasants and Their Markets,* edited by William N. Parker and E. L. Jones. Pp. 73–119. Princeton, 1975.

Mintz, Sidney. "A Note on the Definition of Peasantries." *Journal of Peasant Studies* 1 (1973), 91–106.

Moore, Barrington, Jr. *Social Origins of Dictatorship and Democracy: Lord and Peasant in the Making of the Modern World.* Boston, 1966.

Parker, William N., and E. L. Jones, eds. *European Peasants and Their Markets.* Princeton, 1975.

Pomeranz, Kenneth. *The Great Divergence: China, Europe, and the Making of the Modern World.* Princeton, 2000.

Popkin, Samuel. *The Rational Peasant: The Political Economy of Rural Society in Vietnam.* Berkeley, 1979.

Poston, M. M. *Medieval Economy and Society.* Hammondsworth, 1975.

Redfield, Robert. *Peasant Society and Culture.* Chicago, 1956.

Rösener, Werner. *Peasants in the Middle Ages.* Urbana, 1992.

Schultz, Theodore W. *Transforming Traditional Agriculture.* New Haven, 1964.

Scott, James. *The Moral Economic of the Peasant.* New Haven, 1976.

Scott, Tom, ed. *The Peasantries of Europe from the Fourteenth to the Eighteenth Centuries.* London, 1998.

Shanin, Teodor. *Defining Peasants.* Oxford, 1990.

Slicher van Bath, B. H. *The Agrarian History of Western Europe, 500–1850.* London, 1963.

Smith, Thomas C. *The Agrarian Origins of Modern Japan.* Stanford, Calif., 1959.

Vries, Jan de. *Dutch Rural Economy in the Golden Age, 1500–1700.* New Haven, 1974.

Wolf, Eric J. *Peasants.* Englewood Cliffs, N.J., 1966.

JAN DE VRIES

PERSONAL SERVICES. Economic historians have not yet fully investigated the upkeep and beautification of the face and body. The history we do have tells the story of tensions between home care and the development of dedicated public spaces for pampering. In the eighteenth century, personal services that had previously been the prerogative of the aristocracy started to cater to a growing market of consumers. From their original positions in the homogeneous European court society, purveyors of grooming adapted to both the growing needs of the middle classes and to a multiplicity of cultural and ethnic aesthetics. As Western ideals of beauty and hygiene spread under Imperialism and globalization in the nineteenth and twentieth centuries, the services rendered were standardized and sanitized in the hands of multinational corporations. Today, home dyes and electric razors compete with hairdressers, barbershops, and beauty salons for the discretionary income of fashionable men and women.

Precursors to Modern Services. Hairdressers, barbershops, and beauty salons are all fairly recent inventions of our consumer society. Yet the precursors to these services can be found in the preoccupation with beauty and fashion of Ancient civilizations. The Egyptians trained female slaves to dress hair, apply tattoos, and provide waxing services. Male Romans counted on the *tonsor* (hairdresser) to cut, curl, and dye their hair and apply makeup, while barbers were essential when beards were not in fashion. In Tokugawa Japan (1603–1868) servants were especially valuable if they could makeup and massage their mistresses. Similarly, in medieval and early modern Europe, shaving and hairdressing were essential skills for servants of the aristocracy.

The development of powerful guilds in the Middle Ages institutionalized the professions of dentists, barbers, and wig makers. All three were initially part of the guild of surgeon-barbers in France and England. French wig makers developed their own guild in 1665 when the fashion of wearing wigs returned, establishing themselves as powerful and wealthy controllers of fashion. By 1673, barbers were prohibited from performing the bloodlettings and operations of surgeons. They were relegated to shaving and selling hair products, thereby losing control of more remunerative work. Dentistry was also labeled as an insignificant subcategory of the surgical profession. Tooth pullers in the early modern period often plied their trade in public squares, turning the extraction of rotten molars into a carnival show, further diminishing their reputations as real doctors. By the end of the eighteenth century, however, dentistry had become professionalized in both Europe and the United States. Wealthy patients demanded not just the extraction of teeth, but their replacement, repair, and cleaning. By the nineteenth century, dentistry became integrated within the medical world, distancing it from other personal services.

The eighteenth century saw a revolution in consumer habits due to the development of a stable middle class, which meant the spread of personal service beyond the homes of the elite. Beautification became more widely available in public spaces, transforming practices that had previously been hidden in the homes of the aristocracy. Though the feminine toilette remained a private ritual for both the middle and upper classes, men's grooming took place in dedicated shops. A struggle ensued among trained artisans over who would control the newfound wealth of customers. Wig makers consolidated their power by controlling an increasing amount of masculine spending on their looks, while catering to a multitude of social classes, including artisans and manual workers. Over the course of the century, English wig prices fell from 140 pounds to one guinea for a common wig. In the world of even more profitable feminine toilettes, female hairdressers lost their monopoly, toppled by the newly canonized profession of male hairdressers, whose reputations depended on their creative genius rather than their suitability. Léonard, Marie Antoinette's hairdresser, created such towering and expensive hairdos that many women slept sitting up to preserve them longer. Caricatures and criticisms of the period often blamed hairdressers and wig makers for the inordinate spending on luxuries by Europe's consumer classes.

The simplification of styles at the end of the eighteenth century, which was sped up in France by the Revolution (1789), considerably altered the services offered, forcing artisans either to adapt to changing tastes or go bankrupt. Shorter hairstyles meant that women performed their toilettes themselves and in little time. With the popularity of natural hair, men too no longer needed to spend hours at the wig maker. When facial hair became popular in the late nineteenth century, barbers were also at a loss for clients. To face these changes, hairdressers, wig makers, and barbers offered new services and products. Barbers trimmed and dyed beards, hairdressers sold hair extensions for women, while wig makers aimed toupees at the vanity of older men. Yet these new services were not highly profitable. In London of the 1880s, a shave cost only ten cents and a trim even less. Overall, nineteenth-century fashions of bourgeois propriety and respectability led to a recession for the business of beauty and pampering.

Beauty Services Gain Respectability. A second revolution in services started in the late nineteenth century. In tandem with the growth of a mass consumer society, personal services became both more respectable and accessible. In the United States, this development was first and foremost created by a group of entrepreneurial women. Elizabeth Arden (1884–1966) and Helena Rubinstein (1870–1965) were early rivals in the creation of luxury beauty parlors that brought private rituals into a public but highly feminized space. Madame C. J. Walker (1867–1919) and Annie Turnbo Malone (1869–1957) capitalized on the African-American market for hair care products,

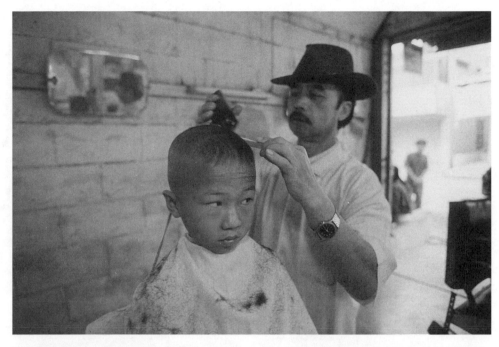

PERSONAL SERVICE. Barber at work, Chiang Sean, Thailand, 1997. (© Mike Yamashita/Woodfin Camp and Associates, New York)

emphasizing the beauty of black womanhood. In Rochester, New York, Martha Matilda Harper (1857–1950) created the first salon franchise in 1890, which expanded into a chain of 350 locations whose goal was to turn poor women into business owners. Late-nineteenth-century industrialization, urban growth, and immigration forced women to look for jobs. These new beauty shops capitalized on this available workforce by transforming hairdressing and cosmetology into respectable feminine occupations. Employment as an agent for a beauty salon was profitable and flexible work for uneducated, rural women, which also helped to build personal links between businesses and their clientele.

After World War I, the market for cosmetics boomed. By 1929, Americans spent 700 million dollars annually. Small-scale businesses were replaced by large corporations with national distribution chains promoted by new means of advertising in newspapers, in magazines, and especially on the radio. In this consumer boom, makeup and other cosmetics became part of a mass-market femininity for the first time in America. Previously a representation of sinful sexuality, lipstick was adopted by 90 percent of American women by 1948. The creation of mass-market cosmetics, hair dyes, and even hand-held hair dryers by the early twentieth century made it possible for women to do much of their beautifying at home. Similarly, the 1895 invention of the safety razor with disposable blades by Gillette allowed men to feel secure shaving themselves, inaugurating

the slow death of the corner barbershop. With the development of the stainless-steel blade in the 1960s, shaving became a veritable industry, with total sales in the United States during the decade totaling 300 million dollars.

Salons and New Services. New inventions in the industry, however, meant that neither sex could completely ignore the services offered by salons. For instance, in 1906, Karl Nestlé, a German hairdresser living in London, unveiled his electrical heating device to create permanent curls, though it was not without the danger of electrocution and burns until the 1920s. In 1941, the chemical thioglycolic acid was found to be the perfect solution to the dangers of electric curlers. Adopted by L'Oréal (founded by Eugene Schuller in 1907), this method soon became the safest means of achieving curls. It remains the main ingredient of the modern permanent. Hair dyes were also made safe with the discovery of double-process bonding in 1920, allowing everyday women to become Hollywood blondes. Though only 7 percent of American woman dyed their hair in 1950, by the 1970s, 70 percent altered their hair color either in salons or with home-dyeing kits.

Changing fashions also helped beauty salons develop new services. For instance, the popularity of tanning in the 1920s and the disappearance of gloves in the 1930s led to a demand for waxing, tanning, manicures, and pedicures. New customers were enticed to try these services by a steady decline in prices for pampering. Not surprisingly, a drop in prices and increased competition among salons led to a refeminization of the profession. In American cities, the number of women hairdressers and beauty-shop workers more than tripled from 1920 to 1930. By 1935, women made up 89 percent of workers in urban personal services, earning sixty-three cents to their male colleague's dollar and only thirty-six cents if they were African American. This feminization of the market continues today, matched by a decline in the amount of money women are willing to spend in salons in comparison to their own ministrations.

After World War II, European-style salons spread to Asia. In Japan, spending on beauty services from 1921 to 1994 increased from 500,000 to 923 million yen. Japanese cosmetics companies, in particular Shiseido, dominated not only their national market (the second largest after the United States) but also made large inroads into other Asian markets, such as Taiwan, Hong Kong, and Mainland China. In Taiwan, European-style beauty salons, offering privacy and a multitude of services, competed with traditional Chinese baths. In other parts of the world, Europeans brought their ideals of beauty with the forces of colonization. After the colonization of Egypt by the British in 1883, conquerors opened beauty salons that soon catered to local elites. In other parts of Africa, the culture of personal services stayed more traditional. In urban West Africa, small, locally owned barber and hairdressing shops promised customers haircuts with Western names (Michael Jordan, Boeing 747). Despite the popularity of these styles and the preponderance of European colonial products (such as Petrol Hahn hair lotion), the incorporation of Western ideals into African traditions indicates the strength of local culture, rather than the spread of multinational corporations and their products.

Cosmetic Surgery. The standardization of beauty, however, has become a fundamental aspect of Western culture. First developed in India in the sixth century BCE, reconstructive surgery was not discovered in Europe until the late eighteenth century. Respectable doctors, however, felt that tampering with the human face for purposes of beautification was a sin against God and thus only utilized this science in cases of illness and injury. Cosmetic surgery came into its own in the late nineteenth century as part of a movement toward racial integration and eugenics. After the successes of reconstructive surgery during World War I and the perfection of anesthetics, the narcissistic and foolhardy aspects of surgery were firmly replaced by a belief in self-improvement, including the possibility of better wages and social connections. By the 1950s, physical alterations had become an acceptable aspect of beauty culture; in one year alone, 5.6 billion dollars was spent on operations. The transformation of the "racial" nose, specifically Italian or Jewish, became a common coming-of-age ritual for young girls in the 1960s. As women en-

tered the business world in greater numbers in the 1970s, they could afford to buy their own beauty, including the enlargement of breasts and the erasing of visible signs of aging to fit with the growing cult of youth. Surgeons sold themselves as the solution to the problems of modern life. Surgery spread beyond the United States, bringing with it the ideals of white hegemonic beauty. After World War II, many Japanese women adopted the practice of eyelid surgery, while Vietnamese women modeled their breast enhancements on playboy centerfolds in an attempt to attract American husbands.

Today's market for personal services remains an unstable sector. As profits in sales of hair products, cosmetics, and toiletries increase, providers of services have to revolutionize their fields in order to entice new customers and keep old ones. A continued acceptance of physical transformation (be it through surgery, exercise, or cosmetics) provides an ever-growing market for development. Yet within this movement toward a homogeneous enactment of beauty there still remain spaces for individual statements and small businesses to thrive. Western personal services have always depended on non-Western traditions (such as massage and shampoos, both from India) and alternative styles (such as tattoos and piercings) for their fundamental survival. It is likely that this exchange of aesthetics and services will continue to both contradict and reinforce the growing globalized economy of beauty.

BIBLIOGRAPHY

Corson, Richard. *Fashions in Hair: The First Five Hundred Years*. London, 1965. An overview that contains interesting anecdotes about hairdressing.

Frasko, Mary. *Daring Do's: A History of Extraordinary Hair*. New York, 1994. A general illustrated history of hair fashions.

Gilman, Sander L. *Making the Body Beautiful: A Cultural History of Aesthetic Surgery*. Princeton, 1999. An important overview with special stress on the late nineteenth century.

Haiken, Elizabeth. *Venus Envy: A History of Cosmetic Surgery*. Baltimore, 1997. Focuses on twentieth-century effects of race and gender on perceptions of beauty.

Hargreaves, Anne S. *White as Whales Bone: Dental Services in Early Modern England*. Leeds, U.K., 1998. A very complete history of the professionalization of British dentistry.

Jones, Colin. "Pulling Teeth in Eighteenth-Century Paris." *Past and Present* 166 (Feb 2000), 100–145. A humorous cultural history of the first French postmodern tooth-puller.

King, Roger. *The Making of the "Dentiste," 1650–1760*. Aldershot, U.K., 1998. A professional history of French dentistry.

Martin, Morag. "Consuming Beauty: The Commerce of Cosmetics in France, 1750–1800." Ph.D. diss. Irvine, 1999. A history of changing cosmetic fashions and their implication for business practices.

McKnight, Gerald. *The Skin Game: The International Beauty Business Brutally Exposed*. London, 1989. An investigation of the promises and prices of the contemporary cosmetics industry.

Piess, Kathy. *Hope in a Jar: The Making of America's Beauty Culture*. New York, 1998. The development of a late-nineteenth-century cosmetics market led by women entrepreneurs and the social acceptance of makeup on a mass scale in the twentieth century.

Plitt, Jane R. *Martha Matilda Harper and the American Dream: How One Woman Changed the Face of Modern Business.* Syracuse, N.Y., 2000. Business history of Rochester entrepreneur and developer of modern chain stores.

Scranton, Philip, ed. *Beauty and Business: Commerce, Gender, and Culture in Modern America.* New York, 2001. Collection of essays addressing the commodification of beauty.

MORAG MARTIN

PERU. *See* American Indian Economies; Andean Region; *and* Spain, *subentry on* Spanish Empire.

PEST CONTROL. The first records of concerted agricultural pest control are forty-five hundred years old: by 2500 BCE, Sumerians were using sulphur compounds to control insects and mites. Botanical insecticides, mercury, and arsenical compounds were being used in China in 1200 BCE. In 200 BCE, the Roman politician Marcus Cato advocated oil sprays for pest control. The first record of biological control comes from China, where in 300 CE predatory ants were used to control caterpillars and beetles in citrus and bamboo crops. The aid of the church was invoked in the fifteenth century: cutworms were excommunicated and banished by the archbishop of Berne in 1476; and the high vicar of Valence tried caterpillars for their crimes, found them guilty, and banished them. In the 1730s, control through cultivation techniques began when farmers planted crops in rows to facilitate weed removal; and crop rotation was introduced, which whether deliberately or not, became a form of pest control. Around 1900, disease-resistant varieties of cotton were bred, and in 1942 a strain of wheat resistant to the Hessian fly was introduced. This brief history indicates not only that pest control has been part of agriculture for a very long time, but also that many different types of pest control have existed, chemical controls having the longest history and plant breeding being the most recently introduced.

Throughout the twentieth century, the dominant pest control technology was the chemical pesticide. Early modern breakthroughs began with the use of Paris Green to attack phylloxera in French vineyards. Lead arsenate was introduced as a general pesticide in the 1890s and lead sulphate as a selective (broad leaf) herbicide in 1896. Synthetic organic compounds began to be used in the 1930s and 1939 saw a major breakthrough: the insecticidal properties of dichlorodiphenyltrichloroethane, or DDT, were discovered. The compound was initially introduced as a delousing agent in the U.S. Army, but its diffusion to a wide variety of applications was very rapid. It was so effective that, following World War II, a project to eliminate malaria by eradicating its carrier mosquitoes was launched. A similar landmark event took place in 1942 with the intro-

duction of the hormone-based herbicide 2,4-D. Both of these chemicals, and the families of related chemicals subsequently developed, were extremely effective and very inexpensive. They were widely embraced because they appeared to mark an enormous technological and economic breakthrough in pest control in agriculture. Not only were the new pesticides widely adopted by farmers, but the pesticide approach was also very rapidly seen as the place where research would yield large benefits: a major shift in the locus of research in entomology away from the general biology of insects and toward the testing of pesticides took place in the late 1930s and 1940s. The entire agricultural system came to be built around this approach: farmers adopted the technology quickly; basic science moved in this direction; chemical firms made large profits in this area and invested heavily in research and development; and policy came to assume that this was the only technology being used.

While great strides were made in increasing effectiveness and reducing cost, there were some unexpected side effects: as early as 1946, DDT-resistant houseflies were reported in Sweden. This was only the beginning of what became a serious resistance problem. Insects developed resistance very rapidly (a major reason for the failure to eliminate malaria). By the mid 1960s, another problem emerged: the chemicals were too stable. Unlike modern pesticides, which break down in days or weeks, DDT and its relatives remained stable for years. Thus, as they were absorbed by plants, they were eaten and moved through the food chain. Birds in particular were badly affected, producing eggs with soft shells, for example. Rachel Carson's *Silent Spring* drew attention to this problem and began a movement to investigate the perils of the chemical approach to pest control and search for alternatives. By the 1970s, countries began imposing widespread bans on DDT, but the chemical approach remains dominant. The use of pesticides continues to grow. Other approaches—cultivation techniques, predator pests, insect pheromone traps, selective insecticides—are all available and have been used for centuries. In 1967, the term "integrated pest management (IPM)" was introduced to describe a systemic, more ecological approach to pest control, one that used all of the available means of control. In spite of widespread belief that chemical pesticides may be causing serious problems, these alternatives have been extremely difficult to introduce.

The breakthroughs in the mid-twentieth century put chemical technology on the road to rapid improvements. Based on this foundation, it was successful in capturing essentially the entire market for pest control. Consequently, its competitor, IPM, had no way to demonstrate its virtues and no resources with which to improve on them. The positive feedbacks that drove this outcome are learning, scale, and coordination.

Chemical companies invested heavily in research and development of the pesticide technology, maintaining and improving its effectiveness. In contrast, research on IPM, having to do with plant and pathogen ecology, was done almost entirely in the public sector. In the year 2000, farmers continued to express uncertainty as to whether IPM could work for them.

Large fixed costs in the form of research and development and economies of scale in the production of inputs favor a technology, in this case chemical control, which has many users.

Finally, coordination problems make transitions from chemicals to IPM difficult. A single farmer cannot shift because his activities can hurt neighbors using different technologies and vice versa. Typically, cases of successful transition, for example, among cotton growers in the southern United States or citrus farmers in Israel, involve significant government intervention.

The chemical control strategy seems deeply entrenched, in spite of its problems and in spite of the fact that many economic studies of IPM find it to be as profitable as a technology. In the mid 1980s, this message began to affect policy. India and Malaysia adopted IPM as ministerial policy in 1985; Germany in 1986; Denmark and Sweden, at least implicitly, the next year; and the Netherlands in 1991. As successes with IPM continue slowly to be noticed, and as the difficulties with chemical control are publicized, it may be that a shift from one technology to another will take place. If so, this will be an important case in the history of technology in which an entrenched technology is supplanted by one that had been largely forgotten.

[*See also* Agriculture, *subentry on* Technological Change; *and* Crop and Plant Diseases.]

BIBLIOGRAPHY
Carson, Rachel. *Silent Spring*. Boston, 1962.
Cowan, Robin, and Philip Gunby. "Sprayed to Death: Path Dependence, Lock-In, and Pest Control Strategies." *Economic Journal*, 106 (May 1996), 521–542.
Huffaker, C., and Messenger, P., eds. *Theory and Practice of Biological Control*. New York, 1976.
Luckman, W. H, and R. L. Metcalf, eds. *Introduction to Insect Pest Management*. New York, 1982.
Woods, A. *Pest Control: A Survey*. London, 1974.

ROBIN COWAN

PETROLEUM INDUSTRY. *See* Oil Industry.

PHILADELPHIA. William Penn founded Philadelphia in 1681 as a capital city for a proprietary colony that would serve as a haven for persecuted Anglican Quakers. A rich hinterland, an enterprising merchant community, and ready markets for the goods processed and crafted in the city transformed Philadelphia into a major commercial entrepôt. By the time delegates convened in the city in 1776 to write the Declaration of Independence and a decade later the Constitution for the new republic, Philadelphia had become second only to London in both the volume and value of the products shipped in and out of its port. Philadelphia's commercial fortunes plummeted, however, in the early nineteenth century as the city lost trade to its chief rival, New York. Rather than enter a long-term period of economic stagnation, the city embarked on a new direction that would mark its history for the next 150 years. It became a major manufacturing center.

Chronicling Philadelphia's rise to industrial supremacy is difficult since no single invention, businessperson, event, or circumstance can be designated as a prime mover. Thousands of initiatives have to be noted since industrialization occurred in the city as a steady mushrooming of varied enterprise. The individual efforts do add up to a whole, and at least four features characterized Philadelphia's industrial structure: product diversity; a diversity of work settings; specialization in products and processes; and the prevalence of small-to medium-sized family-owned-and-managed businesses.

A number of factors contributed to Philadelphia's particular industrial history. An abundance of skilled labor allowed for custom production. The absence of major waterfalls initially limited the building of large-scale, fully mechanized factories. Philadelphia's custom producers further chose not to compete with major firms in other cities who manufactured cheap, standardized goods; their small size afforded a flexibility that allowed them to shift into new product lines and profit in niche markets. Finally, Philadelphia's Quaker commercial elite tended to invest their savings in further trade, banking, canal and railroad construction, and mining, rather than in local industry. This created a capital scarcity for manufacture in the city, another limit on large-scale enterprise, and a vacuum that enterprising native-born and immigrant skilled men could fill in creating their relatively small custom manufactories. Even Philadelphia's famous large firms, such as Baldwin Locomotive, Stetson Hat, and Midvale Steel, thrived on specialty production.

The first significant changes in the city's industrial history occurred in the 1920s with declines in textile and garment manufacture and shipbuilding, although new production of radios, televisions, and electrical appliances sustained manufacturing employment. Industrial production declined precipitously after World War II, with factory closings leading to a loss of 350,000 jobs within three decades' time. Philadelphia's custom manufacturers—slow, resistant or unable to react to a mass consumer market—failed to compete with standardized producers of goods elsewhere in the country and abroad. Population decline

PHILADELPHIA. Southeast Corner of Third and Market Streets, Philadelphia (c. 1798–1800). Drawn, engraved, and published by Thomas Birch (1779–1851) and William Russell Birch. (Wallach Division, The New York Public Library/Art Resource, NY)

accompanied loss of industry—the city's population fell by 30 percent—and with a faltering tax base and rising social welfare costs, fiscal crises marked Philadelphia in the late twentieth century. White-collar and service-sector employment grew, with notable increases in the health and higher-education sectors, but abandoned factory buildings and vacant lots in the city's once proud industrial neighborhoods overshadowed the gains for Philadelphia's downtown office district.

BIBLIOGRAPHY

Licht, Walter. *Getting Work: Philadelphia, 1840–1950*. Cambridge, Mass., 1992.

Scranton, Philip. *Proprietary Capitalism: The Textile Manufacture at Philadelphia, 1800–1885*. New York, 1983.

Weigley, Russell, ed. *Philadelphia: A 300-Year History*. New York, 1982.

WALTER LICHT

PHILIPPINES. Before the Spanish occupation began around 1565, Filipinos lived in small, separate coastal communities called *barangay*s averaging thirty to fifty families each. The 1565 Filipino population is estimated at 1 to 1.25 million. The communities relied on their natural resource endowments, and their technology did not include draft animals or plows. No central or regional authority existed; government and markets were local, a chief headed each *barangay*, and social life was organized by kinship.

The four social castes were chiefs, freeborn people, commoners, and servants and slaves. Freemen and commoners owned land, and commoners delivered a portion of their crops to their masters who were chiefs or freemen, similar to the system of feudal Europe. The *barangay* economy was closely linked to water, with native homes arranged in a linear fashion along rivers rather than in clusters. Boat-making technology was well developed, cotton was spun and woven for clothing, and gold was worked into various qualities. Fowl, goats, swine, and carabao were raised, and fishing was abundant. Coconuts, rice, and millet were fermented into liquor. Other food staples included bananas, jackfruits, tubers, and rice, which was grown on several islands but with extremely rudimentary technology. House lots were owned by occupant families, and fields were strips behind the houses. There was also an undivided tract communally owned by the *barangay*. Lands were transferred through inheritance or barter and could be pledged as security for debts, with the debtor losing his or her land via nonpayment. Barter of commodities among the *barangay*s was rare.

Spanish Colony. The basic structure of the colonial economy was established during the conquest period, the

1560s to 1700. The laws declared that, since the king had paid for the voyages to the Philippines as well as the expenses of the regime and the churches, the natives had to pay tribute to him in return. So the conquerors could collect the tribute more easily, they reorganized the conquered natives into pueblo-parishes and gave each family an equal tract of land. This placed all natives into a single class of small farmers. The system of *real hacienda*, the king's estate, meant that the king owned all lands, while natives had no formal property rights. They could not sell the land they worked, and failure to work the land for two years led to loss of tenancy rights. Grants of land were given to the church, called friar haciendas, and to Spanish conquistadores.

The church brought native families from districts that had not yet been organized into pueblos to become renter-sharecroppers. They had to work the land for subsistence, with rice as the main crop, as well as pay tributes to the regime and to the church. The few Spaniards in the Philippines lived in cities and viewed themselves as gentlepeople, not farmers. Without assigned workers, their lands remained idle or were returned to the church or the king. The pueblo-parish system was further organized into *encomiendas*, in which natives paid tributes in exchange for protection and religious instruction. *Encomiendas* varied in size from one-fourth of a pueblo to an entire pueblo. These were kept by the king or were granted to the church or to conquistadores as private *encomiendas*.

Under the system of the *real hacienda* there were no public revenues or public accounting systems in the Philippines. Instead, all revenues were raised and spent on the account of the *real hacienda*, and a yearly subsidy known as the *real situado* was sent from the king's treasury in Mexico. The king's revenues were fixed at proceeds from the tributes; sale, auction, or lease of offices; monopolies, fines, or forfeitures; and taxes on salaries of a number of offices appointed by the king. Unlike the Dutch and British colonial authorities, which developed colonial agriculture to produce the raw materials their home industries manufactured into finished goods for world trade, the Philippine colony extracted any income above the tributes from the Manila-Acapulco galleon trade, which consisted of shipments of silver bullion from Mexico that were exchanged in Manila for Chinese goods.

The harshness of the private *encomiendas* led to a population decrease from 1588 to 1700. In 1718 the king ruled that all private *encomiendas* would be reincorporated into the king's estate, and population began to rise again, reaching its preconquest level by the 1750s. The land system began to change as population grew, since the increasing number of pueblo families led to the division of the equal-sized family parcels. Additionally, while borrowing against the land was illegal since all lands formally belonged to the king, borrowers and lenders devised agreements called *sanlangbili* to get around this law. Many families lost their fields to usurious loans from a growing native upper class of officeholding natives and Chinese mestizo traders and to usurpation by the friar haciendas. The landless families became sharecroppers to either the moneylenders or the friar haciendas. This enabled the upper class to engage in pueblo and intraprovince trade with the surplus from their debtors' fields. Natives protested the loss of their fields and refused to pay their tributes.

In 1778 King Charles III sent Governor General Basco y Vargas to institute a new economic order in the Philippines. Basco developed a "general economic plan" to create a political, civil, and moral revolution that would lead to economic progress. Agriculture would be the key sector, producing large-scale cultivation for self-sufficiency and export crops to increase the country's wealth. There were only a few Spaniards in the Philippines by this time, as most of the old grantees had left in the 1740s and 1750s, when the galleon trade declined. Basco wanted those who remained to invest their capital in plantation operations. He awarded prizes and honors for contributions to agriculture, such as cultivation of cinnamon, pepper, nutmeg, indigo, cotton, and mulberry trees. There were also awards for ideas that advanced technology, such as operations of silk, cotton, hemp, linen, or tin factories and new inventions.

By developing its own agriculture, commerce, and industry, the Philippines could reduce imports and begin to export. Basco considered the galleon trade irrational, as it amounted to receiving silver from Mexico only to deliver it to Chinese traders. The Real Compañía de Filipinas was chartered in 1785 to open trading opportunities among Manila, Asian ports, Mexico, and Spain, easing the restrictions on foreign trade. It also was intended to promote export agriculture and manufacture of Filipino products, to bring foreign artisans to the Philippines, and slowly to phase out the galleon trade. However, none of the Spanish colonists purchased the compañía shares reserved for them, leaving business operations to other Spaniards who were unfamiliar with colonial society.

The general economic plan did not succeed in disseminating much new useful knowledge in agriculture. No new technology was implemented in the harvests of cotton, sugar, indigo, or abaca, so these products were of low quality. This problem was worse for the plants introduced into cultivation as the natives did not know how to process these crops and were not taught improved methods for planting. They were given cash advances from the compañía to plant crops that were not suited to the locality or for which there was no market demand. However, mestizo and native upper-class families who had gained land through *sanlangbili* were successful at planting small lots of cash crops, such as sugar, indigo, cotton, coffee, and black pepper.

After 1750 population began to increase, resulting in large pueblos. Occupational diversity became possible as domestic trading increased. By the early 1800s many pueblos had market days on which cloth, iron bars, hardware, and tools could be traded for staple foods. In 1813 the galleon trade was abolished, but this did not lead to the desired shift of Spanish capital into agriculture. In 1832 a French medical officer in Manila, Paul de la Gironière, started the first successful sugar plantation. Following his example, Spaniards in the Philippines finally turned to plantation agriculture in the 1830s but soon abandoned it amid competition from native planters. The Real Compañía dissolved in 1834, leaving the Philippines open to world trade without an industrial sector. Foreign trade was financed by trading houses from the United States, Great Britain, Germany, France, and Switzerland. The relationships between local planters and foreign trading houses determined the composition of exports, primarily sugar, tobacco leaf, cigars, abaca fiber, indigo, coffee, and cotton. Cigars were the only product not exported in its raw form.

Spanish Province. In 1850 the Philippines were declared a province of Spain, replacing the system of *real hacienda*. For the first time the government developed a budget, in which 50 percent of the expenditures went to the Finance Department, which spent over five million pesos to collect ten million pesos in revenues, 95 percent from tributes, customs duties, and monopolies. Land was easy to acquire from the *realangas*, land that was never given as a grant or organized into pueblos, but there was no capital or credit system.

The country evolved into a dual economy. Upper-class Filipinos rose into the planter class and produced most of the exported goods, and unschooled natives worked plantations. The large-scale plantations led to new technology in roads, dikes, and canals; improved seed varieties; carpentry shops; and machinery. However, agriculture and industry were still backward, held back by the large foreign demand for unprocessed agricultural produce. Philippine sugar was considered the worst quality in the world market and commanded the lowest price, and the only finished products for export were cigars, produced by hand. Small-scale family farms were still the dominant use of land.

In August 1896 the Filipino revolution against Spain broke out. The Filipinos declared victory in September. In January 1899, an independent Filipino Republic was established with the aims of dismantling the old system, gaining social, political, and economic foundations for egalitarianism, and achieving modernization in technology. In the new economic system domestic trade was taxed, and farmers who worked the land were given title to it under a cadastral system. Land reform was achieved through

redistribution of the friar lands. However, this regime was quickly out of power, as an American victory was declared in the Spanish-American War in May 1898. President William McKinley ordered a U.S. military occupation, and the United States created the economy of special relations.

U.S. Influence. After the ensuing war ended, the U.S. government set out to expand American trade in the Philippines. Americans saw the Philippines as a market for U.S. exports, such as agricultural machinery and manufactured and processed goods, and established tariffs to favor U.S. products. These policies were intended to create an economic system of private enterprise. Within the economy a new system for internal and customs revenues was designed. The internal revenue system simplified the Spanish system of head taxes by raising the tax on luxury items and decreasing the rate on necessary items, shifting the tax burden from the poor. The Americans also attempted to instate a land tax for the first time in Philippine history, but this met with landowner resistance and was suspended for five years. The decision of whether or not to reinstate it was passed to provincial governments, most of whom kept the tax.

The Payne-Aldrich trade law of 1909 provided for partial free trade between the United States and the Philippines. Imports rose almost twenty million pesos, and by 1916 the United States was the principal importer and exporter. Revenues from import duties fell, so for the first time more funds came from internal taxes than from customs receipts.

In 1934 the Tydings-McDuffie Act established the Commonwealth of the Philippines, which provided for a ten-year transition period to independence. The country would have a constitution and be self-governing, but laws affecting immigration, foreign trade, and currency would require approval by the U.S. president. The trade provisions of the act favored the United States. Tariffs on Philippine exports to the United States grew steeper over the ten years, while U.S. goods had unrestricted entry. This regime achieved little growth for the economy from 1900 to 1909, followed by accelerated but uneven growth until the Great Depression of the 1930s.

The U.S. government achieved some success with the modernization of the infrastructure, such as government, public health, and education, as well as industrialization of export commodities. However, the Americans neglected the traditional agricultural sector, the source of livelihood for the majority of natives. Rice cultivation alone engaged the largest part of the labor force, but technology in this field was not expanded. Instead, rice prices were kept artificially low through imports, while only 25 percent of arable land was cultivated.

Land reform was also unsuccessful, as the United States maintained the status quo in landlord tenant relations.

MANILA. Philippine Stock Exchange, 1996. (© Catherine Karnow/Woodfin Camp and Associates, New York)

The rapid increase in population, brought about through improvements in public health, put added pressure on the land, creating a labor surplus and worsening the position of tenants. The area under cultivation more than tripled from 1903 to 1935 owing to U.S. demand for cash crops and an increasing population. But the proportion of farms worked by their owners decreased, and disparities in the distribution of wealth increased. Limits were set on the size of land tracts that could be purchased, ostensibly to protect Filipino lands from foreigners but actually in response to the U.S. beet sugar lobby's fear of competition. Prerequisites to land titling made it almost impossible for small farmers to title their parcels. The disadvantages of tenants and small farmers did not change during the U.S. occupation. Agrarian unrest fueled the leftist and communist movements of the rest of the century.

On 8 December 1941 Japan launched a surprise attack on the Philippines. The Japanese military authorities immediately organized the Council of State to direct civil affairs until they declared the Philippines an independent republic in October 1943. Most of the Philippine elite collaborated with Japanese political institutions, but they were opposed by effective guerrilla activity. The U.S. general Douglas MacArthur, with the help of guerrilla forces, defeated the Japanese in September 1945.

The Philippines suffered enormous loss of life and capital. The Philippine people prepared for independence on 4 July 1946 amid severe inflation and food shortages. Despite political independence, the Philippine economy remained dependent on U.S. markets, and the ties of special relations were not easily severed. In 1946 the U.S. Congress passed the Bell Act, which provided for free trade until 1954, after which tariffs would be increased 5 percent annually until 1974. Additionally quotas would be set for Philippine products, while there would be no restrictions on U.S. imports. U.S. citizens were granted equal economic rights with Filipinos in the exploitation of natural resources. In 1955 the trade agreement was renegotiated, extending the progressive tariffs on Philippine goods.

The political scene of the 1960s and 1970s was dominated by President Ferdinand Marcos, elected president for two terms and then a virtual dictator. During his first term the government improved the quality of life through public works projects, such as roads, bridges, schools, health centers, and irrigation facilities, which also provided benefits for his friends. Part of his platform was a land reform program, but it was never implemented because the landowner elite was politically powerful. During the first years of martial law, declared in 1972, business confidence rose, and the economy benefited from increased stability.

From 1973 to the early 1980s the GNP rose, the inflation rate fell, and dependence on imported oil was reduced through energy substitution measures. However, problems arose as the largest and most productive enterprises were gradually brought under the control of Marcos's personal allies. They were granted monopolies in manufacturing, construction, and financial services and were given huge government subsidies if the enterprises became unprofitable. The millions of Filipinos in the traditional cash crop sector suffered seriously from these arrangements. They could only sell to the sugar and coconut monopolies, and they received less than the world price for their crops. Land reform measures aimed to transfer lands to farming families, but the laws were filled with loopholes and had little impact.

During the martial law period foreign investment terms were liberalized, and Japan challenged the United States as a major participant in the Philippine economy. Nontraditional exports, such as textiles, footwear, electronics, and fresh and processed foods, were initiated. In 1981 martial law formally ended, but the subsequent New Republic program established by Marcos was simply an extension of the crony-dominated New Society. Inflation and unemployment rose, and the GNP contracted between 1983 and 1985 as domestic and foreign investment fell. Economic uncertainty worsened due to the 1983 assassination of Marcos's main opponent Benigno Aquino. The People's Power movement, supported by millions of rural, working-class, middle-class, and professional Filipinos, united behind Aquino's widow Corazon Aquino. In 1986 Corazon Aquino became president of the Republic of the Philippines.

The 1992 election of Fidel Valdez Ramos, Aquino's former defense secretary, marked the beginning of a turnaround in the Philippine economy. Ramos deregulated traditionally protected industries and opened them to competition, liberalized the entry of foreign investors, and relaxed banking rules. Exhibiting dramatic growth by 1994 and 1995, the economy finally looked poised to compete with its more successful Southeast Asian neighbors. These hopes were set back with the Asian financial crisis in 1997, which caused a slowdown in the Philippine economy. However, Ramos's economic reforms ensured that the country weathered the regional crisis in better shape than most of its neighbors.

BIBLIOGRAPHY

Baldwin, Robert E. *Foreign Trade Regimes and Economic Development: The Philippines.* New York, 1975.

Comyn, Tomas. *State of the Philippine Islands.* London, 1821.

Corpuz, O. D. *An Economic History of the Philippines.* Quezon City, Philippines, 1997.

Jenkins, Shirley. *American Economic Policy toward the Philippines.* Stanford, Calif., 1954.

Mallat, Jean. *The Philippines: History, Geography, Customs, Agriculture, Industry, and Commerce of the Spanish Colonies in Oceania.* Manila, Philippines, 1983.

Steinberg, David Joel. *The Philippines: A Singular and a Plural Place.* 2d ed. Boulder, 1990.

PHILIPS FAMILY. Halfway through the eighteenth century (specific dates are unknown), the German merchant Philip Philips settled in the Dutch town of Veenendaal. In 1790, his son Benjamin Philips (1767–1854) moved to Zaltbommel aan de Waal, where he continued his father's business in tobacco and textiles. Benjamin Philips married Lea Hartogh, and they had twelve children. Seven of Benjamin's eight sons moved away from Zaltbommel and settled as cigar producers or coffee and tobacco merchants in Maastricht, Liège, Brussels, and Offenbach. The eldest son, Lion Philips (1794–1886), remained in Zaltbommel to eventually take over the family business. In 1820, Lion Philips married Sophie Presburg, whose sister was Henriette Presburg, Karl Marx's (1818–1883) mother. The pattern of the coffee and tobacco enterprise continued in the next generation. The two eldest of Lion Philips's five sons moved to Aachen to go into the cigar business. Meanwhile, the third son, Benjamin Frederik David Philips (1830–1900), remained in Zaltbommel.

Although Benjamin Frederik David Philips, who used the name Frederik, stayed active in the coffee and tobacco business, he also ventured into other areas. He funded the Frederik Philips Bank in 1871. For a short time, he also exploited—albeit unsuccessfully—the local gas plant, apart from his banking affairs. In spite of this failure, the Rotterdam municipal board appointed him a member of a committee of specialists to advise on the extension of the gas concession. The committee's assignments led Frederik Philips to London, where he studied the progression of electric lighting. A few years later, Frederik's eldest son, Gerard Philips, also became familiar with the progression of electric lighting in Scotland.

Gerard Leonard Frederik Philips (1858–1942) graduated from Delft University in 1883 as a mechanical engineer. After working in a Dutch shipyard for a year, he in 1884 moved to Glasgow, the shipbuilding center of Europe at the time. In the Scottish capital, he became interested in electric lighting applications, which were booming as a result of the recent invention of the incandescent lamp. This interest motivated him to study electric science at the Glasgow College of Science and Arts. From 1884 to 1887, he also participated in the Glasgow University research group run by the renowned physicist Sir William Thomson (1824–1904), later known as Lord Kelvin. After these studies, Gerard Philips started a career at the Anglo American Brush Electric Light Corporation Ltd. in London. His work for this company, which produced incandescent lamps and ran large light projects in Europe, gave him experience in the still young electric light industry. In 1889, Gerard Philips and his father Frederik Philips developed a plan to found a lamp factory in the Netherlands in cooperation with Brush. This plan was terminated as a result of a legal battle involving Thomas Edison's basic patent that forced Brush to end its lamp production.

The electric lamp factory, the fifth in the Netherlands, still came into existence. In 1891, Gerard Philips founded the firm Philips & Company in Eindhoven with his father's financial aid. Aside from the financial base, which was built from the family capital, the production process designed by Gerard Philips, yet discovered by Brush, formed the solid technical basis for the enterprise. His production method was suitable for large-scale production, and it was by far not as labor-intensive as the complicated process Edison and his followers used. In 1895, Philips needed a commercial manager, because he focused mainly on technical management. This help came from his brother Anton Frederik Philips (1874–1951), who was sixteen years younger than Gerard.

Anton Philips successfully constructed a widespread European sales agencies network, which enabled the company to export the main part of the production. Considering the small Dutch domestic market, export was the core of the strong growth Philips & Company achieved in the early twentieth century. When the firm was converted into a public limited company (NV) in 1912, it was the largest employer in the Netherlands and was Europe's third-largest producer of incandescent lamps. The Philips family retained control over the company through its possession of priority shares in the holding company NV Philips Gemeenschapplijk Bezit. In 1914, NV Philips Gloeilampenfabrieken became the first Dutch enterprise to set up a scientific research laboratory. This laboratory soon developed into one of the biggest industrial laboratories in the world. After Gerard Philips retired from business in 1922, Anton Philips was appointed general manager. Anton set in motion a diversification process, which made the enterprise grow into one of the most important electron tube and radio set producers in Europe. At the same time, Philips founded its own sales and production companies in most European countries and in South America. In 1939, Anton Philips passed the company's management on to his son-in-law P. F. S. Otten (1895–1969), who was in his turn succeeded by Anton Philips's son F. J. Philips (1905–). Under their management, the company exploited new grounds, like telecommunication, industrial systems, computers, and semiconductors. H. A. C. van Riemsdijk (1911–), Anton's second son-in-law, was the last member of the Philips family who managed Philips Electronics as its president. In 1977, van Riemsdijk stepped down as president to become chairman of the board of directors. The Philips family has contributed to the development of industry and banking in the Netherlands and in other European countries since the eighteenth century. Nevertheless, its members mainly influenced the electrotechnical industry in the twentieth century through Philips Electronics.

BIBLIOGRAPHY

Blanken, Ivo J. *The History of Philips Electronics N.V.,* vol. 3, *The Development of N.V. Philips' Gloeilampenfabrieken into a Major Electrical Group.* Zaltbommel, Netherlands, 1999.

Blanken, Ivo J. *The History of Philips Electronics N.V.,* vol. 4, *Under German Rule.* Zaltbommel, Netherlands, 1999.

Bouman, P. J. *Anton Philips, de mens, de ondernemer.* 2d ed. Utrecht, 1966.

Philips, F. J. *45 Years with Philips.* Poole, Dorset, England, 1978.

Gielkens, J. *"Was ik maar weer in Bommel," Karl Marx en zijn Nederlandse Verwanten.* Utrecht, 1977.

Heerding, A. *The History of N.V. Philips' Gloeilampenfabrieken,* vol. 1, *The Origin of the Dutch Incandescent Lamp Industry.* Cambridge, 1986.

Heerding, A. *The History of N.V. Philips' Gloeilampenfabrieken,* vol. 2, *A Company of Many Parts.* Cambridge, 1988.

IVO J. BLANKEN

PHILLIPS CURVE. Expressed as an equation and graphed between Cartesian coordinates, the Phillips curve depicts an inverse relationship between inflation and unemployment. David Hume (1752), Henry Thornton (1802), Thomas Attwood (1819, 1831–1832), John Stuart Mill (1833), Irving Fisher (1926), Jan Tinbergen (1936, 1951), Lawrence Klein and Arthur Goldberger (1955), and A. J. Brown (1955) had already analyzed the relationship, the last five with charts and equations; but only the New Zealand economist A. W. Phillips (1958) drew the curve and fitted it to the data. Because he was the first to do so, Richard Lipsey, Paul Samuelson, and Robert Solow named the curve for him. Phillips thought he had found a permanent empirical relationship, but the inflationary experience of the 1970s and 1980s revealed the relationship to be temporary and fleeting. It vanishes when the economy fully adjusts to the inflation. At that point, inflation loses its stimulative powers, and the Phillips curve becomes a vertical line at the natural rate of unemployment.

Hundreds of textbooks and articles trace the evolution of the Phillips curve. First came Phillips's 1956 price-change version

$$p = f(Y - Y^*) \tag{1}$$

expressing the rate of price inflation, p, as a function of the excess demand that drives it, this excess demand being measured by the gap, or difference, between actual and potential output, $Y - Y^*$. Next came his famous 1958 wage-change version

$$w = f(U) \tag{2}$$

relating the rate of wage inflation, w, to the excess demand for labor as measured by the unemployment rate, U. It was this equation that Phillips fitted so successfully to the British data in a series of charts that captured the profession's attention.

There followed Samuelson and Solow, who, capitalizing on the idea that wage inflation equals price inflation in a stationary economy with zero productivity growth, graphed the 1960 price-change Phillips curve

$$p = f(U) \qquad (3)$$

Here was the version that economists in the 1960s and 1970s interpreted as offering a stable, enduring trade-off or menu of alternative inflation–unemployment combinations from which the policy authorities could choose. The curve seemed to promise policymakers that it would hold still or stay put so that they could permanently lower unemployment at the cost of higher stable rates of inflation, but this promise proved illusory. When the authorities tried to move along the curve to find the best inflation–unemployment combination, it shifted upward and to the right.

With the curve revealing itself to be neither fixed nor enduring but rather subject to shifts, economists added a vector of variables, Z, to account for the shifts. Incorporated into the shift-adjusted equation

$$p = f(U) + Z \qquad (4)$$

the Z vector featured such variables as past rates of inflation (a catch-up factor in wage demands), measures of trade-union militancy, unemployment dispersion, demographic factors, and the like.

When these explanatory variables proved inadequate to their task, Milton Friedman and Edmund Phelps replaced them with inflationary expectations, p^e, manifestly the most potent force shifting the curve. Observing that unemployment fluctuated about its equilibrium, or labor-market-clearing, level, Friedman and Phelps also expressed unemployment, U, as the deviation from its natural equilibrium rate, U_N. Thus was born the celebrated 1968 expectations-augmented Phillips curve

$$p = f(U - U_N) + p^e \qquad (5)$$

or

$$p - p^e = f(U - U_N) \qquad (5a)$$

This version says that: (1) the trade-off is between unemployment and unexpected inflation, $p - p^e$, rather than actual inflation, p; (2) the trade-off vanishes when expected inflation adjusts to actual inflation; and (3) unemployment returns to its natural equilibrium rate at this point such that no trade-offs remain to be exploited.

Provided that expectations adjust to actual inflation with a lag, the equation also implies the accelerationist notion that policymakers can permanently peg unemployment below its natural rate by continually raising the inflation rate so that it always stays a step ahead of expectations and frustrates their attempts to catch up. In short, the equation, while ruling out permanent trade-offs between unemployment and the rate of inflation, nevertheless implies a permanent trade-off between unemployment and the rate of acceleration of inflation.

The expectations-augmented Phillips curve has another gloomy implication. Embodying the notion that people revise their inflation expectations downward in adaptive, error-learning fashion only when actual inflation turns out to be lower than expected, the equation implies that disinflation might be too costly to pursue. Should the authorities seek to eradicate inflationary expectations—an absolute necessity for any successful disinflationary policy—they would have to force actual inflation below expected inflation in order to induce the latter to adjust to the former as it converged on the desired target rate. To achieve such disinflation, the authorities would apply contractionary measures to raise unemployment above its natural level. The resulting excess unemployment would put downward pressure on the actual rate of inflation, to which the expected rate would adjust with a lag. Through this long and painful error-learning adjustment process, both actual and anticipated inflation eventually would be squeezed out of the economy, albeit at the cost of much lost output and employment. Small wonder that some advised that it was better to learn to live with inherited inflation than to fight it.

Nobel laureate Robert Lucas of the University of Chicago put these fears to rest. He replaced adaptive expectations with rational expectations in the Phillips curve. He and other new classical economists showed that if people form their expectations rationally rather that adaptively, disinflation need not be a painful, drawn-out process. Rational expectations meant that people would take into account all systematic, and therefore predictable, future disinflationary policy actions and incorporate them into their inflation forecasts. Provided that policymakers conducted policy in a systematic, credible fashion, actual and expected rates of inflation and disinflation would coincide such that no gap would develop between them. Without a gap, there would be no need for excess unemployment to generate one. Inflation, actual and expected, would be brought to its target level with no cost in terms of excess unemployment.

This conclusion proved to be a bit too facile and sanguine. In a world in which wages and prices are to some degree sticky or inflexible such that markets fail to clear instantaneously, even rationally expected disinflation would incur some unemployment cost. Still, the relatively painless disinflation achieved in the United States in the 1990s fits the profile of a Phillips curve augmented with rational rather than adaptive expectations.

The history of the Phillips curve teaches four lessons. One of them is the validity of Steven Stigler's law of eponymy, according to which no scientific discovery is named for its original discoverer; Phillips was far from the first to recognize and analyze the inflation-unemployment relationship associated with his name. More important are the three policy lessons taught by history. First, empirical regularities break down as soon as policymakers try to exploit them (Goodhart's law). The Phillips curve is no exception. Second, there are no long-run inflation-unemployment trade-offs to exploit. Policymakers cannot permanently peg unemployment at disequilibrium levels; attempts to do so produce ever-worsening inflation or deflation. Third, expansionary and contractionary policies affect unemployment only temporarily. The effect vanishes when prices adjust, and all that remains is a changed rate of inflation.

BIBLIOGRAPHY

Blaug, Mark. "The Phillips Curve." In *Economic Theory in Retrospect.* 5th ed., pp. 676–685. Cambridge, 1997. A superbly accessible textbook account of the history of the Phillips curve.

Friedman, Milton. "Nobel Lecture: Inflation and Unemployment." *Journal of Political Economy* 85.3 (1977), 451–472. Friedman's description of the natural-rate hypothesis and the expectations-augmented Phillips curve. Explains why the curve may become upward-sloping.

Humphrey, Thomas M. "Part V: The Phillips Curve." In *Money, Banking, and Inflation: Essays in the History of Monetary Thought,* pp. 205–247. Aldershot, U.K. and Brookfield, Vt., 1993. Contains essays on: the evolution and policy implications of Phillips-curve analysis, recent developments in that analysis, the early history of the Phillips curve, and David Hume's and Henry Thornton's seminal early contributions to Phillips-curve analysis.

Lipsey, Richard G. "The Place of the Phillips Curve in Macro Economic Models." In *Stability and Inflation,* edited by A. R. Bergstrom et al., pp. 49–75. New York, 1978. The best explanation of how and why the Phillips curve came to be incorporated into Keynesian macro models. A godsend for students and teachers.

Phillips, A. W. "The Relation Between Unemployment and the Rate of Change of Money Wage Rates in the United Kingdom, 1861–1957." *Economica* 25 (1958), 283–299. The paper that started it all.

Santomero, A., and J. Seater. "The Inflation Unemployment Trade-Off: A Critique of the Literature." *Journal of Economic Literature* 16.2 (1978), 499–544. An exhaustive review of the controversy over the Phillips curve.

Solow, Robert M. "Down the Phillips Curve with Gun and Camera." In *Readings in Money, National Income, and Stabilization Policy,* edited by Ronald L. Teigen, pp. 140–157. Homewood, Ill., 1978. Reflections on the Phillips curve by the economist who, together with Paul Samuelson, introduced it to researchers in the U.S.

THOMAS M. HUMPHREY

PIGS have been a part of human diets and communities for millennia. In economic terms the pig's prime appeals as a food source are its plasticity, its ability to put on weight prior to slaughter (feed-to-meat conversion ratios as high as 80 percent in piglets and 27 percent in adults), and its ability to adapt to conditions from near total neglect to intensive husbandry. As Zeder (Nelson, 1998) noted, "They can out-produce other livestock animals in numbers of offspring and meat per individual, and their meat has the highest fat and caloric content of any domesticate." At the end of the twentieth century pigs were major dietary sources on all populated continents. However, pigs are not simply caloric inputs to human economic systems.

Domestication of Pigs. Pig utilization as a food resource predates its domestication. Wild boars were hunted across a wide swath of temperate Europe and Asia. Archeologists have dated swine domestication in southwestern Asia before the seventh century BCE, and during China's Yang Shao period (5000 BCE). Debate continues over the exact timing of this development and whether European and Asian hogs originated in the same domestication. Pigs were among the later animals domesticated because they are not easily herded and, as omnivores, they compete with their owners for food resources. They are found in settled, not nomadic, societies. Swine raising has not always been linked with food production but also occurred in association with ritual/religious mass swine killings.

Domesticated pigs have been raised in settings from single animals kept in a privy or a farmer's home to small "herds" kept as part of larger food production operations. Some medieval European abbeys had upward of a thousand pigs under their swineherds' control and kept extensive records on management and feeding regimes, which included penning and controlled feeding. Most pigs, until recent decades, were raised in small operations and were allowed to roam and root for food or constrained and fed household waste and grains.

Regional Aspects of Pig Utilization. Pigs were not native to the Americas but were introduced by Spanish conquistadores. (The peccary, a similar animal but not part of genus *Sus,* may have been in domestication's early stages at the time of conquest.) Swine were a mobile food source and occasionally were freed by explorers departing the islands. Later arrivals often found larger, if somewhat scragglier, herds. These pigs' descendants were distributed across Central America and northern South America. Pigs currently are not as important a meat source in South America; cattle supply most animal protein. Pork is a more important food in Asia and Europe than in the Americas or Africa. On the former continents it comprises more than 50 percent of meat consumed.

Early European settlers brought swine to North America. Clearing virgin forest required heavy labor commitments and pigs were generally turned loose to forage. They were shot like game or collected, confined, and fattened just prior to slaughter. As more time became available for fencing, hogs were less frequently left to root. The early 1800s saw the North American reintroduction of several English varieties and the evolution of a more purposeful system of husbandry. (The English had been purposefully breeding swine for several decades.). Large-scale nineteenth-century migration to the American Midwest and the development of corn-based agriculture helped lead to the growth of a porkpacking industry in the Mississippi and Ohio river valleys. (Corn is the near-perfect food for fattening and firming pigs just prior to slaughter.). They help explain the rise of several urban meatpacking centers, including Cincinnati, Chicago, and Saint Louis. Cincinnati packers developed a "disassembly line," later perfected in larger operations farther west, increasing packing productivity and serving as an "assembly line" precursor. Commercial slaughtering regularized the collection and processing of byproducts, including leather, soap, candles, glue, buttons, dried blood fertilizer, lubricants, lighting oil, and brushes—"everything but the squeal."

Fatback was the prime animal protein source for American slaves in noncoastal areas. Standard weekly rations for adult male field hands included 3.5 pounds of salt pork. More easily preserved than beef, pork was the meat of choice for sailing crews, army regiments, and settlers migrating to the western United States prior to mechanical refrigeration. American hog size and composition have varied over time. Animals in the late 1700s and early 1800s were much larger than their recent counterparts as demand for lard fell with rising petroleum distillation, vegetable oil manufacturing, and consumer demand for leaner meats.

Recent Trends in Commercial Hog-Raising Operations. In the twentieth century's last two decades centralized hog-raising facilities have developed in North America. Pork production increased slightly between 1970 and 1993 (to about 17 billion pounds annually) but the number of hog farms fell by more than two-thirds. A similar downward trend of smaller magnitude is evident in the number of hog-slaughtering plants. The growth of "industrial" hog raising has increased utilization of medical and genetic methods to generate desired hog structure and meat-generating capability. While cost-effective, large-scale farms raise concerns for the hogs and their home communities, as under intensive feeding and housing regimes, swine exhibit higher mortality levels and more aggressive behaviors. Such facilities generate unprecedented amounts of waste, the handling and disposal of which is a serious concern. Global operations characterize the integrated production/slaughtering/distribution firms that increasingly control much of the developed world's pork supply.

Nonfood Uses of Pigs. The addition of a rapidly reproducing, extremely efficient feed-to-meat converter to the stable was not the only economic benefit of pig domestication in East Asia. Use of the pigsty-privy, in which pigs consume human waste and other vegetable matter, converting both into meat and fertilizer while reducing the potential spread of human-to-human parasites, increased agricultural and human productivity. Swine's other nonconsumption-based agricultural uses include clearing soil prior to planting ("hogging down a field"), fungi hunting, and trampling seed into the ground following the sower.

Mythologically viewed both as a symbol of death and a symbol of life, swine have recently become walking medical supply stores, providing replacement heart valves and insulin. Current research evaluates pigs as human organ-transplant donors, taking advantage of the lower likelihood of animal-to-human disease transmission than with primate organs. While these uses add to the pig's importance as a product, they have the secondary benefit of conserving the recipient's human capital.

BIBLIOGRAPHY

Clutton-Brock, Juliet. *Domesticated Animals from Early Times*. Austin, 1981.

Donkin, R. A. "The Peccary—With Observations on the Introduction of Pigs to the New World." *Transactions of the American Philosophical Society* 75.5 (1985).

Heiser, Charles B. *Seed to Civilization*. San Francisco, 1981.

Mellen, Ida M. *The Natural History of the Pig*. New York, 1952.

Nelson, S. M., ed. "Ancestors for the Pigs: Pigs in Prehistory." *MASCA Research Papers in Science and Archaeology*, vol. 15. Philadelphia, 1998.

Sims, John A., and Leslie E. Johnson. *Animals in the American Economy*. Ames, Iowa, 1972.

Towne, Charles W., and Edward N. Wentworth. *Pigs, from Cave to Cornbelt*. Norman, Okla., 1950.

Ucko, Peter J., and G. W. Dimbleby. *The Domestication and Exploitation of Plants and Animals*. Chicago, 1969.

Walsh, Margaret. *The Rise of the Midwestern Meat Packing Industry*. Lexington, Ky., 1982.

Warren, Wilson J. *Struggling with Iowa's Pride: Labor Relations, Unionism, and Politics in the Rural Midwest since 1877*. Iowa City, 2000.

TIMOTHY CUFF

PILKINGTON FAMILY of English glassmaking entrepreneurs.

William Pilkington (1800–1872), son of a Lancashire doctor and liquor merchant, joined the St. Helens Crown Glass Company in 1826 as a silent partner. Following a dispute, William assumed control in 1828. A year later, brother Richard (1795–1869) joined the firm, creating Pilkington Brothers.

During the late 1830s and early 1840s, with other firms reducing production of window glass, Pilkington expanded, owing to an advantageous cartel quota and a generous overdraft account from a Lancashire bank. When the trade recovered, Pilkington was one of the three largest British glassmakers. The 1850s saw further expansion, with rolled plate glass, for mirrors, added to its products. The firm moved to secure supplies of critical inputs, acquiring coal mines and a chemical plant. After the import tariff on window glass was reduced in 1845, Pilkington faced intense foreign competition from continental European producers, forcing some retrenchment.

A second generation of Pilkington family managers William (Roby) (1827–1903), William Windle (1839–1914), Thomas (1835–1925), and Richard (1841–1908)—took control in 1865 and began revitalizing the firm. The product line was extended by entry into the cast plate glass industry in 1873. Most important, the firm adopted Siemens continuous-tank furnaces during the 1870s, before other British glassmakers. This technology turned manufacturing of window glass and rolled plate glass into continuous-flow processes, permitting substantial scale economies. The firm expanded its sales organization, and began to cultivate foreign markets to maintain its domestic output. After 1894, Pilkington and Chance Brothers were the only surviving British window-glass-making firms; by 1903, Pilkington was the sole British producer of plate glass.

The early twentieth century witnessed additional investments in mechanization and electrification. Pilkington developed improved processes for manufacturing and grinding plate glass, but fell behind competitors in failing to develop a similar process for window glass. This failure signaled wider problems. The firm's growing size and complexity made its commitment to "personal capitalism," with ownership and management firmly controlled by family members, increasingly outmoded.

By 1931, the company was in crisis. Profits had plunged, and two third-generation Pilkingtons, Austin (1871–1951) and Cecil (1875–1966), in charge since the early 1920s, resigned. E. H. Cozens-Hardy (1873–1956) assumed the directorship and effected a reorganization. A new executive committee introduced auditing and financial-control systems, and the finance and personnel departments expanded. Finally, nonfamily managers joined the board, and greater emphasis was placed on recruiting talented engineers and administrators from outside Pilkington. To improve departmental coordination, committees of directors and midlevel managers were established for finance, sales, technical issues, and personnel matters. Later, a separate research and development department was created.

Over time, Pilkington's performance rebounded. After World War II, expansion continued with strong demand for glass from the construction and automobile industries. Led by Harry (1905–1983) and Alastair Pilkington (1920–1995), the firm developed the revolutionary "float" process, which produced high-quality plate and sheet glass without expensive grinding and polishing machinery. Its early-1960s introduction made Pilkington the world's leading glassmaker. In 1970, the company went public, but control remained in family hands until the 1980 retirement of Alastair Pilkington as director.

BIBLIOGRAPHY

Barker, T. C. *The Glassmakers. Pilkington: The Rise of an International Company, 1826–1876.* London, 1977.

Chandler, Alfred D., Jr. *Scale and Scope: the Dynamics of Industrial Capitalism.* Cambridge, Mass., 1990.

THOMAS GERAGHTY

PIRACY. Forcible exchange has recurred and coexisted with peaceful trade in maritime economies throughout history. Acts of violence committed on the sea to capture goods and to hold people for ransom or for sale as slaves have been recorded from ancient times. Thus as early as the epics (early Iron Age), Odysseus is shown resorting to such predatory maritime acts. The term *pirate* (from the Greek *peiratés*, meaning "one who makes attempts or attacks") appears around the second century CE. At about the same time, Cilicians, Ligurians, and Illyrians made a living from coastal piracy on what are today the southern coast of Turkey and the Riviera and Adriatic coast of Italy. Throughout the ninth century CE, the Vikings of Scandinavia sent their male youths to engage in remote seasonal raids on the Frankish Atlantic coast, where they sailed up the main rivers and plundered towns and monasteries.

From sea to sea and age to age, there are common patterns and similar episodes that are at once picturesque, violent, and sordid. Pirate operations were usually limited in time and scale. Ruse and swiftness were of essence. Small crafts operating near the coasts would strike at a merchant ship carrying valuable cargo and affluent passengers when it was in a vulnerable position. In the age of sail, this meant being engaged while in a narrow strait, hugging a treacherous promontory, facing contrary winds or momentarily becalmed. Pirates would also land in order to raid commercial fairs and places of pilgrimage that, at certain times of the year, attracted wealth, or, short of a better prey, they attacked isolated and defenseless coastal communities. They used limited capabilities in situations that gave them temporary advantage. They also needed land bases, to which they could retreat, dispose of their cargoes, and initiate contacts to obtain ransoms. As a result, they often had duplicitous relationships with local populations—extorting or terrorizing them at one moment, while playing Robin Hood at another.

Pirates belonged to the microcosmos of working men at sea: poor, illiterate, often press-ganged, working in precarious and exploitative conditions. Their narratives and statements in court give insights into rough all-male communities that have been the subject of romantic fiction in many places since antiquity. They have appeared, at times, as social rebels, a rudimentary notion of equality inferred from their loose chain of command and practice of dividing their bounty among their number. At the same time, with their verbal excesses and eccentricity in dress, by living it up and spending it all, they frequently exhibited self-delusion, an exaggerated sense of freedom, and plain psychopathic cruelty. ("I am a free prince, and I have much authority to make war on the whole world," says Captain Avery, a legendary figure in one of the best-known early-eighteenth-century pirates' narratives.) By rejecting social rules, pirates stood implicitly against ordered (and bigendered) communities.

Historically, the antisocial character of the pirate provided the basis for the legal framework used to repress him. Roman law defined the pirate as *hostis humani generis* and his offense as an attack on the law of nations (*jus gentium*). Rome wielded this notion of universal justice against pirates in achieving naval supremacy in the Mediterranean in the two first centuries CE. It justified an empire in policing its boundaries and was accepted by conquered territories as a benefit of the Pax Romana. After the disintegration of the Roman Empire, independent port cities of the western Mediterranean as well as the Byzantine Empire in the eastern Mediterranean retained the Roman law on piracy. In practice, these cities seem to have relied more often on networks of correspondence and watchtowers (evidence of both have been preserved) to ward off Catalan, Saracen (Moorish), Pisan, and Genoese pirates. In the twelfth century, in a context of political fragmentation that made policing the sea impossible, piracy appeared with the commercial expansion of Baltic and northern merchant cities and of English and French ports. Breton, Norman, Welsh, and Cornish pirates—lacking the rich export merchandise of a Bordeaux or a Plymouth— threatened regular traffic between main ports.

While piracy continued to be framed by Roman law, its practice received a new impetus from privateering, which had its origins in the Western medieval practice of private war. Feudal political organization recognized the customary right of local authorities to act against the indiscriminate taking of property, as well as plundering and kidnapping on the sea. Established sovereigns issued licenses to privately owned and armed ships to attack vessels that had robbed them and to capture their goods in reprisal. Privateering (or *corse*, a medieval word for a military campaign of plundering) developed on a large scale in the Mediterranean between 1450 and 1550. Venice lost its primacy to Spanish, French, and Italian ports as the Ottomans conquered the whole eastern and southern Mediterranean from Istanbul to Morocco (i.e., the former Byzantine Empire and the Arab-speaking regions, albeit with only nominal rule in parts of the latter). On all sides, for centuries, fleets of specialized attack ships were outfitted by local merchants and licensed by the local political authority to venture on the high seas. In the Turkish sphere, the most active were the so-called Barbary corsairs of Tripoli, Tunis, and Algiers; among Christians, there were religious and military orders such as the Knights Hospitable of Malta or the Knights of Saint Stephen, operating from Pisa. The enemy was the pirate, but he was also, conveniently, the "other" in religious terms, in conflict pitting Christians against Muslims and Protestants against Catholics.

Between 1500 and 1700, port communities sponsored thousands of adventurous merchants and explorers who sailed out into the Atlantic in pursuit of new routes, commercial goods, and riches. The patterns of European piracy spread to remote seas, from the Caribbean, North America, and the Pacific, to South Africa, Madagascar, and the Gulf of Bengal. The English, French, and Dutch captains who, like John Hawkins in the 1560s to 1590s, undertook these "privateering voyages" to the Spanish Main were overwhelmingly Protestant. To the Spaniards, they were pirates, defying empires on their margins and breaking into established circuits. The Dutch privateers sponsored by the West Indies Company (founded in 1621) which defended entrepôt trade against the Iberian monopoly, were similarly regarded by the Spaniards. Accusatory semantics—later deconstructed by the historiography of a postcolonial age—were the rule as long as an empire lasted: a challenged metropolis insisted on the legitimacy of its power by labeling rebel colonists as pirates. During the Revolutionary era (1770–1820), the English considered North American insurgents attacking metropolitan commerce to be pirates, as did the Spaniards the *corsarios insurgentes* operating under the flags of newly proclaimed Colombian and Rioplatense republics.

In the seventeenth century, western Europe states, newly expanding mercantilists, asserted their growing power by curbing piracy among their own subjects. It was part of their efforts to control shipping lanes, establish trading companies, and organize merchant fleets. The freelance entrepreneurs who in the previous century helped open new trading routes and found colonies were tracked down as pirates by the English and French mercantilist states, which granted privileges to wealthy merchants of their main ports to attract them into their orbit. Campaigns to suppress piracy—the terms in themselves denote wellorchestrated political operations—led to the punishment of a few (like the notorious Captain Kidd, tried and hanged in London, 1701) and the pardoning of many more. To "cleanse the sea" and then grant pirates pardon appears to have been the usual policy against them, as for example, in the Low Countries, whose North Sea fishing fleet suffered from assaults of Norman and Scottish pirates during the sixteenth century.

At the same time, piracy was kept alive by the hegemonic aspirations of merchant empires, which brought European states into continuous confrontations at sea. After 1650, England and France, which could not afford standing navies, regularly licensed privateers to fight each other. Privateering proved to be "a nursery for pyrates against the peace," as Defoe put it. War had the effect of liberating the American colonies from the domination of metropolitan merchants, establishing a de facto freedom of trade that went hand in hand with privateering. As long as monopolies

PIRATES. Off the coast of the Riau Islands, South China Sea, 1998. (© Mike Yamashita/Woodfin Camp and Associates, New York)

went along with commercial wars, piracy simply fluctuated according to the degree of a state's authority at sea. Piracy periodically surfaced in the faraway regions of empires, a sign of their chronic difficulties in policing the sea.

When a state attempted to impose a new stringent policy, it could upset the delicate balance between central authority and local tolerance, disturbing the existing arrangements between coastal traders and the local population that had developed. Interlopers could then become aggressive and turn into pirates. In the eighteenth century, endemic Caribbean smuggling made up for the undersupply and exorbitant prices imposed by the main metropolitan ports. When this grew into a full-blown contraband trade, Spain acted on the warranties of the Treaty of Utrecht (1713) to establish naval patrols and special fleets of corsairs, in a vain attempt to curb such trade. Smugglers whose business was disturbed resisted with arms and resorted to forced exchange or extortion, that is, to piracy.

Piracy reappeared where political authority collapsed altogether and created a vacuum. In the Caribbean of the 1820s, for instance, contemporaries spoke of "anarchy on the seas." The "Black Republic" of Haiti, which had won its independence from France militarily in 1804 but was not recognized until 1825, was submitted to a blockade by the main powers. Its coastal traders turned into pirates to supply the country. After 1814, Spanish colonial authorities made Cuba the center of royalist counterinsurgency. They recruited privateers but soon proved unable to equip and control them. These corsairs then continued to operate on

their own. They found convenient bases in officially neutral entrepôts, such as the nearby Dutch colony of Saint Thomas, and their prizes were particularly welcome in the chronically undersupplied Cuban region of Oriente. This regional dynamic was to have long-standing consequences. It was the presence of European navies in Caribbean waters, putatively to curb Cuban piracy, that led the United States to proclaim the Monroe Doctrine (1823).

The patterns of piracy observable in the Atlantic world from the Middle Ages to the nineteenth century have parallels on other seas, among Asian peoples or between Asians and Europeans. During the thirteenth century, East Asia provides a clear case of how the intrusion by pirates into an established trading network led to the creation of a new one. The *wāko* (meaning "Japanese bandits") spread along Korean and then Chinese coasts, challenging the Ming rulers and beginning a remarkable Japanese expansion toward mainland Asia that brought them eventually to Java and Manila. During this process, the efforts of the Ming dynasty demonstrate how piracy fluctuated in response to the degree of a state's authority at sea. Between the fourteenth and seventeenth centuries, rulers sought repeatedly to impose strict controls over the dynasty's international trade. This threatened the activities of the Japanese merchants that had penetrated the Chinese coasts along with their Chinese partners. The conflict came to a climax when defensive Japanese raids against a ruinous state policy of a declining imperial power led to a rash of kidnappings and plundering from the coast of Cheking in the north to

Fukien in the south. At the beginning of the nineteenth century, the Chinese Ching dynasty faced a confederation of several thousand pirates along the South China coast and, following a practice seen in the Atlantic world, ended the conflict by pardoning them.

The case of Indonesia illustrates how piracy provided a mechanism for shifts in political control and commercial hegemony. Aggressive seafarers were at the origin of the Malay sultanates established in Indonesia, along with the country's Islamization in the fifteenth century, as it became part of the Islamic trading network that stretched from the coast of East Africa to the China Sea. European intrusion and naval control shifted this regional dynamic. After 1840, when the British displaced Dutch commercial hegemony, they restrained Malay seafarers, who remained pirates instead of becoming possible founders of a maritime state. In the Indian Ocean, the Malabar sailors who defended the southern coasts of India for the Mughal emperor in the sixteenth century were treated as pirates by the Portuguese, who claimed a commercial monopoly in that sea. This pattern emerges again with the second European imperialist expansion during the nineteenth century. For example, the Qawasim, seafarers from a commercial emirate, refused to cede to English control over the entry to the Persian Gulf.

A major change occurred in the history of piracy when a declaration "on maritime law in time of war," signed in 1856 by the former belligerents of the Crimean War, abolished privateering. Having established standing navies to project their power more effectively, the main Western states sought to remove the legal basis for putting war and trade in the same hands, a practice that had helped keep piracy alive. The legal reason given—"that maritime law in time of war [had] long been [uncertain] and the subject of deplorable disputes"—succinctly recognized an old reality: accusations of piracy and actions against it were essentially a legal rationalization of political goals. Political authorities employed the concept to justify establishing or retaining exclusive control over maritime routes or sources of commodities and to dispute the legitimacy of similar claims and actions by others. In so doing, they attempted to project law into a space—the sea—between states.

Because of the limits of documentation, the economic significance of piracy has proven difficult to assess historically. The records of local authorities that licensed privateers and taxed their sales allow some quantitative estimates of the damages inflicted by commercial warfare at sea to individual ports and the limited duration of privateering licenses. The Spanish corsairs in Dunkirk (1629–1638) during the Thirty Years' War and those of Guadeloupe (French Antilles) during the Revolutionary wars (1793–1801) seem to have been the most efficient of their times. Privateering also seems to have made positive contributions to maritime economies in wartime, under conditions that gave legal cover to port cities returning to a predatory form of trade. During the sixteenth and the seventeenth centuries, when corsairs were active on all sides, the vitality of the Mediterranean trade strongly suggests privateering helped attract investments and create jobs, stimulate shipbuilding and the production of provisions and naval equipment, supply local markets, put cash in circulation, and ensure revenues to local authorities. Although the English Lloyd's Company (established in the late seventeenth century) insured Indiamen from European ports, these ships were only a fraction of maritime traffic overseas and were unlikely prey for most of the privateers. On the whole, data provided by insurance records are not a good source for the age of piracy.

In the words of seventeenth-century essayist Daniel Defoe, "The pirate destroys all government and all order, by breaking all those ties and bonds that unite people in a civil society under any government." In the nineteenth century, these traits—defiance of established power, contempt for human life and property—led to the application of the concept of "piracy" in the publishing world; and in the twentieth century, it was extended to the air and then to cyberspace. However, there is still no authoritative definition of piracy within the rule of law. Humanity, against whom pirates are said to be acting, is not a wielder of law—states are—and there is no supranational entity with coercive authority to enforce the law against offenders. The consensus in international law (the various conventions that bind states to a limited degree) is to restrict acts qualifying as piracy to the sphere of private law—outside the normal jurisdiction of a state—without state authority and with private, not political, intent. This leaves out most of what has been significant in the long history of piracy: in the nexus of commercial and political aspirations that characterized the phenomenon, what was legally considered piracy depended on the authority that made the law in the first place.

BIBLIOGRAPHY

Al-Qasimi, Sultan Muhammad. *The Myth of Arab Piracy*. London, 1986.

Andrews, Kenneth R. *Trade, Plunder, and Settlement: Maritime Enterprises and the Genesis of the British Empire, 1480–1630*. New York, 1984.

Defoe, Daniel. *A General History of the Robberies and Murders of the Most Notorious Pyrates*. London, 1724; reprint, New York, 1972.

Gray, Todd. "Turkish Piracy and Early Stuart Devon." *Reports of the Transactions of the Devonshire Association for the Advancement of Science* 121 (1989), 151–179.

Gungwu, Wang. "Merchant without Empires: The Hokkien Sojourning Communities." In *The Political Economy of Merchant Empires*, edited by James D. Tracy, pp. 400–421. Cambridge, 1991.

Hughson, Shirley Carter. *The Carolina Pirates and Colonial Commerce, 1670–1740*. Baltimore, 1894; reprint, New York, 1973.

Julien, Charles-André. *Les Français en Amérique pendant la première moité du XVIe siècle.* Paris, 1946.

Lombard, Denys, and Jean Aubin, eds. *Marchands et hommes d'affaires asiatiques dans l'Océan Indien et la mer de Chine, 13e-20e siècles.* Paris, 1988.

Mathew, David. "The Cornish and Welsh Pirates in the Reign of Elizabeth." *English Historical Review* 39 (1924), 337–348.

Murray, Diane. *Pirates of the South China Coast, 1790–1810.* Stanford, Calif., 1987.

Ogelsby, J. C. M. "Spain's Havana Squadron and the Preservation of the Balance of Power in the Caribbean, 1740–1748." *Hispanic American Historical Review* 49 (1969), 473–488.

Ormerod, Henry A. *Piracy in the Ancient World.* Liverpool, U.K., 1924; reprint, New York, 1987.

Pearson, M. N. *Merchants and Rulers in Gujarat: The Response to the Portuguese in the Sixteenth Century.* Berkeley, 1976.

Pennell, Richard C., ed. *Bandits at Sea: A Pirates Reader.* New York, 2001.

Pérotin-Dumon, Anne. "The Pirate and the Emperor: Power and the Law on the Seas, 1450–1850." In *The Political Economy of Merchant Empires,* edited by James D. Tracy, pp. 196–227. Cambridge, 1991.

Rediker, Marcus. *Between the Devil and the Deep Blue Sea: Merchant Seamen, Pirates, and the Anglo-Maritime World, 1700–1750.* New York, 1987.

Ritchie, Robert C. *Captain Kidd and the War against the Pirates.* Cambridge, Mass., 1986.

Rumeu de Armas, Antonio. *Piraterías y ataques navales contra las islas Canarias.* Madrid, 1946–1950.

Tarling, Nicholas. *Piracy and Politics in the Malay World: A Study in British Imperialism in Nineteenth-Century South-East Asia.* Melbourne, 1963.

Tenenti, Alberto. *Piracy and the Decline of Venice, 1580–1615.* Berkeley and Los Angeles, 1967.

ANNE PÉROTIN-DUMON

PIRENNE, HENRI (1862–1935), Belgian historian, professor at the University of Ghent (1886–1930).

Pirenne's scholarly work, including important editions of texts, established the study of economic history in Belgium, but his career also had a more public aspect. He saw the modern Belgian state as the natural result of historical evolution rather than, as some Flemish nationalists argued, an artificial creation that subordinated Flanders to French speakers. His *Histoire de Belgique* (7 vols., Brussels, 1899–1932) traced the history of the principalities that eventually comprised Belgium from their medieval beginnings through 1914. The work was a great popular success that contributed to the growth of a Belgian national consciousness. Pirenne's internment in Germany during World War I became a *cause célèbre* that heightened his public visibility. Most of his postwar works were interpretive syntheses, notably his *Economic and Social History of Medieval Europe* (English translation, London, 1936, originally a chapter in Gustave Glotz's *Histoire Générale,* Paris, 1933).

Although Pirenne published important studies of the rural economy, he is best known for his work on medieval towns. In *Belgian Democracy: Its Early History* (Manchester, 1915, originally *Les anciennes démocraties des Pays-Bas,* Paris, 1910), he traced urbanization in the Low Countries through the seventeenth century. Pirenne also generalized from the Flemish example to broader theories of comparative urbanization. In *Medieval Cities: Their Origins and the Revival of Trade* (Princeton, 1925), based on a series of lectures given in the United States, Pirenne formulated the "mercantile settlement" theory of urban origins, according to which the towns developed in response to economic rather than political or institutional forces. More pointedly in the posthumously published *Mohammed and Charlemagne* (London, 1939, originally *Mahomet et Charlemagne,* Brussels, 1937), Pirenne argued that urban life in northern Europe ended when the Muslims ended commercial shipping in the Mediterranean in the seventh and the eighth centuries, a view known still as the "Pirenne thesis." He thus saw a sharp economic contrast between the Merovingian and Carolingian periods. Recent work has shown that the volume of trade in luxury goods diminished more than Pirenne thought between the fourth and the sixth centuries and did not end in the seventh, but his view that the Germanic migrations did not end commercial activity has been sustained.

Pirenne thus saw the European cities as creations of long-distance trade that was reborn in the late tenth and the eleventh centuries. He argued that city and village were different in kind and thus rejected the notion that towns evolved from the trading functions of agrarian settlements, a view rejected by historians today. He considered itinerant merchants, not natives of the locality, to be responsible for the revival of trade. They eventually settled in suburbs outside a castle or another structure, which provided protection but fulfilled no economic role except demand for goods traded by the merchants who lived in the suburbs. The towns were thus binuclear, dominated by a new class, the bourgeoisie, which derived its income from trade and industry and thus seriously weakened the control of statecraft and production by the church and the nobility. The radical opposition of interests of suburb and fortification eventually caused the townspeople to become independent of the lords of the fortification, developing their own law and institutions. Pirenne saw capitalism originating in the Middle Ages as a generally positive force for freedom in a feudal world. Pirenne's theses of urban origins and evolution, although modified in detail, have continued to provide a basic structure around which debate has centered.

BIBLIOGRAPHY

Havighurst, Alfred, ed. *The Pirenne Thesis: Analysis, Criticism, and Revision.* 3d ed. Lexington, Mass., 1976.

Hodges, Richard. *Dark Age Economics: The Origins of Towns and Trade, A.D. 600–1000.* New York, 1982.

Hodges, Richard. *Mohammed, Charlemagne and the Origins of Europe: Archaeology and the Pirenne Thesis.* Ithaca, N.Y., 1983.

Lyon, Bryce. *Henri Pirenne: A Biographical and Intellectual Study.* Ghent, 1974.

Verhulst, Adriaan. "The Origins of Towns in the Low Countries and the Pirenne Thesis." *Past and Present* 122 (1989), 1–35.

DAVID M. NICHOLAS

PLANTATION SYSTEM. The central components of plantation agriculture are the concentration of the factors of production (land, labor, and capital) in the hands of a small social and political elite, which in many places is considered to have constituted a planter class. The main features included access to land, usually on a large scale, the production of staple crops for external markets and otherwise for redistribution beyond the confines of the individual agricultural units, and the use of coercion, often through slavery, as the principal means of obtaining labor. In most plantation systems, the domestic market for wage labor was either absent or peripheral to the organization of labor, with one result being the highly uneven distribution of income. Hence the control of land was skewed in favor of a relatively few large-scale entrepreneurs, aristocracy, state officials, religious orders, and others who dominated politics and society, while agricultural production was highly labor intensive. The use of slave labor is often important in plantation systems, yet the distinguishing characteristics emphasize the tendency toward monoculture and production for markets, whether international or regional; the control of land, often as private property; and relatively low technological investment relating to the labor intensity of production. Although plantations were often oriented toward external, specialized markets, the needs of local markets also had to be satisfied, which was often achieved through secondary production on small farms on the estates.

The existence or absence of plantations is a controversial topic that is in part a problem of definition. If *plantation* is used to refer to large-scale agriculture employing slave or other forms of coerced labor and even wage labor under some conditions, then it is a general term that applies to most large estates. In most plantation systems, work was organized in gangs, and this was true in many situations in Africa and elsewhere, not just in the Americas. Such organization depended upon the existence of individuals who had access to land and labor or who commanded the capital that could acquire these factors. The term distinguishes the cultivation of land in large aggregates from small-scale farming by peasants. In fact there were numerous small and middle-sized estates, so agricultural production usually fell on a continuum from large estates to small farms. The specialization involved in plantation production could involve outputs that more than fed the slave producers and required a distributional system for agricultural surplus, either through the market mechanism or some comparable means of redistribution. These characteristics of large-scale agricultural production make the adoption of *plantation* as a descriptive term appropriate for many parts of the world, not just the Americas.

Plantation systems have existed in many places historically, particularly wherever slavery was common. Indeed there is a high correlation between the incidence of slavery and the use of slave labor in production on agricultural lands, whether in classical Rome, the medieval empires of the western Sudan, the Caribbean, or the southern United States. The characteristics of these different systems depended upon the nature of local and international markets, the types of crops being grown, and the ideological and political setting. The plantations of the French and British Empires tended to be more capitalist and entrepreneurial, while those in Portuguese and Spanish spheres tended to be more patriarchal, as was also the case in Muslim areas of West Africa. Conditions varied again in Southeast Asia, where plantations were operated by European chartered companies. However, there was great variation in the terms and conditions of work, depending upon whether plantation systems were expanding or stagnant, usually related to international politics and the economy. Technological change was often retarded because of the reliance on slave and other forms of compulsory labor. Nonetheless there were important technological advances in the production of some crops, such as the sugar mill and cotton ginning, that facilitated the expansion of plantation production.

Large-scale agricultural estates that can be called plantations have existed since antiquity, hence an important distinction should be made between classical and modern forms of estate production. In the modern period plantations were most highly developed as a system in the Americas, where the use of enslaved labor transported across the Atlantic from western Africa was an essential feature of the system. The combination of productive factors was unique, drawing on available land in the Americas, sources of labor principally from Africa, and capital largely from western Europe and developing into a global system of production and trade. The plantation systems of the Americas were especially tied to international markets from their inception and were highly dependent on these markets in the eighteenth and nineteenth centuries. However, plantation systems also developed to satisfy regional markets, such as the market in grain and cotton along the desert edge of West Africa or, in the case of clove production in East Africa in the nineteenth century, largely for markets in the Middle East and India.

Americas. This transatlantic system of plantation agriculture traces its origins to the Mediterranean and especially to the spread of sugar production. Sugar was transferred from the Iberian countries to various islands off the African coast, especially São Tomé, but not the African mainland itself. Instead, sugar jumped the Atlantic and became the staple crop in northeastern Brazil and on the islands of the Caribbean in the European colonies of England, France, the Netherlands, Spain, Portugal, and Denmark. Sugar rapidly depleted the agricultural productiveness of land, hence expansion in production required access to new land, which spread the crop throughout the Caribbean and to Pernamabuco and Bahia in Brazil. Sugar lent itself to a plantation regime because of the intense labor required in harvesting and the need to boil the cane immediately after it was cut to avoid the rapid loss of sugar content. Subsidiary industries, especially the production of molasses and rum, were by-products of sugar output. Moreover the need for livestock to run the mills and move cane promoted the development of subsidiary activities to service estates. Planters experimented with other crops besides sugar, and depending upon terrain, rice, indigo, tobacco, and other crops also were grown.

The expansion of the plantation system was a moving frontier, from early beginnings in Hispaniola and Pernambuco, to Bahia, to Barbados by the middle of the seventeenth century, and from there to other small islands in the Caribbean that were controlled by the English, French, and Dutch. The major expansion in sugar occurred in the eighteenth century, especially in the French colony of Saint Domingue and in English Jamaica, with the smaller islands of Martinique, Guadeloupe, Barbados, and Antigua also important. The revolution in Saint Domingue in the 1790s and the establishment of independent Haiti destroyed the plantation economy there, and British withdrawal from the slave trade after 1807 altered the nature of the labor supply in the British sphere. In the nineteenth century sugar production expanded considerably in Cuba, where the massive importation of enslaved Africans and the introduction of railroads and steam-powered sugar mills enabled the expansion. This broad pattern of expansion reveals two important features of plantation systems. First, plantations tended to be founded on frontiers where land was plentiful, and second, changing technology had an important impact on expansion, both through more efficient ways of moving enslaved labor across the Atlantic and in the introduction of industrial methods such as in Cuba. Despite technological investment, compulsory labor was still common on the agricultural frontier, where new estates were established.

One important feature of plantation systems was the relative degree to which the owners of estates were absent and often lived far from their domains. Although many small and medium-sized planters lived in residence, the largest plantations were often run by agents and overseers who were employed by the owners, who either lived in Europe or who owned more than one estate and only visited individual properties as required. The level of absenteeism varied, however, with owners more likely to live on their estates in Brazil than in some parts of the Caribbean. Plantation ownership involved an extensive reliance on credit, both in the purchase of enslaved Africans and in the sale of crops, so patterns in land control were characterized not only by problems of absentee landowners but also by the transfer of holdings through bankruptcy, the division of estates through inheritance, and the acquisition of more than one estate by large proprietors. Moreover there was a close relationship between land grants and political patronage. In colonial Brazil and in the Spanish colonies, land was often given at the benevolence of the state, obtained through inheritance, and hence was less likely to be obtained through purchase.

Although sugar was the dominant crop of the plantation in America, there were other staples that were grown under plantation conditions. These other crops included indigo, tobacco, rice, and increasingly tree crops, especially coffee but eventually also bananas and other fruit. In the nineteenth century cotton became particularly important in the United States. There was a strong correlation between the harshness of the slavery regime and the type of crop that was produced. Tobacco had to be treated carefully, while sugar had to be processed fast. Moreover it should be noted that there was always a subsidiary-economy to the plantation sector, and plantation systems were in fact diversified, with some reliance on secondary production, including crafts and other crops for local consumption.

The expansion of the plantation system in North America and the movement of the plantation frontier into the Mississippi Valley and Texas requires special comment. The emergence of cotton as the principal plantation crop in the United States occurred after the termination of the transatlantic slave trade in 1807, and plantation development relied on internal sources of enslaved labor among the population already in North America. Not only the type of crop but also the availability of labor determined the structure of the plantation system. The system in the United States was capital intensive, requiring heavy investment in land as well as labor. Although cotton was the main cash crop, plantations usually rotated crops, also growing grain, indigo, legumes, and other commodities, and planters sometimes practiced intercropping.

The plantation systems of tropical America varied considerably in terms of the size of plantation holdings and the diversity of the local economy. In most places smallholders established niches in the production of subsidiary products and services. Many of these individuals were born locally and developed what came to be known as "creole" societies, forming the basis of more diverse economies, despite the dominance of large plantations.

The organization of plantations underwent dramatic change at the time slaves were emancipated. Many estates declined, shifted to livestock production, and otherwise attempted to sustain viability through sharecropping and tenant farming arrangements with the formerly servile population. The decline in sugar production in the Caribbean in the postemancipation period is striking. Alternate forms of labor, including indentured labor from India, were tried but with only marginal success. New plantations did emerge, however, for the production of tropical fruit, especially bananas but also pineapples, and this production depended upon the immigration of contract labor, including migrant labor within the circum-Caribbean. In the United States sharecropping and tenant-farming arrangements predominated after the Civil War, and thereafter large-scale agriculture increasingly relied on technology-intensive production, avoiding a reliance on cheap labor.

Africa. Although the trend in plantation development produced the movement of labor from Africa to the Americas to till land available there, there were related developments on the African shores of this Atlantic world, and a significant proportion of the enslaved workers taken to the Americas worked in urban settings, on smallholdings, and in mines and were not subjected to the plantation regime. Moreover some plantations were established in Africa and were related to the transatlantic plantation system, especially in Angola and in scattered places elsewhere. Finally, the demand for new agricultural products, especially palm oil and palm kernels, led to the development of an indigenous plantation sector in some parts of West Africa in the nineteenth century. The introduction of various tree crops, including coffee, cocoa, rubber, and kola, at the end of the nineteenth century resulted in the great increase in these estates, especially in southern Nigeria, Ghana, and Ivory Coast. The use of slaves and pawns on these estates suggests a reliance on compulsory labor that is comparable to other plantation systems.

Plantations involving slave labor should not be considered a unique characteristic of slavery in the Americas. In fact large-scale agriculture, involving proprietary rights over land and the use of enslaved populations or other forms of compulsory labor, were common in Africa. Such large-scale agricultural estates, often using slavery and sometimes corvée labor, were common in the western and central Sudan, at least since the medieval empires of Songhay and Kanem-Borno dominated this region. Sometimes referred to as slave "villages," these estates ranged in size from a few score to hundreds and even thousands of people. Slaves often worked in the main fields in gangs under overseers, in patterns that were comparable to the organization of labor on plantations in the Americas in the same period. It should be noted that plantations in the Islamic regions of western Africa, particularly in the Sokoto Caliphate and other Muslim states in the nineteenth century, emerged in parallel with the evolution of slavery in the Americas, although this Islamic tradition of plantation organization reflects developments that were largely independent of the transatlantic slave trade.

Plantation production in the Islamic regions of the western and central Sudan was similar to that in the Americas with respect to the amount of land under cultivation and the concentration of land in units that could be worked on a large scale. As in the Americas, plantations were far from uniform. Muslim-owned plantations were sometimes small and compact, but others consisted of dispersed holdings, where slaves moved among fields that could be some distance apart. Overseers were often trusted slaves or former slaves; some masters resided on their estates for only a portion of the year if at all. Punishment for failure to work adequately or for other reasons was often whipping, exposure to the sun, and in extreme cases sale.

The crops grown on plantations in the western and central Sudan included grain, particularly bulrush millet and sorghum, cotton, tobacco, and indigo. The concentration of agricultural production in the rainy season left slaves who had been settled on estates for some time to work on their own account during the long dry season, paying regular amounts of money to their masters in the local currency, cowries in the Sokoto Caliphate and cloth strips in the far western Sudan. Some slaves engaged in irrigated farming on lowlands or worked in long-distance trade. Slaves often had access to separate plots of land for their own use, as was also common in many parts of the Americas. While these practices varied widely in the Islamic regions of western Africa, the installation of Muslim governments generally encouraged the spread of practices that incorporated slaves into society.

There were three types of plantations in the Muslim states of Africa. First, there were those belonging to aristocratic families, often deriving from land grants made at the time of the initial holy war, or jihad, that led to the founding of the state. The jihad leadership wrote numerous books and treatises on land tenure. As Islamic law was interpreted, land was distributed among the victorious Muslims. Second, there were smaller plantations developed by merchants and other wealthy commoners, many of whom were immigrants, officials awarded land as an inducement to settle in return for annual homage and political support. These land grants often came with some form of tax exemption. Third, there were official estates, administered by royal slaves, that belonged to the government. Slaves on these royal estates technically belonged to the emirs and other officials and could not be sold. Slave girls from all types of plantations were selected for concubinage, however, and strong boys were pressed into the military or administrative service.

Plantations were a central feature of Islamic countries in the western and central Sudan. State policy promoted demographic consolidation and expansion through the enslavement of independent or rebellious communities. Annual raiding and jihad thereby generated a steady stream of the newly enslaved or reenslaved. Plantation development depended upon this influx of slaves. In connection with this military policy as it was implemented in the Sokoto Caliphate and other Muslim states, frontier garrisons were settled at fortified towns that became the nuclei of agricultural and craft production. Land grants and favorable taxation were then implemented to encourage nomadic cattle herders to settle down. They were enticed further by the prospect of exploiting slave labor recruited through annual military campaigns into areas not subjugated or against communities considered to be in arrears in tax payments. Frontier settlements thereby became centers of slave-based agricultural production.

The similarities and differences that characterize plantation slavery in different places and different times suggest that plantations should be viewed comparatively, although care must be taken not to force the different experiences into an unwarranted connection with the legacy of slavery in the Americas. Plantation development also occurred along the East African coast in the nineteenth century, for example. There, immigrant Arabs from Oman and local Swahili invested heavily in slaves to grow cloves, coconuts, grain, and other goods for export. The most important plantation centers were on the islands of Zanzibar and Pemba and along the mainland coast, especially around Malindi and Mombasa. Although slaves worked in a regimented fashion characteristic of other plantation systems, various Islamic practices tempered the institution and thereby helped provide a distinctive feature to this plantation system. These practices included extensive concubinage, the use of slaves in the military, emancipation of slaves according to Muslim custom, and the propagation of Islam among slaves. In short, despite the pull of market forces in the Indian Ocean, the institution of slavery and therefore the plantation system developed their own characteristics. Plantations were also established on Mauritius and Bourbon as well as other islands in the Indian Ocean along lines that were similar to the Caribbean colonies. Plantations were also established in Malaysia and Indonesia.

Methods of plantation management varied, and in some cases slaves lived in what appeared to outsiders as villages under headmen or overseers, who supervised agricultural production for the slave owner. Farming was done on a common field for the master, but slaves often had access to small garden plots, and there were specifically designated times when slaves could work on their own. Except for the output of slave gardens, masters controlled the distribution of crops, which were either sold or used within their households. Tree crops, such as kola nuts and shea nuts, were gathered. As in other places absenteeism was common on the big plantations that belonged to the aristocracy and wealthier merchants. Some estates were attached to political positions, which could mean that influential slave officials benefited from plantation output. Many other plantations were quite small, however, and masters and their families often worked in the fields alongside their slaves.

Despite similarities with plantation agriculture in the Americas and elsewhere, plantations in the Muslim states of West Africa had many distinctive features. Slavery as an institution was different. Plantation slaves should be considered as occupying one end of a continuum of servile relationships that dominated Muslim society. Although plantation slaves were often worse off than those in the households of small producers, craftspeople, livestock herders, and others, the lack of a racial barrier and the different socioreligious heritages of the Islamic state were important mediating influences. Cultural and physical distinctions were exploited to establish a line between slave and free, and facial and body markings were used as identification. Color, however, was relatively unimportant. The ideological framework diverged from patterns found in the Americas, too. Emancipation was not only possible but was encouraged. Although plantation slaves probably benefited from Islamic codes less than other sections of the slave population, deathbed grants and self-purchase still held out the possibility of freedom for many slaves.

Market forces in the Islamic savanna of West Africa were of a regional rather than a worldwide nature, unlike those in the plantation areas of the Americas and East Africa. Slaves were as likely to be obtained through raids and warfare and redistributed among the aristocracy as purchased on the open market. These tributary and raiding relationships contrast sharply with those in the Americas, where slaves were only obtained through the market. The distribution of plantation crops was also less developed in West Africa than in either the Americas, East Africa, or Southeast Asia in large part because of constraints in transport that prevented integration with the world market. Instead, the plantation sector was oriented toward a regional economy that acted as a focal point for economic development within West Africa as a whole. In contrast, American and East African plantations were appended to the European and Indian Ocean economies, and these plantation sectors catered to overseas demand and not to local or regional markets.

BIBLIOGRAPHY

Cooper, Frederick. *Plantation Slavery on the East Coast of Africa.* New Haven, 1977.

Curtin, Philip D. *The Rise and Fall of the Plantation Complex: Essays in Atlantic History.* 2d ed. New York, 1997.

Dunn, Richard. *Sugar and Slave: The Rise of the Planter Class in the English West Indies, 1624–1713.* New York, 1973.

Genovese, Eugene D. *The Political Economy of Slavery.* New York, 1965.

Greaves, Ida C. "Plantations in World Economy." In *Plantation Systems of the New World,* edited by Vera Rubin et al., pp. 13–23. Washington, D.C., 1959.

Greenfield, Sidney. "Slavery and the Plantation in the New World." *Journal of Inter-American Studies* 11 (1969), 44–57.

Knight, Franklin W. *Slave Society in Cuba during the Nineteenth Century.* Madison, Wis., 1970.

Lombardi, John V. "Comparative Slave Systems in the Americas: A Critical Review." In *New Approaches to Latin American History,* edited by Richard Graham and Peter H. Smith, pp. 156–174. Austin, 1974.

Lovejoy, Paul E. "Plantations in the Economy of the Sokoto Caliphate." *Journal of African History* 19.3 (1978), 341–368.

Lovejoy, Paul E. *Transformations in Slavery: A History of Slavery in Africa.* 2d ed. Cambridge, 2000.

Malowist, Marion. "Les débuts du système de plantations dans la période des grandes découvertes." *Africana Bulletin* 10 (1969), 9–18.

Mandle, Jay R. "The Plantation Economy: An Essay in Definition." *Science and Society* 36 (1972), 49–62 .

Meillassoux, Claude, ed. *L'esclavage en Afrique précoloniale.* Paris, 1975.

Mintz, Sidney. "The Plantation as a Socio-Cultural Type." In *Plantation Systems of the New World,* edited by Vera Rubin et al., pp. 42–59. Washington, D.C., 1959.

Phillips, U. B. *American Negro Slavery: A Survey of the Supply, Employment, and Control of Negro Labor as Determined by the Plantation Regime.* Baton Rouge, La., 1966.

Rubin, Vera, and Arthur Tuden, eds. *Comparative Perspectives on Slavery in New World Plantation Societies.* New York Academy of Sciences, no. 292. New York, 1977.

Schwartz, Stuart. *Sugar Plantations in the Formation of Brazilian Society: Bahia, 1550–1835.* Cambridge, 1985.

Steward, Julian. "Perspectives on Plantations." In *Plantation Systems of the New World,* edited by Vera Rubin et al., pp. 5–12. Washington, D.C., 1959.

Wagley, Charles. "Plantation America: A Culture Sphere." In *Caribbean Studies: A Symposium,* edited by Vera Rubin, pp. 3–13. Seattle, 1957.

Wolf, Eric R., and Sidney Mintz. "Haciendas and Plantations in Middle America and the Antilles." *Social and Economic Studies* 6 (1957), 380–412.

PAUL LOVEJOY

POLAND *[This entry contains three subentries, on the economic history of Poland during the early and medieval periods, early modern period, and modern period.]*

Early and Medieval Periods

The first chronicler of Polish history, Gallus Anonymous, in the early twelfth century, contended that Poland was barely known to the rest of Europe, because it was situated apart from the main routes that Christian pilgrims followed, so that only a few merchants passed through it. This observation would have been even more appropriate for the preceding centuries, when there had been little incentive for exchange between the various Slavic groups, who differed little in their lifeways and material culture. From the ninth century onward, however, some economic stimuli had come into Poland from the periphery, transmitted by a transit trade that provided regional rulers with the means to maintain strongly armed retinues (Pol., *drużiny*) silver coins from the Muslim world, as well as weapons and luxury goods. Consequently, Mieszko the Old (c. 960–992 CE), ruling over Great Poland, strove to gain access to the Baltic Sea and to the transcontinental trade routes in Silesia and Little Poland. Some commerce began to develop from tribute and taxes paid in food (chiefly grain) and products from the forest lands (honey, wax, furs); but the most lucrative of all was the slave trade, whose supply depended on military hostages. The end of Polish military expansion and then the loss of Pomerania and Silesia under Mieszko II (1025–1034 CE) created the need to intensify domestic resources. The Piast dynasty established a system of compulsory services that obligated the free rural population to work part of their time for the benefit of the monarchy. This system, organized around the ducal castles and courts, has survived in the numerous place names that reflect the medieval spectrum of common occupations—various crafts, food production, animal breeding, services for the nobility, forestry, mining—those like Bartodzieje ("honey-collectors"), Piekary ("bakers"), Świnary ("swineherds"). According to some estimates, some 250 local markets functioned in this era for the exchange of food and simple products. Taverns, as elsewhere in Europe, served as brokerage houses, and they assisted in augmenting the circulation of coinage.

Despite the elaborate nature of this exchange system, it actually impeded the local development of skilled crafts and free markets. It also failed to provide the requirements for a growing social elite (both ecclesiastical and secular), which increasingly acquired control over much of the land that had once belonged to the monarchy. Consequently, the monarchy began to decline in both economic and political power, from the late eleventh century onward. The economic patterns that had been evolving in western Europe then spread eastward, beginning with Poland (which led to a process of local colonization that changed the basic social, legal, and economic structures of eastern Central Europe). For both rural and urban settlements, colonists were recruited from the West—especially Germans, Flemings, and Dutch—by special managers (Lat., *locatores*), who acted as agents of the great landowners (but they bore the actual expenses and risks of settlement themselves). When an enterprise was successful, a *locator* gained local office, especially as village mayors (*sculteti*) and town governors (*advocati*). The colonists (Lat., *hospites*, the "guests"), who were acquainted with the more advanced methods of Western agriculture and land surveying, were granted various privileges, according to the Teutonicor German laws (Lat., *ius Theutonicum*), whose most important elements included freedom from services traditionally owed to the monarchy, and the *ius emphyteuticum*, which provided them with a hereditary title to their lands, subject only to an annual, fixed quit-rent. The colonists were free to dispose of their outputs, to sell them on the market, thereby promoting the development of a growing economy based on a division of labor and the circulation of coined money. At the same time, the old castle-towns (Pol., *grody*) were transformed, and many new towns were founded. As a symbol of their new economic alignment, the towns established large market places in their centers: the citizens, chiefly craftsmen and traders, served as customers for the neighboring peasant producers. These new urban communities enjoyed special privileges and an inner autonomy, one of them being the right to form their own guilds.

As the benefits of the German laws were applied to Polish villages, and as immigration from western Europe increased, all these measures promoted an increased economic differentiation and the mobilization of resources. The growth in settlements incorporated large wooded, mountainous, or marshy regions, with a systematic proliferation of villages, water mills, market places, and towns along the main lines of communication—and these processes of economic growth were neither impeded by the thirteenth-century disintegration of Poland into quasi-autonomous duchies nor by the ravages of the Mongol invasions by the followers of Genghis Khan. The regional dukes, striving to increase their incomes, continued to promote the colonization schemes of enterprising individuals and institutions, especially those of religious orders (led by the Cistercians, a Christian monastic order that followed strict Benedictine rule). Meanwhile, the urgent necessity of providing compensation for the Mongol depredations actually brought a great degree of economic "modernization" to southern Poland.

Thus, during the mid- to late-fourteenth century, when western Europe suffered a major demographic and then agrarian crises, Poland was able to expand its colonization movement farther to the east. As is now known, most of Poland was spared the ravages of bubonic plague, which had spread through fleas on rats that entered port cities on trade ships and which had proved so devastating to western Europe. Studies confirm that Poland's population continued to grow and did not contract the Black Death during this era. At that time, the development of Polish lines of commercial communication linked the trade of western Europe with the Black Sea area. From the early fifteenth century, a far greater area of eastern Europe was reached by traders from Poland, especially after Poland's union with Lithuania (*de facto* in 1430; then formally in 1569), an empire that went from the Baltic to the Black Sea.

During the late Middle Ages, the Jews, who had for some time been acting as coiners and administrative servants, were invited into Poland to serve the court during the reign of King Kazimierz the Great (1332–1370). Yet most of the Jewish families came as fugitives from the West and were engaged in various crafts and trade. After settling in towns and villages, they sometimes suffered discrimination at the hands of town authorities and the Catholic church. They had to depend on the sympathy of the monarchs, who, nevertheless, also permitted some towns to exercise privileges that effectively excluded them from urban life.

General political conditions, especially the reunification of Poland and the rise of the Piast dynasty, beginning in the early fourteenth century, had provided a framework for the social and economic advancement of the gentry, most of whom had acquired small estates in return for their military services. With subsequent subdivisions of holdings through inheritance and various adverse economic and social circumstances, many of the gentry faced economic subjugation by the greater magnates and social rivalry by alien knights and from many of the free peasantry (especially the village mayors). For long periods, many of the gentry did not differ substantially from the wealthier peasantry in their lifestyles. Nevertheless, many still enjoyed their status as members of the nobility (Pol., *szlachta*), which as a whole gradually acquired various economic privileges at the expense of both the towns and the peasantry, at least until the sixteenth century. These included the abolition of their own taxes, their expanding control over much cultivated land, and the imposition of increasing servile labor obligations (Pol., *robot*) on the peasantry. Such circumstances permitted and promoted the establishment of their manors, chiefly to produce grain, much of it for export by sea to western Europe; that maritime grain trade was especially facilitated when Poland won secure access to the Baltic, by the Peace of Torun in 1466.

BIBLIOGRAPHY

Davies, N. *God's Playground: A History of Poland*. 2 vols. New York, 1982.

Fedorowicz, J. K., ed. and trans. *A Republic of Nobles: Studies in Polish History to 1864*. Cambridge, 1982.

Gieysztor, A., ed. *History of Poland*. Warsaw, 1968.

Górecki, P. *Economy, Society, and Lordship in Medieval Poland*. London, 1992.

Knoll, P. *The Rise of the Polish Monarchy: Piast Poland in East Central Europe, 1320–1380*. Chicago, 1972.

Modzelewski, K. "The System of the *Ius Ducale* and the Idea of Feudalism: Comments on the Earliest Class Society in Medievel Poland." *Quaestiones Medii Aevi* 1 (1977), 71–99.

Topolski, J. *An Outline History of Poland.* Warsaw, 1986.

Zientara, B. "Socio-economic and Spatial Transformation of Polish Towns during the Period of Location." *Acta Poloniae Historica* 34 (1976), 57–84.

CHRISTIAN LÜBKE

Early Modern Period

Polish-Lithuanian state of the sixteenth to eighteenth centuries that embraced large territory. In 1580, it covered 865,000 square kilometers; in 1634, 990,000 square kilometers. The population in 1650 was estimated at 11 million. That means the average density was about eleven persons per square kilometer. It was a rural country; about 80 percent of the population lived in the countryside. Polish peasants in the sixteenth century were forced into serfdom and obliged to work on the fields of their lords without any compensation. Poland was well poised to become a major exporter of agricultural products to western Europe, where the demand for food was growing quickly.

About the year 1600, the size of an average manor farm in Poland was 120 acres (50 hectares). Agriculture and stock breeding by the nobles progressed at the expense of the ancient forests, marshes, and wastelands. Average grain yields in 1600 were 6 to 7 quintals (1 quinta = 100 kilograms) per hectare (2.47 acres) for rye and wheat, 7 to 8 quintals for barley, and 4 to 6 quintals for oats. This level of production met the needs of the gentry, the home market, and the rapidly growing demand from abroad. By the first half of the seventeenth century, grain exports stood at more than 100,000 lasts (1 last = 2,000 kilograms) a year. The profits from the sale of grain went mostly to the nobility, which spent freely on luxury items, building activities, and culture—hence the flourishing of the Polish Renaissance and Baroque.

As the manor grew, more labor was required from the serfs. Yet despite the increasing restrictions and burdens, the sixteenth century saw no real deterioration in the situation within Polish villages. Enterprising peasants grew extra grain to sell on the local market and were able to invest their income in new tools and livestock. They produced enough to feed their family and to sell, and they could even employ poorer neighbors as paid workers.

Urbanization began in the Middle Ages. By the end of the sixteenth century, there were almost seven hundred urban centers in Poland; by the middle of the seventeenth century, nine hundred. However, only eight cities then exceeded 10,000 inhabitants. Gdańsk had 50,000 inhabitants by the end of the sixteenth century and, between 70,000 and 100,000 in the first half of the seventeenth century. Warsaw's population rose from 6,000 in the sixteenth century to 20,000 to 30,000 in the middle of the seventeenth century. Kraków had a population of 28,000; Poznań,

20,000; Toruń, 12,000; Elblag, 15,000; Lublin, 8,000 to 10,000; and Lwów, about 20,000. There were 148 towns with between 600 and 2,000 inhabitants, while there were 567 boroughs with 500 to 600 inhabitants. About 75 percent of all towns were founded and owned by magnates and rich nobles, which resulted in their deep subordination to the nobility. Approximately 90 percent of all urban centers were focused on both commercial and manufacturing activities, linked to the needs of the local market. Their inhabitants were also often engaged in rural pursuits—cultivating gardens and fields, raising cattle and pigs. Crafts were numerous in bigger towns. (In the first half of the seventeenth century, Gdańsk had seven thousand workshops; Kraków, about seven hundred.) There were some centers of specialized production, such as the mining towns of Wieliczka, Bochnia, and Olkusz in Little Poland or the textile producing centers in Great Poland (Bojanowo, Szlichtyngowo, Leszno, and Rawicz). Towns, located on the Vistula River grew to be important centers of grain trade. But Polish nobles tried to monopolize the sale of agricultural and forest products directly in Gdańsk. They also used this occasion to buy imported industrial goods to the detriment of Polish local production and local craftsmen. This fact resulted in the unfavorable structure of the Polish foreign trade in early modern period. The exchange consisted of imports of industrial and luxury goods and exports of raw materials and agricultural products. However, long-distance land trade took on a different character: Based on the network of international fairs developed on Polish territories, it served as intermediary in east-west commerce (oriental wares, silks, rugs, Russian furs, and Moldavian cattle in exchange for Western industrial products).

The economic decline of Polish territories began in the seventeenth century with monetary troubles (1618–1621, 1655–1656, 1659–1666) and the decrease in demand for Polish grain on international markets. The decline was also linked to the negative results of serfdom. Wars and epidemics in the middle of the seventeenth century and again in the beginning of eighteenth century aggravated the situation. The population fell by half. A revival began only in the second half of the eighteenth century as the population rose again to 11 million. Some magnates and rich nobles tried to improve their estates by releasing peasants of compulsory work. Instead, peasants had to pay rent to the landowners. The king and the magnates organized factories to produce textiles, arms, luxury goods, etc. The network of towns had been reconstructed; urban population at the end of the eighteenth century was about 17 to 20 percent of the country's total. The population of Gdańsk, however, was only about 50,000, and the productivity of its harbor declined by half in comparison with the first half of the seventeenth century. Other towns (Poznań, Kraków) experienced slow demographic and economic improvement. The capital city of Warsaw rose quickly, reaching some 100,000 inhabitants and becoming a metropolis with abundant trade, banking, and manufacturing. This promising economic development, however, was matched by Poland's political dismemberment in the partitions of 1772, 1792, and 1795 and the loss of its independence.

The partitions brought economic disaster. A large number of factories went bankrupt, and rent reform was checked. Polish territories were subjected to an intensive fiscal exploitation. The economic links between the three parts of the country (Russian, Prussian, and Austrian) ceased to exist, and the exchange died. Agriculture suffered particularly, because of the low prices of grains and the decline of its exports. General impoverishment caused the decrease of home markets. The participation of the nobles in the armed uprisings against the partitioning powers ended with the confiscation of their estates. Impoverished towns were losing their city rights. Many turned into villages. Urban population decreased. In 1802, Warsaw had only 64,000 inhabitants. In 1800, Gdańsk had only 42,000.

Despite the continuing unfavorable political situation, the second half of the nineteenth century witnessed a revival of the economy. The total population rose from 23 million in 1846 to 51 million in 1911. The number of Warsaw inhabitants rose from 276,000 in 1872 to 845,000 in 1913, of Łódź from 50,000 to 459,000. The whole urban population grew from 748,000 in the years from 1857 to 1861 to 4,802,000 in the years from 1909 to 1910—that is, from 5.6 percent to 18.5 percent of the total population. The development of a modern economy became possible after the abolition of serfdom and the enfranchisement of peasants (in the Prussian zone from 1811 to 1823, in the Austrain zone in 1848, and in the Russian zone in 1864). Agrarian reforms replaced the old three-fields system with crop rotation and introduced the use of fertilizers and modern agricultural equipment as well as the use of hired labor.

The social differentiation of the countryside population resulted in the great movement of gentry and peasants to the towns, which furthered industrialization. Several industrial centers developed in the Russian zone, especially textile factories in Łódź, Bialstok, and Żyrardów; their production was destined mostly for Eastern markets. In Upper and Cieszyn Silesia (Prussian zone) mining and metallurgical industries flourished, while the Poznań region featured the food processing industry and production of agricultural machines. In the mid-nineteenth century, railways were built linking Warsaw with Vienna and Saint Petersburg, and Silesian towns and Kraków with Berlin. The growth of banking and industrial companies strengthened the bourgeoisie (mostly of German and Jewish origin) and gave birth to the class of workers. Despite these changes, Poland remained a rural country with about 75 percent of the population engaged in agriculture and 70 percent of national income produced by agricultural activities.

World War I (1914–1918) had a disastrous impact on the Polish territories, since 90 percent of the country had been affected by military operations. In 1918, the industrial output was only half of the prewar level. In the agricultural sector, buildings and stocks were destroyed and livestock depleted. Trade was disorganized, and the railway and road networks were destroyed. A high inflation rate and the impoverishment of society completed this sad picture.

BIBLIOGRAPHY

Bogucka, Maria. "Amsterdam and the Baltic Trade in the First Half of the Seventeenth Century." *Economic History Review* 2d series 26.3 (1973), 433–447.

Bogucka, Maria. "The Monetary Crisis of the XVIIth Century and Its Social and Psychological Consequences in Poland." *Journal of European Economic History* 6.1 (1975), 137–152.

Bogucka, Maria. "Polish Towns Between the Sixteenth and Eighteenth Centuries." In *A Republic of Nobles: Studies in Polish History to 1864*, edited by Jan K. Fedorowicz, pp. 135–152. Cambridge, 1982.

Bogucka, Maria. "The Network and Functions of Small Towns in Poland in Early Modern Times." In *Gründung and Bedeutung kleineren Städte in nördlichen Europa der frühen Neuzeit*, edited by Antoni Mączak and Christopher P. Smout, pp. 219–233. Wiesbaden, 1991.

Długoborski, Wacław. "The Pre-Capitalistic and Early-Capitalistic Iron Industry in Poland." *Studia Historiae Oeconomicae* 5 (1970), 191–214.

Drozdowski, Marian Marek. "The Urbanisation in Poland in the Years 1870–1970." *Studia Historiae Oeconomicae* 9 (1974), 223–246.

Gieysztorowa, Irena, "Guerre et régression en Masovie aux XVIIe et XVIIIe siècles." *Annales E.S.C.* 13.4 (1958), 603–629.

Jezierski, Andrzej. "The Problems of the Economic Growth of Poland in the 19th Century." *Studia Historiae Oeconomicae* 9 (1974), 121–140.

Jezierski, Andrzej, ed. *Economic History of Poland in Numbers.* Warsaw, 1994.

Kalinowski, Wojciech. *City Development in Poland up to the Mid-19th Century.* Warsaw, 1966.

Kieniewicz, Stefan. *The Emancipation of the Polish Peasantry.* Chicago, 1969.

Kitzwalter, Tomasz. "Polish Landed Gentry of the Mid-19th Century and Modernisation." *Acta Poloniae Historica* 62 (1990), 135–169.

Kołodziejczyk, Ryszard. "The Bourgeoisie in Poland in the 19th and 20th Centuries Against the European Background." *Studia Historiae Oeconomicae* 5 (1970), 215–230.

Landau, Zbigniew, and Jerzy Tomaszewski. *Wirtschaftsgeschichte Polens 19. und 20. Jh.* Berlin, 1986.

Mączak, Antoni. "Export of Grain and the Problem of Distribution of National Income in the Years 1550–1650." *Acta Poloniae Historica* 18 (1968), 75–98.

Mączak, Antoni. "The Balance of Polish Sea Trade with the West (1565–1646)." *Scandinavian Economic History Review* 18.2 (1970), 107–142.

Mączak, Antoni. "Agriculture and Livestock Production in Poland. Internal and Foreign Markets." *Journal of European Economic History* 1.3 (1972), 363–389.

Mączak, Antoni. *Money, Prices, and Power in Poland, 16th–17th Centuries.* Aldershot, U.K., 1995.

Małecki, Jan Maria. "The Vistula River and Poland's Trade in the 16th and 17th Centuries." *Journal of European Economic History* 6.1 (1977) 323–341.

Małecki, Jan Maria. "Der Aussenhandel und die Spezifik der sozial-ökonomischen Entwicklung Polens im 16. und 17. Jh." In *Schichtung und Entwicklung der Gesellschaft in Polen und Deutschland im 16. und 17. Jh.* edited by Marian Biskup and Klaus Zernack, pp. 21–41. Wiesbaden, 1983.

Misztal, Stanisław. "Changes in Distribution of Industry in the Area Poland in the Years 1860–1965." *Studia Historiae Oeconomicae* 5 (1970), 231–242.

Purchla, Jacek. "La main d'oeuvre dans l'industrie textile dans les provinces polonaises au XIXᵉ siècle." *Problems in Textile Geography.* 7 (1993), 63–79.

Szczygielski, Wojciech. "Die ökonomische Aktivität des polnischen Adels im 16.-18. Jh." *Studia Historiae Oeconomicae* 2 (1967), 83–101.

Topolski, Jerzy. "Economic Decline in Poland from the Sixteenth to the Eighteenth Centuries." In *Essays in European Economic History (1500–1800),* edited by Peter M. Earle, pp. 127–142. Oxford, 1974.

Topolski, Jerzy. "Sixteenth Century Poland and the Turning Point in European Development." In *A Republic of Nobles: Studies in Polish History to 1864,* edited by Jan K. Fedorowicz, pp. 74–90. Cambridge, 1982.

Wyrobisz, Andrzej. "Mining in Medieval and Modern Poland." *Journal of European Economic History* 5.3 (1976), 757–762.

Wyrobisz, Andrzej. "Functional Types of Polish Towns in the 16th–18th Centuries." *Journal of European Economic History* 12.1 (1983), 69–103.

Żytkowicz, Leonid. "The Peasant's Farm and the Landlord's Farm in Poland from the 16th to the Middle of the 18th Century." *Journal of European Economic History* 1.1 (1972), 135–154.

MARIA BOGUCKA

Modern Period

In the autumn of 1918, Poland regained its independence. With an area of 388,400 square kilometers (which, after annexation of Zaolzie, taken from Czechoslovakia in 1938, increased to 389,700 square kilometers), Poland had a population of 27.4 million in 1921, and 35.1 million people in 1939. Over 60 percent supported themselves by agriculture, as part of an agricultural-industrial society in interwar Poland.

After reestablishing its independence, Poland attempted to reunite its three previously partitioned zones, which *inter alia* required gradually bringing uniformity to legislation, monetary circulation, the transport system, and tariffs, as well as establishing a nationwide market. Unification processes were hindered by significant differences in economic development of particular partitioned zones. The zone previously under Prussian occupation was the most advanced; the Russian zone in the eastern borderlands was the least developed. There also had to be reconstruction of the economy (about 10 percent of national assets were destroyed as a result of war). Because of the weakness of private capital, the main responsibility for the reconstruction of industry rested with the state. Efforts to finance the establishment of an administration and an army, the war against Soviet Russia, and the reconstruction of ruins led to a huge budgetary deficit, which was covered by the inflationary emission of money.

In the years 1919 through 1922, moderate inflation had a positive impact on the economic situation. In the summer of 1923, hyperinflation occurred, causing a decline in real wages and salaries and producing an economic crisis, which lasted until February 1926. Afraid of further negative economic and political effects of hyperinflation (a decisive factor being the threat of worker radicalization), the Prime Minister and Treasury Minister Władysław Grabski carried out a financial reform in April 1924 and introduced the Polish zloty, based on gold, which replaced the Polish mark (1 dollar = 5.18 zl). The next budgetary deficit and a strong deficit in balance of trade in 1925 resulted in the collapse of the zloty. Improvement of the world economy in the years 1928–1929 led to strong economic growth in Poland, which resulted in a large increase in industrial production, a decrease in unemployment, and an increase in prices of agricultural products. In October 1927, a new parity of the zloty was determined, based on an international stabilizing load (1 dollar = 8.91 zl). The influx of foreign capital into Poland increased in that period (in 1929 foreign capital controlled 33 percent of joint-stock companies, whereas in 1939 it controlled 40 percent, the highest participation being in oil mining, power stations and waterworks, banks, and insurance).

In the autumn of 1929, Poland fell into the Great Economic Depression, which lasted until 1935. As a result of the crisis, the prices of agricultural products dropped by 66 percent compared to the year 1928, and industrial production fell by 41 percent in 1932 (the year of the most severe industrial crisis) compared to the year 1928. Unemployment in urban areas amounted to about one million people and exceeded the number of those employed in large and medium industries. The excess population in rural areas (agrarian overpopulation) was estimated to be between 2.5 and eight million people. Among European countries, Poland was one of the most seriously affected by the crisis, which *inter alia* was caused by mass withdrawal of foreign capital invested in previous years and bad economic policies (such as a deflationary monetary policy, unrestricted outflow of capital, and adoption of an active anticrisis policy no earlier than 1932). In the years 1933–1936, Poland was a member of the gold bloc.

In 1936 Deputy Prime Minister Eugeniusz Kwiatkowski introduced a policy that would shore up the economic conditions, namely, financing investments in the defense industry by the public sector. These efforts were concentrated mainly in the area of the Central Industrial District (located in the central part of the country), which had been created in 1937 (embracing about 15 percent of the country). Over 100,000 new jobs were created in that region.

MODERN POLAND. Audi cars on a delivery truck, Warsaw, 1994. (© John Eastcott/Yva Momatiuk/ Woodfin Camp and Associates, New York)

Industrial production rapidly increased in that period, but agriculture still faced difficulties due to an inability to reach precrisis price levels, as well as another agricultural crisis, in the autumn of 1938. Financial difficulties forced the government to implement currency control in April 1936. Between 1936 and 1939, the state's role in the economy increased significantly.

During the interwar period, Poland managed to repair war damage, to pass uniform economic legislation, and to create new industrial branches, which had not existed in the Polish territory before 1918 (defense industry, electromechanical industry, etc.). Nevertheless, Poland remained behind Western European countries, and the gap was increasing.

On 1 September 1939 Poland was attacked by Germany, and on 17 September was invaded by the Soviet army; and the country's territory was divided between Germany and the Soviet Union (after the outbreak of the German-Soviet war, the whole territory of Poland was occupied by the Nazis). Part of the Polish land was added directly to the German-Reich, with the remaining part becoming an entirely subordinate territory called Generalna Gubernia (Government General). All factories and larger estates owned by Poles and Jews were confiscated, without reparation, in the territories included in the Reich. Later confiscation included a majority of the craft businesses and a portion of the farms owned by peasants. In Government General, the range of confiscates was lower. Polish territo-

ries were included in the German division of labor, which resulted in the physical liquidation of factories that the Reich deemed unnecessary. Industrial production dropped rapidly with the exception of mining and the armaments industry. Agriculture was burdened with ever increasing compulsory contributions of products, with the producers receiving only symbolic payments. In the territories incorporated by the Reich, the German mark was introduced; whereas in Government General, the Emission Bank in Poland, created by the occupants, was issuing the zloty (called the Cracow zloty). In the areas annexed by the Reich, wages received by Poles were kept at a starvation level, with a drastic decrease in the standard of living. Poles in Government General also suffered, as their wages were frozen at the 1939 level, and prices were rising rapidly owing to the inflationary policy of the Emission Bank in Poland.

About six million Poles and Jews living in Poland in 1939 lost their lives during the war, 10 percent of them killed in warfare and 90 percent victims of terror and extermination. An estimated five million were murdered by the Germans, and about one million were killed or died in the Soviet Union. Polish material losses amounted to about 38 percent of national assets.

After World War II, Poland fell into the Soviet sphere of influence. That resulted *inter alia* in relocation of the country's borders. The Soviet Union annexed Polish eastern territories (more or less up to the river Bug). In compensation,

Poland received territories in the north and west, which had been part of the German Reich before the war (up to the line of the Lusatian Nysa and Odra rivers). The country's area decreased to 322,600 square kilometers, with a population of 23.9 million (which by 1998 had increased to 38.7 million, with 38 percent in rural areas). Poland lost areas with a dominant agricultural character, and gained more urbanized and industrialized ones. However, these developed areas had been ruined by both war operations and mass removal of remaining assets to the Soviet Union. Reshaping the borders led to mass migrations. In accordance with the Potsdam Treaty, the Germans were removed from Poland. As part of agreements between Poland and the Soviet Union, Ukrainians and Belorussians were replaced by Polish reemigrants from territories annexed by the Soviets. The postwar migratory movement embraced several million people.

The new government gradually introduced socioeconomic reforms. The agricultural reform act became effective on 6 September 1944, partitioning all estates with an area exceeding fifty hectares of arable land or one hundred hectares of total area. Peasants received land as a symbolic payment. Agricultural reform resulted in a slight improvement in rural welfare. On 3 January 1946 an act for the nationalization of industry was issued. It allowed the state to take over all large- and medium-size private enterprises, but foreign owners received reparations. Banks in Poland were not subjected to nationalization, but the private ones, except the two largest, were set for liquidation in 1946. The process of taking over private wholesale and to some extent retail trade by the state and cooperatives began in 1947. Collectivization of agriculture started in 1948, but until its cessation in 1956 it managed to embrace only 10 percent of the land.

In the years from 1945 to 1989 the Polish economy followed quasi "cycles." Directly after the Communist takeover (in 1945–1946) and just after subsequent changes of the ruling blocs (in October 1956, December 1970, and December 1980), economic policy focused on the improvement of living conditions. Emphasis on consumer goods industries, agriculture, and housing was central to the economic programs (in 1945–1948, 1956–1958, 1970–1973, and 1980–1989). Under the influence of the Soviet Union and as a result of the distribution of tasks within the Council for Mutual Economic Aid (COMECON), such proconsumption policy soon was replaced by "intensive, socialist industrialization" (1948–1953, 1958–1968, 1973–1976). In these periods, priorities of the programs were in investments aimed at the development of heavy and defense industries, metallurgy, and mining (mainly coal mining). This was done at the expense of consumer needs and the standard of living of a part of the population. This policy produced many barriers in the economy, such as shortages of many products, a deficit in electric energy, and poor transportation capabilities; so the pace of investment in heavy industry had to be slowed in favor of regulation of the economy. By mutual agreement that time was described as an "economic maneuvre" (1953–1956, 1968–1970, 1976–1980). As a rule, however, the pace of changes and regulation of the economy, as well as of increases in the standard of living, was rather slow, eventually leading to outbreaks of social tension (in June 1956 in Poznań; in December 1970 and December 1980 on the coast) and moving the country ahead into a proconsumption stage.

Between 1945 and 1989 Poland became an industrial-agricultural country. Economic development based on restrictive-distribution rules was extensive, and industry was characterized by low labor efficiency and a high level of material consumption. Poland's industry was not competitive with the industries of Western countries. Unemployment was eliminated during that period; and, compared to the interwar period, the standard of living grew significantly, except for white-collar workers.

In 1989, after the communists lost power, Poland began an economic transformation, resulting *inter alia* in implementation of a market economy, privatization of enterprises (with significant foreign participation), liquidation of deficit enterprises, and development of trade with Western countries with lessening trade exchange with former partners from the COMECON countries. Social costs of the transition have been very high, as for forty-five years (1945–1989) the Polish economy was functioning within the distribution of labor imposed by the Soviet Union. Consequently, a lot of enterprises have lost their markets, with a resultant decline in manufacturing and an increase in unemployment, up to about 2.5 million people in the urban areas. However, it is generally believed that, compared to other post-Communist countries, Poland has made significant progress in this transformation.

BIBLIOGRAPHY

The literature on the Polish economy in English is rather sparse. Some publications edited between 1945 and 1989 may not be entirely unbiased. A few basic publications in Polish are also supplied, representing a wide range of sources.

Alton, Th. P. *Polish Postwar Economy*. New York, 1955.

Bobińska, Celina, and A. Pilch, eds. *Employment-Seeking Emigrations of the Poles World-Wide: Nineteenth and Twentieth Centuries.* Kraków, 1975.

Drewnowski, Jan, ed. *Crisis in the East European Economy: The Spread of the Polish Disease.* London, 1982.

Górecki, Roman. *Poland and Her Economic Development*. London, 1935.

Karpiński, Andrzej. *Twenty Years of Poland's Economic Development 1944–1964.* Warsaw, 1964.

Landau, Zbigniew, and Jerzy Tomaszewski. *The Polish Economy in the Twentieth Century*, translated by Wojciech Roszkowski. London, 1985. A bibliography.

Landau, Zbigniew, and Jerzy Tomaszewski. *Gospodarka Polski między-wojennej*, vol. 1, *W dobie inflacji 1918–1923*; vol. 2, *Od Grabskiego do Piłsudskiego*; vol. 3, *Wielki kryzys 1930–1935*; vol. 4, *Lata interwencjonizmu państwowego 1936–1939*. Warsaw, 1967, 1971, 1982, 1989.

Landau, Zbigniew, and Jerzy Tomaszewski. *Zarys historii gospodarczej Polski 1918–1939*. 6th ed. Warsaw, 1999.

Łuczak, Czesław. "Basic Assumptions of the Economic Policies of Nazi Germany and Their Implementation in the Occupied Poland." *Studia Historiae Oeconomica* 11 (1976), 193–213.

Łuczak, Czesław. *Polityka ludnościowa i ekonomiczna hitlerowskich Niemiec w okupowanej Polsce*. Poznań, Poland, 1979.

Montias, J. H. *Central Planning in Poland*. New Haven, 1962.

Taylor, J. *The Economic Development of Poland 1919–1950*. Ithaca, N.Y., 1952.

Yakowicz, J. V. *Poland's Postwar Recovery: Economic Reconstruction, Nationalization and Agrarian Reform in Poland after World War II*. Hicksville, N.Y., 1979.

ZBIGNIEW LANDAU

POLANYI, KARL (1886–1964), Hungarian-American economic historian and anthropologist.

The most influential work of Hungarian native Karl Polanyi was *The Great Transformation: The Political and Economic Origins of Our Time* (Boston, 1957 [originally published in 1944]), begun in England and finished while Polanyi, a student of primitive, archaic, and industrial economic histories, was a faculty member of Bennington College, in the United States. The book's primary objective was to make sense of the Great Depression and the rise of fascism. Focusing on the period of English history from the enclosures (peaking in the 1790s) to the repeal of the Corn Laws (1846), *The Great Transformation* tells a two-part story. One part explains how the demands of the nascent machine age dovetailed with laissez-faire ideology to convince the government to implement a legal framework conducive to competitive capitalism. The second part examines the unintended consequences of this new system and shows how society, in reacting to these consequences, effectively dismantled the system. So, contrary to common interpretation, *The Great Transformation* is not the transition into but rather the transition out of competitive capitalism, a transformation completed by the 1930s.

Unfortunately, confusion does not end with the title. Polanyi's term for competitive capitalism was *market society*, which is a system where all resources are mobilized with unconstrained price-making markets. This self-regulating market system is not merely a collection of markets, the likes of which have been around since antiquity. Rather, the self-regulating market system is a peculiar institutional structure in that it divorces the entire set of provisioning institutions from the rest of culture. Since provisioning is fundamental to survival and social reproduction, the creation of an institutional framework that divorces economy from society renders society subservient—hence, a "market [-determined] society."

The self-regulating market system was also a utopian endeavor. It focused exclusively on providing a steady flow of inputs to the machines of the emerging industrial era, motivated solely by fear of starvation and pursuit of profit. To believe that labor (people) and land (nature) could be allocated effectively by this single motive, without regard for protection, security, or sustainability, was every bit as utopian (if less appealing) as Marx's "from each according to ability, to each according to need." Ignoring security produced widespread social costs, destroying communities and imperiling both people and ecosystems, which in turn led spontaneously and almost immediately to "social protective responses." This is Polanyi's double movement: the first part of the movement is the extension of the market; the second part is the social reaction to curb the resulting social ("external") costs. Contrary to the neoliberal view, Polanyi's argument is that the self-regulating market system was the wellspring of damages to people, communities, and the natural environment. Even capital underwent a double movement, as the pain inflicted on industry owners and bankers by deflations and depressions led to widespread pressures for protection from the business cycle; hence, strong central banks were established, and the gold standard was abandoned.

Polanyi also points out that the so-called laissez-faire system did not occur spontaneously; rather, like all human-devised systems, it had to be instituted. The 1834 Poor Law Reform, most notorious to Polanyi because it treated people (labor supply) to the uncushioned trauma of the self-regulating market system, was one piece of the puzzle—one piece of legislation in a thoughtful, coherent design for competitive capitalism. Although laissez-faire was by design, the social protective responses to market society's unintended consequences were spontaneous, unplanned reactions: "*Laissez-faire* was planned; planning was not" (p. 141).

Although Polanyi's economic history could be considered 180 degrees from the "early" Douglass North, North's Nobel Prize lecture and his more recent work emphasize that economic theory alone cannot explain economic history (institutions matter). Disagreement persists, however, in North's insistence that scarcity is universal, in contrast to Polanyi's view that scarcity is also a function of the institutional structure. If there is one point more worth taking from Polanyi than any other, it is that all economies function within a human-created institutional structure.

BIBLIOGRAPHY

Dalton, George, ed. *Primitive, Archaic, and Modern Economies: Essays of Karl Polanyi*. Garden City, N.Y., 1968. Edited by a Polanyi student and economic anthropologist, who advocates Polanyi's "substantive" approach to study of non-Western economies. Particularly succinct essays are Chapters 4 and 7.

Mayhew, Anne. "Review of Karl Polanyi, *The Great Transformation: The Political and Economic Origins of Our Time.*" Economic History Services. <http://www.eh.net/bookreviews/library/polanyi.shtml> An accessible, succinct essay. Mayhew's subtitle, "Markets to Market to Protection . . . ," captures Polanyi's version of history, with the second, singular noun "market" referring to the self-regulating system of markets (market society).

McRobbie, Kenneth, ed. *Humanity, Society and Commitment: On Karl Polanyi.* Montreal, 1994. A small book of nine essays. Particularly good are Chapter 1, on Polanyi's economic history lectures at Columbia, and Chapter 6, on Polanyi's advocacy of socialism, which he defined as the conscious subordination of the market system to democratic society.

McRobbie, Kenneth, and Kari Polanyi Levitt, eds. *Karl Polanyi in Vienna: The Contemporary Significance of "The Great Transformation."* Montreal, 2000. Includes several good essays on the perils of globalization and economic transition.

Polanyi, Karl. *The Livelihood of Man,* edited by Harry W. Pearson. New York, 1977.

Polanyi-Levitt, Kari, ed. *The Life and Work of Karl Polanyi.* Montreal, 1990. Rich in biographical information and historical context of Polanyi's work.

Stanfield, J. R. *The Economic Thought of Karl Polanyi: Lives and Livelihood.* New York, 1986. Scholarly analysis of Polanyi as institutional economist in the tradition of Thorstein Veblen and John R. Commons.

JAMES A. SWANEY

POLLUTION. The word *pollution* comes from two Latin words: *pollutionem,* meaning defilement, and *polluere,* meaning soiling. Popularly, pollution is the term given to the waste products of consumption and production activities that are discharged into the natural environment—the earth's atmosphere, water bodies, and lands. Pollution can also come from natural processes such as the particulate matter and toxic gases from a volcanic eruption or ash from forest fires. This article's focus is on human sources.

Pollution arises because of the natural laws of thermodynamics. Matter cannot be destroyed, it merely changes form. For example, the combustion of fossil fuels produces energy plus waste products such as carbon dioxide, nitrogen, and sulfur oxides. These wastes can range from relatively innocuous compounds that are readily absorbed by the natural environment to long-lived toxics that accumulate in the tissues of living organisms and the physical environment.

Pollution arises from ignorance and negative externalities. "Pollution, like fraud, is something you impose on others against their will so that you can perhaps gain financial advantage" (Nicholas Ridley, British environment secretary under Margaret Thatcher, as quoted in Francis Cairncross, *Costing the Earth,* Boston, 1992). A negative externality (or external diseconomy) exists whenever the well-being of some agent, individual, or firm is adversely affected by the actions of another agent that are not transferred into the market prices of goods and services, and no compensation is made by the generating party to the affected party. Waste flows by themselves may not create negative externalities. If a waste product is absorbed or neutralized by natural forces, and no diminution of well-being occurs, no externality arises. Note, however, that human well-being may be defined quite broadly to include concern not only for one's own welfare, but that of others, including nonhuman species. If a waste product destroys an ecosystem, people may feel harmed even if they do not directly consume the products of that ecosystem. For example, the destruction of a coral reef by an oil spill may make people feel worse off, even if they never see that reef.

Externalities arise because of the presence of one or both of two characteristics: nonexclusion and nonrivalness. A good or an activity that is nonexcludable is one where it is impossible, impractical, or very costly for one agent to maintain exclusive control over its use. Once the good is supplied to one agent, it is available to all within an area defined by political boundaries and/or geography. This can also be called a technological interdependency between agents or jointness in supply. In the case of waste products, a negative or undesirable good, one person's release of wastes, is also "consumed" or enters into the utility or production function of others because of proximity or technology; and this will be more likely, the larger the population density of a given region. Note, however, the complexity of this situation: Waste generation clearly increases with population, and externalities rise with population density because of a greater likelihood of nonexclusion; however, higher population densities may be needed for pollution control technologies to be cost-effective, owing to economies of scale in the provision of a public good. Nonrivalness is subtly different from nonexclusion. A good is a nonrival in consumption if one person's consumption does not diminish the amount available to another. An example is noise: an airplane flying above a city generates noise pollution that all under its path share equally. Urban smog is shared by all who live in the city.

These characteristics explain why externalities and thus pollution arise. Economic analysis can also explain why some forms of pollution persist although others become internalized by actions taken by agents. The key factor is the existence and the nature of property rights to the natural environment. When property rights are held by individuals (private property rights) or the community acting jointly (community or common property), the negative externality is likely to be internalized. Pollution persists when there are no effective property rights to the natural environment. This situation is called open access. Private property rights over an environmental resource give the holder(s) exclusive rights to use that resource as they see fit (subject to other laws or agreements of behavior in the community). The property-right holder(s) can enjoy the exclusive use of their property and prevent others from interfering with that enjoyment. Nonexcludability no longer pertains. If another agent attempts to violate the right by releasing waste products that affect the private-right holder, the holder can use legal means to stop the pollution or demand compensation. A similar story can be told for community property where the community acts as a single agent to protect its joint interests against polluters from outside the community. Under open access, no one has a property right to the natural environment. There is thus no way to prevent all from using the environment as a waste depository. Pollution will occur when the ability of the natural environment to absorb these waste products is exceeded by their volume or cumulative emissions, and everyone will be worse off but unable to stop the pollution without some form of collective agreement and powers of enforcement. This typically requires the formation of a government or other institutions with powers to regulate the amount of waste being released and, hence, to control pollution.

Controlling Pollution. The optimal level of pollution in society is found where the marginal benefit of releasing waste products equals the marginal damages from those wastes. The marginal damage curve shows the incremental damages incurred by the agent, such as adverse health effects, losses in production, and ecosystem damages. The marginal benefit curve can be viewed as the incremental profits (or utility) gained by the agent releasing the waste for each unit discharged into the environment. Reducing waste will then require either reductions in production of the polluting activity or investing in methods of abating or controlling the wastes so they do not enter the environment. Those being harmed by pollution can also make defensive expenditures that mitigate the impact of the pollution on them.

Societies can reach the optimal level of pollution in three fundamental ways: by negotiation and voluntary agreements not coerced by the state, by actions taken by governments or other institutions, or by technological changes that mitigate the pollution or introduce substitutes that eliminate the polluting activity or good. Government actions can be in the form of command-and-control policies that restrict outputs or inputs or prescribe specific behaviors and technologies, or policy instruments that rely on pricing the polluting activities, such as taxes, subsidies, and establishing markets in pollution rights.

Historically, the predominant methods of internalizing pollution externalities have involved voluntary actions, technological advancements, and command-and-control policies. This is so for both market-based and centrally planned economies; no form of government has been found to be superior to another in addressing pollution ex-

ternalities. The key factors giving rise to persistent pollution problems—open access and informational gaps—are independent of political structure.

There have been and continue to be many examples where pollution has not been internalized, however. The historical examples presented below suggest conditions necessary to internalize pollution externalities and possible actions to be taken. At least five factors come into play. First, all agents involved must have information about the pollutant. The pollution problem must be identified—what is the pollutant, where does it come from, how much is there, and what does it do to people and the environment? If agents do not know that they are being harmed by a pollutant or do not agree about sources and impacts, taking steps to reduce waste flows by individuals or state actions will be difficult, if not impossible. Second, an assignment of property rights is crucial. If property rights can be defined over the environmental resource, voluntary agreements become feasible. With no property rights (i.e., open access), agents can free-ride on any voluntary agreement; if I reduce my wastes and you do not reduce yours, you still benefit from a marginally cleaner environment and pay nothing. Open access thus inhibits negotiations over voluntary waste control. State intervention then becomes the only viable method of internalizing pollution.

Third, transaction costs of negotiation (among private agents or state-to-agent or among states), monitoring, and enforcement must not be prohibitive. Transaction costs are likely to rise as the number of agents involved increases, they are more dispersed in the region, and the size and the characteristics of generators and recipients of the pollution are more asymmetric. If agents are affected differently by the pollutant, it will be much harder to reach a solution because a uniform level of pollution may not be efficient for all. Thus, the characteristics of the pollutant itself will also be a factor. Pollutants that are uniformly mixed and affect all parties in the same way will be easier to address than those that are spatially differentiated; their impact on agents depends on geography, climate, degree of urbanization, and other factors. Pollutants that come from known sources that are stationary in location (point sources) are easier to negotiate over and regulate than sources with no fixed location (nonpoint sources), or pollutants that appear in multiple media (air, water, soils) in complex forms. Pollutants that spill over political boundaries are difficult to address because nation-states are involved in deciding what actions to take. Fourth, the state of technology plays a key role in both the generation and the amelioration of pollution. Pollution from horses used as transportation in urban areas disappeared when the new technology of the internal combustion engine emerged. This ended one form of pollution, but gave rise to another. One could imagine, however, a technological development that significantly reduced most kinds of pollution (e.g., solar energy instead of fossil fuels). The development of new technologies can make it feasible to remove pollutants from the environment (e.g., water purification devices, scrubbers to clean gas emissions from stacks). Finally, a stable political environment—a consistent form of government and lack of upheavals such as wars—assists in addressing pollution problems.

Examples throughout human history help explain the persistence of pollution over time. The historical causes of pollution are identical to the factors that contribute to its presence in modern economies. Initially, pollutants were in the form of human and animal wastes that contaminated water supplies and soils and contributed to air pollution. Extensive agricultural production in many civilizations led to erosion and salinization of soils, rendering them unfit for future cultivation. Mining led to contamination of soils and water by by-products of extraction and processing. Pollution became more acute and widespread as populations grew and became urbanized. Industrialization changed production technologies and introduced different types of pollution—chemical pollutants, air pollution from fossil fuel combustion (first coal, then oil products), and more.

Human and Animal Waste: A Source of Air and Water Pollution. In fourteenth-century Paris, 300,000 animals per year were slaughtered and their carcasses left in the street. Eighteenth-century cities contained piles of human and animal excrement mixed with rotting garbage, which often blocked streets. In 1858, the smell of excrement and garbage become so bad in London that the House of Commons was disbanded. When the French writer Jacques Caille visited Rabat in the early nineteenth century, he observed that "the streets of the city often show a layer of liquid mire more than ten centimetres deep. When waste matter has been removed it is thrown into the sea; or often it is simply heaped up at the gates to the city, where it forms a veritable cess pool" (Ponting, 1991). A French visitor in Isfahan in 1694 noted that the streets were filled with mud and that "This great filthiness is still further increased by the custom of throwing dead animals, together with the blood of those killed by butchers on to the squares and of publicly relieving oneself wherever one happens to be" (Ponting, 1991).

The source of pollution was known in all these cases, but in an open-access environment, solutions were a long time in coming. Although there is scattered evidence of a market solution in the form of sales of human and animal excrement as manure to farmers, this solution was incomplete. Much of the waste remained in the cities. In addition, using human feces as fertilizer spreads intestinal diseases, worms, and flukes, and thus the solution to one pollution problem led to another. The problem with regulating the disposal of wastes was that identifying and prosecuting individual violations was costly and at the same time ineffective unless nearly universal compliance was achieved. The problem was exacerbated because these wastes were largely nonpoint sources until people installed sanitation facilities in their dwellings.

Public policies to provide clean water began with piping in water from rural rivers and lakes and the substitution of well water for river water (e.g., Paris stopped using water from the Seine in 1852 in favor of the large artesian well at Grenelle). Water-treatment facilities were developed in the latter part of the nineteenth century. In addition, effective underground water systems evolved along with cheaper and better sanitary facilities in homes (e.g., the invention of the toilet). In sum, technical advances were the key to possible government intervention in the form of regulations and water-treatment facilities.

Coal Burning and Air Pollution. Air pollution arising from the switch from wood to coal as a source of fuel dates from the Middle Ages in England. Severe air pollution from this source began in London in the sixteenth century, with the pollution appearing as dense fog. In the 1840s in Manchester, close to 60 percent of working-class children died before the age of five, a rate twice that of rural areas. The deaths were attributed largely to extensive coal burning. The average number of hours of sunshine in central London between 1920 and 1950 was nearly 20 percent less than in outer parts of the city less affected by coal smoke. In December 1952, over four thousand deaths were attributed to air pollution caused by coal burning. Government regulations in 1956 restricted the types of fuel that could be burned in cities; and by 1970 the amount of smoke in the air over London had fallen by 80 percent, and the amount of December sunshine had increased by 70 percent.

Air pollution is an open-access problem. Actions taken by individuals are limited to using protective devices such as face masks and air purifiers or moving to cleaner regions. Here again, the source of the pollution and its effects were known for centuries before institutional responses occurred. The solution took the form of government intervention and technical change that resulted in the discovery and the use of alternative sources of fuel. Pollution from coal fell when oil and natural gas were substituted for it. Would the introduction of cheaper fuels by itself have been enough to reduce air pollution to acceptable levels? Probably not, given the coordination problem involved in the simultaneous switching to other fuels. Would government regulations have been effective if cheap alternatives to coal not been available? Again, probably not, or there would have been regulations in the nineteenth century accompanying the widespread introduction of government controls in other areas of economic

POLLUTION. *Source of the Southwark Water Works*, etching by George Cruikshank (1792–1878). John Edwards, owner of the Southwark Water Works, sits on a dome in the middle of the dark and murky Thames River, holding a trident with drowned animals on the prongs as sludge from sewers pours in from both sides. The City of London and Southwark are in the background. (Courtesy of the National Library of Medicine, Bethesda, Maryland)

activity (e.g., public education, child labor, and factory safety).

Industrial Waste and Pollution. Industrial pollution was small-scale and local until the advent of large and concentrated populations and large industrial outputs. Early examples include mining and refining of gold, which requires the use of mercury and lead—a problem in the Roman Empire; tanning of leather, which used large quantities of acid, lime, alum, oil, and mercury, which, together with the remains of the hides, were often disposed of in local rivers; cotton dyeing and sugar refining, which polluted water; and linen bleaching (in 1582 Dutch authorities stopped the dumping of bleach into canals), fumes from alum factories, and ammonia fumes from cement works.

Solutions in these cases took the form of command-and-control regulations to restrict output or require the use of technologies to reduce emissions or make them less harmful when the pollution resulted in air, water, and soil degra-

dation to the larger community. In cases in which the costs of pollution were primarily borne by the producers (e.g., "mad hatters" from mercury poisoning of tannery workers) the cure involved private decisions to change production methods, once the source of the problem was understood.

Acid rain, which was first identified in Manchester in the 1850s, subsequently has become a problem in many parts of the world. The causes of acid rain are complex and took time to be understood. Burning of fossil fuels plus smelting of sulfide iron ores are the main sources of sulfur dioxide in the atmosphere. The burning of fossil fuels also oxidizes nitrogen to produce nitrogen oxides. In the atmosphere these oxides turn into sulfuric and nitric acids, and interaction with precipitation yields acid rain. Acidity is measured on a pH scale where 7.0 is neutral. Normal precipitation is slightly acid at a pH of 5.7. Levels of acid rain with a pH of 2.1 (vinegar has a pH of 2.4) have been observed on a number of occasions. On at least one occasion a pH reading of 1.5 was observed (battery acid has a pH of 1).

Acid rain destroys the stone work in buildings and destroys fish and plant life in streams, rivers, and lakes, in part by promoting higher concentrations of heavy toxic metals. Global sulfur dioxide production increased from approximately 10 million tons per year in 1860 to 50 million tons in 1910 to over 150 million tons by the 1970s. Cleaner technologies have resulted in a fall in sulfur dioxide emissions from the Organization for Economic Cooperation and Development (OECD) countries since the 1970s. World production is still increasing, however, with high concentrations in eastern Europe, Russia, China, and other industrializing countries.

Regulatory responses to acid rain came 120 years after the problem was first identified, owing to information gaps and the open-access character of the pollution. In fact, debates about the causes and the environmental impact of acid rain continued until the 1980s. The responses included legal sanctions against polluters, technological standards, and, more recently, the use of tradable discharge permits for point sources of sulfur dioxide emissions in the United States. These solutions have not always been successful: a technological standard used in the 1960s was to require emitters to install higher waste gas stacks. This improved air quality locally but led to greater dispersion of the acid-forming compounds over larger regions of the country. This illustrates the key role of information gaps in forming effective policies to reduce the impact of pollution.

Recent Industrial Pollution. Since World War II, most industrial pollution resulted from the burning of fossil fuels and heavy industrial production, such as that of iron and steel, other metals, and chemicals. Since then, other serious pollution problems have derived from the increased manufacturing of synthetic chemicals. Many of them are highly toxic and also resistant to degradation by natural processes; so they accumulate in the environment. Examples of their appearance include: the switch from soap to detergent (phosphates), and using synthetic fibers in place of natural fibers; pesticides and polychlorinated biphenyls (PCBs); industrial accidents releasing toxic chemicals (e.g., dioxin released in a 1976 explosion at Sevsco in Northern Italy); leakage from toxic waste dumps; nuclear accidents (Chernobyl in Ukraine in 1986); and chlorofluorocarbons, which contribute to the destruction of the earth's ozone layer.

Institutional and individual responses are under way, but many externalities remain. The usual factors are at work: incomplete understanding of the problem, lack of agreement on the nature of the threat and how best to combat it, open-access resources, solutions that involve high transaction costs in the form of transnational policies, and the hope for future technological cures that will be significantly cheaper than solutions currently available (e.g., using renewable energy instead of fossil fuels).

Global climate change, arising from emissions of greenhouse gases (carbon dioxide, methane, nitrous oxide), exemplifies these problems. The global atmosphere is an open-access resource. Greenhouse gases are uniformly mixed pollutants, creating a worldwide externality; emissions released at any origin will increase global atmospheric concentrations. It would take a significant majority of the world's governments to agree to reduce greenhouse gas emissions before any single country would lower its emissions, because of the enormous free-rider problem; and there is no effective world government to implement and enforce policies. An attempt at a global solution began in the late 1990s when many of the world's countries adopted a framework agreement called the Kyoto Protocol. Each signatory to the protocol set its own policies and target for reduction of greenhouse gases to be met by 2008 to 2012; but the protocol does not become binding unless at least fifty-five signatory countries ratify it, and these countries represent 55 percent of carbon dioxide emissions released in 1990. It is not necessary, or desirable, to require that 100 percent of potential signatories (or 100 percent of the world's countries) ratify the protocol in order for it to become binding. A rule of complete consensus would give each country, in effect, veto power over the agreement. This would create a "holdup" problem wherein each country could demand the aggregate benefit from reduced pollution in exchange for its signature. The implied transaction costs might easily block progress in reducing global warming. There are many examples of this general phenomenon throughout history. A specific case is the English enclosure movement. McCloskey (1975) argues that when unanimous agreement in the village was required in order to transform scattered strips of arable land into more efficient consolidated holdings, little progress was made toward enclosure as individual villagers held out for a disproportionate share of the benefit. Their ability to bargain in this way was eliminated with the advent of parliamentary enclosure laws that required three-quarters (later two-thirds) approval. As a result, enclosure proceeded at a rapid rate.

This agreement has been difficult to achieve. Scientific uncertainty about the links between greenhouse gas emissions and climate change is a significant barrier to action. Although a large number of scientists argue for causality, there are many skeptics. Also, there will be large numbers of "winners" and "losers" from any policy designed to reduce emissions. The losers represent large industrial sectors of economies, namely, fossil fuel energy producers and users. Some of the winners are small island nations that might be under water if global warming occurred. In political power, the losers often outweigh the winners.

As of January 2003, 104 countries had ratified the protocol, contributing approximately 44 percent of total carbon dioxide emissions produced in 1990. Even if the threshold were passed, enforcement of the targets would remain a problem.

Pollution is an enduring problem. "Since human beings have inhabited the earth, they have generated, produced, manufactured, excreted, secreted, discarded, and otherwise disposed of all manner of waste" (Melosi, 1981, p.1). Easy cases to address are those where people quickly understand the problem and can "fix it" because the transaction costs of changing behavior, finding substitutes, or prohibiting production and use of compounds are not high. Sometimes investigators find a technological solution only to discover a new set of problems. The historical record illustrates the path society takes to address pollution. Society first must recognize and understand the problem, then develop property rights and institutions and/or technologies to address it, and, finally, overcome transaction costs so that people can agree to concrete actions in the form of regulations or private initiatives. This process can be very lengthy.

BIBLIOGRAPHY

Brander, James A., and M. Scott Taylor. "The Simple Economics of Easter Island: A Ricardo-Malthus Model of Renewable Resource Use." *American Economic Review* 88.1 (March 1998), 119–138.

Jacobson, Judith E., and John Firor. *Human Impact on the Environment: Ancient Roots, Current Challenges.* Boulder, Colo., 1992.

McCarthy, Tom. "The Coming Wonder? Foresight and Early Concerns about the Automobile." *Environmental History* 6.1 (January 2001), 46–74.

McCloskey, D. "The Economics of Enclosure: A Market Analysis." In *European Peasants and Their Markets*, edited by W. Parker and E. Jones. Princeton, 1975.

Melosi, Martin V. *Garbage in the Cities.* College Station, Tex., 1981.

Ostrom, Elinor. *Governing the Commons: The Evolution of Institutions for Collective Action.* Cambridge, 1990.

Ponting, Clive. *A Green History of the World.* London, 1991.

Simmons, Ian G. *Environmental History: A Concise Introduction.* Oxford, 1993.

Tainter, Joseph. *The Collapse of Complex Societies.* Cambridge, 1988.

Weiss, H., M. A. Courty, W. Wetterstrom, F. Guichard, L. Senior, R. Meadow, and A. Curnow. "The Genesis and Collapse of Third Millennium North Mesopotamian Civilization." *Science* 261.5122 (August 1993), 995–1004.

NANCY OLEWILER AND CLYDE REED

POOR LAWS. England was unique in eighteenth-century Europe in possessing a statutory, tax-based Poor Law. Financed by a local property tax (the poor rate) and dependent on the services of unpaid local officials, it was a distinctive feature of English society that had its origins in the sixteenth century. The key piece of legislation had been the great Elizabethan Poor Law of 1601, which codified existing laws and enshrined the twin purposes of assisting the "impotent" (the old, the sick, and the infirm) and setting the "able-bodied" poor to work. Although modified by an occasional statute, this national welfare framework prevailed for over two centuries until superseded by the Poor Law Amendment Act of 1834. By contrast, Ireland and Scotland did not have formal statutory poor-relief systems until 1838 and 1845, respectively.

Eighteenth Century. What became known after 1834 as the Old Poor Law was highly decentralized, based on the parish as the basic unit of organization, under the supervisory eye of the county magistracy and only ultimately responsible to Parliament. In terms of relief practice, its chief hallmark was its face-to-face character. Overseers of the poor usually knew those they relieved, especially in the small village communities that generally made up the fifteen thousand, mostly rural, parishes. Many historians portray this as a relatively generous welfare system. Poor relief was used to sustain individuals and families at various times in the life cycle: childhood, widowhood, infirmity, and old age. Besides unemployment relief and pensions for the elderly, eighteenth-century overseers' accounts commonly contain payments for rent, food, fuel (coals), boots and shoes, clothing, lying-in expenses (such as childbed linen and payments to the midwife), and burial costs (laying-out, shrouds, grave digging). A picture emerges of a wide-ranging paternalism, which extended to the management of the local labor market, the fixing of wage rates, the fostering of parish orphans, the apprenticing of young persons, and the support of single-parent families.

The image of a generous welfare system is derived from research heavily biased toward the southern counties. Elsewhere in the country the situation could be quite different. Per capita relief expenditures were much lower in the "high wage/pastoral" counties of the north and the west than in the "low wage/arable" counties of the south and the east. For example, in 1802–1803, Lancashire had the lowest pauper:population ratio in the country at 6.7 percent, compared to a southern county such as Sussex at 22.6 percent. In Lancashire wage rates were higher, there was less seasonality in the labor market, and alternatives to poor relief such as allotments, smallholdings, and cottage industry were more common. Regional variations in the practice of poor relief undermine any notion of a uniform *national* Poor Law. However, it was poor-relief practice in the southern counties that became the focus of acute national anxiety in the later eighteenth and early nineteenth centuries and eventually led to a radical reform of the entire welfare system.

Old Poor Law in Crisis. Advancing commercialism, population increase, and economic dislocation from about 1760 on created a crisis of paternalism in which the existing

Poor Law was perceived as a major problem. In particular, a long-term increase in wheat prices encouraged landowners to seek the enclosure of previously marginal land such as wastes and commons. This involved the loss of centuries-old common rights of grazing and gathering vital to the economy of the poor, and without which the laborer had little alternative to the seasonal variations of waged farm work. Influenced by paternalist assumptions about the right to relief, deterioration in the economic conditions of the laborers led to an expansion of welfare provision. The Poor Law authorities in most rural parishes in the south of England responded to underemployment by increasing out-relief to the able-bodied.

Rural parishes employed various methods to relieve poor able-bodied laborers: allowances-in-aid-of-wages, payments to laborers with large families, payments to seasonally unemployed agricultural laborers, the roundsmen system, and the labor rate. Allowances-in-aid-of-wages were potentially the most generous of these methods since they were intended to subsidize the weekly income of laborers' families (both employed and unemployed), adjusted according to the price of bread and the number of children in the family. The most famous example of the allowance mechanism was the bread scale adopted by the magistrates at Speenhamland in Berkshire in May 1795. However, historians have generally moved away from the view that a "Speenhamland system" characterized poor relief during this period. In fact, allowances were a temporary expedient adopted during subsistence crises brought on by harvest failures and high food prices, and preferred by farmers as an alternative to raising laborers' wages. Much more common were child allowances typically paid to laborers' families with four or more children. However, the major form of poor relief in rural parishes from 1795 to 1834 was an unemployment benefit to seasonally unemployed agricultural laborers. The amount paid was often predetermined and fixed somewhat below the going wage rate. Variant forms of the unemployment benefit were the so-called roundsmen system, in which the parish subsidized wages, and the labor rate, which allowed farmers to employ pauper labor in lieu of the payment of the poor rate.

The apparent shift within the relief system toward providing social security for unemployed men and their families and subsidizing the family income of those on low wages may have made sense in terms of paternalist traditions of reciprocity and deference, but it was an affront to the moral as well as the economic sensibilities of a new generation that increasingly accepted the philosophy now known as classical political economy. Under the influence of new ideas, many contemporaries came to regard the English Poor Law as dangerously generous. From Joseph Townsend's hostile *Dissertation on the Poor Laws* (1786)

onward, a debate raged that taxed the minds of some of the greatest intellectuals of the day, among them Edmund Burke, Thomas Malthus, and Jeremy Bentham, plus a host of pamphleteers and essayists. In this debate the concept of pauperism rather than poverty emerged as the central issue. Poverty was regarded as the "natural" state of the majority of mankind required to labor for subsistence, an immutable condition and not a proper subject for human assistance. It was only those unable to labor for their subsistence who should be relieved as paupers. Pauperism emerged as a moral as well as economic problem: how could authorities relieve the genuinely indigent without discouraging self-reliance and demoralizing the laborer?

The debate leading up to 1834 took place in an intellectual climate in which the ideas of Adam Smith, and the political economists who followed in his wake, were forging economic doctrines for a commercial society. Among these, the major influence upon social policy came in the shape of Malthus's *Essay on the Principles of Population* (1798). The implications for the Poor Law were evident. Not only allowances to the able-bodied but all forms of poor relief should be condemned for their presumed contribution to population growth and other harmful economic and moral effects. Malthus developed his critique into an argument for the abolition of all poor relief, starting with the next generation of children so as gradually to nurture prudential habits as opposed to habitual dependency. This effort could be assisted by discriminating charity and self-help. Parallel to such arguments were the ideas on poverty and pauperism emerging from the revival of evangelical thought—what Hilton (1988) has called Christian economics. This philosophy linked competition and the market to moral and spiritual growth. Since individuals were personally responsible for their own salvation, the sustenance of a laborer merely because of his poverty was in contravention of the laws of God. To remove this unthinking paternalism would be to restore the natural order, and to foster self-denial, spiritual growth, and moral virtue. This combination of natural theology and political economy influenced the politics of liberal Toryism, which gave parliamentary support to the Whig reform of the Poor Laws in 1834.

In the eyes of the critics, the Poor Laws of England were responsible for a variety of evils. Outdoor relief, in general, and allowances-in-aid-of-wages, in particular, were the prime target. Rising poor rates, increasing unemployment, falling wage rates, higher food prices, improvident marriages, and a rising birth rate were among the charges against a system that came under attack as an "engine of pauperisation." Since the 1960s, economic historians have largely refuted these criticisms of the effects of the Old Poor Law. As already seen, allowances-in-aid-of-wages were less widespread than contemporaries thought. Moreover,

Blaug (1963) maintained that allowances were too meager to constitute a viable alternative to gainful employment. His chief point was that the Old Poor Law was, in essence, a device for dealing with the problem of surplus labor in the lagging rural sector of a rapidly expanding but still underdeveloped economy. Rather than causing economic dislocation, poor relief developed in response to economic circumstances. Subsequent research has supported this view, showing for example that relief expenditures fluctuated and relief policies changed in correspondence with unemployment levels.

Reform of the Poor Laws. Whatever the conclusions of the modern economic historians, contemporary opinion assumed that the administration of relief rather than the underlying economic conditions was behind the rising tide of pauperism. There were several parliamentary inquiries into the practice of poor relief before the commission appointed in 1832, the most influential being the Select Committee of the House of Commons of 1817. Its report fully accepted the demoralization thesis about out-relief, and, following Malthus, came close to recommending abolition but held back on grounds of practical expediency rather than on any principled defence of a discredited system. Finally, it fell to the 1834 report to come up with a scheme offering to meet the aspirations of the abolitionists while satisfying the doubts of those who feared such a drastic solution.

Why did reform of the Poor Laws (rather than abolition) become such an urgent political issue in the 1830s, leading to the appointment of a royal commission and the introduction of a new system of public relief? The welfare system had become increasingly expensive, and its costs may have hit disproportionately hard in agricultural districts because the value of gross rentals of farm land, which were related to many assessments for the poor rate, had risen much more slowly than welfare costs. However, it is unlikely that, on its own, this was a sufficient issue to persuade Parliament of the need for Poor Law reform. It was also a question of public order and class relations on the land. The so-called Captain Swing disturbances of 1830–1831 affected well over fourteen hundred parishes, mainly in southern and eastern England. Riots, machine breaking, and rick-burnings, accompanied by petitions and protests over wages, poor-relief levels, and the introduction of new machinery, were concentrated in counties with a high per capita relief expenditure. Contemporaries were convinced that reform of the relief system might restore social stability by disciplining an increasingly unruly agricultural labor force. Assertions by laborers that they had a right to an "adequate" or a "fair" subsistence caused particular alarm.

After passage of the momentous Parliamentary Reform Bill of 1832, the reforming Whig ministry of Prime Minister Earl Grey appointed a Royal Commission for Inquiring into the Administration and Practical Operation of the Poor Laws. Two years later, the Report of the Poor Law Commission (written largely by two of the commissioners, Edwin Chadwick and Nassau Senior) was the inspiration behind the New Poor Law of 1834. The report is a consistent polemic against the out-relief of the able-bodied male. It pays scant attention to other categories—the sick, the elderly, children, and so on. However, instead of the pessimism of the Malthusians, the report expresses an optimism about the possibilities of reforming the system to achieve the same ends. A distinction was to be drawn between poverty and indigence. Poor relief was to be confined to the indigent, and any benefits paid to those in work were to cease. Moreover, deterrent conditions were to be imposed on the receipt of poor relief to make it more unattractive to applicants. The chief of these conditions was that relief should not contravene the principle of "less eligibility": that the "situation" of the pauper "on the whole shall not be made really or apparently so eligible as the situation of the independent laborer of the lowest class." With the desire to restore a differential between benefit and employment, the only relief to be offered the able-bodied male was entry to a "well regulated" workhouse and a regime of hard labor and "strict discipline," which it was believed would be "intolerable to the indolent and disorderly."

New Poor Law. The 1834 Poor Law Amendment Act set up national machinery to implement the report's key principles of reform. Administrative responsibility was given to a central authority authorized to issue orders and regulations on relief practice to locally elected boards of guardians. Parishes were to be grouped together into some six hundred Poor Law Unions. However, the Poor Law Amendment Act did not simply translate the 1834 report into practice. Despite the intentions of the reformers, subsequent official policy was the result of compromises between central and local interests, which, as had been the case before 1834, varied both between and within regions. This does not mean that there were no national trends, but those national characteristics were not to be found uniformly expressed across the country.

Historians are by no means in agreement about the impact of the New Poor Law, especially over the first thirty years or so of its operation. A central issue is the extent to which the reformed system was successful in achieving its primary aim, the abolition of out-relief to the able-bodied male. In particular, a series of local studies since the 1960s has stressed the continuity between the pre- and post-1834 periods and the absence of uniformity in the New Poor Law, highlighting the range of local variation and the continued possibility that localized interests could subvert as well as resist the orders of the central authority in London. Also, they have pointed to the persistence of pre-1834 practices after midcentury, including precisely those severely criticized in the Poor Law Report. However, the diversity of relief practice under the New Poor Law was in large part a consequence of concessions by the central authority in the 1840s and 1850s over the crucial issue of out-relief to the able-bodied in the face of large-scale unemployment and a campaign of resistance to the New Poor Law in the industrial districts.

In the second half of the nineteenth century, the New Poor Law evolved into a complex as well as a diverse relief system. It was designed to deal with the phenomenon of rural underemployment and to restore the social fabric in the countryside; but it was problems of structural unemployment, urban poverty, and the casual labor market that the relief system faced by the 1860s. In the 1840s and 1850s, traditional responsibilities for women, children, and the aged poor were reinforced by the assumption that, although much out-relief to adults was in support of insufficient earnings, these groups were marginal to the labor market. In the face of an apparent rise in relief costs in the 1860s, an officially endorsed "crusade against out-relief" (phrase used by S. and B. Webb) was conducted in some urban unions to cut rising relief costs. In this campaign the workhouse test was forced on groups (chiefly able-bodied female applicants) that even the writers of the 1834 report never had in mind. Paradoxically, the attempt to use the welfare system to force women into the labor market after 1870 was accompanied, in some of the larger towns and cities, by more expensive provision in larger pavilion-style workhouses, which were turning the general mixed workhouse into a series of specialist institutions for the sick and the infirm, children, and the elderly. Indeed, reforms in the 1860s went some way to creating a public hospital system in London and some larger cities. However, this should not lead one to accept unquestioningly the Webbs's "deterrence to treatment" model of relief policy. Specialization could also be for punishment, as was increasingly the case for the vagrant, who faced increasingly harsh treatment in the casual ward of the workhouse. Rather it exemplifies an increasing diversity in approach according to the moral category in which classes of applicant were placed.

Those moralizing aspects generally associated with Victorian attitudes to the poor were most explicit in official welfare policy after the 1860s. They evolved alongside the more utilitarian assumptions of 1834. Making character a factor in granting relief enhanced the stigma of pauperism and intensified hostility to poor relief among the "respectable" working class. Moreover, the increasing emphasis upon distinctions between "deserving" and "undeserving" applicants implied that the poverty of the former was due to socioeconomic forces beyond their control. This line of thinking extended even to the case of the able-bodied male when the "Chamberlain Circular" of 1886 (Joseph Chamberlain, as president of the Local Government Board, was responsible for poor relief) encouraged the relief of the "bona fide" unemployed outside the auspices of the Poor Law. Such policies undermined the utilitarian simplicities of 1834 and laid the foundations for broader concepts of state responsibility in the future.

After 1850, the Poor Law was of declining significance as a provider of welfare. Although there are no entirely adequate statistics, it is safe to say that the proportion of the population assisted by state welfare fell consistently below likely levels of poverty. This did not perturb Poor Law officials since the purpose in 1834 had been to create a flexible labor market and to encourage self-reliance rather than welfare dependency. However, in the 1880s and 1890s evidence mounted of a vast reservoir of poverty, which the Poor Law never touched. This was beginning to generate concern across society about the apparently intractable problem of poverty, for which poor relief seemed an increasingly inadequate instrument. In the following decades the Poor Law lost credibility, and the state pursued alternative strategies such as national insurance. Nevertheless, the Poor Law and its institutions lingered until finally replaced in the reforms of the 1940s that created the modern British welfare state.

[*See also* Poor Relief.]

BIBLIOGRAPHY

Blaug, Marc. "The Myth of the Old Poor Law and the Making of the New." *Journal of Economic History* 23 (1963), 151–184. A watershed in the economic history of the nineteenth-century Poor Law; influenced a generation of subsequent work, much of which is discussed by Boyer (1990).

Boyer, George R. *An Economic History of the English Poor Laws, 1750–1850*. Cambridge, 1990. An authoritative general study of the economic characteristics of English poor relief during an era of change; essential reading.

Brundage, Anthony. *The English Poor Laws, 1700–1930*. London and New York, 2002. An authoritative chronological survey.

Checkland, S. G., and E. O. A. Checkland, eds. *The Poor Law Report of 1834*. Harmondsworth, 1974. A modern edition of the famous report that provided the framework for the New Poor Law, this edition includes a useful introduction by the editors.

Crowther, Margaret A. *The Workhouse System: The History of an English Social Institution, 1834–1929*. London, 1981.

Digby, Anne. "The Labor Market and the Continuity of Social Policy after 1834." *Economic History Review* 28 (1975), 68–83. Includes evidence of the survival of Old Poor Law practices and undermines the idea of a revolution in poor relief in 1834.

Harris, Jose. *Private Lives, Public Spirit: A Social History of Britain, 1870–1914*. Oxford, 1993. A general history, with an excellent chapter on later Victorian social theory and approaches to poverty.

Hilton, Boyd. *The Age of Atonement: The Influence of Evangelicalism on Social and Economic Thought, 1785–1865*. Oxford, 1988. Explores the relationship between religious ideas and the success of economic doctrines; contains much of relevance on the Poor Laws.

Himmelfarb, Gertrude. *The Idea of Poverty: England in the Early Industrial Age*. London and Boston, 1984. Contains valuable chapters on the political economy of the Poor Laws in the age of Adam Smith and Thomas Malthus. Has much to say about the moral and economic dimensions of "pauperism"; a widely read and influential study.

Kidd, Alan J. "How the Webbs Wrote Their History of the English Poor Laws." *Economic History Review* 40 (1987), 400–417. Includes a critical evaluation of the pioneer historians of the English Poor Laws.

Kidd, Alan J. *State, Society, and the Poor in Nineteenth-Century England*. London and New York, 1999. A general account that covers charity and self-help as well as poor relief.

King, Steven. *Poverty and Welfare in England, 1700–1850: A Regional Perspective*. Manchester, 2000. Argues that regional differences characterized the operation of the Poor Laws both before and after 1834. In this the north was less generous than the south.

Lees, Lynn Hollen. *The Solidarities of Strangers: The English Poor Laws and the People, 1700–1948*. Cambridge, 1998. Argues that the Poor Laws were an important element in the "economy of makeshifts" and concentrates as much on individual narratives as Poor Law policy.

Marshall, John D. *The Old Poor Law, 1795–1834*. 2d ed. London, 1985. Useful discussion of the historical debates arising from Blaug's insightful study.

Poynter, John R. *Society and Pauperism: English Ideas on Poor Relief, 1795–1834*. London, 1969. Contains the fullest account of the long debate over the Poor Law that culminated in the reform of 1834. Shows how close Parliament came to the abolition of all relief as Malthus had recommended.

Rose, Michael E., ed. *The English Poor Law, 1780–1930*. Newton Abbott, 1971. Documents with valuable editorial commentary.

Snell, K. D. *Annals of the Labouring Poor: Social Change and Agrarian England, 1660–1900*. Cambridge, 1985. Generally useful with a good chapter on poor relief that portrays generous provision under the Old Poor Law—compare with King (2000).

Webb, Sidney, and Beatrice Webb. *English Poor Law Policy*. London, 1910. This remains the most useful of the Webbs's books on the Poor Laws. It was written as part of their research for the Royal Commission on the Poor Laws of 1905–1909.

Webb, Sidney, and Beatrice Webb. *English Poor Law History, Part I: The Old Poor Law*. London, 1927.

Webb, Sidney, and Beatrice Webb. *English Poor Law History, Part II: The Last Hundred Years*. 2 vols. London, 1929. The most detailed of the Webbs's histories. Despite their flaws (see Kidd, 1987), these volumes, and that on the Old Poor Law, remain basic texts for the serious student of English poor relief.

Williams, Karel. *From Pauperism to Poverty*. London and Boston, 1981. Includes a large and very useful appendix of statistical tables and graphs relating to the nineteenth-century Poor Law.

Winch, Donald. *Riches and Poverty: An Intellectual History of Political Economy in Britain, 1750–1834*. Cambridge, 1996.

ALAN J. KIDD

POOR RELIEF. An inclusive definition of poor relief should encompass all forms of aid, charity, and public assistance to the poor. In reality, the dominant role of central governments in the relief of poverty since the early twentieth century has served to obscure the extent to which there exists in all complex societies a "mixed economy of welfare," in which the state is only one of several constituent parts. Thus, in modern Western societies, tax-funded public welfare benefits and services play a greater role than at any previous time in history. Yet even today, they stand alongside the activities of voluntary nonprofit agencies organized on a philanthropic or mutual-aid basis, the informal welfare networks and services of household, kin, and community, and the commercial provision of private goods such as savings, insurance, and pensions. Looked at in less institutional terms, survival for the poor means making the best of an "economy of makeshifts" (Hufton, 1974), mixing earned income (of all sorts) with savings and loans, the support of family and neighbors, the claiming of welfare benefits, and the help of charity.

"Poverty" is not a universal concept. Its usage and meaning differ across time. However, its modern configuration as an economic phenomenon, along with various discourses about it, originated with the rise of the market in western Europe from the later medieval period onward. The experience of poverty is especially associated with certain points in the life cycle and with particular risks. Thus childhood, unemployment, sickness, disability, and old age can be precarious times and events in the lives of individuals and communities. Each of them can be accompanied by a loss of resources and potential or actual dependency upon others. These times and events are most likely to pose a threat to survival if the individual is unprotected by attachment to a group with conventions about, and mechanisms for, assistance on occasions of need. This group can be as confined as the family or as inclusive as the welfare state. It is the exclusion from all such attachments that makes the individual most vulnerable. Thus in the so-called economy of makeshifts it is best to possess as many attachments as possible. Clearly, exposure to want is a cultural condition as well as an economic phenomenon. A society's approach to the welfare of others is determined by such things as its ideas of economic causation and individual rights, or the dominance of certain versions of these ideas. In the twentieth century, the emergence of welfare states in most Western societies marked a shift in the balance of welfare, ceding the state a larger role as provider of welfare benefits. In general, this development was underpinned by a notion of poverty that conceived individuals as citizens with social as well as civil rights.

Before the state welfare programs of the twentieth century, poor relief was the chief mechanism for dealing with poverty. Despite its many guises and purposes it rarely aspired to do more than relieve destitution—to provide a safety net by which the poor could maintain a bare subsistence. However, it dealt with the poor in a variety of ways and often sought to categorize them so as to treat them differently according to type. Much of this approach had rational economic intentions; but poor relief was never purely an economic instrument, and a society's approach to welfare is intrinsically linked to its pattern of power relations and its normative values, especially its view of human

POOR RELIEF. *Virgin of the Tailors*, painting (1533) by Bonifazio de' Pitati. (Accademia, Venice/ Cameraphoto/Art Resource, NY)

purposes. The spread of capitalist relations, from the later Middle Ages onward, encouraged economic motives; but princes and urban elites equally wanted social stability for its own sake and hungered for power and prestige. Poor relief was an instrument of political as well as economic plans. Furthermore, although secular authorities played an increasing role, it must be remembered that all Western societies before the modern era were essentially religious in ideology and institutional structure. There was a general drift from clerical to lay control, but the church and voluntary religious bodies continued to play a major role in relief at least until the eighteenth century.

Medieval Times. The church was the chief source of poor relief during the Middle Ages. Up to a third of ecclesiastical revenues might be allotted to the support of the poor in each parish. Additionally, the church managed charitable donations to monastic orders, and the monasteries were a regular source of relief to the poor. Alms were distributed to wandering beggars at the monastery gates, and infirmaries housed the sick and disabled and offered shelter to those on pilgrimages. Initially, the laity channeled their charity through the church and its monastic

foundations; but during the twelfth century, urban elites began to establish their own hospitals, almshouses, leper houses, and other charitable institutions. Moreover, the rise of the mendicant orders encouraged the custom of giving alms directly to those who asked for assistance.

The theory of poor relief evolved in line with the commercialization of what still remained essentially a feudal society. From the twelfth century onward, the early development of a market economy began to foster increased respect for property based in monetary wealth. It also produced a concept of poverty that distinguished between the voluntary or spiritual poverty of the holy ascetics, who chose their degradation in an imitation of Christ, and that of the involuntary, secular poor, whose social position was ordained by God. The sanctification of voluntary poverty, however, encouraged a degree of compassion toward all supplicants for alms. There was another reason why giving to beggars was common during the medieval centuries (and after): the medieval theory of charity decreed that almsgiving and donations to the church were necessary for the redemption of the sinner, for whom riches and power were portrayed as a moral burden. The poor, however, were perceived merely as the necessary objects of this charity. In what amounted to an "alms contract," the poor were required to pray for the souls of their benefactors in return for the gift of charity. The process became ritualized as the duty of benevolence was worked out through giving to support religious and lay institutions.

Whether much of this benefited those who were not poor by choice is doubtful. The rural poor were largely untouched by charity and remained dependent upon customary rights in the manorial system. Moreover, the penetration of a money-based economy into village life and the population growth of the twelfth and thirteenth centuries greatly increased economic insecurity in rural areas. Even in the towns, those most likely to be assisted were the so-called shame-faced poor, impoverished members of the social elite who were singled out for preferential treatment. The rest of those in need were subject to a growing set of criteria, which would become familiar accompaniments of poor relief over the centuries to come. As Tierney (1959) demonstrated, the "decretist" theologians of the twelfth century categorized supplicants as the "honest poor," who solicited alms through necessity, and the rest, whose unworthy or fraudulent claims could be safely rejected. Alms to the undeserving were decreed to be harmful since the prayers of the undeserving could not be relied on, and the reciprocal character of the "alms contract" thus would be abrogated. These ideas gained credence, and the crowds of beggars, their arms outstretched for aid, who gathered outside churches and littered the streets during festivals and feast days could be freely ignored by the passerby. In fact, the most likely recipients of poor relief in the later medieval town were those considered least able to subsist without aid: the infirm and disabled, orphan children, and the elderly. These "deserving" cases received more or less permanent aid in institutions funded by rich and powerful benefactors. Medieval hospitals provided temporary shelter and distributed food to the needy, and were not providers of medical care in any modern sense.

Sixteenth and Seventeenth Centuries. Poor relief in the postmedieval centuries became enmeshed in the continued growth of a market economy in parts of Europe, but also in the rise of the modern state. Governments attempted to regulate the labor market, civil authorities assumed responsibility for administering institutional relief, and communities made attempts to organize compulsory poor rates to finance growing relief expenditures. Despite the increased role of the state, religious and voluntary bodies continued to play a major role in European relief mechanisms. Underlying these changes was a new view of poverty that emphasized the obligation to work and drew a connection between destitution and idleness. This attitude culminated in the writings of the sixteenth century reformers but had originated in reaction to the Black Death and

the crisis of the fourteenth century, when labor shortages and demands for higher wages led governments across western Europe into (ultimately unsuccessful) attempts to fix wage rates, enforce employment contracts, and impede the passage of migrant labor. Central to these measures were repeated statutes against so-called sturdy beggars, that is, the able-bodied poor, who should be forced to work. The giving of charitable alms was to be restricted to the "impotent" poor, those incapacitated by age or infirmity. Thus the late medieval shift against the "undeserving" beggar was hardened into statute law, and the first intervention of the state into social welfare was marked by repression. The repression of mendicancy remained a chief aim of official policy into the sixteenth century; but from the 1520s and 1530s on, the economic management of poor relief by civil authorities was the major theme in welfare reform across western Europe.

Population pressure, harvest failures, epidemics, and underemployment provoked a relief crisis during the second quarter of the sixteenth century, which was marked by a revolution in welfare provision affecting up to sixty towns and cities and involving a hitherto unprecedented intervention by the state in social welfare. The degree of state intervention was most marked in northern and central Europe and least evident in Spain, Italy, and France; but there were common purposes across the whole of western Europe. In attempts to exclude vagrants, begging was prohibited. In addition, the duty to work was encouraged, and schemes often were promoted to set the able-bodied to work. Municipal authorities gathered funds for the relief of the poor (in "common boxes"), and the law was invoked to enforce the collection of a poor rate from citizens. Several economic historians have concluded that these developments enabled the authorities to use poor relief as a mechanism to regulate the labor market (Geremek, 1994; Lis and Soly, 1979). According to this view, the new poor-relief policies served the needs of an emerging mercantile economy and permitted urban elites to control the supply of labor. Poor-relief payments to underemployed workers in seasonal or casual labor markets allowed the maintenance of a crucial labor reserve during downturns in trade. Poor relief was used to retain essential workers who otherwise might have starved or migrated; relief was reduced or removed when trade revived. Such a pattern was characteristic of an economy in which seasonal and cyclical fluctuations in the demand for labor were common. Thus a key role of the state in welfare policy was the management of economic insecurity.

A tradition inherited from the nineteenth century links this development to the Reformation and to Protestantism. Max Weber, one of the founding fathers of sociology, linked Protestantism with the work ethic and the rise of the capitalist spirit (*The Protestant Ethic and the Spirit of Capitalism*,

London, 1930) and the pioneer economic historian R. H. Tawney identified it with the "new medicine for poverty" (*Religion and the Rise of Capitalism*, London, 1926). Indeed, the doctrines of Luther undermined the redemptive value of charity as good works, and Calvinist distinctions between the elect and the reprobate encouraged a harsh view of the poor. Moreover, many of the towns of the early Reformation enthusiastically adopted the secularization of poor relief. However, twentieth-century historians have successfully undermined this connection by pointing to contemporaneous Catholic examples of reform in cities such as Ypres, Nîmes, Lyons, and Venice (Davis, 1975; Pullan, 1976). Although there were differences between Protestant and Catholic approaches that reveal cultural as well as economic factors at work, there was a new common approach to poor relief in which perhaps only Spain was the exception. Spain resisted the new medicine for poverty in the name of Catholic orthodoxy; religious movements continued to dominate Spanish poor relief although they did generate new charitable initiatives. In Granada, Cordoba, and other towns, Saint John of God and his followers established hospitals for the lowliest as well as the most respectable of the poor. Indeed, even though charities remained central to poor relief in Catholic Europe, they generally fell under secular control and often adopted the new approaches. Although their purposes might be spiritual, they often displayed a willingness to discriminate on economic and moral grounds between applicants. The persistence of charitable relief is particularly important when it is remembered that the municipal poor-relief schemes were generally short-lived, as they were either responses to specific economic crises or became themselves too expensive to maintain. The sheer scale of demands made upon the schemes sometimes exhausted funds. It is too neat a picture to envisage a network of regularly operating centralized relief programs across time. The only state that came close to such a model was England.

English Poor Relief. During the sixteenth century, England developed the most systematic poor relief of any state in Europe, codified in the Elizabethan Poor Law (1597 and 1601), which required poor persons either to support themselves or to apply to their own parishes of settlement for aid. Overseers of the poor in each parish determined eligibility for relief and levied parish poor rates on property owners. Justices of the peace validated the rolls and compelled payments from those who failed to contribute. Various local experiments, many of them modeled on the workhouse established in London's Bridewell hospital in the 1550s, inspired Parliament to make parish overseers responsible for organizing work for the able-bodied poor; but many parishes simply gave "outdoor relief" to the unemployed without "setting them on work." The English Poor Law system of the seventeenth and eighteenth centuries is generally regarded as unique in its national scope, its comparative uniformity, and relative generosity. It reflects, and may even have contributed to, a pattern of economic growth and social change in England that set it apart from the rest of Europe as early as 1700 (Slack, 1988; Solar, 1995). European models, especially the mixture of institutional and outdoor relief in the English Poor Laws, greatly influenced poor-relief provision in colonial America. There was no national system, however; and vagrancy laws plus limited state responsibility for the non-able-bodied, accompanied by a preference for voluntary charity, characterized the welfare policy of American Society until the twentieth century.

Paupers. Besides the economic rationale of labor management, there were powerful noneconomic reasons why poor relief was provided. In an era when social stability was frequently threatened by political unrest and social disorder, poor relief enabled civil authorities to cope with short-term crises such as those caused by trade slumps, food shortages, and disease epidemics. Moreover, up to the nineteenth century most societies had to cope with failing systems of social security on the land as impoverishment led to migration and vagrancy. Authorities tried to deal with vagrancy by exclusion, increasingly harsh punishments, and generally inadequate measures to remove paupers to their places of origin (settlement) where they might legally obtain relief. Since most problems caused by wandering beggars were supposedly caused by idleness, one solution lay in reeducation and the disciplinary regimes of "houses of correction" (bridewells, *rasphuis*). The treatment of the unlicensed beggar as a social deviant requiring correction (generally by exposure to work discipline) was a persistent element in early modern social policy. Ecclesiastical and civil authorities ran these institutions, and in seventeenth-century France they became the defining feature of poor relief (the so-called Great Confinement).

Recently historians have begun to show increased interest in the recipients of poor relief. Whatever the intentions of its providers, such assistance was often vital to the survival strategies of the poor, whose self-help strategies rarely could tide them over more than the slightest of crises. In eighteenth-century Antwerp and nineteenth-century Amsterdam, the poor made rational use of correctional institutions and insane asylums to provide sustenance to family members. (Lis, 1986; van Leeuwen, 2000). In nineteenth-century England, poor women were willing to exploit various private and public resources to supplement inadequate family income, circumventing the official rule that only the impotent poor received help outside the established workhouse. Moreover, applicants for relief adapted to the requirements of the donors that they appear deserving by playing a role in what has been described as the "theatre of charity" (Mandler, 1990).

Industrialization and After. The nineteenth and early twentieth centuries saw rapid industrial advances and unprecedented urban growth, major shifts in patterns of occupation (chiefly from agricultural to industrial and service), greater opportunity for some individuals, and economic insecurity for many. That era witnessed the formation of new social classes, new ideologies, and novel forms of politics and government. It is not surprising for such a "revolutionary" period to be accompanied by a reformulation of social policy. In economic terms, the Poor Law Amendment Act of 1834 in England has been seen by some as the advent of a "liberal capitalist" stage in poor relief. It marked a "liberal break" with the past, as the measure that made the creation of a "free" market in labor a central plank of central government policy (Polanyi, 1944, Rimlinger, 1971). The state was to play an increasing role in the welfare policies of the Western industrial nations, including the United States; and in the age of mass democracy its part would not be limited to poor relief. Ultimately poor-relief policies were subsumed within the structures of the "social welfare state," in which central governments stand committed to the social rights of citizens. However, such notions of entitlement are often contested; and, on a global level, the traditional concept of using poor relief for bare subsistence remains in the forefront, even as idealistic statements of universal rights are linked uneasily with support for development plans and investment strategies.

[See also Poor Laws.]

BIBLIOGRAPHY

Davis, Natalie Z. "Poor Relief, Humanism, and Heresy." In *Society and Culture in Early Modern France*, edited by Natalie Z. Davis. Stanford, 1975. Argues that the poor relief reforms of the sixteenth century cut across confessional boundaries (see also Pullan, 1976).

Geremek, Bronislaw. *Poverty: A History*. Oxford, 1994. Originally written in 1978, long regarded as one of the classics of modern historical writing, and translated into many languages. Puts poverty and poor relief at the center of European history and is strongest on medieval and early modern period.

Hufton, Olwen H. *The Poor of Eighteenth Century France*. Oxford, 1974. The realities of being poor in an underdeveloped economy.

Jutte, Robert. *Poverty and Deviance in Early Modern Europe*. Cambridge, 1994. A very useful general study.

Leeuwen, Marco H. D. van. *The Logic of Charity: Amsterdam, 1800–1850*. London, 2000. A detailed analysis of poor relief in Amsterdam combined with a clearly stated model of relief in preindustrial Europe.

Lis, Catharina. *Social Change and the Labouring Poor: Antwerp, 1770–1860*. New Haven, Conn., and London, 1986.

Lis, Catharina, and Hugo Soly. *Poverty and Capitalism in Preindustrial Europe*. New Jersey, 1979. A powerful analysis of medieval and early modern poor relief from a Marxist perspective.

Little, Lester K. *Religious Poverty and the Profit Economy in Medieval Europe*. London, 1978. A study of the religious ideal of voluntary poverty between 1000 and 1300.

Mandler, Peter, ed. *The Uses of Charity: The Poor on Relief in the Nineteenth-Century Metropolis*. Philadelphia, 1990. See especially the essays by Lees and P. Mandler.

Martz, Linda. *Poverty and Welfare in Habsburg Spain*. Cambridge, 1983.

Mollat, M. *The Poor in the Middle Ages: An Essay in Social History*. New Haven, Conn., and London, 1986.

Polanyi, Karl. *The Great Transformation: The Political and Economic Origins of Our Time*. New York, 1944. A classic of modern economic history; devastatingly perceptive and still challenging. Available in many editions.

Pullan, Brian. "Catholics and the Poor in Early Modern Europe." *Transactions of the Royal Historical Society* 5. 26 (1976), 15–34.

Rimlinger, Gaston V. *Welfare Policy and Industrialisation in Europe, America and Russia*. New York, 1971.

Slack, Paul. *Poverty and Policy in Tudor and Stuart England*. London, 1988.

Solar, Peter M. "Poor Relief and English Industrial Development before the Industrial Revolution." *Economic History Review* 48 (1995), 1–22.

Tierney, Brian. *Medieval Poor Law: A Sketch of Canonical Theory and Its Application in England*. Berkeley, 1959.

Woolf, Stuart. *The Poor in Western Europe in the Eighteenth and Nineteenth Centuries*. London, 1986.

ALAN J. KIDD

POPULAR ENTERTAINMENT. Historically, the scope of popular entertainment ranged from small performances by itinerant showpeople to spectacular events organized by state and church. After the Industrial Revolution, itinerant entertainment declined, especially in England, and was replaced by the growth of a mass entertainment industry. A move from participatory entertainment to spectacle occurred between the late eighteenth century and the early nineteenth century. During the nineteenth century, entrepreneurial activity became prominent in the provision of popular entertainment.

The elimination of open spaces in towns and the increase in factory labor (with a consequent decline in seasonal occupations) also changed the nature of entertainment. Moral, political, and evangelical objections to popular amusements, such as fairs, severely restricted the availability of venues for entertainment during the early nineteenth century. Portable theaters, menageries, circuses, puppet booths, peep shows, exhibitions of "freaks," and waxworks were among the many attractions of the fairs. The demise of London's famous Bartholomew Fair in the 1840s and a number of provincial fairs closed off profitable options and opportunities for seasonal employment.

Circuses and menageries nevertheless survived. Circus entrepreneurs often started with little. Antonio Franconi, the first great French circus proprietor, exhibited trained canaries. The English "Lord" George Sanger exhibited trained birds and mice in a London warehouse. By 1871, through the gradual accumulation of livestock and equipment, Sanger was able to spend £11,000 on the acquisition of Astley's Amphitheatre, the leading equestrian and circus performance venue in London. Earlier, Andrew

Ducrow's equestrian performances were so successful that he cleared £5,000 in a summer season at Astley's during the recession of 1834. At his death, he left property worth £60,000. George Wombwell's success as a menagerie owner originated from the purchase of two boa constrictors for exhibition at a cost of £75, while E. H. Bostock, son of Wombwell's partner, progressed from employment at £2 per week with his mother's touring menagerie to running several touring menageries and circuses and the Olympia, Glasgow, by the early 1900s. The entrepreneurial spirit was also alive in the American circus. James West made a fortune once he realized traveling circuses were more profitable than fixed circuses. The introduction of the canvas tent in 1826 and subsequently the spectacular three-ring circus further enhanced profits. In the nineteenth century, circuses were often run by syndicates, usually involving strong family connections, who controlled a wide range of circus activities and equipment manufacture.

Traveling marionette theaters were popular throughout Europe during the eighteenth and nineteenth centuries. Economical to run, especially as family businesses, they performed in streets and at fairs. However, by the 1870s, the marionette manipulators of France and England were earning around the same as a poorly paid day laborer, although the growth of communications did enhance the range of places to visit for performances. A boom in purpose-built puppet theaters took place from 1860 to 1900, followed by a decline. Such theaters often adjusted admission charges to particular days of the week, but by the 1900s, puppeteers looked elsewhere for employment.

The decline of the nineteenth-century fairs forced puppeteers onto the streets. Street puppeteers could make £4 to £5 per week in the 1820s, especially when half-crown customers ordered private performances outside their houses, but by the mid-nineteenth century this had declined to £2 per week. Other street entertainers were less successful. Henry Mayhew cites a street poet, who earned 3s. in a good week and 1s. or even nothing in a bad one, and three traveling showmen with a bear, a monkey, and two dogs, who each cleared 7s. per week after expenses, making 20s. to 30s. per night in half pences.

The exhibition of "freaks" at fairs and circuses was always profitable. P. T. Barnum's American Museum, which exhibited freaks from 1841 at a 25-cent admission charge, hosted an estimated forty-one million visitors and was a forerunner of the dime shows of the 1870s to the 1900s. Freaks were also exhibited at the great world fairs, amusement parks, and carnivals. With the impact of the 1929 depression on popular entertainment, freak shows declined, and from the 1940s, seriously dwindled in appeal. Some exhibits, however, made good livings. For example, the miniscule General Tom Thumb acquired great personal wealth after Barnum exhibited him in the nineteenth century. Wild animals proved equally exotic in this period but could be costly to purchase and transport (one elephant cost £1,200). Isaac van Amburgh's wild beast show proved profitable from the 1830s, as did the boxing kangaroo at the London Aquarium in the 1890s. Walter Holland, however, lost £7,000 in three days when his attempt to introduce bullfights to London's Royal Agricultural Hall flopped in the mid-nineteenth century.

Fireworks displays were often entrepreneurial. Fireworks became synonymous in Europe with religious and secular celebrations, especially royal progresses and national events. In the eighteenth and nineteenth centuries, they were also a frequent aspect of the amusements offered by pleasure gardens. Charles Brock drew huge crowds for his Crystal Palace fireworks displays (a quarter of a million for his first display in 1866; an average of thirty-five thousand for subsequent exhibitions). The cost of a large display was around £600 at this time. In England, the Explosives Act of 1875 helped regulate the fireworks industry, which previously had been illegal but active since the seventeenth century.

The popular appeal of fireworks was reflected in the huge crowds drawn on 5 November to the Britannia Theatre, Hoxton, for annual representations of *Guy Fawkes* accompanied by William Payne's fireworks. This theater also drew crowds by exhibiting Siamese twins, giants and giantesses, the Tichborne Claimant, and popular acrobats. Music hall acts were also common there. Indeed, the music hall, which developed in the 1830s and 1840s from the "free and easies," pleasure gardens, saloons, and song and supper rooms, became one of the most successful forms of popular entertainment in nineteenth-century England. Although the halls were expensive to run, labor costs were high, and business was unpredictable, they expanded in the middle and final years of the century. By the 1900s, syndicates, formed to meet the high capital demands, developed chains of halls and centralized the industry.

BIBLIOGRAPHY

Bailey, Peter. *Music Hall: The Business of Pleasure.* London, 1986.

Bailey, Peter. *Leisure and Class in Victorian England: Rational Recreation and the Contest for Control, 1839–1885.* London, 1987.

Bogdan, Robert. *Freak Show: Presenting Human Oddities for Amusement and Profit.* Chicago, 1988.

Bostock, E. H. *Menageries, Circuses, and Theatres.* London, 1927.

Brock, Alan St. H. *A History of Fireworks.* London, 1949.

Davis, Jim, ed. *The Britannia Diaries 1863–1875: Selections from the Diaries of Frederick C. Wilton.* London, 1992.

May, Earl Chapin. *The Circus from Rome to Ringling.* New York, 1963.

McCormick, John, and Bennie Pratasik. *Popular Puppet Theatre in Europe.* Cambridge, 1998.

Sanger, Lord George. *Seventy Years a Showman.* London, 1910.

Schlicke, Paul. *Dickens and Popular Entertainment.* London, 1985.

JIM DAVIS

POPULATION. Population is any permanent group of individuals renewing itself through reproduction and migration, structured in a continuous sequence of generations, defined and identified by one or more dimensions of a geographic, political, juridical, ethnic, religious, or cultural nature. Renewal takes place through biological reproduction or social reproduction, which occurs when a group or population gains (or loses) individuals through migration. Theory distinguishes between closed and open populations: in the former renewal is only biological (births); in the latter renewal is both biological and social (migration). Any accidental, occasional, or temporary collection of individuals (the crowd in a stadium, vacationers on the beach, patients in a hospital) although representing a population in technical or statistical terms, is not normally the object of study of history, demography, or genetics. In most cases a population is defined by geographical references—natural, political, or administrative boundaries—but populations are also commonly defined on the basis of religion, language, ethnicity, or other characteristics dictated by convenience or necessity. Most historical analyses refer to geographically defined populations, but in many cases subgroups are treated as populations (urban and rural population; aristocracy and commoners; farmers and laborers; masters and slaves; members of different religious affiliation; speakers of different languages or dialects; individuals belonging to different ethnic groups or castes) with distinctive behaviors in terms of nuptiality, fertility, mortality, or mobility.

Modern counts and censuses have been held regularly since the early nineteenth century (although their origins are much more remote) to assess the size and characteristics of a population. In census practice, a distinction is made between *de facto* and *de jure* or resident population: the first relating to the individuals actually living and working in a given territory even if on a temporary basis, or who happen to be present for other reasons at the moment of the count. The second term relates only to those who have a juridical residential entitlement in the same territory, even if they have emigrated or are usually absent. Another distinction is between urban and rural population, identified with a variety of criteria, the simpler being the one assigning the characteristics of urban to the population living in incorporated townships or cities above a certain size, while labeling everything else rural. A related distinction, between farm and nonfarm (or agricultural and nonagricultural) population is based on the source of the household's income and livelihood or the nature of the prevailing occupation of its members. Institutional population refers to individuals who do not normally live in households, such as soldiers in barracks, patients in hospitals, the indigent in charitable establishments, the religious in convents and monasteries. Merely instrumental

and descriptive are other uses of the term *population*, indicating subsets of individuals with determined biodemographic (sex, age) or social characteristics (marital status, working status), such as male or female population, marriageable population, working age population, and school age population.

Models. Broadly speaking, analysis tries to understand the mechanisms that determine population change and its age structure (relative size of each age group). In any period of time, absolute change is determined by the balance of births and deaths (natural growth) and by the balance of immigration and emigration; in relative terms, these flows are translated into rates, their algebraic sum being the rate of growth (birth rate $= b$; death rate $= d$; immigration and emigration rates i and e, respectively; the rate of growth r being equal to $b - d + i - e$). At any given moment, the age structure is a function of the relative size of the past 100 birth cohorts, of the force of mortality (losses incurred in each cohort between birth and the current year), and of the additions and subtractions operated by migration. Theoretical models illustrate the properties of populations (these are more easily understood when a closed population—no migration—is postulated). The simpler of these models is the stationary population that has a rate of increase equal to zero and an age structure constant in time. An interesting property—known to Edmund Halley (1656–1742) and Leonhard Euler (1707–1783)—is that in a stationary population, in which by definition the birth rate is equal to the death rate, these rates are also equal to the reciprocal of the expectation of life at birth, $e(0)$, or the mean number of years of life of each birth cohort. If b and d are equal to 10 per 1,000, then the expectation of life must been its inverse, or 1000 divided by 10, or 100 years; if—as was the case for many populations before the Industrial Revolution—b and d are equal and comprised between 30 and 50 per thousand, then the corresponding $e(0)$ must vary between 33 and 20 years. Obviously enough, stationarity is an abstract situation and no real population conforms precisely to the model, although some approximate it in the long run. For example, if we postulate a population of a few million (6, for example) at the time of the onset of agriculture some 10,000 years ago, and one of a few hundred million (252, in the estimates of Biraben) in AD 0, the rate of increase on average will have been a tiny 0.06 percent per year, quite close to zero. In a stationary population, the stream of births is constant, and so is the attrition of mortality, so that at every age there is a constant number of individuals, hence the age structure is fixed. As a rule, in a stationary population, the age structure is older the higher the expectation of life is: as an illustration, a population with an $e(0)$ equal to 20 has a mean age of 25 years; if $e(0)$ is 50—as in many Western populations at the beginning of the twentieth century—the mean age is 34; if 80 years—as in modern developed societies—the corresponding mean age is 41.

A more flexible model is that of the stable population, whose foundations can be traced in Euler's works and were later developed by the biologist and demographer Alfred Lotka (1880–1949). A population with fertility and mortality functions (that is, birth rates and death rates by age) that are constant in time develops a fixed-age structure and a constant rate of growth—positive or negative, depending on the levels of mortality and fertility. Many large populations of the past—small ones are often affected by fluctuations and migration and deviate greatly from the stable properties—with no voluntary control of fertility and high mortality were close to stability. In these relatively frequent cases, appropriate models are extremely useful for the interpretation of concrete population trends and characteristics, since the episodic, fragmented, or incomplete information on past populations can be integrated and supplemented by the parameters of a stable population model. Many populations of Europe, for example, between the sixteenth and the eighteenth centuries, have exhibited relatively constant birth rates (between 30 and 40 per thousand) and relatively constant death rates (albeit affected by violent short-term fluctuations), corresponding to an expectation of life at birth between 25 and 35 years. Large populations, such as China's and India's until the mid-twentieth century, have also exhibited stable or quasi-stable characteristics. Much the same thing can be said of many other populations of Africa, Asia, or the Americas before the onset of modernization.

Theory has debated other concepts, such as those of minimum, maximum, or optimum population. Their foundations are different and mainly related to biodemographic considerations for the minimum population, to ecological considerations for the maximum, and to social and economic ones for the optimum. There are minimal size requirements for a population in order to ensure its renewal and continuity: below certain levels (say a few hundred individuals), reproduction can be jeopardized by the scarcity of mating candidates or their randomly distorted age distribution. Moreover, very small populations are vulnerable to violent fluctuations and shocks that might cripple their ability to survive or rebound.

Maximum population relates to the concept of carrying capacity relative to the resources available in a given territory (food, water, space). Estimates are based on a variety of criteria: from categoric pronouncements to mathematical algorithms, from extension of observed population densities to the entire terrestrial surface to methods relying on the availability of a limited resource, generally food. In a recent review of ninety-three estimates of the earth's carrying capacity, from the earliest of Antoni van Leeuwenhoek (1679), Gregory King (1695), and Peter Süssmilch

(1741 and 1765) to contemporary ones, seventeen give a value below 5 billion, twenty-eight between 5 and 10, twenty-four between 10 and 25, and another twenty-four more than 25, with a median value of 10 billion (which, incidentally, is the population that early twenty-first century United Nations projections assign to the world in 2075 under a "medium" fertility scenario). At the beginning of the nineteenth century, the Belgian mathematician Pierre Verhulst incorporated the notion of carrying capacity in the logistic function that describes population change as tending asyntotically to a maximum (K) that is determined by the available resources. The logistic function is a mathematical expression of Malthus's principle, and it was suggested to Verhulst by another Belgian scholar, Adolphe Quételet (1796–1874), under the hypothesis that the sum of the obstacles (natural, related to subsistence) to population growth varies in proportion to the square of the rate of growth.

Optimum population tries to identify the population size that maximizes the welfare of a population. A general idea is that with a given level of capital, resources, and technology, the welfare of a population varies with the increase of the population: when density is very low, welfare is low because too few people are unable to make the most out of the available endowment; when population increases, positive returns to scale and division of labor push welfare up. However, past certain limits, environmental degradation and decreasing returns may set in, pushing welfare down. Determining a theoretical optimum may be possible in a static situation, but is impossible in a dynamic state because population and endowment interact, and because, obviously enough, technology and knowledge are in a continuously dynamic state.

World Population: Until the Neolithic Transition. Estimates of world population growth are based largely on conjectures and inferences, often drawn from nonquantitative information, at least until the eighteenth or nineteenth century. According to Biraben, who has reviewed the literature, prior to the High Paleolithic period (30,000–35,000 BCE) the world population cannot have exceeded a few hundred thousand, reaching a few million around 10,000 BCE, at the onset of the Neolithic period. The gradual transition from hunting and gathering to agriculture was marked, in the general opinion of scholars, by a steady increase of the population as a consequence of the enhanced ability to generate resources. However, the reasons for the acceleration of growth are debated. A classic interpretation is that sedentarization and agriculture secured more stable nutritional patterns, making possible food storage and buffering meteorological vagaries. Survival improved and growth accelerated. Another theory postulates just the opposite: agriculture increased human dependence on a few basic staples (cereal) and the quality of nutrition declined while

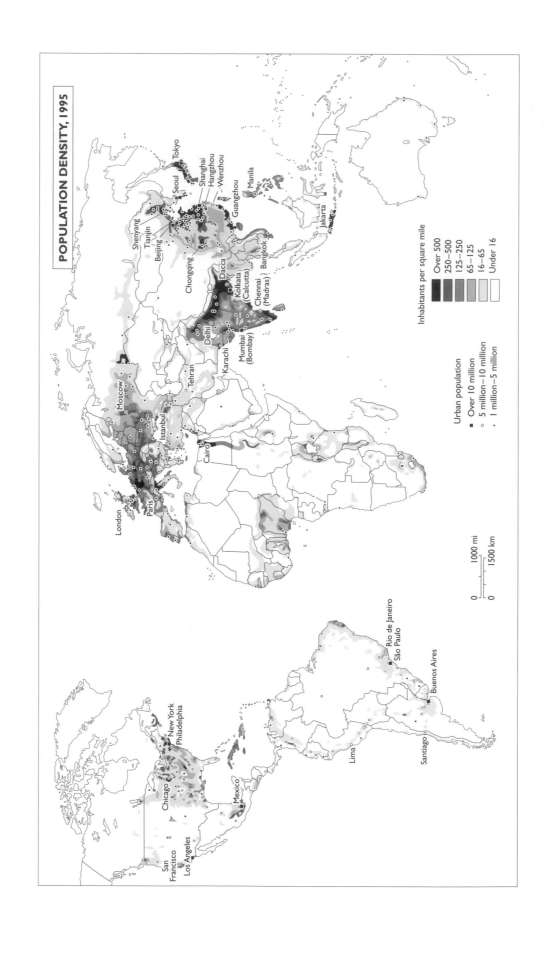

POPULATION DENSITY, 1995

Tokyo
Seoul
Shanghai
Hangzhou
Wenzhou
Guangzhou
Manila
Shenyang
Tianjin
Beijing
Chongqing
Dacca
Kolkata (Calcutta)
Chennai (Madras)
Bangkok
Jakarta
Delhi
Mumbai (Bombay)
Karachi
Tehran
Moscow
Istanbul
Cairo
London
Paris

San Francisco
Los Angeles
Chicago
New York
Philadelphia
Mexico
Lima
Santiago
Rio de Janeiro
São Paulo
Buenos Aires

Urban population
■ Over 10 million
○ 5 million–10 million
• 1 million–5 million

Inhabitants per square mile
Over 500
250–500
125–250
65–125
16–65
Under 16

0   1000 mi
0   1500 km

increased density, domestication of animals, and sedentarization worsened the biopathological conditions and enhanced the transmission of disease. As a consequence, mortality increased, but this increase was more than offset by a higher fertility typical of a sedentary population. In a hunting-and-gathering population, birth intervals are long (through prolonged lactation, regulation of sexual intercourse, and so on), reducing the number of children and enhancing women's mobility; with the transition to agriculture, birth intervals shorten—as observed in twentieth-century !Kung-San in southern Africa—and the birth rate increases. Whichever the explanation, population increased, settlement diffused, and cities developed.

Before the Industrial Revolution. At the beginning of the common era, world population counted 200 or 300 million inhabitants (252 in Biraben's estimates)—about 40 in the Roman Empire, which included most of Europe and parts of Africa and Asia; about 50 in the Chinese Empire; about 35 on the Indian subcontinent. Still the long-run rate of growth, over the preceding millennia had been very low, only a few hundreths of 1 percent per year, and it would remain of the same order of magnitude until the Industrial Revolution. By 1750, world population had increased to a level triple the one reached at the beginning of the common era and not far from 800 million, about 500 million of which were in Asia, more than 100 million were in Europe (excluding Russia), an approximately equal number were in Africa, and less than 20 million were in the Americas.

The relatively low rate of growth over the centuries, apparently not very different on the various continents deserves some comment. The traditional demographic systems were all characterized by very high mortality (with an expectation of life generally lower than 35 years), which was the consequence of a poverty syndrome: poverty of material resources as well as poverty of scientific knowledge. Mortality was mainly a result of transmissible diseases, which accounted for three-fourths or four-fifths of all deaths. Ignorance about the modes of transmission made defenses against disease impossible. Increased urbanization and mobility, although themselves a consequence of a general improvement of the standard of living, supplied ideal conditions for the transmission and diffusion of diseases and epidemics. It follows that even in areas or periods of relative abundance, mortality remained high. Low agricultural productivity, coupled with low levels of trade and oscillations in production—often tied to weather vagaries—determined a high frequency of harvest failures with high prices and falls in consumption and nutritional levels. These crises determined social dislocation, migration to cities, and congestion of charitable institutions—ideal conditions for epidemic outbreaks and mortality crises. The two great world pandemics of plague—

the Justinianean one, which began in the sixth century and terminated in the eighth century, and the one initiated with the Black Plague in Europe in 1348 and that slowly began its retreat from the West in the seventeenth century—determined periods of population decline and stagnation. Between the mid-fourteenth century and the beginning of the fifteenth century, the European population declined by approximately 30 percent, and heavy losses were incurred by African and Asian populations as well.

The high level of mortality was matched by high, largely uncontrolled fertility, which was unable to produce large surpluses of births over deaths. When expectation of life at birth is around 25 to 30 years, more than 50 percent of each birth cohort dies before reaching puberty. High mortality continues through young adult and mature ages, and widowhood, disease, mobility, and separation further reduce the reproductive potential of populations. Under these conditions, the rate of growth over the centuries could only exceptionally exceed a few tenths of 1 percent per year. However, even a slow growth, when land is scarce and productivity stagnant, determines Malthusian pressures on systems that depend on the availability of land in order to provide food, raw materials, and energy. Between 1400 and 1700, Europe's population grew from 52 to 95 million (0.2 percent a year), but the quality of diets deteriorated, prices increased, and numerous sectors of society, such as the landless peasants, faced impoverishment. In Japan, during the Tokugawa period, population stagnated after the beginning of the eighteenth century until the Meiji restoration (1868) in the second half of the nineteenth century. Western European populations developed over the centuries an additional check to fertility and growth through high age at marriage and high levels of celibacy; Japan kept growth in check through abortion and infanticide.

Population change over the centuries or the millennia is not only the consequence of the interaction of biological, natural, or environmental factors that determine the reproductive potential and its checks (diseases, resources, space). Human intervention has been crucial in many episodes of modern population history. European contact with American populations and the slave trade between Africa and America have been crucial for the three continents. European-American contact resulted in a long-term fall of the American indigenous population from precontact levels to a nadir, reached in the seventeenth or early eighteenth century. A recent reassessment of evidence assigns to the continents a population of 43 million at the time of contact. That number fell to little more than 10 million between 1600 and 1700. The causes of the depopulation remain a topic of controversy. The traditional explanation of the demographic catastrophe implies the cruelty and violence of the conquerors, forcible social and economic dislocation of traditional society, and new diseases. This set of explanations came to be known as the Black Legend, and its first proponent was the historian and missionary Bartolomé de las Casas (1474–1566), who was a staunch defender of the cause of the Indians. Recent revisions have raised both the initial estimates of the indigenous population and assigned diseases imported from Europe to a population lacking immunity as the main reason of the demographic catastrophe. Careful analyses are needed in order to assess—for each area and society—the right balanced mix of factors that led to population decline or outright depopulation (as in the Greater Antilles), but the starting episode is European contact. On the other hand, the transatlantic slave trade, which carried an estimated 10 million individuals to America between 1500 and abolition of the slave trade in the early nineteenth century, limited the growth of population in western Africa while giving rise to an important new component of the American population.

The Nineteenth and Twentieth Centuries. World population growth has accelerated considerably since the eighteenth century, reaching 1 billion in 1804, 2 billion in 1927, 3 in 1960, 4 in 1974, 5 in 1987, and 6 in 1999; the rate of growth increased from 0.3 percent in the eighteenth century to 0.5 percent in the nineteenth century, 0.9 percent in the first half of the twentieth century, and 1.7 percent between 1950 and 2000 (with a peak of more than 2 percent in the 1970s). Consensus projections assign to the world population a level close to 9 billion in 2050, implying a further decline in the rate of growth (from 1.6 of the 1990s to 0.3 in the 2040s). Broadly speaking, this cycle of growth must be seen as the overlapping of two different cycles; the first cycle regards the Western world (Europe and the Americas), the second the rest of the world. In Europe and the Americas the cycle initiates with the Industrial Revolution, with a remarkable acceleration of the rate of growth that in the nineteenth century reached 1 percent (as opposed to 0.35 percent for the rest of the world) and slows down in the second part of the twentieth century. It has become customary to call *demographic transition* the process through which mortality and then fertility were reduced from the high pre-nineteenth century levels to the very low levels that currently prevail in Europe, North America, and East Asia. With the Industrial Revolution, the syndrome of poverty (resources and knowledge) was finally broken, and the joint benefits of higher standard of living and increased scientific knowledge are at the basis for declining mortality: at the end of the nineteenth century in several countries of Europe, expectation of life had reached 50 years and was rapidly increasing everywhere. Conceptually, three overlapping sets of factors can be recognized in this process. The first is an increase in per capita material resources, particularly food, and a remarkable decline of subsistence crises and associated mortality crises. This im-

plied an improvement of the standards of nutrition, clothing, housing, hygiene, and of the associated ability to resist disease. The second is the gradual accumulation of knowledge about the factors of microbial transmission—particularly after Louis Pasteur's (1822–1895) discoveries in the 1860s—and its popular dissemination through education and public policies, which enabled individuals to avoid disease. The third and last step involves the development of vaccines and drugs able to prevent or cure disease, a phase that began (after the isolated discovery of vaccination by Jenner in 1798) in the last two decades of the nineteenth century.

The decline of mortality triggers the decline of fertility, through the diffusion of voluntary fertility control. At a very general level of explanation, the decline of fertility is seen as a response to the changing balance of costs and benefits of children, determined by the Industrial Revolution. Costs increase for a number of reasons: declining mortality implies (at a given level of fertility) that more children survive per family; in an urbanizing and industrializing society more investment per child is needed, particularly in terms of education; and mothers must choose between a growing opportunity for gainful employment in the market and the care of the children. Benefits decrease because more modern technology and the shift away from agriculture postpone the age at which children can start being a net source of income for the family. This broad scheme may be useful at a very general level of explanation, since many other factors—particularly those related to the changing sets of cultural values brought about by Enlightenment, the French Revolution, radicalism, socialism—concur in explaining the time patterns and geographical gradient of the decline. Population historians still debate why fertility control began in rural France toward the end of the eighteenth century, and did not begin in industrialized England until nearly a century later. Many scholars believe that changes of values have been more important than cost-benefits considerations. In addition, the view that mortality decline is a necessary antecedent of the decline of fertility is also in dispute, since cases have been adduced where the contrary has happened.

The twentieth century is a continuation of the trend set in motion in the preceding century leading, at its end, to an expectation of life approaching 80 years, a level of fertility below replacement, and rates of natural growth close to zero (at least in Europe). As a result of this fast process of growth, the share of Europe (including Russia) and the Americas in the world population has increased from 21 percent in 1750 to 23 percent in 1800 and 36 percent in 1900. Although South America, under many aspects, has shared characteristics common to the populations of Asia and Africa, it was a recipient, like North America, of a large share of European emigration until the first part of the twentieth century and can be viewed as fully linked to the Western demographic system. Within Europe, the growth of countries at the periphery, like Great Britain and Russia, has been faster than that of older zones of dense settlement, like France, Italy, or Spain.

The second overlapping cycle growth regards the less-favored populations of Asia and Africa (and part of South America). The two most-populous countries, India and China, at mid-twentieth century still had life expectancy below 40 years, as well as uncontrolled fertility, and similar patterns prevailed elsewhere. In these populations, the demographic transition started toward the middle of the twentieth century, when massive transfers of biomedical technologies—new drugs, such as penicillin and sulfa and pesticides, such as DDT—brought about a rapid decline of mortality, more rapid than had ever occurred in the West. Fertility decline lagged behind, initiating a downward course only in the 1970s, while the growth rate reached a peak of 2.5 percent during the 1960s. This was more than double the peak reached in the West in the nineteenth century, and was the direct consequence of the higher fertility prevailing in Asia and Africa (in the West, later age at marriage and high rates of celibacy checked the birth rate even in the absence of fertility control) and of the speedier mortality decline. By the late 1990s, the spread of contraception was reducing fertility everywhere (except in many areas of sub-Saharan Africa), and growth was down almost 1 percent point from its peak of the 1960s. The transition was well on its way.

Population distribution underwent a radical change during the twentieth century. Between 1950 and 2000, Europe's share of the world population declined from 22 to 12 percent, that of North America from 7 to 5 percent; on the increase are Africa (9 to 14 percent), Asia (from 56 to 61 percent), and Latin America and the Caribbean (from 7 to 9 percent). In the first 50 years of the twenty-first century the redistribution will continue with a sharp decline in Europe's weight and a sharp increase in Africa's.

BIBLIOGRAPHY

Boserup, Ester. *The Conditions of Agricultural Growth*. London, 1965. An innovative look at the relationship between population and the economy in agricultural contexts.

Cipolla, Carlo M. *The Economic History of World Population*. Harmondsworth, U.K., 1978. An economic approach to the history of world population.

Cohen, Joel E. *How Many People Can the Earth Support?* New York, 1995. A comprehensive discussion of the relationship between population and the environment, now and in the past.

Cohen, Mark N. *The Food Crisis in Prehistory: Overpopulation and the Origin of Agriculture*. New Haven, 1977. On the Neolithic transition and its demographic implications.

Crosby, Alfred W. *Ecological Imperialism: The Biological Expansion of Europe, 900–1900*. London, 1986. Issues concerning the globalization of biota are presented in a very original way.

Davis, Kingsley. *The Population of India and Pakistan*. New York, 1968.

Haines, Michael, and Richard H. Steckel. *A Population History of North America*. Cambridge and New York, 2000.

Livi-Bacci, Massimo. *The Population of Europe: A History*. Oxford, 1999.

Livi-Bacci, Massimo. *A Concise History of World Population*. Oxford, 2001.

McEvedy, Colin, and Richard Jones. *Atlas of World Population History*. Middlesex, 1985. A good reference book on population size in the various areas of the world.

McNeill, William H. *Plagues and Peoples*. Garden City, N.Y., 1976. On the globalization of diseases and plague in particular.

National Research Council. *Beyond Six Billion: Forecasting the World's Population*. Washington, D.C., 2000.

Sánchez-Albornoz, Nicholas. *The Population of Latin America: A History*. Berkeley, 1974.

Slicher, Bernard van Bath. *The Agrarian History of Western Europe, A.D. 500–1850*. London, 1963. The classic look at the relationship between population and the economy in agricultural contexts.

Smith, David, and Nathan Keyfitz. *Mathematical Demography*. Berlin, Heidelberg, and New York, 1977. An explanation of the historical, mathematical, and methodological foundations of populations and paradigms.

Taueber, Irene B. *The Population of Japan*. Princeton, 1958.

MASSIMO LIVI-BACCI

PORTUGAL *[This entry contains two subentries, an overview and the economic history of Portugal during the Portuguese Empire.]*

An Overview

Portugal, officially the Portuguese Republic, comprises the continental territory (89,000 square kilometers = 35,500 square miles), located in the western Iberian Peninsula, and two archipelagoes, Madeira Islands (800 square kilometers = 310 square miles) and the Azores (2,300 square kilometers = 900 square miles), both in the Atlantic Ocean. The continental territory is bordered by Spain to the north and the east, the Atlantic to the west and south.

The continental territory became Portuguese between the eighth century and the thirteenth, and the archipelagoes (until then not inhabited) were added in the fifteenth. Since being integrated into Portugal, none of these areas has ever ceased to be a Portuguese territory, but other territories—in Africa, Asia, Indonesia, and the Americas—have been under Portuguese sovereignty at various times between 1415 and 1999. None was integrated into Portuguese society and all ultimately passed out of Portuguese control.

Eighth Century to the Sixteenth Century. Portugal began its formal existence as a frontier territory of the Kingdom of Leon (now in Spain) in the ninth century. It became a kingdom in the twelfth century. By the mid-thirteenth century, the continental territory of the Kingdom of Portugal took its general definitive shape, and feudal

PORTUGAL. *Departure from Lisbon for Brazil, the East Indies, and America*. Illustration by Theodore de Bry (1528–1598) from *Americae tertia pars memorabile Brasiliae historiam contines*, chapter 1, p. 313, 1562. (Service Historique de la Marine, Paris/Giraudon/Art Resource, NY)

dependence upon the Kingdom of Leon lapsed. With the end of the conquest of Algarve in 1249, the Moors (who had taken most of Iberia between 711 and 718) were driven back and the kingdom was consolidated as a Roman Catholic country.

Until the 1340s, prosperity predominated and population rose from less than 1 million to nearly 1.25 million. Exports of such commodities as salt and olive oil were developed.

The second half of the fourteenth century was a period of crisis, triggered by the Black Death (bubonic plague) and prolonged by many foreign and civil conflicts. Population dropped to its mid-thirteenth century levels. Devaluations to provide revenue for military expenditure resulted in inflation. The fifteenth century was a period of recovery, fostered by the earliest efforts at seagoing exploration; that led to the formation of the first Portuguese colonial empire, which included a few towns on the coast of Morocco, the Atlantic archipelagos of Madeira and the Azores, and several trade ports on the western coast of Africa. By 1500, population growth rose to mid-fourteenth century levels. At the same time, monetary devaluations were reduced and, by 1500, inflation was tamed.

From the 1490s to the 1570s, Portugal lived its Golden Age as a world power, with a demographic and economic boom at home. By 1600, the population was 2 million. Portugal consolidated the main structures of a modern state, and came to control a huge colonial empire, including part of the Atlantic coast of Morocco; some of the main Atlantic archipelagos; an important number of trade ports and fortresses along the western and eastern coasts of Africa; the coasts of the Indian Ocean, Indonesia, and the Asian coasts of the Pacific Ocean; and some settlements in Brazil. Exportation of such colonial commodities as spices became an important element of the new Portuguese economy.

Late Sixteenth Century and the Seventeenth. According to the traditional view, Portugal's decline began with the 1578 defeat of an intervention in a Moroccan civil war, followed by the Iberian unification in 1580 and the Dutch, English, and French competition for colonial empires in the 1590s. Portugal's prosperity lasted until the 1620s; meanwhile, the core of the Portuguese colonial empire moved to Brazil and sugar began to dominate Portuguese re-exports. Portugal did not escape the so-called crisis of the seventeenth century, when demographic and economic stagnation predominated from the 1620s to 1700, and the bulk of the Eastern empire and part of the African trade ports were lost, mainly to the Dutch. The difficulties within the Western (Spanish) Habsburg Empire led it to increase centralization and taxation, which provoked the 1640 revolution, separating Portugal from it. During the following decades Portugal managed to win the so-called Restoration War against the Habsburgs and to expel the Dutch from northeastern Brazil (occupied since the 1630s).

Eighteenth Century. Portugal's population and economic growth rose again during the eighteenth century. Brazilian gold and Portuguese wines were the main sources of prosperity, and, by 1800, population reached 3 million. The leading role that Portugal had played in Europe's exploration and colonial expansion had ended, so political decadence became a primary concern of the Portuguese elites. Despite economic prosperity, relative backwardness gradually became a national problem. Portugal failed to share in the early waves of European industry that developed into the Industrial Revolution throughout most of western Europe and the new United States of America.

Early Nineteenth Century. The first half of the nineteenth century was a time of great political and social upheavals for Portugal. First, the country was plunged into the struggle between Great Britain and Revolutionary, then Imperial, France (war with France from 1793 to 1795, 1801, and 1807 to 1814, including Portugal's partial occupation (1807–1808, 1809 and 1810–1811). French armies were expelled only with the help of a British expeditionary force. Second, Brazil gradually broke its ties with Portugal: Portuguese monopoly of Brazilian external trade ended in 1808, when the Portuguese government was established in Brazil, fleeing from a French invasion; the formal creation of a Kingdom of Brazil occurred in 1815; Brazil achieved total political independence in 1822, which was recognized by Portugal in 1825. Third, Portugal's internal struggles among the various political groups were ongoing from the 1820s to the 1840s. By that time, a stable monarchic constitutional regime was achieved.

The consequence of these upheavals was that population and economic growth slowed. It was not until 1860, when the population grew to 4 million, that the average standard of living began to improve.

Late Nineteenth Century. Portugal's political and social stabilization, the development of a modern commercial banking system, decisive steps toward the formation of a national economy, and greater integration in the world economy ensured a period of economic growth, that lasted from the 1850s to the 1880s. Some institutional reforms as well as public investment played an important role in Portugal's process of profiting from "catching-up" opportunities. The main institutional reforms included the adoption

of the gold standard (enacted in 1854) and the metric system, with some reduction of protectionism. Public investment provided (or subsidized) a railroad network, paved roads, seaport construction, an electric telegraph network, the beginnings of a telephone network, and a modern postal service. These were financed by borrowing, intended to be paid down by increases in public revenues that resulted from economic growth. The plan failed because fiscal revenues did not grow enough, mainly for political reasons. As a consequence, a financial crisis emerged in the early 1890s, which led to the end of the gold standard in 1891 and a partial suspension of foreign public-debt service in 1892. By 1890, the Portuguese population exceeded 5 million, and the average standard of living was some 50 percent higher than it had been in the 1850s.

Turn of the Twentieth Century. Portugal's main political answer to the difficulties of the 1890s was a reinstatement of protectionism and colonial expansion. Protectionism fostered the revival of cereal grain-agriculture and the development of some industrial sectors—yet that did not result in economic growth until the beginning of World War I in 1914. Thus, the 6 million people living in Portugal then had a standard of living similar to that of 1890, although alternative estimates suggest some increase. Meanwhile, a significant colonial empire had been built in Africa (mainly in Mozambique and Angola), and a huge flow of Portuguese emigrants went to Brazil.

In 1910, the monarchy was overthrown, and a democratic republic was established. The new political situation did not, however, bring new ideas about economic policy.

1914 to 1947. The impact of World War I (1914–1918), the short-term fluctuations of the international economy of the 1920s and 1930s, and World War II (1939–1945) were important to shaping the evolution of the Portuguese society during those years. Political unrest and economic difficulties abounded. Population growth slowed during World War I, but accelerated thereafter; some 8 million people lived in Portugal by the mid-1940s. Real gross domestic product (GDP) growth exceeded population growth. In the immediate post–World War II years, per capita real GDP was nearly 50 percent higher than in 1914.

Portugal remained neutral for almost two years after the outbreak of World War I, then joined to fight against Germany and Austria-Hungary in 1916. The main economic problems faced during the war were shortages and inflation. There were shortages of vital supplies—especially of cereal grains and coal—resulting in a reduction in the level of economic activity. Inflation resulted from the combined effects of external and internal shortages, plus the increase in the money supply, which came from large public deficits. Economic and financial problems led to a sharp rise in state intervention, especially through wartime rationing, which triggered the development of "black markets."

Economic and financial problems remained in the background of Portuguese life from the end of the war until 1924. External shortages were ended with the repeal of the war restrictions, and production gradually recovered to its prewar levels. Administrative controls were dismantled, as were the black markets. Inflation continued as a consequence of external payment problems and a crisis in confidence concerning the value of Portuguese currency. In 1924, the reduction of the deficit, combined with the use of a short-term monetary policy, brought inflation under control.

Financial and economic stabilization were, however, unable to ensure political stability. In 1926, a revolution imposed a military dictatorship, which in 1933 was the beginning of an authoritarian regime that would last until 1974.

The consolidation of financial and economic stabilization was the main concern of the military dictatorship governments. Formal adoption of the gold-exchange standard in 1931 was the last step of this policy.

The Great Depression was not devastating to the Portuguese economy, since there was no significant decrease of GDP; unemployment was absorbed by agricultural and other rural activities. The new Portuguese government implemented a relatively successful response to the challenges of the international economic crisis, combining competitive devaluation with balanced current accounts and public investment.

Portugal remained neutral during all of World War II, although the Allies were allowed to use the Azores as military bases after 1943. The main economic problem of the war years was a shortage crisis similar to that of World War I. The reduction of domestic economic activity was, however, less severe, because of two factors: the exports of tungsten ore and the inflow of capital and remittances. Tungsten-ore exports boomed as the warring nations increased their weapons production. The inflow of capital and remittances came from war refugees who entered the country. The joint effect of the shortage crisis and the balance of payments surplus was, however, inflation.

1947 to 1973. The immediate postwar years were affected by a quick reversal of wartime trends. The shortage crisis ended; foreign trade and production came back to normal levels; inflation ended.

From the late 1940s to the early 1970s, Portugal's economy had uninterrupted growth, which began to close the gap with the most-developed countries. The average standard of living in the early 1970s was four times higher than in the late 1940s. Population growth had decreased during the late 1940s and the 1950s, but the number of people living in Portugal reached 9 million in the early 1960s. During the 1960s and the early 1970s, an emigration boom (mainly to France) caused a slight population decrease to about 8.5 million. Industrialization (especially in the regions of Lisbon and Oporto) was the main economic change, but there was also better human capital, improved efficiency in the banking system, and a greater integration into the world economy. Education had become a priority of public expenditure during the immediate post–World War I years, but the effects of that effort (made by the last governments of the democratic republic) were slow to be felt. After World War II, there was a steady and significant increase in the average level of education among the Portuguese population.

During the interwar years, concentration—as a result of the demise of some of the weaker banks and some mergers—plus the consolidation of the Bank of Portugal as a modern central bank, were the main advances in the Portuguese banking system. Together with the creation of investment banks and a significant expansion of branches, this allowed for a better performance in the role of financial intermediation, especially important after World War II. Portugal was one of the European countries that accepted U.S. aid under the Marshall Plan in 1947. In 1948, it thereby became one of the founding members of the Organization for European Economic Cooperation (OEEC) and, later, a member of the Organization for Economic Cooperation and Development (OECD). Yet Portugal did not immediately join the main world economic organizations that formed after World War II. When the OEEC split into two trading blocks, the European Economic Community (EEC) and the European Free Trade Association (EFTA), Portugal joined EFTA (1960). In 1961, Portugal became a member of the International Monetary Fund (IMF) and the World Bank, and a contracting part of the General Agreement on Tariffs and Trade (GATT) in 1962. In 1961, a free-trade zone and a monetary union between Portugal and its overseas provinces were organized.

During the 1960s, emigrants' remittances and a tourism boom provided a significant surplus in external payments, which again triggered inflation. At the same time, public deficits were incurred because of the colonial war fought in Portuguese Africa against the independence movements within Angola, Guinea-Bissau, and Mozambique. Other significant changes in the international background of the Portuguese economy occurred in the early 1970s: the international abandonment of the Bretton Woods gold-exchange standard, the collapse of Portugal's free-trade zone and monetary union with its colonies, and Portugal's association with the EEC.

Late Twentieth Century. After 1975, the uneasy compromise between colonial empire and European integration was at an end. The authoritarian political regime that supported the compromise was replaced by a democratic regime, after the military coup of 1974. Independence was granted to Guinea-Bissau (1974), Cape Verde, São Tomé and Príncipe, Mozambique, and Angola (1975). Integration into the European Communities was the solution for the future.

During transition there was a breakdown in national economic growth, a huge inflow of refugees from the former colonies (more than a half million people), and the nationalization of key economic sectors and some large firms (which gave rise to a number of public enterprises). Still, these were short-term problems. The last quarter of the twentieth century was characterized by the continuation of Portugal's modern economic growth. By the end of the century, about 10 million people lived in Portugal, with an average standard of living twice that of 1975. Terciarization was the main feature of this period of modern economic growth in Portugal. Various welfare-state policies were introduced, with immediate difficulties for public funds, which soon showed large deficits, thereby accelerating again the inflationary process and bringing significant devaluation to Portuguese currency.

In 1986, Portugal became a member of the European Communities, and participated in the process of European integration, especially those of economic union in 1993 and the monetary union in 1999. During the 1990s, this meant the privatization of most of Portugal's state-owned enterprises, a successful effort to reduce the public deficit, and a curb on inflation and monetary devaluation.

BIBLIOGRAPHY

Fontoura, Paula, and Nuno Valério. "Protection, Foreign Trade, and Economic Growth in Portugal 1840's–1980's: A Long Term View." In *Political Economy of Protectionism and Commerce, 18th–20th Centuries,* edited by Jean-Michel Chevet, Peter Lindert, and John Vincent Nye. Milan, 1994.

Marques, A. H. de Oliveira. *History of Portugal.* 2 vols. New York and London, 1972.

Mata, Eugénia, and Nuno Valério. *História económica de Portugal—uma perspectiva global.* Lisbon, 1993.

Mata, Eugénia, and Nuno Valério. "Monetary Stability, Fiscal Discipline, and Economic Performance: The Experience of Portugal since 1854." In *Currency Convertibility,* edited by Jorge Braga de Macedo, Barry Eichengreen, and Jaime Reis. London, 1996.

Mattoso, José, ed. *História de Portugal.* 7 vols. Lisbon, 1992–1994.

Neves, João César das. *The Portuguese Economy: A Picture in Figures, XIX and XX Centuries.* Lisbon, 1994.

Nunes, Ana Bela, Eugénia Mata, and Nuno Valério. "Portuguese Economic Growth, 1833–1985." *Journal of European Economic History* 18.2 (1989).

Pereira, Pedro Telhado, and Maria Eugénia Mata, eds. *Urban Dominance and Labour Market Differentiation of a European Capital City: Lisbon, 1890–1990.* Boston, London, and Dordrecht, 1996.

Sideri, Sandro. *Trade and Power Informal Colonialism in Anglo-Portuguese Relations.* Rotterdam, 1970.

Valério, Nuno. "The Portuguese National Question in the 20th Century: From Spanish Threat to European Bliss." *In Economic Change and the National Question in Twentieth Century Europe,* edited by Alice Teichova, Herbert Matis, and Jaroslav Pátek. Cambridge, 2002.

NUNO VALÉRIO

Portuguese Empire

Overseas expansion and empire building played a pivotal role in Portugal's history and economy for almost six centuries. The overseas ventures not only dramatically increased revenues but also committed the state to extraordinary and burdensome expenditures involved in developing and defending its overseas holdings. The overall role of the overseas expansion in Portuguese history remains a matter of considerable debate. While overseas trade and revenues contributed to significant periods of prosperity and stability, in the long run they helped to promote the underdevelopment of the Portuguese domestic economy, dependence on foreign capital and diplomatic support, and ossification of the social structures. This interpretation, however, may be too sweeping to apply to the entire period. The recent sustained upsurge in all aspects of Portuguese historiography is bound to yield revisionist conclusions, and caution is necessary in making generalizations.

Overseas Ventures in the Fifteenth and Sixteenth Centuries. The economic potential of overseas ventures first became obvious in the mid-fifteenth century. From West Africa came gold and other valuable commodities plus slaves. Madeira and the Azores offered land for colonization and began to export sugar, wine, dyestuffs, and wheat. The settlement of the Cape Verde Islands in the 1460s and 1470s facilitated trade with Western Africa, whereas the settlement of São Tomé and Príncipe (1490s and 1500s) created a key logistical element in developing the trade in slaves and commodities from the Gulf of Guinea and West-Central Africa. The establishment of trading outposts off the coast of Mauritania, on the Gambia River, and above all the building of the Crown fortress of São Jorge da Mina (now Elmina) in today's Ghana, gave Portugal access to key West African trading networks and sources of gold. The impact on Portuguese foreign trade and royal revenues was dramatic: In the later fifteenth century, overseas commodities rivaled the traditional domestic exports, and income from overseas ventures significantly increased Crown revenues.

The impact of trade with Africa was dwarfed once the Portuguese established themselves in the Indian Ocean during the first two decades of the sixteenth century. A network of fortresses came to control key strategic locations in the Indian Ocean basin, from the coast of East Africa to the Persian Gulf, the shores of the Indian subcontinent, Sri Lanka, the Malacca Straits, and the Indonesian archipelago. In the mid-sixteenth century, the Portuguese established trading relations with China and Japan. Control over the oceanic sea lanes and such key choke points as Ormuz (Persian Gulf) and Malacca (Indonesian Archipelago) gave the Portuguese control of a significant proportion of the

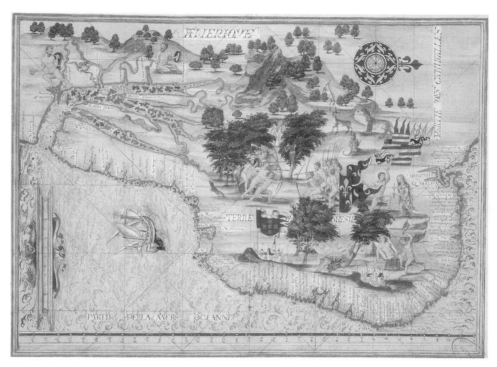

BRAZIL. *Cosmographie Universelle*, painting (1555) by Guillaume Le Testu (c. 1509–1572). (Ministère de la Défense, Vincennes, France/Giraudon/Art Resource, NY)

trade in spices, precious stones, and luxury textiles that had traditionally reached the Near East and Europe through Muslim intermediaries via the Black Sea, the Persian Gulf, and the Red Sea. However, the Portuguese grip was less firm than earlier historians had believed, and particularly after 1550 it was considerably weakened by the revival of a vibrant Muslim and Hindu competition. In the second half of the sixteenth century, Portuguese profits and revenues from Indian Ocean trade began to decline sharply, to the point of deficit according to some observers, partly because of external competition and partly because of the growing costs of shipping and defense. Declining markets in Europe also played a role. Yet while it is true that the Portuguese enterprise in the Indian Ocean suffered in the later sixteenth and early seventeenth centuries, it continued to generate considerable revenue, particularly to private traders.

Overseas expansion certainly was a key factor behind the Portuguese sixteenth-century "Golden Age." Amplifying the late-fifteenth-century trend toward recovery, overseas revenues dramatically boosted the Portuguese economy and royal revenues. Yet, the Portuguese domestic economy also experienced very significant and possibly quite autonomous growth. From the fiscal point of view, however, while the Crown's options to derive revenue from the domestic economy were limited by law and custom, the overseas enterprise presented far fewer constraints.

As soon as overseas expansion began to yield profits in the 1440s, the Crown stepped in to harvest the benefits, either in the form of grants to members of the nobility or through taxation and direct participation in the trade. While economic policies oscillated, the trend during the fifteenth and sixteenth centuries was to claim direct control over the overseas trade or its most profitable components or commodities. Gold, spices, precious stones, and at times slaves, were the goods most often claimed as a royal preserve. The Crown also monopolized those exports that commanded the strongest demand overseas, such as silver and Moroccan textiles. Crown administrators were required annually to assess the books of private merchants and leaseholders in order to determine which aspect of overseas trade was the most profitable and recommend its sequestration for the Crown. The tendency to monopolize overseas trade and administer it directly was particularly strong in the first half of the sixteenth century, but similar attempts continued into the early seventeenth century, and the Portuguese government never ceased regarding its overseas holdings as a strategic source of revenue. From the later seventeenth century onward, however, the Crown relied more on chartered companies and corporations rather than on its own agency.

The Crown's direct trade was organized around overseas outposts that performed both defensive and trading functions. The military and defensive functions were within the mandate of a captain, the commercial function within that of a factor and treasurer. In smaller outposts, the two might be combined. The overseas stations were serviced by monthly or annual fleets dispatched from Lisbon. Lisbon also served as an entrepôt for the marketing and distribution of overseas goods throughout Europe, although in the late fifteenth and in the first half of the sixteenth century Portugal relied heavily on Bruges and then Antwerp in this respect. Bruges and Antwerp also sent to Portugal most of the metals and other goods required for overseas trade.

As far as economic administration was concerned, Lisbon was the focal point of the Portuguese enterprise: All goods coming from overseas were cleared through the central agency handling such trade, the Casa da India e Guiné, which evolved gradually in the course of the fifteenth century and was placed on a firm institutional footing first by Dom João (John) II (r. 1481–1495) and then Dom Manuel I (r. 1495–1521). Dom Manuel's *Regimento da Casa da India e Guiné* served as a blueprint of the Crown's vision of how "state capitalism" should ideally function. This and other documents make it clear, however, that "monopoly" is the wrong term to define the royal overseas involvement. The Crown almost always permitted a considerable degree of private participation, through special licenses, contracts, and leases. Its objective was to maximize revenues, not necessarily to exclude other players.

While the Casa da India originally also performed some administrative functions, the distances involved in maintaining the Portuguese overseas presence demanded a delegation of state powers. In Asia, this led to the creation of the Estado da India, headed by a viceroy or a governor; in the Atlantic Islands and in Brazil, to the implementation of donatory captaincies, rooted in the Peninsular reconquest tradition. The *donatário*, in exchange for territorial holdings, revenue, and judicial powers, would organize settlement and take care of economic development, administration, and defense. In later periods, the donatory rights were either abolished or bought out by the Crown and the *donatários* replaced by state-appointed governors. In either form, these officials played a very important role in economic matters.

The Portuguese "Golden Age" did not necessarily come to an end with the loss of Portuguese independence to Habsburg Spain in 1580. On the contrary, the economic policies of Philip II (r. 1556–1598) and Philip III (r. 1598–1621), the broadening of the joint monarchy's markets, and the availability of American silver needed for Asian trade temporarily strengthened the Portuguese overseas enterprise. However, the amalgamation of the Portuguese and Spanish Empires put an end to Portugal's long policy of neutrality in the European diplomatic arena and made its holdings the target of Spain's enemies, in particular the

Dutch and the French, who launched a series of worldwide attacks against both Portuguese shipping and overseas outposts. With the establishment of the Dutch East India Company and the East India Company at the beginning of the seventeenth century, both the Dutch and the English broke the Portuguese grip on Asian trade; and from the 1620s onward, the Dutch began a systematic and successful campaign of attack and conquest against Portuguese holdings everywhere.

Changes in the Seventeenth and Eighteenth Centuries. Regaining independence in 1640 only made Portugal more vulnerable. Forced to wage war on three fronts—Iberian, Atlantic, and Asian—the new king, John IV (r. 1640–1656), faced the choice of abandoning either the Atlantic or the Indian sphere of interest. Both logistics and the growing economic attraction of Brazil led to the decision to focus the defense there. In the course of the 1640s and 1650s, most of the Portuguese outposts in the Indian Ocean and the Indonesian archipelago fell to the Dutch or were ceded as diplomatic compensation to England, now Portugal's protector. When lasting peace was finally reached with both the Dutch and the Spanish in 1668, Portuguese holdings in Asia were reduced to Goa and a few other enclaves in India, Macao, and Timor.

Holdings on both sides of the Atlantic Ocean were almost lost to Portugal during this period. The Dutch occupied much of the Brazilian coast; and they conquered key Portuguese strongholds in Africa, including Arguim, São Jorge da Mina, São Tomé, and Luanda in Angola, the sources of slaves to Portuguese Brazil. Although due credit must be given to the Portuguese defense effort and the resistance of Lusophone populations against Dutch rule, English diplomatic action played a key role in the survival of the Portuguese Atlantic empire during the mid-seventeenth-century crisis. England, motivated by its rivalry with the United Provinces, protected its interests by championing the international recognition of Portuguese independence at the close of the Thirty Years' War, as well as Portuguese interests in the negotiations resolving the Anglo-Dutch Wars. The Dutch eventually restored to Portugal their conquests in Brazil and most of those in Africa. In return for her support, England was granted key economic privileges in both Portugal and its overseas holdings. This privileged relationship, codified in a series of treaties, lasted into the twentieth century.

The seventeenth-century overseas losses highlighted the key problems of Portuguese economic policy and its socioeconomic consequences. When available, overseas revenues released the Crown from many of the pressures that had previously compelled it to focus on developing the domestic economy and alliances with the cities, as opposed to appeasing the nobility. The overseas ventures provided not only funds for grants to the nobility (as early as 1511 most of the Crown's overseas revenues were assigned to noble pensions and princely appanages), but also opportunities for suitable employment, social promotion, and the personal enrichment of noble families. The grants and personal profits were invested in conspicuous consumption, mostly involving imported luxury goods. This limited the benefits a multiplier effect might otherwise have brought to the Portuguese economy. Lack of domestic capital led to reliance on foreign financiers and prominent foreign merchant families, preparing the ground for Portuguese dependence on foreign capital in the modern era. At the end of the seventeenth century, however, the prosperity brought about by the combined effect of Brazilian agricultural growth, in particular sugar production, and the newly discovered gold deposits in the interior postponed the moment of crisis.

The loss of the Estado da India in the mid-seventeenth century forced a profound transformation of the shape and economy of the Portuguese overseas empire. Its mainstay became the exploitation of large mainland areas on both sides of the Atlantic Ocean, with Brazil as the focal point serviced by the other components of Portuguese Atlantic holdings. Brazilian population grew rapidly in the seventeenth and eighteenth centuries, rising from 150,000 nonnative inhabitants in the mid-seventeenth century to 2,500,000 in 1800 and 3,600,000 in 1819. By 1780, Baía and Rio de Janeiro were respectively the second and third largest cities in Latin America. The most significant demographic factor was the import of African slaves, first to satisfy the overwhelming needs of the sugar plantations, and then, in the eighteenth century, also those of the rapidly expanding mining sector. Brazil alone received over 40 percent of all slaves transported to the Americas, with a pronounced peak in the eighteenth century. However, Portuguese immigration and local population growth also contributed to the rapid demographic expansion.

Charles Boxer (1975) rightly labeled this period the "Golden Century of Brazil," especially when considering the first half of the eighteenth century. The output of sugar plantations was complemented by tobacco and cotton production and extensive cattle ranching in the north. It was, however, the discovery and extensive mining of gold and diamonds in the recently opened interior—Minas Gerais, Goiás, Mato Grosso, Baía, and other areas—that gave the economy an uneven, unstable, but dramatic boost. In the first two decades of the eighteenth century, the exports of gold to Portugal rose to twenty-five metric tons per year, although subsequently they declined to fourteen tons and less. By 1780 the flow of gold had slowed to a fraction of the original volume.

As the gold deposits became gradually exhausted in the second half of the eighteenth century, the Brazilian boom ebbed. The situation was aggravated by the state of the sugar market, which had partly to do with effective demand and overproduction, and partly with the general economic depressions of this period. Expanding cotton and cocoa production eased some of the problems in Brazil, but the overall result still meant significantly lower revenues for Portugal. The Pombaline reforms, intended to change the institutional structures of both the domestic and the overseas economy, encountered serious problems, and the modernization effort largely failed.

From the Nineteenth Century to the Present. In the early nineteenth century, both Brazil and Portugal suffered increasingly from the disruption to trade caused by the Napoleonic wars. After it had become a war zone in 1807, metropolitan Portugal, however, experienced much more direct disruption and devastation, whereas Brazil profited from becoming the seat of the imperial government for more than a decade, with a corresponding relaxation of the previous mercantilist restrictions on its internal development and international trade. The attempt of the mother country to reestablish control over its most prosperous colony led to the declaration of Brazil's independence in 1822.

The loss of Brazil, despite its continued close links with the old metropolis, resulted in yet another profound transformation of the Portuguese overseas empire, now focused on Africa (Mozambique, Angola, São Tomé, a small part of Guinea, and the Cape Verde Islands). Historically, the key business of all these areas had been the slave trade, and their local economies also depended heavily on slave labor. Until the mid-nineteenth century, Brazil readily absorbed all slaves that crossed the Atlantic in spite of British anti-slavery naval patrols. However, Portugal found itself under heavy diplomatic pressure on this issue from its closest ally, Great Britain, and was ultimately compelled to abolish both the slave trade and slave labor in its overseas holdings.

In the second half of the nineteenth century, Portugal's African colonies first stagnated and then scrambled to develop cash crops, grown by dependent labor, to maintain their financial viability. This process went hand in hand with aggressive exploration of the African interior in an attempt to provide evidence of "effective" occupation, a process particularly intense in the 1880s and 1890s during the "Scramble for Africa," when Portugal found itself seriously challenged by Great Britain, Germany, and France over claims to broad territories in West, West Central, and southeastern Africa. Only the onset of the Boer Wars and the British-German rivalry preserved Angola and Mozambique, although Portugal lost its bid for the territory of former Rhodesia. The need to establish an effective claim to the African holdings led to a policy of conquest and "pacification" of the native societies, and thus very costly military campaigns that put the budgets of Angola and Mozambique almost constantly into deficit, despite aggressive economic expansion and the buildup of infrastructure in both areas.

Metropolitan Portugal also experienced problems. Although both the domestic economy and the export sector based on domestic production grew dramatically in the nineteenth century, Portugal faced an accumulating national debt and an unfavorable balance of trade. The modernization effort, largely funded by foreign capital, transformed the infrastructure of the country by the early twentieth century but did not resolve the deep problems stemming from centuries-long reliance on overseas revenues and captive markets. Economic weakness was the most significant factor behind the defeat of Portuguese Republicanism in the 1920s and the acceptance of the fascist regime of António de Oliveira Salazar (1889–1970), whose heavy hand dominated Portugal for forty years.

As minister of finance, Salazar, originally a professor of economics, made it his priority to eliminate budget deficits; and as prime minister, he imposed his vision of an economic order based on the corporatist principle, stimulating the economy through extensive public works, development of agriculture, labor control, regulation of industry, and emphasis on the overseas colonies. This emphasis was as much ideological as pragmatic. Economic exploitation of the colonies became a crucial tool to reduce domestic budget deficits, especially when the remittances of Portuguese emigrants declined during the Great Depression and World War II. The value of the overseas colonies to modern Portugal peaked in the 1950s but at the cost of severe oppression of the native populations, faced with growing numbers of white settlers, forced labor, compulsory cash crop production, and threat of expropriation both at the hands of the state and of the corporations that had been granted extensive concessions and monopolies by the Salazar regime. This oppression stimulated demands for independence from the colonies, a process completed only in the 1970s, following the collapse of the regime and the revolution of 25 April 1974 in Portugal.

Although the Portuguese economy experienced significant growth in the 1960s, a period bracketed by Portugal's accession to the General Agreement on Tariffs and Trade (GATT) in 1962 and the Trade Agreement between Portugal and the European Economic Community (EEC) in 1972, the deep structural problems were not solved by the restoration of democracy in 1974. On the contrary, Portugal faced a series of economic crises, which recurred until 1985. It was only a decade after the April revolution that Portugal embarked on a period of dramatic economic growth, coinciding with the more systematic incorporation of Portugal into the European community. Although Portugal maintains close relations with its former colonies,

particularly in Portuguese Language African Countries (PALOP), its main external trading partners are European. The role of the African markets had declined notably throughout the independence wars era (1961–1974), and plummeted during the troubled postindependence decade, marked by nationalizations, abrogation of preferential trade mechanisms, and the attempted reorientation of the newly independent economies toward alternative trading partners. The subsequent civil wars, particularly in Angola and Mozambique (1977–1992), as well as the accession of Portugal to the EEC in 1986, sealed the changes induced by this trend. Several decades after decolonization, Portugal is a modern, vibrant, prosperous country, having emancipated itself of its dependency on empire. Its former African colonies are not as fortunate: Tormented by civil wars and poverty, their way to recovery has been much slower, despite official claims touting Mozambique as the International Monetary Fund's (IMF) "success story" in Africa.

BIBLIOGRAPHY

The literature on the economic history of Portugal and the Portuguese empire is vast and steadily growing. Portuguese historians have made a remarkably rich contribution to the topic, especially in the last four decades. Since the present work is directed primarily at an English-speaking readership, publications in Portuguese were mostly included only in the absence of coverage in English. It must be pointed out, however, that the majority of works on this topic are written in Portuguese. Some of them, for example, the works of Vitorino Magalhães Godinho, are so fundamental that they cannot be omitted despite the language barrier.

PORTUGAL AND ITS EMPIRE

Marques, António H. R. de Oliveira. *History of Portugal*. 2d ed. New York, 1976. More recent editions of this seminal work exist, but only in Portuguese.

Marques, António H. R. de Oliveira. *Histoire du Portugal et de son empire colonial*. Paris, 1998.

PORTUGAL AND ITS EMPIRE, 1415–1640

Diffie, Bailey W., and George D. Winius. *Foundations of the Portuguese Empire, 1415–1580*. Minneapolis, 1977.

Godinho, Vitorino Magalhães. *Ensaios II*. 2d ed., corrected and enlarged. Lisbon, 1978.

Godinho, Vitorino Magalhães. *Os descobrimentos e a economia mundial*. 2d ed., corrected and enlarged. 4 vols. Lisbon, 1981–1983.

Godinho, Vitorino Magalhães. *Mito e mercadoria, utopia e prática de navegar: Séculos XIII–XVIII*. Lisbon, 1990.

PORTUGAL IN ASIA, 1498–1660

Boyajian, James C. *Portuguese Trade in Asia under the Habsburgs, 1580–1640*. Baltimore, 1993.

Pearson, Michael N. *Port Cities and Intruders: The Swahili Coast, India, and Portugal in the Early Modern Era*. Baltimore and London, 1998.

Subrahmanyam, Sanjay. *The Portuguese Empire in Asia, 1500–1700: A Political and Economic History*. London and New York, 1993.

PORTUGAL, THE ATLANTIC AND BRAZIL, 1500–1822

Boxer, Charles R. *The Golden Age of Brazil, 1695–1750*. 5th ed. Berkeley, Los Angeles, and London, 1975.

Carreira, António. *A Companhia Geral do Grão-Pará e Maranhão*. 2 vols. São Paulo, 1988.

Duncan, T. Bentley. *Atlantic Islands: Madeira, the Azores, and the Cape Verdes in Seventeenth-Century Commerce and Navigation.* Chicago and London, 1972.

Miller, Joseph Calder. *Way of Death: Merchant Capitalism and the Angolan Slave Trade, 1730–1830.* Madison, Wis., 1988.

Pedreira, Jorge Miguel Viana. *Estrutura industrial e mercado colonial: Portugal e Brasil (1780–1830).* Lisbon, 1994.

Schwartz, Stuart B. *Sugar Plantations in the Formation of Brazilian Society: Bahia, 1550–1835.* Cambridge, 1985.

THE ECONOMY OF PORTUGAL AND ITS COLONIES IN THE NINETEENTH AND TWENTIETH CENTURIES

Cervo, Amado Luiz, and José Calvet de Magalhães. *Depois das caravelas: As relações entre Portugal e Brasil, 1808–2000.* Edited by Dário Moreira de Castro Alves. Brasília, Brazil, 2000.

Clarence-Smith, W. G. *The Third Portuguese Empire, 1825–1975: A Study in Economic Imperialism.* Manchester, U.K., and Dover, N.H., 1985.

Corkill, David. *The Portuguese Economy since 1974.* Edinburgh, 1993.

Telo, António José. *Económia e Império no Portugal Contemporáneo.* Lisbon, 1994.

IVANA ELBL

POSTAL SAVINGS. Postal savings systems have been a feature of many European and Asian financial systems, and even played a prominent role in the early-twentieth-century American financial system. Designed to attract and protect the savings of low-income groups, postal savings have relied on the accessibility of local post offices and a government guarantee of deposits to provide banking alternatives to small savers. The increased importance of consumer banking, along with the development of banking institutions such as credit unions, made postal savings systems redundant in many countries. Although notable exceptions such as Japan's postal savings system have flourished, most postal savings systems have either disappeared (e.g., the U.S. system) or become relatively minor financial institutions (e.g., the Swiss system).

Postal savings systems originated in nineteenth-century Europe, at a time when banking institutions were largely oriented toward meeting the needs of commercial entities, not individuals. As the rise of industrial economies led to the development of a working class, the need for banking services appropriate for individuals also developed. A number of institutions arose to meet this need, in particular mutual savings banks, credit cooperatives, and building and loan societies; but perhaps the most basic of these intermediaries was the postal savings system.

Postal savings systems were designed solely to provide a safe repository for the small saver. Meeting this function required access, which was provided by myriad post offices scattered throughout the country, and security, which came from the government guarantee of postal deposits. Unlike the savings banks and other institutions noted above, postal savings systems never provided loans to individuals. The assets of postal savings were either invested in government securities or, as in the case of the U.S. postal savings system, redeposited into solvent national banks.

Because postal savings systems operated with government guarantees, they had a natural advantage over other market-based intermediaries. This led to demands for restrictions on the actions of postal savings systems and to a general view that postal savings systems were anticompetitive. Consequently, most postal savings systems featured limits on the total size of any individual's deposit (in the United States deposits were initially limited to $500, with the limit raised to $2,500 in 1918) and restrictions on the maximum interest rate the system could pay. Postal savings systems were generally viewed as political creations, and as such were often forced to operate with political, rather than economic, constraints.

The U.S. postal savings system provides a nice case in point. Founded in 1910, the impetus for its development was the disastrous Panic of 1907, in which individuals, fearful for the safety of banks, withdrew their deposits in massive numbers. The resultant bank runs crippled the banking system, and calls for reform consumed the political arena. Although Democrats favored instituting deposit

POSTAL SAVINGS. Postal Savings Bank, Vienna, between 1904 and 1906, designed by Otto Wagner (1841–1918). Female genii designed by Othmar Schimkowitz. (Erich Lessing/Art Resource, NY)

insurance, the Republican Party backed a postal savings system, and the Republican victory in the 1908 elections paved the way for its inception.

Because of vociferous opposition by the banking community, the U.S. postal savings system was strictly limited in its operations. With interest rates on bank deposits at approximately 3.5 percent, the postal savings system was allowed to pay only 2 percent on deposits. In spite of the flexible interest rates allowed by some European postal savings systems, Congress did not allow this rate to change with market conditions. Postal deposits, in turn, were to be reinvested at a rate of 2.25 percent in local commercial banks, leaving 0.25 percent to cover the costs of the system.

An interesting feature of the U.S. system was its inclusiveness. The Postal Savings charter declared that accounts could be opened by anyone "ten years of age or over, in his own name, and a married woman in her own name and free from control or interference by her husband." Although women did not yet have the right to vote, they could hold a postal savings account (see Bochnak and Jessup, 1992).

The U.S. Postal Savings System achieved modest success in its early years, with assets of $200 million in 1918, a level it maintained until the onset of the Depression. Following the market crash in 1929 and extensive bank failures in 1930, however, the assets of the postal saving system skyrocketed to $1.2 billion, an amount equal to approximately 10 percent of the banking system. This growth was facilitated both by the government guarantee of postal deposits and by the system's now competitive interest rate (interest at banks having fallen to rates at or below the 2 percent paid by the postal savings system).

Although the original intent was to redeposit postal savings into commercial banks, many banks were unwilling to accept postal deposits because of the mandated 2.25 percent interest rate. Unable to redeposit funds into the banking system, the postal savings administrators increasingly turned to investing in securities. This investment policy decreased the overall money supply and had a particularly devastating effect on housing finance.

Faced with an increasingly precarious banking system, Congress enacted legislation in 1933 setting up a deposit insurance system for banks and savings and loan associations. This action effectively removed a major advantage of postal savings. Although the system would continue for another thirty years, its role became increasingly redundant, and its share of financial assets negligible. The U.S. Postal Savings System was officially terminated in 1966.

Many postal savings systems in other countries remain operative, but most now play minor roles in their financial markets. This reduced role largely reflects the increased availability of savings alternatives and the enhanced role of government banking sector guarantees. An exception to this pattern is the Japanese postal savings system, which has amassed tremendous assets and is the largest financial institution in Japan. With deregulation of the Japanese financial system, it is likely that this dominance will change. Elsewhere, these increasingly anachronistic systems still can play a role in developing economies, as evidenced by Vietnam's recent proposal to start a postal savings system.

BIBLIOGRAPHY
Bochnak, Mary, and Paul Jessup. "A Case for a U.S. Postal Savings System." *Challenge* 35.6 (November/December 1992), 57–59.
Kemmerer, Edwin W. *Postal Savings.* Princeton, 1917.
O'Hara, Maureen, and David Easley. "The Postal Savings System in the Depression." *Journal of Economic History* 33.3 (September 1979), 741–753.
Sprague, Oliver M. W. *History of Crisis under the National Banking System.* National Monetary Commission Report. Senate Doc. No. 538, 61st Cong., 2d Sess. Washington, D.C., 1910.

MAUREEN O'HARA

POSTAN, MICHAEL (1898–1981), economic historian. Born in 1898 at Tighina in Bessarabia, the son of a local proprietor, Michael Postan commenced his higher education in 1914 at the University of St. Petersburg before moving in the next year to study law and economics at the University of Odessa. It was at these premier institutions of pre-Revolutionary Russian higher education, between 1914 and 1917, that he assimilated a profound knowledge of both the economics of the "German School" and contemporary views concerning the "modern" (c. 1689–1917) economic history of Russia. This was to have a marked influence on his subsequent corpus of work. Departing from Ukraine in 1919, he pursued a peripatetic course across Europe to arrive in England at the end of 1920. There he continued his education, enrolling in 1921 at the London School of Economics for a first degree, which he followed in 1924 with a Master's degree. Thus, during the years 1921 to 1926, it was at the premier British school of economics that he studied and was able to assimilate the profound knowledge of neoclassical theory that would have a marked influence on his subsequent corpus of work.

Initially, his work remained firmly rooted within the contemporary institutional framework of the "German School." This had dominated, at that time, the analysis of medieval and early-modern economics and was rooted in an earlier political historiography. Eighteenth-century scholars, who shared with contemporaries that fascination with the architectural and artistic forms of classical antiquity then being re-created in their own times, engaged in the common view (still often expressed today) that the intervening years had seen nothing created of comparable grandeur. The origins of their current state of enlightenment in these matters need be sought no earlier than the Renaissance, when the rediscovery of classical forms reopened the path of learning that was to achieve ultimate realization in the Enlightenment. Subsequently, those who rooted the original formulation of the democratic institutions of their own age in the political ideals and institutional forms of classical Greece reinforced this view. For them, medieval feudalism was a regressive system, interposed between the libertarian institutions of antiquity and their own age.

As late comers to this historical debate, economic historians, whose work first found expression in the studies of the "German School," merely adopted and adapted the existing historiography. For Bloch, Alfons Dopsch, Pirenne, and others the task confronting them was to chart the decay of the institutions of classical antiquity, to examine the origins and nature of the emergent feudal order, and finally to trace its displacement by the institutions associated with an emergent capitalism. Once again, for them medieval feudalism was a regressive system that created a stable-state, low-productivity-level economic system that was transformed only in the sixteenth century by an emergent capitalism. Such a view soon found ready acceptance among Marxist historians. They perceived the regressive nature of the feudal economy as arising from the activities of the dominant landlord class, who squandered the surplus they extracted from the bulk of the population, creating a lack of investment funds so that the latter could not transform their pitiful existence. Only in the sixteenth century, during the "Age of Discoveries," was a new economic system perceived to have been created.

The evolution of "Commercial Capitalism" in western Europe allowed the merchants of that region during the years from 1500 to 1750 to exploit the rest of the world. By such means, they established the beginnings of the European economic supremacy that finally was realized in the "Industrial Capitalism" of the period from 1750 to the present time. These "Structuralist" arguments, moreover, continue to be presented until the present day in a non-Marxian mode by historians who look within the institutional historiography of the "German School" for endogenous factors to explain the processes of economic change. Exceptions to this view will be found in works such as George Grantham's fascinating study on long endogenous fluctuations and the unmaking and remaking of a unified economic space within a relatively constant technological environment during the millennium 300 to 1300 CE. Or, again it may be discerned in the works of medievalists who have made use of the path-breaking "Institutional Economics" of Nobel-Prize-winner Douglass North.

It was within such an analytical framework that Michael Postan first formulated his work in the late 1920s and early 1930s. Successive articles followed each other, on "Credit in Medieval Trade" in 1928, monopoly organization in "The Economic and Political Relations of England and the Hanse (1400–1475)" in 1933, and "The Accumulation of Capital" in 1935. Each described "capitalist" forms and mechanisms employed in the commercial economy of the late Middle Ages.

It was only in the mid-1930s that the three main influences on Postan's thought coalesced in the initial formulation of the thesis that would become the dominant model of medieval economic development. In his study of "The Chronology of Labour Services," published in 1937, he described the institutional changes associated with the process of twelfth- and thirteenth-century demographically impelled extensive agrarian growth. This enjoyed certain parallels with similar changes described in the economic historiography of the Russian economy of the period 1740–1810, where the same forces led to a transition from an *obrok* (money rent) to a *barshchina* (labor service) system of labor management. Working within the same Russian historiographic tradition, he then went on to describe the subsequent agrarian collapse and retreat of economic activity, in his classic study "The Fifteenth Century" in 1939. The institutionally based picture of a stable-state medieval economy presented in the works of the "German School" was now challenged by an implicit, demographically impelled dynamic.

Only the mechanisms underlying this dynamic now had to be revealed. This had to wait some six years (1939–1945), however, during which Michael Postan made a distinguished contribution to the war effort. From 1950–1965, with Postan working latterly with J. Z. Titow, all was revealed. Rising population in the twelfth and thirteenth centuries (described in J. Z. Titow, "Some Evidence of Thirteenth Century Population Growth," *Economic History Review*, 2d Series, 14, 1961) resulted in an extensive pattern of agrarian growth as progressively more land was brought under the plough. This development, however, resulted in the erosion of pasture reserves and a decline in livestock numbers (described in Postan's "Village Livestock in the Thirteenth Century" in 1962). Reduced manuring undermined the fertility of existing arable land and caused acute soil erosion, a process described by J. Z. Titow in *Winchester Yields* (Cambridge, 1972). Per capita land holding and product fell (as revealed in C. N. L. Brooke and M. M. Postan, eds., *Carte Nativorum*, Northants Record Society, 20, 1950), precipitating an acute Malthusian crisis (described in M. M. Postan and J. Z. Titow, "Heriots and Prices on Winchester Manors," 1959). In their view, this Malthusian crisis, commencing in the opening decades of the fourteenth century, and one seen in the context of serious problems of soil erosion, led to a protracted phase of demographic and economic decline that lasted until the very end of the Middle Ages (described in Postan's "Some Economic

Evidence of Declining Population in the Later Middle Ages," 1950). By 1966 the complete model could be displayed in Postan's "Medieval Agrarian Society in its Prime: England" (*Cambridge Economic History of Europe*, vol. 1, Cambridge, 1966).

Acceptance of the thesis by medieval scholars was slow. The late Eleanor Carus-Wilson still presented, in her lectures at the London School of Economics in the early 1960s, the "German School's" institutionally based picture of a stable-state medieval economy. The Postan thesis was tacked on at the end as an exciting "new" hypothesis. Such was not the case among early-modern economic historians. In France, Emmanuel LeRoy Ladurie in his *Peasants of Languedoc* (Urbana, 1977) employed the thesis with great effect. More than a decade earlier, F. J. Fisher in his lectures at the London School of Economics had utilized the model to elucidate sixteenth-century English economic development. A temporal extension of the thesis was under way, just as the concept of a "preindustrial" economy was emerging. Henceforth, in studies such as D. M. Palliser, "Tawney's Century: Brave New World or Malthusian Trap?" (*Economic History Review*, 2d Series, 35, 3, 1982), Postan's demographic cycles were built into a stable-state model extending backward and forward in time between classical antiquity and the Industrial Revolution. Within the context of this modeling and the work of the Cambridge group on early-modern English demographic history, Postan's original work fitted uneasily. It was assimilated only by a speculative adjustment in his 1966 article of absolute population levels in circa. 1300 to five to seven million, with the object of reestablishing an appropriate 1300 and 1688 relativity.

In this form the model continues to hold sway. Studies of markets and commercialization in the medieval economy, most notably Richard H. Britnell's *The Commercialisation of English Society* (Cambridge, 1993) and Bruce M. S. Campbell's *English Seigniorial Agriculture 1250–1450* (Cambridge, 2000), have challenged the Chayanovian basis of Postan's analysis. These discussions have merely served to modify his thesis, which shows no immediate signs of being displaced.

BIBLIOGRAPHY

The following works provide a representative sample of studies of the "German School" of medieval economic history:

Bloch, Marc. *Land and Work in Medieval Europe: Papers by Marc Bloch*, edited by J. E. Anderson. London, 1967.
Bloch, Marc. *Slavery and Serfdom in the Middle Ages: Selected Essays by Marc Bloch*. Translated by William R. Beer. Berkeley, 1975.
Dopsch, Alfons. *Wirtschaftliche und soziale Grundlagen der europäischen Kulturentwicklung aus der Zeit von Cäser bis auf Karl den Grossen*, 2 vols., 2d ed. Vienna, 1923–1924. English (abridged) translation, *The Economic and Social Foundations of European Civilization*. London, 1937.
Pirenne, Henri. *Medieval Cities: Their Origins and the Revival of Trade*. Translated from the French by Frank D. Halsey. Princeton, 1925.
Pirenne, Henri. *Mahommed et Charlemagne*, 2d ed. Paris, 1937. English translation *Mahommed and Charlemagne*. Translated by Bernard Mialle. London, 1939.

For subsequent Marxist studies written within the same historiographic tradition, see the following:

Aston, Trevor H., Charles H. E. Philpin, eds. *The Brenner Debate: Agrarian Class Structure and Economic Development in Preindustrial Europe*. London, 1985.
Wallerstein, Immanuel. *The Modern World System*. Cambridge, 1974.
Wallerstein, Immanuel. *The Capitalist World Economy*. Cambridge, 1979.

Comprehensive collections of Postan's articles, referred to above, will be found in the following:

Postan, Michael M. *Fact and Relevance: Essays on Historical Method*. Cambridge, 1971.
Postan, Michael M. *Essays on Medieval Agriculture and General Problems of the Medieval Economy*. Cambridge, 1973.

IAN BLANCHARD

POST OFFICES AND POSTAL SYSTEMS. *See* Public Utilities, *subentry on* Postal Systems.

POTATO. The potato (*Solanum tuberosum*) is a nutritious tuber that can be grown in various climatic conditions. Domesticated at least seven thousand years ago in the high plateaux of the Andes, it remains an important source of food there. After the Spanish conquest of Peru in the sixteenth century, potato cultivation spread to Europe and other parts of the world. Its subsequent history centers on Europe, which until the twenty-first century produced and consumed most of the world's potatoes. From the mid- eighteenth to the early twentieth century, the potato was instrumental in feeding the rapidly growing population of northern Europe. Increased consumption of the potato was not without risks, as evidenced by widespread and catastrophic failures of the crop in the late 1840s, most notably in Ireland.

For most of its history, the potato was known only along the mountainous spine of South America, from Columbia to Chile. Early settlers domesticated tubers native to the high plateaux and later cultivated two crops per year by selecting more frost-resistant varieties. But the ever-present danger of frost damage made it essential to find a means of stocking potatoes. The solution, the freeze-dried potato, or *chuño*, also became an object of commerce with coastal regions and food for slaves in the Inca silver mines.

The potato was probably first grown in Spain around 1570. During the following century, it spread across Europe and North America, but was generally grown only in gardens—as a botanical or medical curiosity among elites and a minor source of food or fodder. From the late seventeenth century, potatoes were cultivated more widely as a field crop in a variety of regions: along the south coast of Ireland and in Flanders, Zeeland, Alsace, Lorraine,

POTATO. *The Potato Harvest*, painting by Arkady Plastov (1893–1972). (Russian State Museum, St. Petersburg/Scala/Art Resource, NY)

Dauphiné, Rheinpfalz, and Vogtland. War often played a role in stimulating cultivation, either by diffusing knowledge of the crop or by causing shortages of grain that stimulated the search for alternative and more secure sources of food.

Potato cultivation became more widespread in Europe and North America during the early eighteenth century but increased significantly in the later part of the century, as one of many responses to the acceleration of population growth in Europe. As a tuber, the potato could be incorporated into more intensive crop rotations. For those with little land, the hard labor of growing potatoes offered the reward of more calories per hectare. Increased potato consumption had health benefits. Eating both potatoes and cereals diversified the risks arising from crop failures, and, relative to cereals, potatoes were a good source of high-quality protein and vitamins. The downside of depending too heavily on potatoes was that they were difficult to store and costly to transport.

By the mid-nineteenth century, reliance on potatoes for food was characteristic of only a few regions in Europe, notably Ireland, Scotland, and northwest England; Belgium and the Netherlands; the Franco-German border area, including Alsace, the Rhineland, and Baden-Württemburg; the Prussian-Austrian border area, including parts of Saxony, Silesia, Bohemia, and Galicia; and the alpine zones of Switzerland, Italy, and Austria. In most of England, France, Germany, and southern Europe, pota-

toes were a minor element in the diet. Many of the potato-growing regions were upland areas, where cereals were difficult to grow, or were (or had been) centers of linen textile production. Potatoes and flax were intensive crops and had complementary peak labor requirements; domestic production of linen was typically carried out by smallholders.

Ireland stood out from the rest of Europe in its dependence on potatoes. By the 1840s, they accounted for almost a third of the land under crops, a level matched in only a few parts of upland Scotland and Switzerland. The cool, wet Irish climate certainly favored potatoes over cereals; and relatively high prices of land and food, due to agricultural protection in the United Kingdom, pushed the rapidly growing Irish population toward this labor-intensive crop. Irish cereal farmers fed their laborers on potatoes and smallholders used surplus potatoes to feed pigs and chickens, producing large quantities of pork and eggs for export to industrializing Great Britain.

Potato crops throughout Europe were devastated by blight (*Phytophthora infestans*), a fungus that arrived in Belgium with a load of seed potatoes from the United States in 1844. This disease, capable of destroying an entire crop and, depending on the weather, striking year after year, led to failures far more catastrophic than had previously been characteristic of potato or cereal crops. In 1845, the blight hit Belgium, the Netherlands, and adjacent parts of France and Germany most severely. In 1846, it struck throughout northern Europe and, combined with a very poor cereal harvest, led to catastrophic mortality and mass emigration in Ireland.

The persistent effects of the blight—it cut average potato yields by almost half and was tamed only by the introduction of copper sulphate spraying from the 1880s—contributed to falling rural population density in many potato-growing regions of Europe. Yet potato cultivation and consumption expanded markedly during the late nineteenth century in northern Europe. (It was also a period when potatoes started to be eaten in Asia and Africa.) Potatoes became a common feature of the diets of both industrial workers and the middle class. By around 1900, Germans were eating 250 to 300 kilograms (550–660 pounds) per person per year. Increased production and consumption of pork was also tied to the cultivation of potatoes in many countries. Growing potatoes and keeping pigs was one way that small farmers intensified production in response to falling cereal prices. In 1910, potato cultivation was concentrated in Germany, Austria-Hungary, and Russia, which together accounted for about two-thirds of world output and three-quarters of European output. These areas were notable for using potatoes for fodder and in distilling.

During the first half of the twentieth century, the locus of European potato cultivation shifted further east. In western Europe the area under potatoes fell by about a fifth; in eastern Europe it remained more or less stable; and in Russia it almost doubled. Forced procurement of cereals in the Soviet Union encouraged peasants to cultivate potatoes on their private plots. By the 1950s, the Soviet Union alone produced almost two-fifths of world output, and with its satellites almost two-thirds.

In the early 1960s, Europe still accounted for more than 80 percent of world output. France produced more potatoes than the United States, and Poland grew three times as many. Cultivation subsequently declined in Europe, while increasing rapidly in developing countries. In 2000, Europe accounted for less than half of world output and China and India became the first- and third-largest producers. While China fed a third of the crop to animals, elsewhere in Asia and Africa potatoes were primarily a supplementary food for humans. Only in parts of South America and Europe were they the leading food crop. Among the large developed countries, only the United States showed any significant growth in output during the late twentieth century, largely in response to the demand from makers of fried potatoes and other processed products.

[*See also* Famines *and* Irish Famine.]

BIBLIOGRAPHY

Bourke, Austin. *The Visitation of God?: The Potato and the Great Irish Famine*, edited by Jacqueline Hill and Cormac Ó Gráda. Dublin, 1993. Pioneering studies of the potato in Ireland and of the spread of the potato blight.

Cullen, Louis M. "Irish History without the Potato." *Past and Present* 40 (1968), 70–83. Classic statement of the case for population growth as the cause of increased potato consumption in Ireland.

Cullen, Louis M. *The Emergence of Modern Ireland, 1600–1900.* Dublin, 1981. Contains a later, more nuanced interpretation of the Irish diet.

Mokyr, Joel. "Irish History with the Potato." *Irish Economic and Social History* 8 (1981), 8–29. Econometric results that suggest the potato was a cause of Irish population growth.

Ó Gráda, Cormac, ed. *Famine 150.* Dublin, 1997. Contains chapters on the potato in the Irish diet and on the potato famine in Europe; the latter discusses the regional distribution of potato cultivation in Europe.

Ó Gráda, Cormac. *Black '47 and Beyond.* Princeton, 1999. A leading Irish economic historian explores various aspects of the famine of the 1840s.

Rhoades, Robert. *World Geography of the Potato.* Lima, 1990. Useful compendium of information on potato cultivation around the world.

Salaman, Redcliffe N. *The History and Social Influence of the Potato.* Cambridge, 1949. Classic and still valuable work on the history of the potato.

Solar, Peter M. "The Great Famine Was No Ordinary Subsistence Crisis." In *Famine: The Irish Experience, 900–1900*, edited by E. M. Crawford, pp. 112–133. Edinburgh, 1989. Discusses the effect of the blight on crop yields in Ireland and elsewhere in Europe.

Teuteberg, Hans J., and Günter Wiegelmann. "Einführung und Nutzung der Kartoffel in Deutschland." In *Unsere tägliche Kost. Geschichte und regionale Prägung*, 2d ed., edited by Hans J. Teuteberg and Günter Wiegelmann, pp. 93–134. Münster, 1986. The best work on the diffusion of potato cultivation in Germany; contains considerable information on other countries.

Vandenbroeke, Christiaan. "Cultivation and Consumption of the Potato in the 17th and 18th Century." *Acta Historiae Neerlandica*, vol. 5, pp. 15–39. Leiden, 1971. Interpretative essay on the diffusion of potato cultivation and consumption in the Low Countries and France.

Woolfe, Jennifer A. *The Potato in the Human Diet.* Cambridge, 1987. Useful reference on the potato as nutriment.

Zuckerman, Larry. *The Potato.* London, 1999. Popular but well-informed history of the potato in Ireland, England, France, and the United States.

PETER M. SOLAR

POULTRY. Among domesticated animals, poultry and especially chickens are important historically and contemporarily. They (1) provide high-quality meat; (2) can survive in a variety of conditions and on scraps and other low-value foods; (3) furnish another food product, eggs, in addition to meat; and (4) grow to marketable or consumable age rapidly. As a source of protein, the chicken provides high value for its cost. In addition to chickens, which dominate the industry, domesticated poultry include turkeys, geese, ducks, guinea fowl, and pigeons and their nestlings known as squab. Modern domesticated chickens descended from the wild jungle fowl of India. No precise record exists of first domestication, but it occurred more than four thousand years ago. Initially, domesticated chickens were used for cockfighting in Asia, Africa, and Europe; England led in banning the practice in 1849. Europeans were familiar with domesticated turkeys before the Pilgrims consumed their first Thanksgiving dinner. Spanish explorers, who found Aztec and Zuni Indians growing turkeys, took the birds to Spain in 1519. Turkey breeding and consumption spread through Italy, France, and England in the sixteenth century. The Old Testament Bible mentions domesticated geese, though modern geese descended from Eurasian ancestors. Pre-Columbian Indians kept domestic ducks, as did the Chinese two thousand years ago. Waterfowl have tended to be especially popular where rice cultivation thrives. Guinea fowl and pigeons and squabs are popular in particular markets but cannot compete with other domesticated poultry in cost per pound of meat.

Although poultry have a long history of domestication, their production was small-scale and related primarily to local markets and family consumption until the nineteenth century. Nonetheless, as European cities grew, their agricultural supply areas necessarily grew, affecting poultry production. London plea and memoranda rolls and letter books for the fourteenth century describe the punishment of butchers, fishmongers, and poulterers for breaking guild regulations. The guilds and the city regulated sanitary conditions as well as prices. City customs and duties of 1410 distinguished between goods brought into London on foot and those transported in by cart. One hundred eggs brought to the city on (human) foot faced a duty of five eggs, and a load of cheese or poultry paid one halfpenny. A cartload of poultry paid three farthings. These duties suggest that by 1410, London had active poultry and egg markets supplied by farmers outside the city. Bedfordshire and Northamptonshire supplied some of the city's poultry and eggs by the 1600s. Farm wives brought hens, chickens, eggs, and other country items into London for sale, but by the late sixteenth century, they shared the market with middlemen. Poulterers in the city sold at retail. Increasingly, retailers permeated the countryside as they sought to buy directly from suppliers.

Colonial Americans kept chickens for meat and eggs. Relative to modern Americans, the colonials ate little chicken as compared to beef. By the mid-nineteenth century, interest in more effective poultry farming grew. In 1859, Pennsylvania State University began formal instruction in poultry science, which assisted informal efforts at inbreeding, linebreeding, and crossbreeding that had long been used to improve poultry stocks. Poultry diseases also were studied more systematically to reduce their incidence and spread. At least as early as the 1480s, murrain had reduced the stocks of domestic animals around London. The U.S. Department of Agriculture, established in 1862, funded research and became the major source of information about poultry production. The American Poultry Association was founded in 1873 to represent concerns of poultry producers. U.S. researchers, academic and otherwise, set up the Poultry Science Association in 1908.

Despite this activity, poultry production remained relatively small-scale, with urban markets served by local and regional suppliers, until the mid-twentieth century. The problem of breakage and the desirability of freshness made eggs difficult to transport. The small size of poultry made slaughtering, cold storage, and transportation expensive compared to larger meat sources. Warm temperatures and unrefrigerated poultry were a toxic combination. Nonetheless, English producers by the 1920s tried high-volume battery production of poultry and eggs. Commercial producers focused on egg and meat production, but commercial hatcheries spread in the 1920s, signaling more specialization. Larger-scale techniques of poultry production, dominated by chicken and turkey production, became important in the United States after World War II. In addition to more scientific breeding, feeding, and disease control, technology improved in poultry processing with innovations such as mechanical deboners that reduced cost per unit of output. Studies of agricultural production suggest that total factor productivity increased faster in poultry production than in other meat production in the late twentieth century. Larger firms and industry associations experimented with both generic and brand name advertising to expand sales, with evidence that such advertising does help brand name products. Health concerns about red meat also encouraged greater consumption of poultry in the United States. Researchers have found the price elasticity of demand for poultry to be larger than the advertising elasticity, suggesting that industry resources might be better expended on developing cost-reducing technology than on extensive advertising. With larger firms, which took advantage of economies of scale in production, and name brand advertising came increasing concentration of industry, both industrially and locationally. The United States is now the world's leading producer and exporter of chicken and turkey products. As part of the agricultural sector, the poultry industry in many countries has been subjected to government regulation and government protection and subsidies. Because poultry producers buy feed, they are affected by trade protection for domestic grain producers, policies that raise feed prices.

Many modern issues affecting the poultry industry have historical antecedents. Interest in encouraging women in developing countries to raise chickens for meat and egg sale harks back to the farm wife of the nineteenth and earlier centuries. Large-scale poultry firms raise environmental concerns about disposal of poultry litter. Fourteenth-century London regulated the disposal of offal from butchers and poulterers, requiring that waste be carried to the Thames River and deposited at low tide. Use of feed additives and antibiotics to increase size and reduce disease echo London's fifteenth-century concern about the spread of the plague from animals to humans. Today's particularly English animal rights movement is reminiscent of the nineteenth-century movement to ban cockfighting.

BIBLIOGRAPHY

Brester, Gary W., and Ted C. Schroeder. "The Impacts of Brand and Generic Advertising on Meat Demand." *American Journal of Agricultural Economics* 77.4 (1995), 969–979. Representative of the technical, empirical studies for which agricultural economics is known, this article uses data from industry sources, consumer surveys, and grocery store scan device records to examine the effectiveness of advertising what used to be considered a homogeneous product.

Carter, Susan, Scott Gartner, Michael Haines, Alan Olmstead, Richard Sutch, and Gavin Wright. *Historical Statistics of the United States, Bicentennial Edition*. New York, 2000. This is the updated, edited, and electronic CD-ROM version of the historical statistics of the United States.

Fisher, F. J. "The Development of the London Food Market, 1540–1640." *Economic History Review* 5.2 (1935), 46–64.

Heien, Dale. "An Economic Analysis of the U.S. Poultry Sector." *American Journal of Agricultural Economics* 58.2 (1976), 311–316. Another example of the extensive empirical analyses of agricultural economists, this article uses data from the massive collections of the U.S. Department of Agriculture.

Huntington, Ellsworth. "The Distribution of Domestic Animals." *Economic Geography* 1.2 (1925), 143–172.

Mitchell, B. R. *International Historical Statistics: Africa, Asia, and Oceania, 1750–1993*. London, 1998. The author compiles, but does not analyze statistics by country on various kinds of output, including livestock within the agricultural sector for the two and a half centuries covered. What is interesting in comparison with compilations for other continents is the lack of data for poultry in the livestock listings. The author notes that poultry generally cannot be included under the meat heading until the 1950s and 1960s.

Mitchell, B. R. *International Historical Statistics: Europe, 1750–1993*. 4th ed. London, 1998. This compilation provides massive European data by country from existing sources. For only a few countries does data exist on poultry production before 1900.

Mitchell, B. R., with Phyllis Deane. *Abstract of British Historical Statistics*. Cambridge, 1962. This reference volume includes data on livestock, including poultry, but little is reported on poultry before the twentieth century.

Pockney, B. P. *Soviet Statistics since 1950*. New York, 1991. Data on egg production by Soviet republics are included consistently for 1961–1985 and for poultry production for 1941 and 1951–1989. The volume also includes data on state purchases and other disposal of these products.

Sabine, Ernest. "Butchering in Mediaeval London." *Speculum* 8.3 (1933), 335–353. Close reading of public records and account books generates a wealth of information about London livestock treatments, 1300–1500.

U.S. Bureau of the Census. *Historical Statistics of the United States, Colonial Times to 1957*. Washington, D.C., 1961. This volume presents data on many aspects of economic life in the United States, including series on livestock. Notes give the sources for the data, frequently the relevant Census of Agriculture volume. Data on poultry and egg production begin in the first decade of the twentieth century.

ANN HARPER FENDER

POWER, EILEEN (1889–1940), leading founder of economic history.

Remembered today for her popular medieval social histories, *Medieval People* (1924) and *Medieval Women* (1975), Eileen Power was the best-known medieval historian of the interwar years. Together with R. H. Tawney, she transformed economic and social history from a frontier subject into a prominent part of the historical disciplines. She was as famed in her lifetime as were Tawney, G. M. Trevelyan, and Marc Bloch.

Power was born in a suburb of Manchester but was mainly educated at the Oxford High School for Girls. In 1907, with a Clothworkers Scholarship, she enrolled at Girton College, Cambridge. She studied history with Ellen McArthur (an economic historian who worked with William Cunningham) and Winifred Mercier, both leading suffragists. Cunningham established close links between Girton and the London School of Economics (LSE), and Power followed in Lilian Knowles's footsteps and pursued postgraduate research at the LSE. Power took part in the suffrage movement and through friendship was on the fringes of the Bloomsbury group. Awarded a fellowship endowed by Charlotte Shaw, she became one of a pioneer group of women researchers. She also started research on medieval women at a time of a new interest in women and the economy and in women's history more broadly. Power returned to teach at Girton from 1913 to 1920. In 1920, she was awarded the Kahn Travelling Fellowship for a year of world travel. While she was in India and China, she was offered a lectureship in economic history at the LSE. She returned to teach there from 1921 until her death in 1940.

Power's book *Medieval English Nunneries* (1922) and a number of articles on medieval women established her long-standing lead in the field of medieval women's history. She turned her interest more centrally to economic history, and her writing on the medieval and early modern economy was heavily influenced by her experiences in India and China as well as by the new social sciences she encountered at the LSE. She worked closely with Tawney in recasting courses to create a modern curriculum in economic history that was sociological, comparative, cosmopolitan, international, and most important, integrated with the new social sciences. This lifted economic history out of its old framework of economic policy and constitutional development and made it a prominent part of the new LSE with its political engagement and intellectual initiative. Power's novel methodological connection between medieval history and the new social sciences was set out in her well-known inaugural lecture "On Medieval History as a Social Study."

Power's fame was assured with the publication of *Medieval People* (1924), which, together with Tawney's *Religion and the Rise of Capitalism* (1922, 1926), made economic history popular across wide audiences. Power started the Medieval Economic History Seminar with M. M. Postan, her student, and edited with him *Studies in English Trade in the Fifteenth Century* (1933). She inititiated the *Cambridge Economic History of Europe* (1941) and edited the first volume with J. H. Clapham. It was published the year after her death. Power was one of the founders, with Tawney, of the Economic History Society, and she acted as its secretary from its foundation in 1926 until her death. The significance of these initiatives was recognized by Bloch as a movement with parallels to the *Annales* in France. She gave the Ford Lectures in Oxford in 1939, the first woman to do so. These lectures were published after her death as *The Wool Trade in English Medieval History* (1941). The book, which focuses on capital formation, taxation, and international trade, is a classic account of the connections among land, industry, and trade in the medieval period. Power became a corresponding member of the Medieval Academy of America in 1936. She was awarded an honorary doctorate by Manchester University in 1933 and another by Mount Holyoke in the United States in 1937.

Power was passionately committed to the peace movement and hoped a cosmopolitan economic and social history would displace nationalist histories. She wrote a large number of texts for schools, spoke extensively in educational history broadcasts, and was a prominent public lecturer and member of literary London. In the years leading up to her death, she worked on a history of the world but was also part of a prominent anti-appeasement circle in the Labour Party.

Power was a pioneer social historian who drew together history and literature and wrote on novel themes of cultural history and women's history at a time when most medieval history was based in manorial and constitutional history. She developed a comparative and international framework in economic history, using contemporary models of economic and capitalist development in her studies in rural history, English trade, and the wool trade and in her methodological essays.

BIBLIOGRAPHY

Berg, Maxine. "The First Women Economic Historians." *Economic History Review* 45 (1992), 308–329.

Berg, Maxine. *A Woman in History: Eileen Power, 1889–1940*. Cambridge, 1996.

Davis, Natalie Z. "History's Two Bodies." *American Historical Review* 93 (1988), 1–30.

Harris, José. *William Beveridge: A Biography*. Oxford, 1977.

Power, Eileen. *Report to the Trustees, September 1920–September 1921, Alfred Kahn Travelling Fellowship*. London, 1921.

Power, Eileen. *Medieval English Nunneries, c. 1275–1535*. Cambridge, 1922.

Power, Eileen. *Medieval People*. London, 1924.

Power, Eileen. "On Medieval History as a Social Study." *Economica* 12 (1934), 13–29.

Power, Eileen. *The Wool Trade in English Medieval History*. Oxford, 1941.

Power, Eileen. *Medieval Women*, edited by M. M. Postan. Cambridge, 1975.

Power, Eileen, and Rhoda Power. *Boys and Girls of History*. Cambridge, 1926.

Power, Eileen, and R. H. Tawney. *Tudor Economic Documents*. London, 1924.

Power, Eileen, and J. H. Clapham, eds. *The Cambridge Economic History of Europe*, vol. 1. Cambridge, 1941.

Power, Eileen, and M. M. Postan, eds. *Studies in English Trade in the Fifteenth Century*. London, 1933.

Tawney, R. H. "Eileen Power." *Economic History Review* 10 (1940), 91–94.

Thirsk, Joan. "Forward." In *Women in English Society, 1500–1800*, edited by Mary Prior, pp. 1–21. London, 1985.

MAXINE BERG

POWER TECHNOLOGY. One of the key elements of any economy is power. Thus, it is not surprising that power technologies have often been used to periodize the history of technology. Lewis Mumford in *Technics and Civilizations* (1934), for example, used them as a central organizational principle, dividing the history of technology into three broad epochs, each characterized by a dominant motive power: eotechnic (water), paleotechnic (steam), and neotechnic (electricity).

General Attributes. Historically, the development of power technologies, the particular technology chosen by a user, and the impact these technologies had on society were heavily conditioned by eight key attributes—magnitude, density (or compactness), mobility, locational flexibility, reliability, convenience, efficiency, and cost.

Magnitude means the raw amount of power a prime mover can produce. A coal-fired generating plant, for example, produces much more power than a horse.

Density (or compactness) refers to the power a prime mover can produce per unit of size or mass. Steam turbines, for example, are much more compact than traditional reciprocating steam engines because turbines utilize steam at much higher pressures.

Mobility is the extent to which a power technology can be adapted to transportation. Inherently immobile power technologies, such as water wheels, generally have a smaller economic influence than those of comparable magnitude that can be made mobile, such as steam engines.

Locational flexibility pertains to the ease with which a power technology can be sited. Certain power technologies, such as water wheels and windmills, are locationally limited by the nature of their motive force. Others, such as steam engines, because they use fuels easily and economically transported, are geographically more flexible.

Reliability is another key attribute. Technologies dependent on the vagaries of climate and weather, such as wind and water, usually have less inherent reliability than those using fossil fuels. Technologies operating at low temperatures are often more reliable than those operating at high temperatures.

Convenience can also be a critical factor in the choice of power technology. Human muscle is one of the most convenient sources of power since it is readily available at all times. One of the key disadvantages of steam engines was the inconvenience of the long warm-up period required before operation. Internal combustion engines became important, in part, because they had many of the favorable characteristics of the steam engine but could also be started quickly.

Efficiency is the ratio between the power that can be extracted from a machine and the power put into it. Efficiency considerations are often important in choices between power technologies in the same family (for example, between various steam-powered prime movers), but they often play a smaller role in choices between qualitatively different families. For example, even the most primitive water wheels were more efficient, technically, than steam engines, but steam engines became the dominant power technology because other attributes were more important than efficiency, such as locational flexibility, power magnitude, and reliability.

Finally, cost (initial cost, fuel, maintenance) is a critical factor in determining when and if a power technology is adopted. Relatively inefficient undershot water wheels, for example, remained in use for centuries after the discovery of the much more efficient overshot wheels because they were cheaper to construct.

Because each power technology has a different combination of the eight attributes outlined above, the introduction of a new power technology has not usually resulted in the complete displacement of old. Power choices involve complex trade-offs among these attributes, and often economic niches exist where the combined attributes of an older technology remain advantageous.

Animate Power Technologies. The survival of old power technologies even after the emergence of new can be illustrated by considering the earliest human power "technology," muscle. Human muscle can produce no more than about 0.1 horsepower (hp) over extended time. To compensate for this, prehistoric inventors developed various means of power transmission to improve the efficiency of muscular energy. These included ropes and several so-called simple machines, like the lever and wheel and axle. Later, early civilizations combined these techniques with other devices to construct the first autonomous machines, such as the quern, potter's wheel, press, and water-raising devices.

Because of the limited power of human muscle, early civilizations made little effort to concentrate production. Usually little was gained by taking production out of the household and centralizing it. This is not to say that human muscle, properly coordinated, could not generate large amounts of power in combination. Some ancient societies concentrated sufficient muscle power through political and social institutions to construct megaliths, like the pyramids, whose size was matched only in the twentieth century.

The convenience of human muscle and its mobility continued to make it an appropriate power source for many tasks long after stronger and more concentrated forms of power displaced it from many tasks. For example, human muscle is still important in those regions of the world where intensive cultivation of small agricultural plots is the norm for food production. Even in the most advanced technological societies, human muscle remains in use for a myriad of small-power demand tasks, such as bagging groceries.

In the late prehistoric era the domestication of animals provided the first power sources of greater magnitude than human muscle. The key animals were the ox, water buffalo, and horse. The ox and water buffalo could develop about 0.4 to 0.5 horsepower. The horse delivered a bit more but not a full horsepower. In the early 1780s James Watt first gave *horsepower* a quantitative definition so purchasers of his steam engines would have a basis for comparison. However, his value (33,000 foot-pounds per minute), while attainable by a few powerful horses, was substantially beyond a typical horse. This technique insured that users of Watt's engines would not be disappointed by their power output.

Although the horse was significantly faster (by 30 to 50 percent) and slightly more powerful than the ox and water buffalo, it was not, at first, widely used either in agriculture, the dominant productive activity of the bulk of humankind, or in commercial transportation. Two factors account for this. In wet climates, the horse's hoofs were susceptible to damage and deterioration, lessening the horse's reliability. In addition early harnessing inefficiencies limited the horse's power output. When a horse threw his or her weight into a load, the throat-and-girth harness used in antiquity choked the animal. Thus a horse in antiquity could pull only around 25 percent of the load of one in modern times.

The early yokes used on oxen and water buffalos were more anatomically compatible than the early harnessing used on horses, so oxen and water buffalos operated at closer to full efficiency. As a result oxen in most regions (water buffalos in some parts of Asia) were the preferred power source for key agricultural activities, especially plowing, though the slowness of these animals precluded a major role in long-distance transportation.

The emergence of the collar harness and horseshoes transformed the horse into an effective heavy draft animal.

The Chinese used collar harnesses by, at the latest, the fifth century CE. Collar harnesses reached Europe by around 800 CE and attained general use there by perhaps 1200. Collar harnesses increased the useful draft of horses approximately four times over the throat-and-girth harness while simultaneously allowing more effective teaming of horses. Horseshoes, introduced around the seventh century CE, reduced wear on hooves and improved traction and endurance, making horses a more reliable power source. By the nineteenth century a pair of good horses could easily do 25 to 30 percent more fieldwork than a team of four oxen. Moreover, the horse's superior speed extended the range of cultivation and made draft animals more effective at moving goods commercially.

Early Inanimate Power Technologies. The shortcomings of animate power as a means of overland transportation in antiquity made waterborne transportation the preferred method for moving commercial goods over long distances. By at least the end of the fourth millennium BCE, humans had learned to use wind as an aid in moving vessels. Several factors, however, limited the use of wind-powered vessels in antiquity. Because it is not a dense power source, wind required a machine of considerable size (the sails, masts, and hull of a sailing vessel) to capture and transmit enough power to be useful. Because wind was not reliable, sailors could use it effectively only certain times of the year. Finally, the technology used to capture the wind was inefficient. Ancient merchant vessels usually depended on a single square mainsail. This type of rigging generally limited ancient mariners to sailing with the wind.

Fore-and-aft rigs (where the sail ran parallel to the length of the boat instead of perpendicular), which permitted vessels to sail more directly into the wind, appeared in the Indian Ocean centuries before the current era and expanded into the Mediterranean by the first century BCE. However, they were more inconvenient to handle on large vessels and without deep keels (to prevent the wind from moving vessels sideways) had limited effectiveness. Not until the period from 1200 to 1500 CE did both European and Chinese shipwrights significantly improve merchant sailing vessels. In Europe, for example, shipwrights made the wind easier to control (that is, more convenient and efficient) by using multiple masts, subdividing sails into more manageable units, and installing a combination of square and triangular sails to permit efficient sailing both with and into the winds.

The limited density of wind power and the inefficient means of harnessing it restricted its use to waterborne transport in antiquity. The production of agricultural and manufactured goods depended solely on animate power until around 200 to 100 BCE, when craftspeople in western Asia discovered how to tap the energy of falling water.

Waterpower was not a mobile power source, and its use was limited to areas near steadily flowing steams. However, it was a far denser form of power than any other power technology in antiquity. Even early water wheels could develop two to three horsepower, twenty to thirty times the output of a person and around five to ten times the output of an animal, and water wheels could deliver power day and night without rest or feeding.

Technicians quickly developed several forms. Some early watermills depended on horizontally rotating wheels, which transmitted power via a vertical axle directly to millstones. These mills had a relatively low power output, often only around 0.5 horsepower, and low efficiency. Because they did not require gearing and extensive conduits to guide water, however, their cost was low. Vertically situated wheels, with horizontal axles and gearing to transform the plane of rotation from vertical to horizontal, were more widely used. In undershot vertical wheels, water was led beneath the wheel to strike flat blades. The undershot wheel, like the early horizontal wheel, was inefficient. Only around 20 to 30 percent of the energy of the falling water was transformed into mechanical energy at the shaft. The overshot wheel, developed in Europe by, at the latest, the third century CE, was more efficient. In an overshot wheel, water was led by a conduit over the top and deposited into containers, called buckets, built into the circumference. The weight of the water turned the wheel and connected machinery. Overshot wheels delivered two to three times more power for the same amount of water and fall than undershot wheels.

The new, more concentrated form of power represented by the water wheel did not suddenly displace muscle power in antiquity, even in stationary applications for which waterpower was admirably suited, such as grinding grain. Human muscle was less costly. By the third century CE, however, declining populations in the Roman Empire had shifted the balance, and by the fifth century waterpower had come into general use for grinding grain, one of the essential tasks of most societies.

The collapse of Roman rule in western Europe temporarily set back the use of waterpower in that region. But unlike much of Asia, western Europe had an abundance of regularly flowing streams, and unlike China and India, western Europe was chronically underpopulated. Promoted by monasteries, which viewed waterpower as a means to relieve monks from monotonous work and leave more time for prayer and contemplation, waterpower revived and spread steadily in the centuries following the collapse of Roman rule. Moreover waterpower was incorporated into the prevalent social system. Among the feudal dues that many peasants were required to pay was the obligation to grind grain at the lord's flour mill and pay the associated duty, typically one-tenth of the grain ground. By

1086 England alone had nearly six thousand watermills, or one for every fifty households, and flour had become one of the first products whose production was centralized. By 1500 watermills were common fixtures along streams in much of Europe. Later European immigrants carried waterpower to the American continent, and by 1840 approximately fifty-five thousand water-powered mills operated in the United States alone.

Although waterpower was early applied to metallurgical bellows in China, in the West prior to 1000 CE it was largely limited to two uses, grinding grain and raising water. Beginning around 1000, Western millwrights in particular began to expand this list. Using modifications of conventional millstones, by 1500 millwrights had devised ways to grind other materials, such as pepper, mustard, hops, and pottery glazes. By modifying gearing arrangements, they were able to turn large wheel-shaped stones on edge, using them to crush materials like olives and the ingredients for gunpowder. More important, they developed ways of transforming the rotary motion of water wheels into linear motion. The two key devices—cam and crank—were probably known in antiquity but never applied on a large scale. The cam, a projection placed on a water wheel's axle, could be used to raise and drop hammers or stamps equipped with similar projections, converting rotary to reciprocal, straight-line motion. The crank did the same thing more directly. These power transmission devices, adapted to waterpower between 1000 and 1500, greatly extended the number of tasks to which inanimate power sources could be applied. They enabled water wheels to power hammers in fulling mills, paper mills, and ore crushing establishments and to operate saws for cutting wood and bellows for processing metals. The fragmentation of political power in the West, which permitted the rise of a powerful merchant class capable of, and willing to exploit, expanding power technologies for profit, undoubtedly contributed to the rapid expansion and diffusion of these applications.

The technological knowledge developed for waterpower, particularly arrangements of shafts and gears, had broader applications. Persian millwrights as early as the ninth century CE erected simple windmills with blades that rotated in the horizontal plane. These only caught winds coming from a single direction. In the twelfth century European millwrights, drawing from their knowledge of watermills, devised a much different and more versatile form. European windmills had blades that rotated in the vertical plane on a slightly tilted horizontal axle and used shafts and gearing, similar to that of watermills, to carry the kinetic energy of the winds to its machinery. The European windmill could handle variable-direction winds because its blades could be rotated into the wind. The earliest windmills were post mills, so-called because the entire apparatus (blades, power transmission devices, machinery, and housing) was pivoted on a large post. By the fourteenth century European millwrights had developed smock and tower mills, windmills where only the blades and their axle had to be rotated into the wind. The European windmill diffused rapidly, especially along the coasts of the Baltic and North Seas, where winds were relatively reliable and waterpower costly because of the flat terrain.

By 1500 or 1600 Western civilization had become heavily dependent on inanimate power sources, probably the first civilization to move significantly beyond near-total dependence on the sweat of peasants, slaves, or coolies and their animals. By 1750 European engineers were building water wheels and windmills capable of developing forty to fifty horsepower and perhaps more, although averages were still below ten horsepower.

Power Technologies in the Industrial Revolution (1750–1850). By 1700 a few areas of Europe had begun to push existing power technologies up against their natural limits. In England most good power sites along streams within a few miles of major urban areas had been developed, and the list of processes using waterpower continued to grow, increasing the pressure on available sites. The demand for certain products, such as coal, was pushing mines below the water table and increasing the need for more powerful pumping machinery. Because of their locational inflexibility, limited power, or unreliability, existing power sources were increasingly unable to meet industrial needs.

Faced with these problems, British technologists sought a means of converting the thermal energy of coal, which the region had in abundance, into mechanical energy. By 1712 Thomas Newcomen, an ironmonger in southwestern England, had developed a coal-fueled engine that used condensed steam inside a cylinder to create a vacuum. Atmospheric pressure then pushed a piston mounted in that cylinder downward, lifting a pump rod on the opposite side of a rocking beam. Newcomen's atmospheric pumping engine was the first commercially successful device to convert thermal energy to mechanical energy. By midcentury it was in frequent use in British mining districts and had spread to several European countries, but its use was restricted to pumping operations.

Between 1765 and 1785 the Scottish engineer James Watt introduced a host of modifications to Newcomen's engine. He developed means to effectively use the direct pressure of steam rather than the pressure of the atmosphere to move the engine's piston and introduced additional ways (for example, the separate condenser and expansive operation) to reduce steam consumption and thus improve the device's efficiency. Equally important, he modified the engine so it was capable of delivering rotary motion. Watt's engine was more costly than the Newcomen engine, but it was more compact and more

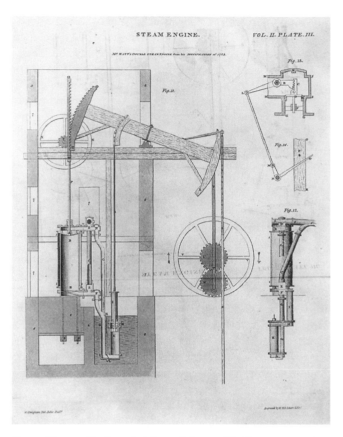

STEAM POWER. Design sketches of James Watt's steam engine, 1822. (Prints and Photographs Division, Library of Congress)

efficient (fuel consumption per unit of power was one-fourth of its previous level). By 1800 Watt's firm alone had manufactured five hundred engines with an average capacity of around twenty-five to thirty horsepower (five times higher than typical watermills, three times that of windmills). Moreover, the largest units by 1800 were capable of developing 100 to 150 horsepower. Steam engines quickly became the power technology of choice in many regions.

Even Watt steam engines were relatively large and heavy for their output and thus incapable of mobility on land. The introduction of high-pressure boilers by Richard Trevithick in England and Oliver Evans in the United States between 1795 and 1805 began the process of transforming the steam engine into a much more dense (compact) power source. As the ratio between weight and power dropped, it became technically possible to use steam for locomotion. Experiments in the first decade of the nineteenth century failed. Combining steam-powered carriages (locomotives) with special "roads" made of iron rails eventually proved the key to success. By the 1830s steam-powered transportation using railroads had provided the first significant advance in land transportation since the domesti-

cation of the horse. By the late nineteenth century the steam-powered railroad had become the standard form of transportation for both passengers and freight in most of Europe and America and had begun to penetrate non-Western countries as well. The first half of the nineteenth century also saw the first successful applications of steam power to waterborne transportation. Steam vessels had largely replaced sail in developed parts of the world by 1900.

The steam engine revolutionized Western technology and society as no previous power technology had. Compared with previous prime movers, animate or inanimate, it could generate more power. Moreover it did not have the limitations of water and wind power. With a good supply of coal (or wood in some instances) it was a reliable power source. It was locationally flexible; steam engines could be used almost anywhere coal could be delivered, agriculture remaining the largest exception. Over the course of the nineteenth century this locational flexibility and the steam engine's greater power encouraged the concentration of production in locations favorable to manufacturing, promoting urbanization. The development of mobile steam power further encouraged industrial concentration, urbanization, and trade, since railroads (or steamships) could bring the necessary goods and raw materials to cities and manufactories and distribute volume-produced goods to wider markets.

Power Technologies in the Late Nineteenth Century. Despite the steam engine's favorable attributes, it had certain inherent disadvantages. It was inefficient in part because the thermal energy of heat, instead of being directly used to produce mechanical power, operated though an intervening fluid (water) heated externally. Moreover steam engines were not convenient for intermittent operation. Steam boilers often required several hours of heating before they could go into operation.

These deficiencies led a number of early nineteenth-century inventors to seek some method of converting thermal energy to mechanical energy by heating air or some other fluid inside the cylinder (internal combustion) so it would act directly against the piston. These attempts failed. The growth of gas lighting in the mid-nineteenth century, however, led several inventors to consider burning illuminating gas (generated from coal) in engine cylinders. Illuminating gas–powered engines potentially had many of the favorable attributes of steam engines (power magnitude, density) plus the additional advantages of higher efficiency (due to internal combustion) and greater convenience of operation, since they could be turned on and off at will. Moreover since gas-powered engines depended on a centralized facility to produce the gas (a city's gas plant) rather than a local boiler for generating steam, potential savings in capital and operating costs existed for small business owners. In the 1870s Nicholas Otto in Germany finally developed a commercially successful engine by working out a system (the four-stroke cycle) of compressing an air-gas mixture in a cylinder before igniting it. Otto engines proved useful to small urban businesses needing the convenience of intermittent operation.

Because Otto engines were compact and powerful, several inventors quickly attempted to transform them into a mobile power source. Success required a denser fuel than illuminating gas and a means for igniting that fuel. In the late 1880s and early 1890s these problems were solved. Gasoline, previously a waste product of the distillation of kerosene from crude petroleum, provided the dense, portable fuel. Timed sparks from storage batteries provided the ignition.

Another form of the internal combustion engine, the diesel engine, designed according to scientific principles and relying on extreme compression of fuel to secure self-ignition, emerged between 1895 and 1910. It ultimately provided an even more compact and efficient, though more expensive, form of internal combustion engine that utilized a different petroleum fraction, fuel oil and was especially suitable to constant power production.

Because both gasoline and fuel oil had a higher energy density than coal and were easier and cleaner to burn, transport, and store, internal combustion engines quickly challenged steam-powered transportation. Because internal combustion engines were a more compact (dense) power technology, for instance, vehicles using them were lighter and did not require the special iron roads of steam-powered locomotives. By 1920 internal combustion automobiles and trucks began to supplement steam-powered railroads for passenger and freight traffic. By 1950 they had displaced them in importance. Diesel engines began to replace steam engines in marine service early in the twentieth century as well. The magnitude, density, reliability, and mobility of internal combustion engine technology also permitted the emergence of commercial air transport toward the mid-twentieth century.

As noted earlier, old power technologies do not usually die with the introduction of new ones. They often have particular attributes that enable them to survive in certain economic niches. Thus the introduction of steam and internal combustion engines did not eliminate waterpower, which retained its importance in certain locales for some fixed manufacturing processes, such as textile production. Hydraulic engineers extended the life of waterpower in these locales by improving steadily the efficiency of water wheels through systematic, quantitative studies and by increasing the technology's reliability through better water management and replacement of wood with iron. At Lowell, Massachusetts, for example, between 1790 and 1840 engineers dammed the Merrimack River and constructed a maze of canals, supplementing this system with reservoirs on the Merrimack's headwaters. By 1840 water-powered textile mills at Lowell were consuming nearly ten thousand horsepower. Similar water-powered complexes existed at other points in North America (Lawrence, Holyoke, Manchester) as well as in Europe (Greenock, Scotland).

Improvements in the water wheel's power density, cost, and efficiency further promoted waterpower's competitiveness. Water acted on only one portion of the wheel at a time on traditional water wheels. Between 1825 and 1835 the French engineer Benoît Fourneyron perfected a rapidly rotating, submerged iron water wheel, called a turbine, in which water acted on the whole wheel simultaneously through carefully designed curved guides and rotor blades. This design improved the water wheel's power density, first cost, and efficiency. The introduction of turbines in a variety of forms between 1840 and 1870 enabled water to remain competitive with steam in regions where coal was not abundant but water was, such as Switzerland, Norway, Canada, and California.

The Emergence of Electrical Power Transmission. By far the most significant development in the late nineteenth century, electrical power transmission originated in the 1870s after electrical technicians developed reasonably efficient methods for converting mechanical into electrical energy with the Gramme generator. By the 1880s it was possible to transmit power commercially by direct current up to several miles for conversion into light. By 1895, with the introduction of alternating current, which permitted the transmission of electrical power at higher voltages with consequent lower power losses, and with the emergence of an effective alternating current motor, it became possible to transmit mechanical power long distances with minimal power losses.

The introduction of electrical transmission had an impact on power technology fully equal to that of the water wheel and the steam engine. For example, it revived interest in waterpower by making it possible to tap falls of water in remote areas and transmit the energy to industrial centers. The key early hydroelectric project involved Niagara Falls, where the combination of water turbines, electrical generators, and high-voltage alternating current enabled power to be generated at Niagara and economically transmitted twenty-five miles to Buffalo, New York, beginning in 1895. This success encouraged imitators. By 1910 coal-poor California was transmitting waterpower electrically hundreds of miles from the Sierra Nevadas to the state's industrial centers in San Francisco and Los Angeles.

Besides giving waterpower a new lease on life, the emergence of electrical power transmission prompted a revolution in steam technology. The growth of electrical power transmission initially created problems for steam engines. Cheap and efficient electrical generators required high

HYDROELECTRIC POWER. View of Lake Lynn Hydroelectric Power House and Dam, Cheat River, Monongalia County, West Virginia, 1968. (Prints and Photographs Division, Library of Congress)

rotational velocities. Traditional reciprocating steam engines, through gearing and belting, could manage this but only with significant power losses and increased vibrations, which reduced engine life. This situation prompted inventors in several countries to renew studies of rotating steam engines. In the 1880s several inventors developed workable, high-velocity rotating steam engines (steam turbines), the most successful by Charles A. Parsons in Great Britain. Parsons turbines used multiple rows of curved blades (like those on a water turbine) set along a horizontally situated shaft to take advantage of the expansion of high-pressure steam. More compact and capable of high velocities with reduced vibrations and of efficiencies equal to or higher than those of traditional steam engines, the steam turbine by the early 1900s had become the prime mover of choice for electrical generation and had even begun to penetrate the marine engine field.

Electrical power transmission was important in another way. It encouraged the concentration of power production and hence the development of progressively larger water-power systems and steam turbine plants. Engineers had long recognized the production efficiencies of large units over multiple small units, but until it became possible to transmit power long distances economically by electricity, such economies of scale were not achievable. Before electrical power transmission, the largest power plants might generate one thousand to two thousand horsepower. By

the mid-twentieth century individual power plants producing millions of horsepower were common.

Electrical power transmission had an even more important impact on manufacturing. As long as power had to be transmitted mechanically by gears, shafts, and belts, manufacturing facilities could not spread far from the engines powering them because of cost and power loses. Machines that consumed large amounts of power had to be located close to the prime mover; machines that consumed less power had to be located on the periphery, regardless of the order in which these machines were needed for any production process. With efficient electrical power transmission, machines powered by electric motors could be located sequentially in the production process, and manufacturing facilities could spread out. The rationally planned mass assembly lines of the twentieth century with plants covering many acres became possible only by the combination of electrical power transmission with more powerful prime movers.

Power Technologies in the Twentieth Century. The twentieth century saw a vast expansion in the scale of use of prime movers developed in the previous two centuries largely because of the diffusion of electrical power transmission. But the century saw the commercial emergence of only two major new power technologies, the gas turbine and nuclear power. Commercial gas turbines emerged out of the need to power military aircraft at high altitudes just preceding and during World War II and drew from the existing technologies of water and steam turbines. Gas turbines proved a more powerful, compact, and reliable technology than reciprocating internal combustion engines at high velocities and altitudes and were most extensively applied to aircraft. However, their higher cost (in fuel and maintenance) and lower efficiency at low speeds limited their applications.

Nuclear power emerged out of weapons programs in World War II as an alternative to coal, fuel oil, and natural gas in producing steam to power steam turbines. As a commercial producer of electricity, nuclear power has not been an unmitigated success. Early predictions that it would be "too cheap to meter" proved false. Problems with maintenance and waste disposal and the cost of safety measures made it difficult for nuclear plants to compete with coal-fired plants, although countries poor in coal and petroleum resources, like France, have turned heavily to nuclear plants. Outside the stationary power area, nuclear power's impact has been limited largely to naval vessels. In these applications certain attributes of nuclear power, such as density (less-frequent need to refuel since nuclear fuels are more concentrated than fossil fuels) and convenience (no need for an air supply to support combustion) outweighed issues of cost and safety.

Some efforts were made in the twentieth century to use renewable energy sources like solar power. Solar power, however, suffers from a number of deficiencies. It is not a dense source of power, hence arrays to collect and store solar energy are usually large and costly. It remains much more expensive than other energy sources, especially coal, petroleum, and natural gas, and its commercial impact so far is miniscule.

For most of the history of power technology, complex trade-offs between the eight attributes mentioned in the introduction (magnitude, density, mobility, locational flexibility, reliability, convenience, efficiency, and cost) had the greatest influence on which power technology was selected for a particular application. As energy issues shifted more into the public forum in the industrialized world, two additional attributes, safety and environmental friendliness, came to the fore. These attributes played little role in power technology before the late twentieth century. Concerns over nuclear power, however, elevated safety to the list of important attributes, and concerns about overcrowding, environmental degradation, and resource depletion added environmental friendliness. These additional factors make choices in the area of power technology more difficult and complex than ever before.

BIBLIOGRAPHY

Butti, Ken, and John Perlin. *A Golden Thread: 2500 Years of Solar Architecture and Technology*. New York, 1980. Best work on historical attempts to tap energy directly from the Sun.

Constant, Edward W. *The Origins of the Turbojet Revolution*. Baltimore, 1981. Covers the emergence of the jet turbine.

Cummins, C. L., Jr. *Internal Fire*, Oswego, Oreg., 1976. An engineering history of internal combustion engines.

Del Sesto, Steven L. *Science, Politics, and Controversy: Civilian Nuclear Power in the United States, 1946–1974*. Boulder, 1979.

Hecht, Gabrielle. *The Radiance of France: Nuclear Power and National Identity after World War II*. Cambridge, Mass., 1998. Excellent study of how political and social pressures influenced the development of nuclear power in France.

Hills, Richard L. *Power in the Industrial Revolution*. Manchester, 1970. Solid overview with emphasis on steam and textiles.

Hills, Richard L. *Power from Steam: A History of the Stationary Steam Engine*. Cambridge, 1989. Good account of the traditional, reciprocating steam engine but with a strong British emphasis.

Hills, Richard L. *Power from Wind: A History of Windmill Technology*. Cambridge, 1994. The most detailed and comprehensive historical account of the history of attempts to tap the winds although with a heavy British emphasis.

Hunter, Louis C. *A History of Industrial Power in the United States, 1780–1930*, vol. 1, *Waterpower in the Century of the Steam Engine*. Charlottesville, Va., 1979. The best and most detailed account of the economic and technical history of water-powered prime movers in the United States.

Hunter, Louis C. *A History of Industrial Power in the United States, 1780–1930*, vol. 2, *Steam Power*. Charlottesville, Va., 1985. Good account of the expansion of steam power in the United States and its impact. A good complement to Hill's account of stationary steam engines.

Hunter, Louis C., and Lynwood Bryant. *A History of Industrial Power in the United States, 1780–1930*, vol. 3, *The Transmission of Power*. Cambridge, Mass., 1991. Covers both mechanical and electrical means of power transmission largely in the United States.

Major, J. Kenneth. *Animal-Powered Engines*. London, 1978. Just about the only extensive study of this type of engine.

Needham, Joseph. *Science and Civilization in China*, vol. 4, pt. 2, *Mechanical Engineering*. Cambridge, 1965. Best source for Chinese contributions to power technology.

Reynolds, Terry S. *Stronger than a Hundred Men: A History of the Vertical Water Wheel*. Baltimore, 1983. Detailed account of the dominant form of water wheel from its inception about 100 BCE to its demise in the nineteenth century.

Scaife, W. Garrett. *From Galaxies to Turbines: Science, Technology and the Parsons Family*. Bristol, Pa., 2000. Much of the work focuses on Charles Parsons's invention and development of the steam turbine; an engineering history.

Smil, Vaclav. *Energy in World History*. Boulder, 1994. A broad overview of the role of energy in human society.

Smith, Norman. *Man and Water: A History of Hydro-Technology*. London, 1976. Although sketchy in many areas, this is the only comprehensive history of waterpower.

White, Lynn. *Medieval Technology and Social Change*. Oxford, 1962. Classic work that discusses, among other things, the interrelationship between changes in power technology (horse, water, wind) and medieval European society.

TERRY S. REYNOLDS

PRICE REVOLUTION. Used to designate a marked and permanent long-term rise in the level of prices, the term Price Revolution usually has meant the price increases that took place in Europe during the sixteenth and seventeenth centuries; but there have been similar transforming price changes at other times, especially during the thirteenth and eighteenth centuries. Economic historians have observed that prices move in cycles, and that different social and economic rhythms combine and influence one another. In the search for these powerful, underlying rhythms, cycles of different chronological length have been detected, and modern computing techniques, above all, time-series, have greatly increased the analytical power at the disposal of the historian. Approaches of this sort will facilitate the comparison of similar phenomena in different periods, and encourage multivariate analysis instead of the monocausal approaches of the past. The European focus also must be adjusted because European prices were linked to developments in the rest of the world.

The price evidence for sixteenth-century inflation in various European countries has long been available, and the data have been used to calculate price indices for individual commodities, generic groups of commodities, and cost of living indices. In England, price and wage indices have been constructed extending over seven centuries. From 1500 to 1600, English prices rose from an index of about 100 to about 500, climbing to about 700 by 1650. Bowden has analyzed cereal, livestock, and industrial prices separately for the period of the Price Revolution.

The continental evidence shows that the Price Revolution was not an exclusively English phenomenon. In 1895, Georg Wiebe showed that, during the sixteenth century, generally rising prices were observable all over Europe, and it was Wiebe who first described the experience as a Price Revolution. For Spain, Earl J. Hamilton demonstrated a similar rise, and argued emphatically for a causal link between the influx of American bullion into Spain and the price rise in that country. Fernand P. Braudel and Frank Spooner have offered a European overview. In Istanbul, prices rose 500 percent between the end of the fifteenth century and the end of the seventeenth century.

Nineteenth- and early-twentieth-century writers generally couched their explanation of these price rises in terms of debasement and/or newly mined bullion, either or both of which should lead to a rise in the money supply. The theoretical basis of this approach, known as Quantity Theory, was refined at much the same time by Irving Fisher in his equation of exchange, $MV = PT$, where M represents the total amount of money in circulation, V the velocity of circulation, P the general price level, and T the total number of transactions. Each of the variables in the equation has been the subject of dispute. Thus, M might include not only the amount of coin in use, but also paper obligations, developing as money as they began to circulate in trade. Gold currencies may be less inflationary than silver of equal value. Even the calculation of the amount of coin in use was not straightforward. Mint output, even if known, could not be simply aggregated, for coins were exported, lost, or worn, and were often passed through the mints several times for recoining.

Neither is the calculation of the price level a simple matter. A cost of living index must be based on the collection of a huge body of price data and accompanied by extensive debate about the inclusion and/or weighting of the items chosen to represent normal consumption in any period. T, the total number of transactions in a given period, is a simple concept, but also one that defies quantification; economists now prefer to replace it with a measurement of gross domestic (or national) product; but, of course, estimating GDP/GNP for historical periods gives rise to much debate. Velocity, also has been much misunderstood. V is a function of the other items in the equation, and attempts to allow for the fact that money can be spent and respent several times over in any given period. However, V cannot distinguish between £100 spent once, and £1 spent one hundred times; so it is a rather blunt instrument. Most important, V cannot be used to measure the relative frequency with which money payments are commonly made. From the Middle Ages until the twentieth century, despite an increase in the use of money V has shown a tendency to fall, chiefly because M has risen. It is a rising money supply that has permitted an increasing use of money, not a rising velocity. Modern formulations of the equation have found V so misleading that its inverse, k, representing the cash balances that people have chosen to hold, is often preferred. In short, the application of the Quantity Theory to historical data has led to some enlightenment and much heated discussion.

In the sixteenth century, Jean Bodin, Sir Thomas Smith, and Gerard de Malynes attributed the rise in prices to the arrival of New World bullion; but this was not the only explanation then current. Indeed, early versions of almost all the alternative explanations subsequently advanced can be traced to the sixteenth century, including enclosures, currency debasement, and population growth. This last, demographic, explanation sprang in part from the view that the stock of money would have accumulated over centuries, so that changes in the annual money supply would be insignificant. This argument proved to be false; for studies of the money stock have shown that it did not, in fact, accumulate over the centuries, but constantly had to be renewed. Nevertheless, an examination of the relationship between population and prices was long overdue.

If population levels rose faster than the productive capacity of the economy, rising demand could have outstripped food supply. This could have generated a rise in food prices, money supply permitting, though not necessarily a rise in the general price level. Indeed, one of the most common fallacies in explanations of the Price Revolution involves such a confusion of changes in relative prices (of individual commodities) with a change in the overall price level. Historical demographers have no doubt that population was rising strongly throughout the sixteenth century; but England's population around 1500 was still far below that of 1300, and improved agricultural techniques and an extension of the cultivated area make it unclear that population growth did, in fact, exceed food production. In particular, the idea that the cultivation of poorer soils led to falling crop yields has not been well demonstrated. Indeed, demographers are increasingly inclined to explain rising population as a consequence, rather than a cause, of general economic growth and rising prices.

Proponents of the demographic explanation of the Price Revolution further argued that the chronology of the price rises in specific countries did not coincide with the arrivals of bullion. New World silver began to arrive in quantity only in the 1540s, but prices began to rise shortly before 1520. There is, however, evidence for a marked increase in European silver production from the late fifteenth century onward, and for the arrival of gold from the Americas before Mexican silver came on stream. Negotiable bills and a market in government annuities also contributed to the growth of the money supply. In England, the Tudor debasement in the middle of the sixteenth century also triggered a major surge in prices, and the same phenomenon began in Turkey in the 1580s. Moreover, since the prices of internationally traded commodities were determined internationally, a purely national perspective may be misleading. In addition, the arrival of bullion in Europe needs to be balanced by an awareness of its reexport in trade to the East.

The relative behavior of the prices of different commodities also is often cited as evidence of a demographic cause. Cereal prices rose more than did those of animal or industrial products, perhaps reflecting increased demand for essential, staple foods, brought about by population growth. However, it is further argued that if prices were moving for monetary reasons, the shift in prices should be general, affecting all prices equally. In fact, although demographic change could alter relative prices, general inflation, whatever its cause, does not act equally across the board. Some associated changes take additional time. Wages characteristically lag price changes. The prices of different commodities rise at differing speeds because of varying elasticities of supply and demand. Whatever the causes of a general price rise, buyers concentrate their spending on essentials, giving rise to changes in relative prices.

The unequal pattern of price rises does not reveal its underlying cause, but it does explain why inflation can have powerful social and political consequences. Inflation created winners and losers, exacerbating social tensions and necessitating the renegotiation of prices, rents, and con-tracts, which called into question many of the fixed assumptions of the status quo. For this reason, the Price Revolution has implications beyond economic history alone. Social developments may also have influenced price movements, as well as being influenced by them. For example, urbanization may have influenced the use of money, affecting velocity and levels of credit. Credit cannot make up for an inadequate money supply since the volume of possible credit is limited by the available supplies of cash; but changes in the organization of credit, the legal structures supporting the money market, and the increasing negotiability of credit instruments all could have influenced M. Finally, it should be noted that an increase in population could have a deflationary impact on the money supply, in that it would increase T, spreading the money supply more thinly over a larger economy. Some recent work therefore has examined deflationary elements at work in the sixteenth century. In this connection the consequences of Elizabeth I's restoration of the sterling silver coinage in 1560 call for further research. Clearly monetary and demographic factors need to be considered together, rather than as mutually exclusive approaches, and the varying impacts of climatic and technological changes also should be borne in mind.

[*See also* Inflation and Hyperinflation *and* Prices.]

BIBLIOGRAPHY

Bowden, Peter. "Agricultural Prices, Farm Profits, and Rents" and "Statistical Appendix." In *The Agrarian History of England and Wales*, vol. 4, edited by Joan Thirsk, pp. 593–695 and 814–870. Cambridge, 1967. Basic price data.

Braudel, Fernand P. *The Perspective of the World*, vol. 3 of *Civilisation and Capitalism, 15th–18th Century*. London, 1985. Pages 71–88 and the references cited there provide an international overview.

Braudel, Fernand P., and Frank C. Spooner. "Prices in Europe from 1450 to 1750." In *Cambridge Economic History of Europe*, vol. 4, *The Economy of Expanding Europe in the Sixteenth and Seventeenth Centuries*, edited by E. E. Rich and C. H. Wilson, pp. 378–486. Cambridge, 1967. A dated interpretation that nevertheless presents a full range of European evidence with much insight. For example, Braudel and Spooner were the first to notice that gold affects prices differently from silver (p. 391).

Challis, Christopher E. *Currency and the Economy in Tudor and Early Stuart England*. London, 1989. Brief but useful summary.

Challis, Christopher E., ed. *A New History of the Royal Mint*. Cambridge, 1992. Provides the essential English mint production figures.

Fisher, Irving. *The Purchasing Power of Money*. New York, 1911. The original formulation of the Quantity Theory of Money.

Flynn, Dennis O. "The 'Population Thesis' View of Inflation versus Economics and History" and "Use and Misuse of the Quantity Theory of Money in Early Modern Historiography." In *Minting, Monetary Circulation, and Exchange Rates*, edited by Eddy van Cauwenberghe and Franz Irsigler, pp. 361–418. Trier, 1984. Quantity Theory for historians.

Hamilton, Earl J. *American Treasure and the Price Revolution in Spain, 1501–1650*. Cambridge, Mass., 1934. Summarizes a number of earlier articles. Dated, but still central because of the importance of Spain and because of Hamilton's unequivocal association of inflation and Spanish American bullion.

Hauser, Henri. *Recherches et documents sur l'histoire des prix en France de 1500à –1800*. Paris, 1936.

Lindert, Peter. "English Population, Wages, and Prices, 1541–1913." *Journal of Interdisciplinary History* 15 (1985), 609–634.

Metz, Rainer. *Geld, Währung und Preisentwicklung: Der Niederrheinraum im europäischen Vergleich, 1350–1800*. Frankfurt, 1990. Investigates possible links between depreciation of money of account and inflation, usefully collecting coin and price data.

Munro, John. "The Central European Mining Boom, Mint Outputs, and Prices in the Low Countries and England, 1450–1550." In *Money, Coins, and Commerce: Essays in the Monetary History of Asia and Europe (from Antiquity to Modern Times)*, edited by Eddy H. G. Van Cauwenberghe, pp. 119–183, vol. 2 of *Studies in Social and Economic History*. Louvain, 1991. Excellent recent statement of monetary approach to the price revolution. See also his home page at <http://www.economics.utoronto.ca/munro5/> for an extensive bibliography.

Outhwaite, R. B. *Inflation in Tudor and Early Stuart England*. London, 1969. Still a valuable introduction.

Pamuk, Sevket. *A Monetary History of the Ottoman Empire*. Cambridge, 2000. Useful recent survey, linking Ottoman phenomena with both East and West.

Phelps Brown, E. H., and S. V. Hopkins. "Seven Centuries of the Price of Consumables Compared with Builders' Wage-Rates." *Economica* 23 (1956), 296–314.

Spooner, Frank. C. *The International Economy and Monetary Movements in France, 1493–1725*. Cambridge, Mass., 1972.

Wee, Herman van der. "Prices and Wages as Development Variables: A Comparison between England and the Southern Netherlands, 1400–1700." *Acta Historiae Neerlandicae* 10 (1978), 58–78.

Wiebe, Georg. *Zur Geschichte der Preisrevolution des XVI und XVII: Jahrhunderts*. Leipzig, 1895. First to speak of a Price Revolution, and to establish its international dimensions.

Wordie, J. R. "Deflationary Factors in the Tudor Price Rise." *Past and Present* 154 (1997), 32–70.

Wrigley, Edward A., and Roger S. Schofield. *The Population History of England, 1541–1871*. London, 1981.

N. J. MAYHEW

PRICES. Price records are one of the most commonly available forms of historical records. For economic historians, price series offer a powerful source of inferential knowledge about changing historical conditions and events, especially in cases where other forms of evidence are lacking. Price data, when combined with evidence on incomes, can be used to gain insights into long-term structural change, changes in standards of living, and alterations in income distribution. Together with the use of econometric techniques, historical price data are also used to measure and investigate market integration at the regional, national, and global levels. Economic historians have observed that prices move in cycles or waves of different chronological lengths, although the specification of these cycles and their causes has been the subject of a good deal of debate. The historical price series are also used as critical evidence in debates among economic theorists. Causes of price changes in earlier periods have been investigated from Malthusian, monetarist, Marxian, Keynesian, agrarian, environmentalist, and other perspectives.

Price records come down to us from ancient civilizations of the Near East, Greece, Rome, India, and China as well as medieval and early modern Europe. One of the earliest examples of price records comes from the ancient city of Babylon, where archaeologists have discovered a vast archive of clay tablets and cylinders on which scribes made almost daily entries of the market prices of six agricultural commodities. These have yielded monthly market series lasting roughly from 500 to 100 BCE. In a recent paper Peter Temin (2002) studied these series to gain insights into the importance of market exchanges in the economies of the ancient world. Using time series methods, he reached the conclusion that these agricultural prices moved in a random walk, that is, they were market prices whose fluctuations reflected the many exogenous shocks, such as major political and military events, experienced by Babylonia (Temin, 2002).

Another important issue into which historical price data can shed new light is market integration at regional, national, continental, and global levels. The theory of market integration in its simplest form stipulates that, as intermarket trade commences, differentials in the prices of commodities tend to decline and eventually disappear. Some of the earliest studies for testing cases of market integration were undertaken with European grain prices. Grain prices tended to converge in northern Europe during the early modern era. (Jacks, 2000). Recently Kevin O'Rourke and Jeffrey Williamson (2002) examined the timing and dynamics of market integration at the global level since 1500. They emphasize that trade volumes may increase because of shifts in demand and supply, but only falling transportation costs and/or trade barriers may bring about price convergence. They conclude that integration of European, Asian, and other commodity markets did not take place until the transportation revolution that began after 1820 (O'Rourke and Williamson, 2002).

Construction of Price Series. Before any such analyses can be undertaken, however, the indispensable raw data needs to be collected. For western and central Europe, this major step was taken by the International Scientific Committee on Price History established in 1929. In the following years François Simiand, Wilhelm Abel, B. H. Slicher van Bath, William Beveridge, N. W. Posthumus, and many other renowned price historians meticulously gathered, organized, and analyzed the price and wage histories from the twelfth century to the present of many of the European cities, compiling sophisticated price series of high quality (Cole and Crandall, 1964). Arguably the most influential project to emerge from this large effort has been that of E. H. Phelps Brown and Sheila Hopkins (1958), who constructed a consumer price index and wage series for construction workers for southern England for seven centuries beginning in 1264. Robert Allen (2002) has united these studies in a common framework by converting all prices to grams of silver and the quantities into metric units, thus arriving at comparable price and wage series for close to twenty European cities. Efforts also have been made in recent years to compile detailed price series for the Middle East, India, East Asia, Latin America, and other regions of the world for the period since 1500. These price studies are also important for comparisons of standards of living in the early modern era. Despite the many problems they present, real wages continue to be the most reliable source of information for standards of living during this period, and the available wage series given in local currencies for different parts of Europe and Asia need to be deflated by consumer price indices. (Phelps Brown and Hopkins, 1958; Allen, 2002).

Global Comparisons. Thanks to the recent studies, we can now begin to discuss the long-term trends in prices not only in Europe but also in other parts of the world from the late medieval era to the present. For example, during the era of the price revolution from 1500 until 1650, Spain and western Europe experienced higher silver inflation than eastern Europe and the Near East. From 1650 to 1750, prices expressed in grams of silver were fairly steady in northwestern Europe, but they declined elsewehere in Europe. The period from 1750 until the end of the Napoleonic Wars was again one of rising prices. As costs of transportation began to decline after 1820, prices in different parts of Europe and the world economy began to move closer to each other. On the basis of these trends, Allen has concluded that in 1800 and even in 1914 the range of prices across Europe was greater than it had been in 1450 or 1500. (Allen, 2002). It is still too early to compare long-term price trends in Europe and Asia in the period before 1800. It appears, however, that European and Asian prices expressed in grams of silver did not necessarily move togeth er in the early modern period.

While prices expressed in grams of silver provide an important vehicle for international and long-term comparisons, prices in different regions or countries were usually expressed in terms of the local or national currency. In Europe and around the Mediterranean from antiquity until after World War I and in many parts of Asia after 1500, local or national currencies were linked to silver or gold or both. The specie content of the currency was determined by the monetary authority that administered the mints. The specie content of the currencies did not stay unchanged, however. As Carlo Cipolla (1963) argued some years ago, one leading cause of reductions in the specie content of the currency or debasements was fiscal. Because decreases in the specie content of the currency reduced the obligations of the local authorities in specie

terms, debasements tended to be more frequent during periods of fiscal difficulties, especially during wars; and furthermore debasements also often furnished substantial mint seigniorage revenues (profits). Even if prices did not always rise in proportion to the decline in the silver content of the currency, debasements did raise the aggregate price level, if not in the short term, certainly in the longer term. There were also more technical reasons associated with the wear and tear and circulation of different types of coinage that tended to reduce the specie content of the currency over the long term. Specie standards thus did not necessarily ensure price stability.

Causes of Price Changes. Ever since the sixteenth century causes of price changes have been the focus of intensive debate among economic theorists and economic historians. The debate on the price revolution of the sixteenth century provides a prominent example of the variety of approaches taken by economic historians in explaining long-term changes in the aggregate price level. The causal linkage between the quantity of money and the aggregate price level stands at the center of these debates. While earlier literature based on the quantity theory of money assumed that demand for money or the inverse of the velocity of circulation was constant or stable, recent studies have emphasized that the determinants of the demand for money need to be examined in a more general framework that includes not only the more obvious factors, such as commercialization and monetization, but also demographic changes and even more broadly social and cultural factors. It would thus be reasonable to expect wide inter-temporal and cross-societal variations in the demand for holding money and velocity of circulation.

Some Italian city-states in the late medieval era and the Dutch, the British, and to a lesser extent the French states in the early modern period began to rely increasingly on taxes and borrowing rather than on debasements to finance budget deficits during periods of fiscal difficulties. The creation and management of the public debt led to a variety of financial innovations and the development of financial markets. These changes contributed to greater price stability in these countries. In many other cases across Eurasia, however, the practice of relying on debasements for fiscal gain continued into the modern era.

An example from outside of western Europe may provide a useful perspective for the causes of long-term price changes in the early modern era. In the Ottoman Empire, which covered a large territory in southeastern Europe and the Near East, fiscally motivated debasements were the most important cause of price increases during the period 1500 to 1914. Prices expressed in grams of silver increased 200 percent, but nominal prices increased by about three hundred times during these four centuries.

PRICES. World War I poster, 1917. (Prints and Photographs Division, Library of Congress)

Prices expressed in grams of silver increased during the period of the Price Revolution until 1650, declined until the early decades of the eighteenth century, and increased again until the middle of the nineteenth century, although around a modestly upward trend. In short the so-called silver inflation contributed to the changes in the overall price level, but its impact paled in relation to that of debasements in the Ottoman case (Pamuk, 2003).

Monetary Regimes. The spread of bimetallism after 1820 and of the gold standard after 1870 tended to bring greater price stability to countries embracing these monetary regimes. Fiscal difficulties and waves of inflation continued, however. As the examples of the Napoleonic Wars, the American Civil War, and World War I demonstrate, even the stronger advocates were prepared to abandon commodity standards under duress. Moreover many countries chose to leave the commodity standards during periods of peace because of economic, fiscal, and political pressures. Some of these later managed to bring their budgets under control and maintain price stability without formally embracing a commodity standard. Countries adhering to bimetallism and later the gold standard experienced moderate decreases in prices during the last quarter of the nineteenth century and then an upward movement until World War I. The international price level in 1914 expressed in terms of gold was not very different from that around 1830. Another period of declining prices was experienced during the 1930s, when prices in dollar terms declined by about one-third in general but with a much more substantial decline in agricultural prices. In those countries issuing inconvertible paper money, on the other hand, the price level depended on fiscal and monetary policies.

The abandonment of the gold standard first during World War I, the failure of the subsequently more limited Gold Exchange Standard during the 1930s, and the shift around the world toward paper money not backed by specie after World War II did not introduce an entirely new element into the picture. Virtually all countries had experimented with inconvertible paper money at one time or another before 1914 (and consider the English example of the "paper pound" from 1797 to 1821). Nonetheless rates of inflation have been higher in the period after 1914. In the United States, whose currency served as the linchpin of the Bretton Woods international monetary system in the post–World War II era, the aggregate price level was roughly the same in 1939 as it had been in 1914. Price increases then averaged about 3 percent per annum until 2000. Inflation rates in the other developed countries were, on the whole, somewhat higher. The developed economies experienced the highest rates of inflation in the aftermath of the oil price increases of 1973. It was in the developing countries that the most striking epiodes of high inflation were experienced during the twentieth century. A large number of these episodes occurred in Latin America after World War II. The twentieth century also witnessed numerous episodes of hyperinflation in which prices increased 50 percent or more per month for more than one year. Most prominent among these were the cases of Austria, Germany, Russia, and others following World War I; Hungary after World War II; and Bolivia and Argentina after 1980. Such high rates of inflation were rare before World War I.

In conclusion, while prices have tended to rise more rapidly since 1914 or 1939, the contrasts with the earlier period should not be exaggerated. The experiences of a large number of countries in the period before 1914 indicate that specie standards did not guarantee a nominal anchor and ensure price stability. Similarly there are examples of countries with inconvertible paper currency that maintained fiscal and monetary discipline and achieved price stability in the period before 1914. Hence the historical record suggests that the most important determinant, in the medium and long term, of the aggregate price level and inflation rate in a given country has not been the monetary regime *per se* but the combination of fiscal and monetary policies and institutions.

[*See also* Inflation and Hyperinflation; Money and Coinage; *and* Price Revolution.]

BIBLIOGRAPHY

Allen, Robert. "The Great Divergence in European Wages and Prices from the Middle Ages to the First World War." *Explorations in Economic History* 38 (2002), 411–447.

Cipolla, Carlo M. "Currency Depreciation in Medieval Europe." *Economic History Review* 15 (1963), 413–422.

Cole, Arthur, and Ruth Crandall. "The International Scientific Committee on Price History." *Journal of Economic History* 24 (1964), 381–388.

Jacks, David. "Market Integration in the North and Baltic Seas." London School of Economics, Working Papers in Economic History No. 55, 2000.

O'Rourke, Kevin H., and Jeffrey G. Williamson. "When Did Globalization Begin?" *European Review of Economic History* 6 (2002), 23–50.

Pamuk, Şevket. "Prices in the Ottoman Empire, 1469–1914." *International Journal of Middle East Studies*, forthcoming.

Phelps Brown, E. H., and Sheila V. Hopkins. "Seven Centuries of the Prices of Consumables Compared with Builders' Wage Rates." *Economica* 23 (1958), 296–314.

Redish, Angela. *Bimetallism: An Economic and Historical Analysis.* Cambridge, 2000.

Temin, Peter. "Price Behavior in Ancient Babylon." *Explorations in Economic History* 39 (2002), 46–60.

Vilar, Pierre. *A History of Gold and Money, 1450–1920.* London, 1976.

ŞEVKET PAMUK

PRINTING INDUSTRY.

The purpose of printing is to produce (and to mass produce) a visible image, most often a written text. The printed text's purpose is to communicate. Until recently, the technology of the printing industry provided the principal means of delivering multiple copies of visible, verbal communication; but the digital revolution has replaced much of the printer's technology and has helped transform the industry into a part of the information industry.

The Beginnings to the Western Invention of Metal Type. Printing began with marks transferred to a surface by means of pressure using seals, stamps, rubbings, and stencils. The earliest printing of any note comes from Asia, in the form of some widely distributed charm scrolls, with images of the Buddha, printed using blocks of wood in eighth-century China (but discovered in Korea). The *Diamond Sutra*, to carry its date 868 CE, is the oldest-known extant book. By the tenth century, the entire corpus of both Buddhist and Confucian scripture had been published by the Chinese in blockbooks (one block of wood carved for each page of text, with some 130,000 pages for the Buddhist scripture). Although individual characters in ceramic type were invented in eleventh-century China, individual characters in wooden type in fourteenth-century China, and bronze type characters were cast as early as the 1160s

in Korea, blockbooks remained in use because of the nature of written Chinese—each type set required as many as 200,000 characters. Eastern printing, often produced in very small editions, was done by means of rubbing—using water-based inks, rather than in a press. Repeated attempts to find links between Eastern printing and that of the medieval West have as yet found no convincing evidence; by contrast, paper's route from China into twelfth-century Italy via the Arabic world is well established.

The Hand Press Period (c. 1450–1800). Strong circumstantial evidence credits the Western invention of printing to the German Johannes Gutenberg, although the details remain obscure. The industry's technological basis was typefounding, the production of interchangeable and reusable metal type for the small character set of the Latin alphabet (twenty-six letters, plus numbers and punctuation marks); these were hand cast in a special mold, adapted from earlier, replica casting molds. The type was then composed by hand (set) on a tray (later a galley) into rectangular pages of text, placed on the bed of a wooden printing press, covered with a layer of an oil-based ink, and rolled under the flat platen of the press, where the ink was transferred from the upper surface of the type onto sheets of paper by the downward pressure of the platen, driven by a handpowered lever and a screw. The type was then stored in bins—one for each character—for the later reuse that would offset the high cost of their manufacture. The printed sheets were folded, gathered, and sewn into finished pamphlets or books; if the sheets were for "jobbing" articles or job printing, they were used flat as notices, posters, banknotes, stamps, cards, or as packaging. The different products of printing were developed and divided into sectors as the industry matured: books from the fifteenth century onward, newspapers and journals from the eighteenth century, advertising and packaging from the nineteenth.

The printing press was adapted from presses used in the wine, papermaking, and cloth industries. Gutenberg's system was to mass produce the types and then mass produce books, thereby considerably decreasing their unit cost. The long-term consequences of the increased availability of books have been hotly debated since Elisabeth L. Eisenstein's *Printing Press as an Agent of Change* (2 vols., Cambridge, 1979). Typefaces (fonts) required long-term investment, but labor, paper, and ink were purchased for each project—with labor and paper costs being approximately equal. Early printers usually undertook the financial risks, and many went out of business quickly, although a few notable dynasties arose.

While the printing industry relied on manpower, it consisted of small firms—often with only a master and two assistants using three or four presses—although there were always exceptions, for example, Anton Koberger in

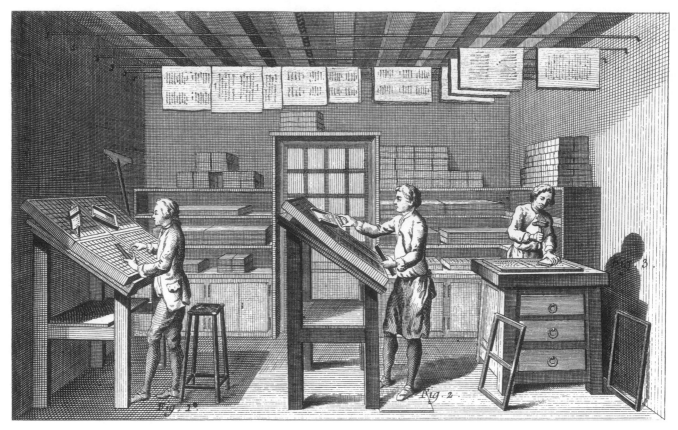

PRINT SHOP. A compositor, at left, picks letters from a typecase to make up lines of text in a composing stick, which he holds in his left hand. A typesetter, at center, places the lines into a narrow tray called a galley. Another typesetter, at right, prepares two pages of type for printing. Plate from Diderot and d'Alembert's *Encyclopédie*, 1762–1772.

fifteenth-century Nuremberg (twenty-four presses) and Christopher Plantin in sixteenth-century Antwerp (twenty-two presses). Successful firms were located in major commercial centers—Venice (fifteenth century), Paris and Antwerp (sixteenth century), Amsterdam (seventeenth century)—not only to facilitate distribution but also to secure financing. For much of this period, the printing industry was inseparable from publishing, and it is debatable whether the two began to separate in the early seventeenth century (see John Feather, *A History of British Publishing*, London, 1988, p. 39) or somewhat later. Early printing was also closely linked to the paper industry and to stationers, who, perhaps above all in Italy, often financed book projects; these largely filled the book needs of both the religious establishments and those of education. When printers first began to organize, they joined the guilds of scriveners (writers of text), which in England became the Company of Stationers in 1557, a body that severely constrained the industry for at least a century, keeping it almost exclusively in London and regulating the size of print runs. Not until the end of the eighteenth century did many firms operate in the provinces, with the exception of the printing associated with both Cambridge University Press and Oxford University Press.

Rapid Changes in the Nineteenth Century. The number of printers in London quadrupled from 1785 to 1850, and there were a few new firms of great size. Clowes and Sons and Eyre and Spottiswoode each employed some four hundred. This pattern continued and, by the mid-1960s, only 0.2 percent employed more than one thousand, while over 60 percent, under twenty-five. Rising costs in London led to relocations (Clowes moved to Beccles, Suffolk, in 1872); thereafter London was decreasingly dominant.

The printing press remained a handpowered, wooden, screw, and flat-platen machine; type was hand cast and set, and paper was hand made until the turn of the nineteenth century, during which most components of the industry became mechanized, and new processes, especially lithography and photography, made significant contributions. Metal type and woodblocks for images delivered ink from raised surfaces (relief), while copper-plate printing delivered ink from sunken surfaces (intaglio); these had served the industry for both text and images. About 1798, printing from a flat surface (planographic) came with lithography.

The lithographic process remained an artistic and jobbing medium until its awkward limestone surface was replaced by zinc, allowing for the development of both a curved printing surface and the faster rotary press of the 1860s—which could then compete with the speed that relief presses had already achieved through a succession of improvements, led by the newspaper sector, especially *The Times* (London).

In the early nineteenth century, an iron press with compound levers had been developed for relief printing by Charles, the third Earl Stanhope, which resulted in increased production and large printed surfaces. By 1810, the German inventor Frederick Koenig powered the press by steam, but lithographic and intaglio presses were not powered until the latter half of that century. Other technical developments of the press automated inking and changed the shape of printing surfaces from flat to curved (both cylindrical and rotary), the feeding of paper from individual sheets to continuous rolls (webs), and the printing from one side to two simultaneously—to meet the speed demanded by daily newspapers. The book-printing sector adopted iron presses, the successors to the Stanhope (such as the Columbian and Albion), but could not justify the investment for many of the other improvements. Paper availability was crucial to printing from its inception, and the Fourdrinier machine, still in use today, replaced hand manufacture of paper early in the nineteenth century. Woodpulp, in the mid-1800s, solved the long search for a viable substitute material in paper making for the often scarce and always costly linen rags. Taxes on paper, in Britain contemporaneously called "taxes on knowledge," decreased progressively, giving considerable boosts to both industries. By mid-century, the manufacture of type faces was mechanized, but the really significant breakthrough came later, with the hot-metal composing machines—the Linotype machine that cast and set lines of lead stags, or strips (1886 at *The New York Tribune*; and thereafter used mostly by newspapers) and the Monotype system that cast and set each character (1897; more useful to book printers). Both combined typecasting with typesetting that was acceptably spaced out to a squared right-edge margin (justified), which eliminated subsequent rehandling of the types. Both systems also used keyboards, a tool that became standard in text preparation.

Photography, invented about 1840, was soon used by the printing industry, since images could be photographically transferred to woodblocks prior to hand engraving. Wood engraving, a late-eighteenth-century adaptation of woodcutting, as well as steel engraving had made images in printed matter economical on a new scale, leading to an increasing use of them in texts (lithographic printing also allowed for the printing of images more easily, although the application came later). Improvements in ink manufacturing increased the use of color. New categories of reading matter were developed, and some were the result of broad socioeconomic changes—for example, the railway novel and popular journalism (the *Illustrated London News*) as levels of literacy rose with wider compulsory state-provided education. Wood engraving as a subindustry ended during the 1890s, as a consequence of chemical processes used to engrave metal blocks. Process-engraved relief-printing blocks for either line drawing or half-tone images still used photographic processes as an intermediate step. In the 1950s it became commercially possible to set text using photography, by means of photocomposition, as developed by the Monotype Corporation and others; a printing surface was produced from a paper or film with a photosensitized layer onto which characters of text were exposed, by means of a laser beam.

Offset printing, which involves printing first to an intermediate surface, then transferring (setting off) the image to the final surface, was developed for lithographic printing onto tin for packaging containers in 1875, then for printing on paper in 1903. Offset printing combined with lithography became the principal method in use throughout the industry during the twentieth century. By the early 1970s, offset lithography and photocomposition had also combined and together finished the industrial use of metal type.

Other Twentieth-Century Developments. Relief printing as well as lithographic printing were improved early in the century, although eventually the metal, presses, pressure, inks, and even the paper would all be challenged as parts of the printing processes in use. Analine printing, patented in 1908 and renamed flexography in 1952, was a new form of relief printing that used rubber plates wrapped around a printing cylinder, with alcohol-based analine colors, initially for the packaging industry. Later developments led to photosensitive polymer-coated metal plates that proved useful for newspapers and inexpensive books. The ancient technique of stenciling had new applications in the commercial use of screen printing (also known as silkscreen, or printing through a porous cloth), especially for jobbing work, textiles, signs, banners, and greeting cards.

Electrostatic printing, or xerography, began in 1938; but the photocopier, developed by the Haloid Company (later Xerox Corporation), did not arrive until the late 1950s. This process is non-impact printing, which transfers a fine powder from an electrically charged surface to paper, using neither ink nor pressure. By the mid-1980s, this technology lay behind the laser printing that is used with computer applications. The changes that computerization has brought to the printing industry are fundamental and as yet hard to assess judiciously. The photocomposition of text was teamed with the computer in the 1960s, although the photographic aspects were replaced in the 1970s by digital storage of the typographic characters (as binary codes), so the process became "imagesetting," which could handle both text and images. By the late 1980s, not only could these be generated, but the arrangement of the pages could be manipulated by software packages for electronic (or desktop) publishing. Such manipulation, originally the province of the printer or compositor, and later the typographer or compositor employed by a publisher, might be undertaken by an author with a computerized pagemaking program. This possibility has resulted in a blurring of the traditional allocation of tasks, because an author, using a keyboard, can compose, correct, format, and transmit the text to a publisher. Ultimately, computerization has led some industry commentators to redefine printing (publishing) as part of the management and dissemination of intellectual property.

Some printing houses, especially R. R. Donnelly & Sons in Chicago with European subsidiaries, have retained their position, by adaptation to digital technology, but from the 1980s onward, the conglomeration of other firms predominated. Along with this technological change came globalization; for a short period, the printing jobs that originated in Europe were printed in Asia. Paper-based printing came to be challenged as the dominant mode of delivery when electronic circuits were seen as possible substitutes for traditional printed products, and the computer screen became an important mode of communication. An electronic book seemed to be the future (Frederick G. Kilgour, *The Evolution of the Book*, New York, 1998), but it has been bypassed by the Internet and the Website. Nevertheless, printed matter in all forms continues to be produced and marketed successfully for both commercial and academic purposes.

[*See also* Book Industry; Magazines; *and* Newspapers.]

BIBLIOGRAPHY

Alford, B. W. E. "Government Expenditure and the Growth of the Printing Industry in the Nineteenth Century." *Economic History Review* 2. 17 (1964), 96–112.

Birch, Philip, ed. *Managing Change in the Printing and Publishing Industry—Strategic Approaches.* Leatherhead, 1994. Discussion by industry leaders of likely changes brought by globalization, the computer revolution, and merger with the information industry.

Febvre, Lucien, and Henri-Jean Martin. *The Coming of the Book: The Impact of Printing, 1450–1800.* London, 1976. Originally Paris, 1958; somewhat oriented to the French book trade. See also more recent works by Martin.

Gaskell, Philip. *A New Introduction to Bibliography.* Oxford, 1972; reissued New Castle, Del., 1996. Technical background to book production; excellent reference bibliography.

Legros, Lucien Alphonse, and John Cameron Grant. *Typographical Printing-Surfaces: The Technology and Mechanism of Their Production.* London, 1916. The main authority for late-nineteenth-century developments.

McKenzie, D. F. "Printers of the Mind." *Studies in Bibliography* 22 (1969), 1–75. This seminal work argues that academic understandings of production patterns had been fictional.

Moran, James. *Printing Presses: History and Development from the Fifteenth Century to Modern Times.* London, 1973.

Moxon, Joseph. *Mechanick Exercises.* London, 1683; 2d ed. by H. Davis and H. Carter. Oxford, 1962. The first printing manual in any language; still extremely valuable, as with Davis and Carter's comments.

Plant, Marjorie. *The English Book Trade: An Economic History of the Making and Sale of Books.* 2d rev. ed. London, 1965.

Steinberg, Sigfrid H. *Five Hundred Years of Printing.* New ed., revised by John Trevitt. London, 1996. A broadly based interpretation and, despite the revision, still shows its mid-twentieth-century origins.

Strauss, Victor. *The Printing Industry.* New York, 1967. American-based snapshot of the postwar but precomputer era.

Tsien, Tusen-Hsuin. *Paper and Printing.* In Joseph Needham, *Science and Civilisation in China*, vol. 5, *Chemistry and Chemical Technology, Part I.* Cambridge, 1985. Definitive treatment of early printing in China.

Twyman, Michael. *Printing, 1770–1970.* 2d ed. London, 1998. Exclusive to Great Britain; unusual in its attention to jobbing printing, with generous illustration. See also Twyman on the history of lithography.

MARGARET M. SMITH

PRIVATE PLOTS. Private plots and private production activities can be found in countries that have collectivized agriculture. The plots exist because of weaknesses in the structure of collective farms, such as inadequate incentives to motivate farmworkers, the inability of managers to supervise workers, and the poor performance of collective farms in producing and raising products, such as livestock, fruits, and vegetables, which are often labor intensive and require farmworkers to take initiative and use judgment.

Private plots first appeared in the 1930s as the USSR's first collective farms encountered difficulties. Communist ideologues considered these private plots to be vestiges of capitalism, and in 1939 private plot activity was restricted. Then World War II brought increased demand for food production, and private plot activity was allowed to increase. After the war, Stalin once more attempted to restrict private plot activity, but by 1958 private activity had expanded again.

Private plots were found in countries that followed the Soviet economic model of collectivized agriculture because these countries had no more success than the USSR in operating collective and state farms. At various times in the last half of the twentieth century, private plots could be found in collectivized agriculture in China, Democratic People's Republic of Korea, Vietnam, Cuba, Yugoslavia, Hungry, Poland, Czechoslovakia, Bulgaria, Albania, and Romania.

The size of private plots varied from country to country, depending in part on population/arable land ratios and on government policies. For example, in the 1970s the average rural household in China cultivated a private plot of about three hundred square meters, which on average constituted about 5 percent of total cultivated land area. While private plots accounted for a small portion of total arable land, the output from these plots, along with such private production activities as the raising of livestock, had significant economic impacts. A large portion of vegetables, fruits, eggs, potatoes, and meat came from private plot activity. This output supplemented household income, provided basic foodstuffs, and provided much-needed protein and essential vitamins and minerals. The output not only helped sustain the rural population, but also found its way into urban areas through marketing arrangements.

Collective farmers faced an unenviable position. Asked to diligently labor in the common fields, they had little say in management decisions but ultimately bore economic risks. Farmers could reduce their risks by allocating some of their free time to tend private plots. By allowing collective farmers to cultivate private plots, rural authorities reduced farmer angst about risk and absorbed labor that otherwise would not have been used effectively. The output increased rural incomes and provided urban areas with much-sought-after fruits, vegetables, and animal protein products.

At the beginning of the twenty-first century, private plots ceased to exist in such countries as Hungary and East Germany, which abandoned collective farms. Other countries, such as Russia, China, Vietnam, and Poland have maintained vestiges of the collective structure and, consequently, retain private plots.

[*See also* Collective Agriculture and Collectivization.]

BIBLIOGRAPHY

Commonwealth Agriculture Bureau. "The Role of Private Plots in Socialist Agriculture." *Annotated Bibliography* No. 7 (1971).

Hedlund, Stephen. *Private Agriculture in the Soviet Union.* London, 1989.

Wadeken, Karl-Eugen. *The Private Sector in Soviet Agriculture.* Berkeley, 1973.

Wadeken, Karl-Eugen. *Communist Agriculture: Farming in the Far East and Cuba.* London, 1990.

Walker, Kenneth R. *Planning in Chinese Agriculture: Socialization and the Private Sector, 1956–1962.* Chicago, 1965.

FREDERICK W. CROOK

PRIVATIZATION. *See* Nationalization and Privatization.

PROCESSING CROPS refers to all operations carried out after the harvesting of food and industrial crops. Some of the initial processing—including grain drying, cleaning, threshing, and winnowing—was carried out on the farm. But in commercial farming, as opposed to subsistence, the greater value-added operations of meal and flour milling for oatmeal and bread (as well as malting, brewing, and distilling for beer and spirits) were always done after the crop was marketed. All industrial crops have required some processing, but most attention in the literature has been given to food-crop processing, particularly flour milling. But starchy root crops like yams, potatoes, and cassava were not milled, and when used as human food, maize and rice were usually eaten as whole grains.

Threshing. From earliest times, threshing and winnowing, the initial separation of grain from the corn and then the separation of grain from its outer covering, were carried out on the farm by hand. This was done in autumn and winter during the slack period of demand for labor for fieldwork. Mechanical threshing began to replace hand threshing in the early nineteenth century, and in some areas of Great Britain it became popular during the Napoleonic Wars. By 1840, the thresher was standard barn equipment on larger farms in labor-scarce districts of Scotland and Northern England. In the later 1840s, the portable steam thresher was improved and replaced hand-, horse-, and water-powered machines. Hand-operated winnowing machines had almost replaced the winnowing fan and shovel before 1840. From the early 1850s, both winnowing and dressing operations were incorporated into the combined steam-driven threshing, winnowing, and dressing machines. By the early 1870s, the flail and horse-driven threshing machines had fallen into disuse in many areas of Great Britain and the United States, and more than three-quarters of British small grain was machine-threshed by portable steam threshers hired from agricultural contractors and larger farmers. Substantial labor saving was gained from the use of machinery. The hand flail allowed a fully fit male to process 0.15 tons of wheat per day, while a 12 horsepower steam threshing machine could do eight times as much. In the twentieth century, the introduction of the gas-driven combine harvester removed the threshing operation from the farmyard to the harvest field.

Milling. Prehistoric people simply laid kernels of grain or nuts on flat stones and pounded them with hand-held stones until they produced meal. The ancient Greeks first replaced hand stones with rotary querns and may have built the first water-powered stone mills to free people from the arduous manual labor of producing flour and meal. The Romans introduced large commercial mills using geared drives, and in medieval Europe watermill technology was developed further. In coastal areas, tidal mills were built to harness the power of the ocean; and after 1180, post windmills became common in places without water power. Small-scale milling machinery was animal powered. Mostly these were horse and donkey mills used on farms to produce fodder.

Initially, stone milling produced a coarse wheat meal containing all parts of the grain mixed together, from which the finer flour was sieved. In the eighteenth century, gradual reduction could be achieved by passing the meal through the same pairs of stones set closer together, or through series of stones set at different heights. This, and improvements in sieving, allowed millers to meet an increasing western European demand for finer, whiter flour after 1750. The first use of steam to provide direct power for stone mills was at the end of the eighteenth century, and around fifty steam engines had been erected in corn mills by the end of 1800. At this time, the major factors encouraging mill owners to convert from water to steam were a large and growing urban market and adequate access to cheap coal.

The change from millstones to roller mills began in Hungary in the 1860s, and the technology was improved in other parts of Europe and the United States. By using a series of graduated porcelain and steel rollers, the entire process was one of gradually reducing the particles of the grain and separating out its different constituents during various stages of continuous milling. Although gradual reduction was possible with stone milling, roller milling had the advantage that it was mechanically more efficient and saved on power consumption as well as labor costs, and also dispensed with the need for regular redressing of the millstones by skilled craftsmen to maintain their cutting efficiency. Prior to 1850 most wheat was milled in the districts where it was grown, but the expansion of the international grain trade after 1850 meant very large wheat mills were built at convenient importing points. This encouraged the establishment of big flour-milling companies in many of the chief seaports of Europe, such as Glasgow, Liverpool, London, Hull, Antwerp, Hamburg, Marseilles, and Venice, as well as in similar firms in America. Because the import of coarse grains for animal food was more diffuse, there was less concentration of this branch of the industry.

Seed Crushing. Egyptian tomb paintings dating back to 3000 BCE record the extraction of oil from seeds by pressing. Over the centuries, a variety of pressing methods evolved, but real efficiency was not available until the invention of the hydraulic press in 1796 by the British engineer Joseph Bramah. In all methods, before pressing, the seed was softened by cooking and then loaded into the press from which the crushed residue was unloaded by hand. After 1900, the invention of the expeller and its improvement over the twentieth century led to its eventually replacing the hydraulic press for seed crushing and oil extraction. In the nineteenth century, most oil was used for industrial purposes, and Great Britain imported large amounts of Argentinian, Indian, and Russian linseed and cottonseed from the Persian Gulf, United States, Egypt,

and India. Linseed oil was used for linoleum and paint manufacture, and cotton oil for soap manufacture. A valuable by-product of the industry was the residual oilcake that was purchased by farmers for cattle feeding. By 1914, Hull, Liverpool, and London became important centers for the industry, but seed crushing was a large industry in New York, New Orleans, and Galveston, as well as several Russian ports. After World War I, linseed and cottonseed declined in importance, but the rise of other oils for human food, particularly copra and palm kernels for margarine, ensured the continued expansion of seed crushing and became the mainstay of the industry.

BIBLIOGRAPHY

Brace, Harold W. *History of Seed Crushing in Great Britain*. London, 1960.

Collins, Edward John T. *Sickle to Combine*. Reading, Pa., 1969.

Gimple, Jean. *The Medieval Machine: The Industrial Revolution of the Middle Ages*, 2d ed., Aldershot, U.K., 1988.

Kuhlmann, Charles Byron. *The Development of the Flour-Milling Industry in the United States: With Special Reference to the Industry in Minneapolis*. Boston, 1929.

Perren, Richard. "Structural Change and Market Growth in the Food Industry: Flour Milling in Britain, Europe, and America, 1850–1914." *Economic History Review* 2d ser. 43.3 (1990), 420–437.

Reynolds, John. *Windmills and Watermills*, New York, 1975.

Storch, John, and Walter Dorwin Teague. *Flour for Man's Bread*. Minneapolis, 1952.

Stuyvenberg, J. H. van, ed. *Margarine: An Economic, Social, and Scientific History 1869–1969*. Toronto, 1969.

Tann, Jennifer. "Corn Milling." In *The Agrarian History of England and Wales, vol. 6, 1750–1850*, edited by G. E. Mingay, pp. 397–415. Cambridge, 1989.

Thompson, Edward P. "The Moral Economy of the Crowd in the Eighteenth Century." *Past and Present* 50 (1971), 76–136.

RICHARD PERREN

PRODUCT SAFETY REGULATION. Public concern over product safety has existed as long as recorded history. The consumer has borne the risks associated with unsafe products through the doctrine of caveat emptor, or buyer beware. In the twentieth century, particularly in its last twenty-five years, the United States and other nations developed significant regulatory controls with respect to product safety. This regulation takes one of three general forms: the provision of information, liability, or the imposition of standards. Although successes are noteworthy, there appears to have been little focus on the net economic benefit of product safety regulation. Government intervention may unnecessarily raise prices and decrease competitive incentives for firms to increase product safety.

Rise and Fall of Caveat Emptor. Markets with adequate information should be capable of internalizing product risks through price and insurance mechanisms. Markets with incomplete or imperfect information, as exists for many consumer goods, may not in general pose a significant safety risk. Media or friends' reports regarding the unsavory taste of a new snack food, or a small wasted purchase, might provide a sufficient correction for informational uncertainties. On the other hand, significant losses from otherwise insignificant purchases, such as infant mortality from choking on small toys, require considerable scrutiny. Product safety legislation should correct for market failures from imperfect or incomplete information that may result in such losses.

Without a clear understanding of a product's (or an occupation's) risk, an individual's decisions will not properly incorporate the risk. With accurate information, consumers will willingly pay higher prices for safer products, and workers will command higher wages for riskier assignments.

Product risks have led to limited attempts at regulation throughout history. Food regulations for sanitation extend back to the Old Testament and ancient Hindu restrictions. Real efforts at regulating consumer safety, however, did not materialize until the end of the nineteenth century. In the United States today, the Consumer Product Safety Commission (CPSC), created in 1972, regulates over fifteen thousand consumer products, and the list does not include the riskiest products, such as alcohol, tobacco, firearms, and vehicles, which are regulated by other agencies.

The question arises of whether protection levels are now higher than an efficient market would produce. Regulation that does not weigh the marginal cost of additional regulation against the marginal benefit of increased safety will not increase economic efficiency. Overregulation may cost consumers more than the additional safety benefits are worth. Regulations, first set in 1972, necessitating flame-retardant pajamas in the United States left parents with a choice between either polyesters that their children found uncomfortable or carcinogen-soaked cotton. These restrictions were not eased until 1996, even though injury data were negligible (Carol Dawson, "CPSC Allows More Choices in Kid's Pajamas," *CPSC Monitor* 3.4, 1998).

An efficient tradeoff between product safety and the cost of regulatory compliance has rarely been the primary focus of regulation. Early regulations, particularly regarding false weights and measures, existed mainly to lower transaction costs between consumers and producers. In many cases, the goal of regulation was to create enough incentive for the producer to provide quality control when reputation effects alone might be insufficient. Fifteenth- and sixteenth-century European food-quality laws worked on this principle; Austrian sellers of spoiled milk had to consume it themselves, and French consumers could pelt egg sellers with any rotten product.

As European trade became increasingly commercialized, rulers prevailed over a shift in legal doctrine intended to smooth transactions. By adopting a rule of caveat emptor, the marketplace came to favor sellers over consumers. Consumers came to bear most of the cost of imperfect information regarding products and occupations. This doctrine held in Europe and North America until the end of the nineteenth century.

The development of mass markets increased both the number of consumers able to purchase prepackaged, mass-produced goods and the number of people working in the industrial sector. This combination led to increased interest and activism in product safety. Some sellers did seek to build a reputation for quality through product branding, as with the introduction of Hire's herb tea (root beer), Heinz ketchup, and Ivory soap in the 1870s. Others found it profitable to reduce quality and endanger consumer safety with products such as chemically treated rancid meat or narcotic medicines. Consequently, both consumers and honest businesses sought regulatory protection at the local level beginning in the 1860s. In 1906, their efforts culminated in passage of the Pure Food and Drug Act and the Meat Inspection Act in the United States. These acts codified the end of caveat emptor in those industries.

Consumer activism since has increased to include safety regulation of toys, clothing, automobiles, and virtually every other product sold in commercial markets. Product liability laws have been developed and strengthened. The threat of regulation may increase safety precautions as much as, if not more than, regulation itself. For example, in the market for recreational scuba-diving apparatus, manufacturers have relied on voluntary standards to avoid direct regulation of their products. Their success is surprising when one notes that scuba diving is considered so risky that it requires its own secondary insurance. The key has been careful industry regulation of sales only to individuals who can prove they have learned the information required for safe use of the breathing apparatus and other gear. This certification process provides a market solution to a set of products with serious consequences of death and injury from misuse. Consumer protection also has developed with industrialization outside Europe and North America. In Korea, the power of consumer activism was first tapped in the early 1900s, but it was aimed at limiting the infiltration of Japanese goods during occupation. By the mid-1960s, rapid industrialization in South Korea led to increased consumer purchasing power and the development of local associations, such as the Korean Housewives' Association, aimed at spreading information, rewarding high quality, and punishing poor quality.

In 1947, the International Organization for Standardization (ISO) began to develop international standards for many consumer products. One major component of these standards, which now cover 140 countries, has been the assurance of safe products. The Organization for Economic Cooperation and Development (OECD) initiated the Committee on Consumer Policy in 1969, and also has made attempts to standardize the collection of injury information and systematize approaches to product safety legislation across nations.

A contributing factor to passage of the 1906 Pure Food and Drug Act and Meat Inspection Act was the publication, in 1905, of Upton Sinclair's *The Jungle*, an investigative novel alleging horrific practices in the Chicago meatpacking industry. The transition from the term *investigative journalism* to *muckraking* that occurred as Sinclair, Ida Tarbell, Lincoln Steffens, and others wrote about the world of big business around them suggests the costs that increased vigilance regarding product safety might have imposed on businesses at the turn of the twentieth century. The high circulation of that era's periodicals, with readership of the top ten American investigative magazines peaking at three million, may have helped to spread a growing concern about market failures due to unsafe products.

Further support for this belief came from the effects of legislation targeted at reducing occupational injury. For example, the fatality rate from rail coupling and braking accidents in 1890 was an astounding five deaths per thousand trainmen, and injury rates were ten times higher. Safety regulation in the form of the 1893 Safety Appliance Act more than halved that rate in less than twenty years. This success began the American call for safety legislation in other occupations, which had not seen such dramatic improvements in risk during the same time period (Aldrich, 1997).

The increase in product safety legislation and product liability regulation reached its peak in the 1970s. In the earlier part of the century, countries regulated high-profile products, including food, automobiles, bicycles, and machinery. In the 1970s, regulation in virtually all OECD nations expanded to cover almost every remaining consumer product. In the United Kingdom, the Consumer Safety Act of 1978 expanded and collected the powers of regulation under existing Consumer Protection Acts begun in 1961. By 1984, France, Austria, Japan, Canada, Australia, Norway, Sweden, Denmark, and Finland all had created regulatory agencies for product safety that covered virtually all products. Germany, the Netherlands, and Switzerland have tended to adapt existing food safety laws to cover nonfood items rather than create new legislation. Although regulations differ significantly across nations, they all rely on a combination of mandatory and voluntary product restrictions and varying degrees of product liability to assure product safety.

Food Safety. Food safety is the oldest of consumer concerns. Early religious laws of several faiths restricted diets to avoid illness and death from poor food quality or preparation. The importance of food safety led to the development of separate regulations to monitor and control safety. Concerns over food safety are evolving from specific threats of illness to longer-term health concerns such as the present concern over the safety of genetically modified organisms. In the United States, the Department of Agriculture, the Department of Commerce, the CPSC, the Environmental Protection Agency, the Food and Drug Administration (Department of Health and Human Services), and the Bureau of Alcohol, Tobacco and Firearms (Department of the Treasury) all create and enforce legislation covering food safety.

Health. Like food, health regulations have long been influenced by safety concerns. Medical licensure should ensure that only knowledgeable individuals treat patients, reducing concerns about imperfect information. Patient safety is paramount to the reputation of not only the individual practitioner but the industry as a whole. The collected writings of Hippocrates of Cos (460–377 BCE) contained not only codes of ethical conduct but also provisions aimed at ensuring this quality. The tradeoff between limiting medical practitioners in order to protect the safety of the consumer and limiting their numbers to restrict occupational entry was apparent even in the fifth century BCE.

From the time of Herodotus until the early twentieth century, medical schools evolved mainly as apprenticeship-oriented, secretive sources of mystical information. The first Western medical school to set up systematic paths of learning as well as general health precepts was established in Salerno, Italy, in the early twelfth century. The Royal College of Physicians in Britain, established in 1518, called for examination of medical practitioners to assure product quality. Finally, in 1858, Britain created the General Medical Council to control admission to the medical register as well as to influence education and medical exams. The American Medical Association (AMA) was founded in the United States around the same time, and proved instrumental in establishing private control of quality through licensing and investigations of quackery. The recent history of medical malpractice suits and increasing liability has also increased the safety precautions taken by the health industry.

The global pharmaceutical industry exists under close scrutiny, due to both the potential harm that could be caused by untested pharmaceuticals and the concentrated market structure of the research-dependent industry. The Pure Food and Drug Act established accountability for labeling and purity of both food and drugs in interstate commerce, but regulations regarding testing came only after the deaths of over one hundred children from an untested sulfa drug (Grabowski and Vernon, 1983). The Food, Drug and Cosmetic Act of 1938 and subsequent amendments form the basis of pharmaceutical regulation today. The heavy costs of testing drugs, combined with the protection of patent laws, have made the pharmaceutical business a high-stakes oligopoly.

Children. Safety regulation regarding children is appealing in great part because (in OECD nations) accidents have traditionally been the largest single cause of death among children between the ages of one and fifteen. Also, since children generally are unable to deduce the full potential consequences of an action, successful product regulation for children should include special care in intended uses plus all potential uses or misuses of the product. Although parents bear the majority of the responsibility for the use of products by their children, information and experience from a broader field that guides legislation may increase safety dramatically.

The OECD member nations determined that the products that cause the majority of accidents for children present the following dangers: poisoning; flammability, burns, and scalds; suffocation and strangulation, falls, and other mechanical hazards; electric shock; drowning; and health hazards from unclean stuffing (filling) material (OECD, 1984). Products that present these hazards have been subject to the greatest legislation, as the pajamas example demonstrates.

The history of product regulation aimed at children's safety parallels that of most consumer goods. For example, standards regarding products often have evolved from voluntary standards into mandatory ones. In Australia, a voluntary standard first existed for child-restraining devices in motor vehicles. This voluntary standard proved ineffective, and became mandatory in 1976 under the Trade Practices Act. From 1956 to 1976, there was a constant-to-slightly-upward trend in infant mortality due to transportation. This reversed itself in 1976; there was a decline from approximately 10.6 infant mortalities per 100,000 from 1976 to 1978 to 6.1 per 100,000 from 1989 to 1991 (Graham Vimpani, "Preventing Unintentional Injuries: Time for a Rethink?" Ninth Asian Congress of Paediatrics, Hong Kong, 22–23 March 1997).

Industrial structure and international trade considerations also affect potential regulation. Firms in industries with a small number of firms can most easily regulate themselves through voluntary standards; indeed they may use the opportunity to collude and increase profits. Products imported from abroad have tended to lead to labeling and other required information and safety standards. Labeling requirements, in particular, may fall on products directly intended for use by children, such as dolls and other toys, or products with which children might interact, including household products, paints, and drugs.

Legislation of various types has made many products safer. In Canada and the United States, mandatory child-resistant containers have led to significant declines in child poisonings, and mandatory crib and pacifier regulations have virtually eliminated strangulation and pacifier choking deaths. Informational campaigns have significantly reduced injuries and fatalities. Particular successes include improved fireworks handling in New Zealand and the United States and reduced traffic accidents in Sweden and Norway.

Additionally, direct regulations have been given extra enforceability through growing product liability. In just the eight years between 1974 and 1982, product liability cases filed in the U.S. district courts increased from about fifteen hundred to almost nine thousand. With regard to civil filings, in 1974 product liability cases represented 1.5 percent of all cases; in 1982 they represented 4.3 percent (Viscusi, 1984). During this period, U.S. liability regulations changed. Until then, product liability rested on whether a manufacturer knew or should have known of the danger of its product (negligence), or whether a manufacturer knew its product was not fit for intended or reasonably expected uses (breach of implied warranty). At the end of the 1970s, regulations moved decidedly from these criteria to strict liability, where a manufacturer was liable for any injuries resulting from a product that was "unreasonably dangerous" without regard for manufacturer intent or contractual limitations.

Other nations are following suit. In Australia, remedies were limited to contract law, or breach of implied warranty, until 1978. Protection to users of a product beyond those directly involved in its sale came with the Trade Practices Act, and recent amendments have increased responsibility to strict liability. In this case, the burden is on the consumer to prove that the defect existed at the time of sale, that an objective consumer would deem the product unsafe against reasonable expectations, and that the injury was sustained because of the defect. Any unreasonable care in use by the consumer may also lower the potential penalty. Restrictions, such as those in Australia, are intended to balance the desire to compensate people injured by defective products with moral hazard incentives for the consumer that might accompany strict liability. Ideally, firms should perceive strict liability as reason enough to enhance their products' safety sufficiently to avoid suits; in reality, these cases happen. Firms, too, have cost incentives to avoid increasing product safety and even to hide cases where they are found liable. This cost incentive proved strong enough that voluntary reporting of accidents and liability rulings was deemed insufficient; in 1991, the United States legally mandated that liability case outcomes be reported to the CPSC.

Transportation. The CPSC reporting mandate does not exist in the United States for most products involved in transportation; they are covered by a separate set of regulations. The history of significant regulation in the transportation industry extends back to shipping and naval concerns, and then rail regulations at the end of the nineteenth century. Much of this regulation, however, focused on occupational safety.

The statistics supporting the need for regulation were convincing; in 1894, the odds of dying as a United States rail employee were an astounding 1 in 428, and of being injured 1 in 37 (Usselman, 1992). The Safety Appliances Act of 1893 was passed to try to reduce these injuries and deaths. However, by 1904, the odds had worsened to 1 out of 357 dead and 1 out of 19 injured. Regulation did not appear to be helping. One plausible explanation for this failure was that the Safety Appliances Act, which targeted technological requirements for coupling devices and brakes, did not target the true safety issues.

Today, regulation in the transportation industry encompasses every aspect of safety and every mode of transportation, from requiring bicycle helmets and the labeling requirements for personal flotation devices to vehicle restraint devices and international airport security.

In the United States, disparate legislative paths for automobiles, highways, airlines, railroads, and shipping converged under the umbrella of the Department of Transportation (DOT), created in 1966. The Federal Aviation Administration, the Federal Highway Administration, the Federal Railroad Association, and the United States Coast Guard are all constituents of the DOT; but the National Transportation Safety Board (NTSB) became independent in 1975. This separation indicates the potential for conflicts between product safety regulation for safety's sake and for the sake of enhancing market power.

The National Highway Traffic Safety Administration (NHTSA), which is within the DOT, was created to target health and safety directly. The agency's mandate was to create regulations that would increase vehicle safety through manufacturer enhancements in technology, and included the ability to force recalls and repairs for safety defects. The administration and its regulations have significantly enhanced automobile safety, but have rarely targeted driver incentives for safety.

Although the roots of automobile safety legislation are at the state level (e.g., drivers licensing and automobile licensing both remain under state jurisdiction), aviation safety legislation has existed at the federal level virtually since the inception of a commercial industry. Civilian pilots recommended registering aircraft and licensing pilots as early as 1912. In 1926 the federal government, through the Air Commerce Act, assumed responsibility for safety regulations and the provision of navigational aids (Priest, 1988).

In the Civil Aeronautics Act of 1938, a single agency was given responsibility for both safety and economic issues.

As the industry continued to grow, and passenger freight increased in volume, the regulatory environment continued to evolve along the dual lines of safety and profitability. In 1958, the Federal Aviation Act created the Federal Aviation Agency (FAA), which is the current regulatory agency for airline safety in the United States; and the Civil Aeronautics Board (CAB) remained the oversight agency for economic issues, including routes and fares, until deregulation of the industry in 1978.

Summary. Caveat emptor has been on the wane since the early years of the twentieth century. Product safety legislation has reduced the risk of injury or death from many thousands of causes, particularly since the acceleration of regulation began in the 1960s. Safety regulations in most developed economies have evolved from extremely limited liability rights in an environment of caveat emptor to sets of overlapping voluntary and mandatory standards and strict liability doctrines. The new regulations, like many of the old ones, are focused on the many complex factors that lead to accidents. The potential for overregulation highlights the need for benefit–cost analysis and comparison in drafting legislation and implementing regulations.

BIBLIOGRAPHY

Aldrich, Mark. *Safety First: Technology, Labor, and Business in the Building of American Work Safety, 1870–1939.* Baltimore, 1997.

Coppin, Clayton A., and Jack High. *The Politics of Purity: Harvey Washington Wiley and the Origins of Federal Food Policy.* Ann Arbor, 1999.

Grabowski, Henry G., and John M. Vernon. *The Regulation of Pharmaceuticals: Balancing the Benefits and Risks.* Washington, D. C., 1983.

Mashaw, Jerry L., and David L. Harfst. *The Struggle for Auto Safety.* Cambridge, Mass., 1990.

Mayer, Robert N. *The Consumer Movement: Guardians of the Marketplace.* Boston, 1989.

Micklitz, Hans-W. "International Regulation on Health, Safety, and the Environment: Trends and Challenges." *Journal of Consumer Policy* 23 (2000), 3–24.

Organization for Economic Cooperation and Development (OECD). *Product Safety: Measures to Protect Children.* Report by the Committee on Consumer Policy. Paris, 1984.

Priest, Curtiss W. *Risks, Concerns, and Social Legislation: Forces That Led to Laws on Health, Safety, and the Environment.* Boulder, 1988.

Rhee, Kee-Choon, and Jinkook Lee. "Review of Consumer Activism in Korea, 1910–1995: A Political-Economic Approach." *Journal of Consumer Policy* 19 (1996), 365–392.

Usselman, Steven W. "The Lure of Technology and the Appeal of Order: Railroad Safety Regulation in Nineteenth Century America." *Business and Economic History* 21 (1992), 90–128.

Viscusi, W. Kip. *Regulating Consumer Product Safety.* Washington, D.C., 1984.

BROOKS KAISER

PROPERTY RIGHTS. Property rights are the bundle of socially sanctioned privileges granted to individuals for the use of valuable resources. They range from defining access and use of natural resources, to defining the nature of market exchange, to outlining work relationships within firms. Further, property rights exist on a continuum, ranging from open access, where no rights exist (usually the source of the "tragedy of the commons"); to informal communal rights, where group members "own" the resource and nonmembers are excluded; to state ownership, a form of communal rights, whereby in theory the government owns the resource and only citizens are granted some right of access; to private property rights, whereby individuals have decision-making authority over access and use. Property rights may be only vaguely delineated with general rules regarding use, and they may be very precisely defined and enforced. Finally, they may be absolute or attenuated by restrictions or regulations and tax levies on the income generated from resource use (Libecap, 1989a). Empirically, property rights rarely have fit one category. Historically, they often have moved across categories in a process of institutional adjustment as economic and political conditions have changed.

Attributes and Efficiency Implications. Regardless of whether rights are held by groups, the state, or private individuals, the ownership of an asset consists of three elements: (a) the right to use the asset (*usus*), (b) the right to appropriate the returns from the asset (*usus fructus*), and (c) the right to change its form, substance, and location (*abusus*). This last attribute is a right to bear the consequences from changes in the value of an asset, and it is the basis for investment and trade. The flexible right of transfer induces an owner to operate with a long-term planning horizon and, thus, to show concern for the efficient allocation of resources over time (Eggertsson, 1990; Furubotn and Richter, 1991, 1997).

These privileges may be outlined through informal, social norms or through more elaborate, written statutes and court rulings. For relatively low-valued assets and/or in cases where the number of parties is small and where there is a history of social interaction, informal local customs are effective in defining and enforcing property rights (Ostrom, 1990). For high-valued assets where new entry is common, increasing the number of competitors with heterogeneous objectives, more formal governance structures, such as legally defined private property rights, are necessary. The movement from informal practices to more formally defined property rights may be smooth, following relative price increases or technological changes (Anderson and Hill, 1975; Davis and North, 1971; Libecap, 1978), or may be contentious (Johnson and Libecap, 1982; Libecap and Johnson, 1980), depending on whether the state supplements or displaces earlier ownership institutions.

Because of their critical impact on production, investment, and trade, property rights have played a key role in the economic performance of societies across history. They assign decision-making authority over scarce resources and allocate the distribution of the resulting benefits and costs. Accordingly, property rights define incentives and time horizons for economic behavior. In general, societies with more secure property rights have out-performed those with weak or insecure property rights, regardless of the underlying stock of natural and human resources (Barro, 1991). There are many examples of resource-rich societies that have had comparatively low levels of economic growth historically (Russia), whereas relatively resource-poor societies have enjoyed much higher levels of economic progress (the Netherlands). When ownership is uncertain, short-time horizons dominate, investment is neglected, trade is reduced, and production is lowered because scarce resources are diverted to defense and predation.

Property rights are political institutions, and the actions taken by government regarding them depend upon the constituencies involved and their relative political power. Throughout economic history and across developed and developing societies today, there has been tension between the efficiency and equity implications of property rights arrangements. The equity effects of more efficient property rights may make them unpopular with certain parties in society. North (1981, 1990) argues that inefficient property rights often were maintained in the interest of influential elites. Opposition by those that benefitted from the old property structure made it very difficult to introduce more efficient property rights in response to new economic opportunities. Stagnant economic growth was the consequence.

For instance, North and Thomas (1973) assert that resistance by the crown to the adoption of new property rights that would facilitate the rise of a commercial class in France and Spain in the late Middle Ages was responsible, at least partially, for the apparent slower economic growth in those countries, relative to England and Holland. In England and Holland, merchants had more political influence, greater security, fewer restrictive regulations, and lower tax levies than existed in their larger European neighbors, where absolute monarchies relied upon a traditional land-owning class to maintain political control. North and Weingast (1989) and Ekelund and Tollison (1997) further describe legal and political innovations in England that strengthened property rights in the late seventeenth century. These changes included important Parliamentary constraints on the power of the king that facilitated the rise of capital markets, hastened the decline of mercantilism, and permitted economic growth to take place in early modern England.

Similarly, Mokyr (1990) cites the oppressive actions by centralized bureaucracies as a reason for the failure of many early, advanced societies in the Middle East and Asia to experience sustained economic growth. Instead, long-term economic growth took place first in smaller, less-centralized western European countries. Those countries competed for mobile artisans, merchants, and entrepreneurs, who were seen as valuable sources of innovation and national wealth. This competition among countries restrained potentially autocratic governments and forced them to adopt property rights, regulatory polices, and taxation regimes that were more supportive of commerce and economic expansion. In a more contemporary examination of the sources of differences in economic growth, Barro (1991, 1996) examines the performance of ninety-eight countries between 1960 and 1985. He argues that the growth rate of real per capita GNP is positively related to measures of political stability, among other variables. Political instability weakens property rights and private investment. Institutions that ensure property rights and market transactions are associated with the more successful countries in his data set.

Mokyr (1990) outlines four distinct processes that underlie economic growth: Investments in both human and physical capital, commercial expansion through trade in goods and inputs, and scale or size effects that bring lower per-unit costs. Each of these factors is dependent upon the nature of property rights. Where property rights are absent or insecure, the incentive to undertake investment in physical and human capital, when the returns are delayed to the future, is reduced. No investing party can be sure that he or she will capture the benefits of those investments. Further, trade is reduced because the basis for voluntary exchange is lacking. Ownership has to be agreed upon before parties will bargain. Demsetz (1967) argues that an assignment of property rights is a prerequisite for markets to facilitate socially valuable exchange and thereby to generate prices that reflect underlying demand and supply. In the absence of market price signals, resources cannot flow smoothly to higher-valued uses as economic conditions change. Moreover, resources will not be allocated effectively over time. When market prices indicate that the present value of resource rents is greater from future, rather than current use, exploitation will be delayed. When property rights and associated market prices are absent, however, there is little information to direct a reallocation or incentive for individuals to postpone resource use to the future.

When rights are very uncertain, the value of production is lowered because parties must focus on short-run objectives (rather than longer-term investment or production that might be more socially valuable), and productive resources must continually be shifted from production to defensive actions. Rent-dissipating violence among competing claimants is possible. When property rights are not well defined, individuals do not consider the full social costs of their activities. Accordingly, the net private and social returns from individual production decisions diverge. Only if property rights are so well defined that private and social net benefits are equalized, will individual economic decisions maximize total wealth, given the existing income distribution and market demand composition. An alternative, although complete, property rights assignment will have a correspondingly different income distribution, demand structure, and production mix. Nevertheless, the output chosen will maximize aggregate wealth under the new rights distribution. In a general efficiency sense, the issue is the completeness of the definition of property rights and not the specific allocation.

American Property Rights. American economic history generally has been one of comparatively secure property rights. American property institutions were modifications of those found in England. In England and throughout Europe, social and economic power largely was derived from land ownership. Land law in England developed in feudalism, which was a means of securing property protection. The vassal, who sought protection from a lord, yielded his land to the lord and became a tenant. There were many layers of feudalism, with the king as lord over all. Gradually, with the decline of feudalism, different kinds of land tenure emerged within English common law that delegated greater authority over land use and income (Cribbet, 1975).

Land was also the most valuable resource in colonial North America. The economy was, after all, natural resource based, largely in farming and fishing. The English system of land ownership that was brought to America was modified to meet the conditions of settling a continent. Restraints on exchange, primogeniture, and other remnants of feudal practices were removed. The trend was to make land like any other marketable commodity that could be bought, sold, and used according to the owner's desires. American property law evolved into a clear system of fee-simple ownership of land (Friedman, 1985). With abundant land open for private claiming by a large segment of the population, many elements of the society viewed the system of property rights as beneficial and just, and they benefitted from the capital gains coming from land sales (Ferrie, 1994; Galenson and Pope, 1989). So long as property owners paid their taxes (duties to the state), their property rights were upheld by the court system and increasingly refined by the government (Libecap, 1978). The practice of establishing clear property rights to land, the most important asset in the economy, created precedents for the subsequent granting of secure property rights to other, less-tangible assets.

The American Constitution is an economic document, designed in part to specify and enforce property rights and to defend them against the arbitrary actions of a powerful state. Articles I, II, and III outline the branches of government and delegate the powers of each, especially the roles of the legislature to make laws that could address property rights concerns and of the courts to arbitrate disputes. In a document that is otherwise short and generally vague, Article I, Section 8, gives Congress power "to promote the Progress of Science and the useful Arts, by securing for limited Times to Authors and Innovators the Exclusive Right to their respective Writings and Discoveries" (Friedman, 1985, 255). The framers clearly understood the importance of property rights in creating incentives for intellectual creativity, invention, and innovation. This section is the basis for patenting law that underlies technological innovation and for intellectual property law that has supported both the writing of articles and books since the eighteenth century, but also, by the late twentieth century, the development of computer Internet software and other related innovations.

Article I, Section 10, is the contract clause that constrains the power of government, which is admonished not to impair "the Obligation of Contracts." Contract stipulations are part of property rights and essential for trade and exchange, and they must be respected and enforceable. Otherwise, the transactions costs of trade will increase and its economic benefits will be reduced. Amendment V guarantees the security of property by asserting that it cannot be taken without due process, and where private property is taken for public purposes, just compensation is required. These are vital restrictions on the power of government to intervene arbitrarily and disrupt private production, investment, or exchange, which were understood by Adam Smith and others in the late eighteenth century as essential for successful economic development (McGuire and Ohsfeldt, 1986, 1989).

The constitutional emphasis on patenting illustrates the emphasis in American property law on promoting the practical adoption of scientific discoveries through clear property rights. Patents were to be granted when the subject had not been previously "invented or discovered," when the applicant was the actual inventor, and when the article was "sufficiently useful and important" to deserve a patent. The United States adopted English law to grant the inventor a monopoly over the invention. This monopoly grant was unusual in American law, and it reflected the esteem in which scientific progress was held (Friedman, 1985). Sokoloff (1988) and Sokoloff and Khan (1990) examine changes in the patent system in the United States in the first half of the nineteenth century to clarify the patenting process and to define the nature of the property rights granted. Americans took advantage of patents to introduce new inventions, especially as markets expanded and new commercial opportunities emerged.

Distributional and Political Issues. The aggregate advantages of a well-defined and enforced property system have never been a mystery. The problem has been in the allocation of property rights. Because property rights to valuable resources, such as agricultural land, urban property, and new inventions, assign wealth and political influence in a society, their distributional implications affect all members of society. For property rights to have any meaning, they must be exclusive to the owner, whether it is the state, a group, or private individuals. Nonowners are excluded from resource-use decisions and from capturing the income drawn from the asset. Accordingly, some parties will see themselves benefitted from a property rights system, whereas others may be harmed. If the rights arrangement is viewed as accessible to nonowners through purchase or other transfers, and if the distribution is seen as relatively equitable or fair (and these perceptions vary across societies and history), then it may have considerable political support. If not, it may face widespread opposition and be vulnerable to forced, violent redistribution. A legal system that defines clear property rights to productive assets has developed historically only where influential constituencies have pushed for such institutional changes. Once a property system has been devised and is supported by a body of law, it becomes part of the society's legal structure and, at that point, more durable. But where property rights have been held with suspicion because of their political and distributional implications, they generally have received less complete legal recognition and enforcement.

The desire to implement or modify property rights in response to new economic opportunities has been a basis for institutional change throughout history. One motivation, associated with agricultural and extractive economies, has been to limit the losses associated with the "tragedy of the commons" (Hardin, 1968) in natural resources. In his influential essay, Hardin described a pasture that was "open to all" and subject to overgrazing because, although each herder privately benefitted from grazing his own animals, the costs of overstocking were spread across all herders. Hence, each herder was motivated to add more animals than would be optimal for the range resource. Hardin was not the first social scientist to call attention to the losses of the common pool. More than a decade before his article, H. Scott Gordon (1954) outlined a similar logic that was extended by Scott (1955) and Cheung (1970). Gordon was concerned about overfishing of common (open-access) fisheries:

> "There appears then, to be some truth in the conservative dictum that everybody's property is nobody's property. Wealth that is free for all is valued by no one because he who is foolhardy enough to wait for its proper time of use will only find that it has been taken by another. . . . The fish in the sea are valueless to the fisherman, because there is no assurance that they will be there for him tomorrow if they are left behind today" (Gordon 1954, 124).

Whether or not a more complete definition of property rights is adopted in response to open-access conditions depends on the magnitude of losses that otherwise would be faced, the nature of bargaining or transactions costs to resolve them, and the costs of defining and enforcing property rights. Capturing a share of the expected gains of institutional change encourages individuals to engage in collective action. The larger and more certain are the expected aggregate gains, the more likely a cooperative solution will be found to create or modify property rights. Historically, there have been cases where collective action was comparatively swift, when the aggregate benefits of agreement were large, distributional conflicts were minimal, and measurement and enforcement problems were small. Measurement and enforcement costs are less for observable, stationary resources, such as agricultural land, where claim boundaries can be marked clearly so that trespass and theft can be quickly determined. With clear boundaries, the range for disputes among rival claimants is narrowed, and fewer resources are needed to arbitrate conflicts. By contrast, costs are higher for migratory, unobservable resources, such as mobile fish stocks and subsurface oil deposits. Violations of property claims are difficult to monitor and to police because ownership boundaries are unclear.

Empirical studies of land use in contemporary developing areas document the importance of property rights for mitigating potential open-access conditions and encouraging investment (Alston, Libecap, and Schneider 1996; Alston, Libecap, and Mueller, 1999; Deacon, 1994; Feder and Onchan 1987; Feder and Feeny, 1991). Deacon compares three possible causes of deforestation—population pressure, growth in income, and insecure property rights—in a cross section of 120 countries between 1980 and 1985. He finds that among the three causes, absent or insecure property rights are the major factor in encouraging rapid harvesting. In their survey of small farmers on the Amazon frontier, Alston, Libecap, and Schneider found that having clear title would increase land values between 20 and 50 percent. Among early settlers to the frontier, informal land allocation and use practices dominated. Land values were too low to justify formal documentation of individual land claims or to justify costly conflict among claimants. With the completion of new roads to market centers in the 1970s, land values rose with declining transportation costs. At that time, informal property rights were no longer sufficient to allow claimants to appropriate potential land rents. With higher population densities and greater competition for control, private enforcement costs rose. Moreover, the parties claiming land were more heterogeneous, and many did not recognize the previous, informal property regimes. To avoid trespassing and other land conflicts, the parties turned to the state for a more formal definition of property rights.

How the state responded, however, depended on political bargaining in the process of more clearly defining and enforcing property laws. Politicians, judges, land agency officials, as well as competing land claimants were involved in the process. Large farmers had different political allies and legal precedents than did small farmers. The resulting political bargaining meant that the rights that emerged diverged from the pattern required for a fully effective institutional arrangement. In some cases, property rights were assigned too late after costly disputes had taken place; in others, overlapping claims were allowed, leading to confused ownership; in still other instances, secure title was provided. This mixture illustrates the complexity of institutional change. Given the primitive state of transportation and the market on the frontier, the conditions reported by contemporary Amazon farmers may be comparable to those on earlier frontiers in North America and perhaps Europe.

There are other historical examples of collective action to define property rights. On the nineteenth-century mining frontier in the American West, prospectors saw the economic consequences of the absence of a recognized mineral rights structure. One of their first activities upon arrival in a region was the drafting of mining camp rules to define and enforce private mineral rights. Moreover, distributional issues were of little concern, at least initially, because the gold and silver deposits were thought to be extensive relative to the number of claimants. Each prospector expected eventually to share in the bonanza. Accordingly, there was rapid agreement on mining camp rules regarding the staking, transfer, and maintenance of individual claims (Libecap 1978, Umbeck 1977).

A consensus that open-access losses are large, however, is not always sufficient to bring about successful institutional change. Many fisheries are classic commons properties, whereby increasing fishing pressure in the absence of property rights to fish stocks brings declining catch per unit of effort and falling incomes. The losses long have been recognized (Higgs, 1982), yet in many cases, private negotiations and government regulation to limit fishing pressure and to increase rents in fisheries have been only marginally successful. In other cases, however, effective action has been taken with adoption of individual transferable quotas (ITQs) (Johnson, 1995). These arrangements, however, generally have been adopted late because of disputes as to what should be done and who should receive property rights. Similarly, open-access losses also have plagued crude oil production in the United States since the first commercial discoveries were made in 1859. Nevertheless, arguments over the distribution of oil reservoir rents resulting from proposed institutional changes have constrained the adoption of both new property rights and regulatory policies (Libecap and Wiggins 1984 and 1985; Wiggins and Libecap 1985).

The division of the gains of institutional change present a key problem in determining whether or not political action to implement changes in property rights will be successful. The questions of who will be excluded and what privileges will be granted those who retain use of the resource must be answered either in small-group negotiations for local, communal arrangements or in broader political negotiations for formal, government intervention. In both settings, negotiating parties attempt to maximize their private net gains from institutional change. They implicitly compare their wealth and political position under the status quo with that offered by the new arrangement. If they do not see themselves made better off, they will oppose significant changes.

Time and precedent play important roles in determining the range of feasible property institutions. Some parties have a vested interest in the status quo and can be expected to oppose change unless they can be compensated in some manner. It may not be possible, however, to improve their welfare and still maintain the advantages of the proposed institutional change. Groups with vested interests may have advantages in political bargaining relative to other groups through lower costs of collective action. Their current position in the system may bind them together to make them a relatively cohesive bargaining group. They also may have beneficial ties to established political processes and leaders. Historically, these advantages have made vested interests effective political lobbyists, biasing institutional change toward maintenance of the status quo.

Any institutional arrangement must consider the wide range of parties involved and the different incentives that they may have in negotiations to define property rights. Depending on the setting, the parties involved may include private claimants, politicians, judges, and bureaucrats. Each has different objectives in devising institutional arrangements. In general, the speed and nature of institutional change to modify property rights will be affected by the number and heterogeneity of the bargaining parties, the distribution of information, as well as legal precedents and social norms. The greater the number of parties, the more claims that must be resolved. Important heterogeneities across the parties in access to information and in production costs, size, wealth, and political experience make consensus more difficult on any property rights modification (Johnson and Libecap, 1982). With limited or asymmetric information regarding the benefits of any adjustment in property rights, parties may be split by honest disagreements or by deception (Williamson, 1975).

Side payments are a way of adjusting shares or property rights to mitigate opposition in negotiations over institutional change. It may not be possible, however, to devise any acceptable side payment that addresses the concerns of key parties who expect to be made worse off. Side payments or political concessions also can modify the property rights arrangement and influence the production gains that are possible. For example, routine exemptions to well-spacing rules and monthly production quotas that were granted by the Texas Railroad Commission to influential small oil producers in the 1930s to secure their political support for oil regulation encouraged excessive capital expenditures and the production of high-cost oil (Libecap 1989b). Whether or not politicians will recognize the demands of certain groups for compensation depends upon a group's political influence and its ability to extract wealth transfers as the price of building a political consensus for the proposed property rights arrangement. These conditions underscore the political nature of property rights institutions.

[*See also* Contract Enforcement and Legal Systems; Inheritance Systems; Patents; *and* Property Rights in Land.]

BIBLIOGRAPHY

Acheson, James M. "The Lobster Fiefs: Economic and Ecological Effects of Territoriality in the Maine Lobster Industry." *Human Ecology* 3 (1975) 183–207.

Agnello, R. J., and L. P. Donnelley. "Property Rights and Efficiency in the Oyster Industry." *Journal of Law and Economics* 18 (1975), 521–534.

Alchian, Armen, and Harold Demsetz. "The Property Rights Paradigm." *Journal of Economic History* 33 (1973), 16–24.

Alston, Lee J., Gary D. Libecap, and Robert Schneider. "The Determinants and Impact of Property Rights: Land Titles on the Brazilian Frontier." *Journal of Law, Economics, and Organization* 12.1 (1996), 25–61.

Alston, Lee J., Gary D. Libecap, and Bernardo Mueller. *Titles, Conflict, and Land Use: The Development of Property Rights on the Brazilian Amazon Frontier.* Ann Arbor, 1999.

Anderson, Terry L., and P. J. Hill. "The Evolution of Property Rights: A Study of the American West." *Journal of Law and Economics* 18 (1975), 163–179.

Barro, Robert J. "Economic Growth in a Cross Section of Countries." *Quarterly Journal of Economics* 106.2 (1991), 407–443.

Barro, Robert J. *Getting It Right: Markets and Choices in a Free Society.* Cambridge, 1996.

Cheung, Steven N. S. "The Structure of a Contract and the Theory of a Non-Exclusive Resource." *Journal of Law and Economics* 13 (1970), 49–70.

Cribbet, John E. *Principles of the Law of Property.* 2d ed., Mineola, N.Y., 1975.

Coase, Ronald H. "The Problem of Social Cost." *Journal of Law and Economics* 3 (1960), 1–44.

Davis, Lance E., and Douglass C. North. *Institutional Change and American Economic Growth.* New York, 1971.

Deacon, Robert T. "Deforestation and the Rule of Law in a Cross-Section of Countries." *Land Economics* 70.4 (1994), 414–430.

DeAlessi, Louis. "The Economics of Property Rights: A Review of the Evidence." *Research in Law and Economics* 2 (1980), 1–47.

Demsetz, Harold. "Towards a Theory of Property Rights." *American Economic Review* 57 (1967), 347–359.

Eggertsson, Thrainn. *Economic Behavior and Institutions.* New York, 1990.

Ekelund, Robert B. Jr., and Robert D. Tollison. *Politicized Economies: Monarchy, Monopoly, and Mercantilism*. College Station, Tex., 1997.

Feder, Gershon, and Tongroj Onchan. "Land Ownership Security and Farm Investment in Thailand." *American Journal of Agricultural Economics* 69 (1987), 311–320.

Feder, Gershon, and David Feeny. "Land Tenure and Property Rights: Theory and Implications for Development Policy." *World Bank Economic Review* 5.1 (1991), 135–153.

Ferrie, Joseph. "The Wealth Accumulation of Antebellum Immigrants to the U.S., 1840–1860." *Journal of Economic History* 54.1 (1994), 1–33.

Friedman, Lawrence M. *A History of American Law*. New York, 1985.

Furubotn, Eirik, and Rudolf Richter. *The New Institutional Economics*. College Station, Tex., 1991.

Furubotn, Eirik, and Rudolph Richter. *Institutions and Economic Theory: The Contribution of the New Institutional Economics*. Ann Arbor, 1997.

Galenson, David, and Clayne Pope. "Economic and Geographic Mobility on the Farming Frontier: Evidence from Appanoose County, Iowa, 1850–1870." *Journal of Economic History* 49.3 (1989), 635–655.

Gordon, H. Scott. "The Economic Theory of a Common Property Resource: The Fishery." *Journal of Political Economy* 62 (1954), 124–142.

Hardin, Garett. "The Tragedy of the Commons." *Science* 162 (1968), 1243–1248.

Higgs, Robert. "Legally Induced Technical Regress in the Washington Salmon Fishery." *Research in Economic History* 7 (1982), 55–86.

Johnson, Ronald N., and Gary D. Libecap. "Contracting Problems and Regulation: The Case of the Fishery." *American Economic Review* 72 (1982), 1005–1022.

Johnson, Ronald N. "Implications of Taxing Quota Value in an Individual Transferable Quota Fishery." *Marine Resources Economics* 10 (1995), 327–340.

Libecap, Gary D. "Economic Variables and the Development of the Law: The Case of Western Mineral Rights." *Journal of Economic History* 38 (1978), 338–362.

Libecap, Gary D. "The Political Allocation of Mineral Rights: A Reevaluation of Teapot Dome." *Journal of Economic History* 44 (1984), 381–391.

Libecap, Gary D. "Property Rights in Economic History: Implications for Research." *Explorations in Economic History* 23 (1986), 227–252.

Libecap, Gary D. *Contracting for Property Rights* New York, 1989a.

Libecap, Gary D. "The Political Economy of Crude Oil Cartelization in the United States, 1933–1972." *Journal of Economic History* 49.4 (1989b), 833–856.

Libecap, Gary D., and Ronald N. Johnson. "Property Rights, Nineteenth-Century Federal Timber Policy, and the Conservation Movement." *Journal of Economic History* 39 (1979), 129–142.

Libecap, Gary D., and Ronald N. Johnson. "Legislating Commons: the Navajo Tribal Council and the Navajo Range." *Economic Inquiry* 18.1 (1980), 69–86.

Libecap, Gary D., and Steven N. Wiggins. "Contractual Responses to the Common Pool: Prorationing of Crude Oil Production." *American Economic Review* 74 (1984), 87–98.

Libecap, Gary D., and Steven N. Wiggins. "The Influence of Private Contractual Failure on Regulation: The Case of Oil Field Unitization." *Journal of Political Economy* 93 (1985), 690–714.

McGuire, Robert A., and Robert L. Ohsfeldt. "An Economic Model of Voting Behavior over Specific Issues at the Constitutional Convention of 1787." *Journal of Economic History* 46.1 (1986), 79–111.

McGuire, Robert A., and Robert L. Ohsfeldt. "Self-Interest, Agency Theory, and Political Voting Behavior: The Ratification of the United States Constitution." *American Economic Review* 79.1 (1989), 219–234.

Mokyr, Joel. *The Lever of Riches: Technological Creativity and Economic Progress*. New York, 1990.

North, Douglass C. *Structure and Change in Economic History*. New York, 1981.

North, Douglass C. *Institutions, Institutional Change, and Economic Performance*. New York, 1990.

North, Douglass C., and Robert Paul Thomas. *The Rise of the Western World: A New Economic History*. New York, 1973.

North, Douglass C., and Barry R. Weingast. "Constitutions and Commitment: The Evolution of Institutions Governing Public Choice in Seventeenth-Century England." *Journal of Economic History* 49.4 (1989), 803–832.

Ostrom, Elinor. *Governing the Commons: The Evolution of Institutions for Collective Action*. New York, 1990.

Scott, Anthony. "The Fishery: The Objectives of Sole Ownership." *Journal of Political Economy* 63 (1955), 116–124.

Sokoloff, Kenneth L. "Inventive Activity in Early Industrial America: Evidence from Patent Records, 1790–1846." *Journal of Economic History* 48.4 (1988), 813–850.

Sokoloff, Kenneth L., and B. Zorina Khan. "The Democratization of Invention During Early Industrialization: Evidence from the United States, 1790–1846." *Journal of Economic History* 50.2 (1990), 363–378.

Umbeck, John. "The California Gold Rush: A Study of Emerging Property Rights." *Explorations in Economic History* 14 (1977), 197–226.

Wiggins, Steven N., and Gary D. Libecap. "Oil Field Unitization: Contractual Failure in the Presence of Imperfect Information." *American Economic Review* 75 (1985) 368–385.

Williamson, Oliver. *Markets and Hierarchies, Analysis, and Antitrust Implications: A Study in the Economics of Internal Organization*. New York, 1975.

GARY D. LIBECAP

PROPERTY RIGHTS IN LAND *[This entry contains two subentries, a historical overview and a discussion of communal control.]*

Historical Overview

Property rights in land consist of the set of formal and informal rights to use and transfer land. Property rights range from open access to a fully specified set of private rights. *Open access* means anyone can use the land regardless of how her use affects the use of others. A full set of private rights consists of: (1) the right to use the land in any manner that one wishes, generally with the caveat that such use does not interfere with someone else's property rights; (2) the right to exclude others from the use of one's land; (3) the right to derive income from the land; (4) the right to sell the asset; and (5) the right to bequeath the land to someone of one's choice. In between open access and private property rights are a host of commons arrangements. Commons arrangements differ from open access in several respects. Under a commons arrangement only a select group is allowed access to the land, and the use rights

PROPERTY TRANSFER. Bill of sale of a field and one house paid in silver; terracotta tablet inscribed in Sumerian script, circa 2550 BCE. (Département des Antiquités Orientales, Musée du Louvre, Paris/ Erich Lessing/Art Resource, NY)

of the commons may be circumscribed. For example, a societal group, such as a village, tribe, or homeowners' association, may allow its members to place cattle in a common pasture but limit the number of cattle any member may put on the commons. A set of rights is only valuable if the rights are enforced. Individuals, social norms, and governments enforce property rights. In more developed and populated societies all three forces play a role, while in less-populated societies governments play less of a role. *Individual enforcement* refers to the efforts individuals exert to maintain their rights. For example, putting a fence around one's land and posting "no trespassing" signs are individual enforcement efforts. *Social norms* refer to the customary beliefs that people in a society hold concerning the use of land. Ostracism is typically the sanction imposed on individuals who do not conform to social norms. Governments enforce property rights through the police and courts.

Determinants and Consequences of the Assignment of Property Rights. Property rights matter because they provide the incentive structure for land use. If land is not scarce, then open access makes sense because there is no point in incurring any costs of specification given that there is an infinite supply of land of equal quality. Only in some sort of Robinson Crusoe world would such conditions prevail. In the real world the degree of scarcity varies.

The more exclusive are rights to the individual or group, the greater the incentive to maintain the value of land. Furthermore more exclusive rights increase the incentive to improve the value of land by increasing its productivity, such as removing rocks or using fertilizers. Having the incentive to invest may not be sufficient to induce investment if individuals are "cash poor." In this situation the ability to invest is aided if land can be used as collateral to secure a loan. In many places this was not possible and indeed is still not possible where mortgage markets are not well developed. Having the ability to sell may lead to better use of land, because sale prices reflect scarcity value, and in the absence of prices, actual scarcity may be difficult to assess. The ability to sell allows those who value it most to purchase it. (Of course it is important to note that in *value* economists include the ability to pay, which historically and today is limited by the degree of development of mortgage markets.)

Ideally property rights to land would become more specific, either to groups or individuals, as the scarcity value of land increases. But this ignores the costs of assigning and enforcing property rights as well as the distributional consequences of the assignment of rights. The importance of more-specific property rights can only be assessed in comparison to less-specific property rights, that is, land does not have any inherent value outside of the property rights structure. Land becomes more valuable when investments are made that increase its productivity, but the investments will not be made unless the right to the return to investment is secure. The following diagram illustrates an ideal assignment and enforcement of property rights.

Suppose the value of land is determined by the value of output produced for the market. Because of transportation costs, the value of otherwise homogeneous land will fall with greater distance from the market. Let line *AB* represent the value of land under open access conditions. At some point *(A)* the land is so remote that it has no market value. One can think of *A* as representing the frontier, where land is abundant and so distant from the market that there is no settlement beyond *A* based on purely economic considerations. As one moves closer to the market, the scarcity value of land increases. At some point *(C)* the value of land would increase with more specific property rights because the rightholder(s) would have an incentive to maintain and increase the value of land. The line *DC* represents the value of land with more specific property rights than the open access conditions with line *BC*. The distance between *DC* and *BC* represents the rent (value) that would be gained by greater specificity. If there were no costs in assigning and enforcing property rights, they would emerge at *C*. Because there are such costs, ideally they would emerge somewhat to the left of point *C*. But political factors play a role, so at times results deviate from

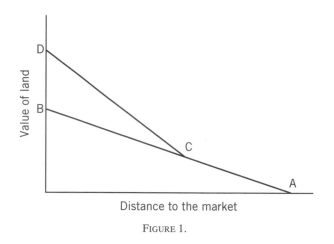

FIGURE 1.

the optimal assignment of rights. Nevertheless, the main points to draw from this illustration are: (1) as land becomes more scarce, a wedge emerges between value under existing open access conditions and more specific property rights; (2) the potential rent from greater specificity has been a potent force in driving the assignment of property rights; and (3) redistributional consequences played out in political arenas have frequently interfered with a pure economic determination of property rights.

Assignment of Property Rights in the British American Colonies. The assignment and development of property rights in the American colonies reflects a mixture of indigenous practices, factor endowments, and institutions brought from Europe. In North America the Native Americans did not treat land as a commodity that could be sold. For example, in the eastern part of what is now the United States, the tribe generally owned the land with individual families or kinship groups having use rights. Land was frequently worked in common by women. Social norms and kinship among the women in the field reduced incentives to shirk. Remnants of commons arrangements, such as the *ejido* systems in Mexico, still persist.

The initial property rights of the colonists in North and South America reflected the prevailing property rights in the countries of their origin. Or as the economic historian Jonathan Hughes remarked, "The colonists did what they knew how to do" (Hughes, 1976, p. 45). In the British North American colonies the initial establishment of rights was feudal in that ultimately one's property rights rested with the crown. In England the feudal system of tenure could be typified as a ladder of obligations and services given and received to those above and below one's position. For example, military tenants received land as a reward for the willingness to fight. The descendants of military tenants inherited the land, provided they paid a fee. This is the origin of the term *fee simple*. Military tenants or "chief tenants" could grant land to those below in return for labor

services. Nonmilitary tenants of the crown had property rights termed *socage*. These rights also enabled the transference of land to heirs, provided a payment was made. Even when land was alienated, the new "owners" took on the obligations of the seller. The colonial term *quitrent* derives from these obligations. The notion was that the rent paid was the only obligation that the new owner incurred, that is, the land was his or hers "quit and free" of other encumbrances. After 1660 England abolished military tenures and only socage remained, but ironically over time people referred to unencumbered socage tenures as "fee simple."

In principle the proprietors of some of the early colonies (for example, Delaware and Maryland) had the right from the crown to establish feudal systems, but because of the abundance of land, tenures everywhere became socage. They were technically socage because the tenure or ownership carried no military obligations, but colonists adopted the parlance of England in calling their property rights fee simple. Over time the colonists abolished the obligations of fees and quitrents (though in some states these lingered into the nineteenth century) along with the royal fifth of any gold or silver on the land.

With respect to inheritances, the colonists deviated more from England. Primogeniture was the norm in England—everywhere but County Kent. This helped maintain large estates and a landed upper class. In the southern colonies primogeniture remained the intestate form of inheritance, but in the northern colonies and middle colonies, with the exception of New York and Rhode Island, multigeniture prevailed. The divergence of the northern and middle colonies from the English tradition can be accounted for by the frontier land conditions faced by the colonists. In particular the importance of motivating all family members in the northern and middle colonies seems paramount. As Joseph Talcott, future governor of Connecticut, remarked in 1699, "Much of our lands remain yet unsubdued and must continue to so without the assistance of younger sons, which in reason can't be expected if they have no part of the inheritance" (Bidwell and Falconer, 1925, p. 63). In the southern colonies, with their greater use of slave and indentured labor (especially compared to the northern colonies), primogeniture helped maintain large agricultural units that could capture the economies of scale associated with monitoring slave labor. Primogeniture also fostered the concentration of wealth, which assisted the elite in the South to maintain political power. It is also important to keep in mind that unless the colonists actively passed legislation to establish multigeniture, primogeniture would rule, because it was the prevailing law in England. So another way of viewing the dominance of primogeniture in the South was that it was less inconsistent with the factor endowments of those in power than was the case of the political interests in the northern and middle colonies. Economic conditions though do not always dominate. Following the Revolutionary War there was a prevailing political sentiment against class-dominated societies. In this spirit all of the states adopted multigeniture by 1798. The system of fee simple and multigeniture enabled rapid settlement in the United States, though the results differed in the North and the South. In the North, until one reached the western Plains, small family farms dominated, whereas in the South a mixture of large plantations along with small family farms prevailed.

Assignment of Property Rights in Brazil by the Portuguese. The factor endowments of the colonies controlled by the Spanish and Portuguese differed, as did the policies promoting the settlement and development of the Spanish and Portuguese colonies. Yet both policies tended to result in large estates. This article only chronicles the development of property rights in Brazil; readers are referred to the references for the land policies in the Spanish colonies and subsequent countries. The Portuguese crown issued its first land policy (*capitanias hereditárias*) in 1532. The crown divided Brazil into fourteen sections, each fifty leagues along the Atlantic Coast with boundaries extending westward. Each *capitanias* (province) was given to a captain, who had complete authority over his land, the only stipulation being allegiance to the crown. This initial land settlement plan fits Hughes's description of path dependence. The crown chose this plan because of its success in settling the Madeira Islands. But given the distance from Portugal and the perceived absence of mineral wealth, the captains were reluctant to invest in their provinces; indeed six of the fourteen captains never took possession of their claims. After the disappointment of this plan in promoting settlement, the crown revoked the rights of the captains and established a governor for the whole colony.

Though Brazil established a governor, there was little incentive offered to settle, and as a result the seventeenth century dawned with scarcely any Portuguese in Brazil. Some scholars have argued that the low population density of Portugal accounts for the absence of settlers. This argument has some merit, but one has to recognize that the most likely migrants did not have the means to pay for their transportation. Unlike the English, the Portuguese and Spanish prohibited indentured servitude. It is worth noting that approximately 70 percent of the free white immigrants to the North American colonies in the seventeenth and eighteenth centuries came as indentures.

The seventeenth century witnessed some settlement of Brazil, mostly in the Northeast, but it was the increased global demand for sugar rather than any policy that altered the incentive to settle. The crown offered large grants of land called *sesmarias* to encourage settlement and pro-

duction. *Sesmarias* are another example of transplanting home institutions. The origins of *sesmarias* date back to 1375. In the late fourteenth century the Portuguese wanted to increase agricultural production and settlement in rural areas of Portugal. The holder of a *sesmaria* had complete property rights over land with the exception of holding the land idle. The purpose of the beneficial use clause was to encourage settlement. Beneficial use as a condition of title remained throughout the history of settlement and continues today, most recently reaffirmed in the Brazilian constitution of 1988. The *sesmaria* system did not stimulate much voluntary migration because in order to petition for a *sesmaria* one had to own the necessary capital for sugar cultivation—money for slaves and sugar mills to process the cane. As a result northeastern Brazil had few settlers from Portugal and many involuntary slaves cultivating sugar. Away from the coast some settlers started cattle ranches to serve the coastal demand, but the ranchers had no formal property rights to the land they used. Initially this did not cause any conflict because land was abundant. In the jargon of economists, there was little demand for title (see Figure 1). The result was that by 1700 Brazil had only about 300,000 inhabitants. After 1700 there was increased exploration following the discovery of gold in the interior. The gold boom lasted until the 1770s, but it did not produce dense settlement. Land remained abundant relative to demand for settlement.

By 1800 Brazil was still a major producer of sugar, but its dominance faded after 1650 with the entry of Dutch production in the Antilles. Because of the settlement spawned by the gold boom and continued small-scale ranching, the population of Brazil had increased to about 3.25 million people. At the same time the United States, with a much smaller land area—this was prior to the Louisiana Purchase and other land acquisitions—had a population of approximately 5.3 million people. With independence in 1822, Brazil abolished the *sesmaria* system, yet curiously it did not put any land policy into place until 1850. Settlers obtained land by *posse* (squatting) and enforced their claims by social norms where land was abundant, such as the frontier areas, or by the potential for force in more settled areas. Though on the frontier small claims emerged, the absence of government enforcement of claims in areas where there was cultivation resulted in the development of large estates known as *fazendas* or latifundia.

The rise of coffee cultivation in the years following independence changed the demand for property rights. Unlike the cultivation of sugar, the cultivation of coffee was accessible to small entrepreneurs. The early coffee producers obtained their claims by squatting, but this increasingly led to conflicts as land values appreciated with coffee prices. Many coffee producers petitioned politicians to clarify land claims. The result was the Land Law of 1850, which legalized all existing *posses* and, perhaps more surprisingly, revalidated all *sesmarias*. Furthermore the statute forbade the future use of *posse* as a means of claiming land, though this was not enforceable. On the frontier squatted claims remained the dominant form of settlement, and generally few settlers contested the claims of squatters. The relative absence of violence was the result of low land values on the frontier coupled with the relative homogeneity of settlers.

The proclamation of Brazil as a republic in 1889 ushered in a new land regime that has remained fairly constant to this day. The policies put in place did nothing to change the high degree of land inequality in Brazil. The principal clauses pertaining to land law include the following: (1) except for boundaries with other countries, public land is in the hands of the state governments; (2) squatters have the right to claim public land and, if put under cultivation, be eligible for a title after one year and one day; and (3) squatters have the right to squat on private land that is not in beneficial use, and if not contested, be eligible for a title after five years. This set of policies led to a fairly systematic settlement of much of Brazil; all regions except the North (Amazon) region had greater than 50 percent of the land area in farms by 1980.

Unlike in North America, a high degree of land conflict accompanied land settlement. Conflicts earlier in the twentieth century resulted from the high degree of squatting, the granting of land by state governors for political favors and sometimes overlapping grants, a lack of a general land office to register land claims, and a slowness in many states in granting titles. The last decade of the twentieth century witnessed a resurgence of land conflicts, largely due to increased squatting on private lands and increased resistance to evictions. The increased resistance resulted from a de facto land reform policy of the government of sometimes expropriating the squatted land from the titleholder and giving it to the squatters. This led to strategic squatting by peasants and increased efforts by landowners to evict. Unfortunately these conflicts stirred up considerable violence and all too frequently resulted in peasants being killed.

Overall the divergence in property rights to land in North and South America emerged early in the settlement process. The result was extremely large farms or ranches in much of South America and small family farms dominating North America, though plantations were important economically and politically in the southern United States from the early eighteenth century until the mid-nineteenth century. The differences in property rights resulted from the initial property rights established by the British, Portuguese, and Spanish; the feasible set of agricultural activities; and the responsiveness of governments to demands for strong property rights to land and demands for redistribution of land.

BIBLIOGRAPHY

Alston, Lee J., Gary D. Libecap, and Bernardo Mueller. "Property Rights and Land Conflict: A Comparison of Settlement of the U.S. Western and Brazilian Amazon Frontiers." In *Latin America and the World Economy since 1800*, edited by John H. Coatsworth and Alan M. Taylor, pp. 55–84. Cambridge, 1998.

Alston, Lee J., Gary D. Libecap, and Bernardo Mueller. "A Model of Rural Conflict: Violence and Land Reform Policy in Brazil." *Environment and Development Economics* 4 (1999), 135–160.

Alston, Lee J., Gary D. Libecap, and Bernardo Mueller. *Titles, Conflict, and Land Use: The Development of Property Rights and Land Reform on the Brazilian Amazon Frontier*. Ann Arbor, 1999.

Alston, Lee J., Gary D. Libecap, and Bernardo Mueller. "Property Rights to Land and Land Reform: Legal Inconsistencies and the Sources of Violent Conflict in the Brazilian Amazon." *Journal of Environmental Economics and Management* (2000).

Alston, Lee J., Gary D. Libecap, and Robert Schneider. "Property Rights and the Preconditions for Markets: The Case of the Amazon Frontier." *Journal of Institutional and Theoretical Economics* 151.1 (1995), 89–107.

Alston, Lee J., Gary D. Libecap, and Robert Schneider. "The Determinants and Impact of Property Rights: Land Titles on the Brazilian Frontier." *Journal of Law, Economics and Organization* 12 (1996), 25–61.

Alston, Lee J., and Morton Owen Schapiro. "Inheritance Laws across Colonies: Causes and Consequences." *Journal of Economic History* 44 (1984), 277–287.

Amaral, Samuel. *The Rise of Capitalism on the Pampas: The Estancias of Buenos Aires, 1785–1870*. Cambridge, 1998.

Anderson, Terry L., ed. *Property Rights in Indian Economies*. Lanham, Md., 1992.

Anderson, Terry L., and Peter J. Hill. "The Evolution of Property Rights: A Study of the American West." *Journal of Law and Economics* 18 (1975), 163–179.

Anderson, Terry L., and Peter J. Hill. "The Race for Property Rights." *Journal of Law and Economics* 33 (1990), 177–197.

Barzel, Yoram. *Economic Analysis of Property Rights*. Cambridge, 1989.

Besley, Timothy. "Property Rights and Investment Incentives: Theory and Evidence from Ghana." *Journal of Political Economy* 103 (1995), 903–937.

Bidwell, Percy Wells, and John I. Falconer. *History of Agriculture in the Northern United States*. Washington, D.C., 1925.

Binswanger, Hans P., and Klaus Deininger. "Explaining Agricultural and Agrarian Policies in Developing Countries." *Journal of Economic Literature* 35.4 (1997), 1958–2005.

Dean, Warren. "Latifundia and Land Policy in Nineteenth Century Brazil." *Hispanic-American History Review* (November 1971), 606–625.

Furtado, Celso. *Formação econômica do Brasil*. Rio de Janeiro, 1961.

Glade, William. *The Latin American Economies: A Study of Their Institutional Evolution*. New York, 1969.

Hughes, Jonathan R. T. *Social Control in the Colonial Economy*. Charlottesville, Va., 1976.

Lima, Ruy C. *Pequena história territorial do Brasil: Sesmarias e terras devolutas*. Pôrto Alegre, Brazil, 1954.

Mueller, Bernardo. "The Economic History, Political Economy, and Frontier Settlement of Land in Brazil." Ph.D. diss., University of Illinois, 1995.

Mueller, Bernardo, et. al. "Land, Property Rights, and Privatization in Brazil." *Quarterly Review of Economics and Finance* 34 (1994), 261–280.

Ostrom, Elinor. *Governing the Commons: The Evolution of Institutions for Collective Action*. Cambridge, 1990.

Ostrom, Elinor, Roy Gardner, and James Walker. *Rules, Games, and Common Pool Resources*. Ann Arbor, 1994.

Platteau, Jean-Philippe. "The Evolutionary Theory of Property Rights as Applied to Sub-Saharan Africa: A Critical Assessment." *Development and Change* 27.1 (1996), 29–86.

Salvucci, Richard J. "Agriculture and the Colonial Heritage of Latin America: Evidence from Bourbon Mexico." In *Colonial Legacies: The Problem of Persistence in Latin American History*, edited by Jeremy Adelman. New York, 1999.

Simonsen, Roberto C. *História econômica do Brasil: 1500—1820*. São Paulo, 1937.

Smith, Henry E. "Semicommon Property Rights and Scattering in the Open Fields." *Journal of Legal Studies* 29 (2000), 131–170.

Stein, Stanley. *Vassouras: A Brazilian Coffee Country, 1850–1900*. Princeton, 1985.

Umbeck, John R. "Might Makes Rights: A Theory of the Formation and Initial Distribution of Property Rights." *Economic Inquiry* 19 (1981), 38–59.

Van Young, Eric. *Hacienda and Market in Eighteenth Century Mexico: The Rural Economy of the Guadalajara Region, 1675–1820*. Berkeley, 1981.

Van Young, Eric. "Mexican Rural History since Chevalier: The Historiography of the Colonial Hacienda." *Latin American Research Review* 18.3 (1983), 5–61.

LEE J. ALSTON AND BERNARDO MUELLER

Communal Control

Property rights in land refer to socially recognized rights to make and enforce decisions about the use of land. One of the property arrangements frequently observed throughout history has been the communal control of land. Various types of communities, ranging from small tribes to large states and from kinship groups to religious networks, have chosen communal allocation and control of property rights in land. For example, the rights to gather wood, grow crops, and graze animals on land have frequently been communally owned.

Communal control of land is not equivalent to open access. A communally owned piece of land is open only to the members of the community, not to outsiders, and the members' own rights are typically restricted. One of the characteristics of a property institution is the community's right to deny interference from the state and members of other communities with the community's right to manage property and also to exclude them from access to community land. In *Structure and Change in Economic History* (1981), Douglass North distinguishes between "common property resources" and "exclusive communal property rights" and relies on the development of the latter to explain the rise of agriculture in human history, "the first economic revolution." Whereas the exclusion of others is not possible for some common property resources, such as air and water, communal rights in land are exercised by the members of a community exclusively. This does not mean, however, that community members have open, unrestricted access to land. To avoid misuse or overuse of land, communities have typically developed various institutions that rationed members' own access to land and regulated who should use the land, when, and for what purposes. For example, a tribal chief, the whole village, or a democratically elected council made and enforced the regulations, making obedience to these regulations a prerequisite to membership in the community.

Open Field System. Perhaps the best-known examples of communal rights in land existed during the European medieval era under the system of agricultural production called the open field system, also known as the common field system. One of the characteristics of the open field system was the division of land between the privately held arable and the collectively owned nonarable land that was used mainly for grazing. Cropping and harvesting decisions on the arable land were made communally. In addition, the arable land reverted to common grazing land when the field was fallow, in a well-defined seasonal cycle. On the nonarable land and when the arable land was fallow, the villagers had common rights to graze their animals, gather firewood, and so on, subject to various regulations. For example, grazing rights were typically attached to land holdings, and a formal court or village meeting made decisions concerning land use.

Communal control of land has been observed in a rich variety of other settings in history. When the Spanish invaders seized the Inca Empire early in the sixteenth century, members of the localized corporate kin groups called the *ayllu*, a unit of Andean social organization above the family, had communal rights in land. Similarly, at the base of the Aztec social order were the tribal clans called the *calpultin*, who lived on the communal land owned by their lineage. Various religious or ideological groups, such as the Israeli kibbutz or nineteenth-century American religious communes like the Shakers and Amana colonies, established networks with communal property. Communal control of land was a significant component of the customary law in indigenous landholding systems in precolonial Africa, and communal rights in land similarly existed in ancient Mesopotamia, the *Kipat* system in Nepal, land communes in the Russian Empire, collective agriculture systems of, for example, China, eastern Europe, and the Soviet Union, and the *mushā'* system observed in Levantine villages in the late Ottoman period.

The wide variety of property arrangements with communal control of land can be categorized according to the status of land in the overall economic system of production and distribution. One possibility is for all property, including land and other productive resources, to be communally owned. In many tribal societies there was little personal property, and land was typically owned by kinship groups. Similarly, religious and secular communes typically controlled labor, capital, and land communally and allowed little personal property. As another possibility, some societies, such as Russian land communes, controlled land communally, even while holding most other property in private. In other cases, mixed or alternating property systems ruled the control of land. In the open field system, village land was divided into two parts, and private land reverted to communal land during the off-season. Similarly, the Tigray of Ethiopia alternated land tenure between private and communal ownership as a way of controlling population growth.

Although we do not always know how and why communities chose communal control of land over its alternatives, it might be possible to distinguish between the intentional choice of communal control of land and its establishment as a "spontaneous order." Intentional choice of communal control could come from a religious, political, or ideological objective. Some communities, such as American religious communes, established communal control of land by starting a new society based on communal principles and making the voluntary acceptance of communal control a prerequisite to becoming a member. In other communities, a group of leaders changed the property arrangement from private to communal control by somehow coercing or persuading other members. Communal control as a spontaneous order, on the other hand, refers to an institution established on the basis of the self-interest of individuals without necessarily making a formal agreement or being subjected to compulsion. That communal control of land was an integral part of the open field system, despite vast differences among places where the open field system was observed, suggests an institution established as a spontaneous order.

Egalitarian principles have been important reasons some communities chose communal control of land. Socialistic societies and religious or secular communes typically considered sharing of wealth and egalitarian distribution of income important objectives and used egalitarian principles in regulating communal rights in land. Although communal control of land thus may have facilitated achieving a more equitable distribution of income, there might be limitations. For example, as the membership of a community grows, a single commune becomes harder to maintain, and communities often react to increasing size by establishing a network of communities. When the communities comprising the network are autonomous, however, inequalities among them are likely to occur. Although maintaining one large commune or introducing a formal redistribution mechanism among communes could eliminate these inequalities, the costs of coordination and motivation may be too high to establish

these mechanisms. Therefore the likelihood of achieving consistent egalitarian objectives through communal control of land might be restricted to single communities with small populations.

Problems and Regulations. The economic literature on property rights has identified several problems likely to arise in a system with communal control of land. One of these problems is the possibility of resource depletion because of overuse of the land, an idea that received widespread attention with the publication of Garret Hardin's classic paper titled "The Tragedy of the Commons," published in *Science* in 1968. If there were no restrictions on land use, each member of the community tended to overgraze or overwork the land to maximize the value of his or her communal rights. In grazing animals, for example, each member of the community would have an incentive to put more and more animals on the communal land, because in doing so he or she would receive the direct private benefits from these animals while other members would bear the costs. Problems of open access, however, should not be confused with problems of communal control. When a community has exclusive rights in land, it has an incentive to monitor the activities of its members to ensure its long-term economic viability. Indeed, as mentioned above, communities have typically instituted mechanisms to regulate the use of communal rights in land. In the open field system, for example, to prevent overgrazing, various restrictions typically were placed on the number and kinds of animals that could be pastured. Although the possibility of free riding still existed, communal regulations greatly reduced the potential for the problem of resource depletion.

The negotiation and enforcement of these regulations, however, can be costly. For example, in systems of property arrangements that require unanimous agreement by community members for adoption of a regulation, the cost of negotiating an agreement can be prohibitively high because each person would have a monopoly right to block the agreement. This creates a potential "anticommons" problem, the inability to use resources productively. When a centralized agent, such as a ruler or an elected council, rather than a decentralized mechanism is used to make decisions, the cost of making decisions can still be high despite lower agreement requirements. Because the coordination of the use of land would require detailed information about such things as technology, resources, and individual preferences, it would be difficult for a centralized agent to decide how best to restrain the use of land. Moreover, even if the cost of making rules might be low, the cost of enforcing them might be high because every member of the community would have an incentive to break the rule and appropriate some private gain at the expense of other members. The community must incur some cost to police the behavior of the members and enforce the rules.

Alternatives. To cope with the high costs of negotiation and enforcement of communal regulations, societies have developed various social institutions. In *Governing the Commons* (1990), Elinor Ostrom studied various long-enduring and self-governing institutional arrangements that societies have developed to manage what she calls "common-pool resources" and the origins and evolution of some of these institutions. Her examples show some of the principles that facilitated members of communities to commit to conforming rules and to monitor each other's conformance. Similarly, complex rules and regulations observed in the open field system and other historical examples of communal control of land show the ways communities developed various institutions to reduce the cost of negotiating and enforcing agreements.

Another potential problem with communal control of land emerges when members of the community till the land jointly as a team. If a community controls production on arable land and distributes output to its members according to rules, such as equal sharing, that do not depend on members' individual efforts, the independence between income and effort creates an incentive problem. Because the incremental revenue produced by additional effort is not directly reflected in a member's income, each member of the community has an incentive to choose suboptimal levels of effort and a "free ride" on the efforts of others. Suboptimal levels of effort by all members then result in an inefficient level of total output. The standard incentive theory thus leads to expectations of communal control of the arable land as less productive than private control, where each member has maximum incentives to work on his or her own land. Others have argued, however, that communities can avoid the incentive problem through social institutions like mutual monitoring, communal work ethic, and behavioral interdependence. For example, studying the productivity of Shaker communes quantitatively in a comparative setting, Metin Coşgel and John Murray (1998) found that, all else being equal, communal farms were as productive as private ones.

Underlying all potential problems that the economic literature on property rights has identified with communal control of land is the free rider problem, the incentive of every member of a community to seek greater private gains at the expense of the rest of the community. As the historical evidence shows, however, communities manage or avoid the problem by developing social institutions that regulate behavior.

[*See also* Common Goods *and* Open-Field System.]

BIBLIOGRAPHY
Bartlett, Roger, ed. *Land Commune and Peasant Community in Russia: Communal Forms in Imperial and Early Soviet Society*. New York, 1990.
Bassett, Thomas J., and Donald E. Crummey, eds. *Land in African Agrarian Systems*. Madison, Wis., 1993.
Coşgel, Metin, and John Murray. "Productivity of a Commune: The Shakers, 1850–1880." *Journal of Economic History* 58.2 (1998), 494–510.
Dahlman, Carl. *The Open Field System and Beyond: A Property Rights Analysis of an Economic Institution*. Cambridge, 1980.
Demsetz, Harold. "Toward a Theory of Property Rights." *American Economic Review* 57 (1967), 347–359.
Ellickson, Robert. "Property in Land." *Yale Law Journal* 102 (1993), 1315–1400.
Field, Barry C. "The Evolution of Property Rights." *Kyklos* 42.2 (1989), 319–345.
Hardin, Garret. "The Tragedy of the Commons." *Science* 162 (1968), 1243–1248.
Keohane, Robert, and Elinor Ostrom. *Local Commons and Global Interdependence: Heterogeneity and Cooperation in Two Domains*. London, 1995.
Libecap, Gary. *Contracting for Property Rights*. New York, 1989.
Neeson, J. M. *Commoners: Common Right, Enclosure, and Social Change in England, 1700–1820*. Cambridge, 1993.
Ostrom, Elinor. *Governing the Commons*. Cambridge, 1990.
North, Douglass. *Structure and Change in Economic History*. New York and London, 1981.
Oved, Yaakov. *Two Hundred Years of American Communes*. New Brunswick, N.J., 1988.

METIN M. COŞGEL

PROSTITUTION. Prostitution may not be the world's oldest profession, but it appears on a list of occupations in Babylon in 2400 BCE. Commercial prostitutes were clearly distinguished from temple prostitutes, women who served—either temporarily or as bonded servants—in temples and whose sexual relations with strangers were thought to bring both parties closer to divinity. Although little is known about Babylonian commercial prostitutes, they seem to have come from recently impoverished farming families, the daughters of men who had lost their land through debt; what they did with their earnings, and whether they helped their parents regain their land, is not known. But it is known that commercial prostitution was commonplace in ancient Greece and ancient Rome, and that most such women came from impoverished rural families; what is not known is what they did with their earnings. But earnings from prostitution were great, and in many of the Muslim parts of Spain, city-states earned revenues from owning and running brothels, staffed by impoverished women about whom little is known. The issue of who would control prostitution—whether its regulation should be done by secular or religious authorities—continued well into the early-modern period, which saw a gradual criminalization of prostitution: it become less of a sin and more of a vice that had to be legislated against.

In the medieval west, prostitution was tolerated. Most medieval prostitution was concentrated in cities. One thirteenth-century writer compared prostitutes to sewers—in a metaphor of urban pollution that was to continue for six centuries—necessary, unpleasant, and best concentrated in one part of a city. Some towns, eager to earn revenue from—and through—prostitutes, set up municipal brothels, regulated and run by the city itself, such as the one in the Venetian Rialto. In other towns, authorities licensed certain taverns and bathhouses for prostitution; such licenses gave the towns revenue and protected women from beatings and rape by customers. In many towns, it was said that prostitutes were foreign women—Flemish women in France and Great Britain, for example—and it is generally thought that these women were unwed mothers or young widows unable to maintain themselves in their homelands. Whether they sent their earnings home or sought to establish themselves were they worked is not known. In many places, prostitutes were made to wear special clothing to distinguish them from other women, but whether this was to stigmatize prostitutes to attempt to keep respectable women from engaging in occasional prostitution is not at all clear. In any case, the lines between respectability and prostitution were often blurred by long-term informal liaisons that ranged from servile relationships, as in concubinage, to formal contractual relations in which women pledged sexual fidelity to a man who was married to someone else.

Prostitution in the Modern Era. The location of prostitution in the realm of vice and illegality framed much of its conduct in the modern era. After 1800, when prostitution came to be thought of as a particularly modern and social evil brought about by the increasing industrialization of part of the world and the conquest of the rest, both the work women did and the earnings they derived from their work were outside the law. But because the moneys with which men paid prostitutes came either from their wages or capital, or from their savings, and because prostitutes often reinvested their earnings in family farms or their own property, it is possible to reconstruct broad, global economic patterns of prostitution since 1800.

Indeed, prostitution tends to become widespread when wage labor becomes a commonplace livelihood for men, often replacing agriculture or crafts. When the demand for male labor is intense, and when male earnings are relatively great, enough self-employed prostitutes—whether on the streets or in their own rooms, working occasionally or for many years—were either tolerated by incipient forms of state control or considered part and parcel of the flow of available labor power. Some of the conventional explanations for the causes of prostitution, the breakdown of families or sex ratios of eight or ten or fifteen men to one women do not explain prostitution in any way, nor are they always accurate, but they are shorthands for the disruption that accompanies a rapid increase in male participation in wage labor.

Brothels and pimps—relationships in which women are someone's employees—tend to develop relatively late in the history of prostitution, the result of attempts to eradicate vice and to save male wage labor from the ravages of women's expropriation strategies. When it became illegal for a women to be self-employed on the street, women began to require the services of men to negotiate the world of law and danger for them. If the streets are in the East End of London or Nairobi, or if the brothels are in Guatemala City or Shanghai or Paris, there are economic and social differences that shape some of the practices that constitute prostitution, but the ways prostitutes do their work, the forms of labor they use when they sell sexual relations, are shaped by the men's incomes and women's relationship to how men earn their incomes.

Types of Prostitution. All the work of prostitutes is reproductive—in fact, they sell that part of themselves—of male energies and family formations. Prostitutes perform tasks that most frequently include conversation, cooked food, toiletries—that restore, flatter, and revive male energies. Prostitutes sell sexual intercourse in a relationship, abrupt or deferential or anywhere in between. The question of why one woman walks the streets when another waits patiently in her room for well-to-do patrons and still another lives and works in a brothel is hardly one of personality, appearance, or upbringing; it cannot be explained by a women's vulnerability to male exploitation. Each of these forms of prostitution are accumulation strategies, each with specific rates of profit and ways of organizing labor time, that suggest not only why women entered prostitution but also what they did with their earnings as prostitutes. Each of these forms has a specific relationship to the women's own social reproduction, whether or not she supports the family into which she was born or into which she married, or uses her income to establish herself as an independent household. In short, whether a woman is on the streets, in her room, or outside her room calling out to passing men, all has to do with the rate of profit she seeks and the amount of time she will devote to earning those profits.

Prostitutes in their own rooms. Women who stay in their own rooms, whether call girls or the self-employed women in their rooms in Nairobi's oldest slum, made the greatest investment of their time and money in prostitution. They have been for the most part historically self-employed. Not only do they work out of their places of residence, or rent a room specifically for their prostitution, but they provide a greater range of services than do practitioners of any other form. Women provide, or have available, food and bathing facilities, and offer these as part of the services offered—and the services for which a man can be asked to pay for when he leaves. In this form, a woman asked to be paid at the end of the visit, not at the beginning,

BROTHEL. Frontispiece by Crispin de Passe to *Miroir des plus belle courtisanes de ce temps* (The looking-glass of the fairest courtiers of these tymes), seventeenth century. (By permission of the Folger Shakespeare Library, Washington, D.C.)

so that a man might pay for all he used, but that contains a great risk: a man might not pay, or might promise to pay next time, or might underpay. In each case, a woman must acquiesce. An argument over money could turn violent, and, more important, neighbors might be unhappy to protect a prostitute next door; a woman would accept little or no money occasionally to protect her ability to prostitute herself from her own room.

Indeed, women who practiced this form of prostitution insisted that these risks were outweighed by the advantages of the form, which was one of slow and steady accumulation. A man might pay very little after a night-long visit, to be sure, but the goal of this form of prostitution was slow and steady accumulation. Whatever a man might pay, he would be encouraged to come again and again, and to establish a regular relationship in which he would not only pay well for a night's visit, but also become a generous source of gifts. Moreover, night-long visits were infrequent in the long weeks between pay packets, but to ensure such a respectable but illicit relationship, a prostitute working out of her own room would do all that she could to not appear to be solely interested in money. This was not simply a self-preserving fiction, it was an identity—a profitable one.

In 1923, the elite "singing girls" of Shanghai protested attempts to register them by marching under banners that read "We sell our voices, not our bodies." Such practices made such prostitutes virtually invisible to police and reformers' surveillance, and despite reformers' obsessions with the number of prostitutes they could not see, prostitutes who worked from their own rooms remained self-employed long after many women on the streets were not. Such apparent passivity masked another strategy altogether, however—a pattern of long-term accumulation in which women earned money to establish themselves as independent heads of households. Such prostitutes in Nairobi invested their earnings in urban property, housing the very labor force who formed their clientele; and as they did so, they often made sure that their kinfolk could not inherit it when they died. Likewise, the census category in Helena, Montana, in the late nineteenth century for such women was "capitalists with rooms."

Streetwalkers. In most conventional wisdom, streetwalkers are considered anything but capitalists; at best they are considered the most vulnerable of prostitutes and at worst they are considered the most degraded and disgraced. Yet the form is not only extremely widespread—it is, after all, the only form of prostitution available to homeless women, including the ubiquitous runaways that reformers from North America to East Africa worried about—it is extremely profitable, which explains why so many women continued to practice this form of prostitution long after they had acquired the wherewithal for a few months' rent. Indeed, women on the streets boasted that this was the best—and the safest—way to earn money from prostitution: Women chose the streets they walked on, and there a careful woman could chose an elite clientele. Nairobi streetwalkers stated that they could tell by the make of a car how much to charge a man. On the streets, often with one's competitors nearby, a women could refuse a man who seemed either threatening or poor; and even though there have been some heinous exceptions, police records from nineteenth-century France or twentieth-century Nairobi, Toronto, and Shanghai indicate that streetwalkers were very rarely victims of violence, compared to women in their own rooms. Nevertheless, there is social stigma to streetwalking, and it was certainly one of the most overtly competitive forms of prostitution. Why would a woman continue this work for more than a few weeks?

Streetwalkers provided the least amount of domestic labor of any form of prostitution. They sometimes took customers to their rooms, but rarely provided food or all the amenities of a night-long visit. They most frequently negotiated the price in advance, thus making the nature of the transaction clear to all parties. Such prostitution, of course, was most profitable if a woman had several customers in one night—generally thought to be the epitome of the humiliation and degradation of prostitutes—and this was precisely the goal of most streetwalkers. Several customers a night, a tidy profit for a few hours' work, and a woman could go home and have the rest of the day to herself, free to attend to childcare. Why would women subject themselves to such repeated indignities? The overwhelming evidence is that streetwalking, with its intense level of accumulation, was the form of prostitution chosen by daughters of agriculturalists, recently impoverished by drought, disease, land laws, and the ravages of invasive state control.

By and large, in Shanghai, on the streets of Honolulu, Elko, Nairobi, Dar es Salaam, London, or Manchester, women who walked the streets did so in order to support, and sometimes bail out, rural households that were facing ruin. The most aggressive prostitution was the behavior of the most dutiful of daughters. Older women who worked as streetwalkers—to the horror of reformers around the world—had the same goals: They were wives and mothers and aunts and sisters who walked the streets to support husbands, children, and daughters.

Homebound prostitutes. The women who sat outside the doors of their homes, or on the porches of the houses in which they rented rooms, or in the windows of their rooms, and waited for men to come to them were called the *wazi-wazi* in Nairobi (from the Swahili word meaning *open,* as in exposed) or *crib prostitutes* in the American West (for the size of their quarters). They actively solicited men but could refuse any customer before he was allowed in the women's room. Worldwide, such prostitutes called out their price to passing men, which other prostitutes saw as a lowering of the overall prices in a neighborhood, and provided few if any domestic services once they took a man to their room. Such prostitutes specialized in brief sexual encounters for which they charged a fixed price, most often maintained at a stable but low rate by the density of prostitutes living in the same building or nearby. Such work was most profitable when the numbers of male migrant laborers skyrocketed, and indeed, prostitutes in Gold Rush San Francisco or in Katsina in Nigeria posted their prices on their doors. This was a form of prostitution favored by women newly arrived in a city—Japanese prostitutes in Hawaii, Jewish prostitutes in New York's Lower East Side in 1900, Tanzanian women in Nairobi during World War II—who had little stake in maintaining the decorum of a given neighborhood and whose interests were in sending money to their far-off homes, not establishing themselves in town right away. By and large, this was the form of prostitution practiced by women from recently impoverished households, women who used the high volume, high profits of the form to restore a family's fortunes. Like streetwalkers, these women did not buy property for themselves where they worked; they bought property—in town or the countryside or even their homeland—for their parents, their brothers, their husbands.

Brothels. Straddling the space between women who waited in their rooms and the women who waited outside their rooms were brothels, and all the labor and economic relations that were obtained in them. Indeed, many madams began as prostitutes with their own rooms, and their property investments were used to rent to prostitutes and to keep brothels. For these women, property ownership and brothel management invariably were forms of independent accumulation, establishing themselves as independent household heads rather than supporting their families. For these women, the greatest profits were not from their own or their employees' sale of sexual relations, but from nonsexual services.

Nineteenth-century brothels in London and San Francisco estimated that their greatest profits came from liquor sales; madams in nineteenth-century Paris realized their greatest profits from renting clothes to their employees. For the women who were their employees, work in a brothel often developed from streetwalking or were recruited from the immigrant women sitting outside their rooms. Invariably, these were women performing family labor, working to support households that could no longer support its young women. Madams in late nineteenth-century Saint Paul, Minnesota, recruited within families, asking women working for them to bring their siblings off the streets to work for them. Teenage brothel prostitutes in Bangkok, often regarded as the world's most exploited prostitutes, sent almost two hundred thousand dollars back to one rural area in 1976.

Prostitution, then, was family labor in which women supported the households into which they were born or, less often, married, or worked to establish themselves as household heads. Their ability to profit from prostitution was shaped by the labor form—or combination of forms—they used in their work, and how that form is embedded into a relationship between migrant labor, the availability of housing, and state intervention.

BIBLIOGRAPHY

Best, Joel. "Careers in Brothel Prostitution: Saint Paul, 1865–1883." *Journal of Interdisciplinary History* 12.4 (1982), 597–619.

Bujra, Janet M. "Women 'Entrepreneurs' of Early Nairobi." *Canadian Journal of African Studies* 9.2 (1976), 213–234.

Guy, Donna. "White Slavery, Public Health, and the Socialist Position on Legalized Prostitution in Argentina, 1913–1936." *Latin American Research Review* 23.3 (1988), 60–80.

Harsin, Jill. *Policing Prostitution in Nineteenth-Century Paris.* Princeton, 1985.

Hershatter, Gail. *Dangerous Pleasures: Prostitution and Modernity in Twentieth-Century Shanghai.* Stanford, Calif., 1999.

Hirata, Lucie Cheng. "Free, Indentured, Enslaved: Chinese Prostitutes in Nineteenth-Century America." *Signs: A Journal of Women in Culture and Society* 5.1 (1979), 3–29.

McCreery, David. "'This Life of Misery and Shame': Female Prostitution in Guatamala City, 1880–1920." *Journal of Latin American Studies* 12 (1987), 333–353.

Phongpaichit, Pasuk. *From Peasant Girl to Bangkok Masseuses.* Geneva, 1982.

Rosen, Ruth. *The Lost Sisterhood: Prostitution in America, 1900–1918.* Baltimore, 1982.

Walkowitz, Judith R. *Prostitution and Victorian Society: Women, Class, and the State.* Cambridge, 1980.

Walkowitz, Judith R. *City of Dreadful Delight: Narratives of Sexual Danger in Late Victorian London.* Chicago, 1992.

White, Luise. *The Comforts of Home: Prostitution in Colonial Nairobi.* Chicago, 1990.

LUISE WHITE

PROTECTIONISM. *See* Commercial Policy, *subentry on* Tariffs.

PROTO-INDUSTRIALIZATION. *See* Domestic Industry.

PROVENCE. Three key features distinguish the medieval economy of the French province of Provence: its urban character, a legacy from the Roman past; its thriving agriculture; and the significant number of free landholders. For the history of Provence during the first half of the Middle Ages, the paucity of sources hinders any analysis of its economic evolution. It seems clear, however, that military disturbances from the incursions of Germanic-Frankish tribes caused less devastation than epidemic disease, from the mid-fifth century to the eighth century. Subsequently, under the first Carolingians, the economy grew, and settlement expanded along the coast and the Rhone and Durance Valleys. Small landholders and aristocratic proprietors on large estates *(villae)* produced a wide variety of goods: wheat, olive oil, wine, meat, fish, and salt. But with the Muslim incursion during the late ninth century and the early tenth century, the unprotected villagers and landlords dispersed into the forests and mountains of Upper Provence.

There, after the liberation of Provence at the end of the tenth century, an economic takeoff and demographic expansion first appeared. At this juncture a distinctive form of feudalism developed. The counts of Provence exercised limited authority over a host of lesser lords, who increasingly imposed bondage on the peasantry, especially in Upper Provence. In Lower Provence, however, significant numbers of landholders remained free, and where intensive agriculture required much labor, peasants secured lifetime or perpetual leases on seigniorial domains. In the thirteenth century, when the counts were intent on reaffirming their power, this land management system spread. Their centralized administration and their activities at the papal court in Avignon from 1309 stimulated commerce and trade. Even earlier, the commercial privileges the port city of Marseille enjoyed until the Mamluk conquest of Acre, made it in 1291 a major Mediterranean center for redistribution of Flemish cloth and exotic products. Urban revival spread to other harbors and cities (Arles, Nice, Aix, Sisteron, Tarascon, and Grasse), spurred by general growth in the Provencal population, which soared to nearly half a million people in the early fourteenth century. By then early signs had appeared of the long economic recession brought by famine, disease, and demographic crisis.

Climatic factors and especially warfare and brigandage caused food shortages throughout the fourteenth century, even after recurring waves of plague seriously reduced the population. Numerous fields and villages were permanently abandoned, with consequences lasting until the fifteenth century. As inhabited areas contracted, population became more concentrated, cattle raising increased, the lease management system spread, and workers flocked to the cities of Lower Provence from Upper Provence and foreign regions. Economic recovery was slower in Provence than in some other regions of southern Europe, Italy especially, and became evident only after 1470. By the end of the fifteenth century traditional and new industries (leather, wool and cloth, silk, paper, glass, and soap) rejuvenated the urban economies, and trade intensified between regions and with neighboring countries.

At the end of the Middle Ages a transformed Provence already manifested conditions that became more prominent during the ancien regime. In particular the gap had widened between Upper Provence, with fewer people in smaller villages, and Lower Provence, with its constellation of large villages and towns. But since the peasant and urban economies were so closely intertwined, the Provencal cities, unlike their Italian counterparts, retained a distinctive rural flavor.

BIBLIOGRAPHY

Baratier, Édouard. *La démographie provençale du XIIIe au XVIe siècle, avec chiffres de comparaison pour le XVIIIe siècle.* Paris, 1961.

Baratier, Édouard. *Enquêtes sur les droits et revenus de Charles d'Anjou en Provence (1252 et 1278).* Paris, 1969.

Baratier, Édouard, ed. *Histoire de la Provence.* Toulouse, 1969.

Coulet, Noël, and Louis Stouff. *Le village de Provence au bas Moyen Âge.* Aix-en-Provence, France, 1987.

Février, Paul-Albert. *Le développement urbain en Provence: De l'époque romaine à la fin du XIVe siècle.* Paris, 1964.

Pryor, John H. *Business Contracts of Medieval Provence: Selected "Notulae" from the Cartulary of Giraud Amalric of Marseilles, 1248.* Toronto, 1981.

F. G. MICHAUD

PRUSSIA. Dominant themes are, first, early modern Prussia's agrarian development, widely seen as establishing a noble landlordism and peasant subjection forming the military-bureaucratic absolutist state's social foundation. Second looms the question of eighteenth-century "mercantilist" commercial-industrial development by government fiat. Third stands the Prussian state's role in nineteenth-century German industrialization and economic unification.

The Rise of the Junkers. Junkers were the medieval nobility who settled the lands of pre-1945 northeastern Germany, from the Elbe River in the west to the southeastern Baltic land of Prussia in the east. The aristocratic Order of the Teutonic Knights conquered Baltic Prussia, which in 1618 fused with a state centered on Berlin to become Brandenburg-Prussia. From 1701 this state was the Kingdom of Prussia, an archipelago of provinces reaching from the lower Rhine to Brandenburg and Pomerania across intervening Polish land to East Prussia.

The Teutonic Knights developed Prussia into a well-documented grid of large-scale demesne farms producing grain and other products for westward export. After the order's 1525 secularization, the demesne farms became ducal estates or passed into the hands of the privatized nobility. In Brandenburg, as elsewhere in East Elbia, the gentry responded to the favorable markets of the "long sixteenth century" by expanding originally modest seigneurial demesnes into large estates. To gain unpaid labor, noble landlords and administrators of similar, newly established princely demesne farms exploited seigneurial authority over freeholding but tribute-bound village farmers to impose new and oppressive labor services, typically three days weekly with a team for full holders and three days of weekly manual labor for smallholders.

Thus arose, in the standard intepretation, a condominium of Junkers and the Brandenburg-Prussian state over an immiserated countryside. When, after 1640, Prussia's Hohenzollern princes undertook absolutist state building, starting with a standing army funded by heavy new rural taxation, they gained the nobility's assent by granting them new exploitative powers over their subjects. The Junkers' export orientation and their villagers' poverty injured bourgeois interests. Their sons entered state service as army officers and high officials, renewing a crown-nobility alliance in a regime rich in military-bureaucratic authoritarianism and poor in civil society autonomy and sturdy yeomen.

Recent research refocuses this picture. Early modern commercialized manorialism earned nobility and crown-estate administrators good incomes, but subject farmers largely evaded personal enserfment and threadbare misery. The new labor services amounted to rent increases following late medieval decline in cash and product rents. Yet, in the period from 1618 to 1806, villagers used their command of scarce labor and animal traction that are indispensable to the cultivation of the aristocratic-princely estates and their access to princely adjudication to resist further increase in feudal rents. The absolutist regime protected them from seigneurial eviction because they were its prime taxpayers. Large estates did not stifle technological innovation and productivity gains. Commercialized manorialism's sixteenth-century emergence produced extensive growth, while eighteenth-century landlords, eager to expand sales and facing subject farmers' resistance to heightened labor services, moved in large numbers to fallow-free, convertible (cereal fodder) agriculture worked increasingly by estate-housed free wage laborers. In the 1807–1816 "peasant emancipation" triggered by Napoleon's 1806 defeat of Prussia, landholding subject villagers gained unencumbered personal freedom and family-sized freehold farms in exchange for land or cash paid their former lordships. Henceforth, until 1945, some two-thirds of East Elbian Prussian farmland lay in villagers'—mainly middle and big family farmers'—hands, while the rest comprised large estates worked by wage labor and increasingly owned by non-nobles. Considering villagers' centuries-long contention with landlords over feudal rent, and their increasingly frequent recourse to the royal law courts, the argument that commercialized manorialism reduced rural commoners to silent submission loses force and with it inferences about Junker landlordism's authoritarian effects.

Sparta of the North. Under kings Frederick William I (r. 1713–1740) and Frederick II "the Great" (r. 1740–1786), government-planned and royally financed economic development reached an intensity rare in absolutist Europe. By Frederick II's death the army, in a kingdom of fewer than 6 million, counted about 250,000 soldiers. Keen on multiplying their subjects' numbers, the Hohenzollern successfully settled hundreds of thousands of foreign colonists on reclaimed land while establishing a productive population of Jews and middle-class French Huguenots in the towns. The extensive crown estates, which with their dependent villages and forests comprised a third or more of the kingdom's land, were leased for renewable six-year terms exclusively to non-noble tenant farmers. These entrepreneurs readily followed government exhortations to productivity-enhancing innovations, creating models of fallow-free convertible farming for the nobility to emulate. The government improved its crown-estate subject farmers' tenures and rents, converting them in large numbers before 1806 into free perpetual leaseholders. Frederick II's army magazines bought and sold domestic grain to maintain tolerable prices for both urban buyers and rural sellers. The government had long opened or closed the land to grain exports according to its assessment of domestic needs despite the Junkers' zeal for free trade.

To supply the army, Frederick William I founded a government-run wool manufactory for uniforms and issued monopolies to private armaments makers. Frederick II greatly expanded the monopoly system, including expensively subsidized silk and porcelain works. He invested heavily in Berlin housing, bestowing new buildings gratis on landowners. Though the state-dependent Royal Bank opened in 1766, Frederick's regime financed its affairs with the help of numerous private bankers, some of them risk-laden "court Jews," and the government-controlled Prussian Seehandlung, a multipurpose commercial and financial institution established in 1772. The eighteenth-century kings accumulated large treasures, which proved useful in war. Frederick II incurred unpopularity by farming Prussian taxes after 1766 to a French-run consortium.

The most successful of eighteenth-century absolutist policies were those aimed at developing the mining and metallurgical industries of the resource-rich province of Silesia, conquered from Austria. Enforcing Frederick's comprehensive government regulation of extractive industries, the royal Mining Corps proceeded to open model mines and foundaries in Upper Silesia, supplying them with steam engine–driven pumps and coke-burning smelting furnaces. The corps also effectively encouraged private entrepreneurship. Although absolutist-subsidized textile or luxury-goods operations sometimes ran at deficits and

disappointed consumers, by 1800 state-patronized wool, linen, and cotton production was considerable. Yet the Mennonite silk manufacturers in Prussia's Rhenish town of Krefeld prospered impressively independent of the state.

Eighteenth-century statistics display rising agricultural output, land and commodity prices, urban and rural population, and tax revenues. Though real wages among the urban unskilled and misfortune-stricken countrypeople were low, living standards for artisan masters and self-sufficient, surplus-selling family farmers, including retired elders, were often good in comparison with the west. Many among the educated and propertied classes lived in comfort and even luxury. Measured against post–Thirty Years' War (1618–1648) conditions, absolutist Prussia had, by the Industrial Revolution's eve, grown markedly richer and more productive.

A Century of Prussian Liberalism. Rejecting Frederick II's rigid statism, late eighteenth-century Prussian intellectuals embraced Adam Smith's teachings enthusiastically. The high officials who dominated the Prussian reform era (1807–1819) restructured state and society in a liberal spirit. Apart from the "peasant emancipation," the reformers proclaimed "industrial freedom" ending guild restrictions, enfranchised the Jewish middle and upper classes, replaced absolutist taxes with new and simplified levies, and initiated a Prussian customs union that by 1834 expanded into the German Customs Union, creating a wide free-trade zone (though Austria stayed aloof). The European great powers' bestowal on Prussia in 1815 of the Rhineland and adjacent Saar and Ruhr coalfields profoundly changed the state's economic structure. In these western regions, steam-driven industry and railroad building broke through in the 1820s and 1830s to an industrialization that, following sharp economic recession in 1844–1848, sustained rapid growth throughout Prussia.

Economic historians long judged the post-1815 state's fostering of technological innovation and capital formation through the investments of the Prussian Seehandlung, the Business Department, and the Mining Corps as growth accelerators and catalysts of industrialization. While state-generated annual net industrial investment reached impressive levels (11–12 percent in the years 1830–1848), it often preempted private investments that otherwise would have occurred. Yet considering that nineteenth-century German industrialization owed its spark to railroad building and associated industries, the state's vigorous championship, after initial conservative indecision, of private railroad construction paid rich dividends.

By the 1840s, criticism of statism was rife among businesspeople. The government's creation of the Customs

Union earned widespread applause, but tariffs long remained too low to protect infant industries from British competition effectively, and restrictions on joint-stock companies and patents impeded growth. After the 1848–1849 revolution, the government largely abandoned its industrial investments and mining regulation. Under the direction of Chancellor Otto von Bismarck's liberal commercial and financial policy maker Rudolf Delbrück (in office 1862–1876), the Prussian government complemented German political unification with modern economic legislation on all fronts, lifting the 1871 German Empire into its meteoric economic ascent.

Prussia's triumphant self-transformation in the new empire brought to a close, as the incorporation of the Rhineland had earlier begun, its history as an independent sociopolitical entity. Its economy was one that, under often enterprising and innovative state direction, adapted successfully through four centuries to new technologies and market opportunities. Despite noble privilege, feudal inertia exerted little influence over Prussian economic history, while the bourgeoisie drew more advantage from cooperation with the princely regime than from fighting it.

BIBLIOGRAPHY

Brophy, James M. *Capitalism, Politics, and Railroads in Prussia, 1830–1870.* Columbus, Ohio, 1998.

Brose, Eric Dorn. *The Politics of Technological Change in Prussia: Out of the Shadow of Antiquity, 1809–1848.* Princeton, 1993.

Diefendorf, Jeffry M. *Businessmen and Politics in the Rhineland, 1789–1834.* Princeton, 1980.

Hagen, William W. "How Mighty the Junkers? Peasant Rents and Seigneurial Profits in Sixteenth-Century Brandenburg." *Past and Present* 108 (1985), 80–116.

Hagen, Willian W. "Seventeenth-Century Crisis in Brandenburg: The Thirty Years' War, the Destabilization of Serfdom, and the Rise of Absolutism." *American Historical Review* 94 (1989), 302–335.

Hagen, William W. "Village Life in East-Elbian Germany and Poland, 1400–1800: Subjection, Self-Defense, Survival." In *The Peasantries of Europe from the Fourteenth to the Eighteenth Centuries,* edited by Tom Scott, pp. 145–190. London, 1998.

Kaufhold, Karl Heinrich. "Leistungen und Grenzen der Staatswirtschaft." In *Preussen: Beiträge zu einer politischen Kultur,* edited by Manfred Schlenke, pp. 106–119. Hamburg, 1981.

Kocka, Jürgen. "Entrepreneurs and Managers in German Industrialization." In *The Cambridge Economic History of Europe,* vol. 7, edited by Peter Mathias and M. M. Postan, pp. 492–589. Cambridge, 1978.

Lee, J. J. "Labour in German Industrialization." In *The Cambridge Economic History of Europe,* vol. 7, edited by Peter Mathias and M. M. Postan, pp. 442–491. Cambridge, 1978.

Melton, Edgar. "*Gutsherrschaft* in East Elbian Germany and Livonia, 1500–1800: A Critique of the Model." *Central European History* 21 (1988), 315–349.

Ogilvie, Shilagh, and Bob Scribner, eds. *Germany: A New Social and Economic History, 1450–1800.* 2 vols. London, 1996.

Tilly, Richard H. "Capital Formation in Germany in the Nineteenth Century." In *The Cambridge Economic History of Europe,* vol. 7, edited by Peter Mathias and M. M. Postan, pp. 382–441. Cambridge, 1978.

Tilly, Richard H. *Vom Zollverein zum Industriestaat. Die wirtschaftlich-soziale Entwicklung Deutschalnds 1834 bis 1914.* Munich, 1990.

Tipton, Frank. *Regional Variations in the Economic Development of Germany during the Nineteenth Century.* Middletown, Conn., 1976.

Treue, Wilhelm. *Wirtschafts- und Technikgeschichte Preussens.* Berlin, 1984.

WILLIAM W. HAGEN

PUBLIC ADMINISTRATION. One of the most prominent features of the twentieth century has been the growth of governments. Governments in rich countries, for whom the best data is available, grew steadily in absolute terms and as a share of gross domestic product (GDP). Governments in poor countries, for whom less data is available for earlier decades, may have grown as well, although the evidence is scanty. From the eighteenth century to the present day in Britain the growth of government has had its proponents and its opponents. There is evidence that larger governments slow the rate of economic growth by taking a larger share of resources from productive sectors of the economy and through onerous regulations that stifle creativity and encourage corruption and inefficiency. There is also evidence that the major difference between poor countries and rich countries is not geography, climate, or natural resources but the institutions that govern their economies, the most important of which is government. Ultimately there is no single resolution of this debate. Some governments are good for economic growth and their citizens' welfare. Some governments are truly horrible, both in retarding economic growth and in development and in causing untold harm and suffering to their citizens.

This essay reviews the history of government administration throughout the world in the twentieth century. Governments are examined from three perspectives: size, structure, and function. Size measures the share of GDP devoted to government revenues and expenditures. Structure measures the allocation of government activity among central or national governments and provincial, state, and local governments. Function measures the type of revenues governments collect and functions on which governments spend. To correlate the growth of government with economic development, each of these measured will be considered in relation to per capita income at the end of the twentieth century using data published by the World Bank and the International Monetary Fund (IMF). The essay then looks back over the entire twentieth century using data on the developed industrial economies. The numbers in the following tables are accurate, but they are averages of averages and therefore are dependent on the countries in the sample and the construction of the quintile groups. Readers who are interested in using this data should consult the original sources.

Size, Structure, and Functions of Government Today. The World Bank and IMF regularly gather and publish statistics on per capita income, economic performance, and government activity in countries around the world. Although there are over two hundred countries, not all report information on all statistics in every year. Complete data on per capita income, central government expenditures as a share of GDP, and provincial, state, and local government expenditures for the years between 1995 and 2000 are available for seventy-four countries. The following tables group countries by income quintiles, that is, by the poorest 20 percent of countries to the richest 20 percent of countries.

In Table 1 per capita income is measured in U.S. 1999 dollars per person as an average of annual per capita income for the years 1995 to 2000 (for years with available data). Total government, central government, and local government expenditures and revenues are calculated as a percentage of GDP (for ease of exposition, provincial, state, and local governments are referred to as "local government"). In the last two columns local government expenditures and revenues are calculated as a share of central government expenditures and revenues. The numbers for each of the quintiles represent the simple averages of each country in the quintile. The countries are not weighted by population, so, for example, India has the same weight as Nepal. Weighted averages and a more complete sample would produce slightly different results.

First, notice the wide distribution of income. Average income in the poorest quintile is $1,260 a year, while it is $16,307 in the richest quintile. The richest country is over fifty times richer than the poorest country. Richer countries have substantially larger governments. Government accounts for 29 percent of GDP in the poorest countries and 53 percent of GDP in the richest countries. This is also true at the different levels of government. Central governments account for 26 percent of GDP in the poorest countries and 35 percent of GDP in the richest countries. Yet provincial, state, and local governments account for only 2

percent of GDP in the poorest countries and 17 percent of GDP in the richest countries.

The strong positive correlation between per capita income and the size of government across countries is just that, a correlation. The fact that rich countries have larger governments than poor countries by itself does not reveal whether larger government causes income to grow or countries with higher incomes decide to spend more on government.

The last three columns of the table provide information on provincial, state, and local governments in these countries. Three important aspects stand out. First, local government expenditures as a share of GDP rise steadily as income rises. Rich countries have bigger governments overall, bigger central governments, and much bigger local governments than poor countries. The richest quintile of countries has central governments that are roughly 50 percent bigger than the poorest quintile of countries, while local government expenditures in the richest quintile are eight times larger than in the poorest quintile of countries, as a percentage of GDP. Second, as income increases across countries, so does the share of government expenditures and revenues undertaken by local, as opposed to central, governments. The local share of central government expenditures and revenues does not rise steadily by income quintile (more on that in a moment), but the richest quintiles have significantly larger local sectors relative to the central government. Third, expenditures are considerably more decentralized than revenues, that is, the local share of central government expenditures is greater than the local share of central government revenues for every quintile. In wealthier countries the central governments collect a larger share of revenues and then transfer funds to local governments through intergovernmental grants, so a larger share of expenditures is undertaken at the local level.

The most obvious reason some countries have more decentralized governments is the physical size of the

TABLE 1. *Size of Government as a Percentage of GDP and by Level of Government, by Income Quintiles, 1995–2000*

	Per capita income	Government expenditures as percentage of GDP	Government revenue as percentage of GDP	Central government expenditures as percentage of GDP	Central government revenues as percentage of GDP	Local government expenditures as percentage of GDP	Local revenues as percentage of central government expenditures	Local expenditures as percentage of central government revenues
Poorest 20 percent	1,260	29	27	26	24	2	7	11
Second 20 percent	2,767	31	28	28	26	3	4	9
Third 20 percent	5,038	37	35	30	26	7	22	32
Fourth 20 percent	9,883	37	34	32	30	5	8	14
Richest 20 percent	16,307	53	54	35	35	17	36	53

SOURCES: "Global Development Finance and World Development Indicators"; *Government Finance Statistics Yearbook*.

country. Large countries, like Argentina, Brazil, Canada, China, India, the Russian Federation, and the United States, must have a local sector because administration of basic government services requires smaller units of government. Many physically smaller countries have no reported local government expenditures or revenues. The most decentralized country in the world is Argentina, where local government expenditures are more than twice central government expenditures. But size cannot explain much of the fiscal decentralization in richer countries. In the richest quintile of countries in this sample, only Singapore reports no local sector, yet the quintile includes countries as physically small as Luxembourg, Belgium, Denmark, and Switzerland. The concluding section considers other explanations for why richer countries have more decentralized governments. Again, correlation is not causation.

The functions of government are divided into two groups: taxes and expenditures. For a larger sample of 110 countries, again using data from the IMF, Table 2 presents the share of all government revenues that comes from various tax sources. This data applies only to central governments. The first column gives per capita income by quintile, and the second column gives the share of total revenues reported as individual functions in the IMF report (the IMF numbers are not broken down completely). The table does not report revenues from all sources, just the most important ones: taxes on income, profits, and capital gains (which are broken down in the next two columns into taxes on individuals and corporations); taxes levied for social security contributions; taxes levied on domestic goods and services; and taxes on international trade and transactions.

The income quintiles in this table are slightly different from those in Table 1 because the sample is larger. High-income countries differ from low-income countries in three important ways. First, although all countries rely on taxes on income, profits, and capital gains, only the richest countries rely heavily on the personal income tax. Second,

taxes levied for social security contributions rise steadily with income. Third, taxes on international trade and transactions decline steadily with income. The figures in Table 2 can be understood in a different way. Taxes levied for social security programs are typically income or payroll taxes, and taxes on international trade and transactions are often tariffs (either per unit or by value) and are much like sales taxes on individual exchanges. In the richest quintile of countries broad-based income taxes (including social security contributions) make up roughly 50 percent of all government revenues, while in the poorest quintile of countries taxes on exchange make up about 60 percent of all government revenues.

On the expenditure side, Table 3 gives expenditures by major function. Reporting of government expenditures is less complete than for revenues. Detailed breakdowns are available for only 70 percent of expenditures in the two poorest quintiles. Poor countries tend to spend a larger share of their budgets on "general public services and public order" and on education, while richer countries tend to spend a larger share of their budgets on health and on "social security and welfare" programs.

Size, Structure, and Functions of Government Historically. Comparable data for the twentieth century is only available for the developed countries of the Western world. Vito Tanzi and Luger Schuknecht (2000) recently compiled statistics on government in the twentieth century. Wherever possible, they report statistics on all governments: national, provincial, state, and local. Table 4 reports revenues in total and by basic revenue types.

As before, these numbers are averages of figures for individual countries and are not weighted by country size, and not all categories of revenues are included in the details of the table. Blank cells in the table occur when no figures are reported by Tanzi and Schuknecht for that year. At the end of the nineteenth century revenues accounted for about 9 percent of GDP in what would become the developed countries of the twentieth century. Over the course of

TABLE 2. *Share of Central Government Revenue by Revenue Source, by Income Quintiles, 1995–2000*

Quintile's Mean Per Capita Income	Share of Detailed Revenues Reported	Taxes on Income, Profits, Capital Gains	Taxes on Individuals	Taxes on Corporations	Taxes on Social Security	Taxes on Domestic Goods and Services	Taxes on International Trade and Transaction
831	90.4	21.0	9.1	9.2	1.7	28.8	29.0
2,053	91.4	22.1	6.2	10.9	5.3	36.3	12.9
3,523	89.9	24.5	7.2	11.1	8.5	25.9	15.6
7,264	95.0	24.6	9.9	11.3	14.7	32.1	7.1
15,594	93.2	31.5	21.2	7.5	20.4	27.1	3.0

Sources: "Global Development Finance and World Development Indicators"; *Government Finance Statistics Yearbook.*

TABLE 3. *Share of Central Government Expenditures by Expenditure Function, by Income Quintile, 1995–2000*

PER CAPITA INCOME	SHARE OF DETAILED EXPENDITURES REPORTED	GENERAL PUBLIC SERVICES AND PUBLIC ORDER	DEFENSE	EDUCATION	HEALTH	SOCIAL SECURITY AND WELFARE
831	68.4	18.8	9.8	16.4	5.3	7.5
2,053	71.2	13.5	9.6	13.3	6.1	11.2
3,523	84.7	18.4	8.7	16.0	9.5	14.1
7,264	82.2	12.7	8.0	13.4	7.2	25.3
15,594	84.1	10.4	8.4	9.9	11.0	31.2

SOURCES: "Global Development Finance and World Development Indicators"; *Government Finance Statistics Yearbook.*

the twentieth century revenues rose from 9 percent to 43 percent of GDP, with the most rapid growth coming before 1980. "Direct taxes" are taxes levied directly on the taxpayer and include taxes on income, taxes on property, and poll taxes, while "indirect taxes" are levied on intermediaries rather than final consumers and include sales taxes, excise taxes, and value-added taxes. Customs revenues are levied on international trade. These numbers are comparable to the numbers in Table 2 for the richest quintile of countries and, as in Table 2, show that in the 1990s the richest countries rely in roughly equal parts on indirect taxes (on the sales of goods and services), direct taxes (on income, profits, capital gains, and property), and receipts from social security contributions. One hundred years earlier government was about a fifth of its current size (as a share of GDP). At the beginning of the twentieth century governments received about a third of their revenues from direct taxes, a third from indirect taxes, and the remainder from customs revenues (taxes on international trade and trans-

actions) and miscellaneous other revenues. The biggest difference in the structure of government revenues in wealthy countries today and a century ago is the importance of social security revenues and the unimportance of customs revenues. In this the poorest countries today (Table 2) look much like the developed countries did a century ago.

Table 5 reports government expenditures as a share of GDP. The table then breaks down expenditures into "real expenditures," that is, expenditures for the purchase of goods and services, and "subsidies and transfers," that is, expenditures that simply transfer income from one group to another. The final column gives government employment as a percentage of total employment. The overall growth of government portrayed in Table 5 mirrors the growth of government in revenues reported in Table 4. Real expenditures grew from about 5 percent of GDP to 17 percent of GDP, a growth matched by the growth of government employment, which rose from 2.4 percent of

TABLE 4. *Government Revenues and Revenue Sources as Percentage of GDP, Developed Countries, 1870 to Present*

	GDP PER CAPITA 1990$	REVENUES AS PERCENTAGE OF GDP	DIRECT TAXES AS PERCENTAGE OF GDP	INDIRECT TAXES, DOMESTIC, AS PERCENTAGE OF GDP	CUSTOMS AS PERCENTAGE OF GDP	SOCIAL SECURITY RECEIPTS AS PERCENTAGE OF GDP
About 1870	2,119	9.3	2.4	3	1.8	
1913	3,723	8.8	2.6	3	1.7	
1920		13.7	3.2	3.4	1.6	
1937		16.6	3.4	4.9	2.2	
1960	9,083	28.7	9.5	11.6		7.1
1980		40.1	13.5	11.8		10.5
1990	20,372	42.2	14		0.8	
About 1996		43.5		13.5		12.1

SOURCE: Tanzi, V., and L. Schuknecht, *Public Spending in the 20th Century.*

TABLE 5. *Government Expenditures, Total and by Type, as Percentage of GDP and Government Employment as Share of All Employment, Developed Countries, 1870 to Present*

	EXPENDITURES AS PERCENTAGE OF GDP	REAL EXPENDITURES AS PERCENTAGE OF GDP	SUBSIDIES AND TRANSFERS AS PERCENTAGE OF GDP	GOVERNMENT EMPLOYMENT AS PERCENTAGE OF ALL EMPLOYMENT
About 1870	10.8	4.6	1.1	2.4
1913	13.1			
1920	19.6			3.7
1937	23.8	11.4	4.5	5.2
1960	28	12.6		12.3
1980	41.9	17.9	21.4	17.5
1990	43	17.4		
1996	45	17.3	23.2	18.4

SOURCE: Tanzi, V., and L. Schuknecht, *Public Spending in the 20th Century.*

employment in the 1870s to 18 percent in 1996. The dramatic shift in the composition of government expenditures came in the growth of subsidy and transfer programs, welfare and social security.

Table 6 shows expenditures for defense, education, health, pensions (including social security), unemployment programs, and interest on government debt as a percentage of GDP for available years. The last column of the table gives total government debt as a percentage of GDP in each year. Government expenditures for defense have not risen over the twentieth century. The bulk of expenditure growth occurred in social services. Education grew from 0.6 to 6.1 percent of GDP, health services from virtually 0 to 6.4 percent, pensions from virtually 0 to 9.6 percent, and unemployment insurance from 0 to 1.6 percent. The growth in these four functions accounts for more than two-thirds of the increase in government expenditures as a share of GDP over the last century.

Putting This into Perspective. The preceding tables contain many numbers in different units from table to table. Table 7 converts per capita government revenues and expenditures into 1990 dollars and enables direct comparisons over the twentieth century. The upper panel of the table presents the Tanzi and Schuknecht data for their sample of developed countries. The lower panel presents the income quintiles from the World Bank and IMF data used in earlier tables. Tanzi and Schuknecht's sample corresponds roughly but not exactly to the top income quintile of the World Bank and IMF data.

The first column gives income per capita in 1990 dollars. The next two columns give per capita revenues and expenditures and the last four columns expenditures on defense, education, health, and social security.

In 1913 the countries in Tanzi and Schuknecht's sample, the richest countries in the world in 2000, had higher average incomes than 40 percent of the countries in the World Bank sample. Yet their governments were smaller in 1913 relative to GDP, about 11 percent of GDP, than the poorest nation's government in 1995, whose revenues and expenditures are between 25 and 30 percent of GDP. In absolute

TABLE 6. *Government Expenditures by Function as Percentage of GDP, Developed Countries, 1870 to Present*

	DEFENSE AS PERCENTAGE OF GDP	EDUCATION AS PERCENTAGE OF GDP	HEALTH AS PERCENTAGE OF GDP	PENSIONS AS PERCENTAGE OF GDP	UNEMPLOYMENT AS PERCENTAGE OF GDP	INTEREST AS PERCENTAGE OF GDP	GROSS DEBT AS PERCENTAGE OF GDP
About 1870		0.6				2.5	47.9
1913	4	1.3	0.3	0.4		2.2	59.2
1920	2.4			1.2		3.1	66.3
1937	3.7	2.1	0.4	1.9	1.3	3.4	78.1
1960	3.4	3.5	2.4	4.5	0.3		
1980	2.5	5.8	5.8	8.4	0.9	3.1	46.4
1990				8.9			60.4
1996	2	6.1	6.4	9.6	1.6	4.5	71

SOURCE: Tanzi, V., and L. Schuknecht, *Public Spending in the 20th Century.*

TABLE 7. *Government Revenues, Expenditures, and Expenditures by Function in 1990 Dollars per Capita*

	YEAR	GDP PER CAPITA IN 1990$	PER CAPITA REVENUES IN 1990$	PER CAPITA EXPENDITURES IN 1990$	PER CAPITA DEFENSE IN 1990$	PER CAPITA EDUCATION IN 1990$	PER CAPITA HEALTH IN 1990$	PER CAPITA SOCIAL SECURITY IN 1990$
Developed	1913	3,723	439	488	149	48	11	15
countries	1960	9,083	2,607	2,543	309	318	218	409
	1990	20,372	8,597	8,760	407	1,243	1,304	1,956
All countries 1995 to 2000								
Poorest 20%		1,260	339	361	33	59	19	19
Second 20%		2,767	785	861	83	114	53	91
Third 20%		5,038	1,758	1,881	137	300	179	265
Fourth 20%		9,883	3,398	3,703	296	496	266	935
Richest 20%		16,307	8,756	8,571	717	849	939	2,675

terms the rich countries in 1913 had governments whose revenues and expenditures were slightly larger in 1990 dollars than the governments of the poorest governments today but far smaller than the governments in any other income quintile. The richest governments in 1913 spent far more on defense than most poor countries in 1995 but considerably less on education, health, or social security than even the poorest countries today.

Generalizations. The seven tables can be summarized in the following generalizations.

1. The size of government, both absolutely and relative to GDP, has grown in most countries over the twentieth century.
2. The majority of the growth in government expenditures is for basic social and human services, such as education, health, social security, and (although detail has not been provided in these tables) highways, police, fire, water and sewage, and justice. Growth in expenditures for defense and interest on debt are not a major source of government growth.
3. Countries that have higher incomes have bigger governments. This relationship for undeveloped countries in 1900 cannot be estimated without more historical information on the sizes of their governments.
4. As per capita income rises with economic growth, the absolute and relative sizes of governments increases.
5. Countries with higher incomes tend to have more decentralized governments. Larger shares of all government expenditures are made at provincial, state, and local levels, and larger shares of all government revenues are collected at provincial, state, and local levels.
6. The collection of revenues tends to be more centralized than the spending of money. Local governments account for a larger share of government expenditures than of government revenues.

These generalizations apply to countries on average. They may not apply to individual countries at specific points in time.

Explanations. There are no simple answers to the questions: Why have governments grown so much in the twentieth century? Why have governments taken on a larger role in providing social services? Do countries with bigger governments experience higher rates of economic growth? Or do economies with higher incomes purchase more services that just happen to be provided by governments? The lack of answers is not for lack of trying. There is a large and impressive literature on the growth of government and on government's impact on economic development. Clear answers are confounded by two facts. First, the relationship between high incomes and large governments is simply a correlation; it tells nothing about what causes high incomes or large governments. It is likely that some third factor causes both income to be high and governments to be large, that the link between economic growth and government size is not directly causal, and that other factors mediate the relationship. Second, while it is tempting to treat all governments as the same, in fact governments differ as widely from one another as people do.

With those caveats in mind, what can be said about the causes of government growth and its relationship to economic development? There are two schools of thought in economics and economic history about these questions. They are not competing schools, indeed they are rather complementary, but they are different ways of thinking about government. One school is associated in economics with the work of James Buchanan (1975) and in economic history with the work of Robert Higgs (1987), Mancur Olson (1982), and J. R. T. Hughes (1977). This school assumes that politicians and government officials are maximizers, just like every other person in the economy. Given the chance, politicians will use their discretionary governmental powers to advance their own interests (where those interests could be monetary, ideological, or personal). Sometimes the interests of the politicians and the society at large converge, sometimes they conflict. Certain types of government institutions, for example democracy, may be better at aligning the interests of the politicians with the interests of the citizens, but in every political system it is inevitable that the politicians will use the mechanism of government to distort the allocation of resources within the economy to favor themselves and their supporters at the expense of the larger public good. In simple terms, the larger government is, the more likely it is that government will do harm. The growth of government can be seen as the result of a gradual and not so gradual accumulation of power over time. Governments tend to accumulate power most rapidly during times of crisis, producing the ratchet effect noted by Higgs.

There is no countervailing "good government" school of thought in economics (more on this shortly). There is, however, a large and influential literature on the determinants of economic growth. In recent years the advent of large data sets on the economic performance of countries in the second half of the twentieth century has enabled economists to estimate the proximate sources of economic growth. While these studies confirm the fact that countries with larger governments have higher incomes, they also show that across countries, when controlling for things like the level of income, countries with larger governments actually grow more slowly. But these studies also show something more powerful and important. If you ask people in different countries what they think about their governments, whether or not they trust their governments and trust each other, the answers are powerfully associated with economic growth. That is, countries with "good governments" and social capital (trust) tend to grow faster. According to this line of thinking, it is the quality, not the size of government, that matters.

"Good governments" can be measured in many ways. One is the measure of "trust" studied by Stephen Knack and Phillip Keefer (1997). Other measures include the openness of the economy, the likelihood that governments will repay their debts, the presence of unbiased judicial institutions, the presence of competitive political parties, and the presence of the rule of law. These and other measures are in the work of Andrei Schliefer and Robert W. Vishny (1998), Ross Levine (1997), and Rafael La Porta, Florencio Lopez-de-Silanes, Andrei Shleifer, and Robert W. Vishny (1999). Measures of good government, either direct or indirect, usually turn out to be an important if not the most important determinant of how fast economies grow.

With a few notable exceptions, countries that were wealthy at the end of the twentieth century had governments at the beginning of the twentieth century that recognized and supported the rule of law and private property rights, repaid their debts, had relatively open borders, and had political competition. An exception is Germany under the Nazis, highlighting how fragile good governments can be.

Most wealthy countries also have federal government structures, that is, government administrations with two or more independent levels of government decision making. Barry Weingast (1995) has argued that decentralized governments may do better at promoting economic growth because intergovernmental competition may promote more efficient government and because independent provincial, state, and local governments may serve as counterweights against inappropriate policies at the central level. Again there are counter examples. The most decentralized country in the world is Argentina, which has fallen from the ranks of the richest countries in the world to the lower half of per capita income over the twentieth century.

This literature agrees with the views of Buchanan and Higgs that government policies are often bad for economic development, as suggested in the title of Shleifer and Vishny's book, *The Grabbing Hand*. On the other hand, this research also agrees with important results in economic history and public finance. The economic historian Douglass North (1981, 1990) argued that institutions, particularly governments, are the key to understanding why most economies do not grow, but some do grow. In public finance, Richard Musgrave (1959) and his students laid out the ways government can make a positive contribution to the economy, and Wallace Oates (1972) demonstrated how fiscal federalism can make government more efficient.

Conclusions. While it would be inappropriate to suggest that a consensus exists among economists and economic historians about why governments grew in the twentieth century and the impact of government growth on economic performance, a few preliminary conclusions can be advanced.

By 1900 a group of countries, less than twenty in number and located primarily in western Europe and North America, had developed political institutions that provided rule of law and secure property rights. These countries also had the highest per capita incomes of the time, and most were well on the way to developing industrial economies. Whether the government institutions that arose in these economies promoted economic development or economic growth promoted the rise of better government institutions is still an open question. With few exceptions, these countries had federal systems of government.

Over the course of the twentieth century the developed countries not only continued to grow economically, but their governments grew faster than their economies. By the end of the twentieth century government revenues and expenditures in these economies accounted for about half of GDP on average, ranging from 35 to 60 percent of GDP. The major growth in expenditures occurred in education, health, social security, and other basic government services in protection, transportation, utilities, and justice. Subsidies and transfers came to play a much larger role in the activities of these governments. On the revenue side, these governments grew to rely less on taxes on international trade and the domestic sale of goods and services and more on taxation of individual incomes.

There is no evidence that bigger government directly promotes economic growth. Instead, using modern data and controlling for factors like incomes, there is evidence that countries with larger governments grow more slowly. On the other hand, countries with high incomes and big governments also appear to have societies in which citizens trust each other and their governments to a greater extent than in other societies. Understanding how the development of good government policies and institutions promotes both the growth of government and of economies is a task for economists and economic historians in the years to come.

BIBLIOGRAPHY

Buchanan, James M. *The Limits of Liberty: Between Anarchy and Leviathan*. Chicago, 1975.
"Global Development Finance and World Development Indicators." World Bank. Available online at <www.Worldbank.org/data/online-databases>.
Government Finance Statistics Yearbook. International Monetary Fund. Vol. 25. 2001.
Higgs, Robert. *Crisis and Leviathan: Critical Episodes in the Growth of American Government*. New York, 1987.
Hughes, J. R. T. *The Governmental Habit*. New York, 1977.
Knack, Stephen, and Phillip Keefer. "Does Social Capital Have an Economic Payoff? A Cross Country Investigation." *Quarterly Journal of Economics* 112.4 (1997), 1251–1288.
La Porta, Rafael, Florencio Lopez-de-Silanes, Andrei Shleifer, and Robert W. Vishny. "The Quality of Government." *Journal of Law, Economics and Organization* 15 (1999), 222–279.
Levine, Ross. "Financial Development and Economic Growth: Views and Agenda." *Journal of Economic Literature* 35.2 (1997), 688–726.
Musgrave, Richard. *The Theory of Public Finance*. New York, 1959.
North, Douglass C. *Structure and Change in Economic History*. New York, 1981.
North, Douglass C. *Institutions, Institutional Change and Economic Performance*. New York, 1990.
Oates, Wallace E. *Fiscal Federalism*. New York, 1972.
Olson, Mancur. *The Logic of Collective Action*. Cambridge, Mass., 1965.
Olson, Mancur. *The Rise and Decline of Nations*. New Haven, 1982.
Shleifer, Andrei, and Robert W. Vishny. *The Grabbing Hand: Government Pathologies and Their Cures*. 1998.
Tanzi, Vito, and Ludger Schuknecht. *Public Spending in the 20th Century: A Global Perspective*. 2000.
Weingast, Barry. "The Economic Role of Political Institutions: Market-Preserving Federalism and Economic Growth." *Journal of Law, Economics, and Organization* 11 (1995), 1–31.

JOHN JOSEPH WALLIS

PUBLIC GOODS. Recognition that provision for some economic needs cannot be left to private markets and individual incentives-based economic decisions is in the work of Adam Smith (1776). But a modern technical description of public goods is best dated from P. A. Samuelson (1954). Samuelson's important paper identified two primary features that distinguish public or collective goods from private or individual goods.

Pure Public Goods. Pure public goods are such that, once available to any member of a specified group, the same quantity or quality is available to every other member at no extra cost. The reasons for this equal availability are, first, that such goods are not used up when enjoyed (nonrivalness) and, second, because, if available to any consumer, they cannot be excluded from any other group member (nonexcludability). Standard examples include the lighthouse beacon that warns all ships (nonexcludable) and whose utilization by one ship in no way reduces its availability to other ships (nonrival). National defense is another example. Once a nation is secure from foreign invaders, all its members are secure. More contemporary examples include protection of pollution-free environments, preservation of natural species, establishment of political freedoms, provision of property rights guarantees by an impartial and universal police and judiciary, and maintenance of the rule of law. Broadly speaking these should be understood to be economic "goods" because all require the deployment of costly resources and yield desirable outcomes. All display the property that their enjoyment by one person in no way diminishes their availability to others to enjoy. Since the amount consumed is independent of the identities of the providers, the interdependence among consumers should be thought of as anonymous. These characteristics of public goods basically precondition all normative analysis of them and imply the theoretical properties of their provision.

The basic dilemma is if every member of a group enjoys a good irrespective of who supplies it, no one acting voluntarily will provide the good—at least no one will provide a sufficient amount of it. Instead, all will have an interest in seeing others pay the supply costs while they enjoy the benefits without making any cost contribution themselves. Every individual, that is, has good reason to free ride—in whole or in part—on the provisions of others. One therefore should anticipate that, for the provision of such public goods, free markets based on individual rationality will fail. This means that the amount or quality of collective goods provision to follow from individual rational behavior will fall short of what the aggregate of individuals in a group desires and in extreme cases will not be supplied at all. Despite the fact that a group is nothing more than the collection of individuals who belong to it, individual rationality, even assuming it to be universal, will not secure the rational collective outcome. Economic analysis suggests that, to achieve an efficient provision of collective goods, an outside agency with coercive powers, such as government, must provide it, imposing its provision upon and exacting payments from those who collectively benefit.

Throughout history kings and princes have carried out some of the functions implied by this social contract, even if they were often coupled to dynastic or other "selfish" considerations of the prince. Among the functions carried out by the Roman Republic and later emperors was the suppression of piracy and the adjudication of commercial disputes, which made commerce possible. Other public goods they supplied were popular entertainment and the formalization of religion. In the postmedieval period the control of epidemics was added to the list of public goods provided by authorities. S. R. Epstein (2000) has argued that the European state played an indispensable role in facilitating the rise of market economies between 1300 and 1750 by enforcing rules and preventing opportunistic behavior and free riding. In the centuries since the Enlightenment this list has grown a great deal. New public goods supplied in modern states include the coordination of measures and standards, the broadcasting of radio and television signals (often cited as a classic public good), and the provision of trustworthy information (all human knowledge has public goods characteristics because it is intrinsically nonrivalrous and exclusion is quite difficult in most cases).

Voluntary Provision of Public Goods. One insight that economic history provides the analysis of public goods is that in the past people have exchanged, produced, consumed, and shared many goods in environments that were not at all mediated by markets and prices and seem to have succeeded, to some degree at least, in overcoming free riding. These ranged from strictly economic transactions to social and political institutions, from medieval guilds and modern labor unions to allocations within families and voluntary philanthropic giving, from public interest lobbying to special private interest favor seeking, from the behavior of professional associations and religions to that of entire nations as they formed alliances. This myriad of applications raises paramount questions of how such groups of people and such organizations achieved their goals. The initial supposition of economists was that, instead of individual rational action, society must rely on government power to enforce individual contribution via coercive taxation and expenditure.

Research by economists and historians informed by the theory of public choice has raised doubts about whether or not coercive governments may have always been the best instrument to correct social inefficiencies stemming from free-rider behavior. The question raised already by the Romans, "who shall protect us from the protectors," needs to be applied to the role of coercive government power in supplying public goods. Government behavior itself is riven by free-rider failures. Historically incompetent and selfish governments have often provided public goods at a level far below what society desired and what was technically feasible. Moreover a plethora of historical research has pointed to the existence of individual unregulated voluntary behavior that provided public goods even though it is characterized by free riding and therefore necessarily in some sense inefficient (Olson, 1965). Authors such as Alexander J. Field (2001), Paul H. Rubin (2002), and Ridley (1996) have all pointed to a large number of examples in which people behaved consistently in an altruistic way, that is, they overcame their narrow individual selfishness and moderated opportunistic free riding. Poor relief before the welfare state depended largely on unforced giving. Volunteer armies, anonymous charitable donations, Stakhanovism (named after a legendary Russian miner who set a record of cutting 102 tons of coal in one shift during the Second Five-Year Plan in the Soviet Union), and successful communal societies (for example, the Israeli kibbutz) are examples of such behavior.

It is often felt that, in overcoming the free-rider problem and enabling the supply of public goods beyond its "rational" minimum, ideology of some sort (whether religious or otherwise) must play a role. Indeed Douglass North has defined ideology as a set of beliefs necessary to overcome free riding. Such ideological considerations present a modification of narrowly defined *homo economicus*, and it may well have genetic origins as Field has argued. Yet there are also more pragmatic economic factors that explain the historical provision of public goods in the absence of coercion. Three factors can explain the degree of success a group has in providing itself with a collective good without government coercion. These are (a) the size of the group, (b) the heterogeneity of its members, and (c) the ability of the group to offer selective incentives to individuals to induce contribution to the collective good. Size matters because, all other things equal, the ability to detect free riders and to pressure them into conforming varies inversely with size (the kibbutzim are predominantly between two hundred and five hundred members). Heterogeneity matters because in heterogeneous groups the likelihood of nonconformism will increase; once a few group members become free riders, others are more likely to follow suit. Selective incentives are ways of getting around the free-rider problem: medals, social prestige, and promises of the next world are all mechanisms to elicit behavior that under "narrow" rational behavior would not occur and would lead to radical underprovision of public goods. Mancur Olson (1965) first recognized this possibility of "selective incentives" as an explanation for why in practice individuals supply anything at all to their public goods group. The voluntary provision model thus has become the paradigm for numerous positive behavioral patterns, including such looming international questions as cooperation among countries in regulating the international economy, controlling pollution, and even fighting terrorism.

Mixed and Impure Public Goods. Often when a collective good is supplied to a group there can be a modifying factor that qualifies or limits its perfect nonrivalness or perfect nonexcludability. One example is local public goods, such as fire protection and sanitation. Theorists have noted that, if such local public goods were provided differentially by different communities and if individuals could choose their communities, then they would reveal their preferences by the locational choices they made and in doing so would solve the public goods provision problem. Such economics of "fiscal federalism," in which people vote with their feet rather than their wallets, has been of much interest to theorists. Historians have found little evidence that the supply of these goods—with the exception of education—has been a major determinant in migration decisions.

There are also mixed public and private goods, as first noted by J. M. Buchanan (1965). Following Samuelson's public goods–private goods distinction, Buchanan proposed that some goods might occupy a position intermediate between the polar categories of pure private and public goods, part public and part private. What is the right size of a group for consumption of a public good when that good can be confined to the members of the group and others excluded? Such groups are sometimes known as public goods clubs. Applications of the idea of public goods clubs ranges from the design of public facilities, such as transport systems or school and health facilities, all the way up to entire nations, viewed in a sense as giant "clubs."

Another fruitful application of the pure public goods paradigm to historical experiences is based on the recognition that individuals may derive multiple benefits from the provision of public goods to their group. When an individual contributes to his or her group, he or she may obtain a private, personal benefit from his or her contribution ("warm glow") as well as provide all members of the group (himself or herself included) with a public benefit. Thus to understand the incentives a country has to clean up the international environment (and therefore to understand the possibilities for collaborative action), note that the implementation of its environmental programs may not only benefit the entire globe (for example, constrain global warming) but also differentially benefit the country itself (for instance, by enhancing tourism). The same idea inspires the analysis of philanthropy by J. Andreoni (1990), where gifts to a particular charity both provide a private "feel-good" benefit to the giver and simultaneously a public benefit to every giver in the public goods group.

Discovery of public goods as a separate category for investigation has produced an explosion of theoretical research into the economics of the public sector. Indeed public goods now provide the first and most fundamental rationale for the role of government in the economy. Before public goods, this role was basically thought to be one of repairing failures in the private sector, along with equity or distributional purposes. Of course the explosion in research has paralleled an enormous relative growth of the public sectors of national economies over the past century. This trend continues, now often focused on international public goods and problems nations have in overcoming their free-riding instincts. In most Western nations the share of government in national expenditure has risen dramatically in the twentieth century. While in 1913 the percentage averaged around 10 percent in most European nations, the percentage was above 40 percent in 1999. Much work by economic historians, especially Jonathan R. T. Hughes, Robert Higgs, and Peter Lindert, has been concerned with explaining this unprecedented expansion.

The importance of public goods in the rise of the modern welfare state is not easy to quantify. It is sometimes believed that the elasticity of expenditures with respect to income is larger than one, so that when nations get richer they tend to spend a disproportionate amount on publicly supplied goods. Many of the areas in which twentieth-century governments have encroached on what was traditionally the domain of the private sector are publicly supplied but do not count as pure public goods; instead some other market failure is usually cited. Investment in human capital, the provision of health care, and various forms of insurance (including pensions) are all areas in which neither the nonrivalness nor the nonexcludability criteria hold for individuals, though in many countries they are largely or exclusively supplied by the government. Yet it is hard to deny that modern states invest in the education and health of their citizenry and work toward a more equitable distribution of income because it is felt that a better-educated and more equitable aggregate creates a civic society that itself has the nature of a public good. This argument, made most clearly by Peter Lindert (1994), seems an insight more specific to economic historians than to theorists.

[*See also* Environment; Epidemics; Local Public Goods; Natural Resources; Property Rights; Public Administration; Public Health; Public Utilities; *and* Sanitation.]

BIBLIOGRAPHY

Andreoni, J. "Impure Altruism and Donations to Public Goods: A Theory of Warm-Glow Giving." *Economic Journal* 100 (1990), 464–477.

Atkinson, A., and J. Stiglitz. *Lectures on Public Economics.* New York, 1984.

Buchanan, J. M. "An Economic Theory of Clubs." *Economica* 32.1 (1965), 1–14.

Cornes, R., and T. Sandler. *The Theory of Externalities, Public Goods, and Club Goods.* New York, 1996.

Epstein, S. R. *Freedom and Growth: The Rise of States and Markets in Europe, 1300–1750.* London, 2000.

Field, Alexander J. *Altruisticaly Inclined? The Behavioral Sciences, Evolutionary Theory, and the Origins of Reciprocity.* Ann Arbor, 2001.

Higgs, Robert. *Crisis and Leviatan: Critical Episodes in the Growth of American Government.* New York, 1987.

Hughes, Jonathan R. T. *The Governmental Habit Redux.* Princeton, 1991.

Lindert, Peter H. "The Rise of Social Spending, 1880–1930." *Explorations in Economic History* 31.1 (January 1994), 1–37.

Lindert, Peter H. *Social Spending and Economic Growth since the Eighteenth Century.* 2 vols. Cambridge, forthcoming 2004.

Olson, Mancur L., Jr. *The Logic of Collective Action: Public Goods and the Theory of Groups.* Harvard Economic Studies, vol. 124. Cambridge, Mass., 1965.

Rubin, Paul H. *Darwinian Politics: The Evolutionary Origin of Freedom.* New Brunswick, N.J., 2002.

Samuelson, P. A. "The Pure Theory of Public Expenditure." *Review of Economics and Statistics* 36 (1954), 387–389.

Smith, Adam. *Wealth of Nations.* London, 1776.

MARTIN C. McGUIRE

PUBLIC HEALTH. In contrast with the history of medicine, which focuses on the diagnosis and treatment of disease, the history of public health focuses on the actions that communities have taken to avoid the threat of disease and other threats to health and welfare. The history of public health offers an account of how and why governments and other public bodies have responded to threats to health. It also assesses how effective public health measures have been in meeting those threats.

Effect of Disease. The threats posed by disease varied as populations went through the three stages of the epidemiological transition first described by Abdel R. Omran for European populations. The changing nature of these threats is essential for the history of public health from the fourteenth century through the present. The first stage describes the mortality pattern of premodern and early modern European populations. Subsistence crises and epidemics of the plague, typhus, smallpox, and measles caused large spikes in mortality. By the early nineteenth century the West had entered the second stage. Although large year-to-year fluctuations in mortality disappeared, mortality remained high at twenty-four per one thousand. The biggest killer was now tuberculosis. Other infectious diseases, such as typhoid fever, diphtheria, enteritis, and the airborne illnesses bronchitis, pneumonia, and influenza together accounted for one-half of all deaths. By the onset of the third stage in the mid-twentieth century, crude mortality had fallen by two-thirds, and mortality from infectious diseases had fallen by 90 percent. Modern diseases that proved much more difficult to prevent—cancers and diseases of the circulatory system—now accounted for one-half of mortality.

In areas outside of Europe and the temperate zones settled by Europeans, substantially different patterns of disease prevailed. Instead of tuberculosis, malaria, sleeping sickness, yellow fever, and blackwater fever posed the greatest mortality threats. The plague and cholera were endemic in the Indian subcontinent. Mortality from most causes fell substantially during the twentieth century, with the exception of more modest reductions in diseases most directly related to income, including the diarrheal diseases. Effective treatment and vaccination, not just the success of public health measures, accounts for much of the decline that has occurred.

The history of governmental interventions of behalf of public health began with the realization that effective countermeasures could reduce or even eliminate the economic costs of disease. These costs include the catastrophic loss of life, the disruption of commerce, the spillover effects of disease, the impact of disamenities, and the reduced "efficiency" of the working population. The Black Death of the fourteenth century and subsequent epidemics posed such high economic costs that authorities were required to respond. An outbreak of the plague in a community could bring commercial activity to a halt, as those with sufficient resources fled and those remaining faced mortality rates of up to 60 percent. Over the four centuries from 1340, the plague increased mortality in Barcelona by about one-quarter.

As more communities adopted the complete cutoff of trade as a countermeasure to protect themselves from an epidemic of the plague (or later cholera), costs of an outbreak or a threatened outbreak rose. During most of the nineteenth century reports of plague epidemics in the hinterlands repeatedly forced the closure of the port of Bombay and other ports on India's west coast and prevented the travel of Indian pilgrims making the hajj to holy sites in Arabia. Hamburg's merchants faced similar isolation during the cholera epidemic of 1892. Care of the infected could also place a large burden on communities.

In short, infectious disease presents a classic case of an adverse externality. Infection of one individual threatens contagion of others in the community. Efforts to combat the disease will protect the individual as well as diminish the risks of contraction of others within the community and elsewhere. Diseases such as tuberculosis, smallpox, polio, HIV, infant diarrhea, and scarlet fever are all readily transmitted through person-to-person contact, either via the fecal-oral route or through air. Other diseases, such as cholera and typhoid, can be spread over longer distances through contaminated water or food.

By the nineteenth century high mortality rates specific to a region, community or neighborhood were also recognized

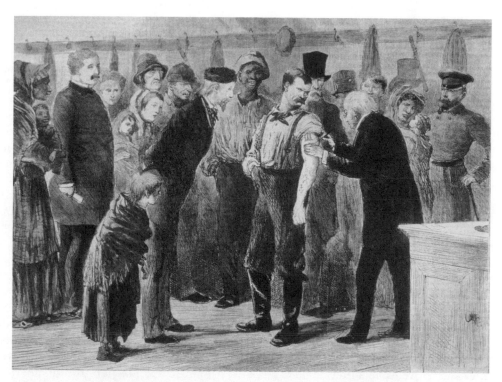

PREVENTIVE MEASURES. A physician giving a vaccination. Drawing by Sol Eytinge, Jr. (1833–1905), *Harper's Weekly*, 16 March 1872, p. 204. (Courtesy of the National Library of Medicine, Bethesda, Maryland)

as a disamenity that could decrease the value of property or raise the cost of attracting labor. Officials in Memphis, Tennessee, Rio de Janiero, and elsewhere realized that yellow fever epidemics posed risks to the long-term attractiveness of their cities to new residents. Disease in the tropics, including malaria and yellow fever, prompted exceptionally high mortality among nonnatives and posed a barrier to plans for imperial expansion. Evidence from England in the 1830s and about 1900 suggests that the risk of high mortality could account for a 10 or 15 percent wage premium.

Finally, from the end of the nineteenth century through the Nazi regime in Germany, public health policies also responded to the threat that disease (both morbidity and mortality) posed to a nation's potential productivity or "national efficiency." Unhealthy individuals in poor physical condition were not fit for military service; this perspective also argued they posed a cost to society as a whole as inefficient workers. The decline in fertility directed public attention to the risks that high infant and maternal mortality posed to the long-term viability of national populations. The loss of life of those in their most productive years, whether due to tuberculosis in 1900 or HIV in 2000, represented both human tragedy and a waste of human capital.

Public Health Strategies. Since the Middle Ages public health strategies have employed a wide range of meas-

ures. Many of them restricted the rights of individuals and property owners and prompted critical changes in the economic role of government in the provision of services. All fundamentally drew on the then-prevalent beliefs about what caused disease. Implementation of them was often the outcome of the interplay of the expense of carrying them out, the distribution of political power, and the distribution of net benefits of change.

The first effective measures to combat an acknowledged threat to public health combated the spread of the plague. The disease is endemic in rodent populations (especially rats). It jumps to human populations when high mortality among the rodent hosts prompts the flea that carries it to seek out new (human) hosts. Contemporaries noted that the plague spread along trading routes and concluded that it was transmitted by contact with those already infected with the disease. After its appearance in Europe during the mid-fourteenth century, the plague gained a foothold in Europe that resulted in periodic epidemics over the next four centuries. Advanced Italian city-states led the counterattack during the fifteenth century with strategies that drew upon a contagionist perspective. Against considerable public resistance and despite their potential expense, these measures gradually became standard practice throughout Europe by the end of the seventeenth century. Potential carriers, which included ships, vehicles, or travelers arriving from areas known to experience an epidemic, were placed under quarantine for a period long enough to ensure that either they were free of the disease or the disease had run its course. Local authorities isolated infected residents with a form of house arrest or moved them to "pesthouses" or "plague hospitals" located outside of the city walls. Personal effects of the infected were either sanitized or burned. During the eighteenth century the Austrian government established an effective *cordon sanitaire* along the two-thousand-kilometer border with the Ottoman Empire to prevent transmission by land routes.

By the end of the eighteenth century the plague had disappeared from all of non-Ottoman Europe. The widespread application of similar measures in the Ottoman Empire apparently contributed to the disappearance of the plague by the 1840s, after five centuries of recurring epidemics. This disease remained endemic in India, Kurdistan, and parts of Yemen into the twentieth century and subsequently established a foothold in Africa and the American West. Historians question whether the anticontagion measures were alone sufficient to eliminate the threat of the plague. Alternative explanations include the spread of brick and stone construction, which denied habitat to the host rodents, and the spread of a related disease (*pseudotuberculosis*) that conveyed immunity to the plague in rodent populations. Authorities adopted similar strategies of isolation during the nineteenth and twentieth centuries for such highly infectious diseases as scarlet fever and polio.

Theories of contagion also informed campaigns to combat smallpox. Discovery of the potential effectiveness of inoculation—and then vaccination with cowpox—at the end of the nineteenth century led to sporadic efforts to vaccinate larger numbers of people in an effort to prevent the spread of the disease. Because of its physical invasiveness and potential for breaking taboos, vaccination faced resistance among varied groups of people. Immigrants in the United States, Hindus in India, and residents of Rio de Janeiro all offered fierce resistance to vaccination campaigns. Comprehensive vaccination of those at risk throughout the world was finally achieved in the 1970s.

Europeans initially responded to the appearance of Asiatic cholera in 1831 with quarantines and isolation in accordance with the contagionist theory. These measures were quickly abandoned as ineffective. During the subsequent epidemics that struck Europe and the Americas over the next fifty years, observers noted that cholera affected some districts of cities more than others. The work of the British statistician William Farr (1807–1883) and others established similar statistical regularities for mortality overall. The realization that mortality had a spatial character prompted the emergence of an environmentalist or lo-

calist approach to explaining the causation of disease. Environmentalist explanations focused either on miasmas (poisonous gases emitted by polluted ground or collections of waste) or on the pollution of groundwater. The British Poor Law commissioner Edwin Chadwick (1800–1890) drew upon the environmentalist perspective to inform his pathbreaking inquiry into sanitary conditions in British towns of 1842. The central tenet of Chadwick's "sanitary idea" was that the construction of centralized water supply and sewage collection systems could significantly reduce urban mortality.

Although in 1855 the British anesthesiologist John Snow (1813–1858) was the first to present solid evidence that cholera was a waterborne disease, his perspective achieved widespread acceptance only at the end of the nineteenth century, after the French chemist and biologist Louis Pasteur (1822–1895) posited the germ theory of disease and the German physician Robert Koch (1843–1910) isolated the cholera vibrio in 1883. The germ theory also confirmed that contaminated water or food could transmit typhoid and reinforced the policy conclusions suggested by the environmentalist approach. It scored an early success in the development of the diphtheria vaccine, which had a major impact on childhood health by the beginning of the twentieth century.

The environmental cleanup that actually occurred rejected Chadwick's unified approach and instead focused initially on providing clean, centrally piped-in water supply to replace the wells and cisterns then in use in virtually all cities. With a lag of ten to twenty years or more, cities then undertook massive investments in comprehensive sewer systems to shift the disposal of human waste to flush toilets using waterborne carriage and disposal at a remote site. The capital investment required for these sanitary investments was substantial, particularly when measured against the resources available to pay for it. The payments for the amortization, interest, and costs of maintenance of these facilities would cost up to four days of work for the German or American unskilled worker at the end of the nineteenth century.

The focus on environmental sources of disease also prompted attention to improving the disposal of other municipal wastes. The bacteriological revolution shifted the focus from testing milk and other foods for impurities to looking for contamination by known bacteria. The realization that contaminated meat and milk could carry tuberculosis after Koch's discovery of the tubercle bacillus in 1882 prompted stricter regulations of slaughterhouses and dairying. Finally, a generalized concern with the adverse effects of crowded living conditions on public health, particularly on tuberculosis, led to comprehensive housing building and use codes, slum clearance, and the construction of public housing. These efforts all took root during the late nineteenth century and became staples of public policy through the latter part of the twentieth century.

By the early twentieth century public health advocates broadened the scope of their efforts to include individual behavior that was deemed harmful to health. This movement, known as the "new public health," traced the cause of high infant mortality to inadequate care by mothers. Education programs, visiting nurses, and infant health centers were all used to persuade mothers about the benefits of breast-feeding, cleanliness in the home, and appropriate diet. As the twentieth century progressed, public health efforts focused on discouraging other unhealthy behaviors, including the use of tobacco and consumption of foods high in fats and cholesterol. Campaigns to improve sanitary practices in developing countries also follow the approach of the new public health.

The germ theory of disease also provided an intellectual foundation for rapid progress in the field of tropical medicine. European interest arose directly from the desire to protect the health of Europeans in African and Asian colonies and eventually to improve the health of colonized peoples as well. Epidemics of sleeping sickness and smallpox could cause rates of mortality in the affected regions of Africa equivalent to the 35 percent experienced during the Black Death in Europe. Malaria and yellow fever also exacted heavy tolls. Following the pioneering work of the physician Ronald Ross (1857–1932), who confirmed in 1897 that the mosquito transmitted malaria, application of the germ theory of disease led to the identification of the insect vectors responsible for the transmission of most tropical diseases by the 1920s.

Colonial governments combated these diseases with a primitive form of quarantine. Local authorities would segregate areas designated for settlement by Europeans from the residential areas of the native population and provide for screens and other forms of protection. Drainage schemes aimed at the mosquitoes that carried yellow fever and malaria were also undertaken, but again initially in areas designated for Europeans. Once they recognized that sleeping sickness could be endemic to locations with certain geographic features or vegetation (such as the shoreline of Lake Victoria), colonial governments pursued policies of forced relocation and controls on settlement. As treatments and vaccinations became available during the twentieth century, more of these diseases were brought under control.

Most of Africa and Asia lagged well behind Europe and North America in providing clean piped water and effective disposal of sewage. Sanitary commissions were established in some communities, and plans were developed. But provision was limited to enclaves of white settlers and perhaps some adjacent districts. Rapid population growth in urban areas of developing countries during the quarter century after independence has raised the cost of providing all residents with the standard of provision found in developed countries. One-third to two-thirds of urban residents in lower-income countries remain without direct access to water supply, and the situation is much worse for access to hygienic toilets and waste disposal systems.

Ongoing Debates. Two important questions are key to the economic history of public health: did public health reform yield large benefits up to 1910, and why did reform take so long to occur? Many historians have argued that public health reform offset the worst excesses of market-driven economic development and urbanization during the nineteenth century; they credit it with the unprecedented decline in urban mortality. Another perspective holds that rising living standards in the wake of economic growth allowed for improved nutrition and increased resistance to tuberculosis and other diseases of the lungs; declines in waterborne diseases that were most amenable to public health measures made only a modest contribution to mortality decline. The higher incomes provided by economic growth also helped fund the construction of these facilities and thus indirectly the decline in mortality. Statistical studies have not resolved this debate. They have found that sanitary improvements and other public health measures cut infant mortality, diarrheal disease mortality, and even general mortality rates. Research also indicates that reduced incidence of diarrheal disease also improved the net nutritional status of the population and could have heightened resistance to tuberculosis and other diseases.

The other debate concerns the halting progress of public health reform during the nineteenth century. A common argument places the blame on the control of government by narrow landlord interests unwilling to take on new expenses. Case studies of German and American cities suggest that along with the high costs of public health measures, the incomes of communities played a critical role in determining when reforms would take place, if at all. In those places where incomes were simply too low, such as in many African and Asian communities today, only a minority of residents would be served.

[See also Food Processing Industry, *subentry on* Food Safety Regulation; *and* Sanitation.]

BIBLIOGRAPHY

Brown, John C. "Public Reform for Private Gain? The Case of Investments in Sanitary Infrastructure: Germany, 1880–1887." *Urban Studies* 26.1 (1989), 2–12.

Cipolla, Carlo M. *Faith, Reason, and the Plague in Seventeenth-Century Tuscany.* Brighton, U.K., 1979.

Ewbank, D. C., and Samuel Preston. "Personal Health Behavior and the Decline in Infant and Child Mortality: The United States, 1900–1930." In *What Do We Know about the Health Transition?* edited by John Caldwell, pp. 116–149. Canberra, 1990.

Goubert, Jean-Pierre. *The Conquest of Water: The Advent of Health in the Industrial Age*. Cambridge, 1989.

Harrison, Mark. *Public Health in British India: Anglo-Indian Preventive Medicine, 1859–1914*. Cambridge, 1994.

Leavitt, Judith Walzer. *The Healthiest City: Milwaukee and the Politics of Health Reform*. Princeton, 1982.

Mokyr, Joel, and Rebecca Stein. "Science, Health, and Household Technology." In *The Economics of New Goods*, edited by Timothy F. Bresnahan and Robert J. Gordon, pp. 143–200. Chicago, 1997.

Omran, Abdel R. "The Epidemiologic Transition: A Theory of the Epidemiology of Population Change." *Milbank Memorial Fund Quarterly* 49.1 (1971), 509–538.

Porter, Dorothy. *Health, Civilization, and the State: A History of Public Health from Ancient to Modern Times*. London, 1999.

Rosen, George. *A History of Public Health*. Baltimore, 1993.

Sabben-Clare, E. E., D. J. Bradley, and K. Kirkwood, eds. *Health in Tropical Africa during the Colonial Period*. Oxford, 1980.

Sheard, Sally, and Helen Power, eds. *Body and City: Histories of Urban Public Health*. Aldershot, U.K., 2000.

Szreter, Simon. "The Importance of Social Intervention in Britain's Mortality Decline c. 1850–1914: A Re-Interpretation of the Role of Public Health." *Social History of Medicine* 1.1 (1988), 1–37.

Wohl, Anthony. *Endangered Lives: Public Health in Victorian Britain*. London, 1983.

Woods, Robert, and John Woodward, eds. *Urban Disease and Mortality in Nineteenth-Century England*. London, 1984.

JOHN C. BROWN

PUBLIC HOUSING AND HOUSING POLICIES.

Public or social housing is defined by Anne Power as housing that is not built for profit and is normally let at below market rents to lower-income groups or to those who are unable to buy a home independently. It is built and managed by a wide range of institutions: local authorities, housing associations, limited dividend companies, workers' cooperatives, and private landlords. But all are regulated in some fashion by the state.

The extent of social housing varies among (and indeed within) societies, with the former USSR and People's Republics and the United States representing the extremes. In the Soviet bloc, housing was regarded as a universal right and the responsibility of the central state. In the USSR in the early 1970s, 80 percent of funds came from state capital investments. The five-story block of flats predominated, relying on prefabricated units and mechanized flow-line assembly. At 5 to 6 percent of family income, rents were low, and allocation was determined by local soviets of working people's deputies on the basis of need for improved housing. Private ownership continued to exist, however, especially in rural areas. Moreover the state increasingly encouraged provision by private cooperatives, though these were often required to follow standard designs and accounted for only 6 to 7 percent of total construction in 1974. The state provided communal facilities and achieved socially mixed neighborhoods, but it exercised little quality control, and blocks often looked shoddy

shortly after they were built and suffered from weather penetration and poor insulation. In East Germany these problems were compounded by the reliance on giant estates. The biggest developments in East Berlin were between thirty-five thousand and sixty thousand units.

By contrast the United States relies on what the President's Commission on Housing referred to in 1982 as "the genius of the market economy." Public housing accounted for only 1 percent of the total stock in 1993, and it is provided for the "permanent poor" or "underclass," particularly black single mothers and the low-income elderly, who have the least chance of finding private rental housing. By the mid-1970s American public housing was "a form of highly stigmatized ghetto housing" and at the "point of near-terminal crisis" (Harloe, 1997). Urban renewal programs inevitably resulted in increased homelessness. Even in the Great Depression, when the private housing market collapsed, the federal government's first priority was to reconstruct private housing finance and to ensure that any public initiative did not compete with the private sector. Consequently the first and arguably only decisive legislative measure in favor of public housing in American history—the 1937 Housing Law, which established local public housing authorities to build, own, and manage housing with generous loans from the federal government—only accounted for 7 percent of housing output between 1938 and 1940.

Housing in western Europe lies between these extremes, regarded as a "limited social right" (Power, 1993) within the orbit of the welfare state. Thus British and Irish law places a statutory duty on local authorities to help the unintentionally homeless, while by the *droit au logement* of 1990, the French state recognized the right to housing of all. In Britain public housing was built and managed directly by local authorities, and at its peak, around 1975, it accounted for nearly one-third of the entire housing stock and housed more than a third of the population. Only Ireland followed the British model of provision. In continental Europe a wider variety of landlords played a social role, most notably in Germany, where social housing companies were required to follow the law of 1940 by which they would operate for the public good and charge only cost rents. French law required public housing to be provided by autonomous bodies because of historical concerns about corruption; state-sponsored but independent landlords therefore arose. These bodies typically accounted for about 20 percent of all housing.

Despite this diversity of provision and scale, scholars have detected a common pattern of development in advanced capitalist countries since the late nineteenth century, with public housing oscillating between "residual" provision and "mass" provision. With the exception of Britain and Ireland, homeownership remained common in rural areas. However, the rapid growth of urban areas resulted

PUBLIC HOUSING. Aerial view of suburban apartment houses, Hungary, 1985. (© Bill Weems/Woodfin Camp and Associates, New York)

in urban housing crises from the 1880s. In most cities into the 1920s, 80 to 90 percent of households rented privately, but this tenure could provide neither the numbers nor the quality of dwellings required. Housing reformers, political parties, and labor movements suggested alternatives ranging from unobstructed market provision to housing by charities, employers, workers' cooperatives, tenant copartnerships, garden city associations, and local authorities. But little progress was made before 1914. For a short period after World War I, faced with acute housing shortages, fears of revolution inspired by the Soviet example, and electoral pressure for postwar social improvements, European governments intervened directly (as in 1919 in Britain, where the central government largely financed local authority building) and indirectly (as between 1917 and 1921 in Denmark, where the state provided loans and subsidies to private builders and building societies as well as local authorities) to promote mass public and private housing for a wide range of urban workers. Intervention in this pe-

riod was temporary and relatively ineffective. State support did not last beyond the 1920s. In Britain, the Netherlands, Denmark, Sweden, France, and Germany no more than 15 percent of families were accommodated in public housing, and public housing increasingly assumed a residual character, offering low-cost dwellings for those on the lowest incomes.

Total war once again revived mass public housing, for similar reasons and for a much longer period (until the mid-1970s). West Germany, for example, emerged from World War II with a massive housing shortage because of war damage and with a communist neighbor. Most European states had turned to industrialized, high-rise construction by the 1960s, attracted by the possibilities of speed, low cost, and the production of large numbers of dwellings in block estates on easily available land on the peripheries of cities. Mass housing in this period was more deeply embedded than previously, recognized by social democratic and conservative governments as part of the postwar welfare state settlement. From the mid-1970s economic and political circumstances changed, and to the present all governments have sought once again to residualize public housing, as in the United States, targeting marginal groups outside the labor market, such as single mothers and the unemployed or, particularly in France and Germany, immigrant workers. Poverty and social exclusion were concentrated on the *grands ensembles* (estates of high-rise flats) in France or peripheral council estates in Britain. By the mid-1980s the latter had become "local subsistence economies, utterly dependent on state benefits" (*Faith in the City*, 1985). Despite this in 1987 the government sought to raise council rents, limit housing benefits, and transfer council properties to housing associations.

The housing needs of the majority of Europe's population were to be met through owner occupation and private rental. The mix varied, as did measures to promote it. But all governments looked primarily to market provision by the 1990s. This was part of a more general restructuring of welfare states and the social bases of politics. However, a complete state withdrawal from public housing seems impossible, not least because of the often unsustainable financial burdens that mortgage repayments place on median earners in increasingly insecure labor markets on the one hand and that financial measures to assist owner occupiers place on governments on the other. This was demonstrated by the British experience in the 1980s. Conservative and Labour governments after 1945 extended mortgage tax relief until the Conservative government began to restrict it from 1988 onward. Despite its commitment to owner occupation, the government had to accept that assisting the tenure was too expensive, distorted investment, and "overheated" the housing market. This was clear in the early 1990s as house prices fell, "negative equity" appeared, and repossessions rose.

The history of housing provision in the capitalist West has led Michael Harloe (1997) to suggest that residual public housing is "normal" under advanced capitalism since the market is unable to provide affordable and decent dwellings for the urban poor. The ideology of democratic citizenship and the political and social imperative to supervise the "underclass" mean that no Western government can rely only on the market economy. Mass public housing for the "respectable" working class and elements of the middle class is for Harloe an "abnormal" form under capitalism, arising when there is a generalized societal crisis or a restructuring of capitalist democracy, as with the creation of welfare states after 1945. At other times mass public housing is "a radical challenge to core capitalist interests" (Harloe, 1997, p. 538). As noteworthy, however, is the historic failure of social democratic regimes to challenge this trajectory, even though the capacity of some owner occupiers to realize capital gains is a major cause of increasing inequality, and the thoughtless demonization of "problem families" contributes to social exclusion, violence, and disorder.

BIBLIOGRAPHY

Baldwin, P. *The Politics of Social Solidarity: Class Bases of the European Welfare State, 1875–1975*. Cambridge, 1990.

Coleman, A. *Utopia on Trial*. London, 1985.

Faith in the City. Report of the Archbishop of Canterbury's Commission on Urban Priority Areas. London, 1985.

Fuerst, J. S., ed. *Public Housing in Europe and America*. London, 1974.

Harloe, M. *The People's Home? Social Rented Housing in Europe and America*. Oxford, 1997.

Malpass, P. *Housing Associations and Housing Policy: A Historical Perspective*. New York, 2000.

Malpass, P., and A. Murie. *Housing Policy and Practice*. Basingstoke, U.K., 1999.

Musil, J. "The Development of Prague's Ecological Structure." In *Readings in Urban Sociology*, edited by R. E. Pahl, pp. 232–259. Oxford, 1968.

Pooley, C. G., ed. *Housing Strategies in Europe, 1880–1939*. Leicester, 1992.

Power, A. *Hovels to High Rise: State Housing in Europe since 1850*. London, 1993.

Ravetz, A. *Council Housing and Culture: The History of a Social Experiment*. London, 2001.

ANDRZEJ OLECHNOWICZ

PUBLIC UTILITIES *[This entry contains five subentries, a historical overview and discussions of electrical supply and networks, gas supply and networks, mass transit, and postal systems.]*

Historical Overview

The past 150 years have witnessed the development of public utility systems in the areas of gas, electricity, telephones, local rail and bus lines, and water and sewerage. Gas and water and sewerage systems were built first, typically during the late eighteenth and early nineteenth centuries for the world's largest cities; and during the mid- to late-nineteenth century for smaller cities. Electricity, telephones, and local transit systems were not developed until the late nineteenth and early twentieth centuries. In the formative stages of development, consumers had to exorbitantly pay high rates for services of often dubious quality. Consequently, only businesses and a handful of wealthy families were able to afford such luxuries. As late as 1880, for example, less than one-quarter of urban residents in the United States were connected to public water systems. Only when extensions in service allowed producers better to exploit economies of scale in production and distribution, did rates fall and become affordable for large segments of urban society.

These new technologies transformed urban life. The introduction of water and sewerage systems helped eliminate waterborne diseases such as cholera, dysentery, and typhoid fever from the developed world. Typhoid, for example, is unheard of in the developed world where clean and safe water is easily accessible, and remains a problem only in those areas that have yet to develop adequate public water systems. Similarly, gas and electricity systems allowed urban dwellers to switch away from using dirtier and more dangerous technologies associated with burning coal, wood, candles, and kerosene. Light derived from either coal gas or electricity was not only cleaner and safer; it also was cheaper and more powerful. A modern-day electric lamp gives off twelve hundred times more light than the earliest forms of lighting.

Three factors make it likely for public utility systems to be heavily regulated and controlled by government authorities. First, public utilities' rates and service are politically salient. Gas, electricity, water, and the like have long been central to the daily operation of most households in the developed world; so, consumers are sensitive to high rates or poor service. This is especially true in the case of water, where failure to provide clean water at an affordable price has contributed to epidemics of typhoid fever and cholera. Historically, in major American and European cities, politicians have been able to garner votes, and in some cases win elections, solely on the promise of delivering lower utility rates.

Second, public utility systems are natural monopolies. Distribution of gas, electricity, water, sewerage services, and so on, is subject to substantial economies of scale; it is inefficient to have duplicate mains or pipelines. Moreover, at least in the case of water and sewerage systems, there also may have been substantial positive externalities in the form of reduced risk of epidemic disease. In this setting, devising institutional structures that promote effective and long-lasting competition among utility companies is difficult. Only in the past twenty years have authorities devised mechanisms that enable consumers to chose from an array of utility providers, particularly in the area of gas and electricity, rather than relying on a single monopoly provider. This has been accomplished by unbundling the supply, transportation, and storage services offered by natural gas and electricity providers.

The third reason why public utility systems are likely to be regulated is related to technology: utility systems are both costly and highly idiosyncratic (for example, once constructed, gas mains have no other use other than distributing gas), so that the owners of such systems are vulnerable to opportunistic behavior on the part of political authorities. Because it is difficult for utility companies to relocate and reconfigure their assets for alternative uses, they are often at the mercy of the local and regional governments that control them. As a result, for much of their history, utility companies have been the victims of regulatory and political extortion. There are many examples of local politicians winning votes from consumers by setting utility rates below cost, or extorting bribes from local utilities by threatening onerous regulatory policies.

This vulnerability has had important implications for the regulatory evolution of public utilities. Given the possibility of regulatory hold-up after they install their mains and wires, private utility companies were initially reluctant to enter urban markets. Only if local politicians could credibly promise not to engage in opportunistic behavior ex post facto did private companies invest. In the absence of such commitments, private companies refused to invest, and local governments were forced to undertake the process of building and operating utility systems themselves. European cities tended to follow the latter course, and typically controlled their local utility systems via municipal ownership. In contrast, local U.S. authorities often made the necessary commitments by going to the other extreme and granting private utility companies lucrative franchises that imposed few constraints on rates and guaranteed the companies monopoly status. Another solution was for local authorities, who had the strongest incentives to engage in opportunistic forms of regulation, to abdicate control to officials in higher governmental jurisdictions, who presumably were more objective than local governments in the regulatory policies they espoused. In the United States, this commitment procedure transferred regulatory power from local city councils to state regulatory commissions, a change that occurred between 1910 and 1930, depending on the state.

[*See also* Public Goods *and* Public Health.]

BIBLIOGRAPHY

Armstrong, Christopher, and H. V. Nelles. *Monopoly's Moment: The Organization and Regulation of Canadian Utilities, 1830–1930*. Philadelphia, 1986.

Blake, Nelson. *Water for the Cities: A History of the Urban Water Supply Problem in the United States*. Syracuse, N.Y., 1956.

Castaneda, Christopher J., and Clarence M. Smith. *Gas Pipelines and the Emergence of America's Regulatory State: A History of the Panhandle Eastern Corporation, 1928–1993*. Cambridge, 1996.

Foreman-Peck, James, and Robert Millward. *Public and Private Ownership of British Industry, 1820–1990*. Oxford, 1994.

Gayle, Dennis J., and Jonathan N. Goodrich, eds. *Privatization and Deregulation in Global Perspective*. Westport, Conn., 1990.

Hughes, Thomas P. *Networks of Power: Electrification in Western Society, 1880–1930*. Baltimore, 1983.

Levy, Brian, and Pablo T. Spiller. "The Institutional Foundations of Regulatory Commitment: A Comparative Analysis of Telecommunications Regulation." *Journal of Law, Economics, and Organization* 10 (1995), 201–246.

Melosi, Martin V. *The Sanitary City: Urban Infrastructure in America from Colonial Times to the Present*. Baltimore, 2000.

Thompson, Carl D. *A Survey of Public Enterprises, Municipal, State, and Federal, in the United States and Elsewhere*. New York, 1925.

Troesken, Werner. *Why Regulate Utilities? The New Institutional Economics and the Chicago Gas Industry, 1849–1924*. Ann Arbor, 1996.

WERNER TROESKEN

Electricity Supply and Networks

Before electricity was supplied as a commodity, telegraph, telephone, and arc lighting utilities used it to supply their services. Arc lighting's brilliant intensity made it unsuitable for most indoor usage. The need for a "subdivided" light eventually led to the development of the incandescent light almost simultaneously by Joseph Swan (1828–1914) in England and Thomas Edison (1847–1931) in the United States. Edison's contribution to the electric power industry went far beyond the light bulb as he developed a complete system to generate electricity centrally and distribute it to consumers. In April 1882, an Edison demonstration system complete with central station and lighting customers was opened in London (Holborn Viaduct). In September of the same year, a permanent system of the same type began operation in New York City (Pearl Street).

Early Network Development. Edison's direct-current technology lacked a means of easily converting the voltage of electric current, a capability necessary for long-distance transmission and the development of large electricity networks. Such networks provide several important economic advantages. Generating stations need not be physically close to consumers, often a requirement for hydroelectricity, which must be generated where nature provides falling water. Although steam plant location is more flexible, these plants are best placed either near large bodies of water that can serve as heat sinks or near supplies of fuel.

Networks that connect dissimilar users of electricity are likely to have steadier usage of electricity over time. Suppose residential electricity use occurs primarily in the evening and industrial use occurs primarily during the day. A network connecting both groups can allow the same generating equipment that supplies industrial users during the day to supply residential users in the evening. By using the generators more fully around the clock (higher "load factor"), less total generating capacity is needed than would be if each group were supplied separately, thus reducing costs.

In order to insure reliability, reserve generating capacity must be maintained to provide power when random events (such as unexpected breakdowns) cause ordinary capacity to be insufficient to meet demand. A network combining many generating stations and users will have a lower variance in these random shortfalls and can thus achieve a desired level of reliability with a lower proportion of capacity devoted to reserve.

Networks provide particular benefits to hydroelectricity. The total amount of power available from a hydroelectric installation varies according to variability in the flow of water. Some of this variation is seasonal and some of it is random. Although hydroelectricity can be quite cheap to generate, users of electricity place enormous value on reliability. A network that interconnects steam and hydroelectric generators can use the steam generators when hydroelectricity is unavailable, thus providing reliability. A large network also offers a large number of potential users for unpredictable "dump" power, which must be used opportunistically. For these reasons, networks have frequently been developed first where hydroelectricity was present.

Despite the enormous advantages of large-scale networks, the United States found it difficult to implement them fully. Although network technology became quite complex, it was always easier for the engineer to design an optimal network than it was to overcome the institutional, legal, and political barriers required to build one. Competitors of Edison, including the U.S. companies Westinghouse and Thomson-Houston, developed alternating current (AC) systems in which transformers could be easily used to convert electricity to high voltage for transmission and back to lower voltage for use. Although a "battle of the systems" raged at the close of the nineteenth century, the networking advantages of AC were insurmountable. The development of interface technologies, such as the rotary converter that converted alternating current to direct current, greatly aided the construction of large networks encompassing existing systems.

Private or Municipal Ownership? Before the turn of the century, the U.S. industry consisted of numerous small independent enterprises. Twenty-five nonexclusive franchises were granted for Manhattan between 1882 and 1900, and twenty-four electric utilities were established in Chicago between 1883 and 1887. The period between 1900 and 1906 saw considerable consolidation in metropolitan areas. Under the leadership of Commonwealth Edison's president, Samuel Insull (1859–1938), who had worked for Thomas Edison and had become the most prominent industry executive of his time, Chicago developed the first modern metropolitan supply network. Insull's success was due to his political skills, his devotion to the newest technology, his unwavering commitment to increased scale in both generation and distribution, and his willingness to take risks.

An early concern in the United States was over the issue of whether electric (and other) utilities should be owned and operated by private for-profit companies or by municipal governments. Municipalities had an advantage in raising money in capital markets since municipal governments could prevent private competition and could guarantee bonds with taxation powers. A study begun in 1905 by the National Civic Federation with individuals on all sides of the issue led to a consensus that if utilities were privately owned, they should operate as protected monopolies whose profits were regulated by state utility commissions. Between 1907 and 1914, most states adopted utility regulation using an evolving methodology originally developed for railroads and unique to the United States. This did not, however, end the argument over the proper ownership of utilities.

Rapid Growth and Increased Power Demands. Both the scale and the output of the U.S. industry grew rapidly. In 1904, for example, the largest turbine-powered generator had a capacity of only 5,000 kilowatts. Eight years later, the largest generator had a capacity of 20,000 kilowatts, and a state-of-the-art power plant probably had a capacity of around 40,000 kilowatts. By 1929, the maximum generator capacity had leapt to 165,000 kilowatts, and a state-of-the-art plant had a capacity of around 610,000 kilowatts. Along with increased generator size came improvements in transmission technology, enabling higher transmission voltages, which increased the carrying capacity of transmission lines. The maximum voltage of transformers ordered from General Electric, the largest producer of electrical equipment in the industry, doubled from 140,000 volts in 1911 to 280,000 volts in 1933. Kilowatt-hour generation in the United States went from 11.5 billion in 1912 to 43.6 billion in 1922 to 79.3 billion in 1932, nearly a sevenfold increase over the two decades. The number of customers increased by a slightly smaller factor, from 3.8 million in 1912 to 23.8 million in 1932, reflecting increased consumption per customer. Generating capacity increased from 5.1 gigawatts in 1912 to 34.4 gigawatts in 1932, a 6.7-fold increase. Because of the growing scale of production technology, this expansion in output occurred without an increase in the number of machines powering generators. In 1912, there were 11,902 electric utility prime movers; in 1932, there were 11,185. The power of the average prime mover had increased from a little more than 630 horsepower to nearly 4,300 horsepower, and the capacity of the generators they powered similarly increased.

The capital appetite of the industry was enormous and forced it constantly into capital markets in a quest for outside financing. Not until after 1914 did the industry's total revenues equal its capital expenditures, and in the 1920s annual gross capital expenditures averaged more than 50 percent of revenue. During the early part of the twentieth century, it was difficult to induce those not actually involved in the running of a company to invest in the company's equity. This cash shortage resulted in many of the suppliers to electric utilities accepting their customer's stock as payment for equipment or services. These stock holdings formed the nucleus of many of the public utility holding companies that were to play a large role in the industry.

Long-distance transmission and large networks in the United States prior to World War I were generally associated with hydroelectricity from the Sierra Nevada Mountains in California and the Appalachians in the Southeast. In both areas, population centers tended to be located a distance from hydroelectric sites. Point-to-point transmission lines later developed into proper networks.

World War I created concern in several countries, including the United States, Germany, and Great Britain, that existing systems were insufficient to meet wartime needs and that both increased generating capacity and improved networks were necessary to meet those needs. Both Germany and the United States created new giant power plants. In the United States, construction of the massive Wilson Dam across the Tennessee River was begun but was unfinished at war's end. In Germany, the Golpa-Zschornewitz plant had similar origins. War enabled the U.S. government to encourage and even mandate interconnections between power companies. That power ended with the war, however, and Americans returned to bickering over whether electric utilities should be publicly or privately owned. This situation contrasted sharply with those in Germany and Great Britain, which had traditions of mixed government-private involvement in the power industry. In the United States, political differences delayed the completion of the Wilson Dam, and the issue of its disposition occupied the U.S. Congress more than any other single issue during the 1920s.

The postwar period saw the development of a regional network in Bavaria and a nationwide grid in Great Britain. The failure of regional networks to develop an optimal form in the United States became apparent in a study by the U.S. Geological Survey in 1921. Authored by William S. Murray, the *Superpower* report showed that better coordination and interconnection among the utilities serving the area between Washington, D.C., and Boston had the potential of saving 40 percent of total costs. Although the report tried to be sensitive to the interests of the existing private utilities, ownership and other institutional barriers prevented the bulk of improvements from being made. An exception was the Pennsylvania–New Jersey Interconnection, constructed in part in response to the huge Conowingo Dam and hydroelectric facility. This became a rare example of an integrated interstate U.S. network involving private power companies under different ownership. In 1956, this network was renamed the Pennsylvania–New Jersey–Maryland Interconnection, and it coordinated the operations of eleven private electric utilities by 1981.

With the primary backing of the new governor, Gifford Pinchot, and his utilities advisor, the Philadelphia engineer Morris Lewellen Cooke, an agency of the Pennsylvania state government released in 1925 another integrated network plan that came to be known as the *Giant Power* proposal. Although it covered only utilities in Pennsylvania, it advocated a complete restructuring of the industry. Independent generating stations sited at coal mines were to compete for customers. Separate transmission companies would operate as common carriers and would connect the mine mouth generators with distributors. Although these distributors could be regulated private companies, new classes of government-owned and cooperative distributors were also to be created to provide service to underserved rural areas. The *Giant Power* proposal made little attempt to accommodate the interests of existing utilities, and it would have sharply reduced the power of the existing regulatory commission. It advocated the use of new technologies its critics argued were untested. It faced considerable opposition from private utility interests and failed to pass the Pennsylvania legislature.

Holding Companies. Public utility holding companies became increasingly important in the United States during the 1920s. In addition to electrical equipment manufacturers, financiers, consulting engineers, and utility executives also formed holding companies. A holding company typically owned a controlling but minority interest in several operating companies or other holding companies. The tendency of multiple layers of holding companies to form enabled some top holding companies to maintain absolute control over operating companies despite miniscule investment in those companies. Unified control enabled holding companies to consolidate a number of smaller companies operating in contiguous territories and led to large regional integrated networks still in operation today, including systems operated by The Southern Company and American Electric Power. Most holding company holdings were not contiguous, however, and the nature of corporate ownership made it difficult to determine who controlled U.S. electric utilities. By the latter part of the decade, many believed that the industry was heading toward a national monopoly, as had already occurred in the telephone industry. Alarmed, the proponents of public ownership succeeded in initiating several government investigations of the utility holding company industry. The

Federal Trade Commission (FTC) between 1928 and 1935 conducted the last of these, the most extensive investigation ever undertaken of any U.S. industry. The reports issued by the FTC revealed widespread exploitation of the regulatory system through excessive service charges, several instances of unstable financial structures, and at least one case of financial mismanagement resulting in criminal charges.

The intervening Great Depression further strengthened the hand of the opponents of private power, including the new President Franklin D. Roosevelt, whose tenure as governor of New York made him a veteran of battles between the advocates of government and private ownership of utilities, and exposed him to Ontario Hydro, a publicly owned utility whose service area was adjacent to New York. Ontario Hydro charged lower prices than nearby privately owned New York utilities and also had a program of rural electrification unlike anything in New York. Ontario Hydro and its leader, the charismatic Adam Beck, had become a lightning rod for both the proponents and opponents of publicly owned utilities in the United States. Expansion of electricity usage became a major goal of the New Deal. Within the first hundred days, the Tennessee Valley Authority (TVA) was established with a broad mandate to develop the Tennessee River basin. The TVA created an integrated hydroelectric system in the Tennessee Valley, sold electricity at low prices—particularly to residential users—pioneered rural electrification in the United States, and eliminated all privately owned power companies in its area. For decades it served as the lightning rod for the controversy over utility ownership. Other New Deal programs subsidized the construction of municipal power systems, encouraged the formation of rural electric cooperatives, and built and operated massive hydroelectric facilities on the Columbia River and elsewhere. Although these policies may have had a positive or neutral impact on the development of electricity networks, the Public Utilities Holding Company Act (PUHCA) of 1935 had a negative impact. This law ordered a massive restructuring of the industry by forbidding any holding company from owning operating companies in more than one state unless those companies had contiguous service territories and were operated as a single utility. All other operating companies had to be divested. Holding companies that continued to exist were required to register with the Securities and Exchange Commission and obtain extraordinary prior approval to issue any securities.

The PUHCA eliminated the major method by which large, integrated regional networks were developing in the United States. The original Administration bill would have ameliorated this somewhat by giving the Federal Power Commission the authority to order utility interconnections and the construction of transmission facilities. This provision was dropped after opposition from state regulators, who feared this would lead to usurpation of their regulatory authority by the Federal agency. Although there was hope that enforcement of the act would result in "trading" of operating companies so that holding companies would acquire systems with contiguous territories, this did not occur.

World Electrification. The 1920s and 1930s saw a worldwide increase in interest on electrification, and several World Power Congresses were held in which delegates from many countries shared information and experiences. The 1933 conference provided statistics that give some insight into the state of world electrification at that time. The four countries with the highest per capita consumption of electricity were Canada, Sweden, Switzerland, and the United States, in that order. Norway did not participate in that conference, but other data suggest its per capita electricity use was substantially higher than Canada's. Despite the emergence of networks, very little electricity was sold internationally. Switzerland did not export electricity to its neighbors, and Canada was a net exporter to the United States. Nevertheless, imported electricity was negligible for all reporting countries. There was considerable variation in how electricity was used at that time. Most electricity appeared to be used for industrial purposes. Although the United States devoted an above-average proportion to homes, offices, shops, and small motors, its proportion was exceeded by the corresponding proportions in seven other countries, including Switzerland, Austria and New Zealand.

Of particular note is the fact that most of the countries participating in the World Power Congress in 1933 provided electricity to a larger proportion of their population than did the United States. Less than 70 percent of Americans lived in areas where electricity was available. By contrast, more than 90 percent of those living in Demark, the Netherlands, Belgium, Switzerland, Luxembourg, France, and Italy were in areas served by electricity. Even those living in Czechoslovakia and Spain apparently had better access to electricity than did Americans.

In the United States, the period from 1945 to 1965 was one in which rapid technological improvement led to falling prices in every year (except 1945–1946), and continued growth in output and consumption. War requirements resulted in increased generation to meet such needs as aluminum production, and some networking improvements were made, including the formation of the Southwestern Power Pool. The fight over utility ownership abated partly because Congress prohibited the TVA from extending its service area and enabled it to borrow funds instead of depending on contentious Congressional action.

World War II ended with the destruction of much of Europe's electric power infrastructure. The French government took over the reconstruction of the industry through the government-owned Électricité de France, which set about a large scale program of construction of hydroelectric facilities and of the reintegration of the systems of some one thousand private utilities that had previously provided electrical service. The utility was a leader in the use of rate structures to encourage electricity consumption patterns to maximize economic efficiency.

A sequence of crises hit the industry after 1965. In that year, a failed relay in Ontario led to a blackout that affected most of the northeastern United States, providing stark evidence of the need for network improvements and leading to the formation of the National (now North American) Electricity Reliability Council (NERC) to help coordinate interutility reliability efforts. The OPEC oil embargo of 1973 and ensuing energy crisis resulted in turmoil for the industry as it faced pressures to switch boiler fuels. Increased national sensitivity to environmental problems had a major impact on the electric power industry that by then was responsible for most of the coal use in the United States.

Nuclear Power. The biggest crisis, however, involved a disastrous experience with nuclear power. Although the industry was initially hesitant to embrace this technology, it faced considerable encouragement from the U.S. government. In hindsight, its reaction was amazing. By the late 1960s, nuclear plants under construction were six times bigger than any in operation. It was an enormous gamble on an untried technology, and it went badly for the industry. Plants routinely ended up costing five to ten times their original estimates. Even more damaging, the estimates of electricity demand used to plan new construction were wrong—in part because of the increases in electricity's price—forcing the cancellation of unneeded plants on which considerable expenditures had already been made. The total capacity of cancelled plants eventually exceeded the capacity of all plants in existence. This ultimately led to a movement to restructure the industry, a change that will accentuate the need for improved network facilities.

Contemporary defenders of nuclear power in the United States place much of the blame for its failure on the system of regulatory oversights to which the U.S industry was subjected. This system, it was argued, force unnecessary duplication in the reviews of the designs of separate plants and imposed significant and expensive design changes after construction was well underway. Nuclear power, in this view, was best handled by France, which had a streamlined regulatory process characterized by preapproved designs. Today, roughly 80 percent of French electricity is generated by nuclear power, the highest per capita generation of any country. Like the United States, however, France also overestimated the future demand for electricity and was forced to cancel much planned capacity.

BIBLIOGRAPHY

Brown, D. Clayton. *Electricity for Rural America: The Fight for the REA*. Westport, Conn., 1980. The definitive history of the REA.

Brown, Frederick, ed. *Statistical Year-Book of the World Power Conference, No. 1, 1933 & 1934*. London, 1936.

Conot, Robert. *A Streak of Luck*. New York, 1979. Classic biography of Edison.

Hargrove, Erwin C. *Prisoners of Myth: The Leadership of the Tennessee Valley Authority, 1933–1990*. Princeton, 1994. Although the entire history of the TVA is covered, this work is mainly concerned with the problems that became apparent starting in the late 1970s.

Hirsch, Richard E. *Power Loss: the Origins of Deregulation and Restructuring in the American Electric Utility Industry*. Cambridge, Mass., 1999. Especially valuable for events in the industry between 1960 and the late 1990s.

Hubbard, Preston. *Origins of the TVA: The Muscle Shoals Controversy, 1920–1932*. Nashville, 1961. The story of Wilson Dam to the beginning of the TVA.

Hughes, Thomas P. *Networks of Power: Electrification in Western Society, 1880–1930*. Baltimore, 1983. A number of case studies involving the development of electricity networks are examined in detail, including the development of electricity supply in Berlin, Chicago, and London.

Hyman, Leonard S. *America's Electric Utilities: Past, Present, and Future*. Arlington, Va., 1985. The views of a stock analyst on utility financing, the holding companies, and nuclear power.

Israel, Paul. *Edison: A Life of Invention*. New York, 1998. Recent scholarly Edison biography.

McDonald, Forrest. *Insull*. Chicago, 1962. Sympathetic and readable biography of one of the most interesting of the electric utility pioneers.

Mitchell, Sidney A. *S. Z. Mitchell and the Electrical Industry*. New York, 1960. Biography of the founder of the Electric Bond and Share Company by his son. Good case study illustrating how holding companies came to dominate the industry.

Nye, David E. *Electrifying America: Social Meanings of a New Technology, 1880–1940*. Cambridge, Mass., 1990. Deals more with the impact of electrification on American life than with the business history of the industry.

Owen, Marguerite. *The Tennessee Valley Authority*. New York, 1973. Many books have been written about the TVA, whose reputation plummeted after this book was written. This is a relatively unbiased but favorable account of the TVA's early history. Earlier books tend to be polemical. Later ones tend to deal with the loss of reputation.

Rudolph, Richard, and Scott Ridley. *Power Struggle: The Hundred-Year War over Electricity*. New York, 1986. The struggle between private and public ownership over electric utilities. The account is more journalistic than scholarly and is sympathetic with the public power side.

Stoler, Peter. *Decline and Fail: The Ailing Nuclear Power Industry*. New York, 1985. A balanced account of the events surrounding the abandonment of nuclear power, this book does not fully analyze the issues of economics and utility planning.

JOHN L. NEUFELD

Gas Supply and Networks

This review of the evolution of gas distribution focuses on three aspects of distribution: technology, social context, and regulation.

Technology. Distributing gas for lighting and heating always has required large and irrevocable investments in mains, pipelines, and other distribution technologies. The nature and geographic scope of these investments, however, has depended on the type of gas being distributed: manufactured coal gas or natural gas.

Manufactured coal gas was used during the nineteenth and early twentieth centuries primarily for lighting and to a much lesser degree for heating. Gaslight was an urban phenomenon. For example, in the United States in 1899, four cities—Chicago, New York, Philadelphia, and Saint Louis—consumed half of all the coal gas produced in the country. In rural areas, kerosene lamps remained the most common form of lighting well into the twentieth century. Moreover, until the late 1870s, lighting with gas was a luxury. In 1870, it would have cost more than 15 percent of the average laborer's income to light a home with gas. Gas companies thus sold primarily to businesses and the wealthy. Competition from other lighting sources, such as kerosene, helped limit the demand for gas; in 1870, it cost much more to light a home with gas than with oil lamps. However, during the late 1870s and early 1880s, technological changes caused large reductions in gas rates. Rate reductions and other factors—gas gave off four times more light than kerosene, and it was cleaner and safer to use—helped expand the market for coal gas. By 1900, some 9 percent of all U.S. families lit their homes with gas, and 35 percent of all families did so by 1920.

Coal gas almost always was distributed through a set of mains specific to a particular city, and investments in gas mains dwarfed the capital investments made by other urban manufacturers. For example, in the two largest cities in the United States in 1890, Chicago and New York, local gas companies owned more than 10 percent of all physical capital invested in their respective cities, a figure not equaled by any other industry. Gas companies put nearly all of their capital underground, in the form of mains. By 1906, Chicago gas companies had laid over two thousand miles of mains. According to one official, it would have taken "10,000 to 15,000 men, working constantly, summer and winter, two years to lay 2,000 miles of mains" (Troesken, 1996). Other sources suggest that during the early 1890s it cost about $135,000, in 1991 dollars, to lay one mile of gas mains.

Why did gas mains cost so much? Although wood and paper were used for mains during the early 1800s, by the late nineteenth century mains were made almost exclusively of cast iron. Engineers advised that they should measure more than four inches in diameter and weigh no less than 220 pounds per twelve-foot length of pipe. Large high-pressure mains, those more than twenty inches in diameter, weighed over a ton. Given the size and the weight of the mains, laborers worked in gangs of twenty or more, placing the mains thirty inches or more below ground to reduce the stress induced by cold weather and heavy traffic. The mains also were pitched to prevent sulfur and tar residuals from building up and clogging them.

During the twentieth century, competition from electricity and natural gas gradually undermined the market for coal gas. Electricity drove consumers away from using gas for light and toward using it for heating and cooking. Electricity was a safer, and eventually cheaper, lighting source than gas. Nonetheless, because people used coal gas for both heat and light, for a long time it remained more popular than electricity. For example, as late as 1916, there were roughly twice as many coal gas consumers in major American and European cities as there were electricity consumers. As electricity eroded the gas-lighting market, natural gas eroded the coal-gas–heating and –cooking market. Natural gas, with two times more heat energy per cubic foot than coal gas, was the superior heating fuel. By the 1960s, residential consumers had stopped using coal gas for either light or heat.

As demand for, and production of, natural gas grew, so too did the networks of mains used to distribute gas. Networks designed for distributing gas within the confines of a particular city, or even portions of a particular city, gradually were incorporated into larger interregional distribution systems. In the United States, large interstate pipelines were built linking supplies of natural gas in Alaska and the southwest with concentrations of population and consumer demand in other regions. By the year 2000, there were nearly sixteen thousand miles of interstate pipelines installed in the United States. Recent estimates suggest that the costs of laying large interstate pipelines were even larger than those associated with laying city-specific mains, as much as five to ten times larger; between 1996 and 2000, the cost of laying one mile of pipe averaged $862,000.

As large interstate pipelines linked regions within the United States, gas supplies in Algeria, Libya, and Russia were linked to concentrations of consumer demand in Europe, Japan, and the United States through the development of vast interregional pipelines and the introduction of a new technology of distribution: liquefied natural gas. Lowering the temperature of natural gas to −260°F reduced its volume six hundred times and allowed it to be transported as a liquid in modified ocean tankers. As with pipelines, shipping liquefied natural gas required large idiosyncratic investments. Cryogenic tankers capable of keeping the gas at −260°F had to be built, as did special receiving terminals to handle the refrigerated tankers. As with pipelines, these distribution systems cost hundreds of millions of dollars.

Social Context. Gas lighting and heating transformed household life in good and bad ways. Before gas, people used coal and wood to fuel their stoves and heat their homes and candles and kerosene lamps for light. These technologies required substantial amounts of household labor. In 1900, the typical urban household using coal stoves had to shovel seven and one-half tons of coal a year; for households using coal-fired furnaces, six tons had to be shoveled into the furnace each year. People often made their own candles and trimmed their own oil lamps; but the oil lamps frequently exploded, burning those trying to light them. Coal gas and natural gas freed housewives and other home laborers from such drudgery and danger. On the other hand, using gas had its own risks. An individual who failed to turn off gas lights before retiring for bed risked death or serious injury; if the gas flame were blown out somehow, the odorless gas eventually would cause asphyxiation. Such deaths were not uncommon during the nineteenth century. However, some cultural historians argue that people were uneasy about becoming dependent on outside, industrial sources for light and heat, rather than being self-sufficient.

More broadly, social historians of technology argue that the diffusion of new technologies is not an inexorable process but is shaped by humanly devised institutions and organizations relating to culture, economics, law, and politics. The introduction of gas light and heat provides a case in point. In *Cities of Light and Heat: Domesticating Gas and Electricity in Urban America*, Mark H. Rose shows how various social constructs influenced gas distribution. In Rose's story, norms about appropriate gender roles shaped the way gas companies marketed their new technologies. One gas company, for example, promoted the use of gas stoves with an advertisement stating: "Where a lady has a day's work to do, the gas range is good for an hour's saving time." Rose also shows that organizations with no direct links to gas companies influenced the diffusion of this new technology. For example, public-school teachers promoted social norms, such as cleanliness and safety, that encouraged future home owners to use gas. Similarly, home builders used gas and electricity as part of larger advertising schemes that promised home buyers quaint stone fences, shelters, parks, and old-fashioned bridges.

Regulation. For most of their existence, gas suppliers and distributors have been regulated in one form or another. Three factors have helped make it likely that gas suppliers will be regulated. First, gas rates and service are politically salient. Because gas was, and continues to be, central to the operation of most households in the developed world, high rates, unusually large increases in rates, or poor service will generate substantial consumer dissatisfaction and political activity. Second, distributing gas is subject to substantial economies of scale; it is not efficient to have duplicate sets of distribution mains. In this context, promoting genuine competition among gas suppliers and distributors is difficult. Third, as the discussion above implies, distributing gas required large and idiosyncratic investments; gas mains were expensive and had no use other than distributing gas—leaving gas distributors vulnera-

ble to political expropriation by regulatory authorities. Simply put, local regulators could extort bribes, or use low rates as a way to win votes, without fear that gas companies in their jurisdiction would exit because it was impossible for gas companies to pick up their mains and move.

For western Europe and the United States, the regulatory history of gas distribution might be divided into four distinct phases:

- Phase I (1790–1880): an early developmental stage, characterized by private ownership and lax regulatory controls.
- Phase II (1880–1900): characterized by a high degree of local, city-level regulation and control, through either municipal ownership or municipal regulation.
- Phase III (1900–1970): characterized by increased regulatory involvement of state or national regulators (as opposed to municipal regulators), through either state/national regulation or nationalized ownership.
- Phase IV (1970–present): characterized by deregulation of private or investor-owned gas companies and privatization of nationalized and municipally owned gas companies.

The lax regulatory environment that characterized the early history of gas regulation was driven by two factors: (1) consumers (because there were so few of them) had relatively little political clout during this period, and (2) local governments were concerned that strict regulations might inhibit private investment. The concern about regulations inhibiting private investment was not unfounded. In the United States, cities and towns that refused to grant generous regulatory franchises to gas companies found themselves without service, and were forced to build and operate municipally owned gas systems.

As the gas industry developed and expanded, the number of consumers grew and so too did their political power. By the late nineteenth century, consumers had become thoroughly dissatisfied with the high rates and the poor service of the private monopolies that dominated local gas markets. In turn, the consumers lobbied local governments for increased oversight and control, which ushered in the period of municipal regulation and ownership. There were sharp national differences in how this process played out, however. Municipal ownership was much more common in England and continental Europe than the United States. By 1900, in England nearly 50 percent of all gas companies were municipally owned, whereas in the United States less than 5 percent of all gas companies were so owned. Instead, U.S. cities and towns relied on municipal regulation.

Now captives of local politics and consumer demands, the gas companies that managed to remain in private hands quickly grew dissatisfied with municipal control and lobbied for regulation by either state or national authorities, who they believed would be less responsive than municipalities to the demands of consumers. The move to the next phase, that of state and national control, was driven in part by this lobbying and in part by technological changes that undermined the efficacy of local control. For example, during the early twentieth century in the United States, gas companies began to ship natural gas through vast interstate pipelines that could not, under the U.S. Constitution, be regulated by state and local authorities. This gave rise to the a series of laws expanding the regulatory powers of the federal government during the 1930s.

The move to deregulation and privatization was driven by two forces. First, there was mounting evidence, much of it originating at the University of Chicago, that public-utility regulation in general and gas regulation in particular were not working as intended; gas companies were charging near-monopoly rates but providing imperfect service. Similar evidence highlighted the poor economic performance of government-owned and -operated enterprises. Second, in a larger era of government belt-tightening and fiscal conservatism, governments deemed it too costly to continue paying for regulatory and ownership systems that delivered dubious benefits.

[*See also* Gas Industry *and* Public Utilities, *subentry on* Historical Overview.]

BIBLIOGRAPHY

Brown, George T. *The Gas Light Company of Baltimore: A Study of Natural Monopoly.* Baltimore, 1936.

Castaneda, Christopher J., and Clarence M. Smith. *Gas Pipelines and the Emergence of America's Regulatory State: A History of the Panhandle Eastern Corporation, 1928–1993.* Cambridge, 1996.

Foreman-Peck, James, and Robert Millward. *Public and Private Ownership of British Industry, 1820–1990.* Oxford, 1994.

Jacobson, Charles David. *Ties That Bind: Economic and Political Dilemmas of Urban Utility Networks, 1800–1990.* Pittsburgh, 2000.

Rose, Mark H. *Cities of Light and Heat: Domesticating Gas and Electricity in Urban America.* University Park, Pa., 1995.

Schivelbusch, Wolfgang. *Disenchanted Night: The Industrialization of Light in the Nineteenth Century,* translated by Angela Davies. Berkeley, 1988.

Stotz, Louis P., and Alexander Jamison. *History of the Gas Industry.* New York, 1938.

Troesken, Werner. *Why Regulate Utilities? The New Institutional Economics and the Chicago Gas Industry, 1849–1924.* Ann Arbor, 1996.

Troesken, Werner. "The Sources of Public Ownership: Historical Evidence from the Gas Industry." *Journal of Law, Economics, and Organization* 13.1 (1997), 1–27.

WERNER TROESKEN

Mass Transit

Mass transit, otherwise known as urban public transport, is generally taken to mean transportation services in towns and cities provided in vehicles that are shared by multiple unrelated people. The services can be provided by road, on rails, or in some cases on water. The definition usually excludes taxicab services, intercity travel, and local services provided in rural areas. The history and fortunes of mass transit are intricately related to developments in transportation technology and also technology's effect on urban structure.

Horsepower. Prior to 1800, towns and cities were compact, and nearly all travel was done on foot or horseback. In some cities the existence of rivers or canals allowed some wealthy residents to live at some distance from the city center and commute by boat (see, for example, the *Diary* of Samuel Pepys). There is also evidence that following development of the harness, horse and oxen carts provided rudimentary systems of public conveyance in towns in the 1700s. However, their widespread use was limited, pending the breeding of larger horses and improvements in the deplorable conditions of the roadways. There appears to be some agreement that the first modern incarnation of a horse omnibus was in Nantes, France in 1825, its initial purpose being to convey the public to a spa on the edge of town. This operation also gave us the name omnibus after the "Omnes Omnibus" sign above the hatter's shop of Monsieur Omnes, which was located near the terminal. Within six years the innovation had spread to Paris, London, New York, and Philadelphia. The physical limitations of horse power constrained the capacity of the vehicles. Consequently prices were high, and service was limited to the middle class. More egalitarian transportation was made possible when the car was placed on rails (in 1835, in New York City), as a reduction in friction allowed use of a larger car and brought more affordable prices. Average speeds also increased, permitting the development of cities with a radius of two to two and one-half miles from their center. For the first time, persons without access to their own horse or carriage could live at some distance from their workplace. This development occurred at the same time that the first railroads started to provide commuter service—albeit with little influence on urban forms because stations had to be spaced far apart, and the termini did not penetrate the centers of most cities.

Electric Traction. Urban transport was limited by the speed and the capacity of the horse. Although steam traction was attempted on the existing horse-car lines, it soon became apparent that faster and higher-capacity services would be possible only if there were grade separation from street level. The first subsurface steam line was introduced in London in 1863, and the first elevated line in New York City in 1868. Although speeds were certainly faster, and congestion at ground level was avoided, these vehicles' smoke and soot were not much of an improvement over the smell and health risks of substantial volumes of horse manure. The use of underground cables to move the cars

PUBLIC TRANSPORTATION. Streetcar in Seoul, Korea, early 1900s. (Frank and Frances Carpenter Collection/Prints and Photographs Division, Library of Congress)

promised a somewhat cleaner alternative (from 1873 on in San Francisco), but the real breakthrough came in 1888 with the first substantial deployment of an electric streetcar (tramway) in Richmond, Virginia. American engineer Frank Sprague (1857–1934) mounted the electrical traction motors on the vehicle's axles and drew electrical feed from an overhead wire. Nine years later in Chicago, Sprague introduced a multiple-unit system whereby one driver could control all the motors on the train, thus starting a revolution.

Transit's Heyday. In the 1890s, existing horse- and cable-car lines were electrified and extended, and electric elevated and subway systems were constructed in the major cities. The resulting higher speeds allowed the new systems to serve areas four to five miles from the city center, which were beyond the reach of the horse bus but closer than the areas served by commuter railroads. Moreover, the high capacity of these systems allowed fares that all could afford. The use of a flat rather than a distance-based fare further encouraged workers to move away from congested and disease-ridden housing that surrounded the commercial centers. This time was perhaps the heyday of mass transit, as the various streetcar lines amalgamated to form large combines that provided transit service, generated electricity, and acted as property developers. It is reasonable to postulate that the only time in its history when transit was profitable was during the period when the companies were actually property developers who provided transit service as a subsidiary business. The development

ments spread beyond Europe and North America as electric subway systems opened in Buenos Aires (1914) and Tokyo (1927).

The dominance of the streetcar/tramway companies was short-lived. Motorbus services started in London in 1904 and New York in 1905. Moreover, private motorcars and shared taxicab, or jitney, services began to nibble at the edge of the market. Jitney and private bus services flourished in the years around the end of World War I, leading the existing transit companies to demand regulation to protect their markets. The consequent regulation came at a price, however. Rather shady pricing and financial dealings by streetcar companies in the 1890s led to public demands for price controls or public ownership. With rising costs, limitations on prices, competition from the car, and a legacy of overcapitalization and overexpansion in the 1890s, many private companies went bankrupt in the 1920s or during the Depression of the 1930s. Public ownership became more widespread. Per capita transit use decreased throughout the twentieth century, but an increase in urban population partly counteracted that decline in the early years of the century, resulting in a peacetime peak in the absolute number of transit riders in the mid-1920s.

Public Ownership and Subsidies. After a boom in transit use during World War II, the financial decline continued in the 1950s, now hastened as prosperity and increasing automobile ownership allowed for the development of low-density suburbs of single-family homes on the edges of traditional cities, away from traditional transit-served corridors. Industry also moved from locations close to rail yards in the center of traditional cities to those close to suburban intercity highways. Social turmoil in the 1960s further hastened the depopulation of older cities. The widespread availability of air-conditioning and the opening up of underpopulated areas of the Americas and Australasia led to the construction of new large cities that were totally automobile-dependent and significantly different in structure from traditional cities. It is frequently argued that nearly all cities that were founded, or expanded rapidly, in the twentieth century developed an urban pattern that consigned transit the role of a fringe mode of transportation. Some older cities (Detroit and Los Angeles are notable examples) became so automobile-dependent that public transit services all but disappeared.

In the short term, operators in traditional cities were able to remain solvent by the substitution of lower-cost trackless trolley buses and motor buses for streetcars/tramways. However, by the mid-1960s, all these gains had been reaped. Public operating subsidies were needed if these operators were to remain solvent. Consequently, the remainder of the industry passed into public ownership, there being a reluctance at the time to provide subsidy funds to private entities. At the same time, many relatively old but secondary cities whose population had grown since the 1940s (Toronto, Stockholm, Rome, Nagoya) demanded that mass-transit rail systems be built to create or preserve high-density downtowns. It became the norm to construct these new systems with public funds. Some authors are of the opinion that many of these systems are overbuilt, and that far greater benefits could be obtained with a resurgence of less-expensive streetcar, now known as light rail transit (LRT), or bus systems. This is equally true in the developing world (São Paulo, Caracas, Hong Kong), where many systems were built with foreign-aid money and with equipment and technology sold by companies in developed countries. For many of the new systems, particularly in North America, actual performance has been disappointing, with higher costs and lower demand than the proponents had claimed.

Deregulation and Privatization. The great expansion of public operating subsidies, particularly in the 1970s, gave rise to the suspicion that much of the funds had been channeled into wage increases for the staff, operating inefficiencies, and the pursuit of political or social goals. Also, the increasing subsidies did not stop the contraction of demand in the face of competition from the automobile. A backlash developed, with some observers looking to the commercial success of the descendants of the jitneys in the form of private minibus services in Kuala Lumpur, Malaysia, and Santiago de Chile. These authors argued that only private enterprise and competition could restore the fortunes of transit.

The British Transport Act of 1985 marked the start of the privatization era for transit. In Britain, formerly publicly owned operators were sold to the private sector. Now routes with high demand are provided commercially at commercial fares. Provision of services that still require subsidies are procured on short-term competitive contracts. Outside of London, entry restrictions were removed from the commercial sector of the market. In London, on the-road competition was not allowed, but now all routes—profitable and unprofitable—are provided by short-term franchises of three to five years. In the 1990s, privatization spread across the developed world, many parts of the former communist world, Asia, and South America. In most cases, privatization followed the London model rather than providing full, unfettered competition. All evidence points to unit-cost reductions of at least 30 percent. By the mid-1990s, privatization was being applied to rail services in addition to bus services. However, with a few exceptions (as, for example, in Denver, Indianapolis, and Phoenix), privatization has not made many inroads in the United States. In some countries such as Jamaica and in many parts of Africa, where unemployment is high and labor costs are low, either legal or illegal owner-operated jitneys have become so numerous and successful that the traditional public operator has been forced out of business. Although some economists have promoted the reintroduction of jitneys in developed countries, high labor costs and low unemployment rates usually have hindered the supply of these services. Indeed, in Britain the minibuses introduced by many companies immediately after deregulation have become less "mini" over time, and now approach the forty-seat vehicles that economists have calculated to be the optimal vehicle size.

The Future. The future of mass transit is unclear. After a century of decline, there may be new signs of hope. The fortunes of many traditional cities rebounded in the 1990s. Ridership is up in New York, London, and other cities for the first time since the 1920s (but not in the British provincial cities that have "enjoyed" the benefits of complete deregulation for fifteen years). Privatization has removed much of the midcentury excesses of regulation and subsidy-induced inefficiencies. The increasing road congestion in many of the more automobile-dominated cities has brought about a demand for the introduction of higher-density living and transit alternatives. Still there seems to be a preference by planners for high-cost rail-based systems rather than lower-cost road-based systems.

Of course, mass transit remains strong in countries with large populations, limited land availability, and/or low incomes that limit private-car ownership. Hong Kong, Singapore, Seoul, Mexico City, and the Japanese cities are strong mass-transit markets and may be expected to remain so for decades to come as driving there becomes almost impossible. Jitneys and shared taxis dominate in the large African cities, and new rail and bus-based systems are being deployed to solve the traffic problems of Bangkok and the Indian subcontinent. From a worldwide perspective, the reports of mass transit's death are very much exaggerated.

BIBLIOGRAPHY

Clutton-Brock, Juliet. *Horse Power: A History of the Horse and the Donkey in Human Societies.* Cambridge, Mass., 1992. Discusses equine forms of transportation prior to 1800.

Garbutt, Paul E. *London Transport and the Politicians.* London, 1985. Illustrates how political influence shaped mass transit from 1960 to 1985.

Glaister, Stephen, ed. *Transport Subsidy.* Newbury, U.K., 1987. A collection of essays discussing optimal levels of subsidies.

Gómez-Ibáñez, José A., and John R. Meyer. *Going Private: The International Experience with Transport Privatization.* Washington, D.C., 1993. A review of the initial stages of privatization.

Kain, John F. "The Urban Transportation Problem: A Reexamination and Update." In *Essays in Transportation Economics and Policy: A Handbook in Honor of John R. Meyer,* edited by José Gómez-Ibáñez, William B. Tye, and Clifford Winston, pp. 359–401. Washington, D.C., 1999. Discusses the decline of transit and critiques the preference for building rail-based systems. Updates an influential 1965 book that Kain coauthored.

Pickrell, Don H. "Rising Deficits and the Uses of Transit Subsidies in the United States." *Journal of Transport Economics and Policy* 19.3 (1985), 281–298. Discusses the diversion of subsidy funds into cost inefficiencies in the 1970s.

Thomson, J. Michael. *Great Cities and Their Traffic.* Harmondsworth, U.K., 1977. Shows how the urban form of cities around the world is related to their transportation system.

Vance, James E., Jr. *Capturing the Horizon: The Historical Geography of Transportation.* New York, 1986. A textbook treatment of the history of transportation. Chapter 5 provides a comprehensive treatment of early urban transportation.

Waters, Alan A. "The Benefits of Minibuses: The Case of Kuala Lumpur." *Journal of Transport Economics and Policy* 13.3 (1979), 320–334. Suggests that a free market could lead to improved service by the return of jitneys. Written by an author who was influential in public-policy decisions of the British government.

IAN SAVAGE

Postal Systems

The postal system, social theorist Francis Lieber observed in 1832, ranked with the printing press and the mariner's compass as one of the three "most effective agents of civilization." By substituting the postal system for gunpowder in Francis Bacon's celebrated technological triumvirate, Lieber highlighted the major role that the postal system— the principal preelectrical long-distance communications technology—by the nineteenth century had come to play in encouraging commerce, fostering political communication, and expanding popular access to knowledge.

This article highlights the significance of postal systems in economic history, with a focus on the period since 1700. For economic historians, postal systems are a neglected topic; many economic history textbooks ignore them altogether. This is unfortunate, since, as the Canadian economic historian Harold Innis demonstrated many decades ago, communication has distinctive attributes, which he termed "biases," that are susceptible to measurement and analysis. Constrained by the scarcity of relevant scholarship, this article is confined primarily to those postal systems that have attracted the most attention—namely, those in Great Britain, the United States, and France.

The Earliest Delivery Systems. The postal systems of the past three centuries have surprisingly little in common with the courier services of antiquity. Most courier services were confined to major administrative centers, and restricted, like the Roman *cursus publicus*, to the transmission of government dispatches. All were ordinarily closed to the general population. For this reason, the *Oxford Classical Dictionary* (New York, 1996), recommends that we characterize these services not as postal systems, but, rather, as "government communication networks."

The first identifiably modern postal systems emerged in medieval Europe to serve the political, diplomatic, social, and commercial needs of government officials, clerics, merchants, and students. By the eighteenth century, these corporate postal systems had been mostly superseded by the national postal systems similar to those of modern times. Large, geographically extensive, and administratively complex, national postal systems have for three hundred years been keystones of the modern information infrastructure. In the nineteenth century, they were often lumped together with the railroad and the telegraph as distinctively modern innovations. By 1900, some American journalists went so far as to call them the greatest business enterprises in the world.

It has long been customary for scholars to characterize mail delivery in the period prior to the railroad and the telegraph as primitive and slow. The limitations of long-distance information flows in the half-century between 1790 and 1840, for example, were a theme of Allan R. Pred's *Urban Growth and the Circulation of Information* (Cambridge, Mass., 1973) and Alfred D. Chandler, Jr.'s, *Visible Hand* (Cambridge, Mass., 1977). These scholars highlighted the indisputable fact that it was not until the 1840s, after the advent of the railroad and the telegraph, that commercial information routinely moved faster than government dispatches in ancient Rome.

The Pace Picks Up. Such a disparaging assessment of pre-1840 mail delivery is open to question. Speed, as Ian Steele demonstrated in his *English Atlantic, 1675–1740: An Exploration of Communication and Community* (New York, 1986), is not a transhistorical norm. In the eighteenth century, a horse express that attained a speed of ten miles an hour was fast. No means of communication, after all, had ever been faster. Beginning around 1800, an

POST OFFICE. London's post office, colored aquatint (1809) by Augustus Pugin (1762–1832). From *Microcosm of London*, 1809–c. 1811. (Prints and Photographs Division, Library of Congress)

impressive speed-up in mail delivery took place, hastened by incremental improvements in the road network and the growing reliance on the stagecoach as a means of conveyance. It was this communications revolution—based on renewable energy sources and utilizing no motive power unknown to the ancients—rather than the alleged slowness of the mails that shaped the popular conception of mail delivery in the generation immediately preceding the coming of the railroad and the telegraph.

Postal systems have often fostered improvements in the means of transportation. In early-nineteenth-century United States, for example, postal subsidies for stagecoach service underwrote the establishment of a rudimentary national system of public transportation. To hasten the movement of the mail, postal administrators coordinated the scheduling of most of the country's stagecoaches. Stagecoach timetables are often overlooked by economic historians. Yet, as sociologist Anthony Giddens has observed, such time-space ordering devices lie at the very heart of modern organizations. Postal policy helps explain why so many stagecoach passengers complained about the bumpiness of their ride: postal revenue funded the vehicles that conveyed the mail but not the right-of-way over which it was conveyed. Postal subsidies also hastened the rise of the British steamship industry in the second half of the nineteenth century and the establishment of commercial aviation in the United States in the 1920s.

Long before the rise of the modern industrial corporation, postal systems were "big business." By 1828, the American postal system, with almost eight thousand offices, was the country's largest civilian employer, a distinction it retained until the 1870s, when it was overtaken by the Pennsylvania Railroad. Especially impressive was the institution's geographical reach. In the 1820s, the American postal system had almost twice as many offices as the postal system in Great Britain, and more than five times as many offices as the postal system in France. This meant that the United States had seventy-four post offices per one hundred thousand inhabitants—far more than the seventeen in Great Britain or the four in France.

Nineteenth-century commentators sometimes described the postal system in language that oddly prefigured recent accolades of praise given to the Internet and the World Wide Web. Postal systems, one American commentator predicted in 1851, would foster geographical expansion, economic prosperity, and political stability: "While printing held forth a flaming torch, to guide the steps of man to a higher and nobler destiny than he had previously known, the establishment of posts, in systematic order, conveyed its benignant rays to the four corners of the globe, penetrating its darkened regions, and equalizing, elevating, and harmonizing . . . the social position and geographical distribution of the people."

Legal Monopolies versus Private Enterprise. Since the seventeenth century, the postal systems of Great Britain, France, and many other countries have enjoyed various privileges that ordinarily included a legally guaranteed monopoly over the transmission of certain kinds of information. In Great Britain, the postal monopoly was originally justified as a surveillance technique; by the eighteenth century, its rationale had come to embrace revenue-generation. In Britain's North American colonies, for example, Benjamin Franklin took great pride in his success as the first colonial postal administrator to return a revenue to the Crown.

In the United States, the postal monopoly became, with the passage of the Post Office Act of 1792, an instrument of civic education. To facilitate the spread of political information, or what is now called news, Congress subsidized the transmission of newspapers and hastened the expansion of the postal network into the thinly settled transappalachian hinterland. Throughout the first half of the nineteenth century, newspapers made up around 95 percent of the weight of the mail, while generating a mere 5 percent of the revenue. To keep the institution self-sustaining, Congress kept letter rates high and retained a monopoly over the transmission of ordinary correspondence. As a consequence, letter writers—mostly merchants living along the Atlantic seaboard—subsidized the transmission of political information to the South and West.

The expansion of the railroad network in the 1830s created a novel communication conduit. Taking advantage of this conduit, entrepreneurs in Great Britain and the United States established nongovernmental mail delivery firms on several high-volume routes. Though it is uncertain how much mail these firms diverted, in certain markets the total almost certainly exceeded 50 percent. In response, legislators enacted laws to buttress the postal monopoly and reduce and simplify the basic letter rate. This reform—"penny postage" in Great Britain; "cheap postage" in the United States—substantially augmented mail volume, just as its proponents had hoped. In addition, it hastened the advent of several familiar postal practices, including mandatory prepayment, mailboxes, and postage stamps.

For much of the twentieth century, postal administrators in Great Britain, France, Germany, and many other countries retained control over what is now called telecommunications. This "postal-industrial complex," as it is sometimes termed, was a formidable institution—and often the largest employer—in many countries in both the developed and the developing world. In the decades preceding World War I, many postal systems also established a parcel post, while some even provided rudimentary banking facilities known as postal savings. Since 1970—spurred partly by new communications technologies and partly by an ideological commitment to deregulation—policymakers in Great Britain, France, and Germany, but not Japan, have severed the links between mail delivery and telecommunications. In so doing, they experimented with the various hybrid institutional forms—partly public and partly private—that characterize most of the world's postal systems in the twenty-first century.

Most present-day postal systems serve a territory roughly congruent with a nation-state. In early modern Europe, in contrast, several postal systems, including the sprawling institution that the Thurn and Taxis family maintained for the Hapsburgs, crossed numerous territorial boundaries. In addition, and in contrast to most national postal systems, the Thurn and Taxis postal system only sporadically monitored the messages that it conveyed. If present-day trends persist and communication networks become increasingly open and global, such cosmopolitan institutions may conceivably become *more* relevant models for the emerging information infrastructure of the twenty-first century than the national postal systems that they preceded.

Economic Influence. Postal systems have exerted an enduring influence on several features of the modern world economy. Most obviously, they furnished precedents for telecommunications regulation. A half-century before the telegraph, as Peter J. Wosh has observed ("Going Postal," *American Archivist*, 61 [1998], 220–239), the American postal system emerged as a crucible for information policy debates on topics ranging from pricing and access to surveillance. It is hardly coincidental that Theodore N. Vail—the visionary telephone executive who during the 1900s made "universal service" a policy goal at AT&T—spent several formative years as superintendent of the Railway Mail Service, or, for that matter, that electronic messages are known not as e-grams but as e-mail.

Among the most influential postal policy precedents has been the uniform pricing scheme that the British postal system adopted in 1840 on the recommendation of Victorian educator Rowland Hill. Having demonstrated that the cost of sorting the mail far exceeded the cost of its transportation, Hill proposed that, regardless of distance, every letter sent within Great Britain pay a uniform fee. Hill's proposal set a precedent that would later be invoked by regulators in many public utilities, including electricity, to justify the deliberate cross-subsidization of high-cost, thinly settled regions. According to economist R. H. Coase, Hill's supposed endorsement of uniform pricing was misleading, since, in fact, Hill had supported uniform rates not to encourage cross-subsidies—a policy that, like the postal monopoly, Hill opposed—but, rather, to match prices more precisely to costs.

Postal systems have long played an indispensable—albeit often unappreciated—role in hastening the creation of national and transnational markets. For centuries, they have facilitated the transmission of price data, purchase orders, promissory notes, and even negotiable currency. By the mid-eighteenth century, German merchants relied on the Thurn and Taxis postal system to secure a steady flow of information on market changes in Brussels and Antwerp. By the 1820s, American farmers received through the mail regular reports on European demand for agricultural staples, such as cotton and wheat. In addition, and no less importantly, American merchants had by this time grown accustomed to enclosing in individual letters as much as $10,000 in cash. Since merchants could neither insure these transactions nor sue the government should their letters go astray, their willingness to assume this risk is eloquent testimony to the high esteem in which the postal system was held. By the early 1850s, American merchants sent $100 million through the postal system every year; prior to the rise of the parcel delivery industry in the late 1830s, the amount may well have been even higher.

The economic significance of postal systems extends far beyond their role in market creation. No genealogy of the information age can overlook the myriad contributions that postal systems have made during the past three-hundred years in expanding popular access to knowledge. Information "came of age," the historian of technology Daniel R. Headrick observed, during the eighteenth-century age of "reason and revolution." Postal systems, as institutional manifestations of the humanitarian promise of the Enlightenment, have—by facilitating the global spread of political information, research reports, technical know-how, and market data—helped lay the groundwork for the ongoing revolutions in politics, science, technology, and industry that are such defining features of the modern world.

BIBLIOGRAPHY

Behringer, Wolfgang. *Thurn und Taxis: Die Geschichte ihrer Post und ihrer Unternehmen.* Munich, 1990.

Campbell, Robert M. *The Politics of the Post: Canada's Postal System from Public Service to Privatization.* Peterborough, Ont. 1994.

Chandler, Alfred D., Jr., and James Cortada, eds. *A Nation Transformed by Information.* New York, 2000. See in particular the essays by Richard D. Brown and Richard R. John.

Coase, Ronald H. "Rowland Hill and the Penny Post." *Economica* 6 (1939), 423–435.

Crew, Michael A., and Paul R. Kleindorfer, eds. *Competition and Innovation in Postal Services.* Boston, 1991. Includes essays on Rowland Hill's contribution as an economist.

Daunton, Martin. *Royal Mail: The Post Office since 1840.* London, 1985. Particularly informative on the twentieth century.

Flichy, Patrice. *Dynamics of Modern Communication: The Shaping and Impact of New Communication Technologies.* London, 1995. Offers a French perspective.

Fuller, Wayne E. *The American Mail: Enlarger of the Common Life.* Chicago, 1974.

Headrick, Daniel R. *When Information Came of Age: Technologies of Knowledge in the Age of Reason and Revolution, 1700–1850.* New York, 2000. Comparative and broadly framed.

John, Richard R. *Spreading the News: The American Postal System from Franklin to Morse.* Cambridge, Mass., 1995. Explores the communications revolution that antedated the railroad and the telegraph; includes citations to unattributed references in this essay.

Noam, Eli. *Telecommunications in Europe.* New York, 1992. Includes a brief survey of nineteenth-century postal policy in Great Britain, France, and Prussia.

Perry, Charles R. *The Victorian Post Office: The Growth of a Bureaucracy.* London, 1992. Includes information on telegraphy and telephony.

Robinson, Howard. *The British Post Office: A History.* Princeton, 1948. Particularly informative on the period between 1640 and 1900.

Sinclair, James. *Uniting a Nation: The Postal and Telecommunication Services of Papua New Guinea.* Melbourne, 1984.

Westney, D. Eleanor. *Imitation and Innovation: The Transfer of Western Organizational Patterns to Meiji Japan.* Cambridge, Mass., 1987. Considers the transfer of British postal practices to Japan.

RICHARD R. JOHN

PUDDLING AND ROLLING. The process of making wrought iron from pig iron by heating and stirring it in the presence of oxidizing agents is called *puddling*. In 1783 and 1784 Henry Cort took out patents for a new method of making wrought iron. His method was a break from the traditional ways of refining iron in Europe; it used coal instead of charcoal, and the iron was shaped by a rolling mill instead of a hammer. With the new method, pig iron was melted down (smelted) in a coal-fired reverberatory furnace, in which the iron did not come in contact with the fuel. While in a molten state, the iron was being refined. The resulting pasty mass of wrought iron was brought from the furnace to a heavy hammer were it was "shingled" into consolidated pieces of iron; these were then reheated in a second furnace before being shaped into bars in a rolling mill.

The new technology was not immediately adopted, although during the 1780s it was tried in a few places. The first trials resulted in an inferior quality of iron made with the puddling and rolling method. Only after improvements had been made to the new technique, at Richard Crawshay's Cyfarthfa ironworks in Wales, did puddling begin to spread in Britain. Puddling was not the first coal-using method to be tried in Britain. From about the 1750s, wrought iron had been made with coal as the fuel; the most important method had been "potting and stamping," and puddling then competed with it and others in the late 1700s. Henry Cort had promoted his new method by stating that puddled iron was superior in quality to the best Swedish iron. Although this was not then the case, the quality of puddled iron was improved and, in the second quarter of the nineteenth century, with the development of "wet-puddling," British iron could compete in the same markets as the top brands of Swedish iron.

British wrought iron production in the late 1780s has been estimated at about 32,000 tons annually, about half coming from coal-using methods. At that time, an additional 50,000 tons were imported. With the expansion of puddling, this changed dramatically. Around 1800, British production amounted to 100,000 tons while imports had declined to less than 20,000 tons. British production continued to rise, and 150,000 tons were made in 1815. Britain then became an important exporter of iron. The development of puddling allowed Britain to move from an iron-importing country to the world's leading iron exporter in about thirty years.

The expansion of Britain's iron exports had an enormous effect on ironmaking, on iron markets in the rest of Europe, and subsequently in the rest of the world. Traditional charcoal-based ironmaking soon declined, and a restructuring of the iron industry occurred in many countries.

Puddling and rolling was introduced to Belgium in the 1820s, and it was soon established in other regions. The introduction of puddling and rolling did not, however, mean the immediate end of charcoal-using methods. These continued to expand in parts of Europe, and even in Britain, where more than fifty charcoal-refining hearths were in use as late as the 1850s.

[*See also* Cort, Henry *and* Metallurgic Industry.]

BIBLIOGRAPHY

Evans, Chris. "Iron Puddling: The Quest for a New Technology in the Eighteenth-Century Industry." *Llafur* 6.3 (1994), 44–57.

Fremdling, Rainer. *Technologischer Wandel und Internationaler Handel im 18. Und 19. Jahrhundert: Die Eisenindustrien in Großbritannien, Belgien, Frankreich und Deutschland*. Berlin, 1986.

Harris, John R. *The British Iron Industry, 1700–1850*. Houndmills, U.K., 1988.

Hyde, Charles K. *Technological Change and the British Iron Industry, 1700–1870*. Princeton, 1977.

GÖRAN RYDÉN

PUTTING-OUT SYSTEM. *See* Domestic Industry.

QUARRIES. Quarries are sites where natural mineral products destined for construction are extracted. The extracted materials may be used without preliminary preparation, like the rocks granite and marble, or may be subjected to a firing for the development of a final product: clay for bricks and tiles, marl for cement, limestone for lime. These rocks are abundant and without great economic value. Their geological prospecting is not subject to a demand for concessions, and their exploitation is tied to an authorization that essentially takes into account respect for the environment. The opening of a quarry requires the needs of a large center of consumption, the existence of a quality material, ease of access to the site of exploitation, and the possibility of transporting the material.

The first quarries date from the Neolithic Age in Europe. Humans of the Paleolithic Age had been simple gatherers of rocks; they had never searched them out by digging into the ground. The Neolithic was the age when populations settled in villages; it was also the time when the first permanent quarries were created. The first professional specializations appeared; here were the first quarriers in the world. The quarries, of flint in layers of chalk or sandstone for making grindstones, when they were underground, comprised vertical wells, sometimes twenty meters deep, and short horizontal galleries. As they were not very productive, they were numerous over several hectares. The flints extracted were the object of an active commerce and of a distant exportation according to the quality of the rock. Most often the raw material was not transported; hewn flints were exported. This presupposes the existence of hewing workshops, the presence of qualified workers, and the economic organization of this commerce.

The great monuments of antiquity, throughout the Mediterranean, were great consumers of rocks. The exploitation of quarries in Egypt took place on the same scale as the monuments that were to be built. During the Middle Empire expeditions counting as many as seventeen thousand men opened quarries between the Nile and the Red Sea, in rock formations of high quality. The essentials of sculpture took place on the premises: obelisks, sphinxes, statues. On the other hand, pyramids like those at Giza were built from rocks extracted nearby and brought by boat over the flooded Nile. The well-preserved cut surfaces of quarries used by the Romans provide information about techniques of extraction. A pickaxe cut lateral grooves around a block, often voluminous (up to ten meters long for the creation of columns), then wedges of wood or iron driven to the bottom of the grooves made the block break off in the back on a plane parallel to that of the front surface. Certain rocks acquired universal renown around the entire Mediterranean basin, such as the marble of the Greek island of Paros, more transparent than that of Carrara.

The middle ages in Europe also consumed the products of quarries in large amounts for the construction of walls around cities and of fortified castles. Gothic churches and then the castles of the Renaissance demanded rocks in smaller quantities (Gothic churches used two times less stone than Romanesque churches) but of more differentiated qualities, each being allocated to a specific place in the building: for the bases of walls, which had to impermeable to rising waters, for the sculpture surrounding the doors and windows, for pavement and the steps of stairways, for the decoration of interior walls. Quarries multiplied and specialized. Used by the Romans, but little exported since the antique port of Luni silted up, the marble of Carrara was once again exploited during the Renaissance. This was its glorious period with the sculptures of Michelangelo, who came himself to the quarries to choose his rocks. All of Europe used Carrara marble during the fifteenth and sixteenth centuries. But this marble suffered an eclipse with the arrival of baroque art, which preferred marbles of lively colors.

In the eighteenth and nineteenth centuries means of communications developed. The construction of roads and of railroads necessitated the creation of a new material that quickly came into great demand: a granulation of ground rocks for lining roads with stones and for making railroad ballast; people were looking for a rock of great mechanical quality that could be extracted with less care to be used broken into little pieces, not for construction or decoration. But luxury stones were still sought, and with the advancement of knowledge in geology, the available products were numerous. The architect Charles Garnier (1825–1898) used dozens of different marbles for the Paris Opéra. As a general rule rocks used for construction were of local origin, but those used for facing or decoration could be exported overseas. The marble of Carrara was now renowned worldwide. It was exported, for example, to Brazil for the construction of the Museum of Fine Arts of Rio de Janeiro. In Paris the little quarter "of the Americas" was that of the former gypsum quarries; the plaster made with this rock was exported as far as Louisiana.

Clay has a long history worldwide. The rock is abundant at the surface and easy to extract. The invention of pottery and later of porcelain, the use of clay tablets as a medium for writing, of bricks, and of tiles are important points in human activity. Much employed in antiquity and the middle ages, brick suffered an eclipse during the classical age in favor of stone but regained importance in the nineteenth century. Clay remains the base material for simple dwellings in all the countries of the world.

Techniques for the exploitation evolved over time. Open quarries were always exploited following the techniques of descending terraces, like a gigantic staircase. The only limit to this exploitation was the height of the successive cut surfaces, which could collapse. The maximum depth was soon reached by two stairways of terraces facing each other, and a quarry that could not grow at the surface had to close. Underground quarries made it possible to follow to great depths the beds exploited at the surface. The oldest of these used the surface technique of descending terraces; this succeeded in digging vast cavities whose ceilings, out of reach, could not be reinforced. This dangerous technique was abandoned in favor of quarries with ascending terraces. The extraction was carried out uphill, exploiting walls and a ceiling that were never too high and could easily be reinforced as soon as the hole filled in with the abundant scraps from the cutting. The horizontal galleries providing access to the quarry quickly became too long; the work of exploitation was then carried out from vertical wells dug through the overlying terrain. Until the appearance of modern excavation equipment, the presence on the surface of layers without economic interest was an obstacle to the extraction of rocks at greater depths. It was also necessary to preserve at the surface vast expanses suitable for cultivation. Many quarries were dug by quarriers who were also farmers and who were able, by this technique, to preserve their fields. Likewise in order to preserve dwellings and to avoid encroaching on lands suitable for construction, cities dug their quarries under their houses.

In the twentieth century the techniques of cutting up rock, practically unchanged since antiquity, were modified: cutting with a wire that turns between several pulleys, percussion hammers powered by compressed air, explosives reserved for the extraction of rocks to be used for lining roads. The exploitation of granite was done with the help of a heat lance that cut rocks by melting them. But the returns were always weak. Rarely greater than 25 percent, they could go as low as 10 percent if one sought, for example, a marble of a specific color. Modern architecture for the most part requires concrete, which remains the greatest consumer of the products of quarries. Beautiful stones make decorative concretes; pieces of marble from Carrara embellish concrete facades of modern buildings. Furthermore, and from time immemorial, monuments and houses have been demolished in order to serve as quarries for the construction of new buildings.

ROMAIN BROSSÉ
Translated from French by Sylvia J. Cannizzaro

R

RADIO AND TELEVISION INDUSTRY *[This entry contains three subentries, a historical overview and discussions of technological change and industrial organization and regulation.]*

Historical Overview

Both radio and television have a long prehistory, stretching back to the seventeenth century but speeding up during the late nineteenth century. The economic history takes off, however, with a relevant nineteenth-century prelude both in telegraphy and telephony. Radio was thought of at first as a substitute for line telegraphy, and the broadcast element inherent in radio transmission and reception was considered a disadvantage. Radio telephony—words, not Morse code—became possible only during the first decade of the twentieth century, although the telephone (1876) had been conceived of at first as a possible source of entertainment as well as or rather than a conveyer of domestic and business messages. Electrophone companies, set up during the 1880s, had objectives similar to those of radio companies forty years later. The most enterprising and sustained project was the Telefon Hirmondo service in Budapest.

The same technologies, global in scope, were predicted before they became practical. Different countries used them in different ways, according to their constitutional, political, economic, social, and educational structures and attitudes. The business pioneer was the Italian Guglielmo Marconi (1871–1937), who arrived in London with a bundle of radio devices in 1896. After exhibiting them to politicians, civil servants, and naval and military officers as well as to scientists and to the public, he launched his Wireless Telegraph and Signal Company a year later. It had an initial capital of £100,000, of which £60,000 in pound shares was held by Marconi himself, who kept a tight control over business operations and treated £25,000 as capital. His first company was followed up in 1900 with the Marconi International Marine Communication Company.

At sea, radio could compete effectively with cable, and Marconi was given wide publicity when he successfully transmitted transatlantic messages across the ocean in 1901. The following year the Marconi Wireless Telegraphy Company of America, registered in 1901, was incorporated. Subsequently other companies were formed, including the Russian Company of Wireless Telegraphs and Telephony in 1908. As the Marconi business operations extended, they raised complex issues, usually concerning patents and relationships with government. Competition intensified too. The German Telefunken Company, subsidized by the state, was the most formidable competitor.

In the United States, where in 1900 telephone usage was far more highly developed than in any other country, the future of broadcasting depended on the success of early experiments with radio telephony. The first invention, however, was British. In 1904 J. A. Fleming, a Marconi Company consultant, devised the thermionic valve, described long before the microchip as "the tiniest little giant in history." Two years later, the American Lee de Forest, who called himself "the father of radio," added a third electrode to Fleming's diode. A Canadian, however, Reginald Fessenden, was the first person to broadcast "a wireless concert," from Brant Rock, Massachusetts, on Christmas Eve, 1906.

In the same year, the Marconi Wireless Telegraph Company of America hired as an office boy fifteen-year-old David Sarnoff (1891–1972), who was on duty as a wireless operator when radio was used in the Titanic disaster of 1912. During World War I, Sarnoff suggested the invention of "a simple 'Radio Music Box' . . . arranged for several different wavelengths" that would enable listeners to pick up radio programs. He foresaw not only the wireless set but the great audience for information and entertainment that radio would attract. In 1919 he became vice president of the Radio Corporation of America (RCA), the product of a radio manufacturers' consortium, but backed by the federal administration as a successor to the wartime pattern of controlled American radio. It took over all the fundamental Marconi patents. Sarnoff became general manager in 1921 and president in 1930.

The war had given an impetus to industrial and operational radio development on both sides of the Atlantic, and with its ending amateur radio enthusiasts—"hams"—many of them organized into wireless societies, hoped to be able to communicate freely with each other, sometimes over great distances. Most of them used crystal sets, which were cheap and easy to make. Legislation had restricted their activities even before the war: In Great Britain and the United States, for example, they had to have licenses.

While hams, many of them using Morse code, not words, formed pressure groups after 1918, a number of entrepreneurs, including newspaper proprietors, saw the possibility of launching radio stations, each with its own call sign. The first was KDKA Pittsburgh, a Westinghouse station, which began broadcasting in 1920 as a promotional measure to sell wireless sets. There was a boom in radio promotion during the early 1920s, without the federal government being involved either in the economics of the system or in its social consequences. When the British government—through the Post Office—sought to avoid "the chaos of the ether" associated with open marketing, a consortium of radio manufacturing companies, including the Marconi Company, set up a British Broadcasting Company with a capital of £100,000. Revenue would be derived from royalties on receiving sets and license fees (required for all listeners), and profits were to be restricted to 7.5 percent per annum.

The Scottish general manager of the company, J. C. W. Reith (1889–1971), appointed after advertisement, was determined that the company should provide a "public service": To restrict its programs to entertainment and to rely on advertising would "prostitute" what was "a universal and extraordinarily cheap medium of communication." Reith was largely responsible for the conversion of the company into a public corporation, still with the same initials—BBC—in January 1927.

Reith believed in what he did not hesitate to call a "brute force of monopoly," on both technical and programming grounds. By 1927, which was also the year the Federal Radio Commission was set up in Washington, however, British and American radio patterns had diverged sharply. The latter relied not on license fees but on advertising and offered mainly entertainment. Between 1927 and 1939 two powerful broadcasting networks were created, the National Broadcasting Company (NBC, 1926), a creation of RCA, and the Columbia Broadcasting System (CBS, 1927), taken over by William S. Paley in 1929. A third network, the American Broadcasting Company (ABC), was formed in 1943. The networks, carefully watching and responding to program ratings, were later to dominate television as well as radio until a breakthrough in cable television in the 1980s. So, too, was the BBC in Britain until it lost its monopoly position in television after fierce parliamentary debates in 1955. Monopoly in sound went later, during the 1970s and 1980s.

Both the American and British systems were easily distinguishable from systems of state-owned radio and later television, as in the Soviet Union and in Germany between 1933 and 1945. There were many hybrid systems also, as in

Canada, and in France the Post Office after 1948 managed a public broadcast system with a number of coexisting commercial stations.

The different radio systems came into international conflict before World War II. The BBC itself, with no government financial backing, had introduced an Empire Service in 1931, and in 1938, faced with hostile propaganda from Italian and German stations, it broadcast its first foreign language programs. A "war of words" was intensified after 1939, which also brought in Japan, where a public broadcasting organization, NHK (Nippon Hoso Kyokai), had been founded on lines close to the BBC in 1926. Extolling "the national spirit" became the NHK's mission after the Japanese-Chinese War of 1937, and in the years between 1939 and 1945 it acquired an international dimension. After the defeat of Germany, Italy, and Japan, their broadcasting systems were remodeled by the victorious allies. German radio and later television were decentralized, Italy acquired a new national broadcasting authority, and in Japan commercial companies competed with a reorganized NHK.

In the United States and Great Britain sound broadcasting had been so well established by 1939 that those engaged in it were anxious to postpone facing up to its challenge. So, too, were other media interests, including the cinema—which had moved from pictures without sound to "talkies" after 1927—and the press. In Great Britain J. L. Baird (1886–1946), working on his own, invented a mechanical mode of televising pictures. It was first demonstrated in 1923, but Baird found it difficult to establish a profitable and reputable business enterprise. When the BBC agreed, with some reluctance, to establish a regular but limited television service in 1936, it settled, after tests, on an electronic mode developed in large-scale laboratories by Electrical and Musical Industries (EMI), founded as the result of a merger in 1931. A year later, Russian-born Vladimir Zworykin invented the first effective "iconoscope," a charge-storage type of transmitting tube.

The rapid spread of television in the United States after 1945 was customer driven. With few programs on offer, the production of television sets rose from 178,000 to fifteen million between 1947 and 1952, when there were more than twenty million sets in use. But by 1948 *Business Week* could already call television "the poor man's latest and most prized luxury." A mass audience was quickly identified, but the programs were for the most part unambitious and cheap, with old films, quizzes, and celebrity shows the staple fare. By contrast in Great Britain the BBC emphasized quality after restoring television in June 1946. The number of television sets rose from 14,560 in March 1947 to more than a million in 1951, and two years later the figure had doubled. There were restrictions on capital spending, however, in a period of austerity and for television

TELEVISION. Secretary of Labor William N. Doak and his secretary, W. W. King, examine a television, Washington, D.C., 1931. (Underwood & Underwood, New York/Prints and Photographs Division, Library of Congress)

enthusiasts progress was too slow. But when the BBC's television monopoly was broken by act of Parliament in 1954, an American model was not followed. An Independent Television Authority was set up to issue company franchises, control advertising, and monitor program standards.

When these changes took place thirty-six million television sets were in use in the United States and only 4.8 million in the whole of Europe, with 4.5 million of these in Great Britain, but a European takeoff was about to begin. A year later, the number of sets in Europe had doubled. By the mid-1960s more than ninety countries had television stations, and the great global audience had reached over 750 million. American television interests were beginning to look abroad increasingly for markets, and in the following twenty years there were signs of what came to be called globalization in the emergence of international conglomerates.

Television did not supplant sound radio, the less expensive medium, which prospered with the development of transistor and mobile radios. Yet in both radio and television there were technological problems with economic consequences. In sound radio, for example, frequency modulation (FM) and the use of Very High Frequencies (VHF), raised questions, as did High Definition Television, developed in Japan, about the distribution of frequencies on the radio spectrum, considered nationally and internationally to be a scarce resource.

Digital technology, which offered a universal code in words, pictures, and numbers for all communications, offered prospects not of scarcity but of cornucopia. Broadcasts, whatever the characteristics of their broadcasting systems, were required in the 1970s and 1980s to face the implications of cable ("the wired city") and satellites, the first of them Telstar in 1962. There was a new emphasis in policy discussions about both radio and television on global links with telecommunications, deregulation, the multiplication of channels for listeners and viewers, and enhanced individual choice. The case for public broadcasting had to be defended in terms of program quality. The great audience itself was increasingly fragmented. The ramifications of the "great web" changed perspectives as well as business strategies. In the process fortunes were made and lost. The economics remained fundamental. The legal and political issues became more complex.

[*See also* Advertising; Film Industry; *and* Information and Communication Technology.]

BIBLIOGRAPHY

Aitken, Hugh G. J. *Syntony and Spark: The Origins of Radio.* Princeton, 1976.

Barnouw, Erik. *A Tower in Babel.* Princeton, 1966.

Barnouw, Erik. *The Golden Web*. Princeton, 1968.

Barnouw, Erik. *The Image Empire*. Princeton, 1970.

Barnouw, Erik. *Tube of Plenty*. Princeton, 1975.

Beninger, James R. *The Control Revolution: Technological and Economic Origins of the Information Society*. Cambridge, Mass., 1986. Explains how the concept of an information society emerged within industrial history.

Briggs, Asa. *The History of Broadcasting in the United Kingdom*, 5 vols. Oxford and New York, 1995. Based on BBC archives and a wide range of secondary sources.

Clarricoats, John. World at Their Fingertips. London, 1967. The world is the world of radio amateurs, the hams.

Derthick, Martha, and Paul J. Quirk. *The Politics of Deregulation*. Washington, D.C., 1989. Examines and discusses changes of outlook in the 1980s.

Douglas, Susan J. *Inventing American Broadcasting*. Baltimore, 1987.

Dutton, William H. *Society on the Line: Information Politics in the Digital Age*. Oxford, 1996. Useful essays with reading lists.

Head, Sydney W. *World Broadcasting Systems*. Belmont, Calif., 1985. A standard account.

Mulgan, Geoff. *Communication and Control: Networks and New Economies of Communication*. Cambridge, 1991. Thoughtful study of radio and television and issues in their evolution.

Noam, Eli M. *Television in Europe*. New York, 1991. A useful summary with a comparative dimension.

Pool, Ithiel de Sola. *Technologies of Freedom*. Cambridge, Mass., 1983.

Smith, Anthony. *The Shadow in the Cave*. London, 1976. An intelligent analysis of communications history by an author who has dealt with other media, including film and the press.

ASA BRIGGS

Technological Change

The central technology of the radio and television industry is the use of electromagnetic waves of specific frequencies for broadcasting audio and video. The theory of electromagnetic waves reached its maturity with the publication of James Clerk Maxwell's *Dynamical Theory of the Electro-Magnetic Field* in 1864, but it would be 1886 before the German physicist Heinrich Hertz conducted a series of experiments that would prove that electromagnetic waves could be radiated through space and detected at a distance from the transmitter. Hertz's experiment soon ignited a rush to design transmitters and detectors that would make wireless communication feasible.

Radio Technology. The first wireless communication system was built by Italian inventor Guglielmo Marconi, who would leverage his patents to transform the Wireless Telegraph and Signal Company, incorporated in England in 1897, into a near monopoly of radio communications until World War I. Marconi's transmitter was conceptually no different than Hertz's, accumulating electricity in a capacitor, accelerating it through a spark gap, and radiating the resulting electromagnetic waves through an antenna. Detection of the electromagnetic pulses was achieved by a coherer, a glass tube containing loose carbon filings that would change their electrical conductivity when exposed to electromagnetic waves. What gave Marconi's system the unprecedented range necessary to commercial operations was the design of its antennas. With no theory on which to rely, Marconi departed from traditional practice by grounding the antennas and by painstakingly experimenting with different configurations, gradually increasing the reach of his signals.

Original spark transmitters broadcast in a vast range of frequencies, making it impossible for two stations to operate in the same geographic area due to interference. The problem was solved by incorporating syntonic circuits, which could filter out undesired frequencies in transmitters and, likewise, make receivers sensitive only to certain frequencies. The concept of syntony, developed by British scientist Oliver Lodge, involves making transmitters and receivers resonant at one frequency only and remains to this day the keystone of radio technology.

Despite ingenious tuning, spark transmitters still radiated waves at many different frequencies, thus using up valuable spectrum space. Moreover, they produced a series of pulses rather than a single, continuous signal. This was sufficient for radiotelegraphy, which required only the ability to detect a signal or its absence, but not for transmitting the human voice. The ability to broadcast modulated sound required a continuous wave, which could only be generated by a continuously oscillating element. The first such oscillators were the radiofrequency alternators, conceived by American inventor Reginald Fessenden and developed at the General Electric company by the Swedish engineer Ernst Alexanderson starting in 1906. The Alexanderson alternators operated on the same principle as power-generating alternators, but by rotating much faster and including several poles on its disks, produced currents that changed polarity over 100,000 times per second instead of the usual 50 or 60. The rapidly oscillating current could be modulated through a microphone and fed to an antenna. It could then be received by crystal detectors, which could receive modulated signals and were beginning to replace coherers. Danish inventor Valdemar Poulsen developed an alternative continuous wave transmitter based on an electric arc, a concept that was perfected by Americans Cyril Elwell and Leonard Fuller. Arc transmitters were produced by the Federal Company and used primarily by the U.S. Navy.

The transmission of voice through radio, however, was still in desperate need of an amplifying device at the receiver, since in its absence all the energy to reproduce the sound had to come from the electromagnetic wave. The triode vacuum tube, invented by American Lee De Forest in 1906 by adding a control grid to a diode rectifying valve, proved to be the component that would provide the needed amplification and drive radio into the home. When it was discovered that the triode vacuum tube could also function as an oscillator, thus making cheaper transmitters possible, the radio industry was ready to reach the vast residential markets. Between 1920 and the end of World War II, vacuum tubes reigned supreme over radio.

Receivers still had to convert radio waves into sound waves, which had a much lower frequency. Reginald Fessenden had to this end conceived the heterodyne principle, which operated by subtracting from the radio signal locally generated waves of slightly less frequency. The principle was incorporated into Edwin Armstrong's superheterodyne circuit, designed during World War I, which is still at the heart of modern radio receivers.

Armstrong also invented frequency modulation, the transmission mechanism used by FM (frequency modulation) radio. Instead of transmitting sound by modulating the amplitude of the carrier wave, FM radio is generated by modulating its frequency. It also uses the VHF (very high frequency) portion of the spectrum, with frequencies of about an order of magnitude higher than AM (amplitude modulation), and its channels are twenty times as wide. The combination of these factors allow FM to be virtually free from interference and to broadcast high-fidelity sound, although at the price of a somewhat prodigal use of spectrum. Despite its technical superiority, FM did not have a large market penetration in its early stages, as it was adamantly opposed by the Radio Corporation of America (RCA), and it was also shifted from its original spectrum allocation by the Federal Communications Commission (FCC) to make room for television channels. However, FM channels were wide enough to accommodate stereo broadcasting, whereas AM channels were not; with the FCC's, approval of a stereo broadcasting system proposed by General Electric in 1961, FM started its rise to eventual market dominance.

The invention of the transistor at AT&T's Bell Labs in 1947 was a watershed moment for the whole electronics industry. Among other properties, transistors could greatly amplify electrical currents using less power and taking up a fraction of the space of a vacuum tube. Transistor receivers could easily fit in an automobile or be even carried in a pocket, a feature that expanded the demand for receivers and consequently the extent of the radio audience.

Television Technology. Conception and research of television technology started in the last quarter of the nineteenth century, soon after the discovery of the photosensitive properties of certain elements, most notably selenium. In addition to the familiar elements of a radio broadcast system, television requires an image-scanning device, such as a camera, and a receiver capable of decoding and reproducing the images. Although the scanning principle evolved in the preelectronic era, signal amplification and image reproduction required electron tubes, and therefore the first television systems did not surface until the 1920s.

The Scottish inventor John Baird is commonly regarded as the father of television, although American Charles Jenkins developed a similar system slightly before Baird, and despite the fact none of the components of those systems were ever commercially viable. Baird and Jenkins relied on mechanical scanning to generate their images, a technique that soon proved inferior to electronic methods and, although widely used in experimental transmissions, would be discarded by the end of the 1930s.

The inventions that would eventually carry television to commercial maturity were Vladimir Zworykin's iconoscope and Philo Farnsworth's image dissector. The iconoscope, developed by Russian-born Zworykin at the RCA laboratories, was the first storage tube, a class of devices that retain image data on an electrically charged layer until it can be scanned by an electron beam. Farnsworth's image dissector, in contrast, did not have storage capabilities, but one of its imaging components proved essential for enhancing the quality of the iconoscope pictures. The combination of both resulted in Telefunken's image iconoscope, which would dominate the camera designs until the 1950s. Better image storage materials and technologies resulted in the image orthicon tubes, developed during World War II as part of remote guidance systems, the vidicon, and the plumbicon, the latter essential in modern color television cameras.

The cathode ray tube (CRT) has always been at the center of television receivers. Used by nineteenth-century researchers to study the properties of the electron, its ability to display images was added around the turn of the century, when the German scientist Karl Braun is credited with adding a phosphor layer that emitted light when hit by electrons. Painstaking experimentation with different light-emitting materials and scanning electron beams resulted in the slow but constant improvement of the CRT, which only at the beginning of the twenty-first century is starting to be replaced by other technologies, such as liquid crystal displays and plasma screens.

Television transmission standards need to take into account the trade-off between picture quality and scarce spectrum bandwidth. Thus, both the American NTSC standards and the European PAL and SECAM adopted interlaced scanning, which broadcasts odd and even lines alternatively, thus cutting in half the required bandwidth at the price of some image flicker. Audio is transmitted using FM, and image data use a form of AM. Television settled itself in the VHF portion of the spectrum. Later demand for more channels prompted the opening of the UHF (ultra high frequency) band, despite its less desirable propagation properties and other technical difficulties.

Experimentation on color television gained speed in the years immediately following World War II, and after an intense contest between RCA and CBS (Columbia

Broadcasting System) to impose their own standards, ended with the adoption of the NTSC color standard, sponsored by RCA. Off to a slow start, color television gained momentum in the mid-1960s, whereas monochrome programming quickly faded into obsolescence. Ingenious signal coding allowed color television to remain within the 6 MHz of bandwidth originally allocated for each monochrome channel, thus allowing backward compatibility with existing monochrome receivers.

A major improvement for television programming was the advent of broadcast video recorders, first introduced in 1956 by the Ampex Corporation. The amount of information in a video signal made storing it in a tape of practical size a significant engineering challenge, which was solved by the use of recording and scanning heads that spin as the tape is pulled by. Whereas previous programming had always been live and what recording existed was conducted on film, magnetic video recording brought an unprecedented flexibility, enabling better planning, reruns, and instant replay capabilities. By the late 1970s, magnetic recording technology had evolved enough for Sony and JVC to introduce two incompatible home video recording systems, a contest in which JVC's VHS system would eventually claim the market. Viewers' favorite programs can now be recorded for future enjoyment, even if they are broadcast at inconvenient times.

Cable, Satellite, and HDTV. As early as 1949, some remote communities began erecting sensitive antennas to capture distant television signals and distribute them by cable to their neighbors. Later enhanced by microwave and satellite distribution, the high bandwidth of cable allows subscribers to receive a great number of channels regardless of their geographic location and without the disadvantages of UHF. The large programming choice and the provision of additional services, such as closed captioning and pay-per-view, propelled cable into a majority of homes in the United States by the mid-1980s.

With the launch of the first commercial communications satellite in 1965 by the Intelsat consortium, intercontinental live television broadcasts became a reality, and soon a growing satellite network provided increasing coverage to each region of the planet. In the 1990s, satellite television became available directly to the end user; its large bandwidth enables it to offer programming superior to cable systems, although the quality of broadcast is sometimes affected by atmospheric conditions.

The quality of air television broadcasts emerged from a compromise to preserve spectrum space, but better definition has been quietly researched for decades. High-definition television (HDTV) systems, pioneered by the Japanese NHK corporation, have been technically feasible since the 1970s. With at least double the amount of lines of standard television and wider screens, they aim to provide an enhanced viewing experience by more closely resembling the definition and aspect ratio of feature movies. However, the enormous bandwidth requirements of HDTV mean that its distribution may only be practical through satellite, and, as long as programming is not expanded, receivers may not become cheap enough to reach the mass market. Moreover, HDTV faces a challenge from EDTV (enhanced definition television), a class of systems that work by enhancing current television standards through computerized methods.

BIBLIOGRAPHY

Abramson, Albert. *The History of Television, 1880 to 1941*. Jefferson, N.C., 1987. Probably the most exhaustive and comprehensive source on early television history, the book is rich in technical detail, as well as in its discussions of patent issues. The large amount of information makes the narrative difficult to follow, though. A follow-up by the same author covering the years 1942 to 2000 is scheduled for publication in 2002.

Aitken, Hugh G. F. *Syntony and Spark—The Origins of Radio*. New York, 1976. An account of the origin of radio technology in the era of radiotelegraphy. The three main chapters examine the technical accomplishments of Heinrich Hertz, Oliver Lodge, and Guglielmo Marconi, as well as their economic impact.

Aitken, Hugh G. F. *The Continuous Wave: Technology and American Radio, 1900–1932*. Princeton, 1985. A follow-up to *Syntony and Spark*, this book examines the origins of continuous wave technology and its implications for commercial radio broadcast. Successive chapters focus on radiofrequency alternators, voltaic arcs, and audion tubes. The emphasis then switches to the formation of the Radio Corporation of America.

Bray, John. *The Communications Miracle: The Telecommunication Pioneers from Morse to the Information Superhighway*. New York, 1995. The book presents a series of vignettes of the most important inventions in the telecommunications industry. Although the subject is not circumscribed to radio and television, and therefore their coverage is rather concise, it provides a general overview of their technical foundations and the inventions that made them possible.

Dupagne, Michel, and Peter B. Seel. *High Definition Television: A Global Perspective*. Ames, Iowa, 1998. An overview of the development of HDTV and the policy problems and conflicts of interest surrounding its implementation in Japan, Europe, and the United States.

Hudson, Heather E. *Communication Satellites: Their Development and Impact*. New York, 1990. A description of the formation and evolution of the major satellite consortia and the impact of satellite service on both the industrialized and developing world. The book could profit from a deeper technological angle, though.

Inglis, Andrew F. *Behind the Tube: A History of Broadcasting Technology and Business*. Boston, 1990. A tour de force by an RCA insider, this book provides a comprehensive overview of almost all technological innovations that shaped both radio and television, as well as characterizations of the major figures and corporations responsible for their implementation. The emphasis is on the production side rather than on the end user, with transmitter and cameras receiving much more attention than receivers.

Levin, Harvey J. *The Invisible Resource: Use and Regulation of the Radio Spectrum*. Baltimore, 1971. A primer on the technical characteristics, usage, and regulation principles of the resource at the heart of radio and television technology. Although slightly dated, this book provides the essentials for understanding the radio spectrum and the problems concerning its allocation.

Rees, David W. E. *Satellite Communications: The First Quarter Century of Service.* New York, 1990. A detailed description of the Intelsat satellite system by a corporate insider, complete with detailed technical accounts of the evolution of satellite capabilities through time. The economic impact of satellite technology is somewhat overlooked, however.

Slotten, Hugh R. "Rainbow in the Sky: FM Radio, Technical Superiority, and Regulatory Decision-Making." *Technology and Culture* 37.4 (October 1996), 686–720. A revision of the early history of FM and the political decisions that shaped its evolution within the radio industry.

Wood, James. *History of International Broadcasting.* London, 1992. Although a study on use and policies of shortwave radio until 1990, the book contains two technical sections that offer a glimpse into the technology of very-long-distance radio broadcasts.

MAURICIO DRELICHMAN

Industrial Organization and Regulation

A relatively recent addition to the methods available for human communication, broadcasting emerged in the 1920s as a product of various scientific discoveries made during the course of the previous century. In less than a century, it has made its mark as a key shaper of social and cultural values, as the locus for political struggle over the dissemination of ideas, and as a technology conducive to the creation of extremely profitable businesses. Along with mass-circulation publications, films, and recorded music, radio and television have emerged as most striking examples of a process of change that can be called the industrialization of culture. In this process, the ancient activities of "telling stories" and transmitting ideas have been absorbed, in part, into the realm of commodity production.

Established as major industries in the twentieth century, both radio and television have been confirmed as key economic sectors for the new millennium, albeit challenged and changed by the newer cable, satellite, and Internet technologies and absorbed into a wider "information economy" as a consequence of the convergence of digital signals in telecommunications, computing, and broadcasting. The considerable growth of the new communications technologies can be attributed to both the increased information needs of a global market and accelerated demand for home-based information and entertainment.

Regulation and Control. In the richer countries of the world, in North America and in Europe, broadcasting emerged during the same decade as the political practice of universal adult suffrage; and its links to the world of politics have remained more than purely coincidental. As a form of communication, it promised to surpass the power of the book and of the printing press; and in its use of the airwaves as a medium of diffusion, it offered to governments a perfect opportunity for public intervention. Consequently, radio and television frequencies have been allocated by governments in most countries at most times, with the exception of periods of civil war. In countries as varied as China, Saudi Arabia, France, and the former Soviet Union, these governments have, at different times, taken a close interest in the political and the cultural content of broadcast programs. Even where governments have taken a relatively "hands-off" or relaxed attitude to the content of broadcasting, they have established a system of "arms-length" regulatory oversight through such bodies as the Federal Communications Commission in the United States and the Broadcasting Council in the Czech Republic.

Although governments themselves are dependent upon the International Telecommunication Union (ITU) for the awarding of national frequencies, they have considerable latitude within their own boundaries for shaping the service. A brief survey of broadcasting in different parts of the world reveals that the conditions attached to awarding of licenses have varied considerably, depending upon the cultural, political, and economic priorities of a given nation-state. Thus licenses might be obtained at virtually no cost and with few license conditions, as in the United States, or at a relatively high price and with quite detailed license obligations regarding the quality and the range of the program service, as in the United Kingdom. Within the limits of their own constitutions and laws, governments are free to build conditions into the license-awarding process; and these provisions may have striking consequences for the quality of the programs, and the profitability of the business.

In liberal democracies, the day-to-day business of broadcasting tends to be conducted at a distance from the state; but—despite the intensification of market liberalism during the 1980s and the emergence of new satellite technologies whose transmission "footprints" cross the boundaries of nation-states—there are still countries where the delivery of broadcasting services is controlled and managed from within a department of state. Direct state control could be found in France until the early 1980s, and continued after that time in Cuba, China, and a number of African and Arab countries. In India, the national broadcaster, Doordarshan, was not removed from the control of the Ministry of Information until 1997.

Financing of Broadcasting. A cursory inspection of the early history of broadcasting reveals that the technologies of the medium in no way determined the economic models adopted for delivery of the service; so an analysis of the economic history of radio and television must engage at some points with the controversies of political economy and with the competing or alternative models of public, private, and voluntary provision. In the United States, for example, broadcasting was developed largely through privately owned and shareholder-based companies seeking to maximize profits through the delivery of a service funded largely by advertising. In the former Soviet Union, by contrast, radio was developed as a state monopoly under the control of the Communist Party, owned and funded directly by the state. In the United Kingdom, a national monopoly in public broadcasting was awarded to a non-profit organization, the British Broadcasting Corporation (BBC), funded through a state-supervised annual levy—the license fee—payable on all radio receivers and subsequently on all television sets. However, unlike the situation in the Soviet Union, much was made of the proposition that the BBC remained operationally independent of the government of the day; and the BBC lost its monopoly status in 1954.

In the new millennium, the delivery of broadcasting services is moving toward a market-led and not a political command-led model, although there remain important differences of emphasis in the organization and delivery of broadcasting in different parts of the world, which reflect continuing and deep-rooted political and cultural differences. The development of television, in particular, has been held back in poorer countries lacking a mass consumer market with its accompanying tax base and advertising revenues. The United Nations Educational, Scientific and Cultural Organization (UNESCO) published estimates of the number of television sets per thousand people in various countries for 1997. Very low numbers are shown for several African and Asian countries, with under 10 sets per thousand for Cambodia, Bangladesh, Ethiopia, and Mozambique, compared with 65 for India, 223 for Brazil, 321 for China, 521 for the United Kingdom, and 806 for the United States.

Although all broadcasting systems face certain common problems in signal distribution and program production (regarding geographical distance, physical terrain, and cost-effective use of resources), four distinct models for the organization of broadcasting can be recognized:

1. Broadcasting services delivered by profit-maximizing companies and funded by either advertising or subscription.
2. Services delivered by a government as a public service and funded by either a system of universal public ownership or general taxation.
3. Services delivered, at a distance from government, by non-profit-making bodies with a public service remit, funded by a compulsory and universal license fee or tax revenue.
4. Services delivered by voluntary and not-for-profit bodies, funded by donations from the users and supporters of the service.

The reality is more complex than this, and inspection of almost any national broadcasting system will reveal examples that draw on more than one of these models. Many of the national and not-for-profit public service broadcasters in Europe, as well as Doordarshan in India, derive a considerable portion of their income from advertising. The famously commercial and profitable U.S. broadcasting system, led by powerful networks such as the Columbia Broadcasting System (CBS) and the National Broadcasting Company (NBC), coexists with a public television system established by the federal government in 1967 to provide an alternative to the dominant commercial model. As a relative newcomer, U.S. public television would attract around 2 percent of the prime-time audience, whereas a European public broadcaster, the BBC, established in the early days of broadcasting, continued to hold about a 40 percent share of the total television audience by the start of the new millennium. Even as the system of public provision remained healthy and attractive in some parts of the world, public monopolies became increasingly unsustainable, finding themselves under growing pressure from commercial cable and cross-border satellite providers. By the end of the twentieth century, this was the case for India, China, and several countries of the Arab world.

Although some audiences value advertising-free radio and television, and some theorists have argued that pressures from advertisers can distort program content, advertising nonetheless remains one of the globally pervasive sources for meeting the costs of program production. Along with the distinction between broadcasting (the right to transmit programs) and production (making programs), an analysis of the role of advertising goes to the heart of the specific characteristics of broadcasting, considered as both a commodity and a business. This is so despite the early reservations expressed even in the United States, where Secretary of Commerce Herbert Hoover declared in 1924: "I believe that the quickest way to kill broadcasting would be to use it for direct advertising. The reader of the newspaper has an option whether he will read an ad or not, but if a speech by the President is to be used as the meat in a sandwich of two patent medicine advertisements there will be no radio left" (Sterling and Kittross, 2002, p. 53).

Although a non-advertising-based system was created in the United Kingdom and persisted until the 1950s, Hoover's belief proved unsustainable in practice in America, and broadcasting rose from taking a 2 percent share of all U.S. advertising revenue in 1930 to a combined radio and television share of 28 percent by 1988. With the considerable expansion of cable and other services over the next two decades, the television share of total advertising expenditure rose to around 38 percent in the United States by 1999 (with a comparable U.K. figure of about 32 percent). Despite the growth of pay-per-view and subscription methods for financing programs, the availability of advertising revenues clearly will remain a key factor in the further expansion of radio and television services.

The role of advertising in the economics of broadcasting has varied in different places at different times, and so also has the relationship between control of program transmission ("broadcasting") and involvement in the making of programs. Some governments have taken the view that broadcasters or advertisers might also be program producers, whereas others have required that, on competitive or cultural grounds, there be some separation of the three activities. Thus, in the early 1970s the U.S. networks were prohibited from owning the programs that they transmitted (except for news and current affairs)—a measure that boosted opportunities for both independent producers and Hollywood studios. In Britain, there have been long-standing regulations preventing advertisers from making (though not from sponsoring) programs. Since 1989, under European Union regulations, broadcasters have had to have at least 10 percent of the programs they transmit made "out-of-house" by independent producers.

There remain some deep-seated differences between countries regarding the role of advertising, the part played by the state, the priority given to public service issues, and the optimum structures for delivering and paying for broadcasting services. However, in almost all countries there has been a move toward more market-sensitive systems, as ratings (the measurement of audience size and type for particular programs) have taken over as the general currency of concern among the broadcasting executives who commission the programs.

[*See also* Advertising.]

BIBLIOGRAPHY

Aufderheide, Patricia. *Communications Policy and the Public Interest: The Telecommunications Act of 1996.* New York and London, 1999. A detailed account of the 1996 U.S. legislation, reflecting some major economic and technological changes in both broadcasting and telecommunications. It contains a wide-ranging set of appendixes, including an abridged version of the act and a variety of public-policy position papers.

Barwise, Patrick, and Andrew Ehrenberg. *Television and Its Audience.* London and Newbury Park, 1988. A still-valuable account of the nature of television with regard to the role of the audience in the economics of the medium.

Blumler, Jay G., and T. J. Nossiter, eds. *Broadcasting Finance in Transition: A Comparative Handbook.* New York and Oxford, 1991. An account of changes in broadcasting finance from a European perspective during a period of major change and expansion.

Briggs, Asa. *The History of Broadcasting in the United Kingdom.* 5 vols. Oxford, 1961, 1965, 1970, 1979, and 1995. Probably the most authoritative and historically detailed account of the history of British broadcasting from its origins in the ethos of the BBC to the emergence and expansion of commercial broadcasting. Volume V takes the study up to 1974; a sixth volume, by Jean Seaton, is in preparation.

Herman, Edward S., and Robert W. McChesney. *The Global Media: The New Missionaries of Corporate Capitalism.* London and Washington, 1997. A critical account of the growth of transnational corporations in the media field, with some reflections upon the perceived negative implications of this growth for national culture and democratic government.

Mosco, Vincent. *The Political Economy of Communication: Rethinking and Renewal.* London and Thousand Oaks, 1996. A widely researched and at times historically inflected account of the political economy of the media, including some reflection upon the perceived tensions between "policy studies" and "cultural studies."

Picard, Robert. *Media Economics: Concepts and Issues.* Newbury Park, Calif., 1989. An overview of some of the key issues in the economics of the media from a largely American perspective.

Price, Munroe E., and Stefaan G. Verhulst, eds. *Broadcasting Reform in India: Media Law from a Global Perspective.* Delhi and Oxford, 1998. A useful collection of essays written from both relatively statist and avowedly free-market perspectives. Extensive appendixes include policy documents, draft legislation, and the Constitution of India.

Sinclair, John, Elizabeth Jacka, and Stuart Cunningham, eds. *New Patterns in Global Television: Peripheral Vision.* Oxford and New York, 1996. A view of global media developed from the vantage point of Australia and therefore from outside of the metropolitan centers of the Northern Hemisphere. This collection contains useful essays on media developments in Australia, Canada, the Arab world, India, and Central and South America.

Smith, Anthony, ed. *Television: An International History.* Oxford, 1995. An overview, by different authors, of the historical development of the medium of television with excellent visual illustrations. The survey includes Africa, Australia, France, Germany, the former Soviet Union, Japan, the United States, the United Kingdom, and the third world.

Sparks, Colin, with Anna Reading. *Communism, Capitalism and the Mass Media.* London and Thousand Oaks, Calif., 1998. A useful and sometimes controversial account of the role of the media in capitalist and communist economies, together with a detailed consideration of changes since 1979 in Poland, Hungary, the Czech Republic, and Slovakia.

Sterling, Christopher H., and John M. Kittross. *Stay Tuned: A Concise History of American Broadcasting.* 3rd ed. Mahwah, N. J. and London, 2002. A detailed overview of the history, technology, and, to some extent, the economics of broadcasting in the United States.

ONLINE RESOURCES

Council of Europe: <http://www.coe.int/> The home page of the Council of Europe provides useful information and debate on the media within the Media Division of the Human Rights section.

Federal Communications Commission: <http://www.fcc.gov/> The home page of the Federal Communications Commission, the key regulatory body for both media and telecommunications within the United States; this site provides access to a wide range of information.

UNESCO: <http://www.unesco.org/> The home page of the United Nations Educational, Scientific and Cultural Organization gives access to the annual statistics on television ownership per thousand of the population throughout the world.

SYLVIA HARVEY

RAILROADS *[This entry contains three subentries, a historical overview and discussions on technological change and industrial organization and regulation.]*

Historical Overview

Railroads are the very symbol of the Industrial Revolution. In the railroads' first century, their primary raw materials were coal and iron, also the primary raw materials of the Industrial Revolution. They brought mechanized power to inland transportation and mobilized the economy. Their financing created modern capital markets. Modern management methods grew up with the railroads. Railroads contributed to economic growth by widening markets and thus promoting scale economies, specialization, and greater comparative advantage. Railroads improved overall transportation productivity, releasing resources for employment in other sectors. Because railroads symbolized so much of the Industrial Revolution, historians and economists, like Walt Rostow and Joseph Schumpeter, pointed to railroads as an indispensable, leading sector for achieving industrialization or the takeoff. But economics Nobel laureate Robert Fogel questioned that view in his book *Railroads and Economic Growth: Essays in Econometric History* (Baltimore, 1964). In any case, the railroads employed the Industrial Revolution's first key innovation, the steam engine. Marrying the steam engine to iron rails allowed the railroad industry, if not the economy, to take off.

Beginnings. Before the application of the steam engine to transportation, moving goods and people had changed little for millennia. Alexander the Great and Napoleon used the same means to move their armies: horses and marching feet. In fact, horses were the source of power on the first railroads.

The first railroads were built to reduce friction because friction wore out roadways, leaving them rutted. The first railroad innovation, the wooden tie, also predates the application of the steam engine. In 1785, William Jessop invented the tie to hold the rail in place above ground. But horses and rails were not completely compatible. Horses require soft footing for traction, but rails require a firm foundation to stay in place.

Before railroads dominated the landscape, transportation relied on highways and water carriage. Inland water carriage meant canals. In the United States, the Erie Canal was a landmark success. It yielded an 8 percent annual return on its construction costs and spawned many imitators. However, these imitators were rarely successful. In contrast to New York's success with the Erie, Pennsylvania's canals were money losers. Speed was a problem. It took longer to go by canal from Liverpool to Manchester than to sail from New York to Liverpool. Turnpikes were not much of an alternative. Besides also being slow, they were small-scale. In Massachusetts, the average turnpike was only twenty miles, and in Pennsylvania, eight turnpikes and three bridge companies served the route between Philadelphia and Pittsburgh. Speed and scale changed with the coming of the steam-powered railroad, but steam engines developed first as stationary applications.

The English inventor Thomas Newcomen developed the first steam engine to pump water out of mines. Another British inventor, James Watt, made significant improvements in the steam engine, but his steam engines were low-pressure designs. Although low-pressure engines were safer to operate, they were too big for practical transportation use. One of Watt's employees, William Murdock, developed a working steam carriage that made an experimental run. Unfortunately for Murdock, Watt and his partner discouraged Murdock from any further experimentation because they feared the danger of high-pressure steam engines. The fear of high-pressure steam engines exploding followed locomotives throughout the early years of railroading. This allowed another English engineer, Richard Trevithick, to attain the honor of inventing the locomotive.

Trevithick worked with high-pressure steam engines, many employed in stationary service. High-pressure steam engines improved the weight-to-power ratio. Trevithick was convinced that high-pressure steam engines applied to iron rails could move heavy loads. In 1804, his locomotive pulled ten tons of iron and seventy men from Pen-y-Darran to Navigation House, a distance of nine miles. However, another twenty years passed before a commercial common carrier adopted the steam-powered locomotive. In 1808, Trevithick deployed his invention as an amusement ride in London, but that venture ended with a derailment. It remained for George Stephenson to build locomotives and guide the railroad's first commercial successes.

Stephenson was uneducated and practically illiterate, but he had innate engineering talent. In 1812, Stephenson became enginewright at Killingworth High Pit, which employed a locomotive developed by another British inventor, John Blenkinsop, to move coal from mine to wharf in Leeds. Blenkinsop's locomotive began operation on 24 June 1812. Stephenson became interested in locomotives and started building his own. When Stephenson heard that a group of Durham Quakers had obtained a parliamentary act to construct a railway from Stockton to Darlington, he lobbied for and received the position of the railway's engineer. This provided the opportunity to deploy his locomotives. The Stockton and Darlington Railway opened on 27 September 1825 and was the first steam-powered common carrier. However, horses initially did most of the hauling. Textile factory owners in the Midlands wanted a better transportation alternative to canal service because canals were too slow and unreliable. This led to the Liverpool and Manchester Railway in 1830. The directors of this railway decided to employ all locomotives and no horses. They set up the Rainhill Trials to choose the best technology. Stephenson's Rocket won the trials, and the Liverpool and Manchester opened on 15 September 1830 with Stephenson as chief engineer.

Stephenson was a visionary in his use of locomotives and his understanding of future railroad operations. He foresaw the inherent conflict between heavy freight, like iron and coal, versus passenger services. Heavy freight requires more durable rails but can travel at relatively slower speeds, while passenger traffic is light and fast. Stephenson's remedy was to have separate railways for freight and passenger service. (This is not quite the way the U.S. Congress in 1971 set up Amtrak, the American passenger railroad, because Amtrak shares the freight carriers' rails.) In one regard, Stephenson was not foresighted. He recommended that railroads be limited to top speeds of forty miles per hour. Even in Stephenson's own lifetime, this became old-fashioned thinking.

Canals could not stave off the railroads' onslaught. The Liverpool and Manchester Railway killed off its canal competitor. Other canals survived in niche markets where speed was not essential. And railroads quickly developed a speed advantage. Horses could at best do ten miles per hour. This was the top speed for coaches, and canals were slower. By 1832, railroads were achieving over fifteen miles per hour. In the 1840s, trains passed forty and began pushing sixty miles per hour. The death knell for coaches came when, in 1838, Parliament shifted mail from coaches to railroads. By that time, the passenger business had left the coaches. A last convert was Queen Victoria, who first used rail service in 1842. Coaches and supporting industries withered away.

As British railroads developed, they relied on private capital and management, but Parliament provided important powers to early railroad development. One such power was land acquisition. Another parliamentary act in 1840 made railroads monopolies on their own lines. This meant no open or shared access, a departure from canals and turnpikes, which were open to all carriers. However, it was too difficult to coordinate locomotive speeds and avoid accidents and congestion on railroads. The telegraph found its first practical application in coordinating railroad operations. The telegraph permitted long-distance and out-of-sight signaling, especially important for safe tunnel operations. The telegraph became the railroads' nervous system.

By the 1840s, English railways apparently were thriving. The companies banded together to coordinate interline movements. In 1842, they formed the Railway Clearinghouse. Because the English railroads were private, there was no central plan. They radiated from London as individual monopolies. They raised their capital privately, and their success led to a speculative bubble in the 1840s. Railroad equities paid dividends and seemed to be as risk-free as government bonds. The companies were the new technology and offered safe, fast transportation to serve the industrial age. In 1843–1844, fifty new schemes were floated and, reminiscent of the 1990s' Internet bubble, projects that would serve no inhabitants (that is, no customers) still had high share prices. George Hudson, the railway king, warned investors that stock prices could also fall, which they did when the Bank of England raised interest rates and punctured the bubble. Railroad mania was repeated in the United States.

Early American Railroads. Although the United States in general had good inland water transportation, some ports were not as fortunate as New York or New Orleans, both at the mouths of major rivers. Baltimore, Boston, and Charleston had relatively poor inland access and thus became early railroad promoters. Baltimore wanted an inland transportation system that would rival the Erie Canal. It did not get that with the Chesapeake and Ohio Canal, because that canal terminated in Alexandria, Virginia, fifty miles to the south. Baltimore merchants boosted the Baltimore and Ohio Railroad, which began operations in 1828 and reached the Ohio River at Wheeling in 1852. Charleston sought to draw cotton exports to its port and promoted the South Carolina Canal and Railroad, which connected Charleston to the Savannah River at Augusta, Georgia. In 1833, this railroad, at 130 miles, was the longest railroad. Overall, there were three thousand railroad miles in 1839, when economic depression paused further expansion.

The 1840s and 1850s experienced a major American railroad expansion in overall mileage and average company mileage. Before this surge, American railroads were usually less than fifty miles in length. Like English railroads, American railroads were knocking out their canal competition. Railroads were straighter, were cheaper to build in rough terrain, did not require water, and were faster. Travel time between New York and Chicago decreased from three weeks to three days from 1800 to 1857. By 1860, the United States had thirty thousand railroad miles, which was then one-half of the world's total railroad mileage. In contrast to English railroads, which had private funding for construction, American railroads got 25 percent of their financing from government sources by 1860.

Resource endowments drove American railroad innovation and differences between American and European railroads. In the nineteenth century, land was plentiful in the United States, but labor was expensive. The reverse was true in Europe. European railroads conserved land and were built straight, while American railroads used more land and adopted more curves. This meant American railroad cars had to adapt to curves, and in 1834 Ross Winans patented the bogie, the swiveling wheel assembly. American railroads also had steeper grades that, when combined with the overall need to save on labor, meant American locomotives had to be more powerful, tolerant of poor tracks, and simple to maintain.

American and British railroads led the evolution of the standard gauge (that is, the space between the rails), which is 4 feet 8.5 inches. Standard gauge is thought to have

MEETING OF GIANTS. The joining of Central Pacific and Union Pacific lines, Promontory, Nevada, 10 May 1869. At center, the engineers shake hands. (Prints and Photographs Division, Library of Congress)

evolved from the lateral space between the wheels on horse wagons, which matched ruts on poor roads. But standard gauge may not have been ideal. Isambard Kingdom Brunel built England's Great Western Railway with a broad gauge of seven feet. He believed this allowed smoother rides from lower carriages and faster speeds. But Britain's other railroads adopted the standard gauge, which meant the Great Western had to adapt to exchange traffic. At first, the Great Western added a third rail, but by 1892 it relented, removed the third rail, and adopted standard gauge. American railroads finished universal standard gauge adoption in 1886.

Prior to railroads, steamboats dominated inland transportation in the United States. The country possessed several major river systems, and steamboats permitted effective travel against the current. In the early nineteenth century, the ubiquity of steamboat travel differentiated the United States from Europe, which relied more on horse-drawn coach. The coach versus steamboat orientation was reflected in train-board passenger accommodations. European railcars had first class compartments, laid out like coaches, that did not initially interconnect. American trains had open parlor cars, reminiscent of steamboat passenger facilities. But in fact the American entrepreneur George Pullman's inspiration for his industry-leading

passenger cars was the luxury hotel lobby. Other American passenger cars had bench seats facing forward like seating on small riverboats, while other (non–first class) European passenger accommodations seemed to be almost an afterthought. Initially, they were open-air cars with benches.

Railroad Development in Other Countries. Railroad development in other countries did not follow a uniform pattern. Politics, geography, or national defense concerns affected the speed and organization of railroad expansion. For example, Belgium was an early adopter, and with railroads it established more firmly its 1830 independence from the Netherlands. Belgium began building railroads after independence so its trade could avoid Dutch ports. Belgian railroads were built to establish economic links with Prussia, France, and England. Because at that time Stephenson's locomotive technology was leading edge, the Belgians became Stephenson's customers. The Belgians also imported rails because they did not have an iron industry to match Britain's. But the importance of railroads to national policy meant the Belgian government built the lines until the first private concession was granted in 1843. From 1843 to 1870, private firms led further railroad expansion. English investors stimulated this private phase. However, some overbuilding occurred, which led the government to intervene again in an effort to keep some lines open and rationalize the system. By 1926, when the national company was formed, over 90 percent of rail mileage was in government control.

French railroad development followed the Belgian pattern with the government directing railroad planning. French railroads were centrally planned because the French did not want railroad development left to the vicissitudes of the free market. The French also were slower to adopt railroads than England or Belgium because French coal reserves were more limited. French leaders worried that the new technology would exhaust its coal resources. However, while France had central railroad planning, in 1838 the French parliament rejected state ownership and construction and instead opted for grants of private concessions. This started on a small scale, as the government granted minor concessions until 1842, when France established the national system. At that time, France designed a system of six major lines that the government granted as private concessions. French railroad development fostered the emergence of domestic iron and steel and then electricity. Railroads in France, as in other countries, allowed productive activities to move to new locations.

Prussia and the rest of Germany followed a different pattern from France or Belgium, in part because of politics and the political division of Germany before 1871. Political concerns made Prussian railroads rely on private entrepreneurship and private capital. As railroads began developing across Europe, the Prussian government was loath to call a parliament to raise taxes for any purpose, even for railroad development support, because such a parliament might provide a means to amplify liberal pressure for political reform. The private Prussian railroads went on to form associations to cooperate on gauges, interconnections, and rates. In other German states, railroad development was haphazard. Some state governments blocked railroad development because they feared trade diversion, but such restraint lasted until railroad development in neighboring states forced a response for development.

As in other countries, German railroad development encouraged development in the domestic iron and coal industries. At first, in the 1830s and 1840s, Germany imported iron from Britain because the German iron industry was relatively backward. But by the 1850s, Germany had developed a more modern industry and was producing its own rails. It even started exporting its output. Germany had better coal reserves than France, but it still imported increasing tonnages of British coal until the brink of World War I because transporting British coal was cheaper than domestic sources. However, the German coal industry was developing so much that the market share of imported British coal started falling in the 1860s.

Prussia also showed how railroads could be exploited for military purposes. It used its railroads to swiftly mobilize its forces against Austria in 1866 and France in 1870. This advantage led to Prussian victories in both wars and ultimate German unification under Prussian leadership. However, the lesson of rapid Prussian mobilization locked the European powers into rail-based mobilization schedules that fatally constrained diplomatic options in 1914.

Italian railroad development was not as successful as that in other countries. It was also somewhat later. Although there was some minor building in the 1840s and 1850s in Tuscany and the Piedmont, it was not until political unification in 1861 that the first real construction boom occurred. Italian topography was not conducive to railroad expansion. The Italian Peninsula, with a mountainous interior and several good ports, provides ample support to water carriage competition for rail. Southern Italy was a high-cost area for rail and was not well integrated into the rest of the industry. Railroads faced relatively high fuel costs in Italy, and government policy inhibited railroad development. The state took 28 percent of railroad revenues, which constrained the companies' incentives to exploit any scale economies. Italian railroads' relatively weak development did not provide much impetus for development of complementary industries like iron and steel. In fact, high tariffs on metal products to protect the domestic industry probably inhibited the growth of metal-user industries like railroads. The only area in Italy that seemed to benefit from railroads was the Po Valley. In contrast, the peninsular trunk lines were costly without providing offsetting social benefits. Italian railroads also brought industrial prominence to Genoa and relative decline to Venice.

Unlike Italy, Russia and the Iberian Peninsula did not have ample water carriage alternatives, so railroad development brought benefits. They also had different gauges from their neighbors. Russia's gauge resulted from the directions of an uninformed American engineer. Spain and Portugal had different gauges from France for defensive purposes. Spain's development was based on imported iron until the 1890s tariffs made imports too expensive. At the same time, 20 percent of Spain's coal production went to domestic railroads. Russian railroad development was also relatively late, and the first line between Saint Petersburg and Moscow was finished in 1854. Railroad development in southern and eastern Europe was constrained by less-favorable factor endowments than in northern and western Europe.

Chinese railroad development brought debates over development versus unemployment and national defense versus foreign exploitation. Chinese officials worried that railroad development would create groups of unemployed transportation workers. Such unemployed workers could prove susceptible and eager accomplices to rebellion

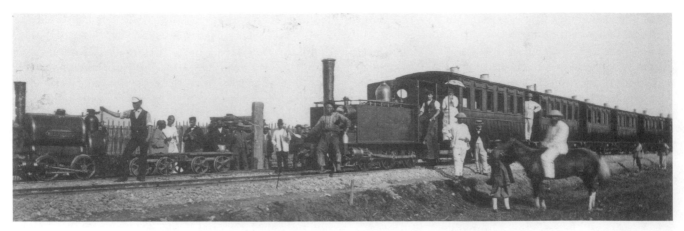

WOOSUNG RAILROAD, CHINA. Enroute from Woosung to Shanghai, late 1800s. (Prints and Photographs Division, Library of Congress)

against the government. With foreign powers grabbing significant chunks of Chinese territory, Chinese officials also worried about whether railroad development would facilitate further foreign exploitation or allow China to better thwart the foreigners. The Boxer Rebellion showed the benefits of rail for defense because the Chinese used rail to move forces to the front swiftly while they tore up the tracks in front of the foreign troops, limiting their speed. China completed its first line, Shanghai to Woosung, in 1876. The foreign powers sought and received railroad-building concessions within their respective influence spheres, first the French and the Russians, followed by the Germans and the British. China had 255 railroad miles in 1894, when this foreign-dominated constructed boom started, and achieved 5,780 miles by 1911. While China was starting and then rapidly expanding its railroads, American railroads were evolving from robber baron stewardship to government regulation and developing modern management techniques along the way.

Robber Barons and the Visible Hand. Matthew Josephson, in his book *The Robber Barons* (1935), claimed nineteenth-century American entrepreneurs and business leaders, including those in the railroad industry, made their fortunes by taxing the public the way medieval barons taxed river traffic. Later economic historians, particularly Arthur Johnson and Barry Supple in *Boston Capitalists and Western Railroads* (1965), provided a more sophisticated and useful analysis. They divided railroad leaders into two groups. The first group had leaders who sought to follow a long-term strategy of reinvesting profits into their properties and developing demand along their lines. Johnson and Supple identified this strategy as developmental. John Murray Forbes and Charles Perkins followed a developmental strategy on the Chicago, Burlington and Quincy Railroad. Johnson and Supple's second group followed a short-run strategy of taking profits by paying out dividends and through security trading. These

were speculators like Jay Gould. Beyond strategies, railroads became the first of the modern industrial corporations because their size and industry economics required new management structures.

Alfred Chandler, in *The Visible Hand* (1978), argued that railroads developed the management structure for the modern industrial corporation. Railroad development and management required civil engineering skills, which prompted a growth in engineering schools in the 1850s and 1860s. More advanced management structures became necessary after 1850, when railroad lengths exceeded fifty miles and created geographically dispersed enterprises. This brought a layered management hierarchy and began the separation of management and ownership. J. Edgar Thomson led the Pennsylvania Railroad through a major management structure innovation, a line and staff organization with divisions. The New York Central Railroad and European railroads generally followed a functional organization plan unlike the Pennsylvania's division structure. Thomson also led the Pennsylvania in developing accounting processes and information, the latter a prerequisite for proper control and administration of a large business. By 1893, largely due to Thomson's leadership, the Pennsylvania administration and organization structure was world premier.

Because railroading was capital intensive, railroads created depreciation and capital accounting to track the flow of funds through the organization. After the U.S. Civil War, Albert Fink led the development of cost accounting. Railroad managers were cost focused because railroads had subunits that were cost centers rather than profit centers and because revenues were tracked corporatewide, not at the section or branch level.

These management innovations led Chandler to pose his basic "visible hand" thesis: management in the large industrial firms, like railroads, replaced the market forces of Adam Smith's invisible hand. However, railroad industry economics also broke the simple boundaries of Smith's model.

Railroads diverged from Smith's typical small firm because they were capital intensive and had high fixed costs. Typically, nineteenth-century railroads had fixed costs that were two-thirds of total cost. High fixed costs created scale economies, which meant railroads could not set prices equal to marginal cost and survive in the long run. Many leading railroad theorists and practitioners, like Charles Francis Adams, Jr., who was both a state regulator and later a railroad executive, did not believe laissez-faire would work for their industry because marginal cost pricing was impractical. In the 1850s, railroads began pricing based on service value rather than cost. They provided volume discounts to large shippers and even secret rebates. In France, railroads followed economist Jules Dupuit's suggestions to maximize returns by setting multiple rates, but the French government intervened to limit the extent of the price discrimination. But as long as American railroads had room to expand and not face much direct competition, they could avoid stresses of "cut-throat" competition or selling above marginal cost but below average cost. The United States experienced a railroad building frenzy from 1868 to 1873 with a 40 percent increase in railroad miles.

During this time, the United States completed its first transcontinental railroad when the Central Pacific and Union Pacific met at Promontory Point, Utah, in 1869. Both railroads received federal land grants and loans to spur their construction. The Central Pacific was led by the banking magnate Chester Crocker, the industrialist Collis P. Huntington, and Leland Stanford, who was later governor of California and founder of Stanford University. They later folded the Central Pacific into their more prominent Southern Pacific system. The Central Pacific had developmental purpose in serving Nevada's silver mines along its way to Utah. The Union Pacific crossed largely barren and unsettled territory to reach Promontory Point, and it was a prime target for speculation and manipulation. The Union Pacific's management created a construction company, Credit Mobilier, to reap profits from building rather than operating the railroad. When the congressman and Union Pacific investor Oakes Ames passed extremely profitable Credit Mobilier stock around Congress, he precipitated a scandal. The scandal broke in 1873, and the resulting congressional investigation brought censure for Ames.

Besides congressional scandal, 1873 witnessed a dramatic collapse in the economy that also had severe implications for railroads and the financial sector. The crash caused a fall in demand and brought severe rate competition. Furthermore, the crash caused the Pennsylvania and other railroads to pause their expansion plans. The crash also forced the Pennsylvania to move its bond business from Jay Cooke's brokerage, which had collapsed with the crash, to the Drexel and Morgan house.

In the 1860s and 1870s, many railroads had formed pools (that is, cartels) to limit price competition, but in 1869 the Pennsylvania tried a new approach by building a system that eventually was controlled through a holding company. Not every railroad saw the virtues of system building as practiced by the Pennsylvania. The Chicago, Burlington and Quincy, a well-managed western railroad, tried to avoid the expense of system building early in the 1870s, but Charles Perkins led them to that strategy after the railroad found itself in competition with Gould, the speculator and master cartel breaker.

Gould was none too fond of cartels. He knew there were profits to be reaped by entering markets dominated by cartels. Whether he was using the Erie to compete with the Pennsylvania and New York Central in the East or the Missouri Pacific against Perkins and the Burlington in the West, Gould was wresting market share and profits from the cartels. Gould's strategies forced railroads to follow the Pennsylvania's approach and build systems. As Chandler argued, these systems became the first large industrial businesses and provided many breakthroughs in management practice.

Railroads encouraged the development of capital markets. They required large and unprecedented amounts of capital, and American railroads had to search abroad for adequate supplies of capital. After the instability brought by the series of revolutions in 1848, Europeans were eager to move capital into the American market. New York exporting firms began dealing in railroad securities. The New York Stock Exchange grew rapidly with the addition of new railroad stocks.

Chandler concluded that railroads provided speedy and reliable transportation that was a prerequisite of the mass production and mass distribution industrial economy. Schumpeter and Rostow concurred and noted railroads' importance as a leading sector. However, cliometric economic historians, led by Fogel, have questioned this analysis and have provided estimates that reduce the railroads' significance.

It's the Steam Engine, Stupid. Fogel measured railroads' contribution to American economic growth by estimating how much more it would have cost the economy to have the level of economic activity in 1890 without the railroads. He pointed out that the vast majority of settlement was within the reach of a steamboat and wagon transportation alternative. He estimated that for agricultural products, the savings were about 3 percent of 1890 GNP. When he expanded the estimate to the whole economy, he estimated that they were between 5 and 10 percent but surmised they were probably closer to the lower figure. He concluded that railroads were not an indispensable contributor to American industrialization. In fact, he posited that the United States may well have developed the internal combustion engine quicker if there had not been railroads.

Indeed, Fogel's findings may not be so surprising when one remembers that both railroads and steamboats relied on a key, perhaps the key, innovation of industrialization, the steam engine. It is inconceivable to imagine the gains from industrialization without the steam engine.

But Fogel's econometrics did unleash a stream of research and controversy. Critics pointed out that Fogel's analysis depended on comparative statics. He compared actual 1890 conditions to hypothesized 1890 conditions without railroads, but this analysis did not account for the fact that without railroads, relative prices and production functions would also change. Other criticism noted that Fogel's analysis assumed railroad prices equaled marginal cost, but this was rarely true because of the way railroads priced. Thus, the actual transportation costs were lower than what Fogel assumed. There was also a problem with assuming elastic long-run supply curves, particularly for canals, which had more constraints than Fogel included in his analysis. Fogel also understated the railroads' contributions to minerals development. The economist Albert Fishlow reviewed Fogel's work and concluded that the actual railroad contribution in 1890 was over 10 percent. However, at 10 percent or even 5 percent, railroads were still an important innovation. It is also important to remember how the railroads contributed to growth compared to the growth trend and not just the absolute level of GNP.

Applying Fogel's technique to analyze the importance of railroad development in other countries highlighted whether inland water transportation was a viable alternative. Countries like Spain and Mexico, which did not have good inland waterway alternatives, produce social savings estimates in the range of 20 to 40 percent of GNP. On the other end of the spectrum are countries like Belgium and Italy, where the social savings estimates are merely a few percentage points of GNP. The United States and the United Kingdom fall more in the middle, with social savings between 3.5 and 11 percent, depending on the base year used in the analysis.

One controversy that cliometric analysis has resolved regards whether or not American railroads were built ahead of demand (that is, ahead of settlement). Fishlow, in *American Railroads and the Transformation of the Ante-Bellum Economy* (1965), found that western railroad building followed settlement and facilitated settlement in neighboring areas. Thus, it was railroad building in Ohio that facilitated settlement in Indiana and Illinois. One exception was the Union Pacific, which was built ahead of demand across an unsettled wilderness to reach its juncture with the Central Pacific at Promontory Point.

Besides facilitating settlement of the American wilderness and lowering transportation costs in developed and developing economies, railroads impacted other industries and even the routines of living. Schumpeter believed that the economy was so transformed; he termed it the "railroadization" of the economy. Consider that railroads standardized something as basic as time, with adoption of standard time. In Britain, the Railway Clearinghouse established the Greenwich time standard in 1880. Standard time came to Germany in 1893. American railroads established the four continental time zones in 1889, although they were not legally recognized until 1918.

Even within developed areas, railroads changed the settlement pattern. Railroads created the suburbs and ended certain enclaves' remote exclusivity. For example, the English middle class began frequenting the seaside towns of southern England.

Railroads' backward linkages were just as impressive because railroad input demands changed the industries that were the sources of those inputs. Their huge demands for capital created the modern capital markets. In 1906, 85 percent of corporate bonds and 50 percent of stock on the New York Stock Exchange were for railroads. Between 1880 and 1910, American locomotives consumed 20 percent of American coal output. In 1860, American railroads consumed 40 percent of rolled iron output, but perhaps more importantly, railroad demands for more durable rails than wrought iron rails pushed the iron industry to produce steel. Steel rails were one-half of American steel output between 1867 and 1891.

By the end of the nineteenth century, railroads had transformed many economies and encouraged development and settlement. In many areas, their contribution may have been replaced by inland water carriage. However, the contribution of that alternative mode would have depended on the steam engine. In any case, the late nineteenth century witnessed the railroads at the pinnacle. American railroad construction peaked in the 1880s, and overcapacity was becoming an endemic problem. At this point, governments began to regulate or nationalize railroads, either to curb their power or to rationalize overbuilt systems.

Regulation, Nationalization, and Decline. Railroad economics contributed mightily to creation of public policies of regulation or nationalization. Because of scale economies, railroads practiced price discrimination, but this upset shippers without competitive alternatives and less elastic demand. Railroads themselves wanted some forum to control the competitive pressure they were under because their system of cartels proved unstable. This instability was caused by chiseling or new entry of someone like Gould. In the United States, the railroads relented and accepted establishment of the Interstate Commerce

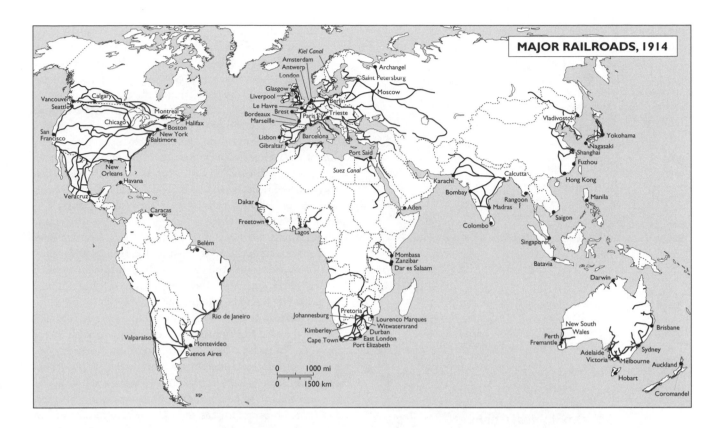

MAJOR RAILROADS, 1914

Commission to regulate the industry. But that body did not prove an agency for enforcing cartel agreements after the courts found cartels in violation of the Sherman Antitrust Act in 1897.

James J. Hill, the last great American builder who opened up the Pacific Northwest when he completed the Great Northern in 1893, sought to control competitive excesses by merging rival roads into big systems. He attempted to unite the Great Northern, Northern Pacific, and Chicago, Burlington and Quincy into an entity called Northern Securities, but President Theodore Roosevelt had his first antitrust success when the Supreme Court broke that entity apart in 1904. During this time, the Progressive Era in the United States, American rate regulation also began to freeze railroad pricing at levels that were not compensatory, as Albro Martin documented in *Enterprise Denied* (1971). Besides providing nonremunerative rates, regulation froze the systems in place. American railroad systems of the 1890s remained basically unchanged in 1945. During World War I, the U.S. government took over the industry when the railroads became hopelessly congested. The government boosted worker pay but held down rates. This constrained the railroads' ability to maintain their property. After the war, when the railroads returned to the private sector, they never achieved a 6 percent return on investment, even in the Roaring Twenties. As highway traffic became more competitive, railroads declined further. In the

1930s, railroads made minimum investments, and traffic fell, with passenger business off 30 percent.

After World War II, Great Britain and France nationalized their rail industries, but the United States maintained its regulatory structure. The building of the interstate highway system, started under President Dwight Eisenhower in the 1950s, accelerated the railroads' decline. Perhaps best embodying this trend were the dire straits of the New York Central Railroad and the Pennsylvania Railroad. In the late 1950s, these previously highly regarded, blue chip companies had to cut back dividends, and their bonds fell to junk status. Their managements decided the solution lay in merger. However, this was a failure. The Penn Central bankruptcy in 1970 precipitated a restructuring of the industry, including a new regulatory regime. The Staggers Act, passed in 1980, deregulated the industry so that eventually over three-quarters of rail traffic became free of rate regulation.

Some industry analysts believed the railroads' future would be best served with high-speed operations. As Stephenson noted in the mid-nineteenth century, that would help passenger operations but not freight. In 1934, the Chicago, Burlington and Quincy employed the first passenger diesel, which reached speeds of one hundred miles per hour. Thirty years later, the Japanese deployed their high-speed Shinkansen train. At the beginning of the twenty-first century, it is not clear that high-speed operations will return rail passenger service to the dominance it enjoyed in the late nineteenth century.

BIBLIOGRAPHY

Chandler, Alfred. *The Visible Hand*. Cambridge, Mass., 1978.

Dale, Rodney. *Early Railways*. Oxford, 1994.

Fishlow, Albert. *American Railroads and the Transformation of the Ante-Bellum Economy*. Cambridge, Mass., 1965.

Huenemann, Ralph William. *The Dragon and the Iron Horse: The Economics of Railroads in China, 1876–1937*. Cambridge, Mass., 1984.

Johnson, Arthur, and Barry Supple. *Boston Capitalists and Western Railroads*. Cambridge, Mass., 1965.

Josephson, Matthew. *The Robber Barons*. New York, 1935.

Klein, Maury. *The Life and Legend of Jay Gould*. Baltimore and London, 1986.

Martin, Albro. *Enterprise Denied*. New York, 1971.

O'Brien, Patrick. *The New Economic History of the Railways*. New York, 1977.

O'Brien, Patrick, ed. *Railways and the Economic Development of Western Europe, 1830–1914*. New York, 1983.

Saunders, Richard, Jr. *Merging Lines: American Railroads, 1900–1970*. DeKalb, Ill., 2001.

Schivelbusch, Wolfgang. *The Railway Journey: The Industrialization of Time and Space in the Nineteenth Century*. Berkeley, 1986.

Wilner, Frank N. *Railroad Mergers: History, Analysis, Insight*. Omaha, 1997.

WILLIAM HUNEKE

Technological Change

A modern railway has been defined as a publicly controlled means of transport possessing four distinctive features: a specialized track, mechanical traction, the accommodation of public traffic, and the conveyance of passengers. However, a long history of development preceded this stage. Basically, a railway is a prepared track that so guides the vehicles running on it that they cannot leave the track. Under this second definition, the germ of the railway can be traced back to Neolithic times when trackways were laid across marshy ground and were formed of transverse planks placed on the surface, held together with longitudinal beams of wood pinned along each side of the trackway. These longitudinal beams would have prevented sledges from slipping off the track. Examples have been found in Germany and Britain, dating from the third millennium BCE to roughly 900 BCE. On Malta, trackways carved into rock dating from the second millenium BCE may have been used to guide vehicles. Across the Isthmus of Corinth, a system for carrying ships or other goods on wheeled cradles guided by grooves cut into the rock was begun by Periander about 600 BCE and remained in use until at least 67 CE. However, none of these early guided ways continued into the modern era.

Another type of guided track originated in metaliferous mines of central Europe, certainly by the fourteenth or fifteenth centuries CE, where heavy ore had to be moved from the working face of the mines to the exterior as the tunneling became deeper and deeper. Two types of guidance system developed. The best known and the most widespread method was laying two parallel planks with a slot between them along the adit into the mine. On the small trucks pushed by hand, a pin called a hund projected downward to engage in the slot and so guide the vehicle. The planks or rails did not extend far beyond the entrance to the mine. The other, possibly earlier, form of medieval railway had a channel or angle rail, which provided the advantage over the other system that the trucks, with their flat-rimmed wheels, could be dragged or pushed more easily in places without rails since they had no protruding guide pin. One of these systems, probably the hund method, was almost certainly brought to the English Lake District by German miners in the 1560s; but the mines were unprofitable and the system had no influence on later British developments. Indeed, these mining guided trackways proved to be a dead-end technology.

Early British Railways. English coal mines are responsible for the next developments, from which can be traced the origins of today's railways. In metaliferous mines, the tunnels were narrow, and the ore was heavy; so the trucks were small. Outside the mines, it was more economical to transport the ore in larger road vehicles. As coal was needed in large amounts for burning in towns and cities away from mining areas, the wagonway proved to be the solution for its distribution. Up to the accession of Elizabeth I, British coal was mined on a small scale to supply local markets; but from 1600 to 1700, there was a startling change, with production increasing roughly fourteenfold. During the eighteenth century, output rose steadily but more slowly than in the preceding decades. Demand for coal stimulated railway development, which, in turn, enabled that demand to be met.

The coalfield to the west of Nottingham was worked extensively throughout the sixteenth century and well into the seventeenth. Coal was taken by carts for consumption in Nottingham or to the River Trent, where it was loaded into barges for broader distribution. Huntingdon Beaumont leased pits in the Strelley area, and between October 1603 and October 1604 laid a two-mile stretch of wagonway with rails to enable his coal to be more accessible for both Nottingham and the Trent. This wagonway or railway is now considered to be an ancestor of the modern railway. Beaumont also had coal-mining interests far to the north in Northumberland and it seems clear that he had the honor of introducing the wagonway to the important coal mining area of the Tyne and Wear. He seems to have built three lines running down to the River Blyth but failed to make a fortune for himself.

Judging by later northern wagonways, Beaumont most likely used wooden rails on which the wagons were guided with wooden flanged wheels and drawn by horses; and the rail gauge is most likely to have been about 4 feet 8 inches. All these features became standard later in Northumberland. The voracious appetite for coal in London was met in the seventeenth and eighteenth centuries by opening up coal mines farther and farther into the hinterland around Newcastle upon Tyne through the use of wagonways on which coal could be transported to riverside staithes for transshipment. Wayleaves had to be arranged with the landowners so that the wagonway could cross other people's land.

Another system of smaller wagons started in the Coalbrookdale area of Shropshire at about the same time as Beaumont in Nottingham, and spread northward to the Whitehaven coal mining area in the Lake District and then into the Scottish lowlands in the 1750s. The importance of this wagonway lay in the use of iron. Iron wheels were being cast at Coalbrookdale before 1730; and since they tended to cut the wooden rails, strips of iron were often nailed on top of the rails where most wear occurred. This practice may also have started at Coalbrookdale in 1767. Cast iron was used but was too brittle; so this method did not become common until after Henry Cort's wrought iron puddling process in 1784. Apparently, it was not until the 1790s that rails made entirely from cast iron came into general use. Then, with cast iron wheels running on cast iron rails, friction was reduced, enabling heavier loads to be hauled.

John Curr of Sheffield claimed that he introduced the cast iron plateway into mines in 1776. This type of rail achieved considerable popularity after 1790 in the Midlands for short lines principally linking coal mines with canals, and in the mountainous coal and iron mining areas of South Wales. Flangeless wheels loose on their axles ran on the flat part of a right-angled plate and were retained on the track by the vertical section. The Penydarren plate-type tram road in South Wales was the scene for Richard Trevithick's first trial of a steam railway locomotive in 1804, which, although the engine itself was successful and won the wager, showed the weakness of this type of rail because its weight broke the plates. By 1810, this type of railway was outmoded. Trevithick demonstrated another steam railway locomotive, the *Catch Me Who Can,* in London in 1808 but did not continue with his pioneering attempts. In 1811, John Blenkinsop designed a four-wheeled steam locomotive for use on the Middleton Colliery Railway in Leeds, with a toothed driving wheel engaging with specially cast rails with cog teeth on one side. In 1812, it became the first steam locomotive in the world put into regular service. Although some other railways were constructed on this principle, it proved to be another dead-end design.

The next steps were taken in the Newcastle area through the development of the steam locomotive. In 1814, William Hedley had his *Puffing Billy* working on the Wylam plate-type wagonway. The weight of the locomotive was spread over eight wheels on a pair of bogies. George Stephenson's *Blucher* followed a little later at Killingworth, an edge railway with flanged wheels, the precursor of the modern system. Stephenson pursued locomotive development over the ensuing years on other lines such as the Hetton Colliery Railway in 1822; yet by 1823 fewer than thirty steam railway locomotives had been built, and not one of them proved to be decisively superior to horse traction.

Modernization. During the 1820s, the railway scene changed dramatically. First there was the introduction of wrought iron rails, which replaced cast iron. Not only was wrought iron stronger, so that there were fewer breakages; but lengths as long as fifteen feet were being rolled, compared with the three-foot length of a cast iron rail, which enabled the permanent way to be made much smoother. It was probably the improved permanent way together with the potential of the steam locomotive that caused such people as Edward Pease and William James to foresee a great future for this mode of transport. In 1821, Pease thought that there would be no difficulty in laying a railroad from London to Edinburgh, which could transport the mail at a rate of twenty miles per hour with steam locomotives. James put forward his first suggestions for an iron railway between Liverpool and Manchester in 1822, on which the use of steam carriages was contemplated. It was confidently expected that conveyance of merchandise between these last two places would be speeded up and the rates of carriage reduced. The first prospectus for the Liverpool & Manchester Railway was issued on 29 October 1824, but the bill for its construction was thrown out of Parliament in 1825. It was necessary to have parliamentary authorization for compulsory purchase of land along which the railway route would pass.

Then, on 27 September 1825, the Stockton & Darlington Railway was opened as a public railway, with Stephenson's locomotives hauling coal and merchandise trains though the passenger traffic was still operated by horses. The Liverpool & Manchester Railway was authorized in 1826, and construction began amid controversy over how the trains should be operated. One faction suggested a series of stationary steam engines pulling the trains by means of ropes. The Stephenson party backed the locomotive. The issue was resolved at the Rainhill Trials in 1829. The *Rocket,* designed by George and Robert Stephenson with a new type of multitubular boiler suggested by Henry Booth, secretary to the Liverpool & Manchester Railway, showed an unprecedented speed of thirty miles per hour and convincingly won the event. It marked a turning point in the history of civilization. At the opening of that railway by the Duke of Wellington on 15 September 1830, all the trains were steam-hauled. The steam railway locomotive had finally triumphed over the horse, and the first true intercity railway was launched.

The Liverpool & Manchester Railway proved to be the Grand British Experimental Railway, which formed the basis for all others. The pace of development of the steam locomotive was incredible. The *Rocket* was soon laid aside, and in 1832 the Stephensons introduced the much steadier and heavier 2-2-2 *Patentee* type. Passengers were soon demanding speeds of no less than twenty miles per hour. The rail track had to be relaid with heavier rails and all the equipment improved, but it soon became clear that railways could compete with turnpike roads, particularly when carrying passengers. The number of passengers wishing to travel on the new railway exceeded all expectations, with 445,047 traveling in the first full year of 1831. Their number alone showed that here was the start of a new transport era, opening with the faster, smoother journeys offered by the railway.

The success of the Liverpool & Manchester Railway convinced others of the viability of the steam intercity railway. Projects were quickly launched on a much larger scale than the 35 miles of that line. There was the London-to-Birmingham line promoted in 1833, a distance of 110 miles. It, together with the Grand Junction Railway (80 miles), linked Birmingham to Liverpool and Manchester, thus providing a rail route to the capital. Brunel's Great Western Railway, with its wide gauge of 7 feet, was authorized in 1835 and opened to Bristol in 1841 (118 miles). By 1850, some 6,559 miles of line had been opened in England and Wales with a sanctioned capital of £288,000,000. In 1912, this mileage had reached 15,000, providing links to virtually every town as well as many villages.

The opening of the Liverpool & Manchester Railway and the subsequent demand for railways across the world gave rise to many new industries, the most obvious in the construction of locomotives. Making railway locomotives required a new engineering approach because they were mobile machines, flexing on the joints of the track but needing to be as light as possible though strong enough to resist the forces generated by the higher speeds. At first, the locomotives were supplied by private firms such as Robert Stephenson & Company in Newcastle, the Vulcan Foundry at Newton le Willows, or Sharp, Roberts & Company in Manchester. Carriages and other rolling stock had to be constructed as well, often by other outside contractors.

With the spread of railways came the need for more powerful locomotives, both to haul longer trains and to tackle more steeply graded mountainous lines. Although locomotives with a pair of single driving wheels sufficed at first, it was soon found to be necessary to have four coupled wheels; and Americans pioneered the use of a four-wheeled bogie beneath the cylinders to give greater stability when rounding curves. The 4-4-0 types were probably the most popular designs for passenger engines in the last part of the nineteenth century, but the more powerful 4-6-0 had been introduced for heavier trains on steeper gradients. There was constant technical improvement, such as the Stephenson valve gear in 1842, which gave greater economy, or the Giffard injector in 1852, which made maintaining the water level in boilers easier.

All the equipment had to be maintained by the railway companies; so each new line had to have its own engineering shops, which created a demand for machine tools capable of meeting required higher standards. Manchester especially developed a thriving machine tool industry. Another industry made signaling equipment as the need for greater safety became increasingly obvious. As improvements such as the Bessemer Converter and the Siemens open hearth process cheapened steel production in the 1860s, this material was quickly taken up by railway companies owing to its better wear characteristics. Parts made from steel such as rails and tires lasted longer and proved to be more economical than iron.

Maintenance workshops also could be used to build locomotives. In the United States, locomotive construction remained in the hands of specialized builders; but in England, the railway companies started to build their own. The two most famous examples are the Great Western Railway Works at Swindon, begun soon after 1835, and the London & North Western Railway Works at Crewe, laid out in 1840. Here and at other similar places, new towns were created with their own houses, schools, and churches in addition to the actual works.

There was equally dramatic expansion in civil engineering. The Liverpool & Manchester Railway had to go over the boggy area of Chat Moss, cross the Sankey Brook on a ten-arched viaduct, and pass through the Mount Olive cutting, hewn out of solid rock, before goods wagons were sent down to the docks by the Wapping tunnel. Although the canal engineers had faced similar problems, railway engineering was carried out on a grander scale than canal engineering, and the Liverpool & Manchester Railway provided a foretaste of what was to come. For example, new types of bridges had to be designed with an ever greater span. Robert Stephenson crossed the Menai Straits between Anglesey and North Wales in 1851 with his tubular Britannia bridge, where the trains ran through the tubes; the longest span here was 460 feet in a total length of 1,380 feet. The cantilever Forth railway bridge near Edinburgh was opened in 1889 with spans of 1,710 feet and a total length of 5,320 feet, not including the approach viaducts.

RAILROAD ROUTES. Map of railway route from Paris to Saint-Germain with a notice explaining the works of art and illustrations of the locomotive machinery and transport cars in use. Colored lithograph, 1837. (Bibliothèque Nationale, Paris/Giraudon/Art Resource, NY) ▶

Carte du Chemin de Fer
de
PARIS À St GERMAIN
Avec une Notice descriptive des Travaux d'Art.
Départ toutes les heures, de Paris & du Pecq, et toutes les demies heures le Dimanche
par A. M. PERROT

VUE DES MACHINES LOCOMOTIVES & DES VOITURES DE TRANSPORT

à Paris, chez Lerri libraire place S.t L.Auxerrois 24.

Worldwide Development. Other countries were quick to follow the British lead. There had been some mineral railways overseas, and the first wooden railway in the United States was built in 1795. Then, in 1828, the Baltimore & Ohio Railroad was begun as horse-drawn railway with wooden rails covered with wrought iron strips. On the European continent, the Wilkinsons laid down minor plateways at Le Creusot in the 1790s for coal and iron production. In the late 1820s, the coal mines in the St. Etienne region, in France, were linked to the rivers Loire and Rhône by various edge railways. The first public railway in Austria was the horse railway built from Linz to Budweis between 1827 and 1832.

However, the success of the *Rocket* and other steam locomotives on the Liverpool & Manchester Railway really quickened the pace of development everywhere. In 1829, the Delaware & Hudson Canal imported four colliery-type locomotives from Britain; but, in 1831, it was the *John Bull*, supplied by Robert Stephenson & Company, based on their successful *Planet* type, to the Camden & Amboy Railway, New Jersey, that really launched the steam railway in America. The first wholly steam-operated railway in the United States was the South Carolina Railroad, which, by 1833, had 136 miles in operation. By 1835, the Baltimore & Ohio was 76 miles long, also entirely worked by steam. In that year, there were 1,000 miles of railway open, which had grown to nearly 9,000 miles by 1850.

The American lines were built cheaply and quickly, with sharp curves, steep gradients, and timber trestle bridges. At first, rails had to be imported from England; it was not until 1844 that they began to be rolled in the United States. Likewise, the first locomotives and rolling stock were British. Firms such as Rothwell, Hick & Rothwell, Bolton, and then Benjamin Hick were supplying locomotives and freight cars to the Pontchartrain Railroad and the New Orleans & Carollton Railroad in the early 1830s. However, Matthias Baldwin in Philadelphia built the first locomotive in America, *Old Ironsides*, in 1831–1832, the forerunner of a vast output. The first bogie locomotive in the United States was built by John B. Jarvis in 1832. This type was soon extended into the classic American 4-4-0 with light bar frames that were the mainstay of motive power in the advance of railroads westward.

The coming of the railroad opened up the western part of America. During the 1850s, the system continued to expand rapidly. Where railways were built into regions still to be settled, grants of public land were made to the railroad companies, which they could sell to recover costs and promote settlement. In this way, throughout much of the United States the railroads came first and settlement later, with towns growing up around railroad stations. By 1860, there were over 30,000 miles of railroad in the United States, and the first transcontinental link-up was achieved at Promontory Point, Utah, in 1869, with a railroad 1,780 miles long. The network continued to spread throughout the nineteenth century, absorbing the energy and the resources of American engineers and manufacturers; and it was not until the final years of this period that American influence began to be felt in other parts of the world.

Elsewhere, British influence constructed most of the early railway lines. Even in France, the first major line, the Paris-to-Rouen line begun in 1841, was engineered by Joseph Locke and built by Thomas Brassey. British influence could be expected throughout the British Empire, as in India, where the first lines were being constructed in the 1850s, and in Australia. It was largely British capital that built the railways to open up the vast mineral deposits in central Africa. More surprising, perhaps, was British involvement in South America, where nearly all the early major lines were at first British-owned and -run, particularly in the Argentine. The railways helped to realize the commercial potential, whether agricultural or mineral, in all these places.

To be successful, the railway had to adapt to local conditions. America's lightly laid lines (mentioned above) were built to the Stephenson rail gauge of 4 feet 8.5 inches. However, potential traffic might not justify such a large railway; and a narrower gauge could have sharper curves more easily constructed in mountainous country. In England, the Festiniog Railway introduced steam locomotives to its 2-foot gauge line in North Wales in August 1863, and passenger services followed in 1865. Such development dramatically demonstrated the practicality of steam locomotives on narrow gauges. However, other countries had been conducting similar experiments. There was the Norwegian government's twenty-four-mile line with a gauge of 3 feet 6 inches from Grundsett to Hamar in 1862, followed in 1864 by others totaling over eighty miles. Gauges of 3 feet 6 inches and one meter became the standard in many countries of southern Africa starting in 1872, in New Zealand in the 1870s, and in Australia from 1865 on, as they were cheaper to construct. Even with a narrower rail gauge, the loading gauge was often more generous than the British, so that narrow-gauge locomotives in, for examples, South Africa might be larger than British ones.

As railways penetrated into mountainous regions, steep gradients were encountered, which were beyond the limits of adhesion working. Blenkinsop's concept of a cogwheel driving through a toothed rail was the answer, but this time the cog rail was placed in the center of the track. The first true rack railway was built in 1868 up Mount Washington, in New Hampshire, as a tourist attraction, but that type of rack rail was not used again. Swiss engineer Niklaus Riggenbach opened his line up the Rigi

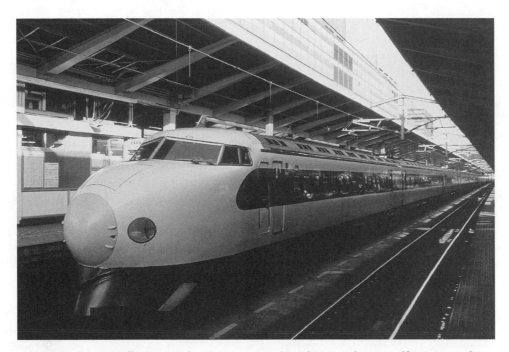

HIGH-SPEED TRAIN. Bullet train, Tokyo Station, 1988. (© Mike Yamashita/Woodfin Camp and Associates, New York)

mountain near Lucerne, Switzerland, in 1871–1873. An improved rack system was developed by Roman Abt in the 1880s, suitable for use on main lines so that steep sections could be climbed with the rack and more level ones worked by adhesion. These rack and adhesion lines took railways into new regions, particularly in Switzerland with, for example, routes to Zermatt and St. Moritz. In India, there was the Nilgiri Railway up to the Nilgiri summer resort, and there was the Trans-Andine Railway in South America.

Starting in the 1880s, electrification further broadened railway communications. In Europe, Werner von Siemens demonstrated a small electric train, which carried passengers around a Berlin exhibition in 1879. Short tourist lines were opened in 1883 by Magnus Volk at Brighton as well as a line at the Giants Causeway, Northern Ireland, which showed electrification's potential. In 1881, von Siemens operated a passenger electric railway one and one-half miles long on the outskirts of Berlin, which was the forerunner of many urban electrified railway and tram routes. The first horse-drawn street tram began operating in New York in 1832. The idea spread first to other American cities, and then Paris in 1855 and Birkenhead in 1860. Steam traction was tried on these trams but never became popular. In Britain, the first electric tramway was opened at Blackpool in 1885. The principle was taken up enthusiastically in the Untied States, not only in cities but also with the vast network of interurban systems developed there.

Electric traction also spread underground, where it was much more suitable than steam. Special steam locomotives had been used on both the Metropolitan and the District railways in London from 1863 on. The opening of the electric City & South London Railway in 1890 launched the era of the deep-level tube railways, improving passenger travel within that city. Electrification also aided urban transport on American elevated street railways, such as those in New York, since it was both clean and cheap. The only elevated railway in Britain was the Liverpool Overhead Railway, opened in 1893 and electrified from the start. At this time, many railway companies resorted to electrification of their suburban lines to meet competition from the electric trams on the streets. Switzerland, with extensive supplies of hydroelectricity, was initiating various forms of electric traction at the turn of the twentieth century, which soon proved suitable for mainline operation.

The development of railways across the world resulted in new forms of transport, especially for passengers, who could travel more cheaply and quickly than ever before. Many took advantage of this opportunity so that excursion and holiday traffic soon developed. Then access to mineral resources that could not otherwise have been exploited was opened up in many countries. This helped to generate supplies of resources that otherwise would have become exhausted and checked the process of industrialization. Agricultural products could be transported more quickly from countryside to town, remaining in better condition through reduced travel times. Wheat grown on the prairies in North America could not have been marketed in Europe without having railways to take it to ports. Thus railways helped to feed major urban areas as well as allowing them to expand. In these and many other ways, railways helped to improve the quality of life and inaugurated a new era in civilization.

BIBLIOGRAPHY

Bagwell, Philip S. *The Transport Revolution from 1770.* London, 1974.
Hills, Richard L., and D. Patrick. *Beyer, Peacock, Locomotive Builders to the World.* Glossop, U.K., 1982.
Lewis, Michael J. T. *Early Wooden Railways.* London, 1970.
McNeil, Ian, ed. *An Encyclopaedia of the History of Technology.* London, 1990.
Morgan, Bryan. *Civil Engineering: Railways.* London, 1971.
Snell, John B. *Mechanical Engineering: Railways.* London, 1971.

RICHARD L. HILLS

Industrial Organization and Regulation

As railroads began to appear during the 1830s, this revolutionary transportation form required new everything. Thus the "Demonstration Period," which lasted until mid-century, involved various efforts to perfect this highly promising transportation form. These efforts included suitable motive power, track gauge, and overall design. Arguably, the prototype carrier was England's privately owned and operated Liverpool & Manchester Railway, which engineer George Stephenson crafted between 1826 and 1830. As the first carrier designed exclusively for steam locomotion and the first substantial railway to rely exclusively on commercial and passenger rather than mineral traffic, the road inspired builders elsewhere, especially in the United States.

Business Organization. Although not readily apparent to the casual observer, the new railroad demanded an appropriate business organization. Since most early carriers in Europe and America were modest in size, the complexity of management was small. Even America's longest carrier (and for a time the world's longest), the South Carolina Canal and Rail Road Company, which stretched 135 miles between Charleston and the Savannah River, had no great difficulties in office management, train operations, or other corporate functions.

Early firms turned logically to other businesses for guidance. Canals in England and stagecoach and steamboat companies in America served as popular models. Pivotal corporate positions included president, secretary, and treasurer. These early railroad leaders were almost always associated with local enterprises; they were bankers, farmers or planters, merchants, and professional men. A future railroad executive might also have had a rich background in business affairs. Take the case of New Yorker Erastus

Corning (1794–1872). This key figure in the 1853 merging of several shortlines that created the New York Central Railroad came from a background that included experience as a bank and insurance company president, nail manufacturer, merchant, and an importer and maker of railroad iron products. The president, perhaps joined by his business colleagues, became the chief promoter for the railroad, seeking private investor commitment, even public backing, and, of course, community support.

These pioneer roads also employed a general manager or someone (sometimes called a superintendent) with major responsibilities. This individual worked with department heads, including those involved in maintenance and daily operations. The general manager might participate in new-line construction, either directly or indirectly, depending on whether the railroad, a wholly owned affiliate, or a private concern handled the project.

Modifications and innovations occurred; some railroads in Europe and America by mid-century had evolved into truly complex and expensive commercial arteries. This growth commonly prompted the managerial decision to split lines into operating divisions. The New York & Erie Rail Road (Erie) spearheaded this drive—a sensible move since in 1851 the company finished a 447-mile route between the Hudson River and Lake Erie. By the end of the nineteenth century, it was common for a single person, the superintendent, to have the authority to make key day-to-day decisions. He was aided by a variety of support staff, including an assistant superintendent; a trainmaster, whose responsibilities involved freight and passenger movements; and a roadmaster, who focused on line maintenance. This divisional superintendent likely reported to a general manager or a top official.

With "system building," which exploded in the United States following the Civil War, some companies really functioned as a collection of associated properties. The New York Central System, for example, consisted of several distinct units, including the Lake Shore & Michigan Southern; Michigan Central; and New York Central & Hudson River. In the case of the Wabash Railroad, for a time, this property, mostly split its operations east and west of the Mississippi River (Saint Louis). Each of these affiliated units, however, customarily contained two or more divisions.

In the field of railroad organization, a trendsetter emerged, the Pennsylvania Railroad (PRR). Although by the 1890s its foremost rival, the New York Central, proclaimed itself to be the "Greatest Railroad in the World," the PRR's equally self-serving motto, "The Standard Railroad of the World," seemed accurate. This Philadelphia-based colossus became the most widely emulated railroad in the world, just as nonrail businesses at home and abroad copied PRR practices. The company, according to

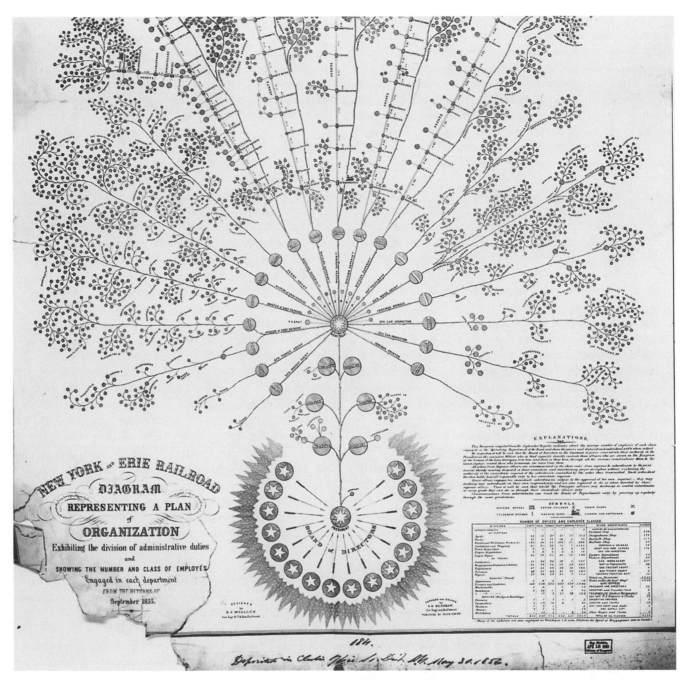

RAILROADS. Bottom half of an 1855 organizational diagram of the New York and Erie Railroad. (Prints and Photographs Division, Library of Congress)

business historian Albro Martin, "had solved just about all of the problems, apparently, that could be solved by clever organization." Management consisted of more than divisional superintendents. There was a bevy of high-ranking executives, including four vice presidents, each with special responsibilities; a chief engineer; head of motive power; general manager; general superintendent of transportation; general superintendent of motive power; and

engineer of branch lines. An array of other officials also supervised hundreds of employees. By 1900, these men collectively considered themselves to be "professionals," working in an arena of ambition-driven men who sought to aid their employer in every possible way.

By the time the PRR had perfected its corporate structure, railroads in other parts of the world that were privately controlled developed similar structures. In those nations where the state or central government owned and operated carriers, they, too, embraced business practices that followed the format of bigger firms, whether an American giant or one of the regional roads in the United Kingdom. The State Railways (the latter-day Nederlandsche Spoorwegen) in the Netherlands, which took shape between 1860 and 1890, possessed a corporate bureaucracy that resembled an American or British concern. Moreover, railroads that operated in its far-flung colonies, most notably in the Dutch East Indies, possessed carbon-copy qualities.

Regulation of the Industry. Although regulation of private or public railroads varied widely and throughout the world, what occurred in the United States was hardly unique. With the maturing of the American railroad corporation that coincided with the full flowering of the Railway Age, leaders of the nation's first great industry attempted to iron out their mutual problems as best they could. Most agreed with J. P. Morgan, Sr. (1837–1913) that competition was good but cooperation was better. By the beginning of the twentieth century, a half-dozen or so "communities of interest" had emerged. Executives like E. H. Harriman (1848–1909) and James J. Hill (1838–1916) gained notoriety for their community of interest activities, creating alliances between their own railroads and others and involving investment bankers and major shippers. Every effort was made to manage the business efficiently and profitably, yet there might be criticisms, especially from reformers who believed that the dominant carriers were "anticompetitive" and acted "against the public interest."

Even before the advent of these communities of interest, Americans began to fuss about railways. Early on citizens worried that their communities might be missed by the iron horse; after all, the railroad commonly offered dependable transportation where before none had existed. The function of government, and it was usually state government, involved providing attractive charters and at times direct financial support (usually purchase of bonds or stock) to these fledgling enterprises. If it became apparent that a railroad would not be constructed through a particular area because the private sector was either unwilling or unable, residents might demand that politicians respond with public assistance. Illinois represents an American state that not only granted charters to railroad promoters but actually entered the business itself. In 1837, lawmakers passed the Internal Improvement Act, which resulted in the partial construction of the Northern Cross Railroad, a project intended to bisect the state at its midsection. Public authorities, however, completed a substantially shorter line, a poorly constructed 57-mile road that opened in 1842. The Northern Cross, which cost taxpayers $750,000, languished; and on 26 April 1847, the state auctioned it off for a paltry $21,100. Politicians decided that the private rather than the public sector was better suited for rail construction and management. Fortunately, investor-owned projects developed rapidly, and by 1860 Illinois claimed a substantial rail network.

Granger Laws. Once the iron horse had shattered the isolation of a particular state or region, there began complaints about a host of matters, usually involving rates for freight and passenger service. The feeling developed that "the public" was at the mercy of "monopolists." These alleged individuals were enormously unpopular; in fact, Americans harbored a long-standing hatred of monopoly, whether in royal, private, or public hands. Prior to 1860, a few states, led by New Hampshire and Massachusetts, had created public regulatory commissions, but more powerful ones emerged after the Civil War, often the result of the so-called "granger" agitation, which was especially powerful in the upper Midwest. Consisting of a coalition of farmers, merchants, and commercial groups, grangers usually sought to reduce rates and end long- and short-haul discriminations. They pressed hard for the creation of state commissions with powers to protect their legislative accomplishments. Their victories were impressive. The most dramatic one came in Wisconsin with the Potter Act of 1874. This controversial statute arranged freight and passenger traffic into classifications and established maximum rates for items within each category. Generally, it ended the common practice of carriers setting a greater rate per ton mile and per passenger mile for the shorter haul. The Potter measure also created a three-member board of railroad commissioners to implement its provisions. Unquestionably, this type of legislation set a precedent of inflexibility in rates, especially for freight, and it accepted their assumption that "reasonable" charges were based solely upon distance. Lobbying from railroads and a growing public feeling that extreme granger laws were wrong-headed, resulted in repeal of the most restrictive ones, including the Potter Act. Nevertheless, in 1877 the U.S. Supreme Court in the landmark case of *Munn* v. *Illinois* upheld the constitutionality of these granger statutes.

Yet, the U.S. Supreme Court subsequently reversed itself in terms of the constitutionality of an important aspect of the Granger laws. If a state-controlled rate affected interstate commerce, an illegal action had occurred. The high court's decision of 1886 in *Wabash, St. Louis, & Pacific* v. *Illinois* ruled that the shipments in question, which traveled on an interstate rather than intrastate basis, could not be regulated by Illinois or any other state since the Constitution gave exclusive jurisdiction over interstate commerce to the federal government.

Birth of the Interstate Commerce Commission. Since the public would not abandon its desire to have rate competition, the Wabash decision precipitated Congressional action. This was somewhat surprising because railroad rates, especially for freight, were in decline, even though some carriers had attempted to stop unbridled competition through pools and other arrangements. In 1887, federal politicians endorsed a Senate study, the Cullom Committee report, that condemned discrimination in railroad rates, urged remedial legislation, and recommended a commission to provide supervision. The result was the Interstate Commerce Act that launched federal regulation of railroads. The enforcement agency, the Interstate Commerce Commission (ICC), had the power to see that all rates were "just and reasonable." Moreover, the ICC was to protect consumers against discrimination between persons or places, no traffic pooling was to occur, and charges for short hauls could not exceed those for long ones.

Although the ICC troubled most railroad leaders and their associates, fears shortly diminished. Attorney General Richard Olney (1835–1917), a member of the Cleveland administration, for one, privately told an industry executive that the ICC would surely take the railroad's point of view and might well become a barrier between a carrier and its disgruntled patrons. Olney may not have been fully clairvoyant, but the ICC generally failed to meet the expectations of reformers. Partly because certain wording of the 1887 act was vague and partly because the federal courts took the position that the ICC did not have the power to fix rates for the future (that is, in place of rates held illegal) or to enforce the long-and-short-haul clause, the measure was virtually nullified. The U.S. Supreme Court decision in 1897 of *ICC* v. *Cincinnati, New Orleans, and Texas Pacific Railway Co.* drove the final nails into the ICC's coffin in terms of rate regulation.

Reformers, however, did not abandon their desire to bring railroads under the public's thumb. As a result of the cataclysmic depression of the 1890s, America experienced an intense and extensive period of massive housecleaning, commonly known as the Progressive Era. Since the Railway Age had become fully established, consumers continued to complain about aspects of the relationship of the nation's first big business with the "public." Not only did state progressive leaders lash out at carriers, commonly demanding ad valorem taxation of railroad property, they wanted Congress to do more.

A harbinger of national reform came in 1903. A major piece of federal regulation, the Elkins Act, outlawed any departure by a railroad from its published tariff. Since this measure made all forms of rate-cutting and rebates illegal, the railroad industry mostly applauded its passage. Progressives, too, seemed pleased.

More Acts of Regulation. Cooperation, however, between railroad executives and political progressives did not extend to a Congressional reform bill introduced by progressives James Hepburn. Backed by reformers nation-wide, the Hepburn Railway Rate Act of 1906 reversed some of the policies established by federal courts, thus dramatically strengthening the ICC. The statute did much, including allowing the ICC to specify the legal maximum when rates were found to be unreasonable. Minimum rates, though, could not be prescribed. Moreover, the Hepburn Act gave the ICC jurisdiction over industrial railroads and private car lines and empowered it to control divisions of rates and charges made for switching and for special services rendered by shippers. It also contained the "commodities clause" that forbade railroads to haul (except for their own use) goods they had themselves produced. This reform statute also provided stiff penalties for delay and falsification in the submission of reports to the ICC.

From the industry's perspective, more bad news came in 1910 with the Mann-Elkins Act. This triumph of political progressivism made significant changes in the 1887 legislation. The ICC could now suspend proposed rate increases, for a stated period, while it determined their legality. The statute placed the burden of justifying higher rates on the carriers. This became the first peacetime legislation that permitted the federal government to establish de facto price ceilings on a single industry.

Before the Progressive Era ran its course, other pieces of regulation affected the railroad enterprise. Two measures signed during the waning months of the Taft administration had considerable impact: the Panama Canal Act of 1912 and the Valuation Act of 1913. The former made it unlawful for any railroad under the Interstate Commerce Act to own, operate, or control any water carrier operating through the canal, "or elsewhere." Passed in the name of competition, this law dealt a severe blow to coordinated rail-water service. The latter act directed the ICC to conduct a comprehensive evaluation of the nation's railroads. Progressives considered railroads to be greatly overcapitalized, and they did not want them to receive revenues based on inflated paper values. The Valuation Act caused the Division of Valuation to balloon into a gigantic fact-gathering bureaucracy. The process eventually consumed $48 million of public and $152 million of railroad funds in a vain quest to create workable guidelines that would establish appropriate rates for every carrier.

Although progressivism subsided after the United States entered World War I, a dramatic control nevertheless took place. Difficulties coordinating freight traffic and other wartime concerns prompted Congress in late 1917 to "federalize" much of the industry. The twenty-six months of federal control that followed became a nightmare for rail managers; traffic patterns became disrupted and portions of the plant and equipment deteriorated for lack of proper maintenance.

On 1 March 1920, Washington returned the railroads to their owners. Soon thereafter Congress passed the

Transportation Act of 1920 that sought to cartelize the industry. Particularly significant were features to equalize the rate of return among carriers. The law directed the ICC to prepare a set of consolidation plans whereby strong and weak roads would be merged. The statute also contained an elaborate, albeit controversial, plan for equalizing earnings between the powerful and not-so-powerful roads. Generally, the act disappointed everyone involved. The consolidation plan, most of all, fizzled; strong systems had no desire to be saddled with helpless lines.

Regulation of the railroad industry continued to be tweaked, although by the 1920s the transportation environment was undergoing radical change. Competition from automobiles, buses, trucks, and even airplanes had ended what monopolies railroads had theoretically enjoyed. Moreover, older forms of transportation, pipelines and water transportation, experienced rejuvenation. These competitive trends meant that railroad regulatory statutes needed to be reconsidered since nothing in them had anticipated the impact of modal competition. Although at times railroad management suffered from forms of ossification, some executives in this new competitive environment redefined their properties as transportation companies, adding buses and truck service where the law permitted. The Transportation Act of 1940 attempted to establish a national transportation policy, one that would provide "fair and impartial regulation of all modes of transportation." But this measure hardly upset the status quo.

Modern Regulatory Era. Finally, in the late 1950s politicians launched the "modern" regulatory era. The first piece of important legislation came with the Transportation Act of 1958. A key provision permitted carriers to abandon unprofitable passenger trains and trackage. Then a national railroad crisis developed with the bankruptcy of the Penn Central Transportation Company in 1970 and was followed by the failure of several Northeastern and Midwestern roads. Congress responded by creating the National Railroad Passenger Corporation (Amtrak) in 1971, the Regional Rail Reorganization Act of 1973, the Railroad Revitalization and Regulatory Reform Act of 1976, and also in 1976 the quasi-public Consolidated Rail Corporation (Conrail). Tax dollars poured into the industry. Then in 1980 the all-important Staggers Act became law. It ended the absolute control of the ICC over maximum and minimum freight rates and granted carriers additional rate-making rights. These statutes collectively deregulated the industry in such a way as to give it freedom of action, which it had not possessed since the nineteenth century. Staggers, especially, ushered in a new day for carriers, allowing management to be more creative with rates, service, and the like. By the twenty-first century, not only had the ICC closed its

doors, but the old-style railroad executive who belonged to the "cult of the operating man," that is, a railroad official too tradition-bound to ever become a dynamic leader, had largely disappeared. This "leaner and meaner" industry became an important departure from its regulatory past.

In some ways, other industrialized nations replicated the American pattern of public supervision. The British experience, for example, holds strong similarities. In 1889 Parliament passed the Regulation of Railways Act; during the World War I era (1914–1921), railroads fell under the control of the government's Railway Executive Committee; and 123 separate carriers amalgamated into the "Big Four" (Great Western, London Midland & Scottish, London & North Eastern ,and Southern) in 1923. Then in 1948 nationalization occurred, creating British Rail. Modal competition subsequently prompted the "Beeching Report" that after 1963 led to massive line abandonments and service cut-backs. Finally, in 1994 privatization took place with formation of investor-owned Railtrack, which although in bankruptcy currently controls the track and infrastructure of the remaining railway network. Whether in Great Britain, the United States, or elsewhere, there have long been changing organizational and regulatory developments in the railroad industry.

BIBLIOGRAPHY

Adams, Charles Francis, Jr. *Railroads: Their Origins and Problems.* New York, 1878

Beck, Gerald. *Alternative Tracks: The Constitution of American Industrial Order, 1865–1917.* Baltimore, 1994.

Benson, Lee. *Merchants, Farmers, and Railroads: Railroad Regulation and New York Politics, 1850–1887.* Cambridge, Mass., 1955.

Chandler, Alfred D., Jr., ed. *The Railroads: The Nation's First Big Business.* New York, 1965.

Chandler, Alfred D., Jr. *The Visible Hand: The Managerial Revolution in American Business.* Cambridge, Mass., 1977.

Daniels, Winthrop. *American Railroads: Four Phases of Their History.* Princeton, 1932.

Hilton, George W. *The Transportation Act of 1958: A Decade of Experience.* Bloomington, Ind., 1969.

Goodrich, Carter. *Government Promotion of American Canals and Railroads, 1800–1890.* New York, 1960.

Grant, H. Roger. *North Western: A History of the Chicago & North Western Railway System.* DeKalb, Ill., 1996.

Kolko, Gabriel. *Railroads and Regulation, 1877–1916.* New York, 1965.

MacAvory, Paul W. *The Economic Effects of Regulation: The Trunk-Line Railroad Cartels and the Interstate Commerce Commission before 1900.* Cambridge, Mass., 1965.

Martin, Albro. *Enterprise Denied: Origins of the Decline of American Railroads, 1897–1917.* New York, 1970.

Martin, Albro. *Railroads Triumphant: The Growth, Rejection, and Rebirth of a Vital American Force.* New York, 1992.

Miller, George H. *Railroads and the Granger Laws.* Madison, Wisc., 1971.

Overbey, Daniel L. *Railroads: The Free Enterprise Alternative.* Westport, Conn., 1982.

Stover, John F. *American Railroads.* Chicago, 1997.

H. ROGER GRANT

REAL BILLS DOCTRINE. The real bills doctrine states that the quantity of money can never be excessive or deficient if issued through bank loans backed by sound short-term commercial paper representing goods in the process of production and distribution. The doctrine contends that if banks lend only against short-term commercial paper, the money stock will be secured by, and will automatically vary in step with, real output so that the latter will be matched by just enough money to purchase it at existing prices. Through the medium of the commercial bill of exchange, output valued at market prices determines the money stock in a real bills regime.

As a rule for stabilizing general prices, the doctrine is either unnecessary or fallacious. It is unnecessary for open economies operating on a commodity (gold) standard or on a regime of convertible currencies and fixed exchange rates. Price levels in such economies are exogenously determined in world markets and need no real bills rule to anchor them. For closed economies and those operating with inconvertible currencies and floating exchange rates—economies in which domestic money stocks determine prices—the rule is fallacious and potentially destabilizing. It is fallacious because, instead of backing each unit of money with a fixed physical quantum of goods, it ties the money stock to the dollar volume of commercial paper, a variable that moves in step with prices and thus the money stock itself. By anchoring each dollar of money to a dollar's worth of commercial paper representing a dollar's worth of output, it sets up a price-money-price feedback loop whose elements are free to contract or expand without limit. The result is that any random upward shock to prices will, by raising the nominal value of goods and hence the nominal volume of commercial paper, increase money's backing and so justify an expansion of its supply. The consequent expansion will further bid up prices and so on ad infinitum in a self-reinforcing inflationary spiral. In short, the doctrine ignores the fact that price increases themselves expand the needs of trade and so justify the monetary expansion necessary to sustain them.

The doctrine's core idea traces back to John Law, who in 1705 proposed a paper currency backed by the nominal value of land. Next came Sir James Steuart, who in 1767 substituted commercial paper for land in Law's formulation. Later, Adam Smith, in his 1776 *Wealth of Nations*, justified the doctrine as a prudent guide for bankers making loans in a convertible currency regime. During the Napoleonic Wars, antibullionist defenders of the Bank of England extended the doctrine to an inconvertible currency regime. Seeking to exonerate the bank from blame for the wartime inflation that followed the suspension of convertibility in 1797, the antibullionists denied that the bank had caused inflation since it had issued money only against real bills of exchange and so had merely responded to the needs of trade.

Henry Thornton, in his 1802 *Paper Credit of Great Britain*, exposed the fallacy of this position by observing that rising prices require an ever-growing volume of loans and money just to finance the same level of real transactions. Inflation, by raising the needs of trade, thereby induces the very monetary expansion necessary to sustain it, and the real bills criterion fails to limit movements in the quantity and the value of money. Thornton also enunciated a point later made famous by Knut Wicksell, namely, that business loan demands become insatiable when the loan rate of interest lies below the expected rate of return on the use of the borrowed funds. In such circumstances, the supply of eligible bills offered as collateral for loans becomes limitless, and the real bills criterion constitutes no bar to overissue.

Despite these criticisms, the real bills doctrine survived and prospered in nineteenth-century banking tradition. Renamed the law of reflux (according to which monetary overissue is impossible because excess notes and deposits return instantaneously to the banks for conversion into coin or repayment of loans), the doctrine reappeared in the famous currency school–banking school controversy in the mid-nineteenth century. In particular, the banking school asserted that the needs of trade automatically regulate a convertible currency such that a legally mandated gold cover is unnecessary.

The twentieth century saw the doctrine written into the 1913 Federal Reserve Act, which authorized regional Federal Reserve (Fed) banks to rediscount real bills or "eligible paper" for member banks seeking to obtain reserves with which to accommodate business loan demands. The doctrine gained impetus in the 1920s when Fed officials discovered how to control the offer of bills through means other than the rediscount rate. Open-market operations constituted the key instrument here. Such operations, by initially affecting reserves, induced offsetting member-bank borrowing or repayment at the discount window, leaving total reserves unchanged. Since member banks borrowed only against real bills, the Fed, through open-market operations, could influence the volume of borrowing and thus the quantity of bills seeking discount. Rises in borrowing and bills discounted signaled the occurrence of open-market sales and thus restrictive policy. Conversely, falls in the level of borrowing and bills clamoring for discount constituted a sign of open-market purchases and expansionary policy. Bills and borrowing equally measured the impact of open-market policy. For this reason, borrowing entered the real bills doctrine as an indicator of monetary ease or tightness. This borrowing indicator and its partner, the level of market interest rates, led the Fed astray in the early years of the Great Depression. These indicators signaled wrongly that policy was easy, when the opposite was true.

Finally, the real bills doctrine also underlay the Reichsbank's policy of issuing astronomical sums of money to satisfy the needs of trade at ever-rising prices during the German hyperinflation of 1922–1923. The Reichsbank insisted on pegging its discount rate at 12 percent (later raised to 90 percent) when market rates of interest were well over 7,000 percent per annum. As Henry Thornton might have predicted, this huge rate differential made it extremely profitable for commercial banks to rediscount bills with the Reichsbank and to lend the proceeds, thereby producing additional inflationary expansion of the money supply and further upward pressure in interest rates. However, the authorities showed no recognition of this inflationary sequence. Instead, they repeatedly stated that their duty was passively to supply upon demand the growing sums of money required to mediate real transactions at skyrocketing prices. Citing the real bills doctrine, they refused to believe that issuing money on loan against genuine commercial bills could be inflationary.

Having learned the lessons of the past, today's central bankers tend to reject the real bills doctrine for all the reasons cited above; but their main ground for rejection is the doctrine's contention that the money stock must vary procyclically with real activity rather than countercyclically as economic stabilization requires.

BIBLIOGRAPHY

Glasner, David. "The Real Bills Doctrine in the Light of the Law of Reflux." *History of Political Economy* 24 (1992), 201–229.

Green, Roy. "Real Bills Doctrine in Classical Economics." In *The New Palgrave Dictionary of Money and Finance*, vol. 3, edited by Peter Newman, Murray Milgate, and John Eatwell, pp. 300–303. London and New York, 1992.

Humphrey, Thomas M. "The Real Bills Doctrine." In *Money, Banking and Inflation: Essays in the History of Monetary Thought*, pp. 21–31. Aldershot, U.K., and Brookfield, Vt., 1993.

Humphrey, Thomas M. "Monetary Policy Frameworks and Indicators for the Federal Reserve in the 1920s." Federal Reserve Bank of Richmond Working Paper No. 00-7. 2000. Describes the Fed's employment of the real bills doctrine as a framework for policy analysis in the 1920s.

Laidler, David. "Misconceptions About the Real Bills Doctrine: A Comment on Sargent and Wallace." *Journal of Political Economy* 92 (1984), 149–158.

Mints, Lloyd W. *A History of Banking Theory*. Chicago, 1945. The standard and for many years the definitive critique of the real bills doctrine.

West, Robert C. *Banking Reform and the Federal Reserve, 1863–1923*. Ithaca, N.Y., 1977. Describes how the real bills doctrine came to be written into the Federal Reserve Act.

THOMAS M. HUMPHREY

REGULATION *[This entry contains five subentries, a historical overview and discussions of control of prices, of quantity, of quality, and of entry and exit.]*

Historical Overview

Regulation may be discussed from several perspectives. For example, it could be taken to mean any legitimate and controlling requirements, whether governmental (as in criminal law or intellectual property) or private (the codes of good conduct practiced by a trade association). If so, then the entire history of law and of private control would be fair game. This article looks at a much narrower field, providing a general survey of both public and private attempts to regulate behavior in the economic or commercial sphere of social life.

Three very broad periods are considered. The first dates from the first recorded legal code (Code of Hammurabi, c. 1750 BCE) to circa 1600 CE, roughly the end of the Middle Ages. The second period extends from the onset of the modern capitalistic, industrial economies in the seventeenth century CE until the late twentieth century. The third period includes the modern economy from approximately the late 1970s until today.

The era stretching from the beginning of settled agriculture and urban life to the end of the Middle Ages might be characterized as one in which there was no clear difference between the state and the private economy. Although governments established and enforced boundary rights for land, contractual rights for trade and employment, the regulation of prices, and the issuance and enforcement of regulations of weights and measures designed to foster orderly markets, governments were also the principal economic actors from the Code of Hammurabi until the beginning of the Age of Exploration.

There is no clear dividing line in historical time between nonindustrial and industrial economies, but one can observe in the late Middle Ages the beginnings of two important developments that led to the more modern history of governmental regulation: a broader scope for private initiative and the rise of the nation-state and its attendant, mercantilism. Trade broadened, and cities grew as market entrepôts. Protection (largely private) of professional training and status arose, through guilds and other restrictions on entry into defined professions. Perhaps to preserve orderly markets but certainly to reward loyal backers, governments regulated entry into lines of business. Also governments everywhere established requirements that merchants charge a "just price" and determined legitimate selling hours and places of sale. With the rise of the nation-state, governments began to practice regulation designed—as in the mercantile system forcefully attacked by Adam Smith—to enrich the nation.

Market regulation in its modern dress is a product of the late Industrial Revolution. The economic world created by that technological and organizational revolution put old businesses and settled patterns of behavior at risk. Insofar as governments responded to those upheavals, they tended to do so in a haphazard manner—that is, addressing a particular problem rather than acting pursuant to a coherent theory of the appropriate relationship between the economy and the state.

The modern field of economics did not begin to provide a principled basis for regulation until late in the nineteenth century. Moreover, when it did begin to study regulation, some time passed before the theoretical basis for regulation was clear. Socialists argued that regulation should be so thoroughgoing that private institutions virtually disappeared. Other economists argued that regulation should be used to prevent, among other things, "ruinous competition." Even though regulation of powerful industries such as electrical utilities, power companies, railroads, banks, telecommunications, and others had proceeded from the 1890s on, a clear theoretical basis for that regulation did not appear till the 1950s and 1960s, when the welfare-economic analysis of market failure and market imperfection and the field of industrial organization with its analysis of such topics as marginal-cost pricing (first articulated in the 1840s) and rate-of-return regulation provided an academic basis for the sorts of regulation then being practiced, and for their reform.

During the twentieth century, regulation designed to foster competition and curb anticompetitive forces was common, having begun in the United States with the Sherman Antitrust Act in 1890. Almost every country either nationalized its public utilities or allowed them to be private and investor-owned but closely regulated by governmental commissions. Generally, price controls became less common, save in times of emergency such as a war or a political "crisis," as in energy or health-care markets. Many countries practiced entry controls into what were deemed vital industries or those affected with national security, such as telecommunications, radio and television, health, and defense. There were also continuing private controls on entry, as in licensing requirements for attorneys and physicians, regulations sometimes enforced through state enforcement mechanisms.

The surge of regulatory interventions that had begun in the developed economies in the late nineteenth century and expanded in the aftermath of the Great Depression and World War II began to slow and then recede in the last decades of the twentieth century. Led by the United States, many of the developed countries began to dismantle their regulatory structures. For example, many governments stopped the close regulation of entry and exit in the airline industry (or the nationalization of their airlines) in favor of a policy of relatively free entry and exit.

As the old forms of regulation were ebbing, a new form of regulation was growing. This "new regulation" focused on areas of social and economic life that had previously not been the subject of governmental attention—the environment (especially water and air pollution), workplace safety and nondiscriminatory access to the workplace, housing, and other assets and opportunities. These regulations took justification from the need to regulate external effects and information flows. In both of these forms of regulation, an important development was the replacement of so-called command-and-control regulation with marketlike instruments. An example is the attempt to reduce the amount of nitrous oxide emissions by requiring emitters to have emissions permits and allowing market transactions in those permits, an innovation of environmental regulation in the early 1990s in the United States.

The process of deregulation of particular industries had an even wider echo in national economic policies. For instance, a decades-long experiment with national ownership of certain central social assets—an experiment that went furthest in the People's Republic of China, the Union of Soviet Socialist Republics, and central and eastern European countries—came to a stunning end in the late 1980s and the early 1990s with the collapse of the Berlin Wall (and its division of Germany into West and East) and the dissolution of the Soviet Union. For the developing countries, there was also a turn from heavily regulated to lightly regulated economies—a turn called the "Washington consensus" that deeply affected the lending policies of the international aid agencies.

At the beginning of the twenty-first century, there are new challenges for regulatory policy. Two forces in particular merit notice: globalization and technological changes in information generation and dissemination. "Globalization" refers to a great increase in cross-border commercial interactions. Since 1947 the system of international trading rules, administered first by the General Agreement on Tariffs and Trade and since 1995 by the World Trade Organization, has fostered the sale of an ever-increasing share of world output in goods and services across national borders. Because globalization exposes national economies to heightened competition, and because membership in the WTO greatly restricts a nation's ability to impose restrictions on foreign competitors, there has been a profound lessening of the abilities of national governments to regulate their own providers of goods and services. An important effect of this trend has been an attempt to replace national regulation with international regulatory agreements. One example is the convergence of different national systems for intellectual-property protection onto a single model; another example is the attempt to reach agreement on international environmental regulations on such matters as acid rain and greenhouse gases. The pharmaceutical industry has been a particular source of friction under globalization, with prices and availability of drugs difficult to control in the developing countries by the companies that hold patents to those pharmaceuticals in the developed countries.

Another important challenge to national regulatory systems is rapid technological change in the information industries. For example, the remarkably rapid rise of digital technology in the last two decades of the twentieth century has presented the developed economies, in particular, with new challenges that may call forth new regulatory paradigms. For example, there are concerns about whether the incentive to engage in creative endeavors can be preserved, given that, for instance, music and writing can be easily copied across the Internet. Such regulation of the Internet as exists is frequently self-regulation agreed to by the users rather than imposed on users by governmental agents.

BIBLIOGRAPHY

Breyer, Stephen. *Regulation and Its Reform*. Cambridge, Mass., 1984.

The Avalon Project at Yale Law School "Code of Hammurabi." <http://www.yale.edu/lawweb/avalon/medieval/hammenu.htm>.

Finley, Moses I. *The Ancient Economy*. 2d ed. Berkeley, 1985.

Hughes, Jonathan R. T. *The Governmental Habit: Economic Controls from Colonial Times to the Present*. New York, 1977.

Kahn, Alfred. *The Economics of Regulation: Principles and Institutions*. Cambridge, Mass., 1988.

Kearney, Joseph D., and Thomas W. Merrill. "The Great Transformation of Regulated Industries Law." *Columbia Law Review* 98 (1998), 1323.

McGraw, Thomas K. *Regulation in Perspective: Historical Essays*. Cambridge, Mass., 1982.

Sunstein, Cass R. *After the Rights Revolution: Reconceiving the Regulatory State*. Cambridge, Mass., 1990.

THOMAS S. ULEN

Control of Prices

Economists have, for at least two hundred years, been extremely skeptical of governmental attempts to regulate prices. There are both theoretical and practical reasons for this skepticism. In theory attempts to regulate prices are likely to lead to the inefficient use of resources. For example, an attempt to keep the price from rising above a certain level that is below the equilibrium level will induce consumers to demand more of the good than suppliers are prepared to supply. The resulting excess demand can induce inefficient nonprice methods of allocation, such as waiting lines, and substitution away from the regulated good or service and toward other goods or services that, in the absence of price regulation, would not be so attractive. On a practical level, governmental attempts to regulate prices are likely to consume so many resources in the process as to seriously hamper the functioning of the economy. Friedrich Hayek long ago noted that price in the unregulated market is an extraordinarily efficient method of disseminating vital information to independent decision makers about the social value of resources. Unregu-

lated competitive market prices capture and disseminate information more efficiently than any alternative.

There are, however, some sound economic reasons for regulating prices. Economists have long recognized that, for those goods and services for which certain market imperfections are present, the control of prices may lead to an increase in socially desirable use of those goods and services. Consider a good, such as immunization against an infectious disease, that generates external benefits. In an unregulated competitive marketplace, consumers will choose, from their own individual-welfare-maximizing point of view, exactly the right number of immunizations; but from a social-welfare-maximizing point of view, they will choose too little of the external-benefit-generating service. To induce the socially optimal amount of immunization, government should reduce the price of immunization through subsidization of private provision or below-cost public provision. Elementary school education provides just such an external benefit; since the 1840s in the United States, local governments have provided public education at no or very low cost, probably on these grounds.

Governments have regulated the prices of private monopolies (and sought to break up those monopolies). They also have tried to control the prices charged by those who generate external costs so as to bring private and social costs more closely into alignment. For instance, those who negligently or deliberately impose harm on others may be assessed damages to compensate their victims—a form of price control that seeks to induce future potential wrongdoers to internalize the costs they may impose on others and, therefore, to increase their prices. Also governments have sought to control the price of public goods, such as national defense, fireworks, some natural resources, and information, in an effort to improve social well-being.

Governments may seek to control prices for noneconomic reasons. During a national emergency, such as war or famine, the government may believe that limiting prices to an affordable level is necessary to ensure broad access to scarce goods and services and to prevent rioting. Wartime has almost invariably been a period in all societies in which the authorities have sought to keep the prices of necessities relatively low and those of luxuries relatively high.

Since the rise and spread of Islam in the seventh century CE, Islamic governments have sought to control one particular price, the rate of interest, on the ground that the Qur'ān forbids the charging of interest for the loan of money, probably as a method of preventing merchants from abusing the poor. Similarly, the Christian world interpreted the biblical injunction against usury as one forbidding excessive rates of interest (a proscription that lingered into the late-twentieth-century United States) and also called on merchants and rulers to adhere to a "just price." Under the English doctrine of *assumpsit*, which dates from at least the thirteenth century, those in "public callings" had to take on all business presented to them and had to do so at reasonable rates. Somewhat later in England and in almost all the Western world, governments strictly regulated the rates charged to customers in such public occupations as baking, innkeeping, tavernkeeping, grain storage, public transportation, and the like. There was no clear theoretical understanding of such instances of price control; rather, the goal probably was simply to prevent sharp dealing and undue advantage taking by merchants in prominent industries.

Today price control is commonly part of a policy of controlling inflation. Typically, governments include the control of wages and other incomes as part of such a policy. Episodes of hyperinflation in Germany in the 1920s contributed to the rise of the National Socialist Party and led to broad wage and price controls. To counteract hyperinflation after World War II, the Allied occupiers of the Axis powers imposed wage and price controls. Chancellor Ludwig Erhard of West Germany scrapped wage and price control in the early 1950s, to the horror of the American occupiers but with desirable results. Other countries, notably in Latin America, had episodes of hyperinflation in the 1970s and 1980s that their governments unsuccessfully sought to bring under control, in part through wage and price controls. Recently, a rapid rise of health-care costs has led, so far unsuccessfully, to calls for the imposition of price controls on health care.

The United States has had experiences with all these forms of price and income control: during World War II, as part of the Wage Stabilization Board; during the Korean War, from 1950 to 1953; and during the Nixon Administration, from 1971 to 1974. One part of these attempts that typically lasted after the other controls lapsed was rent control, which has always proved popular among renters, however harmful its other effects.

Wage restraints have been a common form of price control. Republican Rome forbade the payment of any compensation to lawyers. Medieval guilds regulated the wages of apprentices. Most modern societies, largely for political reasons, establish minimum wages for all workers. There has been such a minimum in the United States since the passage of the Fair Labor Standards Act of 1938.

The most principled and effective method of price regulation has been that associated with the regulation of natural monopoly. The modern era of regulation generally and of prices specifically can be dated, at least in the United States, from the U.S. Supreme Court's opinion in *Munn v. Illinois*, 94 U.S. 113 (1877). In that opinion Chief Justice Waite found an Illinois statute regulating certain prices (grain storage rates) to be constitutionally permissible. More generally, he held, using an old English legal formulation, that the state could regulate any business "affected with a public interest." In theory this formulation could apply to most private businesses, but in practice it has been largely confined to the regulation of common carriers, businesses formerly covered by the doctrine of *assumpsit*. The new principle of regulation emboldened the U.S. federal government to pass the Interstate Commerce Act in 1887, which established the first administrative agency, the Interstate Commerce Commission.

Economists, who had not theretofore defined the circumstances in which regulation would be efficient, responded by defining "natural monopoly" and elaborating a theory of regulation and methods for implementing the theory. In economic theory, a natural monopoly is not the same as what the law has meant for eight centuries by "common carrier," but there is a connection. A natural monopoly is a firm with declining average costs over the relevant range of demand. This situation frequently occurs because fixed costs loom large in the total costs of the firm, as is often the case with public utilities and other capital-intensive enterprises. Because of declining average costs, the total costs of production would, in theory, be lower if a single firm provided the good or service. However, a single firm, if unregulated, would restrict output and raise price so as to achieve monopoly profits. This makes the case for governmental regulation of natural monopolies, as more fully described below.

After the creation of the first administrative agencies in the late nineteenth and early twentieth centuries, most countries struggled for a long period to determine how best to effect regulation of natural monopolies. By the 1950s, administrative practices, as embodied in the United States by the Administrative Procedures Act of 1946, had settled upon rate-of-return regulation as the prevailing method of regulating natural monopolies. In rate-of-return regulation a commission collects information on the costs of the regulated industry, including the amount of invested capital, and determines a price that the industry may charge per unit of good or service such that the investors earn a normal rate of return on their investments. Often the regulator allows the regulated industry to charge different prices to different classes of customers or at different times of the day, month, or year.

Rate-of-return regulation, like regulation generally, is in retreat. One important reason is that many natural monopolies are disappearing. Many public utilities, such as long-distance air and rail transportation and telecommunications, are being deregulated altogether as new technologies convert those industries from natural monopolies into competitive industries.

The rise of relative economic sophistication in the developed countries and the demise of the socialist model of governance have created a presumption against wage and price controls as effective or efficient methods of public policy. Although political forces will always be present and powerful and will no doubt argue in the future for a renewal of price regulation, the control of prices seems to be largely a historical phenomenon.

[*See also* Antitrust; Energy Regulation; Environment, *subentry on* Environmental Policies and Regulation; Product Safety Regulation; and Regulation, *subentries on* Control of Entry and Exit, Control of Quality, *and* Control of Quantity.]

BIBLIOGRAPHY

Butterworth, John. *A Theory of Price Control and Black Markets*. Avebury, U.K., 1994.

Demsetz, Harold. "Why Regulate Utilities?" *Journal of Law and Economics* 11 (1968), 55.

Galbraith, John Kenneth. *A Theory of Price Control*. Cambridge, Mass., 1980.

Hayek, Friedrich Von. "The Use of Knowledge in Society." *American Economic Review* 35 (1945), 519.

Hughes, Jonathan. *The Governmental Habit*. New York, 1977.

Kahn, Alfred. *The Economics of Regulation: Principles and Institutions*. Cambridge, Mass., 1988.

Kearney, Joseph D., and Thomas W. Merrill. "The Great Transformation of Regulated Industries Law." *Columbia Law Review* 98 (1998), 1323.

Notermans, Ton. *Money, Markets, and the State: Social Democratic Economic Policies since 1918*. Cambridge, 2000.

Pencavel, John. "The American Experience with Incomes Policies." In *Incomes, Policies, Inflation, and Relative Pay*, edited by J. L. Fallick and R. F. Elliott. London, 1981.

Pollard, Maurice, and Peter Mathias, eds. *The Cambridge Economic History of Europe: The Industrial Economies: Development of Economic and Social Policies*. Cambridge, 1989.

Postan, M. M., ed. *The Cambridge Economic History of Europe: The Agrarian Life of the Middle Ages*. Cambridge, 1966.

Viscusi, W. Kip, John M. Vernon, and Joseph E. Harrington, Jr. *Economics of Regulation and Antitrust*. 3d ed. Cambridge, Mass., 2000.

Weitzman, Martin L. "Prices vs. Quantities." *Review of Economic Studies* 41 (1974), 477.

THOMAS S. ULEN

Control of Quantity

Governmental regulation of the quantity of output emanating from a particular firm or from an industry is relatively rare, with some notable exceptions. There is no technical reason for reluctance to regulate quantity of output or of input; regulators can just as easily regulate one as the other, subject to the conditions identified by Weitzman for preferring price regulation to quantity regulation. Rather, the central reason for the reluctance seems to be that quantity restrictions have long been recognized as one of the hallmarks of monopolization and collusion. For example, the Organization of Petroleum Exporting Countries (OPEC) has, with the help of its members' governments, successfully restricted crude oil production since the 1950s. The cartel had spectacular success at cutting production quantities

in 1973 and again in 1979—sharp reductions undertaken largely for political, not economic, reasons—so that the world price for a barrel of crude oil tripled in the course of just a few years. Most governments shun quantity regulation because they have been far more interested in ending rather than fostering monopoly and collusion.

A notable exception to governmental reluctance to regulate quantity has been the circumstance in which a government has sought to foster anticompetitive behavior. Cartels are notoriously unstable; there is a strong incentive for the members of the collusion to promise to restrict output so as to raise price and increase joint profits, but an equally strong incentive for each cartel member to try secretly to violate the quantity restriction and make even greater profits. One effective way to reduce the incentive for cartel members to cheat on quantity restriction is for governments to make the quantity restriction binding through regulation. Generally, it is easier for governments to detect and enforce violations of the collusive agreement than for private members to do so.

An example of governmental regulation of quantity being used to foster anticompetitive ends is that of crude oil production in Texas. From the 1930s to the mid-1970s, the Texas Railroad Commission, operating under a broad grant of authority to regulate state public utilities in the public interest, set and enforced quantity restrictions on crude petroleum production in the state of Texas. The price of crude oil was determined on world markets, but Texas production was such a small fraction of total world output that decisions by Texas producers could not affect world price. Therefore, the restriction of output by the Texas Railroad Commission simply served to enrich oil producers in that state through means that, if undertaken privately, would have constituted an antitrust violation.

There have been numerous other examples of quantity regulation. Governments frequently have restricted the quantity of certain goods during a national emergency, such as in war or after a natural disaster. For example, governments in the developed countries limited the quantity of gasoline that individuals could consume in response to the 1973 OPEC oil embargo. Typically, however, such quantity restrictions end as soon as the emergency ends. Several governments—the socialist and communist economies—have practiced quantity restriction not for particular industries but for the entire economy. The end of such governance has also led to an end of the thorough style of planning that characterized those economies.

The presumption against quantity regulation also is evident in a remarkably successful multilateral system of regulating international trade. Article XII of the General Agreement on Tariffs and Trade (since 1995 called the World Trade Organization) prohibits the use of quotas on imports by members of that organization. It has been a well-known policy of that organization since its founding in 1947 to convert quantitative trade restrictions into tariff duties and then to work to reduce the tariff duties. That, for example, is precisely the strategy that the WTO has, since 1995, embarked upon to reduce quantitative restrictions on the international trade in agricultural goods.

An interesting recent development in price-versus-quantity regulation has occurred in the United States with regard to environmental regulation. From the 1960s, when regulation of air and water pollution began in earnest, to the late 1980s, most regulation of the environment was price-based. That is, polluters paid a price or tax for quantities of pollution that the regulators detected. Particular quantitative limits on certain pollutants were rare. Rather, the theory was that the price charged to a polluter—if that price were set properly—would cause the polluter to internalize the amount of its external cost and lead it to reduce the pollution to a net social-benefit-maximizing level.

It proved quite difficult for the regulators to set the pollution tax correctly and to detect the amount of effluent being generated by individual polluters; so the U.S. Environmental Protection Agency, at the behest of economists, tried a different regulatory strategy. The regulators believed that they could establish, monitor, and enforce quantitative limits for particular pollutants in particular regions of the country. In a system first proposed in 1990 and implemented in 1994, the EPA determined the total amount of tonnage of sulfur dioxide that it would allow to be emitted throughout the country in 1995. The agency then gave 110 of the country's most polluting power plants an entitlement to issue a share of that total amount of sulfur dioxide. If a plant produced less of the pollutant than it was entitled to produce, it was allowed to sell to other polluters (or to any other willing purchaser, such as an environmental group) the unused portion of its entitlement. If a plant wanted to produce more sulfur dioxide than it had entitlements to generate, then it had to purchase entitlements to pollute from some plant that was under its allotment. The total value of exchanges of these permits recently exceeded $600 million per year.

The system created an incentive for polluters to install scrubbers and other low-pollution production technologies. Although there is still some controversy about the efficiency of the tradable-permit program, it apparently has caused a 30 percent reduction in the amount of sulfur dioxide. This success has caused the exploration and implementation of tradable-permit systems for other pollutants, such as ozone in 1999 among twelve Northeastern states and a variety of permit systems for different pollutants in parts of California.

[*See also* Antitrust; Energy Regulation; Environment, *subentry on* Environmental Policies and Regulation; *and* Regulation, *subentries on* Control of Entry and Exit, Control of Prices, *and* Control of Quality.]

BIBLIOGRAPHY

Baumol, William J., and Wallace Oates. *The Theory of Environmental Policy.* 2d ed. Cambridge, 1988.

Vietor, Richard H. K. "Government Regulation of Business." In *The Cambridge Economic History of the United States*, vol. 3, *The Twentieth Century*, edited by Stanley L. Engerman and Robert E. Gallman. Cambridge, 2000.

Viscusi, W. Kip, John M. Vernon, and Joseph E. Harrington, Jr. *The Economics of Regulation and Antitrust.* 3d ed. Cambridge, Mass., 2000.

Weitzman, Martin L. "Prices vs. Quantities." *Review of Economic Studies* 41 (1974), 477.

THOMAS S. ULEN

Control of Quality

Consumers have a difficult time acquiring and judging information about the quality of some of the goods and services available to them. In the parlance of modern economics, there is often an informational asymmetry between buyers and sellers regarding product quality. For example, grain may appear to be dry and of high quality, but parts of the load may be of an inferior grade. Or a piece of art sold as the work of a famous master may be a copy. These and related difficulties have often given rise to fraud, in which sellers try to "palm off" goods of an inferior quality as being goods of a superior quality.

The root of the problem, as economists have long known, is that information is a peculiar good. It is frequently a public good—nonrivalrous in consumption and costly for profit-maximizing producers to identify and charge consumers. As a result, unregulated markets tend to supply a socially suboptimal amount of information. Governments have recognized this problem since at least the seventeenth century and have taken steps to see that societies receive the appropriate amount of information.

This can occur either through the direct governmental provision of information—as when government operates research laboratories, such as the National Institute of Medicine in the United States—or the governmental subsidization and regulation of the private provision of information—as in the recognition of intellectual property rights. To minimize fraudulent sales and encourage consumers to trust merchants, governments and private organizations have long sought to regulate the quality of output. Since the time of the Code of Hammurabi, for instance, the regulation of weights and measures has been commonplace.

There have been additional methods by which societies have sought and continue to seek to ensure the quality of commercial goods and services. Note first that honest merchants have long wanted to make it feasible for consumers to trust their assurances of quality. So, there are many historical examples of self-regulation by suppliers in which they have tried to guarantee quality. One time-honored method was for each merchant to establish a reputation as honest and as a producer of a high-quality output. To the extent that this was successful, a merchant could then transfer that good reputation to a family member or a purchaser by passing or selling the business to them. In some instances it was the organizer of a market fair who undertook to guarantee the quality of the goods sold by individuals at his fair, so that the reputation for quality attached to a particular marketplace, and the presumption was that those individual sellers who came to Scarborough Fair were honest. Additionally, some trades organized themselves so as to provide, among other things, quality assurance. Medieval craft guilds, for instance, controlled entry into certain skilled professions, such as printing or carpentry, in part to be able to assure customers that if they hired members of the guild, they would receive high-quality goods and services.

Modern professional licensing procedures—as for accountants, physicians, and lawyers—follow the same pattern of guaranteeing minimum quality standards. Also, some private companies offer to verify the safety and other qualities of products. Since 1894, Underwriters Laboratory, for example, has provided an independent safety-testing service and a certification procedure for commercial products in the United States and Europe. For the most part, producers seek out UL on a voluntary basis—without being legally obliged to do so.

Throughout history, the state has also adopted direct methods of regulating quality. Private law has always allowed those who have received a good or service that was not what they reasonably believed that they had bargained for to seek a remedy from the seller—through, for example, a breach-of-contract action or an action for fraudulent conveyance. Moreover, consumers who were injured by a commercial product could proceed against the manufacture on a theory that the product was defectively designed or produced or that the warnings of danger from the use of the product were defective. However, until about 1915, most courts in the developed world protected manufacturers from these actions, claiming that the consumers had to be in privity of contract with the manufacturer (i.e., to have purchased directly from the manufacturer rather than from an independent retailer) before they could mount such an action. However, since the early part of the twentieth century, courts have been far more expansive in allowing injured consumers to seek recovery from the manufacturer of a defective product. As a result, sellers have long had an incentive to avoid private lawsuits by speaking nonfraudulently about the qualities and powers of their goods and services and by designing and manufacturing safe products.

Another method by which the state encouraged quality in products was by recognizing the right of a producer to have an identifying mark on his output and to punish those who misused that distinctive mark. Economists believe that trademarks are an important inducement for producers to invest in improving the quality of their output because they reduce the search costs that consumers incur in selecting goods and services. Archaeologists have found evidence of producers' identifying marks on goods that are four thousand years old and that have come from China, India, Persia, Egypt, Rome, Greece, and elsewhere. Until relatively recently in human history, the protection of these trademarks was largely a matter of private self-help rather than through formal law. A United States court decided the first trademark infringement case in 1825, and Congress did not enact the first federal trademark statute until 1870, an act that the U.S. Supreme Court struck down as being beyond the constitutional powers of Congress. Congress enacted a second trademark law in 1881 that avoided the deficiencies of the 1870 act. U.S. trademark law currently stems from the Lanham Act of 1946. As an indication of how egregious that law finds trademark infringement to be, the Lanham Act entitles a successful plaintiff in an infringement case to recover three times his actual losses. There has been an international agreement to recognize trademarks since the Madrid Agreement of 1891, but the United States agreed to join the relatively weak international recognition efforts only in the late 1990s.

Direct governmental regulation of the quality of output through administrative agencies has been relatively rare. Traditional rate-of-return regulation for public utilities generally did not include much attention to the quality of the service that the utility was providing, merely that the service was available. The central reason is that the regulation of quality is expensive. It is relatively straightforward to regulate price and quantity because the regulatory goals are easy to specify and, therefore, relatively easy to check. But it is difficult to quantify quality and, therefore, difficult to enforce.

There were, however, important exceptions to this general observation that regulators tend not to regulate quality. What distinguishes the following two examples of vigorous quality regulation is that they involve the sale of goods and services where there are severe informational asymmetries between consumers and producers and the value of truthful information is very high. Consider the regulation of the safety of food and drugs. While there had been earlier limited and haphazard governmental attempts to regulate food safety, it was not until the passage in 1906 of the Food and Drug Act by the U.S. Congress that the modern regulation of food and drugs began. The U.S. Food and Drug Administration (FDA), which has counterparts in nearly every country, requires food manufacturers to reveal the contents of their products on their labels and imposes substantial premarket safety tests on such products as pesticides and pharmaceuticals. Another important exception to the proposition that regulators tend not to regulate quality is the regulation of information associated with the issuance and sale of shares in publicly traded business organizations. Associations of stockbrokers had, since the founding of various European stock exchanges and the New York Stock Exchange in the late eighteenth century, imposed restrictions on themselves that were like the licensing restrictions of other professionals. The hope was that these restraints on stockbrokers would induce them to evaluate the prospectuses and financial statements of companies seeking to sell securities, leading to the elimination of excessively risky company shares.

This system of indirect regulation served the modern developed economies well so long as the number of investors purchasing stocks was small and the number of companies selling shares was limited. But when those numbers increased, a different form of regulation was necessary. The Securities and Exchange Act of 1933 required listed organizations to provide certain standardized basic financial information to investors and prohibited deceit, misrepresentation, and fraud in the sale of securities and created the federal Securities Exchange Commission to provide continued oversight and enforcement.

The newer forms of governmental regulation—so-called "social regulation"—pay much more attention than did traditional theories of regulation to quality issues. For example, the U.S. Occupational Safety and Health Administration (1973) pays special attention to workplace safety issues, such as the presence of toxic chemicals in the workplace. The U.S. Environmental Protection Agency (1964) regulates water and air quality and checks for the presence of toxic and hazardous substances.

BIBLIOGRAPHY

Breyer, Stephen. *Regulation and Its Reform.* Cambridge, Mass., 1984.
Peltzman, Sam. "The Economic Theory of Regulation after a Decade of Deregulation." In *Brookings Papers on Economic Activity: Micro-economics 1989,* edited by Marin Neil Baily and Clifford Winston, pp. 1–41. Washington, D.C., 1989.
Posner, Richard A. "Theories of Regulation." *Bell Journal of Economics and Management Science* 5 (Autumn, 1974), 335–358.
Shapiro, Sidney A., and Joseph P. Tomain. *Regulatory Law and Policy: Cases and Materials.* 2d ed. Charlottesville, Va. 1998.
Sunstein, Cass R. *After the Rights Revolution: Reconceiving the Regulatory State.* Cambridge, Mass., 1990.
Viscusi, W. Kip, John M. Vernon, and Joseph E. Harrington, Jr. *Economics of Regulation and Antitrust,* 3d ed. Cambridge, Mass., 2000.

THOMAS S. ULEN

Control of Entry and Exit

For all but the last several centuries of history, decisions on entry into and exit from the production of goods and services were largely state matters. The village elders decided who would be allowed to conduct trade with those living across the water; the king decided who would be the exclusive licensee for the importation of tobacco from his colonies; the royally designated private guild was given control over who could be a printer and what they could print; the emperor designated who was to be the exclusive tax collector in particular regions of his empire; and the shogun licensed exclusive rights to produce war materiel for his loyal vassals. And just as the award of these economic favors was the exclusive jurisdiction of the ruler, so, too, was their removal. Changes in the identity of the ruler or alterations in the lists of those who were favored at court could cause sudden and dramatic exits from the production of goods and services, including perhaps the loss of the lives of the previous provider, his family, and employees.

These patterns applied to enterprises of size and of which we have historical record. But hidden from our certain knowledge were small enterprises whose entry-and-exit regulations were minimal. These included small landholdings whose principal aim was to generate only enough output for the occupiers of the land and for whom production for the market was irregular and small scale. Continuation of these enterprises depended on an unbroken line of male heirs, inheritance being the principal form of entry. Exit occurred through migration, trauma (such as early death or conquest), and, increasingly, sale.

In addition, as villages gave way to towns and cities, there were small local non-farming enterprises—such as bakeries, stables, inns, and ironmongeries—that prospered and failed according to the fortunes of the localized market more than to the good graces of the central government or political favor.

These patterns of control of entry and exit began to change with the onset of modern growth in western Europe in the fifteenth century. The slow rise of the marketplace, of democracy, and of broader (first national, later international) patterns of trade changed the goals and methods of the regulation of entry and exit.

Modern microeconomics argues strongly in favor of free entry and exit from economic activity as one of the best guarantors of social welfare. Indeed, since the early part of the twentieth century, economists have appealed to "perfect competition" as the hallmark of a welfare-maximizing market. And since at least 1890, when the U.S. Congress passed the Sherman Antitrust Act, governments have labored to create conditions of competition. Other countries—and such emerging federations as the European Union—have followed this practice, so that one may say that for the last hundred years there has been a general consensus in favor of fostering competition and against centralized control of entry and exit into economic activity.

The four- or five-hundred-year path to this consensus was gradual, not sudden. Nor could one truthfully say that even in the developed countries there are not important instances of centralized and politicized influences on entry and exit. All that one can confidently maintain is that those influences on entry and exit decisions are less than they have been in the past—often significantly less.

Consider that entry into many labor markets since the fifteenth century has been regulated—either directly by the state through licensing requirements or by some private entity delegated to do so by the state. For example, admission to the highly prestigious Chinese administrative bureaucracy was through a state examination that was so rigorous that it selected only the best and the brightest, not necessarily those with political connections. An even earlier example is that only members of certain families could serve as priests or rabbis in certain religions (such as the descendants of Levi in Judaism). The medieval guilds in Europe established entry conditions into many professions, both as a self-serving means of limiting competition and as a means of assuring minimal quality of those within the profession. Modern professions, such as law and medicine, illustrate these same conditions. In the United States, for instance, one can become an attorney in any of the fifty states or the District of Columbia only after graduating from a law school approved by the American Bar Association (the trade group of licensed attorneys) and after passing an entrance examination administered by the state Supreme Court or bar association. Modern antitrust law is alive to the possibility that these entry limitations might have anticompetitive effects and have whittled away at those aspects (such as price collusion and anti-advertising pacts) through vigorous prosecution. Entry into personal services markets in most countries is still likely to be governed by training and licensing regulations administered by the state or by a private entity empowered by the state.

The greatest innovation in entry regulation was the general incorporation laws of the mid-nineteenth century. Most business organizations until the mid-nineteenth century were (and even today are) proprietary (owned by an individual or a family) or partnerships. There were a few larger business entities, called "corporations," that had special privileges conferred by the state. Among those privileges, the most important was that of "limited liability," by means of which the state guaranteed investors in the firm that they would almost never be liable for any losses of the corporation other than the extent of their investment. This had great attraction to investors over, say, a partnership, in which the partners are liable for all the debts incurred by the organization and so allowed for larger numbers of investors. These and the other privileges of incorporation were so extraordinary that until the early nineteenth century in the United States and several decades later in western Europe, the corporate form of business organization required a special charter from the government. These "special incorporation laws" necessitated, at a minimum, making a strong case to the legislature that the charter was in the public interest, that the people responsible for the operation of the corporation were upstanding citizens, and that there would be no foreseeable draw on public resources for the successful operation of the enterprise. Not only was the granting of special charters for the corporate form of organization rare, but the consideration of petitions for those charters was a significant burden on legislative time.

Largely to save on that legislative burden, New York State passed the first "general incorporation" statute in 1811. Other states followed, though slowly, so that by 1850 the corporate form was available in every state, although for limited purposes. Not until 1875 or so was the corporate form available for every legitimate business purpose. (See Romano, 1993, for an account of the ensuing competition among various states in the United States for the business of incorporating businesses.) These acts laid out the general powers of a corporation, the general requirements that a successful applicant must fulfill, the annual franchise tax and other responsibilities, and so on. Under these acts, anyone seeking to incorporate could do so by fulfilling the requirements and applying to the Secretary of State of the state in which he chose to incorporate.

Entry into certain industries deemed to have special significance continues to be limited by additional regulations. For example, one cannot typically simply start a public utility (in such industries as telecommunications or the provision of electricity, water, or transportation), a television or radio station, or a hospital without securing from the relevant governmental authority a certificate of "public convenience and necessity." Here, as with professional licensing, there is an unfortunate mix of sensible public policy and possible self-dealing by those already in the business. Similarly, monopoly sports leagues—for example, national football associations—typically govern closely the entry (and exit) of franchises, ostensibly in order to control the joint product that they produce (sports entertainment) but possibly so as to protect themselves from competition from other leagues.

An egregious example of entry limitation that almost certainly feathered the nests of entrenched firms occurred in the United States between 1935 and 1975. For those forty years, the federal Civil Aeronautics Board refused to allow any entry into long-haul passenger airline travel in the United States. (Similar restrictions applied to such other public utilities as interstate telecommunications and interstate trucking. Other countries besides the United States tended to have government-owned public utilities.) Then in the late 1970s and early 1980s, these restrictions

CONTROL OF ENTRY AND EXIT. Lisle Blackbourn and Joe Stydahar, head coaches of the Green Bay Packers and the Chicago Cardinals, and Buddy Parker, the mentor of the Detroit Lions huddle during a draft meeting of the National Football League, 27 January 1955. (Associated Press/Library of Congress)

(and the regulatory agencies that implemented them) ended. The result was a significant wave of entry into those previously restricted markets, the exit of some inefficient older, protected companies (such as Pan American Airways), and a dramatic fall in the real price of airline, trucking, telecommunication, and other previously regulated services.

The regulation of exit has been, until the last two hundred years, much less significant than the regulation of entry. Private enterprises came and went as business conditions, conquest, climate, and politics dictated. But the rise of the modern business organization necessitated legal intervention. Corporations, as we have seen, attract many investors; they also typically have many creditors in addition to their shareholders—for example, secured creditors, who extend loans to purchase equipment and build plants and take a security interest in the assets that they help the firm to purchase, and unsecured creditors, who loan money simply against the legal obligation to repay. When a corporation begins to fail, it is unable to meet the obligations to all its creditors. This may trigger a rush among the creditors to grab as many assets of the corporation as they can so as to receive as large a portion of the value of the debts the corporation owes them as possible. Bankruptcy law seeks to prevent this grab and to substitute a more orderly method of dealing with this

common pool problem. Although there are Roman antecedents of bankruptcy law, England did not have a law of bankruptcy until 1542. The U.S. Congress passed the first bankruptcy act in 1800, but that law was not "permanent" until the Bankruptcy Act of 1898.

Bankruptcy, which can, generally speaking, take the form of a liquidation of the enterprise's assets (so-called "Chapter 7" bankruptcy in the United States) or reorganization of the enterprise ("Chapter 11" bankruptcy in the United States), provides an orderly method of allowing a business to exit an industry or to have breathing space in which to seek to reorganize itself. Many of the newly developing economies and the transition economies have adopted bankruptcy statutes that are modeled on those of the developed countries.

BIBLIOGRAPHY

Barton, Benjamin. "Why Do We Regulate Lawyers?: An Economic Analysis of the Justifications for Entry and Conduct Regulation." *Arizona State Law Journal* 33 (2001), 429.

Curran, Christopher. "Regulation of the Professions," In *The New Palgrave Dictionary of Economics and the Law,* edited by Peter Newman, pp. 247–254. London, 1998.

Friedman, Milton. *Capitalism and Freedom,* pp. 137–160. Chicago, 1962.

Jackson, Thomas. *The Logic and Limits of Bankruptcy Law.* Cambridge, Mass., 1986.

Romano, Roberta. *The Genius of American Corporate Law.* Washington, D.C., 1993.

Young, S. David. *The Rule of Experts: Occupational Licensing in America.* Washington, D.C., 1987.

THOMAS S. ULEN

RELIGION. Religion bulks large in the history of civilizations; presumably, therefore, it has influenced economic life and development. The most celebrated theory on religion's economic implications—the Weber thesis—bears on the most important event in modern economic history, the Industrial Revolution, and is the subject of a separate article. Here we need only note that, in Weber's view, it is no accident that the Industrial Revolution originated in western Europe after the Protestant Reformation. For Weber, the ascetic ethic of Reformed Christianity inculcated values intrinsic to modern capitalism—favoring investment rather than consumption, and the relentless pursuit of profit—which revolutionized economy and society.

Critics have accused Weber of missing the point. Some estimates attribute nearly 90 percent of income growth in England and the United States after 1780 to technological innovation, not mere capital accumulation. However, profit maximization entails innovation—if profitable innovations are available. Can religion affect this variable?

Religion and Technology. Lynn White argued that it did. Since at least 1000 CE, western Europe's propensity for innovation has been striking; by the end of the Middle Ages, its technology had outstripped all rivals, including Byzantium, Islam, and China. He attributed this to the West's unique moral enthusiasm for machines. Drawing on illustrations in medieval manuscripts, White pointed to a persistent pictorial association between Christian virtue and advanced technology (including the windmill, eyeglasses, and the rotary grindstone). The innovation he most stressed was the mechanical clock, both as a feat of engineering and for its social and moral connotations: the clock became the standard iconographical symbol of temperance, which (though of classical pagan origin) was by the later Middle Ages the most admired virtue of Latin Christendom. Temperance signifies measure, and clocks measure time and human life. (The word *measure*, significantly, connotes both measurement and moderation or restraint.) The clock as a symbol of virtue endorses a punctual, regular, reliable, almost bourgeois lifestyle. In the later Middle Ages, clocks became ubiquitous in western European churches and cities; in the fourteenth century, Oresme compared the universe to a clock and God to a clockmaker.

Like others, White also emphasised the unique (Judeo-)Christian understanding of the relationship between God, man, and nature. The creator-God transcends nature, which contains nothing of the divine; He created man in His image and commanded him to rule nature in accordance with the divine will. Nature is thus an object of human manipulation, essentially a human resource. By contrast, Plato's typically Greek view sees the world as alive, ensouled, and divine, while in China (as Weber remarked) modern technology was inhibited by fear of offending the spirits believed to inhabit the natural world. The Christian view, according to White, cleared the way for technology. (Somewhat puzzlingly, he alternated between excoriating this as "the roots of our ecological crisis," and celebrating it as the source of "the dynamism of Western culture.") Technology, however, is not identical with the dominative attitude to nature, which David Landes has dubbed the "Faustian ethic"; it is, in Weber's terms, the rational (that is, effective) domination of nature. (Faust was a magician, not a technologist.) The West's rationalism does not derive from its Judeo-Christian roots (notwithstanding a notable hostility to magic in Judaism and Protestant Christianity), but from classical pagan, especially Greek, thought—even if Christianity was able to incorporate Greek rationalism by defining reason as a gift of God. However, the attitude of the Greek philosophers toward labor, trade, and what came to be called the mechanical arts was notoriously contemptuous. The Judeo-Christian attitude was different: as White pointed out, the Decalogue commands men to labor six days of the week, as did God Himself. Thus, he suggested, Western thought evaluated economic activity most positively when Judeo-Christian attitudes prevailed. Yet Judaic culture was no more conducive to technological progress than was Greek philosophy: on the contrary, it was, especially in its Rabbinic phase, profoundly traditionalist and legalistic. The roots of the West's technological ethos must lie elsewhere.

Relevant here are Christian interpretations of the Biblical Fall of Man. God gave Adam dominion over nature. In prelapsarian times, nature cooperated willingly: Adam's labor in Eden (as a gardener) was not toilsome, but a pleasure. The catastrophe of the Fall ended this happy state: among other woes for humankind, nature became recalcitrant and could be made to supply human needs only by harsh labor. Adam's seed must toil to live, as a punishment for sin. Yet all was not lost. For Augustine, the function of human bodily labor is to serve man's rational soul; and the "arts" (that is, the mechanical arts) aid this function. One possible implication is most significant: technological progress serves to counteract the devastating consequences of the Fall. By the thirteenth century, this idea was explicit in Vincent of Beauvais's *Speculum maius*: fallen man, though he can be redeemed only through Christ, can begin to raise himself through knowledge, including the mechanical arts (Male, 1910). It came to full fruition in the thinking of Francis Bacon, prophet of modern science and technology.

Bacon's influence. Bacon is best known as the eloquent champion of empirical science based on inductive methods. Two further points, however, require emphasis: the utilitarian (and therefore technological) purpose of Baconian science, and its religious justification—above all, the connection between them. Bacon famously enjoined men to seek knowledge "for the glory of the Creator, and the relief of man's estate." Man is fallen because of Adam's sin. That sin, Bacon stressed, was unnecessarily to seek moral, not natural, knowledge: the latter not only glorifies God, it can "repair" man's loss of dominion over nature, and even holds out hope that his state "might . . . be restored to . . . the sovereignty and power which [man] had in the first state of his creation." Bacon strikingly reversed the medieval hierarchy of liberal and mechanical arts, urging philosophers to learn from the practical knowledge of artisans and imitate, but also systematize, the methods by which it is acquired. Works, Bacon significantly asserted, are the test of knowledge as of faith. He gave his program a strongly millenarian tinge by applying to "this autumn of the world" the "prophecy of Daniel": "Many shall pass to and fro, and science shall be increased." This he saw already beginning in "the opening of the world by navigation and commerce" and "the further discovery of knowledge."

Bacon's great influence began not in his lifetime but during the Puritan ascendancy after 1640. Puritans saw the millennium foreshadowed by their own triumphs and were highly receptive to Bacon's message, repeatedly invoking his authority and his millennial hopes for science and technology, and citing the prophecy in Daniel. Robert Merton, too, has documented the important role of Puritans in seventeenth-century British science. Science entered the cultural mainstream with the foundation of the Royal Society, whose second Charter (1663) echoes Bacon by dedicating its labors to the glory of God the Creator, and the advantage of the human race. The Society abandoned millennialism, but the program remained. Thomas Sprat, founding member and first historian of the Society, compares it to Solomon's House, an ideal institution imagined by Bacon in his unfinished utopia, *New Atlantis,* as "dedicated to the study of the works and creatures of God, knowledge of causes . . . and the enlarging of the bounds of human empire, to the effecting of all things possible."

Any argument implicating religion in the unique economic development of the West must explain why Eastern Christendom was not so affected. Orthodox Christianity never experienced a Protestant Reformation; but according to Lynn White and others, the contrast between the two Christian civilizations is far older—older, perhaps, than the formal schism of 1054. In Greek Christianity, the influence of classic Greek culture was considerably greater, including the philosophers' depreciation of technology, economic activity, and the active life generally. Comparing the universe to a clock as Oresme does, or to a machine, as do later medieval Latin clerics, was unacceptable in the East; mechanical clocks, which proliferated in Western churches, were banned from Orthodox ones. The Eastern Church happily accepted the Gospel story of Martha and Mary at face value, as teaching the inferiority of the active life to the contemplative; Western theologians struggled to vindicate Martha. These contrasts, White argues, are symptomatic.

Islam. Orthodoxy apart, the world religion closest to Latin Christianity is Islam. Islamic civilization, in the medieval period and even later, was among the most impressive in the world, politically, culturally, economically, and technologically. Why did it not make the breakthrough into industrialism and sustained economic growth?

In some ways, Islam resembles Christianity; in others it is strikingly different. Like Christianity, Islam combined Judaic monotheism and classical Greek culture, but in Islam the two never became a unity. To religious orthodoxy, Greek-inspired philosophy and science—despite brilliant achievements over some centuries—appeared foreign, even an enemy, to be fought and eventually suppressed. Before 1000 CE, with the "closing of the gate of *ijtihad,*" the corpus of Islamic doctrine was declared complete, and an end decreed to creative interpretation and development of the holy texts. According to al-Ghazālī, one of the greatest and most influential of Muslim theologians, the concept of natural causality (basic to Western science) is an unacceptable denial of God's omnipotence. Only God knows the future. The power of such views was illustrated when, in 1580, a group of *ulema* (Muslim clerics) procured the destruction of the Ottoman Sultan's observatory in Galata (founded three years earlier) as a sacrilegious attempt to penetrate God's secrets, which they blamed for an outbreak of plague.

That this version of Islam prevailed was not preordained but reflected the balance of power. In Islam, however, issues of power are integral to religion. Islam has never recognized any distinction of principle between what is God's and what is Caesar's. Furthermore, whereas Christianity's world-historical role depended on its adoption by the Roman state (after several centuries during which it had time to mature its principles) Islam very quickly created an extensive empire by force of arms. For this rapid triumph there was, Weber argued, a price to pay: Mohammed had to make significant concessions to the values of the Bedouin warrior-chiefs and tribes on whom his success depended. A warrior nobility, Weber noted, is not naturally the carrier of a prophetic religion, unless it "directs its promises to the warrior in the cause of religion," that is, bases itself on war against infidelity. Thus Islam became essentially a warrior religion whose goal was "subjugation of unbelievers [by] the faithful." Although the centuries have greatly complicated and supplemented this ethos, the ideal of the warrior who conquers or dies for the faith remained significant and had economic implications, indicated below.

Mohammed was at once religious, military, and political leader, as were his successors the Caliphs and, later, Sultans. The typical Muslim state blended autocracy with imperialism (based on patrimonial bureaucracy and prebendal feudalism, in Weber's terminology). It was geared to, and indeed depended on, military conquest. Imperialist expansionism is no historical rarity, but the peculiarity of Islamic imperialism is that it was religiously mandated, and perhaps the more successful for that. Also, it was an essential ingredient of the political system (the ruler rewarded and secured the loyalty of the politico-military class with grants of conquered land) and of its economic achievements, which owed little to asceticism or hostility to consumption. When military expansion ended, so did economic expansion.

The Muslim state was also autocratic, untrammeled by any rule of law, and exhibited an arbitrariness and unpredictability unconducive to rational economic activity. Yet law was important in Islamic society. Its formulation was in the hands of the *ulema*, who were both jurists and theological scholars, and the recognized guardians of religious orthodoxy. Thus the law was religious law. It was not hostile to the activity of the merchant, or even to the pursuit of profit; nevertheless, the fact that, for example, the regulations governing the Ottoman guilds were part of religious law made it hard to adapt them to changing circumstances. In theory, religious law was unchangeable; in practice, the result was not that it did not change, but that no systematic or rational method of change was recognized. Four distinct "orthodox" juristic schools were acknowledged, any accredited member of which could issue a *fatwa* (authoritative opinion)—again making for an uncertainty and unpredictability unconducive to the needs of commerce. In theory, also, the law enunciated by the *ulema* should be applied by the Caliph or other ruler; in practice, no adequate means were available to enforce this. An autonomous area of secular law under the ruler's control was recognized de facto; and eventually the *ulema*, conscious of their dependence on the ruler, abandoned even the pretence of control, enunciating the doctrine that, because "tyranny is better than anarchy, he whose power prevails must be obeyed." The typical Muslim ruler, therefore, enjoyed a power so absolute that Weber uses the term *sultanism* for the "ideal typical" system of unfettered, arbitrary, and capricious authority.

East versus West. Such a system was not propitious for economic development, above all because of the lack of security for private property, which was exposed to arbitrary exactions and seizure by political authorities. The contrast here with western Europe is great; but not with the situation in non-Islamic Asiatic empires, such as China. One might therefore ask whether religion is really so significant in this (very crucial) respect; arguably, the great difference between West and East has instead been a matter of the much more powerful political position in the West of the merchant class (or bourgeoisie). However, the latter too may be related to religion.

What is usually called the "Weber thesis" concerns the causal relationship between ascetic Protestantism and modern Western capitalism. There is, however, a second Weber thesis, concerning the unique position of the European city. Compared with their Islamic, Chinese, and Indian counterparts, European cities, not only in antiquity but also in the Middle Ages, enjoyed much greater independence and powers of self-government. Likewise, European guilds enjoyed much greater autonomy than, for example, those of the Ottoman Empire, which were largely controlled by the Sultan's government. This status of European cities and guilds is, otherwise expressed, the political power of the European bourgeoisie—a power sufficient to make it a useful ally of European monarchs against troublesome feudal nobles and thus able to exercise genuine political influence. Secure property rights are one consequence of this; others are recognition of an autonomously developed business law, the "law merchant," including a law of contract; finance of governments by regular and predictable taxation rather than arbitrary exactions; and representative assemblies in which the commercial classes shared power.

Why, however, were western Europe's commercial classes so much more influential than their equivalents elsewhere? According to Weber, in part, because they were Christians. Crucially, Christianity (unlike its Judaic progenitor) is individualistic and universalistic, centered on the individual's salvation, obligations, and relationship to God. It thus devalues, is even hostile to, and therefore weakens, older particularistic solidarities, especially ties of kinship and family. Thus, it clears the way for a new kind of solidarity, such as that of the Western city. The concept and reality of *citizenship* were unique to the West, according to Weber. In other great civilizations, the city was only a geographical location, without emotional or political reality. The cities of China and Islam were amalgamations of clan and tribal groups, not unified communities. The contrast between Christianity and Chinese religion in relation to family ties is striking: the family is absolutely central to Confucian piety (as indicated by the phrase "ancestor worship"—sometimes said to be misleading; but in this respect it does not mislead). Islam's failure to override familistic solidarities seems more puzzling, since Islam, like Christianity, is individualistic and universalistic, in principle at least. It seems, however, that its early dependence on the Bedouin (for whom tribal solidarity was central) has been more influential here, even in the long run. In Indian civilization the urban population was fragmented and weakened not by family or blood ties, but by the Hindu caste system.

China. Notwithstanding the political weakness of its cities and merchants, China was for centuries a world leader in economic and technological progress—so much so, that its later stagnation and even regression constitute a historical puzzle. According to the economic historian E. L. Jones, "China came within a hair's breadth of industrializing in the fourteenth century"; yet, by the fifteenth, the government had banned all maritime trade. Others date the onset of decline from 1300 or even earlier: it may even originate in the era of China's greatest economic achievements, the Song dynasty (960–1279 CE). Both religion and government are implicated—indeed, in Chinese Confucianism (or rather neo-Confucianism) the two are inextricably fused. The famous Chinese mandarinate (government by scholar-bureaucrats) was initiated by the emperor T'ai Tsu (r. 960–976), to wrest power from his military commanders. Over time, the solidification of the neo-Confucian worldview as a state-backed orthodoxy seems eventually to have stifled economic progress. In contrast to the dominative attitude so often attributed to Christianity, the Confucian (and equally, Taoist) sees the world—natural and human—as a finely adjusted organic unity: man's duty is to adjust to this harmony and preserve it from any disturbance that might bring disaster to nature and society. Social conflict could both cause and arise from cosmic disharmony; hence any innovation that might induce it should, if possible, be avoided. As these views became pervasive, the Chinese state, which earlier frequently sponsored technological innovation and economic enterprise, became the disseminator and enforcer of an antitechnological, antiscientific and antimercantile culture (the ban on maritime commerce seems to have been influenced by Confucian arguments that trade demeaned the emperor). Chinese government, after the Song reforms, became notably centralized and autocratic (a development in which the Confucian doctrine of the emperor's heavenly mandate played its part) and was staffed by a Confucian scholar-gentry oriented to an exclusively literary and moral culture. Appointment to the mandarinate depended on examinations in the Confucian classics, to which the rigidly controlled state education system was also geared. Original or critical thinking appears to have been frowned upon. What emerged was a combination of autocracy and traditionalism largely unconducive to economic progress.

Although Chinese neo-Confucianism did not and perhaps could not bring forth the modern world, it has more recently shown itself well capable of adjusting to the modern economy. Leaving aside Japan (discussed below), the most impressive economic success in the late twentieth century is found in countries of Chinese or quasi-Chinese Confucian culture, or countries (such as Thailand and Malaysia) harboring significant Chinese minorities, whose economic role has been out of all proportion to their size. Arguably, Confucianism's intense familism, once a handicap, can now be an advantage. The family-based firm may flourish, by drawing upon a global scientific, technological, legal, and economic infrastructure, which Confucianism could not itself create. Confucianism familism also (some argue) provides a socially (and therefore economically) valuable moral infrastructure, now dangerously weak in the hyper-individualist West.

Japan. The first non-Western society to industrialize was, of course, Japan, after the Meiji Restoration in 1868. Just as impressive was Japan's rapid economic recovery after World War II, which made the country a world economic leader. Confucianism has been important in Japan for many centuries, but, sharing the religious arena with the native Shinto and various forms of Buddhism, was never so dominant as in China. Importantly, it also operated in a completely different political context from the Chinese—a state typically dominated not by a bureaucratic autocracy but by feudal warriors, the Samurai. Since this class took the lead in the modernization and industrialization of Japan after 1868, the Samurai ethic (*Bushido*, "the way of the warrior") and its religious elements and connections are central to understanding Japanese economic history. As Robert Bellah has stressed, this was an ethic quite unlike the "romantic militarism of the . . . European nobility": rather, it was strikingly ascetic, sober, and self-disciplined, qualities shared with, and reinforced by, the Zen Buddhism that was widespread in Samurai ranks. There are, indeed, striking parallels between Zen and the "ascetic Protestantism" credited with such a crucial role in the rise of Western capitalism by the Weber Thesis. According to Hugo Munsterberg, a defining feature of Zen is its rejection of "the traditional paraphernalia of Buddhism—the sacred texts, the worship of images, the chanted ritual," in favor of inner experience. Zen made a "cult of austerity" and of frugality, shunning the temptations of worldly possessions. Again according to Munsterberg, Zen permeated the thoughtways not only of the Samurai, but also, more indirectly, of Japanese culture generally (*vide* the celebrated restraint of the Japanese aesthetic sensibility).

Another notable feature of the Samurai ethic was the enormous emphasis placed on loyalty—to the warrior's lord (for whom he should be prepared to die), not only as an individual, but also as the representative of his fief, embracing his retainers as a collectivity. The Samurai loyalty ethic significantly modified Japanese Confucianism, which in the Tokugawa period preceding the Meiji Restoration enjoyed a powerful resurgence, in part state sponsored, and disseminated not only through the education system to the Samurai class that staffed the bureaucracy, but also more widely through a society that was becoming increasingly literate. This did not turn Japan into a replica of China; rather, its effect seems to have been to modify the Samurai ethic in a more collectivist direction, and spread this Confucianized version of *Bushido* more widely through society. Filial piety, so central to Chinese Confucianism, was and is highly valued in its Japanese version; but it never displaced from preeminence the ethic of loyalty to one's superior as the representative of one's collectivity. It even strengthened the loyalty ethic by giving it a religious tinge, and investing it with the emotional intensity of family ties, so that Japanese firms have been able to count on a very remarkable degree of loyalty from their employees. The obverse of this has been an acceptance by Japanese corporate managers of an obligation for the welfare of inferiors (employees) going far beyond what is normal in the West. As the twenty-first century has begun with the Japanese economy in some disarray, however, many features of its quasi-Confucian industrial system (notably guaranteed lifetime employment) have been coming under severe pressure from the ruthless logic of the global market.

[*See also* Monasteries *and* Weber Thesis.]

BIBLIOGRAPHY

Bacon, Francis. *The Advancement of Learning and New Atlantis.* London, 1906. Originally published in 1605 and 1627, respectively.

Bacon, Francis. *The New Organon and Related Writings.* Indianapolis and New York, 1960. Originally published in 1620. Includes *The Great Instauration.*

Bellah, Robert N. *Tokugawa Religion: The Values of Pre-Industrial Japan.* Boston, 1957.

Dore, Ronald P. *Education in Tokugawa, Japan.* London and Ann Arbor, 1984.

Hill, Christopher. *Intellectual Origins of the English Revolution.* London, 1972. The title is misleading. The bulk of the text concerns science, medicine, and the ideas of Francis Bacon.

Hooykaas, Reijer. *Religion and the Rise of Modern Science.* Edinburgh, 1972. A lucid general survey.

Inalcik, Halil. *The Ottoman Empire: The Classical Age, 1300–1600,* translated from the Turkish by Norman Itzkowitz and Colin Imber. New Rochelle, N. Y., 1989. See in particular Chapter 18, "The Triumph of Fanaticism."

Jones, Eric L. *The European Miracle.* Cambridge, 1981. Compares economic development in Europe and Asia.

Landes, David S. *The Unbound Prometheus: Technological Change and Industrial Development in Western Europe from 1750 to the Present.* Cambridge, 1969.

Male, Émile. *L'art religieux du XIIIe siècle en France: Étude sur l'iconographie du moyen age et sur ses sources d'inspiration.* Paris, 1910.

Merton, Robert. *Science, Technology, and Society in Seventeenth-Century England.* New York, 1970. Originally published in 1938 in *Osiris: Studies on the History and Philosophy of Science, and on the History of Learning and Culture* 4.2, 360–632.

Mokyr, Joel. *The Lever of Riches: Technological Creativity and Economic Progress.* New York and Oxford, 1990.

Munsterberg, Hugo. *Zen and Oriental Art.* Tokyo and Rutland, Vt., 1965. See especially Chapters 6 and 7 on Japanese architecture and gardens.

Ovitt, George, Jr. *The Restoration of Perfection: Labor and Technology in Medieval Culture.* New Brunswick and London, 1987. Focuses on theology.

Rodinson, Maxime. *Islam and Capitalism.* Harmondsworth, 1977. Translated by Brian Pearce. Originally published in French by Éditions du Seuil, Paris, 1988. A scholarly Marxist argument for the economic irrelevance of religion.

Schacht, Joseph, ed., with C. E. Bosworth. *The Legacy of Islam.* 2d ed. Oxford, 1974. See especially Chapter 5 on "Economic Developments," Chapter 4 on "Politics and War," and Chapter 9, "Law and the State."

Turner, Bryan. *Weber and Islam: A Critical Study.* London, 1974. Of interest mainly for its discussion of the Islamic state and its economic repercussions.

Weber, Max. *The City.* London and New York, 1958. Translated by Don Martindale and Getrud Neuwirth. Originally published in *Archiv für Sozialwissen-schaft und Sozialpolitik* 47 (1921) and later in *Wirtschaft und Gesellschaft,* vol. 2 (Tübingen, 1956). See especially Chapter 2, "The Occidental City."

Weber, Max. *The Sociology of Religion.* London, 1965–1966. Translated by Ephraim Fischoff from the 4th ed. Originally published in 1922 as "Religionssoziologie," from Weber's magnum opus, *Wirtschaft und Gesellschaft.* See especially Chapters 6, 13, and 16.

Webster, Charles. *The Great Instauration: Science, Medicine, and Religion, 1626–1660.* London, 1975. A very full discussion of the Baconian and Puritan influence.

White, Lynn, Jr. *Machina ex Deo: Essays in the Dynamism of Western Culture.* Cambridge, Mass., 1968. See especially Chapters 4, 5, and 6.

White, Lynn, Jr. *Medieval Religion and Technology: Collected Essays.* Berkeley, 1978. See especially Chapters 12, 14, and 19, and the author's introduction.

MICHAEL LESSNOFF

RENT SEEKING is a socially costly pursuit of wealth transfers. Perhaps most visible when it takes place within a certain political order, the practice is ubiquitous whenever competition takes place for a fixed prize. The concept, invented by Gordon Tullock (1967) and expounded independently by Anne Krueger (1974) in the context of international trade, describes a loss to society from monopoly in addition to the so-called deadweight loss. The latter, the Harberger triangle, is commonly understood as loss due to any price above marginal cost and is associated with tolls, tariffs, and excise taxes in addition to monopoly prices (above marginal cost).

Rent-seeking losses are societal reductions in welfare associated with attempts by individuals or interest groups to secure monopolization of markets by competing for "artificial rents." These losses may include spending on lawyers or lobbying, or any other expenditure necessary to obtain a fixed prize. Legal and lobbying resources are deflected from positive-sum employments to, at best, zero-sum activities. The waste is the opportunity cost of positive-sum employment of lobbying resources in other parts of the economy. Empirically the costs may be small or large. Individuals whose rents are being dissipated want to minimize costs. Those who stand to benefit (e.g., lobbyists) want rent-seeking costs to be large. Actual results are determined by the source of property rights control in any given economy.

The use of real resources to obtain a rent transfer from one group of (generally poorly organized) market participants to a group (often well organized and smaller in number) with intense interests in obtaining the monopoly prize creates social wastes and limits exchange. The wastes of rent seeking—wealth dissipation—are in contrast to the pursuit of profits and wealth production. A Schumpeterian monopolist directs resources to most valued ends and, in the process, makes profits, thus creating wealth. A competitive process, as long as entry is not barred, ensures that new and competing products or product dimensions reduce price–cost margins and economic profits through time. Society's welfare is thereby maximized, in contrast to the dissipation of resources and wealth experienced through rent seeking.

The rent-seeking paradigm has undergone a number of extensions and qualifications since its invention (see McCormick and Tollison, 1981; Tollison, 1997). Many of the innovations turn on how the process of rent seeking takes place over time, including important work on rent dissipation, rent capitalization, defensive rents (McChesney, 1987), and so-called transitional gains gaps (Tullock, 1971). In relating the theory to history and historical institutions, no extensions are more important than those integrating the rent-seeking process as practiced by interest groups to economic regulation and institutional change. Two contributions are of primary relevance. Rather than simply assuming that regulation was, normatively, in the public interest, George Stigler (1971) began to develop a positive theory of institutional change by arguing that political systems were rationally devised and rationally employed to capture the regulatory apparatus. Industry demands regulation in Stigler's version; and the state supplies it through subsidies, entry control, suppression of substitutes or complements, by price fixing and other means. The political process through which politicians are able to sell regulations for votes and resources makes it unlikely that the public interest will prevail. Characteristics of the voting process, most particularly the fact that the voters need an agent and cannot vote themselves on marginal issues, lead to all kinds of agency problems. Only strongly felt preferences of majorities and minorities are registered. Some voters, even a large number, remain rationally ignorant since the pro rata effect on them of particular forms of regulation is perceived to be small or nonexistent.

Sam Peltzman (1976), in a generalization of Stigler's theory, developed a model including the marginal trade-offs by politician-regulators in an interest-group setting, accounting for both producers' and consumers' surplus distributions. Net demanders of regulation, represented by interest groups of any kind, were wedded to politician-suppliers of regulation in a general theory integrating economic factors with the political process. Rent seeking is the essence of the process through which regulations appear (and disappear). Those who seek regulation, typically well-organized smaller groups, in the form of taxes, tolls, regulated rates, or tariffs are willing to invest resources to get it. Those injured by such economic controls, typically larger numbers of voter-consumers, will invest up to the amount of their interest in preventing such regulation. The point is that the resources devoted to rent seeking—lobbying, legal expenses, and so on—are wasted resources from the standpoint of society. In this non-Marxian process, consumers or any other group can "win." The trick of the politician-regulator (monarch or dictator) is to balance regulatory favors of one group against the other; but in doing so property rights, incentives, and the volume of exchange are altered so that wealth creation is reduced.

Rent seeking—with its waste of expenditures to obtain privileges—riddles the process that with some specification of exogenous and endogenous variables actually becomes a theory of government or institutional-historical change. Rents and potential rents emerge through technological change that can support new regulations, deregulations, or a cycle of interventions. Once some political metric and constitutional conditions are assumed (monarchy, democracy, and so on), the theory of rent seeking along with particular forms of self-interested behavior is capable of explaining some important aspects of historical processes.

Rent-Seeking Behavior and Economic History. Competition for fixed prizes must have occurred from the very beginnings of humankind. There are undoubtedly numerous and important examples of rent-seeking activity in primitive and early societies. Monarchy, authoritarian rule, and dictatorships—systems that punctuated ancient, medieval, and early modern worlds—are ripe cultures for rent seeking. Specialized studies, some of a neoclassical/public-choice flavor, abound. Roman taxation is a good case study. Although the data are incomplete Levi (1988), for example, attempts to explain forms of revenue collection over critical episodes of Roman history. In particular, she argues that "tax farming" and other methods of collecting revenue under the empire were a function of constraints on emperors' relative bargaining power, their discount rates, and transaction costs. There was, however, clearly a rent-seeking component when ancient rulers decided on how, what, and whom to tax, and what and whom to spend on and benefit. The political clout of particular interest groups (demanders and suppliers of regulation, taxation, and income distributions) and their relative power to obtain privileges or to resist taxation through time was a crucial factor. Opportunistic political and economic behavior on the part of dictators or government bureaucrats in Rome and in the provinces, together with a host of alternative transaction costs in tax collection or regulatory enforcement, determined the success of rent seeking and the course of economic growth and development.

The dissolution of the Roman Empire and substantive conquests of Rome and its foreign possessions and associated institutions led to two critical developments having enormous importance for the future of Western civilization and economic growth. The first of these was the rise of feudal estates, which exemplified new relations between land, labor, and capital. The second was the rise of Christianity, first as a fledgling competitor in religious belief against late Greek and Roman varieties of gnosticism and later, after the tenth century, as a supranational government with implications for economic growth in western Europe. Both of these developments have received attention in the emerging neo-institutionalist and rent-seeking literature.

Changes in relative input prices making labor relatively more expensive than land, created by the great European plagues, undoubtedly had a profound impact on feudal institutions, especially land-tenure systems. However, territorial rent seeking by aristocrats and others was accompanied by waxing and waning of the power of the Roman Catholic Church, an institution that was as rationally worldly as it was otherworldly in character. The Roman church developed a "market" for "assurances of eternal salvation," elevating venality to new heights. This organization sought to extract wealth from secular society and to dominate civil authority in myriad ways—suppressing heresy through violence and intimidation, regulating credit markets to its own benefit, and striving to monopolize medieval religious dogma. The church, as a kind of supranational government, clashed with the rent-seeking proclivities of secular authorities, including feudal aristocrats, town governments, and other nascent civil interests. These clashes clearly affected economic growth and development in particular parts of western Europe (Ekelund et al., 1996).

The ascendance of the nation-state in the mercantile period brought new levels of rent seeking to civil governments. In a pioneering study, historian Frederic C. Lane (1958) investigated organized violence and its effects upon the economic motives and behavior of Renaissance governments in exacting tribute from merchants for protection. Later Ekelund and Tollison (1981, 1997) described the impact of Crown rent seeking in the domestic and international economy on political and economic institutions. In England the result was a transfer of power to Parliament, with less power to the monarch. They describe in some detail the political process through which rent seeking and property rights transfers were accomplished. The neoinstitutional orientation of "mercantilism" was chiefly accomplished by analyzing (a) how jurisdictional problems, of a largely self-interested nature, between the royal court system and the common-law courts created shifts in the locus of political power and economic authority between the monarch and democratic institutions (the Parliament); and (b) how agency problems between the monarch and enforcement mechanisms within the British economy (especially among the local sheriffs) led to de facto internal deregulation. The sequence was that rent-seeking activity altered property rights through the political process, and property rights changes created new incentives that altered the direction of economic activities, having implications for growth and the nature of the economic and political system. In particular, the Parliament was not at the time particularly suited to supply regulation, both internal and external, owing to high coalition and enforcement costs.

This straightforward argument was embellished in an emphasis on whether the new and emerging regime in England produced "credible commitments" in fiscal developments after the Civil War, the Restoration, and the Glorious Revolution (North and Weingast, 1989). However, the "modern world" might not have arrived had other conditions not been obtained. For twenty or more years after the Revolution of 1688, there were both domestic and foreign demands for the return of the Catholic monarchs in the line of Stuart succession, namely, the Jacobites supporting James II (and later the "Pretender," James III). Focusing on the effects that these dramatic developments had in the capital markets, Wells and Wills (2000) develop an econometric technique to analyze threats to the institutional structures described in earlier contributions. They conclude that stock market reactions, embryonic though the stock market was, were clear harbingers of the credible commitments that were required of new institutions leading to modern capitalism. These historical changes were, in part at least, brought on by cracks in the rent-seeking apparatus of the English monarchs. They occurred, moreover, as an unintended consequence of self-interested activity.

The institutional evolution of other nations also has been described with a rent-seeking model of regulation and governance. Although English institutions developed in such a manner as to provide stability and growth, the French mercantile state (under Colbert) languished through a highly developed internal system of rent seeking. Incredibly intricate systems of regulation and control, along with no-nonsense enforcement by *intendants* in the provinces helped provide revenue for a corrupt French monarchy. "Luxury" productions proliferated while economic growth languished. If anything, the Spanish experience with rent seeking was even more debilitating than the French for the course of economic growth in the modern world.

The decline of mercantilism in England and its persistence (and even strengthening) in countries such as France and Spain is thus to be explained, at least in part, by the dissipation of wealth through wasted resources and altered incentives in rent-seeking activities. Such recent seeking, of course, took place against the backdrop of internal and external conflict, legal codes restricting the ownership of property, Inquisitions, and the emergence of Protestantism. The Council of Commerce in France (Schaeper, 1983), espousing an "industrial policy" and rent-seeking cartels, restricted exchange in seventeenth-century France. Likewise, rent-seeking by the Spanish and Portuguese Crowns, retarded growth against the backdrop of similar institutional rigidities to exchange and wealth creation (North, 1991; Ekelund and Tollison, 1997).

Modern Economic History and Rent Seeking. The concept of rent seeking, as suggested above, has been integrated into a general theory of regulation featuring interest-group competitions for the prize of politically granted restrictions. This overarching modern study of "institutional economics" includes not only rent-seeking behavior as an integral part of the theory but, owing to the fact that altered rules through rent seeking must affect property rights and incentives, the property rights literature as well. As such, the theory of rent seeking has become a prominent part of an emerging neo-institutional economics through which specific historical institutions may be analyzed. In a generalized framework, Mancur Olson (1982; 1996) identified rent-seeking as a primary cause of the rise and fall of nations. Put quite simply, the older the society, the longer wealth-restricting institutions retard economic exchange and growth. Growth, in this view, is a function of historical experience with rent seeking through some political structure (Ades and Glaser, 1995; Shleifer and Vishny, 1998).

Studies identifying the rise and fall (and perhaps the rise again) of particular institutions and of the welfare implications of such episodes are also of critical importance in interpreting modern historical experience. The emergence of railway regulation in the United States, its heyday, and its decline, together with the costs of regulation (when effective), may be analyzed with rent-seeking concepts and interest-group arguments. Likewise, the history of antitrust may be given a rent-seeking interpretation (McChesney and Shughart, 1995). Historical examples, involving the timing of and reasons for the emergence of child labor legislation (Davidson et al., 1995), the rent distributions of Occupational Safety and Health Administration and Environmental Protection Agency regulations (Bartel and Thomas, 1987), rent seeking and property rights restrictions in the optometry market (Hass-Wilson, 1986), the vicissitudes of telecommunications deregulation (Kaserman et al., 1993), and myriad other historical changes in economies, are all brought to life through the modern neo-institutional theory, of which rent seeking is a part. As such, the concept of rent seeking has become an important tool, especially when used with modern neoclassical economics, for analyzing economic history and the evolution of institutions.

BIBLIOGRAPHY

Ades, Alberto F., and Edward L. Glaeser. "Trade and Circuses: Explaining Urban Giants." *Quarterly Journal of Economics* 110 (1995), 195–227.

Bartel, Ann P., and Lacy G. Thomas. "Predation through regulation: The Wage and Profit Effects of the Occupational Safety and Health Administration and the Environmental Protection Agency." *Journal of Law and Economics* 30 (1987), 239–264.

Davidson, Audrey B., E. Davis, and Robert B. Ekelund, Jr. "Political Choice and the Child Labor Statute of 1938: Public Interest or Interest Group Legislation?" *Public Choice* 82 (1995), 85–106.

Ekelund, Robert B., Jr., and Robert D. Tollison. *Mercantilism as a Rent-Seeking Society.* College Station, 1981.

Ekelund, Robert B., Jr., and Robert D. Tollison. *Politicized Economies: Monarchy, Monopoly, and Mercantilism.* College Station, 1997.

Ekelund, Robert B., Jr., et al. *Sacred Trust: The Medieval Church as an Economic Firm.* New York, 1996.

Hass-Wilson, Deborah. "The Effect of Commercial Practice Restrictions: The Case of Optometry." *Journal of Law and Economics* 29 (1986), 165–186.

Kaserman, David L., John W. Mayo, and Patricia L. Pacey. "The Political Economy of Deregulation: The Case of Intrastate Long Distance." *Journal of Regulatory Economics* 5 (1993), 49–63.

Krueger, Anne O. "The Political Economy of the Rent-Seeking Society." *American Economic Review* 64 (1974), 291–303.

Lane, Frederic. "The Economic Consequences of Organized Violence." *Journal of Economic History* 18 (1958), 401–417.

Levi, Margaret. *Of Rule and Revenue.* Berkeley, 1988.

McChesney, Fred S. "Rent Extraction and Rent Creation in the Economic Theory of Regulation." *Journal of Legal Studies* 16 (1987), 101–118.

McChesney, Fred S., and William F. Shughart II, eds. *The Causes and Consequences of Antitrust: The Public Choice Perspective.* Chicago, 1995.

McCormick, Robert E., and Robert D. Tollison. *Politicians, Legislation, and the Economy: An Inquiry into the Interest-Group Theory of Government.* Boston, 1981.

North, Douglass C. "Institutions and Economic Growth: An Historical Introduction." *World Development* 17 (1991), 1319–1332.

North, Douglass C., and Barry R. Weingast. "Constitutions and Commitment: The Evolution of Institutions Governing Public Choice in Seventeenth-Century England." *Journal of Economic History* 49 (1989), 803–832.

Olson, Mancur. *The Rise and Decline of Nations: Economic Growth, Stagflation, and Social Rigidities.* New Haven, Conn., 1982.

Olson, Mancur. "Big Bills Left on the Sidewalk: Why Some Nations are Rich and Others Poor." *Journal of Economic Perspectives* 10 (1996), 3–24.

Peltzman, Sam. "Toward a More General Theory of Regulation." *Journal of Law and Economics* 19 (1976), 211–240.

Schaeper, Thomas J. *The French Council of Commerce, 1700–1715: A Study of Mercantilism after Colbert.* Columbus, Ohio, 1983.

Shleifer, Andrei, and Robert W. Vishny. *The Grabbing Hand: Government Pathologies and Their Cures.* Cambridge, 1998.

Stigler, George J. "The Theory of Economic Regulation." *Bell Journal of Economics and Management Science* 2 (1971), 137–146.

Tollison, Robert D. "Rent seeking." In *Perspectives on Public Choice*, edited by D. C. Mueller, pp. 506–525. Cambridge, 1997.

Tullock, Gordon. "The Welfare Costs of Tariffs, Monopolies and Theft." *Western Economic Journal* 5 (1967), 224–232.

Tullock, Gordon. "The Costs of Transfers." *Kyklos* 4 (1971), 629–643.

Wells, John, and Douglas Wills. "Revolution, Restoration, and Debt Repudiation: The Jacobite Threat to England's Institutions and Economic Growth." *Journal of Economic History* 60.2 (2000), 1–24.

ROBERT B. EKELUND

RETAIL TRADE. Retailing has a fundamental significance in the economic life of communities, ancient and modern. Retailing forms the essential cog in the process of transferring goods and information about them from producers to final consumers and in enabling the flow of information back again. As Geoffrey Crossick and Serge Jaumain have stressed, (1999, p. 3) "Retail distribution constitutes an immediate point of intersection between economy, culture and daily life." However, the study of retailing has, for long, been a much neglected subject in historical research.

In economic history, as in other disciplines, the tradiional concern has been with assessing moments of change in retail evolution at the expense of continuity. The key concern has been to understand capitalist commodity markets with the emphasis on mass consumer markets and the distribution of machine mass-produced goods. Consequently, interest has focused on the mid-nineteenth century onward in western Europe and North America, at the expense of understanding retail systems of earlier periods and other places. Recent research into earlier periods, however, has revealed the significance of the retailing of basic household goods to all levels of the population in nonindustrialized societies. Such research broadens our understanding of the importance of retailing and opens up the issues of continuity and the impact and relative significance of change.

The standard trajectory established by retail and business historians is that fixed-shop retailing took over from markets, fairs, and peddlers in the eighteenth century, to be eclipsed in turn by large-scale retailing in the mid-nineteenth century, at which point new techniques were seen as necessary to sell mass quantities of goods to mass consumers. Focus of attention has been placed on new and unusual forms of retailing, technological innovations, and organizational change.

While economic historians have been interested in placing these "transformatory" elements within broader pictures of economic and social change, cultural studies have sought to extrapolate their impact on consumers, interpreting new femininity, passivity, and fashion-based acquisitiveness as a consequence of these new forms. This latter perspective reinforced the perceived watershed between industrial and preindustrial consumption and has emphasized the power of the innovative retail site over the long-term experience consumers possessed in all periods.

The effect of the emphasis on the new and the unusual also has led to the marginalizing of research into petty retailing and itinerant selling, which, rather than dying out, have run alongside the evolution of large-scale retailing and have often accounted for a far greater percentage of retail activity.

Ancient and Medieval Systems. There is ample evidence of the activity of retailing, rather than ad hoc barter, from ancient times. The economic life of ancient Babylonia was a complex of activities based on a market system, even if this was not the same self-regulating mechanism of capitalist economies. The chief marketplace of Babylon formed a distinctive landmark, and in most streets of the city stalls sold foodstuffs, ceramics, and cloth, and shops sold more expensive wares. Market areas containing stalls and shops existed across all continents in the ancient world, even where money economies did not exist. Pictures of market scenes with the sale of foodstuffs and manufactured goods regulated by officials appear in the Egyptian Old Kingdom Tombs dating from 2500 to 2400 BCE. In imperial Rome, Trajan's Forum contained about 150 shops on various levels, and the buildings of Pompeii, covered by volcanic ash in 79 CE, reveal hundreds of examples of fixed shops with counters and open, street-fronting windows, including some large shops on two floors and even "fast-food" outlets.

In the medieval period, markets—especially covered markets and market halls—thrived and gave rise to some dramatic retail architecture, such as the halls of Bruges and Ypres begun in the early 1200s, and the cotton market and bazaar in Jerusalem, dating from 1329. Other forms of retail architecture included arcaded streets that protected shops beneath and created areas for sociable shopping, and covered off-street areas, much like bazaars, housing sometimes hundreds of tiny shops selling wares of all kinds. Fixed shops continued to cluster around market sites, a symbiotic relationship that has continued to the present day.

Fairs should not be neglected in this period as important retail and wholesale sites. Many fairs were large, of great renown, and of international standing, such as the Leipzig fair. Fairs drew consumers from the poorest to the wealthiest, including royalty, and the appeal was as much for the entertainment of the site as for purchasing.

Regulation and Guilds. Peddlers and other itinerant tradespeople were regulated by civil authorities in the medieval period. As Laurence Fontaine (1996) has shown, peddling dynasties could be widespread across Europe, reaching into even the remotest areas, such as the Alps or Scandinavian uplands. These peddling operations were managed by long lines of credit, were ready to diversify their wares, and provided a valuable and dependable service to customers.

In medieval Europe, retailing was regulated by guilds that stipulated who could open shops or run stalls, set conditions for the selling of goods, and established the regulation of apprenticeships. Much of medieval retail regulation aimed to ensure measures and quality (underlining the long standing of the battle against adulteration in the history of customer rights in retailing), but, most particularly in the case of foodstuffs, regulation also was used to keep prices to the final consumer reasonable, to manage the distribution of food, and to prevent hoarding and local shortages. The power of guilds (if not their presence) weakened over time, most particularly in England, and many of the regulatory functions were taken over by civil authorities. Relaxations on the rules of apprenticeship allowed more unskilled workers to enter the retail trade, while petty shopkeeping stood outside guild regulation, encouraging expansion throughout the period. Small shops were easy to set up and were untaxed; the front room of any house could easily be converted. Most shops sold items from a variety of producers, local and distant.

The Early Modern Period. Throughout the seventeenth and eighteenth centuries, consumer markets expanded in Europe, particularly in Britain, France, and Holland. New goods appeared from the East as a result of increased trading and colonization, and copying these imports at home resulted in innovation in production and lower costs to the consumer. Populations increased, and transportation and distribution, especially with the stagecoach system, improved.

Fairs and markets continued in importance, but the majority of consumer purchases were now made from fixed shops. Hoh-cheung and Lorna Mui (1989) have shown that fixed-shop retailing increased in the seventeenth and eighteenth centuries in England, and they calculate that there was the same percentage of shops per capita in the mid-eighteenth century as in 1951. Branch shops or subsidiary outlets already were appearing and were used to tap new markets and spread risk. Elite shopping areas developed as towns were remodeled and older markets and street stalls were relocated. In a more prosperous climate, consumers, including working people, proved themselves able and keen to experiment and expand their purchasing activities. However, the expansion in retailing in traditional trades was even greater than in new and fashionable goods. Such research has overturned the concept of a consumer revolution in late-eighteenth-century England in favor of a picture of steady long-term change, and work on other European countries is now growing.

The theory of the late-eighteenth-century consumer revolution has come under much criticism for its emphasis on female acquisitiveness and the powerful role of fashion. Despite interest in the new and fashionable, the vast majority of shopping continued for basic household items, although now many more goods were able to be bought in their finished state than previously.

Fixed shops were stocked from a complex network of suppliers, from wholesalers to merchants, other retailers, and subcontracting systems. The shop itself was a dedicated sales environment, unconnected with any making or processing activities. Innovations and adaptations appeared over the seventeenth and eighteenth centuries in shop layout, design, service, and sales techniques. Sash glazing was introduced into shops from the late-seventeenth century, fascia boards and shop fronts changed with fashions in style, and shop windows increased in size. Service-oriented interiors sported glass display cases, display boards, gilding, columns, chairs, and mirrors. In fast-selling shops, goods were piled high and flamboyantly in interiors dominated by long counters for processing sales. Advertising techniques included an integrated system of trade cards, bill heads, handbills, signs and fascia board, all sporting the shop symbol acting as the business logo. Evidence from large-scale retailers at the end of the eighteenth century shows the introduction of techniques such as fixed pricing, changing displays, sales, self-service, and showrooms, and sometimes interiors on a dramatic, aristocratic scale. Producers such as Wedgwood and Boulton made use of mail order and outrider systems and nationwide newspaper advertising, as well as conventional retailing.

The Nineteenth Century. The focus of history of retailing in the nineteenth century has been one of the evolution of large-scale organizations appearing across western Europe and North America, tied to population increase, urbanization, and a widening variety and increasing standardization of goods. The gap in research still lies with small-scale retailing in the period. The growth of large-scale retailers in the nineteenth century did not necessarily hinder small-scale shopkeeping, where the pattern was also one of expansion. Small-scale retailers became more focused on servicing lower-income consumers, who very often could not take full advantage of large-scale retailing such as department stores, multiples, or cooperatives.

The cooperative movement began in northern England in the 1840s and sought to serve the poor by dividing profits among loyal customers in the form of dividends. Cooperatives used branch shops and vertical integration, and included a wholesale side, but were vulnerable to competition.

The growth of multiples—shops with large numbers of subsidiaries—began with shops retailing foodstuffs. These retailers introduced new methods of distribution, making

RETAIL TRADE. Shoppers browsing at New York's R. H. Macy and Company department store the week before Christmas, 1942. (Marjory Collins/Prints and Photographs Division, Library of Congress)

use of improved product transportation, storage (especially freezing), and the expanding railway networks.

Department stores have undergone many different stages of development, emerging from the larger, successful drapery shops in Britain and France, where the many different classes of cloth were separated into specialist departments by the 1830s. Rather than a sudden and shocking appearance, department stores expanded gradually, as adjacent properties were gradually bought up and incorporated. Between individual department stores there were considerable differences in clientele, publicity, range of merchandise, and styles of management. Yet what was new and distinctive about the stores in general was their combination of certain elements on an extensive, capital-intensive level: large-scale buildings, lavish displays and interior designs, intensive advertising, mail order, home delivery, and fixed pricing.

From 1890 to 1914, department stores underwent another phase of expansion, with internal restructuring and sometimes complete rebuilding. New symbols of modernity were introduced, including elevators, cash registers, and the use of novel building materials. More services were added, such as restaurants and concerts. A final key phase of change after 1914 was mainly organizational, including the amalgamation of firms.

Much has been made of the impact of the early department stores on their customers, and stores have been studied in terms of gender, modernity, cultural consumption, and social anxiety. Department stores achieved a huge symbolic presence in the late nineteenth century. Their size and their investment in the latest technical innovations, coupled with the loudly voiced, though unfounded, fears of small retailers, meant that the department store came to stand for many of the social anxieties troubling European societies of the time. However, the department store was less novel and consumers far more experienced than contemporary debates have suggested.

The Twentieth Century. In the early twentieth century, adaptation and new developments in the large-scale retail sector continued. *Prix uniques* shops, or single-price stores, imported into Europe in the interwar period (1918–1939) from the United States, successfully challenged department stores. Prix uniques offered low prices and were less focused on service, but they provided a wide range of goods in a single establishment. Prices rose conventionally in a series of clear steps, thus avoiding expensive ticketing operations and speeding up sales processing.

In the 1930s, "scientific" methods of selling and advertising became popular in retailing in the United States, spreading to Europe in the 1950s. These innovations (escalators, new lighter and brighter interior designs, island counters, modern fonts in signage), acted as symbols of modernity, as previous innovations did in the nineteenth-century department store. Design trends of such currency were suitable for the sale of new electrical goods now available at affordable prices: radios, refrigerators, and later, freezers and automatic washing machines. The idea of "rational" retailing also affected management processes; John Lewis department stores had an Intelligence Department surveying where savings in time and money could be made. As always, such shifts in image allowed other retailers to make a feature of the opposite image and to trade on tradition, reputation, and old-fashioned service.

The 1950s and 1960s was the era of supermarkets and retail conglomerates, operations that responded to consumers' needs to shop quickly and efficiently. The key was to reduce interaction with shop staff and to increase levels of self-service. All food in supermarkets was displayed ready-packed, shifting the burden of knowledge and decision making to customers alone. The ethos of self-service spread in the 1960s and 1970s, affecting most kinds of retail outlets, so that most shops came to use this technique to some degree in the Western world by the late twentieth century. In terms of the individual customer's experience of shopping, self-service represents perhaps the most significant change in sales methods since medieval times.

Despite the general trend toward self-service, some large shops, especially department stores, have continued to trade on their ability to give informed service. Likewise, not all Western countries have embraced large-scale retailing—in Italy, regulation favors small shopkeeping. Change and innovation in small shops is still constant, with the fashion boutique of the 1960s and the minimalist displays of designer clothes shops today as prime examples.

In the second half of the twentieth century, the shopping mall and the shopping precinct, with its pedestrianized areas, created new areas for socializing and shopping. Innovations in retailing in the later twentieth century focused on further management rationalization; the computerization of stock management and introduction of bar coding. New retail forms keep on appearing, such as warehouse, factory, farm, thrift, and catalog shops, each appealing to different consumer requirements. Budget, bulk-buy shops such as Matalan and Kmart started expanding into countries around the world, joining other large-scale retail companies in the trend toward globalization. The targeting of underdeveloped countries by global companies has caused considerable concern about the survival of local retail ventures, local cultures, and the sustainability of world resources. New forms of retailing continue to excite interest as to fundamental change in the retail scene, such as the arrival of Internet shopping. However, as Internet shopping has shown, success is not always assured, and suitable for the sale of only certain products.

BIBLIOGRAPHY

Benson, John, and Gareth Shaw, eds. *The Evolution of Retailing Systems, c. 1800–1914.* Leicester, London, and New York, 1992.

Benson, John, and Gareth Shaw, eds. *The Retailing Industry.* 3 vols. London, 1999.

Bronner, Simon, ed. *Consuming Visions: Accumulation and Display of Goods in America, 1880–1920.* New York, 1989.

Campbell, Bruce, and Richard Britnell. *A Commercialising Economy: England 1086 to c. 1300.* Manchester, 1995.

Coquery, Natacha. *L'hôtel aristocratique: le marché du luxe à Paris au VIIIe siècle.* Paris, 1998.

Cox, Nancy. *The Complete Tradesman: A Study of Retailing, 1550–1820.* Aldershot, U.K., 2000.

Crossick, Geoffrey, and Serge Jaumain. *Cathedrals of Consumption.* Aldershot, U.K., 1999.

Davis, Dorothy. *A History of Shopping.* London, 1966.

Fontaine, Laurence. *History of Pedlars in Europe.* Cambridge, 1996.

Glennie, Paul. "Consumption within Historical Studies." In *Acknowledging Consumption: A Review of New Studies*, edited by Daniel Miller pp. 164–203. London and New York, 1996.

Hoh-cheung and Lorna Mui. *Shops and Shopkeeping in Eighteenth Century England.* Montreal, 1989.

Keene, Derek. "Shops and Shopping in Medieval London." In *British Archaeological Association Conference Transactions for the Year 1984*, vol. 10, *Medieval Art: Architecture and Archaeology in London*, edited by Lindy Grant. pp. 29–46. London, 1990.

Larke, Roy. *Japanese Retailing.* London and New York, 1994.

Morris, Meaghan. "Things to Do with Shopping Centres." In *Grafts: Feminist Cultural Criticism*, edited by S. Sheridan. London, 1988.

Sargentson, Carolyn. *Merchants and Luxury Markets: The Marchands Merciers of Eighteenth-Century Paris.* London, 1996.

Walsh, Claire. "Shop Design and the Display of Goods in Eighteenth-Century London." *Journal of Design History* 8.3 (1995), 157–176.

Westerfield, Ray. *Middlemen in English Business.* London, 1968.

Wrigley, Neil, and Michelle Lowe, eds. *Retailing, Consumption and Capital: Towards the New Retail Geography.* Harlow, 1996.

CLAIRE WALSH

RETIREMENT. Retirement can be defined as the permanent withdrawal of an individual from his or her normal paid employment. For much of the twentieth century, retirement overwhelmingly affected men and involved the termination of work in the sixth decade of their lives. However, patterns of retirement are now becoming more complex, and thus harder to define: for example, some individuals return to employment, some experience "phased" or "flexible" retirement (by continuing to work part time, or in a less-demanding occupation), and, of course, many notionally retired individuals perform informal or voluntary work that has economic value, even if it is not recorded as such. In the last thirty years, the average age of retirement has steadily fallen in all industrialized societies. When combined with improving longevity, this is resulting in a longer period of leisure in old age, and it is increasingly affecting women, as their economic activity rates increase. Retirement normally involves reliance on a state, occupational, or private pension plan, rather than earnings. It has thus been a major reason for the establishment of modern welfare states. For example, in Great Britain, pensions and other social security payments to retirees absorb one-half of the entire social security budget (which, in turn, amounts to nearly one-third of all public expenditure).

Retirement has existed far back into human history. But before the twentieth century, it was generally confined to a small, wealthy minority who were economically self-sufficient, or to those supported by a limited number of occupational pension plans. For the majority of the population—engaged predominantly in agricultural labor— formal paid work was reduced in intensity in old age, until physical incapacity forced a complete cessation of employment. In nineteenth-century Great Britain, the main source of income for such old people was the Poor Law. In many parishes, outdoor relief would be paid as a supplement to the diminishing earnings obtained from work. It is significant that, until 1890, the English Poor Law placed all paupers aged sixty and above in the category of "aged and infirm." Evidence, such as that collected by the poverty investigator Charles Booth (1840–1916) showed that reliance on the Poor Law rapidly increased past the age of sixty-five. This older form of retirement was essentially "infirmity" retirement, whereas the unfolding of the twentieth century was accompanied by the emergence of "jobless" retirement. Thus, over the past one hundred years, old age has become synonymous with retirement.

The fall in the economic activity rates of older men in advanced industrial societies since the late nineteenth century has been very striking. In Great Britain in 1881, 73.6 percent of males aged sixty-five and above were defined by the census as "gainfully occupied"; by 1951, this had fallen to 31.1 percent; and by 1991, it was only 8.7 percent. In the United States, 68.3 percent of men aged sixty-five and above were economically active in 1890; by 1950, this had fallen to 41.4 percent; and by 1990 it was 16.3 percent. In contrast, American women aged sixty-five and above have slightly increased their low economic-activity rates, from 7.6 percent in 1890 to 8.6 percent in 1990. Similar long-run trends can be observed in all industrialized societies, though with subtle differences in timing.

Explanations of Retirement. On the surface, it is paradoxical that increasing proportions of older men should have withdrawn from formal paid employment concurrently with presumed improvements in their health status (which should also have improved working capacity) and changes in the labor process, which have made work lighter and less physically demanding. The reasons for this paradox have engendered some debate among social historians.

Broadly speaking, explanations of the spread of retirement over the past one hundred years have tended to suggest a decline in either the supply of older workers, or the demand for the labor of older workers. Few serious social historians would accept only one of these positions; the differences are those of emphasis between them. The former set of explanations views human agency as crucial in explaining "retirement behavior" and would classify retirement as a consumer good, analogous to paid holidays, a shorter working week, and greater leisure time. One such model, popular in the 1950s and 1960s was "disengagement theory." This model suggested that older people gradually withdrew from active life, including participation in the labor market. More recently, there has been an examination of the effect of economic incentives, such as accumulated wealth and savings, enabling individuals to withdraw from work, or the enticements of state and private pension schemes. Again, it is possible to argue that cultural factors have played a part, and that the twentieth century saw the growth of a "retirement tradition," a "retirement expectation," or an "early-exit culture" in popular attitudes.

By contrast, "demand-side" explanations suggest that the major factor triggering off modern "jobless" retirement, and sustaining much of its progress, was the interrelated set of changes experienced by advanced industrial economies from the late nineteenth century onward, characterized by larger units of production (notably, the joint-stock company) with more "scientific" management regimes, greater precision in job grading, and a more intense scrutiny of the productivity of individual workers. Mandatory retirement was a way of dispensing with older workers who were judged—in the aggregate—to be of decreasing value in a more technology-intensive economy. Essentially, older workers became progressively "de-skilled" and lost their industrial worth. Over the past one hundred years, older workers have tended to be concentrated in long-established, declining industries (notably manufacturing and agriculture) where, on retirement, they have not been replaced; by contrast, newer industries, such as electronics and service-based enterprises, have always had much more youthful age structures. This viewpoint contends that the rate of decline in the economic activity of those aged sixty-five and above has been strongly related to economic changes. For example, in Great Britain the recession-hit 1930s saw a rapid decline, but in the boom years of the 1960s, the decline was minimal. Again, during World War II, heavy industry in both Great Britain and the United States expanded rapidly, drawing older workers back into employment. In the United States, there was a 30 percent increase in the number of men aged sixty-five and above in the labor force between 1940 and 1945; and the postwar economic boom (partly stimulated by the Korean War) meant that between 1940 and 1950 their economic activity rates remained virtually unchanged (at just over 41 percent).

There are strengths and weaknesses in both models. "Supply-side" explanations have become more popular with the reemergence of free-market economics since the 1980s, and have some pertinence when applied to middle-class retirees on generous occupational pension plans. However, they rather presuppose a world of perfect rationality, in which citizens can make "intertemporal life cycle choices" in their own interests and can operationalize their "tastes and preferences." Such complex econometric modeling of human behavior is less convincing when applied to the majority, whose contract of employment is usually terminated by their employer, and who suffer a marked income and consumption shortfall on retirement. The "pension as incentive" argument is historically unconvincing: in the United States, the first federal social security pension payments were made in 1940—by which time 58 percent of the total decline in the economic activity rates of men aged sixty-five and above between 1880 and 1990 had already taken place. In Great Britain, the fall in the economic activity rates of older men commenced nearly three decades before the 1908 Old Age Pensions Act; changes in the value of the basic state pension do not correlate with the rate at which retirement spread; the economic activity rates of women aged sixty to sixty-four increased in the two decades after the women's pensionable age was lowered to sixty in 1940, from 14.1 percent in 1951 to 28.8 percent in 1971; and by the turn of the twenty-first century, two-thirds of British men have given up work by the age of sixty-four, a year before they receive the state pension. "Demand-side" explanations can appear too economically deterministic and unable to capture the complex mix of causal factors, but they do fit with the view of contemporaries that "worn-out" older workers were being displaced—against their will—in increasing numbers.

A plausible combination of "supply" and "demand" explanations would hold that structural economic factors triggered off modern mass retirement, but at a later stage the withdrawal from work around the age of sixty-five became embedded in popular expectations, thereby accelerating the process. Thus, in all advanced industrial economies, trades unionists, labor organizations, and pensioners' pressure groups campaigned for improved state pensions as a recognition of the economic plight of older workers displaced from the labor market.

However, measuring the complex mix of human agency and contextual economic factors behind the "retirement decision" is methodologically very difficult. For example, ill health has long been used as a socially acceptable justification for de facto unemployment in late middle age and old age. The rise in disability benefit claims in many advanced industrial societies over the past thirty years cannot necessarily be taken as evidence of declining health status among older workers, but has also been caused by the structural changes in those economies that have displaced older workers. In response, governments have liberalized the conditions for receipt of such benefits. "Early-exit incentives," encouraging early retirement, are often designed to get rid of unwanted older workers who cost more to employ than their productivity justifies. Again, employees may be required, as part of their contract of severance and as a condition of their receiving enhanced benefits, to define their retirement as "voluntary" where it was in fact impelled by an employer's desire to achieve workforce downsizing. Such was the case in the United States in the 1980s.

Pensions. In the nineteenth century, a few occupation pension schemes existed (such as that for civil servants in Great Britain). By the late nineteenth century, state pension schemes had come onto the political agenda in several industrialized societies. Three of the earliest state pension schemes were those introduced in Germany in 1889, Denmark in 1891, and New Zealand in 1898. In late-nineteenth-century Great Britain, the commencement of modern retirement engendered public concern over the plight of the impoverished "worn-out" older worker; employers increasingly viewed mandatory retirement as economically and managerially desirable; and removing the aged from the Poor Law by a system of state pensions was seen as a way of facilitating its reform. The first Old Age Pensions Act was passed in 1908, providing five shillings (twenty-five pence) per week to all citizens aged seventy and above, subject to a means test and other conditions. This scheme was tax funded and noncontributory, and particularly benefited women (who made up nearly two-thirds of these first pensioners). Further significant legislation followed in 1925, when the age of eligibility was lowered to sixty-five and a partial shift to contributory funding was put into effect. The 1946 National Insurance Act made the state pension universal and contributory; and in 1975, the State Earnings Related Pension Scheme was introduced (and subsequently cut back). In the United States, a movement for federal old-age pensions existed in the first three decades of the twentieth century but made little headway until the economic depression of the 1930s. By 1932, seventeen U.S. states had old-age pension laws, but benefits were meager and coverage poor. Federal pensions were finally introduced by the 1935 Social Security Act, as part of the New Deal, and first payments were made in 1940. Old-age assistance was also made available from 1936. Subsequent amendments—particularly those introduced in 1950 and in the early 1970s—improved coverage and value.

The large proportion of public expenditure absorbed by state pensions in all advanced industrial societies has given rise to periodic concerns over the fiscal costs of an aging population. In Great Britain, the population aged sixty-five and above has risen from 1.5 million in 1901 (5 percent of the total population) to 9.3 million today (16 percent). Projections suggest that this proportion may increase by one-third, once the entire "baby boom" generation has moved into retirement, to 21 percent in 2041. But this assumes a continued low birth rate and little immigration. A previous wave of concern over the "graying" of the British population (in the late 1930s) turned out to be a false alarm, due to a rise in the birth rate. Much of the concern focuses upon the likely worsening of the "dependency ratio" of pensioners to workers, but there are alternative interpretations: for example, the ratio will improve if more women enter work and expand the labor force. Nevertheless, concerns over aging populations in the future have led governments in nearly all advanced industrial societies to reform their pension schemes.

A frequently debated question is whether state pensions have discouraged families from taking care of their older relatives. The extent of such family support in the past is difficult to measure, but some contemporary investigations in Great Britain (for example, by Charles Booth) showed that in the nineteenth century, younger relatives found it financially very difficult to support their aged parents. Support by family, neighbors, and almshouses was considerable in the United States before federal Social Security. Pensioners are more likely to live alone now than in the past—for example, in Great Britain, 7 percent of people aged sixty-five and above lived alone in 1950, and now it is 35 percent—but this may be part of a general trend in all industrialized societies toward more independent living, manifested in the growth of single-person households.

The New "Retirement Agenda." The profound economic transitions that have affected Western economies since the early 1970s have had a major impact on retirement. Many postwar commentators thought that retirement at age sixty-five had become a social norm that would remain unchanged. Yet from the early 1970s, male "early" retirement has inexorably spread down the age structure. Thus in Great Britain, the economic activity rates of men aged fifty-five to fifty-nine remained fairly constant between 1951 and 1971 (actually increasing slightly, from 95.0 percent to 95.3 percent); by 1994, however, only 76.1 percent were economically active. For men aged sixty to sixty-four, the respective rates were 87.7 percent (1951), 86.6 percent (1971), and 51.2 percent (1994). By late 1998, almost one-third of British men aged fifty to sixty-four had no paid work, and most of these had given up looking for a job. Economic activity tails off with rising age after the age of fifty: by the age of sixty, only 58 percent of British men are employed. The gender differences in changing labor market demand are striking. Older British women aged fifty-five to fifty-nine have experienced increasing eco-

nomic activity rates since World War II, consequent upon the growth of feminized jobs: for those aged fifty-five to fifty-nine, these have risen from 29.1 percent in 1951 to 50.9 percent in 1971 and 55.7 percent in 1994. Likewise, in the United States the economic activity rates of men aged fifty-five to sixty-four fell from 83.0 percent in 1970 to 67.8 percent in 1990; yet for women aged fifty-five to sixty-four, there was a rise over the same period, from 43.0 percent to 45.2 percent. Workless men in late middle age can now experience a long period between the end of their formal employment and the commencement of "pensioner" status at age sixty-five; this creates considerable problems of self-identity in a culture in which work still confers social status.

In the last ten years, there has been much discussion in industrialized societies about the sustainability of continued male early retirement, particularly when placed against a background of concerns over social security and health-care costs, a future aging population, and persistent skills shortages in the labor market. There has been increasing questioning of whether modern economies can afford to get rid of highly skilled employees solely on the basis of age. The use of such crude "age proxies" is seen as a waste of human capital. In Great Britain, this has led to a renewed interest in the labor market problems of older workers, with consideration of solutions such as retraining, lifelong learning, "welfare-to-work" programs for those aged fifty and above, and policies to combat age discrimination in employment. For example, after much deliberation and consultation, the British Government published a *Code of Practice: Age Diversity in Employment* in 1999, with the goal of encouraging employers to achieve a more "age-diverse" workforce and purge themselves of those "agist stereotypes" that automatically equate old age with industrial obsolescence. However, it is extremely doubtful that age discrimination *per se* has been a major factor. The more likely cause is the decline of stable, "job-for-life" industrial employment (in which older workers have been concentrated), and its replacement by more service-based, insecure, and part-time employment (recruiting younger workers and more women). Significantly, the United States has had an Age Discrimination in Employment Act since 1967; this has been steadily extended in coverage to the extent that mandatory retirement is now virtually abolished in all but a small number of occupations. While this legislation has given older American workers much valuable protection in the workplace, it has been unable to prevent the downsizings and plant closures that have diminished job opportunities for older men in the last twenty years. For example, of one million American workers aged fifty-five and above who were displaced from the labor force in 1995–1997, only 56 percent had been reemployed by February 1998. Postindustrial labor markets are becoming patterned in an increasingly complex way, with pronounced mismatches of skill, region, gender, and age. Redundant steelworkers aged in their late fifties are not being rehired in new computer-based industries. For older workers to be reemployed, a restimulation of manufacturing would be required, and this is unlikely to take place.

The sociology of old age has also been profoundly affected by the spread of early retirement. In the last ten years, postmodern theories of aging have suggested that the life-course is becoming increasingly blurred with the removal of the familiar markers of aging (including "age-sixty-five" retirement). If health status improves, "active middle age" may henceforth extend for some forty years—from the fourth decade of life to the eighth—and this will profoundly reshape social identities. Others have pointed to the emergence of new contradictions in attitudes to old age—between, on the one hand, the optimistic, "use-it-or-lose-it" approach, which argues that good health, happiness, and ability to work can be sustained well past the age of sixty-five, and, on the other, the more pessimistic view of a growing mass of workless citizens at the top end of the age structure, imposing an enormous fiscal burden on younger cohorts. A vitally important question facing all advanced industrial societies is whether the trend to earlier retirement can be reversed, and in answering this question a proper understanding of the long-run history of retirement is crucial.

[*See also* Income Maintenance, *subentry on* Social Insurance.]

BIBLIOGRAPHY

Aaron, Henry J., and Gary Burtless, eds. *Retirement and Economic Behavior.* Washington, D.C., 1984.

Burtless, Gary, ed. *Work, Health and Income Among the Elderly.* Washington, D.C., 1987.

Costa, Dora L. *The Evolution of Retirement: An American Economic History, 1880–1990.* Chicago, 1998.

Disney, Richard, Emily Grundy, and Paul Johnson, eds. *The Dynamics of Retirement: Analyses of the Retirement Surveys.* London, 1997.

Graebner, William. *A History of Retirement: The Meaning and Function of an American Institution, 1885–1978.* New Haven, 1980.

Haber, Carole, and Brian Gratton. *Old Age and the Search for Security: An American Social History.* Bloomington, Ind., 1994.

Hannah, Leslie. *Inventing Retirement: The Development of Occupational Pensions in Britain.* Cambridge, 1986.

Hushbeck, Judith C. *Old and Obsolete: Age Discrimination and the American Worker, 1860–1920.* New York, 1989.

Kohli, Martin., et al., eds. *Time for Retirement: Comparative Studies of Early Exit from the Labour Force.* Cambridge, 1991.

Laczko, Frank, and Chris Phillipson. *Changing Work and Retirement: Social Policy and the Older Worker.* Philadelphia, 1991.

Lazear, Edward P. "Why Is There Mandatory Retirement?" *Journal of Political Economy* 87.6 (1979), 1261–1284.

Macnicol, John. *The Politics of Retirement in Britain, 1878–1948.* Cambridge, 1998.

Phillipson, Chris. *Reconstructing Old Age: New Agendas in Social Theory and Practice.* London, 1998.

Thane, Pat. *Old Age in English History: Past Experiences, Present Issues.* Oxford, 2000.

JOHN MACNICOL

RHINE. Among the great rivers of Europe, the Rhine (Rhein, Rhin, Rijn) occupies a special position. Besides the pleasantness of its medieval heritage, symbolized best by the string of castles overlooking the river on the stretch between Mainz and Coblenz, the Rhine owes its special place to the fact that, over the centuries, it was a contested border between France and Germany. The Rhine's significance as one of the main central European transportation arteries seems of lesser importance at first glance. This, however, is a myopic view at best, for even today the Rhine ranks as one of Europe's busiest inland waterways.

Geography. From its source in the Swiss Alps to its North Sea mouths, the Rhine covers a length of about 1,000 kilometers (620 miles). Becoming a more noticeable body of water only after having left Lake Constance, through which it flows, the Rhine's navigability sets in some 30 kilometers (19 miles) east of Basel. Thereafter, it flows for nearly 700 kilometers (434 miles)—initially by means of a side canal—through France and Germany, passing such major cities as Mannheim, Mainz, Cologne, Düsseldorf, and Duisburg, Europe's busiest inland port. At Duisburg, the Rhine-Herne Canal opens a gateway to the northwestern German canal system and connects the Rhine with major German seaports such as Emden, Bremen, and Hamburg. Shortly after having crossed the Dutch border, the Rhine splits into three navigable branches (Waal, Neder-Rijn, and IJssel), which extend the main river to the major Dutch ports. On its way to the North Sea, the Rhine takes in a number of navigable tributaries, most importantly Neckar, Main, Moselle, and Ruhr. With the opening of the new Main-Danube Canal in 1992, a waterway link exists between northwestern and southeastern Europe.

Navigation. The Rhine has been used for navigation since Roman times. In preindustrial days, vessels were small, rarely extending more than 100 tons of loading capacity. Traffic was hampered by numerous tolls and other charges. In addition, Cologne, Mainz, and Dordrecht possessed staple rights, which meant that goods had to be unloaded there and offered for sale at local markets for a number of days. Next to boats, which had to be pulled upstream by horse or manpower, the rafting of timber to Dutch ports was an important business. Liberalization of traffic began in the wake of the Congress of Vienna in 1815, which proclaimed the internationalization of the major European rivers. Subsequently, an international commission set policy on behalf of the sovereign states through which the Rhine flows.

Although free trade soon became a victim of political nationalism and renewed economic restrictions, Rhine shipping continued to prosper as a result of technical inventions and river improvements. The introduction of steamboats and the towing of barges greatly aided upstream traffic. In 1827, the first Rhenish steamboat company was formed in Cologne, followed in 1838 by a rival firm based in Düsseldorf. The two companies later merged and still exist today under the KD label. The Rhine's quality as a waterway became enhanced by dredging and other constructional improvements. The maximum loading capacity of the largest barges at normal water levels increased from 600 tons in 1850, to 1,400 tons in 1890, and subsequently to 3,500 tons in 1914 on the Rhine's main stretch between the Dutch border and Mannheim. This meant that even smaller oceangoing vessels could reach Rhenish ports.

Economic Performance. As a result of these infrastructural improvements, the volume of traffic on the German stretch of the Rhine increased as well: from an estimated 100 million ton-kilometers (tkm) in 1835, to 2 billion tkm in 1885, to nearly 11 billion tkm in 1913. Most of that increase came as a result of an explosion in bulk-goods traffic of coal, iron ore, and chemical materials in the wake of Germany's "Second Industrial Revolution" of the 1890s. By the early twenty-first century, nearly 40 billion tkm were moved on the Rhine between Basel and the German-Dutch border, attesting to the vitality and continued importance of the Rhine as a European waterway.

BIBLIOGRAPHY
Febvre, Lucien. *Le Rhin: Histoire, mythes et réalités*. Paris, 1997.
Kunz, Andreas, and John Armstrong, eds. *Inland Navigation and Economic Development in Nineteenth-Century Europe*. Mainz, 1995.
Mellor, Roy E. H. *The Rhine: A Study in the Geography of Water Transport*. Aberdeen, 1983.

ANDREAS KUNZ

RHODES, CECIL JOHN (1853–1902), British entrepreneur, minerals mogul, imperialist, and political leader in southern Africa.

Rhodes became one of the wealthiest self-made entrepreneurs in the English-speaking world during the 1880s and 1890s. In 1889, at age thirty-five, he controlled about 90 percent of the world's diamond supply and a large percentage of the Witwatersrand gold mines. Rhodes, only a major figure in the financial and political calculations of Cape Colony, then was catapulted into a position of unquestioned world power and significance. His rise to riches and prominence was rapid and vigorous. Arriving in Africa at age seventeen, from his father's vicarage in Bishop's Stortford, England, to farm cotton, he soon trekked to the newly opened (1870) diamond fields at Kimberley. There he worked small claims (the holes or mines had

been divided up into small plots, termed claims), teamed up with older men to make and sell ice and ice cream to the miners, and shrewdly amassed a small but not staggering financial stake by the time he was twenty-three. Within a few more years, he was a leading diamond digger, owning many claims, but a dozen or so other men in Kimberley were wealthier.

In 1881, Rhodes's charisma carried him into Cape Colony's Parliament. By 1883, he was active in acquiring territory to the north for Cape Colony, and in creating what is now Botswana. In 1886, he joined the rush of miners and capitalists to what is now the Gauteng Province of South Africa, then the Transvaal Republic, where seams of gold had been discovered; no one yet knew the extent of the gold vein or what the prospects were for it. Rhodes and his partners purchased assiduously and, in addition to their large stake in diamonds, soon cornered a large proportion of the better deposits.

In 1888 and 1889, having barely dealt with his new gold properties, and while continuing to play a very large role in the politics of Cape Colony, Rhodes outwitted some other men of fortune and put the Kimberley diamond mines under his unquestioned control.

During the 1890s, Rhodes manipulated the supplies of diamonds, and the share prices of his several mining companies, to maximize the earning potential of his several companies. He became prime minister of Cape Colony and led it for five years. At the same time, he gained an imperial charter for the British South Africa Company, his vehicle for the invasion of the African-ruled lands beyond the Limpopo River. Within a few years, Rhodes ran Rhodesia (now Zimbabwe) and Northern Rhodesia (now Zambia), influenced the destinies of Nyasaland (now Malawi) and Bechuanaland (now Botswana), interfered in Mozambique, raided the Transvaal, and prepared the entire region for the turmoil of the Boer War (1899–1902).

Alongside his entrepreneurial, imperial, and political adventures, Rhodes introduced modern citrus crops and agricultural methods to Cape Colony, fostered modern methods of sheep rearing and disease prevention, sponsored the country's first universities, and backed the inventors and engineers who improved techniques for extracting the gold from the geolithic conglomerates in which it was bound. He also sponsored the construction and extension of railroads and electric telegraph lines to the peripheries of South Africa and throughout southern Africa.

Rhodes never married. He died young, of aortic and heart problems. He left bequests that supported schools, universities, and other institutions of learning and culture in southern Africa. Yet the legacy for which he is best known is the Rhodes Scholarship competition, which sends students from all over the former colonial English-speaking world to the University of Oxford, where he took

CECIL JOHN RHODES. Portrait from *Africa in the Nineteenth Century*, by Edgar Sanderson, London, 1898, p. 248. (Russell and Sons/ Prints and Photographs Division, Library of Congress)

a very undistinguished degree in 1881, after eight years of intermittent study, interspersed between bursts of entrepreneurial hustling in Cape Colony.

BIBLIOGRAPHY

Rotberg, Robert I. *The Founder: Cecil Rhodes and the Pursuit of Power*. New York, 1988. Contains the full account of Rhodes's various activities, with extensive discussion of his political motives and accomplishments. Several chapters focus on his contributions to the economic development and history of diamond and gold mining, of railroad building, and of southern Africa as whole; one shows how Rhodes gained control of the diamond properties.

ROBERT I. ROTBERG

RICARDO, DAVID (1772–1823), English economist.

Ricardo set the theoretical paradigm for classical political economy. After his early days in business, and during his early thirties, he developed a keen interest in economic theory. In 1817, he published *Principles of Political Economy and Taxation*.

Because of his early life in business, during an era now regarded as the onset of a full-fledged Industrial Revolution in Great Britain, Ricardo gained a deep knowledge of how the political economy works. As his chief goal, he sought to derive laws that governed distribution of the national income among the various classes: landowners, workers, and capitalists. In his book, the chapters on value discuss a firm's behavior in terms of the labor theory of value, as derived from or influenced by Adam Smith. Ricardo's laws were later transformed by Karl Marx into the formulas of price accounting. It was observed that when rates of profit are equalized for all products, a rise in the real wage rate creates a fall in the rate of profit. The result is a declining curve called the wage-profit frontier.

The derivation of this frontier assumes that land is homogeneous and plentiful, so that rent is free. When and where land differs in quality, as Ricardo actually assumes, the surplus that remains after wage payments is handed over to the landowners as rent. To discuss this rent theory, Ricardo developed a theory of differential rent; the idea of marginalism thus began with him.

Ricardo made these assumptions: that capitalists do not consume, that workers do not save, but that landowners do consume, while saving rent from their income. The total savings in the economy equals total profits plus savings from rents. On the other hand, he accepted Say's law, which implies, as Keynes later observed, the full employment of labor and capital. The wage fund per worker, in terms of the cost of necessities, provides the real wage rate. Given such wages, full employment ultimately results. Under such circumstances, the rate of profit on the wage-profit frontier is extended in order to admit rent payments; and market prices and rents therefore follow accordingly.

In his chapter on machinery, which was added to the third edition of the *Principles*, Ricardo insisted, however, that a substitution of machines for labor would create unemployment, even though such a proposition contradicts Say's law, which he still adhered to in this chapter. Ricardo's views greatly influenced Walras, especially in his law of income distribution. Thus, in a progressive economy wages per worker tend to decline, rent will rise appreciably, and the rate of profit will fall substantially.

In Ricardo's view, there are two mainstays of the modern economy: free competition and democracy. On the basis of the principle of comparative cost, he advocated free international trade; but in his lifetime democratic systems were still evolving, so that a government's decisions on economic policies were made on such metaphysical bases as Jeremy Bentham's utilitarianism. Ricardo's own contributions to public financial economics were rather thin; discussions on taxes in *Principles* were no more than "applications of the theoretical principles," as Marx stated.

DAVID RICARDO. Portrait by J. R. McCulloch from the frontispiece to *The Works of David Ricardo* (London, 1888). (Prints and Photographs Division, Library of Congress)

Repeal of the Corn Law, which Ricardo ardently advocated, was finally realized after his death. Then agriculture began to decline, though not for another quarter century; and consequently, as he expected, new industries emerged. Thus the success of Ricardian economics led to significant structural changes within the economy. The paradigm of economics changed, after him, to the marginalists.

BIBLIOGRAPHY

Hollander, Samuel. *The Economics of David Ricardo*. London, c. 1979.
Morishima, Michio. *Ricardo's Economics*, Cambridge, 1989.
Ricardo, David. *The Works and Correspondence of David Ricardo*, edited by Piero Sraffa. 11 vols. Cambridge, 1951–1955.

MICHIO MORISHIMA

RICE FARMING. Rice feeds half the world's population. It is the staple food of Asia and is also important in South America. There are two cultivated rices, *Oryza sativa* of Asia and *Oryza glaberrima* of West Africa, but *O. sativa* dominates commerce. It has differentiated into three subspecies. *Indicas* originated in the Asian tropics and subtropics, *japonicas* in the subtropical and temperate zones, and *javanicas* in the equatorial climate of Indonesia. *Indicas* and *japonicas* are the most important. They are also divided into "dry," rain-fed upland and lowland rices, and "wet," irrigated and "floating" deep-water rices. Some can grow in water up to 5 meters (5½ yards) deep, rapidly growing longer as flood waters rise.

The earliest remains of cultivated long-grain *indica* rices were found in northern India, and in eastern China dating back seven thousand years. The oldest round-grain *japonica* rices found in China are dated to about fifty-three hundred years ago. But rice in its cultivated form came late to many parts of Asia, particularly Japan, the Malay Peninsula, and Java. Rice seems to have come to Japan twenty-four hundred to twenty-three hundred years ago from the Yangzi region and was cultivated in the southern island of Kyushu. Rice became the leading crop in the Malay Peninsula about twelve hundred years ago, and irrigated rice reached Java only eight hundred years ago. Rice was not the staple food in Korea until the 1930s. Before rice, diet was based on millets, sorghums, barley, and tubers like the yam and cocoyam. Rice was regarded as a luxury, a superior grain among an array of inferiors. When rice came to an area, it soon replaced the previous staples. It remained dominant even after the introduction of American crops, such as maize, cassava, and sweet potatoes. When it came to South America, rice began to replace these crops even there. *Indicas* were carried from India to the Middle East, North Africa, and even Europe three thousand years ago, and they were taken to East Africa and Madagascar. *Javanicas* also came to Madagascar from Indonesia. The United States received rice from Madagascar in 1685. South America obtained rice from Europe, and so did West Africa, although the indigenous rice *O. glaberrima* is thought to have originated in the Niger delta and spread along the swampy areas of the African coast.

Rice is a member of the grass family, like barley and wheat, and it, too, is an annual. But it is a semiaquatic or swamp crop and gives its best yield with approximately 6 millimeters (¼ inch) of water a day. If water supplies fall below this level, yields are quickly reduced. So irrigation is the best system of growing rice and makes it possible to grow rice continuously on the same land. More than 75 percent of the world's rice is "wet rice" from irrigated fields, most of which are in Asia. Nearly another 20 percent of world rice production comes from lowland areas, where rice is only watered by rainfall. The remaining 5 percent comes partly from rain-fed hill areas and partly from swampy, flooded areas. To provide irrigation, terracing has been built in Java, Sri Lanka, Japan, and northern Luzon in the Philippines, but because rice arrived there comparatively recently, it is thought the terraces were originally built for other crops.

The colonial powers in Asia established agricultural research stations during the nineteenth century, and from 1870 Japan, too, established research stations as part of its thrust for modernization and development. This work continued in the 1920s and 1930s. Building on it, the Ford and Rockefeller Foundations with the Philippine government established the International Rice Research Institute at Los Baños, Laguna, in 1960. Its aim was to preserve existing rice varieties and provide genetic material from which new high-yielding varieties could be raised. This program has been successful and contributed to the "Green Revolution." It created new semidwarf varieties of *indicas*, which matured more quickly, enabling farmers to grow two and three crops a year on the same land. The first of these was IR 8, released in 1966, and by 1994 IR 72 had been released. These new varieties needed better provision of water, fertilizer, and pesticides to grow well, involving additional costs. They increased production in areas where irrigation could be provided, but less was done to improve productivity in the dry rice areas or the great delta areas of Asia, rice's natural home. Even now many Asian farmers produce a yield of only 2 tons per hectare, a small increase over historical levels. Although the latest varieties can produce yields up to 20 tons, this is possible only under perfect conditions, which rarely apply.

The first rice farmers grew their rice in swamps. Subsequently, rice has traditionally been grown in tropical rainfall areas or close to rivers that seasonally overflow their banks. In the monsoon area, the crop cycle starts with the rains. When the soil is muddy enough, the field is turned over. Bullocks are often loosed into the field to churn it up with their hooves. Simple bullock-drawn plows and harrows have been used since ancient times. Where there is no grazing for bullocks, the farmers turn the soil with heavy hoes. These days, small mechanical tillers and tractors are common.

Depending on variety, it takes four to eight weeks for a seedling to grow to about 20 centimeters (8 inches) when it can be transplanted. The advantage of growing the seedlings in a nursery means the main field is available for other crops during these weeks. Transplanting encourages the root system to spread and stimulates extra shoots, which will make more ears of grain. Transplanting is by hand, using the span of the hand as a spacer, a backbreaking task. But regular spacing is ensured, which cannot be said when scattering the seed broadcast. The young plants

RICE FARMING. Scenes of African Americans working in rice fields, Ogeechee River, near Savannah, Georgia, 1867. Illustration by Alfred R. Waud (1828–1891), *Harper's Weekly*, 5 January 1867, p. 8. (Prints and Photographs Division, Library of Congress)

are grown in the flooded field, and if possible the water level is adjusted to the height of the plants. Often the fields are flooded and drained several times for weeding and spreading fertilizer. Lastly, the field is dried for reaping. Then the grain is threshed, dried, and stored.

These traditional methods may be compared with the most up-to-date methods used in the United States, Australia, and Suriname. There the land is plowed and harrowed by tractor, and the seed is sown broadcast by mechanical seeders, which scatter up to 15 meters (about 16 yards). In large fields, seed is sown by aircraft, which covers more than 150 hectares (375 acres) per day. The seed is soaked first to help germination, and fertilizer is mixed with it so that seed and fertilizer are spread together. Airborne techniques were pioneered in the 1920s and 1930s. As the seedlings grow, the land is kept underwater. As harvest draws near, the fields are drained to allow combined harvesters to operate. For small Asian farms, mechanization is a mixed blessing. Most operations of paddy (rice in the husk) production and threshing and drying can be done by hand, and when there is family labor, it is the best approach. Machines save labor, but they do not increase yield per hectare. They are expensive and need servicing, spare parts, and fuel. Even so, small tractors and rotovators are increasingly in use. By overcoming labor shortages, they have encouraged the development of multicropping.

Paddy is milled to remove the husk before it is traded. (An exception is the U.S. trade to South America, where the millers there prefer rough rice, which they can mill to their own requirements.) Long and medium grain dominate international trade, with short grain significant only for Japan, South Korea, Taiwan, and China north of the Yangzi. The rice is graded according to its quality after milling, a crucial feature being the percentage of broken grains. The highest grades are 100 percent unbroken, the quality falling as the percentage of broken grains rises. Husking was originally done by hand using a wooden mortar and pestle, and such methods are still used locally. But rice for the international market must be polished and white, and is processed and bagged at modern mills. Even today, rice is normally traded in 50-kilogram (110-pound) polypropylene bags.

Rice moves to areas where incomes are rising. In 1869, the Suez Canal opened Asia to international investment in plantations and mines, creating work for Indian migrants in Sri Lanka and Malaysia. Chinese laborers went to Malaysia and also Indonesia. As these migrants prospered, much of their increased income was spent on their preferred luxury, rice. The Philippines also began to import rice, and so did China as farmers turned to cash crops. Myanmar, Thailand, and Vietnam saw a vast expansion in commercial rice farming, and Rangoon, Bangkok, and Saigon became great milling centers and exporters. The

steam-driven rice mills there were an early feature of Asian industrialization. Rice also went to Europe, resulting in an international grain market—the rice world linking with the wheat world in India, a producer and exporter of both grains. Globalization of grain prices was a crucial development of the late nineteenth century. American farmers were affected by the monsoon, benefiting from better prices when the monsoon failed. But globalization bore consequences in 1929, when gluts in both grains brought prices down and bankrupted farmers all over the world. This was a major feature of the Depression. Since 1945, the great international rice exporters have been Thailand and the United States, and Vietnam has recently returned to the world market.

BIBLIOGRAPHY

Barker, Randolph, Robert W. Herdt, and Beth Rose. *The Rice Economy of Asia*. Washington, D. C., 1985. Good on developments in rice production since 1945.

Bray, Francesca. *The Rice Economies: Technology and Development in Asian Societies*. Oxford, 1986. Well-presented account of historical developments.

Dethloff, Henry C. *A History of the American Rice Industry, 1685–1985*. College Station, Texas, 1988.

Grist, D. H. *Rice*. 6th ed. London, 1986. The most important study of rice, a compendium covering all aspects of production.

Huke, Robert E., and Eleanor H. Huke. *Rice: Then and Now*. Manila, 1990. Brief but informative.

International Rice Research Institute, Manila. <http://www.riceweb.org> The world's leading rice research institution; contains information on all aspects of rice production, and includes a useful but short historical section.

Latham, A. J. H. *Rice: The Primary Commodity*. London, 1998. A general study with particular attention to trade and commerce.

Latham, A. J. H., and Larry Neal. "The International Market in Rice and Wheat, 1868–1914." *Economic History Review* 36.2 (1983), 260–280.

Swaminathan, M. S. "Rice." *Scientific American* 250.1 (1984), 62–71.

Wickizer, V. D., and M. K. Bennett. *The Rice Economy of Monsoon Asia*. Stanford, Calif., 1941. The classic study of the interwar years. Invaluable even today.

A. J. H. LATHAM

ROAD TRANSPORTATION *[This entry contains three subentries, a historical overview and discussions of technological change and regulation.]*

Historical Overview

Any level of economic activity beyond that of complete self-sufficiency requires the transport of goods between producer and consumer. And some or all of this movement of goods almost always takes place by road. Information also often moves by road. This was especially true before the telephone and the telegraph, but even today face-to-face contact is generally essential for the consummation of business deals and the transfer of technology. The quality and quantity of roads in a region can thus have a major impact on the frequency of exchange of goods and information, the decisions of producers and consumers, technological and organizational innovation, and thus economic growth.

Roads, in the sense of beaten paths, have existed for countless millennia. Aboriginal peoples often removed obstacles from these paths and added rocks or logs to facilitate fording waterways. Though early pathways tended to be on high ground, paths were often worn meters deep over centuries of use. When humans turned toward road construction, they often followed these earlier paths. Many modern roads still do, though the demands of pack animals, wagons, and automobiles and trucks in turn encouraged modifications in route.

The earliest attempts to surface roads with bricks, stones, or other materials date from at least six thousand years ago. All of the earliest civilizations made some attempt at road construction. Roads also connected civilizations, such as the Silk Road between Europe and China (from c. 300 BCE), though these tended to be but beaten paths for much of their extent.

In many cases, early civilizations achieved networks that later deteriorated and only were surpassed in the early modern period. In Europe, the Roman road system is justly famous for achieving a quality and extent not regained for a millennium. In China, the earliest large-scale network in the world was created before the Chou dynasty of 1100 BCE, and the Chou designated five types of roads passable in turn by pack animals, narrow vehicles, and one, two, or three larger vehicles. Later periods saw the deterioration of this road network; an old Chinese saying speaks of roads being good for seven years and then bad for four thousand. The Indus civilization (c. 3000 BCE) used bitumen to bind road bricks together millennia before this substance was used elsewhere. The Maurya Empire of the fourth century BCE built an extensive road network. The Persians (sixth century BCE) built a road network that included a twenty-six-hundred-kilometer road from Susa to Sardis in Asia Minor. In the fifteenth century CE, the Incas built a system of roads, including two north-south roads thirty-six-hundred kilometers in length that included tunnels and vine-based suspension bridges. The Spanish used this system to conquer the Inca Empire speedily.

It is important, when discussing the roads of both ancient and early modern states, to distinguish between roads that served a primarily administrative purpose and those that were well suited to commercial traffic. Roads designed for messengers on foot or horseback might be impassable for heavily burdened pack animals and especially wheeled vehicles. While some Roman roads certainly facilitated commercial traffic, others, because of uneven paving and a reliance on fords rather than bridges, were of limited commercial utility. Chinese roads tended to be less straight and less flat than Roman roads. The Persians established a government postal relay system along their roads, which apparently served both private and governmental purposes. The Susa to Sardis road was generally level but often only a beaten path. The Incas restricted the use of their roads to government messengers.

Britain developed a national system of all-weather turnpike roads in the eighteenth century. On the eve of the Industrial Revolution, it possessed a far better national road network than any other country in the world. France and China, among others, built a few impressive roadways (and failed to maintain these), but their networks were limited. Many countries improved their road networks in the nineteenth century, though the advent of the railway shifted attention away (relatively) from roads. The development of the bicycle and especially the automobile and the truck encouraged another wave of road construction that affected every corner of the world.

Road construction almost everywhere in the world is plagued by the simple fact that natural materials that are easily formed into a smooth surface tend not to be durable (especially when wet) and vice versa. Road construction and maintenance thus has proven an expensive and administratively demanding proposition and has invited experimentation with a diversity of materials and techniques. Special note should be taken of the need for regular maintenance. Many governments have built roads but failed to maintain them.

As roads were improved, the users responded by developing power sources and vehicles suited to the new conditions, which often encouraged further road improvements in turn. Animals were bred for hauling. Horses, which are superior to other animals for road transport in most regions, replaced oxen and other draught animals as haulage opportunities increased. Carriages and wagons that could move faster over smoother surfaces were developed. Even the modern automobile was developed in an environment where ashphalt roads had already been created, though their extent was minimal.

The Economics of Road Transport. Before the advent of the railway, goods with a low value relative to weight, such as coal or grain, generally were moved by water, for the cost per ton-mile by water was usually a fraction of that by road. Rates for road transport were three to four times those of water transport on comparable routes in eighteenth-century England. British goods incurred as great an expense moving thirty miles inland by road as being shipped across the Atlantic to the American colonies. Yet where water transport was unavailable, even bulky goods often moved short distances by road. Even if water transport was available, the higher cost of loading and unloading boats could tip the balance toward road transport over short distances.

TRAVEL ON FOOT. *Morning Fuji,* by Ando Hiroshige (1797–1858), Tokaido series, no. 14, 1833–1834. Two women travelers and a porter carrying their boxes, Hara Station, Japan. (John Cotton Dana Collection/The Newark Museum, Newark, New Jersey/Art Resource, NY)

Passengers and goods with a higher value to bulk ratio, including most finished goods, were generally moved by road transport, which was both faster and more reliable. Highwaymen were usually, but not always, less of a threat than pirates, not to mention wartime press-gangs (road transport often became cheaper than water transport in times of war). Ships at sea were subject to the vagaries of the wind, those on rivers or canals to frost, drought, and flood. Wagons could be stuck in the mud on bad roads but rarely were delayed for long on well-constructed roads. For some goods, like wool, fear of water damage also encouraged the use of road transport. Another advantage of road transport flowed from the small size of wagons relative to boats. It was often easier and less expensive to move small consignments by road, and road transport services tended to be more frequent. Finally, road transport was more flexible. A given road could generally sustain an increase in traffic better than a canal or a port, and draft animals and wagons could be pulled from agricultural uses in the face of a surge in demand.

The railway made inroads into the traditional markets for both road and water transport. It moved bulky goods as easily as water and competed with roads in terms of speed and reliability. But railways could not go everywhere, thus roads retained an important role in moving goods and people door to door. With the advent of the automobile and truck, roads won back from railways a considerable share

of goods and people movement. They are today, as for most of the past, the conduit for the majority of goods traffic by value throughout the world.

The quality of roads largely determined the cost, speed, reliability, and frequency of road transport. Of particular importance here is the type of traffic a road could support. Primitive beaten paths were generally suitable only for people on foot. The use of pack animals required greater care in removing obstacles and limiting grades. Where the use of pack animals was common, special road surfaces were often constructed. Horses can pull some six to eight times as much in a wagon as they can carry on their backs, and similar ratios hold for other draft animals. Thus a huge potential payoff existed for the construction of roads that could support wagon traffic. But this payoff was not easily achieved, for wagons require a smooth road surface and bridges across waterways. Bicycles and automobiles in turn required yet smoother surfaces than wagons, at least if they were to run at high speed.

Indeed, the automobile changed the economics of road transport in many ways. It created a massive demand for more and better roads (and then for such novelties as motels, amusement parks, and drive-in restaurants, which further increased road usage). Governments throughout the world found in gasoline taxes a relatively painless way of making users pay for road construction and maintenance. While at first the emerging technologies of asphalt and concrete road construction were applied to existing roadways, it soon became apparent that the full potential of the automobile could only be achieved with new roads.

The limited-access highway allowed cars to travel in safety at high speeds. Since such highways were exhorbitantly expensive to build across populated areas and since high speeds required the elimination of sharp curves, these new highways often followed quite different routes from their predecessors. While the two most famous examples of such highway systems are the German autobahns of the interwar period and the interstate highway system begun in the United States in the 1950s, governments throughout the world worked toward the development of such networks once automobiles and trucks became common. Governments everywhere have come to grapple with a host of concerns that usually were considered of less import before the automobile, including pollution (though the manure left by horses had become a major urban problem on the eve of the automobile), congestion, safety, and demand forecasting.

The most obvious effect of an improvement in transport services is that noted by Adam Smith. Lowering the cost of transport expands the size of the market and facilitates through regional specialization both an expansion in the scale of establishments and the division of labor within and between establishments (recall that finished goods usually move by road). Further, if transport improvements allow entrepreneurs to ship goods to a large market without having to accompany the goods (as happened with the development of a national network of common carriers in eighteenth-century England), they will be encouraged to produce homogenous goods such as can be sold through catalogs or salespeople with samples. This in turn will encourage the adoption of both centralized workplaces and mechanization. Likewise, transport improvements can facilitate urbanization, for cities depend on the import of provisions and export of goods and services. Increased reliability of transport services reduces the inventory costs associated with organizational forms, such as the modern factory, where workers and machines lie idle in the absence of raw materials. Transport improvements encourage the use of a wider range of raw materials in production. The resulting complexity of output encourages organizational and technological innovation. Transport improvements, and particularly road improvements, make personal travel quicker, less expensive, and more comfortable, encouraging the spread of information about technology, fashion, markets, and methods of organization.

The act of road construction and maintenance is a costly endeavor. Important backward linkages can affect the producers of road materials and road equipment (the use of machines such as rollers and stone crushers has been known for millennia, though road construction only became highly mechanized in the late nineteenth century and even today is carried on with picks and shovels in many parts of the world), and "final demand" linkages

INDIAN CART. Men in a two-wheel horse cart, India, between 1890 and 1923. (Frank and Frances Carpenter Collection/Prints and Photographs Division, Library of Congress)

from the wages paid to road workers. Often a reasonable road is needed to move road materials to the construction site.

Economic historians may for a variety of reasons underappreciate the role of road improvements in encouraging economic growth. First, the very ubiquity of roads serves to deflect attention toward more dramatic developments both within and beyond the realm of transport services. Moreover, it is all too easy to ignore the dramatic differences that can and have existed in road quality and the effects these differences have on the cost, speed, and reliability of road transport. Third, it can be imagined that improvements in road quality are called forth as the level of economic activity increases; in reality a host of economic, administrative, and technological problems must first be solved.

Administration and Finance of Road Transport. Given the potential economic advantages of road improvements, the sluggish and uneven pace of road improvements in world history must reflect in large part the cost and administrative difficulties associated with road construction and maintenance (plus the oft-noted fact that economic development has not always been a primary governmental concern). A handful of distinct means have financed and organized road improvements in human history. Each has advantages and disadvantages. Various factors, such as population density, monetization of the economy, the bureaucratic capability of the government, and the level of economic activity, determined which method of organization was best. The course of institutional change is slow and unpredictable, and the best institutional form for a particular time and place need not be observed in practice. The institutional structure in place at a particular time and place largely determines the degree to which that society achieves road improvements that encourage economic development.

Central Government Finance and Control. This is the most familiar method in the modern world, and it has a long pedigree. The Roman roads were managed centrally, though attempts were made to finance roads from local taxes. Scholars suspect that the road networks of earlier civilizations were also to a large extent centrally directed and financed. The advantage of this approach is that the system can potentially be designed and implemented with the needs of the whole community in mind. Otherwise, locally administered roads may not serve the needs of long-distance travel. However, centralized states are often guilty of building with administrative rather than economic motives. Military motives can loom especially large. From the earliest empires to the interstate highway system in the postwar United States, road improvements have been motivated in large part by a desire to be able to move troops quickly to any point of attack. Roads often radiate from the capital to every corner of the state, forcing transit of goods and people through a crowded metropolis. They may provide limited access to raw materials and may serve poorly the interests of local people. Unless the government has a bureaucratic presence throughout the land, it may not maintain roads properly. Of course, such a system depends entirely on the continuing ability of the state to finance road maintenance. The Roman roads began to crumble as the empire faced difficulty in financing them.

Some mixture of centralized and local control is today common in most developed countries and is widely observed historically. The national government takes on some responsibility for a national network (sometimes in concert with lower levels of government, as with the interstate highway system), and state and local governments manage and finance roads of more localized interest. Though complex jurisdictional negotiations hardly guarantee the best balance between local and national interests, jurisdictional division of responsibilities ensures that each is reflected to some extent. Note that roads between countries require some degree of international cooperation.

Tolls. The key alternative to tax-based finance is to have road users pay for the road. This method is used today in many developed and less developed countries and has been common historically, especially for bridges. Thousands of kilometers of toll roads were built in the United States in the early postwar period. Economic theory suggests that a societal loss is associated with the fact that those people who would benefit from the road by less than the toll cost choose not to use it. Yet there are also costs associated with raising taxes. Certainly for governments that find it difficult or impossible to finance desirable road initiatives, a toll road will generally be judged superior to no road. One advantage of toll finance is that those building and maintaining the road are guided to serve the interests of those who actually use the road. In other words, toll roads are an example of decentralized decision making but one in which the tendency to ignore nonlocal interests is ameliorated. One key problem is the difficulty of collecting tolls. Funds devoted to toll collection are not available for road maintenance. Modern toll roads face little danger of toll evasion, for most modern vehicles lack off-road capability. Still, some police oversight is generally necessary. In the days of wagons, attempts to drive around or through toll gates were more common. Since the problem of evasion is naturally lower in the case of bridges, tolls on bridges have been more common historically.

Tolls by their nature can only be collected once a road is built. Toll roads are only possible, then, if the operators are able to borrow money (or if they are given the right to collect tolls on an existing road). Since the cost of even a short stretch of road is generally beyond the capability of one person to finance, toll roads are generally managed by either local authorities or some sort of corporation. New road construction often requires the exercise of eminent domain, otherwise each landowner along the route may try to obtain the full present value of the roadway in payment. The English Parliament, from the late seventeenth century, allowed the establishment of private turnpike corporations (still a rare institutional form at the time) with the important rights to borrow, charge tolls, and exercise eminent domain. England's colonies inherited this institutional structure, and the (especially northeastern) United States developed an impressive network of turnpike roads in the early nineteenth century.

Charity. The societal benefits of good roads have long been recognized. Bridges in particular were often built by local nobles or religious organizations (especially but not exclusively on routes of pilgrimage) as charitable gestures. Yet the sheer scale of the costs of road construction meant that such charitable endeavors could solve only some of the more serious bottlenecks in road transport; they could not on their own create a national network. Moreover, charitable donations focused on construction. Necessary maintenance was often not provided for.

Statutory labor. Given that road construction was generally labor intensive until the late nineteenth century, one possible solution to the problem of financing road work was to require all citizens to work on the roads. This method has apparently been used in every region of the world, often across millennia. In the United States it was used as late as 1913 in Alabama (replaced in part by prison chain gangs). One obvious drawback is that most citizens lack any special knowledge of road making. Statutory labor was less likely than skilled labor to achieve a proper surface or drainage. Since statutory labor was only compelled at certain times of the year, regular maintenance was impossible, and one rain storm could make a road impassable. Moreover, as with serfs working on demesne land, citizens had an incentive to shirk. Since they often were supervised by an amateur and social equal, shirking was likely even more prevalent than on the demesne. Still, though labor productivity could be quite low, the system was often judged better than nothing when the funds for paid labor were difficult to raise.

BIBLIOGRAPHY

Barker, Theo, and Dorian Gerhold. *The Rise and Rise of Road Transport, 1700–1900.* London, 1993. Discusses how the road fared against the railway in Britain and emphasizes the role of the bicycle in encouraging road improvement.

Flink, James J. *The Automobile Age.* Cambridge, Mass., 1987.

Gregory, John Walter. *The Story of the Road.* London, 1931.

Langdon, John. *Horses, Oxen, and Technological Innovation.* Cambridge, 1986. Analyzes the shift from oxen to horses in thirteenth- and fourteenth-century England.

Lay, Maxwell G. *Ways of the World: A History of the World's Roads and of the Vehicles That Used Them.* New Brunswick, N.J., 1992. The best comprehensive survey, it stresses the technical developments but tries to place roads in a broader social and economic context.

Leighton, Albert C. *Transport and Communications in Early Medieval Europe, AD 500–1100.* Newton Abbott, U.K., 1972.

Li, Lilian. "Integration and Disintegration in North China's Grain Markets, 1738–1911." *Journal of Economic History* 60.3 (2000), 665–699. Discusses the limitations of the early modern Chinese transport system.

Martyn, N. *The Silk Road.* Sydney, 1987.

Needham, Joseph. *Science and Civilisation in China,* vol. 4, *Civil Engineering and Nautics.* Cambridge, 1971.

Pawson, Eric. *Transport and Economy: The Turnpike Roads of Eighteenth-Century Britain.* London, 1977. Shows that these formed a coherent network.

Schreiber, Herman. *The History of Roads: From Amber Route to Motorway.* London, 1961.

Shirley-Smith, Hubert. *The World's Great Bridges.* 2d. ed. London, 1964.

Szostak, Rick. *The Role of Transportation in the Industrial Revolution: A Comparison of England and France.* Montreal, 1991. Discusses the economic impact of transport improvements, the relative advantages of road versus water, and the institutional framework in which improvements occurred.

Szostak, Rick. "The Economic Impacts of Road and Waterway Improvements." *Transportation Quarterly* 50.3 (1996), 127–142. Draws modern policy implications from the experience of eighteenth-century England and the nineteenth-century United States.

Thorburn, Thomas. *Economics of Transport: The Swedish Case, 1780–1980.* Södertälje, Sweden, 2000. Constructs data series on transport expenditures and analyzes the effect of transport improvements on the Swedish economy.

Ville, Simon P. *Transport and the Development of the European Economy, 1750–1918.* New York, 1990. Short survey chapter on roads.

Rick Szostak

Technological Change

By about 7000 BCE, humans domesticated large animals to provide a secure food supply. The castration of domestic cattle to produce the strong and manageable ox began about 5000 BCE. The farmers used their oxen as a power source for such farm duties as plowing ground and preparing it for seeding. Once an animal could be harnessed to pull a plow, it was a relatively simple step to convert the plow into a crude transport device by placing the payload on the shafts and allowing them to drag along the ground. This early truck is called a travois. The dragged sled was a relatively simple extension of the travois concept.

The Wheel. Little need for further transport technology existed while there was nothing to transport. Transport development required a market demand for farmers' produce. That is, society had to change from a subsistence level to a stage in which groups were producing more food of a particular type than they needed themselves. The excess was traded, and that trade demanded freight transport. In response, the efficacy of the travois was improved by placing a crude roller or wheel between the ends of the shaft. Similarly, log rollers were placed under sleds.

The wheel was invented in about 5000 BCE, probably as a piece of technology transfer from the dragged travois and the potters' wheel. The first wheels were made of wood and therefore also depended on the availability of woodworking tools. It was not a simple or inevitable step and was not developed indigenously in the Americas, Australia, Southeast Asia, or southern Africa. Many of the early wheels that have been discovered are about a meter in diameter and are comprised of three planks. Joining them with an axle was the next major step. The first axles were fixed, and the wheels rotated about their axes.

Placing the platform developed for the sled on large wheels gave rise to the cart and the wagon. Two-wheeled vehicles (carts) appeared in about 3000 BCE in Mesopotamia and were used for freight haulage. This was an important breakthrough, as animals can haul loads up to ten times greater than those that they can carry on their backs. The carts were initially hauled by oxen placed on either side of a central shaft and reacting against a crossbar attached to the shaft. Oxen pull from a hump at the back of the neck and have prominent shoulders, so they are relatively easy to harness in this fashion. As cart technology improved, carts became lighter, and some could be hauled by donkeys.

The use of two shafts made cart construction simpler. In about 2500 BCE it was found that carrying the vertical load in the shafts on the ox's back, rather than on its shoulders, increased haulage capacity by 50 percent. These developments and the ever-present need to carry heavier loads favored four-wheeled wagons, which appeared at about this time. Spoked wheels arrived in about 2000 BCE. Steerable wagons and iron tires, which first occurred in about 500 BCE, were important and useful advances but were difficult technologies for many societies to master. Heavy carts and wagons of course required smooth, wide track surfaces, which were still rare, so for the next four thousand years most significant freight haulage was by sea.

The horse was domesticated in about 3000 BCE, but its use for hauling was complicated by the fact that it pulls from forward of the shoulder and can readily be suffocated by a load against its windpipe. A horse therefore requires a carefully structured, padded collar resting on its shoulder. The need for uniform pressure means a horse works best between a pair of shafts, whereas two oxen could work on either side of one shaft. These difficulties meant that the slower-moving ox remained a major source of motive power. Donkeys and similar animals were also used as pack animals. A donkey carried up to fifty kilograms of freight in baskets suspended from its back. From about 2000 BCE, organized convoys of pack animals operated in the Middle East. By 300 BCE these convoys had developed into the elaborate trading caravans that traveled throughout the Middle East and along the Silk Road linking west and east. Genghis Khan developed the caravan concept to its ultimate form, sometimes journeying with mobile houses nine meters wide set on wheels six meters apart.

Personal Travel. During the period of wheeled development, personal travel improved also. This development was particularly driven by the needs of armies and administrators, as it was found that successful war was fruitful in terms of initial booty from and long-term taxation of the subjugated.

Horse riding began in Russia in about 3000 BCE but was not common in the Middle East until about 1000 BCE. It was primarily used for war. Neither saddle nor stirrup had then been invented, so the horse was mainly used for pulling light chariots. As harnessing, particularly the use of bits, improved, the ridden horse supplanted the chariot in about 500 BCE. The horse was far too expensive for ordinary citizens, who traveled for comfort rather than for time savings on slow-moving donkeys. Passengers forced to travel long distances by land and unable to commute by horseback traveled in four-wheeled wagons, which provided some weather protection and avoided the continual rocking motion of two-wheeled carts. Travel speeds were no better than walking.

Early Roads. Although carts and wagons could haul loads of over a ton, most heavy loads were moved by ship as road vehicles were unreliable and roads inadequate. Vehicles can be made and sold for a profit, yet roads must be built and maintained without an obvious income stream. Thus the first major arterial roads were built to aid armies and, after the conquest, the tax collectors and tithe takers. Such roads were built and maintained with the spoils of battle. The Assyrian Royal Road in the Middle East ran from the Mediterranean port of Izmir some 2,500 kilometers to seaports on the Euphrates near Ur. The surface was primitive but adequate. Of more importance were the frequent post houses that provided the slow-moving travelers with places to rest and replenish.

The two major road systems that developed under the conquer and tax model were those of the Chinese (40,000 kilometers of quality roads operating between 1000 BCE and 500 CE) and the Romans (80,000 kilometers of quality roads operating between 334 BCE and 500 CE). These were major "manufactured" or "improved" roads with good running surfaces, manageable alignments, and engineered water crossings. Indeed, the Roman roads were famously overengineered wonders of engineering organization rather than of engineering science. They were nevertheless far inferior to water transport in terms of operating cost and freight capacity. One reason was that the vehicle technology and animal harnessing was still primitive. For example, the Roman harnesses tended to choke the animal,

ITALIAN MAILCOACH. Painting by Heinrich Buerkel (1802–1869). (Staedelsches Kunstinstitut, Frankfurt am Main, Germany/Foto Marburg/Art Resource, NY)

could not handle downhill hauling, and did not permit harnessing animals in line. After the Roman Empire declined, Roman roads rapidly deteriorated without ongoing maintenance. They were quarried for building materials and often were destroyed by locals to prevent their use by plundering invaders. Carts were largely restricted to farm use, and wagons virtually disappeared.

The reappearance of significant road transport required the prior reappearance of strong central administrations to build and maintain the roads. This first occurred in France with Charlemagne in about 800 CE. With the aid of strong central administrations, France maintained its role as the leading national road administration for the next millennium. Whereas earlier roads had been driven by the need to conquer and tax, as Europe emerged from the Middle Ages by 1500 CE the need was more to trade and tax. The farms had once again developed beyond subsistence and were ready to trade, kings needed regular contact with their barons, markets and traveling fairs were major trading activities, bishops needed to visit their priests, and the people needed their pilgrimages and crusades. The key transport criterion was reliability. Nothing traveled faster than walking pace, and loads were under a ton in weight. Certainty of arrival was more important than time of arrival.

The Second Coming of Vehicles. Slowly vehicles improved. The development of farming led to superior horses and better harnessing. Horses were also more readily available. By the thirteenth century, wagons were coming

into common use, and professional carriers were plying the roads. The wagons could carry up to eight tons and travel for eight hours at up to five kilometers per hour. Nevertheless, at the end of the eighteenth century, land transport performance had improved relatively little over the four thousand years since the wagon was first invented. Two obvious needs existed by the time of the Industrial Revolution. One was a better power source than the horse and the ox, and the other was better roads. The world had yet to enter a time when most people traveled frequently or for significant distances. The vast bulk of personal travel was by walking. People lived where they worked, and even the large towns were of walkable dimensions. A small minority of the population with available resources rode horses. All vehicles carrying people were called carriages. In Roman times, the Celts invented four-wheeled carriages with leather strap suspensions, giving some passenger comfort. The technology was then lost for over a thousand years, during which time passenger travel by wagon was slow and uncomfortable. The first semblance of public transport came with the stage coach.

In 1600 CE, carriages were little more than furnished, lumbering wagons carrying up to eight people at walking speed. Iron springs were developed in about 1625, and in the 1660s, Philip di Chiesa, an Italian working in Berlin, produced the first practical vehicle with a suspension, a coach capable of being pulled at faster than walking speed. His "Berliner" coach carried up to sixteen passengers at seventy-five kilometers per day. These so-called "flying" coaches were the first significant transport change since the lighter iron-tired vehicles of 50 CE. Coaches were created by the growing group of independent, skilled artisans flourishing in the new Europe of the Renaissance. By 1750, coaches had replaced horse riding as the preferred intercity personal transport. For instance, personal travel times between London and Bristol, a distance of 180 kilometers, dropped from seven days by post horse in 1558 to twelve hours by mail coach in 1832.

Coach technology also gave rise to urban public transport in the eighteenth century. Blaise Pascal began the first service in Paris in 1662 using horse buses. It was not successful as the buses were too slow and expensive to attract sufficient patronage. Success did not occur until cities began to grow after the Industrial Revolution, creating a wider market. Buses aimed at this lower-income market were introduced in Bordeaux in 1812. Bus design improved dramatically over the next twenty years as the burgeoning cities rapidly increased market demands. The roads were quite rough, and following the example of the developing railways, horse-drawn street rail (trams, street cars, or light rail) was introduced in New York in 1832. Rails flush with the road surface awaited better steel-making practice in 1852. The electric tram began replacing the horse tram in the 1880s, following the invention of the electric generator in 1870. Street public transport had its boom between this period and the end of World War I, when affordable automobiles came on the market. Many cities, in retrospect unwisely, gave the automobile road priority over public transport. Today the bus and tram are experiencing some resurgence owing to improved priority and separate tracks.

A Change in Roads. The next development in transport required improved power sources and better roads. The demand for better roads came first, as the performance of the flying coaches was noticeably impeded by poor road surfaces. The Romans had developed their roads by marshaling the resources of a state focused on conquest and taxation. Such a centralization of commitment did not exist in eighteenth-century Europe. It came closest to realization in France with its history of strong administrations based in Paris. Effective control required good road links with Paris, so it is not surprising that the resurgence in road making occurred in France.

Nicolas Bergier began that revival in 1622 with a translation and application of the Roman road-making manuals. Roman practice was far too expensive, and in 1757 Pierre-Marie Trésaguet made the first steps to modern road making by stressing the importance of drainage and of making each layer in the pavement perform its specific function as effectively as possible. In deference to Roman methods, the base layer of the pavement structure consisted of pieces of quarried stone about two hundred millimeters in size with a flat, narrow side placed on the natural formation.

In Yorkshire, England, an intuitive road maker named Blind Jack Metcalf in the period 1753–1810 produced roads in which the pavement layers were selected with great care. His attention laid many of the seeds of modern practice. From 1801 to 1830 Thomas Telford, an ex-stonemason and famous bridge builder, turned his masonry skills to road making and drew significantly from the work of Trésaguet. In particular Telford had seen that some of the problems of the French could be avoided by using somewhat more cubical blocks, an improvement that came at added cost. He thus applied masonry practice to roads, and his projects, funded by national programs, were effective but expensive. The major road-making breakthrough came with John McAdam, who worked in the south of England in the early part of the nineteenth century. He realized that small (twenty-five millimeter) pieces of broken, angular stone (called "aggregate"), when placed in layers within a pavement, could work as effectively as the elaborate and far more expensive structures of the Romans, the French, and Telford. McAdam's method remains at the core of all modern road making, and the product is called macadam. It was an extraordinary innovation and paradigm shift, producing better and cheaper roads.

When tar (and later, bitumen) became available as a consequence of post–Industrial Revolution manufacturing processes, it was mixed with macadam to produce asphalt. Similarly, the mixing of cement mortar and aggregate produces concrete. Asphalt and concrete are the staple materials used in heavy-duty modern roads and have greatly changed modern road construction. Both materials were around before the twentieth century, but their practical application to road making only occurred with the advent of powerful, steam-powered equipment for manufacturing, moving, and placing the material. The benefits also flowed through to macadam, which was greatly improved when steamrollers became available after 1860.

Modern Transport. By the beginning of the nineteenth century, the road surface was no longer the limit on travel speed or capacity. That limit was imposed by the power supply, predominantly the horse and the ox, which had served for about three millennia. The Industrial Revolution of the eighteenth century provided steam power, and inventors such as Richard Trevithick produced steam-powered vehicles. They were large and lumbering and found few roads suitable for their operation. Other inventors, such as George Stephenson in the 1820s, placed their steam engines on trays with flanged wheels running on steel rails. The age of the railway had arrived, and for the next one hundred years only minimal investment was made in roads. Indeed, without maintenance, many roads deteriorated to a worse condition in 1920 than in 1820.

Forms of bicycle are reported in 1791. As the fruits of the Industrial Revolution became available, the first practical bicycle, using the mechanical advantage that makes the device uniquely attractive, was invented by Kirkpatrick Macmillan in Scotland in 1839. His ideas were lost for twenty years, until Pierre Michaux began making bicycles commercially in Paris in 1861. The modern bicycle with spoked wheels, ball bearings, and pedal chain drive was introduced by Henry Lawson in London in 1877. The bicycle then provided the world's first great democratization of travel. Over the next thirty years cyclists lobbied vociferously for better roads, maps, and other travel facilities.

The automobile, motorcycle, and truck powered by internal combustion were invented between 1885 and 1891. World War I dramatically demonstrated the daily usefulness of internal combustion cars and trucks. Before the 1920s were over, motor vehicle traffic congestion was a problem in many cities. Once again, the road was the transport limit but this time in terms of capacity rather than the quality of the running surface. In fact, the increasingly large trucks did not have a major impact. Truck loads have risen from five tons to over one hundred tons, controlling the individual wheel loads (to between two and four tons) by using more wheels per truck carried on modern suspensions.

Modern Roads. The road response to the swarm of new vehicles began in the United States, where William Vanderbilt in 1906 built a special road, a parkway, on Long Island for car racing. A few more parkways (no intersections and no sharp curves) were built in New York State, but the major impact came with the work of Robert Moses in the 1920s. Similar activities on a smaller scale had been occurring in Germany from 1913, and Moses' work in New York caught the attention of the German engineers. They improved on his principles with design speeds of 150 kilometers per hour and began building the German autobahn system in 1929. In 1933, the program gained the strong support of Adolf Hitler's Nazi government, which saw the program as a trial mobilization embodying Nazi ideals of national character, spirit, strength, and beauty. Coincidentally, it helped soak up Germany's massive unemployment.

The need for a national network of high-quality roads was also recognized in the United States. As in Germany, the initial incentive was not transport economics. In 1922, the U.S. Army produced the Pershing map, which designated where roads of prime military importance were needed. By the mid-1930s, the War Department had identified forty-five thousand kilometers of strategic highways. In 1941, in the midst of World War II, a defense act provided funds for internal road building. Planning and advocacy continued, and in 1956 the United States began building its National System of Interstate and Defense Highways (the interstates). The project, effectively completed in the early 1990s, includes seventy thousand kilometers of freeway. True to their history, all are designed to carry the vehicles of the U.S. Army.

Similar systems developed in France, Germany, and Italy, for example, were not merely road links but were carefully designed networks linking key origins and destinations and bypassing others. Such systems were greatly aided after 1950 by the development of computer-based tools for modeling or simulating traffic on networks, thus allowing assessment of alternate plans and the impact of new developments (that is, new traffic generators and attractors).

High-quality road and bridge building has also occurred throughout the world, although it is often restricted by community opposition to the enormous loss of local amenity caused by roads built to high geometric standards. The incentive for road construction has often come from the demands of the motorist, whose voting power has influenced the allocation of many political budgets. The economic benefits, however, often have flowed to the truck operators. Not surprisingly, rail systems have struggled to compete outside high-density towns.

Road Funding. In terms of rational economics, new roads and bridges should be seen as investments meeting either a social need or passing some benefit-cost filter. Their maintenance, a marginal cost, should be met by direct charges on the users. It is rare to find roads that meet such a simple, rational model. The initial investment is often driven by political or social decisions, and road maintenance is often at the end of the funding priority. Rational links between road benefits and road costs are hard to establish, as the road transport operators are often only linked to the road managers by the bluntest and most indirect of taxing systems.

Road funding has always been a problem. At the beginning of this article, it was stated that most early roads were built for conquest and taxation. When the tax collected was high, it was worth maintaining and improving the roads. Without a strong central administration, this incentive disappears and at the best of times will only support radial roads. Relatively recent examples of such roads were the military roads built by the English in eighteenth-century North America and Scotland. After American Independence, many American statesmen saw their road network as a way of binding the new Republic together. Nevertheless, only one national road was built in the United States prior to the interstate system, and it was abandoned with the advent of steam rail.

From the thirteenth century onward, some notable roads and bridges were built as acts of religious commitment, but it was an unreliable method. When roads were local issues, rather than routes for marching armies, many communities tried the corvée system, in which adjacent property owners were required to donate labor to work on the roads. Although widely tried, it was rarely successful, as the circumstances usually meant that the labor was difficult to obtain, of poor quality, and poorly managed. It was employed in Alabama as late as 1913.

Instead of labor, an alternative was to ask abutting owners to pay for road maintenance. For much of history, the system was difficult to enforce, but in recent times it has found some favor with local governments. An approach with similar difficulties was to apply the tax over the entire local community. With modern taxation methods, it is now one of the most common funding methods. The other common current method uses taxes on the purchase of fuel and vehicles.

The last major method has been by tolls on road users. Records document toll roads in India in 320 BCE. By the eleventh century, tolls on roads, bridges, and city gates were common throughout Europe. Britain legalized the concept of a toll road in 1661. The form was broadened in 1706, when independent trustees were allowed to manage a toll road. The method became widespread despite great public opposition. At its peak in 1830, Britain had 1,116 separate "turnpike" trusts operating about 40,000 kilometers of main roads. In these times, toll evasion was always a major concern. The toll road has had a resurgence, particularly in the United States, France, and Italy. The resurgence is further fueled by the introduction of methods of automatic toll collection, which do not require the vehicle to stop.

Bridges. Bridges in many ways follow a pattern similar to roads. The Chinese and the Romans were excellent bridge builders. As with roads, the Romans were distinguished more by their engineering management than their design subtlety. Many of their semicircular masonry arches, often built in difficult locales, have survived. The technical difficulty of an arch is measured by its span. Roman arches rarely spanned more than thirty meters. By increasing the span to rise ratio from 2 to 5, the Chinese in 590 CE spanned thirty-seven meters. This record stood for 750 years before Italian artisans in 1345 built the Ponte Vechio with a span-to-rise ratio of 7.5 and the Adda River Bridge in 1377 with a span of seventy-two meters. The Ponte Vechio record was not bettered for 400 years; the Adda record lasted 526 years. Clearly the masonry arch had reached its technological limits.

From 280 BCE, a different form of bridge using cables to suspend the bridge deck was developed in China using vine cables. Spans of up to sixty meters were reported in China in 700 CE. Ironworking was common in India and southern China, and the first iron chain suspension bridge was built in Tibet in 1420 CE. It also was the first bridge to employ towers and a flat suspended deck. Fifty-seven similar bridges were constructed by the inventor, Thang-tong Gyalpo.

Iron also led to a major leap forward in the development of the arch and truss. The first metal arch, opened at Coalbrookdale in England in 1781, spanned thirty meters. Coalbrookdale has been called the birthplace of the Industrial Revolution. However, iron made its major impact on truss bridges. The largest timber truss, a seventy-meter span, crossed the Rhine at Reichenau in Switzerland. Timber trusses developed further in the timber-rich regions of the American Northeast. The longest span was a 110-meter structure over the Susquehanna River at McCalls Ferry, opened in 1815. Iron began to be used in trusses in 1840. In a quantum jump, the Quebec Bridge opened with a record 549-meter span in 1917.

In the twentieth century, conventional bridges (less than sixty-meter spans) were largely steel beams or prestressed concrete. Both depended on modern manufacturing and high-quality, controlled materials. The large bridges reverted back to suspension bridges, again as high-quality cables became available from steelmakers. Initially, the bridges were still the classic suspension bridges, but after World War II, German former aircraft designers developed cable-stayed bridges, in which the suspension cables directly support the bridge deck. Such bridges can span up to four hundred meters. However, the largest bridges are still suspension bridges of Thang-tong's style, including the Akashi Straits bridge in Japan, spanning 1,780 meters, that opened in 1991.

Tunnels are difficult and expensive transport facilities to construct and maintain, usually requiring good equipment and superb organization. The first traffic tunnel was a nine-hundred-meter footway built in soft ground under the Euphrates in 2150 BCE. The Romans built a tunnel in hard rock near Naples in 30 BCE. The rock was broken by heating it and then splashing it with cold water. Explosives were first used for tunneling in Saluzzo, Italy, in 1480. Between 1825 and 1843 Isambard and Marc Brunel built the first major soft-ground tunnel. It was 460 meters long and passed under the Thames at Wapping. Tunneling for the London Underground from 1865 onward provided the technology for an outburst of road tunnels under rivers beside major cities, such as New York City's Hudson and East rivers.

BIBLIOGRAPHY

Addison, William W. *The Old Roads of England*. London, 1980.

Agricola, Georgius. *De re metallica*. Translated by Herbert Hoover. New York, 1950.

Albert, Bill. *The Turnpike Road System in England, 1663–1840*. Cambridge, 1972.

Aldcroft, Derek H., and Michael J. Freeman, eds. *Transport in the Industrial Revolution*. Manchester and Dover, N.H., 1983.

Allen, Thomas B. "Xinjiang and The Silk Road's Lost World." *National Geographic* 189.3 (March 1996), 2–43 and 44–51.

Anthony, David, Dimitri Y. Telegin, and Dorcas Brown. "The Origin of Horseback Riding." *Scientific American* 265.6 (December 1991), 44–48A.

Armstrong, Ellis L. *History of Public Works in the United States, 1776–1976*. Chicago, 1976.

Balogun, J. A., R. J. Robertson, et al. "Metabolic and Perceptual Responses whilst Carrying External Loads by Head and by Yoke." *Ergonomics* 29.12 (1986), 1623–1637.

Baron, P. "Transportation in Germany: An Historical Overview." *Transportation Research Part A* 29 (1995), 9–20.

Bokonyi, Sandor. "The Importance of Horse Domestication in Economy and Transport." *Transport and Social Change* 2 (1980), 15–21.

Caro, Robert A. *The Power Broker: Robert Moses and the Fall of New York*. New York, 1974.

Chartres, J. "L'homme et la route." *Journal of Transport History* 2.1 (1981), 65–68.

Dyos, H. J., and Derek H. Aldcroft. *British Transport: An Economic Survey from the Seventeenth Century to the Twentieth*. Leicester, 1969.

Federal Highway Administration. *America's Highways: 1776–1976*. Washington, D.C., 1976.

Field, D. C. "Mechanical Road-Vehicles." In *A History of Technology*, vol. 5, edited by C. Singer, E. J. Holmyard, A. R. Hall, and T. I. Williams, pp. 414–437. Oxford, 1958.

Forbes, R. J. "Roads to c. 1900." In *A History of Technology*, vol. 4, edited by C. Singer, E. J. Holmyard, A. R. Hall, and T. I. Williams, pp. 520–547. Oxford, 1958.

Hey, D. *Packmen, Carriers and Packhorse Roads*. Leicester, 1980.

Lay, M. G. *Ways of the World*. New Brunswick, N.J., 1992.

Leighton, Albert C. *Transport and Communications in Early Medieval Europe, AD 500–1100*. Newton Abbot, 1972.

Villefosse, René Hon de. *Histoire des grandes routes de France*. Paris, 1975.

MAXWELL G. LAY

Regulation

Roads provide the most basic means of transportation and communication. Before canals, railroads, and telecommunications, roads provided the arteries for the flows of commercial trade and military conquest. From ancient times, roads became the focus of government action, because of their strategic and commercial importance.

Ancient Roads. Ancient kings built roads to link their conquests. The Assyrians had a road engineer corps, *ummani*, who built a mountain road for King Tiglath-pileser I (c. 1115–1077 BCE) in 1100 BCE. The Assyrians built the first major arterial road to link Susa (their capital) with Nineveh, and the Mediterranean at Izmir in western Turkey. In 670 BCE, the Assyrian king Esarhaddon (r. 680–669 BCE) ordered road construction to facilitate trade and commerce.

The Persians were also renowned road builders. The Persian Empire required land-based communication because it stretched from modern Iran to the Mediterranean. Cyrus II (c. 585–529 BCE) built roads that allowed the rapid movement of his army. He built roads in Jordan in 550 BCE. Darius I (r. 522–466 BCE) extended Cyrus's road network and implemented a sophisticated postal system that further facilitated imperial integration and administration. Darius's most important project was the Royal Road, which was completed about 500 BCE. The Royal Road extended 2,700 kilometers and had 111 post houses. Postal messengers had priority on the Royal Road and could travel the road's length in ten to twenty days.

Ancient China and India also witnessed road construction that linked imperial domains. In China, road construction began during the Western Zhou dynasty (1066–771 BCE) and a system developed that identified officials responsible for road maintenance. But Chinese road construction took off after 200 BCE during the Qin and Han dynasties. The first emperor, Shi-Huangdi, constructed post roads across his empire and implemented a sophisticated bureaucracy to administer his empire. In 221 BCE, Shi, who is best known for building the Great Wall, initiated an early vehicle-size regulation, standardizing chariot gauge at about 1.5 meters. The Chinese then standardized road widths based on that gauge. Around 750 CE, the ancient Chinese road system peaked at 40,000 kilometers (compared to 80,000 kilometers for the Romans).

By 300 BCE, King Chandragupta (c. 321–297 BCE) of India linked a Susa-Rawalpindi road to a 3,000-kilometer Great Royal Road, which ran southeast to Delhi, terminating at the capital of Patna and the mouth of the Ganges. Chandragupta instituted a ministry to oversee the road.

Roman Roads. Like the Persians, the Romans understood roads' importance for coordinating and administering a vast empire. Realizing the roads' imperial importance, Julius Caesar (100–44 BCE) took the title "Curator Viarum," Director of the Great Roads. His successor Augustus (r. 27 BCE–14 CE) also realized the road system's importance. He commissioned his top general Marcus Agrippa (63?–12 BCE) to map the empire's roads, a process that took twenty years.

Rome's first arterial road was the Via Latina, constructed in 334 BCE to link Rome with Calvi, a recently acquired colony. Calvi grew in significance and Rome began construction of the famous Via Appia (Appian Way) in 312 BCE. Poet Publius Statius (c. 45–96 CE) called it the "Queen of Roads" in 70 CE. However, its construction emptied the public treasury. Rome's road system peaked in 200 CE at approximately 80,000 kilometers. The system circled the Mediterranean and covered western Europe. The Roman army was responsible for road building and maintenance, but road crews were usually made up of convicts and slaves. However, toward the end of the empire, construction ceased and maintenance became solely the responsibility of local citizens. This proved unsatisfactory. Earlier, Augustus had tried to make road funding the responsibility of the local inhabitants, but this was not popular. Imperial funds were still needed.

Romans regulated road widths, vehicle weights, and operating times. But weight limits were widely skirted. The Romans faced the ancient dilemma of the road manager wanting lower weights to limit road wear, while road users want to move the maximum cargo weight. In 438 CE, the Theodosian legal code raised the weight limits for ox and horse wagons. However, the code had a more innovative approach to enforcing the weight limits by also limiting the number of animals per vehicle. In 45 BCE, in an effort to limit congestion, Julius Caesar banned traffic in Rome's city center from 6 AM to 4 PM. Claudius extended this prohibition to all Roman towns in 50 CE. The empire's decline left a moldering system for medieval Europe, although large segments were intact and useful.

Medieval and Renaissance Roads. Early medieval localities viewed roads as a means for invasion, so they obstructed or blockaded old Roman roads at boundaries. Feudal lords also realized that roads could mean freedom for their serfs, so controlling road access was important for controlling subject populations. Charlemagne (742–814 CE) understood roads' significance in empire building. He constructed roads and put them under a central authority. He also instituted a system obligating his subjects to work on road maintenance. This system evolved into the dreaded corvée (forced labor), abolished by the French Revolution in 1791. In the thirteenth century, Genghis Khan (c. 1162–1227) was reopening the Silk Road to support his conquest of China. He established a sophisticated system of couriers and post houses, which helped him control China from his Mongolian homeland. Genghis Khan's Mongolians were superb road builders.

Philip II (r. 1179–1223) led France into a system of central government road construction. Philip began paving Paris when he covered a couple of crossroads to eliminate the putrid stink. France had the leading road system between 1300 and 1900 and had 30,000 kilometers of royal roads centered on Paris. Louis XI (r. 1461–1483) established a national messenger system, Couriers de France, in 1464. The system had post houses set in stages of 20 kilometers and couriers would pass four stages per day. France's Henry IV (r. 1589–1610) revived road building as a means to unify France following the Wars of Religion in 1594. He appointed the first chief inspector of highways. Henry began constructing ring roads around Paris on the site of the old city walls.

Providing the resources for road maintenance was a problem that medieval France and England tried to solve through use of the corvée which subjected vassals to military or other physical duty. It entailed maintaining the roads and bridges of the feudal lord. As feudal obligations ceased to fulfill the maintenance requirements, France added a salt tax in 1591 to generate revenues for road upkeep. In 1555, the English Parliament passed a highway act that required the various parishes to maintain roads, with individual parishioners obligated to provide four days of service annually. In 1654, Parliament allowed parishes to hire road surveyors to supervise the work.

In an effort to maintain their roads, medieval governments followed Roman precedents in regulating road widths and vehicles. Medieval authorities also established traffic regulations and tried to counter criminal activities on the highways. A German traffic regulation in 1200 established right of way based on "right and might," which meant pedestrians yielded to mounted riders, who in turn yielded to wagons. In 1487, Paris declared that galloping through town was "speeding" and was punishable by flogging. In order to limit highway ambushes and robberies, the English statute of Winchester in 1285 declared that 60 meters needed to be cleared on the sides of roads leading to market towns. In fact, English law established that an attack on highway travelers was equivalent to an attack on the king himself. Highway robbery was thus a capital offense.

Early Modern Roads. Highway banditry was a scourge of seventeenth-century England. English highway robbery was almost unique in Europe because England did not have any police or military patrols. Instead, England relied on private action through bounty incentives. The Highwayman Act of 1692 offered a forty-pound bounty upon capture and conviction of a bandit. In fact, the initial highway patrols, known as Bow Street Runners, began in the late eighteenth century as private ventures facilitated at the Bow Street magistrate courts, where the crimes were usually successfully prosecuted.

More mundane traffic regulation continued in this period. In 1722, London's Lord Mayor wanted to insure traffic passage over London Bridge. He instituted rules that traffic must move on the left and that prohibited stopping on London Bridge. However, Robespierre (1758–1794) moved French traffic to the right side. Peasants in France had traditionally moved right to defer to aristocrats' carriages. Robespierre made right-side driving the law. Napoleon (1769–1821) spread this rule across continental Europe, and America adopted it with Pennsylvania's Lancaster Turnpike in 1792. The authorities also passed regulations to reduce congestion.

Pavement continued to be a concern and prompted vehicle weight and wheel restrictions. Because wider tires reduced roadway wear, Parliament passed a law in 1662 requiring 100-millimeter widths. However, this was repealed in 1670 because the wider wheels did not fit the existing ruts. Parliament tried again in 1753 with the Broad Wheel Act, which limited vehicle gauges to 1.65 meters and required a 225-millimeter minimum wheel width and 450 millimeters for very heavy loads. Parliament amended this law in 1755 to allow a 150-millimeter minimum for wagons with fewer than seven horses. Parliament further refined the requirement in the First General Highway Act of 1767, which permitted 225-millimeter widths for vehicles up to seven horses and 400-millimeter widths for vehicles above that. This resulted in the use of conical tires to avoid the regulation. A more economically efficient solution was making vehicles pay fees for roadway wear. In 1555, Dublin had public facilities for weighing vehicles to ascertain correct toll charges. In 1741, a British law allowed British turnpikes to charge extra tolls for loads weighing more than three tons (noblemen exempted). John Wyatt invented a weigh-bridge platform in 1744, which facilitated weighing heavy vehicles; and rights to weigh were auctioned annually. Legal authorities also enacted laws specifying road construction standards. Colonial Virginia passed such a law in 1632.

Funding roads was problematic. France repealed the corvée in 1791 and replaced it with taxes and tolls. Virginia tried a lottery in 1790. New York still had a variation of the corvée, a law requiring free males to provide between one and thirty days annually for roadwork, depending on need and capability. But New York roads were still poor, and there were not enough settlers in rural areas to provide adequate labor. Acquiring resources for adequate road construction and maintenance led many to support a private approach, the turnpike corporation, funded by tolls.

Tolls and Turnpikes. Roadway tolls have an ancient lineage. India had them in 320 BCE. Eleventh-century Europe was quite familiar with tolls, and tollgates are noted in the Domesday Book in 1085. The authorities found it easiest to enforce toll collection on bridges. London Bridge began collecting tolls in 1286 and generated enough revenue to fund its own maintenance plus the construction of Tower, Southwark, and Blackfriars Bridges. In 1274, Edward I (r. 1272–1307) granted toll authority on a road heading north out of London, but the measure did not lead to widespread toll-collecting grants.

The English turnpike era began in 1706 when Parliament passed the first of several turnpike acts, which granted turnpike trustees power to borrow money to improve the roadway and to impose tolls. The private toll road became known as a turnpike. The name derives from military defensive obstructions known as turnpikes, which were long poles with sharp metal tips attached to vertical poles and resembled the pike weapon.

Turnpike tolls were not popular. Riots against turnpikes led George II (r. 1727–1760) in 1734 to impose the death penalty for turnpike gate destruction. This had minimal deterrent impact (e.g., in 1753, Yorkshire and Bristol rioters wrecked about a dozen turnpike gates). English turnpike expansion peaked in the second half of the eighteenth century. Between 1751 and 1771, Parliament passed almost nine hundred separate turnpike acts. England had 40,000 kilometers of turnpikes by the early nineteenth century.

The turnpike era came later to America and was also driven by the need to acquire adequate funding. But economic development played a large role. A corvée-based system did not work in rural American areas with sparse settlement. Improvement sponsors believed that a turnpike corporation provided the means to organize resources necessary for construction and road maintenance. The first U.S. turnpike was the Lancaster Turnpike, which the Pennsylvania legislature chartered in 1792 with a $300,000 capitalization. The Virginia legislature funded a second turnpike, the Little River Turnpike, in 1785, finally completed in 1802. However, this turnpike was exceptional in its being a public venture. American turnpikes were generally organized as private concerns.

While English turnpikes were organized as nonprofit trusts, financed by bonds, Americans created for-profit turnpike companies, funded by an early version of stock, local subscriptions. The turnpike company had several advantages over the previous methods of road construction or maintenance. It could reach beyond a single local town and acquire resources from all the towns it planned to connect. Instead of relying on corvée labor obligations, the company could hire contractors for specific jobs. An important job was the tollkeeper who, besides collecting tolls, provided some local security and local community representation. Turnpike companies were an organizational breakthrough. When a company completed a certain mileage, its charter enabled it to construct a tollgate and start collecting tolls. By the 1830s, American turnpikes reached their zenith.

In 1811, the U.S. federal government began constructing the National Road, which began in Cumberland, Maryland, and reached Wheeling (now West Virginia) in 1818. It reached Zanesville, Ohio, in 1833, but the government began receiving reports of corruption among the road's construction contractors. Furthermore, President Andrew Jackson (1767–1845) vetoed the Maysville Road project in 1830, bringing to an end any federal road schemes until the twentieth century. The National Road had limited support. It reached Vandalia, Illinois, in 1841 and was terminated as a federal project. By this time, the states also had lost enthusiasm for turnpike or road projects. New technology, in the form of first canals and then railroads, began dominating transportation.

The turnpike decline can be traced to several factors. They did not make any money for their investors. They were caught between the difficulty of collecting tolls and the emergence of lower-cost technology, canals and railroads. In the 1830s, turnpike ton-mile rates were ten cents while canal rates were two to three cents. Those customers who did pay turnpike tolls complained when particular turnpikes were not well maintained. This often led to state intervention and suspension of tolls.

Rise of the Automobile. The widespread use of the internal combustion engine provided both increased road demand and a funding source. Governments imposed fuel taxes and registration fees to obtain funds for highway construction and improvements. This was a step toward economically efficient road pricing because these fees were user fees. And the fuel tax was tied to actual use. The U.S. federal government provided aid from general revenues through a series of acts. In 1912, the government provided rural road funds to facilitate postal delivery. A second act, the Federal Highway Act of 1916, provided more general highway aid but was stalled by World War I. The Federal Highway Act of 1921 unleashed a highway construction boom. This legislation restricted funds to a federal highway system linked at state lines and required roadways to be at least 5.5 meters wide. This system comprised 7 percent of total public roads.

Great Britain was slower to develop its highway system. It did not set up a central highways agency until 1909. Part of the problem was the Red Flag Act, which required a person with a red flag to walk in front of motorized vehicles. Parliament passed the act in 1865 to discourage steam-powered highway vehicles. The act was not repealed until 1896.

The increase in highway traffic brought increased traffic regulations. Paris required licenses for drivers of horse carriages in 1867. In 1899, Chicago licensed automobile drivers but banned licenses for anyone requiring glasses. Berlin required hand signals for turns in 1902. Salt Lake City implemented the first modern traffic signals in 1912, and Baltimore had vehicle-activated signals in 1928. In the 1920s, U.S. highway authorities recommended the use of pneumatic tires with maximum weight of 4.5 tons per tire. This has remained standard, with increased weights achieved by adding more tires. The Great Depression witnessed government extending its regulatory reach from licensing and traffic flow to industry regulation.

Regulation, Deregulation and Superhighways. The Great Depression fundamentally changed attitudes. The free market was no longer trusted to provide society's requirements. Economic policy was in a shambles and required overhaul. The Roosevelt administration embraced new economic policies for the economy and for particular industries, including highway carriers.

The Motor Carrier Act of 1935 brought regulation to truckers. However, it affected less than half of the industry because it exempted private carriage and agricultural commodities. Railroads supported motor-carrier regulation because unregulated trucks and buses were diverting higher-value freight and passenger service, leaving railroads with lower-value bulk commodities. In the 1930s, Great Britain also regulated entry and fares in its highway industry, while Germany regulated bus and truck fares.

In the United States, highway regulation lasted fewer than fifty years. Economists highlighted the waste and lack of innovation. The United States deregulated trucking as it was deregulating its railroads in 1980. Great Britain deregulated its truckers as well, but continental Europe and Japan did not follow. They had much invested in their state railway systems and feared that trucking deregulation in the 1980s would create huge rail operating deficits because unleashed highway carriers would divert more traffic from the rails.

Highway carriers in developed countries have a good infrastructure available to them. The foundations for this infrastructure were laid in the interwar period. The fascist dictators built the precursors of the modern superhighway. Benito Mussolini (1883–1945) developed Piero Puricelli's plan for a new Italian highway system. The first autostrada was a 50-kilometer route from Milan to Varese and Lake Como, which opened in 1924–1925. The German autobahn began before Hitler came to power, with a 20-kilometer segment built between Cologne and Bonn in 1929–1932 by the Rhineland province. The Nazis took over all autobahn construction in 1933. Military engineer Fritz Todt (1891–1942) led construction, completing 4,000 kilometers by 1942.

America and Great Britain came later to the building of superhighway systems. The first British motorway came in 1958 with completion of the 13-kilometer Preston Bypass. The United States built parkways, for automobiles only, in the first half of the twentieth century, mostly through the efforts of local governments. The 10-kilometer Long Island Motor Parkway opened in 1908. New York City and Westchester County built the 27-kilometer Bronx River Parkway between 1916 and 1923. Another New York area parkway, the Merritt Parkway, opened in 1939. America's first superhighway was the 270-kilometer Pennsylvania Turnpike, which opened in 1940. It was built with federal support on an abandoned rail line.

President Eisenhower galvanized the country behind the need for an interstate system, which now bears his name. In 1956, Congress passed two acts that authorized and funded the interstate highway system. Congress created a trust fund, maintained by fuel taxes, to provide financing. The system grew to 70,000 kilometers by 1990 and provides road systems, historic contributions to commerce and defense.

BIBLIOGRAPHY

Barron, Hal S. "And the Crooked Shall Be Made Straight: Public Road Administration and the Decline of Localism in the Rural North, 1870–1930." *Journal of Social History* 26 (Fall 1992), 83–104.

Brandon, David. *Stand and Deliver! A History of Highway Robbery.* Stroud, U.K., 2001.

Friedlander, Amy F. *Freight Transport Regulation.* Cambridge, Mass., 1981.

Hartz, Louis. *Economic Policy and Democratic Thought: Pennsylvania, 1776–1860.* Cambridge, Mass. 1948.

Klein, David B., and John Majewski. "Economy, Community, and Law: The Turnpike Movement in New York, 1797–1845." *Law and Society Review* 26 (1992), 469.

Lay, M. G. *Ways of the World: A History of the World's Roads and of the Vehicles That Used Them*. New Brunswick, N.J., 1992.

Scheiber, Harry N. "Federalism and the American Economic Order, 1789–1910." *Law and Society Review* 10 (1975), 57.

Weingoff, Richard F. "A Peaceful Campaign of Progress and Reform: The Federal Highway Administration at 100." *Public Roads* 57 (Autumn 1993), 1.

WILLIAM HUNEKE

ROBERTS, RICHARD (1789–1864), English inventor.

Born on 22 April 1789, at Llanymynech on the borders of England and mid-Wales, Roberts may have received a rudimentary education at the local church school, where the priest recognized his practical abilities and taught him some woodworking and lathe-turning. After working in the local quarries, Roberts was employed as a patternmaker at the Brosley and then the Horseley Iron Works. Trying to avoid being conscripted into the militia, Roberts went first to Liverpool and then to Manchester, seeking work. In Manchester, he helped a wood turner but again had to flee the militia officers and so moved to London, where he was employed for a couple of years by Henry Maudslay as a turner and fitter. Roberts learned from Maudslay the importance of machine tools for producing high-class work.

Roberts returned to Manchester in 1816 and set up his own engineering works, where he manufactured a vast range of inventions, some of which were covered by twenty-five patents over the next forty or so years. He is most famous for inventing the first really successful power loom in 1822, followed by his self-acting spinning mule three years later. A strike of skilled mule spinners caused the mill owners to approach Roberts, to see if he could solve the problem of how to wind on the spun yarn automatically. He refused initially but then agreed. After his first attempt in 1825, which did not succeed to his satisfaction, he patented a quadrant winding mechanism in 1830, which formed the basis of nearly all subsequent mules until the last were built for cotton spinning in 1927. It reduced the skill needed to work these machines and also enabled their size to be increased with more spindles, giving greater productivity.

However, Roberts's major contributions to mechanical engineering lay in his inventions for machine tools. By 1817, he had improved both the gear cutting machine and the metal turning lathe so that their accuracy was increased, making them suitable for medium-scale production. He invented the backgear on the mandrel, thus increasing the range of speeds on the lathe. In the same year, he invented a planing machine, which he developed into a very versatile tool capable of making beveled and spiral shapes as well as flat surfaces. These tools laid the foundation for him to introduce production engineering based on standard templates and gauges, and were the first of a wide range of slotting, shaping, rolling, punching, shearing, and many other machines.

Demand for his looms was such that, by 1825, he was manufacturing eighty each week, which necessitated standardization of production. Roberts adapted standard techniques for the construction of his mules, followed by railway locomotives in the 1830s. The partnership of Sharp, Roberts, begun in 1826, quickly developed into probably the most important mechanical engineering firm in Manchester, with a wide range of textile machines, machine tools, and railway locomotives. These locomotives also were produced to a standard design with high-quality engineering. An export trade to continental Europe soon developed, and demand increased so much that in 1839 the Atlas Works was constructed especially for manufacturing locomotives.

After the partnership was terminated in 1843, Roberts continued to suggest many more inventions in the fields of textiles, horology, shipbuilding, and other industries, but only one of any note, his Jacquard machine in 1847 for punching holes in iron plates, which simplified construction of the tubular bridges at Conway and Menai in North Wales and the Victoria Bridge at Montreal, Canada. Roberts spent most of wealth promoting his shipbuilding schemes unsuccessfully and died in poverty in London on 11 March 1864. Through his work on machine tools, he had raised the standards of mechanical engineering and may be considered the father of production engineering.

BIBLIOGRAPHY

Catterall, G. S. "The Life and Work of Richard Roberts, with Special Reference to the Development of the Spinning Mule." M.Sc. thesis, Manchester University, 1975.

Chaloner, W. H. "New Light on Richard Roberts, Textile Engineer (1789–1864)." *Transactions of the Newcomen Society* 41 (1968–1969).

Dickinson, W. H. "Richard Roberts, His Life and Inventions." *Transactions of the Newcomen Society* 25 (1945–1947).

Hills, R. L. *Richard Roberts, 1789–1864*. Ashbourne, U.K., 2002.

Smiles, S. *Industrial Diography: Iron Workers and Tool Makers*. London, 1879.

RICHARD L. HILLS

ROCKEFELLER, JOHN DAVISON (1839–1937), American entrepreneur in oil and philanthropy.

Rockefeller was born in Richford, New York, to William Avery Rockefeller (1810–1906), a traveling medicine showman, and the pious yet tolerant Elisa Davison Rockefeller (1813–1889). Historians have speculated extensively on how their dichotomous parental roles shaped Rockefeller; but he proved to be his own man, concentrating on developing the analytic skills critical to building important ventures.

The family moved to Cleveland in 1853, and the following year, at age fifteen, John took the standard six-month business curriculum of bookkeeping and penmanship. He then set off resolutely to find a job. Every day for two months he called on potential employers, until one firm, the commission merchants Hewitt and Tuttle, urgently needed a junior bookkeeper. Meticulous in spotting ways to cut costs, as well as a tireless bill collector, in less than two years he parlayed his reputation, $800 in savings, and a loan into a junior partnership in the new firm of Clark and Rockefeller, commodity brokers and shippers.

While handling the accounting, Rockefeller also was quite successful in soliciting business. No glad-handing salesman, he inspired trust by assuring customers about the care given to their products. His ability to earn others' confidence also helped him to obtain loans from Cleveland bankers, critical to tapping the gains from the volume allowed by financing more contracts. By the end of 1862, when oil shipped through the port began to increase noticeably, Rockefeller, then twenty-three, was already one of the wealthiest men in Cleveland.

Clark and Rockefeller built a refinery with Samuel Andrews, who had learned the rudiments of extracting kerosene from crude oil. Rockefeller undertook the new enterprise with entrepreneurial passion, devising ways to cut costs and use waste products. Sensing further savings in a larger refinery, he constantly advocated expansion. When Clark resisted, Rockefeller bought his partner out in 1865, and continued to expand, using borrowed money. He built a second refinery at the end of the year and then a barrel factory and an acid reclamation facility to reduce costs. His Standard Oil company was framed in 1867 and incorporated in 1870. Rockefeller sent his brother William to New York City to manage exports of kerosene, now a sizeable fraction of sales, and to cultivate bankers for financing. He also added Henry Flagler, who became Standard Oil's negotiator with the railroads. Many criticisms of the company have turned on its winning favorable rates, commonly called rebates. There was an economic logic for this; larger shipments of oil allowed the railroads to lower costs for example, substituting tankcars for boxcars carrying barrels of kerosene. In the oft-cited case where Standard Oil was reported to have received rebates for its competitors' oil as well as its own, the company had contracted with the railroads to guarantee regular shipments of oil, well beyond its own production. This allowed the railroads to use what is now called a unit train, one dedicated exclusively to regular round trips between Cleveland and the Atlantic ports. Here Standard Oil was not competing with other Cleveland refineries, but rather it was acting as the distributor, lowering the net cost of all the firms through efficient shipping.

In 1871, the Southern Improvement Company, a cartel initiated by the major railroads, attempted to combine such efficiencies for all shipments of oil. However, it excluded sizable groups of oil producers and, in the resulting uproar, fell apart before it could begin operations. This incident turned Standard Oil and Rockefeller into symbols of massive economic change and power, a view that has persisted for well over a century.

On 1 January 1872 Rockefeller expanded the capital base of the company from $1 million to $3.5 million in order to continue acquiring other refineries. He did not buy competitors just to eliminate competition; each acquisition was assessed on its own merits for Standard Oil, with the owners usually paid more than market value. Because Rockefeller operated more efficiently, sometimes dramatically so, he could pay more for a firm than others could hope to recoup. He usually kept specialty operations, such as lubricants, vaseline, and wax, that could operate on a smaller scale; the smaller and less efficient operations such as kerosene refineries were scrapped. He was always looking for companies with good managers, whom he viewed as the most valuable resource the company could acquire.

In 1882 Standard Oil moved to a trust form of organization. Trusts commonly were regarded as monopolistic arrangements in an industry, used to obtain higher prices and profits, traditionally for such commodities as sugar, rope, and whiskey. However, Standard Oil's major concern was coordinating complex operations across state lines at a time when the incorporation laws had not yet adapted to such developments. More appropriate legal structures, such as those permitted by New Jersey's enactment of holding-company legislation in 1889, would follow; but Standard Oil had to improvise in the meantime. The early 1880s also saw the transfer of most of Standard Oil's executives to New York City. A large new headquarters building was constructed near Wall Street, where the management began crafting an efficient structure out of the various acquisitions. Refineries were consolidated at larger, more efficient locations and tied into new pipelines. To rationalize Standard Oil's operations, Rockefeller created executive committees for each major function, refining and marketing, for example. These working groups gathered information, discussed improvements, and suggested productive investments. This management innovation has been widely followed in large, multifunctional firms ever since then.

In the 1890s Rockefeller became the richest person in the world, sailing past steel magnate Andrew Carnegie. Even after leaving day-to-day management, Rockefeller undertook two major projects that greatly added to his wealth. The first was developing the oil fields around Lima, Ohio, which industry experts had dismissed as too "sour," their sulfur content spoiling kerosene. Rockefeller hired Herman Frasch, to develop a technique for purifying the oil, thereby extending Standard Oil's dominance in oil through the 1890s. Rockefeller also bought large tracts of the Mesabi Range iron ore deposits in northern Minnesota,

Standard Oil had been able to build and maintain a dominant position in its sector through its efficiency. Without that margin of superiority, it could never have become stigmatized as a monopoly; and once that margin began to fade, as it inevitably did by 1911, antitrust efforts became increasingly inappropriate.

In the 1890s, Rockefeller began phasing out of Standard Oil management; so he had about forty years to enjoy his wealth. Predictably, he approached spending his money much as he did creating it, looking for large opportunities that required entrepreneurial creativity instead of simply giving money to established charities. The bulk of the $500 million that he gave away—his son, John D. Rockefeller, Jr. would donate an additional billion dollars—went into medical research and new systems of public health. He founded what is now Rockefeller University, nudging American medical practice toward scientific professionalism; and he initiated programs in public health, notably to eliminate hookworm in the American South.

BIBLIOGRAPHY

Chandler, Alfred D., Jr., and Richard S. Tedlow. "The Standard Oil Company—Combination, Consolidation, and Integration." In *The Coming of Managerial Capitalism, A Casebook on the History of American Economic Institutions*, chap. 14. Homewood, Ill., 1985.

Chandler, Alfred D., Jr. *The Visible Hand, The Managerial Revolution in American Business*. Cambridge, 1977.

Chernow, Ron. *Titan: The Life of John D. Rockefeller, Sr.* New York, 1998.

Hawke, David Freeman. *John D.: The Founding Father of the Rockefellers*. New York, 1980.

Hidy, Ralph W., and Muriel E. Hidy. *History of the Standard Oil Company (New Jersey): Pioneering in Big Business, 1882–1911*. New York, 1995.

Nevins, Allan. *Study in Power: John D. Rockefeller, Industrialist and Philanthropist*, 2 vols. New York, 1953.

Tarbell, Ida M. *The History of the Standard Oil Company*, 2 vols. Gloucester, Mass., 1904.

Williamson, Harold F., and Arnold R. Daum. *The American Petroleum Industry: The Age of Illumination, 1859–1899*. Evanston, Ill., 1959.

GERALD GUNDERSON

JOHN D. ROCKFELLER. (Prints and Photographs Division, Library of Congress)

which experts had regarded as hopelessly low-grade. Rockefeller's usual confidence that such a problem could be solved through innovations in organization and technology again proved correct.

In 1911, capping a long period of criticism of and litigation against Standard Oil, the U.S. Supreme Court ruled that the organization was a monopoly and divided it into independent regional companies. The ruling served mostly as a catharsis for public frustration, having little economic effect. By 1911, oil discoveries in Texas, Russia, and Southeast Asia provided competition. In addition, competitors in Standard's home territory, the Northeastern United States, had always been in close pursuit, borrowing its innovations and, in some cases, pioneering their own.

ROMAN EMPIRE. The Roman Empire comprised the lands of the Mediterranean basin as well as large parts of Europe including Britain. This large landmass was held together for over four centuries (first century BCE–fourth century CE) by a modest but highly professional army, a political system that integrated local authority with an equally modest civil administration under the authority of the emperor, and an imperial and religious ideology that fostered unity and consensus.

The empire was built on a complex mix of regional economies of varying sophistication inherited from the states, cities, tribes, and other entities conquered or annexed by Rome in the first through third centuries CE. Under Caesar and particularly Augustus, a provincial administrative structure was established that permitted more efficient tax collection. This included the establishment of a coinage system involving gold, silver, and bronze coins that allowed for a wide range of monetized transactions, for both state and private commercial purposes. Augustus also regularized the provision of foodstuffs (*annona*) for the city of Rome from the provinces of Africa and Egypt. These actions, combined with the establishment of the rule of law, a common language (Latin), and peace, laid the basis for an empire that by any premodern measure experienced an extraordinary level of economic integration and development for more than two hundred years, and perhaps longer.

However, the need to feed and maintain a permanent, professional army of over 300,000, and the growth of towns between the mid-first and early-third centuries CE seemed to have acted as the chief engines of the empire's economic growth. The provisioning of the Roman army, particularly along the northern frontiers, including Britain, stimulated the construction of serviceable roads and the increased production of crops and animals, craft goods, construction materials, and other commodities in Rome's European provinces. Since the army was paid in coin, the regions directly tied to servicing it became highly monetized.

The Roman government encouraged the development of cities throughout the empire. New towns (*colonia*) comprised of Roman citizens or veterans were established in a number of provinces, especially in the west in the late-first century BCE and the first century CE. During the course of the first and second centuries CE, both new and existing cities experienced an increase in their mean size and population. The growth of urbanism caused a number of fundamental changes in Roman economy and society. First, it raised demand for foodstuffs and was thus a major contributing factor in the expansion and the intensification of agriculture, particularly the production of cereals, olive oil, livestock, and wine. Second, it spawned the growth of a manufacturing sector of the economy, ranging from household production to specialized workshops and cottage industries, to meet growing demand for nonagricultural goods. The ability to meet the increased need for agricultural and manufactured goods was made possible in part through notable technological advances in water lifting, milling, mining, shipbuilding, and the diffusion and the adoption of technology (Wilson, 2002). Finally, the powerful injection of demand provided by cities raised the volume of commercial trade and transport in many parts of the empire (Hopkins, 1980; Harris, 2000).

One symptom of the transformed social and economic environment created by peace, urban expansion, and agricultural growth was modest population growth, chiefly in the western empire, from an estimated forty-five million in

14 CE to sixty million on the eve of the great plague in 164 CE (Frier, 2000).

Taken together, these developments point to an increase in per capita disposable income and by extension a slight growth in per capita and not just aggregate production in the empire. However, as with all political economies, some regions of the Roman Empire remained impoverished or at best stagnant across time. Some arid and mountainous regions in Africa and in central Europe were poor in resources and thus incapable of moving out of low-level agriculture or stock raising. Other areas suffered from being removed from the main communication networks to Rome and the army, and therefore did not benefit from the growth in economic activity associated with supplying the cities and the army.

There were also significant social and cultural constraints on the ability of the Roman economy to perform and grow efficiently and powerfully. Roman concepts of accounting, banking, finance, management, investment, and labor were deeply rooted in premodern agrarian and family-based values that impeded the development of a legal, social, and cultural framework for conducting complex economic transactions, particularly over long distances, similar to that found in the mercantile cities of the emerging nation-states of Europe. However, a comparison with modern, capitalist models of economic growth tends to obscure those aspects of Roman legal, institutional, political, and social structures that allowed for greater consumer, social, and even political freedom throughout the empire (Andreau, 2000). The emperors' effective binding of the senatorial order also raised public confidence in the Roman state and cleared the way for greater political and social mobility among provincial elites. Even though poverty was a reality everywhere, its presence does not preclude the possibility that the quality of life under the empire was perhaps the highest in the history of the ancient Mediterranean world, and remained so until the seventeenth century in Europe.

The globalizing nature of economic growth in the Roman Empire between circa 50 BCE and 250 CE created both benefits and problems. In positive terms, it spawned a hybrid "Roman" culture within a matrix of shared aspirations, values, and beliefs. A citizen of the empire traveling from Britain to the Euphrates in the mid-second century CE would have found in virtually every town along the journey foods, goods, landscapes, buildings, institutions, laws, entertainment, and sacred elements not dissimilar to those in his own community. Although each of these features was shaped by its own particular environmental and cultural milieu, it was the things shared—the commonwealth—rather than the things that divided them that drew the peoples of the empire together into a common union. Although local elites were generally able to share in

APPLE SELLERS. Funerary relief from Arlon, second century CE. (Musèe Luxembourgeois, Arlon, Belgium)

the identity and the benefits of empire, the greatest beneficiaries were those regions with a strong resource base and preexistent complex social and political structures. However, a case can be made for a political culture under the empire that provided for a level of individual liberty, justice, and local autonomy among its population that was unparalleled in the ancient world, and not achieved again in Europe until the modern period.

There is a general scholarly consensus that the Roman economy may have weakened, beginning perhaps as early as the later-second century CE. The supply of coin in the Roman Empire declined in the mid-second century, a change perhaps directly related to a cessation of bullion production at the Spanish mines. This was probably a factor in the debasement of the coinage instituted at the end of the century, and is likely to have had a direct impact on state spending on the military, the *annona*, and construction works (Wilson, 2002). There is also evidence that the plague under Marcus Aurelius contributed to a decline in population and a reduction in trade and transport in the medium term. Whether these events sparked the beginning of a regression in the overall performance of the Roman economy is not certain; but they were followed in the third century by the first serious security threats to the empire, in the barbarian and Persian invasions that penetrated the northern and eastern frontiers and caused widespread upheaval in Gaul, the Danubian provinces, Asia Minor, and the Levant. The attacks temporarily undermined the fiscal stability of the empire and the political and administrative apparatus that tied the cities and provinces to the central state, though there is no indication of permanent damage to the empire's urban and rural infrastructure.

The reestablishment of a secure monetary system and the military and administrative reorganization of Diocletian and Constantine helped restore stability to the empire and its economy. The foundation of a new imperial capital in Constantinople also stimulated economic growth in Greece and the eastern provinces down to the sixth century, as did the breakup of the empire into two parts in the late-fourth century, which saved the east from expending resources in the west where new barbarian invasions in the late-fourth and fifth centuries seriously weakened the region's overall security and economy (Ward-Perkins, 2000a, 2000b). Africa, except for the eastern littoral, continued to perform well until the Vandal invasions, when the cutoff of the *annona* to Rome weakened its strong position as a massive exporter of agricultural and small manufactured goods such as fine tableware. Although precise information is lacking, the real decline or transformation in the fabric of the Roman economy seems to have occurred everywhere in the sixth and seventh centuries (Garnsey and Whittaker, 1998; Ward-Perkins, 2000a, 2000b).

The economy of the Roman Empire, although premodern, underdeveloped, and unstable, was structurally more resilient and innovative than imagined by Finley (1985). Its scale and its performance were unmatched in Europe until the early-modern period. It may have made a false start in the economic history of Europe, but comparison with the modern European experience has too often obscured analysis and understanding of the complex and long-term achievements of the Roman economy.

BIBLIOGRAPHY

Andreau, J. "Commerce and Finance." In *The Cambridge Ancient History*, 2d ed., vol. 11, *The High Empire, A.D. 70–192*, pp. 769–786. Cambridge, 2000.

Bowman, Alan K. "Provincial Administration and Taxation." In *The Cambridge Ancient History*, 2d ed., vol. X, *The Augustan Empire, 43 B.C.–A.D. 69*, pp. 344–370. Cambridge, 1996.

Duncan-Jones, R. P. *Structure and Scale in the Roman Economy.* Cambridge, 1990.

Finley, M. I. *The Ancient Economy.* 2d ed. Berkeley, 1985. Probably the most influential work in shaping current thought on the ancient economy. However, its emphasis on structure over performance and on textual as opposed to archaeological evidence (the essay was written before the boom in archaeology of the ancient economy) led Finley to underestimate the scale and the performance of the Roman economy.

Frier, Bruce. "Demography." In *The Cambridge Ancient History*, 2d ed., vol. XI, *The High Empire, A.D. 70–192*, pp. 787–816. Cambridge, 2000.

Garnsey, Peter. "The Land." In *The Cambridge Ancient History*, 2d ed., vol. XI, *The High Empire, A.D. 70–192*, pp. 679–709. Cambridge, 2000.

Garnsey, Peter, and C. R. Whittaker. "Rural Life in the Later Roman Empire." In *The Cambridge Ancient History*, vol. XIII, *The Late Empire, A.D. 337–425*, pp. 277–311. Cambridge, 1998.

Giardina, A., ed. *Societa romana e impero tardoantica.* 4 vols. Rome and Bari, 1986.

Greene, Kevin. *The Archaeology of the Roman Economy.* London, 1986. The best general treatment of the value of archaeology for Roman economic history.

Greene, Kevin. "Industry and Technology." *The Cambridge Ancient History*, 2d ed., vol. XI, *The High Empire, A.D. 70–192*, pp. 741–768. Cambridge, 2000.

Harris, W. V. "Trade." *The Cambridge Ancient History*, 2d ed., vol. XI. *The High Empire, A.D. 70–192*, pp. 710–740. Cambridge, 2000.

Hitchner, R. B. "The Advantages of Wealth and Luxury. The Case for Economic Growth in the Roman Empire." In *The Ancient Economy: Evidence and Models*, edited by J. Manning and I. Morris. Stanford. Forthcoming.

Hopkins, Keith. "Taxes and Trade in the Roman Empire." *Journal of Roman Studies* 70 (1980), 101–125. Offers an intriguing model of the structure, scale, and performance of the Roman economy.

Hopkins, Keith. "Rome: Taxes, Rents, and Trade." In *The Ancient Economy: Recent Approaches*, edited by Walter Scheidel and Sitta von Reden, pp. 190–230. Edinburgh, 2002.

Horden, Peregrine, and Nicholas Purcell. *The Corrupting Sea. A Study of Mediterranean History.* Oxford, 2000.

Howgego, Christopher. "The Supply and Use of Money in the Roman World." *Journal of Roman Studies.* 82 (1992), 1–31.

Mattingly, David J., and John Salmon. *Economies beyond Agriculture in the Classical World.* London and New York, 2001.

Saller, Richard. "Framing the Debate over Growth in the Ancient Economy." In *The Ancient Economy: Evidence and Models.* edited by J. Manning and I. Morris. Stanford. Forthcoming.

Ward-Perkins, Bryan. "Land, Labour and Settlement." In *The Cambridge Ancient History*, vol. XIV, *Late Antiquity: Empire and Successors, A.D. 425–600*, pp. 315–345. Cambridge, 2000a.

Ward-Perkins, Bryan. "Specialized Production and Exchange." In *The Cambridge Ancient History*, vol. XIV, *Late Antiquity: Empire and Successors, A.D. 425–600*, pp. 346–391. Cambridge, 2000b.

Wilson, Andrew. "Machines, Power and the Ancient Economy." *Journal of Roman Studies* 92 (2002), 1–32.

Whittaker, C.R., and Peter Garnsey. "Trade, Industry and the Urban Economy." In *The Cambridge Ancient History*, vol. XIII, *The Late Empire, A.D. 337–425*. pp. 312–337. Cambridge, 1998.

R. BRUCE HITCHNER

ROMANIA. *See* Balkans.

ROME AND THE PAPAL STATE. The Papal State was a patchwork of lands under the direct or indirect rule of the Roman pontiffs from 756 to 1870 CE. They stretched across the middle of the Italian Peninsula from sea to sea, corresponding to the modern regions of Umbria, Marche, Lazio, and eastern Emilia-Romagna and covering at their apogee about 41,500 square kilometers. They further included the external small dependencies of Benevento in southern Italy (from 1077 to 1860) and the Comtat Venaissin in Provence (from 1274 to 1791). Although the papal claim to temporal power was based on a forged document, the Donation of Constantine, the actual origins of papal sovereignty are in both the gradual rise of papal influence in central Italy vis-à-vis the collapse of imperial authority and the general insecurity of the early medieval centuries, and the church accumulation of extensive estates around Rome, known as the Patrimonium Sancti Petri (the Patrimony of Saint Peter).

Except for sporadic revivals, the actual administration of church territories in central Italy occupied a subordinate role in papal political strategy before the fifteenth century. As a result, throughout the Middle Ages the states remained a mosaic of diverse and autonomous lands with little in common. Romagna, Umbria, and Marche had a number of major towns whose economic development mirrored closely urban developments in Northern Italy and Tuscany. The lack of a single unifying political structure did not constrain economic activity but did foster local independence and fierce internecine competition. Much of the southern provinces of the Papal State instead formed Rome's agricultural belt and consisted largely of feudal estates, most of which were owned by Roman clerical institutions and aristocratic families.

ROME. Markets in the Piazza Navona, painting by Gaspare Vanvitelli (van Wittel) (1653–1736). (Galleria Colonna, Rome/Alinari/Art Resource, NY)

The greatest contribution of the medieval papacy to economic development was in the realm of finance through the promotion of international credit techniques. Since direct papal rule wielded limited authority, the papacy pioneered the erection of a centralized fiscal machinery designed to generate a flow of contributions (commonly known as tithes) from subject territories to Rome. Thanks to the cooperation of Italian and Jewish bankers and money dealers, the papacy mobilized a sizable portion of European ground rents, converting them into liquid capital and thereby contributing mightily to the Italian commercial revolution during the "long thirteenth century" (circa 1180–1320).

The translation of the papacy to Avignon (1309–1377) and the ensuing Great Schism (1378–1417) brought papal authority to a low ebb and the state close to complete disintegration. Substantial changes took place after the return of Martin V to Rome in 1420. Successive Renaissance popes set out to restore the church's territorial domain, at first by means of administrative reorganization, then by means of military repossession culminating in the capture of Bologna in 1506, Perugia in 1540, and Ferrara in 1597. Current historiography recognizes the effectiveness of papal state building in the fifteenth and sixteenth centuries. Authority was increasingly centralized, the provinces were put under the firm control of papal officials, and the administration was rebuilt around six *congregationes* (commissions).

Reassertion of temporal authority in central Italy amounted to a refoundation of the Papal State. This refoundation had the greatest importance for papal political and financial independence but failed to lead to greater economic integration and development of its component parts. Before the eighteenth century, the government in Rome did little to stimulate production and trade, content to regulate the flow of foodstuffs and to secure a steady flow of contributions from the provinces. The state's reservoir of taxable wealth was tapped to support the international role of the early modern papacy and provided the basis for the renovation of papal finance, the most innovative element of which was long-term credit. At first, borrowing was disguised behind the sale of venal offices. In 1526, the emission of the *monte fede* marked the beginning of long-term interest-bearing debt, either in the form of life annuities or perpetual shares (redeemable or nonredeemable), which turned Rome into one of the main money markets in Europe. The ingenuity and dependability of the papal curia failed to improve the economic ills of the papal domains but made a contribution of major importance to the evolution of the management of public finance.

The sixteenth century transformed Rome from a small medieval town into a modern metropolis of over 100,000 inhabitants. Rome mirrored the strengths and weaknesses of the Papal State. As a territorial capital, the city was

TABLE 1. *Population of Rome (1300–1870)*

DATE	POPULATION
ca. 1300	ca. 30,000
1440	30,000–35,000
1526	55,000
1600	102,000
1650	121,000
1700	142,000
1750	158,000
1790	163,000
1870	200,000

SOURCE: Felloni, Giuseppe, "Italy," in *An Introduction to the Sources of European Economic History, 1500–1800*, edited by C. Wilson and G. Parker, pp. 5–7, London, 1980; Ginatempo, Maria, and Lucia Sandri, *L'Italia delle città: Il popolamento urbano tra medioevo e rinascimento (secoli xii–xvi)*, p. 149, Florence, 1990; Insolera, Italo, "Roma," in *Storia d'Italia*, vol. 6, *Atlante*, p. 324, Turin, 1976.

haunted by the legacy of its classical past and by its role as the spiritual center of Christendom. Because of the fragmented nature of the state, Rome did not succeed in becoming the economic heart of the domain, and unlike most other notable European cities, it was never an important productive and commercial center. Rome was unique in the importance of its service sector. Rome thrived as a great clerical bureau, a mart, and a consumption center living off the large numbers of pilgrims, visitors, and prelates. Apart from building, the one true industry of Rome, typical occupations were luxury crafts and service trades. Banking and financial services figured prominently. All of the important banking firms in Italy (notably from Siena, Florence, and Genoa) had branches in Rome. Sellers, vendors, and dealers were legions. According to most estimates, the annual influx of visitors exceeded 100,000 and were many more during jubilee years. In 1600, Rome accommodated no less than half a million pilgrims. The whole city economy was geared to this: 5,614 booths, shops, and inns employed 24,193 people. The primary activity, however, was the clerical administration revolving around the papal bureau and its network of courts and offices. To that hub, the large families of the resident cardinals and the staffs of religious and charitable agencies must be added. Overall, the administrative machinery probably employed between one-fourth and one-third of the city's population at any given time.

[*See also* Roman Empire.]

BIBLIOGRAPHY

Bauer, Clemens. "Die Epochen der Papstfinanz: Ein Versuch." *Historische Zeitschrift* 138 (1927), 457–503.

Delumeau, Jean. *Vie économique et sociale de Rome dans la seconde moitié du XVIe siècle*. Paris, 1957–1959.

Noble, Thomas F. X. *The Republic of St. Peter: The Birth of the Papal State, 680–825*. Philadelphia, 1984.

Partner, Peter. *The Lands of St. Peter: The Papal State in the Middle Ages and the Early Renaissance*. London, 1972.

Partner, Peter. *Renaissance Rome, 1500–1559: A Portrait of a Society*. Berkeley, 1976.

Partner, Peter. "The Papacy and the Papal States." In *The Rise of the Fiscal State in Europe, c. 1200–1815*, edited by R. Bonney, pp. 359–380. Oxford, 1999.

Prodi, Paolo. *The Papal Prince, One Body and Two Souls: The Papal Monarchy in Early Modern Europe*. Cambridge, 1988.

Stow, Kenneth R. *Taxation, Community, and State: The Jews and the Fiscal Foundations of the Early Modern Papal State*. Stuttgart, 1982.

Waley, Daniel. *The Papal State in the Thirteenth Century*. London and New York, 1961.

MAURO CARBONI

RONG FAMILY. During the first half of the twentieth century, the Rongs became the richest businesspeople in China. According to a nationwide audit done by the government of the People's Republic in 1956, the Rongs were worth 60 million Chinese yuan—far more than any other capitalist family in the country. The Rong family made its fortune in cotton textiles and flour. The brothers who founded this industrial empire, Rong Zongjing and Rong Desheng, were born into a merchant family in Wuxi, a city seventy-five miles west of Shanghai, where they grew up with strong ties to their family, lineage, and native place. Their native-place tie was different from loyalty to a hometown or place of birth. All Chinese inherited their fathers' native places (in the same way that they inherited surnames), and Chinese merchants generally preferred to deal with native-place associates rather than other Chinese because they spoke each other's local dialects and expected eventually to return home, where the reputations of their families, lineages, and native places were at stake.

As young men, the Rong brothers faithfully served their native place for twenty-four years (1881–1915) by raising capital through native banks (*qianzhuang*) in Shanghai and remitting it to Wuxi, which, with their help, became China's fifth-most industrialized city in the 1910s. Then in 1915, the Rong brothers broke precedent by founding an industrial enterprise outside Wuxi. Despite opposition from their native-place associates, they opened Shenxin Cotton Mill as an unlimited liability company in Shanghai, and when denied financial support from their native place, they turned for the first time to Shanghai-based Japanese-owned banks that had no ties to their family or anyone else from Wuxi. In 1921, they completed the transfer of authority over their business from Wuxi by opening in Shanghai their General Corporation, another unlimited liability company, which served as headquarters for all of the Rong family's industrial enterprises—Maoxin and Fuxin Flour Mills as well as Shenxin Cotton Mills. Continuing to draw upon Japanese as well as Chinese financing in Shanghai, the Rong brothers raised the number of Shenxin's cotton mills from two to eight: six in Shanghai, one in Wuxi, and one in Hankou. By 1932, Shenxin employed 31,717 workers (the most of any firm in China) who spun yarn on 561,592 spindles (the most of any firm in China) and wove cloth on 5,357 looms (the most of any firm in China except one, the Japanese-owned Kanegafuchi Cotton Mills).

The Rong brothers ran the risk of destroying their native-place network, but even while they aggressively overcame opposition from their native-place associates, they fully included the same associates in the implementation of these policies by appointing them as members of Shenxin's administrative staff in Shanghai, Hankou, and other cities as well as Wuxi. In 1928, for example, of the 957 staff members that they employed, no less than 617—64.5 percent—hailed from Wuxi.

The Rong family provides perhaps the supreme example in Chinese history of entrepreneurs using a Chinese social network to build up large, profitable, and competitive industrial enterprises. The Rong brothers achieved this success not by passively accepting their social network of family members and native-place associates in some classic, unchanging form but by seizing leadership of it and transforming it into a sizable and highly structured business organization.

BIBLIOGRAPHY

Bergère, Marie Claire. *The Golden Age of the Chinese Bourgeoisie, 1911–1937.* Translated by Janet Lloyd. Cambridge, 1989.

Bush, Richard C. *Politics of Cotton Textiles in Kuomintang China, 1927–1937.* New York, 1982.

Chan, Wellington K. K. *Merchants, Mandarins, and Modern Enterprise in Late Ch'ing China.* Cambridge, Mass., 1977.

Coble, Parks M. *The Shanghai Capitalists and the Nationalist Government, 1927–1937.* Cambridge, Mass., 1986.

Cochran, Sherman. *Encountering Chinese Networks: Western, Japanese, and Chinese Corporations in China, 1880–1937.* Berkeley, 2000.

SHERMAN COCHRAN

ROTATING SAVINGS SOCIETIES. "Rotating credit societies" is the collective name for a variety of informal institutions that provide saving and lending services. The acronym ROSCA (rotating savings and credit association) has been used to describe them in many circumstances, but unfortunately also has been connected with lotteries and other, unrelated credit schemes. ROSCAs *per se* are important both for the services they provide and because they illustrate the way people use social ties to develop simple institutions that mitigate problems posed by incomplete markets.

There are several types of ROSCA. To illustrate, consider what seems to be the most common, a "random" ROSCA. There are N people who each want to buy a nondivisible good that costs $C*N$. The N people ("members") commit to meeting once each week. At every meeting each member puts an amount C into a pot. The members draw lots, and the winner gets to take that week's total contributions ($C*N$). At every following meeting, the previous winners still must contribute but cannot win a second time. Eventually every member will have contributed C at each of N meetings, for a total of $C*N$ in contributions, and every member will have won the pot of $C*N$. Thus each member contributes precisely what he or she wins. All members eventually win the pot; they differ only in when they win the pot.

How does the ROSCA provide savings and credit services? The first member to win the pot receives, in effect, a loan from the others equal to $C(N-1)$. He or she repays this loan over the next $N-1$ meetings, at an interest rate of zero. Each successive winner is at first a net lender and then a net borrower. The last person to win the pot lends $C(N-1)$ to the others, again at an interest rate of zero. Thus from the members' viewpoint the ROSCA is both a savings and a lending institution. There are also alternative forms of ROSCAs. In the most common alternative, the bidding ROSCA, the pot is not allocated randomly but goes to the member who pledges the most to the other ROSCA members. These pledges can comprise larger future contributions, gifts, and so on.

The ROSCA clearly improves the economic well-being of its members in the case where they have no access to financial institutions. For simplicity consider the random ROSCA. The last person to win contributes C per period for $N-1$ periods and then wins the amount $C*N$. This stream of contributions is identical to what would happen if he or she put away C per period for $N-1$ periods, saving up to buy the hypothetical nondivisible good. The last winner has the worst outcome from the ROSCA. All earlier winners are strictly better off because of the ROSCA, as they have their $C*N$ earlier than would have been the case had they just saved C per week. For individuals with access to interest-bearing savings or loans, the comparison to the ROSCA is more complicated. For an individual considering participation in a ROSCA, of course, the comparison between the ROSCA and the credit market depends on the terms offered in the credit market.

ROSCAs are most often found among close-knit social groups such as a village or members of an ethnic group (especially in a minority, such as migrants), and so forth. There are two reasons for this. The first is that such people are often excluded from more formal institutions for savings and credit. The second reason is that the ROSCA, to be successful, requires a great deal of trust among all members. Every member of a ROSCA has an incentive to cease making contributions once he or she has won the pot. There are in principle two ways to prevent the group from unraveling in this way. One is to have repeated ROSCAs among the same individuals. Early winners continue to contribute because they want to participate in future ROSCAs. This reputation mechanism, which works for many incentive problems, is relatively weak here because at high rates of discount the present value of future ROSCA participation can be quite low. Another reason not to defect from the ROSCA is the fear of sanctions. Shared bonds of kinship or ethnicity can give ROSCA members a powerful tool against those who would fail to make their contributions. These sanctions could be economic, such as refusing to employ or to purchase from the individual in question, or noneconomic, such as exclusion from social or religious activities. Such sanctions work best among small, well-defined groups, where the option of leaving the group is not very appealing. Both reasons for participating help to explain the popularity of ROSCAs with ethnic minorities and migrants; such people have difficulty obtaining access to the formal credit market, and they have cause to fear exclusion from the social activities of their small group.

The extensive anthropological literature on ROSCAs shows that people use them primarily to save for durable goods. Their basic structure shows that they are not well suited for buffering against income or consumption shocks. Members both lend and borrow in a fixed, rigid time pattern, which is impractical in response to shocks. ROSCAs are also unsuited to financing large, long-term investment, such as the purchase of a farm. The amounts required would entail either very large contributions or an enormous group, both of which would increase the probability that early winners would default on their obligation to the rest of the group.

The existence of ROSCAs as discussed here has been documented in many parts of the globe dating back to at least the late nineteenth century. Shirley Adener and Clifford Geertz, in their early surveys, conveyed the wide distribution and the rich variations of the basic institution across Asia, Africa, and the Americas. ROSCAs have existed for men and for women, for urban and for rural people, and for virtually every occupation and social class. One curious feature of the ROSCA is its apparent absence from European history; there are no clear cases of the institution's existence there although some have inferred the contrary from incomplete descriptions of practices common to occupational or other groups. The lack of European ROSCAs may reflect the strength of other credit institutions or the lack of social ties needed to support the institution.

BIBLIOGRAPHY

Ardener, Shirley. "The Comparative Study of Rotating Credit Associations." *Journal of the Royal Anthropological Institute of Great Britain and Ireland* 94.2 (1964), 201–229.

Besley, Timothy. "Nonmarket Institutions for Credit and Risk Sharing in Low-Income Countries." *Journal of Economic Perspectives* 9.3 (1996), 115–128.

Besley, Timothy, Stephen Coate, and Glenn Loury. "The Economics of Rotating Savings and Credit Associations." *American Economic Review* 83.4 (1993), 792–810.

Geertz, Clifford. "The Rotating Credit Association: A 'Middle Rung' in Development." *Economic Development and Cultural Change* 10.3 (1962), 241–263.

Levenson, Alec R., and Timothy Besley. "The Anatomy of an Informal Financial Market: ROSCA Participation in Taiwan." *Journal of Development Economics* 51.1 (1996), 45–68.

Light, Ivan, Im Jung Kwuon, and Deng Zhong. "Korean Rotating Credit Associations in Los Angeles." *Amerasia Journal* 16.2 (1990), 35–54.

Velez-Ibanez, Carlos G., and Albert Camarillo. "Bonds of Mutual Trust: The Cultural Systems of Rotating Credit Associations among Urban Mexicans and Chicanos." *Journal of American Ethnic History* 5.2 (1986), 72–79.

TIMOTHY W. GUINNANE

ROTHSCHILD FAMILY. Owned and run as a private family partnership, but operating in multiple financial centers, the Rothschild bank was the largest and most powerful financial institution of the nineteenth century.

The original "house" of M. A. Rothschild was founded in Frankfurt by Mayer Amschel Rothschild (1744–1812) in the 1790s. Originally a dealer in coins and other antiquities, Mayer Amschel became broker and later investment manager to William IX (1743–1821), the wealthy Prince (later elector) of Hesse-Kassel. By 1797, Rothschild had already accumulated capital of around £10,000 and was extending credit to a wide range of German clients. When the elector fell out of favor with Napoleon and was driven into exile, Mayer Amschel continued to help him manage his fortune, running the risk of arrest by the French authorities.

None of this was exceptional: Mayer Amschel was just one among many German-Jewish *Hoffaktoren*, "court Jews," offering financial services to petty princes. Nor was his decision to send his third son, Nathan (1777–1836), to England. The rapid growth of industrial textile manufacturing in England attracted numerous German merchants, eager to purchase the new Lancashire fabrics for the continental market. This too became a risky enterprise following Napoleon's imposition of the Continental System. Even Nathan's decision in 1811 to become involved in British war finance was unoriginal. Since the late seventeenth century, British government borrowing—both long-term through the Stock Exchange, and short-term from the money market—had attracted foreign financiers to the City of London. The Rothschilds' mobilization of their continental credit network to relay bullion to the British armies in the field in France in 1814 and 1815, as well as to transfer subsidies to Great Britain's continental allies, was remarkable only for its scale. The risks were commensurate: contrary to legend, Nathan and his five brothers were brought to the brink of insolvency by the news that

Napoleon had been defeated at Waterloo, since they had accumulated gold reserves in the expectation of a prolonged war. Nathan's immense and speculative purchases of British government bonds in the aftermath of Waterloo not only salvaged the situation but also reaped a huge profit. By 1818, the Rothschilds' combined capital amounted to nearly £1.8 million.

Until this point, the Rothschilds' mode of operation had been crude. Their bookkeeping was chaotic. Their correspondence was often intercepted and, although written in *Judendeutsch* (German transliterated into Hebrew characters), deciphered by the Austrian authorities. However, under Nathan's mercurial leadership, and on the basis of the funds they had accumulated during the war, the Rothschilds now began to play a more innovative role, specifically in the integration of the European bond markets.

The system whereby European states funded their budget deficits by selling long-term interest-bearing bonds to an elite of investors through financial intermediaries was well established by 1818. But the loan of that year issued by the Rothschilds on behalf of the Prussian crown was novel in that it was issued simultaneously in multiple markets. The interest was also payable in the market of issue. This corresponded to the unusual form of the Rothschild bank itself. Although it remained a family firm—structured as a partnership between adult male family members—the Rothschild bank took on a multinational character, in that the five brothers were now based in five major European financial and political centers: Frankfurt, Vienna, London, Naples, and Paris.

The success of the Prussian loan and similar transactions for the other great European powers in the 1820s rapidly established the Rothschilds as the dominant force in European financial markets. In terms of capital, they dwarfed their nearest rivals, the Barings. The Rothschilds' operations extended far beyond the European bond markets, embracing a whole range of financial services, including bullion and commodity broking, the discounting of commercial bills, insurance, and even private banking for an elite of aristocratic clients, selected according to their political influence. However, bond issuance and trading remained the Rothschilds' core business. In particular, their multinational structure and the sheer scale of their resources allowed them to conduct a huge and profitable arbitrage business. The acute sensitivity of the bond markets to political events—particularly intimations of revolution or war, both of which implied financial dislocation and an increased default risk—gave the Rothschilds an intense interest in the acquisition and rapid communication of political news. A network of salaried agents and correspondents spread outward from Europe to all the major financial centres of the Old and New Worlds. Their function was as much to transmit news to the partners in Europe as

to engage in commercial transactions. Even so, the Rothschilds were surprised by the 1830 and 1848 revolutions and suffered heavy losses.

Declining public sector deficits in the mid-nineteenth century and defaults by major borrowers in America and Iberia encouraged the Rothschilds to diversify into industrial investment. Mainly at the instigation of James de Rothschild (1792–1868), they acquired major stakes in Austrian, French, Belgian, and Italian railways; mercury mines in Spain; and the ironworks of Witkowitz (Vitkovie) in Moravia.

In absolute terms, the Rothschilds reached their zenith in 1899, when their combined capital (more than £41 million) exceeded that of the five biggest German joint-stock banks put together. In relative terms, however, they were in decline. In part, this reflected the diminishing returns of endogamy: the fourth generation evinced only mediocre financial acumen and was exceedingly risk averse. But the economic and political environment had also become less favorable. The spread of joint-stock banking eventually created comparably large concentrations of capital; more importantly, joint-stock banks were more willing to accept deposits, whereas the Rothschilds persisted in acting more like an investment trust, managing the capital of the Rothschild family alone (and doing so very conservatively). At the same time, the advent of the telegraph and commercial news agencies eroded the advantage the Rothschilds had derived from their network of private agents and couriers. Finally, the unifications of Italy and Germany shifted political power away from Naples, Vienna, and Frankfurt. In the 1840s, the Rothschilds had all but monopolized the markets for French and Belgian government bonds. By the 1890s, there were only a few countries in a similar position of near dependence, notably Brazil and Egypt. Increasingly, the great powers found themselves able to sell long-term bonds directly to the public or via rival intermediaries like post offices, savings banks, or consortia of joint-stock banks. Even Russia—which relied heavily on the Paris market—was never wholly dependent on the Rothschilds.

By the end of the nineteenth century, the extent of the Rothschilds' business empire remained impressive, ranging from Indian railways to South African diamond mines to Caucasian oil fields. They continued to be a crucial part of the "international financial architecture" of the gold-standard era, often acting as intermediaries between the major central banks and the bullion market. Their political power was, however, in decline—a reality belied by the family's increasingly conspicuous consumption and investment, especially in art and real estate, and their acquisition of aristocratic titles and sons-in-law. As amateur diplomats, the Rothschilds worked in vain to avert a military clash between Great Britain and Germany. World War I exposed their strategic Achilles' heel: the absence of a fully

vilification. In the wake of their spectacular rise to preeminence in European finance during the later Napoleonic Wars, there had been innumerable attacks on them, not just by avowed anti-Semites but also by conservative aristocrats, radical democrats, Populists, and socialists—even Zionists. The image recurs in numerous publications of a vast spider's web of money, with the Rothschilds at its center, and politicians, and kings (even popes) entangled around its edges. Recent scholarship, however, has produced a more balanced depiction of their political role.

The Rothschilds were able to achieve a partial—though very far from complete—restoration of their fortunes after 1945. Although the Paris house was nationalized by the government of François Mitterrand in 1981, it has since been reconstituted. Only the original London house of N. M. Rothschild & Sons has survived without interruption. It now forms part of a complex network of Rothschild-controlled companies.

[*See also* Banking, *subentry on* Modern Period.]

BIBLIOGRAPHY

Ferguson, Niall. *The World's Banker: The History of the House of Rothschild.* London, 1998.

NIALL FERGUSON

RUBBER *[This entry contains three subentries, on natural rubber, synthetic rubber, and manufacturing and industrial organization.]*

Natural Rubber

Natural rubber, or latex, can be obtained from various trees and shrubs, though the principal source has been the *Hevea brasiliensis*. When the trunk is cut, latex flows out; hence the name *caoutchouc*, meaning "weeping wood," given by French explorers. From as early as 6 CE, natural rubber was used in tropical America, northeastern India, and Malaya for lining containers, footwear, and clothing, forming torches, and making figures, ornaments, and balls.

European awareness of natural rubber began with Spanish colonization in South America in the fifteenth century. Charles de la Condamine publicized its qualities in 1745 after explorations in Peru. Two years later, François Fresneau supplied the first descriptions of hevea trees plus detailed accounts of methods of tapping and techniques for solidifying latex around clay molds exposed to heat and smoke.

As natural rubber's properties attracted experimental and commercial interest in Europe and the United States, the technological challenge was to render the hard blocks of rubber workable through the addition of solvents. In 1820, Thomas Hancock patented a machine for softening

THE ROTHSCHILDS. Family home in the former Judengasse in Frankfurt am Main, Germany, circa 1900. (Foto Marburg/Art Resource, NY)

fledged Rothschild house in New York. Heavy losses in the financial crises of 1914 and 1931 (the latter largely arising from the collapse and costly rescue of the Rothschild-founded Creditanstalt) drastically reduced the scale of the family's resources. At the same time, the formal ties between the remaining Rothschild houses in London, Paris, and Vienna were dissolved.

The Great Depression, the rise of National Socialism, and the outbreak of World War II brought the Rothschilds to the nadir of their fortunes. The Vienna house was dissolved following the Nazi *Anschluss* of Austria in 1938; the French Rothschilds had to flee Paris after the debacle of 1940; the London office was fortunate to survive the Blitz more or less unscathed. The Nazi war on European Jewry was worse than a return to the days when the family had been incarcerated in the Frankfurt ghetto; now those Rothschilds who fell into the hands of the Nazis risked losing their lives. Yet the family—grotesquely caricatured in the film *Die Rothschilds* (1940)—had grown accustomed to

rubber. The rubber products industry attracted considerable interest during the 1830s. Unfortunately, rubber goods became soft and sticky in hot weather, smelled of chemical solvents, and hardened and cracked if the temperature fell. The key breakthrough was the development of the process of vulcanization, which involved heating a compound of natural rubber, sulfur, and white lead to around 270° F. After this treatment, rubber became durable, allowing the manufacture and use of a wide range of industrial and consumer products. In the United States, Charles Goodyear patented vulcanization in 1844, after more than a decade of experimentation, and he took out several patents overseas, although Hancock managed to register his own patent first in England.

With a secure technology, commercial use of natural rubber expanded rapidly and profitably, with Goodyear's patents, enforced through licensing and aggressive litigation, regulating entry to 1858. Boots and shoes and waterproofed clothing were the major products, but rubber was used for goods ranging from parts in heavy machinery to molded toys and medical and dental supplies. Industrial developments provided new markets, such as electrical insulation and carriage and bicycle tires. Exports of natural rubber increased from 400 tonnes (881,600 pounds) in 1840 to 7,300 tonnes (17 million pounds) in 1870, to 28,000 tonnes (62 million pounds) in 1900 (Barlow, 1978, p. 16). This expansion of supply was achieved through an extension of tapping in the Amazon region of South America, which remained the principal source. In the jungle, individual tappers worked paths among the scattered hevea trees within their designated area, collecting latex from each tree every two or three days and forming it into large balls of smoked rubber. A series of middlemen provided supplies, transport, and credit as the rubber was shipped down river to Belem and then to the United States and Europe. The production and distribution system demonstrated considerable adaptability, drawing in local and metropolitan capital and merchants, to the volatile character of the international rubber trade. Productivity in rubber collection, however, was constrained by the distances between trees and economic incentives to maximize immediate rather than long-term yields. Beginning in the 1870s, high prices prompted the exploitation of rubber-bearing trees and vines in tropical Africa.

A more dramatic demonstration of the ecological impact of empires was the transfer of hevea trees to Southeast Asia in 1876–1877. The idea originated with the British government's India Office. Seeds were shipped secretly from the Amazon; seedlings cultivated at the Kew Botanic Garden were dispatched to Ceylon (present-day Sri Lanka) and Singapore. The project reflected the imagination of imperial officials; commercial interest only materialized from the late 1890s once coffee prices fell.

With the popularity of cycling and later automobiles, the increasing demand for natural rubber stimulated further planting, culminating in a mania for shares in plantation companies in 1909–1910. Plantations were financed by capital from Europe, the United States, and indigenous Chinese merchants. Dunlop, Michelin, and U.S. Rubber pioneered plantation investments by manufacturers. Migrant labor was drawn from southern India, although Chinese plantations generally used their own labor. Because trees took about seven years to mature, Asian output remained minimal in 1910, but by 1915 the region accounted for two-thirds of world output. As prices fell, the old wild rubber areas became marginal producers because the Asian estates were more productive than tapping jungle trees. Smallholding rubber, consisting of small acreages of often densely planted trees, provided its own distinctive low-cost supply. Agency houses supplied credit and trading facilities as well as managing estates, and the Singapore market became more significant with the onset of World War I as American manufacturers traded directly rather than via London dealers.

The potential for natural rubber output to increase rapidly, particularly from the smallholding sector, prompted repeated attempts to regulate supplies, chiefly in the hope of preserving the profitability of European-owned plantations. Thus, planter agitation resulted in the Stevenson Act (1922–1928), designed to limit exports from the British Empire. It was undermined by increasing output from the Dutch East Indies and the smallholding sector along with American plantation investments, notably in Liberia. The international economic collapse of 1929 to 1932 prompted new supply restrictions involving nearly all producers under the International Rubber Regulation Agreement of 1934, which achieved some price stability. In World War II, U.S. and European dependence on imported natural rubber was emphasized when Japan seized control of key producing regions in the Far East. With exports of natural rubber halted, governments, particularly the United States and Germany, promoted the development of synthetic rubbers by major rubber, chemical, and oil corporations. Because the new polymers remained inferior to natural rubber for many products, plantation production revived strongly after 1945. The U.S. government's stockpile of natural rubber acted as a buffer against volatile prices, although political instabilities disrupted output, investment, and productivity, particularly in Malaya. Beginning in the 1970s, radial tires, the impact of higher oil prices on the costs of synthetics, and industrial developments in Asia all contributed to natural rubber's maintaining a market share of between 30 and 40 percent of total production.

BIBLIOGRAPHY

Barlow, Colin. *The Natural Rubber Industry: Its Development, Technology and Economy in Malaysia*. Kuala Lumpur, Malaysia, 1978.

Coates, Austin. *The Commerce in Rubber: The First 250 Years*. Singapore and New York, 1987.

French, Michael J. *The U.S. Tire Industry: A History*. Boston, 1991.

Weinstein, Barbara. *The Amazon Rubber Boom, 1850–1920*. Stanford, Calif., 1983.

MICHAEL FRENCH

Synthetic Rubber

The development of synthetic rubber has been largely governed by the demand for rubber rather than technological innovations. The idea of replacing an important natural material with a synthetic analogue was an audacious one and took many years to perfect. From the outset, both quality and cost were major constraints, and it was difficult for synthetic rubber to compete when the industry was geared to the processing of a natural product, the price of which was often very low.

The synthesis of rubber was made possible by its relatively simple chemical structure. Unlike wool or wood, natural rubber is a polymer with a single repeating unit, a five-carbon hydrocarbon called isoprene. Synthetic rubber technology began in 1879, when the French chemist Gustave Bouchardat heated isoprene with hydrochloric acid to form a rubbery mass. As Bouchardat had obtained his isoprene by distilling natural rubber, the first truly synthetic rubber was made by William Tilden in London three years later. Tilden made his isoprene by cracking turpentine, but the rubbery material was formed only after the isoprene was left to stand for several weeks.

Early Attempts at Synthesis. In the early years of the twentieth century, the Amazonian rubber industry was unable to meet the growing demand for natural rubber from the tire industry. This shortfall stimulated the development of rubber plantations in East Asia and encouraged firms to synthesize rubber. In Great Britain, William Henry Perkin Jr. and Chaim Weizmann at the University of Manchester collaborated with the consulting partnership of Strange and Graham make a form of synthetic rubber from butadiene (a compound similar to isoprene) via butanol. The butanol was produced by the fermentation of starches, with acetone as a by-product. The synthetic rubber project failed, but the fermentation process became an important source of acetone in World War I. The Bayer Company in Germany set up a research program headed by Fritz Hofmann in 1906, and by 1912, it had developed "methyl" rubber. Although methyl rubber was not very suitable for tires, this was the first industrially successful synthetic rubber and was manufactured on a modest scale during World War I.

The postwar fluctuations in natural rubber prices encouraged research into synthetic rubber. Between 1925 and 1932, modest synthetic rubber industries were established in the Soviet Union, Germany, and the United States.

Soviet, German, and U.S. Efforts. The Soviet authorities looked for a method of making synthetic rubber and became aware of the earlier research of Sergey Lebedev, who had made butadiene by passing ethyl alcohol over a catalyst. The early trials were very successful, and factories were set up at Yaroslavl and Voronezh in 1932, at Yefremov in 1933, and at Kazan in 1936. The ethyl alcohol was made from potatoes at a time of great famine in the Soviet Union. By 1940, production had reached forty to fifty thousand tonnes. Originally, the Russians made a weak sodium-polymerized rubber, but with the forced assistance of interned German chemists, the production of Buna S began at Voronezh in 1949. Total Soviet production of synthetic rubber was around 2.3 million tonnes in the late 1980s.

The resumption of synthetic rubber research in Germany coincided with the formation of the German combine IG Farben, formed by the merger of Bayer, BASF, and Hoechst. By the time the research was temporarily halted by the Depression in 1932, IG Farben had already developed two new copolymer rubbers, Buna S (butadiene-styrene) and Buna N (butadiene-acrylonitrile). They were superior to the older synthetic rubbers, but difficult to process on the existing rubber machinery. The butadiene was made from coal-based acetylene. After 1933, the development of synthetic rubber in Germany was increasingly under the control of the Nazi state, which was eager to reduce the imports of natural rubber and to have an alternative source of rubber in wartime. IG Farben erected its first synthetic rubber factory at Schkopau, near Halle, in 1937, and Hüls on the northern edge of the Ruhr followed in 1940. They produced mainly Buna S, which was suitable for tires. At its peak in 1943, the German industry made 110,500 tonnes of Buna S and 3,700 tonnes of Buna N, which was used as a specialty rubber resistant to both oil and chemicals.

The main rival to Buna N was DuPont's neoprene, discovered accidentally by Arnold Collins in 1930 and launched as a specialty rubber in 1937. The large American rubber companies attempted to license IG Farben's Buna rubbers either directly or through IG's American ally, Standard Oil of New Jersey. IG Farben, on the other hand, wanted to collaborate in this field with DuPont. Faced with this impasse, Goodrich brought out its own Ameripol synthetic rubber in June 1940.

In the summer of 1940, the U.S. government became concerned about the safety of America's rubber supplies from German U-boat attack and the Japanese. President Roosevelt created the Rubber Reserve Company (RRC) to stockpile natural rubber, and it was given the task of setting up a synthetic rubber industry in October 1940. The main synthetic rubber was GR-S (Government Rubber-Styrene), the American version of Buna S. Although most of the synthetic rubber was petroleum-based, some of the butadiene monomer was made from ethyl alcohol to placate the farm lobby.

Production of GR-S rose from a minuscule 2,765 metric tonnes in 1942 to 768,139 metric tonnes in 1945, six and a half times German Buna S output at its peak. The polymer plants were separate from the butadiene and styrene production facilities and were all up and running by December 1943. The butadiene-from-alcohol plants started up in the first half of 1943, but the butadiene-from-petroleum plants were delayed, and the alcohol-based plants carried the burden for most of 1944. By 1945, however, as the petroleum-based plants came on stream, GR-S production surged ahead of demand.

Postwar Technology and Production. After the war, the synthetic rubber industry was kept alive because of the threat posed by the Soviet Union, and plants were mothballed rather than scrapped. In October 1948, a superior form of GR-S, called "cold" rubber, was introduced. It was as good as natural rubber for automobile tires, but it was hard to process and was no cheaper than standard GR-S. Even before the Korean War broke out in June 1950, the price of natural rubber had been rising sharply because of heavy buying by the Soviet Union, and the synthetic rubber industry was brought back into full production. GR-S production doubled in 1951 and remained at a high level in 1952 and 1953. Oil-extended rubber—made by combining cold rubber with mineral oil—was introduced to boost synthetic rubber production. The addition of mineral oil also made cold rubber both easier to process and cheaper, thereby enabling the privatization of the industry. The process was begun by Congress in 1953, and the last plant was sold off two years later, concluding one of the most successful publicly owned technological projects in history.

Since the introduction of cold rubber, there have been two major technological innovations. In the mid-1950s, several companies succeeded in making an exact copy of natural rubber. Using the technology developed by Karl Ziegler for the polymerization of ethylene, DuPont made an entirely new type of synthetic rubber from cheap ethylene and propylene in 1961. Neither of these synthetic rubbers offered any serious competition to SBR (styrene-butadiene rubber) in the mass market. American SBR production topped 1.5 million metric tonnes in 1975, but the industry then went into a decline, because the oil crisis made synthetic rubber more expensive relative to natural rubber. For many years, it has remained around 800,000 tonnes. By 1960, synthetic rubber factories had been established in Britain, Italy, France, and Japan. The production of synthetic rubber began in Brazil—the original home of natural rubber—in 1962. Although the Japanese industry soon became a major player, the American industry has retained its dominance. Total world production of all types of synthetic rubber has remained between 10 and 11 million tonnes for many years. By contrast, world production of natural rubber is about 7 million tonnes.

BIBLIOGRAPHY

Herbert, Vernon, and Attilio Bisio. *Synthetic Rubber: A Project That Had to Succeed.* Westport, Conn., 1985. A good overview of the American synthetic rubber program, with numerous tables of statistics.

Hayes, Peter. *"Industry and Ideology: IG Farben in the Nazi Era.* 2d ed. Cambridge, 2000. The best history of the German chemical behemoth during the Third Reich. Provides a good description of the development of Buna.

Howard, Frank A. *Buna Rubber: The Birth of an Industry.* New York, 1947. An inevitably biased account of the development of the synthetic rubber industry by one of the main participants, but containing many interesting details.

Morris, Peter J. T. *The American Synthetic Rubber Research Program.* Philadelphia, 1989. Looks at the research side of the American program and shows how the different parts of the program interacted.

Morris, Peter J. T. "Transatlantic Transfer of Buna S Synthetic Rubber Technology, 1932–1945." In *The Transfer of International Technology: Europe, Japan and USA in the Twentieth Century*, edited by David J. Jeremy, pp. 57–89. Aldershot, U.K. 1992. How Buna S technology was transferred from Germany to America.

Morris, Peter J. T. "Synthetic Rubber: Autarky and War." In *The Development of Plastics*, edited by S. T. I. Mossman and P. J. T. Morris, pp. 54–69. Cambridge, 1994. An overview of the development of synthetic rubber, summarizing the author's research on the German and American synthetic rubber industries.

Morris, Peter J. T. "Ambros, Reppe, and the Emergence of Heavy Organic Chemicals in Germany, 1925–1945." In *Determinants in the Evolution of the European Chemical Industry, 1900–1939*, edited by A. S. Travis, H. G. Schröter, E. Homburg, and P. J. T. Morris, pp. 96–122. Dordrecht, 1998. The development of Buna in the context of the organic chemical industry.

Ross, Davies R. B. "Patents and Bureaucrats: U.S. Synthetic Rubber Developments before Pearl Harbor." In *Business and Government*, edited by Joseph R. Frese, S. J. Judd, and Jacob Judd, pp. 119–155. Tarrytown, N.Y., 1985. A study of the complex relationship between the different companies and the government in the period leading up to 1941.

Solo, Robert. *Across the High Technology Threshold: The Case of Synthetic Rubber.* Norwood, Pa., 1980. A critical study of the American program, which reaches controversial conclusions.

Tuttle Jr., William M. "The Birth of an Industry: The Synthetic Rubber 'Mess' in World War II." *Technology and Culture* 1981 (22), 35–67. A clear analysis of the squabbles that delayed the American synthetic rubber program.

Whitby, G. S., C. C. Davis, and E. R. Dunbrook, eds. *Synthetic Rubber.* New York and London, 1954. The classic textbook on the technology, with a historical chapter and additional historical information in the technical chapters.

PETER J. T. MORRIS

Manufacturing and Industrial Organization

From its origins in the early nineteenth century, rubber manufacturing has mirrored the most significant trends in the industrial economy. These include rapid technological innovations, dramatic changes in product design and manufacturing techniques, increased concentration in some markets, constantly evolving efforts to sell more efficiently, and increasingly global operations. Paradoxically the industry's most important twentieth-century product, the automobile tire, has remained virtually unchanged in appearance and is one of the least glamorous of consumer goods.

Industry Development. The rubber industry emerged in the middle decades of the nineteenth century, when European and American inventors discovered new ways to use crude rubber, made from the sap of *hevea brasilienis*, a tree common to the tropics. Their inventions included calendaring (reinforcing rubber with a textile product), introduced in the 1820s and 1830s, and especially vulcanization (heating rubber with chemical additives to give it permanent form and elasticity), developed by Charles Goodyear between 1839 and 1845. These technical breakthroughs led to a large international trade in crude rubber and to the emergence of firms that produced rubber boots, rainwear, medical supplies, hose, belts, and insulation.

In the late nineteenth century rubber boot and shoe makers, the largest sector of the industry, repeatedly attempted to stabilize prices and limit competition. After many failures, Charles R. Flint, a New York merchant, in 1892 merged the largest American firms, creating the U.S. Rubber Company. Flint absorbed many industrial products makers as well in the following years but continued to run U.S. Rubber as a holding company, making no effort to consolidate operations or achieve operating economies. In the meantime the introduction of the safety bicycle in the 1880s created a new market for the pneumatic tire, invented by John Boyd Dunlop in 1888, which had a separate, inflatable tube inside the tire. The appearance of the clincher rim in the early 1890s simplified repairs and removed a major obstacle to the acceptance of pneumatic tires.

Many industrial rubber goods producers added tires to their product lines in the 1890s. U.S. Rubber soon had as many as four tire plants, and B. F. Goodrich Company of Akron, Ohio, a leading manufacturer of hoses, belts, and related products, developed a large tire department. Its success also created a substantial group of individuals with technical skills who, with the advent of the automobile, made Akron the center of auto and industrial rubber goods production in the United States.

Automobile Tires. In the next decade and a half the automobile tire and the tire industry evolved rapidly, creating enormous competitive pressures. In addition to the established firms, a new group of manufacturers, who were principally tire makers, redefined the industry. Two in particular, Goodyear Tire and Rubber and Firestone Tire and Rubber, both located in Akron and headed by flamboyant entrepreneurs, soon challenged the industry leaders. By expanding rapidly, embracing the latest innovations, developing large factories, and integrating

forward to promote branded products and backward to control raw material supplies, they became the industry leaders. Together with U.S. Rubber and B. F. Goodrich, which embraced many of these innovations as well, they dominated the large original equipment market. Most of the other tire companies either failed or developed niches in the replacement tire market.

In Europe a more subdued version of this process had similar results. By 1920 Dunlop (United Kingdom), Michelin (France), and Pirelli (Italy) had become prominent tire makers. Together with the American "big four," they established sales outlets and manufacturing plants in many European, Asian, and South American countries in the 1920s.

The technological innovations that heightened competition in the industry fell into two categories. First were inventions that improved the durability and reliability of tires. A notable example was the introduction in the 1910s of cotton "cord" in tire plies, which greatly extended tire life. The "straight-sided" tire, also introduced in the 1910s, was easier to change than the clincher and soon became the universal design. Other innovations in the 1920s and 1930s had similar effects on tire quality.

Second were changes in production methods that introduced mass production to tire making. No single innovation or machine was central to this process, though several, such as the Banbury mixer, which combined rubber and chemical additives in an enclosed compartment, and the tire-building machine, which partially mechanized the assembly process, had far-reaching effects. The more fundamental changes were less distinctive. Each new machine or engineering change, introduced separately, created bottlenecks and opportunities that led to more innovation and mechanization. These "compulsive sequences" (in the words of one government study) continued for more than a decade. By employing more capital, materials, and energy, manufacturers increased the speed and output of the factory while reducing the amount of labor required to produce each tire.

The social impact of these changes was also notable. The mechanization of materials handling reduced the incidence and severity of chemical poisoning, while conveyors and other mechanical devices replaced the least-skilled employees and made the work less physically demanding. In the 1920s and 1930s manufacturers employed lower-wage women for a growing number of jobs.

The tire makers were also pioneers in introducing new management systems. All of the major U.S. and European firms embraced the multifunction corporate structure, contemporary scientific management, and welfare capitalism. Goodyear in particular became famous for its extensive benefit programs, Industrial University, and company union.

RUBBER PLANTATIONS. Workers weighing rubber, Brazil, circa 1925. (Frank and Frances Carpenter Collection/Prints and Photographs Division, Library of Congress)

Traditional rubber products were sold through wholesalers, but the growth of auto production encouraged greater specialization. Direct contacts between tire manufacturers and the auto industry accounted for most original equipment sales after 1900, and specialized tire stores soon dominated the replacement market. Other outlets, including company-owned stores, gasoline "service" stations, and chain department stores, became increasingly important in the 1920s and especially in the economically depressed years of the 1930s. A 1926 agreement between Goodyear and Sears set the stage for the new era of retail competition. By supplying Sears with tires at extremely low prices, Goodyear forced other manufacturers to lower their prices and embrace the chain outlets.

The Great Depression devastated the rubber industry, leaving a wake of bankrupt firms, unemployed workers, and barriers to international trade and investment. In the United States it also provoked a rebellion among the industry's production workers (encouraged indirectly by the Franklin D. Roosevelt administration, which promoted collective bargaining to raise wages and stimulate

consumption) and a long period of turmoil in the formerly nonunion industry. During the National Recovery Administration years (1933–1935), rubber workers formed local organizations affiliated with the American Federation of Labor (AFL) and a national union, the United Rubber Workers (URW). In 1936 the URW became a founding member of the Congress of Industrial Organizations, which soon emerged as a militant competitor of the AFL. Tire builders, who performed the most critical and sensitive functions in the tire plants, dominated the tire locals and the URW. Meanwhile Akron workers developed a new strike technique, the sit-down, in 1934 and used it extensively between 1936 and 1938. Strikes, sit-downs, and government promotion of collective bargaining soon led to formal bargaining agreements. Several smaller tire makers agreed to contracts between 1934 and 1937. Firestone and U.S. Rubber followed in 1937 and B. F. Goodrich in 1938; Goodyear held out until 1941.

Synthetic Rubber. The World War II years also introduced important changes to the industry. Japanese military victories in Southeast Asia in 1941–1942 cut off the supply of natural rubber and led the U.S. government to initiate an emergency program to expand synthetic rubber production. By 1943 this effort had alleviated the supply crisis, created a new source of raw material, and enhanced the role of the large corporations, which operated (and later purchased) the synthetic plants. Though wartime restrictions on automobile use forced the manufacturers to convert their factories to other products (Goodyear, for example, became a major aircraft manufacturer), they emerged from the war with greatly improved finances. During the postwar economic boom they expanded tire production, introduced a major new design innovation, the tubeless tire, and addressed the militant unionism of the preceding decade and a half. Since the mid-1930s the manufacturers had aggressively moved production out of Akron, the center of labor unrest. New economic opportunities in the South and West reinforced their determination to find a more docile and less costly labor force. By the 1960s the Upper South had become their favored location.

Industry Upheaval. These innovations paled beside the upheavals of the 1970s, when dramatic changes in market conditions, manufacturing techniques, and tire design shook the industry to its foundations. The principal agent of change was the radial tire, more durable and fuel efficient than the conventional bias ply tire but also more expensive. Radials had become popular in postwar Europe because of higher gasoline prices, but American manufacturers held back, fearful of consumer resistance and lower sales. Their conservatism left them vulnerable to the energy shortages of the 1970s, culminating in the "crises" of 1973–1975 and 1978–1980, which led to a near universal shift to radials. U.S. manufacturers thus had to redesign their plants and install new machinery under the most difficult conditions. Several of the smaller companies failed, B. F. Goodrich and Uniroyal (the former U.S. Rubber) began to reconsider their roles as tire makers, and Firestone suffered a disastrous setback when its radials were shown to be defective.

By the mid-1980s the industry had changed more than at any time since the 1910s. All of the Akron plants and the huge Uniroyal plant in Detroit had closed, and the URW, severely weakened, was forced to merge with the United Steelworkers. In the mid-1980s Uniroyal and B. F. Goodrich combined their tire operations and spun them off as a separate company that performed poorly and was later taken over by Michelin, the leading European radial maker. In the meantime Bridgestone, the leading Japanese company, purchased Firestone; Sumitomo, the second largest Japanese producer, acquired Dunlop; and Continental, a German firm, purchased General Tire, the largest of the second-tier American companies. Together with the expansion of Michelin, these mergers and buyouts were testimony to the severity of the upheavals of the 1970s.

By the end of the twentieth century the industry consisted of a relative handful of small firms in the United States and western Europe producing traditional products, mostly for industry; a growing number of small Asian firms making boots, rainwear, and other consumer goods for export to the West; and a handful of large, globally decentralized firms manufacturing tires. In the United States the industry was relatively dispersed, with most plants in the South and many of them nonunion. The large companies and a new generation of small specialist companies increasingly emphasized the manufacture of polymer products (based on the underlying science), rather than rubber (a specific set of polymers), that included plastics and other substances, which, to lay observers, had little or no connection to rubber.

BIBLIOGRAPHY
Babcock, Glenn D. *History of the United States Rubber Company: A Case Study in Corporate Management.* Bloomington, Ind., 1966.
French, Michael J. *The U.S. Tire Industry: A History.* Boston, 1991.
Jeszeck, Charles. "Structural Change in CB: The U.S. Tire Industry." *Industrial Relations* 25 (Fall 1986), 229–247.
Nelson, Daniel. *American Rubber Workers and Organized Labor, 1900–1941.* Princeton, 1988.

DANIEL NELSON

RUHR. *See* Coal Basins.

RUSSIA [*This entry contains six subentries, on the economic history of Russia during the early and medieval, early modern, and modern periods; during and after communism; and during the Russian Empire.*]

Early and Medieval Periods

The European territory of modern Russia stretches from the Bug River in the west to the Danube in the south to the Volga River in the east—and from the Baltic Sea in the northwest to the Arctic Ocean (the White and Barents Seas). From the fifth and sixth centuries, the Slavs had moved into this region from the southeast, principally via the Carpatho-Danube basin; their core heartland became the Middle Dnieper region. Then, from the seventh century and the eighth, various Balts and Finno-Ugric peoples occupied the western and northern parts of this vast region, respectively. The economic activities of all these peoples were at first restricted by both the natural resources and the climatic conditions. The dense network of the many river valleys that drain these regions initially determined the locations of their settlements—especially for fishing, hunting, and food gathering (e.g., berries, mushrooms, and roots). Because the forests were dense and the marshes mainly impenetrable, the Slavic settlers, who were farmers, struggled to gain adequate land for agriculture. The relatively mild climate to the south of the 55th parallel, however, with its abundant arable soil and scattered forests of pine and oak, offered better, more hospitable lands for both agriculture and animal husbandry. The broad, flat steppe lands adjacent to the Black Sea, which stretch for thousands of kilometers, attracted many pastoral nomadic peoples from eastern Asia: first, the various Hun tribes; then, from the ninth and tenth centuries onward, Turkic peoples.

The emergence of Russia as a viable state was influenced, especially, by the European states to the west and by contacts that were both semimilitary and semicommercial in nature with Scandinavians and Normans—who, in seeking supplies of silver, furs, and slaves—established relatively permanent trading posts along the Russian rivers. The commercial routes that they established came to be known as the Varangian Road, which stretched from Scandinavia to the Byzantine-Greek lands; it was by far the most strategically important and commercially beneficial route to link these far-flung regions. The chief commercial objectives of the Scandinavians and Normans were the following: the Danube basin, which led into the Black Sea, the Crimean Peninsula, and adjacent regions on the northern Black Sea littoral; the city of Thessalonica (modern Thessaloniki, in Greece); and the capital of Byzantium, Constantinople. The Varangian Road established, from the ninth century onward, the major and long-lasting routes of international trade for most of eastern Europe—and thus Russia. From the 860s CE, the Varangian Road influenced the cyclic economic character of the newly emerging Russian state (then called Rus) with its capital at Kiev (in 886 CE; now the capital of Ukraine).

The Rus were originally a retinue of traders, composed chiefly of Scandinavians, (called in Slavic the *druzhina*, or "followers of the prince"). From the ninth and early tenth century, the Rus collected tribute and other payments from the various Slavic groups (the Drevliane, Dregovichi, Krivichi, Sloveni, Viatichi, Severiani, etc.), while traveling with the prince along these trade routes, chiefly during the winter months; this fiscal organization, known as *poludie*, was described by the Byzantine emperor Constantine VII Porphyrogenitus (913–959 CE). During the spring months, the various goods collected during these journeys—beaver furs, white and black fox furs, swords—were placed on boats that plied the River Dnieper. From there, they were taken by Russian merchants to the Black Sea and on to Constantinople for sale or exchange in Byzantine markets that were held during the summer and autumn months. This often sporadic circulation of goods and money (coinage) within these regions continued until the twelfth century, when it was seriously interrupted by incursions of nomads from the steppe lands of Central Asia. Nevertheless, those towns and marketplaces established along the Varangian Road within Russia—Staraya Ladoga, Novgorod, Smolensk, and Belgorod—became and remained significant centers for the handicraft trades, various forms of industry, and commerce. Thereby, a network of both domestic and foreign commercial communications was begun, which has endured until today.

The economic and geopolitical attractions of the Varangian Road offered ambitious Russian princes secure advantages from Byzantium and its allies; these became powerful enough to convince some princes to move the capital from Kiev. Such was the case of Sviatoslav in the late tenth century; he wanted to establish his residence at Pereyaslavets on the Danube, to which, according to the Russian Primary Chronicle, "all the goods flowed: gold from the Greeks, precious cloths, wines and fruits of many kinds; silver and horses from the Bohemians and Hungarians; and from Rus [itself] furs, wax, honey, and slaves." Nevertheless, Kiev still remained the market center for both the domestic and a still flourishing international trade, as well as for Russian industries and arts. Kiev enjoyed the greatest boom years of its economy during the late eleventh century and the early twelfth. By that era, its population had grown, according to various estimates, to some 20,000 or more.

Also flourishing during this era, was Russia's then second largest city, Novgorod, far to the north of Kiev. Its growing prosperity from the 800s into the 1600s was based on its monopolistic "staple" role in governing Russia's trade; it controlled a vast expanse in the north and northwest, dealt with the German trading cities on the Baltic Sea, those that, in the fourteenth century, would organize themselves into the powerful Hanseatic League. In part,

because of that trade, Novgorod and its commercial hinterland had a successful handicraft industry, producing glass beads and rings; glazed vessels and enamelware; jewelry fashioned from amber, bronze, silver, and gold; and ornamental metalwares adorned with filigree work and with niello (deep black enamel inlays made from sulfur alloyed with silver, copper, and/or lead). Many of the craftsmen in Novgorod lived in special residential compounds (in Slavic *dvory*) of the urban elite, producing goods to order from the merchants. In medieval Russia, the basic economic and social unit was the *dvor* (a "family compound" or "homestead"). It functioned as both home and industrial workshop, with extended plots of land for growing basic foods. The structures of the Russian urban economies, not in only the major cities of Kiev and Novgorod but also in the smaller towns—Chernigov, Ryazan, Smolensk, Yaroslavl—consisted of blocks of traders and craftsmen, who were clustered together by street or by district. There is, however, very little evidence of any craft guilds or formal merchant corporations before the late Middle Ages.

The rural economy of early medieval Russia, from the earliest documented era, was based on an agriculture that employed the heavy, wheeled plough, with coulter (the cutting edge) and moldboard. In fact, the introduction of this implement into Carolingian Europe, with revolutionary economic consequences, was due primarily to westward Slavic migrations. If by the late eleventh or the twelfth century, as historians have variously estimated, Russia's population had reached 4.5 million or 5.3 million or even 7.9 million, the overwhelming majority consisted of farming peasants. The bases of Russian rural economies, in the most advanced regions, were arable agriculture and cattle raising—usually in the context of mixed farming, as elsewhere in northern Europe during this era—supplemented by some handicrafts, undertaken during seasons of minimal agricultural activity. The chief crops then grown were a wide variety, including emmer (hard wheat), barley, wheat, millet, spelt, oats, both winter and spring rye, buckwheat, flax, hemp, lentils, peas, beans, and poppyseeds. The major grain crops—rye, wheat, and barley—were cultivated chiefly in the forest zone and the forest-steppe, where oats were less popular. In the Dnieper valley region, the cultivation of barley was often mixed with wheat; to the west, in the warmer Dniester basin, the crops included Spring wheat (mild and dwarf varieties) and, in rotation, rye, oats, millet, peas, and flax. The cultivation of oats as a forage or fodder crop, especially for horses, was particularly significant in the Novgorod region.

In the early medieval era, the two-field system of crop rotations, usually with winter grains followed by a season of fallow, was widespread and the predominant form of arable agriculture. Later, as elsewhere in northern Europe, the three-field system slowly penetrated into this region:

the standard mix was winter grains (rye, wheat) in the first year; summer grains (barley, oats, and leguminous crops like peas and beans) in the second; and a fallow period in the third (thus preceding the ensuing season of winter grains). Successful cultivation under this system depended on the recuperative fallow season (when the soil rested and was restored); a combination of heavy manuring—using manures as fertilizer from animals herded elsewhere (pasture and wastelands)—on the inner fields, with more extensive fallowing on the outer fields, proved to be the most effective. This complex three-field system became the most prevalent, from the fourteenth century and the fifteenth, in the region that is now Ukraine; there, the rich soils of the so-called Black Belt region provided abundant harvests, sometimes with thirty-fold yields. This region, from the 1870s onward—with railroads and steamships—became the veritable "bread basket" for much of Europe. Accompanying that complex rural economy was the productive use of waste lands and woodlands, particularly for forage. Oxen were the primary form of animal power, but horses later became the more coveted draught and status animal (for wagons, carriages, sleds, and riding). Certainly oxen, and other forms of cattle, predominated in the forest-steppe region, while in the northwestern regions cattle were raised along with significant numbers of sheep, goats, and pigs.

In northwestern Russia, the average size of a medieval peasant's holding was a tenure of 5 *dessiatinas* (i.e., about 5.5 hectares) of "good" land, or 6 *dessiatinas* of "middling" land, or up to 8 *dessiatinas* of "poor" lands. In the Novgorod district, the average size of a peasant tenure was 3 *dessiatinas*. The development of specialized commercial horticulture (market gardening) was promoted by the increasing consumption of legumes and other vegetables in many Russian households, along with the standard grains. For most of the population, meat was a luxury reserved for holiday meals. Poultry was raised mainly on the great manorial estates; the medieval texts refer to hens, eggs, geese, and the like that were paid as rents and tributes.

Along with the traditional large settlement towns and the communal villages within large manorial estates. From the fourteenth century onward, the colonization of new territories produced a new type of settlement—the small family farmstead. From the second half of the fifteenth century, rural commerce, although essentially local, became more vibrant, widespread, and active with the demographic recovery. From that era, the proliferation and growth of rural markets and fairs—especially those in the Novgorod, Tver, and Nizhni Novgorod regions—reflected this growth of the commercializing rural economy. A commercialized economy is one that uses money, if in various forms. Some birchbark texts that archaeologists discovered in the early 1950s and onward have been authoritatively dated to the eleventh and twelfth centuries; they indicate that Novgorod and other markets used both squirrel skins and marten skins as money. Although, the initial issue of Russian silver coins can be dated to the late tenth century, under Prince Vladimir in Kiev, various written and archaeological sources attest that both the supply and use of such coins had almost ceased by the turn of the twelfth century (so this period is commonly referred to as a "coinless" one for the Russian economy). The late tenth-century and eleventh-century Varangian circulation of Oriental coins (Muslim) *dirhams*, Byzantine *nomismata*, and some Western *denarii* (Frankish silver pence) was reestablished only much later, in the twelfth century, and in a much smaller volume.

From about the 1140s, Kiev lost its political and economic dominance within Russia to newer centers that were located in the northeast, between the upper Volga and the Oka rivers, in particular to the princes Rostov the Great and to Souzdal; then, from the second half of the twelfth century, to Vladimir. The northeast then developed into the nucleus of medieval Muscovy (with Moscow at its center) as the Grand Duchy of Vladimir. Such changes in urban predominance were due in part to the development of alternative axes of commercial communication, especially to the growth of the Salt Route, from the principality of Galich (later Galicia, in the southwestern extremity of Russia, in the foothills of the Carpathians) along the Great Volga route that went down that river to Astrakhan on the Caspian Sea. Subsequently, from the mid-1300s, the shift of Russia's economic core to its more central regions led to the rise of Moscow as Russia's new political, commercial, and industrial center. In the 1500s, under Ivan IV (the Terrible; 1533–1584), and later, in the seventeenth century; Muscovy expanded, incorporated territory as far to the east as Siberia, and became the Russian Empire in the early eighteenth century.

BIBLIOGRAPHY

Birnbaum, H., and M. Flier, eds. *Medieval Russian Culture*. Berkeley, Los Angeles, and London, 1984. A collection of studies.

Cherepnin, Lev V. "Die Rus' vom 10. bis 14. Jh." In *Handbuch der europaischen Wirtschafts- und Sozialgeschichte*, edited by H. von Kellenbenz, pp. 682–702. Stuttgart, Germany, 1980. The Soviet Russian concept of the main events of Russian medieval history, from the tenth to the fourteenth century.

Fennel, John. *The Emergence of Moscow, 1304–1359*. London, 1968.

Fennel, John. *The Crisis of Medieval Russia, 1200–1304*. London and New York, 1972.

Franklin, Simon, and Jonathan Shepard. *The Emergence of Rus', 750–1200*. London and New York, 1966. Original, systematic research of Russia's political and social history.

Heller, Klaus, *Russische Wirtschafts- und Sozialgeschichte. Der Kiever und die Moskauer Periode (9.–17. Jh.)*. Darmstadt, Germany, 1987. Modern view of the main events of Russian medieval economic history.

Hellmann, Manfred, ed. *Handbuch der Geschichte Russlands*. Wiesbaden, Germany, 1979–1981. Fundamental but arguable Russian history and economics.

Kolchin, Boris A., ed. *Drevnjaja Rus': Gorod, zamok, selo* (Ancient Russia. Town, castle, country). Moscow, 1985. Includes the archaeological materials that provide evidence of the Russian medieval economy, crafts, and industry.

Kulischer, J. *Russische Wirtschaftsgeschichte.* Jena, Germany, 1925. A classic and the former main German handbook on Russian economic history.

Martin, J. T*reasure of the Land of Darkness: The Fur Trade and Its Significance for Medieval Russia.* Cambridge, 1986.

Smith, R. E. F. *The Origins of Farming in Russia.* Paris and The Hague, 1959.

Smith, R. E. F., and D. Christian. *Bread and Salt: A Social and Economic History of Food and Drink in Russia.* Cambridge, 1984.

Vernadsky, George. *Kievan Russia.* New Haven, Conn., 1948. Reprint, 1972. General view of the beginning of Russian history.

MICHAEL BIBIKOV

Early Modern Period

Between 1472 and 1700, Russia expanded at one of the fastest paces of any state in all of recorded history, from 430,000 to 15,280,000 square kilometers (from 172,000 to 6,112,000 square miles). During this time, Moscow increased its control from its Volga-Oka region to include the Novgorod Republic in the northwest and its empire in the north, Smolensk and other areas in the west that had belonged for decades to the Rzeczpospolita (Polish-Lithuanian Commonwealth), Ukraine in the south, and the Urals and Siberia in the east. The population under Moscow's control in this time increased from less than 4 million to perhaps 10 million.

Moscow was able to effect this expansion because of the weakness of its opponents and the extraordinary effectiveness of its government and technologically advanced armed forces. Governmental effectiveness was facilitated by the development of a theory of autocracy in the early sixteenth century, which proclaimed that "in his body, the ruler was a man, but in his authority he was like God." The theory of autocracy legitimized what the government did in the name of the sovereign. The result has been called "the garrison state," in which by 1650 Moscow had nearly complete control over two of the major economic factors, land and labor, and had substantial control over the third, capital, as well.

Throughout this period, Russia perceived that it was under siege. On the western frontier, the major enemies were Poland and Sweden; on the southern frontier were the Tatars, other steppe nomads, and the Ottomans. Any weakness exhibited by Russia was taken by them as a target of opportunity, and liquidation of Russia was one of their primary foreign policy aims. From the south, the Crimean Tatars took advantage of Russia's debilitated state under Ivan the Terrible to burn Moscow in 1571 and its suburbs in 1591. At all other times, the steppe nomads raided Russia ceaselessly in a search for slaves to kidnap. As a result,

Russia (along with Ukraine and Poland) was one of the world's two major "slave reservoirs" (along with Africa). (The word *slave* comes from *Slav*.) Had Moscow not taken effective countermeasures, all of its population would have been sold through the Crimea into the slave markets of the Middle East and the Mediterranean. Those who were not yet enslaved were forced to pay tribute to the Crimeans, which cost the Russian government a million rubles between 1613 and 1650. On the western frontier, the aims were territory as well as booty of all kinds. During the Time of Troubles at the beginning of the seventeenth century, the Poles occupied Moscow and the Swedes seized Novgorod and other northwestern Russian territory.

The garrison state was the product of the first service class revolution, which began with the annexation of Novgorod in the 1470s, mobilized the land to support the army, and by 1649 had created a legally stratified society encompassing almost everyone. Moscow deported the Novgorodian elite and distributed their lands to Muscovite cavalrymen. This was the beginning of the service land (*pomest'e*) system, which rapidly mobilized most of the populated land fund to support the cavalry. The system was formalized legally in 1556, when the government decreed that all populated land had to support military service. This included not only the government's *pomest'e* land but also private, hereditary land (called *votchina*). If the *votchina* owner had more than a specified amount of populated land, he had to render military service as well as provide mounted combat slaves. Thus, the government effectively controlled most of the populated land of Russia.

Russia was primarily an agricultural country with around 85 to 90 percent of the population engaged in farming. Another 2 percent of the population were townsmen, another 2 percent churchmen, perhaps 5 to 10 percent slaves (primarily household, rarely involved in production of any kind), and perhaps 2 percent military and administrative. Even many of the nonfarmers raised much of their own food in gardens at the edge of town. The basic agricultural crops were rye (for humans) and oats (primarily for horses). Slash-and-burn was the basic system of revitalizing the soil, while the three-field system was introduced occasionally when population pressure warranted it (such as in the decades prior to 1550). Rainfall was excessive and the growing season short. The soil in the Volga-Oka region is podzol, an acid soil typically about 3 inches thick. It was cultivated with a wooden scratch plow, the *sokha*. The yields of Russia's crops were pre-Carolingian, in the vicinity of 3:1 (a yield of three for each seed planted).

The cavalrymen depended on the peasants farming their *votchina* and especially their *pomest'e* lands for more than half of the income they needed to support themselves in service, their families, and their slave retinues. The lesser half of their support came from governmental cash payments to buy market commodities such as weapons and horses. Much of that was provided by taxes on the peasantry, plus others. The maintenance of the cavalry, the base of the garrison state, depended on peasants paying rent to their cavalrymen-landholders. In the second half of the fifteenth century, a few monastery debtors were forbidden to move at any time of year except on Saint George's Day (November 26), and in 1497 this was extended to all peasants. As times were comparatively good and there was no perceived population shortage, the Saint George's Day restriction was largely irrelevant until the chaos of Ivan the Terrible's reign, when in many politically strategic places up to 90 percent of the agricultural land was abandoned by its tillers. At this juncture, the government forbade selected peasants to move at all on Saint George's Day. In 1592, this "temporary measure" of the "forbidden years" (which lasted until 1906) was universalized to all peasants, who thereby became enserfed. Simultaneously, a five-year statute of limitations was imposed on the recovery of fugitive serfs to favor magnates who recruited fugitive serfs and government officials running the state south of the Oka and along and across the Volga who wanted Russians to migrate to their regions. For decades, the provincial cavalry actively protested the statute of limitations, which was finally repealed in the Law Code (*Sobornoe Ulozhenie*) of 1649. The *Ulozhenie* also legally stratified the rest of society, thus giving the government control over nearly all of Russia's labor.

The first service class revolution was launched to create the landed cavalry. Around 1550, in response to the requirements of the gunpowder revolution, a semistanding, semiregular infantry was created, the arquebusiers (*strel't-sy*), who were called *musketeers* after the introduction of the musket in the second quarter of the seventeenth century. A major tax was instituted to support them. Also around 1550, the government began to create specific chancelleries (*prikazy*) to manage the land fund and the army, as well as to collect taxes and generate the paperwork involved with the expanding autocratic state. A century later, there were about sixty of these chancelleries, including one to keep track of and regulate the slave population. (Russia was the only country in the world that had a separate bureau in its capital to keep track of slaves.) The government was relatively sophisticated in its monetary policy: It could pay for wars by debasing the currency, but if inflation got out of hand and led to riots, it restored the silver currency to the antebellum level (as in 1662–1663), whereupon prices returned almost immediately to their historical median level.

Beginning in the 1630s for the Smolensk War (1632–1634), the government began to hire mercenaries to introduce linear warfare tactics, and half of the 34,000 troops at Smolensk were members of the new formation regiments.

At the end of the 1640s, preparing for what became the Thirteen Years' War (1654–1667), Moscow again introduced new formation regiments, whose modern cavalry, dragoons, and infantry made the traditional landed cavalry and the increasingly constabulary musketeers obsolescent. In the 1650s, the military establishment (including the dozen chancelleries running various parts of the army) cost around 3.5 million rubles. The median day wage was 4 kopeks per day, and the working male population was around 2 million. The working year was about three hundred days, during which income of 24 million rubles was generated. This would indicate that nearly 15 percent of the total national income was spent on Russian military defense and expansion in this period.

In the Russian service state, most top incomes were established by the government. This included the military and governmental service personnel, who were evaluated and promoted on the basis of merit. The state also set some clerical remunerations, but most were set by the free market, as were incomes of most merchants, tradesmen, and peasants. Quintile income distributions are not available, but wealthy merchants and leaders of the service class, with thousands of serfs on their estates and government salaries of hundreds of rubles, enjoyed luxuries from around the world based on incomes thousands of times higher than those of poor and landless peasants, most slaves, and the urban poor.

As the government concentrated on immediate military concerns during many of the years under review, its relations with the rest of the world had primarily a military focus. In the reign of Ivan III (1462–1505), the government hired military specialists from Italy who introduced bronze artillery casting and the reconstruction of Russia's fortresses. By the 1550s, the center of Western civilization had moved to the North Atlantic, and Russia initiated technology transfers from there. Thus, the mining engineers who blew up the Tatar fortress of Kazan' in 1552—opening Russia's way to the Urals and Siberia—were imported from Holland.

In the seventeenth century, the Russian government arranged numerous technology transfers from the West. This was especially relevant because the Volga-Oka region had (and has) no useful minerals, and the area was poor for agriculture. The Dutchman Andrew Vinius was given a government subsidy and a monopoly to set up a metallurgical industry in 1632 in Tula, the military concentration point on the Oka River facing the steppe to the south where there was a poor grade of bog iron. Glassworks, paper mills, potash works (for dye), and a postal system between Moscow and Vilnius were established by foreigners. Foreign specialists were hired by the dozens in these and other fields, including silk weaving, shipbuilding, munitions manufacture, and astronomy. Medical doctors and pharmacists were hired by the Apothecary Chancellery. Dutchmen established the first "newspaper" in 1621. Explorations for useful minerals were undertaken north of the Volga near Ustiug, where copper, which had been imported from Sweden along with other minerals, was found in the late 1660s. All of these technology transfers and investments were made by the government. The foreigners were supposed to teach the new technologies to the natives, but the monopolies did not allow Russians to compete with the foreigners. Moreover, importing the developed technologies gave Russians little opportunity to understand the systems in order to develop them further. As a result, they were always dependent on additional imports.

A handful of the elite had sufficient funds for technology development but lacked the incentives or permission to spend on anything other than luxury goods, which became a significant import sector even before Peter the Great.

[*See also* Collective Agriculture and Collectivization.]

BIBLIOGRAPHY

Buganov, V. I., ed. *Istoriia krest'ianstva SSSR/Rossii s drevneishikh vremën do 1917 g.* 5 vols. Moscow, 1987–.
Got'e, Iu. V. *Zamoskovnyi krai v 17 veke.* Moscow, 1937.
Hellie, Richard. *Muscovite Society [Readings for Introduction to Russian Civilization].* Chicago, 1967, 1970.
Hellie, Richard. *Enserfment and Military Change.* Chicago, 1971.
Hellie, Richard. *Slavery in Russia, 1450–1725.* Chicago, 1982.
Hellie, Richard, trans. *The Muscovite Law Code (Ulozhenie) of 1649.* Irvine, Calif., 1988.
Hellie, Richard. *The Economy and Material Culture of Russia, 1600–1725.* Chicago, 1999.
Kashin, V. N. *Torgovlia i torgovyi kapital v Moskovskom gosudarstve.* Leningrad, 1926.
Liashchenko, P. I. *History of the National Economy of Russia to the 1917 Revolution.* New York, 1949. An ACLS-sponsored translation of an earlier edition of the 1956 work listed below.
Liashchenko, P. I. *Istoriia narodnogo khoziaistva SSSR.* 3 vols. Moscow, 1956.
Strumilin, S. G. *Ocherki ekonomicheskoi istorii Rossii.* Moscow, 1960.
Ustiugov, N. V. *Solevarnaia promyshlennost' Soli Kamskoi v XVII veke.* Moscow, 1957.
Zaozerskaia, E. I. *Uistokov krupnogo proizvodstva v russkoi promyshlennosti XVI–XVII vekov.* Moscow, 1970.

RICHARD HELLIE

Modern Period

In the course of discussions held from the 1960s to the 1970s, the "pessimist" view of the Russian economic history was dominant. It held that Russia is a backward and highly peculiar country; that its economic development was a function of military requirements; that industrialization was organized by the government in response to the defeat in the Crimean War; that the state and foreign capital were the driving forces of industrialization but failed to substitute for missing factors of economic growth; and that therefore a market economy was not formed and modernization and industrialization ended in failure. The discussions continued in the 1980s and 1990s, but by now the "optimistic" view gained in popularity. The optimists argued that the rates and results of Russian economic development from 1861 to 1913 resembled the Western model; that the country's economy was a real market one; that the prices of goods and production factors were set on the basis of market mechanisms; that the country had brisk commodity and financial markets and actively participated in the international capital market; and that the influx of capital was due to a higher rate of profit. By 1914, the Industrial Revolution had been launched; the reforms of the 1860s had created preconditions for industrialization; the economic role of the state had diminished and was moderate; the country had an adequate corporate legislation; the peasant commune restrained the mobility of manpower and the penetration of bourgeois relations into the countryside, but did not block the formation of an all-Russian labor market or the development of capitalism in the countryside. The Russian market became integrated into the world market, with investment cycles being determined by the situation in Europe, and in the postreform period the standards of living of the population were improving. It became commonly accepted that the period from 1700 to 1917 consisted of three phases: proto-industrialization (1700–1860), when the prerequisites for industrialization were being established; industrialization (1861–1914), when these prerequisites yielded dynamic results; and World War I (1914–1917), when revolution destroyed the existing economic system.

Proto-industrialization. The eighteenth century marked the real beginning of the industrialization process in Russia. Its driving force was industry, which developed from a small-scale home production for the market to a Kaufsystem of production and a putting-out system, whereby a commodity producer becomes a home-based worker engaged in some form of "manufacturing" to modern manufacturing. In the provinces with rich black soil, this development proceeded more slowly; but in the provinces with infertile non-black soil, it was more intensive. The shift to industry was motivated by the lower profitability of agriculture. The state and nobility both supported proto-industrialization. The state took measures to modernize Russia and protect its industry. It patronized home and foreign trade; it also provided secure markets for manufactured goods through procurements by the army, navy, and the new capital city of St. Petersburg. The nobility developed patrimonial industry, engaged in commodity agriculture, and encouraged their peasants to search for additional earnings outside farming. The active role of the state compensated the weak development of the market, capital, hired labor, and the banking system. Whereas nearly 30 manufacturing enterprises appeared in the seventeenth century (at state initiative), this number leaped to 233 in the first quarter of the eighteenth century. Then the initiative shifted from the state to individuals. The state, however, still provided financial support to entrepreneurs, assigned peasants to work in manufactories, and developed the commodity market.

By 1804, the manufacturing industry had nearly 2,402 major enterprises; these increased to 15,388 by 1860. These enterprises employed 14,400 workers in 1725; that figure increased to 95,200 in 1804 and to 565,100 in 1860. The labor force consisted mostly of serfs, who combined agriculture with industry. A dense network of fairs, markets, and trade shops also developed. Trade stimulated the development of credit. In 1733, the government founded the first bank, and opened many more in the second half of the eighteenth century. In 1817, the state created a system of four central and a network of local banks. The first private bank opened in St. Petersburg in 1769. In 1857 there were fifteen such banks, but the total volume of their operations was less than 1 percent of that conducted by state banks. Proto-industrialization proceeded on the basis of serf labor and state participation, with a very limited penetration of capital into the sphere of production; the emerging industrial sector involved an insignificant part of the population: in 1799, about 420,000 workers or 1.2 percent of the entire population were employed in industry and transportation, and by 1860 this figure had only risen to 2.5 million, or 4.2 percent of the population. In agriculture, hired labor was not employed much. Proto-industrialization facilitated the development of industry, hired labor, home and foreign markets, an improvement in the marketability of agricultural produce, growth of the territorial division of labor, separation of industry from agriculture, accumulation of capital, and emergence of banks, as well as the formation of new social strata of workers and entrepreneurs, and the transformation of cities into major commercial, industrial, and financial centers.

Industrialization. The first factory appeared in the textile industry in 1805, and that increased to thirty-nine factories by 1843 and to fifty-seven by 1860. In the 1850s, machines began to replace manual labor at an increasing pace; by 1917, however, the process was not completed. In 1913, in terms of the volume of production, factories surpassed enterprises with manual labor by 1.6 times—7.3 billion rubles as compared with 4.7 billion rubles (here and later on in gold rubles), but in terms of the number of workers, the enterprises using manual labor had 1.7 times as many workers (5.4 million compared with 3.1 million in manufactures). By 1914, industrialization was not complete in either industry or transportation. Russia remained an agrarian country with agriculture barely affected by industrialization. In 1883, the percentage of the agrarian sector in national income was 57 and in 1913 still accounted for 51.4 percent of the national income. In 1897, 70.3 percent of the population were engaged in agriculture and 10.6 percent in industry and transportation. Nevertheless, industry had made great progress. By 1914, home producers still satisfied 56 percent of the demand for machine tools and equipment. The industrial-technical and social basis of capitalism was formed. Industry developed at the same pace as it generally did throughout Europe. Indeed, from 1860 to 1913, the average annual growth rate of the total industrial output was higher in Russia (3.95 percent) than in Europe (2.83 percent), although somewhat less if measured in per capita industrial output (1.75 percent in Russia compared with 1.86 percent in Europe). As a result, the Russian percentage share of world industrial production increased from 7 to 8 percent, although per capita production was 2.2 times lower. A similar pattern emerged in agriculture and transportation. Industrialization in Russia did involve the active participation of both the state and foreign capitals. By 1917, in industry alone, according to different estimates, foreign investment was between 2.0 and 2.2 billion rubles. In 1890, 28 to 29 percent of the capital of commercial and industrial joint-stock companies was foreign. According to some estimates, on the eve of World War I, the total sum of foreign capital in Russia was something on the order of 6.5 to 8 billion rubles. During the war, it increased by an additional 8.5 billion rubles. In 1860, the government reformed the credit system. It abolished old state banks and in their place established the State bank, which then became the country's largest commercial bank. The state also permitted the formation of joint-stock commercial and land banks. In the span of some fifteen years, a modern credit system—based primarily on the private capital of joint-stock banks—was created with government support. By 1914, Russia had 1,476 banks holding capital worth of 1.1 billion rubles; these banks had thus become an important factor in domestic capital formation. Between 1855 and 1889 and from 1909 to 1913, it increased from 7.8 to 12.2 percent of the net national product and became one of the highest in Europe.

The Effects of World War I (1914–1917). The war siphoned off 15 million people from production for military service. As a consequence of German occupation in the western part of the empire, by 1917 central Russia had received 7.76 million refugees. But the war also stimulated industrial expansion: by 1917, large-scale industry employed 2.89 million people—450,000 more than in 1913. By the end of 1916, production exceeded the level of 1913. But output began to decline after the February Revolution: in 1917, it dropped by 55 percent, even though the workforce remained the same. The curtailment of small-scale industrial production began with the onset of mobilization. Because of the war, the percentage of production by

RUSSIAN COUNTRYSIDE. Landowner visiting his estate, painting by P. O. Kovalevsky, nineteenth century. (Tretyakov Gallery, Moscow/Snark/Art Resource, NY)

heavy industry increased from 40 to 56 percent. In 1914–1916, investment in large-scale industry grew, but decreased in 1917. By the end of 1917, the net value of capital stock exceeded the level of 1913 by 16 percent. In 1914, grain production was on the level of 1909–1913; it first increased in 1915 (by 10 percent), but then fell in 1916 (by 13 percent) and still further in 1917 (by another 17 percent). Because of the curtailment of exports, cereal production was sufficient to meet provisioning needs of the population. In 1915, the government introduced fixed grain prices, but rising inflation led to a curtailment of the grain supply. State procurement at fixed prices did not increase grain deliveries; the provision problem was further compounded by the breakdown in the transportation system, making shipment increasingly difficult and leading to a mounting food crisis in 1916–1917 (and an increase in peasant income that persisted until the end of 1917). The impact on urban groups was more complex. In 1914–1916, the real wages of workers employed in defense plants rose, whereas the real wages of white-collar personnel and workers in nondefense plants fell. In 1917, all wages and salaries decreased substantially.

Economic Growth. Reliable estimates of national income are available only for the period of 1861–1913. For the earlier period, economic growth can be judged by the data on goods turnover and on industry and agricultural output. At 1913 prices, the per capita goods turnover was 14.1 rubles in 1753, 35.7 rubles in 1856, 48.3 rubles in 1888, and 67.9 rubles in 1913. The average annual growth of commodity output was 0.91 percent in 1753–1856, 0.95 percent in 1856–1888, and 1.37 percent in 1888–1913. The growth rate of industry and agriculture was lower than that of commodity output because of the increase in the marketable value of agriculture. From 1700 to 1860, the per capita output of agricultural products varied annually, depending on the harvest and market demand, but shows no distinct tendency to increase. From 1861–1870 to 1881–1890, the average annual increase in per capita agricultural output was 0.12 percent, from 1881–1890 to 1912–1913, it was 0.86 percent; the analogous per capita growth in production by large-scale industry rose from 4.36 percent in 1860–1888 to 5.11 percent in 1888–1913. From 1861–1863 to 1881–1883 the per capita national income increased 0.7 percent annually, rising from 1.65 percent between 1883–1887 and 1909–1913, with the highest growth rate in 1889–1904 (3.4 percent per annum). The national income grew faster than the production sector, especially in 1888–1913, since the service sector grew at a faster rate. In short, before 1861, economic growth was very slow, but thereafter sharply accelerated and in due course growth rates increased.

Living Standards. The subject awaits fuller treatment. Western scholars took little interest in the problem, Soviet historians adopted a biased stance and maintained that workers' real wages decreased from the mid-seventeenth century to the 1860s, then increased until 1903–1907, but then dropped steadily until 1917. Before 1913, the real wages of Russian workers were higher than in the West (with the exception of the United States). The growth of real wages by 25–30 percent in 1870–1907 is supported by much evidence; it also correlates with the increase in national income. But the assumption that during the preceding 250 years real wages decreased 7.5 times seems exaggerated and contradicts anthropometric data. In late-nineteenth-century Russia, to sustain themselves biologically, peasants had to spend 54 to 78 percent of their income (including 40–60 percent for foodstuffs) and workers 79 percent (41 percent for foodstuffs); under such

RUSSIAN CAPITAL. Imperial Bank and vicinity, Saint Petersburg. (Bibliothèque Nationale, Paris/ Giraudon/Art Resource, NY)

conditions, stature can serve as a proxy for biological status and well-being. The stature data suggest that the eighteenth century, with the exception of 1725–1744, was unfavorable for the physical well-being of the population (though not to the degree previously assumed), and that the nineteenth and early twentieth centuries (with the exception of 1810–1815 and 1851–1865) were favorable.

Towns and Urbanization. In the seventeenth and early eighteenth centuries, the towns had a substantial population, but townspeople were mainly engaged in farming, with most towns differing but little from villages in their outward appearance or in their public and private way of life. In 1722, the average population of all towns was 4,600; only Saint Petersburg, Moscow, Iaroslavl, and Kaluga had more than 20,000 people. From 1740 to 1860, the urban population decreased from 13 to 9 percent of the total population, because the natural growth of the rural population was higher than that of the urban population and migration of peasants to towns was modest. Before the nineteenth century, the majority of towns (54 percent in the 1790s) were agrarian, and their inhabitants were primarily engaged in farming. During the time from 1800 to 1860, the percentage of agrarian towns decreased to twenty-two and that of industrial and commercial ones increased to fifty-three. After the Great Reforms, urbanization accelerated as a result of the abolition of serfdom and the growing migration of peasants. By 1897, the economic structure of towns changed radically: 2 percent of towns

were commercial, 8.5 percent agrarian, 0.3 percent administrative and military, 89.2 percent a mixed type (with the majority of the population engaged in industry, commerce, and services). The percent of the population residing in towns rose to 15.3 percent in 1914 and nearly 18 percent in 1917.

Village, Peasantry, and Agriculture. Agriculture progressed within the framework of the traditional three-field system. Before 1861, the increase in agrarian production was secured by expanding the land under cultivation; after 1861, the growth came by raising the crop yield. In the 1860s, 96 percent of the sown areas was under grain crops; by 1913, that proportion had dropped to 89.1 percent. The percentage of industrial crops rose to 9.5 and that of fodder crops to 1.4. In 1910, 34 percent of peasant households used improved plowing implements and 11 percent used some kind of agricultural machinery. In 1910, the average peasant household used 1.8 kilograms of fertilizer per hectare of arable land—13 times less than in the United States and 11.5 times less than in England. Russia thus did not experience an agricultural revolution. Progress was slowed by the rural commune, labor ethics, low literacy, serfdom, and other institutional obstacles. The commune entailed collective responsibility, compulsory crop rotation, collective land ownership, and parcelization of land into small strips. Peasant land was not demarcated, making individual farming on communal land impossible. Although this system hampered innovations, it did not entirely preclude them. If the majority of peasants agreed, peasant communes could introduce more effective methods. But peasant agriculture was only one category: in 1905, 25.8 percent of land was in private hands, 35.5 percent under communal ownership, and 39.1 percent belonged to the state, church, and various institutions. In late 1906, the government launched the Stolypin agrarian reform, which gave peasants the right to leave the commune and to receive their shares of communal land as private property and in one separate plot. From that point the enclosure of communal land commenced, a process that had much in common with other European countries. But the world war and 1917 Revolution interceded before that process could be completed. By 1916, 28 percent of peasants had left the commune. The peasants' work ethic encouraged them to satisfy only their minimum requirements. Literacy rose for males (over age nine) from 6 percent in 1797 to 23 percent in 1860, and reached 58 percent by 1917; among females, the literacy rate was lower but rising: 4 percent (1797), 11 percent (1860), and 29 percent (1917). By 1917, the literacy rate in the peasantry was on the level of European Protestant countries in the seventeenth century: 51 percent of males and 22 percent of females.

Serfdom. Serfdom existed in various guises, encompassing state, corporative, or private serfdom—depending on who was the subject of servile relations: the state, a corporation (an urban or rural commune, handicraft workshop, etc.), or an individual. In the early eighteenth century, the entire population was enslaved: the nobility by the state; parish clergy by the state and bishops; tradespeople by the state and urban commune; the state peasants by the treasury and rural commune; seigniorial peasants by the treasury, rural commune, and landlord. Serfdom gradually made way for relations based on personal freedom, agreement, and estate rights. The nobility was emancipated in 1762, the clergy and urban estate in 1785, and the peasantry in three stages: from private serfdom in 1861, from state serfdom in 1861–1905, and from corporative serfdom by the Stolypin reform in 1906–1917.

Demography. From 1700 to 1860, the main demographic characteristics remained stable: east-European nuptuality patterns (early and universal marriage); predominance of multiple families; high nuptuality rates, birthrates, and death rates; high natural population growth (0.81 percent a year); short life span; and the traditional type of population reproduction. From the 1860s onward, nuptuality rates, birthrates, and death rates declined. The mortality rate declined faster than the birthrate; therefore, demographic growth increased to 1.37 percent in 1867–1896 and 1.65 percent in 1897–1913. The transition to birth control started among educated people in more developed Western regions and gradually spread over all regions and among all strata of the population. The late nineteenth century witnessed a demographic transition to the modern pattern of population reproduction, a more effective one from the point of view of material, as well as psychological and physical outlay. In 1851–1913 the average life span increased from 27.1 to 33.5 years.

The Family. During the eighteenth century and until the early twentieth century among all estates, though to a different degree, the family was changing from the multiple or extended family to the nuclear one. The average size of a family decreased from eight to six members. The nuclear family as the main form of the organization of family life came to urban Russia in the mid-nineteenth century—fifty years earlier than in the countryside. After 1861, not only men but women began to work more actively outside the home. But until 1917, the family remained the main production unit. Since production that was based on the household and not on the individual hired labor prevailed, the penetration of capital into production was limited. Hired labor constituted 7 percent of the labor force and 11 percent of the total labor force in 1917.

Russia and Europe. From the early eighteenth century, Russia began to undergo Westernization and from the late eighteenth century became part of the common European cultural, economic, and information sphere. It therefore experienced the same processes, although with a delay and different intensity. Price fluctuations in Russia and in the West indicate the level of contacts. Prior to the eighteenth century, there was no coordination in the dynamics of prices. The price revolution of the sixteenth and seventeenth centuries that spread over Baltic lands, Poland, Sweden, and Austria stopped at the Russian frontier. As a result of asynchronous price fluctuations throughout several centuries by 1700, the level of prices (expressed in grams of precious metals) was seven times lower in Russia than in western Europe. In the eighteenth century, the difference began to close, as Russian prices rose five times in gold and eleven times nominally—more than in the West during several preceding centuries. As a result, the difference in price levels had declined to twofold. In the nineteenth century, Russian and European prices changed in tandem; by the early twentieth century, the gap had fallen to 20–30 percent, reflecting Russia's integration into the world market.

[*See also* Collective Agriculture and Collectivization.]

BIBLIOGRAPHY

Ågren, Maria, ed. *Iron Making Societies: Early Industrial Development in Sweden and Russia, 1600–1900*. Oxford, 1998.

Blackwell, William, ed. *Russian Economic Development from Peter the Great to Stalin*. New York, 1974.

Crisp, Olga. *Studies in the Russian Economy before 1914*. London, 1976.

Falkus, M. E. *The Industrialization of Russia, 1700–1914*. London, 1982.

Gatrell, Peter. *The Tsarist Economy, 1850–1917*. New York, 1986.

Gatrell, Peter. *Government, Industry and Rearmament in Russia, 1900–1914: The Last Argument of Tsarism*. Cambridge, 1994.

Gatrell, Peter. "The First World War and War Communism." In *The Economic Transformation of the Soviet Union*, edited by R. W. Davies et al., pp. 216–237. Cambridge, 1994.

Gerschenkron, Alexander. "Agrarian Policies and Industrialization in Russia, 1861–1917." In *The Cambridge Economic History of Europe*, edited by Peter Mathias and M. M. Postan, vol. 6, part 2, pp. 706–800. Cambridge, 1978.

Gregory, Paul R. *Russian National Income, 1885–1913*. Cambridge, 1982.

Gregory, Paul R. *Before Command: An Economic History of Russia from Emancipation to the First Five-Year Plan*. Princeton, 1994.

Gregory, Paul R., and Robert Stuart. *Russian Soviet Economic Structure and Performance*. 7th ed. Boston, 2001. The book is supplied with voluminous bibliography.

Gurov, Gregory, and Fred V. Cartensen, eds. *Entrepreneurship in Imperial Russia and the Soviet Union*. Princeton, 1983.

Kahan, Arcadius. *The Plow, the Hammer, and the Knout: An Economic History of Eighteenth-Century Russia*. Chicago, 1985.

Kahan, Arcadius. *Russian Economic History: The Nineteenth Century*. Chicago, 1989.

Mironov, Boris N. "Consequences of the Price Revolution in Eighteenth-Century Russia." *The Economic History Review* 45.3 (1992), 457–478.

Mironov, Boris N. "New Approaches to Old Problems: The Well-Being of the Population of Russia from 1821 to 1910 as Measured by Physical Stature." *Slavic Review* 58.1 (Spring 1999), 1–26.

Mironov, Boris N., with Ben Eklof. *The Social History of Imperial Russia, 1700–1917*, vol. 1, 2. Boulder, 2000.

Moon, David. *The Russian Peasantry, 1600–1930: The World the Peasants Made*. London, 1999.

Owen, Thomas. *The Corporation under Russian Law, 1800–1917: A Study in Tsarist Economic Policy*. Cambridge, 1991.

Von Laue, Theodore H. *Sergei Witte and the Industrialization of Russia*. New York and London, 1963.

BORIS N. MIRONOV

Communist Russia

The October Revolution inaugurated one of the most daring and promising social experiments of modern times, establishing a new political, social, and economic system according to a blueprint based on the ideas of Karl Marx (1818–1883) and developed by his followers, notably Vladimir Lenin (1870–1924) and other members of the Bolshevik movement in Russia. Over more than seven decades the communist regime radically transformed the Soviet Union (formally established in 1922), from a mostly rural-agricultural economy, but one with a small modern industrial and urban base (created during the last three to four decades before World War I), into a modern, urban, and industrial economy. The Soviet Union successfully fought and won Nazi Germany as a key member of the Allies, but paid a very high human and economic price. It emerged as a world and an imperial power confronting the West in the Cold War and played this role until the late 1980s. In 1989 a process of disintegration of the Soviet empire began in eastern Europe, and the Soviet Union broke up into fifteen independent states, including an independent Russia. Although the communist economic system had achievements in terms of economic growth, technological modernization and industrialization, the development of social services, and a level of social and economic equality, these gains were bought at the dear price of a dictatorial regime, extremely cruel for decades, mostly but not exclusively under Joseph Stalin (1925–1953), and the denial of most civil and personal liberties. Central planning, nationalization of production assets, and intensive industrialization brought rapid growth and radical structural change initially, but proved unsustainable in the longer run, leading eventually to decreased growth and stagnation. Political and social decay, burdened by a heavy military effort, also contributed to the inevitable change. Mikhail Gorbachev, elected as leader in 1985, started a historical process of radical changes, which were intended initially to reform the system but led to its demise and transformation.

Chronology of Principal Developments. The October Revolution came on the heels of World War I and the defeat of the Russian empire, which brought it to a state of economic decline and political disarray. It brought in its wake a civil war between the communist "reds" and the anticommunist "white" forces, including interventions by other countries. Ideology and war produced a system of war communism, a hybrid of war economy and communist measures: government control; nationalization of key production sectors as a prelude to central planning; centralized grain purchases, including expropriations and rationing; redistribution of land from the nobility to the peasants; and repudiation of all external debts.

The communists won the civil war but at the cost of further economic deterioration, rampant inflation, hunger, and severe shortages. In March 1921, Lenin introduced the New Economic Policy (NEP), a reversal of strategy that included some denationalization of large industry; liberalization of agriculture, food markets, and small and medium enterprises; and inflation stabilization through the introduction of a new currency. External economic relations were encouraged. The NEP lasted until 1928 and helped the Soviet Union recover to the prewar economic level and to stabilize the regime. The period also saw a serious debate on the design of the communist regime and its development strategy. One view supported the concept of balanced growth, at a moderate pace, using the profits of improved agriculture for industrialization purposes. Industrialization should evolve from light, consumer industries to heavy, production industries. Although this strategy assumed active government intervention, including control of the key sectors, it also provided for a relatively liberal economic environment, a continuation of NEP. A second view, following Marxian doctrine, supported

SOCIALISM IN RUSSIA. Bolshevik tracts being distributed on the streets of Petrograd, August 1917. (David King Collection)

rapid growth and industrialization, beginning with machine building and heavy industries, based on self-reliance. Investments should be financed through surpluses extracted from agriculture and forced savings. This strategy called for a stronger authoritarian regime, full nationalization, and central planning. Stalin, who initially supported the first view against Leon Trotsky (1879–1940) and others, adopted the more radical strategy following their expulsion, called off the NEP, and embarked on rapid forced collectivization of agriculture and intensive industrialization. The communist system that evolved lasted with relatively few changes until its demise.

The 1930s, under the guidance of the first five-year plans, was a formative period, as gigantic infrastructure projects and industrial complexes were built, major cities were inhabited, collectivization was enforced, and radical structural changes occurred. Increasing signs of war and the German attack of 1941 forced the economy into increased military production. Military requirements and the initial German conquest of much of the western part of the country forced a gigantic relocation of entire industries to the east, Siberia, and Central Asia. During the war about twenty million people, more men than women, were killed, and the economic infrastructure of the European part of the country was devastated. By 1942 total production declined by more than one-third, but it recovered to nearly 75 percent by 1944. Civilian production, however, declined to 20 percent of the 1940 level in 1942. The labor force, eighty-seven million in 1940, dropped to fifty-five million in 1942 and

seventy-six million in 1944, when more than 17 percent served in the military. The share of gross domestic product (GDP) devoted to the military, 18 percent in 1940, was 70 percent in 1942 and 57 percent in 1944.

A major consequence of World War II was the creation of the Soviet bloc, with expansion of Soviet domination and the Soviet system all over central and eastern Europe, and for a time also over China. The wartime Allies broke up, and the Cold War era started. After a period of reconstruction from the devastation of World War II and the death of Stalin (1953), there had been a significant mellowing of economic and political pressures, manifested in agricultural reforms designed to increase food production and supplies and the country's standard of living. The reform efforts gathered steam during the last years of Nikita Khrushchev (1955–1964) but peaked in a package introduced in 1965 by the new leadership of Leonid Brezhnev and Aleksei Kosygin (1964–1982). These reforms included the introduction of some market principles. Gradually, however, Kosygin's influence in favor of reforms weakened, implementation slowed, and the Soviet Union retreated to a more conservative mode of planning, in a period later termed the era of stagnation, which lasted until after the death of Brezhnev (1982) and the rise of Gorbachev in 1985. Attempts at partial reforms continued, but most failed because of conflicts with basic systemic principles and the system's built-in resistance to change. The year 1965 was a missed opportunity for radical reforms. A sharp rise in the price of energy on the world markets in

1973 and again in 1979, which greatly increased export revenues, and technological achievements in the military and the space program, beginning with the sensational launching of the first artificial earth satellite (*Sputnik*, in 1957), may have created misperceptions and helped to tilt the country's balance against reforms.

Gorbachev, faced with harsh economic difficulties and a heavy military burden, embarked on radical changes. He started with glasnost, (commonly translated as "openness") and perestroika ("reconstruction"). Glasnost introduced some personal and political freedoms and openness, though the dominant role of a somewhat reformed Communist Party was preserved. Perestroika was directed mostly at the economy: central planning was eased and partially decentralized, more decision-making power was granted to enterprises, some price liberalization was allowed, and small businesses and "cooperatives" became legal. The partial nature of these reforms, misguided old-style efforts to immediately resume growth, the poor discipline and fragility of the newly created institutions, and the resistance to change of the bureaucracy, all helped to bring about a deeper crisis characterized by disorganization, shortages, and both repressed and open inflation. Opposition to the changes and these difficulties contributed to a failed coup attempt in August 1991, the resignation of Gorbachev, the end of the Soviet Union, and the start of another era in Russian history.

Structural Changes, Growth, and Equality. The Soviet Union was the largest country in the world in terms of area, stretching from northeastern Europe to the Far East. With its great climatic diversity and abundant natural resources, major waterways, coal, ferrous and nonferrous metals, and timber, it was the second largest producer and consumer of energy in the world. After 1928, when the Soviet Union had recouped the economic losses of World War I and its civil war, its economy was radically transformed from a predominantly rural, agricultural economy to a modern industrial and urban one. In spite of some industrialization in the last years of the Russian empire (in coal, iron and steel, sugar, textiles, and flour mills, with development of a rail network, ports, and financial institutions), in 1926 some 82 percent of the Soviet population remained rural. By the late 1980s almost two-thirds of the population resided in urban areas. Correspondingly, 71 percent of the labor force was engaged in agriculture and 14 percent in manufacturing in 1926; but in the 1980s less than one-fifth of the labor force worked in agriculture, with more than one-third employed in manufacturing. Employment in services grew over the same period, from 15 percent to 37 percent. These very significant changes are consistent in direction with normal patterns of development; but they are quantitatively different from "normal," given the extent of GDP growth. They reflect the socialist development strategy of concentrating investments in manufacturing at the expense of agriculture and of urban infrastructure and services (see below). The decline in agricultural employment and in rural residency was smaller than normal, the rise of employment in manufacturing was larger, and that in services was above normal in public services, education, and health. Marketlike and private services grew very little.

Soviet growth after 1928 was faster than that of some of the developed countries but slower than that of others, including many developing countries, especially in East Asia. Initially the Soviet economy caught up with other countries to some extent, but by the 1970s it had started to lose ground. Still, its 1928 level of GDP per capita stood at around 20 percent of that of the United States and by 1990 had reached 30 percent of the U.S. figure. Soviet growth was achieved through higher rates of investment and higher participation rates of the population in the labor force. High investment rates and a growing military budget left a smaller share of GDP to private consumption (down to 50 percent of GDP), especially during the last two decades. The standard of living of the population improved considerably during the 1950s through 1970s, but the pace of improvements slowed throughout the period and afterward. High work commitments, shortages, rationing of and long lines for consumer goods, arduous and time-consuming household chores exacerbated by poor housing and lack of appliances and of market services, political fears and denial of freedom, all added to the gap between GDP growth and welfare. Higher wage equality, greater spending on social services, and increased economic security compensated somewhat for the difficulties.

The Soviet population grew from 124 million in 1928 (having been 156 million in 1913) to 289 million in 1990. This demographic expansion was the net result of an initially high rate of natural increase that declined sharply over time (less in the Moslem republics), as well as heavy losses suffered during periods of war and the collectivization drive, famine and Stalin's purges (mostly but not exclusively during the 1930s), and border changes. The rate of population growth from all these factors averaged 1.3 percent per year for the entire period, declining from 2.2 percent during the 1930s to 0.75 percent in 1989, with near zero growth in the European regions. In these areas the average age increased, and most families had only one child. The decline in fertility was partly a response of families to pressure to work harder, as well as a result of poor housing and household services.

The communist system was about equality, at least according to the constant declarations of its leaders and the expectations of many onlookers, inside and outside the country. The second part of the communist slogan, "From each according to ability to each according to needs," was "postponed" by Stalin until communism achieved material abundance. He justified wage differentials, determined mostly by the government, according to skills and worker contributions, and this principle prevailed throughout the period. Indeed, wage differentials were very great at the beginning, owing to a vast shortage of skilled and educated workers; but they narrowed over time as technical and higher education spread widely. Most studies found wage differentials in the Soviet Union not significantly narrower than in the welfare states of western and northern Europe, but narrower than in developing countries at a similar level of development. The almost complete nationalization of production left very little private income from assets, which is usually very unevenly distributed. Prices of many basic food items and goods and services (for housing and culture) were heavily subsidized; and the state provided education and health services (almost) free of charge, and social security and pensions to all on a highly equal basis. All these benefits provided all soviets with a minimum acceptable standard of living and raised income equality. For theses reasons the Soviet Union ranked higher on the United Nations' "Human Development Index" than its GDP-per-capita ranking (United Nations, *Human Development Report*, New York, annual).

The above remarks apply only partially to gender differentials. Educational opportunities were open to women, who became the majority of all workers, not only as teachers and nurses but also as physicians, engineers, and economists. Their income, though, stayed at about two-thirds of that of men, as in so many nonsocialist countries. In the Soviet Union this difference was due to the particularly heavy double burden of work and household chores imposed on women, to a male-dominance mentality, and to social discrimination.

A small group made of the political, military, top-managerial, and top-scientific elites enjoyed material privileges of many kinds, not publicly disclosed but a source of envy and cynicism. The country's underground economy, whose volume grew with time, was another source of increasing unofficial inequality.

System of Central Planning. The command economy and its system of central planning delegated to the government almost all the functions of markets. Almost all enterprises were nationalized and managed by government departments. Very little private production was allowed, and thus there were very few small enterprises. Agriculture was mostly collectivized (into kolkhoz) and partly nationalized (into state farms, sovkhoz). The kolkhoz, although formally owned by their members, were also under strict state control. Farmers and others were allowed to till small private agricultural plots, which saved many from hunger during difficult times.

The central committee of the Communist Party formulated the list of major production goals for the following five years and the coming year, and the lower hierarchical echelons of Gosplan, the central planning agency, disaggregated the goals into output targets, down to the individual product and enterprise level. A beehive of bureaucrats, each responsible for the "material balance" of supply and demand of a given product, strived to achieve it, and then to arrange the supply flows and networks and their timing, so that production would proceed smoothly, and shortages would be avoided. Although planning was done mainly in quantities, all products had prices, also determined by Gosplan. These prices, based on a version of the Marxist "labor theory of value," had a limited allocative role of market clearing. They served mostly for aggregation, accounting and control purposes. Plans were made on the basis of upward information flows, beginning with the enterprises and the shops.

Even under conditions of perfect information and with agents that fully identify with the center, such planning is a complex and cumbersome operation, much more time- and brain-consuming than planning by the invisible hand of the market. Yet, real conditions were far from perfect. The planning bureaus were understaffed and even more underequipped; computers were introduced late and were of low quality, as was the software. Information and instructions had to travel great distances through the bureaucratic maze and became distorted and difficult to control and follow. Agents represented their own and their organization's agendas, becoming a source of conflict and distorted reporting. The incentives used to encourage fulfillment of the targets in the annual plans presented to every enterprise were complex yet crude, and thus confusing. The main criterion of success, and the basis for bonuses for both enterprises and their managers, was fulfillment of the output targets. Considerations of costs and efficiency and production of the required assortment of goods received less attention, with underperformance the result. At the same time, fear of high output targets led to underreporting in order to minimize the next year's targets (the "ratchet effect" of Holland Hunter). The response of the system was to make plans "taut" and difficult to fulfill rather than optimal. Underfulfillment became common, and shortages developed. Janos Kornai, a leading scholar of the socialist system, described it as a "shortage economy." Shortages in high-priority areas, such as the military sector, were dealt with by creating a priority system in supplies that "overruled" the plan. The better achievements of the Soviet military sector and its alleged high efficiency were mostly the outcome of such priorities, implemented at exorbitant costs to civilian production.

Planners had to use shortcuts to provide more or less consistent plans on time, and therefore could consider only one or two variants. Inconsistent plans resulted in never ending costly and disruptive *ad hoc* adjustments all year long. It became convenient to plan "from the achieved level" of previous years with minimal structural changes, according to Igor Birman (*Soviet Studies* 30.2 (1978), 153–172). Another deficiency of central planning was that there was no exit mechanism for losing enterprises or obsolete technologies. Such enterprises and technologies, some of which created negative value added, survived with the help of heavy subsidies and "soft" credits (the "soft budget constraint," another Kornai term). The soft budget constraint joined shortages as a major source of the systemic inefficiency of Soviet planning.

The inefficiency of full nationalization and central planning also can be analyzed from the standpoint of property rights. With one distant and somewhat elusive owner or "principal" conveying goals that are not always clear, and a multitude of agents operating in the owner's name from great distances, there is a tendency among agents to usurp segments of the state's property rights and to behave as if they are partial owners or "stakeholders." A reality develops—as happened in this case—of vague diffusion and distribution of property rights, and hence of conflicting actions, inefficiency, and corruption.

The above obstacles created a rigid planning and production system with a very high cost for any change—in the plan, in the supply networks, in timing, and most critically in the introduction of new technologies and innovations. Most of these barriers for change resulted from the system's preferences and incentives for short-term outcomes at the expense of longer-term gains.

Development Strategy and Declining Growth. The downward pressure of the static efficiency of central planning was transformed into dynamic inefficiency through the high cost of change. The same outcome emerged also from the growth strategy adopted by the Soviet Union, a strategy of extensive growth. Growth is extensive when it is generated through adding more inputs to production, more labor and capital, whereas intensive growth results from a more efficient use of a given amount of labor and capital via technological changes, shifts to the production of more profitable products, and other innovations. Extensive growth is exhaustible because the ability to increase the workforce in a given population is bounded, and growth of the capital stock (per unit of output) yields declining returns. Intensive growth is sustainable since there is no limit to innovation, and since mechanisms of the endogenous growth perpetuate the process of innovation. Modern economic growth in market economies is sustainable because of its dominant intensive component, total factor productivity (TFP). The growth strategy under Soviet communism emphasized extensive growth, partly deliberately but partly because of failure to generate innovation.

The Soviet development strategy, based on Marxian growth theory and abundant natural resources, focused on growth maximization via large investments in heavy industry and manufactured goods sectors. Rapid industrialization came at the expense of investments in agriculture and the development of services, considered nonproductive by Marxian doctrine. Labor was maximized through obligating all able-bodied people to work, including women, and by moving people out of agriculture. Low wages provided incentives for two breadwinners in a family. Forced labor, in the millions, served to build projects in remote areas in Siberia and the north. The industrialization drive required many skilled workers, engineers, and so on; so there was a significant effort throughout the country to develop technical and high education.

The share of investment in GDP and the growth rate of capital stock were very high throughout the period by international norms; until the 1970s this was also true of the labor force. Capital and labor together contributed the bulk of per capita growth, as in extensive growth. True, TFP also contributed a fair share during the first part of the period, by filling in the initially broad technological gap and by the structural shift away from agriculture to industry. After 1950, when TFP depended more on domestic efforts, it tapered off and even turned negative, with growth becoming fully extensive and, from about 1970 on, based exclusively on capital. The resulting need to substitute capital for labor further depressed productivity growth.

The inability of the system to generate technological improvements and innovations, or to introduce partial reforms, was one major cause of the decline in growth. Another was exhaustion of the potential for extensive growth, as explained above. With modernization itself causing a decline in population growth, the high rate of participation of women in the labor force and the poor housing conditions and services further depressed fertility. From the 1970s on, most of the additions to the labor force in the Soviet Union came from its Moslem populations. Capital's contribution to productivity sharply declined, and it absorbed an ever increasing share of GDP, leaving a smaller share for other uses, especially consumption. High rates of growth of labor and capital in earlier periods generated lower rates later and expedited the exhaustion of extensive growth. "Haste" at the start was thus self-defeating.

As discussed above, the planning system created negative incentives and bureaucratic barriers to the dissemination of new technologies and innovations. There were also serious barriers to the development of new technologies, or copying them from the West. Although the research-and-development sector was one of the largest such endeavors in the world in terms of human and material resources, it was also run in a command fashion, depressing initiatives from below, the lifeline of innovation. The bulk of the R&D effort was directed to military targets, and the shortage economy prevented most spillovers to civilian production.

Copying from the West was difficult because of the country's limited economic openness and the Cold War.

Additional causes of declining growth over time were growing complexity of the production system that made planning more difficult, deterioration of motivation to work and of discipline, increasing corruption and illegal activities, declining improvements in the standard of living, and weakening of and deteriorating legitimacy of the regime. Collective agriculture, once the cornerstone of the communist system, became the millstone around its neck, pulling it down through growing inefficiency and mounting subsidies. Finally, the requirements of the military sector to preserve the nation's military balance with the West, and to keep the client states loyal, increased significantly—as possibly the final straw that tipped the balance in favor of major change.

Comments. In 1991 Russia became independent of the communist system and embarked on a transition to a democratic society and market economy. A grand social experiment thus ended at the cost of great suffering to many, its hundreds of millions of involuntary guinea pigs. Its legacy was a successful model of early industrialization and modernization, which was emulated by developing countries in the 1950s and 1960s. The social-equality stance of the Soviet system and its early investment in human capital challenged the industrialized countries following World War II and may have played a role in their development of the welfare state. With the Soviet communist variant of socialism gone, debate on the reasons for its failure and the future prospects of socialism will continue, suggesting such causes as misbehavior of eccentric and cruel leaders, the decision to enter the arms race and the Cold War, the authoritarian regime and lack of freedom and systemic economic weaknesses. Although all contributed to its demise, a combination of the last two reasons is the more fundamental flaw of Soviet socialism.

[*See also* Collective Agriculture and Collectivization.]

BIBLIOGRAPHY

Aslund, Anders. *Gorbachev's Struggle for Economic Reform.* 2nd ed. Ithaca, N.Y., 1991.
Bergson, Abram. *The Real National Income of Soviet Russia since 1928.* Cambridge, Mass. 1961.
Bergson, Abram, and Herbert S. Levine, eds. *The Soviet Economy toward the Year 2000.* London, 1983.
Berliner, Joseph S. *The Innovation Decision in Soviet Industry.* Cambridge, Mass., 1976.
Desai, Padma. *Perestroika in Perspective: The Design and Dilemmas of Soviet Reform.* Princeton, 1989.
Easterly, William, and Stanley Fischer. "The Soviet Economic Decline: Historical and Republican Data." *World Bank Economic Review* 9.3 (1995), 341–371.
Domar, Evsey. "A Soviet Model of Growth." In his *Essays in the Theory of Economic Growth*, pp. 223–261. New York, 1957.
Ellman, Michael. *The Destruction of the Soviet Economic System: An Insiders' History.* New York, 1998.
Gregory, Paul R., and Robert C. Stuart. *Soviet and Post-Soviet Economic Structure and Performance.* 5th ed. New York 1994.
Hunter, Holland. "Optimal Tautness in Developmental Planning." *Economic Development and Cultural Change* 9.4 (July 1961), 561–572.
Kornai, Janos. *The Socialist System, The Political Economy of Communism.* Princeton, 1992.
McAuley, Alastair. *Economic Welfare in the Soviet Union: Poverty, Living Standards and Inequality.* London, 1979.
Nove, Alec. *Economic History of the USSR, 1917–1991.* New York, 1993.
Nove, Alec. *The Soviet Economic System.* 3rd ed. Boston, 1986.
Ofer, Gur. "Soviet Economic Growth 1928–1985." *Journal of Economic Literature* 25.4 (December 1987), 1767–1833.

GUR OFER

Post-Communist Russia

In the second half of the 1980s, Mikhail Gorbachev as general secretary of the Communist Party embarked upon a radical reform program, which resulted in increased criticism and opposition, reaching a high in August 1991 when he was overthrown in a coup led by hard-liners who feared a breaking-up of the Soviet Union. The coup failed, mainly due to the public resistance of Boris Yeltsin, who reinstalled Gorbachev as president of the Soviet Union. However, in December 1991, the Soviet Union was dissolved and Yeltsin became president of the Russian Federation.

Nobody anticipated the abrupt collapse of the communist system. The transformation from a centrally planned economic system to a market economy turned out to be far more difficult than the textbook prescriptions would tell and that many Western advisers were proclaiming in the early 1990s. The transformation to a market economy affected the lives of almost 150 million people in Russia alone.

This article first discusses the main economic and institutional developments in the Russian Federation of the last decade of the twentieth century. The following section gives an overview of the main economic indicators and discusses the institutional reforms that have been implemented since the birth of the Russian Federation. The last section deals with privatization and the restructuring of firms and its obstacles.

Main Economic Indicators and Institution Reforms since 1990. Although economic and social reforms already had started in the late 1980s under Gorbachev, it was only in 1992 that a "big bang" program of economic transformation from a centrally planned to a market-based economy began for the Russian Federation. The key elements of such a reform program were price and trade liberalization and the privatization of the state enterprises. Of the transition countries, Russia was one of the first to start the mass privatization program, which was adopted in June 1992, and already in October 1992 the voucher privatization began. The voucher privatization program was completed by July 1994. At this stage the cash-based

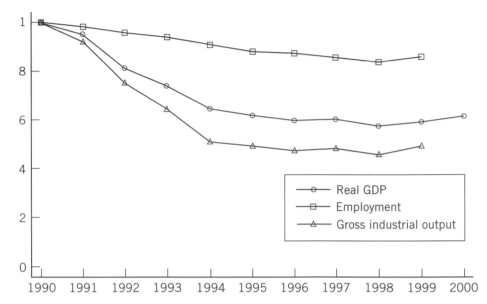

FIGURE 1. The evolution of output and employment in Russia since 1990. SOURCE: EBRD, 2001.

privatization started. During these early, reform years a number of new laws aimed at creating a competitive environment were enacted. In March 1993, a bankruptcy law was enacted, but it took until August 1995 before a law on natural monopolies and a law on joint-stock companies were approved. Furthermore, foreign trade was not completely liberalized until April 1996, more than four years later.

In August 1998, Yeltsin shook the world by defaulting on government bonds. This led to a major banking crisis. As a result, in October 1998 an agency for bank restructuring was established. However, this restructuring proceeded very slowly, and the role of the bank-restructuring agency was minimal since its financial resources and enforcement powers were rather weak. In 1999, a number of new laws, which were aimed at preventing further banking crises, were enacted. By December 1999, Yeltsin resigned as a president, and by March 2000, Vladmir Putin was elected president. In Russia, the reforms that were implemented were often associated with very little real effects, which was mainly due to inconsistencies in terms of economic policies and the emergence of corruption on a relatively large scale.

The substantial debt overhang led to a very loose monetary policy, which resulted in many currency crises and uncontrolled inflation. Consumer prices rose at an annual average rate of 1,526 percent in 1992. Inflation rates remained well above 200 percent during the first four years of economic reforms. Only since 1996 has the annual inflation rate dropped below 100 percent, although the annual average consumer price inflation rate was still 86 percent in

1999 and was expected to be 21.2 percent in 2000 (EBRD, 2001). As a result, barter trade emerged on a relatively large scale in Russia. Given these distortions, it then came as no surprise that the economic situation continued to deteriorate dramatically during this first decade of economic reforms. This is illustrated in Figure 1, which shows the evolution of output and employment in the Russian Federation since 1990.

In Figure 1, the indicators of output and employment are normalized to one in 1990 so that the percentage evolution of output and employment can easily be read from the graph. A first striking stylized fact emerges. Real GDP collapsed in less than four years to 60 percent of its 1990 level, while real industrial output collapsed even more. It was only in the beginning of the twenty-first century that a slight recovery in output began. A second stylized fact is evident in Figure 1. The employment collapse was far less pronounced than the output collapse. Employment collapsed by only 15 percent during this period compared with its pretransition level of 1990. This suggests that labor hoarding, which was prevalent under communism, persisted throughout the transition period of the last ten years of the twentieth century. The fact that aggregate employment did not collapse during this period is an indication that firm restructuring was postponed and that firms continued to have access to soft budget constraints, that is, direct or indirect government subsidies (Commander, et al., 1996). The collapse in output and employment is one of the facts that characterized most of the transition countries; however, only Russia and Ukraine did not experience a recovery a few years in the transition.

Privatization. The Russian privatization program started in October 1992, relatively early compared with other transition economies. The program implied that thousands of companies were given away under the voucher scheme mainly to insiders, (employees and managers). Although cash-based privatization began in July 1994, it affected only a small number of firms. One of the most important of these was the auction of a 2.5 percent stake in Gazprom, which was sold to the German gas consortium Ruhrgas. Privatization did not deliver on its promise. Many economists believed that fast privatization, even though it implied substantial insider ownership, would lead to fast restructuring and better firm performance. Richter and Schaffer (1996) use Russian firm-level survey data of state owned, privatized, and newly established (*de novo*) private firms to investigate firm restructuring and performance in Russia. They find that state-owned enterprises and privatized firms are very similar in their productivity and growth performance. In contrast, *de novo* private firms are fundamentally the most dynamic ones, yielding much better performance. This finding appears in many transition economies (Bilsen and Konings, 1998), and the reason privatization did not better firm performance in the early years of transition can easily be explained by the corporate governance structure of privatized firms.

The labor hoarding of state firms persisted once they were privatized for three main reasons. First, employees became the new owners. Clearly, they were not going to implement restructuring that might imply substantial job loss, thereby threatening their own job security. Second, the persistence of soft budget constraints did not give very strong incentives to firms to engage in deep restructuring. As a consequence, it took a long time before many of the privatized firms engaged in restructuring. Third, the technology in firms was obsolete, and substitution between labor and capital is very difficult. This makes the labor market very rigid, which makes it difficult to absorb economic shocks (Konings and Lehmann, 2001). It was only at the turn of the twenty-first century with the tightening of budget constraints and increased competitive pressure emerging in Russia that we began to see signs of restructuring.

BIBLIOGRAPHY

Bilsen, V., and J. Konings. "Job Creation, Job Destruction, and Growth of Newly Established, Privatized and State-Owned Enterprises in Transition Economies: Survey Evidence from Bulgaria, Hungary, and Romania." *Journal of Comparative Economics* 26 (1998), 429–445.

European Bank for Reconstruction and Development (EBRD). Transition Report Update. London, 2001.

Commander, S., Q. Fan, and M. Schaffer. *Enterprise Restructuring and Economic Policy in Russia*, Washington, D.C., 1996.

Konings, Jozef, and H. Lehmann. "Going Back to Marshall: Labour Demand in Russia." *IZA Discussion Paper*, Bonn, 2001.

Richter, A., and M. Schaffer. "Growth, Investment, and Newly Established Firms in Russian Manufacturing." In *Enterprise Restructuring and Economic Policy in Russia*, edited by S. Commander, Q. Fan, and M. Schaffer, pp. 253–273. Washington, D. C., 1996.

JOZEF KONINGS

Russian Empire

In modern economic literature (e.g., Savel'ev, 1997), the Russian Empire is defined by the historical organization of its geopolitical territory. The empire's economy functioned well and was continually developed. The legal code of the empire was developed by integrating aspects of Roman and Muslim law, the law codes of Lithuania, Magdeburg, Sweden, Austria, and Prussia, and the Napoleonic Code. The traditional organization of the Caucasus in Kazakhstan was retained, but the status of the other parts of empire varied from complete absorption by imperial legislation to protectorates, as was the case with Bukhara and Khiva.

Siberia. The colonization of Siberia, the colonial agricultural borderland of the empire, occurred slowly but steadily after the sixteenth century. According to N. M. Yadrintsev (*Siberia as a Colony*, 1892), "The people of Siberia, because of their desire for wealth, changed from vagrant and nomadic adventurers." Between 1816 and 1897, owing to immigration, Siberia's male population increased by 87.7 percent, from 220,000 to 413,000. As a result of this increase, the proportion of native Siberians fell from 25 percent of the population in 1816 to 15 percent in 1897. This tendency was continued at the beginning of the twentieth century. From the early 1860s to 1917 approximately four million immigrants arrived in Siberia. The regional population, not including the Akmolinsk district (Aqmola), grew from 2.86 million in 1863 to 9.63 million in 1914. During the same period, the amount of land controlled by Siberian natives fell to 29 percent. Similar changes, brought about by the agrarian policies of the government, occurred to native populations in other areas as well, including Bashkiria, Kazakhstan, and Turkistan.

Trade between Siberia and European Russia took place during the Nizhny Novgorod and Irbit fairs. After the opening of the Trans-Siberian Railway, butter, meat, and bread replaced furs, leather, bacon, and wool as the primary Siberian exports. Within twenty years (1894–1913) the export of butter exceeded 600 million rubles. By paying cash for imported goods, Siberians played a large role in the initial accumulation of wealth by the Moscow bourgeoisie and sped up the development of capitalism in the Central Provinces.

Transcaucasia and Northern Caucasus. Kabardia became a part of the Russian Empire in the sixteenth century, Georgia in 1801, and northern Azerbaijan in 1813. In

1828, the empire annexed the former Persian-Armenian provinces around Yerevan (East Armenia). The North Caucasus came under Russian control only in 1864.

In the manifest of 12 September 1801, on the annexation of Georgia to Russia, the emperor Alexander I promised that all taxes would be turned over to the internal civil government of the region. Beginning in 1840 the budget of Transcaucasia was included in the national budget, but no Russian money was in circulation and no imperial financial institutions existed there. The tax system of Transcaucasia also included the payment of chimney money; the total amount of chimney money in the Transcaucasian region in the 1880s was about 2.5 million rubles.

Azerbaijan is among the most oil-rich regions in the world and has a long history of oil production. During the second half of the nineteenth century, the oil-bearing area of Baku produced half of the world's supply. The Rothschilds and the Nobel brothers were the first to provide Russia with technology to develop its Caspian oil resources.

Azerbaijan also occupied an important position in the production of copper ore in the Russian Empire. Of the approximately 15,613,000 *puds* (1 *pud* = 36.11 pounds) of copper ore produced by the 108 mines in operation in Russia in 1902, 8,225,887 *puds* came from the Urals, and 6,631,349 *puds* from the Caucasus. In 1907, Kedabek produced more than a third of the copper ore in Russia.

The communities in the North Caucasus highlands were made up of farmers. With no developed trade, they relied on barter, and patrimonial traditions were strong. The people retained the agricultural traditions that dated to ancient times. In the mountains, stockbreeding prevailed. During the second half of the nineteenth century, however, railroads brought European goods to the North Caucasus and the mountaineers soon developed a new economic system based on their inclusion in the world market, beginning the transition from their traditional culture to a modern one. "Ingush, Chechens, and especially Ossetians can be seen everywhere on the crossroads looking for jobs. No job is beneath their dignity: they can be seen in hotels, public-houses, in noblemen's rooms, at railway stations, in offices, in police stations, as shop boys, etc.," observed Alikhan Ardasenov (*Izbrannye trudy*, 1997, pp. 70–120).

Central Asia. The Kirghiz, Turkmens, and Karakalpaks were cattle breeders and nomads. A significant number of Uzbeks and Tadjiks engaged in irrigation agriculture. By the beginning of the nineteenth century, the three largest Uzbek states of Central Asia, the Bukhara emirate, the Khiva khanate, and the Kokand (Qŭqon) khanate, had strong economies. Trade and crafts grew in the cities of these centralized states. The lands of the Uzbeks, Tadjiks, and Kirghiz were of three categories: those that belonged to the state, those that belonged to the Muslim clergy, and those that belonged to individual owners. When these territories were included in Russia in the mid-nineteenth century, slavery was still in existence; the centers of the slave trade were Khiva and Bukhara. In the 1860s, Central Asia produced raw materials for Russian textile factories, a first step toward the development of the cotton industry in the twentieth century.

Modernization. The abolition of serfdom in 1861 served as a strong impetus for the modernization of the socioeconomic structure of the Russian Empire. The railroads became the tool of control for the huge spaces of Asian Russia, as the regions of Siberia, the Far East, the Caucasus, and Central Asia were called officially after 1880. The Trans-Siberian Railway connected the Baltic Sea with the Pacific, other railways connected the east coast of the Caspian Sea, Bukhara, Samarkand, and Tashkent via Orenburg with Samara and other parts of Russia. Between 1893 and 1902, 4 billion rubles (1 ruble = 50 U.S. cents in 1900) of private money was invested in railway construction and the railway industry. Railroad companies were the main clients of banks before World War I. The largest bank in the country was the Russo-Asiatic Bank; the Siberian Commercial Bank was another leader. Stacheev and Company established branches throughout Siberia, the Far East, and Central Asia. By 1917 Stacheev, with 110 million rubles in shares in different banks, was able to make use of a credit of 220 million rubles.

In 1913, grain production reached its maximum—5 billion *puds* (compared with 3 billion *puds* in 1900). Russia's share of world grain exports was 21.9 percent (compared with 18.4 percent for the United States). However, the greatest profit increases in the pre–World War I years were in stockbreeding (see Table 1). World War I had a disastrous effect on Russia's finances and economy. The resulting situation hastened the end of the Russian Empire.

TABLE 1. *Stockbreeding in Russia and in Other Countries per 100 Inhabitants, 1911–1914 (thousand head)*

	YEARS	HORSES	CATTLE	SHEEP	GOATS	PIGS
European Russia	1914	16.5	23.6	30.2	0.6	10.1
Caucasus	1914	16.0	50.0	97.5	9.0	9.8
Siberia	1914	53.1	66.9	60.3	2.9	17.0
Central Asia	1914	42.0	51.2	185.1	27.5	2.0
Total Russian Empire	1914	20.4	30.2	47.9	3.3	9.9
Canada	1915	37.1	75.1	25.3	—	38.5
USA	1916	21.4	62.2	49.8	3.7	68.9

SOURCE: *Rossija, 1913 god*, Saint Petersburg, 1995, p. 92.

TABLE 2. *Regional Shares of Industrial Manufacturing in the Russian Empire (in percentages)*

REGIONS	1908	1912
Don region and North Caucasus	4.0	5.0
Total European Russia	79.7	78.7
Transcaucasia	5.0	5.7
Siberia	2.7	2.0
Turkestan	1.6	1.5

SOURCE: *Rossija, 1913 god,* Saint Petersburg, 1995, p. 49.

During the period from 1910 to 1913, the rate of growth of industrial manufacturing in Russia was the highest in the world, 6.0 percent, compared with 5.7 percent in the United Kingdom, 4.2 percent in the United States, 4.2 percent in Germany, and 3.9 percent in France. In 1913, Russia constituted 6 percent of world industrial production. Table 2 shows the contributions of the regions of Siberia, Caucasus, and Central Asia to the economy of the empire.

[*See also* Central Asia].

BIBLIOGRAPHY

Ardasenov, Alikhan. *Izbrannye trudy.* Vladikavkaz, Russia, 1997.

Bacon, E. *Central Asians under Russian Rule.* New York, 1966.

Bater, J. H., and R. A. French, eds. *Studies in Russian Historical Geography,* vols. 1–2. London, 1983.

Crisp, Olga. *Studies in the Russian Economy before 1914.* London, 1976.

Damenija, I. Ch. *Istoriographija istorii narodov Kavkaza.* Saint Petersburg, 1996.

Edmondson, Linda, and Peter Waldrou, eds. "Economy and Society in Russia and the Soviet Union, 1860–1930." Essays for Olga Crisp. New York, 1992.

Gatrell, Peter. *The Tsarist Economy, 1850–1917.* London, 1986.

Gregory, P. R. *Russian National Income, 1885–1913.* Cambridge, London, and New York, 1982.

Haxthausen, Baron A. von. *The Russian Empire, its People, Institutions, and Resources.* English ed. 2 vols. London, 1856. Microfilm ed. Ann Arbor, Mich., 1964.

Hosking, Geoffrey. *Russia. People and Empire, 1552–1917.* London, 1997.

Kazmer, Daniel R. *Russian Economic History.* Detroit, 1977.

Kennan, George. *Siberia and the Exile System.* New York, 1891.

Lieven, Dominic. *Russian Empire and Its Rivals.* London, 2000.

Marks, Steven G. *Road to Power: The Trans-Siberian Railroad and the Colonization of Asian Russia, 1850–1917.* Ithaca, N.Y., 1991.

Pearson, R. *Russia and Eastern Europe, 1789–1985: A Bibliographic Guide.* Manchester, 1989.

Savel'ev, P. I., ed. *Imperskii stroi Rossii v regional'nom izmerenii: XIX-nachal0 XX veka.* Moscow, 1997.

Thompstone S. "Russian Imperialism and the Commercialization of the Central Asian Cotton Trade." *Textile History* 26.2 (1995).

Yadrintsev, N. M. *Siberia as a Colony.* Saint Petersburg, 1892.

SERGEI LEBEDEV

RWANDA. *See* Central Africa.

S

SAHARA. The economic history of the Sahara—the plural of *sahra* in Arabic, or "desert"—begins in the third millennium BCE with the gradual emergence of a broad band of arid land stretching from the Atlantic Ocean in the west, to the Nile River and the Horn of Africa in the east. By the time of the construction of the Great Pyramids along the Nile at the beginning of the third millennium BCE, the "deserts" of the Sahara made up the largest dry zone in the world.

Rock art and limited archaeological research suggest that societies in what would become the Sahara were relatively homogeneous, living by hunting and foraging, sometimes combined with vegeculture and limited agriculture. Along the edges of the Sahara and within the desert, three bases for trade emerged. First, desertification promoted greater economic differentiation. Some societies in the desert shifted from hunting and foraging to aquatic foraging, then from aquatic foraging to agriculture around lakes, such as Lake Chad, and in the Senegal, near the Niger, Shari, and Nile River valleys. Among peoples who remained in the more arid reaches of the desert, some came to depend increasingly on herding breeds of goats and sheep that could endure the heat; others clustered around water points, or oases, where on limited expanses of land they turned to irrigation to support intensive agriculture and arboriculture. From the desert edge in the north and south, societies exchanged food products with Saharan trading partners and people circulated among desert societies. Staple resources such as iron, copper, gold, and salt constituted a second basis for exchange. Of these, gold, found in the wooded savanna and forest south of the Sahara, and rock salt deposits, located for the most part deep in the desert, were the most important for Saharan and trans-Saharan commerce. Third, and somewhat later, slave raiding gave rise to commerce in captives—within the Sahara and across it.

While ancient Greek authors such as Herodotus noted a few examples of trade and contact between societies of the Sahara and the Mediterranean basin, such communication was sporadic and indirect. The later Roman record described more regular contact, but concern focused more on protecting the frontiers of empires from the depredations of desert raiders than on fostering exchange.

Saharan caravan trade arose with the appearance of the domesticated camel at the beginning of the Christian era. In the first century CE, camels spread from the Nile valley west to Borkou and north of Lake Chad. By the fourth century, they were common on routes in the eastern Sahara. About this time, too, the use of camels in the western desert gave rise to the trans-Saharan gold trade. The Roman imperial mints in Carthage began to produce coins made of gold from south of the desert; later Muslim rulers in Tunisia (Ifriqiyya) continued this practice. This trade grew in the sixth century, and after the ninth century the spread of Islam into the Sahara laid the foundations for a common mercantile culture. Initially, gold came from mines not too far south of the desert—from Bambuk (in present-day Senegal), Bure (in northwest Guinea), and the Volta region (of Burkina Faso)—which presumes the existence of commercial networks beyond the Islamic frontier. Later, gold from Asante, located farther south in the forest region of present-day Ghana, supplemented these sources. At the height of trade during the medieval period, more than a ton of gold made its way north across the Sahara each year (Austen 1987). Austen also emphasizes the great importance of West African gold for the Mediterranean economy and the maintenance of the balance of payments with South Asia at this time. This prominence declined dramatically with the European discovery of the Americas and the importation of precious metals from across the Atlantic.

In addition to gold, slaves were an important part of Saharan and trans-Saharan commerce. Beginning with a trickle in the ninth century, the flow of people north grew steadily, culminating in the nineteenth century and dropping off in the twentieth century. While a substantial proportion of captives came from West Africa, greater numbers came from farther east in central and eastern Sudan—regions not rich in gold. The demographic loss to sub-Saharan African societies was substantial. Overall, 6 million people were forcibly sent into and across the desert, while at least an equal number perished in initial raids or succumbed to the hardships of travel in the Sahara. On the other hand, for some desert societies, struggling to reproduce themselves in an environment characterized by high rates of infant and general mortality due to disease, famine, and violence, as well as high rates of out-migration, this regular flow of people from the south was crucial for demographic survival. Indeed, it may be argued that the integration of captives into desert societies was essential for the maintenance of the Saharan and trans-Saharan caravan network.

The desert commercial system was a viable economic enterprise for a millennium, and empires both north and south of the Sahara sought to control it—through military, kinship, and religious alliances with the nomadic peoples who dominated the trade routes and oasis stopping points or through outright conquest. The sub-Saharan empires of Ghana, Kanem-Bornu, Mali, and Songhai all launched expeditions into the desert between the eleventh and fifteenth centuries, as did the North African Almohad empire in the thirteenth century and the sultanate of Morocco, which conquered Timbuktu in 1591. On occasion, nomads from the desert—such as the Almoravids of present-day Morocco and Mauritania in the eleventh century—extended their authority to the desert edge and beyond. Although scholars once believed that the appearance of European traders on the West African coast in the sixteenth century sounded the death knell of Saharan trade, recent research suggests that the desert's commercial network—protected by its remote location—thrived, and even expanded, well into the modern era. As late as the 1880s and 1890s, European colonial powers such as France and Great Britain, which by this time controlled the desert edge in both north and south, fretted about commercial competition from Saharan caravans. The construction of railroads and roads from the West African coast to the desert edge in the early twentieth century finally shifted the comparative economic advantage away from Saharan trade.

[See also North Africa.]

BIBLIOGRAPHY

Austen, Ralph A. *African Economic History.* London and Portsmouth, N.H., 1987.

Austen, Ralph A., and Dennis D. Cordell. "Trade, Transportation, and Expanding Economic Networks: Saharan Caravan Commerce in the Era of European Expansion, 1500–1900." In *Black Business and Economic Power,* edited by Alusine Jalloh and Toyin Falola, pp. 114–144. Rochester, N.Y., 2002.

Bovill, E. W. *The Golden Trade of the Moors.* London, 1968.

Bulliet, Richard. *The Camel and the Wheel.* Cambridge, Mass., 1975.

Cordell, Dennis D. *Dar al-Kuti and the Last Years of the Trans-Saharan Slave Trade.* Madison, Wis., 1985.

Daniels, Charles. *The Garamantes of Southern Libya.* Cambridge, 1970.

Gautier, E.-F. *Sahara: The Great Desert.* Translated by Dorothy Ford Mayhew. New York, 1987.

Lovejoy, Paul E. *Salt of the Desert Sun: A History of Salt Production and Trade in the Central Sudan.* Cambridge, 1986.

McIntosh, Roderick James. *The Peoples of the Middle Niger: The Island of Gold.* Oxford and Malden, Mass., 1998.

Newbury, Colin W. "North African and Western Sudan Trade in the Nineteenth Century: A Reevaluation." *Journal of African History* 7.2 (1966), 233–246.

Swanson, John T. "The Myth of the Trans-Saharan Trade during the Roman Era," *International Journal of African Historical Studies* 8.4 (1975), 582–600.

DENNIS D. CORDELL

SAHEL. Derived from Arabic, *sahil* means "border" or "shore." The Sahel refers to the most northern region of sub-Saharan Africa, a relatively narrow ecological zone, some 200 to 400 kilometers (120 to 250 miles) wide, that extends across the continent, from the Atlantic seaboard to the Indian Ocean. The Sahel is a transitional, semiarid zone between the Sahara and the better watered savanna to the south. It forms part of Senegal, Mauretania, Mali, Burkina Faso, Niger, Nigeria, Chad, Sudan, Ethiopia, Eritrea, and Somalia. Although most research on the Sahel concentrates on the region from Lake Chad westward, the themes of human adaptation, state formation, environmental degradation, and periodic drought and famine relate as well to the zone east of Lake Chad.

The climate of the Sahel has fluctuated during the past 20,000 years between relatively sustained dry and wet periods. For the past 2,500 years (c. 500 BCE), the climate has been dry. Research indicates that in the Atlantic Ocean, north of the equator, the lower sea-surface temperatures correlate with lower rainfall patterns in the Sahel. Sea-surface temperatures directly influence the interplay of two large air masses—the warm, moist, maritime tropical air mass that forms in the South Atlantic and the hot, dry, continental air mass that forms over the Sahara. In annual cycles, the maritime air mass moves northward from approximately January to June, then retreats from July through December; the northward movement determines the extent and intensity of rainfall. On average, the Sahel receives 100 to 200 millimeters (4 to 8 inches) of rain, almost all of which falls between June and August. Periodically, the maritime air mass does not move far enough to the north, so the Sahel has a drought. When the continental air mass is on the move, it is referred to as the harmattan, the hot, dry wind; it can carry away significant amounts of the surface soils.

The ecology of the Sahel has been influenced by the Senegal and Niger River systems and by Lake Chad, whose waters attracted early human and animal populations and, later, nomadic pastoralists; this was particularly pronounced in the flood plain of the interior delta of the Niger River (now in Mali). As the annual floods receded, the rich pastures of the region sustained agricultural and seasonal populations, which encouraged their interactions. The Sahel's vegetation consists of low-growing grasses and herbaceous perennials, including acacia trees and baobab trees. The relatively thin vegetation cover does not support the tsetse fly, the vector for trypanosomiasis (sleeping sickness), which is often deadly for cattle. Thus, the Sahel has been a zone of nomadic pastoralism and mixed agro-pastoralism.

Animal and human populations adapted to the oscillating wet and dry cycles and to the Sahel's periodic famines. Before European colonialism, the Sahel farmers developed agronomic regimes that maximized their subsistence security by mixing crops, planting in different fields, raising small livestock, storing grain, and investing in social networks. In drought-prone locales, the farmers sought marriages from communities in better watered locations. The pastoralists moved their herds annually in search of good pasture land, aware that periodically their routes would take them farther afield than usual. Pastoralists and farmers mainly interacted in mutually beneficial ways. After the harvest, farmers welcomed pastoralists to their fields, where their herds could graze and deposit green manure. The farmers exchanged some grain and cloth for hides, milk, and desert products, including salt. The pastoralists, however, needed the farmers more than the farmers needed the pastoralists—during the hot, dry months of the harmattan, the herds' milk supply diminished, so pasturalists then needed grain for their diets. When the climatic or political conditions turned unfavorable for the farmers to exchange their surpluses, the mutually beneficial relations became conflictual. Sahelian farmers moved to defensive positions and developed more complex political organizations. The earliest states in West Africa—Ghana, Takrur, Songhay, and Bornu—were formed in the Sahel, along the zone of interaction between the farmers and pastoralists.

The tenth-century CE formation of states profoundly influenced the economy of the Sahel; it stimulated both urbanization and economic specialization. Specialized long-distance traders, capable of negotiating in various languages and among the different cultures, emerged to service demand for luxuries and ecologically specialized produce. In response to market demand, the farmers and pastoralists of the Sahel expanded production of cloth, grain, and herds. Such urban centers as Timbuktu, Gao, and Kano became important commercial entrepôts and staging grounds for the trans-Saharan trade. Timbuktu also developed into a major center for Islamic higher education. In 1444, with the arrival of the Portuguese off the coast of Mauretania, the Sahel became an enterprise zone with the expansion of the slave trade, which was already servicing demand in North Africa and the Middle East. By the sixteenth century, the Senegal River estuary became a major locale for the emerging transoceanic slave trade, which took Africans in slave ships to Europe and the Americas well into the nineteenth century. Slaves were not the only Sahelian commodities in demand in Europe; as early as the 1400s, European dyers had become aware that dyes took to cloth better when mixed with gum arabic, a substance derived from the acacia trees (*Acacia senegal*) that grew extensively along the northern bank of the Senegal River. The expansion of the European textile industry from the 1600s onward increased demand for gum arabic, the trade of which became governed by complex agreements between the Mauretanian producers, who used slave labor, and the African and Euro-African traders, who operated under French colonial authority.

The Sahel had a sustained arid period from 1790 to 1850, as well as more severe droughts that lasted from twelve to fifteen years in the 1680s, the mid-1700s, the 1820s and 1830s, and the 1910s. Less severe droughts occurred in the 1640s, 1710s, 1810s, and early 1900s. The Sahel had relatively wet phases from the 1500s through the 1700s from 1870 to1895, and in the 1950s. European conquest of the Sahel occurred during the wet phase at the end of the 1800s.

European rule in the Sahel encouraged the expansion of production along the well-established ecological axes. In response to the growing Colonial-era demand for meat in the urban areas along the West African coast, pastoralists and farmers in the Sahel expanded their herds of cattle, sheep, and goats. The large herds put significant pressure on fragile pastures and increased the soil degradation during the annual harmattan. In the 1920s and 1930s, both French and British colonial officials implemented major irrigation projects in the Sahel that sought to use the waters of the Niger River and the Nile to produce cotton for mills in France and England. While neither of these projects succeeded as they had been intended, both led to the significant resettlement of Africans in the Sahel. The relatively wet period of the 1950s and the colonial price incentives for cotton and peanuts encouraged farmers and pastoralists to intensify their activities. In Mali, for example, rain-fed crop production increased by 80 percent from 1952 to 1975. Then from 1940 to 1970, cattle herds in Senegal, Mali, and Niger were expanded by 500 percent and those in Burkina Faso and Mauretania by 300 to 400 percent. Agricultural development in the Sahel resulted in soil and vegetational degradation, and it undermined the well-established forms of subsistence security. Most Sahelian colonies became independent in early 1960s. (The exceptions were Ethiopia, liberated by Britain from Italian occupation in 1941; Sudan, which became independent of Britain in 1956; and Eritrea, which became independent of Ethiopia in 1993.)

When the rains in the Sahel failed from 1968 to 1974, farmers and pastoralists of the region were especially vulnerable to ecological and economic catastrophe. By the early 1970s, some 25 million people faced increased hunger or famine and the loss of their livelihoods or lives. Despite massive international assistance, death rates in the region were enormous and the cattle herds were lost. That drought left the Sahel severely degraded. In the aftermath of the drought, international assistance has tried to help rehabilitate the Sahel and to promote sustainable economic activities. Wetter conditions since the mid-1970s have induced pastoralists to rebuild their herds and farmers to resume their production of export crops. Students of the 1968–1974 drought have come to understand that the event was not merely the result of climate change but the result of economic and cultural changes that had stressed agribusiness and consequently eroded centuries of local agronomic knowledge.

BIBLIOGRAPHY

Binns, Tony, ed. *People and Environment in Africa*. Chichester, U.K., 1995.

Church, R. J. Harrison. *West Africa: A Study of the Environment and Man's Use of It*. New York, 1968.

Copans, Jean, ed. *Secheresses et famines du Sahel*. Paris, 1975.

Grizter, Jeffry A. *The West African Sahel: Human Agency and Environmental Change*. Chicago, 1988.

Lovejoy, Paul, and Stephen Baier. "The Desert-Side Economy of the Central Sudan." *International Journal of African History Studies* 8.4 (1975), 551–581.

Munson, Patrick. "Archaeology and the Prehistorical Origins of the Ghana Empire." *Journal of African History* 21.4 (1980), 457–466.

Nicholson, Sharon. "The Methodology of Historical Climate Reconstruction and Its Application to Africa." *Journal of African History* 20.1 (1979), 31–50.

Roberts, Richard. *Two Worlds of Cotton: Colonialism and the Regional Economy in the French Soudan, 1800–1946*. Stanford, Calif., 1996.

Watts, Michael. *Silent Violence: Food, Famine, and Peasantry in Northern Nigeria*. Berkeley, 1983.

Webb, James. *Desert Frontier: Ecological and Economic Change along the Western Sahel, 1600–1850*. Madison, Wis., 1995.

RICHARD ROBERTS

SALT AND SALT MAKING. From the end of the Neolithic period, humans have sought to enrich their diets with salt, which heightens the flavor of food and provides essential sodium. Eventually they discovered two other important characteristics of salt: its hygroscopic and drying power, and its bactericidal qualities, used in the preservation of hides and the manufacture of leather (shoes, belts, saddles, and shields). Its use as a preservative permitted the manufacture of Roman fish sauce, *garum;* the preservation of animal products (meat, fish, cheese, butter, and eggs); and the manufacture of salted meats (hams and sausages). Wild animals and domestic livestock are salt eaters, especially herbivores (buffalo, camels, and sheep), which consume a great deal of salt.

Salt is well distributed throughout the world. Present in seawater (thirty-five grams per liter), it is more abundant in the warm seas of the tropics and subtropics (for example, the Mediterranean, the China Sea, the Bay of Bengal, and the coasts of Australia and Mexico) than in cold waters (for example, the Baltic). It is also present on the conti-

nents, buried under impermeable soils that protect the layers of rock salt or on the surface in arid climates that form salt lakes. A malleable lightweight rock, salt loses its shape easily and rises from the depths by sliding between other rocks to build domes (diapir folds) that lie just under the surface or to form salt mountains (for example, Cardona in Spain and the Salt Range in Pakistan). Salt is present in all sedimentary basins and in mountain chains, where foldings and upthrusts sometimes lifted it to great altitudes (for example, the region of Salzburg, Austria, the Plateau of Tibet, and the Altiplano region of Bolivia).

Production. Salt is produced by separating it from water or from other rocks. In the Mediterranean climate, salt forms through the work of the sun and the wind in basins filled with seawater running along the shore. People began by enlarging these rocky basins, arranging them to make seawater flow into them; such archaic saltworks still exist in Lebanon, Malta, and the Canary Islands. Creating an artificial installation (salt field, saltworks, or salt pan) requires favorable conditions, flat and impermeable expanses in the vicinity of deltas and estuaries where alluvial deposits create lagoons. The French and Iberian coasts of the Atlantic were favored by tides that naturally filled up the basins. In the Mediterranean, pumping raised the water into the basins. On the Continent, diverse techniques were used, including digging mine galleries in the mountains or breaking away exposed outcroppings of rock salt. On the plains, a simpler technique consisted of drilling a well, harnessing a salt spring, and hoisting it to the surface using elevating machines, a technique adapted to mountains in the twelfth century by injecting soft water through wells into the layers of salt, dissolving the salt, and sending the brine to installations in the valleys through pipes.

The manufacture of salt passes through two stages: dissolution or primary evaporation creates a brine, the evaporation or concentration of which produces salt. Salt is "farmed" at the seaside (using salt pans or salt marshes), "manufactured" through heating with the aide of a combustible (such as wood, peat, coal, gas, or heating oil) in a saltworks. Dependence on energy sources, such as wood, that were quickly exhausted necessitated the invention of technical processes that saved resources: in continental saltworks, processes that copied nature were introduced; graduation buildings *(Gradierwerke)*, for example, captured solar rays and wind. German engineers *(Salinisten)* became masters of these techniques, which they ceaselessly perfected in creating new saltworks. The use of coal in England completely changed the conditions of salt production, making it possible to boil seawater directly by the end of the seventeenth century (as in Northumberland and the Firth of Forth).

Transport and Commerce. Salt was transported everywhere. The principal axes of international transport were

SALT MINES. Engraving (1760) by J. E. Nielson, of a salt mine in Wieliczka, near Kraków, Poland. At top center, workers descend into the mine using cords and support the mine using timber and pillars. At top right, the miners use lifting machines powered by horses. At bottom left, the miners use their tools to break large blocks of salt and cut them into cylinders, each weighing 600 to 800 pounds. At the end of the sixteenth century the mine, which employed 900 workers, produced 26,000 tons of salt. (Collection of J. C. Hocquet)

the great maritime routes, in the Middle Ages, from the islands of the Mediterranean (Cyprus, Sicily, Ibiza, and Cagliari in Sardinia) to Naples, Venice, Pisa, and Genoa; and beginning in the fourteenth century, from the salt pans of the Atlantic coast (Bay de Bourgneuf, and Brouage, Setúbal in Portugal and Cadiz) to the Hanseatic ports of the Baltic, Danzig, Riga, and Reval (present-day Tallinn). Political events such as war compelled the creation of new routes, such as the Dutch route to the archipelago of Cape Verde and the Caribbean. Technical innovation also upset trade routes. Scotland, which in the Middle Ages had been dependent on imports of bay salt from France, in the seventeenth century delivered its white salt to Hamburg and Denmark.

On the Continent, all rivers and waterways were salt routes. Crossing mountains, sailing up torrential valleys, navigating on the calmest lakes, and crossing frozen passes required public authorities to collaborate actively in the maintenance of roads and the construction of bridges, coaching inns, warehouses, and shops to maintain a practicable route and to keep up stocks in Switzerland, the Dolomites, or the Bohemian forest north of Passau. These salt routes were stable through the ages, but industrialization, the use of coal, the discovery of rock salt, and the construction of new means of communication (such as railroads) upset the markets. Bay salt, long dominant in

European commerce, ceded its place to the industrial salts of Cheshire and Lorraine, which took over the markets of northern Europe during the eighteenth and nineteenth centuries.

Salt and Money. Since ancient times, salt making has required heavy investment because it is necessary to build the saltwater marshes on the vast surface protected by dams, equip the salted wells, and build evaporation installation. This work, which precedes production, can take several years to complete. The landowners advance the capital necessary and retain control of the production.

Production, capital, and work. The conversion of salt pans, salt wells, and mines required investments of land and capital. These means of production belonged to large landowners—bishops, large monasteries, and territorial princes who obtained them through public power. For exploitation, modernization, or the renovation of equipment, these landowners raised new capital, which they reimbursed by issuing perpetual loans, such as irredeemable securities and annuities. The well remained the property of the lord, the extracted brine was shared among several people of independent means, such as annuity holders and investors (as in Lüneburg, Halle, Salins, Añana), who entrusted the brine to experts. These salt people had it boiled in lead furnaces installed in small workshops (*sauneries*, brine shops, and salt shops), themselves the property of

SALT PROCESSING. Salt marsh in Guérande, France. Many salt marshes operate using traditional modes of production that have existed since the Middle Ages, such as small family enterprises, manual labor, and multiple harvests using day laborers. (Collection of J. C. Hocquet)

other social groups (such as religious orders, the bourgeois, and merchants), who also received income from their annuities. The salt industry from the end of the Middle ages was weighed down with *rentes* (investments) that burdened costs of production and brought on stagnation (as in Lüneburg and Halle) before the princes confiscated the old saltworks in the eighteenth century to replace them with larger production units more apt to accommodate innovations.

The maritime salt pans that produced solar salt were of two types, Atlantic and Mediterranean. In the first, which provided daily outputs, the exploitation was carried out through a system of familial sharecropping. The second gathered salt one or two times during the summer on a salt march of vast dimensions entrusted to a permanent workforce of several salters who were in charge of the water. They also required numerous seasonal workers hired for the harvest and transport of salt to loading sites. These two statuses, sharecroppers and salaried employees, which appeared in the Middle Ages, were perpetuated into the twentieth century.

Nonfree workers also worked the salt marshes, as in the slave societies of antiquity or in desert saltworks, where black populations bought from black kingdoms and from traffickers from Timbuktu were brought by Tuareg caravanners to numerous saltworks of the Sahara to gather salt sold to the sedentary peoples of the Sahel. In this cycle, the farmers of the Sahel had to provide slaves to the nomads,

who controlled the caravan commerce that brought them their salt. Several other forms of forced labor existed, notably the corvée of peasants (statute labor) to raise seawater to saltworks situated above sea level (as in coastal China), to gather the salt of salt lakes, to support the harvest on Mediterranean salt marshes, and for the cartage of salt on roads (Lorraine in the eighteenth century). These mines had a deplorable reputation, although the air was healthier than that in coal mines, the space less confined, and the work conditions better. On solar salt marshes, the heat and sun beating down on the white surfaces of the crystallizing dishes often were difficult to bear.

Taxation. As a product universally consumed and without effective substitutes but with a narrowly limited production, salt offered a major source of tax revenues. In this sense, salt seemed to serve as any other merchandise, but the Venetians correctly distinguished between "salt" and "merchandise," for salt was unlike any other merchandise. With salt one could acquire all other merchandise. It acted as a standard of value, like a currency, and several civilizations created a "money of salt" (in imperial China, New Guinea, Ethiopia, Tuareg, and Venice in its exchanges with transhumant livestock breeders in the Balkans).

Everyone consumed salt each day but in small quantities. The powers that guaranteed the availability of salt, to guard against speculation by merchants, began by imposing minimal and imperceptible taxes that remunerated its service. Some organized the commerce as a state monopoly (as in Venice). Pressed for money, some states rashly increased the sales price of salt to pay for war, defeat, ransoms, and reconstruction. To guarantee its receipts, the state required populations to purchase salt at state-owned shops, called granaries (as in France and the Papal States). Incapable of administering this dual system of distribution of a product and imposition of heavy taxes, the state entrusted these missions to individuals who bought them at auction. These tax farmers further aggravated the tax burden by reimbursing themselves from it and keeping a large part of the receipts. This unpopular tax (called the *gabelle* in France) provoked an active contraband market as well as its suppression. The heavy salt tax was a low-yield investment for the exchequer, which had to maintain armed troops to prevent tax evasion. The French Revolution abolished the salt tax and all its excesses, but it was soon necessary to reestablish a salt tax paid not by the consumer but by the producers.

Salt Today. Salt is one of the rare products humanity can be assured it will never lack. Dehydration, pasteurization, and freezing have stripped it of its long-uncontested position as exclusive agent of preservation. But humans and animals have never been more numerous, and all consume salt. Nevertheless, salt as food is no longer dominant. Since the inventions of Nicolas Leblanc and the Solvay brothers, who in the nineteenth century made soda from sodium chloride, the chemical industry has used chlorine and sodium to produce several hundred and varied industrial products used daily in homes, automobiles, buildings, cultivated land, meadows, and roads (such as salt for melting snow).

World production of crystallized salt is about 250 million tons, but more and more industry uses saturated brines, that is, liquid salt, the worldwide production of which is nearly 500 million tons. Salt is the object of a active maritime trade organized from tropical countries, such as Mexico, Australia, and Brazil, to industrial countries of the Northern Hemisphere, such as Japan and the Scandinavian countries. The costs of production are low, the costs of transport high, and several countries, such as France, are both importers and exporters, depending on the regional situation with regard to the international market. The principal producers are the most populous countries (China and India), and the power of their chemical industry forces the United States, itself a large producer, to import salt to the ports of the East Coast.

The geography of production is likely to undergo great changes in the next several years. Several large monopolistic groups prefer to develop automated units on the shores of tropical deserts. Nevertheless, several old saltworks committed to the "natural" product and to safeguarding traditional heritage have preserved and even expanded their outlets, as in Brittany in France. Finally, nearly everywhere salt has ceased to be administered as a state monopoly, which was abolished in countries of the European Economic Community (EEC) (such as in Italy and Austria) and in Japan.

BIBLIOGRAPHY

Bridbury, A. R. *England and the Salt Trade in the Later Middle Ages*. Oxford, 1955.

Bufalino, Gesualdo, et al. *Saline di Sicilia*. Palermo, Italy, 1988.

Buschman, J. O. F. *Das Salz, dessen Vorkommen und Verwertung in sämtlichen Staaten der Erde*. 2 vols., Leipzig, 1906–1909.

Choudhury, Sadananda. *Economic History of Colonialism: A Study of British Salt Policy in Orissa*. Delhi, 1979.

Ewald, Ursula. *The Mexican Salt Industry, 1560–1980: A Study in Change*. Stuttgart and New York, 1985.

Eyre, J. D. "Patterns of Japanese Salt Production and Trade." Center for Japanese Studies, Occasional Papers 3 (1952), 15–46.

Forbes, R. J., ed. *Het zout der aarde*. Hengelo, Netherlands, 1968.

Hocquet, Jean Claude. *Le sel et le pouvoir: De l'an mil à la Révolution Française*. Paris, 1985.

Hocquet, Jean Claude. *Chioggia, capitale del sale nel Medioevo*. Sottomarina di Chioggia, 1991.

Hocquet, Jean Claude. et al. *Das Salz in der Rechts- und Handelsgeschichte*. Schwaz, 1991.

Hocquet, Jean Claude, et al. *Hommes et paysages du sel: Une aventure millénaire*. Arles, 2001.

Lovejoy, Paul E. *Salt of the Desert Sun: A History of Salt Production and Trade in the Central Sudan*. African Studies series, no. 46. Cambridge, 1986.

McDougall, Elizabeth Ann. "The Salt Industry in West African History." MA thesis, University of Toronto, 1976.

Multhauf, Robert P. *Neptune's Gift: A History of Common Salt*. London and Baltimore, 1978.

Palme, Rudolf. *Rechts-, Wirtschafts- und Sozialgeschichte der inneralpinen Salzwerke biz zu deren Monopolisierung*. Rechtshistorische Reihe, Bd. 25. Frankfurt am Main and Bern, 1983.

Petanidou, Theodora. *Salt: Salt in European History and Civilization*, Athens, 1977.

Piasecki, Peter. *Das deutsche Salinenwesen, 1550–1650: Invention, Innovation, Diffusion*. Geschichtswissenchaftliche Beiträge, Bd. 104. Idstein, Germany, 1987.

Reyes, Juan Carlos, ed. *La sal en México*. 2 vols. Colima, Mexico, 1995–1998.

Rittel, Hans. *Caravanes du sel*. Paris, 1981.

Tora, Yoshida, ed. *The Aobo Tu: Salt Production Techniques in Ancient China*. Translated by Vogel Hans Ulrich. Sinica Leidensia 27. Leiden, 1992.

Witthöft, Harald. "Struktur und Kapazität der Lüneburger Saline seit dem 12. Jh." *Vierteljahrschrift für Sozial- und Wirtschaftsgeschichte* 63 (1976), 1–117.

JEAN CLAUDE HOCQUET
Translated from French by Sylvia J. Cannizzaro

SAN FRANCISCO. Prior to the gold rush of 1849, San Francisco was a relatively unimportant northern West Coast port. Residents in Monterey and Los Angeles, the centers of government and commerce, viewed San Francisco as little more than the location of the northernmost military presidio and a convenient place to collect hide and tallow from nearby Roman Catholic missions. In

1849, because of its proximity to the mines and its large natural port, San Francisco suddenly became a full-fledged city. Commerce boomed as miners flowed in, and their earnings flowed back to the city's merchants and out on ships to the East Coast. As the gold rush threatened to wind down, mining was given new life in 1859 with the discovery of Comstock Lode, an enormous vein of silver in what would later become western Nevada. By far the largest city in California, San Francisco served as the state's merchant and financial center. Most finished goods were imported although manufacturing sprang up in the city to serve local needs, particularly mining, and agricultural goods such as lumber were regularly transshipped through the port. By 1860, San Francisco was the fifteenth largest city in the United States.

The completion of the Central Pacific Railroad in 1869 exposed San Francisco to the national market and almost immediately plunged the city into a depression, which intensified as the panic of 1873 hit the national economy. The city soon began to revive as a second major silver boom in the Comstock set off a huge speculation in mining stocks, but the collapse of this speculation in 1875 led to the failure of the Bank of California, previously the leading bank in San Francisco. Despite the economic problems of the 1870s, San Francisco had increased its population by more than 50 percent during the decade and by 1880 was the ninth largest city in the United States.

During the remainder of the century, the economy was relatively prosperous. Throughout the state, agriculture—particularly wheat, wine, and citrus—came to be a more powerful economic force than mining. Some of the agricultural products originated in the Central Valley near San Francisco, and much of the remainder went through the city's markets on their way east. With the rise of agriculture and the decline of mining, population growth began to shift toward the southern part of the state. By 1900, San Francisco remained the ninth largest city in the United States, but Los Angeles was now thirty-sixth.

On 18 April 1906, a strong earthquake hit San Francisco, and much of the city burned in an ensuing fire. Modern estimates indicate that the earthquake registered 8.25 on the Richter scale, and that it caused an estimated $500 million (1906 dollars) in damage. The city's recovery was greatly aided by the outbreak of World War I and an associated boom in extractive industries and shipbuilding. The boom collapsed after the war, leaving the city in a depression until 1921. When the results of the 1920 census were released, San Francisco received another blow—Los Angeles was now the largest city on the West Coast and the tenth largest city in the United States, to San Francisco's twelfth.

Having a weaker manufacturing base than many East Coast cities, San Francisco and other West Coast cities actively engaged, and ultimately succeeded, in attracting a significant military presence. In San Francisco, and in the Bay Area generally, political struggles delayed the arrival of significant moneys until the 1930s. By the end of the decade, however, the U.S. Navy had invested one billion dollars in the area, including $650,000,000 in shipbuilding. World War II brought even greater economic prosperity, but at its end a postwar decline. However, the military expenditures of the war and continued expenditures at lower levels had planted the seeds of a technology base that would become increasingly important for San Francisco, the country's fourteenth largest city at the turn of the twenty-first century.

BIBLIOGRAPHY

Bancroft, Hubert H. *History of California.* San Francisco, 1886–1890.
Brechin, Gray A. *Imperial San Francisco: Urban Power, Earthly Ruin.* Berkeley, 1999.
Bronson, William. *The Earth Shook, the Sky Burned.* Garden City, N.Y., 1959.
Dwinelle, John W. *The Colonial History: City of San Francisco.* 4th ed. Reprint. San Francisco [1867] 1978.
Graves, W. Brooke. *San Francisco: A Selected Bibliography on Its History, Government, and Politics.* Washington, D.C., 1968.
Hansen, Gladys C. *San Francisco Almanac: Everything You Want to Know about Everyone's Favorite City.* San Francisco, 1995.
Hittell, John S. *A History of the City of San Francisco and Incidentally of the State of California.* San Francisco, 1878.
Lotchin, Roger. *San Francisco, 1846–1856: From Hamlet to City.* New York, 1977.
Lotchin, Roger. *Fortress California, 1910–1961.* New York, 1992.
Millard, Bailey. *History of the San Francisco Bay Region: History and Biography.* Chicago, 1924.
Senkewicz, Robert M. *Vigilantes in Gold Rush San Francisco.* Stanford, Calif., 1985.

KAREN CLAY

SANITATION *[This entry contains three subentries, a historical overview and discussions of water supply and sewerage and urban drainage.]*

Historical Overview

Sanitation describes the strategies used to provide adequate water for drinking and other household needs and to dispose of household waste (sullage) and human waste (septage). Improvements in sanitation are critical for combating several infectious diseases. Contaminated food or water can transmit cholera and typhoid. Contact with the fecal matter of an infected person can spread diarrheal disease or dysentery. Trachoma and other "hand washing" diseases are most common when water supplies are inadequate to maintain personal hygiene after toilet use. By eliminating odors, flies, and other nuisances associated with large amounts of human and household waste, improved sanitation can also enhance the quality of life in urban areas.

Historically, cities have had a choice between two alternative technologies for supplying water and disposing of waste. The decentralized system has low fixed costs and limited returns to scale. Nearby surface water or springs, shallow wells, and cisterns provide water. Disposal of human waste relies on two methods. Common in Europe and the United States, chamberpots were used in the home and then emptied into a nearby stream or river, onto the street, into a cesspit, or onto a midden (dung heap). As an alternative, privies were located in a courtyard or on the side of the house and emptied directly into a cesspit or nearby stream. Cesspits were cleaned out and reused or simply filled in and replaced with another pit in a nearby location. Other household waste accumulated in dumps and was carted away when convenient. In most cities, surface drainage ditches (covered or uncovered), the remnants of old moats, small streams, and gutters collected runoff. Although in principle household waste was to be disposed of elsewhere, private sewers and privies did empty into surface drainage ditches.

The sanitation revolution of the nineteenth and early twentieth centuries replaced decentralized systems with a central water supply and integrated self-cleansing flushed sewers that disposed of both septage and sullage. These systems also provided drainage. As networked systems, the centralized technologies offered substantial economies of scale and provided water and waste disposal at a marginal cost much lower than decentralized technologies. The centralized technologies also entailed high fixed costs. Developing centralized water and sewer systems according to a unified plan ensures the proper flow of water and disposal of waste.

Decentralized systems can generate external costs in increased morbidity and mortality from sanitation-related infectious diseases. These costs are highest in densely populated urban areas. Throughout history, the low market value of septage and sullage in Europe and America diminished the profitability of collecting it and carting it away from urban areas for use as fertilizer. Most regarded it as a nuisance. Privies that emptied into surface water caused water pollution and led to typhoid or cholera epidemics. Overflowing and porous privy pits and cesspools saturated the surrounding subsoil with decaying human waste. Contamination of nearby shallow wells—the source of water for neighboring households—followed. The sharing of privies by many households reduced the incentive to keep them clean. Periodic efforts to enforce ordinances requiring regular cleaning of privy pits and middens were ineffective. The rapid urbanization in Great Britain and the United States that started in the first half of the nineteenth century placed this system under greater pressure, even as the availability of inexpensive guano fertilizer from Peru after 1820 further reduced the value of urban waste.

Where human waste commanded a high enough price, externalities associated with the decentralized system were kept to a minimum. Consider the case of Japan from the sixteenth through the early twentieth century. The scarcity of arable land ruled out use of the European system of mixed agriculture that relied upon rotations of fodder and food crops and the use of animal manure. Although farmers also used fish fertilizer and composted vegetable matter, human waste provided the primary source of fertilizer. Because it was so valuable, the Japanese developed effective systems for collecting human and household waste in the cities and transporting it to the countryside. Composting waste for several months killed off most bacteria and parasites; farmers distributed the resulting fertilizer in liquid form on cropland. High standards of personal hygiene, including the use of toilet paper in privies and washing hands, diminished the risk of person-to-person transmission of diarrheal disease. A network of surface drains providing for removal of rainwater completed the system.

Most likely, the Japanese system cut the external costs to health associated with the decentralized system. Mortality from diarrheal disease was about the same as in England and Wales in 1900, where the centralized system was already in widespread use. Cholera epidemics were apparently not as severe as in Europe. The system had one drawback. Use of inadequately composted human waste as fertilizer could spread schistosomiasis, a parasitic blood fluke present in the fecal matter of infected individuals, via direct contact in fields. Although the extent of infection in Japan is uncertain, observers have documented severe infestations of schistosomiasis and other soil-born helminths among farmers relying on human waste as fertilizer in paddy agriculture in other East Asian countries, such as China and Korea.

Employing centralized technologies for waste disposal dates back to about 2500 BCE. The small cities of the Indus Valley civilization constructed elaborate covered drains, which also accepted sewage. Many examples of centrally supplied water dating back several millennia can also be found. As the first large ancient city to install both centralized water supply and sewers, Rome set a standard that was not met again until the nineteenth century. Constructed along an old riverbed initially to drain the marshes found in the city, the *Cloaca Maxima* evolved into the main enclosed collector for a network of underground sewers that reached into most neigborhoods by the first century CE. Copious supplies of water available from Rome's system of aqueducts (up to six hundred liters per capita per day) flushed the sewers, although their design meant they also required cleaning by hand. The sewer system ensured efficient drainage of the city and offered the homes of the most privileged residents the luxury of water-borne removal of human waste and ready disposal of wastewater. Although 150 latrines served the public, most of the population continued to rely upon privies and chamber-pots.

After the collapse of the Roman Empire, most European cities reverted to decentralized sanitation technologies. Gradually, technological change enabled the expansion of centralized alternatives. Developed during the sixteenth century, pumps driven by waterwheels offered a notable boost to the potential capacity of centralized water supply systems at a relatively low marginal cost. By granting concessions to private water supply companies using this technology in the seventeenth and eighteenth centuries, such cities as London provided an incentive to provide direct service to a large number of households. The availability of steam-powered pumps after 1800 permitted centrally supplied water systems to go further afield for water and to overcome many of the limitations posed by topography. Installation of central water supply systems in most large British and American cities after 1820 increased the volume of water available to households and industry many times over. Plentiful and inexpensive water also lowered the cost of installing flush toilets, for which the technology had been developed by the early part of the nineteenth century.

By the 1840s, a crisis in sanitation emerged in many American and British cities. The high volume of wastewater overwhelmed decentralized systems of waste removal, even as rapid urbanization pushed up population densities. Toilets that were flushed directly into privy pits caused them to overflow. When the overflow found its way into drainage systems, the risk of human waste polluting the nearest watercourse increased. Epidemics of typhoid fever, cholera (which appeared in Europe and the Americas in the early 1830s), and diarrheal disease resulted from the breakdown of the system.

The English sanitary reformer Sir Edwin Chadwick (1800–1890) first popularized a solution to this crisis. His "sanitary idea" involved installing an integrated system of piped water from a single source and sewers for household wastewater and the water-borne carriage of human waste. Chadwick also favored a closed system. Septage and sullage should be recycled as fertilizer on "sewage farms" rather than being disposed of in the nearest river or lake. Although many cities in both Great Britain and on continental Europe experimented with the closed system, it proved to be so expensive that it was abandoned in favor of less-costly alternatives.

Many communities responded to the risk flush toilets posed to surface water by simply forbidding the disposal of human waste into sewers. Instead, they collected waste from privy pits with pneumatic pumps or they introduced the dry conservancy system, which used a bucket to collect waste, which would then by picked up on a regular basis for disposal outside of the city. The major drawbacks of this approach were the cost of cartage and the unpleasant odor associated with waste removal. Continued use of the privy also meant a heightened risk of exposure to fecal matter, particularly for the large share of urban households that continued to share toilet facilities. Although this alternative remained in place past the turn of the nineteenth century in a number of British cities and on the European continent, households generally preferred the convenience of the flush toilet.

Most communities eventually chose the other alternative of an open system. They accepted both septage and sullage into their sewers and they ignored the problem pollution posed for other communities. They constructed outfall pipes from sewer systems as far as possible from the intake for water supply systems. Eventually, the pollution of surface water prompted most communities to build water filtration plants and then chlorinate water. The open systems eventually proved to be inadequate as sewage and industrial waste increased water pollution. The activated sludge process, which became available shortly before 1914, provided primary treatment of sewage. More sophisticated water treatment technologies were installed later in the century. By the end of the century, massive investments in wastewater treatment systems had begun to undo the damage wrought by decades of dumping untreated household and industrial waste into rivers and lakes.

After 1850, urban sanitation faced new challenges brought about by economic growth and the decline in the real price of packaging materials, such as cloth, glass, paper, and metals. The diminished incentives to conserve and reuse these materials led to rising amounts of household trash and garbage. The reliance on horses for intraurban transportation added to the waste. Cities developed improved methods of hauling away trash and cleaning streets. After the turn of the century, they developed solutions to the problems of solid waste, such as incinerators and sanitary landfills.

By the early twentieth century, cities in Europe, North America, and Australia were well on their way to installing centralized systems of sanitation. Cities in Latin America, Asia, and particularly Africa lagged behind. Colonial governments were generally unwilling to incur the cost of offering the new standard of sanitation to all but enclaves of European residents. In those countries, such as India, where there was a degree of self-government, local representative bodies often resisted the construction of centralized systems because of the high initial outlay. During the twentieth century, efforts to provide a centralized water supply have been most successful in Latin America and Asia. Provision of sewers has lagged far behind. Well over one-third of urban residents of developing countries still used privy pits and cesspools to dispose of human waste at the end of the twentieth century.

One key issue in the debate over the economic history of sanitation reform has been over the relationship between rapid economic development and urban environmental deterioration. Friedrich Engels (1820–1895) first argued in the *Condition of the Working Class in England in 1844* (London, 1892) that unbridled industrialization under the policy of laissez faire was responsible for the crisis in sanitation and high urban mortality found in English cities. This perspective informs most of the subsequent historiography, which argues that the intervention of the public health movement, which campaigned for municipal control of water supplies, the public construction of sanitary sewers, and vigorous regulation of the sanitary conditions of housing, was necessary to overcome the costs of rapid economic development under capitalism. A closer look at this line of argument suggests that economic growth may have both hastened the crisis in sanitation and helped to overcome it. Rising incomes most likely accelerated the breakdown of traditional decentralized systems, but partly because they increased the demand for plentiful, centrally supplied water. Rising incomes facilitated overcoming the high costs of investments in the centralized technologies. Paying for a centralized water supply and sewerage cost a German or American laborer from 3 to 6 percent of his annual earnings at the turn of the nineteenth century. Economic growth—and higher working-class incomes—increased the likelihood that most households would be willing to pay higher rents for upgraded sanitation. By contrast, lackluster economic growth and the resulting poverty in many countries of Africa, Asia, and Latin America poses a major barrier to expanding systems of sanitation. Finally, economic development facilitated the development of markets for municipal credit. These markets were essential for municipal financing of a sanitary infrastructure.

[*See also* Public Goods *and* Public Health.]

BIBLIOGRAPHY

Anderson, Alan D. *The Origins and Resolution of an Urban Crisis: Baltimore, 1890–1930*. Baltimore, 1977.

Brown, John. "Wer bezahlt die hygienisch saubere Stadt? Finanzielle Aspekte der sanitären Reformen in England, USA, und Deutschland um 1910." In *Stadt, Krankheit, und Tod*, edited by Jörg Vögele and Wolfang Woelk, pp. 237–258. Berlin, 2000.

Cain, Louis. *Sanitation Strategy for a Lakefront Metropolis: the Case of Chicago*. Dekalb, Ill., 1978.

Evans, Richard J. *Death in Hamburg: Society and Politics in the Cholera Years, 1830–1910*. New York, 1987.

Macfarlane, Alan. *The Savage Wars of Peace*. Oxford, 1997.

Melosi, Martin V. *The Sanitary City: Urban Infrastructure in America from Colonial Times to the Present*. Baltimore, 2000.

Szreter, Simon. "Economic Growth, Disruption, Deprivation, Disease, and Death: On the Importance of the Politics of Public Health for Development." *Population and Development Review* 23.4 (1997), 693–728.

Wohl, Anthony. *Endangered Lives: Public Health in Victorian Britain*. London, 1983.

JOHN C. BROWN

Water Supply

Providing water to residents and commercial users has long been a fundamental need in urban areas. For thousands of years water supply for those without ready access to surface water or springs has relied upon two alternative technologies. The technologies most suitable for low levels of population density have been wells and cisterns, which are used in areas with low rainfall. These technologies offer no scale economies, but they have the advantage of low fixed costs. Since they rely upon local sources, the cost of conveyance is minimal. The alternative technology is a central water supply system that includes a nonlocal source, conveyance to the locality, and a system of distribution to final users. One of the earliest known applications of this technology was the high-pressure system that supplied the Minoan palace at Knossos on Crete during the seventeenth century BCE.

The Greeks were the first to provide centrally supplied water to a large number of cities. These systems depended upon gravity to convey water through tunnels, open canals, and open viaducts. Fundamental to the long-distance carriage of water was thus an ability to carry out the calculations and measurements necessary to ensure the proper flow. The water supply on the island of Samos, constructed during the sixth century BCE and in use for about one thousand years, conveyed springwater over a distance of 2.4 kilometers to the city. The system supplied each resident with about thirty liters per day. Greek systems also used high-pressure systems that ingeniously took advantage of gravity and the rate of flow to cross valleys without the use of arcades. The inability to control the flow in these systems meant that within the cities elaborate systems of cisterns or "well houses" were needed to store water flowing in by night in order to have an adequate supply to dispense during the daytime at public fountains.

Roman Systems. The Romans are well known for the construction of sophisticated water supply systems. As did the Greeks, the Romans built their water supply systems in response to the domestic and industrial needs of growing urban populations. Until the third century BCE, Roman households relied upon cisterns, fountains, and springs. After that time construction of centrally supplied water became increasingly common. As incomes rose and bathing rituals assumed a greater role in the culture, demand for water for use in public and private baths rose as well. Romans consumed three hundred liters of water per capita

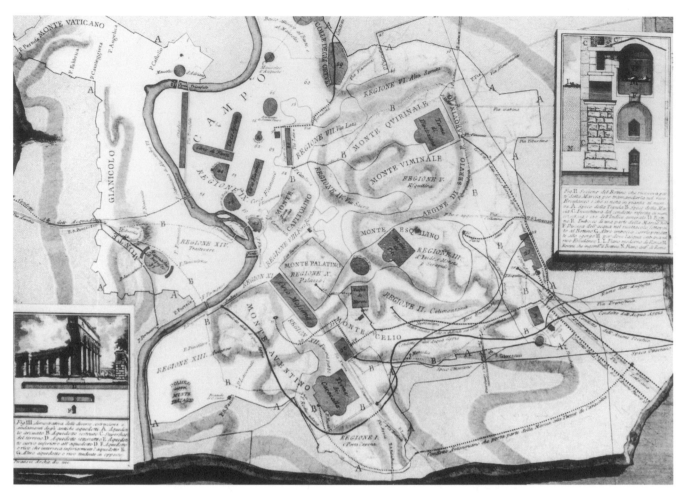

WATER SUPPLY. Map of Rome's aqueducts and the details of their structure, engraving by G. B. Piranesi (1720–1778). (Courtesy of the National Library of Medicine, Bethesda, Maryland)

per day solely for use in baths. Roman systems provided water supply service directly to some privileged households and large housing blocks. In Pompeii most houses had a direct connection to the water supply. Otherwise most water was provided through public fountains. By the middle and later empire periods, most Roman cities had some form of central water supply system.

Because of the high demand for water, Roman systems tapped sources quite far into the hinterland. The system serving Rome that was built up over five centuries eventually relied upon over five hundred kilometers of aqueducts. Although aqueducts conveyed water in tunnels, Roman systems also relied upon aboveground arcades that could span valleys over one hundred meters above ground level. Arcades took up about one-tenth the length of the system serving Rome; the remnants of remaining arcades are today some of the most impressive ruins of Roman construction throughout Europe and the Near East. The capacity of Roman systems was substantial, even by contemporary standards. Per day, Rome's system supplied six hundred

liters per capita, and Pompeii's provided eight hundred liters per capita. The system that supplied Trier, at times the capital of the western empire, had a capacity of one thousand liters per capita per day.

These systems were constructed during an era of peace guaranteed by the military strength of the Roman Empire. With the erosion and eventual collapse of that power, they were vulnerable to damage or outright destruction by hostile forces. By the ninth century most in Europe had been abandoned, although in some parts of the Middle East they continued in use well into the second millennium of the Christian Era.

Medieval Systems. With the destruction of the empire, water supply in European cities reverted to older technologies of wells and cisterns. The upsurge in urbanization of the twelfth and thirteenth centuries led to rising pollution of these sources from rubbish heaps, latrines, and cesspits. Demand also grew for water for industrial uses, such as brewing and tanning. These conditions prompted the construction of systems in Paris, London, and in many important

Italian cities. Urban growth increased the financial resources available for construction of these systems, particularly in wealthier cities, such as Siena and Nuremberg.

Medieval water supply systems relied upon wooden, lead, or earthenware pipes (or conduits) to convey the water from the source—typically a spring or seepage tunnels in a hillside—to one or a few public fountains in the cities. Central European systems would supply a public fountain at the marketplace and a network of other fountains scattered throughout the city. The water supplied was generally of higher quality than well water, but the volume was a tiny fraction of the supply available to Roman cities. One important exception is the system built to serve Seville in the twelfth century, when it was one of the most populous cities of Europe and the principal city of Moorish Spain. Relying upon tunnels built during the time of Roman control, the system provided about twenty-five liters of water per capita per day directly to individual users. Medieval systems could be quite costly to construct, since the absence of fee-simple ownership in land required obtaining complicated agreements for the right of way of the conduits that would be honored by the current owner and all subsequent heirs. Replacement of the wooden pipes in use in central and western European systems was necessary every fifteen years and required tearing up and replacing street pavement.

Early Modern Systems. As the demand for water rose after the sixteenth century, systems using conduits fell into disuse. Cities with access to a convenient source of surface water turned to water-lifting systems that used water-powered piston pumps. These pumps raised the water into a water tower, from which the water was distributed using gravity pressure. The water-lifting systems were widespread in the larger towns of Germany. During the seventeenth and eighteenth centuries private companies granted monopolies by the English Parliament combined the technology of the piston pump with laying wooden pipes to directly serve household subscribers in London. One system built at the London Bridge at the end of the seventeenth century used its four water wheels to supply an amount of water equivalent to twenty liters per day from the River Thames for each of the 0.5 million residents of London. Unfortunately tapping unprotected surface water meant that the water could be quite polluted and of poor quality.

Modern Systems. Despite these advances, most cities still relied primarily upon wells and modest supplies from conduits or piston pumps through the beginning of the nineteenth century. The achievements of the Industrial Revolution, lower-cost iron pipe, and the steam engine fundamentally altered the technology of water supply. Pumps created the potential for the new systems to draw upon much more distant sources than nearby surface water. Cast-iron pipes allowed more flexibility in the design of water conveyance and distribution; they were also more durable than other materials then in use and allowed for more sophisticated control of the flow of water. In England and the United States private firms obtained concessions from local governments (or Parliament) to build systems that supplied piped water directly to households and industrial users. The privately constructed systems served as laboratories for developing the hydrological techniques for identifying adequate sources, perfecting the technology of steam pumps, and finding the best methods for constructing and laying networks of mains and pipes. Most of these early systems served only a fraction of residences, but they did offer considerable savings compared with the most costly alternative, water vendors. The cost per cubic meter of the centrally supplied water in a town such as Portsmouth about 1815 was one-fifteenth the charge for water supplied by a water vendor. In Chartres about 1830 the water supplied by the central municipally owned system cost one-eighteenth of the price of the water vendor. These differentials are on the order of those prevailing in present-day Jakarta. By the mid-1840s a mixture of private and public supply through centralized water systems or wells dominated the water supplies of the larger towns of England. In the United States all cities with a population over fifty thousand had central water supply systems; one-half of these were privately owned. The European continent lagged far behind. The share of French cities of fifty thousand or over that had a system was only one-half, and in Germany it was one-eleventh.

In Europe and the United States the period between 1850 and 1910 marked a break with the halting improvements of the first half of the nineteenth century. For reasons that are still a subject of historical debate, towns began the construction of central water supply systems that offered water piped directly to the household and industrial user. The process was most advanced in the United States and Great Britain, where by the end of the nineteenth century virtually all towns larger than five thousand in population had a centralized water supply. In Germany two-thirds had access to a central supply. The new systems relied upon large wells that tapped groundwater sources, springs, impoundments, and surface water. Use of surface water still ran the risk of epidemics of typhoid or cholera, such as the disastrous cholera epidemic in Hamburg in 1892. Development and then installation of effective filtration systems, monitoring water for known pathogens, and chlorination gradually became standard practices and ensured that these sources also provided pure water.

Per capita consumption of water regained levels that had not been available to European city dwellers for almost two millennia and began to approach current levels of consumption. By about 1910 daily consumption per capita averaged about 110 liters in German cities (versus 160 liters today), 120 liters in English cities (versus 240 today), and 600 liters in larger American cities (versus 480 to 600 liters today). In continental Europe and in England most new waterworks were owned and run by municipalities or water districts. Even in the United States, where private concessionaires typically owned the systems of mass transit and the gasworks, 70 percent of the systems built between 1890 and 1924 were municipally owned. The financing of this rapid expansion of water supply and other infrastructure contributed substantially to the steep increases in municipal debt in Germany and Britain.

Outside of the developed West, investments in central water supply took place primarily during the twentieth century. By 2000 most urban residents in the middle-income countries of Latin American and Asia had access to centrally supplied water. Rapid urban growth in the lower-income countries of Africa and Asia has outpaced their ability to provide residents with water; only one-third to two-thirds have access. The remainder rely upon wells and water vendors. Per capita consumption is about fifty liters per day.

The main debate in the economic history of water supply includes explaining the rapid adoption of central water supply during the last third of the nineteenth century in Europe and the United States. Evidence from the United States and Germany suggests that the diffusion of central water supply systems involved a drop in the threshold size of cities building waterworks and a substantial increase in the unit cost. Per cubic meter costs for systems built in towns under five thousand in population were three times the cost of systems in towns above fifty thousand in population in Germany. Although supply-side explanations have been offered for this development, the decrease in costs because of lower prices of iron would have contributed only a modest impact. Although the increased experience of water supply engineers did diminish the uncertainty associated with building a system, the focus must be on shifts in demand.

Traditional historians of public health have stressed the ability of public health campaigns to increase demand by convincing the public that provision of clean water reduced mortality. In actuality the idea that polluted water transmitted typhoid and cholera gained acceptance only during the last two decades of the century. Other factors played a role. The rising demand of industry for clean water allowed communities to capture scale economies. Evidence suggests that income growth could also push up demands. The limited access to city dwellers in low-income countries in the early twenty-first century suggests that the cost of providing water relative to income poses a significant barrier. Charges for water averaged 10 percent of income for low-income households drawing water from standpipes in Jakarta in the 1990s. Low-income residents of Basel paid closer to 3 or 4 percent of their incomes for an apartment with water supply in the 1880s.

BIBLIOGRAPHY

Blake, Nelson Manfred. *Water for the Cities: A History of the Urban Water Supply Problem in the United States.* Syracuse, N.Y., 1956.

Brown, John C. "Coping with Crisis? The Diffusion of Waterworks in Late Nineteenth-Century German Towns." *Journal of Economic History* 48.2 (1988), 307–318.

Goubert, Jean-Pierre. *The Conquest of Water: The Advent of Health in the Industrial Age.* Cambridge, 1989.

Frontinus Society. *Die Wasserversorgung Antiker Städte.* Mainz, 1987.

Hassan, J. A. "The Growth and Impact of the British Water Industry in the Nineteenth Century." *Economic History Review*, 2d ser. 38.4 (1985), 531–547.

Hodge, A. Trevor. *Roman Aqueducts and Water Supply.* London, 2002.

Magnusson, Roberta. *Water Technology in the Middle Ages: Cities, Monasteries, and Waterworks after the Roman Empire.* Baltimore, 2001.

Melosi, Martin. *The Sanitary City: Urban Infrastructure from Colonial Times to the Present.* Baltimore, 2000.

Smith, Denis, ed. *Water-Supply and Public Health Engineering.* Aldershot, U.K., 1999.

JOHN C. BROWN

Sewerage and Urban Drainage

The issues of urban drainage and sewers relate directly to the ecology and metabolism of the city. From an ecological perspective, construction of the urban-built environment imposed on the natural environment and disrupted natural processes. Cities had to devise methods to dispose of storm waters because of their disruptive effects on commerce and the possibility that they might flood commercial and residential areas. At the same time, cities needed water for a variety of functions, including domestic needs such as drinking and cleaning, industrial purposes, street cleaning, and firefighting. Water supply and wastewater disposal were not originally connected, but they became increasingly linked as cities were forced to decide what sort of disposal system to build for both domestic wastewater and storm water.

The Pre-Industrial City. The first issue cities faced was drainage of storm waters. During the first decades of the nineteenth century, large and medium-sized American cities built infrastructure for their drainage and removal. The construction was motivated by concerns that storm water and flooding would disrupt businesses as well as the belief that stagnant water might give rise to health-threatening miasmas. At the same time, cities were paving downtown streets, reducing their ability to absorb rain and increasing the possibility of flooding. Initially cities built surface conduits to accommodate drainage, but as densities increased, larger municipalities such as New York and Boston constructed underground sewers. During the construction process, they often placed streams in culverts and filled in wetlands in order to increase their land areas. Sewers were first composed of wood, but were soon replaced by conduits constructed of stone or brick. These sewers were usually circular or elliptical in shape and were often large enough for a man to enter for cleaning. Some cities, such as New York (1819), had ordinances that prohibited placing human wastes in the sewers because of the nuisances that could result. Violations of this regulation caused the Common Council to mandate that householders install grates between their drains and the municipal sewer. The majority of nineteenth-century municipalities, however, had no underground drains. Street gutters of wood or stone, either on the side or in the middle of the roadway, provided for surface storm water and occasionally for other wastes. Private householders often constructed drains to the street gutter to remove wastewater from cellars.

Human wastes were disposed of in cesspools and privy vaults. Although many cities had regulations mandating that privies be of a certain depth and constructed of materials such as brick and stone, not everyone honored them. Privies and cesspools ranged from shallow holes in the ground to well-constructed receptacles located close to residences and even in cellars. Privies were supposed to be emptied regularly, but householders frequently let them overflow, so that the ground around them became saturated with wastes. In such situations, householders covered the privies with dirt and dug new ones. In 1829 it was estimated that each day New Yorkers deposited more than 100 tons of excrement into the city's soil.

Most large cities tried to institute periodic cleaning by private scavengers under city contract or by city employees, but services were very inefficient and irregular. The cleaning technology utilized for most of the nineteenth century was labor-intensive and rudimentary—tools consisted of dippers, buckets, and wooden casks. The process created both aesthetic nuisances and health problems, primarily through pollution of groundwater and wells. Scavengers collected the wastes in "night soil carts" and either disposed of them in nearby watercourses or dumps or on farms or sold them to reprocessing plants to be made into fertilizer. In 1880 the wastes of 103 of the 222 U.S. cities listed in the *Social Statistics of Cities*, *Tenth Census* were used on the land.

Piped-in Water and the Origins of the Water-Carriage System. Two factors combined to strain this system of waste disposal and to cause its eventual breakdown and replacement—urban population growth and new urban water-supply systems with the consequent adoption of household water fixtures. The most critical fixture was the water closet or flush toilet. By 1860, about 20 percent of the U.S. population was found in communities of over 8,000 people,

a figure that rose by 1880 to 28 percent. As cities grew larger, population became more concentrated, especially in the original central cores. Transportation restricted the distances that people could live from places of employment and essential urban institutions. Urban density and an explosion of building construction made the existing waste collection system increasingly inadequate. Overflowing privies and cesspools, often close to homes and wells, filled alleys and yards with stagnant water and fecal wastes.

The cesspool–privy vault system of waste collection was further stressed by the adoption of another technology—piped-in water. Until well into the second half of the nineteenth century, most American urbanites depended for their water supplies on local surface sources such as ponds and streams, on rainwater cisterns, or on wells and pumps drawing on groundwater. Water consumption per capita under these supply conditions probably averaged between three and five gallons a day.

The movement in nineteenth-century cities away from a localized and labor-intensive water-supply system to a more capital-intensive system that relied on more distant sources took place primarily for five reasons:

1. Populations increased.
2. More copious water supplies were required for fire-fighting.
3. Water from local sources used for household purposes was often contaminated, tasted and smelled bad, and was suspected as a cause of disease.
4. Water was needed for street flushing at times of concern over epidemics.
5. Developing industries required a relatively pure and constant water supply.

In addition, rising affluence and a desire for convenience undoubtedly increased household demands for water in the middle of the nineteenth century.

In 1802 Philadelphia was the first city to build a waterworks. Other municipalities, such as New York, Boston, Detroit, and Cincinnati, followed and by 1860 the sixteen largest cities in the nation had waterworks, with a total of 136 systems in the country; by 1880 this number had increased to 598. The availability of running water at home caused a rapid expansion in usage, as demand interacted with supply. Chicago, for example, went from 33 gallons per capita per day in 1856 to 144 in 1882; Cleveland increased its usage from 8 gallons per capita per day in 1857 to 55 in 1872; and Detroit went from 55 gallons per capita per day in 1856 to 149 in 1882. These figures reflect unmetered usage and include industrial and other nonhousehold uses, yet they do indicate greatly increased water consumption over a relatively short span of time.

While hundreds of cities and towns installed waterworks in the first three-quarters of the nineteenth century, few of them simultaneously constructed sewer systems to remove the water. They thought the technology was unnecessary, unproved, or too costly. Most cities with waterworks initially diverted wastewater into cesspools or existing storm sewers or street gutters; where not prohibited, householders connected their cesspools to the sewers via overflow pipes.

Especially critical in creating problems was the widespread adoption of the water closet, as families sought the new convenience. Some householders had installed the water closet earlier, using water from cisterns or a local source, but widespread adoption could not take place until piped-in water was available. In cities with waterworks affluent householders were quick to install closets and take advantage of their convenient inside location and comparative cleanliness. For example, in Boston in 1863 (population c. 178,000), there were more than 14,000 water closets out of approximately 87,000 water fixtures. In Buffalo in 1874 (population c. 118,000), 5,191 dwellings were supplied with water and 3,310 with water closets. By 1880, although the data are imprecise, we estimate that approximately one-quarter of urban households had water closets (usually of the pan or hopper type), while the remainder and largely poorer population still depended on privy vaults.

Water closets introduced into homes that were not connected to sewers greatly increased both nuisance problems and sanitary hazards. They were usually connected with cesspools, which were soon overcharged by the increased flow of waste-bearing water. Soil became saturated, cellars were "flooded with stagnant and offensive fluids," and the need for frequent emptying of cesspools and vaults greatly increased. The spreading of feces-polluted water created real and perceived health dangers.

During most of the nineteenth century, physicians generally divided themselves into two groups, contagionists and anticontagionists. Contagionists maintained that epidemic disease was transmitted by contact with a diseased person or carrier. Anticontagionists held that the culprit was vitiated or impure air arising from such conditions as putrefying organic matters, for example, feces, exhalations from swamps and stagnant pools, or human and animal crowding. By the latter half of the nineteenth century, the majority of physicians were anticontagionists. They believed that filthy conditions accelerated the spread of contagious disease, thus underscoring demands for urban environmental improvements. Public health officials viewed overflowing cesspools with water-closet connections as a threat to a healthful environment. As late as 1894, Dr. Benjamin Lee, the secretary of the Pennsylvania State Board of Health, complained that householders persisted in connecting water closets to "leaching" cesspools, thereby distributing "fecal pollution over immense areas and . . . constituting a nuisance prejudicial to the public health."

Some cities attempted to alleviate these hazards by permitting householders to connect their water closets to existing storm sewers, but the latter were poorly designed for waste removal and merely became "sewers of deposit." Another approach, adopted by more than twenty cities, was to use the so-called odorless excavator, a vacuum pump that emptied the contents of cesspools and privies into a horse-drawn tank truck for removal. This "interim" technology, however, adopted between the time that cities turned to piped water systems and the time they installed sewers, was expensive, and still required getting rid of the wastes from the disposal site. Engineers, public health officials, and other sanitarians realized that no existing system was capable of meeting the new demands. Increasingly, in the second half of the nineteenth century, they advocated the water-carriage technology of waste removal as a replacement.

The Water-Carriage System. The water-carriage system of waste removal (or sewerage) was essentially a system that used the wastewater itself as a transporting medium and as a cleansing agent in the pipe. More significantly, it provided a form of urban planning that replaced piecemeal methods of waste removal, particularly the reliance upon cesspools and private sewers consisting of privy vaults. In the 1840s, British sanitarian Edwin Chadwick advocated the adoption of a system of small-pipe sewers made of self-cleansing earthenware that would use the household water supply to dispose of human wastes. A convinced anticontagionist, he believed that odors from decaying organic matter caused the spread of many fatal diseases and that fecal matter had to be transported swiftly from the vicinity of the household. The sewage from this "arterialvenous system," he maintained, could be sold for agricultural purposes. Water-carriage technology, therefore, would provide a system of self-financing health benefits.

Chadwick's system was never fully implemented, but his vision stimulated debate in Great Britain about technology and health and strongly influenced American sanitarians to believe in the benefits of systematic sewerage. The engineers for the earliest sewerage systems in Brooklyn, Chicago, and Jersey City drew heavily on the English sanitary investigations and debates of the 1840s and 1850s, as well as on the actual experience of London with a system of large brick sewers constructed to remedy the sewage pollution of the Thames River. Throughout the remainder of the nineteenth century, visits to sewerage works in cities in Great Britain and Europe were almost mandatory for American engineers involved in planning new sewerage systems. Thus, water-carriage technology provides a good example of the international interchange and transfer of ideas and experience concerning an urban technology.

SUBTERRANEAN ORGANS OF PARIS. The sewers of Paris, c. 2000. (Emmanuel Gaffard)

The system of water-carriage removal of household wastes had a number of important characteristics that sharply differentiated it from the cesspool–privy vault system: it was capital-rather than labor-intensive and required the construction of large, planned public works; it utilized continuous rather than individual batch collection; it was automatic, eliminating the need for human decisions and actions to remove wastes from the immediate premises; and, because of its sanitary and health implications and its capital requirements, it became a municipal rather than a private responsibility.

In the post–Civil War period, professional associations, municipal officials, and citizens' groups held extensive debates and discussions concerning competing wastewater technological systems. These debates often dragged on for years and involved the preparation of a number of engineering reports that addressed the comparative advantages of various forms or designs of waste-disposal technology. Advocates of the water-carriage system argued that the capital and maintenance costs of building sewerage systems would represent a savings for municipalities over the annual costs of collection under the cesspool–privy vault–scavenger systems; that they would lower morbidity and mortality from disease; and that cities that installed them would grow at a faster rate than those without them by attracting population and industry. The opponents of the water-carriage system maintained that water-carriage removal would waste the valuable resources present in human excreta that might otherwise be used for fertilizer; that water-carriage technology would create health hazards, such as contamination of the subsoil by leakage, pollution of waterways with threats to drinking-water supplies and shellfish, and the generation of disease-bearing sewer gas; and that the costs of sewerage systems would create a heavy tax burden. If financed with bonds, they would impose costs on future generations with no voice in the decision.

Sewering the Cities: 1880–1914. In the late nineteenth and early twentieth centuries, American urbanites found that the promised benefits of the technology outweighed the predicted costs, and cities embarked on a massive implementation of sewerage systems. Construction accelerated, especially after the 1870s, and between 1890 and 1909 the miles of sewers in cities with more than 25,000 people had increased from 6,005 to 24,972 miles. Sewers served more than 70 percent of the residents in cities with over 50,000 popu lation. Of the total mileage in 1909, 18,361 miles, or 74 percent, were combined sewers (human and storm wastes in the same pipe) and 5,258, or 21 percent, were separate sanitary sewers; only 1,352 miles of pipe were solely storm sewers.

This immense construction was facilitated by the growth of investment banking, which made supplies of liquid capital more accessible to municipal borrowers. Systems of piped sewerage in the United States were generally funded by a combination of user fees, assessments on abutting property holders, bonds, and general tax revenues.

The choice between separate and combined sewers was an important design question. For the most part, large cities that needed to remove storm water from the streets, as well as household wastewater, installed combined sewers, while smaller cities often constructed sanitary sewers alone, leaving the storm water to run off on the surface. In the 1880s and 1890s, a number of smaller cities installed separate sewers because of the belief, spread primarily by the famous sanitarian Colonel George E. Waring, Jr., that they had superior health benefits when compared with the combined sewers. Waring argued, as had Chadwick, that large combined sewers produced sewer gas by allowing the accumulation of fecal matter, while small-diameter separate sewers speeded the wastes from the vicinity of the household. By 1900, largely because of the work of sanitary engineer Rudolph Hering, most engineers believed that the two sewer designs had equal health benefits, and decisions regarding implementation of one system rather than another were based primarily on cost factors and on the need for subsurface removal of storm water.

The use of combined rather than separate sewers, given the available treatment technology in the late nineteenth and early twentieth century, increased the costs of both wastewater treatment and resource recovery. In addition, the decision had dire consequences with regard to water quality in the future because of combined sewer overflow problems. Most urban policymakers and engineers assumed that dumping raw sewage into streams was adequate treatment because of the self-purifying nature of running water. Although by the 1890s biologists, chemists, and sanitary engineers seriously questioned the validity of this hypothesis, as late as 1909 municipalities discharged 88 percent of the wastewater of the sewered population in waterways without treatment. Where treatment was utilized at the beginning of the twentieth century, it was only to prevent local nuisance rather than to avoid contamination of drinking water downstream.

Health Costs of the System. The disposal of untreated sewage in streams and lakes from which other cities drew their water supplies caused large increases in mortality and morbidity from typhoid fever and other infectious waterborne diseases for downstream users. Bacterial researchers, following the seminal work of Pasteur and Koch, identified the processes involved in such waterborne disease. In the early 1890s, biologist William T. Sedgwick and an interdisciplinary team at the Massachusetts Board of Health's Lawrence Experiment Station clarified the etiology of typhoid fever and confirmed its relationship to sewage-polluted waterways. The irony was clear: cities had adopted water-carriage technology because they expected local health benefits, but disposal practices produced serious externalities for downstream users. This increased morbidity and mortality was an unanticipated result of sewerage technology—a rise in health costs where health benefits had been predicted. Because these costs were often borne by downstream users, however, cities continued to build sewerage systems and to dispose of untreated wastes in adjacent waterways for many years.

Sanitarians and progressive reformers pushed for laws and institutions to deal with the threats to health from urban sewage-disposal practices. One result was the creation of state boards of health (beginning with Massachusetts in 1869) and the passage of legislation to protect water quality. In 1905, the U.S. Geological Survey published its *Review of the Laws Forbidding Pollution of Inland Waters in the United States*, listing thirty-six states with some legislation protecting drinking water. Eight states had "unusual and stringent" laws, usually passed in response to severe typhoid epidemics. Supervision of water quality, whether through merely advisory powers or through stricter enforcement provisions, was usually entrusted to the state boards of health.

Filtration and Disinfection without Treatment. At the turn of the century, the options for dealing with sewage pollution were relatively limited. One was sewage treatment through either sewage farming or intermittent filtration. Both were land-intensive and impractical with the sewage output from the combined systems the great majority of cities used. Another was to secure the municipal water supply from a distant and protected watershed, a course followed by cities such as Newark and Jersey City, both in New Jersey. This approach was more promising in terms of protecting water supplies from contamination. In the late 1890s, another option appeared for cities drawing their water supplies from sewage-polluted rivers. This was water filtration by either slow sand or mechanical filtration. Many inland cities installed mechanical or sand filters in the years after 1897, resulting in sharp declines in morbidity and mortality rates from typhoid fever as well as other diseases.

Water filtration, however, did not remove the sewage from the rivers and lakes, and some health authorities argued that cities should both filter their water *and* treat their sewage, in order to protect both their own water supply and that of downstream cities. Most sanitary engineers took an opposite position, arguing, as did Allen Hazen in his 1907 book, *Clean Water and How to Get It*, that "the discharge of crude sewage from the great majority of cities is not locally objectionable in any way to justify the cost of sewage purification." Hazen maintained that downstream cities should filter their water to protect the public health, and sewage purification should be utilized only to prevent nuisances like odors and floating solids.

By the beginning of World War I, the perspective of the sanitary engineers on disposing of raw sewage into streams had triumphed over that of the "sentimentalists and medical authorities" (sanitary engineer George W. Fuller's characterization) who opposed the use of streams for disposal. Essentially, the engineering position was to use the dilution power of streams to its fullest for sewage disposal, so long as no danger was posed to the public health or to property rights and no nuisance created. Water filtration and/or chlorination could serve to protect the public from waterborne disease.

The practical consequences of this position was that in the period from 1910 to 1930, while the population newly served by sewers rose by over 25 million, the number whose sewage was treated rose only 13.5 million. At the same time, the increase in the population receiving treated water was approximately 33 million. In 1930, not only did the great majority of urban populations dispose of their untreated sewage by dilution in waterways, but their numbers were actually increasing over those who were treating their sewage before discharge. In spite of the increase in untreated sewage, the successes of water filtration and chlorination greatly diminished the incidence of waterborne infectious disease and the earlier crisis atmosphere that had led to the first state legislation had disappeared. Still, waterway pollution became increasingly severe, as untreated municipal discharges were joined by increasing industrial discharges.

Federal Intervention. Important changes in this pattern occurred as a result of New Deal construction programs during the 1930s. Before the 1930s, municipalities paid for all sewer and water construction. During the New Deal, federal Public Works Administration (PWA) funds accounted for 35 to 50 percent of all new sewer and water supply construction. The government's desire to deal with problems of water pollution as well as to provide for unemployment relief provided the impetus for sewer construction. President Franklin D. Roosevelt accelerated investment for sewage treatment facilities by refusing to approve PWA sewer projects that did not provide for waste treatment. Similarly, the Works Projects Administration (WPA) would not construct sanitary sewers unless designed to be compatible with treatment works. By 1938, federal financing had aided in the construction of 1,165 of the 1,310 new municipal sewage treatment plants built in the decade. The population served by sewage treatment increased from 21.5 million in 1932 to more than 46.9 million in 1945. By 1945, 62.7 percent of people living in sewered communities had treated sewage; the rest still disposed of raw sewage into waterways.

In the period after World War II the rate of both sewer building and sewage treatment expanded fairly rapidly, with the greatest increase occurring after federal construction subsidies were provided through the Federal Water Pollution Control Act of 1956. Other water quality acts in the 1960s provided further subsidies, and by 1970 about 120 million people had their sewage treated at a central facility, although raw sewage discharges still occurred in communities with between 15 and 25 million people. During the 1960s and 1970s, the environmental movement helped focus attention on water pollution problems.

Before 1970, all water pollution control efforts, aside from standards regarding water used in interstate commerce (the U.S. Public Health Standards of 1914), were at the state level. In 1970, the Nixon administration created the Environmental Protection Agency. Its divisions related to a variety of pollution issues, including water pollution. The greatest impact on water quality was passage of the Clean Water Act of 1972, which set the goals of attaining water quality in navigable waters suitable for fisheries and for swimming by 1983, secondary treatment in all wastewater-treatment plants by 1988, and zero pollutant discharge by 1995. Other features of the act and subsequent amendments included a focus on technology-based standards and a requirement for federal permits for all point-source pollution dischargers.

While national water quality continues to improve, advances have been much slower, due especially to reductions in the availability of funding, than projected in the 1970s. Neither of the major goals set forth in the Clean Water Act of 1972, for instance, had been reached by 2000. In the meantime, other problems, such as combined sewer overflows, nonpoint pollution, and groundwater pollution—all of which relate to past decisions regarding waste disposal practices and systems—are receiving increasing attention, as the nation continues to struggle with issues of wastewater disposal and water quality in the twenty-first century.

BIBLIOGRAPHY

Cain, Louis. *Sanitation Strategy for a Lakefront Metropolis: The Case of Chicago*. DeKalb, Ill., 1978. A useful study of the history of wastewater-disposal decisions in Chicago.
Goldman, Joanne Abel. *Building New York's Sewers: Developing Mechanisms of Urban Management*. West Lafayette, Ind., 1997. An interesting look at the construction of New York's sewers that explores the development of institutional frameworks for systems management.

Kehoe, Terence. *Cleaning Up the Great Lakes: From Cooperation to Confrontation.* DeKalb, Ill., 1997. A fine study of the struggle for pollution control in the Great Lakes.

Melosi, Martin V. *The Sanitary City: Urban Infrastructure in America from Colonial Times to the Present.* Baltimore, 2000. The most comprehensive study in the literature of municipal waste-disposal practices.

Ogle, Maureen. *All the Modern Conveniences: American Household Plumbing, 1840–1890.* Baltimore, 1997. An insightful exploration of household waste-disposal systems before the construction of centralized sewerage systems.

Platt, Harold L. *City Building in the New South: The Growth of Public Services in Houston, Texas, 1830–1910.* Philadelphia, 1983. A useful case study of infrastructure decision making in a southern city.

Rogers, Peter. *America's Water: Federal Roles and Responsibilities.* Cambridge, 1993. An informative discussion of the evolution of a federal role with regard to water resources.

Schultz, Stanley K. *Constructing Urban Culture: American Cities and City Planning, 1899–1920.* New York, 1989. An informative book on the evolution of city planning ideas and institutions with regard to the building environment.

Tarr, Joel. *The Search for the Ultimate Sink: Urban Pollution in Historical Perspective.* Akron, 1996. A study of urban pollution problems that includes a number of essays on water and wastewater decision making and issues.

JOEL A. TARR

SASSOON FAMILY. The Sassoon family was unique among business dynasties, as their power spanned both the Eastern and Western worlds. The Sassoons flourished for centuries in Baghdad, as leaders of the Jewish community who claimed descent from King David, until the end of the eighteenth century when anti-Semitism spread through the Ottoman Empire. In 1832, David Sassoon (1792–1864), who was born in Baghdad, escaped to Bombay with his wife, Hannah, and two sons, Abdullah or Albert (1818–1896) and Elias (1820–1880), where he opened a counting house and began minor trade with the gulf ports. With his profits, he bought wharfages in Bombay and had capital and interest repaid to him in goods that he could resell for additional profit. The family waited to enter the cotton trade until the first wave of cotton firms figured out the difficulties, often losing money on poorly planned mills.

Elias went to China in 1844 to deal in opium and textiles, two products that made the firm into a powerhouse. David Sassoon and Sons became the most flexible and diversified China traders, trading metals, opium, and cotton for silk, tea, and silver while expanding the spice trade with the Indies. High positions in the firm were reserved for the immediate family. Each son toured such gulf ports as Baghdad and Būshehr to be prepared for a shift in China, and were made almost interchangeable in the business by a constant shuffling of positions. David began two traditions, generous benefaction and loyalty to the British crown, which were continued through the generations.

In 1858, the London branch of the family was established, headed by David's son Sassoon David (1832–1867). The American Civil War led to a huge demand for Indian cotton, and the price rose accordingly. For many mill owners, the sudden wealth led to wild speculation, but the Sassoons quietly invested in property sites that would have a very high value when Bombay began to expand, building office buildings and tenements for factory workers. When the Civil War ended, the cotton price dropped, causing the Bank of Bombay to collapse. Many suffered dramatic losses, but David Sassoon and Sons emerged more powerful because they had avoided stockpiling and suffered only slight losses. They began importing Javanese sugar and rice, as well as investing in local cultivation of tea, in the panic market.

After David's death in 1864, the rivalries between his sons Albert and Elias grew. The latter resigned in 1867 to head his own firm, E. D. Sassoon and Co. He confined his new firm to traditional trading at first, quietly moving into cotton. Meanwhile, David Sassoon and Sons was investing heavily in real estate, building warehouses and docks, but they became absentee landlords as London became the firm's center. E. D. Sassoon, on the other hand, entrenched itself further into Bombay, where they could import from Europe to service the consumer markets of India and East Asia. Shortly before his death in 1880, Elias opened two mills in Bombay. His sons Jacob (1844–1916) and Edward (1853–1924) opened additional mills and streamlined cotton manufacture, installing India's first conveyer belt. By the end of the century, a third of India's half million workers were in cotton, with Sassoon mills among the largest employers. E. D. Sassoon, headed by Jacob, owned six flourishing mills but was experiencing severe competition from Japan. They began to spread their interests to Shanghai and Hong Kong through subsidiaries in public tramways, insurance, laundries, and breweries, while David Sassoon and Sons exercised caution during the uncertain times.

In 1891, opium traffic was condemned by the House of Commons, and the Chinese were growing it themselves and taxing imports. India imposed a tariff on imports to compensate for lost income; but England responded with a heavier excise tax on Indian cotton, and the cotton trade with England dwindled. The Sassoons were among the few firms to survive; and they began to thrive again during World War I, as Bombay was transformed into a port of embarkation. Mills and factories now made tents, books, saddlery, and clothing for the military. Both Sassoon firms also increased the tonnage of foodstuffs shipped to Great Britain.

By 1919, David Sassoon and Sons was flourishing, but a weakness in top personnel was beginning to show. David's grandson Ronald (1895–1924), the firm's hope for chairman, died of a heart attack at age twenty-nine, and without a strong leader to take the initiative, the firm reduced its scope when faced with political upheavals in India. It began to sell properties, reducing the Bombay mills to increase liquid assets. They closed down their Manchester office in 1934, while the Shanghai, Calcutta, and Karachi branches discontinued trading in textiles but maintained offices for transacting import-export business. E. D. Sassoon and Co., on the other hand, expanded their holdings during this period.

In 1921, due to postwar uncertainty in international trade and currencies, as well as higher taxation imposed by British parliament, E. D. Sassoon was incorporated as a private trading and banking company. They funneled assets from England and Hong Kong into their Bombay Trust at good interest rates, which was highly effective at a time of world slump in the cotton demand, India's internal strife, and Japanese industrialization. The Bombay mills continued operation, but other assets were removed from Bombay and invested in the Hong Kong Trust. Edward's son Victor (1881–1961) began to make investments for peacetime Shanghai, despite civil war and Japanese aggression. He bought sites for development as factories and tenements and took over firms making building materials. In 1929, they built the Sassoon House, which contained banks, offices, shopping, and the Cathay Hotel, which soon became a venue for Shanghai's highest society. The Shanghai properties almost tripled in value by 1935.

In 1937, Sino-Japanese War broke out, and the city of Shanghai was brought under the control of the Japanese army. Victor invested capital in American stocks and international bonds to hedge against currency upheavals. The Bombay mills were prepared for capacity output as they would be vital during wartime. The Shanghai properties had increased in value during the war, but the future was uncertain, so Victor began to dispose of them after the war. He established a Bahamian company and sold the mills in 1943, liquidating the Bombay company in 1948. The London, Manchester, and Hong Kong branches of the firm were controlled from Nassau, and the rest of the Shanghai properties were seized by the State Enterprises Company in the newly formed People's Republic of China. Victor's death in 1961 ended the family connection with the company, which was reorganized as a banking company dealing with export finance.

BIBLIOGRAPHY
Jackson, Stanley. *The Sassoons*. London, 1968.
Roth, Cecil. *The Sassoon Dynasty*. London, 1941.

SAVINGS BANKS. *See* Banking, *subentry on* Modern Period.

SAXONY, region in southeastern Germany; formerly an electorate, kingdom, state of the Weimar Republic, and province of East Germany (the German Democratic Republic); the chief city is Dresden, a port on the Elbe River to the north of the Czech border. Saxony (Ger., Sachsen) had a key position in the industrialization process of Germany. As a middle-German state, it had a long tradition of mining and was one of the most densely populated territories in Europe. Unlike in Prussia to its north, Saxon peasants were free individuals who worked their own farms. Beginning in the late 1600s, factories for the production of textiles, porcelain, and glass were developed. From 1793 to 1800, twenty-six factories were founded in Leipzig, twenty in Dresden, and nineteen in Chemnitz, the main cities of Saxony.

When the Industrial Revolution started in England, Saxony became the first German state open to new technology. While the first machines were introduced in Saxony in 1765, machines were used extensively for industrial production only from the 1880s. In 1783, there were only three spinning machines in Saxony; by 1800, there were some two thousand. The first factory to be fully equipped with spinning machines opened in Lössnitz in 1791. After 1800, steam engines were used to power textile machinery, and they were used in the mining industry to pump water out of the mine tunnels. Until 1830, the cotton industry led the industrialization process in Saxony. From 1800 to 1835, machines were mostly imported from England. Inventors and technicians in Saxony, such as Christian Friedrich Brendel, traveled throughout England to obtain knowledge about how to construct such machines; they returned to Saxony and founded machine-building factories. Machine works, such as that of Carl Gottlieb Haubold in Chemnitz (1826), marked the beginning of German industrial development. Industrialization was followed by widespread urbanization in Saxony and the emergence of a working class. The cities of Dresden (66,133 inhabitants), Leipzig (44,806), Chemnitz (21,137), Freiberg (11,054), and Plauen (9,029) then became the biggest of the kingdom. The working class developed out of the peasantry and the artisanal families and, for the most part, the first generation of workers still owned their own houses.

The decades after the September Revolution of 1830 were followed by a transportation revolution. In 1833, Friedrich List published his plan for a national railroad. To realize his dreams, List convinced a number of wealthy Leipzig merchants, including Gustav Harkort, to finance a rail connection between Leipzig and Dresden, which he envisioned as the first step in his plan. When the first train left the station on 7 April 1839, it was Germany's first long-distance rail connection. Leipzig soon became a main junction for the fast-growing rail network—in 1840, it was connected with Halle and Magdeburg, then with Nuremberg and Munich in 1851. The construction of machinery, especially for the rail companies, became the most important part of Saxony's industry, with Chemnitz at its center. Until 1846, about 75 percent of steam engines used in Saxony were produced there. The first German locomotive, the *Saxonia*, was built there. Leipzig became the center of German book printing and the fur trade.

In the late 1800s, Saxony remained an industrialized state with small factories. As late as 1912, the average factory there had only five employees, but changes came rapidly with the approach of World War I, Europe's first mechanized war (1914–1918). The textile industry remained dominant but the metal-processing industry expanded, and new industries, such as chemical and electrical, were introduced—both contributing to the war effort and the nation's needs. Although both World War I and World War II (1939–1945) made great production demands, which were met in devious ways, both wars were lost by Germany and wartime and postwar economic hardships were felt each time. Nevertheless, the industrial sectors were rebuilt and restored. After World War II, Saxony was part of the Soviet Zone, and with the states of Mecklenburg and Thuringia and the provinces of Brandenburg and Sachsen-Anhalt formed the German Democratic Republic in 1949. In 1990, it was united with West Germany, bringing outdated machinery, industrial pollution, and other environmental problems.

BIBLIOGRAPHY

Bramke, Werner. "Die Industrieregion Sachsen. Ihre Herausbildung und Entwicklung bis zum Ende des Zweiten Weltkrieges." In *Industrieregionen im Umbruch*, edited by Rainer Schulze, pp. 291–317. Essen, 1993.

Forberger, Rudolf. *Die Manufaktur in Sachsen. Vom Ende des 16. bis zum Anfang des 19. Jahrhunderts*. Berlin, 1958.

Forberger, Rudolf. *Die Industrielle Revolution in Sachsen, 1800–1861*. 2 vols. Berlin, 1958.

Kiesewetter, Hubert. *Industrialisierung und Landwirtschaft: Sachsens Stellung im regionalen Industrialisierungprozeß Deutschlands im 19. Jahrhundert*. Cologne and Vienna, 1988.

THOMAS ADAM

SCANDINAVIA. *See* Nordic Countries.

SCHLUMBERGER FAMILY. A family of manufacturers from Alsace (France), the Schlumbergers originated in Würtemberg (Germany), and crossed the French border during the Reformation in the mid-sixteenth century. Settling in Mulhouse, they were tanners and then cloth manufacturers, and incorporated themselves into the urban patriarchy. From 1764 on, they were among the main promoters of the industrialization movement that made Mulhouse and Haute-Alsace one of the French poles of the textile (spinning, weaving, and cotton printing) and the

mechanical engineering industries. Several of them took part in the foundation and the activities of a Masonic lodge in Mulhouse in 1809 and the Industrial Society of Mulhouse in 1826. Through the exercise of political mandates and through private initiatives, they distinguished themselves by their civic, religious, and philanthropic commitment.

Among the different descendants of manufacturers settled in Alsace (Mulhouse, Guebwiller, or Ribeauvillé) in the nineteenth century, one stands out: Pierre of Loewenfels (1750–1830), the first of the Schlumbergers to build his fortune in the manufacture of printed calico. In 1810, Pierre's son Nicolas (1782–1867) founded a cotton spinning mill in Guebwiller, and in 1818 established a workshop of mechanical industry specialized in the building of textile machinery: Nicolas Schlumberger & Cie (NSC), still a world leader in the industry. His cousin Jules-Albert (1804–1892) led one of the most important factories of spinning and weaving in Mulhouse, Schlumberger Fils & Cie, which employed twenty-five hundred workers in 1892, and chaired the Chamber of Commerce from 1849 to 1891.

In the twentieth century—while Jean, Nicolas's great-grandson, made a name for himself as a writer on the team of the *Nouvelle Revue Française* (NRF) along with André Gide—Jean's brothers Conrad (1878–1936) and Marcel (1884–1953) perfected a method for electric prospecting of the subsoil that proved effective in searching for oil. In 1934, the brothers created a U.S. branch that became a multinational corporation (Schlumberger Ltd.), employing nearly fifty thousand people in over one hundred countries in 2000. Their brother Maurice (1886–1977) in 1919 founded the Schlumberger bank in Paris, which merged, stepwise in 1945 and 1966, with two very old firms of Parisian high finance to create De Neuflize, Schlumberger, Mallet (NSM)—integrated, since 1977, into the Dutch group ABN AMRO. Marcel's descendants, the brothers Jérôme (born 1934) and Nicolas Seydoux (born 1939), are the respective presidents of the cinema companies Pathé and Gaumont. Jules Albert's descendant Jean (1907–1987), a jeweler who settled in New York and Paris, created jewelry for Schiaparelli and Tiffany, of which he became vice-chairman.

To French historian Michel Hau, the Schlumberger family is a classic example of a "leading family" that, following the examples of the Siemens and Rothschild families, over several generations has been able to rebound successfully and thus to create new profit centers. Like their counterparts, they have developed from a German Judeo-Protestant background, far from any political power. Their rise has been founded not only on educational investment, technical and scientifical mastery, and adjustment to leading industries, but also on family solidarity, an austere way of life, and disdain for property investment. These characteristics have permitted the family to make a very great fortune and have furthered the dynasty's long life.

BIBLIOGRAPHY

Hau, Michel. "Traditions comportementales et capitalisme dynastique: Le cas des grandes familles." *Entreprises et histoire* 9 (1995), 43–59.

Nouveau dictionnaire de biographie alsacienne 33 (1999), 3452–3468.

Schlumberger, Clarisse. *Schlumberger, racines et paysages*. Strasbourg, 1997.

Stoskopf, Nicolas. *Les patrons du Second Empire, Alsace*. Paris, 1994.

Tableaux généalogiques de la famille Schlumberger. Mulhouse, 1953, 1956.

Teissonnière-Jestin, Paulette. "Itinéraire social d'une grande famille mulhousienne: Les Schlumberger de 1830 à 1930." In *Familles industrielles d'Alsace*, pp. 121–213. Strasbourg, 1989.

NICOLAS STOSKOPF

SCHNEIDER, JOSEPH-EUGÈNE (1805–1875), French manufacturer.

As the founder of the Schneider industrial family, Eugène I was able to take advantage of several favorable opportunities. Although born in Bidestroff, the social position of his father Antoine, a notary in Meurthe-et-Moselle, permitted him to study in the high school at Nancy, where he obtained the *baccalauréat* in 1821. He was aided by two influential families. In 1827, he was employed by the Seillière Bank and soon obtained from the manufacturer de Neuflige the management of an ironworks. In 1837, he married de Neuflige's daughter. In December 1836, Seillière and the iron-master Boignes redeemed the bankrupt Le Creusot metalworks, and they entrusted its management to Schneider and his brother, Adolphe. In 1845, after the accidental death of Adolphe, Eugène became the sole manager.

Eugène had attained a relatively good general and professional education. He was only sixteen years old when he passed the *baccalauréat*. He then attended evening courses at the École des Arts et Métiers (industrial arts). In 1854, he was made a member of the Société des Ingénieurs Civils (civil engineers). His interest in innovation was motivated by two journeys to England, in 1840 and 1846. His first engineer, François Bourdon, had invented the steam hammer in 1842.

As one of the most important industrial complexes, Le Creusot had integrated various and complementary domains in metallurgy: the coal mines of Le Creusot, Montchanin, and Decize; the iron mines of Mazenay and Allevard; blast furnaces; the then-new great forge, with its puddling furnaces and rolling mills; and the Martin & Bessemer steelworks. In 1838, the mechanics works constructed the first French locomotive, *Gironde*, as well as steam engines and marine engines. At Chalon-sur-Saône, river barges were built as well as iron frameworks for important structures. The firm was extended beyond France, selling locomotives and marine engines to an international market. The Le Creusot complex included schools as early as 1837. In 1856, courses for workers and managers were added. In 1874, the industrial town had new schools for twenty-two hundred pupils. In 1863, a hospital was built, and housing estates covered the extensive company grounds. In 1867, the Universal Exposition in Paris crowned Schneider's social accomplishments. Contrary to many erroneous ideas, Schneider did not make any cannons before 1870. With the Franco-Prussian War of 1870–1871, and only after a discussion with the French president, was Schneider assigned a new objective—the production of artillery able to compete with that of Krupp's, the German steel firm.

In Second Empire France, Schneider participated in the great affairs of his time. He was regent of the Banque de France in 1854; cofounder in 1864 and president of the Société Générale; vice-president of the P.L.M. railway company; and the first president of the Comité des Forges. He attached the most importance to his political participation: Napoleon III (Louis-Napoléon) had nominated him the first minister of agriculture and trade; in 1852, he became the vice-president of the Corps Législatif, then in 1867, its president.

After his death, two monuments were erected to him. In 1876, the enormous 100-ton steam hammer, to commemorate the apotheosis of technique; and in 1879, the Statue of Gratitude, paid for by the donations of fifteen thousand subscribers.

BIBLIOGRAPHY

Beaud, Claude. "Profit, investissement et croissance chez Schneider et cie au Creusot." *Revue d'histoire économique et sociale* 3 (1977), 452–463.

Beaud, Claude. *"Les Schneider au Creusot: Un modèle paternaliste."* In *Liberalism and Paternalism in the 19th Century*, Tenth International Economic History Congress, pp. 9–18. Louvain, 1990.

Beaud, Claude. "Eugène Schneider." In *Les patrons du Second Empire*, pp. 191–197. Paris, 1991.

Beaud, Claude. "L'innovation dans les établissements Schneider (1837–1960)." *Histoire-Économie-Société* 3 (1995), 501–518.

Silly, J. B. "La reprise du Creusot," *Revue d'histoire de la sidérurgie* 1.1 (1969), 4.12 (1972).

CLAUDE BEAUD

SCHUMPETER, JOSEPH (1883–1950), Austrian-born academic economist, economic historian, historian of economics, social and political philosopher; erstwhile lawyer (Cairo, 1907–1908), Austrian minister of finance (1919), and Biedermann Bank president (1921–1924).

Joseph Alois Schumpeter's school education was in the best classical and aristocratic traditions of the Vienna Theresianum Gymnasium. In 1901, he went on to study law, economics, philosophy, and history in the University of Vienna's Faculty of Law, graduating as *Doctor utriusque juris* in 1906. Later, he was to hold university professorships at Czernowitz (1909–1911), Graz (1911–1921), Bonn (1925–1932), and, finally, Harvard (1932–1950). Peer recognition came through the vast secondary literature his research publications spawned, as well as through his election as president of the Econometric Society (1937–1941) and as president of the American Economic Association (1948).

Schumpeter's career as an academic economist was confirmed with his publication of *Das Wesen und der Hauptinhalt der theoretischen Nationaloekonomie* (The essence and main content of theoretical economics; Munich and Leipzig, 1908). This book, as its title conveys, comprised an exposition and assessment of "the nature and main content of theoretical economics." The formalism of his argument, and the theories on which he chose to focus, forever isolated him from his Austrian contemporaries in economics. That work, and his journal publications of the same period, had a strong methodological orientation, emphasising especially the distinction between static and dynamic analyses in economics. In his substantive argument, he gave prominence to the idea that the free-market capitalist economy is an essentially stable, routinized circular flow of production and exchange characterized by a full-employment, market-clearing general equilibrium.

Contrary to this inert and stable vision, the real economy is observed to be dynamically unstable. Schumpeter's dominant concern was to provide an understanding of this instability, reasoning that it must be explained by some specific disturbance of sufficient force to displace the economy from its inherent equilibrium state. His *Theory of Economic Development*, first published in German (Leipzig, 1912) and later translated into English (Cambridge, Mass., 1934), provided the theoretical foundations for these contrasting visions. His *Business Cycles* (2 vols., New York, 1939), a book of enormous, and arguably excessive, proportions then presented a simplified theoretical version of the theory of cyclical dynamics set out in *Development*. In this later work, the theory was bolstered by prodigious amounts of historical discussion and statistical data illustrating the cycles of instability he found to be endemic to capitalism.

Economic instability is, according to Schumpeter, integral to the processes and the material success of economic development. Saving and capital accumulation that induce growth, to which the majority of economists gave much attention, are of little concern. The economy has the capacity readily to absorb these *quantitative* changes and maintain its essential full-employment equilibrium state. These beliefs set him apart from the burgeoning mainstream of those who adopted the macroeconomics of his *bête noire* from Cambridge, John Maynard Keynes (1883–1946).

Quantitative changes are, Schumpeter argued, analytically separable from the destabilizing forces afflicting capitalism. These forces are attributable to innovation and technological change, undertaken by independent, pioneering entrepreneurs, and funded by generous supplies of bank credit. Moreover, because product, process, and market innovations come in "waves," whipped up in a "gale of creative destruction," the disruptive *qualitative* changes they bring are less readily absorbed by the system than quantitative changes. The consequences are manifested as fluctuations in economic activity and growth, depicted theoretically by Schumpeter in a regularized core of instability referred to as the "primary cycle." This "cycle" highlighted the essential phases of fluctuations, including the innovation-induced prosperity-cum-boom, followed by the beneficial "shake out" of the old, and consolidation of the new, in a recession. The emphasis on technological change and entrepreneurship and their impact on the dynamics of aggregate output and industrial structure, are among Schumpeter's most lasting contributions to our understanding of the economic history of capitalism.

Capitalist dynamism, in the form of business strategies that emphasize entrepreneurial talent and innovation, and the production-cost and product-quality advantages these bring, has become known as Schumpeterian competition. It has been linked to the rise to dominance of large-scale enterprises and the acceptance of monopoly power as necessary characteristics of modern capitalist prosperity. For Schumpeter, such scale and power could be justified if they are built upon and consolidate the material benefits flowing from innovations. He believed that because monopoly positions can be lost as readily as they are won, their use for exploitative purposes is necessarily constrained.

An understanding of economic dynamics, argued Schumpeter, should include its social and political context and recognize its broader consequences. In his most popular work, *Capitalism, Socialism, and Democracy* (New York, 1942), he developed this extended vision of capitalism and provided controversial insights into its fragility and long term prognosis. The book combined the question "Can capitalism survive?" with the reply "No. I do not think it can." But the immanent dynamics that have the potential to bring about its demise, and a possible transition to socialism, were not to be attributed to any ultimate economic stagnation. Recovery from the severest economic depression is always assured. Rather, what would fail in capitalism were the social, cultural, and political supports underpinning its dominant trend of material success. Crucial would be the demise of the entrepreneurial spirit, replaced by the rationalism and routines of managerial bureaucrats. This would be compounded by the open hostility of intellectuals toward the moral-ethical consequences of the system, and by the decay of the traditional political and legal institutions that give capitalism its legitimacy.

Toward the end of his life, Schumpeter turned back to a project that he had begun as a young professor: writing the history of economic doctrines, with particular reference to the development of formal analysis. At the time of his death, he left a gigantic and unfinished manuscript that would be posthumously published as the *History of Economic Analysis* (New York and London, 1954). In the eleven hundred pages of this final legacy, Schumpeter maintained the dogged, opinionated independence of thought and interpretation that had characterized his whole intellectual life.

BIBLIOGRAPHY

BIOGRAPHIES

Allen, Robert Loring. *Opening Doors: The Life and Work of Joseph Schumpeter*. 2 vols. New Brunswick, N.J., 1991.

März, Eduard. *Joseph Schumpeter: Scholar, Teacher, and Politician*. New Haven, 1991.

Stolper, Wolfgang F. *Joseph Alois Schumpeter: The Public Life of a Private Man*. Princeton, 1994.

Swedberg, Richard. *Joseph A. Schumpeter: His Life and Work*. Oxford, 1991.

BIBLIOGRAPHICAL GUIDE

Augello, Massimo M., ed. *Joseph Alois Schumpeter: A Reference Guide*. Berlin, 1990.

GENERAL WORKS

Clemence, Richard V., and Francis S. Doody. *The Schumpeterian System*. Cambridge, Mass., 1950. A comprehensive exposition of Schumpeter's economics, written by two of his former students. Rather lacking in critical insight and prone to exaggerated claims about the veracity of Schumpeter's analyses of capitalism.

Frisch, H., ed. *Schumpeterian Economics*. Eastbourne, U.K., 1982. Presents an editorial introduction and ten high quality papers by a group of recognized Schumpeter scholars. Includes papers on most of the significant themes that constitute Schumpeter's legacy.

Hanusch, Horst, ed. *The Legacy of Joseph A. Schumpeter*. 2 vols. Cheltenham, U.K., 1999. Contains forty-two articles in total, including a number dealing with the reception and impact of Schumpeter's work, dating from 1943 to 1969, as well as later articles on a wide-ranging variety of themes that are current in present-day Schumpeterian scholarship. Most contributors are recognized Schumpeter scholars.

Heertje, Arnold, ed. *Schumpeter's Vision: "Capitalism, Socialism and Democracy" after 40 Years*. New York, 1981. A collection of nine highly informative papers devoted to critically reassessing the theses of Schumpeter's most popular book. Includes contributions from a number of significant Schumpeter scholars.

Oakley, Allen. *Schumpeter's Theory of Capitalist Motion: A Critical Exposition and Reassessment*. Aldershot, U.K., 1990. A critical exposition of Schumpeter's theory of economic development and business cycles that exposes, root and branch, the immanent methodological and substantive limitations of his theoretical project.

Wood, John Cunningham, ed. *Joseph A. Schumpeter: Critical Assessments*. 4 vols. London and New York, 1991. A comprehensive and wide-ranging, but carefully selected, collection of 108 articles published from 1950 to 1988. Included are contributions from a variety of authors, from the unknown to those of world renown, and dealing with virtually every aspect of Schumpeter's life, work, and legacy. Most of the "classical" and "canonical" contributions to the Schumpeterian literature in this period are among the selection.

ALLEN OAKLEY

SCOTLAND. One of the more remarkable success stories in economic history was the rise of the Scottish economy from a marginal and peripheral state to one of the foremost economies in western Europe. Premodern Scotland was a poor and backward economy, held back by an uncertain climate, limited resources, and political instability. Every adult male in medieval Scotland would have had firsthand experience of food shortages and many of actual failure. The last great famines in Scotland came in the 1690s, when in some areas the harvest failed three years out of four, causing severe mortality and migration. Northeast Scotland was worst hit, with perhaps a one-third loss of population. What trade there was, apart from some to the Low Countries or with Ireland, was mostly very local; manufacturing was low in quality and reputation alike.

Economic Transformation. By the late eighteenth century, things were very different. Scottish agriculture was improved beyond recognition and had become a model of best practice for other parts of Europe; remarkably, the modernization of that rural society in the Lowlands created very little unrest. Although textiles was the leading sector, Scotland's economy underwent quite a broad-based transformation, and while it was most marked in the Central Lowlands, it was quite widely experienced elsewhere. Population growth, hitherto fitful and uncertain, from the mid-eighteenth century was sustained decade after decade, prompted by improved economic opportunities and underpinned by the potato rather than medical advances. Urbanization was rapid, notably that of Glasgow, which overtook Edinburgh as Scotland's leading city.

An older tradition held that much of this transformation was due to the Union of 1707, by which Scotland lost its parliament, but obtained unfettered access to English and colonial markets. Studies have shown, however, that there were signs of growth prior to the Union: changes in agriculture; developments in the financial sector, for example, with the foundation of the Bank of Scotland in 1695; and some improvement in manufacturing. Yet it is clear that the inclusion of Scotland within the rapidly expanding British trading empire was of considerable significance, leading to the rise of Glasgow as a center of the European tobacco trade, allegedly due to fraud (or so disgruntled English competitors alleged), but in fact owing more to superior commercial organization. The expansion of the textile sector, especially linen, was aided by quasi governmental regulation through the Board of Trustees and government-funded export subsidy. This proved a proto-industrial springboard for the rapid growth of cotton from the 1770s in the west-central part of Scotland. In contrast, the eastern part of the country retained a commitment to other fibers, such as jute in particular in Dundee. Border areas built a reputation for high-quality woolens—tweed being the most well-known product. Exactly how Scottish the Industrial Revolution in Scotland was is a matter for ongoing debate. Although it did make some use of English entrepreneurship and technology, one unusual feature was the degree to which change was internally financed rather than by inward investment. The process was shaped to an important extent by indigenous Scottish institutions—the law and the church—which were not lost, as the parliament had been by the Union. The role of the Presbyterian church and its parish system in the administration of poor law and education remained of major importance until the later-nineteenth century. What was also significant was the existence of a distinctive educational system from parish and burgh school to university, which put a high premium on literacy at the primary level, provided a flow of clerks and accountants to lubricate the expanding economy, and in the universities was not merely concerned with the niceties of theology but endeavored to relate scientific enquiry to industrial application.

Heavy Industry and Regional Decline. If there is one image that dominates the external perception of industrial Scotland in the nineteenth century, it has been that of the shipyard, central to the takeoff of the heavy industries. There had been a long tradition of coal mining in Scotland—serfdom lingered until 1799—and in iron making, including some isolated big ventures, such as that at Carron, and some experience in shipbuilding, but on only a small scale. All three industries, led by shipbuilding, grew dramatically from the 1820s, a transformation aided and accelerated by the coming of the railways. This transformation involved a break with the past: the rise of the river Clyde to a position of dominance in shipbuilding was based on steam and iron, not wood and sail. By the later nineteenth century, the Clyde was launching two-thirds of the world's tonnage of steam shipping. This success was due to a combination of factors, including driving and innovative entrepreneurship, rising demand, availability of capital, and technological innovation. Growth was eased by a ready supply of skilled and unskilled labor, and the arrival of the Irish proved an asset in economic terms. Many (but not all) Irish settled in the coal- and iron-mining areas of Lanarkshire, arousing considerable hostility and leaving a legacy of sectarianism, which remains yet into the twenty-first century.

The Irish contributed to, although they did not create, problems of bad housing, which became general throughout Victorian Scotland and was not confined to only the larger cities. Housing was notoriously bad in some rural areas, especially in the Highlands, where the regional economy found itself caught between rising population and deteriorating economic opportunity. A wartime boom in kelp and cattle prices came to an end in 1815, and thereafter the region struggled. Highland landlords have been cast as the villains of the piece, held responsible for the general decline in population by a third in many areas of the Highland counties during second half of the nineteenth century, but it is difficult to see how they alone could have arrested or reversed this inexorable regional decline. Emigration, once resisted, became seen as inevitable, and movement out was reinforced by the clearance—sometimes forcible—of surplus population. Guilt and worry that the Highlands could become as disturbed as Ireland over the land issue forced a reappraisal of policy by the state, which increasingly started to intervene. Security of tenure to crofters was granted in 1886, and government subsidy to development was provided in, for example, the Mallaig extension of the West Highland Railway.

Yet for all the importance of the heavy industries, there were other dimensions to the Scottish economy before 1914. There was the continuing strength of agriculture (much less affected by competition from abroad than was true of England); the transformation of such traditional industries as fishing and whisky, allied to the sophistication of the financial sector; and the reputation of Scottish banking, which exercised a considerable influence over policy in England and practice in the colonies. The rise of tourism also became a significant element in the economies of quite a number of seaside and inland resorts. It was not an economy where success was universal, as the decline of cotton manufacturing (except thread) showed, or unstressed: the rise in the later nineteenth century of foreign competition and tariffs alike complicated life for many industries. The banking system, though generally stable, had its hiccups, notably in 1878 when the City of Glasgow Bank collapsed; that the bank's directors went to prison for fraud was little consolation to the many shareholders ruined by unlimited liability. But the momentum of change was positive: Scotland moved from a low-wage economy to one where earnings were on a par with those elsewhere in the United Kingdom, and Scottish money was an important element in the United Kingdom's heavy investment overseas.

War Brings Change. World War I was a watershed. Just when, with the benefit of hindsight, the economy should have been diversifying, demand for ships, sandbags, and other war materials confirmed the old order, and the collapse of the world economy after the boom of 1919–1920 made a shift difficult or impossible. Scotland was overrepresented in the sectors most in difficulty and lacked presence in the new industries, notably the car, where no transition was made to mass production. The consequence was severe unemployment, especially between 1929 and 1933. It was worst in west-central Scotland but was also found in Dundee and Aberdeen, concentrated among the skilled male-working class. Had things been any better in North America, for example, then emigration might have exceeded the astonishing levels of the 1920s when nearly half a million Scots left. Instead, emigration fell to a few thousand.

Few parts of Scotland escaped the brunt of depression, though thanks to its concentration on law, administration, and services, Edinburgh had an unemployment rate half that of the national average—a mere 14 percent in 1932, compared with 30-plus percent for the western part of Scotland. Yet for all the problems of the interwar years, there were real gains for many, as reflected in improvements in health, changes in leisure, and most notably in the provision of housing for lower-income groups. Before 1914, the provision of housing was a function of private capital, and this had left a huge gap at the bottom end of the market. Scottish builders could and did build well, mostly in stone rather than in brick. Middle-class suburbs ringed all the Scottish cities—the "west end"—with their churches, banks, and galleries. Some private companies did provide housing, and decent tenement housing for rent was provided by private investors. But mostly low-income groups were crowded into older property. Even in Glasgow, where municipal socialism was vigorous, as shown in the ownership of water supply and bath houses (the "steamies"), the tramway system, and an imposing City Chambers, no real intervention had been made in the housing market, except to demolish some of the worst slums.

But between 1919 and 1939, some three hundred thousand houses were built in Scotland, of which two-thirds were publicly financed and council owned. Management of the council estates became a key function of municipal authorities everywhere, and a bulwark of Labor Party rule—hence in the 1970s the Thatcher government put through legislation to promote the sale of council housing to sitting tenants, a measure that nevertheless did nothing to arrest the decline of Conservatism in Scotland.

After World War II, the problems of the traditional industries returned in strength. Government policy, especially under the Labor Party, attempted a series of large-scale schemes to locate activities in areas where the existing staples were in decline; the steel plant at Ravenscraig and the car works at Bathgate were but two ventures underpinned by heavy subsidy. Determined efforts were made to arrest the decline of shipbuilding, on which so many related jobs in coal, steel, transportation, and engineering depended, but the process of contraction was only delayed, not arrested. By the late 1990s, only one shipyard was left on the Clyde, one deep pit in all of Scotland, and only a shadow of the steel industry. Whole areas in Lanarkshire and Ayrshire, once at the heart of Scotland's industrial economy, were deindustrialized and derelict. Civil-service jobs were dispersed from the South, for example, the Forestry Commission, but not to these communities.

Employment was shrinking in other traditional industries; in agriculture, thanks in part to mechanization as the horse gave way to the tractor; and in fishing as fewer but bigger and more efficient boats took over the catching, leading to a crisis in fish stocks in the late 1990s. Yet there was substantial growth in local government, in teaching and education, and within the manufacturing sector, notably in computing ("Silicon Glen") and in oil, which transformed both the economic position of Aberdeen and the political fortunes of the Scottish National Party, campaigning under the potent slogan of "It's Scotland's Oil." The discovery of gas and oil in the North Sea and off the Shetlands in the early 1970s created tens of thousands of jobs on the platforms, as well as onshore in construction and supply. Most of the higher-level skilled and supervisory posts were initially filled by imported French, American, and Dutch workers, whose spending power led to an explosion in house prices in the north-eastern part of Scotland. While Scottish industry as a whole, or so many observers considered, did not respond to the challenge as well as it might have done, and the platform construction yards on which so much hope was pinned enjoyed little consistent success, some of the entrepreneurial response was of the highest order, the wood group of Aberdeen being a key example. But this growth was precarious, dependent on the world price of oil remaining high; and when that dipped as it did in the mid-1980s, a factor over which the United Kingdom could exercise no control, the result was immediate depression.

The arrival of multinational enterprise, while welcome, was also a source of instability, raising again the vulnerability of branch enterprises. The problems of being a satellite economy were acute, and only worsened by European Community (EC) measures—certainly necessary for the conservation of fish stocks in the North Sea. Even tourism, which by the 1980s was second only to oil in economic importance and a source of much greater (if less well paid and geographically more widely dispersed) employment, was subject to ebb and flow as exchange rates and political instability could and did take their toll. Information technology altered office routines irretrievably, and when combined with mergers in the banking and financial sector, led to yet more jobs being lost. On the positive side, working from a distance via the Internet began to revitalize the Highlands and islands, though there were acute tensions between those interested in conservation and the scenery—many of whom lived outwith the area and the local crofting community concerned over jobs—as a heated debate over a proposed superquarry on Harris showed. It remains to be seen whether devolution will be positive, negative, or neutral in its economic effects.

[*See also* Great Britain.]

BIBLIOGRAPHY

Campbell, Roy H. *Scotland since 1707: The Rise of an Industrial Society.* 2d ed. Edinburgh, 1985. The standard account of the Scottish economy.

Devine, Thomas M. *The Great Highland Famine: Hunger, Emigration, and the Scottish Highlands in the Nineteenth Century.* Edinburgh, 1988. Examines in depth why the potato failure of the mid-1840s did not have as devastating effects in the Highlands as it did in Ireland.

Devine, Thomas M., and Rosalind Mitchison, eds. *People and Society in Scotland*, vol. 1. Edinburgh, 1988. Contains a variety of articles by leading experts on key aspects of Scottish economic history for the years 1797–1830. Essential.

Dickson, Tony, and James H. Treble, eds. *People and Society in Scotland*, vol. 3. Edinburgh, 1991. Contains a variety of articles by leading experts on key aspects of Scottish economic history for the years 1914–1990. Essential.

Fraser, W. Hamish, and R. J. Morris, eds. *People and Society in Scotland*, vol. 2. Edinburgh, 1990. Contains a variety of articles by leading experts on key aspects of Scottish economic history for the years 1830–1914. Essential.

Payne, Peter L. *Growth and Contraction: Scottish Industry, 1860–1990.* Dundee, Scotland, 1992. A magisterial account of the problems of Scottish industry in the twentieth century.

Saville, Richard. *Bank of Scotland: A History, 1695–1995.* Edinburgh, 1996. A comprehensive account of an institution that has been at the heart of the Scottish financial community for three centuries.

Smout, T. Christopher. *A History of the Scottish People, 1560–1830.* London, 1969. Both informative and a pleasure to read. Particularly strong on the social dimensions to economic change.

Whatley, Christopher. *A Bought and Sold for English Gold?: Explaining the Union of 1707.* Dundee, Scotland, 2001. A measured review of the making of the Union of 1707, and of the role played by economic issues.

Whyte, Ian D. *Scotland before the Industrial Revolution: An Economic and Social History, c. 1050–c. 1707.* London, 1995. A recent survey that presents much original research.

ALASTAIR J. DURIE

SEASONALITY refers to the predictable movements in economic measures, such as production, consumption, and prices that occur periodically during the year. They can be produced by exogenous forces (weather), by cultural institutions (periodic market fairs), or by the combination of the two (the timing of religious festivals to coincide with the harvest). Their effect may be through circumscribing production possibilities, such as the availability of food over the seasons, or through preferences, such as the desire to vacation during good weather.

Seasonal variation is an issue for economic agents for several reasons. Under standard conditions, variation is disliked or inefficient; smoothing consumption produces higher utility if resources can be reallocated cheaply through time. Sharp nonlinearities may make smoothing imperative; for example, Liebig's law holds that the population of a community is determined by the amount of food available in the leanest season (Testart, 1982). Seasonal variation can interact with nonseasonal, random variation to produce disastrous results if bad luck occurs at the wrong time of the year. Institutions designed to address one type of variation may affect the ability of agents to deal with a different source of variation. Storing food to smooth consumption over the year also allows people to absorb an unexpected, temporary shortfall in supply.

Anthropologists, historians, and economists have studied seasonal fluctuations for three reasons. Seasonal fluctuations may explain the existence and development of cultural institutions or economic practices. They may yield insights in how economic agents accommodate other types of exogenous variation, and they may suggest whether a particular class of models is *a priori* plausible. As an example of the last reason, economists have developed models where complementarities in production and preferences make bunching activity at one point in time advantageous. Demonstrating the existence of such complementarities, which can generate multiple equilibria, has been difficult, however. Cooper and Haltiwanger (1993) show that in 1935 the timing of the introduction of new automobiles and the automobile shows moved from the spring to the autumn. While an amendment to the National Industrial Recovery Act signed in January 1935 mandated this change, automakers persisted in introducing new models in the fall after the Supreme Court ruled the act unconstitutional only one-half year later.

For most of human history, the most important source of variation has been the effect of weather on available food supplies, adaptations to which have had broader implications. Primitive hunter-gatherer societies practiced various migratory patterns, including expansive, seasonal migrations. These migrations limited the capability of such societies to develop capital and improve productivity. Some societies faced with sharp seasonal swings in available resources developed storage capabilities. Testart (1982) argues that the ability to hold wealth in hunter-gatherer societies, such as the Native Americans of the Northwest coast, led to the development of cultural institutions similar to those of agricultural societies. Agricultural societies developed a series of strategies to cope with seasonal fluctuations, although even today seasonal malnutrition is a problem in underdeveloped countries. Seasonal malnutrition can have serious developmental consequences, especially if the period of low supply coincides with the period of greatest energy need, such as during the harvest (Sahn, 1989).

One aspect of seasonality that economic historians have stressed is the variation in nonfarm labor supply produced by the seasonal demand for agricultural workers. In

Europe, a large, landless class of workers was idled during the slack periods in agriculture. With their low opportunity costs, entrepreneurs hired the seasonally unemployed to manufacture textiles and other goods for sale using labor-intensive technologies at home. Historians have pointed to this "proto-industrialization" as a precursor to industrialization (Mendels, 1972).

Development in the United States stands in contrast to this European pattern. Sokoloff and Dollar (1997) argue that cottage manufacturing in the United States was rarer and disappeared more quickly than in Europe because inexpensive labor was unavailable, even outside of the harvest season. In the United States, labor was scarce relative to land. As a result, agriculture was more diversified and hence less intensive in the production of grain, whose labor requirements were much more seasonal than other agricultural goods.

A second aspect of seasonality that has been studied is the large variation in interest rates and other financial instruments. Because of the credit and currency needs of the agricultural sector, interest rates rose in the spring and in the fall while reserve-deposit ratios fell, a condition that contemporary analysts described as the "perverse elasticity of the money supply." Miron (1996) argues that such conditions were associated with a significant number of financial panics. With the founding of the Federal Reserve System and the collapse of the gold standard, however, the seasonality in worldwide interest rates was eliminated, and the frequency of panics was lessened. Because other institutions, such as deposit insurance, were developed later to prevent financial panics directly, whether the policy of seasonally smoothing interest rates should be continued and whether it produces such undesirable effects as exacerbated seasonal movements in real output are matters of debate.

Today, the share of output produced by industries that are directly affected by the weather, such as agriculture, fishing, and construction, is much smaller in developed countries than it was in the nineteenth century. Moreover, the degree of seasonality in some industries has probably decreased. The development of steam power reduced the reliance on inland water transportation and power from waterwheels that froze in the winter. Improvements in lighting eliminated the dependence on natural light whose length varies over the year, and improvements in heating and air conditioning allowed operations to continue during extreme temperatures (Kuznets, 1933). Nonetheless, the seasonal variation in GDP remains significant, on average about three times greater than the nonseasonal variation (Beaulieu and Miron, 1992). Year-end holiday gift giving produces a large shift in preferences for consumption goods at the end of the calendar year, and vacations are bunched in a summer month. The observation that some Northern Hemisphere countries vacation in July while others shut down in August—without an obvious reason to prefer one to the other—suggests that agglomeration effects are at work to support the equilibrium of a sharp slowdown in production in that particular month.

BIBLIOGRAPHY

Beaulieu, J. Joseph, and Jeffrey A. Miron. "A Cross Country Comparison of Seasonal Cycles and Business Cycles." *Economic Journal* 102.413 (1992), 772–788.

Cooper, Russell, and John Haltiwanger. "Automobiles and the National Industrial Recovery Act: Evidence on Industry Complementarities." *Quarterly Journal of Economics* 108.4 (1993), 1043–1071.

Kuznets, Simon. *Seasonal Variations in Industry and Trade*. New York, 1933.

Mendels, Franklin F. "Proto-Industrialization: The First Phase of the Industrialization Process." *Journal of Economic History* 32.1 (1972), 241–261.

Miron, Jeffrey A. *The Economics of Seasonal Cycles*. Cambridge, Mass. 1996.

Sahn, David E., ed. *Seasonal Variability in Third World Agriculture: The Consequences for Food Security*. Baltimore, 1989.

Sokoloff, Kenneth L., and David Dollar. "Agricultural Seasonality and the Organization of Manufacturing in Early Industrial Economies: The Contrast between England and the United States." *Journal of Economic History* 57.2 (1997), 288–321.

Testart, Alain. "The Significance of Food Storage among Hunter-Gatherers: Residence Patterns, Population Densities, and Social Inequalities." *Current Anthropology* 23.5 (1982), 523–537.

J. JOSEPH BEAULIEU

SEED AND SEED VARIETIES. The history of the relationship between vegetal seeds and humans evolved in two phases. The first involves the domestication of plants through natural and human selection; the second implies the manipulation of the seeds' quality to generate better yields, given climatic and environmental conditions.

The domestication process consists of growing a plant and, through selection, causing it to change genetically to a form that makes it better able to fulfill human needs. The practice of agriculture began in Mesopotamia around 10,000 BCE. The first crops to be domesticated were varieties of edible seeds: barley, wheat, peas, and chickpeas. In many other parts of the world, seed domestication took place independently. In China, for instance, rice, millet, and soy were domesticated around 7500 BCE. The first farmers selected the quality of seeds that produced the largest or the sweetest fruits. Grains whose stalks had failed to shatter and legumes whose pods had not disintegrated made harvesting easier, and therefore were preferred. These activities amounted to a process of human selection, which permitted the chosen varieties to evolve into the forms we are familiar with today. By the time the Roman Empire was established, the majority of the edible species known today had already been domesticated on the Eurasian continent.

Once domestication was achieved, farmers sought to improve the quality and quantity of the yields by employing better farming technologies and advancing their knowledge of crops. Greeks and Romans recognized the importance of a careful selection of seeds. They knew that seeds should be imported from warm areas to cold regions, where they have softer husk and their germination is faster. Some documents confirm that Romans encouraged experimentation with imported varieties. During the Carolingian era, spelt was the most cultivated cereal in northern Europe, but from the tenth century it began to decline. This was probably because of the extra costs of husking, its lack of adaptability to changes in weather conditions, and its poor resistance to parasites. Wheat became the leading cereal in western Europe because it performed better under all those dimensions. Rye assumed this role in eastern Europe.

The settlement of western and northern parts of Canada and the northern part of the United States involved careful research of the most suitable qualities of grains. In both countries, the harsh climatic conditions required the employment of hard red wheat seeds resistant to drought and cold. The Red Fife was the first hard grain introduced in the United States (in 1850s), whereas in the early colonized East there was a tradition of soft grains. In Canada, the employment of the Marquis quality, in the 1880s, moved the wheat frontier even closer to the Pacific Ocean and the Arctic regions. The employment of these new types resulted in a nearly 30 percent increase in quantity.

In the same years, a major scientific development in biology was achieved that deeply affected agricultural practices. In 1866, the Austrian botanist Gregor Mendel (1822–1884) published his seminal work on genetic heredity. The possibility of controlling the genetics of seeds and generating new varieties particularly responsive to fertilizers—which in the last twenty years of the nineteenth century became available on a large scale—increased the interest in biotechnologies applied to agriculture. At the beginning of the twentieth century, George Harrison Shull (1874–1954), a geneticist of the Carnegie Institute of Washington, a private research institution in New York State, began to study the effects of inbreeding and subsequent crossfertilization in corn. Thanks to Shull's work, by 1909 the basics of breeding hybrid corn were already known. However, producing hybrids was still not commercially feasible because of high production costs. Only in 1923 was the American agriculturalist Henry A. Wallace (1888–1965) able to produce the first commercial hybrid corn and found his own company. During the 1920s, other companies followed Wallace's example and started producing hybrids. By the end of the 1940s, the majority of the corn produced in the United States was hybrid.

The diffusion of hybrid corn in the United States reflected the economic rationality of seed producers and farmers. In the 1950s, economic research confirmed that producers concentrated hybrids' development and sales in areas where expected profits were higher. Similarly, farmers adopted hybrid corn when they generated higher profit opportunities than the traditional open-pollinated varieties. Economic research also showed that the social returns from investments in the research of hybrid corns in the United States yielded very high returns. Given an estimation of all the research expenditures and the net social returns from 1910 until 1955, it has been shown that this endeavor generated approximately seven dollars for every dollar invested.

Hybrid corn was also massively used in Japan, where the limited amount of agricultural land induced farmers to rely on biotechnologies to improve their yields.

A systematic application of more advanced biotechnologies to agriculture began after World War II. New seed varieties—highly responsive to fertilizers—were discovered in the United States and enthusiastically embraced by developing countries, generating the so-called "Green Revolution." High-yielding wheat and corn types were introduced in Mexico during the 1950s with striking results. Mexico was a net importer of wheat immediately after the war, but by 1956 production was sufficient to satisfy internal demand, and the country became a net exporter during the 1960s. This type of wheat also gave excellent results in areas of Asia and Africa. In India, wheat production increased from 12 million tons in 1966 to 47 million tons in 1986. This successful experiment induced breeders to develop new varieties of other crops. High-yielding rice types also were fruitfully introduced in the Philippines during the 1960s. Modern breeders have developed high-yielding qualities of virtually every major crop grown in world. Despite the dramatic increase in yields, the Green Revolution generated many environmental problems. In order to produce the best results, the new varieties required an increasing amount of complementary factors, such as chemical fertilizers and pesticides. Between 1950 and 1990 world fertilizer use increased tenfold. A large-scale employment of chemical factors in agriculture caused many problems of water pollution and endangered the inherent fertility of soils.

BIBLIOGRAPHY

Astill, Greenville, and John Langdon. *Medieval Farming and Technology.* New York, 1997.

Diamond, Jared. *Guns, Germs, and Steel.* New York, 1997.

Griliches, Zvi. "Hybrid Corn: An Explanation in the Economics of Technical Change." *Econometrica* 25.4 (1957), 501–522.

Griliches, Zvi. "Research Costs and Social Returns: Hybrid Corn and Related Innovations." *Journal of Political Economy* 66.5 (1958), 419–431.

Hayami, Yuijiro, and V. W. Ruttan. "Factor Prices and Technical Change in Agricultural Development: The United States and Japan, 1880–1960." *Journal of Political Economy* 8.5 (1970), 1115–1141.

Olmstead, Alan L., and Paul Rhode. "The Red Queen and the Hard Red: Productivity Growth in American Wheat, 1800–1940." *Journal of Economic History* 62.4 (2003), 929–966.

White, K. D. *Roman Farming*. Ithaca, N.Y., 1970.

FABIO BRAGGION

SENEGAL. *See* Sudan, *subentry on* Western Sudan.

SERFDOM. Serfdom as a social relationship has been found in a wide variety of European and Asiatic societies, occurring over a period of almost two thousand years prior to the mid-nineteenth century. Indeed, serfdom has proved to be such an elastic concept as to lead some historians to doubt whether the term has any analytical value. Certainly, in practice, the precise form taken by serfdom cannot be specified in advance but must be established empirically for each particular time and place.

Definition. Like most categories, serfdom can be best understood by what it excludes rather than what it includes. In essence, serfdom involves legal restrictions, in particular on the right of movement, along with economic burdens and a degrading social status that separate serfs from others within their societies who are legally free. Yet, although unfree, the serfs' enjoyment of legal and customary rights and their social existence within stable families and village communities differentiate them from the chattel slaves of the domestic household and the gang slaves of the ancient latifundia and modern plantations. As peasants, whose possession of land, tools, livestock, and family labor meant that they could directly provide their own subsistence, serfs can be further distinguished from both slaves dependent upon rations supplied by their masters and from free laborers dependent upon wages paid by their employers. However, within the peasantry, the legal restrictions imposed on serfs separate them from independent (or "allodial") proprietors, from those who hold by a free hereditary tenure for a fixed and secure rent, and from those peasants who hold by a fixed-term, leasehold tenure whose rent is determined by the market.

In defining serfdom, two different forms of servility need to be distinguished. First, there was personal serfdom, in which servility was a hereditary personal status passed on to all the offspring of a serf, as in the case of the medieval *nativi de sanguine*, the serfs by blood. Such serfs were personally bound to their lord and unable to leave without his permission. They could be bought and sold, with or without their tenements, as happened in thirteenth-century China and in eighteenth-century Russia, despite a law to the contrary there of 1649. Second, there was tenurial serfdom, by which the tenant was bound to his holding but did not pass on that servility to all of his offspring. Both forms of serfdom coexisted in the medieval West, where those who were personally unfree could acquire land that was free, and those who were personally free could take on an unfree holding, along with its associated restrictions and obligations, yet remained free in status and thus able, in theory, to leave to take up land elsewhere. By contrast, in the so-called Second Serfdom, which developed in eastern Europe from the end of the fifteenth century on, each state opted either for tenurial or for personal serfdom. Bohemia and Brandenburg, for instance, chose the former, whereas Poland, Prussia, and Russia, among others, adopted the latter.

In societies where serfdom was personal and inherited by all of the serf's offspring, a far higher proportion of the population became serfs, even among those who were landless, than in societies based on tenurial serfdom. Here, the legal status of serfdom was extended to producers who were not peasants but who nonetheless had obligations to their masters that were not incurred by those producers who were legally free. In eighteenth-century Russia, for example, large numbers of industrial serfs engaged in tasks such as weaving and metalworking. Where they were directly employed by their masters, for instance, in estate "factories," these serfs could expect to be paid lower wages than those received by free wage laborers. If they sold their labor on the market or worked as independent artisans, they owed a quitrent or tax (*obrok*) to their masters, paid from their wages or profits.

History. In western Europe, serfdom evolved gradually from about the second century CE onward as, on the one hand, former slaves were granted plots of land and became tenants, and, on the other, free tenants were tied to the soil by the imperial authorities. In the chaos and collapse of central public power of the Dark Ages, lords acquired increasing jurisdictional powers over their tenants; and growing numbers of free proprietors, willingly or not, granted their holdings to lords and received them back as tenancies. As late as the sixth century, even though tenants were being tied to the soil, labor services seem to have been light. By the ninth century, however, the classic bipartite manor, divided between the "outland" leased to peasants and the demesne "inland," which the lord had kept in his own hand and was worked by labor services (corvée labor), was well established between the Loire and the Rhine, even though estates worked by slave labor or those with no demesne but only tenants rendering rents in kind were also common.

Serfdom seems not to have developed in the Islamic states but was found in Asia. In China, as in the early medieval West, a combination of the elevation of former slaves and the degradation of formerly free peasants who surrendered their land to lords meant that by the tenth century CE much of the population was enserfed and could not move without their lords' permission. In Japan, the peasants were being bound to the soil from the Taika reforms of the mid-seventh century onward although, as in the West, the decline of the central authority and the decentralization of power to the nobility in the eleventh and twelfth centuries also encouraged the development of manorialism.

In most of the West, serfdom was in decline from the eleventh century onward as commercialization, peasant flight to newly colonized land, and rising population saw the gradual enfranchisement of peasants and a shift from labor services toward money rents. In England and Catalonia, the end of serfdom was delayed until the years after the Black Death (1348–1349). In both countries, landlords reacted to contemporary population decline by attempting to reassert their control over the peasants through an intensification of serfdom. However, in Catalonia, the peasants eventually won their freedom through armed, military uprisings (1462–1472, 1484–1486). In England, by contrast, despite uprisings such as the Great Revolt of 1381, the peasants failed to achieve their freedom through acts of armed resistance. Nevertheless, by the "silent revolution" of piecemeal negotiations between lords and peasants, manor by manor, serfdom had virtually disappeared from England by about 1500. In most of the West, serfdom thus retained only a vestigial existence until it was finally abolished following the French Revolution.

Yet even as serfdom in the West was coming to an end, its rise to dominance in eastern Europe was just beginning. In eastern Europe, unlike the medieval West, the state played a central role in the creation, and the eventual abolition, of serfdom. From the late fifteenth to the seventeenth century, a series of decrees issued by diets dominated by the nobility tied the peasants to the soil and introduced uniform national systems of personal or tenurial serfdom. In late-medieval England, in conditions of population scarcity, competition between lords for tenants forced them to recognize the peasants' freedom; in early-modern eastern Europe, by contrast, political cooperation between the lords via the state allowed them to impose serfdom despite similar conditions of low population. The rise of serfdom in eastern Europe usually was accompanied by the enlargement of the demesnes, often at the expense of the peasants, and the imposition of heavy labor services. By the eighteenth century, however, a combination of rising population, high leasehold rents, and cheap wage labor meant that serfdom was no longer so economically attractive for many lords. Nevertheless, the lords themselves showed little interest in formally abolishing serfdom. In eastern Europe, serfdom was ended, as it had begun, by government decree: in 1781, in Austria-Bohemia; in 1862, in Russia; and, finally, in 1864, in Romania, where peasant emancipation meant that, for the first

time in well over a thousand years, Europe was entirely free of serfdom.

In China, hereditary serfdom was ended by decree in the late seventeenth and eighteenth centuries, when the landlords, attracted by new sources of income, and the government, prompted by widespread peasant rebellion, both came to see servility as a cause of social disorder. In Japan, the fixed, hereditary status system developed in the Tokugawa shogunate (1603–1868), by which peasants were, in theory, fixed to the soil, also was officially ended from above, by reforms following the Meiji Restoration (1868). In practice, however, this system had long been eroded from within by the commercialization of rural society.

Explaining Serfdom. An extremely influential interpretation of serfdom is that provided by Karl Marx (1818–1883). Marx contrasted wage laborers under capitalism, who did not themselves possess the means of production and were therefore compelled by economic necessity to sell their labor power to others, with peasant producers who, through effective possession of land, tools, raw materials, and labor power, could provide their own subsistence. Peasants thus seemed to have no economic reason to render "surplus labor" to their lords in the form of rent, which was the basis of the latter's existence as a class. Marx argued that, as a result, the transfer of rent could be effected only by noneconomic means: by coercive sanction, by the legal, political, and military powers embodied in serfdom.

Certainly, serfdom constituted an extra-economic relationship between landlords and peasants. After all, medieval landlords, whether noble or ecclesiastical, possessed not just landed properties but also their own private, manorial courts to which their tenants owed suit, and from which, as in Japan, their unfree tenants had no right of appeal to the public courts. These courts enforced the payment of rents and services along with all the other obligations to which unfree tenants were liable, and from which free tenants were largely exempt. These obligations included tallages paid at the lord's will, death-duties (heriots) owed by tenants, and the various fines that the unfree had to pay, for instance, the *merchet* paid on the marriage of a daughter or the *chevage* paid for permission to leave the manor temporarily. The manorial courts also enforced the lords' economic monopolies to which the unfree, but not the free, were subject. These included the obligation to use the lord's mill to grind corn, a service for which the villeins (the unfree) had to hand over a percentage of their corn (multure).

Freed from such noneconomic pressures, the free tenants in the medieval West typically had rents that were fixed, relatively low, and usually paid in the form of money. In contrast, the obligations of unfree tenants were elastic—determined, in theory, by the will of the lords.

Moreover, these obligations often took the form of heavy-labor services on the lord's demesne, the product of which was consumed by the lord and his household or was sold for his benefit. Such duties were time-consuming and considered degrading; so tenants often were eager to "commute" them into money payments, allowing the lords to replace them with wage labor. The labor services required from the unfree reached their highest levels in early-modern eastern Europe, as in sixteenth-century Brandenburg, where harvest services could be unlimited, or early-eighteenth-century Poland, where a peasant holding could be obliged to provide six or seven days labor per week for the demesne.

In all of these ways, serfs were subject to their lords' extra-economic powers; yet it is problematic to see the serfs' relationship with their lords as purely coercive in nature or as derived simply from an "effective possession" of the means of their own subsistence. After all, serfs acquired such possession only on condition that they rendered particular rents and services to lords who enjoyed a monopoly of landownership. As Marx himself put it, "all rent is based upon the title to land as a right of exclusion," which results from the monopoly enjoyed by certain people over particular pieces of land. In this perspective, the landlords subordinated the peasants and required them to render rents and services on the basis of the latter's separation from the land rather than on the basis of their possession of it. The level of rents and other obligations paid by unfree tenants thus can be viewed as made up of two elements: first, simply the rent paid by the tenant for access to land; and, second, an extra level of payment over and above the market level, which the lords extracted through the use of their legal and coercive powers.

Why then did lords resort to extra-economic means of extracting rents from peasants rather than simply relying on their monopoly possession of land? The most compelling answer is that extra-economic coercion was a response to times of high land-to-labor ratios and low population densities. As Marc Bloch long ago pointed out, had a free market in land prevailed in the late Roman Empire and the early-medieval West, tenants likely would have been able to wrest low rents and favorable terms of tenure from their lords. In the existing circumstances, serfdom was used to bind peasants to the soil in order to provide the lords with tenants and to ensure rents at a higher level than those that would have resulted from a purely "economic" exchange. The advantage of such a system to the lords could be that it then remained in use even when the conditions that had originally given birth to it had long since disappeared.

In eastern Europe too the introduction and the strengthening of servile ties were associated with periods of a scarcity of tenants and of labor. In Poland, for instance, the tying of the peasants to the land in the late fifteenth and early sixteenth centuries was a reaction to the shortage of tenants and labor produced by cessation of immigration from the west and the ease with which peasants could migrate to lands farther to the east. Similarly, the final enserfment of the Russian peasantry in the mid-seventeenth century was associated with a period of depopulation caused by disease, war, and opportunities for flight to newly colonized lands. However, a scarcity of population was never enough *per se* to allow the lords to enforce serfdom. Indeed, in England, as discussed above, the demographic decline of the period circa 1348–1500, when population fell by about one-half, is usually seen as the key factor in bringing about the collapse of serfdom, rather than its intensification. The English peasantry were able to use their newfound scarcity to wring concessions from the lords, demanding an end to the burdens and restrictions of villeinage and their replacement with new forms of free leasehold and copyhold tenure. In practice, therefore, whether the lords were able to take advantage of the scarcity of tenants to enforce serfdom, or the peasants were able to use their scarcity to achieve freedom, depended upon a variety of nondemographic factors, principally the role of the state and the strength of the peasant community in its resistance to lordly demands.

Advantages and Disadvantages of Labor Services. Where lords were able to enforce serfdom, they had to choose between taking rents primarily in the form of money, in kind, or as labor services although, as in China, all three forms of rent could coexist. Certainly, as in medieval Catalonia where demesnes were never an important source of revenue for the lords, the existence of serfdom by no means necessarily meant that lords opted for labor services. Where landlords did impose labor services, they were likely to incur peasant hostility, both because the serfs resented the element of personal monitoring inherent in unpaid work and because the lords' peak demands for labor naturally coincided with those periods, such as harvest time, when the peasants were particularly eager to work on their own land. Labor services thus were often accompanied by foot-dragging by the tenants and, as shown in both medieval England and China, seem to have been significantly less productive than the peasants' work on their own plots or the demesne work performed by hired labor.

Lords thus were most likely to impose labor services at times of high land-to-labor ratios when labor scarcity and high wages meant that it was in a lord's interest to work his demesne with "unpaid" labor services. The true cost of such labor to the lord was the land granted to the tenants who performed these services, a cost that, when land was abundant, was relatively low. A classic example of a labor scarcity that led to the imposition of labor services is provided by Bohemia in the seventeenth century, during the Thirty Years' War, which produced a population decline of over 40 percent, leading to vacant lands, low rents, high wages, and low grain prices. The lords' response here, as in contemporary Hungary, was to increase labor services (*robot*) in order to produce grain for the home and foreign markets without having to employ wage labor. Similarly, in Poland, the wars of the 1650s and 1700–1721 resulted in a doubling of labor services as lords continued with demesne agriculture in a time of depopulation. Labor services were also an attractive option to lords at times when domestic or foreign demand for grain made it profitable to turn to commercial agriculture using "free" serf labor. Similarly, in times of monetary debasement and inflation, it also made sense for lords to receive demesne produce rather than to collect devalued money rents.

Why did lords not try to maintain their incomes in such circumstances by raising money rents rather than by imposing labor services? The most credible answer is that raising money rents was made difficult by the tendency for them to become fixed at customary levels in preindustrial societies (see below). Besides, peasants in societies where land was abundant had no incentive to pay substantial money rents to their lords and could resist demands for extra rent or taxation by holding output to the levels required for their own subsistence, as seems to have happened in late-sixteenth-century Russia. If the lords had wished to extract relatively high levels of rent from unfree tenants, they would thus have been obliged to monitor and supervise the peasants' entire labor time on their plots, in order to ensure the production of surpluses above subsistence levels. The use of labor services, in contrast, guaranteed the lords an income but required them to monitor only that proportion of peasant labor performed on the demesne.

Theory and Reality. That serfs were subject to their lords' very considerable coercive powers might suggest that they were completely at their lords' mercy. In fact, serfs always had various ways of defending themselves against their lords' demands. At the most extreme, this defense could take the form of rebellion and attacks on the persons and property of their landlords, as in the peasant reaction to oppressive landlordism in fourteenth-century China or the uprisings in Hungary in 1735, 1755, 1763–1764, 1784, and 1790. The memory of such revolts helped limit the lords' demands even though, in Hungary, serfdom had actually been introduced in 1514 as a punishment for peasant revolt. But there were other, less dramatic forms of resistance, such as flight, foot-dragging when performing labor services, or instigating various forms of legal action against lords. Another potential source of protection for serfs against their lords was the state. In late-seventeenth- and eighteenth-century Prussia-Brandenburg and Austria-Bohemia, for instance, the central government imposed limits on landlordly exactions in order to ensure its own ability to extract taxation and military service from the peasants although total peasant renders to landlord and state could actually increase in such circumstances.

Perhaps the key defense for serfs against their landlords was the tendency of preindustrial obligations to become fixed by custom. As a result, the reality of social practice was often at odds with the suppositions of legal theory. For instance, in medieval English law, which was modeled on the Roman law of slavery, a villein's terms of tenure were purely arbitrary: he held at the will of his lord, with no protection from the royal courts. Yet, in reality, far from being arbitrary, the villein's burdens of rent, tallage, and services were fixed by local manorial custom; far from being insecure, the villeins enjoyed a de facto hereditary tenure of their land. Indeed, in conditions of growing land shortage, such as those of late-thirteenth- and early-fourteenth-century England or eighteenth-century Hungary, the supposedly arbitrary terms of servile tenure could actually function as a defense against manorial impositions since the rents and obligations levied from customary unfree tenures lagged behind prices and those rents available to landlords from land held on fixed-term leases. In these conditions, landlords who had once used villeinage to raise rents above the economic level now stood to gain by abandoning villeinage and shifting to leasehold tenures that were not subject to custom and whose rents therefore reflected the real demand for land. Serfs, protected by custom, could now accumulate land and property. As is evident in both China and the medieval West, serfs may have had a dishonorable legal status but, compared to slaves, landless laborers, rack-rented leaseholders, or the free tenants of tiny holdings, they were by no means necessarily the poorest or the most insecure members of the rural population.

[*See also* Feudalism.]

BIBLIOGRAPHY

Anderson, Perry. *Lineages of the Absolutist State*. London, 1979.
Bloch, Marc. "The Rise of Dependent Cultivation and Seignorial Institutions." In *The Cambridge Economic History of Europe*, 1st ed., edited by J. H. Clapham and Eileen Power, vol. 1, *The Agrarian Life of the Middle Ages*, pp. 224–277. Cambridge, 1941. 2d rev. ed., edited by M. M. Postan, pp. 235–289. Cambridge, 1966.
Blum, Jerome. "The Rise of Serfdom in Eastern Europe." *American Historical Review* 62 (1957), 807–836.
Blum, Jerome. *Lord and Peasant in Russia from the Ninth to the Nineteenth Century*. Princeton, 1961.
Bix, Herbert P. *Peasant Protest in Japan, 1590–1884*. New Haven, 1986.
Brenner, Robert. "Economic Backwardness in Eastern Europe in the Light of Developments in the West." In *The Origins of Backwardness in Eastern Europe: Economics and Politics from the Middle Ages until the Early Twentieth Century*, edited by D. Chirot, pp. 15–52. Berkeley, 1989.
Bush, M. L., ed. *Serfdom and Slavery: Studies in Legal Bondage*. London, 1996.
Bush, M. L. *Servitude in Modern Times*. Cambridge, 2000.
Carsten, Francis L. *The Origins of Prussia*. Oxford, 1954.
De Ste Croix, Geoffrey E. M. *The Class Struggle in the Ancient Greek World from the Archaic Age to the Arab Conquests*. London, 1981.

Domar, Evsey D. "The Causes of Slavery or Serfdom: A Hypothesis." *Journal of Economic History* 30 (1973), 18–32.

Freedman, Paul. *The Origins of Peasant Servitude in Medieval Catalonia*. Cambridge, 1991.

Hilton, Rodney H. *Class Conflict and the Crisis of Feudalism: Essays in Medieval Social History*. London, 1985.

Millward, Robert. "An Economic Analysis of the Organization of Serfdom in Eastern Europe." *Journal of Economic History* 42 (1982), 513–548.

Millward, Robert. "The Early Stages of European Industrialization: Economic Organization under Serfdom." *Explorations in Economic History* 21 (1984), 406–428.

Nash, Robert C. "The Economy." In *The Seventeenth Century: Europe, 1598–1715*, edited by J. Bergin, pp. 11–49. Oxford, 2001.

Postan, Michael M., ed. *The Cambridge Economic History of Europe*, vol. 1, *The Agrarian Life of the Middle Ages*. 2d ed. Cambridge, 1966.

Pounds, Norman J. G. *An Economic History of Medieval Europe*. 2d ed. London, 1994.

Rigby, Stephen H. *English Society in the Later Middle Ages: Class, Status and Gender*. Basingstoke, 1995.

Rösener, Werner. *Peasants in the Middle Ages*. Cambridge, 1992.

Stone, David. "The Productivity of Hired and Customary Labour: Evidence from Wisbech Barton in the Fourteenth Century." *Economic History Review* 50 (1997), 640–656.

Totman, Conrad. *Japan before Perry: A Short History*. Berkeley, 1981.

S. H. RIGBY

SERICULTURE. Technological change in mulberry growing and silkworm raising is difficult to analyze. There has been no major technological breakthrough comparable to the mechanization in the industrial stages. Of course, the discovery of the "best practice" must have been a long process, full of costly errors, but no historical record has been left. Once discovered, however, the "best practice," especially in silkworm raising, seems to have undergone few if any major changes. There is little difference between the advice of, say, fifteenth-century Chinese textbooks and nineteenth-century Italian ones. Both suggested that mulberries had to be given a lot of fertilizers and that worms had to be kept wellfed, wellsupplied with fresh leaves, and, above all, clean to prevent the spread of diseases.

The major contribution of modern technology to the development of sericulture was in the selection of races of cocoons. It was the almost unintended consequence of the fight against the pebrine. Pebrine is a serious disease because it is both infective and hereditary. Silkworms infected during their life can survive and lay eggs, but their offspring are bound to die before spinning the cocoon. Disease-free eggs could be produced with the so-called cellular technique. Each couple of moths were mated separately in a cell and checked immediately afterward with a microscope. This technique, developed by Pasteur in the late 1860s, saved the European sericulture. The production of eggs became a highly specialized activity, and producing firms soon began to systematically cross-breed different types to obtain the "perfect" hybrid. The latter was never found—in Italy at least—because the interests of farmers and industrialists diverged markedly. In China and Japan, which had never experienced the pebrine, the cellular technique was adopted in the 1890s and in the 1910s, respectively. But Japan learned fast: In 1911, the government set up a National Institute for Silkworm-eggs Production, which three years later produced a new hybrid, the F1. Its use spread fast in the next years. As argued by Yuijro Kyokawa (1984), this innovation improved the quality of the cocoons and, above all, made the production of a homogeneous silk much easier. Homogeneity greatly helped the success of Japanese silk on the world market.

On the other hand, there is evidence that since the 1870s the total factor productivity has been increasing in Japan and probably in other countries as well. Otherwise, it would have been impossible to have an increased production with falling prices of cocoons relative to other agricultural products. The only major innovation seems to have been the widespread adoption of labor-saving techniques in silkworm raising. Instead of feeding them chopped leaves picked from full-sized trees, they were given whole branches with the leaves still attached (branch or tower feeding), cut from smaller plants (mulberry bush). These methods were standard practice in other parts of Asia, such as Bengal or southern China, and spread to Italy and Japan in the late nineteenth century. The amount of labor saved, however, was too small to account for the measured productivity growth. This latter must have been achieved with a number of microinnovations (e.g., more fertilizers for mulberries, better mulberry varieties, better disease prevention).

[*See also* Silk Industry; Silk Road; Textiles; *and* Total Factor Productivity.]

BIBLIOGRAPHY

Beauquais, Henri. *Histoire économique de la soie*. Lyon, 1910. Although in French and probably difficult to find, it still remains a valuable source of information.

Bell, Lynda. "Farming, Sericulture and Peasant Rationality in Wuxi County in the Early Twentieth Century." In *Chinese History in Economic Perspective*, edited by T. Rawski and L. Li, pp. 207–241. Berkeley and Los Angeles, 1992. A short account of the development of sericulture in one of the major producing areas in central China.

Cayez, Pierre. *Métiers jacquard et hauts forneaux aux origines de l'industrie lyonnaise*. Lyon, 1978.

Cayez, Pierre. *Crises et croissance de l'industrie lyonnaise*. Lyon, 1980. These two books are the major recent work on the history of a key weaving area.

Cavaciocchi, Simonetta, ed. *La seta in Europa secc XIII–XX*. Florence, 1993. Proceedings of a conference, with several articles in English.

Cottereau, Alain. "The Fate of Collective Manufactures in the Industrial World: The Silk Industries of Lyons and London, 1800–1850." In *World of Possibilities*, edited by J. Zeitlin and C. Sabel, pp. 75–152.

Cambridge, 1997. A comparison between silk weaving in Lyon and London in the first half of the nineteenth century.

Eng, Robert Y. *Economic Imperialism in China: Silk Production and Exports*. Berkeley, 1986. A general history, critical of the organization of the silk industry and of its role in Chinese development.

Federico, Giovanni. *An Economic History of the Silk Industry, 1830–1930*. Cambridge, 1997. A general overview of the industry, with extensive bibliography.

Feltwell, James. *The Story of Silk*. Sutton, 1990. A simple and readable account of long-term development.

Kyokawa, Yuijro. "The Diffusion of the New Technologies in the Japanese Sericulture Industry: The case of the Hybrid Silkworm." *Hitotusbashi Journal of Economics* 25 (1984), 31–59.

Kyokawa, Yuijro. "The Transformation of Young Rural Women into Disciplined Labor under Competition-Oriented Management: The Experience of the Silk-Reeling Industry in Japan." *Hitotusbashi Journal of Economics* 32 (1991), 49–69. The title is somewhat too narrow, as it deals with technical progress in reeling.

Kumar Bag, Sailendra. *The Changing Fortunes of the Bengal Silk Industry, 1757–1833*. Calcutta, 1989. Focuses on the efforts by the East India Company to improve the quality of Indian silk.

Kuhn, Dieter. "Textile Technology: Spinning and Reeling." In *Science and Technology in China*, edited by J. Needham, vol. 5, part 9. Cambridge, 1988. A detailed analysis of technology, with information on the development of the industry, especially in its early stages.

Li, Lillian. *China's Silk Trade: Traditional Industry in the Modern World*. Cambridge, Mass., 1981. A general overview, dealing mostly with the nineteenth and twentieth century, but with an introduction on the previous history.

Lopez, Roberto S. "The Silk Industry in the Byzantine Empire." *Speculum* 20 (1945), 1–42. A classic article, still the best description of the Byzantine silk industry.

Ma, Debin. "The Modern Silk Road: The Global Raw Silk Market, 1850–1930." *Journal of Economic History* 56 (1996), 330–355. Focuses on the integration of the world market for raw silk, but reports some additional information.

Malanima, Paolo. *La Fine del Primato*. Milan, 1998. A general book on the Italian economy in the seventeenth and early eighteenth century, with estimates of trends in silk output.

Matsui, Sugihiro. *The History of the Silk Industry in the United States*. New York, 1930. Although difficult to find, it is the only comprehensive history available.

Poni, Carlo. "Per la storia del distretto industriale serico di Bologna." *Quaderni Storici* 73 (1990), 93–167. The best case study on a preindustrial silk processing area.

Scranton, Philip. "An Exceedingly Irregular Business: Structure and Process in the Paterson Silk Industry, 1885–1910." In *Silk City: Studies on the Paterson Silk Industry*, edited by P. Scranton, pp. 5–68. Newark, Del., 1985. The only recent work on the economics of silk weaving in the United States.

Shih, Ming S. *The Silk Industry in Ch'ing China*. Ann Arbor, 1976. A short and sometimes confusing book, that nevertheless reports much useful information.

Silberman, Herman. *Die Seide*. Dresden, 1897. Although in German and probably difficult to find, it still remains a valuable source of information.

So, Alvin. *The South China Silk District: Local Historical Transformation and World System Theory*. Albany, N.Y., 1987. Laden with jargon and scarce on information, it is the only recent work on the Canton area.

Sugiyama, Sugihiro. *Japan's Industrialisation in the World Economy*. London, 1988. Includes an extensive chapter on silk.

Giovanni Federico

SETTLEMENT. That early humans were a migratory species, infiltrating most land environments, is unequivocal. The development of more complex forms of culture, material and intellectual, and exploitation of what the land surface had to offer in terms of food, other raw materials, and even psychological nourishment, was linked with the emergence of varied types of settlement. The term bears many shades of meaning, but human dwellings and all associated structures, from humble shelters and scattered compounds, farmsteads and great barns, terraced rows, churches, temples, vast manufactories, office complexes, military establishments, mining camps, squatter hovels, and condominiums are all parts of the physical manifestation of human settlement. Settlement, however, has two fundamental qualities: on one hand, the physical structures are always embedded within an economic system. Based in hunting, gathering, and fishing or production and consumption within a global economy, settlement characteristics are always grounded in the economic and social organization of space. On the other hand, settlement exists in a seamless robe of time. Settlement changes can be seen within a single lifetime: new settlements are founded, new houses added to existing places, or wholly new places planted or developed as need arises, occasionally even new capital cities, such as Brasilia. Conversely, the impact of flood, earthquake, and the devastation of warfare destroy settlements, sometimes beyond replacement. Settlement is always, however, a continuing feature of all human experience, for the home, focusing upon the fire of the hearth and the bed, provides shelter, warmth, protection, and storage. It is a place for the preparation and consumption of food, for the birthing and rearing of children, and for care of the old, the sick, and the injured.

By the third and fourth millennium BCE, cities containing as many as fifty thousand souls existed in a world still largely populated by scattered hunter-gatherer communities using seasonally occupied camps, containing at most a few families. Archaeologically, the earliest cities are attested in Mesopotamia, but a site at Sannai-Maruyama in Japan, occupied between 5000 and 3000 BCE by people of the Jomon culture, also reached city size. The early domestication of plants, generally considered essential for the support of urban concentrations, is now seen to involve both regionally separate innovation as well as the migration of ecologically potent communities, transferring domesticated plants and animals from one region to another. Understanding this past is further complicated by postglacial rises in sea level, leading to the flooding of important areas, such as the Sunda platform, between the island communities of Southeast Asia, and the lower portions of the Arabian Gulf. Nevertheless, the rise of cities and the implosion of social and economic activities that took place within them represent a fundamental line across time.

A city is a container for material structures, dwellings, shrines, open spaces for markets and ceremonies, and the citadels defending the stored movable wealth and for controlling and protecting the people. But cities represent more, for their presence created a fundamental division between the rural and the urban, with all that this implies in terms of human economic activity and psychology, while within them divisions of labor and the emergence of social hierarchies matured.

The recognition of differences in the duration of the occupation of a given site, the small area of land beneath any settlement, is crucial. Ephemeral settlements of a few days, temporary settlements of several weeks, seasonal settlements of some months, semipermanent settlements of some years, and permanent settlements lasting for several generations can be recognized. This classification remains as true today as it is of past conditions, for uneven economic development ensures that the different types coexist over the earth. The permanence of many settlements now seems assured, for even Hiroshima and Nagasaki were reconstructed, but nevertheless permanence remains a concept, not a certainty. The dichotomy between settlement patterns—the ways that settlement entities, isolated dwellings and farmsteads, hamlets, villages, and towns, are distributed both throughout and between regions—and settlement forms, the nature and qualities of the individual entities, are the result of development though many millennia. On a world scale, there are longstanding contrasts reflecting attractive environments, suitability for agriculture, and environmentally more constrained regions, traditionally used for hunting and, when woodland is absent or has been degraded or cleared, by the grazing of domesticated stock. In this we see the contrast between the well-watered and fertile plains and the hill and mountain masses and desert margins. The existence of productive and densely populated core regions and colonizing margins plays an important part in generating local diversity. On a world scale, throughout all time, the impact of conquest and imperialism and the extinguishing of indigenous land rights have frequently imposed layers of wholly new colonial or ideological patterns and forms upon traditional arrangements. However, human ingenuity is such that there are few generalizations about settlement that cannot be challenged by specific cases. We only have to remember the high Andean terraces created by the Incas.

There are deep paradoxes in these observations. Throughout the world, the past has value. In California, where the established Native American past is virtually invisible beneath European landscapes created in the nineteenth and twentieth centuries, only a few limited historically recent survivals are treasured. In Europe, in contrast, nodal points such as Rome, Prague, London, and Istanbul, while retaining powerful contemporary importance, possess character and qualities rooted in the deep well of the past. All, for instance, have great bridges, emphasizing that communication with wider regions was one factor in their development. The newly built bridge near Istanbul serves as a reminder of the role of water transportation in former trade links between Asia and Europe. Nevertheless, the historic qualities, seen in ancient and old buildings, in inherited street patterns, in former market squares and surviving walls, point to the role of the past as heritage. Even amid the fertile plains of Europe, historically dominated by villages, the constraints of private land ownership and a system of local written records have ensured the survival of village plans established nearly a thousand years ago to become the rural suburbs for the burnished residences of bankers and stockbrokers. In a similar way, not only is the life of a nineteenth-century wooden barn in Sweden or a stone farmstead in the north of England prolonged, but past settlement forms and patterns are adapted, revitalized, and absorbed into the present.

[*See also* Internal Migration; International Migration; *and* Settler Economies.]

BIBLIOGRAPHY

Braudel, Fernand. *The Mediterranean and the Mediterranean World in the* Age *of Philip II*. 2d rev. ed. London, 1966.

Chapelot, Jean, and Robert Fossier. *The Village and House in the Middle Ages*. London, 1985.

Harris, David R., ed. *The Origins and Spread of Agriculture and Pastoralism in Eurasia*. Washington, D.C., 1996.

Oppenheimer, Stephen. *Eden in the East*. London, 1998.

Pounds, Norman J. G. *An Economic History of Medieval Europe*. 2d ed. London and New York, 1994.

Roberts, Brian K. *Landscapes of Settlement: Prehistory to the Present*. London and New York, 1996.

BRIAN K. ROBERTS

SETTLER ECONOMIES are those established by migrants who bring institutions from another economy rather than adapt to pre-existing social and economic institutions in their new location. Their own institutions may be heavily adapted, either by the dropping of restrictions or by the accentuation of elements relevant to the new environment; for example, the United States, whose institutions had many British origins, offered greater economic freedom than did the United Kingdom, combined with slavery and its retention for decades after it was abolished in Europe.

Within Western economic history, the term *settler economies* has been primarily applied to the European settled portions of the Americas, Australasia, and Africa. From the sixteenth to the twentieth century, European settlers were attracted to these "empty lands" with expectations of increased wealth. Thus the phenomenon of settler economies was inextricably linked with the emergence of a world economic system centered on Europe, and the growth of such economies accelerated in the nineteenth and early twentieth centuries as this process reached its zenith. Settler economies are likely to have specific features of initial high-income levels, which may be brought back into line with origin country incomes by further labor migration, and of age structures associated with high participation rates and, possibly, high savings rates. Driven by needs of infrastructure or security, the state typically played a far more active developmental role in the new lands than it did within contemporaneous European home economies.

One strand of research literature focuses on the implications of specialization on natural resource exports. The staple approach is especially associated with such Canadian historians as Harold Innis (1930) and W. A. Mackintosh (1923), who analyzed the way the characteristics of successive staple exports (cod, fur, timber, wheat) shaped the pace and nature of Canada's economic development. The English seafarers John Cabot and his son Sebastian discovered both the east coast of Canada and the Grand Banks cod-fishing waters in the early 1500s; the fur trade led to extensive exploration of North America in the 1600s and 1700s but little European settlement; timber led to immigration, because of the excess capacity in the lumber boats of the early 1800s returning to Canada from Europe; and wheat led to sustained economic growth from the mid-1800s, from the beneficial externalities of the family farm for domestic demand, education, and so forth. The settlement of Siberia and the steppes by Russians between the seventeenth and the twentieth century may be analyzed in analogous terms. Douglass North (1961) applied a similar framework—emphasizing U.S. intraregional specialization among the South, the Northeast, and the West—in his cotton-burning export-engine model of economic growth in nineteenth-century United States.

Because settlers typically export the staple product to support their own living standards, based on high levels of imports from their country of origin, the staple theory has included analyses of the international economy—although before 1945, historians often conducted such analyses in terms of imperial history. Since then, economic historians led by Arthur Lewis (1978) and by Kevin O'Rourke and Jeffrey Williamson (1999) have modeled the international factor flows that were associated with the huge migrations of 1870 to 1913, when international capital markets were also well developed. In general, this type of research has found that labor migration played a major role in speeding up the factor price-equalization process, as vast areas were brought into efficient production and the global economy grew at historically unprecedented rates. Global capital markets then reinforced the process, as high investment rates in Canada, Argentina, Australia, and the United-

States during all or part of this period could be supported, irrespective of domestic savings rates. High income levels in successful settler economies were mainly driven by resource abundance, most obviously in gold-rush settings. The age structure of the settler populations, with a preponderance of working age males, reinforced the tendency for high incomes per head, even as an initial economic boom faded. Thus, for example, the Australian economy continued to enjoy the world's highest income per capita even as the economy diversified during the final third of the nineteenth century. Low dependency rates may have led to high savings rates, although this is debated, and its economic impact is unclear if capital remained mobile internationally.

A major differentiating feature between the more and the less successful settler economies appears to be the use made of resource rents. In parts of Latin America, for example, such rents were used to support an elite whose lifestyle was inimical to general economic development—a feudal-style village economy was maintained. In contrast, in Argentina, Australia, Canada, and elsewhere, a conscious strategy of import-substituting industrialization was pursued for several decades at the expense of the resource-abundant export sector; such a strategy incurred short-term resource allocation costs, but it established a modern industrial sector that was initially uncompetitive in world markets but has been capable of transformation. Questions continue to be debated about whether the short-term costs were justified by the long-term benefits, or whether the initial import-substituting phase was a necessary condition for the subsequent growth of more internationally competitive industries. Another differentiating feature has been the extent to which the imported institutions have been modified in ways conducive to economic growth. Mancur Olson (1996) has drawn attention to the importance of such events as translocation in leading to the relaxation of constraints on profit-seeking behavior, so that opportunities become seized rather than ignored (in Olson's graphic imagery, big bills are not left on the sidewalk). The United States provides the best example of that among the economies settled by Europeans since the 1500s. Settlers in both Australia and New Zealand focused more on the social aspects of their British heritage; this resulted in a protective state and a culture of equality for them, which discouraged "tall poppies" in most walks of life other than sport.

The research literature on settler economies has generally paid little attention to settlers' effects on indigenous populations. In less politically correct eras, the New World and Australia were often described as "empty lands" before European settlement. Most economic historians were content to leave the study of native societies to anthropologists, while analyses of the effect of European settlement were conducted mostly by epidemiologists, who studied the flow of pathogens between natives and settlers. The early

Canadian staple theorists were an exception, emphasizing the contrasting impact of the fur trade, which relied on cooperation with native peoples, and of extensive farming, which was incompatible with the native peoples' lifestyles. In this view, the contrast between the relatively benign Canadian treatment of native peoples and the early genocidal U.S. treatment is firmly tied to their differing staple products. Similar analysis could be applied to Australian settlers' brutal treatment of the Aborigines, whose hunting lands were taken for farms and sheep ranching, and to the differing treatment of indigenous populations in the fur and minerals regions of northern Siberia and in the steppelands, where Russian and, later, Soviet authorities killed or displaced millions of nomadic herders to promote settled agriculture. Relations between European settlers and indigenous peoples have been most fraught in the relatively densely settled areas of Africa and Asia, where small numbers of settlers had to coexist with large native populations. In some areas the settlers formed an enclave, which may have had little impact on native lifestyles, while in other areas there were major conflicts over land rights. The outcomes had vastly different implications for social systems in, for example, South Africa, Algeria, and New Zealand—whereas the European settlers were a short-term phenomenon with less lasting impact elsewhere in Africa and Asia.

Settler economies are neither a modern phenomenon nor just a European one. The earliest well-attested settler economies date from the Late Uruk period, of about 3000 BCE, when settlers from the Sumerian civilization moved up the Tigris and Euphrates rivers to establish new cities in northern Mesopotamia. One was Habuba Kabira, a planned city built on a virgin site (now in Syria), which stretches for over a kilometer along the Euphrates River; its construction methods and cultural assemblage were characteristic of southern Mesopotamian cities and were far more sophisticated than anything previously in the northern region. Archaeological finds, such as numeral tablets and clay seals (the hardware of trade) and bevel-rimmed bowls (the major mass-produced good of the era), indicate active trade by the settler economy, probably involving timber, which was then in short supply in southern Mesopotamia. Similar Late Uruk period expansion and settlement along the rivers was found at other sites, such as at Tell Brak and at Nineveh. There has been little attempt to apply theories derived in the context of modern economic history to the settler economies of ancient Mesopotamia or to the Classical-era Mediterranean world, although the well-documented Punic and Greek colonies in southern Italy and elsewhere had many economic similarities to the European colonies of two thousand years later. Analyses of such large-scale migrations or of the medieval settlement of eastern Europe by Western Europeans, tend to focus on the consideration of push and pull factors; they emphasize the population pressures in the regions of origin as much as the benefits to the migrants and the consequences for the new-found lands' economies.

Population pressures and imperialist desires for expansion have also been behind some twentieth-century settler movements, as in Southeast Asia, where Javanese settlers have moved to the outer islands of Indonesia, and in China, where Han Chinese have occupied historically Mongolian, Tibetan, and Uighur lands. The political implications of such economic developments have become more salient as the international community pays increasing attention to the rights of the indigenous peoples—notably Tibetans and East Timorese—in a way that was absent in earlier settler episodes.

[*See also* Economic Development; Economic Imperialism; *and* International Migration.]

BIBLIOGRAPHY

Denoon, Donald. *Settler Capitalism: The Dynamics of Dependent Development in the Southern Hemisphere*. Oxford, 1983.

Diamond, Jared. *Guns, Germs and Steel*. London, 1997. A biologist's perspective on settler economies.

Easterbrook, William, and Hugh Aitken. *Canadian Economic History*. Toronto, 1956. The best synthesis of the staple approach to Canadian economic development.

Hartz, Louis. *The Founding of New Societies*. New York, 1964. Essays on the United States, Latin America, South Africa, Canada, and Australia from a radical perspective.

Innis, Harold. *The Fur Trade in Canada: An Introduction to Canadian Economic History*. Toronto, 1930 (rev. ed. 1956).

Lewis, W. Arthur. *The Evolution of the International Economic Order*. Princeton, 1978. Lectures on the emergence of a global economy since 1850.

Macintosh, William. "Economic Factors in Canadian Economic History." *Canadian Historical Review* 4 (1923), 12–25. The classic early exposition of the staple approach to Canadian economic history.

McLean, Ian. "Saving in Settler Economies: Australian and North American Comparisons." *Explorations in Economic History* 31.4 (1994), 432–452.

North, Douglass. *The Economic Growth of the United States 1790–1860*. Englewood Cliffs, N.J., 1961.

Olson, Mancur. "Big Bills Left on the Sidewalk: Why Some Nations Are Rich and Others Poor." *Journal of Economic Perspectives* 10.2 (1996), 3–24.

O'Rourke, Kevin, and Jeffrey G. Williamson. *Globalization and History: The Evolution of a Nineteenth-Century Atlantic Economy*. Cambridge, Mass., 1999.

RICHARD POMFRET

SEVILLE. Located on the banks of the Guadalquivir River, with fluvial access to the Atlantic Ocean, and the center of a rich agricultural hinterland, Seville underwent numerous transformations under a diversity of rulers and political systems. An important Roman city in antiquity, Seville became a large urban economic center under Islam—certainly the leading city and economic depot in western Andalusia after the demise of the Córdoba caliphate in 1031 CE—and the putative capital of the kingdom of Castile after its conquest by Christian forces in 1248. In the early modern period, at the height of its opulence, the city became a great site for international trade, the gateway to the Americas, and, an economically vibrant industrial and agricultural component of Spain's modern economy.

Agriculture. Seville has long served as the head of a productive agricultural region. During the Islamic era, it reached its highest point under Almohad rule in the twelfth century. The heart of Seville's agricultural production was the Aljarafe region. The cultivation of wheat, various other cereals, wine, spices, and other products benefited from Muslim agricultural advancements, but olives and olive oil were the main staple and the basis of Seville's rural economy.

When the Christians conquered Seville in 1248 and established their rule throughout most of western Andalusia, the region was adversely affected by the departure of large numbers of Muslims and then the expulsion of the Mudejars (Muslims living under Christian rule) after their failed rebellion in 1264. The *repartimiento* of Seville (the partition of lands and houses among Christians that was undertaken by Ferdinand III and Alfonso X in the mid-thirteenth century) gives us a clear portrait of the way in which agricultural production was structured in that period: grain lands, orchards, vineyards, mills, and the profitable olive groves. Nonetheless, in the first century of the Reconquista, the region seldom matched the agricultural output of the Almohad period. Christians, migrating from the north and New Castile into Andalusia, did not have the technical skills to adopt the type of agriculture that was practiced in the south, with its emphasis on irrigation. Their experience with dry farming was useless in the newly conquered lands.

Unlike Valencia in the east, where Christian conquerors kept Muslims in semiservile conditions as agricultural labor, thus permitting the survival of Muslim rural practices and knowledge, the region of Seville experienced a century of demographic dearth and declining agricultural production. The expansion of the transhumance into Extremadura and, eventually, to the pasture lands in western Andalusia somewhat compensated for the decrease in agricultural production, but it was not a solution. The decline of agriculture from about 1250 to 1350 and demographic losses (from the expulsion of the Muslims and the return of many northern settlers to their places of origin) led, to the reemergence of Roman-style latifundia as the quintessential form of rural organization and production in the region. The consequence was the highest percentage of landless agricultural laborers (*jornaleros* or journeymen) in Iberia.

But the Sevillian countryside was too rich and important to suffer any permanent decline. By the late fourteenth century, the city was experiencing remarkable growth and was well under way to becoming the largest city on the peninsula before the opening of the Atlantic trade. This growth required a larger agricultural output, and the traditional staples of the region (grain, wine, and olives) underwent a vigorous revival. Supplying the city and eventually provisioning the great fleets that twice a year plied their trade between Seville and the Americas spurred the development of a profitable rural economy.

Manufacturing, Banking, and Trade. Under the Almohads, Seville became an important commercial center and a substantial exporter of a variety of agricultural and industrial goods. Its large market, the Alcaicería (covered market), served as the base for a far-flung export network. Sevillian products traveled north to Christian Spain and beyond to other western European realms. Textiles (including silks), wrought iron, fruits, spices, wine, and olive oil were the main staples of important north-south economic exchanges. During the Almohad period, Genoese merchants and bankers established a firm foothold in Seville and its countryside, placing the Andalusi economy within the Christian Mediterranean commercial networks. After the Christian conquest, Genoese and other Italian merchants solidified their position in the banking and commercial life of the city.

By the late fourteenth and early fifteenth centuries, Seville had become a thriving and growing city, with about 30,000 inhabitants before the discovery of the New World. With the opening of the Straits of Gibraltar to commercial sailing in the mid-fourteenth century and the deterioration of the land routes leading from Italy to northern France and Flanders (because of the disruptions of the Hundred Year War), Seville became an important link in the new commercial routes connecting Italy with England and Flanders via Iberian ports.

Seville and the Atlantic. With the discovery of the New World, Seville came to play a unique role in the Castilian and Atlantic world economy. All trade with America passed through Seville, and all those wishing to travel or migrate to the New World did so, theoretically, through the city. The Casa de Contratación, located in Seville, regulated and monitored all the traffic and economic exchange between Spain and its maritime colonies. This economic monopoly and the influx of precious metals into Seville propelled the city to new heights. Its population tripled by the late sixteenth century (to over 90,000 inhabitants), turning Seville into a cosmopolitan and chaotic city as well as the capital of Spanish commerce. This new scale brought increased difficulties in supplying the city, and its new wealth led to dazzling displays of opulence.

SEVILLE. View of the port, eighteenth century. (Maritime Museum, Seville, Spain/SEF/Art Resource, NY)

Even when the silting of the Guadalquivir prevented large ships from sailing into Seville—leading to the rise of Cádiz as the terminus for the Indies fleets—Seville did not falter. It remained the administrative center of the Spanish overseas empire and, eventually, of cigar making, publishing, and olive oil production throughout the early modern period. Thus, Seville remained, as it does to this very day, an important agricultural and industrial center.

BIBLIOGRAPHY

Carande, Ramón. *Sevilla, fortaleza y mercado: Las tierras, las gentes y la administración de la ciudad en el siglo XVI*. Seville, 1975.

Carmona Ruiz, María Antonia. *Usurpaciones de tierras y derechos comunales en Sevilla y su "tierra" durante el siglo XV*. Salamanca, 1995.

Collantes de Terán Sánchez, Antonio. *Sevilla en la baja edad media: La ciudad y sus hombres*. Seville, 1977.

García Fernández, Manuel. *El reino de Sevilla en tiempos de Alfonso XI (1312–1350)*. Seville, 1989.

González Jiménez, Manuel. *La repoblación de la zona de Sevilla durante el siglo XIV: Estudio y documentación*. 2d ed. Seville, 1951.

González, Julio. *Repartimiento de Sevilla*. Seville, 1951.

Morell Peguero, Blanca. *Mercaderes y artesanos en la Sevilla del descubrimiento*. Seville, 1986.

Pike, Ruth. *Aristocrats and Traders: Sevillian Society in the Sixteenth Century*. Ithaca, N.Y., 1972.

TEOFILO F. RUIZ

SHANGHAI. In the long history of Chinese civilization, the emergence of Shanghai as China's largest metropolis is relatively recent. Strategically located at the point where the Pacific meets China's longest river, the Yangzi, Shanghai was still a modest cotton handicraft market town with a population of more than two hundred thousand before 1840. Fifty years later, its population exceeded one million, making it China's largest city. By around 1930, it surged to more than three million inhabitants and became the world's fifth- or sixth-largest city at the time.

The economic weight of Shanghai far surpasses that of its population. From 1860 to 1936, Shanghai accounted for more than half of China's foreign trade and one-fifth of its shipping business, becoming the world's seventh largest port in 1931. Also in 1931, Shanghai absorbed 34 percent of the total foreign direct investment (FDI) in China and 67 percent of FDI in manufacturing. In 1933, Shanghai alone was responsible for about 40 percent of the national manufacturing output. By the 1920s and 1930s, Shanghai's financial district boasted Asia's highest concentration of banks, trading firms, currency, stocks, and commodity exchanges.

The rise of modern Shanghai had as much to do with geography as with history. Shanghai's hinterland, the Lower Yangzi delta, had traditionally been China's most economically and culturally advanced region. But before the mid-nineteenth century, Suzhou, which was situated at the base of the Grand Canal, was the major city in the region, and Shanghai was a minor market town on its periphery. The fortune of Shanghai turned when it became a treaty port open to foreign trade under the Treaty of Nanjing, signed after China's humiliating defeat in the Opium War of 1840–1842. The treaty granted Western powers access to Chinese markets as well as extraterritorial rights for their residents within the designated quarters (the so-called areas of International Settlement or Concession) in the treaty port.

But even among all the treaty ports, Shanghai stood out because its colonial authorities were most successful in expanding both the surface area and jurisdiction of their International Settlement over the course of time. By the 1910s, the combined area of International Settlement, which came about through a merger of the British and American quarters, and the French Concession was about 1.5 times the total size of all twenty-three areas of International Settlements in other treaty ports in China. Moreover, the colonial governments managed to impose on their territories a Western-style political system with the tripartite power structure of legislature, administration, and judiciary. They maintained their own troops and police, collected taxes, and built infrastructures, such as roads and port facilities. Shanghai became a defacto city-state, a "nation" within a nation.

The expansion of colonial territories in Shanghai invoked strong nationalist backlash among the Chinese residents. Partly to prevent further colonial expansion, Chinese citizens reorganized and remodeled municipal government in the Chinese part of the city, ironically, after the political institutions in the International Settlement. It was clear that the Western-style political institution did offer stronger rule of law, better enforcement of property rights, and more efficient governance. This strange mixture of three independent governments within one metropolis, combined with its status of neutrality and autonomy, turned out to be a blessing for Shanghai in a tumultuous modern China. Shanghai remained relatively peaceful and more often became a shelter for both Chinese and foreign refugees escaping civil unrest and wars. The city's distinctive multicultural character, freewheeling style of capitalism, and its associated image of decadence and debauchery earned it various legendary names, such as "the Paris in the Orient," or "a Paradise for the Adventurous."

Before 1895, Shanghai remained largely a commercial and trade city. It developed very quickly in the areas of banking, finance, trade, and shipping. But its industrial development, however, was severely constrained by the nature of the treaties that granted foreigners only the right to trade but not to manufacture. The Treaty of Shimoneseki, signed in 1896 following China's naval defeat by Japan, removed this restriction. The defeat also sent a wake-up call to the conservative Qing government. In the early 1900s, the Qing government made a crucial policy switch, instituting a series of reform measures to support private

SHANGHAI. Scene at the docks, between 1890 and 1923. (Burton Holmes/Frank and Frances Carpenter Collection/Prints and Photographs Division, Library of Congress)

enterpreneurship, largely abandoning its earlier policies of direct government sponsorship of industrializing China. These two factors combined to put Shanghai on a course toward becoming a major industrial city. The path became even easier following the outbreak of World War I, which greatly relieved the competitive pressure of manufacturing imports from a war-torn Europe.

Modern manufacturing expanded at a rapid pace after 1896. Undoubtedly, much of China's industrial expansion, which, according to available statistics for 1912–1936, occurred at a stunning annual rate of 9.4 percent, took place in Shanghai. Along with the massive increase in FDI, especially from a rapidly industrializing Japan, was the explosive growth of Chinese enterpreneurhsip. While banks, trading firms, and industrial corporations still clustered in the International Settlement, manufacturing plants tended to locate in the Chinese territory of the city because of its low rent. In 1933, Chinese-owned firms produced twice as much manufacturing output as foreign firms. By the

1920s and 1930s, Chinese entrepreneurs also made successful inroads into modern banking, real estate, foreign trade, and retail service—areas long dominated by foreign capital.

The composition of industrial output, while still dominated by the labor-intensive consumer goods, such as textile and food processing, began to evolve as machinery, chemical, and other producer goods expanded prominently toward the 1930s. The Shanghai-based industrialization also exerted a powerful impact on China, particularly the Lower Yangzi delta. Low value-added industries or sectors of industry began to outmigrate in search of lower factor cost. The massive outflow of industrial capital and entrepreneurship from Shanghai, for example, transformed the once modest market town of Wuxi (in the neighboring Jiangsu province) into China's fifth-largest city. In the 1920s and 1930s, Wuxi became known as "little Shanghai."

Capitalism in Shanghai suffered but nonetheless survived through Japan's full-scale invasion after 1937 and the period of hyperinflation under the rule of the Nationalist Party in the late 1940s. But the Communist takeover in 1950 brought fundamental changes to the city. Soon China's door swung shut again, and Shanghai's once industrial prowess was utilized and expanded under the ambitious state-sponsored industrialization program, with its population swelling to more than ten million by the 1970s. China's economic reform and reopening to the outside world in the late 1970s breathed fresh air into Shanghai. Since 1990, Shanghai has made remarkable progress toward reintegrating into a global economy that is drastically different from the one it had once had to turn its back on fifty years ago.

BIBLIOGRAPHY

Johnson, Linda Cooke. *Shanghai, from Market Town to Treaty Port, 1074–1858.* Stanford, Calif., 1995.
Johnstone Jr., William C. *The Shanghai Problem.* Westport, Conn., 1937.
Murhey, Rhoads. *Shanghai, Key to Modern China.* Cambridge, Mass., 1953.
Rawski, Thomas. *Economic Growth in Prewar China.* Berkeley, 1989.
Xiong, Y. Z., ed. *Shanghai Tongshi.* 8 vols. Shanghai, 1999.

DEBIN MA

SHARECROPPING. Sharecropping is a contract whereby agricultural workers exchange labor for a share of the crop. Despite their basic simplicity the terms of sharecropping contracts can vary enormously. For example, for the worker a contract may include housing, board, garden plots, use of livestock for private purposes, fuel from a woodlot, cash advances, credit at a commissary, *inter alia*. The amount shared can also vary. Moreover, it is important to keep in mind that the fertility of the soil and size of the sharecropped plot may vary. To assert that sharecropping

contracts are inflexible and not subject to economic conditions is a gross misreading of the historical record. In Europe, Asia, and South Africa the term *sharecropping* is used rather loosely and may apply to share tenants and sharecroppers. In the United States there is an economic and legal distinction between sharecroppers and share tenants. In Europe, long-term sharecropping was prevalent in agricultural contracting when labor cultivated vines—for example in Italy and Spain. In areas producing annual crops, as in South Africa, annual sharecropping contracts were the norm but they were frequently renewed.

Sharecropping in the United States. In the United States sharecropping arose after the demise of slavery and was rare outside of the South. It went hand in hand with the production of cotton and tobacco. Emancipation gave slaves their freedom over their labor services but it did not endow them with land or capital equipment. For the most part, plantation owners held on to their land and most of the complementary capital equipment, such as mules, cotton gins, and plows. In addition, former slaves did not have experience in purchasing inputs or selling the output. The question arose: How best should the ex-slaves and plantation owners contract for labor services? Experimentation is the best term for the arrangements tried in the early years following emancipation. The parties tried straight wages per year or per month along with team production whereby a percentage of the output was split among all workers. Contracting for wage workers on the entire plantation did not work out because of the high degree of monitoring labor effort that was required when labor effort was not linked to reward; that is, wage workers were paid by the month regardless of their effort over that month. Contracting with large teams also proved unsatisfactory because of the "free-rider problem." (The free-rider problem refers to people not bearing the full cost of their actions. In the case of agriculture, if a worker stints on his labor effort, causing output to be lower, he only bears the cost according to his share of the output but reaps the entire benefit without working as hard as others).

As a result of dissatisfaction with existing contractual arrangements some plantation owners experimented with paying the head of the household a share of the output on a plot that he (and his family) farmed exclusivity. As with previous arrangements, the plantation owner furnished the work stock, plows, and other capital equipment. The costs of seeds and fertilizers were frequently shared. This form of sharecrop contract proved successful, depending on the endowments of landlords and labor. For young agricultural workers without capital it seemed a better option than working for wages, both because sharecroppers generally made more than wage workers and because it entailed less direct hour-by-hour monitoring, always irksome

SHARECROPPING. Sharecropper at work on a tobacco farm near Manning, South Carolina, 1939. (Marion Post Walcott/Prints and Photographs Division, Library of Congress)

to workers but particularly so in the racist environment following the demise of slavery. On the landlords' side, they were able to dispense with some amount of costly monitoring as well as shift some of the output risk to laborers.

Sharecropping has an important legal distinction from share tenancy. The Georgia Supreme Court in 1872 clearly articulated that sharecroppers are wage workers paid their wages with a share of the crop. The landlord had the right to the crop and owed the sharecropper a share of the output. On the other hand, a share tenant had the right to the crop and owed the landlord a share of the output. This legal distinction mattered when sharecroppers had outstanding debts because the landlord first took his share of the output before the creditor, typically a country merchant, could claim the output as payment for a sharecropper's debt. In addition, share tenants had the right to be on the land at their discretion, whereas the right of occupancy and use of land by sharecroppers was at the discretion of the landlord.

Sharecropping became a more popular form of contracting over time but it never drove the other forms—wage and tenant contracts—out of existence. We do not have systematic evidence on sharecropping until the 1920 Census of Agriculture. Prior to 1920, the census categorized sharecroppers as share tenants. The scattered evidence that we have indicated that sharecropping was increasing relative to other forms of contracting. From a study of plantations in Georgia conducted in 1911, sharecropping contracts accounted for approximately 50 percent of the contracts, tenant contracts represented 35 percent, and wage contracts 15 percent. Alston and Kauffman (1977) published state level estimates of sharecroppers for 1900 and 1910. They found that sharecroppers increased in both census years in the U.S. South. The aggregate number of sharecroppers continued to increase, peaking with the 1930 Census, after which sharecropping began to decline. After the 1960 Census of Agriculture the prevalence of sharecropping decreased to such an extent that the Census no longer collected the number of farms operated by sharecroppers. A convincing explanation is that the advent of the mechanical cottonpicker brought the era of sharecroppers to a close.

The Economic Rationale for Sharecropping. The economic basis of sharecropping (and share tenancy) is that it reduces the monitoring costs associated with wage contracts and redistributes output risk. For many but not all workers with some experience but no capital, sharecropping was a step on the way toward becoming a tenant. Some people have claimed that sharecropping was inefficient, but they were comparing it to a nirvana world of zero monitoring costs. For efficiency the marginal revenue product of labor should be equal to the opportunity cost of labor. In other words, workers will work until the addition to value due to effort is equal to the additional value of their leisure from not working. Because sharecroppers receive only a share of the output they will stop working when the additional amount they receive is equal to the additional value of their leisure. The implication is that sharecroppers will work too little and hence sharecropping is inefficient. The fallacy in the argument is that sharecroppers will work much harder than wage workers, who are paid by a unit of time (hour, day, month, or year). In practice both sharecroppers and wage workers are monitored, but sharecroppers require less monitoring. Because contracts are typically negotiated annually, sharecroppers will work diligently to impress the landlord and have their contracts renewed. The stimulus for increased effort is greater if landlords are able to compare the output of multiple sharecroppers on homogeneous land.

The inefficiency argument also holds for share tenants but the alleged inefficiency would be less because share tenants receive a greater share of the output than sharecroppers and hence would work harder without monitoring. Share tenants do require less monitoring. The reason they received a greater share of the output is because they usually provided their own work stock (generally owned but at times rented). The greater share received represents largely a payment for the tenant's supply of capital, but also a return to the tenant for his human capital, for the lower monitoring costs borne by the landlord, and for the absorption of more risk.

Sharecropping and Poverty. Sharecropping has also been blamed for poverty. This argument is not specific to the United States. Sharecropping has been blamed for the relatively low standards of living of sharecroppers in some countries in early modern Europe (e.g., Italy, France, and Spain) as well as in the highlands in present-day Peru, and in parts of Asia and Africa. It is true that poverty went hand in glove with sharecropping, but not because of any particular aspects arising from the incentives of the contract. Rather, much of the poverty of sharecroppers resulted from a lack of education and living in racial- and/or class-dominated societies. In the United States the agricultural elite in the South benefited from keeping educational expenditures low. (The same argument holds for much of Latin America, Asia, and Africa.) This reduced the opportunities for migration for poor black and white agricultural laborers. In the United States, with poor immigrants flooding into the North until the restrictions on immigration in the 1920s, migration to the North without a skill did not promise a high return. Keeping the supply of labor

large in the South meant that the return to all laborers was low in absolute terms.

The extant evidence indicates that black and white sharecroppers received the same wages, but blacks faced greater hurdles in ascending the agricultural ladder. Because of racism, blacks were more likely than whites to be cheated by unscrupulous landlords or country merchants. Neither black nor white sharecroppers had much hope of legal recourse against a powerful landlord. Of course, competition among landlords for workers more than any fear of the law limited the amount of cheating and helped sharecroppers ascend the agricultural ladder. Not all climbed to owner, but a significant percentage of sharecroppers succeeded. By 1880 25 percent of black farm operators (sharecroppers, tenants, and owners) in the South owned the land that they farmed. Given the starting conditions fifteen years earlier and the social and legal environment, this is a laudable accomplishment.

[*See also* Agricultural Rents; Tenant Farming; *and* Tenant Right.]

BIBLIOGRAPHY

Alston, Lee J., and Joseph P. Ferrie. "Paternalism in Agricultural Contracts in the U.S. South: Implications for the Growth of the Welfare State." *American Economic Review* 83 (1993), 852–876.

Alston, Lee J., and Joseph P. Ferrie. *Paternalism and the American Welfare State: Economics, Politics, and Institutions in the U.S. South, 1865–1965.* Cambridge, 1999.

Alston, Lee J., and Robert Higgs. "Contractual Mix in Southern Agriculture since the Civil War: Facts, Hypotheses and Tests." *Journal of Economic History* 42 (1982), 327–353.

Alston, Lee J., and Kyle D. Kauffman. "Were Postbellum Agricultural Labor Markets Competitive?" *Explorations in Economic History* 38.1 (2001), 181–194.

Alston, Lee J., and Kyle D. Kauffman. "Agricultural Chutes and Ladders: New Estimates of Sharecroppers and 'True Tenants' in the South, 1900–1920." *Journal of Economic History* 57 (1997), 464–575.

Alston, Lee J., and Kyle D. Kauffman. "Up, Down, and Off the Agricultural Ladder: New Evidence and Implications of Agricultural Mobility for Blacks in the Postbellum South." *Agricultural History* 72 (1998), 263–279.

Atack, Jeremy. "Tenants and Yeoman in the Nineteenth Century." *Agricultural History* 62 (1988), 6–232.

Atack, Jeremy. "The Agricultural Ladder Revisited: A New Look at an Old Question with Some Data for 1860." *Agricultural History* 63 (1989), 1–25.

Black, John D., and R. H. Allen. "The Growth of Farm Tenancy in the United States." *The Quarterly Journal of Economics* 51 (1937), 393–425.

Brandt, Karl. "Fallacious Census Terminology and Its Consequences in Agriculture." *Social Research: An International Quarterly of Political and Social Science* 5 (1938), 19–36.

Carmona, Juan, and James Simpson. "The 'Rabassa Morta' in Catalan Viticulture: The Rise and Decline of a Long-Term Sharecropping Contract, 1670–1920s." *Journal of Economic History* 59 (June 1999), 290–315.

Cohen, J. S., and F. L. Galassi. "Sharecropping and Productivity: Feudal Residues in Italian Agriculture, 1911." *Economic History Review* 43 (1990), 646–656.

Ferleger, Louis. "Sharecropping Contracts in the Late-Nineteenth-Century South." *Agricultural History* 67 (1993), 31–46.

Galassi, F. L. "Tuscans and Their Farms: The Economics of Share Tenancy in Fifteenth-Century Florence." *Rivista di Storia Economica* 9 (1992), 77–94.

Hibbard, Benjamin H. "Tenancy in the Southern States." *Quarterly Journal of Economics* 27 (1913), 482–496.

Higgs, Robert. *Competition and Coercion: Blacks in the American Economy, 1865–1914.* Chicago, 1977.

Higgs, Robert. "Race, Tenure and Resource Allocation in Southern Agriculture, 1910." *Journal of Economic History* 33 (1973), 149–169.

Hoffman, P. "The Economic Theory of Sharecropping in Early Modern France." *Journal of Economic History* 44 (1984), 309–319.

Hopcroft, Rosemary L. *Regions, Institutions, and Agrarian Change in European History.* Ann Arbor, 1999.

Irwin, James R., and Anthony P. O'Brien. "Where Have All the Sharecroppers Gone? Black Occupations in Postbellum Mississippi." *Agricultural History* 72 (1998), 280–297.

Jeeves, A. H., and J. Crush. *White Farms, Black Labour: The State and Agrarian Change in South Africa, 1910–1950.* Pietermaritzburg, South Africa, 1997.

Jones, P. J. "Medieval Agrarian Society in Its Prime: Italy." In *The Cambridge Economic History of Europe*, vol. 1, edited by M. M. Postan and H. J. Habakkuk, pp. 340–430. Cambridge, 1964.

Kauffman, Kyle D. "Why Was the Mule Used in Southern Agriculture? Empirical Evidence of Principal-Agent Solutions." *Explorations in Economic History* 30 (1993), 336–351.

Reid, Joseph D., Jr. "Sharecropping as an Understandable Market Response: The Post-Bellum South." *Journal of Economic History* 33 (1973), 106–130.

Reid, Joseph D., Jr. "Sharecropping in History and Theory." *Agricultural History* 49 (1975), 426–440.

Shlomowitz, Ralph. "The Origins of Southern Sharecropping." *Agricultural History* 53 (1979), 557–575.

van Onselen, Charles. *The Seed Is Mine: The Life of Kas Maine, A South African Sharecropper, 1894–1985.* New York, 1996.

Woodman, Harold D. "Post-Civil War Southern Agriculture and the Law." *Agricultural History* 53 (1979), 319–337.

Woodman, Harold D. *New South: New Law.* Baton Rouge, 1995.

Wright, Gavin. *Old South, New South: Revolutions in the Southern Economy since the Civil War.* New York, 1986.

LEE J. ALSTON

SHEEP AND GOATS. Sheep and to a lesser extent goats constituted an important element of a mixed-husbandry system employed by most rural dwellers (*rustici-pagani*) in the Middle Ages and the early-modern period. Organized in ewe-flocks, they provided the rural population with meat (ram-lambs), milk, manure, hides, and coarse wool. In most cases, wool was plucked rather than shorn from the skins of dead animals (wool fells, morlings, shorlings, and lentenware), providing raw materials, after rock spinning, for textile producers of worsteds. Within prevailing patterns of animal husbandry, this was the most stable element in changing conditions, both spatially and temporally, of pastoral land availability. In northern Europe, conditions of abundant pastoral land availability existed universally during the so-called Dark Ages (c. 400–1100 CE) and survived thereafter in western Europe from 1370 to 1520, and in central Europe continuously until circa 1500. Archaeological finds of animal bone, from this period of abundant pasture, suggest a marked subordination of sheep in relation to either cattle or horses in extensive patterns of animal husbandry. In southern Europe, North Africa and Asia Minor, on the other hand, where pastoral activity was restricted to sparse alpine pastures or sun-parched plains, the sheep and goats, capable of feeding on such stunted grass growth, enjoyed a far wider hegemony.

Agrarian Systems. When population pressure led to an extension of arable activity at the expense of pastoral reserves, across northwestern and southern Europe (1100–1370 and after 1520), these pastoral lands had a new economic value. Both arable farmers and their pastoral counterparts assumed a functional division and spatial delineation between these activities. In northwestern Europe, the once seemingly limitless upland and marshland reserves of pastoral land were for the first time (1100–1370) subject to a process of spatial delineation and jurisdictional definition. Such lands, enhanced in value, were divided up between lords and peasants, now functionally differentiated from their counterparts in the plain. The latter had the resources (hay from high-value meadowlands, concentrates in the form of brewing lees, postharvest stubble, and limited common grazing, which was continuously being eroded by the extension of arable land) to maintain necessary stocking levels on their holdings. However, they lacked sufficient land for rearing such stock. Plow animals (horses and cattle, the latter also being the peasants' main source of meat when too old to serve as work animals) had to be purchased.

A reduction in sheep numbers also caused a diminution in available indigenously produced supplies of raw materials for textile production and necessitated buying such wares. The source of such animal products now became upland and marsh grasslands. These years saw in these regions the proliferation of lordly studs and vaccaries (providing horses and oxen, respectively, for draught animals) and great demesne flocks of sheep, which roamed the extensive pastures and were the main source of high-quality wool.

This regionally specialized production of high-quality wool took place within a quite distinct organizational system of flock management. Operating within a genetically heterogeneous and functionally undifferentiated animal population, the production of high-quality wool at this time rested not on the creation of distinct breeds of wool animals but on the development of lordly wether (castrated male sheep) "flying"-flocks. Such flocks, composed of a small breeding element and an extended number of wethers, though able to maintain their size, were not easily expanded or contracted. To enjoy this flexibility in a

SHEEP AND GOATS. Hand scroll by Chao Meng-fu (1254–1322), Yüan dynasty, China. (Freer Gallery of Art, Smithsonian Institution, Washington, D.C.: Purchase, F1931.4)

constantly changing market situation, however, the lord existed in a symbiotic relationship with his peasant neighbors operated on the basis of ewe-flocks. In boom conditions characterized by rising pastoral rents, peasants met their rent obligations by selling the lords their ram-lambs for incorporation into the wether-flock, while maintaining or expanding flock size by the retention of ewe lambs. During slumps, as rents fell, the peasants reduced their sales of ram-lambs, which in these conditions would be raised to grace their tables. The peasants thus continued to satisfy their consumption and cash requirements from a ewe-flock producing meat/cash (ram-lambs), milk, manure, hides, and coarse wool. Such was not the case with demesne "flying"-flocks, which fulfilled the specialized function of high-quality shorn wool production for the "new" specialized European woolen-cloth manufacturers.

In southern Mediterranean Europe the situation was somewhat different. Population growth here (1100–1370 and after 1520) tended to be concentrated in the towns or fortified hill villages. This posed major grain-provisioning problems, which in part at least were satisfied within an international context. Overseas imports of grain to the great cities of Mediterranean Europe, however, rarely if ever comprised more than 10–15 percent of urban consumption. The onus of maintaining urban grain supplies thus tended to fall upon the cities' *contada*, where cereal producers operated within a transhumance system of husbandry. On the eastern, western, and southern borderlands of the region this took place within a nomadic context involving wholesale movements of peoples. Occupying the steppe lands on the margins of the great deserts during the winter seasons, they grazed their flocks of sheep and goats on the extensive but sparse grasslands of these lands, pre-

vailing climatic conditions determining the extent and intensity of their intraregional nomadic movements. With desiccation of this grazing during the summer, however, they were forced to migrate to the adjacent alpine grasslands (in the North African Tell, Anatolian plateau, and Crimean Mountains). Here their flocks grazed and manured the land, ensuring an abundant harvest not only of grain but also of pharmacopoeia the following year.

Within the Mediterranean lands bounded by these nomadic societies, transhumance activity took place in a somewhat different form conditioned by the prevailing feudal systems. The basic functional dichotomy between flock structures, found farther north, repeated itself here. As the eighteenth-century naturalist Guillame Bowles wrote, Spain has "two species of sheep: the first kind whose wool is ordinary, spend their lives in one place, do not change pastures, and return every night to the sheepfold; the others, which have fine wool, travel every year, and after spending the summer in the mountains go down to the warm meadows of the southern parts of the kingdom." (1776, p. 70) Yet, for the first time, this differentiation also had a genetic basis. "Itinerant" sheep since the fourteenth century had been a separate and distinct breed—the merino, a cross-bred Spanish-Berber wool sheep. The organizational deployment of these animals took place in a very different environment from that farther north. On the extensive, underpopulated, and climatically marginal lands of La Mancha, Extramadura, and Andalusia in Spain, or the similar plains of the Morea, Naples, and Sicily where erratic rainfall made intensive tillage extraordinarily precarious, the great seigniorial latifundia provided a home each winter for the vast flocks of sheep. These animals manured the land before their departure in the spring, thus allowing it to be prepared for cropping on the basis of a "field-grass" husbandry.

This system prevented soil erosion by retaining water residue over the summer in the root systems of the extensive grass cover, and it allowed a spatially limited but high-yield (20–30:1 in contrast to the northern European 4:1) agriculture to be practiced. It was complemented by the husbandry practices of the peasant villagers on the fringes on the dry plain, who supplemented their incomes by providing harvest-time labor on the great latifundia. They also practiced an intensive mixed husbandry, supplementing the limited manure supplies provided by sheep folding by utilizing the manure provided by the animals in transit in spring and autumn between the mountains and the plains.

Innovations. Agrarian systems continued to prevail until at least the mid-nineteenth century; but as population numbers increased, there was a tendency for the pastoral reserves of the peasantry to be eroded and the great southern European latifundia to be broken up for an extensive arable regime—with disastrous effects. Only by a shift of animal husbandry to the margins of the continent were most European towns able to maintain their meat supplies and then mainly in the form of cattle rather than sheep or goats. From circa 1470 to circa 1830, great herds of cattle were driven each year from Scotland, Wales, Ireland, Denmark, Hungary, and the lands of the Trans-Pontine steppe to the great European metropolitan centers. Only with the subsequent decline of these overland trades after circa 1830 were wool-sheep introduced alongside peasant breeds into these marginal lands—the merino into New Russia and the Black-face and Cheviot to Scotland in the context of "The Clearances."

From circa 1470 to circa 1830, cattle predominated in these lands. Yet in transit to their point of final consumption, these cattle required feeding grounds, and on arrival at their final destination grazing was needed where they could be fattened up. Such lands in the prevailing agrarian regime were becoming harder to find. Innovation in the form of a system of "up and down" or "convertible" husbandry in northwestern Europe, however, transformed this situation. Sown leys provided a rich grassland sward, which, after heavy stocking, could be broken up by plow, and the heavily manured land produced abundant supplies of cereal (yielding 1:15–20) and cleaning (flax, tobacco) crops. By the eighteenth century this system of husbandry, established in Britain, the northern and southern Netherlands, and south Germany, provided abundant supplies of animal feed (grass, hay, and, where barley provided the basis for a brewing industry, concentrates in the form of lees) for the cattle crossing these lands. Grassland management, however, also required a new mixed-animal-husbandry practice. An even grazing of the rich grassland leys necessitated not only stocking with cattle that fed on long grass but also sheep that cropped the lesser sward.

A new system of flock management emerged. Freed from the necessity of cattle rearing on the new northwestern European "farms," sheep numbers increased and were subject to a process of functional specialization as animals were increasingly bred for meat rather than wool. Wool markets from circa 1470 to circa 1830 were accordingly transformed. Until the eighteenth century, the best-quality wool still came from the transhumance flocks of the Mediterranean lands, which thereafter were supplemented by southern Russian supplies. A lower-quality but more abundant supply of wool was now available from the "new" northwestern farms practicing convertible husbandry. While the burgeoning Netherlands and to a lesser extent British textile manufacturing industries continued to import supplies of high-quality Spanish and later Russian wool, most producers drew on supplies of cheap, lesser-quality local wool, from which they made textiles that at this time established a worldwide hegemony. By the 1830s, however, demand for these raw materials was beginning to outstrip supply, creating a problem that even the extension of sheep farming into new marginal lands could not resolve. As wool (and flax) thus increased in price, textile manufacturers replaced these raw materials with a new one—cotton—a price-elastic commodity that now swept all before it. Wool henceforth lost its primacy in textile markets.

Sheep farming also changed fundamentally. In the context of the emergence of a global economy, the focus of wool production again shifted—to the great merino flocks of Australia and New Zealand, which became the principal supplier of European markets, and to the United States. Subject to a heavy fall in prices, in "free trade" Britain and the Netherlands farmers abandoned the production of wool, henceforth developing new breeds of sheep predominantly for the domestic meat market. Elsewhere in Europe, where farming was protected by tariffs, animal numbers in general and sheep in particular rapidly declined.

[*See also* Livestock Leases; Pastoralism; *and* Wool Industry.]

BIBLIOGRAPHY

Bowden, Peter J. *The Wool Trade in Tudor and Stuart England.* London, 1962.

Bowles, Guillame. *Introduction à l'histoire naturelle et à la géographie physique de l'Espagne.* Translated from the Spanish by Vicomte de Flavigny. Paris, 1976.

Klein, Julius. *The Mesta: A Study in Spanish Economic History, 1273–1836.* Cambridge, Mass., 1920.

Lopez, Roberto S. "The Origin of the Merino Sheep." *Jewish Social Studies Publication* 5 (1953), 161–168.

Power, Eileen. *The Wool Trade in English Medieval History.* Oxford, 1940.

Ryder, Michael Lawson. *Sheep and Man*. London, 1983.
Trow-Smith, Robert. *A History of British Livestock Husbandry to 1700*. London, 1957.

IAN BLANCHARD

SHERMAN ACT. *See* Antitrust.

SIAM. *See* Thailand.

SIEMENS FAMILY. The Siemens company is a global leader in electronics and electrical engineering with a presence in over 190 countries worldwide. Founded in 1847 as the Siemens & Halske Telegraph Construction Company, it was originally a purely family business organized along straightforward lines. Its development was steered by the dominating personality of its founder, Werner von Siemens, and the influence of the Siemens family.

Werner von Siemens (1816–1892) laid the foundations for the company's success through his inventions, and made it into an industry pioneer. His discovery of the dynamo-electric principle in 1866, based on Faraday's work, represented a breakthrough for power generation. However, his importance as an entrepreneur went beyond his formulation of fundamental discoveries; he was a scientist and businessman who developed his inventions into marketable products and overall solutions. The completion of extremely demanding and risky projects such as the construction of the Indo-European Telegraph Line from London to Calcutta and the laying of transatlantic cables gave the company an international reputation.

A significant factor in the company's success was the close-knit network of loyal and capable supervisory employees from within the family who could also fill key positions abroad. This reflected the founder's wish to set up a worldwide enterprise, like that of the Fuggers, that he regarded as his personal realm and a family affair. Thus Werner's younger brothers Wilhelm (1823–1883), and Carl (1829–1906) played outstanding roles in the company. Shortly after it was founded, they established subsidiaries in England and Russia and contributed greatly to the expansion of its international business. All three brothers were knighted: Wilhelm (Sir William) by Queen Victoria of England, Carl by Russian Tsar Nicholas II, and Werner by German Emperor Friedrich III.

Siemens & Halske was the undisputed leader of the German electrical industry until the 1880s, but the industry began to change in response to technological advances. A family business with a limited capital base could no longer compete with stock corporations such as AEG, founded in 1883. However, the family principle and the desire for autonomy and independence led Werner von Siemens to reject the idea of changing the company's legal form, as this would have meant relinquishing family control.

A new orientation had to wait until Werner passed the helm of the company to his sons Arnold (1853–1918) and Wilhelm (1855–1919) and his brother Carl, as personally liable partners. The company was converted into a stock corporation in 1897, but the family continued to be the almost exclusive shareholder. Company articles were reformulated to retain the control previously exercised by the personally liable partners, by binding the managing board to the directives of the chairman of the supervisory board, who was a member of the family. Even after the German Stock Corporation Law came into force in 1937, the traditional form of management was preserved, although legally the chairman's directives were now merely suggestions or recommendations.

The founder's sons followed their father's policy of developing the business with technological innovations. Advances in lighting, medical engineering, wireless communications, and domestic appliances are early examples, which were followed after World War II by developments in components, data systems, automotive engineering, and semiconductors. The company's twin mainstays were communications technology and power engineering (power generation and distribution). The founding of Siemens-Schuckertwerke (SSW) in 1903 by merging the power-engineering activities of Siemens & Halske with Schuckertwerke made Siemens a global industry leader before World War I.

After World War I and the deaths of Werner's two older sons, Arnold (1918) and Wilhelm (1919), the helm of the company passed to Carl Friedrich von Siemens (1872–1941), Werner's third and youngest son. As chairman of the supervisory boards of both parent companies, Siemens & Halske and Siemens-Schuckertwerke, he steered the company during the difficult period of the Weimar Republic and the rise of National Socialism. All his strategic decisions focused on preserving the unity of the company, which limited itself to electrical engineering but handled all that industry's sectors. Siemens again became a global leader in the mid-1920s. Apart from his commitment to the company, Carl Friedrich played a part in national politics as a parliamentary deputy for the German Democratic Party and was involved in numerous business associations. When the National Socialists came to power in 1933, he resigned all his official positions.

When Carl Friedrich died (1941), his nephew Hermann von Siemens (1885–1986) took over as chairman of the supervisory boards of the two companies, a post he held until 1956. However, his room to maneuver was limited by World War II and its aftermath. The postwar reconstruction phase was followed by technological advances, new sectors of activity, and the recovery of traditional export markets, which enabled the company to regain its global position by the mid-1960s. Hermann's nephew and Werner's grandson Ernst von Siemens (1903–1990) was largely responsible for reconstructing Siemens & Halske AG after 1945 and moving its headquarters to Munich. He also merged the parent companies of Siemens & Halske, Siemens-Schuckertwerke, and Siemens-Reiniger-Werke, founded in 1932 as a branch of the electro-medical business, in 1966 to create Siemens AG. A major restructuring program introduced in 1966 was concluded in 1971 when Peter von Siemens (1911–1986), a great-grandson of the founder, became chairman of the supervisory board of Siemens AG, a post he held until 1981.

The history of the Siemens company typifies the development of a family business from a personal enterprise in the era of the company founder, to an entrepreneurial enterprise owned largely by the proprietor family, and then to a managerial enterprise, a large stock corporation with broad public ownership. Although the founding family steered the company's strategic orientation from its beginnings, it continues to be the largest shareholder without playing an active role. The family and its foundations own almost 7 percent of the capital stock. Their interests are concentrated in an asset-management company headed by Peter von Siemens (born 1937), a great-great-grandson of the company founder, formerly a member of the managing board of Siemens AG and now a member of the supervisory board.

BIBLIOGRAPHY

Feldenkirchen, Wilfried. *Werner von Siemens—Erfinder und internationaler Unternehmer*. 2d revised and enlarged ed. Munich and Zurich, 1996. English translation: *Werner von Siemens—Inventor and International Entrepreneur*. Columbus, Ohio, 1994.

Feldenkirchen, Wilfried. *Siemens, 1918–1945*. Munich and Zurich, 1995. English translation: *Siemens, 1918 to 1945*. Columbus, Ohio, 1999.

Feldenkirchen, Wilfried. *Siemens—Von der Werkstatt zum Weltunternehmen*. Munich and Zurich, 1997. English translation: *Siemens—From Workshop to Global Player*. Munich and Zürich, 2000.

Siemens, Georg. *Der Weg der Elektrotechnik: Geschichte des Hauses Siemens*. 2 vols. 2d ed. Freiburg and Munich, 1961. English translation: *History of the House of Siemens*. 2 vols. Freiburg and Munich, 1957. Reprinted, New York, 1977.

Siemens, Werner von. *Lebenserinnerungen*. 18th ed., Munich, 1986. English translation: *Inventor and Entrepreneur—Recollections of Werner von Siemens*. 2d ed., London and Munich, 1966.

Sir William Siemens: A Man of Vision. London, 1993.

WILFRIED FELDENKIRCHEN

SIEMENS-MARTIN PROCESS, a steelmaking method first applied in the 1860s, also known as the acid open-hearth process. It was characterized by pig iron and scrap input to a Siemens furnace. The earlier Siemens process was defined by the use of a reverberatory, regenerative Siemens furnace with pig iron and iron ore input. Reverberatory meant that a low wall inside a long, shallow furnace separated the fuel from the charge. Regenerative meant that hot exhaust gases were used to preheat the fresh air coming into the combustion chamber by piping both flows of air through the same bricks. Hot input air (400°C or more) saved fuel and raised the furnace temperature to the extent that no stirring was required. Charles William Siemens, of the famous German engineering family, had used furnaces like this for glassmaking starting in 1861. The Siemens process could make steel by taking pig iron and iron ore as input.

The Siemens process was improved when French ironmaster Pierre Martin added scrap iron to the bath instead of iron ore. The resulting Siemens-Martin process was developed and patented in the mid-1860s by Pierre Martin and his brother Émile and by C. W. Siemens. Siemens-Martin steel eventually became commercially successful and displaced Bessemer steel. The resulting method, in brief, was to receive liquid pig iron (or melt it) in the furnace, creating a "bath," then add scrap or puddled wrought iron, then add spiegeleisen or ferromanganese, and heat.

The mass-production alternative, the Bessemer converter, blew air through the molten pig iron in a converter to burn away carbon. The key reason Siemens-Martin steel tended to take over from Bessemer was that it was heated at length, usually eight or more hours, whereas Bessemer converters completed a "blow" in nine to fifteen minutes. The Bessemer process was hard to control precisely because it was not possible to sample the charge at an intermediate stage, and a few seconds could make a difference in the final carbon content. In contrast, it was relatively straightforward to control the timing of the Siemens-Martin process and to test the molten metal along the way. This was done sometimes by drawing a small ladleful to form an ingot, allowing it to cool, then hammering the ingot. A culture of refined and scientific control built up around the Siemens-Martin process. Another advantage of the long heating process was that the output was highly homogeneous, whereas Bessemer steel could have variations within it that led to cracking. Indeed, by the late 1880s, Bessemer steel was unwelcome for structural members in U.S. building contracts.

Other controlled ways of making steel existed (cementation, blister, crucible, or shear steel), but these were labor-intensive. A puddled steel had been made in Europe, but its quality was lower.

The Siemens-Martin process required the use of pig iron with little phosphorus content. A later (1878–1879) invention of the Gilchrist-Thomas alkaline adaptation (the basic open-hearth process) could use phosphoric ore. Use of one or the other depended on the ore available.

Because of Siemens-Martin and related inventions, the price of steel fell at least 5 percent a year on average, and the volume purchased rose about 10 percent a year, from the 1860s through the 1890s.

BIBLIOGRAPHY

Burn, Duncan. *The Economic History of Steelmaking, 1867–1939: A Study in Competition.* Cambridge, 1940.

Gordon, J. E. *The Science of Structures and Materials.* New York, 1988.

Landes, David. *The Unbound Prometheus.* Cambridge, 1969.

McHugh, Jeanne. *Alexander Holley and the Makers of Steel.* Baltimore, 1980.

Misa, Thomas J. *A Nation of Steel: The Making of Modern America, 1865–1925.* Baltimore, 1995.

Rosenberg, Nathan. *Inside the Black Box.* Cambridge, 1983.

Stoughton, Bradley. *The Metallurgy of Iron and Steel.* 2d ed. New York, 1911.

Temin, Peter. *Iron and Steel in Nineteenth-Century America.* Cambridge, Mass., 1964.

PETER BENJAMIN MEYER

SILK CULTIVATION. *See* Sericulture.

SILK INDUSTRY *[This entry contains three subentries, a historical overview and discussions of technological change and industrial organization and the state. The bibliography for this entry can be found at the end of the last subentry.]*

Historical Overview

The silk thread is secreted by an insect, the *Bombyx mori*, to protect itself in a cocoon while transforming itself into a moth. The insect, now purely a domesticated creature, must be hatched from eggs produced in the previous season, and raised by feeding it on mulberry leaves until it spins the cocoons. Then the thread is wound up (or "reeled") in hot water, to dissolve the gum that holds the cocoon together. The raw silk is usually strengthened (thrown) by joining and twisting, producing several different types of yarn, which can be used for weft (the tram) and for warp (the organzine). Finally, the silk is woven or otherwise processed to produce cloths, ribbons, knitwear, and whatever else consumers want. Thus, the silk "industry" consists of four distinct stages: the production of cocoons or sericulture (which includes mulberry growing and silkworm raising), the production of silk or reeling, the production of yarn or throwing, and the production of silk wares or weaving. The process has always been highly labor-intensive, and the total world supply of silk and silk wares has usually been artificially constrained by state regulations. The unit price thus has always been high enough to make long-distance trade viable even with the most backward transport technolo-

gies. The history of silk production is deeply entwined with that of trade.

Early Development. Archeological remains from northern China date the origin of silk production to sometime between 2850 and 2650 BCE. China would remain the largest producer and consumer of silk and silk wares until the late nineteenth century. For half this period, about two thousand years, it was also the only producer of raw silk. It exported raw silk and silk wares to neighboring countries, but the export of silkworm eggs was strictly forbidden. The Chinese monopoly broke down during a period of political turmoil around 200–300 BCE. Silkworm eggs were smuggled eastward to Korea, westward to Central Asia, and possibly southward toward India (Bengal). Actually, some early literary Indian sources mention silk production around 1300–1400 BCE, but they probably refer to other species of insects, which produced an inferior type of silk (called tussah). A second wave of diffusion of sericulture started around 300–400 CE, and spread southwards toward Central China (the area around Shanghai); and it also began in Japan, in the central provinces of the Isle of Honshu. In spite of claims by traditional Japanese sources, it is most likely that Japanese silk production was imported from China. About a century later, in 552–556 CE, two monks succeeded in smuggling some silkworm eggs to Byzantium, which was to remain the center of silk production in the Western Hemisphere for some centuries. The Arabs or the Byzantine Empire brought sericulture to Spain in the ninth century and to southern Italy (Sicily and Campany) in the tenth and eleventh centuries. From there, silk production began a slow march northward, reaching north Italy (Piedmont, Lombardy, and Veneto) and southern France in the fifteenth century. The production of raw silk also moved farther south in China, to around Canton, while it disappeared from north China. In the late seventeenth century, silk was produced in most of Asia (especially around Shanghai, and Canton and in central Japan and Bengal), and in all the Mediterranean basin (mainly in north Italy, Provence, and the Bursa area). The geography of the industry would remain almost unchanged until the 1950s.

Until the sixteenth century, the diffusion of throwing and weaving was intimately linked to that of sericulture. It is possible to discern a common pattern. At first, people (or, better, the elites of the society) started to dress in imported silk wares. Then, local artisans began to produce cloths with imported silk for domestic markets or for exports. Their demand for raw material stimulated the development of a local silk supply, which boosted weaving. The pattern was repeated, with some variation, time and again. For instance, Chinese silk (imported via the famous Silk Road) had been woven in Rome and elsewhere in the Mediterranean since 100 CE, well before the beginning of

SORTING OF THE COCOONS. Painting from the *Book of the Silk Industry*, Qing Dynasty, early nineteenth century. (Bibliothèque Municipale, Poitiers, France/Giraudon/Art Resource, NY)

local production. Although weaving was swept away in the western part of the Roman Empire by Barbarian invasions, it survived in the eastern part. For centuries the Byzantine Empire was renowned for its silk and purple cloths. Silk weaving spread back to Europe in the eight or ninth century, brought by Byzantine or Arab artisans, one or two centuries before silk production began. Weaving started in south Italy, then, at the end of the eleventh century, in Lucca (Tuscany), which for two centuries was the main center for production of silk wares in Europe. The silk came still mainly from south Italy, while the local (Tuscan) production began in the late twelfth century, but it never met demand. In the thirteenth and fourteenth centuries, silk weaving developed in all major Italian industrial cities—Florence, Venice, Genoa, Bologna, and Milan; and in due time it was followed by the production of silk in the countryside of each city. After the decline of wool production in the fourteenth century, the silk industry became Italy's most important manufacturing activity.

Widening Markets. Until the late seventeenth and early eighteenth centuries, Italy was both the main producer and the largest processing center of silk. Its silk wares were eagerly consumed in Europe and in the Middle East. However, Italy's position did not go unchallenged. Many Euro-

pean states tried to foster development of the silk industry, and they eventually succeeded. Silk weaving began to spread north of the Alps in the sixteenth and seventeenth centuries, first in France and later in Switzerland, Prussia, and the United Kingdom. It has been estimated that Europe as a whole consumed some twelve hundred metric tons of silk in 1600 and forty-four hundred in 1780. Italy managed to increase its output of silk from a thousand metric tons in 1600 to twenty-eight hundred in 1780. Weaving did not disappear from Italy, as many historians once thought; the domestic consumption of silk may have remained constant. Yet, undeniably, the overall position of Italy in the division of labor had changed. It once was the sole supplier of high-quality cloths, and it became the main provider of tram and organzins to northern European weavers. By 1780, the other Mediterranean countries (Spain, France, Austria, and the Levant—i.e., the Middle East) produced one thousand metric tons of silk, and the balance, about eight hundred metric tons, was imported from Asia.

The production of silk in Italy and in other Mediterranean countries continued to grow quite rapidly until the late 1840s, when total European consumption reached seven to eight thousand metric tons, a third of which was imported from the Far East. Then this growth was suddenly halted by the diffusion of a hitherto unknown silkworm disease, the pébrine, which appeared in France at the end of the 1840s and spread throughout the Mediterranean basin in the 1850s and 1860s. The collapse of Mediterranean output caused imports from the Far East (mainly China) to soar, up to almost two-thirds of European consumption. By the mid-1870s, silk production had recovered in all Mediterranean countries except France and Spain, but imports from Asia did not disappear. On the contrary, the 1870s marked the beginning of a steady rise in production and trade of raw silk that would last until 1929. According to best (but still highly uncertain) estimates, the world output grew threefold from the 1870s to 1930s—from some seventeen thousand metric tons (a quarter of it from the Mediterranean) to more than sixty thousand (only 7 percent from the Mediterranean). World trade soared from eight thousand metric tons in 1873–1875 to almost forty-nine thousand in 1927–1929. In other words, in those sixty years, the trade increased six fold, from less than one-half to three-fourths of output.

The ultimate cause of this boom was growing demand for silk wares in all the industrializing countries of the West, fueled by growth in income and a decline in relative price. World consumption per capita of silk (in weight) grew by 3 to 4 percent annually, much more than that of any other "natural" fiber. The two biggest markets for silk wares were the United Kingdom and, from the 1880s–1890s

DYEING OF SILK. Painting from the *Book of the Silk Industry*, Qing Dynasty, early nineteeth century. (Bibliothèque Municipale, Poitiers, France/Giraudon/Art Resource, NY)

on, the United States. Although Great Britain imported most of its needs from France and other continental countries, most of the American demand for silkworms was satisfied by the domestic industry. By the late 1890s, the United States had overtaken France as the main consumer of raw silk in the West, and since (probably) the 1900s China as the main consumer of silk worldwide. On the eve of the Great Depression, the United States consumed about half the world output.

The increase in total demand was accompanied by a deep change in the nature of the industry. It was transformed from batch production for the elites into mass production for the middle class or even the wealthiest blue collar workers. As said at that time, silk was being "democratized." The process had already started in Europe in the early nineteenth century, but it was greatly accelerated by the development of the U.S. industry. The change affected

demand for raw silk as well. The mass production of silk wares American style needed a medium-quality, but highly homogeneous raw material. Japan specialized in that type of silk, and it came to dominate the U.S. and thus the world market. On the eve of the Great Depression, Japan accounted for two-thirds of world exports, and roughly half of world output. In sixty years, its production had grown thirty-fivefold. China and Italy continued to supply mainly the European countries. Italy produced high-quality silk almost exclusively, whereas Chinese silk ranged from that of the best Shanghai filatures, which matched the Italian quality, to the coarsest hand-reeled silks. The meteoric rise in Japanese production caused the share of the world market of both countries to fall substantially; by the late 1920s, China supplied one-fifth of total world exports, and Italy a mere 10 percent. China's decline was steady, with an increase in total exports probably made possible only by stagnation or decline of domestic consumption. On the contrary, Italy managed to increase its total silk output quite rapidly and to hold onto its world market share until the 1900s. Afterward, its output began to decline, never to recover.

The 1929 crisis hit luxury industries such as silk very hard. The world silk trade fell by roughly one-third, with prices plummeting to one-third of those of the late 1920s. The silk industry did not benefit as many others did from the World War II boom, as silk had very few wartime uses. Nor did the industry recover in the 1950s, mainly because silk was for the first time subject to competition from an artificial fiber, nylon. All three major producers of raw silk were severely hurt. The Italian industry swiftly disappeared in the 1950s to early 1960s, and Italy's weaving industry now relies on imported silk. The once-mighty Japanese industry shrank very quickly, to be saved only by protection on tariffs. Its production is now one-tenth of the 1930s peak, and its silk is used exclusively for domestic consumption. Finally, Chinese exports were reduced for political reasons. The production gap has been only partially filled by growth of output and exports of new producers, in Asia (Thailand, Korea) and elsewhere (Brazil). Only in the 1980s did world silk production return to the pre-World War II quantities, and the total trade is still substantially lower than those levels. Also the location of weaving has changed. The United States is no longer the major world producer; and in Europe century-old production centers such as Zurich and Lyon have disappeared, and others (such as Como) specialize in the top end of the market. A lot of medium- and low-quality silk wares are imported from China and other less-developed countries. On the other hand, the development of artificial fibers has put silk wares back at the top end of clothing markets, although many more people can afford to buy them now, compared to prewar years. Therefore, to some extent, the characteristics and the worldwide geography of silk production are more like the industry of one thousand years ago than that of one hundred years ago.

[*See also* Central Asia; Clothing Trades; Silk Road; *and* Textiles.]

GIOVANNI FEDERICO

Technological Change

This article discusses the reeling, throwing, weaving, and dyeing processes.

Reeling. In principle, reeling equipment can be very simple: a pan of heated water and some sort of reel (maybe a simple stick), for rolling the silk on. If this were the early reeling technology, the silk would be very uneven and defective, a serious drawback. All the defects would have to be corrected later, in throwing and weaving, at high additional cost—and sometimes could not be amended, with the value of the cloth correspondingly diminished. As the quality of silk has always been of paramount importance in the business, many innovations have been designed to improve it. The main ones in preindustrial times were the addition of a crossing (a device to wring water from the yarn) and a treadle (to move the reel), increasing the size of the reel, and reducing the number of cocoons per yarn. With the partial exception of the treadle, all these innovations were quality-enhancing ones. Both the crossing and the large reel aimed at drying the silk as much as possible, and thus at preventing the yarns from sticking together. Using fewer cocoons yielded a thinner and more regular silk, but required more attention and thus more labor per unit of length. Information on the diffusion of these innovations is sparse, and it is impossible to map their adoption with any precision. There were some notable differences among the two major producing areas, Italy and China. In China the size of the thread has remained greater than in Italy, and use of a treadle machine never spread to Europe, where reels were moved by hand. On the whole, however, the basic layout of the reeling basin was quite similar in the two areas. This may have been a coincidence or, as forcefully argued by Kuhn, the result of transfer of technologies from China to Europe.

Two major innovations changed reeling technology in Europe in the eighteenth century. First, basins were gathered in large workshops, so that the workers could be monitored better. The second major innovation, by the Frenchman Albert Gensoul in 1805, was the use of steam. It was first used simply to heat the water, and later, in the 1830s and 1840s, also to move the reels and to stifle moths. In the next century or so, the modern steam-powered equipment was substantially improved. Most early innovations, including the original Gensoul machine, aimed to improve the quality of silk. Steam-reeled silk (called filatures) was more regular, thinner, and better in all respects than hand-reeled silk and was sold at a corresponding premium on the world market. From the 1870s on, innovations aimed primarily at increasing the productivity of labor, by increasing the number of yarns each worker could manage. The combination of higher quality and higher productivity proved irresistible. Over time, all the major silk-producing areas switched to steam-reeling, even if hand-reeling did not disappear. By the 1870s, steam-reeling was largely adopted in the whole Mediterranean basin and had begun to spread in southern China and in Japan. The remaining major producing area, central China, adopted it in the 1890s. Chinese firms copied the Western machinery, but with little or no improvement over time. On the contrary, Japanese producers developed their own technology, less capital-intensive than the Italian one.

However, Italy maintained clear leadership, both in quality of silk and in total factor productivity, until at least the 1920s.

The Italian-style steam-powered machinery was undoubtedly a great advance over the traditional fire-heated basins, but was still semiautomatic. Cocoons were handled by hand, and the necessary skill could be acquired only with some years of intensive training. There was an obvious incentive to mechanize reeling fully, especially because in Italy and Japan wages were increasing as a consequence of economic growth. However, the goal proved quite elusive. Mechanization was a most difficult task, and maybe the investments in research and development were not large enough. The first effective automatic machines were built in Japan on the eve of World War II. They would not spread until the 1950s, first in Japan and later in China and other Asian countries. On the other hand, the automatic machines were not adopted in Italy, where silk reeling was by then almost in a terminal state.

Throwing. It is not definitely known when raw silk began to be thrown, in the modern meaning of the world, before being woven. The earliest archeological evidence of twisted silk yarn in China dates back to the Shang period (c. 1500–1000 BCE). For many centuries, silk was thrown by transferring the thread from one or two fixed reels to a rotating spool, oriented in a different direction (e.g., vertically if the reel was horizontal, and vice versa). The spinner rotated the spindles, by hand, or with a crank or a treadle. The technology was very simple and highly labor-intensive. An obvious way to increase productivity was to have more than one spindle moved by some centralized power source. The first evidence of throwing machines dates back to 1272 or 1276 CE in Lucca (Italy) and to 1313 in China, but in both cases they might have invented much earlier. The two machines differed quite markedly. In the Chinese one (the multiple spindle twisting frame), the motion was transmitted to several spindles with shafts. The illustrations suggest a quite small machine, with dozens of spindles, but they refer to human-powered machines; water-powered ones might have been bigger. On the contrary, in the Italian *mulino da seta* (silk mill, also known as *alla Bolognese*), the whole frame was moving, rotating around its axis, powered by water or animal force; and this rotation was transmitted to spindles.

The subsequent history of throwing technology in the two areas diverged. In China, mechanical throwing of silk seems to have been slowly falling into disuse in the next centuries (or at least there is no direct mention of it), even if these machines were still used for other fibers. A labor-saving device may have not been worth its cost when the population was growing. On the contrary, the *mulini da seta* spread throughout northern Italy and became the standard throwing equipment in the eighteenth century,

producing a much better (more regular) yarn than the hand-spinning devices. The diffusion was probably slower than it might have been, as export of the technology was strictly forbidden. In 1717, in a well-known early case of industrial espionage, the Englishman T. Lombe succeeded in smuggling out the designs and setting up the first working *mulino da seta* outside Italy.

The main limit of the *mulino da seta* was the low speed of the spindles (no more than fifteen hundred rotations per minute), which constrained the growth in product per worker. Higher speeds could be reached only with a radically different machine, the so-called square throwing machine. It appeared in France in the mid-eighteenth century, with its invention traditionally attributed to P. Vaucanson, who might have been only the first to describe it in print. The machine had a fixed frame and moving spindles, with the same principle as the Chinese multiple spindle twisting frame, and may have been inspired by it. The use of a shaft for many spindles still limited the speed; so the final step was the use of a shaft for each spindle. The first cylindrical machines were developed in the United Kingdom in the 1820s. Afterward they spread in all the silk-consuming countries, though more slowly in Italy. Throwing in the Far East remained very backward.

Weaving. The looms used for silk did not differ much in their basic construction from those used for other textiles. However, silk weaving differs remarkably from, say, cotton weaving. Silk is more fragile than other fibers, and the patterns consumers wanted were more complex than the usual ones of a cotton fabric. Some types of woven cloths, the so-called *grandes façonnées*, were real works of art. Their production required a highly skilled weaver and a good assistant. The amount of skilled labor was dramatically reduced by the invention of a special loom by the Frenchman Joseph-Marie Jacquard (1804). The reproduction of the design was entrusted to a sort of pre-punched card, which automatically selected threads of the right color. This device disposed of the assistant, and enabled even a relatively inexperienced weaver to produce highly complex patterns. The Jacquard loom was adopted quickly in the production of patterned cloths, especially in Lyon.

The silk-weaving industry lagged other textiles by at least fifty years in adoption of the power loom. The first attempts started quite early, in the 1820s, but the machine did not take root before the 1860s, and it did not substitute fully for the hand loom before the 1900s. This delay is somewhat puzzling, as the advantages of mechanization were as great for silk as for other fibers. The power loom was twice as productive as the hand loom in the 1870s and 1880s and four times as productive in the 1920s. Furthermore, the power loom could be operated by anyone, including women who had no skill in using it. Its adoption in the silk industry was delayed because the early looms put too much strain on the silk, and because they could weave only the simplest patterns. In fact, the mechanization started much earlier in the United States—which produced mainly standard goods—than in Europe. Only at the end of the nineteenth century did technical progress made it possible to use the power loom for all kind of cloths.

Dyeing. A colorful pattern has always been a distinctive feature of the best silk cloths; so dyeing has always been extremely important in the silk industry. Unfortunately, it is impossible to outline the technical progress, if any, of silk dyeing in preindustrial times because it has always been an empirical and highly secretive process. In the nineteenth century, the silk industry benefited, as did all textiles, from progress in the chemical industry. In a somewhat peculiar way, it benefited even more than other textiles. By the 1870s, silk cloths were being adulterated ("weighted") with other substances, such as lead. At the peak of this practice, in the 1890s and early 1900s, these substances accounted on average for about a third of the total weight of the "silk" cloths produced in Lyon (with peaks up to three quarters). The practice was an (almost) open commercial fraud, but made it possible to cut substantially the prices of cloths—by a quarter on average. "Weighting" thus played an important role in spreading the consumption of silk wares among less affluent people. However, in the long run consumers began to shun the weighted products, and the practice slowly disappeared.

GIOVANNI FEDERICO

Industrial Organization and the State

The evolution of silk industry has been shaped by the contrast between the economics of the business and state intervention. This contrast has by no means been exclusive to the silk industry, but in its case it seems particularly strong. Silk and silk wares have always been tradable commodities, with a relatively simple technology that could have made their production very competitive. Thus, in a (hypothetical) free-trade world, the silk industry would have settled wherever the environment and the resources were most suitable, and these areas could have supplied the whole world's consumption. On the other hand, the industry has been a big business, worthwhile from a mercantilistic perspective, and silk wares have enjoyed a highly symbolic value in many societies. Thus all the "states" (in a broad meaning of the word) have tried to control their production as tightly as possible in an ongoing tug-of-war between the producing states, which have wanted to keep as great a monopoly as possible, and the other states, which have wanted to break the monopoly and start their own production. The whole story of the silk industry can be interpreted as a slow (and incomplete) movement toward its

"ideal" organization and location in a free-trade competitive environment. The first part of this article describes this organization, focusing on differences among sectors and on possible changes brought about by technical progress. The second part discusses the evolution of state intervention.

Industrial Organization. Sericulture has always been, and still is, a small-scale peasant activity, highly competitive by definition. The environment influences the location, but this constraint is not always binding. Mulberries can grow in a wide range of climates, from the semitropical climate of southern China (where trees yielded leaves up to six times a year) to the quite cold one of the Po Valley in northern Italy. Silkworms are quite sensitive to low temperatures, but that problem could be solved with heating, albeit at a substantial cost. Mulberries do not need much land and can grow almost everywhere—on riverbanks, alongside roads, and so on. The key factor for the development of sericulture was the availability of labor. Yet, sericulture has never developed in several environmentally suitable areas—notably the American South. With traditional technology, the production of a kilo of silk (from twelve kilos of fresh cocoons) needed some eighty to one hundred hours of work, most of it in the few final days of silkworm raising. With preindustrial technology, reeling was a followup of sericulture. Cocoons had to be processed immediately after the harvest, before the moth could make its way through the cocoon and leave it unfit for reeling. They were usually reeled by the same peasants who had raised the silkworms; so the production of silk could become established and prosper wherever there was enough labor at the right time of the year. A shortage of labor may have hindered its development in some preindustrial societies where population was scarce, and the primary concern was to grow food.

The silk was sold to merchants (or, in the case of state monopoly, to the state) who organized all further processing. They hired weavers and dyers to produce the cloth, often lending them the loom, and sold the product. This system was highly flexible, and in principle (i.e., without restrictions to access) highly competitive; anyone could have started a business. To be sure, it needed more capital than did sericulture or reeling, both for the instruments (looms, spinning wheels, and above all the "silk mills," etc.) and for financing the purchases of silk. The total amount was not so great, and capital could be borrowed. The key factor was skilled labor. Becoming a silk merchant, a weaver, or a dyer required years of training under the guidance of an expert master. Throwing was less skilled-labor-intensive, and at least in Italy was mechanized quite early (the Italian "silk mills" were among the first factories, in the modern meaning of the word). It nevertheless was located close to weaving, to minimize transaction costs (notably for monitoring). In other words, before industrialization, silk processing would have settled wherever enough technical skills were available—and skills tended to cluster in cities. The entire story of silk weaving is the story of industrial cities (or "industrial districts" in modern jargon), such as Lucca, Bologna, Lyon, Krefeld, and so on. In fact, hand-loom weaving spread to the countryside only in the early nineteenth century, when the average quality of the cloth began to decline. However, unlike the case of agricultural labor, these technical skills were highly mobile. Weavers, dyers, and merchants could, and indeed did, move from one city to another, and their migrations determined the size and the very existence of the silk industry in each of the cities.

Technical progress, mechanization, and the widespread adoption of a factory system in the nineteenth century modified this situation. The leap was particularly great in reeling, traditionally the most "rural" (i.e., backward) of the processes. Peasants started to sell cocoons instead of silk, and their daughters became fulltime industrial workers, who had to adjust to factory discipline and sometimes had to leave their families and live in dormitories. Silk merchants turned into fulltime industrialists, who purchased cocoons, had them processed, and sold raw silk or silk yarns to weaving firms. These changes, however, did not alter the basic characteristics of reeling. It remained a labor-intensive (compared with the rest of manufacturing) and highly competitive industry. In fact, the reeling equipment was highly divisible, and, beyond a quite low threshold, did not entail any economies of scale. The investment was correspondingly small, and it was relatively easy to find the necessary capital. The markets for cocoons and raw silk were well developed, fairly efficient, and on balance quite competitive. Therefore, setting up a reeling firm was simple, and the incumbents had no *a priori* advantages.

In all the major countries there were literally hundreds of reeling firms. Most of them managed one or few plants, with very small clerical and managerial staffs. The exception to this rule was Japan, where a handful of very large companies managed dozens of plants, controlled the supply of cocoons in wide areas, and built their own machinery with in-house technology. The biggest of them, the Katakura Co., in the 1920s produced as much as a half of all of Italy's production, but this amounted to a mere 8 percent of the total Japanese output. Furthermore, the traditional link between sericulture and reeling was loosened but not severed. Cocoons become technically tradable, thanks to the use of steam stoves and in some cases reeling was established quite far from cocoon-producing areas (e.g., in central China in Shanghai). However, moving cocoons was rather expensive, as they were bulkier than silk. Therefore, in the long run the growth in silk production depended on the supply of cocoons, and ultimately on the labor supply in the countryside. L. Nghiep and Y. Hayami ("Mobilizing Slack Resources for Economic Development: The Summer-Fall Rearing Technology of Sericulture in Japan," *Explorations in Economic History* 19 (1979) 163–181) have forcefully argued that the diffusion of a second (summer) and a third (fall) crop alongside the traditional spring crop was instrumental in the increase of Japanese output, and that this happened because Japanese peasants had a lot of spare time to raise silkworms. On the other hand, high wages prevented any development of sericulture and reeling in the United States, and rising wages in industrializing countries, such as France by the 1870s and Italy by the 1900s, caused the silk industry to decline.

The process of mechanization was apparently less dramatic in throwing and weaving than in reeling. In throwing it started quite early and lasted for a long period of time; in weaving it was delayed by technical problems. On the other hand, it had major consequences for the organization of industry because the modern equipment did not require any skill. The workers had only to feed the machines and fix the broken yarns. Hand-loom weavers found their precious skills useless almost overnight, and their number fell rapidly. The new equipment was indeed more expensive than the old, but probably throwing and weaving were relatively less capital-intensive in, say, 1930 than two centuries before. Producers moved to labor-abundant, often rural areas, and erstwhile industrial cities as Lyon became service centers or had to find a different specialization. On the other hand, throwing and weaving equipment was divisible, and barriers to entry were low; so the number of producing firms was high and the competition among them quite strong.

State Intervention. In all its early (and, unfortunately, scarcely known) history, the silk industry was a state enterprise. In an extreme version, which seems to have been adopted in China for some centuries, the whole production cycle, from cocoon to cloth, was operated as a state monopoly. Silk wares were used by the emperor, his family, and the court and were given, as part of their salary, to high-ranking senior officials; but they were not sold to ordinary citizens. A similar organization was adopted in the Byzantine Empire under Justinian (sixth century CE), whose Codex regulated the type and the color of silk dresses according to social status. Later, however, the state loosened its grip a bit. Citizens were allowed to produce and trade silk and silk wares, but only under very tight state control. All exports were subject to state licensing, and internal consumption was still heavily regulated. The export of production secrets was strictly forbidden and punished very severely.

In its second stage, control of the silk industry moved to the producers' and traders' associations, or guilds (the earliest recorded Italian guild, in Venice, dates back to 1256). They set wages and prices of cloths, and controlled production methods, thereby reducing the scope of real competition, and possibly innovation as well. Last but not least, they restricted access to indispensable training, often to sons and relatives of the members, and thus raised the members' earnings. Arguably, the silk guilds wielded more power than those of, for example, cotton. The competition from the (nonorganized) rural workforce was less intense than for cotton, because weaving silk was much more difficult. Furthermore, they could at least try to control the supply of silk, often in cooperation with the authorities. For instance, all the silk produced in the countryside of Bologna had to be sold in the city. The Piedmontese government set up an elaborate system for control of silk production, which included a prohibition against exports of raw silk to foster domestic throwing. Finally, the guilds got the government's cooperation in enforcing the prohibition against their members' migrating and transferring their technical knowledge to competing cities.

At the same time, the immigration of skilled workers was actively sought by any would-be silk-weaving center, by bribing them with privileges, tax exemptions, and money subsidies. These policies were repeated time and again, by medieval Italian cities, and by France under Henry IV at the end of the sixteenth century, as well as the United Kingdom and Prussia in the next century. The efforts extended to the production of raw silk, but with little success. All attempts to develop sericulture in northern Europe failed, and the effort of the British East India Company to transfer European techniques to Bengal from the 1780s to the 1820s was not successful.

The mercantilist policies fell progressively into disrepute, and were abandoned in the early nineteenth century. For instance, the Spitalfields Acts, which regulated silk weaving in London, were abolished in 1824, as was the prohibition on exporting raw silk from Piedmont in 1834. These acts marked the start of a third, and the least intrusive, phase of state intervention. The great boom of the silk industry in the nineteenth century unfolded under a comparatively free-trade regime, so that the localization of the silk industry tended to conform to a pattern of comparative advantage much more closely in those years than before. However, comparatively free did not mean totally free. After a brief spell of almost pure free trade in the mid-nineteenth century, many countries again raised duties on silk yarn and silk wares, in some cases to almost prohibitive levels. Arguably the U.S. industry would have not thrived as much as it did without protection. Even now, trade in silk wares, as in other textiles, is far from free. The protection never extended to raw silk because of the opposition of weavers' lobbies, and sericulture and reeling were actively encouraged by other means. In some cases, such as France from the 1880s on and Japan from the 1950s on, governments tried to stave off the decline of production by subsidizing the producers. Other governments tried to foster the production of silk. The most important case in point is Japan, whose government enacted a wide range of support policies from the 1870s onward. It engineered the importation of reeling technology from France (the famous Tomioka reeling plant, set up in 1872); it set up an elaborate system of quality control for silk exports in the 1860s and 1880s; and, from the 1890s on, it supported technical progress in sericulture. According to conventional wisdom, the state support was instrumental to the growth of the Japanese industry. Some scholars have argued that most of these policies were either irrelevant (e.g., the technological transfer) or positively damaging (e.g., the silk quality-control system), and that only the support of innovation had positive effects.

Summary. By its nature, the silk industry ought to have been a paragon of competition throughout its history. Without state intervention, sericulture and reeling would have been established together in labor-abundant countries. With preindustrial technology, weaving and throwing were highly specialized urban trades, likely to cluster close to consumers. Nineteenth-century mechanization transformed them into run-of-the-mill labor-intensive manufacturing. The industry's worldwide locations should have been quite sensitive to changes in the relative cost of labor, but actual locations were heavily influenced by state intervention. In the long-run this intervention slowed the development of the silk industry and made silk apparel more expensive than it might have been.

BIBLIOGRAPHY

Beauquais, Henri. *Histoire economique de la soie*. Lyon, 1910. Although in French and probably difficult to find, still a very valuable source of information.

Bell, Lynda. "Farming, Sericulture and Peasant Rationality in Wuxi County in the Early Twentieth Century." In *Chinese History in Economic Perspective*, edited by T. Rawski and L. Li, pp. 207–241. Berkeley and Los Angeles, 1992. A short account of the development of sericulture in one of the major producing areas in central China.

Cavaciocchi, Simonetta, ed. *La seta in Europa secc XIII–XX*. Florence, 1993. Proceedings of a conference, with several articles in English.

Cayez, Pierre. *Métiers jacquard et hauts forneaux aux origines de l'industrie lyonnaise*. Lyon, 1978.

Cayez, Pierre. *Crises et croissance de l'industrie lyonnaise*. Lyon, 1980. Cayez's two books are the major recent work on the history of a key weaving area.

Cottereau, Alain. "The Fate of Collective Manufactures in the Industrial World: The Silk Industries of Lyons and London, 1800–1850." In *World of Possibilities*, edited by J. Zeitlin and C. Sabel, pp. 75–152. Cambridge, 1997. A comparison between silk weaving in Lyon and London in the first half of the nineteenth century.

Eng, Robert Y. *Economic Imperialism in China: Silk Production and Exports*. Berkeley, 1986. A general history, very critical of the organization of the silk industry and its role in Chinese development.

Federico, Giovanni. *An Economic History of the Silk Industry 1830–1930*. Cambridge, 1997. A general overview of the industry, with an extensive bibliography.

Feltwell, James. *The Story of Silk*. Sutton, 1990. A simple and readable account of long-term development.

Kuhn, Dieter. "Textile Technology; Spinning and Reeling." In *Science and Technology in China*, edited by J. Needham, vol V, part 9. Cambridge, 1988. A very detailed analysis of technology, with much information on the development of the industry, especially in its early stages.

Kumar Bag, Sailendra. *The Changing Fortunes of the Bengal Silk Industry 1757–1833*. Calcutta, 1989. Focuses on efforts by the East India Company to improve the quality of Indian silk.

Kyokawa, Yuijro. "The Transformation of Young Rural Women into Disciplined Labor under Competition-Oriented Management: The Experience of the Silk-Reeling Industry in Japan" *Hitotusbashi Journal of Economics* 32 (1991), 49–69. Has a somewhat too narrow title, as it deals with technical progress in reeling.

Li, Lillian. *China's Silk Trade: Traditional Industry in the Modern World*. Cambridge, Mass., 1981. A general overview, dealing mostly with the nineteenth and twentieth centuries, but with an introduction to the previous history.

Lopez, Roberto S. "The Silk Industry in the Byzantine Empire." *Speculum* 20 (1945), 1–42. A classic article, still the best description of the Byzantine silk industry.

Ma, Debin. "The Modern Silk Road: The Global Raw Silk Market, 1850–1930." *Journal of Economic History* 56 (1996), 330–355. Focuses on integration of the world market for raw silk, but reports some additional information.

Malanima, Paolo. *La fine del primato*. Milano, 1998. A general work on the Italian economy in the seventeenth and early eighteenth centuries, with estimates of trends in silk output.

Matsui, Sugihiro. *The History of Silk Industry in the United States*. New York, 1930. Although difficult to find, the only comprehensive history available.

Poni, Carlo. "Per la storia del distretto industriale serico di Bologna." *Quaderni storici* 73 (1990), 93–167. The best case study of a preindustrial silk-processing area.

Scranton, Philip. "An Exceedingly Irregular Business: Structure and Process in the Paterson Silk Industry 1885–1910." In *Silk City. Studies on the Paterson Silk Industry*, edited by P. Scranton, pp. 5–68. Newark, N.J., 1985. The only recent work on the economics of U.S. silk weaving.

Shih, Ming. S. *The Silk Industry in Ch'ing China*. Ann Arbor, 1976. A short and sometimes confused book, but reports much useful information.

Silberman, Herman. *Die seide*. Dresden, 1897. Although in German and probably difficult to find, still a very valuable source of information.

So, Alvin. *The South China Silk District: Local Historical Transformation and World System Theory*. Albany, N.Y., 1987. Laden with jargon and short on information, the only recent work on the Canton area.

Sugiyama, Sugihiro. *Japan's Industrialisation in the World Economy*. London, 1988. Includes an extensive chapter on silk.

GIOVANNI FEDERICO

SILK ROAD. Trade routes across Eurasia flourished for three millennia, but only earned an evocative name after they were dead. The phrase *Silk Road*, created by a nineteenth-century German geographer, is really a misnomer. There was never only one route, and silk was not its only good. But it is a useful catchphrase. From circa 1500 BCE to 1500 CE, thriving commerce, accompanied by religious proselytization and artistic and technological exchange, knitted together the Eurasian economy. Unfortunately, all the pilgrims, traders, and adventurers who crossed huge expanses of desert in pursuit of scriptures, profit, or power left more colorful stories than economic analysis. Sparse data are scattered across a multitude of languages and disciplines.

The main route began at Chang-an (now Xi'an), capital of China in the seventh century CE, at one million people the largest city in the world. From there it headed northwest through the Gansu corridor to Dunhuang, center of a thousand cave paintings, where it divided north and south to follow the rim of the terrible Taklamakan desert. Rejoining at Kashgar in East Turkestan, the routes then led west into Transoxania, the land between the Oxus and Jaxartes rivers, then south into India or west to Persia, and on to Rome/Byzantium and Antioch, the terminus on the Mediterranean coast.

Two metaphors may help to sketch its structure. First, think of a large net, composed of many interlocking strings, held up by two or more poles. The poles are the settled agrarian empires: Rome and its successors in the west, China in the east, and India and Persia to the south. These densely populated zones provided the supply-and-demand forces that powered the network. The strings are caravans: heavily loaded camels led by frontier traders of many ethnic types. They cross at nodes of exchange: oases scattered across the grasslands and deserts. A second metaphor invokes the parallels between the grassland steppe and the ocean. Settled empires constitute the mainland, caravans are ships, oases are archipelagoes, and nomads are the denizens of the deep—the only people who can subsist almost entirely off grass and not grain.

Trade depended on a precarious balance between these four cultures. Nomads, in exchange for protection rents (called "tribute" by the Chinese), ensured that traders could cross the steppe safely. The traders needed access to capital and markets supplied by the agrarian civilizations. The agrarian oases supported lodging and restocking points called caravanserai. The rise and fall of trade depended on the military and commercial stability of all the participants. It was a highly profitable, but volatile, enterprise, suitable only for high rollers.

The extremely high transport costs meant that only goods with very high value-to-weight ratios would be carried for profit. Only soldiers could afford bulky goods. Carrying grain from China's northwest to troops at the nearest oasis, a mere fifteen hundred kilometers, cost ten times the original price. For merchants, silk fit the bill perfectly: a mysterious fabric whose production technology China monopolized for two thousand years. Jade from Central

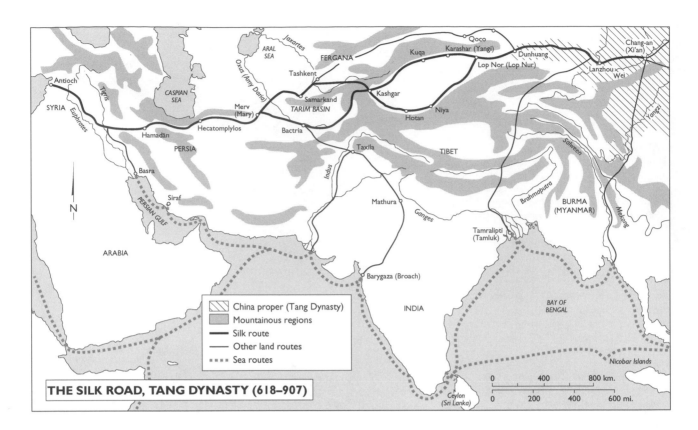

THE SILK ROAD, TANG DYNASTY (618–907)

Asia was another profitable commodity, as were those uniquely self-transporting goods: slaves and horses.

The interaction between nomadic state builders and Chinese empires pumped commodities into the network. Because steppe resources were so dispersed, pastoralists usually struggled with other nomads to support their families. Resources to build a large confederation could only come from outside the steppe, especially from China. Like good bank robbers, nomadic state builders went where the wealth was. As China centralized under a new dynasty, a nomadic state often rose along with it. So the Xiongnu confederation gained strength side by side with the Han Empire from the second century BCE to the second century CE, and the Turks and Uighurs rose with the Tang Empire in the seventh to ninth centuries CE. Both sides gained from this symbiotic, if reluctant, embrace.

China, with its dense population, high-yielding agriculture, and advanced commerce, was self-sufficient in everything but one crucial national security item: horses. The Chinese search for horses turned Chinese eyes to the heart of Central Asia. A military expedition by the Han emperor to obtain the famed "blood sweating horses" of the Ferghana valley returned with only 10 percent of its men and few horses. An easier method was to trade silk for horses at regulated border markets and "tribute missions," where Chinese emperors bought protection from damaging raids, while nomads pretended to submit to the emperor's superior virtue.

Silk, of little use *per se* to the nomads, except for the Khan's robes, served as a fiduciary currency, which they in turn sold to Central Asian merchants in exchange for metals, jewelry, and weaponry. When the China-nomadic protection relationship was stable, goods flowed through the oasis towns, stimulating urban cultures, religious patronage, and mercantile prosperity. But the relationship was vulnerable both to Chinese dynastic decay and the replacement of one nomadic confederation by a newer, rawer set of conquerors. The volatility of these trade cycles surpassed anything known to capitalism, past or present.

Trade in silk goes back at least to the second millennium BCE. Silk textiles from China have been discovered from circa 1500 BCE in Transoxania and circa 1000 BCE in Egyptian tombs. Written records of the first century BCE describe embassies to the Xiongnu bringing marriage alliances and substantial quantities of silk. Payments rose from eight thousand pieces of embroidered silk and six thousand pounds of silk floss to eighty four thousand pieces and seventy eight thousand pounds fifty years later. In the first century CE, Pliny complained that silk imports were draining the Roman empire of hundred million sesterces of silver. As the Xiongnu declined, the Kushan Kingdom in northern Afghanistan became the central nomadic empire guaranteeing the free flow of trade, but with the collapse of the Han Empire in the second century CE, followed by the decline of Rome over the next two centuries, major disruptions broke the chain. Still, communication was secure enough to allow the spread of Buddhism out of India into Central Asia and China in the fourth to seventh centuries CE. Patrons gave Buddhists large bolts of silk; silk wrappings for saints' burials turned up in Christian Europe several centuries later.

The Silk Road was the Internet of antiquity. Every major religious tradition met there, leaving traces of hybridized Buddhism, Zoroastrianism, Manichaeanism, Islam, Confucianism, Judaism, and Nestorian Christianity. Technical knowledge passed freely, if obscurely. Because merchants needed a lingua franca, like Aramaic, or later Sogdian, their information technology enabled Central Asians to record their languages. The Uighurs, Mongols, and Manchus used the Sogdian alphabetic script to create their official records.

With the consolidation of the Tang Empire in the seventh century, followed by the rise of the Uighurs and the powerful Tibetan empire, the trade network reached the peak of its activity. Then a new crusading religious army from the East, the Arabs, arrived, defeating Chinese expansion in 751 CE. Goods still flowed through the competing states, dominated by the trade of horses for silk. The Uighurs even put the Tang emperor back on his throne in order to keep arrangements intact. It was well worth a few kowtows to sell poor horses to the Chinese for twenty-eight bolts of silk and buy better ones in the steppe for 95 percent less.

The next century demonstrated that this luxury trade, although a minuscule portion of the general economy, exerted potent effects. In 840, the new nomadic power in the north, the Kirghiz, crushed the Uighur state, cutting the horse supply to China. As prices shot up to more than forty bolts of silk, the desperate emperor looked to where the domestic wealth was: in tax-exempt Buddhist monasteries. After he defrocked thousands of monks, confiscated lands, and melted down huge bronze statues, Buddhism survived, but lost out as official orthodoxy to the hard-line Confucianists. Truly, for want of several thousand horses, the Buddhist kingdom of China was lost.

The division of China and the steppe into competing regional kingdoms in the tenth century again broke many trading links, while for the first time maritime shipping across the Indian Ocean to Southeast China became a serious competitor. But the Mongol unification in the thirteenth century of nearly the entire Eurasian continent formed the world's largest pacified continental trading zone. Once again, travelers crisscrossed Eurasia; Marco Polo was only one of hundreds of all nationalities. They easily combined the roles of businessman, emissary, explorer, pilgrim, and spy.

Thereafter, the trade routes declined in relative if not absolute volume. In the sixteenth century, the Ming dynasty blocked frontier contact by completing the Great Wall, and no more nomads unified the steppe. Gunpowder weaponry and the opening of the New World sea routes did not end continental trade; it still survived in altered form. More important was the fixing of the Sino-Russian border and the elimination of an independent Mongolian state in the seventeenth and eighteenth centuries. Until 1990, China and Russia firmly partitioned the steppe, leaving no room for the independent nomad and caravan trader.

The collapse of the Soviet Union left in its wake five new independent Central Asian states, plus truly independent Mongolia. New goods—drugs, weapons, and oil—now flow on old routes. Trucks, railroads, and airplanes have replaced camels. China has welcomed the Turkish president's call for reopening the old Silk Roads. Will they have a new global future?

[*See also* Central Asia; Sericulture; *and* Silk Industry.]

BIBLIOGRAPHY

Barfield, Thomas J. *The Perilous Frontier: Nomadic Empires and China.* Cambridge, 1989. The best analytical study.

Beckwith, Christopher I. "The Impact of the Horse and Silk Trade on the Economies of Tang China and the Uighur Empire." *Journal of the Economic and Social History of the Orient* 34.2 (1991), 183–198. Makes the case that China's loss of horse supplies caused the suppression of Buddhism.

Franck, Irene M., and Peter Brownstone. *The Silk Road: A History.* Oxford, 1986. A general survey, with many quotes from travel accounts and good maps.

Frank, Andre Gunder. *The Centrality of Central Asia: Comparative Asian Studies,* vol. 8, pp. 1–57. Amsterdam, 1992. Raises big questions about Central Asia's role in systemic world history.

Liu, Xinru. *The Silk Road: Overland Trade and Cultural Interactions in Eurasia.* Washington, D.C., 1998. Useful focus on silk goods and their religious and economic effects.

Mair, Victor H. "Dunhuang as a Funnel for Central Asian Nomads into China." In *Ecology and Empire: Nomads in the Cultural Evolution of the Old World,* edited by Gary Seaman, pp. 143–164. Los Angeles, 1990. Rich information on this key city of the Silk Road.

Rossabi, Morris. "The 'Decline' of the Central Asian Caravan Trade." In *The Rise of Merchant Empires,* edited by James D. Trocy, pp. 221–271. Cambridge, 1998. Argues that politics, not seaborne commerce, caused the decline of trade in the sixteenth and seventeenth centuries.

PETER C. PERDUE

SINGAPORE is one of the four dynamic, East Asian NIEs (newly industrialized economies) (the other three being South Korea, Taiwan, Hong Kong) that have consistently chalked up high rates of economic growth for a sustained period—at average rates of 9.2 percent in the 1960s, 9.3 percent in the 1970s, 7.5 percent in the 1980s, and 6.1 percent during 1990–1998. Also dubbed Asia's four "dragons," these NIEs are generally scarce in land and poor in natural resources. However, they have managed to overcome their constraints by intensifying their human resource development and by operating export-oriented development strategies. Accordingly, their economic growth depends heavily on manufactured exports. Today, they all have become full-fledged developed economies.

The Smallest Asian Dragon. With a resident population of 3.2 million today, Singapore is the smallest of the four NIEs, but it is also the most economically developed. This by itself is no small achievement for Singapore, which started off with greater adversities than those faced by the other three NIEs. Hong Kong's industrialization in the 1950s was facilitated by the influx of capital, skilled labor, as well as entrepreneurs from China escaping from Communism. Taiwan also benefited from a large number of educated elites and administrators from Mainland China who evacuated with the Kuomintang army to Taiwan in 1950. But Singapore's immigrant population from China and India were largely poor and marginally educated. Hence, for years Singapore's literacy level was the lowest of the four NIEs. Furthermore, whereas both South Korea and Taiwan received substantial American economic aid in the early phases of their industrial takeoff, Singapore had to depend precariously on itself.

In 1960, Singapore started with a per capita gross national product (GNP) of U.S. $440. By 1999, its per capita income of U.S. $29,600 was only slightly below the U.S. level, but well exceeded the average of high-income economies (U.S. $25,700), ranking Singapore as the world's ninth-highest. Singapore today is an economy with low inflation and full employment, cushioned by huge international reserves and zero foreign debt. By all accounts, Singapore's economic development is truly a success story.

Beyond GNP growth, Singapore has also made impressive progress in social areas such as public housing and education. In 1998, 81 percent of the population lived in government-built flats, which were owned by residents. In 1999, just a little more than 50 percent of the relevant age-cohort population were enrolled for tertiary education. For years, Singapore has earned the reputation for being the cleanest city in Southeast Asia.

The Industrialization Process. The story of Singapore's modern economic development is commonly traced back to 1959, when the present ruling People's Action Party (PAP) government under Lee Kuan Yew first took power in the then-self-governing Singapore. Singapore had limited economic growth in the nineteenth century and before and after World War II; but the critical economic transformation associated with industrialization came about only after the end of British colonialism.

Historically, Singapore owed its existence and early developments to its strategic geographical location, which enabled it to develop into a flourishing trading port in Southeast Asia. When the newly elected PAP government came to power in 1959, entrepôt trade activities constituted the mainstay of the Singapore economy, accounting for 18.8 percent of its total GNP, compared with only 8.7 percent from manufacturing. However, by the late 1950s there were clear signs that the entrepôt economy was stagnating and entrepôt activities could no longer be depended upon as the future engine of growth, in part because Singapore's neighbors, out of nationalism, were developing direct trade links with the outside. Above all, the entrepôt economy was simply incapable of generating sufficient jobs to resolve Singapore's acute unemployment, which stood at a hefty 13 percent in 1959.

Singapore's industrialization program, therefore, was mounted rationally and deliberately because Singapore had no other viable options. The basic industrialization program was initiated and managed by the then-Minister of Finance Goh Keng Swee, who has since been credited as the "architect" of Singapore's economic development. Among the measures taken, the UN development expert Albert Winsemius (a Dutch national) was invited to advise the new government, and he recommended the rapid buildup of the manufacturing sector based on a liberal immigration policy to attract foreign skills and a generous incentive scheme to attract foreign investment. A series of legislation, such as the Industries Ordinance, was enacted to promote new industries. The Economic Development Board (EDB) was set up in August 1961 with its primary function of promoting foreign investment and new industries. EDB remains the most important economic agency in the republic to this day.

However, economic growth was quite slow in the first part of the 1960s, partly because Singapore essentially adopted the import substitution type of industrialization strategy. But the main cause may be attributed to domestic political instability, manifested in widespread labor unrest and frequent squabbles with Malaysia. Political uncertainty was further heightened after 1963 when Indonesia, under president Sukarno, launched the *Confrontasi* campaign against Singapore and Malaysia (Greater Malaysia). This deterred foreign investment in Singapore and curtailed its trading activities.

In August 1965, Singapore was separated from Malaysia to become a fully independent state. Economically, the separation was a blessing to Singapore's long-term development, because the loss of Malaysia as a large domestic market quickened Singapore's transition from import substitution to export-oriented development strategies. Singapore was now free to devise its own appropriate tariffs and to expand its global economic linkages. In the short run, however, the separation from its hinterland brought to the fore Singapore's very problem of survival, which was soon aggravated by the shock of the British military's

TABLE 1. *Basic Economic Data, Singapore*

	1960	1970	1980ᵃ	1990	1998	1999ᶜ
Gross Domestic Product						
At Current Market Prices (S$m)	2,149.6	5,804.9	25,090.7	66,464.4	138,529.2	143,981.3
Annual Change (%)	9.9	15.1	11.0	14.2	−1.4	3.9
At 1990 Market Prices, Singapore dollar million (S$m)	—	—	—	—	—	—
Annual Change (%)	8.7	9.4	7.4	9.0	0.4	5.4
Gross Fixed Capital Formation (GFCF)						
At Current Market Prices (S$m)	204.9	1,888.5	10,203.1	21,577.8	51,352.4	46,771.3
GFCF as % of GNP	9.4	32.2	42.4	31.6	34.6	30.2
At 1990 Market Prices						
Annual Change (%)						
Total	—	11.8	6.4	10.3	−6.7	−3.6
Private	—	12.2	7.1	10.0	−9.9	−4.7
Public	—	11.3	3.9	11.1	7.2	0.2
Gross National Saving (S$m)	−52.3	1,129.7	8,251.8	30,008.0	80,626.9	83,567.9
As % of GNP	—	19.3	34.3	43.9	54.3	54.0
As % of GFCF	—	59.8	80.9	139.1	157.0	178.7
Employment						
Employed ('000; Mid-year)	—	644.2	1,073.4	1,537.0	1,869.7	1,885.9
Unemployment Rate (%)(Average)ᵇ	13.0 (1959)	6.0	3.5	1.8	3.2	3.5
Measures of Inflation (Annual Change in %)						
Consumer Price Index	—	5.6	2.7	3.4	−0.3	0.4
Trade						
Total Trade at Current Prices (S$m)	7,554.8	12,289.6	92,797.1	205,012.0	353,626.8	382,431.2
Imports	4,077.7	7,533.8	51,344.8	109,806.0	169,863.5	188,141.6
Exports	3,477.1	4,755.8	41,452.3	95,206.0	183,763.3	194,289.6
Domestic Exports	217.1	1,832.2	25,805.2	62,754.2	105,917.6	116,325.0
Re-exports	3,260.0	2,923.6	15,647.1	32,451.8	77,845.7	77,964.7
Annual Change (%)	4.2	20.2	10.3	11.4	−7.5	8.1
Balance of Payments						
Current Account Balance (S$m)	—	−1,705.8	−3,375.8	5,659.2	35,187.8	36,398.2
Overall Balance (S$m)	—	564.8	1,419.3	9,892.5	4,980.6	7,321.2
Exchange Rate (Per U.S. $)	—	3.0942	2.1412	1.8125	1.6736	1.6949
Official Foreign Reserves						
Total at End of Year (S$m)	—	3,097.9	13,757.7	48,521.3	124,584.4	128,457.0
Ratio-to-Merchandise Imports (Months)	—	4.9	3.2	5.3	8.8	8.2
Public Debt at End of Year (S$m)	—	2,016.6	14,669.5	51,425.6	115,183.4	125,777.1
Domestic	—	1,842.8	13,732.5	51,357.7	115,183.4	125,777.1
External	—	173.8	937.0	67.9	—	—
Debt-Servicing Ratio (%)	—	0.6	1.0	0.2	—	—

ᵃ Annual changes refer to averages for the decade.   ᵇ Data for 1970 and 1980 refer to June.   ᶜ Preliminary.
SOURCES: *Economic Survey of Singapore, 1991 and 1999* (Singapore, Ministry of Trade and Industry).

withdrawal from the state, further depriving Singapore of another important source of income and employment.

The government's responses to the challenges included the introduction of the Employment Act and the Industrial Relations Act in 1968 (to outlaw illegal strikes) to attract more labor-intensive type of foreign investment. To generate more domestic savings for development, the Central Provident Fund (CPF, Singapore's Pension Scheme) rates were also raised. This subsequently became the major source of domestic capital formation.

More significantly, the international economic environment in the late 1960s and the early 1970s, marked by the free flow of capital and technology from the developed world, was exceedingly favorable to outward-looking developing economies. The booming developed countries also allowed easy access to their markets for the labor-intensive manufactured exports from the developing world. Hence, tremendous opportunities were available for Singapore to expand its labor-intensive exports, particularly electronics components.

The Second Industrial Revolution. On the eve of the first world oil crisis in 1973, Singapore had already transformed itself into a throbbing and humming industrial and commercial hub in Southeast Asia, with near-full employment. The oil crisis brought about a brief period of "stagflation"; but the economy quickly resumed its growth momentum through the late 1970s. By 1980, with a per capita GNP of U.S. $4,500 (about 40 percent of the U.S. level), Singapore was classified by the World Bank as an upper-middle-income economy. But as the economy continued to boom on the back of rising, labor-intensive manufactured exports, it soon ran into acute labor shortages, which had to be met with an increasing influx of foreign workers from Singapore's neighboring countries. Policymakers became increasingly concerned about whether the manufacturing sector, with its heavy reliance on low-cost foreign labor and low value-added activities, could in the long run sustain its dynamic role of leading the economy in growth. Furthermore, labor-intensive exports were facing the rising specter of protectionism in developed countries.

Thus, the government took bold measures, one of which was the high-wage policy to force the pace of industrial restructuring (i.e., from labor-intensive activities to more capital-intensive and higher-productivity pursuits). Singaporeans called this the "Second Industrial Revolution." Similar industrial upgrading was also successfully taking place at about the same time in South Korea and Taiwan, albeit with less government intervention.

Economic-restructuring efforts finally bore fruit. By the 1990s, Singapore had developed a viable manufacturing sector, comprising many export-oriented, technology-intensive industries. The economy had also grown more broad-based and resilient because of the rise of a wide range of tradable services, such as banking and finance, communications, and transportation. But the economy has also come to depend heavily on external demand (exports of goods and services) as its source of growth.

Problems in the Next Lap. With the approach of the new millennium, Singapore was pushing hard to develop itself into an "intelligent island" for the emerging information society and knowledge-based economy. As a small compact island with a world-class physical infrastructure and ample financial resources, Singapore has found it relatively easy to develop the required IT (information technology) infrastructure. In fact, 98 percent of all homes are already wired to Singapore One, the island-wide broadband high-capacity network and switches for multimedia applications and communication services. But the new economy has also heightened Singapore's inherent constraints.

The major challenge for Singapore comes from the "software component" associated with the accumulation of human and intellectual capital. Here Singapore, as a tiny country with a small high-level manpower base, faces considerable disadvantages, which cannot be eliminated by liberal immigration of foreign talent. Another problem comes from Singapore's limited domestic capability for innovation and entrepreneurship, or the so-called "technopreneurship." Lacking a culture of creativity, combined with a strong government presence in daily economic life, has slowed Singapore's development in entrepreneurship.

The future is also fraught with considerable political and social uncertainties. How will this small city-state cope with the new political and social landscape created by the globalized knowledge economy? How will Singapore relate to its Southeast Asian neighbors, which are economically and socially lagging so far behind?

BIBLIOGRAPHY

Goh, Keng Swee. *The Practice of Economic Growth.* Singapore, 1977, 1995.

Huff, W. G. *The Economic Growth of Singapore.* Cambridge, 1994.

Lim, Chong-Yah, ed. *Economic Policy Management in Singapore.* Singapore, 1996.

Sandhu, Kernial Singh, and Paul Wheatley, eds. *Management of Success: The Moulding of Modern Singapore.* Singapore, 1989.

JOHN WONG

SINGER, ISAAC MERRITT (1811–1875), American inventor.

Singer was born in Pittstown, Rensselaer County, New York. His parents soon divorced; Singer, unable to get along with his stepmother, at age twelve moved to Oswego, New York, to live with his older brother. He worked in a variety of unskilled jobs for nearly seven years, then had a short apprenticeship—four months—as a machinist. Singer also discovered a passion for the theater and for the next nine years wandered about the country, appearing on stage and using his mechanical creativity to support himself. He developed and patented a rock-drilling machine in 1839, and in 1849 he perfected and patented a carving machine.

In 1851 Singer was in Boston working in a machine shop when someone brought in a Lerow and Blodgett sewing machine for repairs. Learning that there was probably a fortune to be earned if someone could improve current designs, the traditional tale is that Singer immediately fell to the task, sketching a redesigned machine in hours and building it in eleven days. Whether true or not, Singer clearly was the first to bring together the elements that define the modern sewing machine. But Elias Howe held most of the critical patents on sewing machines and soon sued to force all manufacturers, including I. M. Singer & Company, to produce machines under his license. With the challenge from Howe, Singer turned to lawyer Edward Clark (19 December 1811 to 14 October 1882). Unable to pay for Clark's services with cash, Singer agreed to give him a one-third interest in his patents.

Clark, born in Athens, Greene County, New York, graduated from Williams College (1831), read law with Ambrose Jordan, then became his partner. Though without any background in business, Clark soon decided to give all his attention to the sewing machine venture. On 1 January 1852, Singer and Clark established a partnership, I. M. Singer & Company, each owning one-half. Clark took responsibility for legal, financial, and marketing matters, Singer for manufacturing and continuing work to improve the sewing machine. Singer proved his mechanical genius, securing over the next few years twenty-two additional patents for a variety of valuable improvements. After losing to Howe in the patent case in 1854, I. M. Singer, together with other manufacturers, agreed to pool their patents and charge a $15 fee for each machine under license. With some modifications, the pool continued until 8 May 1877, when the last patent in the pool expired.

Clark played a decisive role in the development of the Singer company and American business practice. It was Clark who recognized the importance of controlling the retail operations of the company, developing the branch house network. He also saw huge potential in the "domestic" market for a smaller, lighter machine—the "Turtle Back"—that women could use in the household. To develop this market, Clark conceived of the "hire-purchase" system. The company leased the machine to a customer, counting the lease payments toward the purchase price. At the end of the lease, the customer got title to the machine. Thus, with the McCormick Harvesting Machine Company, Singer was one of the pioneers in the use of credit to extend sales. The Singer approach also required development of a force of canvassers to collect the weekly payments as well as to maintain the machines. This approach soon carried Singer to a dominant position in the industry and led the company to develop one of the most sophisticated accounting systems and business organizations yet seen. It was also Clark who understood the opportunities that European markets offered, and he began the push in 1862 to put Singer machines into those markets, markets it also soon dominated.

Singer and Clark never got along well. The well-educated Clark was a sharp contrast to the poorly educated, highly temperamental Singer. In June 1863, Clark confronted Singer, forcing dissolution of the partnership. In its place came a new company, The Singer Manufacturing Company, 80 percent owned by Singer and Clark. Neither could serve as president as long as the other lived.

Singer withdrew from further involvement with the company, spending most of his remaining years in Europe. A year after Singer's death in 1875, Clark, then sixty-five, returned as company president until his own death in 1882.

BIBLIOGRAPHY

The State Historical Society of Wisconsin has a large collection of Singer company records; there is a second smaller collection at the University of Michigan. The New York Historical Association's Farmers' Museum in Cooperstown, New York, has three collections with Clark papers. Finally, the Greene County Historical Society in Coxsackie, New York, has the Fox-Clark papers.

Brandon, Ruth. *A Capitalist Romance: Singer and the Sewing Machine.* New York, 1977. Offers an engaging biography of Singer.

Davies, Robert B. *Peacefully Working to Conquer the World: Singer Sewing Machines in Foreign Markets, 1854–1920.* New York, 1976. Provides the only extensive scholarly history of the company.

FRED CARSTENSEN

SLASH-AND-BURN FARMING. *See* Swidden Agriculture.

SLATER, SAMUEL (1768–1835), American pioneer of the factory system.

Son of a yeoman farmer, Samuel Slater was born in Belper, Darbyshire, England on 9 June 1768. At age fourteen and one-half years he apprenticed himself to Jedediah Strutt, the owner of a local cotton textile mill and former partner of Richard Arkwright. During his six-year apprenticeship, Slater's mechanical genius developed, along with an ability to manage others that allowed him to become superintendent of Strutt's mill. At the end of his apprenticeship in 1789, Slater emigrated to America in the guise of a farmer in hopes of making his fortune in America's infant textile industry.

Not long after his arrival in New York, Slater formed a partnership with the Rhode Island textile merchants Almy and Brown. Slater was to construct and operate Arkwright machines, Almy and Brown were to supply the money, market the finished product, and give Slater one-half the net profits. Relying on his memory and his remarkable mechanical ability, the twenty-one-year-old Slater worked with Sylvanus Brown, who was a noted worker in wood, and David Wilkinson, who was skilled in the shaping of iron, to produce machines that transformed raw cotton into finished yarn of superior quality. The first cotton mill in America successfully to use the Arkwright machines began operations on 20 December 1790 in Pawtucket, Rhode Island. The machines soon were producing so much yarn that Almy and Brown were swamping the market.

Drawing from his British past, Slater developed a factory system (later known as the Rhode Island System) based upon the customary patterns of the New England village.

SAMUEL SLATER. (Prints and Photographs Division, Library of Congress)

Children between ages seven and twelve years old were the first employees of the mill, working under Slater's strict supervision. Soon he enlisted entire families, who often lived in company-owned housing located near the mills and shopped at company stores. To educate his workers, Slater opened a Sunday School where students of Rhode Island College (later Brown University) taught reading and writing, in the first such program established in the United States.

In 1799, Slater formed his own company, Samuel Slater & Company, and built the White Mill on the Massachusetts side of the Pawtucket River. He enlisted the aid of his brother John, a millwright in England, to help him run that mill while he continued to run the mill he shared with Almy and Brown. By the first decade of the nineteenth century, Slater held part ownership in three factories in Massachusetts and Rhode Island. In 1823, he expanded his interests further by purchasing a mill in Connecticut. He continued to diversify, forming factories to manufacture machinery for many of the New England mills. He also formed a partnership with his brother-in-law to produce iron for use in machinery construction.

Slater's style of management, known as the Slater System, proved to be one of his major weaknesses. His business interests included cotton factories, woolen mills, commission firms, foundries, machine shops, and real estate in several states; but he paid little attention to coordinating and integrating the various concerns. To complicate matters further, Slater was unwilling to delegate authority, choosing to make most of the decisions himself. This approach not only was inefficient but often caused serious delays. When he did delegate responsibility, friendship or kinship—rather than ability—became the defining criterion. Slater emphasized close product–family identification, family participation, and slow, steady long-term growth.

The economic downturn of 1829 forced Slater to rethink his management style. To manage his properties, he engaged the help of his sons and formed a new family partnership, Samuel Slater and Sons. The youngest of the three sons, Horatio Nelson Slater, urged a complete overhaul of the family business, prompting a reorganization of Slater's holdings and a new approach to the growing market economy. New cost-cutting measures were introduced, and slower traditional means of economic growth were abandoned. Subsequently, the firm became one of the leading manufacturing companies in the United States.

In 1833, Slater fell seriously ill. That spring, President Andrew Jackson visited him in Pawtucket and paid him this tribute: " I understand you have taught us how to spin, so as to rival Great Britain in her manufacture; you set all these thousands of spindles to work, which I have been delighted in viewing, and have made so many happy by a lucrative employment." With that, he greeted Slater as the "Father of American Manufactures." Samuel Slater died on 20 April 1835.

BIBLIOGRAPHY

Almy and Brown Papers. Samuel Slater Production Reports and Correspondence. Rhode Island Historical Society, Providence. The collection contains numerous letters and company papers.

Cameron, Edward H. "The Genius of Samuel Slater." *Technology Review* 57 (May 1955), 333–338. The article provides a description of the early days of the Industrial Revolution and Slater's role in America's textile industry.

Cameron, Edward H. *Samuel Slater: Father of American Manufactures.* Portland, Maine, 1960. This good biography was sponsored by Slater's great-grandson.

Gras, Norman Scott Brien, and Henrietta M. Larson. *Casebook in American Business History.* New York, 1939. One chapter gives an excellent discussion of Slater's various business transactions.

Samuel Slater Collection. Baker Library, Harvard University, Cambridge, Mass. This large collection contains the records of Slater's mills and some of his personal papers.

Tucker, Barbara M. *Samuel Slater and the Origins of the American Textile Industry, 1790–1860.* Ithaca, N.Y., 1984. This work is a good case study of Slater's factory system.

White, George S. *Memoir of Samuel Slater, the Father of American Manufactures.* New York, 1966. Reprint of 1836 ed. The author used his personal acquaintance with Slater to provide a description of his influence on the American textile industry.

DIANNE C. BETTS

SLAVE DEMOGRAPHY. There is no consensus among historians about the definition of a "slave society," but if the ratio of slaves to total population is seen as an important element of such a definition, some slave-owning societies historically have more claim than others to be labeled as slave societies. It is probable that in many, if not most, slave-owning societies those owned by others comprised only a small fraction—maybe 10 percent or less—of the total population. In some cases, however, the ratio of slaves to total population was higher, though still less than half, while in a small proportion of cases, slaves comprised a majority of the population. The geographical distribution of slave ownership across societies, therefore, has invariably been highly uneven. In the modern world, slavery has been particularly identified with Africa and the Americas, though it has been prevalent in other continents, notably Asia. Although evidence on slave populations is weaker as one goes back in time, chattel slaves comprised about a third of the populations of colonial Brazil and the antebellum U.S. South, some parts of Africa (including the nineteenth-century Sokoto Caliphate of modern northern Nigeria), and probably the ancient Greco-Roman empires. Only perhaps in the post-Columbian British and French colonies in the Caribbean (and possibly similar island economies, such as Zanzibar) were to be found societies where enslaved people comprised not just a majority but more than 70 percent of the population. As long as slavery existed, West Indian islands, such as Barbados, Jamaica, Saint Domingue, and after 1800 Cuba, were therefore clearly "slave societies." Whether other societies with lower proportions of slaves in their populations should be labeled the same is debatable. Brazil, the United States and the Sokoto Caliphate each had, nevertheless, populations of slaves that, at their maximum, were greater than that for the Caribbean as a whole. Thus, whereas the slave population of the Caribbean reached a maximum of about 1.1 million in 1790, slave populations in Brazil and the Sokoto Caliphate probably peaked at more than 2 million, while the slave population of the U.S. South reached about 4 million in 1860. The United States may not have had the largest slave population in world history—there are suggestions that up to 9 million slaves lived in India during British rule—but on the eve of the American Civil War, it was the largest slave-owning society in the history of the Western world.

Slave Demography in the Americas. Far more is known about the Atlantic slave trade and the history of slave populations in the post-Columbian Americas than about slave demography in other times and places. Whether the demography of American slavery provides useful insights into slave demography more generally is an open question. Although slavery existed in the Americas before the arrival of Europeans, the growth of American slavery after 1500 was dramatic and almost totally dependent on Africans or people of African descent. By 1790, the slave population of the Americas had probably grown to about 3.5 million and, notwithstanding slave emancipation in the French and British Caribbean between 1791 and 1848, probably exceeded 6 million by 1860. In 1790, more than three-quarters of the slaves in the Americas lived outside the United States; by 1860 only one-third did so.

Debate over the growth of the slave population in the Americas has centered on the relative importance of the Atlantic slave trade and of slave reproduction within the Americas. Ratios of slave populations to slave arrivals from Africa suggest, however, that importation of new slaves from Africa was critical in sustaining overall growth in slave population in the Americas, at least until the end of the eighteenth century. Almost 6 million arrivals from Africa between 1500 and 1790 were needed, in fact, to achieve a slave population of perhaps 3.5 million by the latter date. Even with some allowance for slave manumission, notably in Brazil, these statistics point toward a massive failure of slave reproduction in the Americas. Annual rates of natural decrease of population in the West Indies seem in fact to have varied from 2 percent to 5 percent for much of the eighteenth century. In this respect, American slavery was, in historian Barry Higman's phrase, "a demographic disaster area" (Drescher and Engerman, 1998, p. 174). This disaster was compounded, from the point of view of Africans, by horrendous age-specific mortality rates experienced by slaves en route to America. Importation from Africa remained a major factor in supporting continuing slave population growth in the Americas after 1790, with another 3.6 million or so Africans reaching America before 1860, but its relative importance declined in the face of increasing rates of slave reproduction. Crucial to this shift were demographic trends in the United States, where reproduction accounted increasingly for the growth of the slave population before 1807 and almost wholly sustained it thereafter, with natural growth of the slave population of the U.S. South from 1820 to 1860 matching that of the white population. By contrast, slave population growth elsewhere tended, with some exceptions, to remain heavily dependent on slave importation, a point illustrated by the fall of Jamaica's slave population from 1807 to 1834 consequent upon Great Britain's abolition of its slave trade and by continuing low ratios of slave population to slave imports in Brazil.

As long as the Atlantic slave trade existed, therefore, slavery in the Caribbean and Brazil retained an African face, whereas in the United States from the mid-eighteenth century, if not earlier, it had an increasingly Creole one. The degree to which differences in patterns of population growth impacted on the cultural history of slavery in different parts of the Americas has yet to be resolved, but their consequences for population structures is much clearer. Because the slave population of the United States largely grew by natural means, it rapidly assumed a normal age pyramid and sex distribution, with large proportions of children and older people as well as more females than males. By contrast, populations whose growth remained dependent on slave imports from Africa—essentially many of those in the West Indies and Brazil—tended to have age profiles weighted toward young adults. This largely reflected the preference of American buyers for slaves who were fifteen to twenty-five years old, a preference that, probably because of the importance of demand for labor for sugar cultivation, seems to have been consistent through time. Within the fifteen-to-twenty-five-year age group, males in particular were considered "prime" slaves. Shippers of slaves were not always able to satisfy the preferences of American buyers of slaves because changes in African slave supply conditions as well as in oceanic transport costs affected the age and sex composition of the Atlantic slave trade through time. Overall, however, no less than six out of ten of the slaves landing in America between 1650 and 1860 were male. Moreover, most, before 1800 at least, were adult. This pattern of slave shipments allowed American demand for slaves to dovetail to some degree with that within Africa or across the Sahara, where buyers of slaves tended to prefer to females. Nevertheless, the scale of the Atlantic slave trade after 1650 may have helped to skew the sex distribution of the population of parts of Atlantic Africa that were major suppliers of slaves to America. There are also claims that the Atlantic slave trade caused local depopulation in parts of Africa and even hindered African population growth, especially between 1700 and 1850. In this respect, the labor requirements of American plantation societies outside the United States ultimately produced distortions in population patterns on both sides of the Atlantic.

Slave importation reflected, and possibly contributed to, the failure of most American slave populations outside the United States to grow naturally before 1850, but why did the demographic history of slaves in the United States differ from that of most of those elsewhere in the Americas? In common with debates on population growth more generally, discussion of slave reproduction in the Americas has tended to revolve around the relative importance of mortality and fertility rates and the epidemiological, environmental and social factors that affected them. The search for explanations of differences in slave reproduction patterns has involved analysis of census, plantation, and other records, the last including anthropometric evidence that, by permitting the study of slaves' stature, helps to throw light on their nutrition. The search for explanation has also been guided by distinguishing areas of the Americas that focused on sugar cultivation and that attracted the largest slave imports from Africa from other slave-using areas of the Americas. The importance of this distinction is reinforced by evidence of demographic similarities between the sugar-growing sections of Louisiana and the West Indies and of the natural growth of slave populations in parts of Brazil and the Caribbean that focused on activities other than sugar production.

Labor regimes associated with sugar cultivation on large plantations often employing several hundred slaves are, therefore, increasingly seen to hold the key to explaining differences in slave reproduction rates in the Americas. Organized in gangs that required pregnant and nonpregnant women to labor alongside men, slaves on sugar plantations were subjected to perhaps one of the most arduous and brutal work regimes known to modern history. It involved long hours of closely supervised and heavy work, sometimes round the clock, in the field and sugar mill, during a crop season that could extend to more than six months. Outside of work on the sugar crop, slaves also often had to cultivate their own provision grounds. The reward for such efforts, moreover, seems to have been a diet that was probably inadequate nutritionally to both protect the health of slaves and meet the needs of the work effort imposed on them. Although its effects are difficult to quantify, such a lifestyle almost certainly contributed to the high mortality of all age groups of slaves on sugar plantations as slaves were, in Higman's words again, "literally worked to death." Equally, it almost certainly helped to lower fertility rates through its impact on slave family life and mating patterns and the ability or willingness of slave women to bear children. Moreover, indifference by sugar planters to the demographic consequences of the labor regimes over which they presided was arguably possible as long as supplies of fresh labor from Africa were available at a cost lower than that of encouraging slave reproduction. In tandem with a ready supply of slave labor from Africa, the sweet tooth of European consumers seems to have profoundly shaped patterns of slave demography in the Americas.

Slavery Outside the Americas. What, if anything, can the demography of slavery in the Americas after 1500 tell us about slave demography in those other times and places for which little information has survived? Is either of the two patterns of slave demography in the Americas likely to reflect slave demographic experience elsewhere, or are American patterns to be seen as extreme cases of slave demography historically? The latter seems the more plausible answer, thereby underlining perhaps the peculiarities of slave experiences in the Americas after 1500. Though no hard evidence exists, it is difficult to imagine slaves in other societies attaining rates of natural increase comparable to those in the antebellum United States. Indeed, few free populations outside the United States attained such rates of growth before the twentieth century. At the other extreme, there is evidence of gang slavery in the late Roman Republic and the early Roman Empire. It is also worth noting that sugar production spread to the Americas from the Middle East and the Mediterranean, though whether the latter depended on gang slavery is unclear. The possibility that slaves in societies outside the Americas sometimes faced work regimes as brutal and demographically disastrous as those encountered on American sugar plantations cannot be ignored. In addition, slaves were sometimes employed in military activities, no doubt with, at times, severe loss of life. Historically, however, many, if not most, slaves appear to have been employed in units where the employment environment tended to resemble slave-employment conditions in the Americas outside sugar production. This was perhaps particularly evident in Africa itself, where slaves working in small-scale units were also frequently absorbed into the lineage or kinship networks of their owners. The brutal experience of slaves on sugar plantations in the Americas should not mislead us, therefore, into assuming that most slave regimes in history were so costly demographically as that linking Africa with Brazil and the Caribbean before 1860. Nor, however, should the demography of slavery in the United States encourage us to neglect the human and social costs that slavery invariably inflicted on its victims even under the most favorable of demographic outcomes.

[*See also* Slavery *and* Slave Trade.]

BIBLIOGRAPHY

Bergad, Laird. *Slavery in the Demographic and Economic History of Minas Gerais, Brazil, 1720–1888.* Cambridge, 2000.

Drescher, Seymour, and Stanley L. Engerman, eds. *A Historical Guide to World Slavery.* New York, 1998.

Eltis, David, and Stanley L. Engerman. "Fluctuations in Sex and Age Ratios in the Transatlantic Slave Trade, 1663–1864." *Economic History Review* 46 (1993), 308–323.

Fogel, Robert W. and Stanley L. Engerman. *Time on the Cross.* 2 vol. London, 1974.

Higman, Barry. *Slave Populations of the British Caribbean 1807–1834.* Kingston, Jamaica, 1995.

Karasch, Mary C. *Slave Life in Rio de Janeiro, 1808–1850.* Princeton, 1987.

Lovejoy, Paul E. *Transformations in Slavery: A History of Slavery in Africa.* 2d ed. Cambridge, 2000.

Phillips, William D. Jr. *Slavery from Roman Times to the Early Transatlantic Trade.* Minneapolis, 1985.

DAVID RICHARDSON

SLAVERY. Economically, slavery has been most important as an institution by which labor can be extracted from marginalized persons although in many slave-using societies, slaves have had few productive roles. The questions of who is a slave and who is not and of what terms in different languages should be translated as "slave" have often been subject to debate. Generally, definitions of slavery have stressed either the slave as property or the slave as a person withdrawn from kinship structures and thus lacking in social identity. For Dutch ethnographer H. J. Nieboer (*Slavery as an Industrial System*, The Hague, 1910), the slave is property and performs compulsory labor. For Suzanne Miers and Igor Kopytoff (*Slavery in Africa*, Madison, 1977), the African slave is a fictive kinsman. For Orlando Patterson (*Slavery and Social Death*, Cambridge, Mass., 1982), slavery is rooted in "social death"; that is, slavery exists as an alternative to execution, and the slave is a dishonored isolate. In general, these definitions are linked. The property relationship makes it possible to deny the slave any kinship relationship. Conversely, the absence of kinship makes it possible to treat the slave as property and fully exploit his or her person.

Slavery probably originated from the question of what to do with captives. Female captives could always be absorbed as wives and often were. Male captives could be ransomed, killed, or absorbed. Among the American woodland Indians, the alternative was being tortured to death or taken in as a full member of the community. At some point in every society, the decision was made to exploit or sell captives rather than to kill, ransom, or incorporate them. The development of slavery thus was often linked to social differentiation. A society with slaves was by definition a class society. Preconditions were the ability to control the slaves and some reason for exploiting slave labor. Slavery did not usually exist among hunter-gatherers or simple horticultural societies. It existed in almost all complex preindustrial civilizations and among nomads capable of controlling and exploiting slaves.

Nieboer argues that slavery is most likely to develop where land is abundant, labor in short supply, and technology simple. This theory does not explain the origins of slavery, or why slavery is used rather than another form of unfree labor such as serfdom. It is also incorrect for technology; sugar involved increasingly complex machinery, and slaves in Brazil and the United States have been used profitably in industry. However, the theory holds for most highly developed slave systems. Evsey Domar ("The Causes of Slavery or Serfdom: A Hypothesis," *Journal of Economic History* 30 (1970), 18–32) extended Nieboer's formulation to an analysis of serfdom in Russia. Slavery was important in China, but there roles tended to be limited. High population densities meant that anyone who owned land could find labor. Although some powerful persons in early dynasties had very large slaveholdings, most Chinese slaves have been servants, concubines, and entertainers. Similarly, Arabs became major importers of slaves as early as the seventh century, but those slaves were used primarily as servants, concubines, and soldiers. In these and in many Asian societies, slaves were most likely to be found in the homes and palaces of the wealthy and powerful. Some slaves could also achieve power as military leaders or officials, particularly eunuchs. These people were still slaves, but they were wealthy because they were slaves, that is, totally dependent. In many societies, slavery has been a source of dependable supporters of those competing for power and a source of status.

Slave Societies. Moses Finley (*Ancient Society and Modern Ideology*, New York, 1980) has suggested that the first slave society was Greece. By slave society he means a society in which slaves were the major source of productive activity, and slavery shaped culture and all aspects of life. Marxists would refer to such a society as having a slave mode of production. There is no clear evidence that any earlier society depended on sl ave labor, but that does not mean that slavery was unimportant in earlier societies, or that slaves did not engage in productive activity. Slaves were numerous in Ancient Egypt and in early Mesopotamian civilizations. In India, slavery seems to go back to the Aryan conquests, which began about 1750 BCE, and may have existed earlier. Periods of conquest in India and elsewhere often involved massive enslavement. In Mesopotamia and Buddhist Southeast Asia, temples often had large slaveholdings. The Inca of Peru had a class of hereditary agricultural workers, but their role in production was marginal. Almost everywhere, prisoners of war were used on public works.

Finley argued that there were three preconditions to the creation of a slave society: private ownership of land, commodity production and the existence of markets in which surpluses could be sold, and the lack of adequate supplies of labor within the society. Societies have followed different paths to the creation of a slave society. For Athens, it was Solon's reforms. In the fifth century BCE, Athens was already producing for export and had slaves. Faced with social conflict caused by the spread of debt bondage, Solon canceled debts, abolished debt slavery, and granted citizenship to Athenian peasants and artisans. The poorer citizens became the rowers for the Athenian fleet. Landowners dealt with the resultant shortage of labor by purchasing slaves and using prisoners taken in Athenian wars. Slaves also moved into handicraft industries. The result was a society dependent on the constant import of slaves, their productive efforts, and the distinction between slave and citizen. In Athens, the demand created the supply. In Rome, the reverse may have been true. To be sure, slavery already existed when Roman armies began to spread Roman rule. These conquests made huge numbers of slaves available for latifundia created by the consolidation of estates in Italy. Small peasants displaced by this process either joined the urban proletariat or took military service and often ended up as colonists elsewhere in the empire.

The other slave societies cited by Finley were a result of the development of plantations in the Americas. The development of the modern slave plantation dates to the Crusades and the discovery by Venetians and Genoans that they could grow sugar using Arab technology and slave labor. As technology improved and demand for sugar increased, the sugar plantation became the central institution in the development of a capitalist agriculture and a highly regimented form of slavery. Free labor was used in early centuries, as among the Arabs, but increasingly slaves were necessary to grow sugar. Sugar plantations spread from Cyprus to the western Mediterranean, and then, as Iberian sailors moved out into the Atlantic, to islands discovered by them. Madeira and São Tomé became major sugar producers; but by the end of the sixteenth century, Brazil was the world's largest producer. The British settled on Barbados and the French on Saint Christopher in 1627. After experimenting with other crops, both islands shifted into sugar in the 1640s. A major factor was that the Dutch, who had briefly controlled Brazil, were able to provide technology, know-how, and credit. By the early eighteenth century, six nations were cultivating sugar in the West Indies; and for most of them the West Indian colonies were the most important overseas source of wealth and important markets for metropolitan industry.

None of the Atlantic islands suited to sugar had adequate supplies of labor. Some, such as Madeira, were unpopulated. On others, as later in the Americas, enslaved native labor was used; but native peoples often were not used to agricultural labor, and their numbers were speedily reduced by disease. Thus, the possibility of profit depended on finding labor. Both the Atlantic islands and Brazil found that labor largely in Africa. The British in the West Indies tried indentured labor, but indentured laborers from the British isles died almost three times as frequently as African slaves. Furthermore, as wages rose in seventeenth-century Britain, and conditions on sugar plantations became known, it was harder to recruit laborers. A similar history was replicated by other plantation crops: tobacco in the Chesapeake colonies of Virginia and Maryland and rice in South Carolina. Though East European slaves were important in the Mediterranean, African slaves became the primary source of labor, and racist ideologies developed to justify their exploitation. Slave plantations also developed in the Indian Ocean and in parts of the Dutch East Indies, and slaves were used almost everywhere Europeans settled up to the end of the eighteenth century. At the Cape of Good Hope and in the Indian Ocean, many of the slaves were Asian; in Southeast Asia, virtually all of them were.

There were other societies as well within which slave production was important. In some, slaves may have been

SLAVERY. Slaves work and prospect for gold in the mines of the region called Varaguas. Illumination from *Histoire naturelle des Indes*, the "Drake Manuscript," folio 100, late sixteenth century. (Pierpont Morgan Library, NY/Art Resource, NY)

as numerous as in ancient Greece. According to Anthony Reid (*Southeast Asia in the Age of Commerce 1450–1680*, New Haven, 1988), Southeast Asia met Nieboer's and most of Finley's conditions. Population was low, and land was freely available; by the sixteenth century, commodity production was widespread. Wars thus were fought not so much for territory as for slaves. These wars and the resultant enslavement and movement of masses of people were probably a major factor in keeping population densities low. Hence, a circular process evolved, in which low population densities made slaves necessary, leading to wars and the shifting around of conquered peoples, which increased mortality and kept population densities down. Two factors differentiate this case from ancient Greece and Rome and the Americas. First, power was arbitrary and the accumulation of wealth was safe only when it was transformed into a body of retainers and therefore into military power. This meant that property rights were not highly developed. Those who accumulated slaves had to create a balance between political and economic variables. Second, formal slavery coexisted with other forms of social obligation. The most important, debt slavery, is not actual slavery because debt slaves remained attached to a kinship unit and could be freed if they paid their debts.

Slave Supply. Slave societies created a tremendous demand for slaves. Only in Rome did supply precede use. Elsewhere, slave societies tended to be economically dynamic societies in which the profits from the exploitation of slave labor generated expansion. They also tended to have high levels of mortality, especially among the newly enslaved, who often arrived in poor health, were harshly treated, and inevitably had problems in adapting to new environments. There was also a significant demand from societies that were not slave societies but were important slave users. The Chinese market seems to have been fed largely, except during some periods of warfare, by the sale of children by the poor. In many areas, demand was structured by religion. Enslavement of Muslims was forbidden by Islam, and the conditions under which others could be enslaved were circumscribed. On the frontiers of Islam, these restrictions often were ignored, and the prohibition on enslaving Muslims justified enslavement of non-Muslims. This also meant that all slaves were brought in from outside the Muslim world. The same thing is true of Christianity. Even during the centuries when European planters were hungry for labor, Europeans regularly massacred but did not enslave each other.

There was thus a series of slaving frontiers, which moved as people converted to one religion or the other. Ancient Mesopotamian civilizations bought slaves from poorer hill regions. Greek merchants bought slaves from the Black Sea, which continued to supply slaves for Mediterranean peoples for over twenty-five hundred years. In the Middle Ages slaves were produced along the growing frontier of German expansion, but this trade subsided with the conversion of Poland and Lithuania to Christianity. Russia too was a source of slaves for Byzantium and the Muslim world. For Asia, James Warren (*The Sulu Zone*, Singapore, 1981) has described a mobile frontier of seaborne marauders that supplied servants, concubines, and workers for intersecting diasporas of European officials and Chinese merchants in Southeast Asia from the sixteenth to the nineteenth centuries.

African slaving frontiers, however, were unique in that slave trading and slave production became the most important economic activities for many African states. The Portuguese were able to purchase slaves on the West African coast in the fifteenth century, but their numbers were relatively small, rarely over one or two thousand a year and probably mostly people enslaved in local conflicts. As the trade increased, prices rose, and some coastal people became middlemen, pushing trade routes into the interior. Others, who resisted the lure of the trade, found that they had to sell slaves or be threatened by more powerful neighbors. During the second half of the seventeenth century, when demand by West Indian planters pushed prices higher, a series of states emerged in the interior of West Africa that specialized in the production of slaves. During the eighteenth century, over six million slaves were shipped across the Atlantic. Slaves also moved into the Sahara, across the Sahara, up the Nile, and across the Red Sea and the Indian Ocean. Precise data are rare for these other trades, but Austen has suggested that over twelve centuries eight million slaves may have been exported, but various very rough estimates suggest that the slave exports to the Mediterranean, the Middle East, and the Indian Ocean may have been as great as the Atlantic trade, although over a longer period of time.

A major by-product of slaving was the use of slaves within Africa. It is probable that in western Africa during the eighteenth century, as many slaves were kept as were exported, as a result of both increased availability and increased social differentiation. As in Southeast Asia, those who achieved wealth and power found that they had to invest some of their profits in accumulation of followers. This meant slaves for their armies and slave women as concubines, as the mothers of sons, and as rewards for men who served them. Slaveholdings were greatest in and around commercial cities, in Muslim states, in the core areas of slaving states such as Oyo and Asante, and along the desert's edge where slaves produced grain and cloth for exchange with transhumant pastoralists. In these areas, by the nineteenth century slaves often were a majority of the population, a higher percentage than in all of Finley's slave societies except for some of the West Indian islands. Thus, it can be argued that the slave trade created slave societies in Africa by making slave labor available for diverse purposes. In the nineteenth century, after European nations abolished the slave trade and slavery, the trade within Africa actually increased as slaves were directed not to export markets but to the production of palm oil and peanuts in West Africa and to cloves, sesame, and copra in Zanzibar and East Africa.

In many Asian and African societies, debt and poverty often forced people to sell their own children, but, in general, warfare and raiding were the major sources of slaves. The slave trade also provided an incentive for enslavement to be used as a penalty for criminal acts and a temptation to sell deviants, criminals, and political opponents. In slave-producing areas, the cost of slaves was low. Curtin (*Economic Change in Precolonial Africa*, Madison, Wis., 1975) suggests that the price of a slave was often about two times what it would cost to maintain the slave for a year. The importance of the slave trade to participants lay in the importance to them of both slaves and strategic commodities. States often depended on slave warriors to enslave others and on slave farmers to feed court and army. Slaves were exchanged for weapons, for iron that could be used to make weapons, and for commodities that could be distributed to those who served the state. Even in a decentralized society, income from the slave trade was necessary for acquisition of goods essential to the community's defense or adaptation of its economy. For example, among the Balanta of the Guinea coast, iron tools made it possible for the Balanta to shift to cultivation of rice, which produced higher yields from smaller areas and thus made it possible for cultivators to remain close to their walled villages.

The World the Slaves Made. Within slave systems, there was always a contradiction between the legal position of the slave and actual treatment. Legally, slaves were things, property, instruments of other people's will. In a slave caravan, on board a slave ship, sometimes in mines, or on public works, where there was no concern for reproduction, a slave really was a thing, and usually treated harshly. In all slave systems, harsh punishments, fear, and terror were used to maintain discipline. Whipping and sometimes even maiming were common. Nevertheless, most slaves were owned for some purpose. Either the slave lived in a household, and his or her willing service was desired, or the slave worked in a plantation or enterprise, where his or her productivity was important. Slavery gave the master arbitrary power, which in the hands of a sadistic or cruel individual, could be used brutally; but, generally, a concern for productivity forced the slave owner to recognize the slave's humanity. At the simplest level, this reflected itself in slave living arrangements. Slaves preferred small family huts to barracks-like accomodation. They wanted something of their own, and in most slave societies were allotted their own plots, which provided most of their sustenance and sometimes a surplus that could be traded.

In most societies, the slave family had no legal existence. Slaves could accumulate, but they could not bequeath or inherit; children could be sold independently of their mothers and spouses separated. Slaves could not count on their children supporting them in their old age. Slaves did, however, live in family units and have strong familial ties. These families tended to matriarchal, but ties were often broad, with numerous "aunts" and "uncles." Planters ignored these ties at their risk. In addition, slave systems generally involved some kind of "flow-through." Amelioration was possible in all slave systems. Slaves were treated better as they adapted to the system. Those who served faithfully were given privileges or better jobs. In Africa, there was a progression through stages from carefully supervised labor to a kind of sharecropping. There was almost always some manumission. In plantation systems of the Americas and the Indian Ocean, many of those manumitted were former lovers and offspring of their masters, but others were trusted retainers. Only in some parts of the American South was an effort made to restrict manumission, and even there legal fictions made it possible for some outstanding individuals to act as if free. For example, Simon Gray ran a barge business on the Mississippi River. Most modern slave societies had a significant freed slave population and a variety of work regimes.

Slave Work. In the first three centuries of European activity in the Americas, most of the people who crossed the Atlantic were African slaves. The largest number of slaves and the greatest profits were in sugar, which was also the greatest killer as it was grown in places with high disease rates. Unlike most other slave trades, the American trade involved primarily men. Slave prices were so low that it was more economical to buy slaves than to raise them. Although concubinage was common, few slaves were purchased for sexual purposes, and planters were rarely concerned about reproduction. The process of producing sugar was brutal. Units were large because they were built around a sugar mill; or, as in Brazil, there was a series of small farms around a large one. To get the most sugar, it was important to get the cane into the presses and the boiling room as soon as possible after it was cut. The harvest season was long, in some areas seven or eight months, during which slaves worked very long hours, sometimes shifts of eighteen to twenty-four hours. Tired slaves often were killed or permanently maimed by getting arms caught in the presses. Thus, sugar plantations everywhere had high mortality, a low rate of reproduction, and a constant demand for more slaves. The higher mortality of males meant that by 1808 the number of male and female slaves in the British West Indies was roughly equal, and by 1834 women were a majority.

Other crops had a better rate of reproduction. South Carolina rice was cultivated in an area with a poor disease environment, but that probably operated to the advantage of slaves because they generally worked on a task system rather than in gangs and were left alone more than sugar slaves. Coffee, indigo, cacao, and spices were also grown in the West Indies. In mainland North America, the major crops, tobacco and then cotton, had fewer economies of scale than other crops and thus were often cultivated in smaller units. Before Whitney invented the cotton gin in 1793, the largest market for slaves was in tobacco-growing areas of Virginia and Maryland. Most tobacco farms had fewer than twenty slaves. These slaves had to work hard, but the work was less harsh than that in sugar, and their environment was healthier. By the end of the eighteenth century, the Virginia slave population was growing. With cotton, though there were some economies of scale and some very wealthy planters, the average slave owner owned ten slaves. Within all slave systems, a hierarchy of roles developed. Slave drivers directed work gangs, and there were artisans such as masons and carpenters. If there was not enough work, skilled workers were hired out, or they hired themselves out and paid their masters part of their salaries. Urban artisans also often worked on a self-hire system. About a quarter of the slaves in most American systems were not involved in direct production, including house slaves, who worked long hours but had less onerous tasks than field workers.

The end of the slave trade was the beginning of the end for slave systems in the West Indies, but it strengthened slavery in the United States. In both areas, imports ended in 1808. At this time, no West Indian island was reproducing its slave population internally, but Barbados went into a surplus after 1810. For the United States, the slave trade ended just as the cotton boom was beginning. Fueled by the expansion of cotton to Alabama and Mississippi, slave prices tripled between 1800 and 1850. Slaves were valuable property. Although infant mortality remained high and infant health poor, adult slaves tended to be as healthy as their free counterparts, as a result of good nutrition, decent health care, and a favorable disease environment. Therefore, natural increase was able to supply the demand for labor. Over a half-century, there was a massive shift of slave populations from older states. Virginia contained 42 percent of the U.S. slave population in 1790, but by 1860 two-thirds of the slaves in the United States were working in the cotton South.

For economic historians, the most heated questions have been about the profitability of slavery and its efficiency. The nineteenth-century debate on abolition was influenced by a belief that free labor was more productive than slave labor. Eric Williams (*Capitalism and Slavery*, Chapel Hill, N.C., 1944) argued that abolition took place in the West Indies when it did because slavery had served the function of creating a dependent labor force and was declining. Other writers responded that the planters themselves defended slavery vigorously, and that the plantations were still highly profitable at the time of abolition. Furthermore, Cuba and Brazil benefited from British abolition by expanding their slave-based sugar production. Up to the mid-twentieth century, most writers assumed that free labor was more productive than slave labor, and that the slave plantation was a system in decline at the time of Civil War. In 1956, Kenneth Stampp (*The Peculiar Institution*, New York, 1956) claimed that the slave plantation was highly profitable. In 1958, Alfred Conrad and John R. Meyer ("The Economics of Slavery in the Ante-Bellum South," *Journal of Political Economy* 66, 95–130) argued that there was a 10 percent return on investment in slaves, and that it was cheaper to raise a slave than to buy one. Robert Fogel and Stanley Engerman (*Time on the Cross*, Boston, 1974) argued that organization and intensification produced greater efficiency. Put in simpler terms, a slave could be forced to work harder than a free worker, and, because a slave has little choice of leisure or consumption, more could be extracted from him. Using latest statistical methods, Fogel and Engerman calculated that slave farms were 40 percent more efficient than free farms, that in material terms slaves were as well off as free workers, and that the system showed no signs of decline. *Time on the Cross* was vehemently attacked, but most writers accept today that throughout the Americas slave plantations were still productive when slavery was abolished.

Linked to the question of profitability was the question of the contribution of slavery to economic growth. Williams argued that the triangular trade made a major contribution to financing the Industrial Revolution. Although it is now clear that ties to industrialization were limited, profits from the linked trades of slaves, sugar, and supplies contributed greatly to growth of the North American colonies and to accumulation of wealth in the metropolitan areas. For the United States, the question is posed by the different rates of growth of the North and the South. Gavin Wright argued that that the efficiency demonstrated by Fogel and Engerman was based on the ability of the plantation to put more labor into the fields. Slave owners were invested largely in movable capital, human beings, and thus had little commitment to land and local development. As a result, per capita incomes grew, but the South experienced a much slower development of canals and railroads than the North, and a slower rate of population growth. This argument can be extended to the West Indies and northeast Brazil, where the slave economy discouraged free immigration and slave owners often were not interested in development of other resources.

Emancipation and Decline. Islam, Christianity, and Buddhism all sought to limit the exploitation of slaves and encourage humane treatment and manumission; but no systematic attack on slavery was launched before the middle of the eighteenth century. Slavery did decline in a number of areas. Thus, in early Japan, slavery existed, but by 1200, it had virtually disappeared. In Russia, slavery disappeared by the early seventeenth century; but during the eighteenth century, serfdom was transformed by Peter the Great in ways that came to resemble slavery. Probably the best documented decline is in medieval Europe. In the last centuries of the Roman empire, Roman armies were no longer enslaving large numbers of people. Though enslavement increased briefly while the Germanic kingdoms were establishing themselves, the decline of a market economy deprived Roman slave systems of their economic rationale. With retreat into a manorial economy, slaves were gradually converted into serfs, attached to the land but with rights to marriage and to the products of that land. At the same time, free peasants found the protection of the manor desirable, and the two groups merged. Slavery persisted for centuries at various royal courts as well as along various frontiers, but by the twelfth century it had disappeared in much of northern Europe. Slavery continued in the Mediterranean, but at a much reduced level: largely urban, rarely over 10 percent of the population, and mostly servants or workers in petty enterprises.

The eighteenth-century abolition movement rooted in both Christian and Englightenment thought had very rapid successes. The Danes abolished the slave trade in 1792. The French abolished slavery in 1794, but it was reestablished by Napoleon in 1802. Britain and the United States ended the slave trade in 1808, and the British forced most European powers to do likewise, often reluctantly, after the Napoleonic Wars ended. Slavery was abolished by the British in 1833, the French in 1848, and the Americans in 1865. With Brazilian abolition in 1888, it had been eliminated throughout the Western world. During the following twenty years, it was abolished in most European colonies as well as Thailand, China, and Turkey. The question is, why did the abolitionist movement develop when it did, and why was it so successful? For long, it was treated as a pure triumph of virtue. This approach was attacked by Williams, who argued that the logic of abolition was economic. Both arguments are hard to sustain today. The issue is why hard-headed legislators in different countries were persuaded to abolish a profitable institution. The most likely explanations involve the transformation of values linked to industrialization, or the hostility of free labor or groups dependent on it to competition with slave labor.

Emancipation in different areas took place under very different circumstances. Britain and France abolished slavery and compensated slave owners. In the United States, emancipation came as a result of a war the slave owners lost. In Brazil, it came in 1888 as slaves themselves, heartened by earlier small measures, began to take matters into their own hands. In many colonies, it was imposed reluctantly by colonial regimes on slave owners of a different culture. However, there were similarities. In no area was compensation paid to former slaves. The major issue in most areas was control of their labor. In this struggle, policymakers, slave owners, and many abolitionists displayed similar perceptions of the slaves as improvident, lazy, and dependent on the discipline that slavery provided. There was on all sides a fear of vagrancy, hunger, crime and disorder. To control former slaves, the British used Masters and Servants legislation in many parts of the empire. In India in 1843, the British used a formula that other colonial regimes adopted: they simply withdrew the support of the state from slavery. No slave owner could go to court to claim or enforce a master-slave relationship. Colonial regimes adopting the Indian model usually hoped that most slaves would not notice and would continue what they were doing.

Fears of disorder were almost everywhere unjustified. Slaves generally sought two things: they wanted to control their work life and their family life. Generally, the crucial variable was access to land. Where slaves could get land, they left. On Mauritius, where lands were freely available in the interior, almost all of the slaves left the plantations. On Jamaica, where mountainous land was available, female labor was almost totally withdrawn from the plantation, and male labor was reduced. On Barbados, however, all land was owned, and freed slaves had no option but to continue working on the plantation. In colonial Africa, there were massive departures by people who had been enslaved during their own lifetime. In French West Africa, as many as a million went home. In Northern Nigeria and the Sudan, British colonial governors moved strongly to limit similar migrations and keep slaves where they were; but everywhere slaves moved into separate homesteads, and everywhere masters found it necessary to concede increasing autonomy to their slaves. In the United States, a massive effort was made to assist and educate former slaves. Some took over plantations. Others took to the road to look for a better life. With time, the zeal for reform faded, and Southern whites regained control of their political systems. Control over land and credit then became crucial. Most former slaves had no way of buying land. They rejected plantation labor but usually were forced to work as sharecroppers.

In many places, the response of slaves had important long-range consequences. The retreat into the hills of Mauritius was a retreat into subsistence. Planters had less control over Indian indentured workers, many of whom became hawkers, merchants, artisans and landowners. In the United States, slaves won the right to farm for themselves, but were locked into poverty by racism and a lack of land. Generally, though often poor and often exploited, freed slaves were in many ways better off than slave workers. Though privileged royal slaves have often sought to maintain their status and servants have found it useful to nurture client relationships, there is no known case of slave workers or cultivators refusing freedom or seeking a return to slavery.

Slavery is illegal today everywhere in the world, but civil war has led to a return of slave raiding in the Sudan, and slavery still exists in isolated areas of the Mauritanian Sahara. Millions of people are still in some form of captivity. These include children who make rugs in Asia, adults and children in the sex industry, migrant workers in places like the Amazon and the Dominican Republic who are held prisoner, and children forced to work or fight in various civil conflicts. Most are held captive only as long as they are considered useful to their captors.

[*See also* Slave Demography *and* Slave Trade.]

BIBLIOGRAPHY

Austen, Ralph. "The 19th Century Islamic Slave Trade from East Africa (Swahili and Red Sea Coasts): A Tentative Census." In *The Economics of the Indian Ocean Slave Trade in the Nineteenth Century*, edited by W. G. Clarence-Smith. London, 1988.

Austen, Ralph. "The Mediterranean Slave Trade Out of Africa: A Tentative Census." In *The Human Commodity: Perspectives on the Trans-Saharan Slave Trade*, edited by Elizabeth Savage. London, 1992.

Berlin, Ira. *Many Thousands Gone: The First Two Centuries of Slavery in North America*. Cambridge, Mass., 1998.

Cooper, Frederick. *Plantation Slavery on the East Coast of Africa*. New Haven, 1977.

Curtin, Philip. *The Rise and Fall of the Plantation Complex*. Cambridge, 1990.

David, Paul A., Herbert Gutman, Richard Sutch, Peter Temin, and Gavin Wright. *Reckoning with Slavery: A Critical Study in the Quantitative History of American Negro Slavery*. New York, 1976.

Eltis, David. *Economic Growth and the Ending of the Transatlantic Slave Trade*. Oxford, 1987.

Elvin, Mark. *The Pattern of the Chinese Past*. Stanford, Calif., 1973.

Finley, Moses. "Slavery." In *International Encyclopedia of the Social Sciences*, edited by David L. Sills, vol. 14, pp. 307–313. New York, 1968.

Fogel, Robert W. *Without Consent or Contract: The Rise and Fall of American Slavery*. New York, 1989.

Genovese, Eugene. *The World the Slaveholders Made*. New York, 1969.

Genovese, Eugene. *Roll, Jordan, Roll: The World the Slaves Made*. New York, 1974.

Higman, Barry. *Slave Populations of the British Caribbean*. Baltimore, 1984.

Hopkins, Keith. *Conquerors and Slaves*. Cambridge, 1978.

Klein, Martin A, ed. *Breaking the Chains: Slavery, Bondage, and Emancipation in Africa and Asia*. Madison, Wis., 1993.

Lovejoy, Paul. *Transformations in Slavery: A History of Slavery in Africa*. Cambridge, 1983.

Meillassoux, Claude. *The Anthropology of Slavery: The Womb of Iron and Gold*, translated by Alide Desnois. Chicago, 1991.

Morgan, Philip. *Slave Counterpoint: Black Culture in the Eighteenth Century Chesapeake and Low Country*. Chapel Hill, N.C., 1998.

Patnaik, Utsa, and Manjari Dingwaney, eds. *Chains of Servitude: Bondage and Slavery in India*. Chennai, 1985.

Reid, Anthony, ed. *Slavery, Bondage and Dependency in Southeast Asia*. St. Lucia, 1983.

Schwartz, Stuart. *Sugar Plantations in the Formation of Brazilian Society: Bahia, 1550–1835*. Cambridge, 1985.

Sheridan, Richard B. *Sugar and Slavery: An Economic History of the British West Indies, 1623–1775*. Baltimore, 1974.

Solow, Barbara, ed. *British Capitalism and Caribbean Slavery*. Cambridge, 1987.

Solow, Barbara, and Stanley Engerman, eds. *Slavery and the Rise of the Atlantic System*. Cambridge, 1991.

Toledano, Ehud. *Slavery and Abolition in the Ottoman Middle East*. Seattle, 1998.

Wright, Gavin. *The Political Economy of the Cotton South*. New York, 1978.

MARTIN A. KLEIN

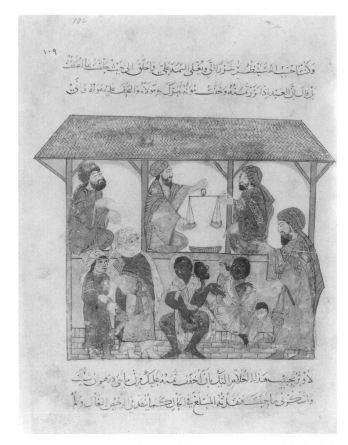

SLAVE TRADE. The thirty-fourth of the *maqamat* (assemblics) of al-Hariri (died 1122) illustrated by Yahya al-Wasiti in 1237. The *maqamat* are a collection of anecdotes featuring a narrator and a witty vagabond called Abu Zayd. This scene, set in Zabid in Yemen, involves the purchase of a slave. "Here is the boy," (says Abu Zayd masquerading as a slave merchant)," . . . I wish to make you fond of the lad by lightening the price for him; so weigh out two hundred dirhams." (Bibliothèque Nationale de France, Paris)

SLAVE TRADE. Wherever societies or states have sought to exploit slave labor, trades in slaves have commonly existed, either to allow the numbers of enslaved people to expand or simply to sustain the size of the enslaved population. Given the widespread reliance on slavery by states or empires throughout history, trafficking in slaves has thus been an important feature of international trade or trade within societies from antiquity onward. Egyptian and Greco-Roman slavery clearly depended on the marketing of slaves, and, while evidence on slave trafficking in Asia and medieval Europe is limited, so too did slavery in Southeast Asia up to the nineteenth century or in parts of the post-Roman Mediterranean world. Slavery was not a condition confined to particular peoples, but large proportions of those sold as slaves in the Mediterranean or in the Middle East came from sub-Saharan Africa. Furthermore, trafficking in slaves in the Red Sea and Indian Ocean largely centered on the forced migration of peoples from East Africa, while the greatest long-distance traffic in enslaved peoples in history—that to the Americas between 1500 and 1870—was exclusively a trade in Africans.

This article concentrates on the post-Columbian, Atlantic slave trade, largely because it is the most well documented and researched of all slave trades. It is worth emphasizing, however, that Africans were not the only victims of slave trafficking in history—many victims of slave traders in Southeast Asia were from the Indonesia archipelago—and that trafficking in enslaved Africans across the Sahara predated the Atlantic slave trade by many centuries. Moreover, trades in enslaved Africans continued and, in the case of East Africa, expanded during and after suppression of the transatlantic trade. The Atlantic trade may, therefore, have been the largest and most concentrated, temporally and racially, ocean-borne traffic in slaves in human history—massively outstripping similar trades across or within other oceans—but it was not an uncommon trade. Only from the perspective of the early-twenty-first-century Atlantic world, with its emphasis on free labor, does the Atlantic slave trade or indeed other trades in enslaved peoples appear exceptional or unusual.

Few aspects of the Atlantic slave trade have attracted more attention among economic historians than its origins, its volume and composition, and its profitability. Each of these issues has been the source of major debate, exposing interests in subsets of issues of broader significance for economic historians. Debate over the origins of the transatlantic traffic has involved consideration of the relative importance of economic and noneconomic factors in promoting its development. Similarly, arguments over the volume of the Atlantic slave trade, while not unimportant in their own right, ultimately relate to wider issues. These include the scale of involvement of African societies in the export slave trade, the human cost of slave trafficking, and the impact of the Atlantic slave trade on African development. Equally, preoccupation with the profitability of slave trading reflects an interest in such related issues as the bargaining positions of African and European traders and the relationship between colonialism, transatlantic slavery, capital accumulation, and European industrialization. In these respects, debates about the Atlantic slave trade have become closely intertwined with investigations of disparities in regional economic development and performance in the Atlantic world during the last five hundred years.

Origins of the Atlantic Slave Trade. Just as slavery underpinned the creation of other empires in history, so the Atlantic slave trade was an integral part of European expansionism from the time of Columbus, a critical outcome of which was colonization of the Americas and exploitation of American natural resources through African labor. European overseas expansion had, of course, both eastward-looking and westward-looking faces, and while European involvement in the shipping of slaves was principally an Atlantic activity, development of the transatlantic traffic in slaves relied heavily on Indian textiles and cowries (or shell money), both major trade goods in western Africa. If goods from the East were important in supplementing European and even American goods in facilitating transactions by Europeans in slaves in Africa, it was demand for labor in the Americas that largely drove the growth of the transatlantic traffic in enslaved Africans from the sixteenth century onward.

Central to rising demand for labor in the Americas was sugar, the cultivation of which was transplanted by Europeans from the Atlantic islands off Europe and Africa first to Brazil by the 1530s and then a century later to the West Indies. Although slaves were employed in a range of other agricultural and nonagricultural activities in the Americas as time went on, as much as 90 percent of the labor time of newly enslaved Africans was probably devoted to producing sugar and its derivatives. The scale and direction of the slave trade thus depended on the labor needs of the sugar plantation complex. This pattern was reinforced by the collapse of local American population levels under European colonization—thus creating an acute imbalance in land-labor ratios that enslaved labor from outside helped to rectify—and by the widespread failure of enslaved populations to sustain themselves naturally. To net demand for slave labor was added replacement demand for labor.

The extent to which economic, political, or ideological factors determined the racial composition of the Atlantic slave trade is an issue of debate. This debate has been reinvigorated by claims that, in strictly economic terms, enslaving Africans was not necessarily the low-cost option. It may, indeed, have been cheaper to resort to coerced European labor. Be this as it may, by the time the sugar revolution took off in the Americas, enslaved Africans were already identified with sugar production in the Mediterranean and Atlantic islands, thereby foreshadowing later developments, based on European capital and African labor, in Brazil and the West Indies. Whatever combination of economic and political factors is used to explain the rise of African slavery in the Americas, however, it was demand for sugar among Europeans that largely accounts for the growth and scale of slave shipments across the Atlantic in the three and a half centuries after 1500.

Slave Trade Volume. Modern attempts to measure the magnitude of the Atlantic slave trade—as well as its temporal and geographical patterns—date from Philip Curtin's "census" of the trade (*The Atlantic Slave Trade: A Census*). Relying on published data, Curtin concluded that, ±20 percent, some 9.4 million enslaved Africans landed in America during the history of the transatlantic slave trade. Curtin did not attempt to estimate the number of slaves taken from Africa, but assuming that 15 percent of those shipped died in transit, Curtin's 9.4 million arrivals figure translates into an estimate of shipments from Africa of, ±20 percent, just over 11 million people. This represented a substantial downward revision of most previous claims about the scale of the Atlantic slave trade and, not unsurprisingly, provoked a wave of new research, based on previously untapped primary sources, on the magnitude of the trades of major slave-carrying nations. Such research has, until now, advanced more rapidly in the case of British, French, and Dutch slave trades than of the Portuguese. Continuing weaknesses in information on the Portuguese trade represents an important deficiency in our knowledge of the Atlantic slave trade, particularly since Portugal had a much longer association with the Atlantic slave trade than other European nations.

Continuing deficiencies in data have not prevented several historians from making new global estimates of the trade. Underpinning these are new estimates of the distribution of the trade among national carriers, as well as across time and space. Notwithstanding improvements in knowledge of numbers of slaves shipped, we still know very little about the total numbers of people in Africa affected by the slave trade or even of the size of the African populations from whom slaves were drawn. In this respect, our knowledge of the demography of the slave trade and thus its impact on Africa still remains very incomplete.

A number of issues have been clarified since Curtin's census appeared. To begin with, whatever problems Curtin faced in making his calculations, his global estimate of the trade has proved remarkably resilient. Most recent assessments suggest that it is unlikely that more than 12 million slaves were taken from Africa to America between 1500 and 1870. Indeed, the most recent recalculation suggests that just over 11 million slaves were taken from Africa to America, 9.6 million of whom reached their destination (Eltis, 2001). The last figure is only marginally higher than Curtin's original estimate. While some historians are likely to remain skeptical of such calculations, assessments of the global dimensions of the Atlantic slave trade now seem to have come full circle.

Atlantic Slave Trade Composition. Research done since Curtin's census has given greater solidity to other quantitative aspects of the transatlantic traffic in slaves. For example, the Portuguese or, more accurately, Portuguese-Brazilians were overall the largest single carriers of slaves, entering the traffic earliest and leaving it late. Second to the Portuguese were the British, who entered the trade consistently only from the 1640s but from 1670 to 1807 carried probably more than 40 percent of all the slaves crossing the Atlantic, eclipsing the Portuguese in the process. Without Parliamentary abolition of British slave carrying in 1807, the British may well have continued to overshadow other slave carriers after that time. Notwithstanding the relative briefness of their involvement in slave carrying, the British carried more than 3 million slaves from Africa and together with the Portuguese, who carried probably more than 5 million, accounted for nearly three-quarters of all the slaves leaving Africa from 1500 to 1870. Of the remaining 2.8 million or so slaves shipped from Africa, perhaps half were carried in French ships, with Dutch, Spanish, mainland North American, and Danish carriers accounting for almost all the rest.

The temporal distribution of slave shipments across the Atlantic was uneven. Before 1650, the number of slaves leaving Africa for America seems to have been no more than five to ten thousand a year. Almost all were taken to Brazil. The sugar revolution in the Caribbean from the 1640s onward combined with further increases in ship-ments to Brazil to produce, however, a huge surge in slave shipments during the following century and a half. By 1780–1800, the number of the slaves entering the transatlantic traffic was eighty thousand or more a year, almost two-thirds being destined for the West Indies and the rest for Brazil. Thereafter, British abolition of slave carrying in 1807 and subsequent efforts to suppress slave carrying by others caused some reduction in the transatlantic slave traffic. Even so, expanding demand for slaves in southeast Brazil and in Cuba helped to ensure that some fifty-five thousand Africans a year were still entering the Atlantic slave trade from 1810 to 1850. Thus, more enslaved Africans were shipped to America after Great Britain abolished its slave trade than during the entire first century and a half of the traffic. Put another way, more than 90 percent of the Africans entering the transatlantic slave trade did so during the two centuries after 1650.

The growth in transatlantic slave shipments in the century or so after 1650 had major repercussions for patterns of slave supply in Africa. Whereas those entering the traffic before 1650 were very largely shipped from areas south of the Congo, increases in shipments after 1650 largely depended on shipments from other parts of Atlantic Africa. Prominent among these additional sources of slaves were the Gold Coast, the Bight of Benin (or Slave Coast) and the Bight of Biafra in West Africa, and the Loango Coast north of the Congo in West-Central Africa. Other parts of Atlantic Africa, such as Senegambia and Upper Guinea, supplied slaves to America, notably from 1750 to 1800, and Southeast Africa was also drawn on as a source of slaves for America from the 1780s onward. Overall, however, West-Central Africa (north and south of the Congo), the Gold Coast, the Slave Coast, and the Bight of Biafra supplied more than 85 percent of the enslaved Africans taken to America from 1500 to 1870. It was the responsiveness to external demand of slave suppliers in these parts of Atlantic Africa that largely accounts for the expansion of slave shipments to America during the two centuries after 1650. It was also, of course, these parts of Africa that bore most of the burdens or costs associated with supplying the Atlantic slave trade.

Profitability and Costs of Slave Trade. The impact of the Atlantic slave trade on Africa has been and remains a major area of debate. It relates to the wider issue of the relationship of the slave trade to regional disparities in economic development in societies bordering the Atlantic Basin since the time of Columbus. It is widely accepted that without coerced labor, commercial exploitation by European colonists of the natural resources of the Americas after 1500 would have been hindered. African slave labor is thus seen to have been crucial to the growth of the plantation complex in the Americas and of the wealth of the American planter class. This complex, in turn, was linked to the emergence of transatlantic trades in sugar and other agricultural products as dynamic elements in the expansion of European international trade and capitalist relations from the mid-seventeenth century onward and thereby as pillars of European industrialization. By contrast, the processes by which enslaved Africans were supplied to America are seen to have inflicted untold damage on the societies from which slaves were drawn. Indeed, for some, the outcome of the Atlantic slave trade was akin to a zero-sum game with European and white American prosperity based on the exploitation of enslaved Africans being associated with systematic depopulation and underdevelopment of Africa. What light does recent research throw on such claims about the slave trade's impact on Africa and Europe?

As the Atlantic slave trade drew mainly on societies bordering Atlantic Africa between the Gold Coast and southern Angola, its impact on Africa was perhaps more limited geographically than is sometimes implied. Even within the regions consistently and heavily involved in supplying slaves to America, moreover, some groups evidently benefited from the trade. With few exceptions, control of the slave supply to Europeans remained in African hands, and the indications are that the bargaining positions of Africans and Europeans were not so unbalanced in favor of Europeans as claims about African underdevelopment might lead one to suppose. On the contrary, during the peak years of the Atlantic slave trade, 1750 to 1850, the terms of trade between Africans and Europeans at the coast tended to favor the former, assisting those who controlled slave exports to increase their real incomes. In this respect, the impact of the Atlantic slave trade on income levels and wealth accumulation in Africa was not wholly negative.

It is difficult not to believe, however, that in any assessment of the balance sheet of participation in the Atlantic slave trade, the gains to Africa were outweighed by the costs. Most of the direct costs of the trade were borne by its immediate victims, many of whom never even reached the coast of Africa or boarded a ship bound for America. Figures on the numbers of slaves shipped, large though they are, are thus likely to understate, perhaps substantially, the private costs to individuals of Africa's involvement in the Atlantic slave trade. To these private costs must also be added the social costs or externalities associated with sustained and large-scale procurement of slaves for export. The burden of such costs almost certainly varied from one locality to another, depending among other things on the mechanisms used to procure slaves. Even so, prolonged exposure of African societies to enslavement activities created distortions in demographic structures (given shippers' preferences for adult males) and, according to some historical simulations, caused depopulation or even population decline. The social implications of these demographic consequences of enslavement activities were compounded by others, notably increased levels of disorder, violence, and insecurity and, in some cases, endemic political instability. It is impossible to measure precisely the social costs to Africa of participation in the slave trade. However, given, the importance often attributed by economists to political stability and social order in promoting economic development and welfare, African participation in the Atlantic slave trade, while profitable to some, almost certainly generated more pain than gain for most of those whose lives were affected by it.

If, on balance, Africa lost by participation in the slave trade, how much did Europe gain? More specifically, what contribution did transatlantic slavery and the slave trade make to promoting European industrialization?

The exploitation of coerced labor and its contribution to wealth accumulation in Europe and North America is a long-running historical theme. For example, Karl Marx (*Capital*, 3 volumes, London, 1959 edition) highlighted the use of slaves to generate surplus value, while J. A. Hobson (*The Evolution of Modern Capitalism*, London, 1906) emphasized how exploitation of serfs and slaves by Italian republics provide the wealth to nurture "capitalistic methods of production at home." Eric Williams (*Capitalism and Slavery*, London, 1944) later applied this type of argument to explain the British Industrial Revolution, his most famous work being described as a study of the role of slavery and the slave trade in providing the capital to finance British industrialization. The fact that Great Britain was both the first industrial nation and the major slave-carrying nation from 1650 to 1807 gives some plausibility to Williams's argument. Its plausibility is further reinforced by evidence of personal and commercial ties between the merchants of Liverpool, the dominant British slave port from 1750 to 1807, and the emergent textile manufacturing capitalists of Manchester, often regarded as the cradle of Great Britain's Industrial Revolution. Superficially at least, Williams's assertion that profits from slavery and the slave trade fertilized British industrialization appears, therefore, to carry conviction. At the same time, it underlines the importance of overseas trade, mercantilism, and colonial expansion to British eighteenth-century economic development, notwithstanding economist Adam Smith's claim in the *Wealth of Nations* (1776) that colonies were a net loss to Great Britain.

Slavery and Industrialization. The fact that from 1500 to 1870 Portugal carried more slaves across the Atlantic but failed to industrialize first has encouraged skepticism of Williams's arguments regarding slavery and industrial capitalism. Evidently, wealth from the slave trade and Brazilian slavery was alone incapable of propelling

Portugal along the road to industrialization. A similar message is implicit in studies critical of specific aspects of Williams's argument in the British context. One issue has been the profitability of the British slave trade and plantation slavery. While yielding respectable and sometimes spectacular private rates of return, these activities were not apparently the financial bonanza implied by Williams. Moreover, comparisons between earnings from slaving voyages, with estimates of eighteenth-century British investment generally or even in specific sectors of the economy, suggest, almost without exception, that slave-trade profits could have contributed at best only small amounts to financing early British industrial expansion. In effect, financing of British industry depended on a range of sources, of which profits from slavery were one. Similar approaches have been adopted—and similar conclusions reached—in analyzing relationships between eighteenth-century British overseas trade in general and colonial trade in particular and demand for British industrial output. The value of such approaches remains controversial, however, not least because they may be weak in explaining economic or structural change. In this context, it is worth noting that slave-produced goods, such as sugar, coffee, and tobacco, helped, for better or worse, to reshape British consumption patterns and to foster the growth of such new institutions as coffeehouses. It is also perhaps not unimportant that the exports needed to pay for these new consumer goods and the slave labor that produced them absorbed increasing proportions of British industrial output in the eighteenth century.

African and colonial markets were significant outlets for British cotton and linen textile manufacturers after 1750. At the same time, the financial needs of trade in sugar and slaves are seen to have nurtured financial innovation in Great Britain, helping to promote London's status as Europe's premier financial center. Such developments in consumption, industry, and finance were not solely or even necessarily principally dependent upon British involvement in transatlantic slavery, but involvement nevertheless helped to promote change in many areas of British economic life. Williams may have overstated the impact of slavery and the slave trade on British industrialization, but those who reject his views run the risk of understating their impact on social and economic change in eighteenth-century Great Britain and perhaps other parts of western Europe.

[*See also* Asiento; Slave Demography; *and* Slavery.]

BIBLIOGRAPHY

Curtin, Philip. *The Atlantic Slave Trade: A Census.* Madison, Wis., 1969.

Drescher, Seymour, and Stanley L. Engerman eds., *A Historical Guide to World Slavery.* Oxford, 1998.

Eltis, David. *The Rise of African Slavery in the Americas.* Cambridge, 2000.

Eltis, David. "The Volume and Structure of the Transatlantic Slave Trade: A Reassessment." *William and Mary Quarterly* 58 (2001), 17–46.

Finkelman, Paul, and Joseph C. Miller eds., *Macmillan Encyclopedia of World Slavery.* 2 vols. New York, 1998.

Inikori, Joseph E. *Africans and the Industrial Revolution in England.* Cambridge, 2000.

Inikori, Joseph E., and Stanley L. Engerman eds. *The Atlantic Slave Trade.* Durham, N.C., 1992.

Klein, Herbert S. *The Atlantic Slave Trade.* Cambridge, 1999.

Manning, Patrick. *Slavery and African Life: Occidental, Oriental, and African Slave Trades.* Cambridge, 1990.

Savage, Elizabeth, ed. *The Human Commodity: Perspectives on the Trans-Saharan Slave Trade.* London, 1992.

Solow, Barbara L. ed. *Slavery and the Rise of the Atlantic System.* Cambridge, 1991.

Thornton, John. *Africa and Africans in the Making of the Atlantic World, 1400–1800.* Cambridge, 1998.

DAVID RICHARDSON

SLAVIC CENTRAL EUROPE. Bohemia, Moravia, and Slovakia comprise a region in the heart of East Central Europe and, despite significant differences in political history, share some common economic and geographic characteristics. The western and northern perimeters of the region are bounded by mountains, spanning the area from the Šumava range in southwestern Bohemia to the Sudeten Mountains in the northwest and the Tatra and Ore Mountains in northern Slovakia. The mountains contain a variety of minerals, including silver, copper, iron, uranium, and in Northwest Bohemia, brown coal. Celtic tribes, who had settled the region by the fifth century BCE, mined these metals even before the arrival of the Slavs in the seventh century. The gentle hills and plains of central and southern Bohemia, the highlands of central Moravia, and the Danube River valley in southern Moravia and Slovakia contain rich agricultural land. Bohemia's trade was oriented historically toward the north via the Vltava (Moldau) and Labe (Elbe) Rivers. The trade of Moravia and Slovakia was oriented traditionally south along the Danube River, which runs through Bratislava, the capital of Slovakia.

During the ninth century, much of the region was united in the Great Moravian Empire, which engaged in trade throughout Central Europe. Slovakia was incorporated into the Hungarian kingdom in 907, while the rulers of Bohemia and Moravia accepted the suzerainty of the Holy Roman Emperor in 1041. Both Hungary and the Bohemian crownlands joined the Habsburg monarchy in 1526. The era from the twelfth century to the fourteenth century was one of increasing prosperity, based on productive agriculture (including aquaculture in southern Bohemia), forestry, crafts, silver mining, and metalworking. German craftspeople and farmers began settling in Slavic Central Europe in the thirteenth and fourteenth centuries.

The prosperity of these years was undermined by changes in trade patterns and politics beginning in the fifteenth century. Jan Hus's (1369–1415) religious reform movement led to the Hussite Wars of the mid-fifteenth century, which solidified the control of the towns and gentry over the government of Bohemia and Moravia. At the same time, however, the urban economy began to decline as European trade became more oriented toward the Mediterranean Sea and the Atlantic Ocean. The silver mines of East Central Europe were exhausted just as Europe became awash in American silver and gold. Thus, even before the outbreak of the Thirty Years' War (1618–1648), the economy of Slavic Central Europe had begun to decline.

The defeat of the Bohemian rebels at the Battle of White Mountain in 1620 brought about significant political, social, and economic changes. The political and economic influence of urban centers was eroded; new feudal burdens were imposed on the peasantry; and a new nobility, which was predominantly German in culture, Catholic in religion, and imperial in loyalty, was established in Bohemia. The traditional view that Czech craft production was decimated after 1620 has been replaced by a clearer understanding that the decline began earlier and that, even during the seventeenth century, craft production continued among Czech, German, Slovak, and Hungarian populations. At the same time, the baroque culture spawned an interest in new technologies and novelties.

Manufacturing was established in some of the urban areas and in the Bohemian and Moravian border regions in the eighteenth century. Textile and glass production were particularly important. Domestic spinning and weaving of wool were common, and members of the nobility also founded manufactories on their estates. The most pressing problem was the status of the serfs, who had become increasingly unproductive, thanks in part to excessive labor dues (known as *robot*), which sometimes required the peasants to work five or six days a week on the lord's estate. Progressive members of the nobility joined scientific agricultural societies, such as the Royal Bohemian Society of Sciences (1769), and sought to reform serfdom so they could adopt new agricultural practices. Some of the worst abuses of serfdom were addressed in the reforms of Maria Theresa (r. 1740–1780) and Joseph II (r. 1780–1790). The patent of 1775 allowed nobles to convert *robot* to monetary payments, although few took advantage of this opportunity because it also provided land to the serfs.

The French Revolution and the Napoleonic Wars helped stimulate the development of manufacturing, particularly during the continental blockade. However, Austria's long involvement in the wars and its many defeats forced the government to declare bankruptcy in 1819. This,

combined with the conservative policies of Francis II (r. 1792–1830) and his foreign minister Clemens von Metternich (governed 1809–1848), prevented further substantive agricultural reform and inhibited industrial development in Bohemia, Moravia, and Slovakia (as well as elsewhere in the monarchy). A small private banking system provided a modicum of financing for industrial development. Steam power was not widespread until the 1860s, when large cotton spinning, weaving, and printing factories were established. Mechanization of textile production was closely tied with the development of the machine and chemical industries in Bohemia and Moravia.

Industrialization. Industrialization began to take off after the abolition of serfdom during the revolutions of 1848–1849. Members of the nobility retained most of their lands and received payments from both the peasants and the government in compensation for the loss of labor services that resulted from the abolition of serfdom. This provided them with substantial capital to invest. In addition, new laws in the 1850s and 1860s made it easier to establish joint-stock companies. New banks, such as the Credit-Anstalt Bankverein (1855) in Vienna and the Böhmische Eskomptebank (1863) in Prague, were founded on the model of the French universal bank and invested in new industries, such as railroads and the refining of beet sugar in Bohemia and Moravia. Municipal savings banks and credit cooperatives also were established, integrating local savings into regional capital markets and investing in local businesses and farms. Investment fever swept Bohemia and Moravia, along with other areas of the Habsburg monarchy, until the stock market crash of 1873 sparked the collapse of many new firms and banks and a depression that lasted until the end of the decade.

Industrial growth resumed in the 1880s. The traditional manufacturing in northwestern Bohemia and northern Moravia was concentrated in textiles (particularly wool and cotton), porcelain, glass, and coal mining. Iron manufacturing was concentrated in the Vitkovice (Witkowitz), Teplice (Teplitz), and Kladno works. The Škoda works in Plzeň (Pilsen) were founded in 1869 to produce machinery and eventually expanded to become one of the monarchy's most important armaments factories. These firms were owned predominantly by Germans, and their management was often controlled by the Viennese great banks.

By the 1890s, pronounced regional and national differences became apparent. Newer industries, such as machine building and agricultural processing (especially sugar refining and beer brewing), were concentrated in the center of Bohemia, where the population was predominantly Czech. These firms received much of their capital from the large Czech banks, such as the Živnostenská banka (Tradesmen's Bank, 1869), located in Prague. Prague's financial markets expanded significantly in the early twentieth century, as the number of Bohemian banks increased from thirteen in 1881 to twenty-three in 1914. Capital of Czech and German Bohemian banks reached 1,899 million crowns, compared with 5,279 million crowns held by Viennese banks (Brousek, 1987, pp. 34–35). Increasing concentration was also apparent in Bohemian and Moravian industry in the early twentieth century.

Labor migration both within the Habsburg monarchy and to industrial centers in Germany and North America accelerated in the late nineteenth century and early twentieth century. As the large coal mining and textile firms in the Bohemian and Moravian borderlands expanded, they often hired inexpensive Czech labor, which migrated to the borderlands from the center of the provinces to compete with the established German labor force. This internal migration exacerbated national conflicts in Bohemia and Moravia. Czech workers also migrated to lower Austria and Vienna, where a significant Czech minority developed by the early twentieth century. Emigration from both the Bohemian crownlands and Slovakia to North America in the late nineteenth century and early twentieth century partially offset the natural increase in population. In 1921, Bohemia had a population of 6.7 million, Moravia 3.3 million, and Slovakia 3 million (Teichova, 1988, p. 4).

Economic Relations between Bohemian Crownlands and Slovakia. The Compromise of 1867, which divided the Habsburg monarchy into Austrian and Hungarian halves, also created separate Austrian and Hungarian economies linked by a Customs Union, which was renegotiated every ten years. Slovakia was fully integrated into the economy of the Hungarian half of the monarchy. The Slovak population was employed predominantly in agriculture, and the few lumber and woodworking firms and grain mills were owned by Hungarians. Most of Slovakia's raw materials were shipped to Budapest for processing, and transportation links were all oriented toward that city. Little direct trade or investment linked Slovakia with Bohemia and Moravia until the first decade of the twentieth century, when Czech banks began to invest in regional Slovak banks and industrial enterprises.

World War I brought the economic and political collapse of Austria-Hungary. In 1918, the regions of Slavic Central Europe were united for the first time since the demise of the Great Moravian Empire. Regional differences in economic development between Bohemia and Moravia on the one hand and Slovakia on the other were among the factors that ultimately undermined the cohesion of the Czechoslovak state.

[See also Czechoslovakia and the Czech and Slovak Republics.]

BIBLIOGRAPHY

Brousek, Karl M. *Die Grossindustrie Böhmens, 1848–1918.* Munich, 1987.

Freudenberg, Herman. *The Waldstein Woolen Mill: Noble Entrepreneurship in Eighteenth-Century Bohemia.* Boston, 1963.

Good, David F. *The Economic Rise of the Habsburg Empire, 1750–1914.* Berkeley, 1984. Examines economic growth rates in the Habsburg monarchy and argues that the monarchy was well integrated and experienced sustained modern economic growth during the nineteenth century. Significant focus on Bohemia and Moravia.

Klima, Arnošt. *Economy, Industry, and Society in Bohemia in the Seventeenth–Nineteenth Centuries.* Prague, 1991.

Rudolph, Richard. *Banking and Industrialization in Austria-Hungary: The Role of Banks in the Industrialization of the Czech Crownlands, 1873–1914.* New York, 1976.

Teichova, Alice. *The Czechoslovak Economy, 1918–1980.* New York, 1988.

CATHERINE ALBRECHT

SLOAN, ALFRED (1875–1966), American manager, engineer, and philanthropist.

Alfred Pritchard Sloan, Jr., transformed General Motors Corporation into the dominant automobile company and the largest and most successful business enterprise in the United States and the world, creating what many observers considered the prototypical business organization of the era and a harbinger of the future. A noted philanthropist, individually or with others, he established the Sloan School of Management at the Massachusetts Institute of Technology; the Alfred P. Sloan Foundation, which emphasized support of science and technology; and what is now the Memorial Sloan-Kettering Cancer Center in New York.

Sloan was born in New Haven, Connecticut, but later moved with his family to Brooklyn, New York. He entered Brooklyn Polytechnic Institute at age eleven and finished his B.S. in electrical engineering at the Massachusetts Institute of Technology in three years, graduating in 1895.

Sloan began work with the Hyatt Roller Bearing Company in New Jersey in 1895, leaving briefly to join a company making refrigeration systems. In 1898, he and a bookkeeper, Peter Steenstrup, borrowed $5,000 from Sloan's father and a friend to save Hyatt from liquidation. With Sloan directing the engineering and operations and Steenstrup the selling (until his departure in 1909), Hyatt became a large, successful supplier of ball bearings to the automobile industry. In 1916, the General Motors founder William Durant bought Hyatt from Sloan and his investors for $13.5 million and put Sloan in charge of United Motors, a group of parts and accessories companies Durant had put together.

In 1918, when General Motors bought the assets of United Motors, Sloan became vice president and a director of General Motors and a member of its executive committee. Frustrated with Durant's management, Sloan almost resigned in 1920. Luckily, soon thereafter, Durant was replaced as president by Pierre du Pont, who served long enough to stabilize the company and who turned over the reins to Sloan in 1923. Sloan served as president until 1946 and as chairman of the board from 1937 to1956.

The impact of Sloan and General Motors on the economic history of the United States and the world has been great. Sloan broke Ford's hegemony and led General Motors to unquestioned leadership of Detroit's "Big Three" by producing a line of cars from economy to luxury models with annual model changes, strengthening the dealer network, instituting highly effective financial policies, and building modern proving grounds and a technical center. Sloan's organizational innovations, which helped General Motors retain its industry leadership for decades after he left, combined decentralized operations with centralized coordinated policies. General Motors gained sales, earnings, and technological leadership and remained profitable when auto sales dropped by 75 percent during the Great Depression. It became the nation's largest private producer of military hardware during World War II and also moved successfully into diesel locomotives and appliances.

Public knowledge of Sloan's work was enhanced by two excellent books. *Concept of the Corporation* (1946), a study of General Motors by the professor and management consultant Peter Drucker, became the cornerstone of the new academic discipline of management. General Motors gave Drucker free access to its management, meetings, and facilities for two years during World War II and virtually complete freedom to publish his findings. Shortly before his death, Sloan published *My Years with General Motors* (1964), considered by some the best business biography ever written. The writing style is objective and matter-of-fact, and Sloan celebrates the achievements of the organization more than his own role. But his intellectual gifts and ability to find and manage diverse talent, address problems creatively, and encourage long-term strategic thinking are clearly displayed. Unlike such individualistic entrepreneurs as Henry Ford, Sloan managed by persuasion, fact finding, presence (such as his frequent visits to dealers), and open discussion rather than by edict and ego.

Within mainline academic economic history, surprisingly little has been written about Sloan or General Motors, especially in leading American journals, in the last fifty years. Three factors probably account for this. First, academic writers of economic history have focused on developing aggregate information on economic performance and in applying economic theory and quantitative methods to questions in economic history. In this context, much of what has been written on General Motors and Sloan is considered business history or management rather than modern economic history.

Second, General Motors and the automobile were so embedded in the American economy by the 1930s that they have been extensively studied on a contemporary basis by professors of economics, political science, history,

ALFRED SLOAN. (Underwood & Underwood, New York/Prints and Photographs Division, Library of Congress)

law, and business and management disciplines. General Motors made frequent appearances in industrial organization, labor history, international trade controversies, and social history and in the work of such scholars as the historian Alfred Chandler and the economist John Kenneth Galbraith on the evolution of large companies and their influence on American capitalism.

Finally, economic historians must wrestle with the question of whether or not successful leaders and institutions contribute to economic progress. Sloan is a case in point. As Drucker has pointed out in *Adventures of a Bystander* (1978), Sloan separated his work as a professional manager from his personal activities. Some authors have claimed he had no personal interests beyond management. As Drucker points out, nothing could be further from the truth. Sloan served on the Council on Foreign Relations and was for decades passionate about politics. He was deeply involved in education, not only via philanthropy but through his work with the General Motors Technical Institute. He was gregarious and had close friends, though not at work. Drucker argued that these activities were relevant to the public's understanding of Sloan's work and General Motors, because the large corporation is enmeshed in American social and political lives. Sloan disagreed and argued that adherence to sound principles of management was the key to continuing success. This argument, ironically, can lead to the conclusion that systems and conditions can more or less automatically produce the leaders needed. Yet the great success of General Motors under this particular leader may itself be persuasive evidence to the contrary.

BIBLIOGRAPHY

Chandler, Alfred D., Jr. *Strategy and Structure: Chapters in the History of the American Industrial Enterprise.* Cambridge, Mass., and London, 1962. One of several influential books by this author on the development of large organizations, this volume includes chapters on both DuPont (which also had a decentralized system) and General Motors, the latter with treatment of the organizational approach taken by both Durant and Sloan.

Drucker, Peter F. *Concept of the Corporation.* New York, 1946. As a relatively young scholar, Drucker was invited to study General Motors from the inside for two years. The book become a classic work on management and began Drucker's rise as a noted management consultant and prolific writer on the management of modern business and its economic, political, and social milieu.

Drucker, Peter F. *Adventures of a Bystander.* New York and Toronto, 1978. The essay entitled "The Professional: Alfred Sloan" offers excellent insights into Sloan, how General Motors worked, and why Drucker was criticized by his academic colleagues in the 1940s for working on a topic (business management) then considered unsuitable for serious economists and political scientists.

Galbraith, John Kenneth. *The New Industrial State.* Boston, 1967. While parts of this book seem dated and deterministic (for instance, the notion that the United States and the Soviet Union would find the form and performance of their economies converging), it takes seriously the magnitude of the economic transformation wrought by General Motors and other large corporations.

McClelland, David C. *The Achieving Society.* Princeton, Toronto, New York, and London, 1961. This book by a psychologist contains only a little material on Sloan, but it makes the case that a society's ability to develop is heavily dependent on its having entrepreneurs with a certain set of psychological characteristics.

Slona, Alfred P., Jr. *My Years with General Motors.* Garden City, N.Y., 1964. This excellent, informative, and influential autobiography is a treasure trove for the reader who wants to know about the rise of General Motors under Sloan's leadership, though it understates the full range of his own interests and contributions.

Sloan, Alfred P., Jr., with Boyden Sparkes. *Adventures of a White-Collar Man.* NewYork, 1941. Sloan's less-formal and shorter book on part of his career, with especially interesting material on his time with Hyatt Roller Bearing Company and his visions for future American growth.

Tedlow, Richard S. *New and Improved: The Story of Mass Marketing in America.* New York, 1990. Chap. 3 of this book on marketing by a Harvard Business School professor is an excellent description of how General Motors used new forms of marketing to surpass Ford.

BRADLEY G. LEWIS

SLOVAKIA. *See* Slavic Central Europe.

SLOVENIA. *See* Balkans.

SMEATON, JOHN (1724–1792), British engineer.

John Smeaton was born at Austhorpe near Leeds, England, on 8 June 1724 and died there on 28 October 1792.

JOHN SMEATON. (Image Select/Art Resource, NY)

His father, an attorney, hoped his son would follow the legal profession and so had him educated at Leeds Grammar School and in 1742 sent him to London to learn law. However, Smeaton had met Henry Hindley, a leading Yorkshire instrument maker, who taught the lad the basic skills of his trade. Smeaton received further instrument training in London with his father's permission and opened a shop for scientific instruments there in 1748. His early experiences gave Smeaton three assets for his later career as a civil engineer: an understanding of the law for the legal background, a practical ability to use tools with an understanding of materials, and a recognition of the need for accuracy in his work, whether in surveying and its instruments or in the presentation of his reports and drawings.

Through the scientific papers he presented, Smeaton was elected a Fellow of the Royal Society in 1753, and this position later helped him raise the status of the engineering profession. He had already carried out a series of experiments on models of wind and watermills to determine their efficiency, and his paper to the society entitled "Experimental Enquiry concerning the Natural Powers of Wind and Water to Turn Mills and Other Machines," in 1759, was recognized as an important scientific achievement both in Britain and on the Continent. Given the Copley medal, the highest award of the Royal Society, the paper showed the best ways of constructing waterwheels and windmill sails to increase their power production.

By then, Smeaton had already begun to alter the direction of his career into what he termed civil engineering. In 1755, he toured part of the Low Countries and, on his return, went to Scotland to survey improvements for navigation on the River Clyde. Then in 1756, the Earl of Macclesfield, president of the Royal Society, recommended Smeaton for reconstructing the Eddystone lighthouse, which had recently burned down. Its successful completion, in 1759, brought Smeaton instant recognition in his new field. Not only had he developed a hydraulic cement, but the construction of the lighthouse was based on scientific principles, grounded in careful, accurate observation.

It was the application of these principles that enabled Smeaton to raise the status of civil engineering to that of a profession, and to have it recognized as such. As part of this change, he instituted the Society of Civil Engineers in 1771, which met as a dining club in London during sessions of Parliament, where experiences could be exchanged, and was a forerunner of later professional institutions.

Smeaton's civil engineering practice ranged widely over many projects: improvements to river navigation, commencing with the Upper Calder, Yorkshire, in 1756, and the Forth & Clyde Canal, starting in 1766, which was the first British canal to cross a watershed; improvements to harbors stretching from Saint Ives in the west to Ramsgate in the east and Rye in the south to Peterhead in the north; fen drainage schemes in Yorkshire and Lincolnshire; bridges at Coldstream, Perth, and elsewhere; and over fifty watermills and windmills. His reports on these and other schemes were considered such important examples for other engineers to follow that they were published posthumously in three volumes in 1812. His papers to the Royal Society followed in a further volume in 1814.

An example of his application of scientific principles to his engineering practice may be seen in the case of a steam engine used to pump water for the New River Company, London. When set to work in 1769, its performance failed to match Smeaton's expectations; so he built and tested a large model at Austhorpe. Although he succeeded in improving the engine's efficiency, he failed to achieve a technical breakthrough like that of James Watt at the same time. Smeaton constructed some important engines, such as those at Long Benton and Chacewater, but he acknowledged the theoretical superiority of Watt's design and realized the advanced engineering skills that would be entailed to construct it. Smeaton introduced the concept of "duty," the amount of water raised by a given amount of coal, which formed the basis of judging the efficiency of steam engines for many years.

The importance of Smeaton's work lay first in the high standards he introduced to many spheres of engineering, which were based on scientific principles. In this way he raised the standing of engineers so that they could be regarded as professionals. In his practice, he improved transport communications around the whole country, enabling the infant Industrial Revolution to spread and develop.

BIBLIOGRAPHY
Skempton, A. W., ed. *John Smeaton, F.R.S.* London, 1981.
Smeaton, John. *A Narrative of the Building and a Description of the Construction of the Edystone Lighthouse.* London, 1791.
Smeaton, John. *Reports of the Late John Smeaton, F.R.S., Made on Various Occasions in the Course of His Employment as a Civil Engineer.* 3 vols. London, 1812.
Smeaton, John. *The Miscellaneous Papers of John Smeaton, F.R.S.* London, 1814.
Smiles, Samuel. *Lives of the Engineers.* London, 1861.

RICHARD L. HILLS

SMITH, ADAM (1723–1790), economist.

Adam Smith played many roles in economic history—economist, jurist, ethicist, rhetorician, observer of trade and commerce, and historian. Although he was active during the early years of industrialization, his writing indicates that he did not realize he was witnessing a fundamental change in production and commerce and the organizational and technological changes that characterized industrialization. Smith's unprecedented works *The Theory of Moral Sentiments* (1759) and *An Inquiry into the Nature and Causes of the Wealth of Nations* (1776) thus were not analyses or predictions of industrialization and its effects but did contain many prescient observations that continue to make him relevant to economic analysis.

Smith's greatest contribution to economics was his integrated system for analyzing human economic behavior and institutions. From natural law to the distinction between justice and beneficence to the role of competition and division of labor in creating gains from trade, to how trade creates growth differentially across societies, to how money facilitates exchange, Smith synthesized human nature, practical empiricism, and economic principles to construct a theoretical foundation for economic analysis.

The idea behind the invisible hand underpins Smith's work. Smith's invisible hand is not a theory of providential design but rather a causal mechanism, a metaphor for spontaneous, unplanned social order. How else can one explain the division of labor or the development and use of money? These features of a complex economy were not planned or intended—they were the unintended consequences of human action. The concept of unplanned order weaves the *Wealth of Nations* together and is a fundamental building block in all of Smith's work. This explanation of the development of social institutions was one of the biggest contributions to thought from the Scottish Enlightenment that came from the works of Smith, David Hume, Adam Ferguson, and others.

Unplanned order as manifested in a self-regulating economy was a novel idea in the eighteenth century; one of the primary roles of the *Wealth of Nations* was a critique of mercantilism. Both European trade and intellectual thought in the century preceding Smith's work were characterized by the belief that increasing one nation's wealth came at the expense of other nations. Mercantilist policy, particularly in countries such as France and Spain, dictated minimizing imports and maximizing exports and keeping as much gold and silver (specie) in the country as possible. These policies required an activist government to regulate and manage the flow of goods and of specie. Smith saw the fallacies in these policies and set out to critique them systematically in the *Wealth of Nations*.

Smith's work laid the foundation for explaining how trade creates value. The ability to trade arises out of specialization and the division of labor. While Smith was not the first to emphasize the importance of the division of labor (William Petty was), it was again his incorporation of it as a fundamental pillar in his system of analysis that was notable. Another fundamental pillar, one that often gets lost in modern policy debates, is the role of cooperation as a fundamental part of mutually beneficial exchange and competition. Similarly relevant is the role competition plays in disciplining market participants more effectively and parsimoniously than external regulation. Smith also articulated the extent to which the division of labor (and therefore gains from trade) is limited by the extent of the market, and the extent of the market is a function of transportation costs and the availability of transport networks. His analysis of the importance of relative transport costs to the interconnection and extension of markets still echoes in the work of modern economic historians (for example, Mark Overton).

In the *Wealth of Nations*, his most influential work, Smith focused on the roles of agriculture, manufacturing, and commerce and their interrelationships to explore how and why some societies are more prosperous than others. In the course of this exploration Smith thoroughly analyzed the separate supply and demand components of trade and market outcomes as well as the interrelationship between them. Furthermore one of the most pioneering elements of this analysis was how he integrated the role of time in price determination. Smith showed how demand effects, particularly unanticipated ones, can cause prices to change quickly (his example was the demand for black crepe cloth right before a public mourning). Then suppliers can adjust output over time to the extent that they find it profitable, and entry and exit occurs to bring the market

ADAM SMITH. Engraving by John Kay (1742–1826). (British Cartoon Collection/Prints and Photographs Division, Library of Congress)

price in line with the "natural price" as determined by wages, rent, and profit (Smith, *Wealth of Nations*, 1976, bk. 1, chap. 7). This articulation of change over time in the price elasticity of demand and supply, or the responsiveness of demand and supply to changes in price, is still one of the basic concepts of economics.

Smith's system of economic analysis existed within a theory of history. Smith held a stage theory of history in which societies move through four general stages. The first two were the hunting and pastoral stages, which were largely nomadic. The third stage, farming, followed and then finally evolved into the commercial stage. In his theory Smith characterized the move from nomadic hunting through pastoralism and farming to commercialism as primarily changing property rights and the ways individuals interacted and defined the institutions of civil society.

Civil society was in many dimensions the object of Smith's study throughout his life, although he is most famous for his economic analysis of the commercial manifestations of civil society. His scholarship and insights on the interplay of human nature, property rights, and the institutions of civil society in creating growth remain fascinating and important.

BIBLIOGRAPHY

Blaug, Mark. *Economic Theory in Retrospect*. London, 1985.

Campbell, R. H., and A. S. Skinner. *General Introduction to an Inquiry into the Nature and Causes of the Wealth of Nations*. Oxford, 1976.

Coase, Ronald. "Adam Smith's View of Man." In *Essays on Economics and Economists*. Chicago, 1994.

Coase, Ronald. "The Wealth of Nations." In *Essays on Economics and Economists*. Chicago, 1994.

Ekelund, Robert B., Jr., and Robert F. Hebert. *A History of Economic Theory and Method*. New York, 1996.

Overton, Mark. *Agricultural Revolution in England: The Transformation of the Agrarian Economy, 1500–1800*. Cambridge, 1996.

Smith, Adam. *An Inquiry into the Nature and Causes of the Wealth of Nations*. (1776). Reprint, Indianapolis, 1976.

Smith, Adam. *The Theory of Moral Sentiments*. (1759). Reprint, Indianapolis, 1976.

West, E. G. *Adam Smith: The Man and His Works*. New Rochelle, N.Y., 1969.

LYNNE KIESLING

SMUGGLING. Smuggling is the covert and usually illegal movement of something into or out of a given place. The place typically but not necessarily is a political jurisdiction that has established the rules regulating such movement. Although most frequently across international borders, smuggling can involve borders within nation-states, for example, cigarettes smuggled from low-tax southern states in the United States to high-tax states. Past (and present) smuggling has involved goods, people, capital, and ideas. It can be illegal movement of these into a political jurisdiction (illegal import or immigration) and also illegal movement of these out of the political area (illegal export or emigration).

Political jurisdictions can restrict trade in goods by outright prohibition or via tariffs, which can be set high enough to prohibit legal exchange of the taxed goods or can be set below the prohibitive level to raise revenue and reduce imports. Tariffs, taxes on imported goods, also have been called customs or custom duties. Political jurisdictions, typically nation states or countries, also can use quotas to restrict flow of goods.

A quota sets a limit on the quantity of the good that is permitted to enter the jurisdiction legally. Generally tariffs or customs are levied to raise revenue for the levying jurisdiction as well as to restrict the flow of goods. A prohibitive tariff, however, raises no revenue because nothing is traded. Quotas generally restrict trade without raising revenue but can be auctioned to interested trading parties, thereby generating funds. Jurisdictions that set quotas or levy tariffs need not and often do not set the same restrictions on all sources of the goods; tariffs and quotas can differ depending upon the export site. Smuggling therefore often involves efforts to evade taxes on goods moving into or out of particular places.

Smuggling can be in goods ready for final consumption but also can involve unprocessed raw materials or intermediate goods. In the latter cases restrictions on trade often limit export of the material from the restricting jurisdiction rather than limiting import into the jurisdiction.

When socioeconomic and political conditions vary considerably across nations and those nations also restrict the emigration and immigration of people, smuggling of humans has happened. In the late twentieth century smuggling of humans occurred when countries limited legal immigration, as in the United States, and when countries limited legal egress, as in the Soviet Union. In historical context the smuggling of humans who were moving voluntarily should be distinguished from the smuggling of enslaved humans. Abolition of the legal slave trade, predominantly in the nineteenth century for western Europe and its former colonies, triggered at least some smuggling of slaves.

The costs of smuggling include the costs of transporting the smuggled item. High transportation costs relative to the value of the item transported limit both legal trade and illegal smuggling. Physical capital equipment and buildings tend to be physically large and bulky and therefore expensive to transport. Smuggling of physical capital might occur but is limited because of transport costs. Smuggling of monetary capital has been easier both historically and in present times. Specie money (gold, silver) and paper money were shipped illegally historically, but the information costs of determining the value of currency likely made the smuggling of specie more attractive than the smuggling of paper assets. Specie could travel in the form of jewelry and other consumer goods, easing smuggling though carrying the risk of theft.

Physical capital and human labor have contributed importantly to the growth of output per person in the world and especially in the Western world. Without new technology, however, growth in output per capita in the modern world would have been significantly lower. New technology has resulted from human ideas and ingenuity in transforming ideas into viable products. Once new technology is developed, copying the new idea is cheaper than reinventing it. Unsurprisingly as technological change led to commercial success and economic growth, interest surged in imitating successful new technologies. Both individual companies and nations sought to preserve their advantages by keeping new technologies secret.

Even before nations developed patent laws to protect individuals and companies from uncompensated use of their inventions, organizations and nation states often restricted the export of ideas embodied in new technology. For

SMUGGLING. Village along the Iraq–Iran border where Iraqi smugglers trade their goods for Iranian clothes and plastics, 1999. (© Mike Yamashita/Woodfin Camp and Associates, New York)

example, guilds in western Europe restricted the flow of gifted craftspeople and machinery to keep secret their production processes. Eighteenth-century England tried to keep innovations in cloth production secret, prohibiting the export of plans for machinery and factory layout, but by the early nineteenth century American cloth producers were able to adapt smuggled British technology to the resource conditions of New England.

By definition smuggling is illegal. Illegal activity generates few records, at least few that are readily accessible. Economic historians have debated the extent of smuggling; the lack of recorded evidence makes empirical study of smuggling and resolution of the debate exceedingly difficult. Economic studies of smuggling have generated principles that suggest where and when smuggling will occur. Smuggling is an adjunct to exchange and trade; people smuggle primarily because it is lucrative. Smuggling therefore is more likely when and where extensive trade crosses political boundaries and where conditions make smuggling profitable.

Long-distance trade likely began with civilization, but its volume, at least according to the best measures currently available, increased dramatically in the eighteenth and nineteenth centuries and centered on western Europe and its colonies. Trade per capita on the eve of World War I was roughly twenty-five times its level at the beginning of the nineteenth century. Of course increase in measured trade might be the result of a reduction in smuggling. The level of trade is unchanged, but what was illegal and unmeasured became legal and measured. Growth of trade alone does not suggest better opportunities for smuggling. As an illegal activity, smuggling can only occur when profitable trade is made illegal; smuggling is much more likely when trade restrictions are onerous. Restrictions on trade that is otherwise unprofitable will not lead automatically to smuggling. Illegal trade is more costly than legal trade because it involves the risk of detection and punishment. If the probability of detection is low or the punishment if caught is mild, smuggling becomes more attractive.

Evading detection generally increases transaction costs, whether from the need to forge documents, bribe inspectors, or use roundabout transport routes. Profit from smuggling depends upon these higher costs as compared to the price that can be received for the smuggled good. That price depends upon the size of the tariff and the elasticity of demand for the product, so a low tariff could raise large revenues for the importing country without inducing smuggling. These principles suggest that smuggling most likely occurred historically with goods that have high value relative to weight and bulk and low price elasticity of demand. Although smuggling of specialized expensive artifacts might depend upon a market populated by a few wealthy people, smuggling probably is more profitable with a large market for less-specialized goods. Detection is less likely when the smuggled good is already traded, and rising incomes for many create a larger market for the smuggled good. It is facilitated with multiple points of entry and exit. Because water transportation historically was much less costly than overland transportation, trade has been associated with sea and river ports. Smuggling thus seems more likely to have occurred into and out of countries with extensive coastlines amenable to landing ships without elaborate docking facilities.

The conditions point to seventeenth- and eighteenth-century western European countries with mercantilist policies as likely places historically for smuggling. Empirical studies have focused on the tea trade into western Europe, especially Great Britain, the trade in tobacco, the trade in sugar and its products between Caribbean colonies and North America, and the trade in cotton during the American Civil War embargo. Fuller knowledge of the extent of smuggling requires careful comparison of company and merchant records and evidence of consumption patterns with official shipping and custom duties records.

In the second half of the twentieth century economic studies of international trade increasingly examined the impact of trade policy on development, especially in poorer regions. Both theoretical economists and policy advisers noted the prevalence of smuggling and the importance of incorporating this phenomenon into models of trade and policy considerations. These studies focused on (1) whether or not smuggling likely increased economic well-being and (2) how smuggling affected government revenues. Theoretical economic models sought to incorporate smuggling into general equilibrium models of trade; whether or not smuggling definitively improved welfare depended, unsurprisingly, upon the particular assumptions made. Though not yielding a unique answer about the welfare impact of smuggling, these models have suggested avenues for empirical study of smuggling. They also have illuminated likely outcomes of trade restriction under different physical and institutional conditions.

Smuggling continues to interest economists in both developed and developing economies. Modern smuggling involves people crossing international borders. It also involves materials, such as plutonium for nuclear weapons, and goods, such as drugs, weapons, and cigarettes. Money capital flows more readily with electronic transfers than it previously has, facilitating smuggling.

BIBLIOGRAPHY

Bhagwati, Jahwrel N., and Bent Hansen. "A Theoretical Analysis of Smuggling." *Quarterly Journal of Economics* 87.2 (1973), 172–187. This often-cited article has spawned the modern theoretical literature on smuggling; it utilizes technical economics to develop its arguments. Professor Bhagwati has written a number of articles on the topic.

Bhagwati, Jahwrel N., and T. N. Srinivasan. "Smuggling and Trade Policy." *Journal of Public Economics* 2 (1973), 377–389. This article examines the policy implications of the theory of smuggling.

Cameron, Rondo. *A Concise Economic History of the World.* New York, 1993. This historical survey does not focus on smuggling, but by examining growing world trade it provides information on the places and times likely to exhibit smuggling.

Cole, W. A. "Trends in Eighteenth-Century Smuggling." *Economic History Review* 10.3 (1958), 395–410. This article focuses on smuggling of tea in trying to estimate the extent of smuggling.

Cole, W. A. "Rejoinder: The Arithmetic of Eighteenth-Century Smuggling." *Economic History Review* 28.1 (1975), 44–49. Professor Cole responds in this article to questions about his calculations in his 1958 article on smuggling.

Lebergott, Stanley. "Through the Blockade: The Profitability and Extent of Cotton Smuggling, 1861–1865." *Journal of Economic History* 41.4 (1981), 867–888.

McClusker, John J., and Russell R. Menard. *The Economy of British America, 1607–1789.* Chapel Hill, N.C., 1985. Although not a history of smuggling, this book extensively examines legal trade in colonial British America and refers to illegal trade and its likely magnitude.

Norton, Desmond A. G. "On the Economic Theory of Smuggling." *Economica* 55.217 (1988), 107–118. This technical article briefly summarizes and then extends modern models of smuggling. It applies the model to smuggling of agricultural goods within the European Economic Community (EEC).

Thursby, Marie, Richard Jensen, and Jerry Thursby. "Smuggling, Camouflaging, and Market Structure." *Quarterly Journal of Economics* 106.3 (1991), 789–814. This article includes theoretical models incorporating industry structure to examine the likely extent of smuggling and its effect on economic welfare. It also refers to numerous other studies, including applications of theoretical models to the smuggling of cigarettes.

Ann Harper Fender

SOCIALISM. *See* Marxism and Marxist Historiography.

SOCIAL MOBILITY. Social mobility is usually taken to refer to the movement of individuals within the stratification system of a society. Most of the contemporary literature deals with social mobility in advanced industrial or postindustrial societies that are primarily stratified along lines of social class (indexed typically by occupation and employment status). The usual focus is thus on movement between social classes, for example, from the working class to the middle class or to elite positions within the society. (There have also been a few studies of income mobility.) It is also usual to make a distinction between inter- and intragenerational social mobility. Intergenerational studies compare the social positions of fathers and sons (or more rarely of fathers and daughters), whereas intragenerational studies compare the social positions of a given individual at different stages of his or her occupational career (for example, comparing first job on entry to the labor market with later jobs).

A completely different (but rarely employed) perspective on social mobility focuses on the movement of particular social groups within a stratification system. For example, an Indian jati (a caste subgroup) might employ various strategies to alter its position within the caste system. One could also study the way in which particular occupational groups have risen or fallen within the stratification system. In *The Blackcoated Worker* (London, 1958), for example, David Lockwood presents evidence indicating that clerks probably had a somewhat higher economic position in the nineteenth and early twentieth century (when literacy was relatively rare and hence their skills were in short supply) than they did at mid-twentieth century. However, most of the established literature focuses on the movement of individuals within a stratification system assumed to be stable over time.

The literature on social mobility has been dominated by two major theoretical concerns: social order and economic efficiency. One tradition, going back at least as far as Karl Marx, sees high rates of social mobility as inhibiting class formation and reducing the likelihood of class conflict. In *Das Kapital*, vol. 3, Marx famously claimed that "the more a ruling class is able to assimilate the foremost minds of a ruled class, the more stable and dangerous becomes its rule," and suggested that high rates of social mobility partly explained the lack of an organized labor movement in the United States. Goldthorpe (1980) has argued that a class with a high level of intergenerational stability will exhibit a greater degree of class solidarity and hence a greater potential for collective action in pursuit of shared political goals than a less stable class.

The second tradition, associated with the functionalist school of sociology, has argued that the "logic of industrialism" will lead to higher rates of social mobility since a competitive industrial society requires that individuals be recruited to occupations on the basis of merit (and more generally of skills and competencies that are relevant to the performance of the job) rather than ascribed characteristics, such as class origins, gender, or ethnicity, that are irrelevant to job performance (Sorokin, 1927; Blau and Duncan, 1967).

Mobility Tables. A great deal of recent empirical research has addressed the question of whether industrialization has in fact led to increased rates of social mobility. Most of this research has been based on sample surveys of the adult population that ascertain the current class position and the class origins (indexed by father's class) of the respondents. From such surveys a mobility table cross-tabulating fathers' and sons' class positions can be derived. Such a table provides a snapshot of mobility. (It should be noted that such snapshots may be misleading because of the dynamic nature of the career process.) By comparing mobility tables from surveys conducted at different dates, or by comparing tables for respondents born in different periods, it is possible to estimate trends over time.

Table 1, a standard mobility table for men, shows the percentages of the total sample (7,286 respondents) that lie in each cell of the table. (Researchers often also use "outflow" tables, which calculate row percentages and thus show the current class positions of respondents from given origins, and "inflow" tables, which calculate column percentages and thus show the origins of respondents currently in particular classes.)

In analyzing mobility tables, sociologists have made an important distinction between absolute and relative mobility. The absolute rate of mobility is the total proportion of the sample that is intergenerationally mobile. The absolute proportions upwardly or downwardly mobile also can be calculated. In Table 1 some 35.1 percent of the sample lie on the main diagonal (running from top left to bottom right) and thus were, at the time of the survey, intergenerationally stable. Therefore, 64.9 percent of the sample were intergenerationally mobile. If the class schema is a straightforward hierarchical one, it can be said that those individuals lying to the left of and below this diagonal were upwardly mobile (since their father's class was lower than their own class), and those lying to the right of and above the diagonal were downwardly mobile. In this table, 42.7 percent were upwardly and 22.3 percent downwardly mobile. (However, the class classification used in this table is not strictly hierarchical, and movements in either direction between the routine nonmanual class and the petty bourgeoisie might best be regarded as sideways movements rather than as movements up or down.)

Relative rates of mobility, on the other hand, indicate the relative chances of people from different class origins of achieving certain (more desirable) destinations and avoiding other (less desirable) ones. They are typically calculated by odds ratios. For example, in the table, the odds that someone from higher salariat origins will stay there rather than move down to the semi- and unskilled manual class are 2.8:0.4 or 7:1. This figure can be compared with the odds of someone from a semi-/unskilled manual origin getting to the higher salariat or staying where he or she is. These odds are 2.7:11.5 or 0.23:1. The odds ratio is thus

TABLE 1. *Male Mobility in Britain (percentages of total sample)*

	SON'S CLASS						
FATHER'S CLASS	HIGHER	LOWER	ROUTINE	PETTY	SKILLED	SEMI- AND UNSKILLED	ALL
Higher salariat	2.8	1.4	0.3	0.7	0.5	0.4	6.1
Lower salariat	2.2	2.1	0.7	0.7	0.9	0.7	7.3
Routine nonmanual	1.4	1.1	0.6	0.5	1.0	0.7	5.3
Petty bourgeoisie	2.3	2.0	1.0	4.4	3.0	2.5	15.1
Skilled manual	4.3	4.3	2.5	2.9	13.7	8.3	36.0
Semi- and unskilled	2.7	2.7	1.5	2.1	9.7	11.5	30.2
All	15.7	13.6	6.6	11.3	28.8	24.1	100

SOURCE: Heath and Payne, 2000, Table 7.4.

30:1 (7/0.23), indicating substantial inequality in relative mobility chances. (An odds ratio of 1:1 would indicate equality in relative mobility chances.) Odds ratios have the convenient mathematical property that they are not affected by the marginal totals, and they thus can tell something about the underlying openness or fluidity of a society, net of structural change.

Absolute rates of mobility tend to be driven to a considerable extent by structural change (reflected in the differing marginal totals in Table 1 for fathers and sons). An industrializing society will tend to have increased "room at the top" and hence an increased rate of upward mobility, as compared with a more static preindustrial society. The marginal totals in the table show that 13.4 percent of the fathers were in the salariat, whereas among the sons this percentage had more than doubled to 29.3 percent. Thus there must have been some net upward mobility in order to fill the vacancies in the expanding salariat. There is a broad consensus that the more economically advanced societies in the second half of the twentieth century had rapidly changing occupational structures with increasing room at the top and hence high rates of net upward mobility. However, it is not entirely clear that this pattern will continue, and it could well be that absolute rates of mobility will start to decline in the near future.

Mobility Trends. Although there is general agreement among scholars about the trends in absolute mobility, there is much more controversy about trends in relative mobility. A particular focus of contemporary research has been on whether fluidity, as measured by odds ratios, has increased as societies have industrialized. Erikson and Goldthorpe (1992) found little sign of increasing fluidity in Britain or in most of the other countries they studied, whereas Ganzeboom and his colleagues (1989), surveying a wider range of countries than Erikson and Goldthorpe, found slow but long-term trends toward increasing fluidity, at a rate of about 1 percent per annum (that is, the odds ratios have been gradually getting closer to 1:1). No studies, however, have suggested that fluidity has been decreasing.

As noted earlier, most contemporary sociological research on social mobility is based on sample surveys. To calculate trends, scholars either have compared the results from different surveys conducted at various points of time (as Ganzeboom and his colleagues did) or have used cohort analyses, comparing the experience of birth cohorts born in different periods (as Erikson and Goldthorpe did). The former method enables one to cover only the second half of the twentieth century since the first usable samples postdate World War II (the earliest used by Ganzeboom and colleagues being a 1947 NORC survey in the United States). The latter method enables scholars to examine trends over the whole of the twentieth century since the oldest respondents in the earlier surveys will have entered

the labor market at the beginning of the century (see, for example, Heath and Payne, 2000, who include a pre-1900 birth cohort). However, birth-cohort analysis makes a number of strong assumptions and may not be a good guide to long-term trends. (In particular, older respondents born in earlier periods may have experienced more career mobility at the time of the survey than have younger respondents; they may also have suffered more attrition, through migration or mortality, which introduces biases.)

A major limitation of the sociological research, then, is that it covers a relatively limited time span that may be too short for an effective evaluation of the logic of the industrialism thesis. Clearly, social surveys cannot be used for earlier periods, but a number of other sources are available, although each has its drawbacks. One method has been to study the social origins of well-documented elites. A good example of this is P. E. Razzell's study of "The Social Origins of Officers in the Indian and British Home Army" (*British Journal of Sociology* 14, 1963, 248–60), which goes back to 1758. Such studies of elite recruitment are tantamount to investigating just one column of the mobility table, and clearly do not permit calculation of overall absolute rates of mobility or odds ratios. These studies are not without interest, however; and a particularly notable one is that of Hollingsworth, who studied the social background of the marriage partners of the peerage over the period 1550–1949, in "The Demography of the British Peerage" (*Population Studies*, supplement to vol. XV111, no. 2). Hollingsworth's data on intermarriage between the peerage and commoners can be thought of as showing trends in marital mobility, and demonstrate a considerable widening of access (implying greater social openness) toward the end of the nineteenth century.

The other major source used has been marriage registers. In Britain, the 1836 Registration of Births, Deaths and Marriages Act required church registers to record the occupations of the partners and their parents. Marriage registers are not without their problems, particularly as their coverage may vary over time as fewer people have married in church. Marriage registers also capture individuals at a relatively early stage of their careers, and class position at marriage may not be a good index of one's eventual class destination. Nevertheless, they represent one of the best sources for studying nonelite mobility. From these records, Miles (1999) has constructed intergenerational mobility tables for that proportion of the adult population that married in church during the nineteenth and early twentieth centuries. He shows that there were increasing rates of upward mobility out of the working class, and that fluidity (as measured by odds ratios) increased considerably toward the end of the nineteenth and the beginning of the twentieth century. Similar conclusions have been reached by Prandy and Bottero (2000), using data provided by members of family-history societies in Britain and Ireland; and, as already noted, the story told by Hollingsworth about marriages into the peerage is also consistent with this conclusion that fluidity increased at the end of the nineteenth century and the beginning of the twentieth. (Heath and Payne's survey-based cohort analysis is also consistent with this conclusion.)

Although the long-term trend toward increased fluidity may be correct for Britain, the functionalist explanation in terms of the requirements of economic efficiency is not necessarily to be preferred. It is quite likely that the trend toward increased fluidity is associated with the growth of bureaucratic employment and formal, meritocratic selection procedures. These procedures have been known in bureaucracies in preindustrial societies (notably in Mandarin China), and their spread in industrial societies may be linked with factors such as the growth of the public sector and not simply with economic pressures *per se*.

There also appear to be long-established differences in national "mobility regimes," which persist despite industrialization. Cross-national studies have shown, for example, that Ireland has exhibited somewhat lower fluidity, whereas Sweden has higher fluidity (Erikson and Goldthorpe, 1992). The explanation for these persisting cross-national differences are not yet clearly established. Political factors such as the long-term dominance of the social democratic party in Sweden may be involved in the explanation of Swedish openness. Cultural factors may also be important, although interestingly the United States, despite its well-documented culture of individualism, does not appear to exhibit a higher level of fluidity than do European societies such as Britain, France, and Germany, with their stronger traditions of collective provision. Another important factor might be actual inequalities of conditions between the social classes. In general, one might expect mobility to be less likely, the greater the social and economic distance is between the classes; so societies with more equal class structures might be expected to exhibit greater social fluidity than those with greater class distance.

BIBLIOGRAPHY

Blau, Peter M., and Otis Dudley Duncan. *The American Occupational Structure*. New York, 1967. A pathbreaking study of social mobility in the United States, developing causal models of the mobility process and using sophisticated statistical techniques (particularly path analysis).

Breen, Richard, ed. *National Patterns of Social Mobility*. Oxford, forthcoming. A major new comparative study of mobility trends in advanced societies.

Erikson, Robert, and John H. Goldthorpe. *The Constant Flux: A Study of Class Mobility in Industrial Societies*. Oxford, 1992. A major cross-national study using high-quality data from twelve first-world countries and applying highly sophisticated quantitative methods (based on loglinear modeling). Comparison of birth cohorts in these surveys suggested that there had been no increase in fluidity.

Ganzeboom, Harry B. G., Ruud Luijkx, and Donald J. Treiman. "Intergenerational Class Mobility in Comparative Perspective." In *Research in Social Mobility and Stratification*, edited by Arne S. Kalleberg, vol. 8, pp. 3–84. 1989. An exhaustive study drawing on every known sample survey to cover recent trends in mobility in thirty-five countries, primarily in the first world but also including Brazil, India, the Philippines and Malaysia. An appendix to the article helpfully gives all 149 mobility tables that the authors have collected. This study uses the same conceptualization of social class as Erikson and Goldthorpe but different statistical methods, making evaluation of these authors' (very different) conclusions difficult.

Glass, David V., ed. *Social Mobility in Britain*. London, 1954. The pioneering study of social mobility based on the first nationally representative sample survey of mobility in 1949.

Goldthorpe, John H. *Social Mobility and Class Structure in Modern Britain*. Oxford, 1980. 2d ed. 1987. The definitive study of social mobility in Britain, using some sophisticated quantitative methods but also explaining the results and methods in a lucid way and relating the findings to the major theoretical issues.

Grusky, David B., ed. *Social Stratification: Class, Race and Gender in Sociological Perspective*. 2d ed. Boulder, 2001. An excellent reader that brings together major articles on class structure and mobility.

Heath, Anthony, and Clive Payne. "Social Mobility." In *Twentieth-Century British Social Trends*, edited by A. H. Halsey, pp. 254–278. London, 2000. A relatively nontechnical introduction to the study of mobility, using birth-cohort analysis to investigate trends over the twentieth century.

Kaelble, Hartmut. *Social Mobility in the 19th and 20th Centuries: Europe and America in Comparative Perspective*. Leamington Spa, 1985. A systematic review both of local studies of mass mobility and of recruitment to the business elite in Europe and America.

Miles, Andrew. *Social Mobility in Nineteenth- and Early Twentieth-Century England*. London, 1999. A major historical study of social mobility using marriage registers. The study gives the national picture of mobility trends and uses the same conceptualizations and statistical methods as used by sociologists such as Erikson and Goldthorpe or Heath and Payne.

Prandy, Kenneth, and Wendy Bottero. "Social Reproduction and Mobility in Britain and Ireland in the Nineteenth and Early Twentieth Centuries." *Sociology* 34.2 (2000), 265–281. Draws on records provided by members of family-history societies to trace trends in social mobility. It uses very different conceptualizations of the class structure and different statistical methods from Miles, but reaches similar conclusions.

Sorokin, Pitirim A. *Social and Cultural Mobility*. Glencoe, 1927. The first major monograph on social mobility, not based on sample surveys or systematic historical details but with great theoretical and empirical range, covering the whole of recorded history and with fascinating detail on, for example, the social background of Roman emperors and medieval popes.

Thernstrom, Stephan. *Poverty and Progress: Social Mobility in a Nineteenth Century City*. Cambridge, Mass., 1964. A pioneering historical study based on the original manuscript schedules of the U.S. censuses.

ANTHONY HEATH

SOCIAL SAVINGS. The American economic historian Robert Fogel coined the term *social saving* in the early 1960s. Fogel used the concept in a professional journal article (1962) and in his pioneering book, *Railroads and American Economic Growth: Essays in Econometric History*

(1964), on the quantitative importance of railroads to the 1890 American economy. The social saving from a technological innovation is the difference between actual national income in a given year and the national income that would have been generated had the economy made the most efficient possible adjustment to the absence of the innovation. Anyone trying to measure the social saving must describe and measure a plausible "counterfactual" economy—one that could have existed in the absence of the innovation.

Fogel argued that agricultural products and other goods could have been moved by expanding use of waterways, wagons, and storage and by extending the system of waterways, with a loss of no more than 5 percent of 1890 gross national product (GNP). In a second influential work *American Railroads and the Transformation of the Ante-Bellum Economy* (1965), Albert Fishlow estimated a social saving of 5 percent of 1859 GNP attributable to railroads, though he used somewhat different methods from Fogel and focused on the developmental contributions of railroads. Over the next two decades, scholars generally found social savings of 10 percent or less for Russia (1907), England and Wales (1865, 1890), France (1872), Germany (1890s), Belgium (1865, 1912), and China (1933). By contrast, social savings estimates for Mexico by John Coatsworth (25 to 39 percent in 1910) and for Spain by Antonio Gomez-Mendoza (11.8 percent in 1878, 18.5 percent in 1912) suggested railroads were crucial in those countries.

Fogel's social saving calculations especially have been controversial. Many traditional economic historians objected altogether to the use of the concept, arguing that it measured what might have happened rather than what did. Fogel and others answered that traditional arguments often implied a counterfactual that no one tested. Among the rising "new economic historians" who were quite comfortable using sophisticated quantitative methods and economic theory, debate focused more on the quality of data, the scope of measurements, and whether or not Fogel's counterfactual accurately depicted the full effects of an economy without railroads. Most of Fogel's critics have been content to argue on one or more of these grounds rather than to calculate new social saving estimates themselves. Jeffrey Williamson, using a seventy-two-equation general equilibrium model connecting all economic variables in a consistent system, estimated the social saving from 1890 U.S. railroads at 21 percent. Even Fogel's critics, however, generally have not endorsed this estimate as more credible.

The attempts to calculate social savings for railroads have added to the knowledge but have highlighted the difficulties in measuring the contributions of ubiquitous technological innovations. Indeed, explicit use of the social saving concept has not been widespread beyond the railroad debate, perhaps because other measures of an innovation's success, such as its social rate of return or its rate of diffusion, are often simpler and will suffice.

[*See also* Technology.]

BIBLIOGRAPHY

Fishlow, Albert. *American Railroads and the Transformation of the Ante-Bellum Economy.* Cambridge, Mass., 1965. This book was a significant contribution to the social saving controversy among new economic historians, but it was less influential that Fogel's work, perhaps in part because Fishlow attempted to measure the actual effects of the railroad rather than using a full "counterfactual" analysis.

Fogel, Robert W. *Railroads and American Economic Growth: Essays on Econometric History.* Baltimore and London, 1964. This book challenged the view that the railroad was an indispensable contributor to nineteenth-century American growth, helping to fuel a major scholarly debate and establishing Fogel's reputation as a daring and creative practitioner of the "new economic history."

Fogel, Robert W. "Notes on the Social Saving Controversy." *Journal of Economic History* 39 (1979), 1–54. Fogel's Presidential Address to the Economic History Association provides an excellent overview of much of the debate that followed his calculation of the social saving from U.S. railroads in 1890.

McClelland, Peter D. *Causal Explanation and Model Building in History, Economics, and the New Economic History.* Ithaca, N.Y., and London, 1975. Some chapters are too mathematical for nonexperts, but there are lucid explanations of how "new economic historians" attack problems in economic history.

BRADLEY G. LEWIS

SOIL AND SOIL CONSERVATION. Human-induced soil erosion occurs whenever and wherever rain or wind hits soil that has been disturbed. The more sloping the land where the disturbance occurs and the more torrential the rain or the stronger the wind, the greater the amount of erosion. Thus road building and urban construction can and do promote significant erosion. But the main source is agriculture, and agriculturally induced erosion and soil conservation practices to control it are the foci here.

Why Is Soil Erosion a Problem? Soil erosion creates two kinds of problems. First, it removes from the soil organic matter and other nutrients needed for plant growth, it reduces the soil depth in which plant roots can grow, and it can reduce the ability of the soil to absorb and retain water. All of these effects tend to reduce the capacity of the soil to produce food and fiber and, on a sufficiently large scale, could threaten the world's food supply. Second, when the soil is washed from a field, it often enters streams as sediment and is deposited in, for example, lakes and reservoirs, where the muddy water damages recreational values, increases the cost of cleaning the water for industrial and residential uses, and by filling reservoirs shortens their useful lives. Sediment deposited in irrigation canals will gradually reduce their capacities, and deposition in rivers will in time raise the river beds enough to promote flooding and increase the cost of dredging the rivers to permit unimpeded river transport.

Methods of Soil Conservation. Farmers and societies have recognized the dual threats of soil erosion for thousands of years and have developed techniques for easing the threats. Basically there are two such techniques, which may be used separately or together. First is manipulation of vegetation on the land. In general the thicker the vegetative cover, the greater the protection against the impact of rain and wind. Thus reforestation of denuded land will greatly reduce the threat of erosion. Leaving residue from the previous crop on the land, a form of so-called conservation tillage, has been shown to reduce erosion on sloping land by 50 to 90 percent relative to the amount of erosion with so-called clean tillage (no crop residue).

The second conservation technique consists of what might be called mechanical measures. Three of these dominate:

(a) building terraces across sloping land to hold the soil in place;
(b) plowing on the contour, that is, across the slope of the field instead of up and down it; and
(c) strip-cropping, which means alternating strips of crops with strips of grass, all on the contour.

Historical Examples. The literature provides a number of examples of the erosion threat and conservation responses to it in ancient civilizations. In his book *Soil Conservation* (1939), Hugh Hammond Bennett, rightly known as the father of soil conservation in the United States, illustrated the two kinds of erosion damage and counter measures taken two thousand and more years ago in North Africa, the Middle East, Central Asia, Italy, and Peru. Bennett asserts, "The construction of irrigated terraces comprised Phoenicia's chief contribution to the agricultural development of the Mediterranean lands" (Bennett, 1939, p. 26). He notes that the remains of irrigated terraces have been found in Palestine and on the slopes of Judea. According to Bennett, political unrest in the second century CE in the Near East eventually led to the destruction of these soil conservation works and the subsequent loss of irrigated land because of the filling of reservoirs and irrigation canals with sediment.

Moving to erosion and soil conservation conditions in the Western Hemisphere a thousand or more years ago, Bennett notes: "In Peru . . . the lands were sloping, and the Incas and their predecessors had developed highly efficient methods of soil conservation [which is to say, terracing] . . . . The earliest terraces show signs of carefully planned construction" (Bennett, 1939, pp. 48–49).

Modern Concerns about Soil Erosion and Soil Conservation. For more than forty years after Bennett wrote,

relatively little research dealt with the soil erosion and soil conservation situation over major areas of the globe. In the 1980s there was a renewal of interest, perhaps reflecting new concerns in the 1970s about the prospect of feeding the world. In 1984 Lester Brown and E. Wolf published *Soil Erosion: Quiet Crisis in the World Economy*, in which they estimated that global-scale excessive erosion (the amount in excess of the amount consistent with maintaining the long-term productivity of the soil) was about 25 billion metric tons annually. They did not discuss in any detail the production impacts or off-farm damages, but the implication was that both were high.

Despite the dire estimate by Brown and Wolf, in the 1980s a consensus emerged among experts in the field of soil erosion that in fact little was known about the extent of global soil erosion and even less about either its on-farm impacts on soil productivity or its off-farm damages (Dregne, 1988; El-Swaify et al., 1982; Nelson, 1988).

In the early 1990s two studies for the first time provided reasonably reliable estimates of the amount of erosion on agricultural land worldwide plus some indication of the resulting damage to on-farm productivity. (Neither study, however, had anything to say about off-farm damages.) The study, published in 1992 by Harold Dregne and N. T. Chou, specialists in dryland agriculture at Texas Tech University, was based on a thorough review of the published and unpublished material on the amount and extent of eroded land in dry areas around the world as well as on the authors' own extensive experience in dryland research. (Drylands are in arid, semiarid, and dry subhumid regions.) Dregne and Chou classified these lands according to their conditions as slightly, moderately, severely, or very severely degraded. Slightly degraded land had suffered a cumulative loss of 1 to 10 percent of its productivity in the undegraded state, moderately degraded land had lost 10 to 25 percent, severely degraded land had lost 25 to 50 percent, and very severely degraded land had lost more than 50 percent of its original productivity.

Another study was done by a team of soil scientists at the Agricultural University at Wageningen in the Netherlands, headed by professor Roel Oldeman. The focus of the study was all agro-ecological zones on a global scale. Some two hundred soil scientists around the world were asked to classify agricultural and forest lands in their regions as slightly, moderately, severely, or very severely degraded, the same degree-of-degradation categories used by Dregne and Chou. The study showed that 23 percent of the area surveyed was degraded to some extent, 7 percent of it slightly so, 10 percent of it moderately, and 6 percent severely or very severely.

Unlike Dregne and Chou, Oldeman and his colleagues did not estimate the percentage loss of on-farm productivity corresponding to each of the four degree-of-degradation

DUST STORM. Scott City, Kansas, April 1935. (Prints and Photographs Division, Library of Congress)

categories. Pierre Crosson (*Soil Erosion and Its On-Farm Productivity Consequences,* 1995) did this, combining the Oldeman data with the respective percentage estimates of productivity loss taken from Dregne and Chou. The weighted average loss across the four degradation categories in the Oldeman study was 5 percent. This is the cumulative erosion-induced loss of global on-farm productivity over the forty-five years from the end of World War II to 1990.

Since this is the only published estimate of its kind, it is not possible to test its reasonableness against any other. It is fair to say, however, that the estimate is much lower than the comparable one implicit in Brown and Wolf or in a study published in *Science* magazine in February 1995 by David Pimentel and his associates. (With respect to Pimentel and associates, see Crosson, 1995a.)

Soil Erosion and Conservation in the United States. Concern about erosion and efforts to control it came to a head in the United States in the mid-1930s, when Congress established the Soil Conservation Service (SCS) in the U.S. Department of Agriculture (USDA). The SCS was headed by Bennett, who for years had argued vigorously that soil erosion was "a national menace" (Bennett and Chapline, 1928). States set up a system of soil conservation districts that provided the institutional mechanism by which the SCS provided technical advice to farmers about the importance of soil conservation and techniques for achieving it. Another agency, also in the USDA, shared the costs of funding these conservation techniques with farmers.

Over the next forty years the USDA invested tens of billions of dollars in soil conservation programs even though there were no solid estimates of how much erosion was actually occurring in the country let alone the scale of its

on-farm productivity losses or the cost of its off-farm impacts. It was not until 1977 that the first quantitative estimates of the actual annual amount of agriculturally induced erosion were made (*Soil, Water, and Related Resources in the United States,* 1980). Comparable estimates were subsequently made in 1982, 1987, 1992, and 1997. The availability of these data stimulated research to estimate erosion-induced losses of cropland productivity. Three models to do this were developed. One, called the Productivity Index (PI) model (1984) was developed by soil scientists at the University of Minnesota; another, the Erosion Productivity Index Calculator (EPIC) model (1989), was developed by soil scientists, hydrologists, and economists at the USDA; and the third was developed by Crosson at Resources for the Future (1986). Each model was used independently to address this question: Should current rates of cropland erosion continue for one hundred years, what would be the impact on cropland productivity at the end of the period? EPIC indicated that productivity would be down 2 to 3 percent, PI showed a decline of some 4 percent, and Crosson's work indicated productivity 10 to 12 percent less than it would be in the absence of erosion. These numbers are far less than almost anyone expected, given the rhetoric about the severity of the erosion threat to the country's agricultural productivity.

None of the three studies dealt with off-farm damages of erosion. The work of Brown and Wolf (1984), Pimentel and colleagues (1995), and others implied that off-farm damages had been high for decades and were not being reduced. All such studies, however, were based on models and anecdotal evidence. These dire scenarios, moreover, were challenged by Stanley Trimble (1999) and Trimble and Crosson (2000), who made three points. First, most local and regional case studies showed marked decreases in off-farm sedimentation over the past six decades. Second, in at least some parts of the United States soil conservation has allowed increased stream stability and improved biological habitat. Third, the amount of sediment transmitted by U.S. streams was only a small fraction of the erosion estimated by the USDA.

Has Soil Conservation Worked? Is the relatively small amount of soil erosion in the United States evidence that the country's farmers have adopted soil conservation on a large scale? There are grounds for believing that it is. In the first place, the billions of dollars the USDA spent over the last six or seven decades in support of soil conservation programs have clearly had a significant impact in persuading farmers to adopt soil conservation practices. But it is unlikely that this is all there is to it. Evidence suggests that farmers themselves have invested significantly in soil conservation. This should not be surprising. In the United States farmers have secure private property rights in their land. This means that within broad limits they can do pretty much what they wish with their land. A corollary is that the farmers themselves reap the benefits from good land management and pay the costs of bad management. For most farmers the land is their most important single asset. It behooves them therefore to protect their land against erosion-induced losses of productivity. This incentive for farmers to invest in soil conservation plus the financial and other assistance provided by the USDA probably explain sufficiently why erosion damages to on-farm productivity are so low in the United States.

This line of argument raises another question: Might farmer incentives to invest in soil conservation also play an important role in explaining why erosion-induced losses of on-farm productivity are low all around the world, as the findings from the study by Oldeman and others indicate? This possibility now can be no more than a hypothesis because of insufficient information about the extent to which farmers in the developing countries of Asia, Africa, and Latin America have firm, enforceable property rights in their land. But the Oldeman results seem strongly to indicate that farmers all around the world have recognized the importance of soil conservation and have invested widely to install such practices on their land.

[*See also* Crop Rotation *and* Fertilizing.]

BIBLIOGRAPHY

Bennett, Hugh Hammond. *Soil Conservation*. New York, 1939.
Bennett, Hugh Hammond, and William Chapline. *Soil Erosion: A National Menace*. Washington, D.C., 1928.
Brown, Lester, and Edward Wolf. *Soil Erosion: Quiet Crisis in the World Economy*. Washington, D.C., 1984.
Crosson, Pierre. Letter to *Science* 269 (28 July 1995a), 461.
Crosson, Pierre. *Soil Erosion and Its On-farm Productivity Consequence: What Do We Know*. Washington, D.C., 1995b.
Dregne, H. "Desertification of Drylands." In *Challenges in Dryland Agriculture: A Global Perspective—Proceedings of the International Conference on Dryland Farming*, edited by P. Unger, T. Sneed, W. Jordan, and R. Jensen. Amarillo, Tex., 1988.
Dregne, H., and N.T. Chou. "Global Desertification: Dimensions and Costs." In *Degradation and Restoration of Arid Lands*, edited by Harold Dregne. Lubbock, Tex., 1992.
El-Swaify, S., E. Dangler, and C. Armstrong. *Soil Erosion by Water in the Tropics*. Honolulu, Hi., 1982.
Lindert, Peter. *Shifting Ground: The Changing Agricultural Soils of China and Indonesia*. Cambridge, Mass., and London, 2000.
Nelson, R. *Dryland Management: The Land Degradation Problem*. Environment Department Working Paper No. 8. Washington, D.C., 1988.
Pimentel, D., et al. "Environmental and Economic Costs and Conservation Benefits." *Science* 267 (24 February 1995).
Pierce, F., R. Dowdy, W. Larson, and W. Graham. "Soil Erosion in the Corn Belt: An Assessment of Erosion's Long-Term Effect." *The Journal of Soil and Water Conservation* 39 (1984).
Soil, Water, and Related Resources in the United States: Status, Conditions and Trends. Part 1. U.S. Department of Agriculture. Washington, D.C., 1980.
The Second RCA Appraisal: Soil, Water, and Related Resources on Nonfederal Land in the United States. U.S. Department of Agriculture. Washington, D.C., 1989.
Trimble, S.W. "Decreased Rates of Alluvial Sediment Storage in the Coon Creek, Wisconsin, 1975–1993." *Science* 285 (20 August 1999), 1244.
Trimble, S.W., and Pierre Crosson. "U.S. Soil Erosion Rates: Myth and Reality." *Science* 289 (2000), 248.

PIERRE CROSSON AND STANLEY TRIMBLE

SOLAR POWER. The sun is responsible for most of the earth's energy. Plant photosynthesis provides the basis for coal and oil. The sun's heat, even indirectly, provides wind and wave power. Solar power, though, is commonly attributed to direct energy from the sun. This happens in two distinct ways: solar thermal and solar electricity. The first uses the sun's heat and is most commonly used for supplying hot water. (One development takes this further to drive steam turbines.) Much more versatile, and the focus here, is the direct conversion of sunlight into electricity, which is known as photovoltaics (PV).

How It Works. Most commonly, silicon is intensely refined to remove impurities. Part of the silicon is then doped with boron, which has excess positive "holes," and part with phosphorous with excess negative electrons. This is what is known as a semiconductor. When light hits the silicon, electrons move between the layers. This energy is then collected by a metal backplate and front grid as electricity.

To withstand the harsh environmental conditions that they operate in, the cells are laminated between protective material and have an expected life of twenty to thirty years.

Past and Present. Despite its rise to prominence in the 1970s and 1980s, this industry can trace its origins more than 150 years to Edmund Becquerel. He observed a

SOLAR POWER. Panels on a farmhouse, Salton Sea, California, 1990. (© Alex Quesada/Woodfin Camp and Associates, New York)

light-dependent voltage between two electrodes in an electrolyte. Albert Einstein united these threads with his theory of the photoelectric effect in 1905, for which he received the Nobel Prize. It was the space program during the late 1950s that provided the catalyst for the industry.

During the mid- to late 1970s, innovation led to cheaper, more efficient solar cells. This, coupled with increased energy efficiency of remote equipment such as telecommunications, led to the viability of solar as a power source, not just for satellites but also for terrestrial applications. This period also witnessed a dramatic rise in conventional fossil-fuel prices and with it the realization that fossil-fuel sources were finite. The space program gave fresh impetus to cost reduction and improvements. Today, most people see solar all around through the form of the humble solar calculator.

Benefits and Uses. Photovoltaics require no fuel and minimal maintenance. As such, the key early uses have been in equipment for remote locations, such as marine navigational aids, telecommunications repeater sites on mountains, and space satellites. At these venues, it is expensive and difficult to bring in fuel or grid power. As a renewable energy source, photovoltaics is environmentally benign. Once manufactured, it does not give off gases, such as carbon dioxide, that lead to global warming.

Solar produces no noise when operating and, providing it has access to light, will generate electricity. This makes it one of the few renewable energies that can be used in the urban area.

Solar, unlike fossil fuels, is most appropriate when used as a distributed technology—that is, generating power where needed. The present PV market has experienced a fairly high and stable increase of more than 15–25 percent per year. Today the annual solar module production is estimated to be about 180 MWp (megawatt peak), still small when compared with conventional generation but growing fast. Although costs have fallen sevenfold since 1981, its cost at present explain the small relative impact.

Solar power is used in four general areas: remote industrial equipment, such as telecommunications devices; rural power systems in the unconnected developing world; consumer devices, such as calculators; and the fastest-growing sector known as grid connect. Here, solar acts as a complement to the standard grid. It is installed on individual buildings to supplement power to the grid. In this case, solar not only acts as an energy source, but it is a part of the building itself. The key drivers for this are the environmental aspects.

Solar is used in every country in the world. In 2000, the world's two largest markets were Japan and Germany. Eighty thousand holiday cottages in Norway use solar lighting. Kenya is just one example of a developing country whose needs are being met in part by solar power, representing two billion of the six billion people in the world who do not have electricity. In developing countries, the issues are macroeconomic. In the developed world it is the strength of state and consumer environmental commitments.

Government and the Environmental Agenda. The environment has become of increasing concern. The most visible manifestation of this is the growth of "green" parties in government. They are within the national governments of Germany, Finland, Italy, and France. Other countries have local and state equivalents. When consumers have a preference, it is for clean, renewable energy, though "at the right price." Thus, government programs are in place in many countries to stimulate the take-up of solar. Although many challenges are still ahead, the Kyoto Treaty was a major world commitment to reducing emissions. Increased use of renewable energy is a common way all nations can help meet the terms of the treaty. Deregulation of energy markets in many countries has provided other opportunities to use solar power. Examples of where support mechanisms are in place to speed take-up include California, Japan (which offers grants), and Germany (which rewards solar owners with a contribution at five times the cost of conventional electricity).

Limitations. The key current limitation to take-up is price. Output and, therefore, final cost of solar electricity varies, depending on geography. For remote villages in Asia and roadside-emergency telephones, it can be the cheapest energy source. For mainstream use and grid-connected users in the developed world, it can be ten to forty times more expensive than conventional electricity. Solar's output is intermittent, which requires backup sources such as grid/batteries for periods of poor nighttime weather. Output per area is still low.

The Future. The focus of the solar industry is a lower-cost and higher-efficiency product to compete further with conventional power sources. Market growth is the key to this. A virtuous cycle of greater production, lower prices, and greater demand has evolved. Technological innovation and government policies will also play key roles. The issue is not whether but how great a role solar will play in the world's future energy supply.

BIBLIOGRAPHY

BP Solar. *BP Solar: The Natural Source for Electricity*. <http://www.bp-solarex.com>. Contains further examples of product applications.

National Renewable Electricity Laboratory. *NREL Online*. <http://www.nrel.gov>

U.S. Department of Energy. *Office of Energy Efficiency and Renewable Energy Home Page*. <http://www.eren.doe.gov>

German Federal Ministry of Economics and Technology. *World-Wide Information System for Renewable Energy Home Page*. <http://wire.ises.org>

Database of State Incentives for Renewable Energy. *DSIRE Home Page*. <http://www-solar.mck.ncsu.edu/dsire.htm> Database of U.S. state assistance.

Global Solar Partners. <http://www.solarpartners.org> Basic educational site.

Canadian Association for Renewable Energies. *Renewable Energy*. <http://www.renewables.ca> Renewable energy news.

MARK HAMMONDS

SOMALIA. *See* Ethiopia.

SOMBART, WERNER (1863–1941), German social scientist and economic historian.

The son of a liberal industrialist, Sombart studied law, history, and political science, first in Pisa and then at the University of Berlin, a stronghold of the younger generation of the German "historical school," who emphasized economics and inductive methods of historical research. In Berlin he attended the seminars of Gustav Schmoller and Adolf Wagner, *Kathedersozialisten* (academic socialists) and founders of the progressive Association for Social Reform. He completed his doctoral thesis, a socioeconomic study of the Roman Campagna, under Schmoller in 1888 and two years later was appointed to a lectureship in political science at the University of Breslau. Viewed as a Marxist by the government and his peers, he was subsequently prevented from accepting chairs in Freiburg, Heidelberg, and Karlsruhe. In 1906 Sombart accepted a post at the new Berlin School of Commerce, but it was not until 1917 that he was called to a chair of economics and political science at the university. By the time he retired in 1931, Sombart had achieved recognition as one of the leading German social scientists of his generation.

Sombart's most influential work, *Modern Capitalism*, first published in 1902 and revised and expanded between 1916 and 1927, sought to explain the origin and spirit of capitalism. Sombart identified the rational calculation of profit as the defining feature of the capitalist economy and traced its origins to late medieval Italy, when the money-making impulse first became widespread through the activities of merchants, retailers, and moneylenders. Sombart's periodization and his view that religion played a minor role in the development of capitalism were contested by Max Weber in *The Protestant Ethic and the Spirit of Capitalism* (1904–1905), which linked the capitalist ethic to Puritanism. The influence of Weber is reflected in the controversial *The Jews and Modern Capitalism* (1911), where Sombart attributed to Judaism the role in the genesis of capitalism that Weber had assigned to Protestantism. In *The Quintessence of Capitalism* (1913), Sombart returned to his original thesis with additional evidence of a capitalistic spirit in pre-Reformation society and religion, and two further studies published in the same year examined how war and luxury consumption contributed to the growth of early capitalism.

Sombart was among the first historians of socialism. His *Socialism and the Social Movement* (1896) went through six German editions and was translated into several languages. In *Why Is There No Socialism in the United States?* (1906) he argued that cheap land and high wages had delayed the development of working-class politics in the United States. A selective form of this argument is often invoked in support of the American "exceptionalism" thesis. During World War I, Sombart began to distance himself from Marxism. Critical of both the Bolshevik Revolution and the Weimar Republic, he had embraced a conservative form of nationalism by the mid-1920s. In *German Socialism* (1934) Sombart expressed sympathy with aspects of National Socialism, though he was critical of its totalitarianism, and his last book, *Vom Menschen* (1938), rejected Nazi racial theories.

BIBLIOGRAPHY

Backhaus, Jürgen, ed. *Werner Sombart (1863–1941): Social Scientist*. 3 vols. Marburg, 1996. Most recent collection of essays assessing Sombart's life, theories, and influence.

Lenger, Friedrich. *Werner Sombart, 1863–1941: Eine Biographie*. Munich, 1994.

Sombart, Werner. *Der moderne Kapitalismus*. 1st ed. 2 vols. Leipzig, 1902. *Der moderne Kapitalismus: Historisch-systematische Darstellung des gesamteuropäischen Wirtschaftslebens von seinen Anfängen bis zur Gegenwart*. 2d ed. 3 vols. Munich, 1916–1927.

Sombart, Werner. *Socialism and the Social Movement*. Translated by Mordecai Epstein. London and New York, 1909. Originally published as *Sozialismus und soziale Bewegung*. 6th ed. Jena, 1908.

Sombart, Werner. *The Jews and Modern Capitalism*. Translated by Mordecai Epstein. New York, 1913. Originally published as *Die Juden und das Wirtschaftsleben*. Leipzig, 1911.

Sombart, Werner. *The Quintessence of Capitalism*. Translated by Mordecai Epstein. New York, 1915. Originally published as *Der Bourgeois: Zur Geistesgeschichte des modernen Wirtschaftsmenschen*. Munich, 1913.

Sombart, Werner. *Why Is There No Socialism in the United States?* Translated by Patricia M. Husbands and C. T. Husbands. London, 1976. Originally published as *Warum gibt es in den Vereinigten Staaten keinen Sozialismus?* Tübingen, 1906.

LAWRIN ARMSTRONG

SOUTHERN AFRICA

SOUTHERN AFRICA *[This entry contains three subentries, on the economic history of southern Africa during the early, colonial, and modern periods.]*

Early Period

Southern Africa was one of the first parts of the world to be occupied by humans. There is clear evidence that, by a million years ago, groups making and using distinctive stone tools were scavenging for plant and animal foods across grasslands and savannas, making temporary camps alongside rivers and pans and under rock overhangs. Over the millennia, this way of life became steadily more sophisticated. Early people learned to make smaller, more specialized implements, using stone and other materials, and passing this knowledge on to others (the cultural transmission of information is accepted as one of the defining features of humanity). People learned the properties of plant foods and their seasonal availability, and how to trap and hunt animals more efficiently. Favorable living places, particularly well-located caves and rock shelters, were visited repeatedly, resulting in stratified occupation layers that have yielded a rich archaeological record of these communities and their economies.

About a hundred thousand years ago, this long-established hunter-gatherer way of life began to change. People living near the coast specialized in collecting the abundant sea foods from rocky shorelines. There is evidence of cooperative behavior, suggesting more sophisticated social organization. Evidence of the deliberate burial of the dead suggests belief in an afterlife and a sophisticated concept of time. There are the remains of ritual activities. Sometime later, a tradition of rock engraving and painting became established, leading to a wealth of sacred sites with complex and distinctive motifs and themes—the longest continual tradition of art yet known. These economic and cultural changes were accompanied by physical changes—the emergence of a fully modern human biology. While there is still debate about the interpretation of these transitions, some archaeologists, combining the evidence from excavations with genetic extrapolations based on DNA studies, have seen these developments in southern Africa as the point of origin for all the world's modern human populations.

A second horizon of change—and one that was to affect radically the economic history of southern Africa—came some two thousand years ago. An array of farming techniques had been developed to the north: sheepherding in the Mediterranean region and North Africa; cattle farming on the margins of the Sahara; and grain cultivation in the Ethiopian highlands and the Sahel belt. These were accompanied, and enabled, by ironworking—new technologies for tools, which allowed forest and savanna to be cleared and fields to be hoed. This new way of life spread steadily southward, displacing or incorporating hunter-gatherer bands. In the drier central and western regions, a nomadic pastoral economy allowed the best use of sparse grasslands and desert margins. In the east, early farmers spread south through the coastal regions and major river valleys, choosing village sites close to good soils or nutrient-rich littoral woodlands. By the middle of the first millennium CE, this transformation was complete. Farming villages were established in Zambia, Zimbabwe, the costal lowlands of Mozambique, and the eastern seaboard of South Africa to the extent of reliable summer rainfall. Herders, measuring their wealth in both cattle and fat-tailed sheep, were living in Botswana, Namibia, the drier western regions of South Africa, and the winter rainfall region of the Cape. Hunter-gatherers, following a much older way of living, had specialized desert and mountain economies, bartering and interacting with both herders and farmers.

As with other parts of the world, the development of the farming way of life initiated an interplay between increased population density, the accumulation of resources, economic specialization and social change. As part of these processes, southern Africa became part of a wider economic region, with growing networks of local barter, and with east-coast traders eager to obtain gold, ivory, animal skins, and other exotic commodities for the Arab and Indian markets. By the early twelfth century, there is clear evidence of urban development in the Limpopo River valley. A series of large villages was followed by concentrated settlements, perhaps housing as many as ten thousand people, of which Mapungubwe is the best-known example. Mapungubwe was a socially stratified town, with the elite living on the hilltop and its graves distinguished by rich grave goods. There were specialized industries, including metalworking and ivory carving, and an economy based on large herds of cattle. Wealth was marked by accumulations of glass trade beads—as rare and valuable in Mapungubwe as was gold in contemporary Europe, and testimony to complex networks of trade via Indian Ocean settlements and coastal dhows.

Mapungubwe's early success as a trading state was the basis for the rise of Zimbabwe. Centered on the high plateau to the north of the Limpopo, early Zimbabwe owed its success to the ready availability of gold and the ability to mine in stopes. Authority was marked by a network of regional centers across the plateau, westward into Botswana and the margins of the Kalahari, and eastward to the Mozambique coastal plain. Each regional center had a distinctive plan, with a central, elite area marked off by stone walling decorated in distinctive designs. It is probable that regional centers controlled mining, large herds of cattle, and the distribution of trade goods.

The largest and best known town in early Zimbabwe is Great Zimbabwe. Many times larger than the regional centers, Great Zimbabwe nonetheless shared the same architectural principles. Building on the ways in which authority was marked at Mapungubwe, the elite were sheltered behind high stone walls on the Hill. A further and extensive complex of stone walling beneath the Hill identified the rest of the town's center, while ordinary people lived in tightly packed clay-and-thatch houses around the periphery of the town. Estimates of population vary between ten thousand and thirty thousand people, sustained by farming and by large herds of cattle. As with Mapungubwe, there is evidence of craft specialization and trade: metal and gold work, hordes of glass trade beads, and porcelain ceramics from Asia. A remarkable set of carved soapstone birds attests to the spiritual life of Zimbabwe and has been interpreted as the markers of individual kings. These and other aspects of Great Zimbabwe allow a direct connection with recent Shona customs, known through oral evidence.

The economic and social complexity of early Zimbabwe is paralleled in contemporary developments further to the south. The beginning of the second millennium was characterized by the expansion of farmers from the coastal plains and river valleys to the higher grassland regions, including those of the southern highveld of South Africa. These developments were enabled by more specialized cattle herding and the accumulation of wealth that this allowed. Extensive complexes of stone enclosures across the high veld attest to dense populations that settled westward to the extent of reliable annual rainfall. There were widespread systems of trade that linked cattle herders with specialized ironworkers in the eastern lowveld and elsewhere. By the middle of the millennium, the historical foundations of contemporary South African communities had been firmly established.

Southern Africa in 1600, then, was economically diverse. In the west, herders and hunter-gatherers, speaking a range of Khoisan languages, moved seasonally across the landscape. In the east, Bantu-speaking farmers grew sorghum and millet, tended livestock, and specialized in iron production and other crafts. The more recent history of these societies had been characterized by the introduction of new crops and livestock, by the possibilities and consequences of long-distance trade, and by the rise and fall of urban centers. Further change was imminent as new traders and raiders pushed inland from the Portuguese settlements on the Indian Ocean coast, and European interests competed for the lucrative sea routes to the East that would lead to colonial settlement at the Cape.

BIBLIOGRAPHY

Deacon, Hilary J., and Janette Deacon. *Human Beginnings in South Africa: Uncovering the Secrets of the Stone Age.* Walnut Creek, Calif., 1999.

Hall, Martin. *Farmers, Kings and Traders: The People of South Africa, 200–1860.* Chicago, 1990.

Hall, Martin. *Archaeology Africa.* Cape Town, 1996.

Huffman, Thomas. N., and John C. Vogel "The Chronology of Great Zimbabwe." *South African Archaeological Bulletin* 46 (1991), 61–70.

Voigt, Elizabeth A. *Mapungubwe: An Archaeo-Zoological Interpretation of an Iron Age Community.* Pretoria, South Africa, 1983.

MARTIN HALL

Colonial Period

In the economic history of southern Africa through the course of the seventeenth to nineteenth centuries, the common theme that animates available analyses concerns the growing links to a world market. This meant, in the first place, access to raw materials: ivory, hides and skins, slaves, land, and mineral products for those accumulating wealth through those links. However, this literature also emphasizes the limits to market impact and the continued importance of inward-looking economies based on meeting survival challenges in an environmentally diverse and often difficult environment.

Through the nineteenth century, however, the impact of the Industrial Revolution, with its intensified search for raw materials that might involve far more processing, became noticeable: the emergence of wine, wool, sugar, and diamonds as export commodities; the rapid growth in import of textiles and metal goods from Europe; the renewed quest for gold. This impact came together with the move, almost complete by 1890, toward colonial subordination of the entire region. The extension of the market and market values contained within it the promise of remarkable economic growth, as well as demographic and social developments. But the reality was charged with upheaval, war, and the destruction of existing ways of life, which placed the benefits in a far more critical light.

Portuguese Beginnings. At the onset of the seventeenth century, small-scale Portuguese intrusions had brought about the creation of a kind of sphere of influence that stretched south and inland from Mozambique Island to the interior central plateau. However, the object of the intrusions, the lucrative Indian Ocean gold trade, remained elusive. Producers abandoned numerous small-scale sites, some of which became in any event exhausted. In 1693, the Changamire rulers ousted the last Portuguese from the plateau. Thereafter, the chief field of their influence lay in the *prazo*s, the Portuguese-designated estates in the lower Zambesi valley, which functioned much like African chiefdoms but retained ties to Portuguese society and exported ivory. Indian commerce was the principal beneficiary.

Hard as it is to trace their spread, this era also saw the entry of new trade goods and, more significantly, new crops, notably maize but also cassava into the northern parts of the southern African region from the west. Andrew Roberts (*A History of Zambia*, London, 1976) gives a sense as well of a gradual process of state formation (Kazembe, Bulozi), which bore some relationship, often indirect and difficult to trace, to control over such resources as ivory, copper, and salt.

Arrival of the Dutch East India Company. From 1600, the southwestern corner of the region attracted a growing amount of transient trade from passing European ships, using Table Bay as a place for refreshment and the acquisition of meat. In 1652, the Dutch East India Company established a permanent settlement at Cape Town as a means of consolidating this commerce. Cape Town became the western gateway to the Indian Ocean commercial world of the company during and after its heyday, but its hinterland simultaneously developed into a distinctive colonial society. Lacking an export attractive to European consumers, the colonial economy grew by provisioning

the fleet, the garrison, and, to a lesser extent, Dutch possessions in the East with meat, grain, and wine. The indigenous population of stock-herding Khoi Khoi were expelled, subordinated, or wiped out through disease while the company imported a total of some sixty thousand slaves from Africa and Asia to work on farms and in the growing urban center of Cape Town. A small number of European settlers multiplied under favorable conditions, struggling as they became stronger to reduce the economic monopoly privileges of the company. At the top of this society stood a small class of what the historian Robert Ross has termed the Cape gentry, usually with very close relations to the company officials.

The settled agrarian economy of the western Cape could not be replicated in the dry, riverless interior, but the eastern and northern frontiers of the colony expanded and were scenes both of intense conflict between settler and indigene as well as of a far-reaching commercial expansion of European goods, notably firearms and of the sale of natural products, such as ivory, hides, and skins. Marginal individuals and their followers were extruded from the colony but were also attracted by possibilities further afield.

British Conquest and Expansion. These pressures intensified after the 1795 British conquest of the Cape (again in 1806 and established by treaty in 1815). The colony was extended far to the east in various stages, while a second focus of British expansion was established around a second commercial entrepôt on the coast at Port Natal in 1842. The wandering farmers, or *trekboere*, had by then established whole new areas of settlement in what became the Orange Free State and the South African Republic, reflecting pressures caused by the growing cost of land and abolition of slavery in the Cape Colony, as well as the lure of attractive resources in the interior. The Great Trek, and those of related people of color, many of whom were called Griqua, were marked by high levels of violence, dispossession, and the taking of captives. Further north, in the lower Zambesi valley, ivory tended to give way to slaves as the major export, and the *prazo*s became increasingly militarized.

Formation of States. These forces meshed with the simultaneous process, again characterized by considerable violence and large-scale human movement, of African state formation, the so-called *Mfecane*. The *Mfecane* process began north of Port Natal with the emergence of the Zulu state and impacted on the entire region, including what is today southern and central Mozambique, Zimbabwe, and Zambia, while armed Khoi and mixed-race pastoral leaders overwhelmed much of Namibia. Imitation of, and resistance to, these states led to the creation of still others such as Lesotho, the Bemba kingdom of northern Zambia, and the revived Bulozi around the upper Zambesi. Few if any of these states were able to master the intensifying commercial pressures. In fact, as possibilities for wage labor emerged, allowing for the acquisition of guns and herds, migrant labor became a striking feature of the regional economy from the middle of the nineteenth century, with a tendency to undermine the authority of patriarchal rulers. In the last imperial phase, the independence of such rulers got in the way of the systematic colonial economic and social order and was more or less deliberately destroyed.

Under British rule, the Cape Colony abolished slavery in 1834, and henceforth its economy operated on a free-labor basis; but the former slaves had almost no access to land, and resources and were essentially proletarianized. Initially, imperial incorporation allowed for the successful development of wine exports, but this did not survive the rise of British free trade with Europe. It was the eastern and northern parts of the colony that connected agrarian production with the world market, through the systematic cultivation of wool-bearing sheep and then ostriches raised for their feathers. In Natal, the introduction of indentured Indian workers after 1860 made it possible for sugar plantations, unable to find a suitable committed local work force, to flourish along the coast.

Diamonds and Gold. However, the great leap forward for capitalism in southern Africa stemmed from the discovery of diamonds on land claimed simultaneously by Griqua and Boer, deep in the interior in 1867. Yet here at Kimberley, it was the British who were able to establish their claims. Over a period of approximately fifteen years, the diamond fields attracted large numbers of migrants from international points of origin, temporary migrants from all parts of the region, including unconquered chiefdoms. Meanwhile, a multitude of small-holding miners and merchant profits gave way to a system of virtual monopoly under the control of the De Beers diamond company. A systematic, hierarchical labor system involved a bifurcated world: a regimented, closed compound system for migrant workers and a structured suburban working-class community for white supervisory and skilled labor. Kimberley became the focus of a substantial regional transportation network, with the railway reaching the coast in 1885. Yet Kimberley was a kind of giant dress rehearsal for the far more earthshaking developments that would follow the discovery of massive, deep gold veins further north and east on the Witwatersrand ridge in the territory of the South African Republic in 1884. This "Mineral Revolution" would herald the economic transformation of the region.

By 1890, major changes could be observed even in the northern part of southern Africa. By this date, Cecil Rhodes (1853–1902), the Kimberley magnate looking to find a second Rand to the north—and also Prime Minister of the Cape Colony—was sponsoring the Pioneer Column to lay political claims to northern Zimbabwe following the ambiguous Rudd Concession negotiated with Lobengula (1836–1894), the Ndebele king, who dominated the south. Extending commercial networks in the Zambesi valley lay behind intensified Portuguese trade and the gradual extinction of slaving. German settlers and prospectors were searching for a viable basis to prop up German colonial rule in South-West Africa, proclaimed in 1884. A dynamic core of capitalist enterprise was taking possession of southern Africa while the turbulent frontiers it spawned swept up every corner of the region. Localized economies either found a purchase in this process or suffered marginalization and worse.

BIBLIOGRAPHY

Alpers, Edward A. *Ivory and Slaves in East Central Africa: Changing Patterns of Trade in the Later Nineteenth Century.* London, 1975.

Beach, David. *Zimbabwe before 1900.* Gweru, Zimbabwe, 1984.

Elphick, Richard, and Hermann Giliomee, eds. *The Shaping of South African Society, 1652–1840.* Cape Town, 1989.

Keegan, Timothy. *Colonial South Africa and the Origins of the Racial Order.* London and Charlottesville, N.C., 1996.

Marks, Shula, and Anthony Atmore, eds. *Economy and Society in Pre-Industrial South Africa.* London, 1980.

Newitt, Malyn. *Portuguese Settlement on the Zambesi.* London, 1973.

Roberts, Andrew. *A History of Zambia.* London, 1976.

Ross, Robert. *Beyond the Pale: Essays on the History of Colonial South Africa.* Hanover, N. H., 1993.

Turrell, Robert V. *Capital and Labour on the Kimberley Diamond Fields, 1871–1890.* Cambridge, 1987.

WILLIAM FREUND

Modern Period

Competition between European powers for colonies (the "Scramble for Africa") and the discovery of the gold reef on the Witwatersrand in 1886 led to the reshaping of the region of southern Africa politically, economically, and socially. The regional center then shifted from Britain's Cape Colony (with its diamond mines, worked from 1870) to the Boer-ruled (Dutch) Transvaal and the fast-growing city of Johannesburg, with its European-financed gold mines—the shift led to the South African War (1899–1902) and Britain's defeat of the Boer alliance of Transvaal and Orange Free State. Britain then ruled the whole of what was South Africa until 1910, when the independent Union of South Africa was established (governed by a white minority on the basis of official anti-blacks discrimination).

In the late 1890s, the rinderpest epidemic hit the herds of southern Africa and decimated livestock, in much the same way that today's human population is being decimated by HIV/AIDS. In 1890, Southern Rhodesia (today Zimbabwe) and Northern Rhodesia (today Zambia) were conquered and ruled by the British South Africa Company. Basutoland (today Lesotho), Bechuanaland (today

Botswana), and Swaziland were also colonized, and transformed largely into reserves of cheap labor for South Africa. The south of Portugal's colony Mozambique became a labor reserve for the South African mines, as did Northern Rhodesia for those of South Africa and the adjacent Katanga region of the Belgian Congo (today the Democratic Republic of the Congo). Central and northern Mozambique were leased by Portugal to three large private companies, for plantations based on conscripted labor. Germany conquered South West Africa (today Namibia) and exterminated more than half its population in the center and the south in war from 1904 to 1907.

For most of the twentieth century, the basis of the southern African economy was migrant cheap black labor, channeled to the mines (and in some cases the farms) by recruiting companies and by the levying of taxes. In Southern Rhodesia, this was called the system of *chibaro*. Wages were paid at the level of a single male worker (rather than to reproduce a family) and, with these workers housed at the mines in regimented compounds, wives and children were expected to survive on their own subsistence agriculture in the rural home areas. White workers, largely recent immigrants, were protected from black competition by job color bars. Gold mining flourished in South Africa and supplied almost 60 percent of South African exports from the 1890s to the early 1980s, but it was less successful in Southern Rhodesia. At its height, South African gold production constituted 25 to 33 percent of world production. From 1906, mining also began in South West Africa, based on cheap contracted migrant labor from Ovambololand to the north.

Both development and underdevelopment continued throughout the region, creating uneven economies, with urban islands of mainly white plenty in a sea of rural black impoverishment. The rail lines tended to link mining centers with the coast. In South Africa, pass laws (where "Natives" had to carry passes to and from cities) inhibited the permanent settlement of the indigenous population in the cities. Permanent urbanization of the indigenous population emerged far less rapidly than that of whites (or of Indians, who lived mainly in Natal, or of "Coloureds" living mainly in Cape Province).

Agriculture was transformed in southern Africa by the emergence of mining-based cities, on the Witwatersrand, in Salisbury and Bulawayo in Southern Rhodesia, and later in the Copper Belt of Northern Rhodesia. In some cases, indigenous producers were the first to respond to the new markets for food. The state rapidly intervened to support and promote white-settler farmers, however, to provide them with cheap land, cheap labor, and branch rail lines. From 1900, the "maize triangle" on the Highveld flourished and became the core of Afrikaner (descendants of Dutch settlers) nationalism. In Southern Rhodesia, settler commercial farming was based on maize and tobacco; its success provided the basis for a self-governing, white-minority-settler colony in 1923. At the same time, Northern Rhodesia was handed by the British South Africa Company to Britain. German settlers were encouraged in South West Africa, and when that country was conquered by South Africa in 1915 (and after Britain defeated Germany in 1918 in World War I) was ruled as a mandate of the League of Nations. On farms throughout the region, labor conditions were difficult, even quasi-feudal. By the 1920s, labor tenancy was the norm on South African farms.

Through most of southern Africa, the migrant labor system and the whites' agriculture were reinforced by the practice of racial macrosegregation—reserving small portions of generally poor land (reserves) for the conquered indigenous population and preventing their land ownership in the white (settler) areas. A patriarchal system in the rural areas was also reinforced by the state, to ensure the subordination of black women. These were the aims of such laws as the Natives Land Act of 1913 in South Africa, strengthened in 1927 and 1936, and of the Land Apportionment Act of 1931 in Southern Rhodesia. A similar system was applied in South West Africa from the 1920s. South Africa expected the transfer from Britain of Basutoland, Swaziland, and Bechuanaland to it, as additional reserves, but that never occurred.

In growing labor disputes, black workers went on strike at mines in South Africa and in Southern Rhodesia after World War I. In 1922, cost-cutting measures by the mine-owners led in South Africa to the Rand Revolt—a strike and uprising by white workers in defense of the job color bar. In 1924, the election of an economically nationalist government in South Africa led to the attempt to promote export agriculture and secondary industry; in agriculture, control and marketing boards were soon established (and, later, in Southern Rhodesia). The South African government also imposed tariffs, to undercut interregional as well as overseas trade. Through these means and the establishment of state industries in iron and steel, for example, it aimed at import-substitution. The South African economy, however, continued to depend on gold for foreign exchange. Then copper mines established in Northern Rhodesia in 1928 grew to dominate that economy. (In the post–World War II boom year of 1953, those mines supplied 16 percent of non–Soviet bloc world production.)

The Great Depression (1929–1940) resulted in general decline and serious unemployment in southern Africa from 1929 to at least 1931. The abandonment of the gold standard, first by Britain in 1931 and then by southern Africa in 1932, allowed gold prices to float and with an increase in price, restored the economy. This upswing was prolonged and was continuous during World War II

MINING IN SOUTH AFRICA. Men working 2,000 feet underground in the Kimberley Diamond Mine, South Africa, between 1890 and 1905. (Frank and Frances Carpenter Collection/Prints and Photographs Division, Library of Congress)

(1939–1945). Secondary industry developed then in South Africa, and tractors began to transform agriculture. In Southern Rhodesia, secondary industry was also stimulated and overtook mining by 1947 in its contribution to Gross Domestic Product. During the war, mass urbanization and proletarianization of the blacks in South Africa (and to a lesser extent in Southern Rhodesia) had led to the rise of squatter settlements. A big strike movement of black workers occurred in wartime South Africa and, in 1946, there was a large but severely repressed strike by black mineworkers. During the war, the South African government had hesitatingly and ambiguously eased its segregation policy. In Southern Rhodesia, a railworkers strike in 1945 spread to Northern Rhodesia, and in April 1948, there was a general strike of 100,000.

Fear of black proletarianization led to the victory of the Nationalist party (NP) in the South African election of 1948, the implementation of policies of apartheid (a rigid government-sponsored form of racial segregation), and the effective administration of South West Africa as a fifth province of South Africa. Partly in reaction to apartheid, the Federation of Northern and Southern Rhodesia and Nyasaland (today Malawi) was established in 1953 by the British government, on an ostensible program of "racial partnership." The economic boom in the advanced industrial countries from 1950 to 1975 fostered the growth of the South African manufacturing industry, behind tariff barriers on the basis of import-substitution; this was, however, "peripheral industrialization" that relied on foreign exchange produced by the primary sector (gold, agriculture) to pay for imports of producer goods. In the 1960s, there was massive foreign investment and unparalleled economic growth in South Africa, which became an industrial powerhouse. In the 1990s, South Africa accounted for four-fifths of the value of southern Africa's production.

In the 1950s and 1960s, white Afrikaners (descendants of Dutch and German settlers, speakers of Afrikaans, a language that developed from seventeenth-century Dutch) became entrepeneurs and joined the largely English-speaking captains of business. In the 1950s, the Nationalist government in South Africa attempted to restructure the black labor force, with a minority permitted to urbanize permanently and the rest remaining on reserves as migrant labor. In those years, there were mass protests against apartheid in South Africa, but the main black organizations were banned in 1960. Armed struggle was launched against the government in 1961. During the 1960s the National party launched its program of social engineering and forcibly removed millions of blacks from urban and white rural areas; it also declared a program for self-government of Bantu homelands (Bantustans), the former Native reserves. Liberals in South Africa placed their hopes for the ending of apartheid on the rationalizing imperatives of economic growth; the radical historians, however, pointed to the parallel rapid growth and the implementation of apartheid, and they argued that apartheid served the interests of capitalism.

African nationalists in the Federation described its "partnership" as that of the (white) rider and the (black) horse, and, by organizing mass action produced its dissolution in 1963. That was followed by the independence of Nyasaland as Malawi and the independence of Northern Rhodesia as Zambia in 1964. White settlers in Southern Rhodesia unilaterally declared independence from Britain in 1965, which led to the launching of a guerrilla war by black African nationalists. Bechuanaland became independent as Botswana in 1966, Basutoland as Lesotho in 1966, and Swaziland as Swaziland in 1968. The sporadic attempts by South Africa, throughout the century, to get them from Britain had decisively failed.

During the 1960s, the region was thus divided between white-ruled South Africa, South West Africa, Southern Rhodesia, Mozambique, and Angola, and the black-ruled Zambia and Malawi. In South West Africa, South Africa attempted to impose an ethnic "homelands" policy. Then guerrilla struggles erupted in Mozambique, Angola, South West Africa, and Southern Rhodesia. While Malawi sought the path of friendship with the white South, Zambia did not. The state began to nationalize production in Zambia and, by 1978, controlled 80 percent of the economy; its attempts to diversify the economy and narrow the urban-rural income gap met, however, with limited success.

By the early 1970s, and with the world economic recession of 1974, the South African economy entered crisis. Essentially, its low-paid domestic market could not sustain further import-substitution; nor could it achieve the economies of scale to break into world markets in manufactured goods. Despite the short-lived gold boom at the start of the 1980s—when prices rose to U.S. $800 and more an ounce—the consequence was manifested in slowing direct foreign investment, periodic balance-of-payments crises, an increase in debts to foreign banks, rising unemployment, and a slowing of growth. By the late 1980s, the South African economy was stagnant.

SOUTHERN AFRICA. Workers in the Premier Diamond Mine at Cullinan, near Pretoria, South Africa, 1962. South Africa's diamond industry, which began in the mid-1800s, produces more than 90 percent of the world's natural diamond wealth. (Hamilton Wright/*New York World-Telegram* and the *Sun* Newspaper Photograph Collection/Prints and Photographs Division, Library of Congress)

Angola and Mozambique in 1975, following democratization in Portugal, became independent, and both followed an economic policy of extensive nationalization. In South Africa, a wave of strikes from 1972 to 1974 and a national youth revolt in 1976 (encouraged by the independence of the Portuguese colonies) heralded a popular uprising and a workers' strike movement that grew in intensity through the 1980s; it fundamentally tipped the balance of power from white to black. The urbanization of blacks also increased, through both individual and collective defiance of the pass laws. Massive informal settlements of shack-dwellers were soon outside most major cities and towns. Reforms by the South African pro-apartheid government, concerning labor, race, and pass laws, and the introduction of a new constitution were all seen as "too little and too late." In 1986, amid revolutionary upsurge, the South African government finally abolished the pass laws, which had sustained the hated migrant labor system.

Southern Rhodesia became independent as Zimbabwe in 1980, after negotiations, presided over by Britain, between its government and guerrilla leaders. In the same year, the South African Development Coordination Council was launched by non–South African states in the region, to try to integrate their economies and reduce their dependence on South Africa—that met with very little success. The Zambian economy entered crisis, resulting from the fall in the copper price. Angola and Mozambique were devastated by the activities of rebel black armies that were supported by the South African government. The only country that prospered in southern Africa in the 1980s was Botswana, based on revenues from diamond mining. The World Bank and the International Monetary Fund (IMF) intervened in Zambia and later Zimbabwe, to impose structural adjustment programs.

The economic and political crisis in South Africa led to a campaign of sanctions, which took effect in 1985, when implemented by major international banks, as a result of the revolutionary upsurge. At the end of the 1980s, South Africa negotiated the independence of South West Africa as Namibia, whose economy in the 1990s remained based on mining that was dominated by foreign companies. For Namibia, independence was a prelude to the establishment of negotiations between the South African apartheid government and the (unbanned) liberation movement organizations, a move compelled by the growing political and economic crisis. In 1994, the first democratic election was held in South Africa; it was won by the African National Congress headed by Nelson Mandela. White minority rule had come to an end in southern Africa.

In the 1990s, Angola and Mozambique rapidly shed state ownership of the economy. Angola remained disrupted by civil war, rendering more than 2 million people homeless. Mozambique grew rapidly until devastated by floods in 2000. In South Africa, there was a certain recovery in economic growth; the post-1994 government introduced a neoliberal policy called Growth, Employment and Redistribution (GEAR)—its goals liberalization of trade, privatization of industry, and the decrease of the budget deficit with the aim of attracting foreign investment to promote growth. The effects, however, were severe job losses, of some 1 million from 1994 to 2000. Gold mining, particularly, was severely hit, from the low gold price; in 2000, for the first time, platinum overtook gold as the foreign exchange earner. The New Technology came to South Africa during the 1990s, creating the "digital divide" between major centers and the countryside. HIV and AIDS were said by the United Nations to be growing in the southern African region faster than anywhere else in the world: by 2000, nearly one-third of the population of Botswana was estimated to be HIV positive. In the 1990s, two huge dams were completed in Lesotho, to supply water to the massively growing urban population of the Witwatersrand. Agriculture remained the mainstay of the economy in many countries in Southern Africa, and severe inequalities persisted throughout the region. Mozambique, Malawi, Zambia, and Lesotho are classified as lowest income countries by the United Nations, while South Africa has one of the highest indices of income inequality in the world.

Zimbabwe, Angola, and Namibia sent troops in 1999 to prop up the president of the Congo. In Zimbabwe in 2000, against severe crisis in the economy and the threat of the rise of an opposition party, the Movement for Democratic Change, President Robert Mugabe supported the mobilization of war veterans to seize land from white farmers.

BIBLIOGRAPHY

Bond, Patrick. *Elite Transition: From Apartheid to Neoliberalism in South Africa*. London, 2000.

Bonner, P., P. Delius, and D. Posel, eds. *Apartheid's Genesis, 1935–1962*. Johannesburg, South Africa, 1993.

Davies, R. H. et al. *The Kingdom of Swaziland: A Profile*. London, 1985.

Fine, Ben, and Z. Rustonjee. *The Political Economy of South Africa*. Johannesburg, South Africa, 1996.

Gay, John, et al., eds. *Lesotho's Long Journey*. Maseru, Lesotho, 1995.

Gelb, Stephen, ed. *South Africa's Economic Crisis*. London, 1991.

Green, R. H. *Namibia: A Political Economic Survey*. Brighton, U.K., 1979.

Halpern, Jack. *South Africa's Hostages: Basutoland, Bechuanaland, Swaziland*. Baltimore, 1965.

Hobart Houghton, D. *The South African Economy*. London, 1964.

Horwitz, Ralph. *The Political Economy of South Africa*. London, 1967.

Lipton, Merle. *Capitalism and Apartheid*. Hants, U.K., 1986.

Marais, Hein. *South Africa, Limits to Change: The Political Economy of Transition*. London, 1998.

Murray, Martin J. *South African Capitalism and Black Political Opposition*. Cambridge, Mass., 1982.

Murray, Martin J. *South Africa: Time of Agony, Time of Destiny*. London, 1987.

Murray, Martin J. *The Revolution Deferred: The Painful Birth of Post-apartheid South Africa*. London, 1994.

Nattrass, Jill. *The South African Economy: Its Growth and Change.* Oxford and Cape Town, 1981.

Nattrass, Nicoli, and E. Ardington, eds. *The Political Economy of South Africa.* Oxford and Cape Town, 1990.

Omar, Gasan, et al., eds. *An Introduction to Namibia's Political Economy.* Cape Town, South Africa, 1990.

Phimister, Ian. *An Economic and Social History of Zimbabwe, 1890–1948: Capital Accumulation and Class Struggle.* London, 1987.

Picard, L. A. *The Evolution of Modern Botswana.* London, 1985.

Saul, John, and Stephen Gelb. *The Crisis in South Africa: Class Defense, Class Revolution.* London, 1981.

Simson, Howard. *Zambia, a Country Study.* Scandinavian Institute of African Studies. Uppsala, Sweden, 1985.

Stoneman, Colin, ed. *Zimbabwe's Inheritance.* London, 1981.

Sylvester, C. N. *Zimbabwe: The Terrain of Contradictory Development.* London, 1991.

Worden, Nigel. *The Making of Modern South Africa: Conquest, Segregation and Apartheid.* Oxford, 1994.

MARTIN LEGASSICK

SOUTH SEA BUBBLE. *See* Business Cycles *and* Financial Panics and Crashes.

SOVIET UNION. *See* Central Asia *and* Russia.

SPAIN *[This entry contains three subentries, on the economic history of Spain during the early and medieval periods, the Spanish Empire, and modern times.]*

Early and Medieval Periods

In the Middle Ages, there was no Spain. The Iberian Peninsula was divided into entities that were not politically integrated until Bourbon rule in the eighteenth century. These regions—northern Castile, Aragon, Catalonia, Valencia, Andalusia, the Basque country, Galicia, and Granada—followed the rugged contours of Iberia's topography. Geography and climate shaped the patterns of socioeconomic organization and economic development.

Northern Spain. The region extending from Galicia west to the Pyrenees Mountains received abundant rain. Verdant valleys, high mountains, and ample harbors supported a dairy economy, livestock tending, fruit trees, cereal growing, and vineyards. After the Muslim invasion in 711 CE, the region, at first isolated, was drawn into a symbiotic relationship with Muslim al-Andalus in the south. Population growth in the northern valleys led to settlement into the fairly deserted plains of Leon and Castile during the eighth and ninth centuries. This marked the beginnings of the so-called Reconquest, which was spurred by social and economic transformations of mountain areas rather than by ideological or religious factors. The north was a land of free peasants. They often held small

plots of land from secular or ecclesiastical lords in long-term leases or for life. By the eleventh century, the popularity of the Christian pilgrimage to St. James of Compostela brought thousands of pilgrims from north of the Pyrenees. Many stayed, which led to the emergence of the first urban centers—Burgos, Sahagún, Leon, Compostela (800–1000 CE)—the rise of the bourgeoisie, and trade with the South and trans-Pyrenean regions. When the kings of Castile repopulated the Bay of Biscay area in the late twelfth century, its ports served as entry points for a lively trade with Flanders (now Belgium) and England. The patterns of trade were fixed quite early. Castile exported raw products (tallow, hides, honey, and, after 1300, iron and wool) and imported manufactured products (textiles, finished goods, and salted fish). This trade marked a shift from the hitherto dominant commercial links between northern Castile and al-Andalus to a more international commercial structure. Coins began to circulate in earnest after the twelfth century, a sign of the growing sophistication of economic exchanges.

Central Spain. South of the western spurs of the Pyrenees lay the great plains of Old and New Castile. With little precipitation and long winters, Old Castile was a land of dry farming, specializing in cereal grains and vineyards. Livestock on the plain was herded between summer and winter pastures. After the conquest of western Andalusia in the 1230s and 1240s, the transhumance (long-distance movement of herds) (the Mesta) sought new pastures in Extremadura and western Andalusia, creating new economic links between northern Castile-Leon and the south. As in northern regions, there were large monastic and noble estates but peasants had the usufruct (right of use) of their lands. This did not mean that peasants were exempt from paying excessive dues; but nowhere in the western kingdoms is there evidence of widespread servile tenure. In towns—especially in Burgos—merchants served as intermediaries for a profitable trade in textiles. Their profits allowed the mercantile elites to gain political and social control of northern cities after the 1250s and to receive numerous privileges from the Crown. In other cities, such as Avila and Sepúlveda, land rents and the income from the transhumance led to the rise of urban oligarchies throughout the realm. By the thirteenth century, small-scale manufacturing (of mostly low-quality textiles) spread to Avila, Soria, and other cities on the plain. In Toledo, even after the Christian conquest in 1085, the city retained some of its fabled Muslim artisanal production (fine ironworks, leather, textiles).

Southern Spain. Under Muslim rule, Andalusia experienced great prosperity. Córdoba and Seville became important manufacturing centers, producing silk textiles, ironwork, and luxury items. Agriculturally, the Muslims implemented a sophisticated system of irrigation (inherited from the Romans) and animal husbandry. The cultivation of winter wheat, olive trees, grapes, oranges, other fruits, some spices, and rice (in the east) made the region rich. The Arabs revolutionized agriculture and their innovations—vertical mills and norias, wheels for drawing water—changed the face of southern Spain. Moreover, until the mid-thirteenth century and the Christian conquests, al-Andalus served as the terminus for far-flung commercial networks. These networks linked Iberia with the eastern Mediterranean and with Central Africa in lively economic exchanges. Jews and Muslims played an important role in the economic life. Many Jews were traders, merchants, financiers, tax collectors, and tax farmers throughout the kingdom into the late fourteenth century; along with Muslims, they served other key economic functions as artisans, shopkeepers, farmers, masons, and doctors.

After the 1250s, most of western Andalusia was back in Christian hands. Muslims were expelled from the region in the 1260s, but the Christians were, on the whole, incapable of keeping Muslim economic structures alive. The expansion of the transhumance into the south and the scarcity of population brought serious economic upheavals (inflation, declining agricultural productivity, depopulation) to all of Castile until the fifteenth century. Only in the late fourteenth century did Andalusia begin to recover, led by Seville's growth as the leading peninsular city. Seville remained an important entrepôt. In other cities, most notably Jaén, silk cloth production flourished, though usually in Mudejar hands. Unlike in the North, the latifundia predominated in the South. Most peasants were landless daily workers. This fairly consistent pattern of landholding was transported to the New World by the Conquistadors from the region.

Eastern Spain. The Crown of Aragon consisted of three distinct regions—Aragon, Catalonia, and Valencia. Aragon proper resembled Castile in its topography. It was dominated through most of the Middle Ages by noblemen and ecclesiastical lords; its vast Muslim rural population toiled the land under almost servile conditions. In some regions of Catalonia (Old Catalonia) peasants were enserfed under harsh conditions from the 1200s to the late 1400s. Catalonia's rich valleys, cereal fields, and vineyards thrived in the temperate climate of the Mediterranean. But the region was dominated by the great city of Barcelona, which, from the eleventh century onward, was one of the great commercial centers of the western Mediterranean. To the southeast, the agriculturally rich lands of Valencia were tended by skilled, irrigation-wise, Muslim peasants, even after the Christian conquest in the early 1200s. With a large horticultural production, rice, sugar cane, and other semitropical products, the kingdom of Valencia was one of the most prosperous Iberian regions in the late Middle Ages. Its capital city Valencia dominated long-distance trade and surpassed Barcelona as a commercial center in the fifteenth century.

The Economy of Spain. Throughout the Middle Ages, Spain did not have an integrated economy. Castile had few dealings with Aragon, Valencia, or Barcelona. Its commercial links were with the textile-producing Low Countries, especially after the 1350s, when the export of recently improved merino wools became the lifeline of the realm, particularly with the steeply rising cost of English wool and the disruptions of the Hundred Years' War on English-Flemish relations. In the east, Catalonia and Valencia became commercial rivals; Aragon remained rural and backward. Agriculturally, however, these regions shared the same traditional Mediterranean practices: the Roman plow; the biannual two-field rotation system; the focus on cereal growing and vineyards. Iberian soils were too thin for the northern heavy plough or for the three-field rotation of crops. Throughout the peninsula, with some exceptions, the family was nuclear; inheritance was partible and included females. From the 1200s onward, this practice somewhat curbed the nobility's tendency to consolidate land holdings into contiguous estates and to create entailments. In the countryside, the oscillation between property fragmentation and consolidation was paralleled by the tension between communal and private ownership.

In such cities as Burgos, Barcelona, Seville, and Valencia, the profits garnered from long-distance trade led to the formation of entrenched oligarchies which, by the late Middle Ages, these were acquiring noble rank. Guilds did not prosper in Iberia, and they did not play the political role they did elsewhere in Europe. In medieval Spain, especially in Castile, the differences between city and country were not as sharp as they were in some other European countries; urban centers held jurisdictional and economic ties with their vast hinterlands. At the close of the Middle Ages, Barcelona suffered a precipitous decline while Castile came increasingly to depend on its exports of wool and, after 1521, of bullion.

[*See also* Latifundia.]

BIBLIOGRAPHY

Dufourcq, Charles Emmanuel, and Jean Gautier-Dalche. *Histoire économique et sociale de l'Espagne chrétienne au Moyen Age*. Paris, 1976.

Constable, Olivia R. *Trade and Traders in Muslim Spain: The Commercial Realignment of the Iberian Peninsula, 900–1500*. Cambridge, 1994.

García de Cortázar, José Angel. *La sociedad rural en la España medieval*. Madrid, 1988.

Glick, Thomas F. *Islamic and Christian Spain in the Early Middle Ages: Comparative Perspectives on Social and Cultural Formation*. Princeton, 1979.

Munro, John H. "Wool Price Schedules and the Quantities of English Wools in the Later Middle Ages." *Textile History* 9 (1978), 118–169.

Munro, John. "Medieval Woollens." In *The Cambridge History of Western Textiles*, edited by David Jenkins. Cambridge and New York, 2001.

Ruiz, Teofilo F. *Crisis and Continuity: Land and Town in Late Medieval Castile*. Philadelphia, 1994.

Vicens Vives, Jaime. *An Economic History of Spain*. Translated by F. M. López Morillas. Princeton, 1969.

Vicens Vives, Jaime, ed. *Historia de España y América. Social y económica.* 2 vols. Barcelona, 1972.

TEOFILO F. RUIZ

Spanish Empire

The overseas expansion of Castile and Portugal was a manifestation of the economic and political vitality of fifteenth-century Europe. It is not clear whether or not the Iberian economies that emerged from the crisis in the fourteenth century had already achieved a division of labor that prompted a search for raw materials to support expanded exports. But from 1450 onward the expansion of this trade increased the demand for gold and led Iberian mariners to explore the West African coast in search of new gold supplies. The increasing demand by European aristocracies for spices used in preserving food encouraged the search for a new passage to the Orient, while the Ottoman presence in Asia Minor hampered Venetian trade. There were also some strictly Iberian motives for the outward push. In Castile medieval growth based on feudal territorial expansion, fueled by the Reconquesta, was reaching its national limits by the mid-fifteenth century. Andalusian nobles then turned their attention to the fishing waters off the North African shore. Along with the nobility, the crown and the church—which called the enterprise a crusade—also showed interest in exploration of the African coast and in conquest of the Canary Islands. This conquest, begun in 1405, was completed during the reign of Ferdinand and Isabella. Genoese bankers and merchants, who lent money to the Spanish monarchs, also took an interest in the endeavor. Soon a plantation economy based on the production of sugar was organized on the islands.

Discovery and Conquest. In 1492 the conquest of Granada and Christopher Columbus's discovery of America adhered to the same expansive logic of an economy and a social organization that had made territorial expansion its fundamental base, hence the "feudal character" of Spain's overseas expansion. This has given rise to the idea that America was initially exploited by a backward and archaic society that was not equal to the challenge of empire, while in fact this was not at all the case. The discovery of America was the result of Spanish sailors' increasingly systematic observations of ocean currents and winds. Since the fifteenth century the Iberian Peninsula had been a proving ground for navigation techniques. The concurrence of advances in cartography and mathematical calculations, borrowed from the Muslim and Jewish cultures, with the practical experience gathered over several decades, were important components of the process. The caravel, a synthesis of northern and Mediterranean ship design, and the use of the compass enabled mariners to venture further from the coasts and to estimate their positions on the high seas with great accuracy.

If the Iberian kingdoms were well prepared for the initial discovery, they were no less prepared for the conquest, for navigating between the different parts of their empires, or for the colonization and control of the territories. The centuries of reconquest of Iberian territories from the Moors and the subsequent repopulation (and navigation) spawned the military and maritime know-how that, together with the internal divisions of the indigenous societies in the New world, explain the dizzying pace of expansion. Once the Atlantic routes were established and the Caribbean Islands came firmly under Spanish control, Hernán Cortés extended the crown's dominion over the Aztec confederation in Mexico. In 1536 the Pizarro brothers took possession of Peru, the center of the Inca Empire, and mounted expeditions to Chile and El Plata, which, since Ferdinand Magellan's 1519 journey, could also be reached from the Atlantic. Expansion was more difficult in the distant Philippines, discovered by Magellan in 1521. But the discovery of the contratradewinds and the Kuro-Sio current by the cosmographer Friar Andrés de Urdaneta (1565) paved the way for a trade route that linked the islands to Spain's American base at Acapulco.

Spanish institutions also helped address the great problem faced by all empires: the financing of the conquest and control of the new territories. The desire of the crown, which was to limit the autonomy of the colonists; the provisions of the papal bulls issued by Alexander VI in 1493; and the strength that the pronative position of people like the Montesinos fathers Las Casas and Vitoria eventually gained in Castile prevented making the outright enslavement of the Indians the basis of this process. Meanwhile the enormous cost prevented the crown from exercising direct control of the process. Consequently the conquest came to be based on a system of *capitulaciones* reminiscent of certain peninsular medieval institutions, whereby the different captains, following agreements with the king, could obtain credits from private financiers (often Genoese or Germans) with which to undertake their colonizing enterprises. Once a territory was conquered, the crown granted the colonists privileges, authority, and tax-raising powers to compensate them for their efforts and to enable them to repay the borrowed funds. The system was completed by the granting of *encomiendas*, whereby groups of Indians paid tribute to their conquerors, and of *repartimientos*, by which they were obliged to work for wages.

Thus the crown externalized costs and risks in exchange for concessions of authority and privileges. Institutions, such as the *ayuntamientos* and *municipios* (local authorities), the *audiencias* (courts), viceroys (alter egos of the king in colonial governments), and so forth, helped organize the territory and secure the power of the monarch, and the viceroys and *audiencias* also counterbalanced the influence of the conquistadores, the conquerors. Castile's universities furnished specialized jurists and theologians to the bureaucracies that governed the New World.

In the Americas the Spaniards encountered a rich variety of peoples and civilizations. From the sparsely populated areas of California, inhabited by hunting and gathering peoples, to those of eastern Patagonia, populated by hunters and fishers, there was a highly diverse ensemble of peoples with quite different economies, but only a few engaged systematically in agriculture. Among the agriculturalists were the Aztec confederation of Mexico, which had a large population, forcing Malthusian problems; the Mayan culture of Guatemala and the Yucatán, which was undergoing a process of political decay, possibly because it had reached the limit in the relation of resources and population; and the Inca civilization of the Andes. Sophisticated agriculture and systems such as nonmercantile redistribution and reciprocity, which reflected a complex administrative organization, permitted the exchange of goods from different areas.

Demographic Changes. The initial impact of the conquest and colonization was a demographic decline accompanied by profound economic and social changes. This gave rise almost immediately to the famous "black legend" about Spain, which held that war, taxes, and a brutal overexploitation of the Indian had been the cause of the decline. Some years ago studies (for example, those of Cook and Borah) pointed to a demographic crisis, in which the population of the central Mexican *meseta* (plateau) fell from 25 million to only 2.6 million in 1568, and this appeared to corroborate those allegations. Despite the opposition of Father Las Casas and despite the "New Laws" (1542) enacted by the monarchy, the intensive exploitation of labor by the *encomenderos*, who were more keen to reap immediate profits than to ensure the reproduction of the workforce, may well have contributed to this phenomenon. Abuses in the application of the *repartimientos* and systems such as that of the *mite* (an Inca institution that obliged all Indians to supply labor to the emperor), as applied in the mines in Peru, must have had similar effects. The relocation of entire peoples, the use of "reciprocity" for one's own benefit and without giving anything in return (in contrast to the practice of the Incas, who redistributed tax monies among the different regions, the taxes collected by the Spaniards were not used to the benefit of the native population), the imposition of monogamy, and forced conversion to Christianity all influenced the birthrate and the circulation of goods and appeared to indicate a systematic destruction of the aboriginal, preconquest societies.

However, more recent research suggests a more nuanced view, and more importantly it poses the problems in less black-and-white terms. New calculations suggest that the estimates of pre-Columbian population figures may have been exaggerated and that the demographic disaster, while substantial, was less severe than formerly believed. In addition an ecological component of the contact between the cultures is now recognized. If it was from the Americas that diseases such as syphilis and crops like potato and corn came to Europe, the Europeans brought plants, microbes, and animals that had a negative impact on the New World's immunological and ecological systems. Work in the mines was especially destructive, not so much because of its rigors as because of the inadequate nutrition of the miners.

At all events the result was not the complete disappearance of the indigenous society and its substitution by entirely new economic and social structures (in contrast to what occurred in North America in the nineteenth century). The continual intermarriage of Spaniards with Indian women gave rise to a process that, along with native demographic decline, changed the ethnic composition of the continent. Soon there appeared, in a population of mixed-blood people (not only in the biological sense but also in the social), an elite of "Creoles" (biologically mixed-blood people with Spanish fathers who had been born to the earliest colonists), who held sway over the indigenous population but among whom there were increasing social differences.

The relations of Spanish colonists and Creoles with the crown were by no means harmonious. Anxious to dominate the emerging local elites, the king strengthened institutions such as the *audiencias* by naming Spaniards direct clients, combating the power of the *encomenderos* and intensifying the latter's links with the indigenous people, who retained the status of "vassals of the king." The relation between the crown and the church, which advocated a program of evangelization based on the mere substitution of religious beliefs instead of a more thorough acculturation, were unstable and occasionally conflictive.

Trade. In New Spain and Peru the mining economy expanded rapidly until 1630 thanks to the introduction of silver refining by amalgamation with mercury. Forced labor was used in some areas, wages were paid in others, and mining activities were controlled indirectly by powerful groups of silver dealers and mercury brokers. The development of cities, depopulation, the growing difficulties faced by the *encomenderos*, and the establishment of great haciendas, which often marketed their own production,

SPANISH EMPIRE. Map of the silver mines at Potosí, Bolivia. The first mine as opened in 1545. Pen and ink drawing with watercolor, eighteenth century. (Archivio generale de Indias, Seville, Spain/Scala/Art Resource, NY)

brought an important change to the American economy. This change occurred at the same time that forced trade reached its peak among the natives, who were obliged to pay their taxes in coin. A tax-gathering apparatus was created that, through levies on local trade (such as the *alcabala*) and on mining, filled the annual silver fleets destined for Seville.

Measured by the volume of goods, colonial trade was small in macroeconomic terms. At the end of the sixteenth century it amounted to scarcely 2 percent of Castile's GNP. It is also worth noting that Spain's economic growth substantially antedated American colonization and that many regions, especially some of those under the crown of Aragon, had only an indirect and limited contact with the Atlantic trade. This is not to suggest that colonial trade was inconsequential, especially to Castile, or that Castile's economy was merely "semiperipheral," a relay in the transport of raw materials to Europe and in the export of European manufactured goods to the colonies. It is certainly true that the Castilian economy had one of its foundations in the export of raw materials, and from midcentury European industrial goods made up a large part of the Sevillian loadings. But such simplifying generalizations are belied by the rapid industrial growth of some cities, often thanks to import substitutions evident until 1570–1580; by the fact that Spain was Europe's third most urbanized area even in 1600; and by the notable development of inland cities.

The impact of America on the Spanish economy was sudden. The arrival of American treasure in Seville, where the Casa de Contratación (1503) monopolized colonial trade, the large profits it furnished, and the increase in the coinage and circulation of money it fostered fueled trade on the Iberian Peninsula (among Castile, Aragon, and Portugal) and trade between Spain and the rest of Europe. At the same time large profits accrued to Genoese, German, and Castilian merchants involved in the trade. Although there is still controversy over the concrete mechanisms that may explain the phenomenon, the impact of growing monetary circulation on prices seems clear. The revenues to the crown from the empire were never large in proportion to the total tax revenues of Castile (only at the end of the century did they attain the exceptional figure of 25 percent), but for the Spanish Habsburgs, American treasure had the great advantage of being free from the interference of the *cortés* (parliament) of Castile. This allowed complex credit maneuvers with European banking houses and financed the crown's military needs in its far-flung domains. Meanwhile, to the extent that America buttressed Castile's protagonism in that "composed monarchy" of an international character that constituted the so-called "Spanish Empire," it also led to a growing sclerosis of political and social institutions, which were thus able to withstand the strains derived from a process of economic development and social change begun in the fifteenth century that was similar to that taking place elsewhere in Europe.

Seventeenth Century. The seventeenth century brought changes in both the Spanish and the American economies and hence in the relations between them. A crisis in mining has been mentioned as well as a decline in colonial trade that may have occurred in parallel to a recession on the peninsula itself. But today both ideas are being freshly examined. Some authors have recalled that the exhaustion of certain mines was accompanied by the opening of new ones. Morineau's figures for arrivals of silver in Europe show, except for the middle years of the century, a degree of continuity inconsistent with the idea of a "general crisis" in America. One must also consider that a significant proportion of the trade was conducted directly with Asia via the Philippines and in the "Manila Galleon." It is evident, on the other hand, that the internal economic development, the need for food and raw materials associated with economic development and with mining, the establishment of large agricultural operations, and the development of the colonial bureaucracy led to the creation of autonomous mercantile circuits within the Americas that absorbed some of the flow of metals. They also led to the spread of smuggling, to the benefit of other powers and to the detriment of the monopoly regime, that was often responsible for the difficulties and high costs of the official trade flows. All this relaxed the ties with the metropolis and shunted off an important part of the silver. It explains the lack of correlation between the quantities of metal reaching Europe and the increasingly exiguous official figures for landings in Spain.

Thus the situation was not so much a crisis as a recomposition of the colonial economy, whose control from the metropolis became increasingly problematic. This fact has a parallel in the social and political spheres. The accession by members of the Creole oligarchy to public offices, the concept of such offices as opportunities for profit, and the growing power of the church in some areas increasingly undermined the power of the crown and increased smuggling and administrative corruption.

There are also some nuances with regard to the Iberian Peninsula. There is no doubt that interior regions of Castile underwent a period of recession of both production and population. But colonial problems could not be blamed for this crisis. One may also argue against Hamilton's theory that the arrival of precious metals pushed up wages and aborted Castile's industrial development. Indeed the problems stemmed from the rigidity of the Spanish economic and social structures, which had been the basis of the Habsburg Empire. In addition a restructuring of the peninsular economy centered on the expansion of the coastal region, whose slowness (but not absence) speaks of economic recession. The "seventeenth-century crisis" definitely led to the decline of inland cities (except Madrid) and to the loss of competitiveness of peninsular industry and trade, which strengthened the hands of the European merchants who were active in Seville from the end of the sixteenth century. Together with Spanish naval and military decay, this decline led to the growing interference by foreigners in the monopoly regime and to a rise in smuggling. At the end of the seventeenth century, when the hub of overseas trade had shifted from Seville to Cadiz, the crown, whose revenues from incoming silver had notably declined, was obliged to bear the cost of protecting an empire with a high degree of administrative corruption and in which the greatest profits were carried off, either directly or via intermediaries involved in colonial trade in Seville or Cadiz, by French, Dutch, English, Flemish, and Italian merchants, who shunted to their own countries the portion of the incoming silver that does not appear in the records of precious metals in Seville.

Eighteenth Century. The Bourbons sought to remedy this situation within the context of the new mercantilist doctrines, which called for stricter control of the colonies, in a period during which the struggle for world markets and the fostering of colonial demand for goods from the metropolis became essential features of international economic relations. But as American participation in world silver production increased and with it the interest of other countries in trading with the Americas, this proved a frankly difficult enterprise.

Defense spending was enlarged, and a royal army led by officers from peninsular Spain was created. The church was more strictly controlled, and administrative reform was undertaken, including the creation of a royal bureaucracy that could limit the power of the Creole elites. The crown tried to curtail colonial manufacturing activity, to revive intercolonial trade, and to stimulate demand for Spanish goods. Consulates and trading companies were established to break the monopoly of the merchants of Seville, Cadiz, Mexico, and Lima. In 1777 the Compañía de Filipinas was founded in a bid to reorient toward Spain the transpacific trade between Manila and American ports. In 1764 other peninsular ports were allowed to take part in colonial trade, which helped a number of Spanish regions develop industries. All this was accompanied by reforms in the navy and the tax system intended to combat smuggling, to achieve tighter control of the silver shipments, and to pay for the reforms themselves. These policies raised the costs of protection and supervision, but they also increased the crown's share of colonial profits. The redistribution of those profits broadened the invigorating impact on the peninsular economy.

These measures acted in concert with the autonomous dynamics of the American economy. The revival of interior trade, the development of cities, and the growing exports (not only to Spain) of colonial goods, such as cacao, sugar, tobacco, hides, cotton, and dyes, further enlivened an increasingly prosperous plantation economy. Poor regions and those that previously played secondary roles in the operations of trading circuits, for example, Río de Plata, Venezuela, and Cuba, took on a new importance. All this must have been noticed in the metropolis. America was one of the keys to enlarging revenues for the crown, not only because of the growing volume of silver shipments, which were taxed both as mining products and as trade, but also because of the burgeoning revenues from customs duties on the trade (and monopoly) of American goods in Spain (tobacco, cacao, sugar, and so forth) and their reexport to other European countries.

There was also an increase in Spain's exports to the Americas, including those of manufactured goods, though these remained relatively small. At the end of the century regions such as Galicia, Cantabria, Catalonia, and Valencia were benefiting from this trade and from the import and redistribution of American goods. The collateral effects of such trade could be perceived in the vigor of coastal merchant groups, in the strengthening of trading links with the interior, and in shipbuilding, insurance, and credit. All contributed to the internal development of the peninsular economy.

But there were limits to the structural changes that took place in the Spanish economy. The rise in revenues for the crown did not bring about a profound tax reform or a financial revolution, so the wars at the end of the century seriously debilitated the treasury. In macroeconomic terms the colonial market continued to have only a marginal importance for the Spanish economy. Exports and reexports to the colonies amounted to scarcely 2 percent of the GNP, and among them the proportion of Spanish industrial goods was small, composed chiefly of foreign goods finished on the peninsula. The reforms had failed to eliminate other countries' expanding trade with the American colonies because of the lesser competitiveness of the Spanish economy. The weakness and rigidities of the agrarian economy and the obstacles to the formation of a domestic market meant the positive impact of colonial trade was canceled out or was confined to coastal areas.

Nineteenth Century. However, the Bourbon reforms were decisive in another way. By restricting the maneuverability of the colonial oligarchies (which had gained economic power and social influence), the reforms sowed discontent among them. Imbued with the new liberal spirit and in light of the power vacuum and the political convulsions brought on by the Napoleonic wars, the oligarchies' discontent led to independence in 1824. All that remained under Spanish dominion in the Americas were Puerto Rico and Cuba. In the latter, which was officially a Spanish province and duly represented in the *cortés*, the local oligarchy remained loyal to the crown because of its large proceeds from the production and sale of coffee and sugar

and its fears of a slave revolt. In the Pacific, Spain also retained the Marianas, Carolinas, and Palaos Islands as well as the Philippines, where there was no alternative to the influence of Spanish religious orders.

Traditionally the loss of the colonies has been regarded as a major setback for the Spanish economy. Current historical research challenges this notion, noting the relatively small weight of the empire in macroeconomic terms. However, tax revenues did decline steeply with the loss of the "American treasures" and the concurrent reduction of proceeds from customs duties. This impoverishment of the state led to the definitive crisis of the old regime, and the large national debt marked the history of Spain in the nineteenth century. However, domestic productive sectors withstood the loss of the colonies relatively unscathed. Even before independence local industries, especially in Catalonia, became increasingly competitive in the domestic market, and this process was accelerated in the 1820s. The reduction of exports of agricultural goods was offset by the formation of the domestic market and by the expansion of wheat and flour exports to Cuba. Thanks to this trade and its proceeds, cities such as Santander witnessed the rise of a new mercantile bourgeoisie.

Surprisingly the liberal Spanish regime opted to strengthen the church's control of the Philippines—the state paid the salaries of some clerics—as the sole manner of maintaining control over the colony. There were attempts to reorient the islands' economy toward the metropolis via the promotion of tobacco cultivation and mining while also trying to supplant the Chinese in foreign and domestic trade. Only at midcentury were major reforms instituted that, along with the opening of the Suez Canal in 1865 and the development of the telegraph and mail service, heralded change. However, criticisms of regular clergy by lay clergy and the upsurge of an embryonic Philippine bourgeoisie and intellectual community, which took a critical view of the metropolis (with the support of Spanish intellectuals), upset the delicate balance of power. A series of conflicts, not initially of a nationalist character, led to revolt and United States intervention in 1898.

In the nineteenth century Cuba underwent an extraordinary expansion of sugar output, in close parallel to the increase of the black population, which had as a reverse side the import of Spanish products in a monopoly regime. This monopoly and Spain's connivance in the slave trade preserved the links between the Cuban sugar economy (sugar displaced coffee as the basis of the island economy) and Spanish governments. This alliance weakened as the owners of sugar mills had to confront a decline in the price of sugar, an increase in the cost of slaves, and growing debts to peninsular slave dealers. From the 1860s onward the Spanish monopoly clashed with the growing orientation of the Cuban economy toward the United States, to which agricultural products were exported in exchange for manufactured goods. At the same time Creole plantation owners began to accept the idea of a gradual abolition of slavery, although the adult black population was obliged to work on the sugar plantations for a time. After the Civil War in the United States, these problems were accentuated in a war, whose outcome in 1898 brought the abolition of slavery, the political independence of Cuba and Puerto Rico, and as in the Philippines, the strong presence of U.S. economic interests in the area.

Twentieth Century. With the loss of Cuba, Puerto Rico, and the Philippines, Spain's colonial empire was gone. But the twentieth century saw the projection of Spanish interests in Morocco (a Spanish protectorate between 1912 and 1956). More recently independence was achieved in other areas in Equatorial Guinea (conceded by Portugal in 1778 and given independence in 1979) and the Spanish Sahara (recognized by Portugal in 1509 and made independent in 1975), which constituted (leaving aside the current North African enclaves of Ceuta and Melilla) the last vestiges of the old empire.

BIBLIOGRAPHY

Attman, A. *American Bullion in the European World Trade, 1600–1800.* Gotëborg, 1986.
Bethell, L., ed. *The Cambridge History of Latin America*, vol. 2, *Colonial Latin America*. Cambridge, 1984.
McAlister, L. N. *Spain and Portugal in the New World, 1492–1700.* Minneapolis, 1984.
Morineau, Michel. *Incroyables gazettes et fabuleux métaux.* Cambridge, 1985.
Pérez Herrero, P. *America Latina y el colonialismo europeo. Siglos XVI–XVIII.* Madrid, 1992.
Wallerstein, I. *The Modern World System.* 3 vols. New York, 1974–1988.
Yun-Casalilla, B. "The American Empire and the Spanish Economy: An Institutional and Regional Perspective." In *The Cost and Benefits of European Imperialism from the Conquest of Ceuta, 1415, to the Treaty of Lusaka, 1974*, edited by P. O'Brien and L. Prados de la Escosura. *Revista de Historia Económica* 16.1 (Winter 1998), pp. 123–156.

BARTOLOMÉ YUN-CASALILLA
Translated from Spanish by Dwight Porter

Modern Spain

Modern Spanish history displays a full-circle evolution from a dynamic, medium-sized monarchy in the late Middle Ages to exactly the same by the beginning of the twenty-first century. In between, Spain became the largest world empire of its time, only to lose this empire in stages and to contract, by 1950, to a medium-sized country: closed, backward, and not at all dynamic. The rise and fall of a major power like Spain is an enduring object of reflection, offering lessons for current and future generations. The major interpretations of economic success and decline must pay careful attention to the Spanish experience because of its changing fortunes and the long-lasting

consequences of an ill-designed set of institutions. In this entry, I will focus on internal developments.

Spain under the Catholic Kings. There was nothing special about 1479 but for the coincidence of Isabella of Castile and Ferdinand of Aragon obtaining full and undisputed access to each of their crowns. More important was their marriage in 1469, for it had long-lasting consequences in Spanish and world history. They represented the last medieval and the first modern monarchy—Ferdinand being the model for Machiavelli's prince. Most notable was their dynastic policy. They married all their sons and daughters with neighboring kingdom heirs to achieve their basic family goal: to survive and expand. Out of this policy they obtained, in two or three generations, the huge empire of Charles I (known as Charles V outside of Spain) and of Philip II.

To keep themselves and their dynasty in power, they behaved as modern monarchs. They built a bureaucratic administration: They closely monitored the nobles, kept an eye always opened to popular opinion, and they were generous with the merchants and bankers that helped them. But, above all, they focused on a policy of military expansion—the perennial solution to galvanize a country in the making. The conquests of Granada in 1492, Canary Islands in 1496, and Navarre in 1512 were major landmarks. The discovery, in 1492, of new lands by Columbus—to be named America—was less impressive initially, although it quickly became clear that it was an epochal event. The early awareness is reflected in the Tordesillas Treaty between Spain and Portugal (1494), through which a division of the world was accepted—allowing the Portuguese to colonize Brazil in the following decades. When Ferdinand and Isabella sensed some opposition, they focused criticisms against the Jews, who were banned from Spain in 1492, a few months after Granada was conquered. Earlier on, the monarchy put in motion the Inquisition (1480), a fearsome religious police and judiciary.

Table 1 provides a summary of the economic development of Spain from 1500 to 2000.

The Sixteenth Century. The sixteenth century was the golden age of Castile. Two kings reigned through most of the century—Charles V (1516–1556) and his son Philip II (1556–1598). They inherited a wide array of lands and titles and found themselves governing a worldwide empire. In the homeland of this empire, Castile, population grew quickly, recovering from the epidemics and civil strife of the late Middle Ages. It was an expanding period for the whole economy of Spain, and for each of its regions. The only exception was the former kingdom of Granada, which suffered both from its abandonment as de facto capital of the kings and from the suppression of the *moriscos* revolt in 1570. Throughout the century, Castilians, mainly from the southwest regions, emigrated by the thousands to the

TABLE 1. *Spain: Main Economic Variables, 1500–2000*

	1500	1590–1600	1700	1800	1900	1950	2000
Population (in millions)	4.8	6.8	7.5	11.0	18.6	28.1	40.7
GDP (in million pesetas)*	60.0	277.2	562.7	2,200	10,649	182,417	100,894,843
GDP per head (in pesetas)	12.50	40.76	75.03	200.0	572.5	6,492	2,478,989
Prices[a] (1,500 = 100)	100	439	742	1,432	1,475	13,983	737,883
Real GDP (in million constant pesetas)	60.0	63.14	75.85	153.7	722.0	1,305	13,674
Real GDP per head (in constant pesetas)	12.50	9.29	10.11	13.92	38.82	46.43	336.0
State income[b] (in million pesetas)	2.33	29.76	24.4	203.3	973.6	20,358	40,845,070
State income (in million constant pesetas)	2.33	6.78	3.29	14.19	66.01	145.6	5,535
State income, per capita (in constant pesetas)	0.48	1.00	0.44	1.28	3.55	5.18	136.0
State income, per GDP unit (in percentages)	3.9	10.7	4.3	9.2	9.1	11.2	40.5
Openness (in percentages)[c]	—**	—	3[d]	6[e]	11	3	23
			—	14[e]	24	7	54
Urbanization (percentage of total)[f]	8.3	23.9[g]	9.0	24.0[h]	29.3	50.7[i]	70.0
		13.2		14.7[h]	21.0	42.0[i]	64.0
Agrarian population (percentage of employed)	—	—	—	65.3	64.8	47.6	6.8
Life expectancy at birth (years)	—	—	c. 25	28.1	34.8	62.1	78.7
Two major towns (in thousands of people)	Granada 75	Seville 135	Madrid 140	Madrid 168	Madrid 540	Madrid 1,618	Madrid 2,939
	Seville 45	Toledo 80	Seville 72	Barcelona 100	Barcelona 533	Barcelona 1,280	Barcelona 1,504

*1 peseta = 4 reales; 1 euro = 166.386 pesetas
**—indicates no data
[a] 1500–1900, Consumer Price Index; 1900–2000, GDP deflator
[b] 1500–1700, Castile crown income; 1800, Spanish crown income
[c] First row, X/GDP; second row, (X+M)/GDP
[d] 1720
[e] Excluded transit trade
[f] First row, population in towns of more than 5,000 inhabitants; second row, population in towns of more than 10,000 inhabitants. From 1787 onward the definition becomes tighter: the data refer to "entities," excluding towns with disseminated population
[g] Mid-sixteenth century
[h] 1787
[i] 1960

SOURCES: *Anuario Estadístico de España;* Bairoch, P., J. Batou, and P. Chèvre, *La populations des villes européennes, 800–1850;* Ballesteros, E., "Una estimación del coste de la vida en España, 1861–1936," pp. 363–395; Barquín, R., "Primera aproximación al coste de la vida en España, 1815–1860," pp. 303–315; Bilbao, L. M., "Ensayo de reconstrucción histórica de la presión fiscal en Castilla durante el siglo XVI," pp. 37–61; Comín, F., "Sector público," pp. 395–460; Feliu, G., *Precios y salarios en la Cataluña moderna,* vol. 1; García-Sanz, A., "Repercusiones de la fiscalidad castellana en los siglos XVI y XVII," pp. 15–24; *Informe económico;* Kamen, H., *The War of Succession in Spain 1700–1715;* Martínez Vara, T., "Una estimación del coste de la vida en Santander, 1800–1860," pp. 87–124; Merino, J. P., *Las cuentas de la Administración Central española, 1750–1820;* Nadal, J., *La población española (siglos XVI a XX);* Nicolau, R., "Población"; Pérez-Moreda, V., "Spain's Demographic Modernization, 1800–1930," pp. 13–41; Pérez-Moreda, V., and R. Rowland, "La péninsule ibérique," pp. 463–484; Prados de la Ecosura, L., "La evolución del comercio exterior, 1790–1929," pp. 133–154; Prados de la Escosura, L., "La pérdida del imperio y sus consecuencias económicas en España," pp. 253–300; Prados de la Escosura, L., *El progreso económico de España, 1850–2000;* Reher, D.-S., "Ciudades, procesos de urbanización y sistemas urbanos en la Península Ibérica, 1550–1991," pp. 1–28; Reher, D.-S., and E. Ballesteros, "Precios y salarios en Castilla la Nueva: La construcción de un índice de salarios reales, 1501–1991," pp. 101–151; Tafunell, X., "Urbanización y vivienda"; Tena, A., "Sector exterior"; Vries, J. de, *European Urbanization, 1500–1800;* Yun, B., "The American Empire and the Spanish Economy: An Institutional and Regional Perspective," pp. 123–156.

newly conquered America, while northwest regions like Aragon and Catalonia received immigrants from southern France. Urbanization (for towns with more than 10,000 inhabitants) went up from 8 to 13 percent, while towns with population over 5,000 remained stable or even declined. Some towns grew much larger: Seville, Toledo, Madrid, but also Valencia, Barcelona, and many others. Although there is a lack of reliable figures on the sector distribution of population, the evidence points to a move from agrarian activities to industrial and, mainly, to services, particularly in Old and New Castile and Andalusia.

There was a spectacular expansion of commerce, originating in the booming American trade. From the beginning, Castile imposed a complete monopoly on this trade. Every good and every person had to be declared and registered at the Casa de Contratación in Seville—a system that lasted until 1717. As the incoming trade expanded regularly both in volume and in value, and its value was high (gold and silver accounted for the largest part of the entries), the surrounding economy and all the Castilian economy enjoyed a growth in demand. The internal supply was slow to react to this increased stimulus. Consequently, Seville attracted traders from all over Europe who offered the goods and services requested by the newly discovered continent. Initially, as precious metals were not allowed to be exported, prices rose quickly within Castile, at a yearly rate of 2 percent. The rise continued after 1566, although at a lower rate once it became easier to export gold and silver. Castilian prices rose to become the highest in Europe. It was the homeland of the "price revolution." Real wages also went down quickly.

With increasing income from the West Indies, the monarchy found itself strong enough to accept all the military challenges derived from its world commitments. Charles V and Philip II spent most of their time with their armies, battling all over Europe to defend their territories and their principles. It was expensive: For the period with better evidence—Philip II—the monarchy's expenditures multiplied by four. Revenues had difficulty keeping pace with military expenditures. The resulting gap was bridged with credit. The Habsburg kings became the major players in the credit market. Their demands mobilized the entire credit network all through Europe. When money was available to pay for debts (i.e., the American treasuries arriving at Seville), everything was fine. When money was unavailable, all turned to black. Royal debts were not paid, and a chain of defaults destroyed the whole fabric of social and personal trust. The successive fiscal emergencies of the Crown touched every social class: private bankers and traders, but also artisans and peasants. The distortions were high and had increasingly disruptive effects on efficiency and resource allocation. In general, the advanced and dynamic groups of the Castilian economy were those most taxed, while the privileged classes resisted much better. No wonder that the Castilian economy showed declining symptoms after the 1570s.

The Seventeenth Century. Everything went wrong for most of the seventeenth century. Philip III (1598–1621) and Philip IV (1621–1665) were involved in wars and revolts all over the world. They made an enormous effort to keep their heritage in their hands, but at a cost that became unaffordable. While the sixteenth century provided the monarchy with increasing revenue from the American colonies, the seventeenth century was disappointing. The attacks from regular or irregular enemies became increasingly well organized, and this reduced the regularity with which the annual Spanish silver fleet arrived in Seville. Smuggling became easier as it became more rewarding to avoid the cumbersome fleet system. By midcentury, a good part of the gold and silver exported from America to Europe evaded Seville entirely, moving directly to Amsterdam or other non-Habsburg ports.

The Castilian economy was unable to keep pace with the king's financial needs, and both suffered under the weight of taxes and debts. Because the financial needs were always urgent and the monarch's liquidity nonexistent, the Crown became increasingly indebted to bankers. Offering credit to the Crown could be lucrative, but it carried great risks as well, and many bankers were ultimately ruined.

The recourse to taxpayers was inevitable. Castilian artisans and traders could not pay more—they were being crushed under the fiscal pressure. Urbanization was suffering, suggesting that economic decline was at work. As Castilians were heavily taxed, the king—by initiative of his prime minister, the count-duke of Olivares—asked the other kingdoms to contribute to the imperial effort. Portugal, which joined the monarchy in 1580, revolted and left in 1640. In the same year, Catalonia attempted to separate from Castile. Even Andalucia was the center of a major revolt (1641). There were also revolts in the Italian territories as well as the Dutch revolt that lasted eighty years, from 1568 to 1648. The European-wide Thirty Years' War was the Habsburg Crown's last gigantic effort.

By the mid-seventeenth century, Philip IV had to accept his defeat and withdraw from many of his international commitments. Once this was done, it became possible to introduce some order in the Crown finances. This began during the late seventeenth century. Smoothing and reducing the Crown's needs was most helpful for everybody. The last forty years of the century were much quieter and also much more prosperous. Altogether, the economic outcome of the century was poor. Population stagnated or perhaps, as recent research suggests, increased slightly after a sharp decrease until midcentury. For the second half, all the evidence is clear: The peripheral regions increased their population figures, while the central ones stagnated. The phenomenon affected both the North Atlantic and the Mediterranean regions. The switch from a centripetal to a centrifugal trend was profound. It also reflected changes in economic activity, since early in the century, the northern regions enjoyed demographic growth mainly because of the diffusion of new crops, such as maize. The Mediterranean and southern regions switched to vineyards because of the growing demand from northwestern Europe.

Castile failed to recover until well into the next century. For Spain as a whole, urbanization rates decreased until 1750. A number of towns also declined—even Madrid, the new capital since 1560, which had enjoyed fast growth until the mid-seventeenth century.

The Eighteenth Century. The death of Charles II (1665–1700), who died without a direct heir, plunged Spain into a succession crisis. Philip of Bourbon, nephew of Louis XIV, was the preferred candidate of Charles's last will. Such a change of dynasty worried the many European states that had fought for two centuries against the power of the Habsburg Empire. They were not eager to assist in a concentration of power in the hands of the Bourbon family, controlling both France and the Spanish Habsburg legacy. An alternative candidate, Archduke Charles of Austria, gained broad support, and soon two groups of imperial powers—the Franco-Spanish and the Anglo-Dutch—were at war for more than a decade. The results, decided at the Utrecht peace treaty (1713), were twofold. The European powers recognized Philip V (1700–1746) as sovereign of Spain; when the archduke Charles became German emperor (1711), he lost his international support. This meant the start of a centralized government within Spain, as the regions loyal to Charles, the former members of the Aragon Crown, lost (since their defeat) all their constitutions. But the Spanish Crown had to accept the loss of its European territories (several Italian states, Burgundy, and the Low Countries) and the liberalization of American trade. In effect, the British Crown acquired the right to send one ship per year to Spanish America and to supply slaves.

At home, the Bourbons were good at introducing sound administration and strong centralization, following the French principles of the day. After the long civil war, there was order and peace within the country. State administration was unified. The Spanish economy recovered once the state was no longer a burden. This lasted until the French and Revolutionary Wars of the turn of the century.

Spain entered the eighteenth century as an agricultural economy with declining manufacturing and trade sectors. This peaceful and well-policed century was congenial to economic growth and structural change. Trade expansion was a goal for the monarchy. Internal frontiers (except for the Basque country) were abolished as a consequence of the defeat of the Aragon Crown in the succession war. This triggered increased trade between Castile and Aragon, much to the profit of the losers, who had a much smaller economy. The state invested in ports, channels, and highways as well as in the improvement of urban facilities. The monarchy devoted time and effort to fully recover control of the American empire. The Casa de Contratación was relocated to Cádiz to provide better service to and better control over the arriving fleets. By 1765, a major decision was made: the Free Trade Decrees. These decrees did not introduce free trade but broke the monopolies of Cádiz and Veracruz by adding ports in both Spain and America that were allowed to participate in colonial trade. The profits of the monopoly trade were diffused to many more urban and regional areas. It provided a strong backing to trade and economic growth for the three decades that followed. The growth of internal, colonial, and foreign trade provided new markets for agricultural and manufactured Spanish goods and also for Spanish services (freight, insurance, import-export, banking, and so on).

Meanwhile, the enlightened governments of the second half of the eighteenth century promoted manufacturing activities in an attempt to provide new sources of income to a growing number of peasants. The peasants were increasingly competing with sheep owners—many of them associated with the influential *mesta*, the institution of the main livestock owners—over land and its use. It was a traditional conflict. Since the Middle Ages, Castile specialized in sheep raising and wool exports. Population expansion always created conflicts for this business. It had happened in the sixteenth century and again in the eighteenth. The disagreements over land increasingly dominated economic and social life and began to have a serious effect on political life. The enlightened reformers designed a number of new, more liberal laws, but failed to apply them. Their first move was to free the price of bread, which was previously under control. This provoked a revolt (the *Motín de Esquilache*), as a poor harvest triggered a quick rise in prices.

The economic outcome of the century is clearly positive, although there are many symptoms of stagnation by the end of the century. The agrarian expansion reached its maximum perhaps toward the 1770s. The French wars drained or froze a lot of private and public resources during the last decade of the century.

The Nineteenth Century. The Spanish defeat at Trafalgar meant the end of the Spanish Empire's rule over the central and south Atlantic Ocean. One disaster beckoned another. After the defeat by the British navy came the French invasion of Spain. Both were epochal events, evidenced by the important monuments built at the central squares of the United Kingdom and France. The French invasion was the end of early modern Spain. The monarch stepped down, the state almost dissolved, and Spain became the battlefield of many players. The economy was ruined during the war years. The privileged classes—the church and aristocracy—were also ruined, as was the state. Only the peasants took some advantage of the powers' weakening state. They occupied many *mesta*, sheep-growing lands, and expanded their crops. They ceased to pay rents to their lords. But they had to pay taxes in cash or in kind to many armies (French, British, guerrillas, or Cádiz constitutional government).

For some decades, until the 1840s, the problem of state income was of paramount importance and interfered with public policy. Although major arrangements were introduced—the disentailment of church lands, fiscal reform that included the liquidation of church tithe and its takeover by state taxes, and the refinancing of the external debt—the treasury question remained the hottest one until the end of the nineteenth century. It altered the proper development of economic and public policies, which substituted pro-growth character for short-term extra revenue.

The social conflicts concerning agricultural property found an unexpected solution during the French occupation (1808–1814). The numerous armies fighting on Spanish soil placed a heavy burden on all available resources, which were taxed in kind and on the spot. The extensive sheep-grazing lands were dramatically reduced in size. Spanish peasants expanded villages and introduced a new crop—the potato, in response to a growing demand from the armies. Once the war was over, the *mesta* became extremely weakened. The early nineteenth century saw the assertion of peasants against farmers.

The land question remained central in Spanish life as, for the whole century, most of the major social and economic reforms were related to real property. The liberal political programs were normally oriented to the disentailment of all lands—disentailment from the church (and all its constituents), from the municipalities, from the Crown, and even from the same aristocrats who managed to get rid of the *mayorazgo* institution that prevented them from selling their own land. In a land-hungry country with growing population, the *desamortización* (disentailment) was a success. It attracted a considerable amount of funds, and it enabled further agrarian expansion. In this sense, the main thrust of the Spanish economy for the century between, say, 1770 and 1870 was the demand for land and how it was satisfied. Thanks to this, the Spanish population of some 9 million was able to double. It also meant the end of traditional wool exports. Nevertheless, this move did not generate any technological improvement. It was produced under a stable production function.

The early development of Spanish industrialization started in the manufacture of Catalan cotton textiles during the eighteenth century. Cotton textile manufacturers there sold to their own expanding regional market, Spanish markets—opened with the abolition of internal frontiers—and to the newly opened colonial American market. With the French wars, the loss of the empire, and the complete opening of Spanish markets to French and British goods, Catalan manufacturers underwent a severe crisis. By the early 1830s, a new generation of entrepreneurs, usually heirs of the former manufacturers, was willing to adopt the newly developed technologies. The first attempts took place during the 1830s, but it was during the two following decades (1840–1860) when an industrial revolution occurred in Catalan textile manufacturing.

Since the end of the first Carlist war (a civil war between defenders of the ancien régime and of the new liberal régime, lasting from 1833 to 1839), the attempts to industrialize the country were many, mainly along the Mediterranean coast. By 1854–1856, a new government, probusiness and in favor of developmental policies, provided new laws to speed up railway building, investment banking (of the *Crédit Mobilier* type), and issue and commercial banking. Some 4,500 kilometers (2,790 miles) of railway tracks were built in ten years, and an entire banking system was developed from scratch. This dynamism compensated the industrial backlash owing to the U.S. Civil War and the resulting world cotton shortage.

Nevertheless, railways were less profitable than expected, and a major financial crisis occurred in 1866. Many investment banks had to close as well as some issue banks. Railway building stopped for some ten years. A new liberal government came into office by 1868, providing the last series of liberal legislation: freedom to incorporate companies; a new tariff, much less protectionist than ever (following a declining trend that started in 1841); a new liberal regime for mine property and operation; and a number of other liberal laws. The railways were increasingly used to export agricultural goods. Mining development reacted quickly to the new legal framework. For some twenty years, Spain attracted large amounts of French, British, and Belgian investment in mining and metallurgy. Textile factories also enjoyed some good years because of internal agrarian prosperity. The optimism of the time was reinforced when France started the tariff war with Italy and turned to Spain to compensate for the phylloxera-induced decline of French wine production. The peak came in 1882. Thereafter, a stock market crisis in France, followed by a prolonged agricultural crisis, plunged Spain into economic depression. In response, industrialists and agrarian owners pressed for increased protection. They received it in various steps, mainly by the inclusion of the Caribbean colonies—Cuba and Puerto Rico—within the Spanish tariff zone (but only one way) and by raising the tariff in 1891. This was the end of the free-trade trend in Spain.

The Cuban war (1895–1898), both a colonial war and a conflict with the United States, was a significant moment. As Spain was defeated, this meant the end of any significant colony (but for small territories in Africa) and the assertion of a much more inward-looking development policy. The treasury was able to repay the country's debts quickly, adopting a tough monetary policy and fiscal reform. Nevertheless, the brake on the Spanish economy was such as to prevent Spain from sharing in the globalized economy of the Belle Époque. Spain sent relatively few emigrants to the New World and received relatively little foreign capital. Growth was modest in the quarter century previous to World War I.

The Early Twentieth Century. The outbreak of World War I was a major shock to the Spanish economy. The foreign-oriented sectors—mining and Mediterranean agriculture—suffered, while the industrial regions—Catalonia and the Basque Country as well as other industrial districts—and the Asturias coal mining community enjoyed unprecedented prosperity. Exports to the European allies, mainly France, and to overseas markets boomed, while the home market was supplied almost entirely by Spanish producers. Spain switched to a situation of de facto autarchy (imports were difficult to obtain) with unrestricted access to foreign markets. The stock of foreign capital invested during the previous century was bought back by Spaniards. A whole generation was fascinated by the high moment of national pride associated with these developments. Spain came out of the war and the immediate postwar years of political and social turmoil with increased income per capita, increased wages, a modern banking system, and a significant amount of gold in the Bank of Spain. All of this triggered quick growth in the 1920s, as well as a first wave of interregional internal migration, from the ruined mining and agricultural regions to the newly developed urban and industrial districts such as Barcelona, Bilbao, and Madrid. By 1930, the Spanish economy was in good shape. Unfortunately, the next generation suffered.

The international economic crisis coincided in Spain with the end of the Alfonso XIII (1902–1931) monarchy and the advent of a republican regime (1931) that started to develop advanced social policies. After a couple of years in the opposition (1933–1935) and two defeated revolts (1934) of the most radical groupings, the center-left Republicans and the leftist parties won the 1936 election. This triggered the Franco conspiracy against the republic (July 1936) and the start of the Civil War. It was an almost three-year-long war, featuring a social revolution on the Republican side, but also international isolation. Franco was much more focused on winning the war and getting international credit and provisions. He managed to do so efficiently and won the war in 1939, a few months before Hitler invaded Poland. Franco's new regime went hand in hand with Adolf Hitler and Benito Mussolini. He established a military-run economy, geared toward autarchy because of ideological and political reasons. When Nazi Germany was defeated, Franco's situation became desperate. The former Allies decided to boycott Spain—a move that Franco exploited to reassert his leadership and to intensify autarchy. A closed, state-directed economy was at work during the 1940s and in the 1950s, although to a lesser extent. Its outcome was poor.

The Late Twentieth Century. The Franco regime took note of the success of European postwar recovery and co-operation. The Korean War and the cold war changed his international position completely. From being a friend of Hitler and Mussolini, he became a fierce opponent of Communism. The United States approached Franco's regime, and they signed an important agreement in 1953 on military defense and economic assistance. Meanwhile, the regime cautiously relaxed its autarchic foreign economic policy, introducing a system of multiple exchange rates that was a de facto devaluation. As autarchy was relaxed, the balance of payments suffered pressure. Some market-oriented ministers and high-ranking officers took advantage of the situation to force a decisive opening of Spain to the international economy and an abandonment of autarchic policies. This was achieved in 1959 with the stabilization plan that introduced a dramatic shift in economic policy. Spain joined all the international economic organizations (International Monetary Fund, the World Bank, General Agreement on Tariffs and Trade, Organisation for Economic Cooperation and Development), devaluated the peseta, fixed its exchange rate and declared convertibility, opened manufacturing to foreign investment, abolished a large number of market intervention bodies, and, generally speaking, adopted free-market economy criteria while keeping monetary supply under control.

The plan was a complete success, allowing for the economic "miracle" of the following fourteen years. The huge wave of tourism and direct foreign investment, coupled with the upsurge of emigration to western European countries, provided Spain with large inflows of foreign currency that was used to import capital goods on a grand scale. The modernization of the economy grew at a yearly rate of 7 to 8 percent gross domestic product (GDP) per capita—the most important growth period in Spanish economic history. Nevertheless, the liberalization move was partly repressed when, by 1964, an indicative planning policy was implemented that switched public funding to capital- and energy-intensive firms and sectors.

The oil crisis hit Spain in a delicate moment, coinciding with a period of labor unrest, government instability, and the weakened health of Franco, who died in 1975. His government felt unable to pursue tough monetary policies or to consider a high increase in domestic oil prices. Spain's economy then depended on expanding energy-intensive industries, and efforts to defend this strategy caused inflation to rise quickly, reaching a dangerous 40 percent by mid-1977.

When the first democratic elections (June 1977) allowed the emergence of a fully responsible democratic government, a major economic program was designed with full support from all the democratic parties. Devaluation and monetary control were combined with inflation control

MODERN SPAIN. View of the industrial section of Bilbao, 1984. (© Frank Fournier/Woodfin Camp and Associates, New York)

and with the deployment of the welfare state and direct taxation. These agreements, known as *Pactos de la Moncloa*, are the founding economic and social consensus of Spanish democracy. Unfortunately, the second oil shock came directly thereafter and was much tougher for Spaniards than the first. The total increase in price was immediately transferred to consumers. As wages had also been rising, many manufacturing firms were completely unable to cope with the new state of affairs and had to close. In four years (1979–1982), unemployment rose dramatically. The manufacturing crisis also reached the banking sector, which was deeply involved in heavy industry.

The new socialist government, in office since late 1982, pursued a moderately liberal economic policy, liberalizing the operation of a number of markets, including the labor market. The socialists also bet strongly for full integration in the European Economic Community (EEC). Spain's entrance to the EEC on 1 January 1986 is a major landmark in Spanish history and in its opening to international markets. The transition period lasted for seven years and was more intense than previously thought, as it coincided with an EEC liberalization move: the approval of the Single Act. From 1986 to 1990, Spain enjoyed a sizable increase of direct foreign investment, allowing for high growth rates after a decade of economic stagnation.

The crisis of 1990–1993 was dramatic for Spain. The effort to enter the European Monetary System in 1989 proved to be demanding and perhaps untimely. The pressure of the international economic crisis, combined with German efforts to pay for reunification, pushed some currencies to devaluation. The Spanish peseta underwent three devaluations between 1992 and 1993. Eventually, it gained competitiveness as European markets opened fully and plans for European monetary integration were launched with the Maastricht Treaty. This was the most fortunate combination.

From 1994 to 1998, growth was accelerating while inflation was reduced. Interest rates came down, easing new investment, expanding consumption, and reducing public spending. The entrance into the new European currency—the euro—was a historic achievement for the Spanish economy, as it provided international integration into a high-income group of countries and a series of rules of good economic behavior. All in all, Spanish GDP per head has been catching up with EEC and European Union (EU) averages. At the same time, the country has improved in all the other factors that are captured in measures of well-being such as the Human Development Index. The Spanish position there is clearly among the most advanced nations in the world.

BIBLIOGRAPHY

Carreras, Albert, ed. *Estadísticas históricas de España, siglos 19–20.* Madrid, 1989.

Coll, Sebastián, and José I. Fortea. *Guía de fuentes cuantitativas para la historia económica de España.* 2 vols. Madrid, 1995, 2002.

Comín, Francisco. *Historia de la Hacienda pública*, vol. 2, *España, 1808–1995.* Barcelona, 1996.

Comín, Francisco, Mauro Hernández, and Enrique Llopis, eds. *Historia económica de España, siglos 10–20.* Barcelona, 2002.

Fontana, Josep. *La Quiebra de la monarquía absoluta, 1814–1820: La crisis del Antiguo Régimen en España*. Barcelona, 1971.

Jover, José María, ed. *Historia de España Menéndez Pidal*, vols. 19 (sixteenth century); 23 (seventeenth century crisis); 28 (late seventeenth and mid-eighteenth centuries); 30 (1759–1834); 33 (1834–1900); 37 (1898–1931, 1984); 41 (1939–1975). Madrid, 1989–1996.

Marcos, Alberto. *España en los siglos XVI, XVII y XVIII: Economía y sociedad*. Barcelona, 2000.

Martín-Aceña, Pablo, and James Simpson, eds. *The Economic Development of Spain since 1870*. Aldershot, U.K., 1995.

Nadal, Jordi. *El fracaso de la revolución industrial en España, 1814–1913*. Barcelona, 1975.

Nadal, Jordi. *La población española, siglos 16–20*. Barcelona, 1984.

Pamuk, Sevket, and Jeffrey G. Williamson, eds. *The Mediterranean Response to Globalisation before 1950*. London, 2000.

Prados de la Escosura, Leandro. *De Imperio a Nación: Crecimiento y atraso económico en España, 1780–1930*. Madrid, 1988.

Prados de la Escosura, Leandro. *El progreso económico de España, 1850–2000*. Madrid, 2001.

Reher, David S. *La familia en España: Pasado y presente*. Madrid, 1996.

Ringrose, David R. *Madrid and the Spanish Economy, 1560–1850*. Berkeley, 1983.

Ruiz Martín, Felipe. *El Banco de Es paña: Una historia económica*. Madrid, 1970.

Sánchez-Albornoz, Nicolás, ed. *The Economic Modernization of Spain, 1830–1930*. New York, 1987.

Simpson, James. *Spanish Agriculture: The Long Siesta, 1765–1965*. Cambridge, 1995.

Thompson, I. A. A., and B. Yun, eds. *The Castilian Crisis of the Seventeenth Century: New Perspectives on the Economic and Social History of Seventeenth-Century Spain*. Cambridge, 1994.

Tortella, Gabriel. *Banking, Railroads, and Industry in Spain, 1829–1874*. New York, 1977.

Tortella, Gabriel. *The Development of Modern Spain: An Economic History of the Nineteenth and Twentieth Centuries*. Cambridge, Mass., 2000.

Vicens-Vives, Jaume. *An Economic History of Spain*. Princeton, 1967.

ALBERT CARRERAS